FRENCH COMPUTING DICTIONARY

THIRD EDITION

French-English
English-French

FRENCH COMPUTING DICTIONARY

THIRD EDITION

French-English
English-French

S.M.H. Collin
Francoise Laurendeau
Bernard Mouget

BLOOMSBURY

A BLOOMSBURY REFERENCE BOOK

www.bloomsbury.com/reference

Originally published by Peter Collin Publishing
as *English-French / French-English Dictionary of Computing and Information Technology*

First published 1991
Second edition published 1996, 2000
Third edition published 2004

Bloomsbury Publishing Plc
38 Soho Square, London W1D 3HB

British Library Cataloguing-in-Publication Data
A catalogue record for this book is available from the British Library

ISBN 0 7475 6992 4

Text Production and Proofreading
Katy McAdam, Edmund Wright, Heather Bateman, Cécile Guinard, Emma Harris, Sarah Lusznat, Louise Miller

All papers used by Bloomsbury Publishing are natural, recyclable products made from wood grown in well-managed forests. The manufacturing processes conform to the environmental regulations of the country of origin.

Text processed and computer typeset by Bloomsbury
Printed and bound in Finland by WS Bookwell

Preface

Languages change rapidly, and this new edition of the dictionary brings in many new words and expressions in English and French, while the original text has been widely revised. The aim of this dictionary is to give the user a basic vocabulary of terms relating to computers and information technology in French and English, with translations into the other language.

The vocabulary covers the main areas of computer technology, including hardware, software, programming, networks, and peripherals, together with many applications where computers are used; information technology in general, telecommunications, TV and radio, desk-top publishing, graphics and design, e-mail and the Internet; these are the situations in which the user may frequently require translations from one language into the other.

The dictionary covers not only international usage, but in some cases identifies words and expressions where American and British usages differ.

The dictionary gives many examples of usage, both to show how the words are used in context and how they can be translated. The examples are supplemented by short quotations in both languages from newspapers and magazines from all over the world; these show the worldwide applications of the two languages.

Préface

Cette nouvelle édition revue et corrigée a subi une mise à jour importante. Notre but est de vous offrir le vocabulaire essentiel de la langue de l'informatique qui s'est beaucoup enrichie au cours des dernières années, aussi bien en français qu'en anglais.

Outre les mots du langage courant employés dans le quotidien de l'informatique et de la micro-informatique, vous trouverez le vocabulaire des ordinateurs (matériels, logiciels, programmation, périphériques, réseaux, etc), celui des applications multiples se rapportant au traitement des données (télécommunications, infographie, PAO, etc), et des innovations plus récentes (CD ROM, messagerie électronique, Internet, etc).

Les exemples très nombreux sont des outils précieux qui permettent d'aider à résoudre les problèmes de traduction de cette langue spécialisée qui évolue sans cesse.

De multiples citations tirées de la presse spécialisée du monde anglophone et francophone vous permettront de mieux saisir le sens des mots dans leur contexte.

COMMENT UTILISER CE DICTIONNAIRE

Notre dictionnaire se veut clair et facile à utiliser.

Les entrées apparaissent en caractères **gras** et, après chaque terme anglais, la prononciation est indiquée.

Les différentes catégories grammaticales sont introduites par ■.

Lorsqu'un terme a plusiers significations, celles-ci sont précédées d'un numéro (1, 2, etc). Pour chaque terme, les traductions principales sont indiquées en premier et, lorsqu'il y en a plusieurs pour un même terme, elles sont suivies d'un exemple afin d'expliquer l'usage du terme.

Les explications entre parenthèses permettent de mieux comprendre la signification du terme traduit, dans le cas où le terme pose problème ou lorsqu'il peut être interprété de plusieurs manières.

Certaines entrées sont suivies d'extraits de journaux ou de revues spécialisées, délimités par un cadre, qui apportent un complément d'information sur l'usage du terme en question.

Les abréviations ont été réduites au minimum, en voici la liste:

f	féminin
fpl	féminin pluriel
m	masculin
mpl	masculin pluriel
UK	anglais britannique
US	anglais américain
vi	verbe intransitif
vr	verbe pronominal
vt	verbe transitif

USING THE DICTIONARY

The dictionary aims to provide a clear layout which will help the user find the required translation as easily as possible.

Each entry contains a headword in **bold** type, followed by a pronunciation in the case of English headwords.

Within the entry different parts of speech are introduced by ■.

Different meanings are introduced by numbers (1, 2, etc). Within each meaning division main translations are grouped together first, if there is more than one, followed by examples showing how the headword is used in context.

Glosses in brackets clarify the exact meaning of a word that is being translated, in cases where the meaning is less familiar or the word has more than one possible interpretation.

Boxes after an entry contain extracts from magazines or journals giving more in-depth information on how the word is used.

As far as is possible, abbreviations are not used in the dictionary, with the exception of the following:

f	feminine
fpl	feminine plural
m	masculine
mpl	masculine plural
UK	British English
US	American English
vi	intransitive verb
vr	reflexive verb
vt	transitive verb

FRANÇAIS-ANGLAIS
FRENCH-ENGLISH

A

A *abrév* A

A (anström) *abrév* Å

A: (*lecteur de disque*) A:

abandonner *verbe* **1.** *vt* to abandon **2.** *vt* to exit **3.** *vt* to quit ◇ **si vous quittez votre feuille de calcul sans la sauvegarder, il vous sera impossible de la récupérer** once you have abandoned your spreadsheet, you cannot retrieve it again

abandonner prématurément *verbe* to abort

à base de caractères *adjectif* character-based

à base de procédure *adjectif* procedural

aberration *f nom* **1.** aberration **2.** distortion ◇ **déformation** *ou* **distorsion** *ou* **aberration de l'image** image distortion

à bit significatif *adjectif* bit-significant

abonné *mf nom* subscriber

à bouton-poussoir *adjectif* pushbutton

abréviation *f nom* abbreviation ◇ **dans le texte, on a remplacé le terme processeur par l'abréviation 'proc'** within the text, the abbreviation 'proc' is used instead of processor

ABS *nom* ABS

abscisse *f nom* x-coordinate

absorber *verbe vt* to absorb

absorptance *f nom* absorptance

absorption *f nom* absorption

ACC *nom* accumulator *ou* accumulator register ◇ **stockez les 2 octets de données dans les registres A et B et exécutez l'instruction 'add' – vous obtiendrez le résultat dans l'accumulateur** store the two bytes of data in registers A and B and execute the add instruction – the answer will be in the accumulator

accéder à *verbe* to access ◇ **elle a accédé au fichier (informatique) de l'employé stocké sur l'ordinateur** she accessed the employee's file stored on the computer

accéder à une adresse *verbe* to address

accélérateur *m* **graphique** *nom* graphics accelerator

accélération *f* **de la souris** *nom* mouse acceleration

accepté, -ée d'avance *adjectif* pre-agreed

accepter *verbe vt* to accept ◇ **il a accepté le devis de l'imprimeur** he accepted the quoted price for printing ◇ **il n'a pas accepté** *ou* **il a refusé le poste de programmeur qu'on lui offrait** he did not accept the programming job he was offered

accès *m nom* access ◇ **accès** *m* **à un système par personne non autorisée utilisant un mot de passe valide** piggyback entry ◇ **accès** *m* **gratuit au système WAIS** free WAIS ◇ **accès** *m* **sur demande à la mémoire paginée** demand fetching ◇ **après avoir découvert qu'il faisait du piratage, on lui a interdit l'accès au système** after he was discovered hacking, he was barred access to the system ◇ **avoir accès à quelque chose** to have access to something ◇ **avoir accès à un fichier informatique** to have access to a file of data ◇ **il a accès à de nombreux fichiers confidentiels** he has access to numerous sensitive files ◇ **interdire (à quelqu'un) l'accès à un système** to bar access to a system ◇ **l'accès instantané au disque RAM a été bien accueilli** the instantaneous access of the RAM disk was welcome ◇ **sans accès à l'ordinateur** hands off ◇ **support à accès direct** direct access storage device (DASD) ◇ **théorique accès à l'ordinateur** hands off

accès *m* **à distance** *nom* remote access

accès *m* **aléatoire** *nom* random access

accès *m* **à l'ordinateur principal (par l'intermédiaire d'un micro)** *nom* mainframe access

accès *m* **asynchrone** *nom* asynchronous access

accès *m* **au débit primaire** *nom* basic rate access

accès *m* **au disque** *nom* disk access

accès *m* **cyclique** *nom* cyclic access

accès *m* **de base** *nom* basic rate interface

accès *m* **direct** *nom* **1.** direct access **2.** random access

accès *m* **direct à la mémoire** *nom* **1.** direct memory access **2.** DMA

accès *m* **direct à la mémoire par vol de cycle** *nom* DMA cycle stealing

accès *m* **instantané** *nom* instantaneous access

accès *m* **multiple asservi à la demande** *abrév* DAMA ■ *nom* demand assigned multiple access

accès *m* **non autorisé** *adjectif* access-barred

accès *m* **parallèle** *nom* parallel access

accès *m* **par ligne commutée** *nom* dial-up access

accès *m* **par niveau d'opération** *nom* share-level access

accès *m* **partagé** *nom* shared access

accès *m* **primaire** *nom* **1.** PRI **2.** primary rate interface

accès *m* **rapide** *nom* rapid access

accès *m* **sélectif** *nom* random access

accès *m* **séquentiel** *nom* **1.** sequential access **2.** serial access ◇ **méthode d'accès séquentiel en file** queued sequential access method (QSAM) ◇ **méthode d'accès séquentiel indexé en file** queued indexed sequential access method (QISAM)

accès *m* **simultané** *nom* concurrency

accessoire *m nom* accessory ◇ **il existe de nombreux accessoires pour cet ordinateur individuel très populaire** this popular home computer has a large range of accessories ◇ **plusieurs accessoires, dont un capot d'insonorisation, sont fournis avec l'imprimante** the printer comes with several accessories, such as a soundproof hood

accessoire *m* **de bureau** *abrév* DA ■ *nom* desk accessory

accessoires *mpl nom* ancillary equipment

accessoires *mpl* **de jeux** *nom* gaming gear

accidentel *adjectif* accidental

accolade *f nom* bracket

accolades *fpl plural noun* **1.** braces **2.** curly brackets *ou* curly braces

accord *nom* deal ◇ **accord** *m* **automatique des vitesses de transmission** automatic speed matching

accorder *verbe vt* to match ◇ **accord d'impédance** impedance matching ◇ **charge accordée** *ou* **équilibrée** matched load

accordeur *m* **d'impédance** *nom* cable matcher

accrochage *m nom* lock up

accro *m* **de l'informatique** *nom* nerd

accumulateur *m nom* accumulator *ou* accumulator register ◇ **stockez les 2 octets de données dans les registres A et B et exécutez l'instruction 'add' – vous obtiendrez le résultat dans l'accumulateur** store the two bytes of data in registers A and B and execute the add instruction – the answer will be in the accumulator

accumuler *verbe vt* to accumulate

accusé *m* **de réception** *nom* (*de message envoyé par courrier électronique*) receipt notification

accusé *m* **de réception négatif** *abrév* NAK ■ *nom* negative acknowledgement

accusé *m* **de réception positif** *nom* **1.** ACK **2.** affirmative acknowledgement

accuser réception *verbe* **1.** to acknowledge **2.** (*d'un message*) to acknowledge

achat *m* **grand public** *adjectif* B2C

achats *mpl* **en ligne** *nom* electronic shopping

achats *mpl* **sur Internet** *nom* electronic shopping

acheminement *m nom* **1.** data routing **2.** hierarchical routing **3.** routing ◇ **protocole RIP (d'acheminement de l'information)** routing information protcol (RIP)

acheminement *m* **des messages** *nom* message routing

acheminement *m* **dynamique** *nom* adaptive routing

acheminement *m* **présélectionné** *nom* fixed routing

acheminer *verbe vt* to channel

achèvement *m nom* completion

à connecteur compatible *adjectif* plug-compatible

à couches multiples *adjectif* multilayer

acoustique *adjectif* acoustic

acquisition *f nom* acquisition

acquisition *f* **de données** *nom* data acquisition

actif *adjectif* active

action *f nom* action ◇ **action** *f* **d'appuyer sur deux touches en même temps** chord keying ◇ **action** *f* **d'inclure le message d'origine** quoting ◇ **champ (d'action)** action field

action *m* **en retour** *nom* feedback

ActionMedia (*nom de marque*) ActionMedia

actionné, -ée par événement *adjectif* event-driven

actionner une touche *verbe* to key

activé *adjectif* **1.** enabled **2.** event-driven ◇ **activé par une seule touche** single key response

activé, -ée par reconnaissance des données *adjectif* data-driven

activer *verbe* **1.** *vt* to activate **2.** *vt* to arm **3.** *vt* to enable **4.** *vt* to select ◇ **valider** *ou* **activer un circuit intégré** chip select (CS)

adaptateur *m nom* **1.** adapter *ou* adaptor **2.** adapter plug **3.** adaptor ◇ **adaptateur** *m* **de canal de transmission de données** data adapter unit ◇ **adaptateur** *m* **graphique couleur haute définition Targa™** Targa ◇ **l'adaptateur du câble permet de relier le scanner à une interface SCSI** the cable adapter allows attachment of the scanner to the SCSI interface ◇ **le câble de liaison entre le scanner et l'adaptateur est compris** the cable to connect the scanner to the adapter is included in the package

adaptateur *m* **d'écran** *nom* display adapter

adaptateur *m* **de l'ordinateur hôte** *nom* host adapter ◇ **le câble qui relie le scanner et**

l'adaptateur de l'ordinateur hôte est fourni the cable to connect the scanner to the host adapter is included

adaptateur *m* **de terminal** *nom* terminal adapter

adaptateur *m* **de vitesse de transmission** *nom* baud rate generator

adaptateur *m* **d'interface de communication** *nom* communications interface adapter

adaptateur *m* **femelle/mâle** *nom* sex changer

adaptateur *m* **graphique** *nom* graphics adapter

adaptateur *m* **maître** *nom* bus master adapter

adaptateur *m* **mâle/femelle** *nom* sex changer

adaptateur *m* **VGA** *nom* VGA

adaptation *f nom* adaptation ◇ **adaptation** *f* **automatique de la fréquence vidéo** automatic mode ◇ **l'adaptation de l'oeil pour répondre à différents niveaux de luminosité** *ou* **de brillance** the adaptation of the eye to respond to different levels of brightness

adaptation *f* **automatique de la fréquence vidéo** *nom* automatic frequency switching

adaptation *f* **automatique du mode vidéo** *nom* **1.** automatic frequency switching **2.** automatic mode

adapté à un ordinateur *adjectif* intimate

adapter *verbe* **1.** *vt* to adapt **2.** *vt* to condition ◇ **peut-on adapter cet ordinateur pour les disquettes 5,25 pouces?** can this computer be adapted to take 5.25 inch disks?

addition *f nom* **1.** addition **2.** sum

addition *f* **destructive** *nom* destructive addition

additionnel *adjectif* **1.** add-in **2.** additional **3.** add-on

additionner *verbe vt* to add ◇ **l'addition de chacune des colonnes du tableau donne un sous-total** in the spreadsheet each column should be added to make a subtotal

additionneur *m nom* adder ◇ **additionneur** *m* **à retenue automatique** carry look ahead

additionneur *m* **à deux entrées** *nom* half adder ■ *adjectif* two-input adder

additionneur *m* **à trois entrées** *nom* **1.** full adder **2.** three input adder

additionneur *m* **binaire** *nom* **1.** BCD adder **2.** binary adder

additionneur *m* **complet** *nom* **1.** full adder **2.** three input adder

additionneur *m* **DCB** *nom* BCD adder

additionneur *m* **parallèle** *nom* parallel adder

additionneur *m* **séquentiel** *nom* serial adder

additionneur-soustracteur *m nom* adder-subtractor

addition *f* **sans retenue** *nom* addition without carry

à deux dimensions *adjectif* two-dimensional

à distance *adjectif* remote ◇ **appel de procédure à distance** *ou* **appel RPC** remote procedure call (RPC) ◇ **(système de) lancement de tâches à distance** remote job entry (RJE) ◇ **les utilisateurs peuvent imprimer leurs rapports sur des imprimantes à distance** users can print reports on remote printers

administrateur *m nom* administrator

administrateur *m* **de base de données** *nom* DBA

administrateur *m* **de réseau** *nom* **1.** network administrator **2.** system administrator

Adobe (*développeur de logiciel*) Adobe Systems

Adobe Acrobat (*nom de marque*) Adobe Acrobat

adoucir *verbe* **1.** *vt* to deaden **2.** *vt* (*par addition de pixels*) to dither

adressable *adjectif* addressable ◇ **dans le nouveau système d'exploitation, la totalité des 5Mo de RAM installée est adressable** with the new operating system, all of the 5MB of RAM is addressable

adressable au niveau du pixel *adjectif* dot addressable

adressable par le contenu *adjectif* content-addressable

adressage *m nom* addressing

adressage *m* **abrégé** *abrév* abb. add.

adressage *m* **absolu** *nom* absolute addressing

adressage *m* **associatif** *nom* **1.** associative addressing **2.** content-addressable addressing

adressage *m* **augmenté** *nom* augmented addressing

adressage *m* **binaire** *nom* bit addressing

adressage *m* **de page** *nom* page addressing

adressage *m* **de registre** *nom* register addressing

adressage *m* **direct** *nom* direct addressing

adressage *m* **immédiat** *nom* immediate addressing

adressage *m* **implicite** *nom* implied addressing

adressage *m* **indexée** *nom* indexed addressing

adressage *m* **indirect** *nom* **1.** deferred addressing **2.** indirect addressing **3.** second-level addressing

adressage *m* **inhérent** *nom* inherent addressing

adressage *m* **particulier** *nom* inherent addressing

adressage *m* **simplifié** *abrév* abb. add.

adresse *f nom* address ◇ **adresse** *f* **origine** (*de la première instruction d'un programme*) program origin ◇ **c'est l'adresse à laquelle les données commencent** this is the address at which the data starts ◇ **chaque mot mémoire distinct a sa propre et unique adresse** each separate memory word has its own unique address ◇ **liste d'adresses** address list ◇ **notre fichier contient les adresses de deux mille sociétés en Europe** we keep an address list of two thousand businesses in Europe ◇ **protocole de résolution d'adresse** *ou* **protocole ARP** address resolution protocol (ARP) ◇ **zone d'adresse** address window

adresse *f* **abrégée** *nom* abbreviated address

adresse *f* **absolue** *nom* **1.** absolute address **2.** actual address **3.** machine address **4.** real address

adresse *f* **absolue de la cellule** *nom* absolute cell reference

adresse *f* **à un niveau** *nom* one-level address

adresse *f* **calculée** *nom* **1.** address translation **2.** generated address **3.** synthetic address

adresse *f* **courante** *nom* current address

adresse *f* **d'accumulateur** *nom* accumulator address

adresse *f* **de base** *nom* **1.** base address **2.** presumptive address

adresse *f* **de cellule** *nom* cell address

adresse *f* **de contrôleur de périphérique** *nom* device address

adresse *f* **de destination** *nom* destination address

adresse *f* **de lancement** *nom* initial address

adresse *f* **de pile** *nom* stack address

adresse *f* **de piste** *nom* track address

adresse *f* **de premier niveau** *nom* first-level address

adresse *f* **de référence** *nom* reference address

adresse *f* **de référence directe** *nom* direct reference address

adresse *f* **de réseau** *nom* network address

adresse *f* **de retour** *nom* return address

adresse *f* **de site** *nom* **1.** host address **2.** host number

adresse *f* **de site internet** *nom* **1.** Internet address **2.** Internet number

adresse *f* **de sous-réseau** *nom* subnet address *ou* subnet number

adresse *f* **des ports d'entrée/sortie** *nom* I/O address

adresse *f* **d'exécution** *nom* execution address

adresse *f* **d'instruction** *nom* instruction address

adresse *f* **directe** *nom* **1.** immediate address **2.** one-level address **3.** zero-level address

adresse *f* **d'octets** *plural noun* byte address

adresse *f* **effective** *nom* effective address

adresse *f* **explicite** *nom* explicit address

adresse *f* **générée** *nom* generated address

adresse *f* **immédiate** *nom* **1.** immediate address **2.** zero-level address

adresse *f* **indexée** *nom* **1.** index **2.** indexed address

adresse *f* **initiale** *nom* initial address

adresse *f* **Internet** *nom* **1.** host number **2.** Internet address **3.** Internet number **4.** IP address

adresse *f* **IP** *nom* **1.** dot address **2.** Internet protocol address

adresse *f* **machine** *nom* **1.** absolute address **2.** real address

adresse *f* **origine** *nom* **1.** origin **2.** presumptive address

adresse *f* **paginée** *nom* paged address

adresse *f* **physique** *nom* physical address

adresse *f* **primitive** *nom* presumptive address

adresse *f* **réelle** *nom* **1.** absolute address **2.** actual address **3.** first-level address **4.** real address

adresse *f* **relative** *nom* **1.** floating address **2.** floating symbolic address **3.** indirect address **4.** offset value *ou* offset word **5.** relative address

adresse *f* **secondaire** *nom* subaddress

adresse *f* **spécifique** *nom* specific address

adresse *f* **symbolique** *nom* **1.** floating symbolic address **2.** symbolic address **3.** tag

adresse *f* **URL** *nom* uniform resource locator

adresse *f* **valide** *nom* valid memory address

adresse *f* **virtuelle** *nom* virtual address

adresse *f* **Web** *nom* **1.** universal resource locator **2.** URL ◇ **l'adresse URL de la page d'accueil de la maison Peter Collin Publishing est la suivante: http** *or or* **www.pcp.co.uk** the URL of the Peter Collin Publishing home page is 'http://www.pcp.co.uk'

à échelle variable *adjectif* scalable

aérographe *m nom* airbrush ◇ **nous avons utilisé l'aérographe pour créer un effet de nuage dans cette image** we used the airbrush tool to create the cloud effects in this image

à espacement constant *adjectif* monospaced

affaiblissement *m nom* attenuation

affaiblissement *m* **d'insertion** *nom* insertion loss

affaires *fpl* **électroniques** *nom* e-business

affectation *f nom* assignment

affecter *verbe* **1.** *vt* to allocate **2.** *vt* (*la valeur 1 à un bit*) to set ◇ **affecter une zone de mémoire à une tâche** to assign ◇ **fréquence assignée** *ou* **allouée** assigned frequency

affecter à *verbe* to assign ◇ **deux PC ont été affectés à la préparation des étiquettes** two PCs have been assigned to outputting the labels

affecter d'un signe négatif *verbe* to negate ◇ **la valeur négative** *ou* **l'inverse de 23,4 est –23,4** if you negate 23.4 the result is –23.4

affichage *m nom* **1.** (*sur écran*) display **2.** gas discharge display *ou* gas plasma display **3.** readout ◇ **cette horloge a un affichage numérique** the clock has a digital readout

affichage *m* **à cristaux liquides** *nom* **1.** LCD **2.** LCD screen **3.** liquid crystal display

affichage *m* **alphanumérique** *nom* alphanumeric display

affichage *m* **composite** *nom* composite display

affichage *m* **couleur** *nom* colour display

affichage *m* **de caractères** *nom* character display

affichage *m* **de données** *nom* information output

affichage *m* **destructif** *nom* destructive readout

affichage *m* **de texte** *nom* character display

affichage *m* **d'une page** *nom* page display

affichage *m* **d'une partie de page** *nom* part page display

affichage *m* **électroluminescent** *nom* electroluminescent display

affichage *m* **en positif** *nom* positive presentation

affichage *m* **graphique** *nom* graphic display

affichage *m* **noir sur fond blanc** *nom* positive display

affichage *m* **(au) plasma** *nom* plasma display

affichage *m* **PostScript™** (*nom de marque*) Display PostScript™

affichage *m* **réduit** *nom* part page display

affiché, -ée à l'écran *adjectif* on-screen

afficher ◇ **afficher une image par déplacement horizontal** pan

afficher à l'écran *verbe* to call up ◇ **on a affiché à l'écran les adresses des clients** all the customers addresses were called up ◇ **rappelez le fichier précédent à l'écran** call up the previous file

affirmatif *adjectif* **1.** affirmative **2.** positive

affirmation *f nom* assertion

AFIPS *abrév* AFIPS

AFX (*logiciel*) Apple file exchange

agenda *m nom* planner ◇ **agenda mural** wall planner

agenda *m* **électronique** *nom* electronic agenda

agent *m nom* agent

agent *m* **de transfert de messages** *nom* **1.** message transfer agent **2.** MTA

agent *m* **mandataire** *nom* proxy agent

agent *m* **utilisateur** *nom* **1.** UA **2.** user agent

agglomérer (des données) *verbe* to gather write

agir en tant que modérateur *verbe* to moderate

à grande échelle *adjectif* large-scale

agrandir au plein écran *verbe* to maximise *ou* to maximize

agrégat *m nom* aggregate

agrégat *m* **de données** *nom* data aggregate

aide *f nom* help ◇ **aide en ligne** *ou* **aide contextuelle** context sensitive help ◇ **aides** *mpl* **à la programmation dans un langage déterminé** language support environment

aide *f* **au diagnostic** *nom* diagnostic aid

aide *f* **en ligne** *nom* online help

aide *f* **en ligne liée au contexte** *nom* context-sensitive help

aiguillage *m nom* switch

aimant *m nom* magnet

aimanté *adjectif* magnetic

AIX (*nom de marque*) AIX

ajouter *verbe* **1.** *vt* to add **2.** *vt* to append **3.** *vt* to insert ◇ **avec les touches de fonction, il est facile d'ajouter ou de supprimer du texte** adding or deleting material from the text is easy using function keys ◇ **les producteurs de logiciels ont ajouté un nouveau progiciel de gestion à leur gamme de produits** the software house has added a new management package to its range of products ◇ **si vous tapez la commande DOS 'COPY A+B', vous annexé le fichier B au fichier A** *ou* **vous ajoutez le fichier B à la suite du fichier A** if you enter the DOS command COPY A+B, the file B will be appended to the end of file A

ajustement *m nom* adjustment

ajuster *verbe* **1.** *vt* to centre **2.** *vt* to fit **3.** *vt* to regulate **4.** *vt* to tune

à la main *adverbe* manually

à la volée *adverbe* on the fly

album *m* **de croquis** *nom* (*Apple Macintosh utility*) scrapbook ◇ **nous conservons le logo dans l'album (de croquis)** we store our logo in the scrapbook

alerte *f* **réseau** *nom* network alert

alerteur *m* **bloqué** *nom* stuck beacon

alerteur *m* **d'évènement** *verbe* to beacon

alerteur *m* **d'incident** *verbe* to beacon

à l'état de repos *adjectif* quiescent

algèbre *f nom* algebra

algèbre *f* **booléen** *nom* Boolean logic

algèbre *f* **booléenne** *nom* Boolean algebra

algèbre *f* **de Boole** *nom* **1.** Boolean algebra **2.** Boolean logic

ALGOL *m nom* ALGOL

algorithme *m nom* **1.** algorithm **2.** hashing function

algorithme *m* **d'ancienneté** *nom* (*des pages de mémoire paginée*) least recently used algorithm ■ *abrév* LRU

algorithme *m* **de chiffrement** *nom* cryptographic algorithm

algorithme *m* **de compression** *nom* compacting algorithm

algorithme *m* **de cryptage** *nom* cryptographic algorithm

algorithme *m* **d'effacement de lignes cachées** *nom* hidden line algorithm

algorithme *m* **de la page la moins récemment utilisée** *nom* least recently used algorithm

algorithme *m* **de pagination** *nom* paging algorithm

algorithmique *adjectif* algorithmic

à l'heure *adverbe* per hour

alias *m nom* alias ◇ **le système d'exploitation utilise l'alias COM1 pour désigner le port série à l'adresse 3FCh** the operating system uses the alias COM1 to represent the serial port address 3FCh

alignement *m nom* alignment ◇ **alignement** *m* **de la tête de lecture** head alignment

alignement *m* **automatique des virgules** *nom* automatic decimal adjustment

alignement *m* **de la tête de lecture** *nom* head alignment

aligner *verbe* **1.** *vt* to align **2.** *vt* to centre **3.** *vt* to range

aligner à gauche *nom* range left

alimentation *nom* **1.** feed **2.** power **3.** power supply **4.** single sheet feed ◇ **alimentation** *f* **de secours de la mémoire** memory backup capacitor ◇ **alimentation** *f* **du papier** paper feed ◇ **alimentation** *f* **feuille à feuille** cut sheet feeder ◇ **bloc d'alimentation** power supply unit (PSU) ◇ **voyant d'alimentation** power LED

'...l'alimentation est assurée par une pile au lithium de 6V ou 4 piles au manganèse de 1,5V' [*Science et Vie*]

alimentation *f* **automatique du papier** *nom* auto advance

alimentation *f* **auxiliaire** *nom* battery backup

alimentation *f* **du papier en continu** *nom* continuous feed

alimentation *f* **feuille à feuille** *nom* sheet feed

alimenter (en courant électrique) *verbe* to power ◇ **l'écran est alimenté par le transformateur du PC principal** the monitor is powered from a supply in the main PC ◇ **(appareil) qui marche** *ou* **qui fonctionne (à l'électricité, etc.)** which is powered (by)

alimenter en papier *abrév* FF ■ *verbe* to form feed

alinéa *m nom* **1.** indent **2.** indentation

aller (de ... à) *verbe* to range ◇ **la gamme des produits de la société va du micro portatif au gros ordinateur multiposte** the company's products range from a cheap lapheld micro to a multistation mainframe

aller à rebours *verbe* **1.** to backtab **2.** to backtrack

allocation *f nom* allocation

allocation *f* **de mémoire** *nom* **1.** memory allocation **2.** storage allocation

allocation *f* **de ressources** *nom* resource allocation

allocation *f* **dynamique** *nom* dynamic allocation

allocation *f* **dynamique de canal** *nom* adaptive channel allocation

allocation *f* **dynamique de la mémoire** *nom* dynamic storage allocation

allouer *verbe* **1.** *vt* to allocate **2.** *vt* to assign ◇ **le système d'exploitation a alloué** *ou* **attribué presque toute la mémoire principale au tableur** the operating system allocated most of main memory to the spreadsheet program

allumer *verbe vt* to power up

ALPHA™ *nom* (*élément d'un processeur développé par Digital Equipment Corporation*) ALPHA

alphabetique ◇ **classer des données en ordre alphabétique** alphasort ◇ **classer des données par ordre alphabétique** alphasort

alphagéométrique *adjectif* alphageometric

alphamosaïque *adjectif* alphamosaic

alphanumérique *adjectif* **1.** alphameric **2.** alphanumeric

alphaphotographique *adjectif* alphaphotographic

alpha *m* **test** *nom* alpha test

alpha test *m nom* alpha ◇ **le nouveau logiciel en est au stade alpha** the new software is still in an alpha product stage ◇ **stade alpha** alpha stage

altération *f nom* distortion

altération *f* **de données** *nom* data corruption

altérer *verbe vt* to corrupt ◇ **une baisse de tension durant l'accès au disque peut altérer** *ou* **corrompre les données** power loss during disk access can corrupt the data

alternance *f nom* alternation

alterner *verbe vi* to alternate

ambiant *adjectif* ambient

ambigu *adjectif* ambiguous

ambiguïté *f nom* ambiguity

âme *f nom* core

amélioration *f nom* enhancement

améliorer *verbe vt* to upgrade

America Online (*fournisseur de service internet le plus grand du monde*) America Online

à mode caractère *adjectif* character-orientated

amorçage *m nom* **1.** booting **2.** boot up

amorçage *m* **à chaud** *nom* warm boot

amorçage *m* **automatique** *nom* auto-boot

amorce *f nom* **1.** bootstrap *ou* bootstrap loader **2.** head ■ *abrév* IPL ■ *nom* leader

amorcer un système *verbe* to boot ◇ **après avoir mis l'ordinateur en route, insérez la disquette de lancement** *ou* **d'amorçage** after you switch on the computer, insert the boot disk

amorce *f* **théorique** *nom* seed

amortir *verbe vt* to deaden ◇ **les capots** *ou* **les hottes d'insonorisation servent à amortir** *ou* **atténuer le bruit des imprimantes** acoustic hoods are used to deaden the noise of printers

amortissement *m nom* decay ◇ **délai d'amortissement d'un signal** decay time ◇ **un amortissement court donne un son très aigu** with a short decay, it sounds very sharp

amovible *adjectif* **1.** exchangeable **2.** movable **3.** removable ◇ **disque dur amovible** exchangeable disk storage (EDS) ◇ **un disque dur amovible** a removable hard disk

ampère *m* **(A)** *nom* **1.** ampere **2.** amp

amplificateur *m nom* amplifier ◇ **amplificateur à faible bruit** low noise amplifier ◇ **amplificateur audio** *ou* **(d')audiofréquence** audio amplifier ◇ **classe d'amplificateur** amplifier class

amplificateur *m* **de ligne** *nom* line driver

amplificateur *m* **de signal** *nom* **1.** line driver **2.** regenerator

amplificateur *m* **intermédiaire** *nom* repeater

amplification *f nom* amplification ◇ **augmentez l'amplification** *ou* **le gain du signal d'entrée** increase the amplification of the input signal ◇ **l'amplification est si grande qu'elle cause une distorsion du signal** the amplification is so high, the signal is distorting

amplifier *verbe vt* to amplify ◇ **le signal reçu doit être amplifié avant d'être traité** the received signal needs to be amplified before it can be processed ◇ **téléphone amplifié** *ou* **à écoute amplifiée** amplified telephone

amplitude *nom* **1.** amplitude **2.** magnitude ◇ **amplitude d'un signal** signal magnitude ◇ **distorsion d'amplitude** amplitude distortion ◇ **modulation d'amplitude (MA)** amplitude modulation (AM)

> '…l'amplitude des échos renvoyés renseigne sur la nature des tissus traversés et l'axe X, sur leur position' [*Techniques hospitalières*]

analogique à digital *adjectif* analog to digital

analogique modulé *adjectif* pseudo-digital

analogique-numérique *adjectif* analog to digital

analogique/numérique *abrév* A/D ■ *adjectif* A to D

analogue *m nom* analog ◇ **appareil analogique** *ou* **dispositif analogique** analog device ◇ **multimètre analogique** analog multimeter (AMM)

analyse *f* **cryptographique** *nom* cryptanalysis

analyse *f* **de données** *nom* data analysis

analyse *f* **de réseau** *nom* network analysis

analyse *f* **de systèmes** *nom* systems analysis

analyse *f* **du chemin critique** *nom* critical path analysis ◇ **méthode du chemin critique** critical path method (CPM)

analyse *f* **du trafic** *nom* (*sur une ligne*) traffic analysis

analyse *f* **lexicale** *nom* lexical analysis

analyse *f* **(de) mémoire** *nom* dump

analyse *f* **numérique** *nom* numerical analysis

analyse *f* **syntaxique** *nom* syntax analysis

analyseur *m nom* **1.** analyser **2.** parser

analyseur *m* **de circuit** *nom* circuit analyser

analyseur *m* **de ligne** *nom* line analyser

analyseur *m* **de réseau** *nom* sniffer

analyseur *m* **d'état de logique** *nom* logic state analyser

analyseur *m* **d'image** *nom* image processor

analyste *m&f nom* analyst

anamorphosé *adjectif* anamorphic

ancrage *m* **(du pointage)** *nom* grid snap

Andorre *abrév* ad

angle *m nom* angle

angle *m* **d'écran** *nom* screen angle

angström *m nom* angstrom

animation *f nom* animation

animation *f* **en temps réel** *nom* real-time animation

animation *f* **image par image** *nom* frame-based animation

animation *f* **sur ordinateur** *nom* computer animation

anneau *nom* **1.** logical ring **2.** ring ◇ **anneau** *m* **de Cambridge** Cambridge ring

anneau *m* **collecteur** *nom* backbone ring

anneau *m* **de contre-rotation** *nom* counter-rotating ring

anneau *m* **de sites** *nom* web ring

annexer *verbe vt* to append ◇ **si vous tapez la commande DOS 'COPY A+B', vous annexé le fichier B au fichier A** *ou* **vous ajoutez le fichier B à la suite du fichier A** if you enter the DOS command COPY A+B, the file B will be appended to the end of file A

annoncer *verbe vt* to announce *ou* to

annonciateur *m nom* annunciator

annotation *f nom* annotation

annotation *f* **typographique** *nom* markup

annuaire *m nom* directory

annulation *f nom* **1.** cancellation **2.** file deletion

annuler *verbe* **1.** *vt* to cancel **2.** *vt* (*commande*) to undo **3.** *vt* to undo ◇ **caractère d'annulation** cancel character (CAN) ◇ **vous venez de supprimer un paragraphe, vous pouvez annuler cette action avec l'option 'annuler' (undo) du menu Edition** you've just deleted the paragraph, but you can undo it from the option in the Edit menu

anode *f nom* anode

anomalie *f nom* error

anonymiseur *m nom* anonymiser *ou* anonymizer

ANSI (*nom de marque*) ANSI

antémémoire *m nom* **1.** cache **2.** RAM cache

antémémoire *m* **d'instructions** *nom* instruction cache

anticrénelage *m nom* dejagging

anti-crénelage *m nom* anti-aliasing

antirebond *m nom* de-bounce

anti-repliement *m nom* anti-aliasing

antislash *m nom* backslash

Apache™ HTTP *nom* Apache™ HTTPD

à panne douce *adjectif* soft-fail

à panne partielle *adjectif* soft-fail

aperçu *m* **avant impression** *nom* **1.** page preview **2.** previewer **3.** print preview ◇ **la fonction intégrée 'aperçu avant impression' permet à l'utilisateur de vérifier s'il s'est glissé des erreurs** the built-in previewer allows the user to check for mistakes

à petite échelle *adjectif* small-scale

à plat *adjectif* flatbed

à plusieurs niveaux *adjectif* multilevel

apparaître ◇ **qui n'apparaît pas sur le texte imprimé** invisible

appareil *m nom* **1.** device **2.** unit ◇ **appareil** *m* **en bon état de marche** functional unit

appareil *m* **analogique** *nom* analog *ou* analogue

appareil *m* **d'entrée/sortie** *nom* I/O device

appareil *m* **dispositif de sortie** *nom* output device

appareil *m* **périphérique** *nom* peripheral equipment

appareil photo *m* **numérique** *nom* digital camera

appareil *m* **simple** *nom* simple device

appel ◇ **appel** *m* **à émettre à tous les terminaux d'un site** site poll ◇ **durée** *f* **d'un appel** call duration ◇ **personne** *f* **qui fait un appel téléphonique** caller

appel *m* **à tonalité multifréquence** *nom* **1.** DTMF **2.** dual tone multi-frequency

appel de contrôle *m* **d'état** *nom* status poll

appel *m* **de fonction** *nom* function call

appel *m* **de macro imbriqué** *nom* nested macro call

appel *m* **de page sur demande** *nom* demand paging

appel *m* **de procédure à distance** *nom* **1.** remote procedure call **2.** RPC

appel *m* **de procédure asynchrone** *abrév* APC ■ *nom* asynchronous procedure call

appel *m* **d'un sous-programme** *nom* subroutine call

appeler *verbe* **1.** *vt* to call up **2.** *vt* to invoke **3.** *vt* to poll ◇ **dès réception d'une entrée, on appelle la première fonction** after an input is received, the first function is called up ◇ **rappelez le fichier précédent à l'écran** call up the previous file

appeler un programme *verbe* to call

appel *m* **récursif** *nom* recursive call

appel *m* **RPC** *nom* **1.** remote procedure call **2.** RPC

appel *m* **sélectif** *nom* polling

appel *m* **sélectif de groupe** *nom* group poll

Apple Computer Corporation (*société qui fabrique des ordinateurs*) Apple Computer Corporation

AppleScript (*nom de marque*) AppleScript

Appleshare (*nom de marque*) Appleshare

applet *m nom* applet

AppleTalk™ (*protocole de communication*) AppleTalk™

application *f nom* application ◇ **application** *f* **pour le système Apple Macintosh HyperCard stackware** (*application for Apple Macintosh HyperCard*) stackware ◇ **application** *f* **qui tolère toutes les erreurs possibles** hazard-free implementation ◇ **circuit intégré spécialisé** *ou* **sur mesure** *ou* **circuit spécifique à une application (ASIC)** application specific integrated circuit (ASIC) ◇ **interface de programmation d'application** *ou* **API** application programming interface (API)

application *f* **active** *nom* active application

application *f* **client** *nom* client application

application *f* **partagée** *ou* **sur serveur** *nom* server-based application

application *f* **propre au réseau** *nom* network-intrinsic application

applications *fpl* **informatiques** *plural noun* computer applications

application *f* **verticale** *nom* vertical application ◇ **votre nouveau progiciel pour gérer une boutique de fleuriste est une bonne application verticale** your new software to manage a florist's is a good vertical application

application *f* **Web** *nom* web application

apprendre (quelque chose) *verbe* to master

apprentissage *m* **assistée par ordinateur** *nom* computer-based training

apprentissage *m* **assisté par ordinateur** *nom* **1.** CAT **2.** CBT **3.** computer-aided training

apprentissage *m* **géré par ordinateur** *abrév* CML ■ *nom* computer-managed learning

approbation *f* **du BABT** *nom* BABT approval

approvisionnement *m* *nom* supply

approvisionner *verbe vt* to supply

appuyer (sur une touche) *verbe* to hit

A propos de... About...

araignée *f nom* (*moteur de recherche*) spider

arbitrage *m* **bus** *nom* bus arbitration

arborescence *f nom* spanning tree

arborescence *f* **chaînée** *nom* threaded tree

arborescence *f* **en puits** *nom* sink tree

arborescence *f* **optimale** *nom* minimal tree

arbre *m nom* tree ◇ **(structure en) arbre** tree structure

arbre *m* **binaire** *nom* **1.** binary tree **2.** btree

arbre *m* **de décision** *nom* decision tree

Archie *nom* Archie

architecture *f nom* **1.** architecture **2.** topology ◇ **architecture** *f* **étendue multimédia** CD-ROM/XA ◇ **architecture** *f* **orientée vers l'objet** object-orientated architecture ◇ **l'architecture en pelure d'oignon de cet ordinateur consiste en un noyau central, une couche système d'exploitation, une couche langage de bas niveau et enfin une couche programmes (d') utilisateur** the onion skin architecture of this computer is made up of a kernel at the centre, an operating system, a low-level language and then the user's programs

architecture *f* **à bus multiples** *nom* multiple bus architecture

architecture *f* **client-serveur** *nom* client-server architecture

architecture *f* **d'échange de documents** *nom* document interchange architecture/document content architecture

architecture *f* **de description de document** *nom* DCA

architecture *f* **de micro-ordinateur** *nom* microcomputer architecture

architecture *f* **de processeur scalaire** (*de Sun Micosystems*) Scalar Processor Architecture ■ *nom* SPARC

architecture *f* **de réseau** *nom* SNA

architecture *f* **de réseau SNA** *nom* Systems Network Architecture

architecture *f* **de système d'application** (*de IBM*) SAA ■ *nom* Systems Application Architecture

architecture *f* **d'ordinateur** *nom* computer architecture

architecture *f* **DPA** *nom* **1.** demand protocol architecture **2.** DPA

architecture *f* **du contenu des documents** *nom* document content architecture

architecture *f* **d'un circuit intégré** *nom* chip architecture

architecture *f* **d'un microprocesseur** *nom* microprocessor architecture

architecture *f* **d'un ordinateur** *nom* computer organisation *ou* computer organization

architecture *f* **d'un réseau** *nom* network architecture

architecture *f* **d'un système** *nom* **1.** computer architecture **2.** computer organisation *ou* computer organization

architecture *f* **en pelure d'oignon** *nom* onion skin architecture ◇ **cet ordinateur possède une architecture en pelure d'oignon comprenant un noyau central, un système d'exploitation, un langage de bas niveau et le programme utilisateur** the onion skin architecture of this computer is made up of a kernel at the centre, an operating system, a low-level language and then the user's program

architecture *f* **en tranches** *nom* bit-slice architecture *ou* bit-slice design ◇ **le processeur en tranches utilise quatre processeurs à 4 bits pour réaliser un processeur à 16 bits** the bit slice design uses four 4-bit word processors to construct a 16-bit processor

architecture *f* **étendue multimédia** *nom* CD-ROM Extended Architecture

architecture *f* **(de bus) ISA** *nom* Industry Standard Architecture

architecture *f* **ISO/OSI** *nom* International Standards Organization Open System Interconnection

architecture *f* **MCA** Micro Channel Architecture

architecture *f* **MIMD** *nom* **1.** MIMD **2.** multiple instruction stream-multiple data stream

architecture *f* **MISD** *nom* **1.** MISD **2.** multiple instruction stream-multiple data stream

architecture *f* **multiflux d'instruction – monoflux de données** *nom* **1.** MISD **2.** multiple instruction stream-single data stream

architecture *f* **multiflux d'instruction – multiflux de données** *nom* **1.** MIMD **2.** multiple instruction stream-multiple data stream

architecture *f* **orientée vers l'objet** *nom* object architecture

architecture *f* **ouverte** *nom* open architecture

architecture *f* **SIMD** *nom* **1.** SIMD **2.** single instruction stream multiple data stream

architecture *f* **SISD** *nom* **1.** single instruction stream single data stream **2.** SISD

architecture *f* **SNA** *nom* SNA

architecture *f* **SPARC** (*de Sun Micosystems*) Scalar Processor Architecture ■ *nom* SPARC

archivage *m* **sur ordinateur** *nom* electronic filing

archiver *verbe vt* to archive

archives *f nom* archive

ARCnet *nom* attached resource computer network

à recherche logique *adjectif* logic-seeking

arête *f* **dorsale** *nom* backbone

argument *m nom* **1.** arg **2.** argument

argument *m* **décisif** *nom* deciding factor

argument *m* **de ligne de commande** *nom* command line argument

arithmétique *f* **à modulo** *nom* modulo arithmetic

arithmétique *f* **à virgule fixe** *nom* fixed-point arithmetic

arithmétique *f* **externe** *nom* external arithmetic

arithmétique *f* **interne** *nom* internal arithmetic

armer *verbe vt* to arm

arrangement *m* **binaire** *nom* bit pattern

arrêt *m nom* **1.** halt **2.** termination ◇ **arrêt** *m* **dû à une défaillance de l'appareil** machine check

arrêt *m* **anormal** *nom* abend

arrêt *m* **automatique** *nom* auto stop

arrêt *m* **conditionnel** *nom* conditional breakpoint

arrêt *m* **de l'impression** *nom* print pause

arrêt *m* **désordonné** *nom* disorderly close-down

arrêt *m* **dynamique** *nom* dynamic stop

arrêter *verbe* **1.** *vt* to abort **2.** *vt* to close **3.** *vt* to inhibit **4.** *vt* to shut down ◇ **interrompez** *ou* **arrêtez l'exécution du programme, avant qu'il efface d'autres fichiers** abort the program before it erases any more files

arrêt *m* **inattendu** *nom* hangup

arrêt *m* **pour manque de papier** *nom* form stop

arrêt *m* **programmé** *nom* programmed halt

arrêts *mpl* **de tabulation** *plural noun* tabulation stops

arrêt *m* **total** *nom* **1.** dead halt **2.** drop dead halt

arrière-guichet *m nom* back office

arrière-plan *m nom* background ◇ **le nouveau processeur graphique permet de manipuler indépendamment les images d'arrière-plan et d'avant-plan ainsi que les plans-objets** the new graphics processor chip can handle background, foreground and sprite movement independently

arrondi *m* **au plus près** *nom* rounding

arrondir par défaut *verbe* to truncate ◇ **3,5678 tronqué** *ou* **arrondi par défaut à 3,56** 3.5678 truncated to 3.56

arrondissement *m nom* rounding

arrondissement *m* **de caractère** *nom* character rounding

arséniure *m* **de gallium** *nom* gallium arsenide

artefact *m nom* **1.** artefact *ou* artifact **2.** artifact

article *m nom* **1.** article **2.** record ◇ **articles** *mpl* **dans un fichier** record count ◇ **il a écrit, pour le journal local, un article concernant le groupe d'utilisateurs** he wrote an article about the user group for the local newspaper ◇ **votre article** *ou* **enregistrement contient divers champs regroupés sous une même rubrique** your record contains several fields that have been grouped together under the one heading

articles *mpl* **de consommation** *plural noun* consumables ◇ **il faut inclure les câbles pour imprimantes et le papier sous la rubrique 'consommables'** put all the printer leads and paper under the heading 'consumables'

ascenseur *m nom* elevator

ASCII *nom* **1.** American Standard Code for Information Interchange **2.** ASCII

à semi-conducteur *adjectif* solid-state ◇ **laser transistorisé** *ou* **à semi-conducteur** solid-state laser

assemblage *m nom* **1.** assembly **2.** character assembly **3.** linking

assemblage *m* **adaptatif de paquets** *nom* adaptive packet assembly

assembler *verbe* **1.** *vt* to assemble **2.** *vt* to join ◇ **des erreurs de syntaxe repérées au cours de l'assemblage du programmme source** syntax errors spotted whilst the source program is being assembled ◇ **il y a un certain délai pendant lequel s'effectue l'assemblage en code objet du programme** there is a short wait during which time the program is assembled into object code ◇ **les pièces de l'unité de disque sont fabriquées au Japon, mais l'assemblage se fait en France** the parts for the disk drive are made in Japan and assembled in France

assembler un programme *verbe* to assemble

assembleur *m nom* **1.** assembler **2.** assembler program **3.** language assembler **4.** original equipment manufacturer

assembleur *m* **absolu** *nom* absolute assembler

assembleur *m* **croisé** *nom* cross-assembler

assembleur/désassembleur *m* **(de paquets)** *nom* packet assembler/disassembler

assembleur-désassembleur *m* **de paquets** *abrév* PAD

assembleur *m* **deux passes** *nom* two-pass assembler

assembleur *m* **macro** *nom* macro assembler *ou* macro assembly program

assembleur *m* **une passe** *nom* **1.** one-pass assembler **2.** single-pass assembler ◇ **ce nouvel assembleur une passe travaille très vite** this new one-pass assembler is very quick in operation

assembleuse *f nom* collator

assertion *f nom* assertion

asservi aux codes CTRL *adjectif* (*générés par la touche contrôle*) control-driven

assigner *verbe vt* to assign

assigner à *verbe* to assign

assistance *f* ◇ backup

assistance *f* **technique** *nom* technical support

assistance *f* **technique pour un système** *nom* system support

assistant *m* **numérique personnel** *nom* personal digital assistant

assistant *m* **personnel de communication (APC)** *nom* PDA

assistant *m* **virtuel** *nom* virtual assistant

assisté,-ée par ordinateur *adjectif* computer-aided

assisté par ordinateur *adjectif* computer-assisted

association *f* **de sécurité** *nom* Ipsec *ou* IP Security

association *f* **française de normalisation (AFNOR)** *nom* **1.** American National Standards Institute **2.** British Standards Institute

Association *f* **française de normalisation (AFNOR)** *abrév* BSI

associer *verbe vt* to bind

assortir *verbe vt* to match

assourdir *verbe vt* to deaden

assurance *f* **qualité dans le domaine du génie logiciel** *nom* software quality assurance

assurance *f* **qualité logiciel** *abrév* SQA

astérisque *m nom* asterisk

asynchrone *adjectif* **1.** async **2.** asynchronous **3.** unclocked ◇ **appel de procédure asynchrone** asynchronous procedure call (APC) ◇ **commutation temporelle asynchrone** asynchronous transfer mode (ATM) ◇ **interface pour communication asynchrone** asynchronous communications device interface (ACDI); asynchronous communications interface adapter (ACIA) ◇ **mode asynchrone équilibré** asynchronous balanced mode (ABM) ◇ **mode asynchrone équilibré étendu** asynchronous balanced mode extended (ABME) ◇ **mode de transfert asynchrone** *ou* **mode ATM** asynchronous transfer mode (ATM) ◇ **serveur de communication asynchrone** asynchronous communications server (ACS)

ATA Fast *nom* ATA Fast

ATAPI *abrév* ATAPI

ATD *nom* ATD

atelier *m* **de reliure** *nom* Bindery

atelier *m* **flexible** *nom* **1.** flexible manufacturing system **2.** FMS

Athlon XP (*nom de marque*) Athlon XP

à titre d'information *nom* FYI

ATM (*nom de marque*) Adobe Type Manager

à tolérance de panne *adjectif* fault-tolerant

atome *nom* atom

'...dans un atome, la plupart des électrons tournent autour du noyau et leur mouvement de rotation suffit encore à engendrer un champ magnétique' [*Science et Vie*]

atomique *adjectif* atomic

à *f* **touches** *adjectif* pushbutton

atouts *mpl plural noun* assets

à trois dimensions *adjectif* **1.** 3D **2.** three-dimensional

attaque *f nom* attack ◇ **enveloppe d'attaque** attack envelope

attaque *f* **par saturation** *nom* denial-of-service attack

atteindre un niveau maximum *verbe* to peak ◇ **la tension a atteint le niveau maximum de 1200 volts** the power peaked at 1,200 volts

attente *f nom* waiting state

atténuation *nom* attenuation ◇ **atténuation** *f* **de signal par perte d'alignement** gap loss ◇ **avec un câble trop long, l'atténuation du signal provoquera des erreurs de données** if the cable is too long, the signal attenuation will start to cause data errors

'...le taux d'atténuation des signaux, compris entre 50 et 200 décibels par kilomètre, est encore trop élevé' [*Informatique et bureautique*]

atténuer *verbe vt* to deaden ◇ **les capots** *ou* **les hottes d'insonorisation servent à amortir** *ou* **atténuer le bruit des imprimantes** acoustic hoods are used to deaden the noise of printers

atterrissage ◇ **atterrissage** *m* **de la tête de lecture** head crash

attractif *adjectif* sticky

attractivité *f nom* stickiness

attribuer *verbe vt* to allocate ◇ **le système d'exploitation a alloué** *ou* **attribué presque toute la mémoire principale au tableur** the operating system allocated most of main memory to the spreadsheet program

attribut *m nom* attribute ◇ **cet attribut contrôle la couleur de l'écran** this attribute controls the colour of the screen

attribut *m* **d'archivage** *nom* archive attribute *ou* archive bit

attribut *m* **d'écran** *nom* **1.** display attribute **2.** screen attribute

attribut *m* **de fichier** *plural noun* file attribute

attribution *f nom* allocation ◇ **attribution de bandes de fréquences** *ou* **de longueurs**

d'ondes band allocation ◇ **la nouvelle attribution de bandes de fréquences permettra d'avoir un plus grand nombre de canaux de transmission** the new band allocation means we will have more channels

attribut *m* **lecture seule** *nom* read only attribute

attributs *mpl nom* (*d'un fichier, d'un objet*) properties

attributs *mpl* **programmables** *plural noun* selectable attributes

attribut *m* **système** *nom* system attribute

audible *adjectif* audible

audio *adjectif* audio

audit *m* **informatique** *nom* audit

augmentation *f nom* increment

augmenter *verbe* **1.** *vt* to ascend **2.** *vt* to increment ◇ **le compteur est incrémenté à chaque instruction exécutée** the counter is incremented each time an instruction is executed

augmenter l'échelle *verbe* to scale up

au même niveau *adjectif* flush

à une pile de secours *adjectif* battery-backed ◇ **dans ce portable, le lecteur de disquettes est remplacé par une mémoire CMOS dont le fonctionnement est assuré par une pile auxiliaire** battery-backed CMOS memory replaces a disk drive in this portable ◇ **la carte RAM peut être équipée, en option, d'une pile de secours** the RAM disk card has the option to be battery-backed

au niveau binaire *adverbe* bitwise

auquel on peut se fier *adjectif* reliable

au repos *adjectif* **1.** idle **2.** quiescent

auteur *m nom* author

authentification *f* **de messages** *nom* authentication of messages

auto- *préfixe* self-

autobalayage *m nom* auto scan

autocommutateur *m* **privatif (raccordé au réseau public)** *nom* private branch exchange

autocommutateur *m* **privé** *abrév* PBX

autocorrecteur *adjectif* self-correcting

autodiagnostic *m nom* self-diagnostic

autoexec.bat *nom* AUTOEXEC.BAT

automatique *adjectif* hands off

autonome *adverbe, adjectif* off-line

autonomie *f* **des données** *nom* data independence

autopsie *f nom* post mortem

autorépondeur *m nom* autoresponder

auto-réponse *f nom* auto-answer

autorisation *f nom* authorisation *ou* authorization

autorisation *f nom* clearance ◇ **vous n'avez pas l'autorisation d'accéder à ce processeur** you do not have the required clearance for this processor

autorisation *f* **d'accès** *nom* **1.** access authority **2.** permission

autorisation *f* **de copie (d'un logiciel)** *nom* software licence

autorisation *f* **de copier** *nom* **1.** ATC **2.** authorisation to copy

autorisation *f* **de dupliquer** *nom* **1.** ATC **2.** authorisation to copy

autorisation *f* **en temps réel** *nom* real-time authorisation *ou* real-time authentication

autorisé *adjectif* legal

autorité *f* **de certification** *abrév* CA ■ *nom* certificate authority

autotest *m nom* automatic checking

autotest *m* **à la mise sous tension** *nom* power on self test

A/UX (*nom de marque*) A/UX

auxiliaire *(m&f) nom* **1.** auxiliary **2.** backing ■ *adjectif, nom* backup ■ *adjectif* standby ■ *nom* standby

avalanche *f nom* avalanche ◇ **photodiode à avalanche** avalanche photodiode (APD)

à valeur ajoutée *adjectif* value-added ◇ **réseau à valeur ajoutée** *ou* **réseau à intégration de service (RIS)** value-added network (VAN) ◇ **revendeur à valeur ajoutée** *ou* **revendeur à intégration de service** value-added reseller (VAR)

avancé *adjectif* **1.** sophisticated **2.** state-of-the-art ◇ **un programme de PAO évolué** *ou* **avancé** a sophisticated desktop publishing program

avance *f* **rapide de papier** *nom* slew

avancer d'un pas *verbe* **1.** to increment **2.** to step

avance *f* **technologique** *nom* sophistication

avantages *mpl plural noun* assets

avatar *m nom* avatar

avec alimentation automatique de papier *adjectif* paper-fed

avec configuration invalidée *adjectif* configured-off *ou* configured-out

avec configuration multimédia *adjectif* multimedia-ready

avec configuration validée *adjectif* configured-in

avec connexion *adjectif* connection-oriented

avec contrainte de vitesse du processeur *adjectif* processor-limited

avec dessins *adjectif* patterned

avec fonction courrier *adjectif* mail-enabled

avec motifs *adjectif* patterned

avec toutes les options *adjectif* fully-populated

avec un marqueur d'énumération *adjectif* bulleted

avertir *verbe vt* to warn ◇ **il a averti les opérateurs de saisie d'une surcharge possible du système** he warned the keyboarders that the system might become overloaded

avertisseur *m* **(sonore)** *nom* howler

aveugle *adjectif* blind

avis *m* **de réception** *nom* receipt notification

avis *m* **de série V** *nom* V series ◇ **norme V22 bis (transmission en duplex à 1200 bits par seconde en émission et réception)** V.22 BIS ◇ **norme V23 (transmission en semi-duplex à 75 bits par seconde en émission et 1200 bits par seconde en réception)** V.23 ◇ **norme V24 (circuits d'échange entre système central et terminal)** V.24 ◇ **norme V25 bis (équipement d'appel et de réponse automatique sur le réseau public commuté)** V.25 BIS ◇ **norme V26 (transmission à 2400 bits par seconde sur des lignes louées)** V.26 ◇ **norme V26 bis (transmission en semi-duplex à 2400 bits par seconde en émission et 1200 bits par seconde en réception sur le réseau public commuté)** V.26 BIS ◇ **norme V26 ter (transmission en duplex à 2400 bits par seconde en émission et 1200 bits par seconde en réception sur le réseau public commuté)** V.26 TER ◇ **norme V27 (modem à 4800 bits par seconde sur lignes louées)** V.27 ◇ **norme V27 bis (transmission à 4800 bits par seconde en émission et 2400 bits par seconde en réception sur lignes louées)** V.27 BIS ◇ **norme V27 ter (transmission à 4800 bits par seconde en émission et 2400 bits par seconde en réception sur le réseau public commuté)** V.27 TER ◇ **norme V32 terbo (pseudo-norme mise au point par AT&T, et autres, qui permet une transmission à 19200 bits par seconde)** V.32terbo ◇ **norme V42 bis (compression de données avec contrôle d'erreurs V42)** V.42 BIS

avoir accès à *verbe* to access

avoir lieu *verbe* to occur

axe *m nom* **1.** axis **2.** spindle

axe *m nom* axis

axe *m* **d'abscisse** *nom* x-axis

axe *m* **de l'ordonnée** *nom* y-axis

axe *m* **des abscisses** *nom* horizontal axis

axe *m* **des ordonnées** *nom* vertical axis

axe *m* **des X** *nom* x-axis

axe *m* **des Y** *nom* y-axis

axe *m* **des Z** *nom* z-axis

azimut *m nom* azimuth

B

b *abrév* b

B *abrév* B ■ *symbole* B

B: (*lecteur de disque*) B:

bac *m* **à feuilles** *nom* bin ◇ **bac inférieur** (*pour papier d'une imprimante*) lower bin ◇ **bac supérieur** (*de papier d'imprimante*) upper bin ◇ **corbeille** recycle bin

bac *m* **à papier** *nom* **1.** bin **2.** paper tray

bac *m* **d'alimentation pour enveloppes** *nom* envelope feeder

bac *m* **de recyclage** *nom* Recycle Bin ◇ **pour détruire un fichier ou un dossier, traînez-le jusqu'à l'icône 'corbeille' ou encore appuyez sur la touche 'supprimer'** if you want to delete a file or folder, drag it onto the Recycle Bin icon or press the Delete key

backbone *m* *nom* backbone ring

BACKUP *nom* BACKUP ◇ **ce programme permet aux utilisateurs de sauvegarder les fichiers du disque dur en une seule opération** the program enables users to back up hard disk files with a single command ◇ **la comptabilité de la société a été sauvegardée sur disque en cas d'incendie** the company accounts were backed up on disk as a protection against fire damage

badauder *verbe vi* to lurk

bague *f* **d'autorisation d'écriture** *nom* write-permit ring

baie *f* *nom* **1.** bay **2.** drive bay

baie *f* **(pour cartes)** *nom* frame

baie *f* **avec guide-cartes** *nom* rack ◇ **(carte) montée dans un rack** *ou* **dans une baie avec guide-cartes** rack-mounted

bail *m* **(de location)** *nom* lease

baisse *f* *nom* brown-out

baisser *verbe vt* to fade

balayage *m* *nom* **1.** scan **2.** scanning ◇ **balayage de trame** raster scanning ◇ **dispositif de lecture par balayage** scanning device ◇ **la vitesse de lecture par balayage est de 1,3 pouces par seconde** throughput is 1.3 inches per second scanning speed ◇ **un balayage a fait apparaître les données périmées** the scan revealed which records were now out of date

balayage *m* **d'écran** *nom* television scan

balayage *m* **dirigé** *nom* directed scan

balayage *m* **en dehors des limites** *nom* overscan

balayage *m* **entrelacé** *nom* interlaced scanning

balayage *m* **hors champ** *nom* overscan

balayage *m* **progressif** *nom* progressive scanning

balisage *m* *nom* flagging

balise *f* *nom* **1.** carry bit **2.** flag **3.** indicator flag

baliser *verbe vt* to flag

banc *m* **d'essai** *nom* **1.** benchmark **2.** test bed

bande *nom* band ◇ **bande** *f* **vierge** blank tape ◇ **n'utilisez jamais un modem en bande de base sur une ligne téléphonique normale** do not use a base band modem with a normal phone line ◇ **téléphone bibande** two-band telephone

> '...la bande de fréquence destinée à la radiodiffusion par satellite est la bande des 12 GHz' [*Electronique Radio Plans*]

bandeau *m* **publicitaire** *nom* banner *ou* banner advertisement *ou* banner ad

bande *f* **de base** *nom* baseband *ou* base band ◇ **les réseaux locaux en bande de base peuvent avoir des longueurs de câbles d'environ 300m au maximum** base band local area networks can support a maximum cable length of around 300m ◇ **réseau local en bande de base** baseband local area network

bande *f* **de fréquence intercalaire** *nom* guard band

bande *f* **de mouvements** *nom* change tape

bande *f* **de protection** *nom* guard band

bande *f* **de texte non formaté** *nom* unjustified tape

bande *f* **de travail** *nom* scratch tape

bande *f* **idiote** *nom* unjustified tape

bande *f* **latérale résiduelle** *nom* **1.** vestigial side band **2.** VSB

bande *f* **magnétique** *nom* **1.** cassette tape **2.** magnetic tape **3.** mag tape

bande *f* **multipiste** *nom* band

bande *f* **originale** *nom* **1.** magnetic master **2.** master tape

bande *f* **papier** *nom* **1.** paper tape **2.** punched tape

bande *f* **papier perforée** *nom* punched tape *ou* punched paper tape

bande *f* passante *nom* bandwidth ◇ **bande passante** telephone bandwidth is 3100Hz ◇ **la bande passante de câble à fibres optiques est plus étendue que celle des anciens câbles en cuivre et peut transmettre les données à des vitesses plus grandes** this fibre-optic cable has a greater bandwidth than the old copper cable and so it can carry data at higher speeds

bande *f* perforée *nom* **1.** perforated tape **2.** punched tape

bande *f* sans paramètres d'impression *nom* unjustified tape

bande *f* vidéo *nom* video tape

bandothèque *f nom* tape library

bannière *f nom* marquee

banque *nom* bank

'...le petit disque (CD-ROM) permet aux professionnels d'accéder à des banques de données tout en restant dans l'environnement bureautique' [*Micro Systèmes*]

banque *f* de canaux *nom* channel bank

banque *f* de données *nom* **1.** databank **2.** information retrieval centre

banque *f* de mémoire *nom* memory bank ◇ **une carte d'extension possède une banque de mémoire de 128Ko constituée de 16 puces** an add-on card has a 128KB memory bank made up of 16 chips

banque *f* virtuelle *nom* Internet banking

barette *f* de mémoire de type SIMM *nom* SIMM

baril *m nom* barrel

barre *f nom* bar ◇ **barre de menu** menu bar

barre *f* de défilement *nom* scroll bar ◇ **je sais ainsi que je suis au milieu du document** the marker is in the middle of the scroll bar so I know I am in the middle of the document

barre *f* de défilement horizontal *nom* horizontal scrollbar

barre *f* de menu *nom* action bar

barre *f* de sélection *nom* (*du menu*) highlight bar

barre *f* d'espacement *nom* space bar

barre *f* des tâches *nom* **1.** Desktop taskbar **2.** taskbar

barre *f* d'état *nom* status bar

barre *f* de titre *nom* title bar

barre *f* d'outils *nom* **1.** button bar **2.** toolbar

barre *f* oblique *nom* slash

barre *f* oblique inverse (\) *nom* backslash

barre *f* omnibus *nom* bus bar

barrette *f* de connexion du terminal *nom* terminal strip

barrette *f* de type SIP *nom* single in-line package

bas *m nom* foot ◇ **il a signé au bas de la lettre** he signed his name at the foot of the letter

bascule ◇ **bascule *f* de type JK** JK-flip-flop

basculement *m nom* context-switching ◇ **basculement *m* (de programme)** swap

basculement *m nom* (*de programme*) swapping

basculer *verbe* **1.** *vi* to swap **2.** *vi* to toggle

basculer (des données) *verbe* to exchange

bas *m* de casse *nom* lower case

bas *m* de gamme *adjectif* low-end

base *f nom* **1.** base **2.** foot ◇ **base *f* de la pile** stack base

base *f* 2 *nom* base 2

base *f* 8 *nom* **1.** base 8 **2.** octal scale

base *f* 10 *nom* base 10

base *f* 16 *nom* base 16

base *f* binaire *nom* base 2

base *f* d'adressage *nom* address base

base *f* décimale *nom* base 10

base *f* de connaissances *nom* knowledge base

base *f* de données *nom* database ◇ **responsable de base de données** database administrator (DBA)

base *f* de données active *nom* active database

base *f* de données à structure de champs libre *nom* free form database

base *f* de données de réseau *nom* network database

base *f* de données des adresses et des domaines (dans Internet) *nom* domain name system

base *f* de données en ligne *nom* online database

base *f* de données hiérarchisées *nom* hierarchical database

base *f* de données intégrée *nom* integrated database

base *f* de données linéaire *nom* (*non relationnelle*) flat file database

base *f* de données physique *nom* physical database

base *f* de données relationnelle *nom* **1.** plex database **2.** relational database *ou* relational database management system

base *f* de données Whois *nom* whois

base *f* de numération *nom* radix ◇ **le nombre hexadécimal est à base 16** the hexadecimal number has a radix of 16

base *f* de registre *nom* Registry

base *f* de temps *nom* time base

base *f* de temps réduite *nom* fast time-scale

base *f* de transmission *nom* base station

base *f* hexadécimale *nom* base 16

base *f* horaire TMSF *nom* **1.** TMSF time format **2.** tracks, minutes, seconds, frames time format

base *f* **octale** *nom* base 8

basse *f* **définition** *nom* low resolution

BAT *nom* BAT

batterie *f* **au lithium-ion** *nom* lithium-Ion battery

batterie *f* **au nickel-cadmium** *nom* NiCad

batterie *f* **au nickel-méta-hydrure** *nom* NiMH

batterie *f* **de mémoire de type SIMM** *nom* single in-line memory module

batterie *f* **de serveurs** *nom* server farm

baud *nom* baud

'...même si un bps n'est pas un baud (unité de mesure de la vitesse de modulation, et non du débit), on parle parfois de baud à la place de bps' [*Mon PC Multimédia*]

bavure *f nom* bleed

benchmark *m* **Dhrystone** *nom* Dhrystone benchmark

besoins *mpl plural noun* requirements

bibliothèque *f nom* library ◇ **consultez le catalogue de la bibliothèque pour obtenir les renseignements bibliographiques** look up the bibliographical details in the library catalogue ◇ **les éditeurs ont vérifié toutes les références à la bibliothèque locale** the editors have checked all the references in the local library

bibliothèque *f* **de bandes** *nom* tape library

bibliothèque *f* **de fonctions** *nom* function library

bibliothèque *f* **de graphismes** *nom* graphics library

bibliothèque *f* **de liens** *nom* Bindery

bibliothèque *f* **de logiciels** *nom* **1.** program library **2.** software library

bibliothèque *f* **de macros** *nom* macro library

bibliothèque *f* **de programmes** *nom* **1.** program library **2.** software library

bibliothèque *f* **de programmes d'entrée/sortie** *nom* input/output library

bibliothèque *f* **des routines d'applications** *nom* run-time library

bibliothèque *f* **DLL** *nom* dynamic link library

bibliothèque *f* **d'un système** *nom* system library

bibliothèque *f* **dynamique de liens** *nom* dynamic link library

bibliothèque *f* **dynamique des liens** *nom* DLL

bibliothèque *f* **graphique** *nom* graphics library

bibliothèque *f* **Winsock** *nom* **1.** socket driver **2.** Winsock

bidimensionnel *adjectif* two-dimensional

bidirectionnel à l'alternat *nom* HD ■ *abrév* HDX

bidirectionnel *m* **simultané** *abrév* fdx *ou* FDX ■ *nom* full duplex

biffure *f nom* strikethrough

bifurcation *f* **logique** *nom* switch

binaire *adjectif* binary ◇ **arbre binaire** binary tree (btree) ◇ **communication synchrone binaire** binary synchronous communications (BSC) ◇ **dans un mot à quatre bits, l'échelle binaire est 1,2,4,8** in a four bit word, the binary scale is 1,2,4,8 ◇ **les instructions du programme sont stockées dans le fichier binaire** the program instructions are stored in the binary file ◇ **nombre binaire** binary number ◇ **votre lettre est un fichier texte et non pas un fichier binaire** your letter is a text file, not a binary file

'...ces tensions sont ensuite codées en numération binaire: 011 pour 3 volts, 101 pour 5 volts, etc.' [*Science et Vie*]

binauralité *f nom* binaural sound

BIND *nom* BIND

binette *f nom* smiley

BinHex *nom* BinHex

bio-ordinateur *m nom* biocomputer

BIOS *m nom* BIOS

bipolaire *adjectif* bipolar ◇ **transistor à jonction bipolaire** bipolar junction transistor (BJT)

bistable *adjectif* bistable

bit *abrév* b ■ *nom* **1.** binary **2.** binary bit **3.** binary digit **4.** bit **5.** bit **6.** start bit **7.** start element ◇ **bit de poids (le plus) faible** least significant bit (LSB) ◇ **bit de poids (le plus) fort** *ou* **bit significatif** most significant bit (MSB) ◇ **bits** *mpl* **de description de couleur** colour bits ◇ **bit significatif** significant bit ◇ **bits par pixel** bits per pixel (BPP) ◇ **(nombre de) bits par pouce** bits per inch (bpi) ◇ **(nombre de) bits par seconde (bps)** bits per second (bps) ◇ **la recherche du sixième bit d'un octet contenant un caractère ASCII détermine si le bit significatif indique un caractère en majuscule ou en minuscule** testing bit six of a byte containing an ASCII character is bit significant and determines if the ASCII character is upper or lower case ◇ **leur débit est de 60 000 bits par seconde sur une liaison parallèle** their transmission rate is 60,000 bits per second (bps) through a parallel connection

'...sur une surface de 1 centimètre carré, ils savent faire tenir 100 (cent) millions de bits ou unités de base d'information, 1 ou 0 par exemple' [*Le Point*]

bit *m* **d'archivage** *nom* archive attribute *ou* archive bit

bit *m* **d'arrêt** *nom* **1.** stop bit **2.** stop element

bit *m* **de code** *nom* code bit

bit *m* **de contrôle** *nom* **1.** check bit **2.** service bit

bit *m* **de parité** *nom* parity bit

bit *m* **de poids faible** *nom* **1.** least significant bit **2.** LSB

bit *m* **de poids fort** *nom* **1.** most significant bit **2.** msb *ou* MSB **3.** weighted bit

bit *m* **de protection** *nom* **1.** bozo bit **2.** guard bit

bit *m* **de report** *nom* carry bit

bit *m* **de signe** *nom* **1.** sign bit **2.** sign indicator

bit *m* **de synchro** *nom* sync bit

bit *m* **d'état** *nom* status bit

bit *m* **indicateur** *ou* **indicateur binaire** *nom* flag bit

bit *m* **le moins significatif** *nom* **1.** least significant bit **2.** LSB

bit *m* **le plus significatif** *nom* most significant bit ◇ **le bit le plus significatif dans un mot de huit bits représente 128 en numération décimale** the most significant bit in an eight bit binary word represents 128 in decimal notation

bit *m* **lourd** *nom* weighted bit

bitmap *m nom* bitmap

bit *m* **marqué** *nom* dirty bit

bit *m* **masque** *nom* mask bit

BitNet *m nom* BitNet

bits *mpl* **par pixel** *nom* **1.** bits per pixel **2.** BPP

bits *mpl* **par pouce** *nom* **1.** bits per inch **2.** BPI *ou* bpi

bits *mpl* **par seconde** *nom* **1.** bits per second **2.** bps **3.** bps rate ◇ **leur débit est de 60 000 bits par seconde sur une liaison parallèle** their transmission rate is 60,000 bits per second (bps) through a parallel connection

bit *m* **supplémentaire** *nom* overhead bit

BIX *nom* BIX

blanchir *verbe vt* to wipe ◇ **si vous reformatez, vous détruirez toutes les données du disque** *ou* **vous blanchirez le disque** by reformatting you will wipe the disk clean

blindage *m nom* RF shielding

blindage *m nom* shield

blinder *verbe vt* to shield ◇ **câble en paires torsadées blindé** shielded twisted pair (STP) cable ◇ **câble en paires torsadées non blindé** *ou* **sans blindage** unshielded twisted pair (UTP) cable

bloc *m nom* **1.** bank **2.** block **3.** boot block **4.** boot record **5.** frame ◇ **bloc** *m* **d'enfichage** (*de câble de réseau local*) punch-down block

blocage *m nom* lock up

bloc *m* **d'alimentation** *nom* **1.** power pack **2.** PSU

bloc *m* **de bits** *nom* bit block

bloc *m* **de caractères** *nom* character block

bloc *m* **de données** *nom* data block

bloc *m* **de données de contrôle** *nom* control block

bloc *m* **d'entrée** *nom* input block

bloc-diagramme *m nom* block diagram

bloc *m* **d'identification** *nom* **1.** header **2.** header block

bloc-notes *m nom* **1.** notepad **2.** scratchpad

bloc-notes *m* **d'écran** *nom* screen notepad

bloc *m* **paragraphe** *nom* (*de mémoire*) paragraph

blogage *m nom* blogging

blogosphère *f nom* blogosphere

blogue *m nom* **1.** blog **2.** weblog

blogueur *m nom* blogger

Blue Book Ethernet *nom* Blue Book Ethernet

Bluetooth (*nom de marque*) Bluetooth

BNF étendu *nom* extended Backus-Naur-Form *ou* extended BNF

bobine *f nom* spool

bobine *f* **acoustique** *nom* voice coil

bobine *f* **d'enroulement** *nom* **1.** pickup reel **2.** take-up reel

bobine *f* **de réception** *nom* take-up reel

bobine *f* **d'induction** *nom* **1.** choke **2.** inductor

bobine *f* **ouverte** *nom* open reel ◇ **bande sur bobine ouverte** open reel tape

bobine *f* **réceptrice** *nom* **1.** pickup reel **2.** take-up reel

bogue *m&f nom* bug

bogue *m&f* **de l'an 2000** *nom* millennium bug

boîte *f nom* wiring closet

boîte *f* **à outils** *nom* **1.** toolbox **2.** Toolbox

boîte *f* **à outils Macintosh** *nom* **1.** toolbox **2.** Toolbox

boîte *f* **aux lettres électronique** *nom* electronic mailbox

boîte *f* **aux messages électroniques** *nom* mailbox *ou* mail box

boîte *f* **de cristal pour CD** *nom* CD caddy

boîte *f* **de dialogue** *nom* dialog box

boîte *f* **de jonction** *nom* junction box

boîte *f* **de liste** *nom* drop-down list box

boîte *f* **de listes** *nom* combo box

boîte *f* **de message** *nom* message box

Boîte *f* **de réception** *nom* InBox

boîte *f* **noire** *nom* black box

boîtier *m nom* **1.** caddy **2.** housing ◇ **quand on a laissé tomber l'ordinateur, son boîtier s'est abîmé** the computer housing was damaged when it fell on the floor

boîtier *m* **à simple rangée de connexions** *abrév* SIP

boîtier *m* **de câblage intelligent** *nom* intelligent wiring hub

boîtier *m* **plat** *nom* flat pack

boîtier *m* **pour cartes d'extension** *nom* expansion box

boîtier *m* **pour CD** *nom* CD caddy

bombe *f nom* bomb
bombe *f* **logique** *nom* **1.** logic bomb **2.** time bomb
bond *m nom* hop
bord *m nom* edge
bord *m* **avant** *nom* leading edge
bord *m* **d'alignement** *nom* aligning edge
bord *m* **de référence** *nom* aligning edge
bord *m* **d'introduction** *nom* leading edge
bordereau *m nom* form
bordure *f nom* **1.** border **2.** edge
bordure *f* **d'écran** *nom* screen border
borne *f nom* terminal
borne *f* **d'entrée** *nom* source
borne *f* **de raccordement** *nom* **1.** barrel **2.** terminal ◇ **bloc de raccordement** terminal block
borne *f* **interactive** *nom* kiosk
borne *f* **positive** *nom* positive terminal
bornes *fpl* **d'un tableau** *plural noun* array bounds
boucle *f nom* loop ◇ **boucle** *f* **avec retour automatique à zéro** self-restoring loop ◇ **film en boucle** loop film ◇ **réseau en anneau** *ou* **en boucle** loop network
boucle *f* **analogique** *nom* analog loopback ◇ **boucle analogique avec autotest** analog loopback with selftest
boucle *f* **avec retour automatique aux paramètres de départ** *nom* self-resetting loop
boucle *f* **avec retour automatique à zéro** *nom* self-resetting loop
boucle *f* **conditionnelle FOR...NEXT** *nom* for-next loop ◇ **pour X=1 à 5: imprimer X: calculer la valeur suivante de X – le résultat imprimé sera 1 2 3 4 5** for X=1 to 5: print X: next X – this will print out 1 2 3 4 5
boucle *f* **conditionnelle 'WHILE'** *nom* while-loop
boucle *f* **continue** *nom* endless loop
boucle *f* **d'attente** *nom* wait loop
boucle *f* **de correction** *nom* loopback
boucle *f* **de fond** *nom* **1.** looping program **2.** loop program
boucle *f* **de maintien** *nom* holding loop
boucle *f* **de modification** *nom* modification loop
boucle *f* **de programme** *nom* **1.** looping program **2.** loop program
boucle *f* **de récurrence** *nom* daisy chain recursion
boucle *f* **de rétroaction** *nom* loopback
boucle *f* **de temporisation** *nom* timing loop
boucle *f* **d'itération** *nom* **1.** looping program **2.** loop program
boucle *f* **emboîtée** *nom* nested loop
boucle *f* **fermée** *nom* closed loop
boucle *f* **imbriquée** *nom* nested loop
boucle *f* **infinie** *nom* endless loop
boucle *f* **intérieure** *nom* inner loop
boucle *f* **principale (d'un programme)** *nom* main loop
boucle *f* **sans fin** *nom* **1.** continuous loop **2.** endless loop **3.** infinite loop
boule *f* **de commande** *nom* trackball
bouton *m nom* **1.** (*d'une souris ou d'une manette de jeu*) button **2.** button **3.** contrast **4.** dial **5.** knob ◇ **bouton de densité** density dial ◇ **il y a deux boutons au bas de la ligne d'état, sélectionnez le bouton de gauche pour annuler l'opération et le bouton de droite pour continuer** there are two buttons at the bottom of the status line, select the left button to cancel the operation or the right to continue ◇ **pour ajuster la luminosité de l'écran, tourner le bouton placé à l'arrière du moniteur** the brightness can be regulated by turning a knob at the back of the monitor ◇ **pour obtenir la station de radio, tournez ce bouton** to tune into the radio station, turn the dial ◇ **si l'impression est trop pâle, réglez le bouton de densité (d'impression) sur le noir** if the text fades, turn the density dial on the printer to full black ◇ **tourner le bouton marche** *or* **arrêt** turn the on/off knob ◇ **utilisez la souris pour placer le curseur sur l'icône et démarrez l'application en appuyant sur le bouton de la souris** use the mouse to move the cursor to the icon and start the application by pressing the mouse button
bouton *m* **de ré-initialisation** *nom* reset button *ou* reset key
bouton *m* **droit** *nom* (*de la souris*) right-hand button
bouton *m* **OK** *nom* OK button
bouton *m* **radio** *nom* radio button
bouton *m* **Soumettre** *nom* submit button
bozo *m nom* bozo bit
bps par seconde *nom* bps rate
branche *f nom* branch
branchement *m nom* **1.** branch **2.** jump instruction **3.** leg **4.** unconditional branch *ou* unconditional jump *ou* unconditional transfer ◇ **le poste défectueux est connecté sur ce branchement** the faulty station is on this branch
branchement *m* **conditionnel** *nom* **1.** case branch **2.** conditional branch **3.** conditional jump
branchement *m* **conditionnel à zéro** *nom* jump on zero ◇ **l'instruction de branchement conditionnel à zéro teste l'indicateur zéro** the jump on zero instruction tests the zero flag
branchement *m* **d'un programme** *nom* program branch
brancher *verbe vt* to branch ◇ **brancher un ordinateur portatif sur une station d'accueil** to dock

brancher sur *verbe* to connect
bras *m* **de lecture** *nom* actuator
bras *m* **de lecture/écriture** *nom* access arm
bricolage *m nom* kludge *ou* kluge
bricolé,-ée *adjectif* kluged
brillance *f nom* brightness
brillant *adjectif* brilliant ◇ **il utilise un blanc brillant pour les mises en valeur** he used brillant white for the highlights ◇ **le fond est d'un rouge brillant** the background colour is a brilliant red
broche *f nom* pin ◇ **il faut une fiche à trois broches pour connecter** *ou* **brancher le système sur le secteur** use a three-pin plug to connect the printer to the mains
brosse *f nom* brush
brouillage *m nom* **1.** garbage **2.** interference **3.** noise
brouillon *m nom* rough copy
bruit *m nom* **1.** impulsive noise **2.** noise ◇ **bruit thermique** thermal noise ◇ **marge de bruit** *ou* **limite de tolérance au bruit** noise margin ◇ **température de bruit** noise temperature
bruit *m* **ambiant** *nom* ambient noise
bruit *m* **de fond** *nom* **1.** ambient noise **2.** babble **3.** background noise ◇ **les autres appareils placés autour de cet équipement produiront un fort bruit de fond** the other machines around this device will produce a lot of background noise ◇ **niveau de bruit de fond** *ou* **de bruit ambiant** ambient noise level
bruit *m* **de saturation** *nom* saturation noise
bruit *m* **parasite** *nom* jabber
bruits *mpl* **de quantification** *nom* quantising noise
brûlage *m* **d'écran** *nom* screen burn
brûlage *m* **laser** *nom* ablation
brûler une PROM *verbe* to blast
brut *adjectif* unformatted ◇ **texte brut** unformatted text
bug *m nom* bug
bulle *f nom* bubble-help
bureau *m nom* **1.** bureau **2.** desktop ◇ **nous confions notre correspondance à un bureau de secrétariat local** we farm out the office typing to a local bureau
bureau *m* **de poste** *nom* post office
bureau *m* **de traitement de texte** *nom* word-processing bureau
bureau *m* **électronique** *nom* paperless office
bureau *m* **sans papier** *nom* paperless office
bureautique *f abrév* OA ■ *nom* office automation
bureautique *f* **intégrée** *nom* integrated office
bus *m nom* **1.** bus **2.** highway ◇ **asservi à un bus** bus slave ◇ **bus d'entrée** *or* **sortie** input/output data bus (I/O bus) ◇ **Ethernet est un réseau qui utilise une topologie en bus** Ethernet is a network that uses the bus topology; token ring uses a ring topology
bus *m* **A** *nom* A-bus
bus *m* **AGP** *nom* AGP
bus *m* **Apple Desktop** (*nom de marque*) Apple Desktop Bus
bus *m* **AT** *nom* AT-bus
bus *m* **bidirectionnel** *nom* bi-directional bus
bus *m* **central** *nom* bus
bus *m* **d'adresses** *nom* **1.** address bus **2.** address highway
bus *m* **d'arbitrage** *nom* contention bus
bus *m* **de chaîne** *nom* daisy chain bus
bus *m* **de commande** *nom* control bus
bus *m* **de données** *nom* data bus
bus *m* **de mémoire** *nom* memory bus
bus *m* **d'entrée** *nom* **1.** data input bus **2.** DIB
bus *m* **de transfert de données** *nom* data highway
bus *m* **d'expansion** *nom* expansion bus
bus *m* **d'extension** *nom* expansion bus
bus *m* **d'interface banalisé** *nom* **1.** general purpose interface bus **2.** GPIB
bus *m* **d'interface Hewlett Packard** *abrév* HPIB
bus *m* **d'interface HP** Hewlett Packard Interface Bus
bus *m* **d'interface universel** *nom* **1.** general purpose interface bus **2.** GPIB
bus *m* **d'un micro-ordinateur** *nom* microcomputer bus
bus *m* **(d') entrée/sortie** *nom* **1.** input/output bus **2.** I/O bus
bus *m* **IEEE** *nom* IEEE bus
bus *m* **local** *nom* local bus ◇ **les cartes d'extension les plus rapides se placent dans ce connecteur local bus** the fastest expansion cards fit into this local bus connector
bus *m* **local PCI** *nom* **1.** PCI **2.** peripheral component interconnect
bus *m* **local VESA** *nom* **1.** VESA local bus **2.** VL-bus *ou* VL local bus
bus *m* **MCA** (*de IBM*) Micro Channel Bus
bus *m* **Micro-Channel** (*de IBM*) Micro Channel Bus
bus *m* **multiplexé** *nom* multiplexed bus
bus *m* **partagé** *nom* shared bus
bus *m* **principal** *nom* A-bus
bus *m* **(de type) S-100** *nom* S100 bus *ou* S-100 bus
bus *m* **série** *nom* daisy chain bus
bus *m* **USB** *nom* **1.** universal serial bus **2.** USB
bus *m* **VLB** *nom* VL-bus *ou* VL local bus
but *m nom* objective
but *m* **(visé ou atteint)** *nom* goal

C

cabestan *m nom* capstan

câblage *m nom* **1.** cable plant **2.** cabling **3.** wiring ◇ **il a fallu refaire le câblage du système** the wiring in the system had to be replaced

câblage *m* **permanent** *nom* hardwired connection

câblage *m* **structuré** *nom* **1.** structured cabling **2.** structured wiring

câble *m nom* **1.** cable **2.** landline **3.** lead ◇ **câble** *m* **à fibres optiques de 100–140 microns de diamètre** Type 5 ◇ **câble audio** audio cable ◇ **câble** *m* **blindé non torsadé de 4 fils, en deux paires** Type 8 ◇ **câble** *m* **en paire(s) torsadée(s) sans blindage** UTP cable ◇ **câble vidéo** video cable ◇ **télévision câblée** *ou* **le câble** cable télévision *ou* cable TV

câble *m* **à fibres optiques** *nom* fibre optic cable *ou* fibre optic connection

câble *m* **blindé** *nom* shielded cable

câble *m* **coaxial** *nom* co-axial cable *ou* coax

câble *m* **de branchement** *nom* drop cable

câble *m* **de connexion série** *nom* modem eliminator

câble *m* **de dérivation** *nom* **1.** branch cable **2.** drop cable

câble *m* **de liaison directe** *nom* modem eliminator

câble *m* **d'entrée** *nom* input lead

câble *m* **de raccordement** *nom* patch cord

câble *m* **en paires torsadées blindé** *nom* shielded twisted pair cable

câble *m* **en paires torsadées sans blindage** *nom* unshielded twisted-pair cable

câble *m* **en paire(s) torsadée(s)** *nom* twisted-pair cable ◇ **câble en paire(s) torsadée(s) blindé** *ou* **avec blindage** shielded twisted pair (STP) cable ◇ **câble en paire(s) torsadée(s) non blindé** *ou* **sans blindage** unshielded twisted pair (UTP) cable

câble *m* **jaune** *nom* thick-Ethernet

câble *m* **noir** *nom* thin-Ethernet

câble *m* **optique** *nom* fibre optic cable *ou* fibre optic connection

câble *m* **plat** *nom* **1.** ribbon cable **2.** tape cable

câbler *verbe vt* to wire

câble *m* **ruban** *nom* **1.** ribbon cable **2.** tape cable

câbles *mpl nom* cabling ◇ **les câbles de haute qualité vont permettre à l'utilisateur d'obtenir un taux de transfert de données très élevé** using high-quality cabling will allow the user to achieve very high data transfer rates

câble *m* **UTP** *nom* unshielded twisted-pair cable

cache *f nom* **1.** cache **2.** cache memory **3.** matte

cache *m* **d'instructions** *nom* instruction cache

cacher *verbe vt* to conceal

caddie *m* **en ligne** *nom* shopping basket *ou* shopping cart

cadence *f nom* tempo

cadence *f* **de répétition d'un caractère** *nom* repeat rate

cadran *m nom* dial ◇ **impulsion de cadran** dial pulse

cadre *m nom* **1.** border **2.** bounding box **3.** framework ◇ **on a d'abord établi le cadre** *ou* **la structure du programme** the program framework was designed first

cadrer *verbe* **1.** *vt* to crop **2.** *vt* (*une image*) to crop

cadre-réponse *m nom* response frame

café *m* **Internet** *nom* Internet café

cage *f* **de Faraday** *nom* Faraday cage

caisson *m* **de basse** *nom* sub-woofer

calculateur *m nom* **1.** computer **2.** electronic digital computer

calculateur *m* **analogique** *nom* analog computer

calculatrice *f* (*à Microsoft Windows NT*) Calculator ◇ **il a calculé la remise sur sa calculatrice** he worked out the discount on his calculator ◇ **j'ai besoin d'une pile pour ma calculatrice de poche** my pocket calculator needs a new battery

calculatrice *f* **programmable** *nom* programmable calculator

calcul *m* **binaire** *nom* binary arithmetic

calcul *m* **des déformées intermédiaires** *nom* tweening ◇ **en utilisant le procédé de transformation sérielle nous pouvons montrer comment une grenouille se métamorphose en princesse, en cinq étapes** using tweening, we can show how a frog turns into a princess in five steps

calcul *m* **des dimensions** *nom* dimensioning ◇ **le calcul des dimensions du tableau se fait à ce niveau-ci** array dimensioning occurs at this line

calcul *m* **d'une adresse** *nom* address computation

calcul *m* **en double précision** *nom* **1.** double-length arithmetic **2.** double-precision arithmetic

calcul *m* **en virgule flottante** *nom* floating point arithmetic ◇ **dans un calcul en virgule flottante, le nombre 56,47 serait écrit 0,5647 puissance 2** the fixed number 56.47 in floating-point arithmetic would be 0.5647 and a power of 2

calculer un complément *verbe* to complement

calcul *m* **ultra-rapide** *nom* **1.** cruncher *ou* crunching **2.** number crunching

camelote *f nom* junk

canal *m nom* **1.** channel **2.** input/output channel **3.** secondary channel

canal *m* **alpha** *nom* alpha channel

canal *m* **banal** *nom* common carrier

canal *m* **dédié** *nom* dedicated channel

canal *m* **d'entrée/sortie** *nom* I/O channel

canal *m* **de retour** *nom* **1.** backward channel **2.** reverse channel

canal de transfert d'information *m nom* information transfer channel

canal *m* **de transmission** *nom* communications channel

canal *m* **de transmission de données** *nom* data channel

canalisation *nom* **1.** channelling **2.** conduit **3.** duct ◇ **les câbles de liaison de tous les terminaux sont acheminés par conduite métallique** *ou* **par canalisation métallique** *ou* **sous gaine métallique jusqu'au centre informatique** the cables from each terminal are channelled to the computer centre by metal conduit

'*nf*'

canal *m* **MIDI** *nom* MIDI channel

canal *m* **numérique** *nom* digital channel

canal *m* **principal** *nom* primary channel

canal *m* **universel de transmission par blocs** *abrév* UBC ■ *nom* universal block channel

canon *m* **à électrons** *nom* **1.** electron gun **2.** gun

C ANSI *nom* ANSI C

CAO *nom* CAD ◇ **tous nos ingénieurs travaillent sur des stations de CAO** all our engineers design on CAD workstations

> '...la CAO (conception assistée par ordinateur) est l'ensemble des procédés de création, de calcul, de description d'objets virtuels à l'aide d'un ordinateur' [*Science et Vie Micro*]

capacitance *f nom* capacitance

capacitatif *adjectif* capacitative *ou* capacititive

capacité *nom* **1.** capacitor **2.** capacity **3.** channel capacity **4.** microprocessor addressing capabilities ◇ **capacité** *f* **de traitement de données** EDP capability ◇ **condensateur variable** *ou* **capacité variable** variable capacitor ◇ **qui dépasse la capacité de qc** out of range

> '...la gamme propose un choix de disques durs d'une capacité de 20Mo à 660Mo' [*L'Ordinateur Individuel*]

capacité *f* **d'adressage** *nom* **1.** addressability **2.** addressing capacity

capacité *f* **de calcul arithmétique** *nom* arithmetic capability

capacité *f* **de mémoire** *nom* **1.** addressing capacity **2.** memory capacity **3.** storage capacity

capacité *f* **d'émulation** *nom* emulation facility

capacité *f* **de production** *nom* producing capacity

capacité *f* **de saut** *nom* skip capability

capacité *f* **de transfert** *nom* bandwidth ◇ **bande passante** telephone bandwidth is 3100Hz ◇ **la bande passante de câble à fibres optiques est plus étendue que celle des anciens câbles en cuivre et peut transmettre les données à des vitesses plus grandes** this fibre-optic cable has a greater bandwidth than the old copper cable and so it can carry data at higher speeds ◇ **la largeur de bande d'un téléphone est de 3100Hz L** *or* **(c)** telephone bandwidth is 3100Hz

capacité *f* **d'un circuit** *nom* circuit capacity

capacité *f* **maximale** *nom* maximum capacity

capacité *f* **non formatée** *nom* unformatted capacity

capacité *f* **théorique absolue** *nom* absolute maximum rating

capitale *f nom* uppercase

capot *m nom* hood

capteur *m nom* sensor ◇ **le processus est contrôlé par une batterie de capteurs** the process is monitored by a bank of sensors ◇ **le signal de sortie du capteur varie suivant la température** the sensor's output varies with temperature

capteur *m* **de données à traiter** *nom* milking machine

capteur *m* **d'image** *nom* image sensor

capteur *m* **d'images** *nom* grabber

capteur *m* **d'image vidéo** *nom* frame grabber

capture *f* **d'écran** *verbe* to screen capture ■ *nom* **1.** screen grab **2.** screen shot

capture *f* **de son** *nom* sound capture

capturer *verbe vt* to capture ◇ **capturer des images vidéo une à une** to step frame ◇ **le logiciel permet d'éditer les images capturées** the software allows captured images to be edited

◇ **un scanner peut habituellement capturer des images à une résolution de 300 points par pouce (ppp)** scanners usually capture images at a resolution of 300 dots per inch (dpi)

caractère *m nom* character ◇ **(ordinateur) à mode caractère** character orientated (computer) ◇ **caractère** *m* **indiquant d'aller à la ligne** new line character ◇ **(nombre de) caractères par pouce** characters per inch (cpi) ◇ **le bouton vert vous permet de sélectionner 10 ou 12 caractères par pouce** you can select 10 or 12 cpi with the green button ◇ **le code ASCII est le code de caractères le plus fréquemment utilisé** the ASCII code is the most frequently used character coding system ◇ **l'imprimante à marguerite imprime un caractère à la fois** a daisy-wheel printer is a character printer ◇ **oblique (d'un caractère)** character skew

caractère *m* **ASCII** *nom* ASCII character

caractère *m* **à valeur numérique** *nom* numeric character

caractère *m* **blanc** *nom* space character

caractère *m* **clignotant** *nom* flashing character

caractère *m* **complet** *plural noun* fully formed character

caractère *m* **d' accusé de réception** *nom* acknowledge

caractère *m* **d'accusé de réception** *nom* acknowledge character

caractère *m* **d'alarme** *nom* bell character *ou* BEL

caractère *m* **d'annulation** *nom* cancel character ◇ **le logiciel émet automatiquement un caractère d'annulation suite à une erreur** the software automatically sends a cancel character after any error

caractère *m* **d'échappement** *nom* escape character

caractère *m* **de contrôle** *nom* **1.** check character **2.** control character

caractère *m* **de contrôle de périphérique** *nom* device control character

caractère *m* **de contrôle de précision** *nom* accuracy control character

caractère *m* **de contrôle d'impression** *nom* print control character *ou* print control code

caractère *m* **d'écran** *nom* display character

caractère *m* **de déplacement** *nom* shift character

caractère *m* **d'effacement** *nom* **1.** delete character **2.** erase character

caractère *m* **de fin de page** *nom* page break

caractère *m* **de rappel du curseur** *nom* backspace character

caractère *m* **de redirection** *nom* (*sous DOS*) redirect operator *ou* redirection operator

caractère *m* **de redondance** *nom* redundant character

caractère *m* **de rejet de bloc** *nom* (*dont les données sont mauvaises*) block ignore character

caractère *m* **de remplissage** *nom* **1.** fill character **2.** gap character **3.** ignore character **4.** NUL character **5.** null character **6.** pad character

caractère *m* **de requête** *nom* **1.** enquiry character **2.** inquiry character

caractère *m* **de retour arrière** *nom* backspace character

caractère *m* **d'espace** *nom* blank character

caractère *m* **d'espacement** *nom* space character

caractère *m* **de substitution** *nom* substitute character

caractère *m* **de suppression** *nom* delete character

caractère *m* **de synchro** *nom* sync character

caractère *m* **de synchronisation** *nom* synchronous idle character

caractère *m* **d'identification** *abrév* ID ■ *nom* **1.** identification character **2.** identifier

caractère *m* **d'instruction** *nom* instruction character

caractère *m* **d'interrogation** *nom* inquiry character

caractère *m* **espace** *nom* space character

caractère *m* **graphique** *nom* graphics character

caractère *m* **interdit** *nom* forbidden character *ou* forbidden combination

caractère *m* **joker** *nom* wild card *ou* wild card character

caractère *m* **non autorisé** *nom* illegal character

caractère *m* **nul** *nom* **1.** idle character **2.** NUL character **3.** null character

caractère *m* **programmé par l'utilisateur** *plural noun* user-defined character

caractère *m* **réservé** *nom* reserved character

caractère *m* **retour arrière** *abrév* BS

caractères ◇ **caractères** *mpl* **dans une chaîne** catena

caractères *mpl* **alphanumériques** *plural noun* **1.** alphanumeric characters **2.** alphanumerics

caractères *mpl* **alphanumériques acceptés** *plural noun* (*sur un écran vidéotex*) blast-through alphanumerics

caractères *mpl* **codés binaires** *plural noun* binary coded characters

caractères *mpl* **d'appel sélectif** *plural noun* polling characters

caractères *mpl* **de contrôle d'impression** *nom* printer control characters

caractères *mpl* **d'imprimerie** *nom* type ◇ **ils ont changé de police de caractères et composé l'en-tête en italique** they switched to italic type for the heading

caractères *mpl* **Dingbat™** *nom* Dingbat™

caractères graphiques espacés *plural noun* separated graphics

caractères graphiques séparés *plural noun* separated graphics

caractères *mpl* **gras** *nom* bold face

caractères *mpl* **inversés** *plural noun* reverse characters

caractères *mpl* **mis en évidence** *nom* highlight

caractères *mpl* **par pouce** *nom* cpi ◇ **le bouton vert vous permet de sélectionner 10 ou 12 caractères par pouce** you can select 10 or 12 cpi with the green button

caractères *mpl* **par seconde** *nom* cps

caractère *m* **spécial** *nom* **1.** special character **2.** special sort

caractères *mpl* **spéciaux** *nom* Dingbat™ ◇ **pour insérer une marque de copyright, utilisez les caractères spéciaux** *ou* **Dingbat** to insert a copyright symbol, use the Dingbat font

caractères TrueType™ (*nom de marque*) TrueType

caractère *m* **tab** *nom* tab character

caractéristique *f nom* **1.** attribute **2.** characteristic

caractéristique *f* **essentielle** *nom* prime attribute

caractéristique *f* **principale** *nom* key feature

CardBus CardBus

caret *m nom* caret

carnet *m* **d'adresses** *nom* address book

carte *f nom* board ◇ **(carte de) circuit imprimé** printed circuit board (PCB)

carte *f* **accélératrice** *nom* accelerator board *ou* accelerator card

carte *f* **à coder en encre magnétique** *nom* mark sensing card

carte *f* **à connecteur** *nom* **1.** edge board **2.** edge card

carte *f* **adaptateur** *nom* adapter card

carte *f* **à encoches marginales** *nom* edge notched card ■ *adjectif* notched

carte *f* **à mémoire** *nom* **1.** chip card **2.** smart card

carte *f* **à puce** *nom* **1.** chip card **2.** smart card

carte *f* **audio** *nom* sound card

carte *f* **audio Sound Blaster™** (*nom de marque*) Sound Blaster

carte *f* **bus** *nom* bus board

carte complètement garnie (de composants) *adjectif* fully-populated

carte *f* **connecteur** *nom* bus

carte *f* **contrôleur de disques** *nom* disk-controller card

carte *f* **contrôleur de disquettes** *nom* disk-controller card

carte *f* **courte** *nom* short card

carte *f* **d'accélération** *nom* accelerator board *ou* accelerator card

carte *f* **d'affichage monochrome** *nom* MDA

carte *f* **de capture vidéo** *nom* video capture board

carte *f* **de circuit imprimé** *nom* **1.** card **2.** circuit board **3.** circuit card ■ *abrév* PCB

carte *f* **de disque dur** *nom* hard card

carte *f* **demi-longueur** *nom* half card

carte *f* **de montage sans soudure** *nom* breadboard

carte *f* **d'entrée analogique** *nom* analog input card

carte *f* **de police de caractères** *nom* font card

carte *f* **de sortie analogique** *nom* analog output card

carte *f* **de taille réduite** *nom* short card

carte *f* **d'extension** *nom* **1.** add on board **2.** expansion board **3.** expansion card

carte *f* **d'extension de bus** *nom* bus extender *ou* bus extension card

carte *f* **d'extension de mémoire** *nom* expanded memory board

carte *f* **d'extension multifonction** *nom* multifunction card

carte *f* **d'extension sans mémoires** *nom* bare board

carte *f* **d'interface** *nom* interface card

carte *f* **en-tête** *nom* header card

carte *f* **entièrement équipée** *adjectif* fully-populated

carte *f* **fax** *nom* fax card *ou* fax adapter *ou* fax board

carte *f* **fille** *nom* daughter board

carte *f* **graphique** *nom* graphics adapter

carte *f* **graphique étendue** *nom* extended graphics array

carte *f* **intelligente par contact** *nom* contact card

carte *f* **interface de réseau** *nom* network interface card

carte *f* **(d') interface MIDI** *nom* MIDI interface card

carte *f* **logique** *nom* **1.** logic board **2.** logic card

carte *f* **magnétique** *nom* **1.** magnetic card **2.** personal identification device **3.** smart card

carte *f* **maîtresse** *nom* master card

carte *f* **MCGA** *nom* **1.** MCGA **2.** multicolour graphics adapter

carte *f* **mémoire** *nom* memory board

carte *f* **mémoire sans composants** *nom* bare board
carte *f* **mère** *nom* **1.** motherboard **2.** system board
carte *f* **modem** *nom* internal modem
carte *f* **multimédia** *nom* multimedia card
carte *f* **nue** *nom* bare board
carte *f* **overlay** *nom* overlay card
carte *f* **PC** *nom* PC Card
carte *f* **PCMCIA** *nom* PCMCIA card
carte *f* **perforée** *nom* **1.** punch card **2.** punched card
carte *f* **Plug and Play™** *nom* (*qui ne demande pas de configuration*) plug and play
carte *f* **PNP** *nom* plug and play
carte *f* **RAM** *nom* RAM card
carte *f* **réseau** *nom* network adapter
carte *f* **(interface de) réseau** *nom* NIC
carte *f* **réseau banalisée** *nom* general purpose interface adapter
carte *f* **réseau universelle** *nom* general purpose interface adapter
carte *f* **son** *nom* **1.** audio board **2.** sound card
carte *f* **son AdLib™** *nom* AdLib™
cartes *fpl* **programme** *plural noun* program cards
carte *f* **vidéo** *nom* **1.** video adapter **2.** video board **3.** video controller
carte *f* **vidéo à grand débit** *nom* full-motion video adapter
carte *f* **vidéo pleine animation** *nom* full-motion video adapter
cartouche *f* *nom* **1.** cartridge **2.** magnetic tape cartridge
cartouche *f* **de bande** *nom* tape cartridge
cartouche *f* **de bande magnétique** *nom* **1.** magnetic cartridge **2.** magnetic tape cassette
cartouche *f* **de disque dur** *nom* disk cartridge
cartouche *f* **de disquette** *nom* flexible disk cartridge
cartouche *f* **de données** *nom* data cartridge
cartouche *f* **de jeu** *nom* game cartridge
cartouche *f* **d'encre** *nom* ink cartridge
cartouche *f* **de police de caractères** *plural noun* cartridge fonts
cartouche *f* **de toner** *nom* toner cartridge
cartouche *f* **RAM** *nom* RAM cartridge ◇ **vous pouvez augmenter la mémoire de l'imprimante en enfichant une cartouche RAM supplémentaire** you can increase the printer's memory by plugging in another RAM cartridge
cartouche *f* **ROM** *nom* ROM cartridge
case *f* **à cocher** *nom* check box
cassette *f* *nom* **1.** cassette **2.** cassette tape **3.** tape cassette ◇ **il faut copier vos données sur une cassette de sauvegarde** you must back up the information from the computer onto a cassette ◇ **vidéocassette** video cassette
cassette *f* **compacte numérique** *nom* **1.** DCC **2.** digital compact cassette
cassette *f* **de bande magnétique** *nom* magnetic cassette
cassette *f* **informatique** *nom* data cassette
cassette *f* **mémoire à bulles magnétiques** *nom* bubble memory cassette
cassette *f* **numérique** *nom* digital cassette
catalogue *m* *nom* catalogue
cataloguer *verbe vt* to catalogue
catastrophe *f* *nom* catastrophe
catégorie *f* **1** *nom* Category 1
catégorie *f* **2** *nom* Category 2
catégorie *f* **3** *nom* Category 3
catégorie *f* **4** *nom* Category 4
catégorie *f* **5** *nom* Category 5
cavalier *m* *nom* jumper ◇ **sur cette imprimante, la police de caractères peut être sélectionnée par cavalier** the printer's typeface is jumper-selectable
cc *nom* cc
CCD *abrév* CCD
CD ◇ **cd** *m* CD ◇ **de qualité CD** CD quality ◇ **tapez CD DOCS pour entrer dans le sous-répertoire DOCS** type in CD DOCS to move into the DOCS subdirectory
CD *m* **audio** *nom* **1.** compact disc-digital audio **2.** red book audio
CD-audio *m* *nom* CD-audio
CD-E *m* *nom* CD-E
cd *m* **effaçable** *nom* CD-E
cd *m* **enregistrable** *nom* CD-R
CD-I *m* *nom* CD-I
cd *m* **inscriptible** *nom* CD-R
cd *m* **interactif** *nom* **1.** CD-I **2.** CD-i
CD *m* **interactif** *nom* compact disc-interactive
cd *m* **non réinscriptible** *nom* CD-WO
CD-Photo *m* *nom* PhotoCD
CD-R *m* *nom* CD-R ◇ **un lecteur de CD-Rom standard peut lire un CD-R mais il faut un graveur pour inscrire des données sur le CD-R** a CD-R disc can be played in any standard CD-ROM drive but needs a special CD-R drive to write data to the disc
CD *m* **réinscriptible** *nom* **1.** CD-RW **2.** compact disc erasable
CD-ROM *m* *nom* CD-ROM ◇ **CD-ROM à architecture étendue** CD-ROM/XA
CD-ROM *m* **mode 1** *nom* CD-ROM mode 1
CD-ROM *m* **mode 2** *nom* CD-ROM mode 2
CD-ROM *m* **réinscriptible** *nom* CD-ROM Re-Writable
CD-ROM *m* **XA** XA

CD-ROM/XA *nom* CD-ROM Extended Architecture

'...le CD-ROM est un support technologiquement stable, fiable et de moins en moins cher' [*Micro Systèmes*]

'...contrairement à l'idée reçue, les coûts d'une diffusion de l'information sur support CD-ROM sont globalement inférieurs à ceux d'une impression papier' [*Micro Systèmes*]

CDRTOS *nom* CDRTOS

CD-RW *m nom* CD-RW

CD-vidéo *m nom* **1.** CD-video **2.** video-CD

CD-WO *m nom* CD-WO

Cello *m nom* Cello

cellule *f nom* **1.** cell **2.** element

cellule *f* **binaire** *nom* binary cell

cellule *f* **d'ancrage** *nom* anchor cell

cellule *f* **de contrôle des couleurs** *nom* colour cell

cellule *f* **de mémoire** *nom* **1.** memory cell **2.** store cell

cellule *f* **de travail** *nom* active cell

cellule *f* **magnétique** *nom* magnetic cell

cellule *f* **vide** *nom* blank cell

centile *m nom* percentile

centrale *f* **de transmission** *nom* base station

central *m* **téléphonique** *nom* exchange

centre *m* **de commutation** *nom* switching centre

centre *m* **de commutation des données** *nom* data switching exchange

centre *m* **de recherche documentaire** *nom* information retrieval centre

Centre *f* **Européen pour la Recherche Nucléaire** *nom* CERN

centre *m* **miroir** *nom* mirror site

centrer *verbe vt* to centre ◇ **sur quelle touche faut-il appuyer pour centrer l'en-tête?** which key do you press to centre the heading?

centre *m* **serveur** *nom* information retrieval centre

centre *m* **terminal de paiement** *nom* payment gateway

ce que vous voyez est ce que vous obtenez *nom* WYSIWYG

ce que vous voyez est tout ce que vous obtenez *nom* WYSIAYG

certificat *m nom* **1.** certificate **2.** digital certificate

certificat *m* **d'homologation** *nom* certificate of approval

cesser de fonctionner *verbe* to crash ◇ **la tête de lecture du disque a cessé de fonctionner** *ou* **s'est plantée et il se peut que les données soient perdues** the disk head has crashed and the data may have been lost

CF (Compact Flash) *abrév* CF

CGI *nom* common gateway interface

CGM *nom* computer graphics metafile

chaînage *m nom* chaining

chaînage *m* **arrière** *nom* backward chaining

chaînage *m* **de données** *nom* data chaining

chaînage *m* **en amont** *nom* backward chaining

chaîne *f nom* **1.** chain **2.** daisy chain **3.** (*série de caractères*) string ◇ **chaîne** *f* **de caractères qui se termine par le caractère nul** null terminated string ◇ **langage SNOBOL (de traitement et de manipulation de chaîne)** string orientated symbolic language (SNOBOL)

chaîne *f* **de caractères** *nom* **1.** catena **2.** character string

chaîne *f* **de caractères alphabétiques** *nom* alphabetic string

chaîne *f* **de caractères alphanumériques** *nom* alphanumeric string

chaîne *f* **de caractères ASCIIZ** *nom* ASCIIZ string

chaîne *f* **de caractères interdite** *nom* forbidden character *ou* forbidden combination

chaîne *f* **de caractères numériques** *nom* numeric string

chaîne *f* **de commandes** *nom* command chain

chaîne *f* **d'éléments de données** *nom* data element chain

chaîne *f* **d'initialisation** *nom* initialisation string *ou* initialization string

chaîner *verbe vt* to concatenate

chaîne *f* **vide** *nom* **1.** blank string **2.** null string

chambre *f* **blanche** *nom* anechoic chamber

chambre *f* **sans écho** *nom* anechoic chamber

chambre *f* **sourde** *nom* anechoic chamber

chambre *f* **stérile** *nom* clean room

champ *nom* field ◇ **intensité de champ** field strength ◇ **le dossier 'employés' possède un champ 'âge'** the employee record has a field for age ◇ **transistor à effet de champ (TEC)** field effect transistor (FET)

'...certains champs comportent plusieurs options non visibles dans ce menu; pour les visualiser, vous utilisez la touche de fonction F1' [*L'Ordinateur Individuel*]

'...le champ magnétique apparaît donc comme créé par le mouvement de particules électrisées' [*Science et Vie*]

champ *m* **binaire** *nom* binary field

champ *m* **bloc-notes** *nom* comment field

champ *m* **calculé** *nom* calculated field

champ *m* **clé** *nom* key field

champ *m* **d'adresse** *nom* **1.** address field **2.** operand field

champ *m* **de contrôle** *nom* control field

champ *m* **de données** *nom* data field

champ *m* **de longueur déterminée** *nom* fixed-length field

champ *m* **de longueur fixe** *nom* fixed-length field

champ *m* **de signe** *nom* signed field

champ *m* **de taille fixe** *nom* **1.** constant length field **2.** fixed field

champ *m* **de tri** *nom* sortkey *ou* sort field ◇ **les commandes ont été triées suivant leur date en designant le champ date comme clé de tri** the orders were sorted according to dates by assigning the date field as the sortkey

champ *m* **d'opérande** *nom* operand field

champ *m* **d'opération** *nom* operation field

champ *m* **label** *nom* label field

champ *m* **magnétique** *nom* magnetic field

champ *m* **mémo** *nom* memo field

champ *m* **non protégé** *nom* unprotected field

champ *m* **protégé** *nom* protected field

changement *m nom* **1.** crossover **2.** modification

changement *m* **d'adresse en mémoire** *verbe* to memory edit

changement *m* **d'application** *nom* context-switching

changement *m* **de banque de mémoire** *nom* bank switching

changement *m* **de bloc de mémoire** *nom* bank switching

changement *m* **de police de caractères** *nom* font change

changement *m* **graduel** *nom* phased change-over

changement *m* **progressif** *nom* phased change-over

changer d'adresse *verbe* to relocate

changer de place *verbe* **1.** to move **2.** to swap

changer le nom *verbe* to rename ◇ **sauvegarder le fichier mais changez-en le nom et appelez-le CLIENT** save the file and rename it CLIENT

changeur *m nom* changer ◇ **changeur (de disques) automatique** record changer

changeur *m* **de genre** *nom* **1.** gender changer **2.** sex changer ◇ **il est possible de relier tous ces périphériques en utilisant seulement deux câbles et un changeur de genre** you can interconnect all these peripherals with just two cables and a gender changer

char *m nom* char

charge *f nom* charge

charge *f* **de travail** *nom* workload

charge *f* **d'une pile** *nom* battery charging

charge *f* **électrique** *nom* electric charge

chargement *nom* loading ◇ **chargement** *m* **en fonction du taux d'activité** activity loading ◇ **chargement** *m* **et exécution** load and go; load and run ◇ **le chargement (d'un programme) peut être assez long à effectuer** loading can be a long process

charger *verbe* **1.** *vt* to charge **2.** *vt* to load **3.** *vt* to set ◇ **faire un chargement dispersé** *ou* **éclaté** to scatter load

'...pour charger plusieurs fichiers en une seule opération, séparez le nom de chaque fichier par un espace' [*L'Ordinateur Individuel*]

charge *f* **statique** *nom* corona

chargeur *m nom* **1.** loader **2.** RAM loader ◇ **chargeur de programme de lancement** initial program loader (IPL)

chargeur *m* **absolu** *nom* absolute loader

chargeur *m* **automatique** *nom* automatic loader

chargeur *m* **binaire** *nom* binary loader

chargeur *m* **de cartes perforées** *nom* hopper

chargeur *m* **de programme de lancement** *nom* initial program loader

chargeur/éditeur *m* **de liens** *nom* linking loader

chariot *m nom* carriage ◇ **les opérateurs de saisie trouvent que la touche de retour de chariot est mal placée** the carriage return key is badly placed for touch-typists ◇ **retour de chariot** carriage return (CR) ◇ **retour de chariot** *or* **retour à la ligne** carriage return/line feed (CR/LF)

chariot *m* **piloté par ordinateur** *nom* buggy

châssis *m nom* **1.** chassis **2.** wiring frame

châssis *m* **avec guide-cartes** *nom* frame

châssis *m* **sous tension** *nom* hot chassis

chaud *adjectif* hot

chauffer *verbe vt* to overheat ◇ **il se peut que le système (sur)chauffe dans une pièce qui n'est pas climatisée** the system may overheat if the room is not air-conditioned

chef *m* **du service informatique** *nom* data processing manager ■ *abrév* DPM ■ *nom* system manager

chemin *m nom* **1.** data path **2.** path **3.** route ◇ **le chemin choisi ne s'est pas révélé le plus direct puisque de nombreux noeuds étaient occupés** the route taken was not the most direct since a lot of nodes were busy

chemin *m* **complet** *nom* full path

chemin *m* **d'accès** *nom* access path

chemin *m* **d'accès (DOS)** *nom* path

chemin *m* **de sauvegarde** *nom* backup path

cheminement *m nom* route

chemise *f nom* folder

chercher *nom vt* find ◇ **chercher et remplacer** search and replace ◇ **chercher et remplacer globalement** global search and replace

chercher et remplacer *nom* find and replace

cheval *m* **de Troie** *nom* Trojan Horse

chevauchement *m nom* **1.** lap **2.** overlap

chiffrage *m nom* **1.** cipher **2.** data encryption **3.** encryption

chiffre *m nom* **1.** check digit **2.** check number **3.** cypher **4.** digit **5.** number **6.** numeral ◇ **la base de numération décimale utilise les chiffres 0123456789** the decimal number system uses the digits 0123456789 ◇ **le chiffre décimal 8** *ou* **la décimale 8** the decimal digit 8 ◇ **un numéro de téléphone de huit chiffres** a phone number with eight digits *ou* an eight-digit phone number

chiffre *m* **binaire** *nom* **1.** binary **2.** binary digit **3.** bit

chiffre *m* **de poids faible** *nom* **1.** least significant digit **2.** low-order digit **3.** LSD ◇ **6 est le chiffre le moins significatif du nombre 234156** the number 234156 has a low-order digit of 6 ◇ **bit le moins significatif** *ou* **de poids faible** least significant bit (LSB)

chiffre *m* **de poids fort** *nom* **1.** high order **2.** most significant digit *ou* most significant character **3.** MSD

chiffre *m* **de remplissage** *nom* gap digit

chiffre *m* **en exposant** *nom* superior number

chiffre *m* **inacceptable** *nom* unallowable digit

chiffre *m* **indicateur de signe** *nom* sign digit

chiffre *m* **le moins significatif** *nom* **1.** least significant digit **2.** low-order digit **3.** LSD ◇ **6 est le chiffre le moins significatif du nombre 234156** the number 234156 has a low-order digit of 6

chiffre *m* **le plus significatif** *nom* most significant digit *ou* most significant character

chiffrement *m nom* encryption

chiffre *m* **non admissible** *nom* unallowable digit

chiffre *m* **non affectable** *nom* unallowable digit

chiffre *m* **non autorisé** *nom* unallowable digit

chiffre *m* **octal** *nom* octal digit

chiffrer *verbe* **1.** *vt* to encipher **2.** *vt* to encrypt ◇ **le message chiffré** *ou* **crypté peut être transmis par téléphone sans que personne ne puisse le lire** the encrypted text can be sent along ordinary telephone lines, and no one will be able to understand it ◇ **nos concurrents ne peuvent lire nos fichiers qui sont en langage chiffré** our competitors cannot understand our files – they have all been enciphered

chiffres *mpl* **arabes** *plural noun* Arabic figures ■ *nom* Arabic numbers *ou* Arabic figures *ou* Arabic numerals

chiffres *mpl* **romains** *plural noun* Roman numerals

CHIPS *nom* Clearing House Interbank Payment System

chipset *m nom* chip set

choc ◇ **choc** *m* **de la tête de lecture contre le disque** head crash

choix *m plural noun* bells and whistles

chroma *f nom* **1.** chroma **2.** chrominance ◇ **contrôle chromatique** chroma control ◇ **détecteur chromatique** chroma detector

chrominance *f nom* **1.** chroma **2.** chrominance

chronomètre *m nom* timer

chute *f* **de tension** *nom* **1.** brown-out **2.** power loss

CIE *nom* CIE

circuit *nom* **1.** circuit **2.** trunk ◇ **caractéristique d'un circuit** circuit grade ◇ **circuit** *m* **à très haut niveau d'intégration** jumbo chip ◇ **circuit** *m* **de liaison directe** null modem ◇ **(carte de) circuit imprimé (CI)** printed circuit board (PCB) ◇ **circuits numériques commutés** circuit switched digital circuitry ◇ **circuit** *m* **spécifique à une application** application specific integrated circuits ◇ **niveau de bruit d'un circuit** circuit noise level ◇ **réseau à commutation de circuits** circuit switched network

'...le circuit imprimé pourra être gravé, d'après le dessin proposé, soit par un procédé photographique, soit en recopiant ce dessin à l'aide de pastilles et de rubans' [*Electronique pratique*]

'...en dernier lieu, on implantera les circuits intégrés' [*Electronique pratique*]

circuit *m* **à coïncidence** *nom* coincidence circuit *ou* coincidence element

circuit *m* **à délai de réponse de l'ordre de la nanoseconde** *nom* nanosecond circuit

circuit *m* **analogique** *nom* analog gate

circuit *m* **antirebond** *nom* de-bounce circuit

circuit *m* **combinatoire** *nom* combinational circuit

circuit *m* **composite** *nom* **1.** composite circuit **2.** hybrid circuit

circuit *m* **crypté** *nom* (*de protection de logiciel*) dongle

circuit *m* **de calage** *nom* clamper

circuit *m* **de commande du bus** *nom* bus driver

circuit *m* **de commutation** *nom* switching circuit

circuit *m* **de décision** *nom* decision circuit

circuit *m* **de données** *nom* data circuit

circuit *m* **de numérisation des signaux** *nom* DSP

circuit *m* **disposé en série** *nom* series circuit

circuit *m* **DSP** *nom* DSP

circuit *m* **duplex** *nom* duplex circuit

circuit *m* **électronique** *nom* nanocircuit

circuit *m* **équilibré** *nom* balanced circuit

circuit *m* **ET** *nom* **1.** AND circuit *ou* AND element **2.** AND gate **3.** coincidence gate *ou* coincidence circuit *ou* coincidence element

circuit *m* **hybride** *nom* hybrid circuit

circuit *m* **imprimé** *abrév* PC ■ *nom* printed circuit *ou* printed circuit board

circuit *m* **intégré** *nom* chip ■ *abrév* IC ■ *nom* integrated circuit

circuit *m* **intégré de carte vidéo** *nom* video interface chip

circuit *m* **intégré d'entrée/sortie en parallèle** *nom* parallel input/output chip

circuit *m* **intégré générateur de son** *nom* music chip ◇ **synthétiseur de son** music synthesizer

circuit *m* **intégré spécialisé** *nom* application specific integrated circuits

circuit *m* **intégré sur mesure** *nom* application specific integrated circuits

circuit *m* **logique** *nom* **1.** gate circuit **2.** logic circuit

circuit *m* **logique à trois états** *nom* three state logic

circuit *m* **logique complexe** *nom* gate array

circuit *m* **logique non connecté** *nom* **1.** ULA **2.** uncommitted logic array

circuit *m* **logique programmable** *nom* PLA ■ *abrév* PLD ■ *nom* **1.** programmable logic array **2.** programmable logic device

circuit *m* **mixte** *nom* hybrid circuit

circuit *m* **multipoint** *nom* multidrop circuit

circuit *m* **NON** *nom* NOT gate

circuit *m* **NON-ET** *nom* NAND gate

circuit *m* **numérique** *nom* digital circuit

circuit *m* **OU** *nom* OR gate

circuit *m* **OU exclusif** *nom* **1.** anticoincidence circuit *ou* anticoincidence function **2.** nonequivalence gate

circuits *mpl* **intégrés à application spécifique** *plural noun* ASIC

circuit *m* **tampon** *nom* buffer

circuit *m* **virtuel** *nom* virtual circuit

circulaire *adjectif* cyclic

circularité *f nom* circularity

circuler *verbe vi* to circulate

citation *f nom* quotation

citer *verbe vt* to quote

classe *f nom* class

classe *f* **enveloppante** *nom* wrapper

classement *m nom* indexing

classement *m* **énumératif** *nom* enumerated type

classer *verbe* **1.** *vt* to order **2.** *vt* to sort ■ *nom vt* sort ◇ **classer les adresses en** *ou* **par ordre alphabétique** to sort addresses into alphabetical order

classer des documents *verbe* to file

classer par ordre alphabétique *verbe* to alphabetise *ou* to alphabetize

classer par ordre d'importance *verbe* to rank

classer par rang *verbe* to rank

classeur *m nom* folder

clavier *nom* **1.** keyboard **2.** pad ◇ **clavier AZERTY (utilisé surtout dans les pays francophones)** *ou* **clavier français accentué** AZERTY keyboard ◇ **clavier tactile** *ou* **à effleurement** touch-sensitive keyboard ◇ **contrôle de clavier** *ou* **d'utilisation de touches par scanning** keyboard scan ◇ **terminal entrée** *or* **sortie** *ou* **émetteur** *or* **récepteur à clavier** keyboard send/receive (KSR)

'…bien que la souris soit supportée, la totalité des fonctions peut être exécutée à partir du clavier' [*L'Ordinateur Individuel*]

clavier *m* **à effleurement** *nom* **1.** tactile keyboard **2.** touch-sensitive keyboard

clavier *m* **alphanumérique** *nom* alphanumeric keyboard

clavier *m* **à membrane** *nom* membrane keyboard

clavier *m* **à mémoire tampon** *nom* key rollover

clavier *m* **ANSI** *nom* ANSI keyboard

clavier *m* **ASCII** *nom* ASCII keyboard

clavier *m* **AT** *nom* AT-keyboard

clavier *m* **à touches programmables** *nom* soft keyboard

clavier *m* **auxiliaire** *nom* keypad

clavier *m* **aveugle** *nom* blind keyboard

clavier *m* **AZERTY** *nom* azerty keyboard

clavier *m* **de téléscripteur** *nom* ASR keyboard

clavier *m* **DVORAK** *nom* Dvorak keyboard

clavier *m* **émetteur/récepteur** *nom* ASR keyboard

clavier *m* **étendu** *nom* enhanced keyboard

clavier *m* **hexadécimal** *nom* hex keypad

clavier IBM AT IBM AT keyboard

clavier IBM PC IBM PC keyboard

clavier *m* **interactif** *nom* interactive keyboard

clavier *m* **PC/AT** *nom* PC/AT keyboard

clavier *m* **PC/XT** *nom* PC/XT keyboard

clavier *m* **QWERTY** *nom* QWERTY keyboard

clavier *m* **rapide** *nom* key rollover

clavier *m* **relié à un terminal** *nom* terminal keyboard

clavier *m* **sensitif** *nom* tactile keyboard

clavier *m* **tactile** *nom* **1.** tactile keyboard **2.** touch-sensitive keyboard

clavier *m* **XT** *nom* XT keyboard

claviste *m&f nom* keyboarder

clé *f nom* key

clé *f* **(d'identification)** *nom* key

clé *f* **à usage unique** *nom* one-time pad

clé *f* **de chiffrage** *nom* **1.** cipher key **2.** cryptographic key

clé *f* **de codage** *nom* cipher key

clé *f* **de contrôle** *nom* check key

clé *f* **de cryptage** *nom* **1.** cipher key **2.** cryptographic key

clé *f* **de protection** *nom* protection key

clé *f* **de recherche** *nom* **1.** key **2.** search key ◇ **nous avons sélectionné les enregistrements en utilisant le mot DISK comme clé de recherche** we selected all the records with the word DISK in their keys

clé *f* **de tri** *nom* sortkey *ou* sort field ◇ **les commandes ont été triées suivant leur date en designant le champ date comme clé de tri** the orders were sorted according to dates by assigning the date field as the sortkey

clé *f* **d'index** *nom* index key

clé *f* **d'un code** *nom* (*de cryptage et décryptage*) key ◇ **gestion de clé** key management ◇ **tapez la clé et vous pourrez décoder le dernier message** type this key into the machine, that will decode the last message

clé *f* **électronique** *nom* dongle

clef *f nom* key

clé *f* **primaire** *ou* **principale** *nom* primary key

clic *nom* click ◇ **clic** *m* **témoin de touche** key click ◇ **un clic (sur la souris) vous permet de vous déplacer dans les textes et graphiques** you move through text and graphics with a click of the button

> '...par un simple clic sur un bouton, on se trouve dans la structure de la base, la procédure concernée s'affichant sur l'écran' [*L'Ordinateur Individuel*]

clic et mortier *adjectif* bricks-and-mortar

clic *m* **et mortier** *nom* clicks-and-mortar

clic *m* **publicitaire** *nom* click through

client *m nom* client

clignotement *m nom* blinking

clignoter *verbe vi* to flicker

clip *m nom* video clip

clip-art *m nom* clip-art

cliquer *verbe vi* to click ◇ **cliquer sur le bouton droit (de la souris)** *ou* **effectuer un clic droit** to click on the right button (of the mouse) *ou* to right click ◇ **cliquer sur le bouton gauche (de la souris)** *ou* **effectuer un clic gauche** to click on the left button (of the mouse) *ou* to left click ◇ **cliquer sur Rechercher** click (on) Search ◇ **double-cliquer** to double-click ◇ **utilisez la souris pour agrandir le cadre: cliquez à l'intérieur des limites du cadre et glissez jusqu'à la position voulue** use the mouse to enlarge a frame by clicking inside its border and dragging to the position wanted

> '...avec la souris, il suffit de pointer et de cliquer' [*L'Ordinateur Individuel*]

cliquer à l'aide du bouton gauche (de la souris) *verbe* to left-click

cliquer sur le bouton droit de la souris *verbe* to right-click

clone *m nom* clone ◇ **il existe des clones de tous nos modèles et tous sont plus performants** higher performance clones are available for all the models in our range ◇ **ils ont copié notre nouveau modèle d'ordinateur et commercialisé un clone qui se vend beaucoup moins cher** they have copied our new personal computer and brought out a cheaper clone

clôture *f* **de session** *nom* logging off

CLS *nom* (*de vidage d'écran*) CLS

cluster *m nom* cluster

cluster *m* **perdu** *nom* lost cluster

CMIS *nom* CMIS

CMOS *nom* CMOS

COBOL *nom* **1.** common business orientated language **2.** common ordinary business-oriented language

> '...le COBOL étant le langage de programmation des applications de gestion le plus répandu au monde' [*L'Information professionnelle*]

codage *m nom* **1.** cipher **2.** coding **3.** encoding

codage *m* **anticopie** *nom* copy protection

codage *m* **binaire** *nom* binary encoding

codage *m* **binaire à adresse absolue** *nom* specific coding

codage *m* **bipolaire** *nom* bipolar coding

codage *m* **de Hamming** *nom* Hamming code

codage *m* **direct** *nom* direct coding

codage *m* **en ligne directe** *nom* straight-line coding

codage *m* **indépendant** *nom* interframe coding

codage *m* **relatif** *nom* relative coding

codage *m* **spécifique** *nom* specific coding

codage *m* **treillis** *nom* trellis coding

code *nom* **1.** code **2.** Hamming code **3.** overhead ◇ **code** *m* **de détection et correction d'erreurs** error checking code ◇ **code** *m* **de fin de support (de données)** EM ◇ **code** *m* **d'instruction imbriqué** embedded code ◇ **code postal** post code; *US* zip code

> '...le code est une suite de trois nombres de 1 à 16, ce qui donne 4096 façons différentes de choisir son numéro secret' [*Electronique pratique*]

code *m* **absolu** *nom* **1.** absolute instruction **2.** actual code

code *m* **accéléré** *nom* optimised code *ou* optimized code

code *m* **action** *nom* action code

code *m* **adresse** *nom* address code

code *m* **à facettes** *nom* faceted code

code *m* **amélioré** *nom* optimised code *ou* optimized code

code *m* **à quatre caractères** *nom* fourcc *ou* four-character code
code *m* **à rapport constant** *nom* constant ratio code
code *m* **à rapport de bits fixe** *nom* constant ratio code
code *m* **assimilable par machine** *nom* machine-readable code
code *m* **AT** *nom* attention code
code *m* **à un niveau** *nom* one-level code
code *m* **balise** *nom* flag code
code-barre *m nom* bar code
code *m* **barres** *nom* universal product code
code *m* **BCH** *nom* **1.** BCH code **2.** Bose-Chandhuri-Hocquenghem code
code *m* **binaire** *nom* binary code
code *m* **binaire à 8 bits** *nom* **1.** EBCDIC **2.** extended binary coded decimal interchange code
code *m* **binaire absolu** *nom* **1.** absolute code **2.** specific code
code *m* **binaire réfléchi** *nom* cyclic code
code *m* **biquinaire** *nom* biquinary code
codec *m nom* coder/decoder
code *m* **chaîné** *nom* chain code
code *m* **chiffré** *nom* **1.** cipher **2.** cipher system
code *m* **compacté** *nom* compact code
code *m* **confidentiel** *nom* signature
code *m* **correcteur (d'erreur)** *nom* error correcting code
codec *m* **vidéo** *nom* video codec
code *m* **d'accès** *nom* **1.** access code **2.** authorisation code
code *m* **d'alerte** *nom* (*envoyé à un terminal à distance*) wake-up code
code *m* **d'arrêt** *nom* stop code
code *m* **d'assemblage** *nom* assembly code
code *m* **d'authentification de message** *nom* message authentication code
code *m* **de base** *nom* **1.** basic code **2.** skeletal code
code *m* **de caractères** *nom* character code
code *m* **de caractères interne** *nom* internal character code
code *m* **décimal réfléchi** *nom* cyclic decimal code
code *m* **de commande** *nom* order code
code *m* **de contrôle de bloc** *nom* block code
code *m* **de contrôle d'impression** *nom* print control character *ou* print control code
code *m* **de cryptage RSA** *nom* RSA
code *m* **de déplacement** *nom* shift code
code *m* **de fin anormale** *nom* abend code
code *m* **de fin d'adresse** *nom* end of address ■ *abrév* EOA
code *m* **de fin de bloc** *nom* end of block ■ *abrév* EOB
code *m* **de fin de document** *nom* end of file
code *m* **de fin de données** *nom* end of data ■ *abrév* EOD
code *m* **de fin de fichier** *abrév* EOF
code *m* **de fin de la bande (magnétique)** *nom* end of tape
code *m* **de fin de la transmission** *nom* end of transmission
code *m* **de fin de ligne** *nom* end of line ■ *abrév* EOL
code *m* **de fin de message** *nom* end of message ■ *abrév* EOM
code *m* **de fin d'enregistrement** *nom* end of record ■ *abrév* EOR
code *m* **de fin de support (de données)** *nom* end of medium
code *m* **de fin de tâche** *nom* end of job ■ *abrév* EOJ
code *m* **de fin de texte** *nom* end of text ■ *abrév* EOT
code *m* **de fin de transmission** *abrév* EOT
code *m* **de fonction** *nom* function code
code *m* **de Gray** *nom* **1.** cyclic code **2.** Gray code
code *m* **de Huffman** *nom* Huffman code
code *m* **de marquage** *nom* tape code
code *m* **de paramétrage** *plural noun* non-printing code
code *m* **de perforation** *nom* **1.** punched code **2.** tape code
code *m* **de redondance** *nom* redundant code
code *m* **(indicateur) d'erreur** *nom* error code
code *m* **détecteur d'erreur** *nom* **1.** error detecting code **2.** self-checking code
code *m* **d'exploitation** *nom* operating code
code *m* **d'identification** *nom* ID code
code *m* **d'identification de message** *nom* **1.** MAC **2.** message code authentication
code *m* **d'identification de périphérique** *nom* device code
code *m* **d'identification de touche** *nom* scan code
code *m* **d'instruction** *nom* **1.** computer code **2.** machine code
code *m* **d'instruction à adresse directe** *nom* single address code
code *m* **d'instruction à adresse unique** *nom* single address code
code *m* **d'interruption** *nom* abend code
code *m* **direct** *nom* direct code
code *m* **d'opération** *nom* **1.** command code **2.** operation code **3.** order code
code *m* **EBCDIC** *nom* **1.** EBCDIC **2.** extended binary coded decimal interchange code
code *m* **échappement** *nom* **1.** ESC **2.** escape code

code *m* **élémentaire** *nom* basic code
code *m* **en chaîne** *nom* chain code
code *m* **en langage machine** *nom* machine code
code *m* **erroné** *nom* false code
code *m* **exécutable** *nom* object code
code *m* **horaire de la SMPTE** *nom* SMPTE time code
code *m* **incomplet** *nom* skeletal code
code *m* **intermédiaire** *nom* intermediate code
code *m* **interprétatif** *nom* interpretative code
code *m* **machine** *nom* actual code
code *m* **multiadresse** *nom* multiple address code
code *m* **N dont M** *nom* M out of N code
code *m* **numérique d'une touche** *nom* key number
code *m* **objet** *nom* object code
code *m* **opération** *nom* op code
code *m* **optimisé** *nom* optimised code *ou* optimized code
code *m* **optimum** *nom* **1.** minimal latency coding **2.** optimum code
code *m* **ouvert** *nom* open code
code *m* **page en vigueur** *nom* active code page
code *m* **paramétrable** *nom* skeletal code
code *m* **paramétrique** *plural noun* nonprinting code
code *m* **personnel** *nom* **1.** ID code **2.** signature
code *m* **(binaire) plus 3** *nom* excess-3 code
code *m* **polynomial** *nom* (*de détection d'erreur par algorithme de calcul*) polynomial code
code *m* **précompilé** *nom* precompiled code
code *m* **pur** *nom* pure code
coder *verbe* **1.** *vt* to code **2.** *vt* to encode
code *m* **réfléchi** *nom* reflected code
code *m* **résultat** *nom* result code
codes *mpl* **à chiffres significatifs** *plural noun* significant digit codes
codes *mpl* **(auto)correcteurs** *plural noun* self-correcting codes
codes d'instruction *plural noun* instruction codes
code *m* **source** *nom* source code
code *m* **source libre** *adjectif* open source
code *m* **spécifique** *nom* specific code
codes *mpl* **significatifs** *plural noun* significant digit codes
code *m* **support** *nom* skeletal code
code *m* **symbolique** *nom* **1.** symbolic code **2.** symbolic instruction
code *m* **temporel** *nom* time code
code *m* **temporel longitudinal** *nom* **1.** longitudinal time code **2.** LTC
code *m* **temporel MIDI** *nom* MIDI time code
code *m* **temporel vertical** *nom* **1.** vertical interval time code **2.** VITC
code *m* **universel de produits** *abrév* UPC
codeur *m nom* coder
codeur/décodeur *m nom* CODEC
coeur *m nom* core
coïncidence *f* **inexacte** *nom* pseudo-random
Collage *m* **spécial** *nom* Paste Special
collecte *f* **de données** *nom* data collection
collecteur *m* **de données** *nom* **1.** data sink **2.** sink ◇ **dissipateur thermique** *ou* **radiateur à ailette(s)** heat sink
coller *verbe* **1.** *vt* to paste **2.** *vt* to splice ◇ **après avoir coupé ce paragraphe à la fin du document, je peux le coller ici** now that I have cut this paragraph from the end of the document, I can paste it in here ◇ **colleuse de film** *ou* **de bande** splicing block ◇ **couper** *or* **coller** cut-and-paste ◇ **utilisez de la colle ou du ruban gommé pour raccorder les extrémités (du film)** you can use glue or splicing tape to splice the ends
collision *f nom* collision
colocalisation *f nom* co-location
colonne *f nom* column ◇ **additionner une colonne de chiffres** to add up a column of figures ◇ **écrivez le total au bas de la colonne** put the total at the bottom of the column ◇ **le prix comprend une imprimante 80 colonnes** an 80-column printer is included in the price
colonne *f* **double** *nom* dual column
colorier *verbe vt* to paint
COM1 *nom* COM1
combiner *verbe* **1.** *vt* to coalesce **2.** *vt* to merge
combler *verbe vt* to fill
Comité *m* **Consultatif International Télégraphique et Téléphonique** *nom* CCITT
Comité *m* **National de Normalisation de la Télévision** *nom* NTSC
Comité *m* **pour l'avancement des systèmes télévisés** *nom* ATSC
commande *nom* **1.** command **2.** keyword **3.** order **4.** process control ◇ **commande** *f* **CHCP** (*de changement de page de code*) CHCP ◇ **commande** *f* **CHDIR (de changement de répertoire)** CHDIR ◇ **commande** *f* **CHKDSK (de contrôle de lecteur de disque)** CHKDSK ◇ **commande** *f* **CLOSE** CLOSE ◇ **commande** *f* **de décalage dans le registre** accumulator shift instruction ◇ **commande** *f* **de retour à la situation de départ** revert command ◇ **commande d'interruption (de programme)** interrupt command ◇ **commande** *f* **DIR** DIR ◇ **processeur de codes de commande** order code processor (OCP) ◇ **RUN est la commande d'exécution du programme** the command to execute the program is RUN ◇ **tapez la commande DIR pour obtenir la liste des fichiers** type the command

'DIR' to get the list of files ◇ **utilisez la commande DIR pour afficher la liste des fichiers du disque et ajoutez l'argument de ligne A: pour les fichiers du disque A:** use the command 'DIR' to view the files on disk, add the command line argument 'A:' to view the files on drive A:

commande *f* **CASE** *nom* case

commande *f* **CD** *nom* (*de changement de répertoire)*) change directory

commande *f* **conditionnelle** *nom* conditional statement

commande *f* **de branchement conditionnel** *nom* case

commande *f* **de canal** *nom* channel command

commande *f* **de chariot** *nom* carriage control ◇ **les codes de commande de chariot peuvent être utilisés pour faire avancer le papier de deux interlignes** carriage control codes can be used to move the paper forward two lines between each line of text

commande *f* **de conversion CAST** *nom* cast ◇ **pour convertir une variable de type nombre entier en une variable de type caractère, utilisez la commande CAST** to convert the variable from an integer to a character type, use the cast command

commande *f* **d'édition** *plural noun* edit command

commande *f* **de formatage** *nom* template command

commande *f* **DEL** *nom* DEL

commande *f* **de stabilisation du signal** *nom* (*après échantillonnage*) hold ◇ **en veille** on hold

commande *f* **de tabulation** *nom* tabbing order

commande *f* **d'exécution** *nom* Run command

commande *f* **d'invalidation d'interruption** *nom* disable interrupt

commande *f* **effacer** *nom* DEL ◇ **pour effacer tous les fichiers avec l'extension BAK, entrez la commande DEL** *ou* **.BAK** to delete all files with the extension BAK, use the command DEL *ou* .BAK ◇ **pour effacer un mot à l'écran, appuyez plusieurs fois de suite sur la touche DEL** *ou* **sur la touche Suppr** to remove a word from the screen, press the DEL key repeatedly

commande *f* **et instruction d'édition** *nom* editing term

commande *f* **GOSUB** *nom* GOSUB

commande *f* **imbriquée** *nom* embedded command

commande *f* **interne** *nom* internal command

commande LOAD HIGH *verbe* to load high

commande *f* **MD (de création de répertoire)** *nom* **1.** make directory **2.** MD ■ *abrév* MKDIR

commande *f* **numérique** *abrév* NC ■ *nom* numerical control

commande *f* **numérique directe** *nom* **1.** DDC **2.** direct digital control

commande *f* **numérique par calculateur** *nom* computer numerical control

commandé par les codes CTRL *adjectif* control-driven

commande *f* **point** *nom* dot command

commande *f* **RD** *nom* **1.** RD **2.** (*d'effacement de répertoire*) remove directory

commande *f* **rm** *nom* (*de suppression d'un sous-répertoire sous DOS*) rm

commande *f* **Run** *nom* Run command

commandes *f nom* line control ■ *plural noun* operating instructions

commandes *fpl* **numériques de machines-outils** *nom* CNC

commande *f* **supprimer** *nom* DEL

commentaire *m nom* **1.** annotation **2.** comment **3.** narrative ◇ **en BASIC il est possible d'inclure des commentaires à la suite de l'instruction REM** BASIC allows comments to be written after a REM instruction

commerce ◇ **commerce** *m* **effectué aux moyens de télévision interactive** T-commerce

commerce *m* **électronique** commerce ■ *nom* e-commerce

commerce *m* **électronique** *ou* **e-commerce** *nom* electronic commerce

commercialiser *verbe vt* to release

commision ◇ **commission** *f* **qui approuve et certifie les matériels de télécommunication avant leur mise en service dans le Royaume-Uni** BABT ◇ **si vous développez un nouveau modem, vous devrez obtenir l'approbation du BABT avant de le commercialiser** if you design a new modem, you must have BABT approval before you can sell it

commission *f* **(ANSI) T1** *nom* T1 committee

communauté *f* **virtuelle** *nom* **1.** community **2.** virtual community

communication ◇ **personne** *f* **qui demande une communication** caller

communication *f* **à faible débit** *plural noun* low-speed communications

communication *f* **asynchrone** *nom* asynchronous communication

communication *f* **en arrière-plan** *nom* background communication

communication *f* **non prioritaire** *nom* background communication

communication *f* **par câble** *plural noun* line communications

communications *fpl* **groupées** *nom* batched communication

communication *f* **synchrone binaire** *nom* **1.** binary synchronous communications **2.** BSC

commutateur *nom* switch ◇ **ajoutez le commutateur '*or* W' à la commande DIR (sous DOS) pour afficher le répertoire sur toute la largeur de l'écran** add the switch '/W' to the DOS command DIR and the directory listing will be displayed across the screen ◇ **commutateurs** *mpl* **chaînés** ganged switch ◇ **commutateurs** *mpl* **en série** ganged switch ◇ **série de commutateurs** *ou* **commutateurs en série** switch train

commutateur *m* **à bascule** *nom* DIP switch ■ *abrév* FF ■ *nom* **1.** flip-flop **2.** toggle switch ◇ **commutateur à bascule de type D** D-flip-flop

commutateur *m* **DIP** *nom* DIP switch

commutation *f nom* switching

commutation *f* **de cellules** *nom* cell relay

commutation *f* **de circuit** *nom* circuit switching

commutation *f* **de paquets** *nom* packet switching

commutation *f* **de secours** *nom* switched network backup

commutation *f* **du clavier** *nom* figures shift

commutation *f* **numérique** *nom* digital switching

commutation *f* **par paquets** *adjectif* packet-switched

compactage *m nom* packing

compacter *verbe vt* to concentrate ◇ **les données compressées** *ou* **comprimées ont pu être transmises à peu de frais** the concentrated data was transmitted cheaply

compact Flash *nom* compact Flash

Compaq™ (*fabricant d'ordinateurs*) COMPAQ

comparaison *f* **logique** *nom* logical comparison

comparateur *m nom* comparator

compatibilité *f nom* compatibility ◇ **compatibilité** *f* **avec un système de niveau inférieur** downward compatibility ◇ **OS** *or* **2 possède une fenêtre de compatibilité qui permet de faire tourner les applications sous DOS** OS/2 has a compatibility box to allow it to run DOS applications

compatibilité *f* **d'affectation** *adjectif* assignment compatible

compatibilité *f* **de logiciel** *nom* program compatibility

compatibilité *f* **du matériel** *nom* hardware compatibility

compatible *adjectif* compatible ■ *nom* compatible ■ *adjectif* compliant ◇ **compatible avec des logiciels écrits pour d'autres systèmes** software compatible ◇ **compatible avec système de niveau supérieur** upward compatible

compatible à l'enfichage *adjectif* pin-compatible

compatible avec un système de niveau inférieur *adjectif* downward compatible

compatible Hayes *adjectif* Hayes-compatible

compatible IBM *adjectif* IBM-compatible

compatible LTT *adjectif* TTL-compatible

compatible PC *adjectif* PC-compatible

compilateur *m nom* compiler *ou* compiler program

compilateur *m* **croisé** *nom* cross-compiler

compilateur *m* **d'optimisation** *nom* optimising compiler

compilateur *m* **d'un langage évolué** *nom* language compiler

compilateur *m* **natif** *nom* native compiler

compilateur *m* **originel** *nom* native compiler

compilation *f nom* compilation

compilation *f* **de programme** *nom* program compilation

compilation *f* **et exécution** *nom* compile and go

compiler *verbe vt* to compile ◇ **déboguez votre programme avant de le compiler** debug your program, then compile it ◇ **il faut beaucoup de temps pour faire la compilation avec cette ancienne version du programme** compiling takes a long time with this old version ◇ **les programmes BASIC compilés sont plus rapides que la version interpréteur** compiled BASIC programs run much faster than the interpreter version

complément *m adjectif* add-on ■ *nom* **1.** add-on **2.** complement ◇ **on trouve les compléments en remplaçant les 1 par des 0 et les 0 par des 1** the complement is found by changing the 1s to 0s and 0s to 1s

complément *m* **à 1** *nom* one's complement ◇ **le complément à 1 de 10011 est 01100** the one's complement of 10011 is 01100

complément *m* **à deux** *nom* two's complement

complément *m* **à dix** *nom* ten's complement

complément *m* **à la base** *nom* radix complement

complément *m* **à neuf** *nom* nine's complement

complémenté *adjectif* (*nombre binaire, etc.*) complemented

complément *m* **restreint** *nom* diminished radix complement

composant *nom* **1.** chip **2.** element

> '...les deux composants sont logés dans des boîtiers DIL en céramique ou plastique' [*Electronique*]

composant *m* **de très petite dimension** *nom* microdevice

composant *m* **de type SIP** *nom* single in-line package

composant *m* **OCX** *nom* OCX

composant *m* **VBX** *abrév* VBX

composé *adjectif* compound

composer *verbe vt* to set ◇ **le texte est (composé) en Times romain corps 12** the text is set in 12 point Times Roman

composer à la suite *verbe* to run on ◇ **le texte peut courir sans alinéa** the line can run on to the next without any space

compositeur *m nom* typesetter

composition *f* **au cadran (rotatif)** *nom* pulse-dialling

composition *f* **automatique de lettres types** *nom* automatic letter writing

compresser *verbe vt* to concentrate ◇ **les données compressées** *ou* **comprimées ont pu être transmises à peu de frais** the concentrated data was transmitted cheaply

compression *f nom* **1.** compression **2.** packing ◇ **compression** *f* **d'image avec perte de qualité** lossy compression ◇ **compression** *f* **d'image sans perte de qualité** lossless compression

compression *f* **asymétrique** *nom* asymmetric compression

compression *f* **de disque** *nom* disk compression

compression *f* **de données** *nom* **1.** data compacting **2.** data compression **3.** data reduction

compression *f* **de texte** *nom* text compression

compression *f* **d'image** *nom* image compression

compression-extension *f nom* companding

compression *f* **fractale (d'images)** *nom* fractal compression

compression *f* **spatiale** *nom* intraframe coding

compression *f* **symétrique** *nom* symmetrical compression

compression *f* **vidéo** *nom* video compression

compression *f* **vidéo asymétrique** *nom* asymmetric video compression

comprimer *verbe* **1.** *vt* to concentrate **2.** *vt* to reduce ◇ **les données compressées** *ou* **comprimées ont pu être transmises à peu de frais** the concentrated data was transmitted cheaply

comptabiliser *verbe vt* to account

compte *m nom* account ◇ **si vous êtes un nouvel utilisateur, vous devez demander à l'administrateur de vous ouvrir un compte** if you are a new user, you will have to ask the supervisor to create an account for you

compte *m* **d'affaires** *nom* merchant account

compteur *m nom* **1.** counter **2.** timer

compteur *m* **binaire** *nom* binary counter

compteur *m* **de boucles** *nom* loop counter

compteur *m* **de programme** *abrév* PC

compteur *m* **de répétitions** *nom* repeat counter

compteur *m* **d'inscription** *nom* program address counter

compteur *m* **d'instruction** *nom* **1.** instruction counter **2.** program counter

compteur *m* **incrémenteur/décrémenteur** *nom* up/down counter

compteur *m* **ordinal** *abrév* SCR

compte *m* **(d') utilisateur** *nom* user account ◇ **j'ai un nouveau compte d'utilisateur sur ce réseau, mais j'ai oublié mon mot de passe** I have a new user account on this LAN but I cannot remember my password

CompuServe™ (*fournisseur d'information*) CompuServe

CON *nom* CON

concaténation *f nom* concatenated data set

concaténation *f* **de chaînes** *nom* string concatenation

concaténer *verbe* **1.** *vt* to catenate **2.** *vt* to concatenate

concentrateur *m nom* **1.** active hub **2.** concentrator **3.** hub **4.** smart wiring hub

concentrateur *m* **10base-T** *nom* concentrator

concentrateur *m* **de données** *nom* **1.** data concentrator **2.** milking machine

concentrateur *m* **de réseau** *nom* concentrator

concentrateur *m* **empilable** *nom* stackable hub

concentrer *verbe vt* to concentrate ◇ **concentrer un rayon lumineux sur une lentille** to concentrate a beam of light on a lens

concepteur *m nom* developer

concepteur *m* **de logiciel** *nom* software developer

conception *f nom* system design

conception *f* **ascendante d'un programme** *nom* bottom up method *ou* bottom up programming

conception *f* **assistée par ordinateur** *nom* **1.** CAD **2.** computer-aided design **3.** computer-assisted design ◇ **tous nos ingénieurs travaillent sur des stations de CAO** all our engineers design on CAD workstations

conception *f* **de produits** *nom* product design

conception *f* **économique** *nom* least cost design

concevoir *verbe vt* to devise

conçu,-e par ordinateur *adjectif* computer-generated ◇ **images conçues sur ordinateur** *ou* **images de synthèse** *ou* **graphismes** computer-generated graphics

condensateur *m nom* capacitor ◇ **condensateur céramique** ceramic capacitor ◇ **condensateur électrolytique** electrolytic capacitor ◇ **condensateur non électrolytique** non-electrolytic capacitor ◇ **condensateur variable** *ou* **capacité variable** variable capacitor ◇ **microphone à condensateur** capacitor microphone

condensation *f nom* packing

condenser *verbe vt* to concentrate

condition *f nom* **1.** condition **2.** *vt* condition ◇ **adaptez les données brutes à un format standard** condition the raw data to a standard format

condition *f* **d'alerte** *nom* alert condition

condition *f* **d'arrêt** *nom* halt condition

condition *f* **d'entrée** *nom* entry condition

condition *f* **d'erreur** *nom* error condition

condition *f* **initiale** *nom* initial condition

conditionnel *adjectif* conditional

conditionner *verbe* **1.** *vt* to condition **2.** *vt* to pack

conducteur *m nom* conductor ◇ **le cuivre est un bon conducteur** copper is a good conductor of electricity

conductibilité *f nom* conduction

conductible *adjectif* conductive

conduction *f nom* conduction ◇ **conduction (d'électricité) par broches de contact (en) or** the conduction of electricity by gold contacts

conduire *verbe vt* to conduct ◇ **conduire l'électricité** to conduct electricity ◇ **le cuivre est bon conducteur (d'électricité)** copper conducts well

conduit *m nom* duct

conduite *f nom* **1.** channelling **2.** conduit **3.** duct ◇ **les câbles de liaison de tous les terminaux sont acheminés par conduite métallique** *ou* **par canalisation métallique** *ou* **sous gaine métallique jusqu'au centre informatique** the cables from each terminal are channelled to the computer centre by metal conduit

confidentialité *f nom* privacy ◇ **cryptage de l'information pour en assurer la confidentialité** privacy transformation

confidentialité *f* **de l'information** *nom* privacy of information

confidentialité *f* **des données** *nom* privacy of data

CONFIG.SYS *nom* CONFIG.SYS ◇ **si vous installez une nouvelle carte adaptateur sur votre PC, il faudra ajouter une nouvelle commande dans le fichier CONFIG.SYS** if you add a new adapter card to your PC you will have to add a new command to the CONFIG.SYS file

configuration *f nom* **1.** configuration **2.** map **3.** topology ◇ **configuration** *f* **d'un programme à plusieurs branches** multithread

configuration *f* **de la mémoire** *nom* memory map

configuration *f* **d'entrée/sortie** *nom* I/O mapping

configuration *f* **de registre** *nom* register map

configuration *f* **de réseau** *nom* networking ◇ **cette société informatique est une société britannique spécialisée en réseaux** this computer firm is a UK networking specialist

configuration *f* **de réseau** *nom* network topology

configuration *f* **du matériel** *nom* hardware configuration

configuration *f* **d'un connecteur** *nom* pinout

configuration *f* **d'une base de données** *nom* database mapping

configuration *f* **en étoile** *nom* star topology

configuration *f* **logique** *nom* logic map

configuration *f* **MIDI** *nom* MIDI mapping

configuration *f* **MIP** *nom* MIP mapping

configuré *adjectif* configured-in

configuré en mémoire *adjectif* memory-mapped ◇ **chaque pixel de cet écran configuré en mémoire a une adresse allouée, ce qui permet au processeur d'y accéder directement** a memory-mapped screen has an address allocated to each pixel, allowing direct access to the screen by the CPU

configurer *verbe* **1.** *vt* to configure **2.** *vt* to set up ◇ **ce terminal est configuré pour l'affichage de graphiques** this terminal has been configured to display graphics ◇ **délai de configuration** *ou* **d'installation** set-up time ◇ **dès qu'il a été configuré par l'ingénieur, le nouvel ordinateur a bien fonctionné** the new computer worked well as soon as the engineer had set it up ◇ **il suffit de configurer l'ordinateur individuel une seule fois, à l'achat** you only have to configure the PC once – when you first buy it ◇ **option de configuration** set-up option

configurer en réseau *verbe* to network ◇ **ils exploitent un réseau de micros** they run a system of networked micros ◇ **les postes de travail ont été reliés en réseau plutôt que d'être utilisés indépendamment** the workstations have been networked together rather than used as standalone systems ◇ **programme transmis sur (tout) un réseau de télévision** networked TV programme

confirmation *f* **positive** *nom* (*d'un message*) affirmative acknowledgement

conjonction *f nom* **1.** conjunction **2.** meet

conjonction *f* **logique** *nom* **1.** AND operation **2.** coincidence operation

connaissance *f* **exhaustive** *nom* global knowledge

connaissance *f* **globale** *nom* global knowledge

connecté, -ée en permanence *adjectif* always on

connecter *verbe* **1.** *vt* to link **2.** *vt* to switch

connecter à *verbe* to connect

connecteur *m nom* **1.** connector **2.** empty slot **3.** (*d'un transistor à effet de champ*) gate **4.** joystick port ◇ **le connecteur attaché au câble s'adapte sur tout port série standard** the connector at the end of the cable will fit any standard serial port ◇ **l'ordinateur familial possède un port (pour manette de) jeu** a joystick port is provided with the home computer

connecteur *m* **à enfichage dirigé** *nom* polarised edge connector

connecteur *m* **AUI** *nom* AUI connector

connecteur *m* **à une seule position d'enfichage** *nom* polarised plug

connecteur *m* **à un seul bord d'enfichage** *nom* polarised edge connector

connecteur *m* **BNC coaxial** *nom* BNC connector

connecteur *m* **DB** *nom* **1.** data bus connector **2.** DB connector

connecteur *m* **de câble** *nom* cable connector

connecteur *m* **de carte** *nom* **1.** card edge connector **2.** edge connector

connecteur *m* **de fibres optiques** *nom* fibre connector

connecteur *m* **de réseau RJ45** *nom* RJ-45

connecteur *m* **de type D** *nom* D-type connector ◇ **le port série du PC utilise un connecteur à neuf broches de type D** the serial port on a PC uses a 9-pin D-type connector

connecteur *m* **en D** *nom* **1.** data bus connector **2.** DB connector **3.** D-type connector ◇ **le port série du PC utilise un connecteur à neuf broches de type D** the serial port on a PC uses a 9-pin D-type connector

connecteur *m* **en T** *nom* T connector

connecteur *m* **en T BNC** *nom* BNC T-piece connector

connecteur *m* **femelle** *nom* female connector

connecteur *m* **IEC** *nom* IEC connector

connecteur *m* **mâle** *nom* male connector

connecteur *m* **mâle à deux broches** *nom* jumper

connecteur *m* **MIDI** *nom* MIDI connector

connecteur *m* **PCMCIA** *nom* PCMCIA connector

connecteur *m* **RJ11** *nom* RJ-11

connecteur *m* **ST** *nom* ST connector

connectif *m nom* connective

connectivité *f nom* connectivity

connectivité *f* **JDBC** *abrév* JDBC

connectivité JDBC (*nom de marque*) Java Database Connectivity

connexion *f nom* **1.** contact **2.** nexus **3.** switching ◇ **avec connexion directe** direct connect ◇ **le circuit ne fonctionne pas parce que la connexion est encrassée** the circuit is not working because the contact is dirty

connexion *f* **à chaud** *nom* **1.** hot plugging **2.** hot swapping

connexion *f* **active** *nom* active link

connexion *f* **avortée** *nom* aborted connection

connexion *f* **directe** *nom* direct connection

connexion *f* **en chaîne** *nom* daisy-chaining ◇ **la connexion en chaîne réduit le câblage** daisy-chaining saves a lot of cable

connexion *f* **enroulée** *nom* wire wrap

connexion *f* **fiable** *nom* reliable connection

connexion *f* **fixe** *nom* hardwired connection

connexion *f* **Megastream™** Megastream

connexion *f* **montée en cascade** *nom* cascade connection

connexion *f* **parallèle** *nom* parallel connection ◇ **leur débit de transmission est de 60 000 bits par seconde en connexion parallèle** their average transmission rate is 60,000 bps through parallel connection

connexion *f* **par ligne commutée** *nom* dial-up connection

connexion *f* **pour transmission de données** *nom* data connection

console *nom* **1.** console **2.** operator's console **3.** remote console **4.** remote device **5.** station ◇ **console** *f* (*avec écran et clavier, des compatibles IBM PC*) CON ◇ **console de jeu** play station *ou* playstation ◇ **la console comporte un périphérique d'entrée, soit un clavier, et un périphérique de sortie, soit une imprimante ou un écran** the console consists of input device such as a keyboard, and an output device such as a printer or CRT

> '...le groupe espère bien profiter de sa position stratégique pour transformer ses consoles de jeu en terminaux de communication' [*L'Express*]

console *f* **de jeu** *nom* **1.** game console **2.** games console

console *f* **système** *nom* system console

consommables *mpl plural noun* consumables

consommer *verbe vt* to use ◇ **l'appareil consomme beaucoup trop d'électricité** it's using too much electricity

consortium *m* **W3C** *nom* **1.** W3C **2.** World Wide Web Consortium

constant *adjectif* constant ◇ **débit binaire constant** constant bit rate (CBR) ◇ **le moteur du lecteur de disque tourne à une vitesse constante** the disk drive motor spins at a constant velocity ◇ **vitesse angulaire constante** constant angular velocity (CAV) ◇ **vitesse constante**

constant velocity ◇ **vitesse linéaire constante** constant linear velocity (CLV)

constante *f nom* **1.** constant **2.** one element

constante *f* **de réadressage** *nom* relocation constant

constitution *f* **de file d'attente** *nom* scheduling ◇ **établissement d'un horaire de programme de télévision** *ou* **radio** programme scheduling

constitution *f* **de pile d'interruptions** *nom* interrupt stacking

constructeur *m* **de matériel informatique** *nom* OEM

consultation *f nom* hit

consultation *f* **de table** *nom* look-up

consultation *f* **d'une table de référence** *nom* table lookup

consulter une base de données sans autorisation *verbe* to browse

consultez donc le manuel! *abrév* RTFM

contact *m nom* **1.** contact **2.** PIN ◇ **épreuve de contact** contact print ◇ **(film) négatif contact** contact negative

contact *m nom* hit ◇ **cette clé (de recherche) produit trois contacts** there are three hits for this search key ◇ **courte perturbation sur la ligne** hit on the line ◇ **il n'a fallu que quelques secondes pour trouver la réponse** *ou* **pour obtenir les données** there was a hit after just a few seconds

contact *m* **en or** *nom* gold contact

contacter *verbe vt* to contact

contact *m* **intermittent** *nom* dry contact

contact *m* **sec** *nom* dry contact

contention *f nom* contention

contenu *m nom* content

contenu *m* **de registre** *nom* register map

contenu *m* **vidéo sur Internet** *nom* streaming video

contexte *m nom* context ◇ **l'exemple démontre l'emploi du mot dans son contexte** the example shows how the word is used in context

continuer *verbe vt* to resume

continuité *f nom* continuity

contournage *m nom* contouring

contraindre *verbe vt* to constrain

contrainte *f nom* restriction

contraire *m nom* inverse ◇ **le contraire de vrai est faux** the inverse of true is false

contraste *nom* contrast ◇ **ce bouton vous permet de régler la luminosité et le contraste** the control allows you to adjust brightness and contrast

> '...les jeux d'ombres d'un objet en mouvement, mais restant à la même distance de la caméra, provoquent des variations de contraste que l'objectif cherche constamment à suivre' [*Audio Vidéo*]

contrat *m nom* deal ◇ **il se sont mis d'accord sur un contrat global comprenant le développement d'un logiciel, la personnalisation du matériel et la formation du personnel** they agreed a package deal, which involves the development of software, customizing hardware and training of staff

contrat *m* **de maintenance** *nom* **1.** maintenance contract **2.** service contract

contrat *m* **forfait** *nom* package deal

contrat *m* **global** *nom* package deal ◇ **il se sont mis d'accord sur un contrat global comprenant le développement d'un logiciel, la personnalisation du matériel et la formation du personnel** they agreed a package deal, which involves the development of software, customizing hardware and training of staff

contrôle *m nom* **1.** control **2.** service **3.** (*vérification*) verification ◇ **contrôle** *m* **de la frappe des touches** keystroke verification ◇ **contrôle** *m* **de périphérique par caractère** device character control ◇ **unité de contrôle (de processus)** control unit (CU) ◇ **vérification et validation** *ou* **contrôle et validation** verification and validation (V & V)

contrôlé, -ée par une souris *adjectif* mouse-driven

contrôle *m* **à distance** *nom* remote control

contrôle *m* **cyclique** *nom* cyclic check

contrôle *m* **d'accès** *nom* access control

contrôle *m* **d'accès au support** *abrév* MAC ■ *nom* media access control

contrôle *m* **de bloc de caractères** *nom* block character check

contrôle *m* **de caractère** *nom* character check

contrôle *m* **de cohérence** *nom* consistency check

contrôle *m* **d'écran ANSI** *nom* ANSI screen control

contrôle *m* **de dépassement de capacité** *nom* overflow check

contrôle *m* **de données** *nom* data control

contrôle *m* **de flux d'informations** *nom* information flow control

contrôle *m* **de gain automatique** *nom* **1.** AGC **2.** automatic gain control

contrôle *m* **de l'alimentation** *nom* power monitor

contrôle *m* **de la production** *nom* production control

contrôle *m* **de liaison de données** *nom* data link control

contrôle *m* **de liaison de données de haut niveau** *nom* high-level data link control

contrôle *m* **de ligne de communication** *nom* communications link control

contrôle *m* **de ligne de transmission** *nom* communications link control

contrôle *m* **de mise en communication** *nom* handshake I/O control

contrôle *m* **de numérisation** *nom* test numeric

contrôle *m* **de parité** *nom* parity check

contrôle *m* **de parité paire** *nom* even parity *ou* even parity check

contrôle *m* **de parité paire-impaire** *nom* odd-even check

contrôle *m* **de parité verticale** *nom* vertical parity check

contrôle *m* **de qualité** *nom* quality control

contrôle *m* **d'erreurs** *nom* error control

contrôle *m* **des canaux d'accès** *nom* access channel control

contrôle *m* **de sécurité** *nom* security check

contrôle *m* **de séquence** *nom* sequence check

contrôle *m* **de transfert** *nom* **1.** transfer check **2.** transfer control

contrôle *m* **de travaux groupés en pile** *nom* stacked job control

contrôle *m* **d'exécution des tâches** *nom* job statement control

contrôle *m* **d'inférence** *nom* inference control

contrôle *m* **du flux (de données)** *nom* flow control

contrôle *m* **en cascade** *nom* cascade control

contrôle *m* **et exécution d'interruption** *nom* interrupt servicing

contrôle *m* **et validation** *nom* **1.** V & V **2.** verification and validation

contrôle *m* **horizontal** *nom* horizontal check

contrôle *m* **numérique** *nom* numerical control

contrôle *m* **par écho** *nom* echo check

contrôle *m* **par le récepteur** *nom* backwards supervision

contrôle *m* **par modulo-n** *nom* modulo-N check

contrôle *m* **par redondance cyclique** *abrév* CRC ■ *nom* cyclic redundancy check

contrôle *m* **par redondance longitudinale** *nom* longitudinal redundancy check

contrôle *m* **par redondance verticale** *nom* **1.** vertical redundancy check **2.** VRC

contrôle *m* **par relecture** *nom* read back check

contrôle *m* **par retour** *nom* feedback control

contrôle *m* **par totalisation** *nom* summation check

contrôler *verbe* **1.** *vt* to monitor **2.** *vt* to regulate **3.** *vt* to test **4.** *vt* to verify ◇ **il contrôle** *ou* **suit le progrès des programmeurs débutants** he is monitoring the progress of the trainee programmers ◇ **l'appareil contrôle chaque signal de sortie** the machine monitors each signal as it is sent out

contrôle *m* **sur reste** *nom* residue check

contrôleur *m* *nom* **1.** controller **2.** supervisor

contrôleur *m* **d'accès** *nom* access controller

contrôleur *m* **d'affichage** *nom* display controller

contrôleur *m* **de base** *nom* basic controller

contrôleur *m* **de cache** *nom* cache controller

contrôleur *m* **de communication** *nom* communications control unit

contrôleur *m* **d'écran** *nom* display controller

contrôleur *m* **de disque** *nom* disk controller

contrôleur *m* **de disque IDE** *nom* **1.** IDE **2.** integrated device electronics *ou* integrated drive electronics

contrôleur *m* **de disquettes** *nom* **1.** disk controller **2.** FDC **3.** floppy disk controller

contrôleur *m* **d'émetteur/récepteur asynchrone universel** *nom* UART controller

contrôleur *m* **d'entrée/sortie** *nom* input/output controller

contrôleur *m* **de périphérique** *nom* **1.** PCU **2.** peripheral control unit

contrôleur *m* **de réseau** *nom* network controller

contrôleur *m* **de sauvegarde par domaine** *nom* backup domain controller

contrôleur *m* **de terminal** *nom* terminal controller

contrôleur *m* **d'imprimante** *nom* printer's controller

contrôleur *m* **d'interface** *nom* breakout box

contrôleur *m* **d'interface de périphérique** *nom* peripheral interface adapter

contrôleur *m* **d'interruption programmable** *nom* programmable interrupt controller

contrôleur *m* **DMA** *nom* (*accès direct à la mémoire*) DMA controller

convention *f* *nom* convention

convention *f* **BNF** *nom* Backus-Naur-Form

convergence *f* *nom* convergence

conversationnel *adjectif* interactive

conversion *f* *nom* conversion

conversion *f* **automatique asynchrone/synchrone** *nom* autosync

conversion *f* **binaire-décimale** *nom* binary-to-decimal conversion

conversion *f* **d'affectation** *nom* assignment conversion

conversion *f* **décimale-binaire** *nom* decimal-to-binary conversion

conversion *f* **de code** *nom* code conversion

conversion *f* **de données** *nom* data translation

conversion *f* **de fichier** *nom* file conversion

conversion *f* **de signaux** *nom* **1.** signal conditioning **2.** signal conversion

conversion *f* **de support** *nom* media conversion

conversion *f* **d'une onde en numérique** *nom* waveform digitisation

convertibilité *f nom* convertibility

convertible *adjectif* convertible

convertir *verbe vt* to translate

convertisseur *m nom* **1.** conversion equipment **2.** conversion program **3.** converter **4.** convertor

convertisseur *m* **analogique-numérique** *nom* **1.** ADC **2.** analog to digital converter **3.** A to D converter **4.** digitiser *ou* digitizer

convertisseur *m* **analogique-numérique parallèle** *nom* flash A/D

convertisseur *m* **bande magnétique/carte perforée** *nom* tape to card converter

convertisseur *m* **de normes** *nom* standards converter

convertisseur *m* **numérique-analogique** *nom* **1.** DAC **2.** d/a converter **3.** digital to analog converter **4.** D to A converter

convertisseur *m* **numérique-analogique à accès aléatoire** *nom* random access digital to analog converter

convertisseur *m* **série/parallèle** *nom* serial to parallel converter

convertisseur *m* **texte/signal vocal** *nom* text-to-speech converter

convivial *adjectif* user-friendly ◇ **c'est un appareil vraiment convivial** *ou* **extrêmement facile à utiliser** it's such a user-friendly machine ◇ **comparée à la version précédente, celle-ci est très facile à utiliser** *ou* **très conviviale** compared with the previous version this one is very user-friendly

convivialité *nom* usability ◇ **nous avons étudié les tests de convivialité et trouvé que l'interface (graphique) GUI est plus facile à maîtriser pour les débutants que les lignes de commandes** we have studied usability tests and found that a GUI is easier for new users than a command line

'...toutefois, ce que le logiciel gagne en convivialité pour le débutant, il le perd en rigueur' [*Science et Vie Micro*]

cookie *nom* cookie

'...les cookies sont des codes qu'un serveur enregistre temporairement sur votre disque dur pour vous identifier et pouvoir réutiliser vos coordonnées dans un but commercial' [*Internet Pratique*]

coordination *f nom* coordination

coordination *f* **inductive** *nom* inductive coordination

coordonnée *f* **horizontale** *nom* x-coordinate

coordonnées *fpl plural noun* coordinates ■ *nom* x-y

coordonnées *fpl* **absolues** *plural noun* absolute coordinates

coordonnées *fpl* **cartésiennes** *plural noun* cartesian coordinates

coordonnées *fpl* **polaires** *nom* polar coordinates

coordonnées *Fpl* **relatives** *plural noun* relative coordinates

coordonnée *f* **verticale** *nom* y-coordinate

copie *f nom* **1.** COPY **2.** replication

copie *f* **archivée** *nom* archived copy

copie *f* **carbone** *nom* carbon copy

copie *f* **corrigée** *nom* (*d'un bloc de données*) after-image

copie *f* **d'archives** *nom* archived copy

copie *f* **de bobine à bobine** *nom* reel to reel

copie *f* **de fichier** *nom* (*sur disque dur*) swap file

copie *f* **de sauvegarde** *nom* **1.** backup **2.** backup copy **3.** backup version **4.** security backup

copie *f* **d'original** *nom* protection master

copie *f* **finale** *nom* clean copy

copie *f* **illégale** *nom* **1.** bootleg **2.** pirate copy

copie *f* **miroir** *nom* **1.** disk duplexing **2.** disk mirroring **3.** duplexing

copie *f* **pirate** *nom* pirate copy

copie *f* **piratée** *nom* **1.** bootleg **2.** pirate copy

copie *f* **pour archivage** *nom* file copy

copier *verbe* **1.** *vt* to copy **2.** *vt* to dump ■ *adjectif* master ◇ **ces diapos et photos sont les supports intermédiaires qui doivent être recopiés sur le vidéodisque** those slides and photographs are the intermediate materials to be mastered onto the video disk

copier à l'identique *verbe* to mirror

co-processeur *m nom* coprocessor

coprocesseur *m* **graphique** *nom* **1.** blitter **2.** graphics coprocessor

coprocesseur *m* **mathématique** *nom* **1.** maths chip **2.** maths coprocessor

coquille *f nom* literal

corbeille *f nom* **1.** Recycle Bin **2.** trashcan ◇ **pour détruire un fichier ou un dossier, traînez-le jusqu'à l'icône 'corbeille' ou encore appuyez sur la touche 'supprimer'** if you want to delete a file or folder, drag it onto the Recycle Bin icon or press the Delete key

co-résident *adjectif* coresident

coroutine *f nom* coroutine

corps *m nom* type size

corps *m* **de la boucle** *nom* loop body

corps *m* **d'un programme** *nom* body

corps *m* **d'un texte** *nom* body ◇ **corps (d'un caractère)** body size ◇ **dimension (en points) du corps d'un texte** body size

corps *m* **du texte** *nom* matter ◇ **imprimé** printed matter ◇ **imprimé** *ou* **matériel publicitaire** publicity matter

corps *m* **principal (d'un programme)** *nom* main body

correcteur *m* **d'erreurs ARQ** *nom* ARQ

correction *f nom* **1.** hot fix **2.** *vt* (*mise à jour*) update ◇ **le document original et le document corrigé se trouvent tous les deux sur disquettes** we have the original and updated documents on disks

correction *f* **automatique d'erreurs** *nom* automatic error correction

correction *f* **d'erreur en cours de transmission** *nom* forward error correction

correction *f* **d'erreurs** *nom* **1.** data cleaning **2.** error correction

correction *f* **d'erreurs ARQ** *nom* automatic repeat request

correction *f* **d'erreurs par retransmission** *nom* backward error correction

correction *f* **provisoire** *nom* patch

correspondant *m nom* called party

corrigé *m nom* update

corriger *verbe* **1.** *vt* to edit **2.** *vt* to update

corrompre *verbe vt* to corrupt ◇ **une baisse de tension durant l'accès au disque peut altérer** *ou* **corrompre les données** power loss during disk access can corrupt the data

corrompu *adjectif* corrupt

corruption *f nom* corruption

corruption *f* **de données** *nom* data corruption ◇ **la corruption de données sur la disquette a rendu un des fichiers impossible à lire** data corruption on the disk has made one file unreadable

couche *f nom* layer ◇ **couche** *f* **de phosphore** phosphor coating

couche *f* **application** *nom* application layer

couche *f* **binaire** *nom* (*dans une image graphique*) bit plane

couche *f* **d'adaptation ATM** *abrév* AAL ■ *nom* ATM adaptation layer

couche *f* **de liaison de données** *nom* data link layer

couche *f* **épaisse** *nom* thick film

couche *f* **mince** *nom* thin film

couche *f* **phosphorée à grande persistance** *nom* long persistence phosphor ◇ **les écrans à faible fréquence de balayage ont besoin de phosphore à longue persistance pour éviter l'instabilité de l'image** slow scan rate monitors need long persistence phosphor to prevent the image flickering

couche *f* **physique** *nom* physical layer

couche *f* **présentation** *nom* presentation layer

couche *f* **réseau** *nom* network layer

couches *f nom* ATM layers

couche *f* **session** *nom* session layer

couche *f* **transport** *nom* transport layer

couleur *f* **achromatique** *nom* achromatic colour

couleur *f* **d'affichage** *nom* display colour

couleur *f* **de premier plan** *nom* foreground colour

couleur *f* **intense** *nom* saturated colour

couleurs *fpl* **normalisées** *plural noun* standard colours

coupe *f* **(d'un mot)** *nom* division

coupe *f* **de mot (en bout de ligne) et justification** *f nom* hyphenation and justification ◇ **un programme de coupe de mots et justification établi aux Etats-Unis ne peut être utilisé pour un texte en anglais britannique** an American hyphenation and justification program will not work with British English spellings

coupe *f* **d'un mot** *nom* **1.** (*en bout de ligne*) hyphenation **2.** (*en bout de ligne*) word break

coupe-feu *m nom* firewall ◇ **nous avons mis en place un coupe-feu sur notre intranet pour empêcher l'accès non autorisé aux données de la société par l'intermédiaire de l'Internet** we have installed a firewall in our intranet to prevent hackers accessing company data via the internet link

coupe *f* **impropre** *nom* bad break

couper *verbe* **1.** *vt* to cut **2.** *vt* to scissor

couper et coller *nom vt* cut and paste

couper un mot et justifier *verbe* to hyphenate justify

couplage *m nom* linkage

couplage *m* **de la téléphonie et de l'informatique** *abrév* CIT ■ *nom* **1.** commercial Internet exchange **2.** computer-integrated telephony **3.** computer-telephony integration **4.** CTI

coupleur *m nom* coupler

coupleur *m* **acoustique** *nom* acoustic coupler

coupure *f nom* **1.** breakup **2.** cut **3.** deletion ◇ **les éditeurs ont demandé à l'auteur de faire plusieurs coupures dans le dernier chapitre** the editors asked the author to make several deletions in the last chapter ◇ **les éditeurs ont demandé de faire des coupures au premier chapitre** *ou* **de réduire le premier chapitre** the editors have asked for cuts in the first chapter

coupure *f* **automatique des mots** *nom* automatic hyphenation

coupure *f* **d'alimentation de l'ordinateur** *verbe* to power dump

coupure *f* **de courant** *verbe* to power dump ■ *nom* power failure

courant *m* **alternatif (CA)** *nom* alternating current

courant *m* **continu** *abrév* DC ■ *nom* direct current

courant *m* **contrôlé** *nom* regulated power supply

courant *m* **électrique** *nom* electric current

courant *m* **régulé** *nom* regulated power supply

courant *m* **transitoire** *nom* power transient

courbe *f nom* **1.** chart **2.** plot

courbe *f* **d'apprentissage** *nom* learning curve

courbe *f* **de Bézier** *nom* Bézier curve

Courier *nom* Courier

courriel *m nom* email *ou* e-mail

courriel *m* **vidéo** *nom* v-mail

courrier *m nom* email *ou* e-mail

courrier *m* **électronique** *nom* **1.** email *ou* e-mail **2.** mail

courrier *m* **non sollicité** *nom* unsolicited mail

courrier *m* **postal** *nom* snail mail

courrier *m* **sans intérêt** *nom* unsolicited mail

courrier *m* **vocal** *nom* voicemail

coût *m* **de connexion** *nom* connect charge

couvrir d'encre *verbe* to ink

crash *m nom* crash ◇ **crash** *m* **du disque dur causé par la tête de lecture** head crash

crasse *f nom* drop in

création *f nom* **1.** generation **2.** origination ◇ **la création de la maquette demandera plusieurs semaines** the origination of the artwork will take several weeks ◇ **on utilise l'ordinateur pour créer des images** *ou* **pour la création d'images (de synthèse)** the computer is used in the generation of graphic images

création *f* **de fichier** *nom* file creation

création *f* **de liens** *nom* linkage ◇ **éditeur de liens** linkage editor

création *f* **de modèles de programmes** *nom* modelling

création *f* **de programme** *nom* program generation

créé, -ée par ordinateur *adjectif* computer-generated

créer *verbe* **1.** *vt* to author **2.** *vt* to generate **3.** *vt* to originate ◇ **créer une image à partir de données numériques** to generate an image from digitally recorded data

créneau *m nom* expansion slot ◇ **enfichez la carte d'extension dans l'emplacement libre** insert the board in the free expansion slot

créneau *m* **inutilisé** *nom* empty slot

créneau *m* **pour message** *nom* message slot

crénelage *m nom* aliasing ■ *plural noun* jaggies

crête *f nom* peak ◇ **veillez à ce que la tension de crête ne dépasse pas 60 watts sinon l'amplificateur surchauffera** keep the peak power below 60 watts or the amplifier will overheat

creux *m nom* pit

cristal *nom* crystal

'...le groupe électronique nippon est parvenu à réaliser un écran à cristaux liquides qui, contrairement aux écrans usuels, garantit sous tous les angles de vision une image nette et une haute définition' [*Electronique*]

critique *adjectif* mission-critical

crochet(s) *plural noun* square brackets

cross-assembleur *m nom* cross-assembler

crucial, -e *adjectif* mission-critical

cryptage *m nom* **1.** cipher **2.** encryption ◇ **cryptage** *ou* **code chiffré à clé publique** public key cipher ◇ **standard de cryptage de données** data encryption standard (DES)

cryptage *m* **à clé public** *nom* public key cipher system

cryptage *m* **à clé publique** *nom* public key encryption

crypter *verbe* **1.** *vt* to encipher **2.** *vt* to encrypt ◇ **le message chiffré** *ou* **crypté peut être transmis par téléphone sans que personne ne puisse le lire** the encrypted text can be sent along ordinary telephone lines, and no one will be able to understand it

cryptographie *f nom* cryptography

cryptographique *adjectif* cryptographic

CSS *nom* cascading style sheet ■ *abrév* CSS

Ctrl *nom* **1.** control key **2.** CTR *ou* CTRL *ou* Ctrl

CTRL *nom* CTR *also* Ctrl

cumulateur *m nom* **1.** addend **2.** augmenter

curseur *m nom* **1.** cursor **2.** insertion point

curseur *m* **adressable** *nom* addressable cursor

curseur *m* **(en) bâton** *nom* I-beam

curseur *m* **d'entraînement** *nom* drag image

curseur *m* **destructif** *nom* destructive cursor

curseur *m* **en I** *nom* I-beam

curseur *m* **en pavé** *nom* block cursor

curseur *m* **non destructif** *nom* non destructive cursor ◇ **l'écran devient rapidement illisible lorsqu'on utilise le curseur non destructif** the screen quickly becomes unreadable when using a non-destructive cursor ◇ **lecture non destructive** non-destructive readout (NDR)

curseur *m* **secondaire** *nom* ghost cursor

cXML *nom* cXML

cyber- *préfixe* cyber-

cybercafé *m nom* cybercafé

cyberespace *m nom* cyberspace

cybernétique *f nom* cybernetics

cybersquattage *m nom* cybersquatting

cyberterrorisme *m nom* cyberterrorism

cycle *m nom* **1.** cycle **2.** refresh cycle ◇ **cycle** *m* **de rotation des fichiers de sauvegarde** grandfather cycle ◇ **disponibilité** *f* **dans le cycle** cycle availability ◇ **vol** *m* **de cycle** cycle stealing

cycle *m* **CPU** *nom* CPU cycle

cycle *m* **d'affichage** *nom* display cycle

cycle *m* **de contrôle** *nom* control cycle

cycle *m* **de lecture** *nom* read cycle

cycle *m* **de lecture d'une instruction** *nom* fetch cycle

cycle *m* **de lecture/écriture** *nom* **1.** read/write cycle **2.** R/W cycle

cycle *m* **de lecture/exécution** *nom* fetch-execute cycle

cycle *m* **de l'unité centrale** *nom* CPU cycle

cycle *m* **de machine** *nom* machine cycle

cycle *m* **de mémoire** *nom* memory cycle

cycle *m* **de vie d'un logiciel** *nom* software life cycle

cycle *m* **d'exécution** *nom* **1.** execute cycle **2.** execution cycle

cycle *m* **d'horloge** *nom* **1.** clock cycle **2.** CPU cycle

cycle *m* **d'instruction** *nom* instruction cycle

cycle *m* **d'opération** *nom* operation cycle

cycle *m* **fonctionnel** *nom* action cycle

cycle *m* **principal** *nom* major cycle

cyclique *adjectif* cyclic ◇ **contrôle de redondance cyclique** cyclic redundancy check (CRC)

cylindre *m* *nom* **1.** cylinder **2.** drum

D

DAC RAM *nom* RAMDAC

daemon *m nom* daemon

dataglove *m nom* data glove

datagramme *m nom* datagram

date *f nom* date ◇ **j'ai bien reçu votre message en date d'hier** I have received your message of yesterday's date ◇ **la date de création de ce fichier est le 10 juin** the date of creation for the file was the 10th of June

date *f* **et heure** *nom* date-time

date *f* **ordinale** *nom* Julian date

d'avance *préfixe* pre-

DCA *nom* DCA

DDE *nom* dynamic data exchange

de basse résolution *plural noun* low-resolution graphics *ou* low-res graphics

débit *nom* **1.** data transfer rate **2.** throughput ◇ **débit** *m* **binaire de transmission de données** data signalling rate ◇ **débit** *m* **par défaut** (*d'un modem*) default rate ◇ **débit** *m* **réel de transfert de données** actual data transfer rate ◇ **limité par le débit des données** output-bound; output-limited

débit *m* **binaire** *nom* **1.** bit rate **2.** debit

débit *m* **binaire constant** *abrév* CBR ■ *nom* constant bit rate

débit *m* **binaire disponible** *nom* **1.** ABR **2.** available bit rate

débit *m* **corrigé en bps** *nom* bps rate adjust

débit *m* **de base (d'un RNIS)** *nom* BRA

débit *m* **de transmission** *nom* baud rate

débit *m* **d'une ligne** *nom* line speed

débit *m* **d'une voie de transmission** *nom* channel capacity

débit *m* **maximal de transmission** *nom* maximum transmission rate

débit *m* **moyen (de transmission)** *nom* medium speed

débit *m* **théorique** *nom* (*de données dans un canal*) aggregate line speed

déboguer *verbe* **1.** *vt* to debug **2.** *vt* to troubleshoot ◇ **il faut plus de temps pour déboguer un programme que pour en créer un** debugging takes up more time than construction ◇ **ils ont mis des semaines à déboguer le système** they spent weeks debugging the system

débogueur *m nom* debugger

débogueur *m* **symbolique** *nom* symbolic debugger

débordement *m nom* spillage

débordement *m* **négatif** *nom* underflow

débrancher *verbe* **1.** *vt* to disconnect **2.** *vt* to unplug ◇ **ne déplacez pas le système sans l'avoir d'abord débranché** do not move the system without unplugging it ◇ **n'oubliez pas de débrancher (le câble de) l'imprimante avant de la changer de place** do not forget to disconnect the cable before moving the printer ◇ **vous n'avez qu'à déconnecter le lecteur et en brancher un nouveau à sa place** simply unplug the old drive and plug-in a new one

DEBUG *nom* DEBUG

de bureau *adjectif* desktop

début *nom* start ◇ **début** *m* **de fichier** head ◇ **(code de) début de texte** start of text (SOT *ou* STX)

débutant *m nom* newbie

début *m* **de fichier** *nom* beginning of file

début *m* **d'enregistrement** *nom* home record

début *m* **d'en-tête** *nom* start of header

début *m* **de texte** *abrév* SOT ■ *nom* start of text ■ *abrév* STX

début *m* **d'une page** *nom* head of form ■ *abrév* HOF

décade *f nom* decade

décalage *m nom* **1.** float **2.** lag ◇ **faire un décalage vers la gauche** shift left ◇ **le décalage est perceptible sur les lignes téléphoniques internationales** time lag is noticeable on international phone calls

décalage *m* **à gauche** *nom* left shift

décalage *m* **arithmétique** *nom* arithmetic shift

décalage *m* **circulaire** *nom* **1.** circular shift **2.** end about shift **3.** ring shift

décalage *m* **de fréquence** *nom* dual clocking

décalage *m* **logique** *nom* **1.** logical shift **2.** non arithmetic shift

décalage *m* **vers la droite** *nom* shift right

décaler *verbe vt* to shift

déchiffrage *m nom* decryption ◇ **le décryptage** *ou* **le déchiffrage se fait à l'aide de l'or-**

dinateur pour assurer une plus grande rapidité decryption is done using hardware to increase speed

déchiffrer *verbe* **1.** *vt* to decipher **2.** *vt* to decrypt **3.** *vt* to de-scramble

décibel *m abrév* dB

décibel *m* **(dB)** *nom* decibel

décimal *m* **codé binaire** *nom* binary coded decimal

décimal *m* **codé binaire (DCB)** *nom* BCD

décimal *m* **codé binaire naturel** *nom* natural binary coded decimal

décimale *f* **condensée** *nom* packed decimal

décision *f* **logique** *nom* logical decision

déclaration *f nom* **1.** declaration **2.** declarative statement **3.** execute statement **4.** input statement

déclaration *f* **d'affectation** *nom* assignment statement

déclaration *f* **de confidentialité** *nom* privacy statement

déclaration *f* **de procédure** *nom* procedure declaration

déclaration *f* **de remarque** *nom* **1.** (*dans un programme en BASIC*) REM **2.** (*dans un programme en BASIC*) remark

déclaration *f* **d'une variable locale** *nom* local declaration

déclarer *verbe vt* to declare ◇ **au début du programme X a été déclaré égal à 9** he declared at the start of the program that X was equal to nine

déclenché, -ée par interruption *adjectif* interrupt-driven

déclenché par bascule de front d'impulsion *adjectif* edge-triggered

décoder *verbe vt* to decode

décodeur *m nom* **1.** decoder **2.** de-scrambler

décodeur *m nom* decode unit

décodeur *m* **d'adresses** *nom* address decoder

décodeur *m* **d'instruction** *nom* operation decoder

décodeur *m* **d'instructions** *nom* instruction decoder

de compatibilité ascendante *adjectif* backwards compatible

décompilateur *m nom* decompiler

décompilation *f nom* decompilation ◇ **compilation et décompilation incrémentielles** incremental compilation and decompilation

décompresser *verbe* **1.** *vt* to decompress **2.** *vt* to unpack ◇ **cette routine permet de décomprimer les fichiers archivés** this routine unpacks the archived file

décompression *f nom* decompression

décomprimer *verbe vt* to unpack ◇ **cette routine permet de décomprimer les fichiers archivés** this routine unpacks the archived file

décondenser *verbe vt* to unpack

déconnecter *verbe* **1.** *vt* to disconnect **2.** *vt* to unplug ◇ **vous n'avez qu'à déconnecter le lecteur et en brancher un nouveau à sa place** simply unplug the old drive and plug-in a new one

de constructeur *adjectif* intimate

de contrôle *adjectif* supervisory

de côté client *adjectif* client-side ◇ **application client** client side application

découper *verbe* **1.** *vt* to crop **2.** *vt* (*la bordure d'une image*) to crop **3.** *vt* to partition

de courte durée *adjectif* transient

décrémenter *verbe vt* to decrement ◇ **le contenu du registre a été décrémenté à zéro** the register contents were decremented until they reached zero

décrire un cercle *verbe* to circulate

décrochage *m nom* holdup

décryptage *m nom* decryption ◇ **le décryptage** *ou* **le déchiffrage se fait à l'aide de l'ordinateur pour assurer une plus grande rapidité** decryption is done using hardware to increase speed

décrypter *verbe vt* to decrypt

de démarrage *adjectif* bootable

dédié *adjectif* dedicated ■ *nom* special purpose ◇ **il n'y a qu'un poste dédié** *ou* **réservé aux graphiques sur ce réseau** there's only one dedicated graphics workstation in this network ◇ **ligne téléphonique spécialisée** *ou* **dédiée** dedicated line

déduction *f nom* inference

défaillance *f nom* **1.** (*totale*) crash **2.** fault **3.** glitch **4.** malfunction **5.** problem **6.** program crash ◇ **les données ont été perdues par suite d'une défaillance du logiciel** the data was lost due to a software malfunction

défaillance *f* **de l'ordinateur** *nom* equipment failure

défaillance *f* **du matériel** *nom* **1.** equipment failure **2.** hard failure **3.** hardware failure

défaillance *f* **induite** *nom* induced failure

défaillance *f* **provoquée par une cause externe** *nom* induced failure

défaut *adjectif* default ■ *nom* fault ◇ **le système d'exploitation permet à l'utilisateur de choisir le lecteur par défaut** the operating system allows the user to select the default drive ◇ **par défaut** *ou* **implicite** *ou* **intrinsèque** *ou* **prédéterminé, -ée** by default

> '...le gestionnaire d'écran par défaut correspond aux écrans EGA (vous n'avez donc rien à faire si vous possédez un tel écran)' [*L'Ordinateur Individuel*]

défaut *m* **(de magnétisation)** *nom* drop out

défaut *m* **d'alignement** *nom* skew

défaut *m* **de surface** *nom* scratch ◇ **cette rayure rend la lecture du disque impossible** this scratch makes the disk unreadable
défaut *m* **d'horloge** *nom* hazard
défilement *m* **(du texte sur l'écran)** *nom* display scrolling
défilement *m* **horizontal** *nom* horizontal scrolling
défilement *m* **vertical** *nom* vertical scrolling
défiler ◇ **faire défiler un texte ligne à ligne sur l'écran** roll scroll
défini, -e d'avance *adjectif* predefined
définir *verbe* **1.** *vt* to assign **2.** *vt* to define **3.** *vt* to set up ◇ **toutes les variables ont été définies lors de l'initialisation** all the variables were defined at initialization
définir de nouveau *verbe* to redefine ◇ **nous avons redéfini les premiers paramètres** we redefined the initial parameters ◇ **redéfinir la fonction d'une touche** *ou* **reprogrammer une touche** to redefine a key
définissable par l'utilisateur *adjectif* user-selectable
définition *nom* **1.** definition **2.** resolution ◇ **avec un écran haute définition on obtient un affichage de 640 par 450 pixels** the high resolution screen can display 640 by 450 pixels ◇ **définition** *f* **de balayage** scanning resolution ◇ **définition de l'image** image resolution ◇ **haute définition** high resolution (hi-res)

> '...ces super-consoles peuvent manier en un temps plus réduit davantage d'informations, et donc présenter des jeux avec une meilleure définition graphique' [*L'Express*]

définition *f* **de cellule** *nom* cell definition
définition *f* **de l'affichage graphique** *nom* graphic display resolution
définition *f* **de l'écran** *nom* display resolution
définition *f* **et standards de qualité d'un logiciel** *nom* software specification
définition *f* **maximum** *nom* limiting resolution
déflecteurs *mpl plural noun* deflection yokes
déflexion *f nom* deflection
déflexion *f* **de rayon** *nom* beam deflection
déformation *f nom* **1.** aberration **2.** distortion ◇ **déformation** *ou* **distorsion** *ou* **aberration de l'image** image distortion
déformer *verbe vt* to distort
DEFRAG *nom* DEFRAG
défragmentation *f nom* defragmentation
défragmentation *f* **de fichier** *nom* file defragmentation
défragmenteur *m nom* defragmentation utility
dégradation *f nom* degradation
dégradation *f* **de l'image** *nom* image degradation
dégradation *f* **douce** *nom* graceful degradation
dégradation *f* **limitée** *nom* graceful degradation
dégradation *f* **progressive** *nom* graceful degradation
dégradé *m nom* gradient
de grande vitesse *adjectif* high-speed
dégrouper *verbe vt* to unpack ◇ **dégrouper les éléments d' un bloc** deblock
de haute précision *plural noun* high-spec
de haute technologie *plural noun* high-spec
délai *m nom* **1.** contention delay **2.** gate delay **3.** interval **4.** propagation time
délai *m* **d'attente** *nom* wait time
délai *m* **de configuration** *nom* setup time
délai *m* **de conversion** *nom* sense recovery time
délai *m* **de propagation** *nom* propagation delay ◇ **le délai de propagation dans une voie de communication produit une distorsion du signal** propagation delay in the transmission path causes signal distortion
délai *m* **de retour de ligne** *nom* blanking interval
délai *m* **de retour vertical** *nom* vertical blanking interval
délai *m* **d'installation** *nom* setup time
délai *m* **d'inversion** *nom* turnaround time
délai *m* **moyen** *nom* average delay
de l'heure *adverbe* per hour
déliasser *verbe vt* to decollate
déliasseuse *f nom* decollator
délimiter *verbe vt* to delimit
délimiteur *m nom* delimiter
délimiteur *m* **de données** *nom* data delimiter
démagnétiser *verbe* **1.** *vt* to bloop **2.** *vt* to degauss **3.** *vt* to demagnetise *ou* to demagnetize ◇ **il faut démagnétiser les têtes de lecture** ***or*** **écriture une fois par semaine pour obtenir une performance optimale** the R/W heads have to be degaussed each week to ensure optimum performance
démagnétiseur *m* **de tête** *nom* head demagnetiser
demande *f abrév* ENQ ■ *nom* **1.** enquiry **2.** inquiry ◇ **(fonction) interrogation** ***or*** **réponse** *ou* **demande** ***or*** **réponse** inquiry/response (function)
demande *f* **d'entrée/sortie** *abrév* IORQ
demande *f* **de répétition automatique** *nom* **1.** ARQ **2.** automatic repeat request
demande *f* **d'interruption** *nom* interrupt request
demander la ligne *verbe* to bid ◇ **le terminal a dû demander trois fois la ligne avant d'obtenir un créneau sur le réseau** the termi-

nal had to bid three times before there was a gap in transmissions on the network

démarcation *f nom* demarcation

démarrage *m nom* start

démarrage *m* **à froid** *nom* **1.** cold boot **2.** cold start

démarrage *m* **automatique** *nom* auto start

démarrer à froid *verbe* **1.** to coldboot **2.** to deadstart **3.** to hardboot

demi- *préfixe* semi-

demi-additionneur *m nom* half adder

demi-additionneur *m* **binaire** *nom* binary half adder

demi-carte *f nom* half card

demi-intensité *fpl adjectif* half-intensity

demi-mot *m nom* half word

demi-octet *m nom* nybble *ou* nibble

demi-teinte *f nom* halftone

démo *f nom* demonstration software

démodé *adjectif* out of date

démodulation *f nom* demodulation

démonter *verbe vt* to takedown

démultiplexeur *verbe vt* to demultiplex ■ *nom* demultiplexor

déni *m nom* denial

de niveau *adjectif* flush ◇ **la couverture est rognée de niveau avec les pages** the cover is trimmed flush with the pages

densité *f nom* density

densité *f* **binaire** *nom* bit density

densité *f* **de caractère** *nom* character density

densité *f* **de caractères** *nom* pitch

densité *f* **de données** *nom* (*sur un support physique*) packing density

densité *f* **de mémoire** *nom* storage density

densité *f* **d'enregistrement** *nom* recording density

densité *f* **des composants** *nom* component density

densité *f* **du trafic** *nom* traffic density

dépannage *m nom* corrective maintenance

dépassé *adjectif* out of date

dépassement *nom* underflow ◇ **dépassement** *m* **de capacité de la caractéristique** characteristic overflow

dépassement *m* **de capacité** *nom* overflow

dépendant *adjectif* dependent ◇ **procédé dépendant des résultats** *ou* **relié aux résultats d'un autre procédé** a process which is dependent on the result of another process

dépendant, -e du matériel *adjectif* hardware dependent

dépendant de la vitesse du processeur *adjectif* processor-limited

déplacement *m nom* **1.** displacement **2.** float **3.** relocation

déplacement *m* **de bit** *nom* (*en mémoire*) bit blit

déplacement *m* **de bloc** *nom* (*en mémoire*) block move

déplacement *m* **dynamique** *nom* **1.** dynamic relocation **2.** dynamic relocation program

déplacement *m* **statique** *nom* static relocation

déplacer *verbe* **1.** *vt* to drag **2.** *vt* to move **3.** *vt* to relocate **4.** *vt* to shift ◇ **cette donnée est déplacée au cours de l'exécution** the data is relocated during execution ◇ **déplacer de mémoire auxiliaire en mémoire centrale** to roll in ◇ **se déplacer sans quitter le secteur** (*avec un téléphone*) to roam

de pointe *adjectif* state-of-the-art

dépôt *m nom* deposition

dépouiller *verbe vt* to strip

de recherche *adjectif* searchable

de redondance *adjectif* redundant

de réserve *nom* standby

dérivation *f nom* bypass ◇ **il y a dérivation automatique lorsqu'une des machines tombe en panne** there is an automatic bypass around any faulty equipment

dériver (de) *verbe* to derive

dernier entré, dernier sorti *adjectif* **1.** last in last out **2.** LILO

déroulement *m* **du menu** *nom* action bar pull-down

dérouleur *m nom* **1.** magnetic tape transport **2.** tape transport

désactiver *verbe vt* to disarm

désaffecter *verbe vt* to deallocate ◇ **lorsque vous appuyez sur la touche** *ou* **le bouton de ré-initialisation, toutes les ressources sont désallouées** when a reset button is pressed all resources are deallocated

désaligné *adjectif* nonaligned

désallouer *verbe* **1.** *vt* to blast **2.** *vt* to deallocate ◇ **lorsque vous appuyez sur la touche** *ou* **le bouton de ré-initialisation, toutes les ressources sont désallouées** when a reset button is pressed all resources are deallocated

désassembler *verbe vt* to disassemble

désassembleur *m nom* disassembler

descripteur *m nom* descriptor

descripteur *m* **de fichier** *nom* file descriptor

description *f* **de projet** *nom* outliner

déselectionner *verbe vt* to deselect

désembrouiller *verbe* **1.** *vt* to decode **2.** *vt* to de-scramble

désembrouilleur *m nom* de-scrambler

design *m* **économique** *nom* least cost design

désinstaller *verbe* **1.** *vt* to takedown **2.** *vt* to uninstall ◇ **procédure de désinstallation** uninstall procedure

d'espacement proportionnel *adjectif* proportionally spaced
dessin *m* *nom* **1.** pattern **2.** picture
dessin *m* **au trait** *nom* line drawing ◇ **on trouve dans ce livre des dessins (au trait) et des illustrations en demi-teinte** the book is illustrated with line drawings and halftones
de supervision *adjectif* supervisory
de surveillance *adjectif* supervisory
détecter *verbe vt* to sense ◇ **le programme a pu détecter l'état du connecteur** the condition of the switch was sensed by the program
détecteur *m* *nom* sense switch
détecteur *m* **de virus** *nom* **1.** virus checker **2.** virus detector
détecteur *m* **d'onde porteuse** *nom* **1.** data carrier detect **2.** DCD
détection *nom* (*électronique*) sense ◇ **détection** *f* **de bordures** edge detection
détection *f* **automatique d'erreurs** *nom* automatic error detection
détection *f* **de collision** *nom* collision detection
détection *f* **d'erreurs** *nom* **1.** error detection **2.** error trapping
détection et correction d'erreurs *nom* error detection and correction
détection *f* **et correction d'erreurs** *nom* EDAC
de temps en temps *adjectif* periodic *ou* periodical ■ *adverbe* periodically
détérioration *f* *nom* corruption
détérioration *f* **de données** *nom* data corruption ◇ **les coupleurs acoustiques sont plus susceptibles aux détériorations de données que les modems branchés directement sur la ligne** acoustic couplers suffer from data corruption more than the direct connect form of modem
détériorer *verbe vt* to corrupt
détermination *f* **de l'ordre de priorité** *nom* scheduling ◇ **établissement d'un horaire de programme de télévision** *ou* **radio** programme scheduling
déterministe *adjectif* deterministic
détruire *verbe* **1.** *vt* to delete **2.** *vt* to erase **3.** *vt* to kill **4.** *vt* to scrub **5.** *vt* to wipe ◇ **détruire des données par superposition d'écriture** to overwrite ◇ **détruisez tous les fichiers avec l'extension .BAK** scrub all files with the .BAK extension ◇ **les nouvelles données ont remplacé les anciennes (par superposition d'écriture)** the latest data input has overwritten the old information ◇ **si vous reformatez, vous détruirez toutes les données du disque** *ou* **vous blanchirez le disque** by reformatting you will wipe the disk clean
de type 'flatbed' *adjectif* flatbed
développement *m* **d'un logiciel** *nom* software development
développement *m* **d'un programme** *nom* program development
développeur *m* **d'application** *nom* application developer
développeur *m* **de logiciel** *nom* software developer
déverminage *m* *nom* burn-in
déverminer *verbe vt* to debug
déverrouiller *verbe vt* to unlock
déviation *f* *nom* **1.** alternate route **2.** deflection
déviation *f* **de rayon** *nom* beam deflection ◇ **dans un tube à rayons cathodiques, la déflexion du faisceau est effectuée par un champ magnétique** a magnetic field is used for beam deflection in a CRT
dévier *verbe vt* to deflect
dézipper *verbe vt* to unzip
DHCP *nom* dynamic host configuration protocol
diagnostic *m* *nom* **1.** diagnosis **2.** system check
diagnostic *m* **(de cause) de défaillance** *nom* problem diagnosis
diagnostic *m* **de dysfonctionnement** *nom* malfunction routine
diagnostic *m* **de localisation de défaillance** *nom* fault diagnosis
diagnostic *m* **de localisation de panne** *nom* fault diagnosis
diagnostic *m* **d'erreurs** *nom* error diagnosis
diagnostiquer *verbe vt* to diagnose
diagramme *m* *nom* **1.** chart **2.** schema
diagramme(s) *m(pl) plural noun* presentation graphics
diagramme *m* **à secteurs** *nom* pie chart
diagramme *m* **circulaire** *nom* pie chart ◇ **l'attribution de mémoire est indiquée sur ce diagramme circulaire** the memory allocation is shown on this pie chart
diagramme *m* **de flux de données** *nom* data flow diagram
diagramme *m* **de réseau** *nom* network diagram
diagramme *m* **de Veitch** *nom* Veitch diagram
diagramme *m* **de Venn** *nom* Venn diagram
diagramme *m* **d'opérations** *nom* flowchart
diagramme *m* **d'un circuit** *nom* circuit diagram ◇ **le programme de CAO peut tracer le circuit très rapidement** the CAD program will plot the circuit diagram rapidly
diagramme *m* **en bâtons** *nom* **1.** bar chart **2.** columnar graph
diagramme *m* **en camembert** *nom* pie chart
diagramme *m* **fonctionnel** *nom* functional diagram
diagramme *m* **logique** *nom* **1.** logical chart **2.** logic flowchart

dialecte *m nom* dialect
dialogue *m nom* **1.** conversation **2.** dialog **3.** dialogue *ou* dialog ◇ **fenêtre de dialogue** dialogue box
dialogué *adjectif* interactive
dialoguer *verbe vt* to chat
dialoguer (avec) *verbe* to converse
dialogue *m* **vidéotex** *nom* interactive videotext
diamant *m* **de lecture** *nom* stylus
DIANE *nom* direct information access network for Europe
diaphonie *f nom* (*causée par l'interférence*) crosstalk ◇ **il y avait une telle diaphonie que le signal était illisible** the crosstalk was so bad, the signal was unreadable
diaphonie *nom* babble

'...sa gamme d'appareils s'est grandement élargie avec, en particulier, un suppresseur de diaphonie' [*Audio Tech*]

diaphragme *m nom* diaphragm
diaporama *m nom* slide show
diapositive *f nom* **1.** slide **2.** transparency ◇ **projecteur de diapositives** *ou* **de diapos** slide projector
dibit *m nom* dibit
dichroïque *adjectif* dichroic
dictionnaire *m nom* dictionary
dictionnaire *m* **de synonymes** *nom* thesaurus
dictionnaire *m* **par thèmes** *nom* thesaurus
dictionnaire/répertoire *m* **de données** *nom* data dictionary/directory
didacticiel *m nom* courseware
diélectrique *adjectif* dielectric
différence *f* **de potentiel** *nom* potential difference
différentiel ◇ **modulation** *f* **différentielle dynamique par impulsions et codage** adaptive differential pulse code modulation
diffusion *f nom* **1.** broadcast **2.** diffusion
diffusion *f* **individuelle** *nom* unicast
diffusion *f* **parallèle** *nom* parallel broadcast
diffusion *f* **sur tout un réseau** *nom* networking
digital *adjectif* digital
dimension *f nom* **1.** dimension **2.** size
dimension *f* **de l'écran** *nom* screen size
dimension *f* **d'une unité d'information** *nom* item size
dimension *f* **d'un fichier** *nom* file length
dimension *f* **d'un item** *nom* item size
dimension *f* **d'un registre** *nom* register length
dimension *f* **d'un tableau** *nom* array dimension
dimensionner *verbe vt* to size
dimensions *fpl plural noun* measurements
diminuteur *m nom* subtrahend
DIN *nom* **1.** Deutsche Industrienorm **2.** DIN
diode *nom* diode ◇ **diode électroluminescente** light-emitting diode (LED)

'...petit clavier auxiliaire où chaque touche est accompagnée d'une diode' [*Audio Tech*]

'...des diodes électroluminescentes permettent de contrôler si l'installation s'est effectuée correctement' [*Electronique*]

diode *f* **électroluminescente** *nom* **1.** LED **2.** light-emitting diode
direct *adjectif, adverbe* direct
directement *adjectif, adverbe* direct
directement *m* **enfichable** *adjectif* plug-compatible
directeur, -trice du service informatique *nom* data processing manager
directeur, -trice *m,f* **du service informatique** *nom* computer manager
directeur, -trice *mf* **du service informatique** *nom* system manager
direction *f* **du flux** *nom* flow direction
directive *f nom* directive
Director (*de Macromedia*) Director
DirectSound (*nom de marque*) DirectSound
discret *adjectif* discrete ◇ **le mot de données est formé de bits discrets** a data word is made up of discrete bits
discrimination *f* **d'appels** *nom* call discrimination
disjonction *f nom* **1.** disjunction **2.** exjunction
dispersion *f nom* dispersion
Display PostScript™ (*nom de marque*) Display PostScript™
disponibilité *f* **d'adressage** *nom* addressing capacity
disponibilité *f* **de mémoire** *nom* addressing capacity
disponible *adjectif* configured-in
disposé en couches *adjectif* layered
disposer *verbe vt* to network
disposer en mosaïque *verbe* **1.** to tessellate **2.** to tile
disposer en tableau *verbe* **1.** to tab **2.** to tabulate ◇ **en appuyant sur la touche de tabulation en début de ligne, pour se placer à la colonne 10, la liste se trouvait parfaitement alignée** the list was neatly lined up by tabbing to column 10 at the start of each new line ◇ **la règle de tabulation indique les marges de gauche et de droite** a tab rack shows you the left and right margins
dispositif *nom* **1.** device **2.** microdevice **3.** unit ◇ **dispositif** *m* **de mise hors tension automatique** automatic power off ◇ **dispositif** *m* **de protection contre la copie** copy protection ◇

dispositif *m* **de protection d'écriture** (*de fichier*) file protect tab ◇ **il arrive qu'une protection anticopie défectueuse entraîne la détérioration du disque dur** a hard disk may crash because of faulty copy protection ◇ **le nouveau programme ne sera pas protégé contre la copie** the new program will come without copy protection

dispositif *m* **à champ programmable** *nom* field programmable device

dispositif *m* **à couplage de charge** *nom* charge-coupled device

dispositif *m* **à couple de charge** *abrév* CCD

dispositif *m* **additif** *nom* add-on

dispositif *m* **additionnel** *nom, adjectif* add-in ■ *nom* add-on ◇ **carte additionnelle** *ou* **carte d'extension** add-in card

dispositif *m* **antiparasite** *nom* suppressor

dispositif *m* **à semi-conducteur** *nom* **1.** semiconductor device **2.** solid-state device

dispositif *m* **audio auxiliaire** *nom* auxilliary audio device

dispositif *m* **auxiliaire** *nom* **1.** auxiliary device **2.** safety net

dispositif *m* **CCD** *nom* charge-coupled device

dispositif *m* **d'accès** *nom* facility

dispositif *m* **d'actualisation** *nom* (*d'un système*) retrofit

dispositif *m* **d'affichage** *nom* readout device

dispositif *m* **d'alignement** *nom* aligner

dispositif *m* **d'appel automatique** *nom* ACU

dispositif *m* **d'arrêt** *nom* automatic power off

dispositif *m* **de cadrage** *nom* aligner

dispositif *m* **de contrôle** *nom* monitor

dispositif *m* **d'effacement** *nom* eraser

dispositif *m* **de pointage** *nom* pointing device

dispositif *m* **de pointage absolu** *nom* absolute device

dispositif *m* **de pointage relatif** *nom* relative pointing device

dispositif *m* **de positionnement** *nom* aligner

dispositif *m* **de retour/d'appel** *nom* answer/originate *ou* answer/originate device

dispositif *m* **de routage** *nom* router

dispositif *m* **de secours** *nom* **1.** safety net **2.** standby

dispositif *m* **de sécurité** *nom* safety net ◇ **en cas de panne d'électricité, nous avons un onduleur qui peut prendre la relève** if there is a power failure, we have a safety net in the form of a UPS

dispositif *m* **de stockage** *nom* storage device

dispositif *m* **écran** *nom* readout device

dispositif *m* **électronique actif** *nom* active device

dispositif *m* **électronique armé** *nom* active device

dispositif *m* **électronique d'identification** *nom* personal identification device

dispositif *m* **externe** *nom* external device

dispositif *m* **mémoire** *nom* storage device

dispositif *m* **mémoire pour spoule** *nom* spooler

dispositif *m* **MIDI** *nom* MIDI device

dispositif *m* **supplémentaire** *nom, adjectif* add-in ■ *nom* add-on

dispositif *m* **transfert électronique de fonds** *nom* EFT

dispositif *m* **universel** *nom* **1.** universal device **2.** universal device

disposition *f nom* keyboard layout

disposition *f* **de fichier** *nom* file organisation

disposition *f* **des broches** *nom* pinout

disque *nom* disk

> '...le disque dur fait désormais partie du quotidien: il est devenu un élément indispensable, voire vital, du poste de travail' [*L'Ordinateur Individuel*]

disque *m* **à traiter** *nom* milk disk

disque *m* **CD** *abrév* CD

disque *m* **CD-ROM** *nom* CD-ROM

disque *m* **cible** *nom* target disk

disque *m* **compact** *abrév* CD ■ *nom* **1.** compact disc **2.** disc

disque *m* **compact à lecture seule** *nom* **1.** CD-ROM **2.** compact disc ROM

disque *m* **compact audionumérique** *nom* CD-audio

disque *m* **compact enregistrable** *nom* recordable CD

disque *m* **compact interactif** *nom* **1.** CD-I **2.** CD-i

disque *m* **compact non réinscriptible** *nom* **1.** CD-ROM **2.** CD-WO

disque *m* **compact photo** *nom* PhotoCD

disque *m* **compact réinscriptible** *nom* CD-RW

disque *m* **d'amorçage** *nom* boot disk

disque *m* **de lancement** *nom* boot disk

disque *m* **de quatre-vingts pistes** *nom* eighty-track disk *ou* 80-track disk

disque *m* **de sauvegarde** *nom* backup disk

disque *m* **de travail** *nom* work disk

disque *m* **d'exploitation** *nom* master disk

disque *m* **dur** *nom* **1.** hard disk **2.** hard disk drive **3.** hard drive **4.** rigid disk ◇ **(unité de) disque dur de 6,4 Go** a 6.4GB hard drive

disque *m* **dur amovible** *nom* **1.** disk cartridge **2.** exchangeable disk storage

disque *m* **dur fixe** *nom* fixed disk storage

disque *m* **dur interne** *nom* internal hard disk

disque *m* **dur Winchester** *nom* Winchester disk *ou* Winchester drive

disque *m* **DVD** *nom* DVD

disque *m* **fixe** *nom* fixed disk

disque *m* **formaté par logiciel** *nom* (*word-porcessing*) soft-sectored disk

disque *m* **inscriptible** *nom* recordable CD

disque *m* **laser** *nom* laser disc

disque *m* **magnétique** *nom* magnetic disk

disque *m* **magnéto-optique** *nom* magneto-optical disc

disque *m* **mémoire** *nom* RAM disk

disque *m* **non formaté** *nom* unformatted disk

disque *m* **optique** *nom* **1.** magneto-optical disc **2.** optical disk

disque *m* **optique transitif** *nom* transmissive disk

disque *m* **optique WORM** *nom* (*permettant une seule écriture et des écritures multiples*) write once, read many times memory

disque *m* **original** *nom* magnetic master

disque *m* **OROM** *abrév* OROM

disque *m* **RAM** *nom* **1.** RAM disk **2.** silicon disk

disque *m* **relais** *nom* milk disk

disque *m* **sectorisé par logiciel** *nom* soft-sectored disk

disque *m* **serveur** *nom* network drive

disque *m* **simple** *nom* platter

disque *m* **souple** *nom* diskette ■ *abrév* fd *ou* FD ■ *nom* **1.** flexible disk **2.** floppy disk *ou* floppy

disque *m* **transistorisé** *nom* solid state disk

disquette *f nom* diskette ■ *abrév* fd *ou* FD ■ *nom* **1.** flexible disk **2.** floppy disk *ou* floppy **3.** storage disk

disquette *f* **3,5<">** *nom* microfloppy

disquette *f* **3,25** *nom* minidisk

disquette *f* **5,25 pouces** *nom* minifloppy

disquette *f* **à simple densité** *nom* single density disk

disquette *f* **à simple face** *abrév* SSD

disquette *f* **d'amorçage** *nom* boot disk ◇ **après avoir mis l'ordinateur en route, insérez la disquette de lancement** *ou* **d'amorçage** after you switch on the computer, insert the boot disk

disquette *f* **de 3,5 pouces** *nom* minidisk

disquette *f* **de 5,25 pouces** *nom* minifloppy

disquette *f* **de fontes** *nom* font disk

disquette *f* **de huit pouces** *nom* eight-inch disk *ou* 8-inch disk

disquette *f* **de nettoyage des têtes** *nom* head cleaning disk

disquette *f* **de polices de caractères** *nom* font disk

disquette *f* **de sauvegarde** *nom* backup disk

disquette *f* **d'exploitation** *nom* system disk

disquette *f* **double densité** *nom* double density disk

disquette *f* **(à) double face** *nom* double-sided disk

disquette *f* **non compatible** *nom* alien disk

disquette *f* **non formatée** *nom* unformatted disk

disquette *f* **réversible** *nom* flippy

disquette *f* **simple face** *nom* single-sided disk

disquette *f* **système** *nom* **1.** startup disk **2.** system disk

disque *m* **vidéo** *nom* videodisc

disque *m* **vidéo numérique** *nom* DVD ◇ **graveur de DVD** DVD writer ◇ **lecteur de DVD** DVD drive; DVD player ◇ **lecteur de DVD-ROM** DVD-ROM drive

disque *m* **vierge** *nom* blank disk

disque *m* **virtuel** *nom* **1.** silicon disk **2.** virtual disk

disque *m* **Winchester amovible** *nom* removable Winchester disk

dissimuler *verbe vt* to conceal

dissipateur *m* **thermique** *nom* heat-sink

distance *f* **de Hamming** *nom* **1.** Hamming distance **2.** signal distance

distance *f* **entre signaux** *nom* **1.** Hamming distance **2.** signal distance

distance *f* **sur l'axe des X** *nom* x distance

distance *f* **sur l'axe des Y** *nom* y-distance

distorsion *f nom* distortion ◇ **déformation** *ou* **distorsion** *ou* **aberration de l'image** image distortion

distorsion *f* **d'un signal** *nom* breakup

distorsion *f* **en barillet** *nom* pincushion distortion

distorsion *f* **en coussinet** *nom* pincushion distortion

distorsion *f* **en oreiller** *nom* pincushion distortion

distribuer *verbe vt* to distribute

distribution *nom* distribution ◇ **centre de distribution** distribution point ◇ **distribution** *f* **automatique des appels** automatic call distribution

distribution *f* **automatique d'appels** *nom* ACD

dividende *m nom* dividend

diviser *verbe* **1.** *vt* to divide **2.** *vt* to segment ◇ **diviser un nombre par quatre** (*math*) to divide a number by four ◇ **vingt-et-un divisé par trois égale sept** (*math*) twenty-one divided by three gives seven

diviser en secteur *verbe* to sector ◇ **formatage de secteurs (d'un disque)** (disk) sector formatting

diviseur *m nom* divisor

division *f nom* **1.** division **2.** partition

division *f* **avec paramètres d'identification** *nom* (*d'un programme en COBOL*) identification division

dizaine *f nom* decade

DLL *nom* DLL ◇ **le traitement de texte appelle le vérificateur d'orthographe stocké dans la bibliothèque DLL** the word-processor calls a spell-check program that is stored as a DLL

DMA *nom* DMA

DNS *nom* domain name system

d'occasion *adjectif* **1.** second hand **2.** second user

document *nom* **1.** document **2.** standard document *ou* standard form **3.** standard paragraph **4.** standard text ◇ **document** *m* **créé à partir de paragraphes standard** boilerplate

document *m* **associé** *nom* associated document *ou* associated file

documentation *f nom* documentation ◇ **documentation** *f* **relative à l'utilisation d'un programme** program documentation

document *m* **circulant** *nom* turnaround document

document *m* **composite** *nom* compound document

document *m* **d'origine** *nom* source document

documenter *verbe vt* to document

document *m* **monté** *nom* boilerplate

document *m* **original** *nom* source document

document *m* **RFC** *nom* **1.** request for comment **2.** RFC

document *m* **Web** *nom* webpage

Dolby (*capture de son*) Dolby

Dolby Digital™ (*nom de marque*) Dolby Digital™

Dolby system™ (*nom de marque*) Dolby system™

domaine *m nom* domain

domaine *m* **de premier niveau** *nom* top-level domain

domaine *m* **public** *abrév* PD ■ *nom* public domain

domaines *mpl* **adjacents** *plural noun* adjacent domains

donnée(s) ◇ **à données erronées, résultats erronés** garbage in garbage out ◇ **des données douteuses produisent des résultats douteux** garbage in garbage out

donnée *f* **absolue** *nom* atom

donnée *f* **de contrôle** *nom* test data

donnée *f* **descriptive** *nom* physical parameter

données *nom* **1.** data **2.** information ◇ **données** *fpl* **extraites directement de la mémoire cache** cache hit ◇ **restitution de données** information retrieval (IR) ◇ **stockage et restitution de données** information storage and retrieval (ISR)

données *fpl* **agrégées** *nom* data aggregate

données *fpl* **alphanumériques** *nom* alphanumeric data

données *fpl* **analogiques** *nom* analog data

données *fpl* **brutes** *nom* raw data

données *fpl* **constantes** *nom* fixed data

données *fpl* **de base** *nom* master data

données *fpl* **de commande** *nom* control data

données *fpl* **de contrôle** *nom* **1.** control **2.** control data

données *fpl* **d'entrée** *nom* input

données *fpl* **de sortie** *nom* computer output

données *fpl* **de transmission en continu** *nom* streaming data *ou* streaming protocol

données *fpl* **de type général** *nom* abstract data type ◇ **la pile est une structure de données de type général, elle peut stocker des données de tous types** the stack is a structure of abstract data types, it can store any type of data

données *fpl* **graphiques** *nom* graphic data

données *fpl* **incrémentielles** *nom* incremental data

données *fpl* **non traitées** *nom* raw data

données *fpl* **numériques** *nom* digital data

données *fpl* **numérisées** *nom* digital data

données *fpl* **partiellement traitées** *nom* semi-processed data

données *fpl* **permanentes** *nom* **1.** fixed data **2.** master data

données *fpl* **relatives** *nom* relative data

données *fpl* **saisies** *nom* input

données *fpl* **scalaires** *nom* scalar data

données *fpl* **structurées** *nom* data aggregate

données *fpl* **variables** *nom* variable data

donner les renseignements appropriés *verbe* to document

donner une instruction *verbe* to order

dopage *m* **par diffusion** *nom* diffusion

dopant *m nom* dopant

dopé *adjectif* doped

DOR *nom* digital optical recording

dorsale *f* **inversée** *nom* inverted backbone

DOS *nom* DOS ◇ **lancez le (système) DOS après la mise en route de l'ordinateur** boot up the DOS after you switch on the PC

dossier *m nom* **1.** file **2.** folder ◇ **insérer (un document) au dossier** to place (something) on file

dossier *m* **commun** *nom* shared folder

dossier *m* **partagé** *nom* shared folder

dossier *m* **préférentiel** *nom* blessed folder

dossier *m* **système** *nom* system folder

double *m nom* **1.** (*avec carbone*) carbon copy **2.** COPY ■ *adjectif* dual ■ *nom* replication ■ *adjectif* two-part ◇ **station à double connexion (sur réseau FDDI)** dual attachment station *ou* dual attached station (DAS)

double *m* **chronométrie** *nom* dual clocking

double-clic *m nom* double-click

double densité *f abrév* DD

double *m* **densité** *nom* double density

double *m* **frappe** *nom* double strike

double *m* **précision** *nom* double precision

doubler (un film) *verbe* to dub

DoubleSpace (*nom de marque*) DoubleSpace

doublet *m nom* doublet

doubleur *m* **d'horloge** *nom* clock doubler ◇ **le nouveau processeur d'Intel a un doubleur d'horloge en option qui permet de doubler ses performances** the new CPU from Intel has an optional clock doubler that will double performance

double *m* **vitesse** *nom* double speed

douce *adjectif* soft

douille *f nom* socket

doux *adjectif* soft

DRAM synchrone *nom* synchronous DRAM

drapeau *m nom* **1.** flag **2.** sentinel

drapeau *m* **d'archivage** *nom* **1.** archive attribute *ou* archive bit **2.** archive flag

drapeau *m* **de dépassement de capacité** *nom* **1.** overflow bit **2.** overflow flag

droits *mpl* **d'accès** *plural noun* access rights

duplex *m nom* duplex

duplicateur *m* **de port** *nom* port replicator

duplication *f nom* replication

duplication *f* **de données sur un disque miroir** *nom* **1.** disk mirroring **2.** duplexing

dur *adjectif* hard

durée *f nom* execute time ◇ **durée** *f* **d'exécution (d'un programme)** run-duration

durée *f* **d'assemblage** *nom* assembly time

durée *f* **de compilation** *nom* compilation time

durée *f* **de vie** *nom* lifetime ◇ **ce nouvel ordinateur a une durée de vie de quatre ans** this new computer has a four-year lifetime

durée *f* **de vie d'un dispositif d'impression** *nom* print life

durée *f* **de vie d'une imprimante** *nom* print life

durée *f* **de vie d'un système** *nom* system life cycle

durée *f* **d'exécution** *nom* (*d'un programme*) run-time *ou* run duration

durée *f* **d'une panne** *nom* fault time

durée *f* **moyenne de bon fonctionnement** *nom* **1.** mean time between failures **2.** mean time to failure **3.** MTBF **4.** MTF

durée *f* **moyenne de rétablissement** *nom* MTTR

durée *f* **moyenne de temps de bon fonctionnement entre les défaillances** *nom* mean time between failures

d'utilisation facile *adjectif* **1.** simple to use **2.** user-friendly

DVD *m nom* digital versatile disc

DVD *m* **audio** *nom* DVD-A

DVD *m* **inscriptible** *abrév* DVD-R ■ *nom* DVD-Recordable

DVD-RAM *m nom* DVD-RAM

DVD *m* **réinscriptible** *nom* DVD+RW

DVD-ROM *m nom* DVD-ROM ◇ **lecteur de DVD-ROM** DVD-ROM drive

DVD+RW *m nom* DVD+RW

DVD *m* **vidéo** *nom* digital videodisc

DVD-vidéo *m nom* DVD-video

DX *suffix* DX

dyade *f nom* **1.** doublet **2.** dyad

dynamique *adjectif* dynamic ◇ **amplitude dynamique** dynamic range ◇ **microphone dynamique** dynamic microphone

dysfonctionnement *nom* malfunction ■ *adjectif* malfunctioning ■ *nom* problem

> '…la première branche du réseau dut être recâblée à la suite de dysfonctionnement' [*L'Information professionnelle*]

écarteur *m* **de bande** *nom* lifter

échangeable *adjectif* exchangeable

échange *m* **de données entre unité centrale et périphérique** *nom* peripheral transfer

échange *m* **de données informatisé** *nom* EDI

échange *m* **de trames** *nom* frame relay

échange *m* **d'informations entre unité centrale et périphérique** *nom* peripheral transfer

échange *m* **dynamique de données** *nom* DDE

échange *m* **dynamique des données** *nom* dynamic data exchange

échanger *verbe* **1.** *vt* to exchange **2.** *vt* to swap

échantillon *m nom* sample ◇ **la prise d'échantillon toutes les trois secondes a révélé une augmentation** the sample at three seconds showed an increase

échantillon *m* **à 8 bits** *nom* 8-bit sample

échantillon *m* **à 16 bits** *nom* **1.** 16-bit sample **2.** 24-bit sample

échantillonnage *m* **de qualité** *nom* acceptance sampling

échantillonner *verbe* **1.** *vt* to sample **2.** *vt* to strobe

échantillonneur *m nom* sampler

échantillonneur-bloqueur *m nom* sample and hold circuit

échappement *m nom* escapement

échelle *nom* scale ◇ **intégration à grande échelle** large scale integration (LSI) ◇ **intégration à moyenne échelle** medium scale integration (MSI) ◇ **intégration à petite échelle** small scale integration (SSI) ◇ **intégration à super grande échelle** super large scale integration (SLSI) ◇ **intégration à très grande échelle** very large scale integration (VLSI) ◇ **mise** *f* **à la bonne échelle d'un système informatique** rightsizing

échelle *f* **binaire** *nom* binary scale ◇ **dans un mot à quatre bits, l'échelle binaire est 1,2,4,8** in a four bit word, the binary scale is 1,2,4,8

échelle *f* **de gris** *nom* grey scale

écho *m nom* echo ◇ **chambre à écho** echo chamber ◇ **suppresseur d'écho** *ou* **dispositif anti-écho** echo suppressor

éclater *verbe vi* to deblock

éclateur *m* **de feuilles** *nom* burster

E

e-commerce *m nom* e-commerce

économiseur *m* **d'écran** *nom* screen saver

écran *nom* **1.** display **2.** screen **3.** shield **4.** storage tube **5.** video display ◇ **coin** *m* **gauche supérieur de l'écran** cursor home ◇ **écran** *m* **avec définition supérieure à 1024x1024 pixels** megapixel display ◇ **écran** *m* **avec texte en noir sur fond blanc** paper-white monitor ◇ **image d'écran** screen image ◇ **neige** *f* **sur l'écran** snow ◇ **qu'on ne peut pas faire défiler sur l'écran** non scrollable

'…il s'agit d'une machine sans clavier, de la classe et de la puissance d'une station de travail et équipée d'un écran qui est au moins de la taille d'une page' [*Science et Vie Micro*]

'…les écrans tactiles permettent de sélectionner la fonction désirée, sans apprentissage préalable, par simple pointage d'un menu sur un écran' [*Electronique (Suisse)*]

écran *m* **(de visualisation)** *nom* monitor ◇ **écran multistandard** multi-scan *ou* multi-sync monitor

écran *m* **à cristaux liquides** *nom* **1.** LCD **2.** LCD screen **3.** liquid crystal display

écran *m* **à cristaux liquides rétroéclairé** *nom* backlit display

écran *m* **à matrice active** *nom* active matrix display

écran *m* **à matrice passive à double balayage** *nom* dual-scan display

écran *m* **à micropointes** *abrév* FED ■ *nom* field emission display

écran *m* **analogique** *nom* analog display

écran *m* **à plasma** *nom* gas discharge display *ou* gas plasma display

écran *m* **asservi** *nom* slave tube

écran *m* **à transistors à couches minces** *nom* **1.** TFT screen **2.** thin-film transistor screen

écran *m* **à tube cathodique** *nom* cathode ray tube

écran *m* **brouillé** *nom* bleed

écran *m* **d'aide** *nom* help screen

écran *m* **de démarrage** *nom* startup screen

écran *m* **de quatre-vingts colonnes** *nom* eighty-column screen *ou* 80-column screen

écran *m* **de texte** *nom* text screen

écran *m* **de visualisation** *nom* **1.** display screen **2.** display unit ■ *abrév* VDU ■ *nom* visual display terminal *ou* visual display unit

écran *m* **divisé** *nom* split screen

écran *m* **d'une ligne** *nom* single line display

écran *m* **électroluminescent** *nom* electroluminescent display

écran *m* **électrostatique** *nom* electrostatic screen

écran *m* **(à affichage) graphique** *nom* graphics VDU

écran *m* **magnétique** *nom* magnetic screen

écran *m* **monochrome** *nom* monochrome monitor

écran *m* **multisync** *nom* multifrequency monitor

écran *m* **multisynchrone** *nom* **1.** multifrequency monitor **2.** multisync monitor

écran *m* **numérique** *nom* **1.** digital display **2.** digital monitor

écran *m* **partagé** *nom* split screen ◇ **nous utilisons le mode d'écran partagé pour comparer le texte en cours de travail à un texte de référence conservé en mémoire** we use split screen mode to show the text being worked on and another text from memory for comparison

écran *m* **plat** *nom* **1.** flat panel **2.** flat screen

écran *m* **pleine page** *nom* full-size display

écran *m* **RVB** *nom* RGB display *ou* RGB monitor

écran *m* **tactile** *nom* touch screen

écran *m* **TFT** *nom* **1.** TFT screen **2.** thin-film transistor screen

écran *m* **vidéo avec clavier** *nom* video terminal

écran *m* **virtuel** *nom* virtual screen

écran *m* **visuel** *abrév* VDU ■ *nom* visual display terminal *ou* visual display unit

écrire un programme *verbe* to program

écriture *f* **chiffrée** *nom* cipher

éditer *verbe vt* to edit ◇ **il y a plusieurs touches d'édition – celle-ci permet de reformater le texte** there are several special edit keys – this one will re-format the text

éditer sous forme de liste *verbe* to list ◇ **lister (les lignes d'instruction d') un programme** to list a program

éditeur *m nom* **1.** editor **2.** editor program ◇ **éditeur de liens** linkage editor

éditeur *m* **d'écran** *nom* screen editor

éditeur *m* **de programme** *nom* program editor

éditeur *m* **de programme source** *nom* source editor

éditeur *m* **d'images** *nom* image editor

éditeur *m* **d'onde** *nom* waveform editor

éditeur *m* **EDLIN** *nom* EDLIN

éditeur *m* **ligne à ligne** *nom* line editor

édition *f* **après calculs** *nom* post-editing

édition *f* **après compilation** *nom* post-editing

édition *f* **électronique** *nom* **1.** desktop publishing **2.** electronic publishing

edlin *nom* EDLIN

edu (= établissement éducatif) *suffix* edu

effaçables *adjectif* soft

effacement *m nom* deletion

effacement *m* **des lignes cachées** *nom* hidden line removal

effacer *verbe* **1.** *vt* to clear **2.** *vt* to delete **3.** *vt* to erase **4.** *vt* to kill **5.** *vt* to overwrite **6.** *vt* to rub out **7.** *vt* to scrub **8.** *vt* to wipe ◇ **effacer en masse** bulk erase ◇ **tapez CLS pour effacer** *ou* **faire disparaître ce qu'il y a sur l'écran** type CLS to clear the screen

effacer un fichier *verbe* to zero

effaceur *m* **magnétique** *nom* **1.** degausser **2.** demagnetiser *ou* demagnetizer

effectué -ée par étapes *adjectif* staged

effectué -ée par paliers *adjectif* staged

effectuer ◇ **effectuer un décalage vers la droite** right shift ◇ **effectuer un déplacement de bit en mémoire** blit

effectuer un blogue *verbe* to blog

effectuer un branchement *verbe* to jump

effectuer un clic *verbe* to click ◇ **cliquer sur le bouton droit (de la souris)** *ou* **effectuer un clic droit** to click on the right button (of the mouse) *ou* to right click ◇ **cliquer sur le bouton gauche (de la souris)** *ou* **effectuer un clic gauche** to click on the left button (of the mouse) *ou* to left click

effectuer une copie de bloc *verbe* to block-copy

effectuer une nouvelle compilation *verbe* to recompile

effectuer une partition *verbe* to partition

effectuer une suppression de bloc *verbe* to block-delete

effectuer un traitement *verbe* to process ◇ **le traitement des données sera assez long** processing all the information will take a long time ◇ **nous avons traité les données** we processed the new data

effet *m* **de cascade** *nom* ripple-through effect

effet *m* **de mémoire** *nom* memory effect

effet *m* **de moiré** *nom* moiré effect

effet *m* **d'escalier** *nom* aliasing ■ *plural noun* jaggies

effet *m* **Hall** *nom* Hall effect ◇ **commutateur à effet (de champ) Hall** Hall effect switch

effet *m* **transitoire** *nom* transient

égal *m nom* peer

égalisateur *m* **paramétrique** *nom* parametric equaliser

égalité *f nom* equality

égratignure *f nom* scratch

éjecter *verbe vt* to junk

électricité *f nom* electricity ◇ **les frais d'électricité constituent un élément important des coûts de production** electricity prices are an important factor in the production costs

électricité *f* **statique** *nom* static electricity

électroluminescence *f nom* electroluminescence

électroluminescent *adjectif* **1.** electroluminescent **2.** electroluminescing ◇ **l'écran est recouvert d'une couche électroluminescente** the screen coating is electroluminescent

électromagnétique *adjectif* electromagnetic ◇ **interférence électromagnétique** electromagnetic interference (EMI) ◇ **spectre électromagnétique** electromagnetic spectrum

électronique *f nom* electronics

électrophotographique *adjectif* electrophotographic

électrostatique *adjectif* electrostatic ◇ **haut-parleur électrostatique** electrostatic speaker

élément *m nom* **1.** building block **2.** element **3.** unit

élément *m* **(d'un champ)** *nom* member

élémentaire *adjectif* **1.** elementary **2.** primary ◇ **section élémentaire de câble** elementary cable section

élément *m* **arithmétique étendu** *nom* extended arithmetic element

élément *m* **binaire** *nom* **1.** binary **2.** binary bit **3.** binary digit **4.** bit

élément *m* **dans un tableau** *nom* array element

élément *m* **d'arrêt** *nom* **1.** stop bit **2.** stop element

élément *m* **de données** *nom* **1.** data element **2.** data item

élément *m* **de menu** *nom* menu item

élément *m* **de programme** *nom* program item

élément *m* **de structure** *nom* overhead ◇ **les numéros de lignes sont des éléments de structure en BASIC** the line numbers in a BASIC program are an overhead

élément *m* **d'image** *nom* available point

élément *m* **d'image (sur l'écran)** *nom* display element

élément *m* **d'un code** *nom* code element

élément *m* **d'un signal** *nom* signal element ◇ **l'élément signal de ce système est une courte impulsion de tension qui représente un 1 binaire** the signal element in this system is a short voltage pulse, indicating a binary one

élément *m* **final d'une arborescence** *nom* leaf

élément *m* **fusible** *nom* fusible link

élément *m* **logique** *nom* logic element

élément *m* **logique composé** *nom* compound logical element

élément *m* **logique multiple** *nom* compound logical element

éléments *mpl* **CPU** *plural noun* CPU elements

éléments *mpl* **de l'unité centrale** *plural noun* CPU elements

éléments *mpl* **en vrac** *nom* bag

élimination *f* **des zéros** *nom* **1.** zero compression **2.** zero suppression

éliminer *verbe vt* to filter

éloigné *adjectif* remote

e-mail *m nom* email

emballement *m nom* thrashing

emballer *verbe vt* to pack ◇ **les disquettes sont présentées sous emballage plastique** the diskettes are packed in plastic wrappers

emboîtage *m* **de dossiers** *nom* tree of folders

emboîtement *m nom* interleaving

emboîter *verbe vt* to nest

embrouiller *verbe vt* to scramble

embrouilleur *m nom* scrambler

émetteur *m nom* **1.** sender **2.** send-only device ■ *abrév* TX

émetteur-récepteur *m nom* ASR

émetteur/récepteur *m nom* transceiver ◇ **émetteur** *or* **récepteur radio** radio transceiver

émetteur/récepteur *m* **à clavier** *nom* **1.** keyboard send/receive **2.** KSR

émetteur/récepteur *m* **synchrone asynchrone universel** *nom* USART

émetteur-récepteur *m* **synchrone universel** *nom* universal synchronous asynchronous receiver/transmitter

émetteur/récepteur *m* **synchrone universel** *nom* USRT

émetteur-récepteur *m* **universel asynchrone** *nom* **1.** UART **2.** universal asynchronous receiver/transmitter **3.** universal synchronous receiver/transmitter

émettre des impulsions *verbe* to pulse

émettre une impulsion *verbe* to strobe

émettre un signal *verbe* **1.** to signal **2.** to strobe

émission *f* **de signaux par canaux indépendants** *nom* separate channel signalling

émission-réception *f nom* automatic send/receive

émoticon *m nom* emoticon

émoticône *m nom* emoticon

emplacement *nom* **1.** response position **2.** site ◇ **emplacement** *m* **de rangement** bucket

emplacement *m* **(de lecteur de disque)** *nom* drive bay

emplacement *m* **(de mémoire)** *nom* location ◇ **(prise de vue) en extérieur** on location ◇ **les extérieurs (d'un film)** location shots ◇ **les extérieurs pour ce programme ont été tournés en Espagne** the programme was shot on location in Spain

emplacement *m* **de lecteur de disque** *nom* bay

emplacement *m* **de mémoire** *nom* store location

emplacement *m* **pour carte PCMCIA** *nom* PCMCIA slot

emplacement *m* **protégé** *nom* protected location

employer *verbe vt* to use

empreinte *f nom* (*d'un faisceau*) footprint

émulateur *m nom* emulator

émulateur *m* **intégré** *nom* integrated emulator

émulateur *m* **intégré au circuit** *nom* in-circuit emulator ◇ **cet émulateur intégré au circuit sert à tester le contrôleur de la disquette, en simulant le fonctionnement d'un lecteur de disquettes** this in-circuit emulator is used to test the floppy disk controller by emulating a disk drive

émulation *f nom* emulation ◇ **émulation** *f* **de terminal VT** VT-terminal emulation

émulation *f* **de terminal** *nom* terminal emulation

émulation *f* **d'imprimante** *nom* printer emulation ◇ **cette émulation permet à mon imprimante NEC d'émuler une imprimante Epsom** this printer emulation allows my NEC printer to emulate an Epsom

émuler *verbe vt* to emulate ◇ **une imprimante laser qui peut émuler une série d'autres imprimantes de bureau** laser printer which emulates a wide range of office printers

en attente *nom* sleep

en bolo-bolo *adjectif* greeked

en bon état de marche *adverbe* up ◇ **ils ont sûrement trouvé la source du problème puisque l'ordinateur fonctionne à merveille** they must have found the fault – the computer is finally up and running

encadrement *m nom* border

encapsulation *f nom* encapsulation

encapsulé *adjectif* encapsulated

enceinte *f* **acoustique** *nom* **1.** baffle **2.** loudspeaker

enchaînement *m nom* **1.** chaining **2.** linking

enchaîner *verbe* **1.** *vt* to catenate **2.** *vt* to chain **3.** *vt* to concatenate ◇ **plus de 1000 articles ou chapitres peuvent être enchaînés à l'impression** more than 1,000 articles or chapters can be chained together when printing ◇ **relier en série** *ou* **en chaîne** *ou* **en cascade** to daisy-chain

encodage *m nom* encoding

encodage *m* **adaptif** *nom* adaptive compression

encodage *m* **ARLL** *nom* advanced run-length limited

encodage *m* **en quadrature** *nom* quadrature encoding

encodage *m* **magnétique** *nom* magnetic encoding

encodage *m* **Manchester** *nom* Manchester coding

encodage *m* **RLE** *nom* RLL encoding

encodage *m* **RLL** *nom* run-length limited encoding

encoder *verbe vt* to encode

encodeur *m nom* encoder ◇ **encodeur de couleurs** colour encoder

encodeur *m* **de bandes magnétiques** *nom* magnetic tape encoder

encodeur *m* **des touches** *nom* keyboard encoder

encombrement *m nom* **1.** congestion **2.** (*d'un ordinateur*) footprint **3.** form

en cours d'utilisation *adjectif* active

encre *f* **en poudre** *nom* toner

encre *f* **magnétique** *nom* magnetic ink

en différé *adverbe, adjectif* off-line

en direct *adjectif, adverbe* direct ◇ **appeler** *ou* **téléphoner en direct** to dial direct ◇ **vous pouvez appeler New York en direct depuis Londres** you can dial New York direct from London if you want

enduction *f nom* deposition

enduit, -e d'un dopant *adjectif* doped

énergie *f nom* power ◇ **mode économie d'énergie** power-saving mode

Energy Star *nom* Energy Star

en état de marche *adjectif* working

en faux texte *adjectif* greeked

en fonction du contexte *adjectif* context-sensitive

engorgement *m nom* overrun

en grande quantité *adjectif* quantity

en langage machine *adjectif* **1.** computer-readable **2.** machine readable

en ligne *adverbe, adjectif* online

en mode décroché *adverbe* off-hook

en mode LIFO *nom* push-down list *ou* push-down stack

en panne *adjectif, adverbe* down ◇ **l'ordinateur est tombé en panne deux fois au cours de l'après-midi** the computer system went down twice during the afternoon

en paquets *adjectif* bursty

en passant par *preposition* via

en pavé *verbe* to tile

enregistrement *m nom* **1.** addition record **2.** chained record **3.** fault trace **4.** log **5.** logging **6.** logical record **7.** record **8.** recording ◇ **bande audionumérique** *ou* **bande audio** DAT tape ◇ **ce programme permet l'enregistrement (automatique) des erreurs** features of the program include error logging ◇ **cet enregistrement contient toutes leurs coordonnées** this record contains all their personal details ◇ **enregistrement d'appels** (*téléphone*) call logging ◇ **enregistrement** *m* **de données** (*automatique et chronologique*) data logging ◇ **enregistrement** *m* **de longueur fixe** fixed-length record ◇ **enregistrement** *m* **de modifications** change record ◇ **enregistrement** *m* **de mouvements** change record ◇ **enregistrement** *m* **des suppressions** deletion record ◇ **enregistrement** *m* **d'une transaction** transaction record ◇ **enregistrement** *m* **par faisceau électronique** (*sur microfilm*) electron beam recording ◇ **enregistrements** *mpl* **dans un fichier** record count ◇ **enregistrement** *m* **sur bande audionumérique** DAT ◇ **l'enregistrement sur bande audionumérique produit un son de très haute qualité** DAT produces a very high quality sound ◇ **programme de gestion d'enregistrements** *ou* **de fichiers** records management ◇ **votre article** *ou* **enregistrement contient divers champs regroupés sous une même rubrique** your record contains several fields that have been grouped together under the one heading

enregistrement *m* **actif** *nom* active record

enregistrement *m* **analogique** *nom* analog recording

enregistrement *m* **automatique des erreurs** *nom* error logging ◇ **ce programme permet l'enregistrement (automatique) des erreurs** features of the program include error logging

enregistrement *m* **d'activité** *nom* activity trail

enregistrement *m* **de données** *nom* data record

enregistrement *m* **de fin** *nom* (*de fichier*) trailer record

enregistrement *m* **de longueur variable** *nom* variable length record

enregistrement *m* **de nom de domaine** *nom* **1.** domain name registration **2.** name registration

enregistrement *m* **des chemins d'accès** *nom* access path journalling

enregistrement *m* **des détails** *nom* amendment record

enregistrement *m* **(automatique) des états d'incidents** *nom* failure logging

enregistrement *m* **des modifications** *nom* amendment record

enregistrement *m* **des mouvements** *nom* amendment record

enregistrement *m* **de tête** *nom* leader record

enregistrement *m* **par faisceau électronumérique (sur microfilm)** *nom* EBR

enregistrement *m* **physique** *nom* physical record

enregistrements *mpl* **sélectionnés** *nom* recordset

enregistrement *m* **sur bande audionumérique** *nom* digital audio tape

enregistrement *m* **sur couche polymérisée** *nom* dye-polymer recording

enregistrement *m* **sur disque magnétique** *nom* magneto-optical recording

enregistrement *m* **sur disque magnéto-optique** *nom* magneto-optical recording

enregistrement *m* **sur support magnétique** *nom* magnetic recording

enregistrement *m* **unique** *nom* unit record

enregistrer *verbe* **1.** *vt* to deposit **2.** *vt* to log **3.** *vt* to post **4.** *vt* to read in **5.** *vt* to record **6.** *vt* to write ◇ **changeur de disques automatique** record changer ◇ **enregistrer les appels** (*téléphone*) to log calls ◇ **enregistrer sous** to save as

enregistreur *m nom* recorder

enregistreur *m* **(chronologique)** *nom* logger

enregistreur *m* **bobine à bobine** *nom* reel to reel recorder

enregistreur *m* **cumulatif d'erreurs par unité d'entrée/sortie** *nom* SDR

enregistreur *m* **d'appels** *nom* call logger

enregistreur *m* **de bandes** *nom* magnetic tape recorder

enregistreur *m* **de sons** (*de Microsoft Windows*) Sound Recorder

enroulement *m nom* horizontal wraparound

enseignement *m* **assisté par ordinateur** *nom* CAI ■ *abrév* CBI ■ *nom* **1.** computer-aided instruction **2.** computer-assisted instruction **3.** computer-assisted learning **4.** computer-based learning

ensemble *m nom* set ■ *plural noun* SET

ensemble *m* **des tâches en cours d'exécution** *nom* job mix

ensemble *m* **des travaux en cours d'exécution** *nom* job mix

ensemble *m* **référentiel** *nom* universal set

en série *adverbe* sequentially ■ *adjectif* serial ■ *adverbe* serially ◇ **entrée** *or* **sortie (en) série** serial input/output (SIO)

en service *adjectif* busy

en-tête *m nom* **1.** header **2.** heading **3.** headline **4.** tape header

en-tête *m* **de bloc** *nom* block header

en-tête *m* **de fichier** *nom* **1.** file header **2.** header

en-tête *m* **de message** *nom* message header

en-tête *m* **préétabli (gardé en mémoire)** *nom* form flash

en texte muet *adjectif* greeked

entité *f nom* entity

entraînement *nom* feed ◇ **entraînement** *m* **de la bande papier** paper tape feed

'...un moteur commande l'entraînement du film' [*Science et Vie*]

entraînement *m* **automatique du papier** *nom* auto advance

entraînement *m* **du papier par picots** *nom* tractor feed

entraînement *m* **par picots** *nom* sprocket feed

entraînement *m* **(du papier) par picots** *nom* pinfeed

entrance *f nom* fan-in

entre blocs *adjectif* interblock

entrée *f nom* **1.** data entry **2.** entering **3.** entry **4.** input ■ *abrév* i/p *ou* I/P ◇ **entrée** *f* **dans un journal de bord** log ◇ **limité par la vitesse d'entrée des données** input-limited

entrée *f* **à partir de microfilm** *nom* CIM

entrée *f* **de ligne** *nom* line in

entrée *f* **directe de données** *nom* **1.** DDE **2.** direct data entry

entrée *f* **en temps réel** *nom* real-time input

entrée *f* **parallèle/sortie parallèle** *nom* **1.** parallel input/parallel output **2.** PIO

entrée *f* **parallèle/sortie série** *nom* **1.** parallel input/serial output **2.** PISO

entrée *f* **par lecture de microfilm** *nom* CIM

entrée *f* **principale** *nom* main entry

entrée *f* **série/sortie parallèle** *nom* serial input/parallel output ■ *abrév* SIPO

entrée *f* **série/sortie série** *nom* serial input/serial output

entrée série/sortie série *abrév* SISO

entrée/sortie *f nom* input/output

entrée(s)/sortie(s) *f(pl) nom* I/O ◇ **limité par le débit d'entrée** *or* **sortie** I/O bound

entrée/sortie *f* **configurée en mémoire** *nom* **1.** memory-mapped input/output **2.** memory-mapped I/O

entrée/sortie *f* **en série** *nom* **1.** serial input/output **2.** serial transmission ■ *abrév* SIO

entrée/sortie *f* **graphique** *nom* GINO

entrée/sortie *f* **(en) parallèle** *nom* **1.** parallel input/output **2.** PIPO

entrée/sortie *f* **utilisant une mémoire tampon** *nom* buffered input/output

entrefer *m nom* **1.** air gap **2.** gap **3.** head gap

entrelaçage *m* **binaire** *nom* bit interleaving

entrelaçage *m* **de caractères** *nom* character interleaving

entrelacement *m nom* interleaving

entrelacement *m* **de secteurs** *nom* sector interleave

entrelacer *verbe* to interlace

entrepôt *m* **de données** *nom* data warehouse

entreprise à entreprise *adjectif* B2B

entreprise *m* **de diffusion d'informations grand public** *nom* common carrier

entrer *verbe* **1.** *vi* to enter **2.** *vi* to input **3.** *vi* to read in ◇ **entrer** *ou* **inscrire un nom sur une liste** to enter a name on a list

entretenir *verbe* **1.** *vt* to maintain **2.** *vt* to refresh ◇ **bien entretenu, -e** well maintained

entretien *m nom* **1.** maintenance **2.** upkeep

en trop *adjectif* redundant

en valeur absolue *adjectif* unsigned

enveloppe *f nom* envelope ◇ **détection d'enveloppe** envelope detection ◇ **enveloppe d'attaque (d'un signal)** (*amplitude*) attack envelope ◇ **(temps de) propagation d'une enveloppe** envelope delay

enveloppe *f nom* envelope

environnement *m nom* **1.** environment **2.** platform ◇ **ce logiciel ne fonctionne que dans un environnement IBM** this software will only work on the IBM PC platform

environnement *m* **de développement de programme** *nom* program development system

environnement *m* **graphique WIMP** *nom* **1.** (*avec fenêtre, icône, souris, pointeur*) WIMP **2.** (*avec fenêtre, icône, souris, pointeur*) window, icon, mouse, pointer

environnement *m* **MOO** *nom* **1.** MOO **2.** multiuser domain, object-oriented

environnement *m* **MUD** *nom* **1.** multiuser domain **2.** multiuser dungeon

environnement *m* **universitaire** *nom* campus environment

envoi *m nom* dispatch *ou* despatch

envoi *m* **de mails** *nom* messaging ◇ **envoi de messages (écrits)** *ou* **de mails** text messaging

envoi *m* **de messages** *nom* messaging ◇ **envoi de messages (écrits)** *ou* **de mails** text messaging ◇ **envoi de photos (par téléphone)** photo messaging ◇ **messagerie** text messaging

envoi *m* **différé** *nom* store and forward

envoi *m* **par la poste** *nom* mailing ◇ **envoi de prospectus publicitaires** mailing shot ◇ **établir un fichier d'adresses** to build up a mailing list ◇ **l'envoi (par la poste) de prospectus publicitaires** the mailing of publicity material ◇ **prospectus envoyé par la poste** mailing piece ◇ **publicité directe** *ou* **mailing** direct mailing ◇ **publipostage** direct mailing ◇ **son nom figure sur notre fichier d'adresses** his name is on our mailing list

envoyer par fax *verbe* to fax *ou* to FAX ◇ **j'ai faxé les documents** *ou* **j'ai envoyé les documents par télécopie à notre bureau de New York** I've faxed the documents to our New York office

envoyer par télécopie *verbe* to fax *ou* to FAX ◇ **j'ai faxé les documents** *ou* **j'ai envoyé les documents par télécopie à notre bureau de New York** I've faxed the documents to our New York office

envoyer un accusé de réception *verbe* to acknowledge

envoyer un message croisé *verbe* to cross-post

envoyer un message d'un ton (particulièrement) agressif *verbe* to flame

éphémère *adjectif* transient

épine *f* **dorsale** *nom* backbone

épreuve positive *adjectif* (*photographie*) positive

épreuves *fpl* **pour évaluation des performances** *nom* benchmark problem

EPS *nom* encapsulated PostScript ■ *abrév* EPS

EPSF *nom* encapsulated PostScript file ■ *abrév* EPSF

épure *f nom* blueprint

équation *f* **de Mandlebrot** *nom* Mandlebrot set

équation *f* **machine** *nom* machine equation

équilibrage *m* **des colonnes** *nom* column balance

équilibrage *m* **des lignes de transmission** *nom* balanced routing

équilibre *m nom* balance ◇ **le logiciel de PAO permet à l'utilisateur de juger du bon équilibre** *ou* **de la bonne disposition d'une page** the DTP package allows the user to see if the overall page balance is correct

équilibre *m* **des couleurs** *nom* colour balance

équilibrer *verbe vt* to match ◇ **charge accordée** *ou* **équilibrée** matched load

équilibreur *m* **de ligne** *nom* line adapter

équilibreur *m* **d'impédance** *nom* **1.** balun **2.** line adapter

équipé, -ée d'une pile auxiliaire *adjectif* battery-backed ◇ **la carte RAM peut être équipée, en option, d'une pile de secours** the RAM disk card has the option to be battery-backed

équipement *m nom* standby equipment

équipement *m* **de traitement de formulaires** *nom* form handling equipment

équipement *m* **de transition** *nom* bridgeware

équipement *m* **de transmission de données** *nom* data communications equipment ■ *abrév* DCE

équipement *m* **de vérification automatique (EVA)** *nom* **1.** ATE **2.** automatic test equipment

équipement *m* **informatique** *nom* installation

équipement *m* **interfacé HDLC** *nom* high-level data link control station

équivalence *f nom* equivalence

équivalence *f* **logique** *nom* equivalence function

équivoque *adjectif* ambiguous

éraflure *f nom* (*sur un disque*) scratch

ergonomique *adjectif* user-friendly

erreur *nom* **1.** error **2.** fault **3.** hard error **4.** hazard ◇ **codes de correction d'erreurs** error correcting codes ◇ **codes de détection d'erreurs** error detecting codes ◇ **détection et correction d'erreurs** error detection and correction (EDAC) ◇ **erreur** *f* **de lecture momentanée** transient read error ◇ **erreur** *f* **imputable à un composant défectueux** component error ◇ **il a fait une erreur de total** he made an error in calculating the total ◇ **(signal d')interruption sur (une) erreur** *ou* **sur (un) incident** error interrupt ◇ **les techniciens essayent de corriger une erreur de programmation** the technical staff are trying to correct a programming fault ◇ **le taux d'erreur est inférieur à 1%** the error rate is less than 1% ◇ **message de diagnostic d'erreur** diagnostic (error) message ◇ **nous estimons qu'il y a une erreur fondamentale dans la conception du produit** we think there is a basic fault in the product design ◇ **par erreur** in error *ou* by error ◇ **un pli ou une déchirure dans une page peut être la cause d'une erreur de balayage** *ou* **d'un balayage incorrect** a wrinkled or torn page may be the cause of scanning errors

erreur *f* **absolue** *nom* absolute error

erreur *f* **à l'exécution** *nom* run-time error

erreur *f* **au démarrage** *nom* cold fault

erreur *f* **au départ** *nom* initial error

erreur *f* **à valeur moyenne nulle** *nom* balanced error

erreur *f* **catastrophique** *nom* catastrophic error

erreur *f* **causée par le support** *nom* media error

erreur *f* **consciente** *nom* conscious error

erreur *f* **critique** *nom* critical error

erreur *f* **d'ambiguïté** *nom* ambiguity error

erreur *f* **d'arrondi** *nom* **1.** approximation error **2.** rounding error *ou* round-off error **3.** truncation error

erreur *f* **de balayage** *nom* scanning error

erreur *f* **de compilation** *nom* compilation error ◇ **les erreurs de compilation provoquent l'interruption inopinée de la tâche** compilation errors result in the job being aborted

erreur *f* **d'écriture** *nom* write error

erreur *f* **de données** *nom* data error

erreur *f* **de lecture** *nom* read error

erreur *f* **de logiciel** *nom* soft error

erreur *f* **de quantification** *nom* quantisation error

erreur *f* **de refus** *nom* rejection error

erreur *f* **de rejet** *nom* rejection error

erreur *f* **de substitution** *nom* substitution error

erreur *f* **détectée** *nom* detected error

erreur *f* **de trame** *nom* frame error

erreur *f* **de transmission** *nom* transmission error

erreur *f* **de troncature** *nom* **1.** rounding error *ou* round-off error **2.** truncation error

erreur *f* **d'exécution** *nom* execution error

erreur *f* **due à l'ordinateur** *nom* computer error

erreur *f* **équilibrée** *nom* balanced error

erreur *f* **fatale** *nom* **1.** catastrophic error **2.** fatal error

erreur *f* **générée (par des arrondis)** *nom* generated error

erreur *f* **héritée** *nom* inherited error

erreur *f* **impossible à corriger** *nom* unrecoverable error

erreur *f* **inexplicable** *nom* gremlin

erreur *f* **intermittente** *nom* intermittent error

erreur *f* **irrécupérable** *nom* unrecoverable error

erreur *f* **logique** *nom* logical error

erreur *f* **(causée par la) machine** *nom* machine error

erreur *f* **momentanée** *nom* transient error

erreur *f* **non détectée** *nom* undetected error

erreur *f* **notifiée** *nom* detected error

erreur *f* **passagère** *nom* transient error

erreur *f* **permanente** *nom* **1.** permanent error **2.** solid error

erreur *f* **persistante** *nom* solid error

erreur *f* **propagée** *nom* propagated error

erreur *f* **qui se propage** *nom* propagating error

erreur *f* **récupérable** *nom* recoverable error

erreur *f* **relative** *nom* relative error

erreur *f* **réparable** *nom* recoverable error

erreur *f* **sémantique** *nom* semantic error

erreur *f* **sporadique** *nom* sporadic fault
erreur *f* **transmise** *nom* inherited error
erroné *adjectif* **1.** corrupt **2.** false
escalade *f nom* hill climbing
esclave *m nom* slave
espace *m nom* **1.** gap **2.** space ◇ **espace** *m* **disponible insuffisant** (*dans la pile*) stack overflow
espace *m* **adresse** *nom* address space
espace *m* **d'adressage simple** *nom* flat address space
espace *m* **d'adresse segmenté** *nom* segmented address space
espace *m* **d'affichage** *nom* display space
espace *m* **de manoeuvre** *nom* workspace
espace *m* **de nommage** *nom* namespace
espace *m* **de travail** *nom* **1.** work area **2.** workspace
espace *m* **entre blocs** *nom* block gap
espace *m* **interbloc** *nom* block gap ■ *abrév* IBG ■ *nom* **1.** interblock gap **2.** interrecord gap
espace *m* **mémoire de l'image** *nom* image storage space
espace *m* **mémoire réservé à l'usage d'un utilisateur** *nom* private address space
espacement *m nom* pitch
espacement *m nom* space
espacement *m* **des pixels** *nom* dot pitch
espacement *m* **entre les mots** *nom* interword spacing
espacement *m* **proportionnel de caractères** *nom* intercharacter spacing
espace *m* **neutre** *nom* (*séparant deux fichiers*) file gap
espacer *verbe vt* to space
espaces *mpl nom* spacing ◇ **il y a quelques lignes o— les espaces sont très inégaux** the spacing on some lines is very uneven
espace *m* **sans rupture** *nom* non breaking space
esprit *m nom* sprite
esquisse *f nom* outline
essai *m nom* **1.** operation trial **2.** program testing **3.** test **4.** test run ◇ **un essai fera tout de suite apparaître les erreurs** a test run will soon show up any errors
essai *m* **à blanc** *nom* **1.** (*d'un programme*) desk check **2.** dry run
essai *m* **comparatif** *nom* benchmark
essai *m* **en boucle** *nom* loopback test
essai *m* **non destructif** *nom* non destructive test
essentiel *adjectif* prime
estampille *f nom* time stamp
estompage *m* **en fonction de l'éloignement** *nom* depth cueing
ET *nom* AND function
établir *verbe vt* to preset
établir de nouveaux paramètres *verbe* to redefine ◇ **j'ai reprogrammé cette touche pour obtenir un 5** I have redefined this key to display the figure five when pressed ◇ **nous avons redéfini les premiers paramètres** we redefined the initial parameters ◇ **redéfinir la fonction d'une touche** *ou* **reprogrammer une touche** to redefine a key
établir des liens *verbe* to bind
établir une protection des accès mémoire *verbe* to fetch-protect
établir une transition *verbe* to bridge
établir un pont *verbe* to bridge
étape *f nom* **1.** stage **2.** step
étape *f* **d'un travail** *nom* job step
état *m nom* condition ◇ **état** *m* **logique bas** logical low ◇ **état** *m* **logique haut** logical high
état *m* **commande** *nom* (*d'un modem prêt à recevoir des commandes*) command state
état *m* **connecté** *nom* connect state
état d'attente ◇ **état** *m* **sans attente** zero wait state
état *m* **d'attente** *nom* **1.** wait condition **2.** wait state
état *m* **de configuration** *nom* configuration state
état *m* **de latence** *nom* **1.** wait condition **2.** wait state
état *m* **désactivé** *nom* disarmed state
état *m* **logique** *nom* logic state
état *m* **prêt** *nom* ready state
état *m* **stable** *nom* stable state
état *m* **stationnaire** *nom* steady state
étayer *verbe vt* to back up ◇ **il a apporté tout un dossier pour étayer sa réclamation** he brought along a file of documents to back up his claim
éteindre *verbe vt* to shut down
étendue *f nom* (*choix*) range ◇ **étendue** *f* **de la zone de balayage** scan length
Ethernet *m nom* (*norme IEEE 802.3 de réseau*) Ethernet
Ethernet *m* **à paire torsadée** *nom* twisted-pair Ethernet
Ethernet *m* **câble fin** *nom* thin-Ethernet
Ethernet *m* **câble fin (et bon marché)** *nom* cheapernet
Ethernet *m* **câble lourd** *nom* thick-Ethernet
EtherTalk (*nom de marque*) EtherTalk
étiquetage *m nom* labelling
étiqueter *verbe vt* to label
étiquette *f nom* **1.** label **2.** (*informatique*) tag ◇ **chaque fichier peut être identifié rapidement par son étiquette de trois lettres** each file has a three letter tag for rapid identification

étiquette *f* **de volume** *nom* volume label *ou* volume name

étiquette *f* **extérieure** *nom* external label

étiquette *f* **interne** *nom* inlay card

étiquette *f* **perforée** *nom* punched tag

étiquettes *fpl* **en continu** *plural noun* continuous labels

étoile *f nom* (*caractère d'imprimerie*) asterisk

étouffer *verbe vt* to deaden

étranger *adjectif* alien

être accroché dans une boucle *verbe* to hang

être en colère *verbe* to shout

être en dérangement *verbe* to malfunction

être en marche *verbe* to run

être en tête de liste *verbe* to head ◇ **mon fichier était en tête de la file d'attente** the queue was headed by my file

être expert *verbe* to specialise

être spécialiste *verbe* to specialise

étude *f* **de faisabilité** *nom* feasibility study

étude *f* **des coûts** *nom* cost analysis

évaluation *f nom* measurement

évaluation *f* **des performances** *nom* benchmarking

évaluer ◇ **évalué en cycles possibles par unité de temps** duty-rated

événement *m nom* event

évolué *adjectif* sophisticated ◇ **un programme de PAO évolué** *ou* **avancé** a sophisticated desktop publishing program

exact *adjectif* precise

exactitude *f nom* **1.** accuracy **2.** precision

examiner (quelque chose) attentivement *verbe* to scan ◇ **il a cherché Teddington sur la carte** he scanned the map for Teddington ◇ **l'appareil peut scanner jusqu'à 300 points par pouce** the machine scans at up to 300 dpi resolution ◇ **le fax balaye l'image et la numérise avant transmission** a facsimile machine scans the picture and converts this to digital form before transmission

exception *f nom* exception ◇ **rapport d'exceptions** *ou* **d'anomalies** exception report

excès *m nom* spillage

excitation *f nom* impulse

exclusion *f nom* exclusion

exclusion *f* **réciproque** *nom* **1.** inequivalence **2.** symmetric difference

EXE *nom* exe

exécuter *verbe* **1.** *vt* to execute **2.** *vt* to run ◇ **exécuter qc en mode points** (*une image*) bitmap ◇ **le nouveau progiciel peut être utilisé sur notre PC** the new package runs on our PC ◇ **n'arrêtez pas la vérification de l'orthographe en cours de route** do not interrupt the spelling checker while it is running

exécuter (des instructions) en pipeline *verbe* to pipeline

exécution *nom* **1.** execution **2.** run ◇ **exécution** *f* **d'un programme d'édition** editing run ◇ **exécution** *f* **d'un programme une instruction à la fois** step through

exécution *f* **d'un programme** *nom* **1.** computer run **2.** machine run **3.** program execution **4.** program run

exécution *f* **pas à pas** *adjectif* single step

exigences *f plural noun* requirements

EXIT *nom* EXIT

expansion *f nom* expansion

expédition *f nom* despatch

expert, -e *nom* **1.** networking specialist **2.** specialist

'...les systèmes experts sont les premiers produits de l'intelligence artificielle' [*L'Ordinateur Individuel*]

explication *f nom* comment

exploitable par l'ordinateur *adjectif* machine readable ◇ **le disque garde en mémoire des données en langage machine** *ou* **sous une forme exploitable par l'ordinateur** the disk stores data in machine-readable form

exploration *f* **de données** *nom* data mining

exporter *verbe vt* to export ◇ **pour utiliser ces données avec dBase, il faut les exporter sous la forme d'un fichier de format dBase** to use this data with dBASE, you will have to export it as a DBF file

exposant *m nom* **1.** biased exponent **2.** characteristic **3.** superior number **4.** superscript ◇ **la valeur de l'exposant du nombre à virgule flottante 1,345 x 10[[SUP]]3 est 3** the floating point number 1.345 x 10[[SUP]]3, has a characteristic of 3

exposant *m* **binaire** *nom* binary exponent

exposé *m* **d'un problème** *nom* problem definition

expression *f nom* expression

expression *f* **absolue** *nom* absolute expression

expression *f* **binaire d'un caractère** *nom* character representation

expression *f* **logique** *nom* logical expression

exprimer ◇ **exprimer son mécontentement en écrivant un message en majuscules** shout

extension *f nom* expansion ◇ **extension** *f* **du nom du fichier** filename extension ◇ **l'extension SYS ajoutée au nom du fichier indique qu'il s'agit d'un fichier système** the filename extension SYS indicates that this is a system file ◇ **NuBus™, extension de bus à 96 connecteurs utilisé par les Macintosh de Apple** NuBus

extension *f* **BAK** *nom* BAK file extension

extension *f* **BAT** *nom* BAT file extension

extension *f* **BMP** *nom* BMP ◇ **ce logiciel de peinture permet l'importation de fichiers BMP** (*extension d'un fichier graphique*) this paint package lets you import BMP files

extension *f* **COM** *suffix* com

extension *f* **de la mémoire** *nom* memory expansion

extension *f* **enfichable** *nom* plug-in unit

extensions *fpl* **multimédia** *plural noun* multimedia extensions

externaliser *verbe vt* to outsource

extinction *f nom* decay

extracode *m nom* extracode

extracteur *m nom* extractor

extraction *f nom* retrieval

extraire *verbe* **1.** *vt* to extract **2.** *vt* to pull **3.** *vt* to read **4.** *vt* to retrieve ◇ **nous pouvons extraire les dossiers qui doivent aller à la composition** we can extract the files required for typesetting ◇ **on utilise cette commande pour extraire la liste de tous les noms qui commencent par S** this command will retrieve all names beginning with S ◇ **voici les informations extraites au cours de cette recherche** these are the records retrieved in that search

extraire un clip *verbe* to clip ◇ **un clip de l'accident a été passé aux informations** there was a clip of the disaster on the news

extranet *m nom* extranet

F

fabricant *m* **de produits à connecteurs compatibles** *nom* PCM

fabricant *m* **de produits (à connecteurs) compatibles** *nom* plug-compatible manufacturer

fabrication *f nom* production

fabrication *f* **assistée par ordinateur** *nom* CAM ■ *abrév* CAM ■ *nom* **1.** computer-aided manufacture **2.** computer-assisted manufacture

fabrication *f* **de prototype** *nom* prototyping

fabrication *f* **en série** *nom* mass production ◇ **fabrication en série de moniteurs** *ou* **de calculatrices** mass production of monitors *ou* of calculators

fabriquer sur commande *verbe* to customise *ou* to customize

façade *f nom* bezel

facile à utiliser *adjectif* user-friendly ◇ **c'est un appareil vraiment convivial** *ou* **extrêmement facile à utiliser** it's such a user-friendly machine ◇ **comparée à la version précédente, celle-ci est très facile à utiliser** *ou* **très conviviale** compared with the previous version this one is very user-friendly

facilité *nom* facility ◇ **facilité** *f* **de traitement électronique de données** electronic data processing capability

facilité *f* **d'utilisation** *nom* usability

fac-similé *m nom* facsimile copy

facteur *m nom* factor ◇ **facteur** *m* **de déplacement** (*d'une adresse relative*) float factor

facteur *m* **de bloc** *nom* blocking factor

facteur *m* **décisif** *nom* deciding factor

facteur *m* **de forme** *nom* form factor

facteur *m* **d'élimination** *nom* elimination factor

facteur *m* **de silence** *nom* omission factor

facteur *m* **d'imbrication** *nom* interleave factor

facteur *m* **d'omission** *nom* omission factor

factorielle *f nom* factorial ◇ **la factorielle de 4 (qui s'écrit 4!) ou 1x2x3x4 est 24** 4 factorial (written 4!) or 1x2x3x4 equals 24

factoriser *verbe vt* to factorise *ou* to factorize

faible résolution *f nom* lo-res

faiblir *verbe vi* to fade

faire ◇ **ce programme permet aux utilisateurs de sauvegarder les fichiers du disque dur en une seule opération** the program enables users to back up hard disk files with a single command ◇ **elle a enregistré le programme de télévision sur une bande vidéo et l'a visionné le lendemain soir** she recorded the TV programme on video tape and replayed it the next evening ◇ **faire défiler ligne à ligne sur l'écran** roll scroll ◇ **faire défiler un texte point par point** smooth scroll ◇ **faire jouer (une bande nouvellement enregistrée)** replay ◇ **faire une copie de sauvegarde** back up ◇ **faire une nouvelle mise en pages** repaginate ◇ **faire une offre groupée** bundle ◇ **faire une superposition d'écriture et détruire les données en mémoire** overwrite ◇ **faire un traitement de texte sur ordinateur** word-process ◇ **il a repassé la bande** *ou* **il a remis la bande** he replayed the tape ◇ **la comptabilité de la société a été sauvegardée sur disque en cas d'incendie** the company accounts were backed up on disk as a protection against fire damage ◇ **la mise en page a été refaite avec une nouvelle largeur de ligne** the text was repaginated with a new line width ◇ **la société ne s'est pas souciée d'effectuer la maintenance de routine de son matériel** the company failed to carry out routine maintenance of its equipment ◇ **le premier essai du prototype de lecteur de disquettes a été un échec** the prototype disk drive failed its first test ◇ **les nouvelles données ont remplacé les anciennes (par superposition d'écriture)** the latest data input has overwritten the old information ◇ **ne pas faire quelque chose** fail ◇ **on lit facilement les fichiers après traitement de texte** it is quite easy to read word-processed files

faire apparaître *verbe* **1.** to pop **2.** to reveal

faire avorter *verbe* to abort

faire circuler *verbe* to distribute

faire clignoter *verbe* to flash

faire coïncider *verbe* to register

faire défiler *verbe* **1.** to pass **2.** to scroll ◇ **l'ascenseur est situé au milieu de la barre de défilement** the marker is in the middle of the scroll bar so I know I am in the middle of the document

faire disparaître de l'écran *verbe* to zap ◇ **il a tapé CONTROL Z pour vider l'écran** he pressed CONTROL Z and zapped all the text

faire disparaître progressivement *verbe* to fade out

faire du pipeline *verbe* to pipeline

faire du piratage informatique *verbe* to hack

faire écho *verbe* to echo

faire fonctionner *verbe* to operate ◇ **savez-vous comment fonctionne le standard téléphonique?** do you know how to operate the telephone switchboard?

faire l'analyse grammaticale *verbe* to parse

faire l'analyse syntaxique *verbe* to parse

faire l'essai *verbe* to pilot ◇ **ils font l'essai du nouveau système** they are piloting the new system

faire l'habillage d'une illustration *verbe* to run around

faire marche arrière *verbe* **1.** to backtrack **2.** to reverse

faire monter *verbe* to bring up

faire passer *verbe* to replay ◇ **il a repassé la bande** *ou* **il a remis la bande** he replayed the tape

faire suivre *verbe* to forward

faire un alinéa *verbe* to indent ◇ **comptez deux espaces pour l'alinéa du premier paragraphe** the first line of the paragraph is indented two spaces

faire un audit *verbe* to audit

faire un balayage *verbe* to scan ◇ **le fax balaye l'image et la numérise avant transmission** a facsimile machine scans the picture and converts this to digital form before transmission

faire un brûlage d'écran *verbe* to burn in

faire un chargement éclaté *verbe* to scatter-load

faire un clic *verbe* to click ◇ **cliquer sur le bouton droit (de la souris)** *ou* **effectuer un clic droit** to click on the right button (of the mouse) *ou* to right click ◇ **cliquer sur le bouton gauche (de la souris)** *ou* **effectuer un clic gauche** to click on the left button (of the mouse) *ou* to left click

faire un échange *verbe* to exchange

faire une concaténation *verbe* to catenate

faire une copie de bloc *verbe* to block-copy

faire une déclaration *verbe* to declare ◇ **au début du programme X a été déclaré égal à 9** he declared at the start of the program that X was equal to nine

faire une lecture sélective *verbe* to scatter-read

faire une multidiffusion *verbe* to multicast

faire une recherche *verbe* to search

faire un essai *verbe* to test

faire une tabulation arrière *verbe* to backtab

faire une vérification orthographique *verbe* to spellcheck

faire un fondu *verbe* to fade out

faire *m* **un ordinogramme** *verbe* to flowchart *ou* to

faire un pas *verbe* to step

faire un raccord *verbe* to splice ◇ **utilisez de la colle ou du ruban gommé pour raccorder les extrémités (du film)** you can use glue or splicing tape to splice the ends

faire un scannage *verbe* to scan ◇ **l'appareil peut scanner jusqu'à 300 points par pouce** the machine scans at up to 300 dpi resolution

faire un scanning *verbe* to scan ◇ **l'appareil peut scanner jusqu'à 300 points par pouce** the machine scans at up to 300 dpi resolution

faire un spoule *verbe* to spool

faire un test *verbe* to test

faire un zoom *verbe* to zoom

faisabilité *f nom* feasibility

faisceau *nom* beam ◇ **dans un tube à rayons cathodiques, la déflexion du faisceau est effectuée par un champ magnétique** a magnetic field is used for beam deflection in a CRT ◇ **dédoublement du faisceau** beam diversity ◇ **largeur d'un faisceau** *ou* **d'un lobe** beam width

'...un faisceau lumineux de longueur d'onde inférieure à 950nm ne sera détecté que par la photodiode supérieure et sera entièrement absorbé par celle-ci' [*Opto électronique*]

faisceau *m* **de fibres optiques** *nom* bundle

faisceau *m* **de jonction** *nom* trunk

faisceau *m* **d'électrons** *nom* electron beam

faisceau *m* **d'image** *nom* picture beam

faisceau *m* **électronique** *nom* electron beam

fait, -e sur mesure *adjectif* custom-built

famille *f nom* family

fatal *adjectif* terminal

fausse *adjectif* false

fausse erreur *f nom* false error

faute *f nom* **1.** error **2.** fault ◇ **la secrétaire doit avoir fait une faute de frappe** the secretary must have made a typing error

faute *f* **de syntaxe** *nom* **1.** grammatical error **2.** syntactic error **3.** syntax error

faux *adjectif* false

fax *m nom* **1.** facsimile transmission **2.** fax *ou* FAX ◇ **modem avec fonction télécopie** *ou* **télécopieur-modem** *ou* **fax-modem** *ou* **fax** *or* **modem** fax-modem ◇ **notre fax est tout à côté du standard téléphonique** the fax machine is next to the telephone switchboard ◇ **nous enverrons les plans par télécopie** *ou* **par fax** we will send a fax of the design plan

faxer *verbe vt* to fax *ou* to FAX

feedback *m nom* feedback ◇ **boucle de feedback** *ou* **de réaction** *ou* **de rétroaction** feedback loop ◇ **rétroaction négative** *ou* **feedback négatif** negative feedback

femelle *adjectif* female

femto- *préfixe* femto-

femtoseconde *f nom* femtosecond

fenêtrage *m nom* windowing

fenêtre *f nom* window ◇ **environnement graphique WIMP (avec fenêtre, icône, souris, pointeur)** window, icon, mouse, pointer (WIMP) ◇ **le système d'exploitation permet d'afficher d'autres programmes simultanément dans des fenêtres différentes** the operating system will allow other programs to be displayed on-screen at the same time in different windows ◇ **plusieurs postes de travail à distance sont connectés au réseau, chacun disposant d'une fenêtre sur le disque dur** several remote stations are connected to the network and each has its own window onto the hard disk

fenêtre *f* **active** *nom* active window

fenêtre *f* **bloc-notes** *nom* screen notepad

fenêtre *f* **d'accès** *nom* (*d'un disque ou d'une disquette*) access hole

fenêtre *f* **d'application** *nom* application window

fenêtre *f* **de commande** *nom* command window ◇ **la fenêtre de commande est une seule ligne au bas de l'écran** the command window is a single line at the bottom of the screen

fenêtre *f* **de compatibilité** *nom* compatibility box

fenêtre *f* **d'édition** *nom* edit window

fenêtre *f* **de menu** *nom* **1.** pop-down menu **2.** pop-up menu

fenêtre *f* **de message** *nom* pop-up window

fenêtre *f* **de texte** *nom* text window

fenêtre *f* **d'interrogation** *nom* query window

fenêtre *f* **d'une ligne** *nom* strip window

fenêtre *f* **étroite** *nom* thin window

fenêtre *f* **fille** *nom* child window

fenêtre *f* **inactive** *nom* inactive window

fenêtrer *verbe vt* to window

fenêtres *fpl* **en cascade** *plural noun* cascading windows

fenêtre *f* **splash** *nom* splash screen

fenêtre *f* **textuelle** *nom* text window

fermé *adjectif* hard

fermer *verbe* **1.** *vt* to close **2.** *vt* to shut down

fermeture *f* **de session** *nom* logging out ■ *verbe* to logoff ■ *nom* logout

fermeture *f* **en fondu** *nom* fade out

ferrite *f nom* ferrite

feuille *f nom* **1.** coding form **2.** coding sheet

feuille *f nom* sheet ◇ **alimentation feuille à feuille** (single) sheet feed

feuille *f* **(de papier)** *nom* leaf

feuille *f* **de style** *nom* style sheet

feuille *f* **de travail** *nom* worksheet

fiabilité *f nom* **1.** hardware reliability **2.** reliability ◇ **ce produit a réussi tous les tests de fiabilité** the product has passed its reliability tests ◇ **il est reconnu pour sa fiabilité** it has an excellent reliability record

fiabilité *f* **d'un logiciel** *nom* software reliability

fiable *adjectif* reliable

fibre *f nom* fibre

fibre *f* **Ethernet** *nom* fibre Ethernet

fibre *f* **optique** *nom* **1.** optical fibre **2.** optic fibre

fibre *f* **optique monomodale** *nom* single mode fibre

fibre *f* **optique monomode** *nom* monomode fibre

fibre *f* **optique multimode** *nom* multimode fibre

fiche *f nom* **1.** jack *ou* jack plug **2.** plug ◇ **la fiche est fournie avec l'imprimante** the printer is supplied with a plug

fiche *f* **complémentaire de bus** *abrév* BEC

fiche *f* **téléphone pour modem** *nom* data jack

fichier *nom* **1.** Bindery **2.** content-addressable file ◇ **fichier** *m* **de mouvements** *ou* **de modifications** *ou* **de mise à jour** movement file ◇ **fichiers** *mpl* **à accès aléatoire** random access files

> '...pour créer un nouveau fichier, exécutez la commande 'Nouveau document'' [*L'Ordinateur Individuel*]

> '...en apparence, rien n'est plus simple que de copier un fichier sur disquette, puis d'utiliser cette disquette sur un second ordinateur' [*Action PC*]

fichier *m* **à accès séquentiel** *nom* **1.** sequential file **2.** serial file

fichier *m* **à champs délimités** *nom* delimited-field file

fichier *m* **actif** *nom* active file

fichier *m* **ancêtre** *nom* ancestral file

fichier *m* **annexé** *nom* attachment

fichier *m* **archives** *nom* archive file

fichier *m* **ASCII** *nom* ASCII file

fichier *m* **associé** *nom* associated document *ou* associated file

fichier *m* **audio** *nom* **1.** audio file **2.** sound file

fichier *m* **auto-extractible** *nom* self extracting archive

fichier *m* **avec ajouts** *nom* add file

fichier *m* **bidimensionnel** *nom* flat file

fichier *m* **binaire** *nom* binary file ◇ **votre lettre est un fichier texte et non pas un fichier binaire** your letter is a text file, not a binary file

fichier *m* **binaire exécutable** *nom* COM file

fichier *m* **bureau** *nom* desktop file

fichier *m* **chaîné** *nom* **1.** chained file **2.** threaded file

fichier *m* **chronologique** *nom* journal file

fichier *m* **COM** *nom* COM file ◇ **pour démarrer le programme, tapez le nom du fichier COM à l'invite MS-DOS** to start the program, type the name of the COM file at the MS-DOS prompt

fichier *m* **COMMAND.COM** *nom* COMMAND.COM

fichier *m* **commun** *nom* shared file

fichier *m* **composite** *nom* compound file

fichier *m* **compressé** *nom* zip file

fichier *m* **contigu** *nom* contiguous file

fichier *m* **cookie** *nom* cookie

fichier *m* **d'adresses** *nom* mailing list ◇ **son nom figure sur notre fichier d'adresses** his name is on our mailing list

fichier *m* **d'application** *nom* application file

fichier *m* **de champ de taille constante** *nom* fixed-field file

fichier *m* **de champ de taille fixe** *nom* fixed-field file

fichier *m* **d'échange permanent** *nom* permanent swap file

fichier *m* **d'échange temporaire** *nom* temporary swap file

fichier *m* **de commandes** *nom* **1.** (*de traitement par lots*) batch file **2.** command file ◇ **ce fichier de commandes (de traitement par lots) est utilisé pour économiser du temps et des efforts lorsqu'on effectue une tâche de routine** this batch file is used to save time and effort when carrying out a routine task

fichier *m* **de configuration** *nom* configuration file

fichier *m* **de contrôle de tâche** *nom* job control file

fichier *m* **de données** *nom* data file

fichier *m* **de données externe** *nom* external data file

fichier *m* **délimité par virgule** *nom* comma-delimited file ◇ **à partir de toutes bases de données on peut soit importer des données d'un fichier délimité par virgule, soit en exporter vers le fichier** all databases can import and export to a comma-delimited file format

fichier *m* **de manoeuvre** *nom* scratch file

fichier *m* **de mise à jour** *nom* **1.** addition record **2.** change file

fichier *m* **de mouvements** *nom* **1.** change file **2.** update file

fichier *m* **d'enregistrement des blocs** *nom* block list

fichier *m* **de pointeurs** *nom* pointer file

fichier *m* **de première génération** *nom* grandfather file

fichier *m* **de programme maître** *nom* master program file

fichier *m* **de référence** *nom* **1.** authority file *ou* authority list **2.** reference file

fichier *m* **de sauvegarde** *nom* backup file

fichier *m* **de sortie** *nom* output file

fichier *m* **des registres** *nom* register file

fichier *m* **de tâches à exécuter** *nom* job file

fichier *m* **de témoins** *nom* cookie file

fichier *m* **de transactions** *nom* transaction file

fichier *m* **de travail** *nom* **1.** scratch file **2.** work file

fichier *m* **de travaux** *nom* job file

fichier *m* **de troisième génération** *nom* son file

fichier *m* **DIF** *nom* DIF file

fichier *m* **DLL** *nom* DLL file

fichier *m* **d'ordinateur** *nom* computer file

fichier *m* **en annexe** *nom* attachment

fichier *m* **en boucle** *nom* circular file

fichier *m* **(d') entrée/sortie** *nom* I/O file

fichier *m* **exécutable** *nom* executable file

fichier *m* **fils** *nom* son file

fichier *m* **(graphique) GIF** *nom* GIF file

fichier *m* **GIF animé** *nom* animated GIF

fichier *m* **grand-père** *nom* grandfather file

fichier *m* **graphique** *nom* graphics file

fichier *m* **indexé** *nom* indexed file

fichier *m* **INF** *nom* INF file

fichier *m* **informatique** *nom* computer file

fichier *m* **INI** *nom* INI file

fichier *m* **intermédiaire** *nom* intermediate file

fichier *m* **inversé** *nom* inverted file

fichier *m* **joint** *nom* attachment

fichier *m* **journal** *nom* log file

fichier-journal *m* *nom* journal file

fichier *m* **Lisez-moi** *nom* readme file

fichier *m* **localisation** *nom* country file

fichier *m* **maître** *nom* master file

fichier *m* **MIDI** *nom* MIDI file

fichier *m* **mis à jour** *nom* update

fichier *m* **(de) mouvements** *nom* detail file

fichier *m* **objet** *nom* object file

fichier *m* **ouvert** *nom* open file

fichier *m* **OVL** *nom* overlay

fichier *m* **parent** *nom* parent folder

fichier *m* **partagé** *nom* shared file

fichier *m* **PCX** *nom* PCX file

fichier *m* **père** *nom* father file

fichier *m* **permanent** *nom* **1.** master file **2.** permanent file

fichier *m* **PIF** *nom* **1.** PIF **2.** program information file

fichier *m* **plat** *nom* flat file

fichier *m* **Postscript encapsulé** *abrév* EPSF

fichier *m* **PostScript encapsulé** *nom* encapsulated PostScript file

fichier *m* **principal** *nom* master file

fichier *m* **programme** *nom* program file

fichier *m* **RIFF** *nom* RIFF file

fichiers *mpl* **cachés** *plural noun* hidden files

fichiers *mpl* **dans une file d'attente** *nom* file queue

fichiers *mpl* **en mémoire** *nom* file store

fichier *m* **série extensible** *nom* extending serial file

fichier *m* **signature** *nom* signature file

fichiers *mpl* **mélangés** *plural noun* cross-linked files

fichier *m* **son** *nom* sound file

fichier *m* **source** *nom* source file

fichiers *mpl* **sources** *nom* source book

fichier *m* **subdivisé** *nom* partitioned file

fichier *m* **sur disque** *nom* disk file

fichier *m* **sur disquette** *nom* disk file

fichier *m* **texte** *nom* text file

figer *verbe vt* to freeze ◇ **figer une image** *ou* **faire un arrêt sur image** to freeze (frame) ◇ **le processeur d'image peut figer une image de télévision** the image processor will freeze a single TV frame

fignoler un programme *verbe* to tweak

fil ◇ **2 fils en paire torsadée pour liaison téléphonique** Type 3 ◇ **4 fils, de plusieurs brins chacun, en deux paires** Type 6 ◇ **4 fils, en deux paires de fils solides avec blindage tressé** Type 1 ◇ **12 fils, en six paires, pour transmission de la voix** Type 2

fil *m nom* wire

fil *m* **conducteur** *nom* lead

fil *m* **de charge statique** *nom* corona wire

fil *m* **de mise à la masse** *nom* earth wire

fil *m* **de presse** *nom* newswire

fil *m* **de terre** *nom* earth wire

file ◇ **file** *f* **d'attente** (*des tâches ou des travaux à exécuter*) job queue; job stream ◇ **file** *f* **d'attente des tâches à exécuter** task queue ◇ **file** *f* **d'attente qui fonctionne sur le principe 'premier entré premier sorti'** FIFO queue

file *f* **d'attente** *nom* **1.** (*de demandes de service*) channel queue **2.** (*de données à transmettre*) channel queue **3.** queue **4.** waiting list ◇ **les périphériques tels que les imprimantes laser sont reliés en ligne et les fichiers sont gérés par un système de file d'attente automatique** output devices such as laser printers are connected on-line with an automatic file queue

file *f* **d'attente (de périphériques)** *nom* device queue

file *f* **d'attente à deux entrées** *nom* double ended queue

file *f* **d'attente à deux extrémités** *nom* double ended queue

file *f* **d'attente à l'impression** *nom* print queue

file *f* **d'attente des données d'entrée** *nom* input work queue

filet *m nom* **1.** bar **2.** line **3.** rule

filet *m* **ultrafin** *nom* hairline rule

filière *f nom* path

filtrage *m* **bilinéaire** *nom* bilinear filtering

filtrage *m* **des adresses sources** *nom* source address filtering

filtre *nom* filter ◇ **filtre** *m* **de sélection du signal maximal** auctioneering device ◇ **filtre passe-bas** low pass filter ◇ **filtre passe-haut** high pass filter

filtre *m* **antireflets** *nom* glare filter

filtre *m* **d'amélioration du contraste** *nom* contrast enhancement filter

filtre *m* **dichroïque** *nom* dichroic filter

filtre *m* **passe-bande** *nom* bandpass filter

filtre-peigne *m nom* comb filter

filtrer *verbe vt* to filter

> '...vous pouvez installer un logiciel qui filtrera tous les messages non sollicités' [*Internet Pratique*]

fin *f nom* completion ◇ **fin** *f* **de document** end of document

fin *f* **(de fichier)** *nom* end

fin *f* **anormale** *nom* **1.** abend **2.** abnormal end **3.** abnormal termination ◇ **une commande** *ou* **un signal d'interruption venant d'une imprimante défectueuse a provoqué une fin anormale de traitement** an interrupt from a faulty printer caused an abend

fin *f* **de liste** *nom* tail

fin *f* **de message** *nom* tail

fin *f* **de page** *nom* page break

fin *f* **de paragraphe** *nom* hard return

Finder™ (*interface graphique d'utilisateur de Apple Macintosh*) Finder

fin *f* **de texte** *abrév* ETX

fin *f* **prématurée** *nom* abnormal end

Firewire (*nom de marque*) Firewire

firmware *m nom* **1.** firmware **2.** system firmware

fixe *adjectif* constant

fixer *verbe* **1.** *vt* to mount **2.** *vt* to preset **3.** *vt* to set

flasheur *m nom* (*imprimerie*) output bureau

flèches *fpl* **de défilement** *plural noun* scroll arrows

flot *m nom* stream

flot *m* **de bits** *nom* bit stream

flot *m* **de données** *nom* data stream

flottant *adjectif* floating ◇ **accent flottant** floating accent ◇ **ce modèle est livré avec un processeur à virgule flottante installé** this model includes a built-in floating point processor ◇ **courant flottant** floating voltage ◇ **le processeur à virgule flottante accélère la vitesse de traitement des logiciels graphiques** the floating point processor speeds up the processing of the graphics software ◇ **notation à virgule flottante** floating point notation ◇ **opération en virgule flottante** floating point operation (FLOP) ◇ **virgule flottante** floating point

flottement *m nom* swim

flou *m nom* blur

flux *m* **continu** *nom* **1.** continuous data stream **2.** stream

flux *m* **de données** *nom* data flow

flux *m* **de données de sortie** *nom* output stream

flux *m* **magnétique** *nom* magnetic flux

flux *m* **simple d'instructions, flux multiple de données** *nom* **1.** SIMD **2.** single instruction stream multiple data stream

flux *m* **simple d'instructions, flux simple de données** *nom* **1.** single instruction stream single data stream **2.** SISD

foire *f* **aux questions** *nom* FAQ ■ *plural noun* frequently asked questions

folding *m nom* folding

folioter *verbe vt* to page

fonction *f nom* **1.** bead **2.** equivalence function **3.** flag event **4.** function ◇ **cette machine de traitement de texte possédait une fonction correction orthographique** *ou* **possédait un correcteur orthographique mais n'était pas équipée d'éditeur intégré** the word-processor had a spelling-checker function but no built-in text-editing function ◇ **fonction** *f* **de disjonction** NEQ function; nonequivalence function

fonction *f* **bibliothèque** *nom* library function

fonction *f* **complément** *nom* NOT function

fonction *f* **d'Ackerman** *nom* Ackerman's function

fonction *f* **d'agrégation** *nom* aggregate function

fonction *f* **de chaîne** *nom* string function

fonction *f* **de disjonction** *abrév* NEQ

fonction *f* **de globalisation** *nom* aggregate function

fonction *f* **demande/réponse** *nom* inquiry/response

fonction *f* **d'équivalence** *nom* equivalence function

fonction *f* **de traitement de texte** *nom* text-editing function ◇ **une fonction traitement de texte est intégrée au programme** the program includes a built-in text-editing function

fonction *f* **d'intersection** *nom* **1.** AND function **2.** coincidence function

fonction *f* **d'union** *nom* join

fonction *f* **incorporée** *nom* built-in function

fonction *f* **interrogation/réponse** *nom* inquiry/response

fonction *f* **logique dédiée** *nom* dedicated logic ◇ **la logique dédiée réduit le nombre de puces** dedicated logic cuts down the chip count

fonction *f* **logique spécialisée** *nom* dedicated logic

fonction *f* **NAND** *nom* NAND function

fonctionnement *m* **automatique** *nom* unattended operation

fonctionnement *m* **en tandem** *nom* working in tandem

fonctionnement *m* **itératif automatique** *nom* automatic sequencing

fonctionner *verbe* **1.** *vt* to perform **2.** *vi* to run ◇ **l'ordinateur fonctionne jusqu'à dix heures par jour** the computer has been running ten hours a day ◇ **n'arrêtez pas la vérification de l'orthographe en cours de route** do not interrupt the spelling checker while it is running

fonction *f* **NI** *nom* **1.** neither-nor function **2.** NOR function

fonction *f* **NON** *nom* NOT function

fonction *f* **NON-ET** *nom* **1.** alternative denial **2.** NAND function **3.** NOT-AND

fonction *f* **NON-OU** *nom* **1.** neither-nor function **2.** NOR function

fonction *f* **OR** *nom* **1.** OR **2.** OR function

fonction *f* **OU** *nom* **1.** OR **2.** OR function

fonction *f* **OU exclusif** *nom* anticoincidence circuit *ou* anticoincidence function

fonctions *fpl* **arithmétiques** *plural noun* arithmetic functions

fonctions *fpl* **complémentaires** *plural noun* assets

fonctions *fpl* **de service** *plural noun* services

fonctions *fpl* **graphiques** *nom* graphics kernel system

fonctions *fpl* **graphiques GKS** *nom* GKS

fonction *f* **standard** *nom* standard function

fonction *f* **valeur absolue** *nom* ABS

fond *m nom* **1.** background **2.** background colour ◇ **fond** *m* **de panier** backplane ◇ **le modem est sensible au bruit de fond** the modem is sensitive to background noise ◇ **un texte en noir sur fond blanc est moins fatigant pour la vue** black text on a white background is less stressful for the eyes

fondamental *adjectif* primary ◇ **couleurs fondamentales** *ou* **primaires** primary colours

fond *m* **de panier d'un micro-ordinateur** *nom* microcomputer backplane

fonderie *f* **de silicium** *nom* silicon foundry

fondre *verbe vt* to coalesce

fondu *m* **enchaîné** *nom* **1.** AB roll **2.** dissolve

fonte *f nom* **1.** character set **2.** face **3.** font **4.** typeface

fonte *f* **logicielle** *nom* soft font

fonte *f* **non résidente** *nom* soft font

fontes *fpl* **résidentes** *plural noun* resident fonts

fonte *f* **téléchargeable** *nom* soft font

fonte *f* **vectorielle** *nom* vector font

format *m nom* **1.** format **2.** record layout ◇ **l'imprimante peut accommoder tous les formats jusqu'au quarto** (*de papier*) the printer can deal with all formats up to quarto

formatage *nom* normalisation *ou* normalization

'...le formatage consiste donc à poser des marques sur la couche magnétique de la disquette' [*Science et Vie Micro*]

formatage *m* **de bas niveau** *nom* low-level format

formatage *m* **de disque** *f nom* disk formatting

formatage *m* **de disquette** *f nom* disk formatting

formatage *m* **de secteur de disque** *nom* disk sector formatting

formatage *m* **non destructif** *nom* safe format

format *m* **ASF** *nom* **1.** active streaming format **2.** ASF

format *m* **audionumérique CD-I** *nom* CD-i digital audio

format *m* **AVI** *nom* AVI

format *m* **BCNF** *nom* Boyce-Codd normal form

format *m* **condensé** *nom* packed format

format *m* **d'adresse** *nom* address format

format *m* **d'affichage** *nom* display format

format *m* **de bande** *nom* tape format

format *m* **de cellule** *nom* cell format ◇ **le format de cette cellule est justification à droite et caractères gras** the cell format is right-aligned and emboldened

format *m* **de cellule ATM** *nom* ATM cell format

format *m* **d'échange format** *nom* basic exchange format

format *m* **de code machine** *nom* machine code format

format *m* **d'écran** *nom* **1.** display format **2.** screen format

format *m* **d'écran de saisie** *nom* form ◇ **il a été facile de former les opérateurs à l'utilisation de ce nouveau logiciel, parce que les formats d'écran ressemblent aux rapports d'impression existants** it's been easy to train the operators to use the new software since its display looks like the existing printed forms

format *m* **de données** *nom* data format

format *m* **de fichier** *nom* file format

format *m* **de fichier (de) constructeur** *nom* proprietary file format ◇ **vous ne pouvez pas lire ce fichier de tableur parce que mon logiciel le sauvegarde en format (de) constructeur** you cannot read this spreadsheet file because my software saves it in a proprietary file format

format *m* **de fichier graphique** *nom* graphics file format

format *m* **de fichier graphique Targa™** *nom* Targa

format *m* **de fichier image** *nom* **1.** tag image file format **2.** TIFF

format *m* **de fichier natif** *nom* native file format

format *m* **de fichier (de) propriétaire** *nom* proprietary file format ◇ **vous ne pouvez pas lire ce fichier de tableur parce que mon logiciel le sauvegarde en format (de) constructeur** you cannot read this spreadsheet file because my software saves it in a proprietary file format

format *m* **de langage symbolique** *nom* symbolic-coding format

format *m* **de message** *nom* message format

format *m* **d'encodage** *nom* encoding format

format *m* **d'enregistrements** *nom* record format

format *m* **DIF** *nom* data interchange format

format *m* **d'impression** *nom* print format

format *m* **d'instruction** *nom* instruction format

formaté, -ée d'avance *adjectif* preformatted ◇ **disquette préformatée** a preformatted disk

format *m* **écran large** *nom* widescreen display

formater *verbe* **1.** *vt* to format **2.** *vt* (*un nombre, une donnée*) to normalise *ou* to normalize ◇ **on utilise des feuilles de style pour formater les documents** *ou* **mettre les documents en forme** style sheets are used to format documents

formateur *m* **de données de sortie** *nom* output formatter

format *m* **FIF** *nom* **1.** FIF **2.** fractal image format

format *m* **GIF** *nom* graphics interface format

format *m* **initial** *nom* native format

format *m* **interne** *nom* internal format

formation *f* **à l'aide de didacticiel** *nom* programmed learning

formation *f* **assistée par ordinateur** *nom* **1.** CAL **2.** CBL **3.** computer-aided learning **4.** computer-assisted training

formation *f* **assistée par système expert** *nom* intelligent tutoring system

format *m* **normal** *nom* normal format

format *m* **normal Boyce-Codd** *nom* Boyce-Codd normal form

format *m* **PDF** *nom* **1.** PDF **2.** portable document format

format *m* **RIFF** *nom* RIFF

format *m* **RTF** *nom* **1.** rich text **2.** rich text format ■ *abrév* RTF

format *m* **standard** *nom* normal format

format *m* **TIFF** *nom* **1.** tag image file format **2.** TIFF

format *m* **variable** *nom* **1.** variable format **2.** V format

format *m* **vidéo AVI (de Microsoft)** *nom* audio/video interleaved

format *m* **vidéo Vxtreme™** *nom* (*utilisé sur le Net*) Vxtreme

forme *nom* pattern ◇ **forme** *f* **primitive** graphics primitive

forme *f* **de Backus-Naur** *nom* BNF

forme *f* **d'impression** *nom* form

forme *f* **normale** *nom* normal form

forme *f* **normalisée** *nom* normalised form

forme *f* **primitive** *nom* primitive

formulaire *m* *nom* **1.** application form **2.** form

formulaire *m* **de programmation** *nom* program coding sheet

formule *f* *nom* **1.** expression **2.** formula ◇ **traducteur de formule** *ou* **langage FORTRAN** formula translator (FORTRAN)

FORTRAN *nom* formula translator

forum *m* *nom* **1.** forum **2.** newsgroup

forum *m* **de discussion** *nom* **1.** chat group **2.** discussion group

fourche *f* **de ressources** *nom* resource fork

fourchette *f* *nom* **1.** range **2.** span

fourchette *f* **normale** *nom* normal range

fournir *verbe vt* to supply ◇ **ils ont signé un contrat pour fournir des informations en ligne** they have signed a contract to supply on-line information ◇ **l'ordinateur vient de chez un fournisseur connu** the computer was supplied by a recognized dealer

fournisseur *m* *nom* supplier ◇ **nos fournisseurs japonais ont ouvert un entrepôt en Angleterre** our Japanese suppliers have set up a warehouse in England ◇ **un fournisseur de pièces pour ordinateurs** a supplier of computer parts ◇ **un fournisseur d'unités de disques** *ou* **de lecteurs de disquettes** a supplier of disk drives *ou* a disk drive supplier

fournisseur *m* **d'accès à l'Internet (FAI)** *nom* service provider

fournisseur *m* **d'accès secondaire** *nom* secondary service provider

fournisseur *m* **de service internet** *nom* Internet service provider

fournisseur *m* **de services applicatifs** *nom* application service provider ■ *abrév* ASP

fournisseur *m* **de services Internet** *nom* **1.** access provider **2.** ISP

fournisseur *m* **d'information** *nom* content provider

fournisseur *m* **d'informations** *nom* (*à base de CMIS et de CMIP*) information provider

fourniture *f* *nom* supply ◇ **ils ont signé un contrat pour la fourniture de papier pour imprimante** they signed a contract for the supply of computer stationery

foyer *m* *nom* focus

fractale *f* *nom* fractal

fraction *f* *nom* fraction

fraction *f* **binaire** *nom* binary fraction ◇ **la fraction binaire 0,011 est égale à un quart plus un huitième (ou trois huitièmes)** the binary fraction 0.011 is equal to one quarter plus one eighth (i.e. three eighths)

fractionnement *m* *nom* fragmentation

fragment *m* *nom* fragment

fragmentation *f* *nom* fragmentation

fragmentation *f* **de fichier** *nom* file fragmentation

frais *mpl* **d'accès au système** *nom* access charge

frappe *f* *nom* **1.** keystroke **2.** stroke ◇ **(nombre de) frappes par heure** *ou* **frappes** *or* **heure** keystrokes per hour ◇ **il peut saisir un texte au rythme de 3500 frappes** *or* **heure** he keyboards at a rate of 3500 keystrokes per hour ◇ **vitesse de frappe** keystroke rate

fraude *f* **informatique** *nom* **1.** (*passible du tribunal correctionnel*) computer crime **2.** (*passible du tribunal correctionnel*) computer fraud

fréquence *f* *nom* tempo

fréquence *nom* frequency ◇ **convertisseur de fréquence** frequency changer ◇ **(système) de modulation par déplacement** *ou* **décalage de fréquence** frequency shift keying (FSK) ◇ **diviseur de fréquence** frequency divider ◇ **domaine fréquentiel** *ou* **de fréquence** frequency domain ◇ **fréquence** *f* **de boucle** speed of loop ◇ **fréquence** *f* **de rafraîchissement de la mémoire RAM** RAM refresh rate ◇ **gamme de fréquences** frequency range ◇ **la principale fréquence d'horloge est de 10MHz** the main clock frequency is 10MHz ◇ **modulation de fréquence (MF)** frequency modulation (FM) ◇ **réponse en fréquence** frequency response ◇ **variation de fréquence** frequency variation

> '...pour avoir une chance d'obtenir un filtre fonctionnant à une fréquence d'horloge assez élevée (quelques dizaines de hertz), il est nécessaire d'écrire le programme en langage machine' [*Electronique Applications*]

fréquence *f* **critique de fusion** *nom* critical fusion frequency

fréquence *f* **de balayage** *nom* scanning rate

fréquence *f* **d'échantillonnage** *nom* **1.** sample rate **2.** sampling rate

fréquence *f* **(de balayage) de lignes** *nom* line frequency

fréquence *f* **de porteuse** *nom* carrier frequency

fréquence *f* **de rafraîchissement** *nom* refresh rate

fréquence *f* **d'horloge** *nom* **1.** clock frequency **2.** clock rate **3.** clock speed

fréquence *f* **d'horloge du bus** *nom* bus clock speed

fréquence *f* **d'horloge du processeur** *nom* microprocessor timing

fréquence *f* **d'horloge du processeur central** *nom* CPU clock speed

fréquence *f* **d'images** *nom* full-motion video

fréquence *f* **radio** *nom* **1.** radio frequency **2.** RF *ou* R/F

FTP *m* **anonyme** *nom* anonymous FTP

fusion *f nom* **1.** document assembly **2.** document merge **3.** file collating

fusion *f* **de fichiers** *nom* file merger

fusionner *verbe* **1.** *vti* to coalesce **2.** *vti* to join **3.** *vti* to merge

G

G *préfixe* giga-

gabarit *m nom* template

gain *m nom* gain ◇ **contrôle de gain** gain control

gain *m* **automatique** *nom* automatic gain

gaine *f nom* cladding ◇ **la fibre optique sera moins performante si sa gaine est endommagée** if the cladding is chipped, the fibre-optic cable will not function well

galet *m* **presseur** *nom* head wheel

gamme *f nom* **1.** family **2.** range ◇ **gamme de fréquences** frequency range ◇ **la transmission par téléphone accepte des signaux dans la gamme de fréquences 300 à 3400 Hz** the telephone channel can accept signals in the frequency range 300 – 3400Hz

gamme *f* **de produits** *nom* **1.** product line *ou* product range **2.** product range

gamme *f* **des audiofréquences** *nom* audio range

gamme *f* **de valeurs** *nom* number range

gamme *f* **normale** *nom* normal range

gant *m* **de données** *nom* data glove

gant *m* **électronique** *nom* data glove

garder *verbe vt* to hold

garnir de zéros *verbe* to zerofill

garnir une carte *verbe* to populate

générateur ◇ **générateur** *m* **de programme d'édition de rapport** report program generator ◇ **générateur** *m* **de son** sound chip

générateur *m* **d'application** *nom* **1.** application generator **2.** program report generator

générateur *m* **de caractères** *nom* character generator ◇ **on peut utiliser une ROM comme générateur de caractères pour obtenir les différentes polices** the ROM used as a character generator can be changed to provide different fonts

générateur *m* **de caractères d'écran** *nom* display character generator

générateur *m* **de caractères fac-similés** *nom* facsimile character generator

générateur *m* **d'effets vidéo** *nom* DVE

générateur *m* **de liens** *nom* linkage software ◇ **les graphiques et le texte sont assemblés sans l'aide d'un générateur de liens** graphics and text are joined without linkage software

générateur *m* **de nombres aléatoires** *nom* random number generator

générateur *m* **de nombres pseudo-aléatoires** *nom* pseudo-random number generator

générateur *m* **de programme** *nom* program generator

générateur *m* **de programmes** *nom* generator

générateur *m* **de rapport** *nom* report generator ■ *abrév* RPG

générateur *m* **de renvois** *nom* cross-reference generator

génération *f nom* **1.** data origination **2.** generation ◇ **le fichier père est un fichier de sauvegarde de première génération** the father file is a first generation backup

génération *f* **de nombres aléatoires** *nom* random number generation

génération *f* **d'ordinateurs** *nom* computer generation

génération *f* **d'un système** *nom* **1.** sysgen **2.** system generation

générer *verbe vt* to generate

générer un hash code *verbe* to hash

générique *adjectif* generic

génie *m* **logiciel** *nom* software engineering

géométrie *f nom* geometry

gestion ◇ **gestion** *f* **de l'alimentation** power management ◇ **gestion** *f* **de l'utilisation de l'énergie** power management

gestion *f* **avancée de la mémoire étendue** *nom* enhanced expanded memory specification

gestion *f* **bus** *nom* bus arbitration

gestion *f* **d'accès au disque** *nom* disk access management

gestion *f* **d'accès aux données** *nom* data access management

gestion *f* **de base de données** *nom* database management system *ou* database manager

gestion *f* **de défaillance** *nom* fault management

gestion *f* **de données** *nom* data management

gestion *f* **de fichiers** *nom* file management *ou* file management system

gestion *f* **de file d'attente** *nom* queue management *ou* queue manager ◇ **il s'agit d'un nou-**

veau logiciel de spouling avec gestionnaire de file d'attente intégré this is a new software spooler with built-in queue management

gestion *f* **de mémoire** *nom* **1.** memory management **2.** memory management unit

gestion *f* **de réseau** *nom* network management

gestion *f* **des erreurs** *nom* **1.** error handling **2.** error management

gestion *f* **de tâches** *nom* task management

gestion *f* **de texte** *nom* text management

gestion *f* **de travail SMT** *nom* station management

gestion *f* **informatique de l'apprentissage** *abrév* CMI ■ *nom* computer-managed instruction

gestionnaire *nom* **1.** event handler **2.** handler **3.** manager **4.** peripheral driver ◇ **gestionnaire** *m* **de passerelle CMOT** CMOT ◇ **gestionnaire** *m* **de polices et d'accessoires de bureau** Font/DA Mover ◇ **gestionnaire** *m* **de segment de recouvrement** overlay manager ◇ **le code du gestionnaire de l'unité de disque se trouve dans la bibliothèque** the disk drive handler code is supplied in the library ◇ **l'utilisateur qui clique sur le bouton de la souris lance un message qui est pris en charge par le gestionnaire d'événements** if a user clicks a mouse button this generates a message which can be acted upon by the event handler

gestionnaire *m* **de données** *nom* data administrator

gestionnaire *m* **de fichier** *nom* file manager

gestionnaire *m* **de fichiers HPFS** *nom* **1.** high performance filing system **2.** HPFS

gestionnaire *m* **de liste de diffusion** *nom* **1.** listserv *ou* listserver **2.** listserver **3.** majordomo

gestionnaire *m* **de mémoire étendue** *nom* **1.** EMM **2.** expanded memory manager **3.** extended memory manager

gestionnaire *m* **de mémoire paginée** *nom* **1.** EMM **2.** expanded memory manager

gestionnaire *m* **de message d'avertissement** *nom* notify handler

gestionnaire *m* **d'enregistrements** *nom* records manager

gestionnaire *m* **de paquets** *nom* packet scheduler

gestionnaire *m* **de périphérique** *nom* **1.** device handler **2.** driver

gestionnaire *m* **de périphérique de réseau** *nom* network device driver

gestionnaire *m* **de périphérique installable** *nom* installable device driver

gestionnaire *m* **de police Adobe** (*nom de marque*) Adobe Type Manager

gestionnaire *m* **de priorités** *nom* priority scheduler

Gestionnaire *m* **de programmes** *nom* Program Manager

gestionnaire *m* **de routage** *nom* router

gestionnaire *m* **d'erreurs** *nom* error handler

gestionnaire *m* **d'espacement intelligent** *nom* intelligent spacer

gestionnaire *m* **d'espaces** *nom* spacer

gestionnaire *m* **de tâches** *nom* scheduler

gestionnaire *m* **de texte** *nom* text manager

gestionnaire *m* **de transition** *nom* bridge

gestionnaire *m* **de transmission** *nom* communications executive

gestionnaire *m* **d'icônes-objets** *nom* Object Packager

gestionnaire *m* **d'imprimante** *nom* printer driver

gestionnaire *m* **d'interruption** *nom* interrupt handler

gestionnaire *m* **d'interruptions** *abrév* IH

gestionnaire *m* **ORB** *nom* Object Request Broker ■ *abrév* ORB

gestionnaire *m* **personnel d'information (GPI)** *nom* **1.** personal information manager **2.** PIM

gestionnaire *m* **Web** *nom* webmaster

GFLOPS *nom* gigaflop

GIF (*nom de marque*) GIF

giga- *préfixe* giga-

gigabit *m nom* gigabit

gigaflop *m nom* gigaflop

gigahertz *m abrév* GHz ■ *nom* gigahertz

giga-octet (Go) *abrév* Gb ■ *nom* gigabyte

> '...il supporte des capacités mémoire pouvant aller jusqu'à 4 giga-octets' [*L'Ordinateur Individuel*]

gigue *f nom* jitter

GINO *nom* graphical input output

glissement *m* **à gauche** *nom* left shift

glisser *verbe* **1.** *vi* to drag **2.** *vi* to slot ◇ **la disquette s'insère** *ou* **se glisse dans l'une des deux fentes du lecteur de disquettes** the disk slots into one of the floppy drive apertures ◇ **pour agrandir un cadre, vous cliquez à l'intérieur de ses limites et vous glissez jusqu'à la position voulue** you can enlarge a frame by clicking inside its border and dragging to the position wanted

glisser et cliquer *verbe* to drag and click

glisser et déposer *verbe* to drag and drop ◇ **traînez l'icône document jusque sur l'icône traitement de texte puis lâchez le bouton de la souris, le système démarrera le programme et chargera le document** drag and drop the document icon onto the word-processor icon and the system will start the program and load the document

global *adjectif* global

glyphe *m nom* glyph

gobo *m nom* matte

Google (*nom de marque*) Google

graduel *adjectif* staged

grammaire *f nom* grammar

grandeur *f nom* **1.** magnitude **2.** size ◇ **taille** *ou* **grandeur** *ou* **format de la page** page size

grandeur *f* **scalaire** *nom* scalar value

grand modèle *m* **(de mémoire des processeurs INTEL)** *nom* large model

grands objets *mpl* **binaires** *nom* **1.** binary large object **2.** blob

granularité *f nom* granularity

graphe *m nom* plot

graphe *m* **à aires** *nom* area graph

graphe *m* **de relation** *nom* derivation graph

graphe *m* **exprimé en coordonnées** *nom* coordinate graph

graphe *m* **planar** *nom* planar

graphique *nom* chart ■ *adjectif* graphic ■ *nom* schema ◇ **enregistreur graphique** chart recorder ◇ **représentations graphiques** graphic images

'…les langages graphiques permettent la présentation de résultats sous forme de graphiques plus ou moins riches' [*L'Information professionnelle*]

graphique *m* **à barres** *nom* bar graph

graphique *m* **accéléré** *nom* accelerated graphics port

graphique *m* **orienté objet** *plural noun* object-oriented graphics

graphiques *mpl* **contigus** *plural noun* contiguous graphics

graphiques *mpl* **de basse définition** *plural noun* low-resolution graphics *ou* low-res graphics

graphiques *mpl* **haute définition** *nom* **1.** high resolution graphics **2.** HRG ◇ **la carte graphique haute définition contrôle jusqu'à 300 pixels par pouce** the HRG board can control up to 300 pixels per inch

graphiques *mpl* **interactifs** *plural noun* interactive graphics ◇ **le jeu (électronique) 'les envahisseurs de l'espace' présente d'excellents graphiques interactifs** the space invaders machine has great interactive graphics, the player controls the position of his spaceship with the joystick

graphisme *m* **par balayage de trame** *nom* raster image processor

graphismes *mpl nom* graphics ◇ **graphisme généré à l'aide d'une tortue** turtle graphics ◇ **la présentation graphique a été préparée avec une tortue** the charts were prepared using turtle graphics ◇ **les graphismes tels que diagrammes en bâtons, diagrammes circulaires, etc.** graphics output such as bar charts, pie charts, etc.

graphismes *mpl* **vectoriels** *nom* vector graphics *ou* vector image

grappe *f nom* cluster

grappe *f* **de données perdues** *nom* lost cluster

graver *verbe* **1.** *vt* to burn **2.** *vt* to burn in

grille *f nom* **1.** flowchart stencil **2.** flowchart template **3.** grid

grille *f* **d'aide de clavier** *nom* **1.** keyboard overlay **2.** key overlay ◇ **sans la grille d'aide, je ne saurais jamais quelle touche de fonction je dois utiliser** without the key overlay, I would never remember which function key does what

gros ordinateur *m nom* **1.** large-scale computer **2.** mainframe *ou* mainframe computer

groupage *m* **adaptatif de données** *nom* (*en correction d'erreur MNP*) adaptive packet assembly

groupe *m nom* **1.** bank **2.** discussion group **3.** group ◇ **ce traitement de texte est orienté sur les groupes de travail et comporte un passerelle de messagerie électronique dans le menu courant** this word-processor is workgroup enabled which adds an email gateway from the standard menus ◇ **groupe** *m* **de données qui se répètent de façon périodique** repeating group ◇ **groupe** *m* **de projet** (*relié par réseau ou messagerie*) workgroup ◇ **un groupe de mini-ordinateurs traite toutes les données brutes** a bank of minicomputers process all the raw data

groupe *m* **(d'utilisateurs)** *nom* group

groupe *m* **3** *nom* Group 3

groupe *m* **à répétition** *nom* repeating group

groupe *m* **code** *nom* code group

groupe *m* **de 2 chiffres binaires** *nom* dibit

groupe *m* **de caractères** *nom* group

groupe *m* **de contrôle** *nom* control group

groupe *m* **de discussion** *nom* newsgroup

groupe *m* **de fichiers (connexes)** *nom* file set

groupe *m* **de mots** *nom* **1.** group **2.** (*d'une transmission en parallèle*) word serial

groupe *m* **de programmes** *nom* **1.** group **2.** program group

groupe *m* **de travail** *nom* workgroup

groupe *m* **de travail IETF** *nom* **1.** IETF **2.** Internet engineering task force

groupe *m* **d'icônes** *nom* group

groupe *m* **d'intérêt particulier** *nom* SIG

groupe *m* **d'intérêt spécial** *nom* special interest group

groupe *m* **d'octets** *nom* gulp

groupe *m* **d'utilisateurs** *nom* user group ◇ **j'ai trouvé la solution au problème en me renseignant auprès des autres utilisateurs rencontrés à la réunion des membres du groupe** I found how to solve the problem by asking people at the user group meeting

groupe *m* **fermé d'usagers** *nom* closed user group
groupe *m* **fermé d'utilisateurs** *nom* CUG
groupe *m* **MPEG** *nom* MPEG
grouper *verbe* **1.** *vt* to gather write **2.** *vt* to group
groupe *m* **témoin** *nom* control group
groupe *m* **X/OPEN** *nom* X/OPEN
GUI *nom* **1.** graphical user interface **2.** GUI
guichet *m* **automatique bancaire** *nom* **1.** ATM **2.** automated teller machine
guide *m* *nom* column guide
guide-bande *m* *nom* tape guide
guide *m* **de l'utilisateur** *nom* user's manual
guide *m* **élémentaire** *nom* primer
guillemets *plural noun* (*signe typographique*) inverted commas ■ *nom* quotation marks ■ *plural noun* quotes
guillemets simples *plural noun* single quotes

H

habillage *m nom* skin
habillage *m* **automatique** *nom* autoflow
habiller *verbe* **1.** *vt* to populate **2.** *vt* to skin
half duplex *nom* HD
hampe *m nom* ascender
harmonique *f nom* harmonics
hartley *m nom* hartley
hash code *m nom* hash code
haut *m* **de casse** *nom* uppercase ◇ **M majuscule** upper case M
haut de gamme *adjectif* high-end
haute définition *f nom* high-resolution *ou* high-res
haute *f* **fidélité** *nom* high fidelity
haute *f* **résolution** *nom* hi-res
haute résolution *f nom* high-resolution *ou* high-res
haute technologie *f adjectif* high-tech ■ *nom* high technology
haut-parleur *m nom* loudspeaker
Hayes Corporation™ (*fabricant de modems*) Hayes Corporation
héritage *m nom* inheritance
hertz *m nom* hertz ■ *abrév* Hz
heure *f* **avancée** *nom* daylight saving time
heure *f* **d'entrée** *nom* entry time
heure(s) *f(pl)* **de pointe** *nom* peak period
heuristique *adjectif* heuristic ◇ **un programme heuristique exploite ses actions et décisions antérieures** a heuristic program learns from its previous actions and decisions
Hewlett Packard™ (*fabricant d'ordinateurs*) Hewlett Packard ◇ **bus d'interface HP** Hewlett Packard Interface Bus (HPIB) ◇ **langage de contrôle d'imprimante HP** *ou* **langage HP-PCL** Hewlett Packard Printer Control Language (HP-PCL)
hexadécimal *abrév* H
hiérarchie *f nom* hierarchy
hiérarchie *f* **des données** *nom* data hierarchy
hiérarchie *f* **des mémoires** *nom* memory hierarchy
hiérarchique *adjectif* hierarchical
hiérarchisé *adjectif* hierarchical
hi-fi *f nom* high fidelity
High Sierra *nom* High Sierra
histogramme *m nom* histogram
histogramme *m* **en colonnes** *nom* columnar graph
historique *m nom* history
hologramme *m nom* **1.** hologram **2.** holographic image
horizontale *f nom* x direction
horloge *f nom* clock
horloge *f* **à quartz** *nom* quartz clock *ou* quartz crystal clock
horloge *f* **à relance automatique** *nom* delta clock
horloge *f* **centrale** *nom* main clock
horloge *f* **delta** *nom* delta clock
horloge *f* **de synchronisation d'un système** *nom* system clock
horloge *f* **du bus** *nom* bus clock
horloge *f* **du processeur central** *nom* CPU clock
horloge *f* **en temps réel** *nom* real-time clock
horloge *f* **extérieure** *nom* external clock
horloge *f* **externe** *nom* external clock
horloge *f* **maîtresse** *nom* **1.** master clock **2.** timing master
horloge *f* **numérique** *nom* digital clock
horloge *f* **principale** *nom* master clock
horloge *f* **programmable** *nom* programmable clock
horloge *f* **relative** *nom* relative-time clock
hors connexion *adverbe, adjectif* off-line
hors de contrôle *adjectif* out of control
hors de portée *adjectif* out of range
hors ligne *adverbe, adjectif* off-line ◇ **avant de remplacer le papier de l'imprimante, assurez-vous que l'imprimante est hors ligne** *ou* **off-line** before changing the paper in the printer, switch it off-line
hors service *adjectif* dead
hôte *m nom, adjectif* host
hotte *f nom* **1.** acoustic hood **2.** sound hood
HP *abrév* HP
HSV *abrév* HSV
hub *m nom* hub
hub *m* **actif** *nom* active hub
huit bits *adjectif* eight-bit *ou* 8-bit

hyper- *préfixe* ultra-

HyperCard™ (*système de base de données*) HyperCard

hypermédia *m nom* hypermedia

HyperTalk™ (*langage de programmation*) HyperTalk

HyperTerminal *nom* HyperTerminal

hypertexte *m nom* hypertext ◇ **dans cette page hypertexte, cliquez sur le mot 'ordinateur' et vous obtiendrez la définition du mot 'ordinateur'** in this hypertext page, click once on the word 'computer' and it will tell you what a computer is ◇ **document hypertexte** hypertext document

I

IANA *f abrév* IANA ■ *nom* Internet Assigned Numbers Authority

IBM 1. (*corporation de produits éléctroniques*) IBM **2.** International Business Machines

IBM PC (*nom de marque*) IBM PC

IBM PS/2 (*nom de marque*) IBM PS/2 *ou* IBM Personal System/2

IBM-XT (*nom de marque*) IBM XT

icône *f nom* **1.** icon *ou* ikon **2.** ikon ◇ **cliquez deux fois sur l'icône Machine à écrire pour accéder au traitement de texte** click twice over the wordprocessor icon – the picture of the typewriter ◇ **l'icône du programme graphique à la forme d'une petite palette** the icon for the graphics program is a small picture of a palette

icône *f* **d'application** *nom* application icon

icône *f* **de groupe** *nom* group icon

icône *f* **d'entraînement** *nom* drag image

icône *f* **de police de caractères** *nom* suitcase

icône *f* **de programme** *nom* program icon

icône *f* **non ciblée** *nom* no-drop image

icône *f* **non compatible** *nom* no-drop image

ICSA *nom* NCSA

identificateur *abrév* ID ■ *nom* **1.** identifier **2.** identifier word **3.** label ◇ **identificateur** *m* **de l'utilisateur d'un site** finger

identificateur *m* **unique** *nom* unique identifier

identification *f abrév* ID ■ *nom* identification

identification *f* **automatique des numéros d'appel** *nom* ANI

identification *f* **de fichier** *nom* file identification

identification *f* **d'un terminal** *nom* terminal identity

identifier *verbe vt* to sense

IEE *abrév* IEE

IEEE *abrév* IEEE

illégal *adjectif* illegal

illustration *f nom* picture

illustrations *fpl plural noun* pix

iMac (*ordinateur personnel développé par Apple Macintosh*) iMac

image *f nom* **1.** frame **2.** image **3.** picture ◇ **distorsion de l'image** image distortion ◇ **(algorithme de compression d'image) PIC** picture image compression (PIC) ◇ **porteuse d'image** *ou* **de signal vidéo** image carrier

image *f* **binaire** *nom* bit image

image *f* **circonscrite** *nom* enclosed object

image *f* **cliquable** *nom* imagemap

image *f* **complète** *nom* frame ◇ **fréquence de l'image** frame frequency ◇ **image vidéo** video frame ◇ **la mémoire image peut servir à l'affichage des images météorologiques transmises par satellite** the frame store can be used to display weather satellite pictures ◇ **la télévision britannique utilise une fréquence de 25 images par seconde** *ou* **25 images** *or* **seconde** in the UK the frame frequency is 25 fps ◇ **le processeur d'images permet de figer une image** *ou* **de faire un arrêt sur image** with the image processor you can freeze a video frame ◇ **le processeur d'images permet le stockage d'une image vidéo dans une mémoire image intégrée de 8 bits** the image processor allows you to store a video frame in a built-in 8-bit frame store ◇ **mémoire image** frame store ◇ **saut d'image** frame flyback

image *f* **de bibliothèque** *nom* clip-art

image *f* **de première génération** *nom* first generation image

image *f* **directe** *nom* direct image

image *f* **en arrière-plan** *nom* background image

image *f* **fantôme** *nom* ghost

image *f* **figée** *nom* freeze frame

image *f* **fixe** *nom* still

image *f* **GIF transparente** *nom* transparent GIF

image *f* **hors champ** *nom* off-screen image

image *f* **monochrome** *nom* black and white

image *f* **orientée en film** *adjectif* cine-oriented

image *f* **originale** *nom* first generation image

image *f* **par seconde** *nom* frames per second

imagerie *f* **de synthèse** *nom* imaging

imagerie *f* **documentaire** *nom* document image management

imagerie *f* **médicale** *nom* imaging

imagerie *f* **numérique CD-I** *plural noun* CD-i digital imaging

images *fpl plural noun* pix

images *fpl* **par seconde** *nom* fps
images/seconde *nom* fps
imageur *m nom* film recorder
imageuse *f* **film** *nom* image setter
image *f* **vectorielle** *nom* vector scan
image *f* **virtuelle** *nom* virtual image
imaginer *verbe vt* to picture ◇ **essayez de visualiser l'implantation avant de commencer à dessiner** try to picture the layout before starting to draw it in
imbrication *f nom* interleave
imbriqué,-ée *adjectif* interleaved
imbriquer *verbe vt* to nest
impasse *f nom* deadlock *ou* deadly embrace
impédance *f nom* impedance ◇ **accord d'impédance** impedance matching ◇ **désaccord d'impédance** impedance mismatch ◇ **l'accord d'impédance entre un émetteur et un récepteur réduit au minimum la perte de puissance des signaux transmis** impedance matching between a transmitter and a receiver minimizes power losses to transmitted signals
implantation ◇ **implantation** *f* **des touches sur un clavier** key matrix
implanter *verbe vt* to plant
implication *f nom* implication
important *adjectif* significant
importer *verbe vt* to import ◇ **il est possible d'importer des images d'un logiciel CAO dans un programme de PAO** you can import images from the CAD package into the DTP program
imposer ◇ **ce document de diffusion restreinte ne doit pas être rendu public** the document is restricted, and cannot be placed on open access ◇ **imposer une contrainte à quelque chose** restrict
imprégner d'encre *verbe* to ink
impression *f nom* **1.** print **2.** printing ◇ **une imprimante graphique avec une résolution de 600 dpi fournit une bonne qualité d'impression** a desktop printer with a resolution of 600dpi provides good print quality
impression *f* **à passages multiples** *nom* multipass overlap
impression *f* **d'étiquettes** *nom* labelling
impression *f* **en arrière-plan** *nom* **1.** background printing **2.** print spooling
impression *f* **en différé** *nom* **1.** deferred printing **2.** off-line printing **3.** print spooling
impression *f* **hors ligne** *nom* off-line printing
impression *f* **par imprimante autonome** *nom* off-line printing
impression *f* **par spouling** *nom* print spooling
impression *f* **thermique** *nom* electrosensitive printing
imprimante *nom* printer ◇ **imprimable** *ou* **qui peut être lu, -e** *ou* **accepté, -ée par l'imprimante** printer-readable ◇ **imprimante à bulle d'encre** bubble-jet printer ◇ **imprimante** *f* **à diodes** LED printer ◇ **imprimante** *f* **qui fonctionne sur port parallèle** parallel printer ◇ **imprimante recto** *or* **verso** duplex printer ◇ **langage PCL** *ou* **jeu de commandes de contrôle d'imprimante PCL** printer control language (PCL)

> '...imprimantes à aiguilles, à jet d'encre, à laser, thermiques: les technologies d'impression progressent et les choix de matériels se diversifient' [*L'Ordinateur Individuel*]

imprimante *f* **à aiguilles** *nom* stylus printer
imprimante *f* **à bulle d'encre** *nom* bubble jet printer
imprimante *f* **à caractères pleins** *nom* solid font printer
imprimante *f* **à chaîne** *nom* chain printer
imprimante *f* **active** *nom* active printer
imprimante *f* **à définition des blancs** *nom* white writer
imprimante *f* **à définition des noirs** *nom* black writer
imprimante *f* **à jet d'encre** *nom* ink-jet printer ◇ **les technologies du jet d'encre couleur et du transfert thermique sont concurrentielles** colour ink-jet technology and thermal transfer technology compete with each other
imprimante *f* **à jet d'encre thermique** *nom* thermal inkjet printer
imprimante *f* **à laser** *nom* laser printer
imprimante *f* **Apple LaserWriter™** LaserWriter
imprimante *f* **à sublimation thermique** *nom* **1.** dye-sublimation printer **2.** thermal transfer *ou* thermal wax *ou* thermal wax transfer printer ◇ **la nouvelle imprimante à sublimation thermique peut fournir une image couleur avec une définition de 300 ppp** the new dye-sublimation printer can produce colour images at a resolution of 300dpi
imprimante *f* **à transfert d'encre** *nom* write black printer
imprimante *f* **à transfert LCD** *nom* **1.** crystal shutter printer **2.** LCD shutter printer **3.** liquid crystal display shutter printer
imprimante *f* **à transfert thermique** *nom* thermal transfer *ou* thermal wax *ou* thermal wax transfer printer
imprimante *f* **à tulipe** *nom* thimble printer
imprimante *f* **bidirectionnelle** *nom* bi-directional printer
imprimante *f* **caractère (par caractère)** *nom* character printer
imprimante *f* **couleur** *nom* colour printer
imprimante *f* **d'enveloppes** *nom* envelope printer

imprimante *f* **de réseau** *nom* network printer

imprimante *f* **d'étiquettes** *nom* label printer

imprimante *f* **d'ordinateur** *nom* computer printer

imprimante *f* **électrostatique** *nom* **1.** electrographic printer **2.** electrostatic printer

imprimante *f* **graphique** *nom* **1.** graphics printer **2.** printer-plotter

imprimante *f* **graphique HP LaserJet** Hewlett Packard LaserJet

imprimante *f* **ligne à ligne** *nom* line printer

imprimante *f* **locale** *nom* local printer

imprimante *f* **matricielle** *nom* **1.** dot-matrix printer **2.** matrix printer **3.** stylus printer **4.** wire printer

imprimante *f* **non partagée** *nom* local printer

imprimante *f* **par défaut** *ou* **implicite** *nom* default printer

imprimante *f* **par page** *nom* page printer ◇ **cette imprimante matricielle n'est pas une imprimante page, elle n'imprime qu'une ligne à la fois** this dot-matrix printer is not a page printer, it only prints one line at a time

imprimante *f* **sans impact** *nom* non impact printer

imprimante *f* **série** *nom* serial printer

imprimante *f* **thermique** *nom* **1.** electrothermal printer **2.** thermal printer

imprimante *f* **thermique à étincelle** *nom* spark printer

imprimante *f* **xérographique** *nom* xerographic printer

imprimer *verbe vt* to print ◇ **cette imprimante a un débit de 60 caractères** *or* **seconde** the printer prints at 60 characters per second

imprimer la file d'attente *verbe* to despool

imprimeur *m nom* **1.** output bureau **2.** printer ◇ **on doit envoyer le livre chez l'imprimeur la semaine prochaine** the book will be sent to the printer next week

impulsion *nom* **1.** impulse **2.** pulse ◇ **générateur d'impulsions** pulse generator ◇ **modulation d'impulsion** pulse modulation ◇ **modulation d'impulsions en amplitude (MIA)** pulse amplitude modulation (PAM) ◇ **modulation d'impulsions en durée (MID)** pulse duration modulation (PDM) ◇ **modulation d'impulsions en largeur** *ou* **en durée (MIL** *ou* **MID)** pulse width modulation (PWM) ◇ **modulation d'impulsions en position (MIP)** pulse position modulation (PPM) ◇ **modulation par impulsions et codage (MIC)** pulse code modulation (PCM)

> '...d'un point de vue pratique, ce codage qui ne fait appel qu'aux chiffres 1 et 0 est traduit en impulsions électriques (les 1) séparées par l'absence de signal (les 0)' [*Science et Vie*]

impulsion *f* **d'horloge** *nom* clock pulse

impulsion *f* **électrique** *nom* strobe

impulsion *f* **électronique** *nom* electronic pulse

impulsions *fpl* **de synchronisation** *plural noun* **1.** synchronisation pulses **2.** sync pulses

inaccessible *adjectif* out of range

incertitude *f* **causée par une erreur** *nom* error ambiguity

incident *m nom* fault

inclinaison *f nom* skew

inclusion *f nom* **1.** embedding **2.** inclusion

incompatibilité *f nom* noncompatibility

incompatible *adjectif* incompatible ◇ **en essayant de relier les deux systèmes, ils ont trouvé qu'ils étaient incompatibles** they tried to link the two systems, but found they were incompatible

inconditionnel *adjectif* unconditional

incorporé *adjectif* built-in

incorrect *adjectif* false

incrément *m nom* increment ◇ **augmentez l'incrément à trois** increase the increment to three

incrémentation *f nom* increment

incrémenter *verbe vt* to increment ◇ **le compteur est incrémenté à chaque instruction exécutée** the counter is incremented each time an instruction is executed

incrustation *f* **couleur** *nom* chroma key

indépendance ◇ **indépendance** *f* **de l'environnement de travail** platform independence

indépendant *adjectif* device-independent

indépendant, -e du constructeur *adjectif* vendor-independent

index *m nom* index

indexation *f nom* **1.** index build **2.** indexing

indexation *f* **sur ordinateur** *nom* computer indexing

index *m* **complet** *nom* dense index

index *m* **de cycle** *nom* cycle index

index *m* **des fichiers** *nom* file index

indexer *verbe vt* to index

index *m* **général** *nom* main index

index *m* **hash code** *nom* hash index

index.html *nom* index.html

index *m* **inversé** *nom* reverse index

index *m* **principal** *nom* main index

indicateur *m nom* **1.** flag **2.** indicator **3.** indicator flag **4.** rogue value **5.** run indicator

indicateur *m* **binaire zéro** *nom* zero flag ◇ **si le résultat est zéro, l'indicateur zéro est activé** if the result is zero, the zero flag is set

indicateur *m* **de colonne** *nom* (*dans un traitement de texte*) column indicator

indicateur *m* **de contrôle** *nom* check indicator

indicateur *m* **de contrôle de parité** *nom* parity flag
indicateur *m* **de contrôle spécial** *nom* rogue indicator
indicateur *m* **de fonction** *nom* role indicator
indicateur *m* **de retenue** *nom* carry flag
indicateur *m* **de signe** *nom* sign indicator
indicateur *m* **d'état** *nom* **1.** condition code **2.** device status word
indicatif *m* **littéral** *nom* index letter
indicatif *m* **numérique** *nom* index number
indice *m nom* **1.** inferior figure **2.** subscript
indice *m* **d'absorption** *nom* absorptance
indice *m* **de position** *nom* index
indice *m* **d'équivalence de la sonnerie** *nom* **1.** REN **2.** ringer equivalence number
indiquer *verbe vt* to mark
indisponible *adjectif* configured-off *ou* configured-out
inductance *f nom* inductance
inducteur *m nom* **1.** choke **2.** inductor
induction *f nom* induction ◇ **bobine d'induction** induction coil
induire *verbe vt* to induce
industrie *f* **de matière grise** *nom* knowledge industry
infecter *verbe vt* to infect
inférence *f nom* inference
infini *m nom* infinity
inflagiciel *m nom* bloatware
info-bulles *f nom* ToolTips
infographie *fpl plural noun* **1.** computer graphics **2.** raster graphics
infographie *f* **à adressage binaire** *plural noun* bit-mapped graphics
infographie *f* **interactive** *plural noun* interactive graphics
infographie *f* **par points** *plural noun* bit-mapped graphics
informaticien, -ienne analyste *nom* systems analyst
information *f nom* information ◇ **réseaux d'information** *ou* **réseaux informatiques** information networks ◇ **service (fournisseur) d'information** *ou* **agence d'information** information provider (IP) ◇ **source d'information** information provider (IP) ◇ **technologies de l'information** information technology (IT)
informations *fpl* **de rebut** *nom* garbage
informations *fpl* **sans intérêt** *nom* garbage ◇ **à données erronées, résultats erronés** *ou* **des données douteuses produisent des résultats douteux** garbage in garbage out (GIGO)
informatique *nom* **1.** computing **2.** data processing **3.** informatics **4.** information technology ◇ **connaissances** *fpl* **en informatique** computer literacy ◇ **qui ne possède aucune connaissance informatique** computer illiterate
informatique *f* **défensive** *nom* defensive computing
informatique *f* **répartie** *nom* **1.** DDP **2.** distributed data processing **3.** distributed processing
informatisation *f nom* computerisation *ou* computerization
informatiser *verbe vt* to computerise *ou* to computerize
infrarouge *m nom* infrared
infrastructure *f nom* infrastructure
ingénierie *f* **assistée par ordinateur** *nom* **1.** CAE **2.** computer-aided engineering **3.** computer-assisted engineering
ingénierie *f* **de la connaissance** *nom* knowledge engineering
ingénieur *m* **d'après-vente** *nom* field engineer
ingénieur *m* **de l'entreprise** *nom* resident engineer
ingénieur *m* **de maintenance sur site** *nom* field engineer
ingénieur *m* **d'entretien** *nom* field engineer
ingénieur *m* **de produit** *nom* product engineer
ingénieur *m* **informaticien** *nom* computer engineer
ingénieur *m* **logiciel** *nom* software engineer
ingénieur *m* **programmeur** *nom* software engineer
inhiber *verbe vt* to inhibit
inhibition *f* **du signal** *nom* blanking ◇ **délai de retour de ligne** (*d'une image*) line blanking interval ◇ **impulsion d'inhibition du signal** blanking pulse
ininterrompu de données *nom* continuous data stream
initialisation *f nom* initialisation *ou* initialization
initialiser *verbe* **1.** *vt* to initialise *ou* to initialize **2.** *vt* to set up
injecter ◇ **injecter du texte** (*dans un cadre PAO*) flow text
inscrire *verbe vt* to register
insensibilité *f nom* noise immunity
insérer *verbe vt* to load ◇ **insérer dans une fente ou dans une ouverture** to slot ◇ **la disquette s'insère** *ou* **se glisse dans l'une des deux fentes du lecteur de disquettes** the disk slots into one of the floppy drive apertures
insertion *f* **(sur un clavier français)** *nom* Ins key
insertion *f* **d'espaces** *nom* quadding
installation *f nom* installation
installation *f* **simplifiée** *nom* abbreviated installation

installer *verbe* **1.** *vt* to install **2.** *vt* to set up ◇ **délai de configuration** *ou* **d'installation** set-up time

instance *f nom* instance

instantané *m nom* snapshot

instruction *f nom* **1.** command **2.** control statement **3.** instruction **4.** order **5.** program statement **6.** statement ◇ **appel** *m* **d'instruction anticipé** pre-fetch ◇ **instruction à deux adresses** two-address-instruction ◇ **instruction** *f* **à n adresse(s) plus une** n-plus-one address instruction ◇ **instruction à trois adresses** three-address-instruction ◇ **instruction de branchement** *ou* **de saut** jump instruction ◇ **ligne multi-instruction** multi-statement line ◇ **l'instruction PRINT est un opérande employé dans cette version BASIC pour l'affichage des données suivantes** the instruction PRINT is used in this BASIC dialect as an operand to display the following data ◇ **macro-instruction** macro instruction ◇ **registre d'adresse d'instruction** instruction address register (IAR) ◇ **registre d'instruction** instruction register (IR)

instruction *f nom* program instruction

instruction *f* **à adresse directe** *nom* one-address instruction

instruction *f* **à adresse unique** *nom* **1.** one-address instruction **2.** single address instruction

instruction *f* **absolue** *nom* **1.** absolute instruction **2.** actual instruction

instruction *f* **à deux adresses** *nom* two-address instruction

instruction *f* **à deux adresses plus une** *nom* two-plus-one-address instruction *ou* two-plus-one instruction

instruction *f* **à n adresse(s) plus une** *nom* n-plus-one instruction

instruction *f* **à quatre adresses** *nom* four-address instruction

instruction *f* **arithmétique** *nom* arithmetic instruction

instruction *f* **à trois adresses** *nom* three-address instruction

instruction *f* **à un opérande** *nom* single operand instruction

instruction *f* **'chercher'** *nom* get

instruction *f* **composée** *nom* compound statement ◇ **le débogueur ne peut agir sur les instructions composées** the debugger cannot handle compound statements

instruction *f* **conditionnelle** *nom* conditional statement

instruction *f* **(d'opération) conditionnelle** *nom* discrimination instruction

instruction *f* **d'affectation** *nom* assignment statement

instruction *f* **dans sa forme initiale** *nom* unmodified instruction

instruction *f* **d'appel** *nom* call instruction

instruction *f* **d'arrêt** *nom* **1.** (*dans un programme*) breakpoint halt **2.** (*dans un programme*) breakpoint instruction **3.** halt instruction **4.** stop instruction

instruction *f* **de base** *nom* **1.** basic instruction **2.** presumptive instruction **3.** primitive **4.** reference instruction

instruction *f* **de branchement** *nom* **1.** branch instruction **2.** GOTO **3.** jump **4.** transfer command

instruction *f* **de commande** *nom* control statement

instruction *f* **de contrôle** *nom* control instruction ◇ **la prochaine instruction de contrôle vous donnera les italiques** the next control instruction will switch to italics

instruction *f* **de décalage** *nom* shift instruction

instruction *f* **de décision** *nom* decision instruction

instruction *f* **de déplacer un bloc** *nom* move block

instruction *f* **de lecture d'une instruction** *nom* fetch instruction

instruction *f* **d'entrée** *nom* entry instruction

instruction *f* **d'entrée dans la pile** *nom* non-synchronous sound *ou* non-sync sound

instruction *f* **d'entrée/sortie** *nom* input/output instruction

instruction *f* **de procédure** *nom* narrative statement

instruction *f* **de remplissage** *nom* **1.** blank instruction **2.** dummy instruction **3.** non operable instruction **4.** no-op instruction *ou* no op **5.** null instruction **6.** waste instruction

instruction *f* **de saut** *nom* **1.** branch instruction **2.** GOTO **3.** jump **4.** skip instruction

instruction *f* **de superviseur** *nom* executive instruction

instruction *f* **de surveillance** *nom* supervisory instruction

instruction *f* **de transfert** *nom* transfer command

instruction *f* **d'extraction** *nom* extract instruction

instruction *f* **d'invalider la justification** *nom* justify inhibit

instruction *f* **directe** *nom* direct instruction

instruction *f* **directive** *nom* directive statement

instruction *f* **d'origine** *nom* presumptive instruction

instruction *f* **effective** *nom* effective instruction

instruction *f* **ELSE** *nom* else rule

instruction *f* **en code** *nom* machine code instruction

instruction *f* **en langage machine** *nom* **1.** machine code instruction **2.** machine instruction

instruction *f* **(d') entrée/sortie** *nom* I/O instruction

instruction *f* **factice** *nom* **1.** non operable instruction **2.** no-op instruction *ou* no op

instruction *f* **'GET'** *nom* get

instruction *f* **GOTO** *nom* GOTO

instruction *f* **IF** *nom* IF statement

instruction *f* **IF-THEN-ELSE (de branchement conditionnel)** *nom* IF-THEN-ELSE

instruction *f* **immédiate** *nom* immediate instruction

instruction *f* **indexée** *nom* indexed instruction

instruction *f* **ineffective** *nom* do-nothing instruction

instruction *f* **multiadresse** *nom* multi-address *ou* multi-address instruction

instruction *f* **non autorisée** *nom* illegal instruction

instruction *f* **nulle** *nom* **1.** non operable instruction **2.** null instruction

instruction *f* **PEEK** *nom* (*de lecture directe de la mémoire*) peek ◇ **vous devez utiliser l'instruction PEEK 1452 pour examiner le contenu de la mémoire à l'emplacement 1452** you need the instruction PEEK 1452 here to examine the contents of memory location 1452

instruction *f* **POKE (d'insertion)** *nom* poke

instruction *f* **primitive** *nom* **1.** basic instruction **2.** presumptive instruction

instruction *f* **sans effet** *nom* do-nothing instruction

instructions *fpl* **de lancement** *plural noun* initial instructions

instructions *fpl* **d'initialisation** *nom* log in script

instruction *f* **SI** *nom* IF statement

instruction *f* **sinon** *nom* else rule ◇ **si X=20 imprimer 'X égale 20' sinon imprimer 'X différent de 20'** IF X=20 THEN PRINT 'X is 20' ELSE PRINT 'X not 20'

instructions *fpl* **instructions initiales** *plural noun* initial instructions

instructions privilégiées *plural noun* privileged instructions

instruction *f* **vide** *nom* no-op instruction *ou* no op

instrument *m nom* instrument

intégration *nom* **1.** embedding **2.** integration ◇ **intégration à grande échelle** large scale integration (LSI) ◇ **intégration à moyenne échelle** (*de 10 à 100 composants par CI*) medium scale integration (MSI) ◇ **intégration à petite échelle** small scale integration (SSI) ◇ **intégration à très grande échelle** (*de 5000 à 50 000 composants par CI*) very large scale integration (VLSI) ◇ **intégration à ultra grande échelle** (*au-delà de 100 000 composants par CI*) ultra large scale integration (ULSI)

> '...l'intégration de textes, tables et graphiques au sein d'un document est dynamique' [*Informatique & Bureautique*]

intégration *f* **à grande échelle** *nom* **1.** large-scale integration **2.** LSI

intégration *f* **à moyenne échelle** *nom* medium scale integration ■ *abrév* MSI

intégration *f* **à petite échelle** *abrév* SSI

intégration *f* **à petite échelle f** *nom* small scale integration

intégration *f* **à très grande échelle** *nom* **1.** very large scale integration **2.** VLSI

intégration *f* **de systèmes** *nom* systems integration

intégration *f* **parfaite** *nom* seamless integration

intégration *f* **sans hiatus** *nom* seamless integration

intégration *f* **sur tranche de silicium** *nom* wafer scale integration

intégré *adjectif* **1.** built-in **2.** inbuilt **3.** integral ◇ **ce logiciel possède un système de correction d'erreurs intégré** this software has inbuilt error correction ◇ **la carte adaptateur intégrée rend l'appareil compatible IBM** the built-in adapter card makes it fully IBM compatible ◇ **l'ordinateur est équipé d'un disque dur intégré** the computer has a built-in hard disk ◇ **puisque les lecteurs de disquettes et le modem sont intégrés, l'encombrement est réduit** the integral disk drives and modem reduce desk space

intégré, -ée au circuit *adjectif* on-board

intégré, -ée à une puce *nom* on chip ■ *adjectif* on-chip ◇ **le processeur utilise un logiciel de lancement intégré à la puce, pour permettre le chargement rapide des programmes** the processor uses on-chip bootstrap software to allow programs to be loaded rapidly

intégré -ée *adjectif* integrated

intégrer *verbe vt* to merge ◇ **le système assure l'intégration automatique du texte et des illustrations dans le document** the system automatically merges text and illustrations into the document

> '...le circuit intégré se présente sous forme d'un boîtier comportant 16 broches 'dual in line' (2 rangées de 8). La broche no 16 est affectée au 'plus' alimentation tandis que la broche no 8 est à relier au 'moins'' [*Electronique pratique*]

intégrité *f nom* integrity ◇ **intégrité d'un fichier** integrity of a file

intégrité *f* **des données** *nom* data integrity

Intel™ (*corporation de produits éléctroniques*) Intel

Intel 8086 (*nom de marque*) Intel 8086

Intel 8088 (*nom de marque*) Intel 8088

Intel 80286 (*nom de marque*) Intel 80286

Intel 80386 (*nom de marque*) Intel 80386

Intel 80486 (*nom de marque*) Intel 80486

Intel Indeo (*nom de marque*) Intel Indeo

intelligence *f nom* intelligence ◇ **intelligence économique** business intelligence (BI)

intelligence *f* **artificielle** *nom* **1.** AI **2.** artificial intelligence **3.** machine intelligence

intelligence *f* **répartie** *nom* distributed intelligence

intelligent *adjectif* intelligent

Intel MMX (*nom de marque*) Intel MMX

Intel Pentium (*nom de marque*) Intel Pentium

Intel Pentium Pro (*nom de marque*) Intel Pentium Pro

intensité *f nom* intensity

intensité *f* **de la couleur** *nom* colour depth

intensité *f* **de trafic** *nom* traffic intensity

interactif *adjectif* interactive ◇ **ce logiciel multimédia interactif permet à l'utilisateur de faire de la musique avec un programme de synthétiseur** this interactive multimedia title allows a user to make music with a synthesizer program

interactivité *f nom* interactivity

interbloc *adjectif* interblock ◇ **espace interbloc** interblock gap (IBG)

intercalé *adjectif* interleaved

interclasseuse *f nom* collator

interconnexion *f nom* interconnection

interconnexion *f* **de systèmes ouverts (aux normes ISO)** *nom* **1.** open system interconnection **2.** OSI

interdire l'écriture *verbe* to write protect

interdit *adjectif* access-barred

interface *nom* **1.** channel adapter **2.** interface **3.** interfacing ◇ **adaptateur d'interface** interface adapter ◇ **bus d'interface universelle** *ou* **bus GPIB** general purpose interface bus (GPIB) ◇ **interface** *f* **de programmation d'application de services téléphoniques** TSAPI ◇ **interface MIDI** MIDI interface (card) ◇ **interface** *f* **numérique pour instruments de musique** musical instrument digital interface ◇ **interface série** serial interface ◇ **interface universelle** *ou* **interface GPIA** general purpose interface adapter (GPIA)

> '...ce produit est une interface qui, placée entre le lecteur de disquettes et son contrôleur, interdit physiquement l'écriture sur la disquette mais en autorise la lecture' [*Le Monde informatique*]

interface *f* **API** *nom* application programming interface

interface *f* **aux normes EIA** *nom* **1.** EIA interface **2.** electronics industry association interface

interface *f* **d'adaptation périphérique** *nom* PIA

interface *f* **de commande** *nom* command interface

interface *f* **de commande de média** *nom* media control interface

interface *f* **de contrôle** *nom* command interface

interface *f* **de ligne de commande** *nom* command line interface

interface *f* **d'entrée/sortie** *nom* input/output interface

interface *f* **de programmation** *nom* API

interface *f* **de programmation d'application** *nom* application programming interface

interface *f* **de programmation d'application de services téléphoniques** *nom* telephony services application programming interface

interface *f* **de programmation d'applications de messagerie** *nom* MAPI

interface *f* **de programmation d'application téléphonique** *abrév* TAPI ■ *nom* telephony application programming interface

interface *f* **de terminal** *nom* terminal interface

interface *f* **de transition** *nom* bridge

interface *f* **d'imprimante** *nom* hard copy interface

interface *f* **ESDI** *nom* **1.** enhanced small device interface **2.** ESDI

interface *f* **Fast-SCSI** *nom* Fast-SCSI

interface *f* **graphique d'utilisateur** *nom* graphical user interface

interface *f* **homme machine** *abrév* HMI

interface *f* **homme/machine** *nom* **1.** human-computer interface **2.** human-machine interface **3.** man machine interface **4.** MMI

interface *f* **HSSI** *nom* **1.** high-speed serial interface **2.** HSSI

interface *f* **hybride** *nom* hybrid interface

interface *f* **MIDI** *nom* musical instrument digital interface

interface *f* **normalisée de messagerie** *nom* **1.** vendor-independent messaging **2.** VIM

interface *f* **ODBC** *nom* **1.** ODBC **2.** open database connectivity

interface *f* **ODI** *nom* open datalink interface

interface ODI (*de Novell*) ODI

interface *f* **parallèle** *nom* **1.** parallel interface **2.** parallel port

interface *f* **parallèle de type Centronics** *nom* Centronics interface

interface *f* **pour communication asynchrone** *nom* **1.** ACIA **2.** asynchronous communications interface adapter

interface *f* **pour terminal** *nom* terminal interface ◇ **le contrôleur de réseau possède 16 interfaces pour terminaux** the network controller has 16 terminal interfaces

interfacer *verbe* to link

interfacer avec *verbe* to interface

interface *f* **SCSI** *nom* **1.** SCSI **2.** (*se prononce 'scousi'*) small computer systems interface

interface *f* **SCSI-2** *nom* SCSI-2

interface *f* **standard** *nom* standard interface

interface *f* **système/utilisateur** *nom* user interface

interface *f* **téléimprimeur** *nom* teleprinter interface

interface *f* **TWAIN™** *nom* TWAIN

interface *f* **Ultra-2 SCSI** *nom* Ultra-2 SCSI

interface *f* **Ultra SCSI** *nom* Ultra SCSI

interface *f* **utilisateur** *adjectif* front end

interface *f* **utilisateur conviviale** *nom* friendly front end

interface *f* **utilisateur/machine** *nom* **1.** human-computer interface **2.** human-machine interface **3.** MMI

interface *f* **Wide-SCSI (SCSI large)** *nom* Wide-SCSI

interférence *nom* interference ◇ **atténuation (du signal) due à l'interférence** interference fading ◇ **empreinte d'interférence** interference pattern ◇ **interférence constructive** constructive interference ◇ **interférence destructive** destructive interference ◇ **interférence** *f* **induite par une autre machine** induced interference ◇ **tolérance à l'interférence** interference immunity

interférence *f* **de fichiers** *plural noun* cross-linked files

interférence *f* **électromagnétique** *nom* **1.** electromagnetic interference **2.** EMI

interférences *fpl* **logiques par seconde** *nom* **1.** LIPS **2.** logical inferences per second

interférences *fpl* **radio** *nom* garbage

interfoliage *m* *nom* interleaving

interfolié -ée *adjectif* interleaved

interlignage *m* *nom* **1.** leading **2.** line feed

interligne *m* *nom* **1.** leading **2.** line spacing ◇ **nous utilisons un pont local pour connecter les deux réseaux (locaux) du bureau** we use a local bridge to link the two LANs in the office

interlude *m* *nom* interlude

Internet *m* *nom* Internet

interopérabilité *f* *nom* interoperability

interpolation *f* *nom* interpolation

interprétatif *adjectif* interpretative

interpréter *verbe vt* to interpret

interpréteur *m* *nom* **1.** interpreter **2.** language interpreter

interpréteur *m* **de commande** *nom* shell

interpréteur *m* **de commandes** *nom* command interpreter

interréseau *m* *nom* Internetwork

interrogation *f* *nom* **1.** enquiry **2.** inquiry **3.** polling ◇ **caractère de requête** *ou* **d'interrogation** inquiry character (ENQ) ◇ **(fonction) interrogation** *or* **réponse** *ou* **demande** *or* **réponse** inquiry/response (function)

interrogation *f* **de fichier** *nom* file interrogation

interroger *verbe* **1.** *vt* to interrogate **2.** *vt* to poll

interrompre *verbe vt* to abort ◇ **interrompez** *ou* **arrêtez l'exécution du programme, avant qu'il efface d'autres fichiers** abort the program before it erases any more files ◇ **on a interrompu le programme en appuyant sur la touche rouge** the program was aborted by pressing the red button

interrruption ◇ **interruption** *f* **de traitement pour transfert de données** data break

interrupteur *m* **de reprise** *nom* hardware reset

interrupteur *m* **temporaire** *nom* momentary switch

interruption *f* *nom* **1.** break **2.** interrupt ◇ **brève interruption** *f* **de transmission de données** (*due à un défaut du support magnétique*) data check ◇ **demande d'interruption** interrupt request (IRQ) ◇ **gestionnaire d'interruption** interrupt handler (IH) ◇ **interruption** *f* **du processeur** processor interrupt ◇ **interruption** *f* **en chaîne** daisy chain interrupt ◇ **interruption** *f* **générée par logiciel** software interrupt ◇ **interruption obligatoire** *ou* **qui ne peut être invalidée** *ou* **qui ne peut être masquée** non-maskable interrupt (NMI) ◇ **interruption** *f* **provenant d'une machine** hardware interrupt ◇ **interruption** *f* **qui peut être invalidée** maskable interrupt ◇ **interruption** *f* **sur une erreur** error interrupt ◇ **j'ai résolu le problème en appuyant sur les touches CTRL et Interruption** I stopped the problem by pressing Ctrl-Break

interruption *f* **activée** *nom* armed interrupt

interruption *f* **anormale** *nom* **1.** abend **2.** abnormal end ◇ **en cas de panne, la perte de données sera minimale grâce au nouveau programme de récupération des fichiers suite à une interruption anormale** if a fault occurs, data loss will be minimized due to the improved abend recovery program

interruption *f* **contrôlée** *nom* transparent interrupt

interruption *f* **d'appel** *nom* polled interrupt

interruption *f* **d'entrée/sortie** *nom* input/output interrupt

interruption *f* **(de contrôle) de parité** *nom* parity interrupt

interruption *f* **de service (d'un appareil)** *nom* outage

interruption *f* **d'intervention** *nom* attention interruption

interruption *f* **d'inversion** *nom* reverse interrupt

interruption *f* **non masquable** *abrév* NMI

interruption *f* **obligatoire** *nom* non maskable interrupt

interruption *f* **prématurée** *nom* **1.** abend **2.** abnormal end

interruption *f* **prioritaire** *nom* priority interrupt

interruption *f* **qui ne peut être invalidée** *nom* non maskable interrupt

interruption *f* **qui ne peut être masquée** *nom* non maskable interrupt

interruption *f* **transparente** *nom* transparent interrupt

interruption *f* **validée** *nom* armed interrupt

interruption *f* **vectorisée** *nom* vectored interrupt

intersection *f nom* **1.** conjunction **2.** intersection

intersection *f* **logique** *nom* **1.** AND operation **2.** coincidence operation

intervalle *m nom* **1.** gap **2.** interval ◇ **il y a eu un intervalle entre le moment où on a appuyé sur la touche et la mise en marche de l'imprimante** there was an interval between pressing the key and the starting of the printout

intervalle *m* **blanc entre deux enregistrements** *nom* record gap

intervalle *m* **d'appels** *nom* polling interval

intervalle *m* **de classe** *nom* class interval

intervention ◇ **sans intervention manuelle** hands off

intra-image *f nom* intra *ou* intra frame

Intranet *m nom* intranet

introduction *f nom* input

introduction *f* **(de données)** *nom* entering

introduire *verbe* **1.** *vt* to input **2.** *vt* to load **3.** *vt* to put **4.** *vt* to read in ◇ **introduire le bac inférieur** load lower bin

introduire (des données) *verbe* to enter ◇ **les données ont été saisies** the data has been entered

intrus *m nom* intruder

inutilisable *adjectif* dead

invalide *adjectif* illegal

invalider *verbe vt* to disarm

inverse *m nom* inverse

inversé *adjectif* reverse ◇ **alors que la notation conventionnelle s'écrit: (x-y) + z, la notation polonaise inversée s'écrit: xy – z+** normal notation: (x-y) + z, but using RPN: xy – z+ ◇ **notation polonaise inversée** reverse Polish notation (RPN) ◇ **suivant la notation polonaise inversée, trois plus quatre moins deux s'écrit 3 4 + 2 – = 5** three plus four, minus two is written in RPN as 3 4 + 2 – = 5

inverser *verbe* **1.** *vt* to invert **2.** *vt* to negate **3.** *vt* to reverse ◇ **la valeur négative** *ou* **l'inverse de 23,4 est –23,4** if you negate 23.4 the result is – 23.4

inverseur *m nom* inverter

inverseur *m* **de courant** *nom* inverter

inversion *f nom* **1.** inversion **2.** negation ◇ **il y a inversion du chiffre binaire dans le complément à un** the inversion of a binary digit takes place in one's complement

inversion *f* **binaire** *nom* bit flipping

inversion *f* **chiffres** *nom* figures shift

invisible *adjectif* invisible

invitation *f nom* invitation ◇ **(signal d') invitation à transmettre** invitation to send (ITS)

invitation *f* **à émettre** *nom* invitation to send ■ *abrév* ITS ■ *nom* polling

invite *nom* **1.** cue **2.** prompt ◇ **invite** *f* command prompt ◇ **MS-DOS affiche normalement l'invite (de commande) C:\> pour indiquer qu'il est prêt à traiter les commandes entrées par l'utilisateur** MS-DOS normally displays the command prompt C:\> to indicate that it is ready to process instructions typed in by a user

invite *f* **DOS** *nom* (*à taper une commande*) DOS prompt

invite *f* **du système** *nom* system prompt

invite *f* **point** *nom* dot prompt

inviter à émettre *verbe* to poll

IRQ *nom* IRQ

ISO *abrév* ISO

isolateur *m nom* isolator

isolation *f* **de canaux** *nom* channel isolation

isoler *verbe vt* to isolate

italique *(m) nom* italic ◇ **les notes de bas de page sont toutes en italique** all the footnotes are printed in italics ◇ **le titre est en italique souligné** the headline is printed in italic and underlined ◇ **tapez CTRL I pour imprimer les italiques** hit CTRL I to print the text in italics

itération *f nom* iteration

itinéraire *m nom* route

-ive *adjectif* **1.** native **2.** negative **3.** positive **4.** private **5.** productive ◇ **ligne privée** *ou* **réservée** *ou* **privative** private line ◇ **rétroaction négative** *ou* **feedback négatif** negative feedback

JK

jack *m nom* jack *ou* jack plug
jambage *m* **(descendant)** *nom* descender
jauge *f* **de charge** *nom* meter – power supply
Java™ (*de Sun Micosystems*) Java
Java Script (*nom de marque*) JScript
jeton *m nom* token
jeton *m* **de contrôle** *nom* control token
jeu *nom* set ■ *plural noun* SET
'...une station de travail portable achitecturée autour d'un processeur à jeu d'instructions réduit Mips' [*Le Monde informatique*]
'...deux ans auparavant, le marché des jeux vidéo à domicile était encore l'un des plus florissants de l'industrie du jouet' [*L'Express*]
jeu *m* **de caractères** *nom* character set
jeu *m* **de caractères disponible** *nom* alternate character set
jeu *m* **de caractères nuls** *nom* null set
jeu *m* **de circuits** *nom* chip set
jeu *m* **de commandes AT** *nom* AT command set
jeu *m* **de commandes de contrôle d'imprimante** *nom* PCL
jeu *m* **de commandes de contrôle d'imprimante PCL** *nom* printer control language
jeu *m* **de commandes Hayes AT** *nom* Hayes AT command set
jeu *m* **de composants** *nom* chip set
jeu *m* **de composants MCA** *nom* MCA chipset ■ Micro Channel Architecture chipset
jeu *m* **d'instructions** *nom* instruction repertoire *ou* instruction set
jeu *m* **d'instructions d'un microprogramme** *nom* microprogram instruction set
jeu *m* **électronique** *nom* computer game
jeu *m* **étendu de caractères** *nom* extended character set
jeu *m* **(de cartes) objet** *nom* object deck
jeu *m* **original** *nom* **1.** source deck **2.** source pack
jeu *m* **vidéo** *nom* video game
joindre *verbe vt* to append
joker *m nom* question mark
jonction *f nom* junction
jonction *f* **en T** *nom* T junction
journal *m nom* journal ◇ **les enregistrements modifiés ont été ajoutés au fichier maître et inscrits au journal des modifications** the modified records were added to the master file and noted in the journal
journal *m* **de bord d'un système** *nom* system log
joystick *m nom* joystick
JPEG++ *nom* JPEG++
juke-box *m nom* (*lecteur de CD-ROM qui fait passer le disque choisi*) jukebox
justification *f nom* justification ◇ **un programme de coupe de mots et justification établi aux Etats- Unis ne peut être utilisé pour un texte en anglais britannique** an American hyphenation and justification program will not work with British English spellings
justification *f* **à droite** *nom* right justification
justification *f* **à gauche** *nom* left justification
justification *f* **verticale** *nom* vertical justification
justifier *verbe* **1.** *vt* to justify **2.** *vt* to range ◇ **justifier le texte** align
justifier (la pile) *verbe* to justify
justifier à droite *verbe* to right justify
justifier à gauche *verbe* to left justify
K *symbole* K
K56flex (*nom de marque*) K56flex
Kermit *nom* Kermit
kilo *symbole* K ■ *préfixe* kilo
kilobaud *m nom* kilobaud
kilobit *m abrév* **1.** KB *ou* Kb **2.** Kbit ■ *nom* kilobit
kilobit *m* **par seconde** *nom* Kbps
kilobits *mpl* **par seconde** *nom* kilo bits per second
kilohertz *m abrév* KHz ■ *nom* kilohertz
kilo-mot *m nom* kiloword
kilo-octet *m abrév* **1.** KB *ou* Kb **2.** Kbyte ■ *nom* kilobyte
kilowatt *m abrév* KW
kit *m* **de nettoyage pour écran** *nom* screen cleaning kit
kit *m* **d'extension de micro-ordinateur** *nom* microcomputer development kit
Klamath™ (*nom de marque*) Klamath
K-mot *m abrév* KW

L

label *m nom* **1.** field label **2.** field name **3.** file label **4.** label **5.** quasi-instruction **6.** tape label ◇ **les programmes en langage BASIC contiennent plusieurs labels dont la numérotation des lignes** BASIC uses many program labels such as line numbers

label *m* **de fin de bande** *nom* tape trailer

label *m* **de fin de fichier** *nom* trailer

label *m* **de qualité** *nom* label

label *m* **de volume** *nom* volume label *ou* volume name

label *m* **d'identification** *nom* **1.** header label **2.** (*sur le support magnétique*) interior label

label *m* **interne** *nom* interior label

laisser ◇ **laisser courir le texte** run on ◇ **le texte peut courir sans alinéa** the line can run on to the next without any space

lambda-calcul *m nom* lambda calculus

lampe *f* **témoin** *nom* activity light

lancement *m nom* **1.** booting **2.** boot up **3.** launch ◇ **le lancement du nouvel ordinateur individuel se fera avec six mois de retard** the launch of the new PC has been put back six months ◇ **le lancement du réseau aura lieu en septembre** the launch date for the network will be September

lancement *m* **automatique** *nom* **1.** (*d'un système*) auto-boot **2.** auto start

lancement *m* **du système à chaud** *nom* warm boot

lancer *verbe vt* to launch ◇ **lancer qc sur le marché** to release ◇ **on a lancé le nouvel ordinateur personnel au Salon de l'Informatique** the new PC was launched at the Personal Computer Show ◇ **on lance le traitement de texte avec un double clic sur cette icône** you launch the word-processor by double-clicking on this icon

lancer un système *verbe* to boot

lanceur *m* **de programme de chargement** *nom* initial program header

langage *nom* language ◇ **langage** *m* **C** (*de programmation orienté objets*) C ◇ **langage de bas niveau** *ou* **langage peu évolué** low-level language (LLL) ◇ **langage de haut niveau** *ou* **langage évolué** high-level language (HLL) ◇ **langage** *m* **de programmation orienté objets C++** C++ ◇ **langage de requête** *ou* **d'interrogation** query language (QL) ◇ **traduction** *f* **d'un langage en un autre langage** language translation

langage *m* **ADA** *nom* ADA

langage *m* **adaptable** *nom* extensible language

langage *m* **adapté à la procédure** *nom* procedure-orientated language

langage *m* **adapté au problème** *nom* problem-orientated language

langage *m* **algébrique** *nom* algebraic language

langage *m* **algorithmique** *nom* **1.** ALGOL **2.** algorithmic language

langage *m* **auteur** *nom* authoring language

langage *m* **chaîné** *nom* threaded language

langage *m* **COBOL** *nom* COBOL

langage *m* **(de programmation structurée) COMAL** *nom* common algorithmic language

langage *m* **commun** *nom* **1.** common language **2.** computer-independent language

langage *m* **d'accès** *abrév* DAL ■ *nom* data access language

langage *m* **d'application** *nom* **1.** application orientated language **2.** job orientated language ■ *abrév* POL

langage *m* **d'application temps réel CORAL** *nom* CORAL

langage *m* **d'assemblage** *nom* **1.** assembler language **2.** assembly language **3.** base language

langage *m* **d'assemblage pour microprogramme** *nom* microprogram assembly language

langage *m* **de balisage** *nom* markup language

langage *m* **de balisage SGML** *nom* **1.** SGML **2.** Standard Generalized Markup Language

langage *m* **de balisage WAP** *nom* WAP markup language

langage *m* **de base** *nom* BASIC ◇ **débit de base (d'un RNIS)** basic rate access (BRA) ◇ **méthode d'accès direct de base** basic direct access method (BDAM) ◇ **méthode d'accès séquentiel de base** basic sequential access method (BSAM) ◇ **satellite de système de contrôle de base** basic control system satellite

(BCS) ◇ **système d'exploitation de base** basic operating system (BOS)

langage *m* **de base de données** *nom* database language

langage *m* **de bas niveau** *abrév* **1.** COL **2.** LLL ■ *nom* low-level language

langage *m* **déclaratif** *nom* declarative language

langage *m* **de commande** *nom* **1.** command language **2.** control language

langage *m* **de commande de tâche** *nom* **1.** JCL **2.** job control language

langage *m* **de commande d'imprimante** *abrév* HP-PCL

langage *m* **de commande numérique** *nom* APT ■ *plural noun* automatically programmed tools

langage *m* **de compilation** *nom* compiler language

langage *m* **de conception de programme** *abrév* PDL ■ *nom* program design language

langage *m* **de constructeur** *nom* native language

langage *m* **de contrôle** *nom* (*de périphériques*) command control language

langage *m* **de contrôle d'imprimante HP** Hewlett Packard Printer Control Language

langage *m* **de définition de données** *nom* data description language

langage *m* **de description de données** *nom* DDL ◇ **plusieurs des avantages d'un langage de description de données vient du fait qu'il s'agit d'un langage de deuxième génération** many of DDL's advantages come from the fact that it is a second generation language

langage *m* **de description de page** *nom* page description language ■ *abrév* PDL

langage *m* **de haut niveau** *nom* high-level language *ou* high-level programming language

langage *m* **de haut niveau BASIC** *nom* **1.** BASIC **2.** beginner's all-purpose symbolic instruction code

langage *m* **de haut niveau BCPL** *nom* BCPL

langage *m* **de manipulation de données** *nom* data manipulation language ■ *abrév* DML

langage *m* **de procédure** *nom* **1.** procedural language **2.** procedure-orientated language

langage *m* **de programmation** *nom* programming language

langage *m* **de programmation APL** *nom* **1.** APL **2.** A programming language

langage *m* **de programmation de description de page** *nom* page description programming language

langage *m* **de programmation évolué** *nom* high-level language *ou* high-level programming language

langage *m* **de programmation PL/M** *nom* PL/M

langage *m* **de programmation structurée COMAL** *nom* COMAL

langage *m* **de quatrième génération** *abrév* 4GL ■ *nom* fourth generation language

langage *m* **de requête** *nom* **1.** QBE **2.** query by example **3.** query language **4.** SQL **5.** structured query language

langage *m* **de résolution de problème** *nom* problem-orientated language

langage *m* **de script** *nom* scripting language ◇ **ce logiciel de communication possède un langage de script qui me permet de composer le numéro d'appel et de débuter la session automatiquement** this communications software has a scripting language that lets me dial and log in automatically

langage *m* **de synthèse** *nom* synthetic language

langage *m* **d'interrogation** *abrév* QL

langage *m* **documentaire** *nom* algebraic language

langage *m* **en pelure d'oignon** *nom* onion skin language

langage *m* **évolué** *abrév* HLL

langage *m* **extensible** *nom* extensible language

langage *m* **fondamental** *nom* BASIC

langage *m* **FORTH** *nom* FORTH

langage *m* **FORTRAN** *nom* FORTRAN

langage *m* **graphique** *nom* graphic language ◇ **ce langage graphique permet de tracer lignes, cercles et graphes en une seule opération** this graphic language can plot lines, circles and graphs with a single command

langage *m* **graphique Hewlett Packard** Hewlett Packard Graphics Language ■ *abrév* HPGL

langage *m* **HP-PCL** Hewlett Packard Printer Control Language

langage *m* **HTML** *nom* **1.** HTML **2.** hypertext markup language

langage *m* **informatique** *nom* computer language

langage *m* **interne** *nom* internal language

langage *m* **interprété** *nom* interpreted language

langage *m* **LISP** *nom* **1.** LISP **2.** list processing

langage *m* **LOGO** *nom* **1.** LOGO **2.** logo

langage *m* **machine** *nom* **1.** internal language **2.** machine language **3.** machine language

langage *m* **Modula-2** *nom* Modula-2

langage *m* **multidimensionnel** *nom* multidimensional language

langage *m* **multiniveau** *nom* multidimensional language
langage *m* **natif** *nom* native language
langage *m* **naturel** *nom* natural language
langage *m* **non procédural** *nom* non-procedural language
langage *m* **objet** *nom* **1.** object language **2.** target language
langage *m* **(de programmation) OCCAM** *nom* OCCAM
langage *m* **orienté objet** *nom* object-oriented language
langage *m* **PASCAL** *nom* PASCAL
langage *m* **PCL** *nom* **1.** PCL **2.** printer control language
langage *m* **Perl** *nom* Perl
langage *m* **PILOT** *nom* PILOT
langage *m* **PLAN** *nom* PLAN
langage *m* **POP 2** *nom* (*de traitement de listes*) POP 2
langage *m* **PROLOG** *nom* **1.** programming in logic **2.** PROLOG
langage *m* **QBE** *nom* **1.** QBE **2.** query by example
langage *m* **SNOBOL** *nom* **1.** (*de traitement et de manipulation de chaîne*) SNOBOL **2.** (*de traitement et de manipulation de chaîne*) string orientated symbolic language
langage *m* **SQL** *nom* **1.** SQL **2.** structured query language
langage *m* **standard** *nom* **1.** BASIC **2.** machine-independent language
langage *m* **symbolique** *nom* symbolic language
langage *m* **universel** *nom* machine-independent language
langage *m* **(d')utilisateur** *nom* user-operated language
langage *m* **VBA** (*nom de marque*) Visual Basic for Applications
langage *m* **VBScript** *abrév* VBScript ■ (*nom de marque*) Visual Basic Script
langage *m* **VRML** *nom* **1.** ActiveVRML **2.** Live3D **3.** virtual reality modelling language **4.** VRML
langage *m* **WML** *nom* **1.** wireless markup language **2.** WML
langage *m* **XHMTL** *nom* **1.** extensible hypertext markup language **2.** XHTML
langage *m* **XML** *nom* **1.** extensible markup language **2.** XML
langue *f nom* language ◇ **il parle plusieurs langues européennes** he speaks several European languages ◇ **langue étrangère** foreign language
langue *f* **d'arrivée** *nom* target language
langue *f* **source** *nom* source language
LAN Manager™ (*de Microsoft*) LAN Manager
LAN Server™ (*de IBM*) LAN Server ■ *nom* LAN server
laptop *m nom* laptop *ou* laptop computer
large bande *nom* broadband ◇ **radio à large bande** broadband radio
large bande *f nom* wideband ◇ **modulation de fréquence à large bande** wideband frequency modulation (WBFM)
largeur *f* **de bande agréée** *nom* aggregate bandwidth
largeur *f* **de bande à la demande** *nom* bandwidth on demand
largeur *f* **de bande audio** *nom* sound bandwidth
largeur *f* **de bande autorisée** *nom* aggregate bandwidth
largeur *f* **de bande de fréquence** *nom* bandwidth ◇ **bande passante** telephone bandwidth is 3100Hz ◇ **la bande passante de câble à fibres optiques est plus étendue que celle des anciens câbles en cuivre et peut transmettre les données à des vitesses plus grandes** this fibre-optic cable has a greater bandwidth than the old copper cable and so it can carry data at higher speeds ◇ **la largeur de bande d'un téléphone est de 3100Hz L** *or* **(c)** telephone bandwidth is 3100Hz
largeur *f* **de bande vidéo** *nom* video bandwidth
largeur *f* **de page (en caractères)** *nom* page width
largeur *f* **d'une ligne** *nom* measure ◇ **mètre (à ruban)** tape measure
laser *nom* laser ◇ **communication par rayon laser** laser beam communications ◇ **enregistrement par rayon laser** laser beam recording (LBR)

> '...grâce à un laser à semi-conducteur émettant une lumière bleue (au lieu de l'infrarouge proche), le diamètre du faisceau est réduit de moitié (0,4 micron), ce qui double la densité d'information du disque' [*Science et Vie Micro*]

LaserJet LaserJet
la société *f* **IBM** *nom* Big Blue
latence *f nom* wait time
lecteur, -trice *nom* **1.** drive **2.** logical drive **3.** (*personne*) reader **4.** stylus **5.** tape drive ◇ **lecteur** *m* **de CD** CD-ROM drive ◇ **lecteur** *m* **de disque quadruple vitesse** quad-speed drive ◇ **lecteur** *m* **de disquettes à double face** double-sided disk drive ◇ **lecteur** *m* **de disquettes de huit pouces** eight-inch drive ◇ **l'unité de disque logique F: stocke des données sur une section de l'unité de disque du serveur** the logical drive F: actually stores data on part of the server's disk drive

> '...en introduisant la carte dans le lecteur, les trois chiffres sont lus par un dispositif optique approprié' [*Electronique pratique*]

lecteur *m* **à double vitesse** *nom* double-speed drive

lecteur *m* **(de disque) à tête de lecture fixe** *nom* fixed head disk *ou* fixed head disk drive

lecteur *m* **C:** *nom* C: drive

lecteur *m* **CD** *nom* CD Player

lecteur *m* **de badges** *nom* badge reader ◇ **le lecteur de badges garantit que seules les personnes autorisées ont accès à la salle des ordinateurs** a badge reader makes sure that only authorized personnel can gain access to a computer room

lecteur *m* **de bandes audionumériques** *nom* DAT drive ◇ **la sauvegarde du réseau est assurée par un lecteur de bandes audio(numériques)** we use a DAT drive as the backup device for our network

lecteur *m* **de bandes magnétiques** *nom* **1.** magnetic tape reader **2.** tape reader

lecteur *m* **de bandes perforées** *nom* paper tape reader

lecteur *m* **de cartes** *nom* card reader

lecteur *m* **de cartes magnétiques** *nom* **1.** magnetic card reader **2.** magnetic strip reader **3.** mark sense reader

lecteur *m* **de cartes perforées** *nom* punched card reader

lecteur *m* **de cartouches** *nom* cartridge drive

lecteur *m* **de CD-ROM** *nom* **1.** CD-ROM drive **2.** CD-ROM player

lecteur *m* **de disque(s)** *nom* disk unit

lecteur *m* **de disque courant** *nom* current drive

lecteur *m* **de disque/disquette** *nom* disk drive

lecteur *m* **de disque dur** *abrév* HDD

lecteur *m* **de disquette** *abrév* FDD

lecteur *m* **de disquette(s)** *nom* **1.** floppy disk drive **2.** floppy disk unit

lecteur *m* **de disquette local** *nom* local drive

lecteur *m* **de disquette non partagé** *nom* local drive

lecteur *m* **de disquettes non compatibles** *nom* alien disk reader

lecteur *m* **de documents** *nom* document reader

lecteur *m* **de marques magnétiques** *nom* mark sense device

lecteur *m* **de nouvelles** *nom* news reader

lecteur *m* **de ruban de papier** *abrév* PTR

lecteur *m* **externe** *nom* external disk drive

lecteur *m* **implicite** *nom* default drive

lecteur *m* **monolithique** *nom* monolithic driver

lecteur *m* **multidisque** *nom* multi-disk reader

lecteur *m* **multidisques** *nom* alien disk reader

lecteur *m* **optique de caractères** *nom* **1.** OCR **2.** OMR **3.** optical character reader

lecteur *m* **optique de codes barres** *nom* **1.** optical bar reader **2.** optical wand

lecteur *m* **optique de codes-barres** *nom* bar code reader

lecteur *m* **optique de marques** *nom* optical mark reader

lecteur *m* **optique de microfilms pour entrée de données sur ordinateur** *nom* FOSDIC

lecteur *m* **par défaut** *nom* default drive ◇ **le système d'exploitation permet à l'utilisateur de choisir le lecteur par défaut** the operating system allows the user to select the default drive

lecture *f nom* **1.** reading **2.** sense ◇ **lecture optique** optical reading

lecture *f* **anticipée** *nom* look-ahead

lecture *f* **audio en transit** *nom* streaming audio

lecture *f* **destructive** *nom* **1.** destructive read **2.** DRO

lecture *f* **d'instruction** *nom* fetch

lecture/écriture *f abrév* R/W

lecture-écriture *f* **directe** *nom* demand reading/writing

lecture-écriture *f* **sur demande** *nom* demand reading/writing

lecture *f* **hélicoïdale** *nom* helical scan

lecture *f* **non destructive** *nom* NDR

lecture *f* **non-destructive** *nom* non destructive readout

lecture *f* **numérique** *nom* digital read-out

lecture *f* **optique de données numériques** *nom* DOR

lecture *f* **par balayage** *nom* scanning ◇ **balayage de trame** raster scanning ◇ **dispositif de lecture par balayage** scanning device ◇ **il faut au scanner 9,9 secondes pour lire un document de 8,5 x 11 pouces** its scanning speed is 9.9 seconds for an 8.5 inch by 11 inch document ◇ **la vitesse de lecture par balayage est de 1,3 pouces par seconde** throughput is 1.3 inches per second scanning speed ◇ **récepteur à recherche de signal** scanning radio receiver ◇ **scanner** scanning device ◇ **scanneur** scanning device

lecture *f* **régénératrice** *nom* regenerative reading

légal *adjectif* legal

légende *f nom* **1.** bubble-help **2.** caption ◇ **les légendes sont (imprimées) en italique** the captions are printed in italics

léger *adjectif* lightweight ◇ **un ordinateur léger qui tient facilement dans une valise** a lightweight computer which can easily fit into a suitcase

légère chute *f* **de tension** *nom* sag

lettre *f* **de l'unité de disque** *nom* **1.** drive designator **2.** drive letter *ou* drive designator

lettre *f* **d'identification du lecteur** *nom* **1.** drive designator **2.** drive letter *ou* drive designator

lettre *f* **numérale** *nom* numeric character

lettre *f* **piégée** *nom* letter bomb

lettres *fpl* **de l'alphabet** *nom* alphabetic character set

lettre *f* **standard** *nom* **1.** form letter **2.** repetitive letter **3.** standard letter

lettre *f* **type** *nom* **1.** form letter **2.** repetitive letter **3.** standard letter **4.** template

LH *verbe vt* to load high

liaison *nom* **1.** communications link **2.** connectivity **3.** landline **4.** line **5.** link **6.** linkage **7.** linking ◇ **liaison** *f* **en grappe de plusieurs périphériques** clustering ◇ **liaison** *f* **optique pour transmission de données** optical data link ◇ **liaison** *ou* **transmission par satellite** satellite link ◇ **pour une transmission plus rapide, vous pouvez utiliser la liaison directe avec le gros ordinateur** to transmit faster, you can use the direct link with the mainframe

liaison *f* **(entre plusieurs machines/dispositifs)** *nom* interconnection

liaison *f* **active** *nom* active link

liaison *f* **à fibres optiques** *nom* fibre optic cable *ou* fibre optic connection ◇ **les câbles à fibres optiques permettent de placer les noeuds jusqu'à un kilomètre l'un de l'autre** fibre optic connections enable nodes up to one kilometre apart to be used

liaison *f* **de données** *nom* data link

liaison *f* **de données en chaîne** *nom* data chaining

liaison *f* **directe entre canaux** *nom* channel-to-channel connection

liaison *f* **directe par câble** *nom* direct cable connection

liaison *f* **infrarouge** *nom* infra-red link

liaison *f* **point à point** *nom* point to point

liaisons *fpl* **redondantes** *nom* network redundancy

liaison *f* **T1** *nom* T1 link

liaison *f* **T2** *nom* T2 link

liaison *f* **T3** *nom* T3 link

liaison *f* **terre/satellite** *nom* uplink

libération *f* **anticipée du jeton** *nom* early token release

libérer *verbe* **1.** *vt* to deallocate **2.** *vt* (*de l'espace dans la mémoire*) to free **3.** *vt* (*un bloc de mémoire ou un fichier*) to release ◇ **libérer une partie de la mémoire** blast

libérer la ligne ◇ **libérer la ligne lorsque la transmission est terminée** clear

liberté d'accès à l'information *nom* freedom of information

libre *adjectif* free ■ *nom* free ◇ **indexage libre** free indexing ◇ **ligne libre** free line

licence *f* *nom* licence ◇ **ce logiciel est fabriqué sous licence** this software is manufactured under licence

licence *f* **de site** *nom* site licence ◇ **nous avons négocié longtemps pour obtenir une licence de site pour les 1200 employés du siège** we have negotiated a good deal for the site licence for our 1200 employees in our HQ

licence *f* **d'utilisation** *nom* run-time licence

licence *f* **d'utilisation d'un logiciel** *nom* licence agreement

lien *m* *nom* link ◇ **tests** *mpl* **de contrôle de liens** link trials

lien *m* **actif** *nom* hot link

lien *m* **hypertexte** *nom* **1.** hot link **2.** hotword **3.** hyperlink

liens *mpl* **multiples PPP** *nom* **1.** MPPP **2.** multi-link point to point protocol

lier *verbe vt* to catenate

ligne *f* *nom* **1.** bar **2.** line **3.** row ◇ **avec broches disposées en ligne** in-line ◇ **charge d'une ligne** line load ◇ **courant transitoire d'une ligne** line transient ◇ **délai de retour de ligne** line blanking interval ◇ **dernière ligne** *f* **d'un paragraphe isolée en tête de page** widow ◇ **dispositif de fin de ligne** line terminator ◇ **impédance de ligne** line impedance ◇ **ligne** *f* **de jonction des symboles d'un ordinogramme** flowline ◇ **l'imprimante ne réussit pas très bien à imprimer les lignes très fines** the printer has difficulty in reproducing very fine lines ◇ **une ligne pointillée sépare les entrées les unes des autres** each entry is separated by a row of dots ◇ **unité d'extension d'une ligne** line extender

ligne *f* **(de texte)** *nom* line

ligne *f* **active** *nom* active line

ligne *f* **analogique** *nom* analog line

ligne *f* **à retard** *nom* delay line

ligne *f* **à retard acoustique** *nom* acoustic delay line

ligne *f* **à retard au mercure** *nom* mercury delay line

ligne *f* **banalisée** *nom* common carrier

ligne *f* **commutée** *nom* analog line

ligne *f* **d'abonné numérique** *nom* **1.** digital subscriber line **2.** DSL

ligne *f* **d'abonné numérique à débit asymétrique** *nom* **1.** ADSL **2.** Asymmetric Digital Subscriber Line

ligne *f* **d'accès** *nom* access line

ligne *f* **de balayage** *nom* **1.** scan line **2.** scanning line

ligne *f* **de base** *nom* base line

ligne *f* **de code** *nom* code line

ligne *f* **de commande** *nom* (*d'un programme*) command line

ligne *f* **de commande (d'un programme)** *nom* command line

ligne *f* **d'écran** *nom* display line

ligne *f* **de location** *nom* leased line

ligne *f* **de produits** *nom* **1.** product line *ou* product range **2.** product range

ligne *f* **de programme** *nom* line

ligne *f* **de référence** *nom* guide bar

ligne *f* **de sélection d'un circuit intégré** *nom* chip select line

ligne *f* **d'état** *nom* **1.** information line **2.** status line

ligne *f* **de transmission rapide** *nom* fast line

ligne *f* **de validation d'un circuit intégré** *nom* chip select line

ligne *f* **d'information** *nom* information line

ligne *f* **d'instruction d'un programme** *nom* program line

ligne *f* **d'interruption** *nom* interrupt line ◇ **ce modèle de connecteur d'imprimante utilise une ligne d'interruption pour avertir l'unité centrale qu'il est prêt à recevoir des données** this printer port design uses an interrupt line to let the CPU know it is ready to receive data

ligne *f* **d'une matrice** *nom* row

ligne *f* **d'un tableau** *nom* row

ligne *f* **équilibrée** *nom* balanced line

ligne *f* **guide** *nom* guide bar

ligne *f* **louée** *nom* leased line

ligne *f* **multi-instruction** *nom* multi statement line

ligne *f* **objet** *nom* subject line

ligne *f* **par minute** *abrév* LPM

lignes cachées *plural noun* hidden lines

lignes *fpl* **de contrôle** *plural noun* bus control lines

lignes de transmission de données *plural noun* bus data lines ◇ **Ethernet est un réseau qui utilise une topologie en bus** Ethernet is a network that uses the bus topology; token ring uses a ring topology

lignes *fpl* **par minute** *nom* lines per minute

lignes *fpl* **spécialisées** *nom* scheduled circuits

ligne *f* **téléphonique** *nom* telephone line

ligne *f* **téléphonique dédiée** *nom* dedicated line

ligne *f* **téléphonique spécialisée** *nom* dedicated line

ligne *f* **terrestre** *nom* landline

limitateur *m nom* limiter

limite *f nom* **1.** boundary **2.** edge

limite *f* **de page** *nom* page boundary

limite *f* **limite** *fr* **l'utilisation (de quelque chose)** *nom* restriction

limité par les entrées *adjectif* input-bound

limiter ◇ **limité par le traitement** *ou* **avec contrainte de vitesse du traitement** process bound

limiter l'accès *verbe* to restrict

limiter l'utilisation de qc *verbe* to restrict ◇ **ce document de diffusion restreinte ne doit pas être rendu public** the document is restricted, and cannot be placed on open access

limites *nom* limits ◇ **limites** *fpl* **de la bande des audiofréquences** audio range

limiteur *m nom* transient suppressor

limiteur *m* **de tension** *nom* surge protector

linéaire *adjectif* linear ◇ **antenne linéaire** linear array ◇ **circuit intégré linéaire** linear integrated circuit ◇ **fonction linéaire** linear function ◇ **l'expression Y = 10 + 5X – 3W est une fonction linéaire** the expression Y = 10 + 5X – 3W is a linear function ◇ **l'expression Y = (10 + 5X[[SUP]]2) n'est pas une fonction linéaire** the expression Y = (10 + 5X[[SUP]]2) is not a linear function

linéarisation *f nom* tracing

linéarité *f nom* linearity

l'informatique *f nom* computer science

Lingo (*nom de marque*) Lingo

LIPS *nom* **1.** LIPS **2.** logical inferences per second

lire *verbe* **1.** *vt* to read **2.** *vt* to scan **3.** *vt* to sense ◇ **cette instruction va lire le premier enregistrement du fichier** this instruction reads the first record of a file

lissage *m nom* Gouraud shading

lissage *m* **de courbes** *nom* anti-aliasing

listage *m nom* **1.** listing **2.** source listing ◇ **listage** *ou* **listing d'un programme** a program listing

listage *m* **de mémoire** *nom* memory dump

listage *m* **d'un programme source** *nom* source listing

liste *plural noun* contents ■ *nom* **1.** exception dictionary **2.** list ◇ **liste** *f* **en chaîne** chain list

liste *f* **approuvée** *nom* moderated list *ou* moderated mailing list

liste *f* **chaînée** *nom* **1.** chained list **2.** linked list

liste *f* **circulaire** *nom* ring

liste *f* **complète** *nom* dense list

liste *f* **concaténée** *nom* **1.** chained list **2.** linked list

liste *f* **d'actions** *nom* action list

liste *f* **de contrôle d'accès** *nom* access control list

liste *f* **de diffusion** *nom* automatic mailing list

liste *f* **de référence** *nom* **1.** authority file *ou* authority list **2.** reference list

liste *f* **déroulante** *nom* drop-down list box

liste *f* **descriptive** *nom* description list

liste *f* **des décisions de montage** *nom* edit decision list

liste *f* **des droits d'accès** *nom* ACL

liste *f* **des emplacements disponibles** *nom* uncommitted storage list

liste *f* **des emplacements non alloués** *nom* uncommitted storage list

liste *f* **des fonctions** *nom* capability list

liste *f* **des modifications** *nom* journal ◇ **les enregistrements modifiés ont été ajoutés au fichier maître et inscrits au journal des modifications** the modified records were added to the master file and noted in the journal ◇ **revue spécialisée** *ou* **revue savante** learned journal

liste *f* **des possibilités** *nom* capability list

liste *f* **des ressources disponibles** *nom* available list

liste *f* **d'inclusion** *nom* opt-in mailing list

liste *f* **d'interdictions** *nom* stop list

liste *f* **d'un programme d'assemblage** *nom* assembly listing

liste *f* **du texte source** *nom* source listing

liste *f* **en boucle** *nom* circular list

liste *f* **non approuvée** *nom* unmoderated list

liste *f* **non autorisée** *nom* unmoderated list

liste *f* **ordonnée** *nom* ordered list

lister *verbe vt* to list ◇ **lister (les lignes d'instruction d') un programme** to list a program

liste *f* **séquentielle** *nom* linear list

liste *f* **vide** *nom* null list

listing *m nom* **1.** computer listing **2.** listing **3.** printout **4.** program listing ◇ **le directeur des ventes a demandé un listing des commissions d'agents** the sales director asked for a printout of the agents' commissions ◇ **listage** *ou* **listing d'un programme** a program listing

littéral *m nom* literal

livre *m nom* book ◇ **ce livre existe en édition brochée et en édition cartonnée** the book is available in paperback and hard cover ◇ **ils peuvent imprimer des livres qui ont jusqu'à 96 pages** they can print books of up to 96 pages

livre *m* **d'adresses** *nom* address book

livre *m* **électronique** *nom* **1.** ebook **2.** electronic book

LLL *nom* low-level language

local *adjectif* local ◇ **les cartes d'extension les plus rapides se placent dans ce connecteur local bus** the fastest expansion cards fit into this local bus connector

localisation *f* **(automatique) de panne** *nom* fault detection

localisé *adjectif* local

localiser *verbe* **1.** *vt* to base **2.** *vt* to locate **3.** *vt* to track ◇ **avez-vous réussi à localiser l'erreur de programmation?** have you managed to locate the programming fault?

localiser et réparer une panne *verbe* to troubleshoot

lockout *m nom* lockout

logiciel *m nom* **1.** anti-virus software **2.** application program **3.** communications package **4.** software ◇ **assurance qualité d'un logiciel** software quality assurance (SQA) ◇ **concepteur de logiciel** software writer ◇ **l'éditeur multifenêtre est utilisé pour créer et éditer les programmes d'application** the multi-window editor is used to create and edit applications programs ◇ **logiciel d'application** *ou* **progiciel** applications software ◇ **logiciel** *m* **de protection** file protection ◇ **logiciel** *m* **inclus à l'achat d'un ordinateur** bundled software ◇ **logiciel** *m* **multifenêtre** (*de traitement de texte*) multi-window editor ◇ **logiciel** *m* **qui est grand consommateur de mémoire** memory-intensive software ◇ **logiciels** *mpl* **téléchargés à la vente** soft goods

logiciel *m* **à base de menu** *nom* menu-driven software

logiciel *m* **adapté aux exigences du client** *nom* bespoke software

logiciel *m* **à échelle variable** *nom* (*adaptable au nombre d'utilisateurs*) scalable software

logiciel *m* **anthropomorphique** *nom* anthropomorphic software

logiciel *m* **antivirus** *nom* vaccine

logiciel *m* **auteur** *nom* authoring software *ou* authoring system

logiciel *m* **avec menu** *nom* menu-driven software

logiciel *m* **commun** *nom* common software

logiciel *m* **convivial** *nom* user-friendly software

logiciel *m* **d'agenda** *nom* scheduler

logiciel *m* **d'animation** *nom* animation software

logiciel *m* **d'application** *nom* application software

logiciel d'application *ou* **progiciel** *m nom* applications software

logiciel *m* **d'application spécialisée** *nom* single function software

logiciel *m* **d'archivage** *nom* filing system

logiciel *m* **de bureautique** *nom* **1.** business package **2.** business system

logiciel *m* **de calendrier** *nom* calendar program

logiciel *m* **de calendrier de groupe** *nom* network calendar program

logiciel *m* **de commande** *nom* handler ◇ **le code du gestionnaire de l'unité de disque se trouve dans la bibliothèque** the disk drive handler code is supplied in the library

logiciel *m* **de commande ANSI** *nom* ANSI driver

logiciel *m* **de commande de périphérique** *nom* **1.** device driver **2.** device handler **3.** driver

logiciel *m* **de communication** *nom* communications software

logiciel *m* **de communication TOPS** *nom* TOPS

logiciel *m* **de compression de disque** *nom* disk compression software

logiciel *m* **de comptabilité** *nom* **1.** accounting package **2.** accounts package

logiciel *m* **de comptabilité-gestion** *nom* **1.** business package **2.** business system

logiciel *m* **de création de document Web** *nom* webpage design software

logiciel *m* **de déboguage** *nom* debugger

logiciel *m* **de démonstration** *nom* demonstration software

logiciel *m* **de dessin** *nom* **1.** drawing program **2.** paint program

logiciel *m* **de développement** *nom* development software

logiciel *m* **de diagnostic** *nom* diagnostic program

logiciel *m* **de diagnostic de la mémoire** *nom* memory diagnostic

logiciel *m* **de formatage** *nom* formatter

logiciel *m* **de formatage de texte** *nom* text formatter ◇ **on utilise le formatage de texte comme programme de base de PAO** people use the text formatter as a basic desk-top publishing program

logiciel *m* **de formatage d'impression** *nom* print formatter

logiciel *m* **de gestion** *nom* **1.** management information service **2.** management information system

logiciel *m* **de groupe (de travail)** *nom* **1.** groupware **2.** workgroup software

logiciel *m* **de l'entreprise** *nom* enterprise software

logiciel *m* **d'émulation de terminal** *nom* terminal emulation software

logiciel *m* **de navigation** *nom* browser ◇ **fenêtre du navigateur** browser window

logiciel *m* **de peinture** *nom* paint program ◇ **j'ai fait une esquisse de notre nouveau logo en utilisant cette palette graphique** I drew a rough of our new logo with this paint program

logiciel *m* **de pilotage à distance** *nom* remote control software

logiciel *m* **de plan de travail** *nom* scheduler

logiciel *m* **de présentation (de document)** *nom* presentation software

logiciel *m* **de prise de contrôle à distance** *nom* remote control software ◇ **ce logiciel de prise de contrôle à distance travaille sous Windows et me permet d'utiliser de chez moi le PC de mon bureau relié par modem** this remote control software will work with Windows and lets me operate my office PC from home over a modem link

logiciel *m* **de récupération de fichiers** *nom* (*après incident*) file-recovery utility ◇ **il est impossible de retrouver un fichier perdu sans l'aide d'un logiciel de récupération de fichiers** a lost file cannot be found without a file-recovery utility

logiciel *m* **de réseau** *nom* **1.** common software **2.** networking software **3.** network software

logiciel *m* **de saisie par balayage** *nom* scanning software

logiciel *m* **de scanning** *nom* scanning software

logiciel *m* **de traitement de l'image** *nom* image processing software

logiciel *m* **de traitement de texte** *nom* word-processor

logiciel *m* **de transition** *nom* **1.** bridge **2.** bridgeware

logiciel *m* **d'extension/d'optimisation (de navigateur)** *nom* plug-in

logiciel *m* **en version bêta** *nom* beta software

logiciel *m* **espion** *nom* spyware

logiciel *m* **(de création) graphique** *nom* graphics software

logiciel *m* **gratuit** *nom* freeware

logiciel ICQ (pour messagerie instantanée) (*pour messagerie instantanée*) ICQ

logiciel *m* **intégré** *nom* integrated software

logiciel *m* **libre** (*nom de marque*) Linux

logiciel *m* **microprogrammé** *nom* firmware

logiciel *m* **non compris** *nom* unbundled software

logiciel *m* **non inclus à l'achat d'un ordinateur** *nom* unbundled software

logiciel *m* **paramétrable** *nom* parameter-driven software

logiciel *m* **paramétré** *nom* parameter-driven software

logiciel *m* **paramétrique** *nom* parameter-driven software

logiciel *m* **partagé** *nom* common software

logiciel *m* **piraté** *nom* pirate software

logiciel *m* **pour réseau** *nom* networking software

logiciel *m* **résident** *nom* **1.** memory-resident software **2.** resident software

logiciel *m* **sur mesure** *nom* bespoke software

logiciel *m* **système** *nom* system software

logiciel *m* **(de) système sur puce** *nom* firmware

logiciel *m* **téléchargé** *nom* telesoftware ■ *abrév* TSW

logique *f nom* logic ■ *adjectif* logical ◇ **circuit logique en réseau** logic array ◇ **circuit logique en réseau non connecté** uncommitted logic array (ULA) ◇ **circuit logique en réseau programmable** *ou* **logique câblée programmable** programmable logic array (PLA) ◇ **(nombre d') inférences logiques par seconde** *ou* **LIPS** logical inferences per second (LIPS) ◇ **le raisonnement logique peut être simulé par une machine intelligente** *ou* **un système expert** logical reasoning can be simulated by an artificial intelligence machine

logique *f* **à n niveau(x)** *nom* n-level logic

logique *f* **binaire** *nom* logic

logique *f* **câblée** *nom* hardwired logic

logique *f* **combinatoire** *nom* combinational logic

logique *f* **de reconnaissance** *nom* recognition logic

logique *f* **des ordinateurs** *nom* computer logic

logique *f* **ECL** *nom* **1.** ECL **2.** emitter-coupled logic

logique *f* **floue** *nom* fuzzy logic *ou* fuzzy theory

logique *f* **I2L** *abrév* IIL ■ *nom* integrated injection logic

logique *f* **ILL** *abrév* IIL ■ *nom* integrated injection logic

logique *f* **informatique** *nom* computer logic

logique *f* **intégrée à injection** *abrév* IIL ■ *nom* integrated injection logic

logique *f* **LTT** *nom* TTL logic

logique *f* **négative** *nom* negative-true logic

logique *f* **numérique** *nom* digital logic

logique *f* **positive** *nom* positive logic

logique *f* **séquentielle** *nom* sequential logic ◇ **si l'entrée dans le circuit séquentiel logique est 1101, la sortie sera toujours zéro (0)** if the input sequence to the sequential logic circuit is 1101 the output will always be zero (0)

logique *f* **symbolique** *nom* symbolic logic

logique *f* **transistor-transistor** *nom* TTL logic

logique *f* **transistor-transistor (LTT)** *nom* **1.** transistor-transistor logic **2.** TTL

logo *m nom* **1.** LOGO **2.** logo

logotype *m nom* **1.** LOGO **2.** logo

loi *f* **A** *nom* A law

loi *f* **de Shannon** *nom* Shannon's Law

loi *f* **Informatique et Libertés** *nom* Data Protection Act

longueur *f nom* **1.** block length **2.** length

longueur *f* **de ligne (en caractères)** *nom* line width

longueur *f* **de page** *nom* page length

longueur *f* **d'onde** *nom* wavelength

longueur *f* **d'une ligne** *nom* line length

longueur *f* **d'un enregistrement** *nom* record length

longueur *f* **d'un fichier** *nom* file length

longueur *f* **d'un mot** *nom* **1.** data word length **2.** word length

longueur *f* **du nom d'un fichier** *nom* length of filename

lot *m nom* batch ◇ **mode de traitement par lots** *ou* **par paquets** (processing data in) batch mode

Lotus™ (*développeur de logiciel*) Lotus

louer *verbe vt* to lease ◇ **la société a pour politique de louer son matériel** the company has a policy of only using leased equipment ◇ **la société loue tous ses ordinateurs** the company leases all its computers

ludo-éducatif *m nom* edutainment

lumière *f nom* light ◇ **conducteur de lumière** light conduit ◇ **il faut éviter de placer l'écran sous une lumière trop forte** the VDU should not be placed under a bright light ◇ **lumière cohérente** *ou* **monochrome** coherent light ◇ **lumière ultra-violette** *ou* **rayonnement ultra-violet** ultra-violet light (UV light) ◇ **lumière visible** visible light

luminance *f nom* luminance ◇ **signal de luminance** luminance signal

luminosité *f nom* brightness ◇ **un bouton vous permet de régler la luminosité et les contrastes** a control knob allows you to adjust brightness and contrast

M

Mac *m nom* Mac
MacBinary™ (*nom de marque*) MacBinary
machine *nom* machine ◇ **(instruction** *ou* **donnée) en langage machine** *ou* **exploitable par l'ordinateur** machine-readable ◇ **épreuve de machine** machine proof ◇ **le disque garde en mémoire des données en langage machine** *ou* **sous une forme exploitable par l'ordinateur** the disk stores data in machine-readable form ◇ **machine** *f* **dédiée au traitement de bases de données** database machine ◇ **(logiciel) propre à la machine** *ou* **sur mesure** *ou* **de constructeur** *ou* **adapté à l'ordinateur** machine-intimate ◇ **(logiciel) standard** *ou* **universel** *ou* **qui fonctionne sur la plupart des ordinateurs** *ou* **indépendant de la machine** machine-independent
machine *f* **de Babbage** *nom* analytical engine
machine *f* **de traitement de texte** *nom* word-processor
machine *f* **de Turing** *nom* Turing machine
machine *f* **intelligente** *nom* intelligent device
machine *f* **nue** *nom* clean machine
machine *f* **virtuelle** *nom* virtual machine ■ *abrév* VM
Macintosh (*nom de marque*) Macintosh
macro *f nom* macro ◇ **assembleur pour macrolangage** macro assembler *ou* assembly program ◇ **macro** macro instruction ◇ **macro-assembleur** macro assembler *ou* assembly program ◇ **macro-instruction** macro instruction
macro(-) *préfixe* macro-
macrocode *m nom* macro code
macrocommande *f nom* macro command
macrodéfinition *f nom* macro definition
macro-élément *m nom* macroelement
macro-expansion *f nom* macro expansion
macro-instruction *f nom* **1.** macro **2.** macro call **3.** macroinstruction ◇ **macro-instruction** macro instruction
macrolangage *m nom* macro language
macro-ordinogramme *m nom* macro flowchart
macroprogrammation *f nom* macro programming
macroprogramme *m* **de régulation** *abrév* MCP
macrovirus *m nom* macro virus
magazine *m* **électronique** *nom* e-zine
magazine *m* **en ligne** *nom* webzine
magnétique *adjectif* magnetic ◇ **mise au point magnétique** magnetic focusing ◇ **orage magnétique** magnetic storm ◇ **reconnaissance de caractères magnétiques** *ou* **en encre magnétique** magnetic ink character recognition (MICR)
magnétiser *verbe vt* to magnetise *ou* to magnetize

> '...le champ ainsi créé magnétise les particules métalliques prisonnières de la surface du disque, forçant l'alignement de leurs pôles' [*Science et Vie Micro*]

magnétophone *m* **à cassette** *nom* cassette recorder
magnétoscope *m nom* **1.** VCR **2.** video cassette recorder **3.** video tape recorder **4.** VTR
mail *m nom* **1.** email *ou* e-mail **2.** text message
mailing *m nom* mailing ◇ **publicité directe** *ou* **mailing** direct mailing
maille *f nom* mesh
main *f nom* hand ◇ **petite visionneuse (qu'on tient à la main)** hand viewer ◇ **téléphone mains-libres** hands-free telephone
maintenabilité *f nom* maintainability
maintenance *f nom* **1.** maintenance **2.** software maintenance **3.** upkeep ◇ **service d'assistance technique sur le lieu de travail** *ou* **maintenance sur site** on-site maintenance ◇ **télémaintenance** remote maintenance
maintenance *f* **corrective** *nom* **1.** corrective maintenance **2.** remedial maintenance
maintenance *f* **courante** *nom* housekeeping
maintenance *f* **curative** *nom* remedial maintenance
maintenance *f* **de fichier** *nom* file maintenance
maintenance *f* **de ligne** *nom* line conditioning
maintenance *f* **d'un programme** *nom* program maintenance
maintenance *f* **du parc clients** *nom* customer engineering
maintenance *f* **préventive** *nom* preventive maintenance

maître *m adjectif* master ◇ **programme de commande de l'ordinateur maître** master control program (MCP)

maître *m* **de poste** *nom* postmaster

maître *m* **d'un bus** *nom* bus master ◇ **l'adaptateur maître du bus du réseau a un débit de transfert beaucoup plus élevé que l'ancien** the bus master network adapter provides much faster data throughput than the old adapter

majuscule *nom* uppercase ◇ **qui distingue les majuscules des minuscules** case sensitive

majuscules *fpl plural noun* **1.** block capitals **2.** block letters **3.** capitals *ou* caps

mal fonctionner *verbe* to malfunction ◇ **quelques-unes des touches du clavier ne fonctionnent déjà plus très bien** some of the keys on the keyboard have started to malfunction

manche *m* **à balai** *nom* joystick

manette *f nom* paddle ◇ **manette de jeu** games paddle

manette *f* **de jeu** *nom* **1.** gamepad **2.** joystick

manipulateur *m* **de bloc** *nom* block device

manipulateur *m* **d'interruption** *nom* trap handler

manipulation *f* **(de données/d'images)** *nom* manipulation ◇ **un gestionnaire de base de données ultra-rapide permet la manipulation d'une très grande quantité de données** a high-speed database management program allows the manipulation of very large amounts of data

manipulation *f* **binaire** *nom* bit manipulation

manipulation *f* **de blocs** *nom* block operation

manipulation *f* **de texte** *nom* text manipulation

manipulation *f* **d'octets** *nom* byte manipulation

manipuler *verbe vt* to manipulate ◇ **un processeur d'images qui peut capturer, afficher et manipuler les images vidéo** an image processor that captures, displays and manipulates video images

mantisse *f nom* mantissa ◇ **la mantisse du nombre 45,897 est 0,897** the mantissa of the number 45.897 is 0.897

mantisse *f* **binaire** *nom* binary mantissa

manuel *adjectif* hands on

manuel *m* **(d'utilisation)** *nom* manual

manuel *m* **d'installation** *nom* installation manual

manuel *m* **d'utilisation** *nom* **1.** instruction manual **2.** operations manual **3.** user guide

manuel *m* **d'utilisation élémentaire** *nom* primer

manuellement *adverbe* manually ◇ **l'alimentation en papier de l'imprimante se fait manuellement** the paper has to be fed into the printer manually

maquette *f nom* **1.** artwork **2.** dummy **3.** mock-up **4.** model ◇ **il nous a fait voir la maquette du nouveau centre informatique** he showed us a model of the new computer centre building ◇ **la maquette a été envoyée au flashage** the artwork has been sent for filming

marché *m nom* deal

marche *f* **à suivre** *nom* procedure ◇ **la procédure est expliquée dans le manuel d'utilisation** the procedure is given in the manual ◇ **voici la marche à suivre pour retrouver des fichiers perdus** you should use this procedure to retrieve lost files

marcher *verbe vi* to perform

marge *f nom* margin ◇ **fixer** *ou* **paramétrer une marge** to set a margin ◇ **les marges de droite et de gauche sont les espaces blancs de chaque côté d'une page** the left margin and right margin are the two sections of blank paper on either side of the page ◇ **lorsque vous taperez le contrat, n'oubliez pas de laisser des marges très larges** when typing the contract leave wide margins

marge *f* **d'agrafage** *nom* binding offset

marge *f* **de reliure** *nom* binding offset

marge *f* **d'erreur** *nom* margin of error

marge *f* **de sécurité** *nom* safety margin

marge *f* **intérieure** *nom* gutter

marguerite *f nom* printwheel

marketing *m* **d'affiliation** *nom* affiliate marketing

marketing *m* **viral** *nom* viral marketing

marquage *m nom* flagging

marquage *m* **de limites d'un fichier** *nom* boundary punctuation

marquage *m* **mnémotechnique** *nom* key strip

marque *nom* mark ◇ **marque** *f* **qui permet de retrouver facilement une partie du programme** bookmark

marque *f* **de cadrage** *nom* crop mark

marque *f* **de début d'adresse** *nom* address mark

marque *f* **de début de bande** *nom* beginning of tape marker ■ *abrév* bot *ou* BOT ■ *nom* BOT marker

marque *f* **de début de mot** *nom* word marker

marque *f* **de début d'enregistrement** *nom* **1.** beginning of information mark **2.** BIM

marque *f* **de mot** *nom* word mark

marque *f* **de sélection d'un bloc** *nom* (*de texte*) block mark

marque *f* **espace** *nom* mark space

marque *f* **logique** *nom* mark

marquer *verbe vt* to mark ◇ **intervalle de marquage** (*entre des signaux*) marking interval ◇ **marquer en encre magnétique** to mark sense

marquer un bloc *verbe* to mark block

marqueur *m nom* **1.** device flag **2.** flag **3.** marker **4.** sentinel

marqueur *m* **de bloc** *plural noun* block marker

marqueur *m* **de fin de liste** *nom* **1.** nil pointer **2.** rogue value **3.** terminator

marqueur *m* **de groupe** *nom* group mark *ou* group marker

marqueur *m* **d'énumération** *nom* bullet

marqueur *m* **de paragraphe** *nom* paragraph marker

marteau *m* **d'impression** *nom* print hammer

masquage *m nom* masking

masque *m nom* **1.** filter **2.** mask ◇ **on se sert d'un masque ou d'un stencil pour reproduire le tracé du circuit du transistor sur le silicium** a mask or stencil is used to transfer the transistor design onto silicon

masque *m* **de saisie** *nom* form ◇ **il a été facile de former les opérateurs à l'utilisation de ce nouveau logiciel, parce que les formats d'écran ressemblent aux rapports d'impression existants** it's been easy to train the operators to use the new software since its display looks like the existing printed forms

masque *m* **de séparation** *nom* aperture mask

masque *m* **de sous-réseau** *nom* **1.** address mask **2.** subnet mask

masque *m* **d'interruption** *nom* interrupt mask

masque *m* **filtre** *nom* shadowmask

masquer *verbe* **1.** *vt* to conceal **2.** *vt* to mask ◇ **les lignes qui n'apparaissent pas sont masquées par cet algorithme** the hidden lines are concealed from view with this algorithm

matériau *m nom* material ◇ **contrôle d'approvisionnement en matériaux** materials control ◇ **l'or est le matériau idéal pour la fabrication des connecteurs électriques** gold is the ideal material for electrical connections ◇ **matériaux synthétiques** synthetic materials

matériau *m* **ferromagnétique** *nom* ferromagnetic material

matériau *m* **semi-conducteur de type N** *nom* n-type material *ou* n-type semiconductor

matériel *m nom* **1.** formatter **2.** network hardware **3.** networking hardware

matériel *m* **commun** *nom* common hardware

matériel *m* **de secours** *nom* auxiliary equipment

matériel *m* **informatique** *nom* **1.** hardware **2.** installation

matériels *mpl* **annexes** *nom* ancillary equipment

mathématique *adjectif* mathematical ◇ **modèle mathématique** mathetical model ◇ **sous-programme mathématique** mathematical subroutine

mathématiques *f nom* mathematics

maths *f nom* **1.** math **2.** maths

matière *f* **grise** *nom US* wetware

matriçage *m nom* mastering

matrice *f nom* matrix

matrice *f* **à fond noir** *nom* black matrix

matrice *f* **de caractères** *nom* character matrix

matrice *f* **de points** *nom* dot matrix

matrice *f* **de relation** *nom* matrix

matrice *f* **d'impression à haute définition** *nom* enhanced dot matrix

matrice *f* **graphique** *nom* matrix

matrice *f* **réduite** *nom* sparse array

matrice *f* **Z** *nom* z buffer

mauvaise coupe *f nom* bad break

mauvais fonctionnement *adjectif* malfunctioning

mauvais fonctionnement *m nom* problem

mauvais secteur *m nom* bad sector

maximal *adjectif* maximum ◇ **fréquence maximum** *ou* **maximale utilisable** maximum usable frequency

maximum *m nom* maximum ■ *adjectif* maximum ◇ **amplitude maximum enregistrée** maximum reading ◇ **fréquence maximum** *ou* **maximale utilisable** maximum usable frequency

MCA 1. (*nom de marque*) MCA **2.** (*système de détection d'erreurs*) Microcom Networking Protocol

mécanique *adjectif* mechanical

mécanisme *m nom* mechanism ◇ **le mécanisme du lecteur ne semble pas fonctionner très bien** the drive mechanism appears to be faulty ◇ **l'imprimante possède un mécanisme très simple** the printer mechanism is very simple

mécanisme *m* **d'accès** *nom* access mechanism

mécanisme *m* **d'arrêt** *nom* shut-off mechanism

media *plural noun* media ◇ **le produit a beaucoup fait parler de lui dans les medias** *ou* **a suscité un grand intérêt médiatique** the product attracted a lot of interest in the media *ou* a lot of media interest

média *m plural noun* media ◇ **analyse des médias** media analysis *ou* media research ◇ **couverture médiatique** media coverage ◇ **le produit a beaucoup fait parler de lui dans les medias** *ou* **a suscité un grand intérêt médiatique** the product attracted a lot of interest in the media *ou* a lot of media interest ◇ **les médias** the media ◇ **nous avons eu une bonne couverture médiatique pour le lancement du nouveau modèle** we got good media coverage for the launch of the new model

média interactif *plural noun* interactive media

Media Player (*nom de marque*) Media Player

MediaServer (*nom de marque*) MediaServer

méga *m nom* meg ◇ **l'ordinateur a un disque de quatre-vingt-dix mégas** this computer has a ninety-meg hard disk

méga- *préfixe* mega-

mégabit *m* **(Mb)** *nom* megabit

mégabits *mpl* **par seconde** *abrév* Mbps ■ *nom* megabits per second

mégaflops *m nom* **1.** mega floating point instructions per second **2.** megaflop

mégahertz *m nom* megahertz

mégaoctet *m abrév* **1.** MB **2.** Mbyte

méga-octet *m nom* meg

méga-octet *m* **(Mo)** *nom* megabyte

meilleur choix *m nom* best fit

meilleure affectation *f* **en mémoire** *nom* best fit

mémento *m* **de fonction des touches de clavier** *nom* **1.** keyboard overlay **2.** key overlay

mémoire *nom* **1.** high density storage **2.** memory **3.** storage **4.** store ◇ **emplacement de mémoire** memory location ◇ **la bande magnétique constitue une mémoire séquentielle d'une grande capacité** magnetic tape is a high capacity serial memory ◇ **l'écran peut être comparé à une mémoire qui demande à être rafraîchie, il doit être balayé régulièrement pour éviter de présenter des images instables** the CRT display can be thought of as regenerative memory, it requires regular refresh picture scans to prevent flicker ◇ **mémoire** *f* **à accès aléatoire** random access device ◇ **mémoire à accès rapide** fast access memory (FAM) ◇ **(dispositif) mémoire à couplage de charge** charge coupled device (CCD) memory ◇ **mémoire** *f* **adressable par le contenu** search memory ◇ **mémoire adressable par son contenu** content-addressable memory ◇ **mémoire** *f* **cache premier niveau** L1 cache ◇ **mémoire** *f* **cache second niveau** L2 cache ◇ **mémoire** *f* **circulante** circulating storage ◇ **mémoire** *f* **de format courant** local format storage ◇ **mémoire** *f* **dynamique** circulating storage ◇ **mémoire** *f* **laser sur couche haute définition** emulsion laser storage ◇ **mémoire morte** *ou* **mémoire ROM** read only memory (ROM) ◇ **mémoire** *f* **morte programmable effaçable par ultraviolet** ultraviolet erasable PROM ◇ **mémoire paginée** paged memory ◇ **mémoire** *f* **qui demande à être rafraîchie** regenerative memory ◇ **mémoire** *f* **qui fonctionne sur le principe du premier entré premier sorti** FIFO memory ◇ **mémoire** *f* **qui ne peut être effacée** (*MS-Windows*) nonerasable storage ◇ **mémoire** *f* **tampon (de clavier) chronologique à n positions** n-key rollover ◇ **mémoire** *f* **tampon de capacité** elastic buffer ◇ **mémoire vive** *ou* **mémoire RAM** random access memory (RAM) ◇ **mémoire volatile** volatile storage ◇ **registre d'adresse en mémoire** memory address register (MAR); store address register (SAR) ◇ **registre de mémoire tampon** memory buffer register (MBR) ◇ **registre des données en mémoire** memory data register (MDR); store data register (SDR) ◇ **taille de la mémoire** storage size ◇ **une bande papier perforée est une mémoire qui ne peut être effacée** paper tape is a nonerasable storage ◇ **une RAM dynamique demande à être rafraîchie toutes les 250ns** dynamic RAM is regenerative memory – it needs to be refreshed every 250ns ◇ **unité de gestion de la mémoire** memory management unit (MMU) ◇ **utilisation** *f* **incomplète de la mémoire** (*laissant des zones vides*) checkerboarding ◇ **utiliser une mémoire tampon** buffer

> '...d'autres constructeurs ont adopté des cartes de mémoire vive permanente comme mémoire de masse sur des portables légers' [*L'Ordinateur Individuel*]

mémoire *f* **à accès aléatoire** *nom* **1.** random access memory **2.** random access storage

mémoire *f* **à accès direct** *nom* **1.** DASD **2.** direct access storage device **3.** primary memory **4.** RAM **5.** random access storage ◇ **vous pouvez augmenter la mémoire de l'imprimante en enfichant une cartouche RAM supplémentaire** you can increase the printer's memory by plugging in another RAM cartridge

mémoire *f* **à accès intermédiaire** *nom* **1.** IAM **2.** intermediate access memory

mémoire *f* **à accès rapide** *nom* **1.** fast access memory **2.** rapid access memory

mémoire *f* **à accès sélectif** *nom* random access storage

mémoire *f* **à accès séquentiel** *nom* **1.** SAM **2.** sequential access storage **3.** serial-access memory **4.** serial storage

mémoire *f* **à bulles magnétiques** *nom* **1.** bubble memory **2.** magnetic bubble memory

mémoire *f* **à condensateur** *nom* capacitor storage

mémoire *f* **à couches minces** *nom* thin-film memory

mémoire *f* **à couplage de charge** *nom* **1.** CCD memory **2.** charge-coupled device memory

mémoire *f* **acoustique** *nom* **1.** acoustic memory **2.** acoustic store

mémoire *f* **à double accès** *nom* dual port memory

mémoire *f* **adressable par le contenu** *nom* searching storage

mémoire *f* **adressable par son contenu** *nom* content-addressable memory *ou* content-addressable storage

mémoire *f* **aléatoire** *nom* RAM

mémoire *f* **à lecture seule** *nom* read only

mémoire *f* **à ligne à retard** *nom* delay line store

mémoire *f* **à liste permutée** *nom* nesting store

mémoire *f* **annexe** *nom* shadow memory *ou* shadow page

mémoire *f* **à semi-conducteur** *nom* **1.** semiconductor memory **2.** solid-state memory device

mémoire *f* **associative** *nom* **1.** associative memory **2.** associative storage **3.** parallel search storage **4.** searching storage

mémoire *f* **à supraconducteur** *nom* cryogenic memory

mémoire *f* **audio wavetable** *nom* wavetable

mémoire *f* **à un niveau** *nom* one-level store

mémoire *f* **auxiliaire** *nom* **1.** auxiliary memory **2.** auxiliary storage *ou* auxiliary store **3.** backing memory **4.** backing storage **5.** backing store *ou* backing storage *ou* backing memory **6.** secondary memory **7.** secondary storage **8.** slave cache **9.** slave store ◇ **je vais augmenter la capacité de mémoire auxiliaire en ajoutant un deuxième lecteur de disquettes** by adding another disk drive, I will increase the backing store capabilities

mémoire *f* **avec tampon** *nom* buffered memory

mémoire *f* **banale** *nom* working store

mémoire *f* **basse** *nom* low memory

mémoire *f* **'bloc-notes'** *nom* scratchpad memory

mémoire *f* **bloc-notes** *nom* working store

mémoire *f* **cache** *nom* **1.** cache **2.** cache memory **3.** RAM cache

mémoire *f* **cache asynchrone** *nom* asynchronous cache

mémoire *f* **cache d'un disque** *nom* disk cache

mémoire *f* **cache intégrée à une puce** *nom* on-chip cache

mémoire *f* **cache synchrone** *nom* synchronous cache

mémoire *f* **capacitive** *nom* capacitor storage

mémoire *f* **CCD** *nom* **1.** CCD memory **2.** charge-coupled device memory

mémoire *f* **centrale** *nom* **1.** CM **2.** core memory **3.** core store **4.** main memory **5.** main storage **6.** primary memory

mémoire *f* **centrale rapide** *nom* fast core

mémoire *f* **commune** *nom* (*à toutes les applications sous Windows*) global memory

mémoire *f* **contenant des fichiers** *nom* file storage

mémoire *f* **conventionnelle** *nom* **1.** base memory *ou* base RAM **2.** conventional memory **3.** standard memory

mémoire *f* **cryogénique** *nom* cryogenic memory

mémoire *f* **d'archivage** *nom* archive storage

mémoire *f* **de base** *nom* base memory *ou* base RAM

mémoire *f* **de commande** *nom* **1.** control memory **2.** control ROM

mémoire *f* **de données** *nom* data storage

mémoire *f* **de grande capacité** *nom* mass storage

mémoire *f* **de lancement** *nom* bootstrap memory

mémoire *f* **de masse** *nom* **1.** backing storage **2.** backing store *ou* backing storage *ou* backing memory **3.** mass storage

mémoire *f* **d'entrée** *nom* input storage

mémoire *f* **de tabulation** *nom* tab memory

mémoire *f* **de traitement frontal** *nom* foreground processing memory

mémoire *f* **d'extension** *nom* **1.** extended memory **2.** extension memory

mémoire *f* **d'image linéaire** *nom* linear frame buffer

mémoire *f* **d'images optiques** *nom* scanner memory

mémoire *f* **d'instruction** *nom* instruction storage

mémoire *f* **dynamique** *nom* **1.** dynamic memory **2.** dynamic storage

mémoire *f* **dynamique permanente** *nom* permanent dynamic memory

mémoire *f* **EAPROM** *nom* **1.** EAPROM **2.** electrically alterable programmable read-only memory **3.** electrically alterable read-only memory

mémoire *f* **EAROM** *nom* EAROM

mémoire *f* **écran** *nom* screen memory

mémoire *f* **EEPROM** *abrév* EEPROM ■ *nom* electrically erasable programmable read-only memory

mémoire *f* **EEROM** *abrév* EEROM ■ *nom* electrically erasable read-only memory

mémoire *f* **électrostatique** *nom* electrostatic storage

mémoire *f* **EPROM** *abrév* EPROM ■ *nom* erasable programmable read-only memory

mémoire *f* **EROM** *nom* erasable read-only memory

mémoire *f* **étendue** *nom* **1.** expanded memory **2.** extended memory

mémoire *f* **étendue EMS** *nom* **1.** EMS **2.** expanded memory system

mémoire *f* **externe** *nom* **1.** external memory **2.** external storage *ou* external store

mémoire *f* **fixe** *nom* control memory ■ *abrév* ROM

mémoire *f* **flash** *nom* **1.** flash memory **2.** flash ROM

mémoire *f* **haute** *nom* **1.** high memory **2.** (*UMB*) shadow RAM **3.** upper memory

mémoire *f* **image** *nom* video memory

mémoire *f* **image de page** *nom* page image buffer
mémoire *f* **imbriquée** *nom* interleaved memory
mémoire *f* **ineffaçable** *nom* nonerasable storage
mémoire *f* **intermédiaire** *nom* intermediate storage
mémoire *f* **interne** *nom* **1.** internal memory **2.** internal store
mémoire *f* **interne à accès immédiat** *nom* **1.** IAS **2.** immediate access store
mémoire *f* **(à) laser sur couche haute définition** *nom* laser emulsion storage
mémoire *f* **lecture/écriture** *nom* read/write memory
mémoire *f* **locale** *nom* local memory
mémoire *f* **magnétique** *nom* **1.** magnetic memory **2.** magnetic storage
mémoire *f* **morte** *nom* read only memory
mémoire *f* **morte à fusibles** *nom* fusible read only memory
mémoire *f* **morte auxiliaire** *nom* sideways ROM
mémoire *f* **morte masquée** *nom* masked ROM
mémoire *f* **morte programmable** *nom* **1.** programmable read only memory **2.** PROM
mémoire *f* **MOS** *nom* MOS memory
mémoire *f* **non volatile** *nom* non volatile storage *ou* nonvolatile store
mémoire *f* **non-volatile** *nom* non volatile memory ◇ **la mémoire à bulles est une mémoire non volatile** bubble memory is a non-volatile storage
mémoire *f* **optique** *nom* **1.** optical memory **2.** optical storage
mémoire *f* **optonumérique** *nom* photodigital memory
mémoire *f* **partagée** *nom* shared memory
mémoire *f* **(de) périphérique** *nom* peripheral memory
mémoire *f* **permanente** *nom* **1.** nonerasable storage **2.** permanent memory
mémoire *f* **physique** *nom* physical memory
mémoire *f* **principale** *nom* **1.** central memory **2.** CM **3.** main memory **4.** main storage **5.** primary storage
mémoire *f* **programmable** *nom* programmable memory
mémoire *f* **(de) programme** *nom* program storage
mémoire *f* **PROM** *nom* programmable read only memory
mémoire *f* **protégée** *nom* protected storage
mémoire *f* **qui contient un microprogramme** *nom* microprogram store
mémoire *f* **RAM** *nom* **1.** conventional memory **2.** RAM **3.** random access memory
mémoire *f* **RAM en mode page** *nom* page-mode RAM
mémoire *f* **RAM incomplète** *nom* partial RAM
mémoire *f* **RAM partielle** *nom* partial RAM
mémoire *f* **RAM statique** *nom* static RAM
mémoire *f* **rapide** *abrév* FAM
mémoire *f* **réelle** *nom* real memory
mémoire *f* **ROM** *nom* read only memory
mémoire *f* **ROM effaçable** *nom* **1.** erasable read-only memory **2.** EROM
mémoire *f* **ROM effaçable électriquement** *abrév* EEROM ■ *nom* electrically erasable read-only memory
mémoire *f* **ROM fantôme** *nom* phantom ROM
mémoire *f* **ROM programmable, modifiable électriquement** *nom* **1.** electrically alterable programmable read-only memory **2.** electrically alterable read-only memory
mémoire *f* **ROM programmable électriquement** *abrév* EPROM
mémoire *f* **ROM programmable et effaçable** *abrév* EPROM ■ *nom* erasable programmable read-only memory
mémoire *f* **ROM programmable et effaçable électriquement** *nom* EAROM ■ *abrév* EEPROM ■ *nom* electrically erasable programmable read-only memory
mémoire *f* **séquentielle** *nom* serial memory ◇ **la bande magnétique constitue une mémoire séquentielle d'une grande capacité** magnetic tape is a high capacity serial memory
mémoire *f* **séquentielle indexée** *nom* indexed sequential storage
mémoire *f* **statique** *nom* **1.** static memory **2.** static storage
mémoire *f* **sur disque** *nom* **1.** disk memory **2.** disk storage
mémoire *f* **tampon** *nom* buffer
mémoire *f* **tampon de clavier** *nom* rollover
mémoire *f* **tampon d'écran** *nom* screen buffer
mémoire *f* **tampon de données** *nom* data buffer
mémoire *f* **tampon de l'image** *nom* image buffer
mémoire *f* **tampon d'entrée/sortie** *nom* I/O buffer
mémoire *f* **tampon de transmission de données** *nom* **1.** communications buffer **2.** data communications buffer
mémoire *f* **tampon d'image** *nom* frame buffer
mémoire *f* **tampon dynamique** *nom* dynamic buffer

mémoire *f* **tampon hors champ** *nom* off-screen buffer

mémoire *f* **temporaire** *nom* **1.** erasable storage **2.** temporary storage **3.** working store

mémoire *f* **transistorisée** *nom* solid-state memory device

mémoire *f* **vidéo** *nom* **1.** video memory **2.** video RAM **3.** video random access memory *ou* video RAM

mémoire *f* **(tampon) vidéo** *nom* video buffer

mémoire *f* **vidéo à accès aléatoire** *nom* VRAM

mémoire *f* **virtuelle** *nom* **1.** virtual memory **2.** virtual storage

mémoire *f* **vive** *nom* **1.** RAM **2.** random access memory

mémoire *f* **vive à sortie de données étendue** *nom* EDO memory

mémoire *f* **vive dynamique** *nom* dynamic RAM

mémoire vive *f* **dynamique** *nom* dynamic random access memory

mémoire *f* **vive dynamique synchrone** *nom* SDRAM

mémoire *f* **vive dynamique synchronisée** *nom* synchronised dynamic RAM

mémoire *f* **vive non volatile** *nom* NVRAM

mémoire *f* **vive non-volatile** *nom* non-volatile random access memory

mémoire *f* **volatile** *nom* volatile memory *ou* volatile store *ou* volatile dynamic storage

mémoriser *verbe vt* to memorise *ou* to memorize

mentionner *verbe vt* to quote ◇ **en cas de réclamation, mentionnez toujours le numéro de lot qui apparaît sur le boîtier de l'ordinateur** when making a complaint please quote the batch number printed on the computer case ◇ **il a cité des chiffres mentionnés dans le journal** he quoted figures from the newspaper report

menu *nom* menu ◇ **barre de menu** menu bar ◇ **menu** *m* **de contrôle de commandes** control menu ◇ **menu déroulant** drop down menu

menu *m* **actif** *nom* active menu

menu *m* **contextuel** *nom* right-click menu

menu *m* **déroulant** *nom* **1.** drop-down menu **2.** pop-down menu **3.** pull-down menu ◇ **on affiche le menu déroulant en cliquant sur la barre de menu au sommet de l'écran** the pull-down menu is viewed by clicking on the menu bar at the top of the screen

menu *m* **principal** *nom* main menu

menu *m* **Programmes** *nom* Programs menu

message *nom* message ◇ **code d'authentification de message** message authentication code (MAC) ◇ **commutation de message** message switching ◇ **le message READY signifie que le système est prêt à recevoir des instructions** the prompt READY indicates that the system is available to receive instructions ◇ **message** *m* **d'invitation à faire qc** prompt ◇ **message (écrit)** *ou* **mail** text message ◇ **messages** *mpl* **reçus** incoming traffic ◇ **message 'unmount' (qui indique que le disque n'est pas utilisable, que le disque a été retiré)** unmount ◇ **MS-DOS affiche normalement l'invite (de commande) C:\> pour indiquer qu'il est prêt à traiter les commandes entrées par l'utilisateur** MS-DOS normally displays the command prompt C:\> to indicate that it is ready to process instructions typed in by a user ◇ **numérotation des messages** message numbering

message *m* **(écrit)** *nom* text message

message *m* **à une seule adresse** *nom* single address message

message *m* **avec accusé de réception** *nom* acknowledged mail

message *m* **chiffré** *nom* ciphertext

message *m* **crypté** *nom* ciphertext

message *m* **d'alerte** *nom* **1.** alert **2.** alert box

message *m* **d'avertissement** *nom* notification message

message *m* **de diagnostic** *nom* diagnostic message

message *m* **d'erreur** *nom* **1.** error box **2.** error message

message *m* **diffusé** *nom* broadcast message

message *m* **d'interrogation** *nom* query message

message *m* **d'intervention** *nom* action message

message *m* **d'invitation** *nom* cue

message *m* **d'ordre** *nom* command message

message *m* **électronique** *nom* email *ou* e-mail

message *m* **intégré** *nom* built-in message

message *m* **publicitaire sans intérêt** *nom* spam ◇ **filtre (pour bloquer les messages non sollicités)** anti-spam

message *m* **reçu** *nom* incoming message

message *m* **retourné** *nom* bounce

messagerie *f nom* **1.** BBS **2.** bulletin board *ou* bulletin board system **3.** message board **4.** messaging ◇ **messagerie** text messaging

messagerie (électronique) *adjectif* mail-enabled

messagerie *f* **électronique** *nom* **1.** CBMS **2.** electronic mail **3.** email *ou* e-mail **4.** mail

messagerie *f* **instantanée** *abrév* IM ■ *nom* instant messaging

messagerie *f* **vocale** *nom* voicemail

messagerie *f* **X400** *nom* MHS

mesure *f nom* measure

mesure *f* **de surface** *nom* square measure

mesurer *verbe vt* to measure ◇ **prendre des mesures pour éviter quelque chose** to take measures to prevent something happening

mesures *f* **de sécurité** *plural noun* safety measures

métabit *m nom* metabit

métacompilateur *m nom* metacompiler

métacompilation *f nom* metacompilation

métafichier *m nom* metafile ◇ **le système d'exploitation utilise un métafichier où sont rangées les données qui définissent l'emplacement de chaque fichier sur le disque** the operating system uses a metafile to hold data that defines where each file is stored on disk

métalangage *m nom* metalanguage

métalangage *m* **BNF** *nom* Backus-Naur-Form

métalangage *m* **BNF étendu** *nom* **1.** EBNF **2.** extended Backus-Naur-Form *ou* extended BNF

méthode *nom* **1.** procedure **2.** technique ◇ **méthode** *f* **d'accès à test de porteuse et détection de collision** carrier sense multiple access-collision detection ◇ **méthode** *f* **de gestion de la file d'attente** queued access method ◇ **méthode** *f* **de pagination** (*de la mémoire*) paged-memory scheme ◇ **méthode** *f* **du dernier entré premier sorti** last in first out ◇ **méthode** *f* **du premier entré premier sorti** first in first out

méthode *f* **ascendante** *nom* hill climbing

méthode *f* **brutale** *nom* brute force method

méthode *f* **BTAM** *nom* basic telecommunications access method

méthode *f* **d'accès** *nom* access method

méthode *f* **d'accès à test de porteuse et détection de collision** *nom* CSMA-CD

méthode *f* **d'accès direct de base** *nom* basic direct access method

méthode *f* **d'accès séquentiel de base** *nom* basic sequential access method ■ *abrév* BSAM

méthode *f* **d'accès séquentiel en file** *nom* **1.** QSAM **2.** queued sequential access method

méthode *f* **d'accès séquentiel indexé** *nom* indexed sequential access method ■ *abrév* ISAM

méthode *f* **d'accès séquentiel indexé en file** *nom* **1.** QISAM **2.** queued indexed sequential access method

méthode *f* **d'accès séquentiel indexé multiclé(s)** *nom* **1.** keyed sequential access method **2.** KSAM

méthode *f* **d'adressage** *nom* addressing method

méthode *f* **d'archivage** *nom* filing system

méthode *f* **de classement** *nom* filing system

méthode *f* **d'effacement** *nom* eraser

méthode *f* **de gestion, accès et transfert de fichiers** *nom* FTAM

méthode *f* **de Monte Carlo** *nom* Monte Carlo method

méthode *f* **du chemin critique** *abrév* CPM ■ *nom* critical path method

méthode *f* **du dernier entré premier sorti** *adjectif* LIFO

méthode *f* **du premier entré premier sorti (FIFO)** *nom* FIFO

méthode *f* **FTAM** *nom* **1.** file transfer access and management **2.** FTAM

méthode *f* **LIFO** *adjectif* **1.** last in first out **2.** LIFO

méthode *f* **mini/maxi** *nom* minmax

méthode *f* **PERT** *nom* program evaluation and review technique

mettre ◇ **mettre des données dans la pile** put ◇ **mettre en mode majuscule or minuscule** normalise ◇ **mettre un nouveau produit sur le marché** release

mettre à jour *verbe* **1.** to reveal **2.** to update

mettre à la poubelle *verbe* to junk

mettre à la terre *verbe* to earth ◇ **tous les appareils doivent être mis à la terre** all appliances must be earthed

mettre à niveau *verbe* to upgrade ◇ **les trois modèles offrent des possibilités de mise à niveau sur site** all three models have an on-site upgrade facility

mettre au point *verbe* **1.** to calibrate **2.** to debug **3.** to fine-tune **4.** to focus **5.** to tune **6.** to tweak ◇ **une mise au point très précise améliore la vitesse de dix pour cent** fine-tuning improved the speed by ten per cent

mettre en évidence *verbe* to highlight

mettre en facteur *verbe* to factorise *ou* to factorize

mettre en forme *verbe* to format ◇ **mis en forme à l'impression** to post-formatted ◇ **on utilise des feuilles de style pour formater les documents** *ou* **mettre les documents en forme** style sheets are used to format documents

mettre en marche *verbe* **1.** to activate **2.** to bring up **3.** to operate **4.** to power up ◇ **en appuyant sur la touche CR, on met l'imprimante en marche** pressing CR activates the printer

mettre en mémoire *verbe* **1.** to memorise *ou* to memorize **2.** to store

mettre en mémoire auxiliaire *verbe* to deposit

mettre en page *verbe* to page

mettre en place *verbe* **1.** to install **2.** to load ◇ **ce système est facile à mettre en place et à utiliser** the system is easy to install and simple to use ◇ **mise** *f* **en place de liens (à l'aide d'un éditeur de liens)** to linkage editing ◇ **mise en place d'une dérivation** bridging

mettre en registre *verbe* to deposit

mettre en route *verbe* **1.** to coldboot **2.** to deadstart **3.** to hardboot **4.** to set up

mettre en surbrillance *verbe* to highlight

mettre hors tension *verbe* to power down

mettre sous tension *verbe* to power up

MHz *nom* megahertz

micro *m nom* **1.** micro **2.** microcomputer **3.** microphone ◇ **micro(phone) à aimant mobile** moving coil microphone ◇ **micro(phone) dynamique** dynamic microphone

micro- *préfixe* micro-

microcassette *f nom* microcassette

microcircuit *m nom* microcircuit

microcode *m nom* microcode

microcycle *m nom* microcycle

microélectronique *f nom* microelectronics

micro-instruction *f nom* **1.** microcode **2.** microinstruction

micromètre *m nom* **1.** micrometre **2.** micron

micron *m nom* **1.** micrometre **2.** micron

micro-ordinateur *m nom* microcomputer

microordinateur *m* **à carte unique** *nom* single-board microcomputer

micro-ordinateur *m* **de commande** *nom* microcontroller

micro-ordinateur *m* **de contrôle** *nom* microcontroller

micro-ordinateur *m* **de contrôle à puce unique** *nom* single-chip microcontroller

microordinateur *m* **monocarte** *nom* single-board microcomputer

microphone *m nom* microphone

microphone *m* **cardioïde** *nom* cardioid microphone

microprocesseur *m nom* **1.** microdevice **2.** microprocessor **3.** microprocessor unit ◇ **le microprocesseur en tranches utilise quatre processeurs à 4 bits pour réaliser un microprocesseur à 16 bits** the bit-slice microprocessor uses four 4-bit processors to make a 16-bit word processor ◇ **microprocesseur** microprocessor unit (MPU)

microprocesseur *m* **en tranches** *nom* bit-slice microprocessor *ou* bit-slice processor

microprogrammation *f nom* microprogramming

microprogramme *m nom* microprogram

microseconde *f nom* microsecond

Microsoft™ (*corporation de produits éléctroniques*) Microsoft

Microsoft Exchange (*à Windows 95*) Microsoft Exchange

Microsoft Exchange Server (*à Microsoft Windows NT*) Microsoft Exchange Server

Microsoft Fax (*à Windows 3.1 et 95*) Microsoft Fax

Microsoft Internet Explorer Microsoft Internet Explorer

Microsoft Network Microsoft Network

Microsoft Outlook (*nom de marque*) Microsoft Outlook

Microsoft Outlook Express (*nom de marque*) Microsoft Outlook Express

Microsoft Windows Microsoft Windows

micro-traumatismes *mpl* **répétés** *nom* **1.** cumulative trauma disorder **2.** repetitive strain injury *ou* repetitive stress injury ■ *abrév* RSI

MIDI *nom* MIDI

migration *f nom* migration

migration *f* **de données** *nom* data migration

migrer *verbe vi* to migrate

milli- *préfixe* milli-

milliampère *m* **(mA)** *nom* **1.** mA **2.** milliampere

milliard *m nom US* billion ■ *abrév* bn

millier *m* **d'instructions par seconde** *nom* **1.** kilo instructions per second **2.** KIPS

million *m* **de millions** *nom* billion

million *m* **d'instructions par seconde** *nom* **1.** million instructions per second **2.** MIPS

million *m* **d'opérations en virgule flottante par seconde** *nom* **1.** megaflop **2.** MFLOPS

milliseconde *f nom* millisecond

mini *m préfixe* mini- ■ *nom* minicomputer

miniaturisation *f nom* miniaturisation *ou* miniaturization

minidisque *m* **dur (de type Winchester)** *nom* miniwinny

minimiser *verbe vt* to minimise *ou* to minimize

mini-ordinateur *m nom* **1.** mini **2.** minicomputer

miniprogramme *m nom* applet

minuscule *f nom* lower case

minuter *verbe vt* to time

mirroring *m nom* **1.** disk mirroring **2.** duplexing

mise *f* **à jour** *verbe* to release ■ *nom* update

mise *f* **à jour corrective** *nom* maintenance release ◇ **la mise à jour corrective de ce programme de base de données, version 2.01, corrige le problème des marges** the maintenance release of the database program, version 2.01, corrects the problem with the margins

mise à jour *f* **d'un fichier** *nom* file update

mise *f* **à jour dynamique** *nom* dynamic update

mise *f* **à jour en cascade** *nom* (*dans un tableur à la suite d'un changement de valeur dans une cellule*) ripple-through effect

mise *f* **au point** *nom* **1.** adjustment **2.** calibration ◇ **il faudrait vérifier la manette de commande qui reste parfois coincée** I think the joystick needs adjustment as it sometimes gets stuck ◇ **la luminosité a besoin d'un réglage** the brightness needs adjustment

mise *f* **en commentaire** *nom* comment out

mise en évidence *nom* emphasis

mise *f* **en forme de signaux** *nom* signal conditioning

mise *f* **en majuscule** *nom* capitalisation *ou* capitalization

mise *f* **en mémoire** *nom* **1.** file storage **2.** instruction storage **3.** storage ◇ **mémoire volatile** volatile storage ◇ **taille de la mémoire** storage size

mise *f* **en mémoire de données** *nom* data storage

mise *f* **en orbite** *nom* launch ◇ **le lancement du nouvel ordinateur individuel se fera avec six mois de retard** the launch of the new PC has been put back six months ◇ **le lancement du réseau aura lieu en septembre** the launch date for the network will be September

mise *f* **en page** *nom* page setup

mise *f* **en page(s)** *nom* **1.** layout **2.** page layout ◇ **les designers travaillent à la mise en pages de la nouvelle revue** the design team is working on the layouts for the new magazine ◇ **présentation assistée par ordinateur (PréAO)** computerized page layout

mise *f* **en pages** *nom* **1.** page makeup **2.** pagination

mise *f* **en place** *nom* installation ◇ **il n'a fallu que quelques heures pour mettre l'équipement en place** the installation of the equipment took only a few hours

mise *f* **en place d'un drapeau** *nom* flagging

mise *f* **en position de transport de la tête** *nom* head park

mise *f* **en réseau** *nom* (*d'ordinateurs*) networking ◇ **cette société informatique est une société britannique spécialisée en réseaux** this computer firm is a UK networking specialist

mise *f* **en route** *nom* **1.** cold boot **2.** cold start **3.** start ◇ **(code de) début de texte** start of text (SOT *ou* STX)

mise *f* **en route automatique** *nom* auto start

mnémonique *m nom* mnemonic

mobile *adjectif* movable

modal *adjectif* modal

mode *nom* mode ◇ **mode** *m* **de transmission bidirectionnelle à l'alternat** either-way operation ◇ **mode** *m* **d'exécution d'instructions en pipeline** instruction pipelining ◇ **mode point** *ou* **mode bit-map** bit-map mode ◇ **pour saisir un texte, appuyer d'abord sur cette touche de fonction qui met le terminal en mode alphanumérique** when you want to type in text, press this function key which will put the terminal in its alphanumeric mode

Mode 1 *nom* Mode 1

Mode 2 *nom* Mode 2

mode *m* **actif** *nom* active state

mode *m* **affichage** *nom* display mode

mode *m* **alterné** *nom* alternate mode

mode *m* **à marche arrière** *nom* backward mode

mode *m* **à rebours** *nom* backward mode

mode *m* **asynchrone** *nom* asynchronous mode

mode *m* **AT** *nom* AT mode

mode *m* **avant-plan** *plural noun* foreground mode

mode *m* **bande dessinée** *adjectif* comic-strip oriented

mode *m* **brut** *nom* raw mode

mode *m* **bruyant** *nom* noisy mode

mode *m* **caractère** *nom* character mode

mode *m* **commande** *nom* command mode

mode *m* **conversationnel** *nom* **1.** conversational mode **2.** interactive mode

mode *m* **d'adressage** *nom* addressing mode

mode *m* **d'adressage à matrice active** *nom* all points addressable mode

mode *m* **de contrôle** *nom* control mode

mode *m* **défilement** *nom* scroll mode

mode *m* **de traitement par lots** *nom* batch mode

mode *m* **de traitement par paquets** *nom* batch mode

mode *m* **de transfert asynchrone** *nom* **1.** asynchronous transfer mode **2.** ATM

mode *m* **d'exécution** *nom* execute mode

mode *m* **dialogué** *nom* **1.** conversational mode **2.** interactive mode

mode *m* **différé** *nom* deferred mode

mode *m* **direct** *nom* **1.** direct mode **2.** raw mode

mode *m* **(d') entrée** *nom* input mode

mode *m* **graphe** *nom* plotting mode

mode *m* **graphique** *nom* graphics mode

mode *m* **immédiat** *nom* immediate mode

mode *m* **insertion** *nom* insert mode

mode *m* **interactif** *nom* **1.** conversational mode **2.** interactive mode

modèle *nom* model ■ *adjectif* model ◇ **le nouveau modèle B remplace le modèle A** the new model B has taken the place of model A ◇ **modèle** *m* **de fonte de caractères** outline font ◇ **modèle** *m* **moyen** (*de gestion de mémoire, pour processeurs Intel 8086*) medium model ◇ **voici notre dernier modèle** this is the latest model

modèle *m* **COM** *nom* COM

modèle *m* **compact** *nom* compact model

modèle *m* **conceptuel** *nom* conceptual model

mode *m* **lecture** *nom* reader level

modèle *m* **DCOM** *nom* DCOM

modèle *m* **de caractères** *nom* **1.** face **2.** typeface

modèle *m* **de composant JavaBeans** (*de Sun Micosystems*) Java Beans

modèle *m* **de (gestion des accès à la) mémoire** *nom* memory model

modèle *m* **de référence OSI** *nom* ISO/OSI model

modèle *m* **DOM** *nom* DOM

modèle *m* **mathématique** *nom* mathematical model

modèle *m* **réduit** *nom* model

modèle *m* **stochastique** *nom* stochastic model

modèle *m* **structuré** *nom* structured design

modéliser *verbe vt* to model

mode *m* **local** *nom* local mode

mode *m* **loupe** FatBits

modem *nom* **1.** *US* dataset **2.** modem *ou* MODEM **3.** modulator/demodulator ◇ **le modem viewdata reçoit à 1200 bauds et transmet à 75** the viewdata modem uses a 1200/75 split baud rate ◇ **modem** *m* **à deux vitesses** (*réception et émission*) split baud rate ◇ **(signal de modem) prêt à transmettre** *or* **recevoir** dataset ready (DSR)

'...le modem permet la transmission de données informatiques par l'intermédiaire d'une ligne téléphonique classique' [*Science et Vie Micro*]

modem *m* **à appel automatique** *nom* dial-in modem

modem *m* **à distance de transmission limitée** *nom* limited distance modem

mode *m* **masque** *nom* form mode

modem *m* **avec fonction rappel** *nom* call back modem

modem *m* **câble** *nom* cable modem

modem *m* **compatible Bell** *nom* Bell-compatible modem

modem *m* **de courte portée** *nom* short haul modem

modem *m* **demandeur** *nom* originate modem

modem *m* **de retour de réponse** *nom* answer modem

modem *m* **en bande de base** *nom* base band modem ◇ **n'utilisez jamais un modem en bande de base sur une ligne téléphonique normale** do not use a base band modem with a normal phone line

modem *m* **externe** *nom* external modem

modem *m* **half duplex** *nom* half-duplex modem

modem *m* **intégré** *nom* integrated modem

modem *m* **logiciel** *nom* software modem

modem *m* **pour réseau local** *nom* limited distance modem

modem *m* **sans fil** *nom* wireless modem

modem *m* **télécopieur** *nom* fax modem

mode *m* **multi-utilisateur** *nom* free running mode

mode *m* **octet** *nom* byte mode

mode *m* **protégé** *nom* **1.** privileged mode **2.** protected mode

mode *m* **rafale** *nom* (*de transmission de données*) burst mode

modérateur *f nom* moderator

mode *m* **réactif** *nom* reactive mode

mode *m* **remplacement** *nom* replace mode

mode *m* **réponse** *nom* answer mode

mode *m* **séquentiel** *nom* sequential mode

mode *m* **sortie** *nom* output mode

mode *m* **synchrone** *nom* synchronous mode

mode *m* **texte** *nom* text mode

mode *m* **visualisation** *nom* display mode

modificateur *m nom* modifier

modificateur *m* **de numéro** *nom* dial modifier

modificateurs *mpl plural noun* print modifiers

modification *f nom* **1.** adjustment **2.** change **3.** modification **4.** patch ◇ **les modifications apportées au système permettent de l'utiliser sur un réseau local d'entreprise** the modifications to the system allow it to be run as part of a LAN

modification *f* **d'adresse** *nom* address modification

modification *f* **d'une instruction** *nom* instruction modification

modifier *verbe vt* to modify ◇ **il faudra modifier le logiciel pour pouvoir l'utiliser sur un PC** the software will have to be modified to run on a small PC ◇ **le clavier a été modifié pour le marché européen** the keyboard was modified for European users ◇ **nous utilisons une version modifiée du programme d'édition de lettres types** *ou* **de publipostage** we are running a modified version of the mail-merge system

modifier les codes d'un programme *verbe* to recode

modulaire *adjectif* modular

'...la quatrième version offre désormais un environnement intégré et permet la programmation modulaire' [*Informatique & Bureautique*]

modularité *f nom* modularity ◇ **la modularité du logiciel ou du matériel permet de modifier le système** the modularity of the software or hardware allows the system to be changed

modularité *f* **de la mémoire** *nom* granularity

modulateur *m nom* modulator ◇ **modulateur-démodulateur** *ou* **modem** modulator/demodulator (modem)

modulation *f* **d'amplitude** *abrév* AM ■ *nom* amplitude modulation

modulation *f* **d'amplitude en quadrature** *abrév* QAM

modulation *f* **d'amplitude en quadrature (MAQ)** *nom* quadrature amplitude modulation

modulation *f* **de fréquence** *verbe* to FM ■ *nom* frequency modulation

modulation *f* **différentielle dynamique par impulsions et codage** *nom* ADPCM

modulation *f* **MIC à détection différentielle** *nom* DPCM

modulation *f* **par impulsions et codage (MIC)** *nom* **1.** PCM **2.** pulse-code modulation

modulation *f* **par impulsions et codages (MIC)** *nom* differential pulse coded modulation

module *nom* **1.** bead **2.** building block **3.** chapter **4.** module ◇ **un module d'interface analogique multifonction contient un convertisseur analogique-numérique et un convertisseur numérique-analogique** a multifunction analog interface module includes analog to digital and digital to analog converters

> '...ce logiciel est intégré, ce qui signifie qu'il possède différents modules (au nombre de quatre) ayant chacun une vocation propre: traitement de texte, tableur et graphiques, gestion de fichiers et rapports, communication' [*L'Ordinateur Individuel*]

module *m* **chargeable Netware** NetWare Loadable Module

module *m* **d'accompagnement** *nom* coroutine

module *m* **de gestion d'unité** *nom* **1.** virtual device driver **2.** VxD

module *m* **de mémoire à double rangée de connexion** *nom* dual in-line memory module

module *m* **de mémoire à double rangée de connexions** *nom* DIMM

moduler *verbe vt* to modulate

modulo *m nom* modulus

modulo-n *m nom* modulo-N

molette *f* **de pressage** *nom* head wheel

molette *f* **de serrage** *nom* pinchwheel

monaural *adjectif* monoaural

moniteur *m nom* **1.** monitor **2.** monitor unit **3.** video monitor

moniteur *m* **à fréquence fixe** *nom* fixed-frequency monitor

moniteur *m* **analogique** *nom* analog monitor

moniteur *m* **couleur** *nom* colour monitor

moniteur *m* **de télévision** *nom* television monitor

moniteur *m* **intégré** *nom* firmware monitor

moniteur *m* **multibalayage** *nom* multisync monitor

moniteur *m* **multistandard** *nom* multi-scan monitor

moniteur *m* **numérique** *nom* digital monitor

moniteur/téléviseur *m nom* television receiver/monitor

moniteur *m* **TTL** *nom* TTL monitor

monnaie *f* **électronique** *nom* digital cash

mono *préfixe* mono-

monochrome *adjectif, nom* monochrome ◇ **adaptateur (monochrome) MDA** *ou* **carte MDA** monochrome display adapter (MDA)

montage *m nom* assembly ◇ **il n'y a pas de notice de montage pour aider à la mise en place de l'ordinateur** there are no assembly instructions to show you how to put the computer together ◇ **montage** *m* **d'un document à partir de paragraphes standard** (*à partir de paragraphes standard*) boilerplating

montage *m* **en différé** *nom* **1.** off-line editing **2.** online editing

montage *m* **en série** *nom* series circuit

montage *m* **vidéo** *nom* video editing

monté, -ée en série *adjectif* ganged

monté, -ée sur carte de circuit *adjectif* on-board

monté, -ée sur supports *adjectif* rack mounted

monter *verbe* **1.** *vi* to ascend **2.** *vt* to assemble **3.** *vt* to mount ◇ **les puces sont montées dans des prises de la carte de circuit imprimé** the chips are mounted in sockets on the PCB

monter un disque *verbe* to mount

morphage *m nom* morphing

mort *adjectif* dead

MOS *nom* metal oxide semiconductor

MOS à canal P *nom* p-channel metal oxide semiconductor

(disposition *f* **en) mosaïque** *nom* tile

mosaïque *f nom* mosaic ■ (*nom de marque*) Mosaic

MOS canal P *nom* PMOS

mot *m nom* **1.** computer word **2.** word ◇ **(nombre de) mots par minute** words per minute (wpm *ou* WPM)

mot *m* **actif** *nom* hotword

mot *m* **adresse** *nom* address word ◇ **plus le mot adresse est long, plus la mémoire adressable de l'ordinateur augmente** a larger address word increases the amount of memory a computer can address

mot-clé *nom* **1.** descriptor **2.** key **3.** keyword ◇ **le mot computer est un mot-clé en informatique** computer is a keyword in IT ◇ **mot-clé en contexte** keyword in context (KWIC) ◇ **mot-clé et contexte** keyword and context (KWAC) ◇ **mot-clé hors contexte** keyword out of context (KWOC)

> '...développé en LISP et récrit en COBOL, ce programme fonctionne par repérage des mots-clés' [*L'Ordinateur Individuel*]

mot-clé *m* **en contexte** *nom* KWIC

mot-clé *m* **et contexte** *nom* KWAC

mot-clé *m* **hors contexte** *nom* KWOC

mot *m* **de commande** *nom* control word

mot *m* **de contrôle** *nom* control word

mot *m* **de données** *nom* data word

mot *m* **de longueur fixe** *nom* fixed-length word

mot *m* **de passe** *nom* **1.** access code **2.** authorisation code **3.** password **4.** user ID ◇ **l'utilisateur doit d'abord taper le mot de passe pour avoir accès à la base de données** the user has to key in the password before he can access the database ◇ **protégé, -ée par mot de passe** password-protected

mot *m* **de quatre bits** *nom* quadbit

mot *m* **d'état d'entrée/sortie** *nom* input/output status word

mot *m* **d'état d'un processeur** *nom* processor status word

mot *m* **d'état du programme** *nom* **1.** program status word **2.** program status word register

mot *m* **d'identification** *nom* identifier word

mot *m* **d'index** *nom* index value word

mot *m* **double** *nom* double word

moteur *m nom* engine

moteur *m* **à pas** *nom* stepper motor *ou* stepping motor

moteur *m* **de base de données** *nom* database engine

moteur *m* **de recherche** *nom* search engine

moteur *m* **d'inférence** *nom* inference engine *ou* inference machine

motif *m nom* pattern

mot *m* **instruction** *nom* instruction word ◇ **les fabricants du CPU ont décidé que l'instruction JMP servirait à indiquer un branchement** *ou* **un saut** the manufacturers of this CPU have decided that JMP will be the instruction word to call the jump function

mot *m* **long** *nom* double word

mot *m* **machine** *nom* machine word

Motorola™ (*fabriquant des composants électroniques*) Motorola

mot-paramètre *m nom* parameter word

mot *m* **par minute** *nom* words per minute

mot *m* **principal** *nom* keyword

mot *m* **réservé** *nom* reserved word

mots *mpl plural noun* display highlights

mots *mpl* **mis en évidence** *nom* highlight

mots *mpl* **par minute** *nom* WPM *ou* wpm

mouture *f nom* build ◇ **c'est la dernière mouture du nouveau logiciel** this is the latest build of the new software

mouvement *m nom* **1.** movement **2.** transaction ◇ **traitement de mouvements** *ou* **de transactions** transaction processing (TP)

mouvement *m* **de rotation (transmis manuellement)** *nom* spindling

mouvements *mpl nom* traffic

moyen *adjectif* medium ■ *nom* medium ◇ **un système informatique de taille moyenne** a medium-sized computer system

moyenne *f nom, adjectif* mean

moyenne *f* **de temps de bon fonctionnement entre les défaillances (MTBF)** *nom* MTBF

moyenne *f* **de temps requis pour réparation** *nom* mean time to repair

moyenne *f* **pondérée** *nom* weighted average

MP3 *nom* **1.** MP3 **2.** MPEG audio level 3

MS *abrév* MS

MS-DOS (*nom de marque*) MS-DOS

MSN (*nom de marque*) MSN

multi- *préfixe* multi-

multicolore *adjectif* multicolour

multicouche *adjectif* multilayer

multidimensionnel *adjectif* multidimensional

multidisque *adjectif* multi-disk

MultiFinder™ *nom* MultiFinder

multifonction *f adjectif* multifunction *ou* multifunctional ◇ **un module d'interface analogique multifonction contient un convertisseur analogique-numérique et un convertisseur numérique-analogique** a multifunction analog interface module includes analog to digital and digital to analog converters

multiligne *f adjectif* **1.** multiline **2.** multiple line

multimédia *adjectif* multimedia ◇ **console multimédia** multimedia terminal ◇ **fichier multimédia** multimedia file ◇ **message multimédia** multimedia mail

multiniveau *adjectif* multilevel

multiplate-forme *adjectif* **1.** cross-platform **2.** multi platform

multiple *adjectif* multiple

multiple précision *nom* multiprecision

multiples fraudes *f* **de peu de valeur** *nom* salami technique

multiplet *m nom* gulp

multiplexage *nom* dataplex

> '...il est à remarquer que le multiplexage de 12 canaux vidéo sur une seule fibre est une première avec la qualité de transmission obtenue' [*Opto électronique*]

multiplexage *m* **dynamique** *nom* dynamic multiplexing

multiplexage *m* **(par répartition) en fréquence** *nom* **1.** FDM **2.** frequency division multiplexing ◇ **le multiplexage en fréquence permet de transférer 100 appels téléphoniques sur un seul câble** using FDM we can transmit 100 telephone calls along one main cable

multiplexage *m* **en longueur d'onde** *nom* wavelength division multiplexing ■ *abrév* WDM

multiplexage *m* **hétérogène** *nom* heterogeneous multiplexing

multiplexage *m* **homogène** *nom* homogeneous multiplexing

multiplexage *m* **par répartition dans le temps (MRT)** *nom* **1.** TDM **2.** time division multiplexing

multiplexage *m* **temporel** *nom* **1.** TDM **2.** time division multiplexing

multiplexer *verbe vt* to multiplex

multiplexeur *m nom* **1.** multiplexor **2.** MUX

multiplicande *m nom* **1.** icand **2.** multiplicand

multiplicateur *m* ier ■ *nom* multiplier

multiplication *f nom* multiplication ◇ **la multiplication de 5 par 3 donne 15 comme résultat** the multiplication of 5 and 3 equals 15 ◇ **signe de la multiplication** multiplication sign (x)

multiplier *verbe vt* to multiply

multipoint *adjectif* multipoint

multiprocesseur *m abrév* MPS ■ *nom* multiprocessor

multiprogrammation *f nom* **1.** concurrent programming **2.** multiprocessor interleaving **3.** multi-programming system

multitâche *nom* multitasking

'...les participants auront cinq jours pour apprendre à utiliser un ordinateur dans un environnement multitâche et multi-utilisateur' [*Informatique & Bureautique*]

multi-tâche *adjectif* multitasking

multitâche *f* **en temps partagé** *nom* preemptive multitasking

multitonalité *f* **discrète** *nom* **1.** discrete multi-tone **2.** DMT

multitraitement *m nom* concurrent processing

multivoie *adjectif* (*protocole d'accès au réseau*) multichannel

N

NAND *nom* NOT-AND

nano- *préfixe* nano-

nanoseconde *f nom* nanosecond

nappe *f nom* ribbon cable

Napster (*nom de marque*) Napster

natif *adjectif* native

navigable *adjectif* navigable

navigateur *nom* browser ◇ **fenêtre du navigateur** browser window

'...rappelons que seul un navigateur est capable actuellement d'afficher correctement le contenu des sites Web puisque ceux-ci font appel à un langage particulier (le HTML)' [*Micro Pratique*]

navigateur *m* **Explorer™ (de Microsoft)** (*à Windows 95*) Explorer™

navigateur *m* **WAP** *nom* WAP browser

navigateur *m* **Web** *nom* **1.** Internet Explorer **2.** web browser

navigation *f nom* browsing

navigation *nom* navigation

'...deux logiciels se partagent la quasi-totalité du marché de la navigation sur Internet' [*Micro Pratique*]

naviguer *verbe vt* (*sur Internet*) to surf

'Quarterdeck, réputé pour ses utilitaires propose ici une trousse d'outils pour naviguer sur Internet' [*l'Ordinateur Individuel*]

négatif *adjectif* negative ◇ **accusé de réception négatif (NACK)** negative acknowledgement (NAK *ou* NACK) ◇ **rétroaction négative** *ou* **feedback négatif** negative feedback

négation *f nom* **1.** denial **2.** (*fonction logique*) negation

négation *f* **connexe** *nom* joint denial

négociation *f* **informatisée** *nom* program trading

NetBIOS *m nom* (*système/noyau de base pour gérer les entrées et sorties de réseau*) NetBIOS

nétiquette *f nom* netiquette

NetScape (*développeur de logiciel*) NetScape

Netscape Navigator (*nom de marque*) Netscape Navigator

NetShow (*système audio et vidéo*) NetShow

nettoyage *m* **de données** *nom* data cleaning

nettoyage de fichiers *m nom* file cleanup

nettoyage *m* **de mémoire** *nom* garbage collection

nettoyer *verbe* **1.** *vt* to clean **2.** *vt* to zap

NetView™ (*de IBM*) NetView

NetWare™ (*de Novell*) NetWare

neutre *adjectif* neutral

Newton (*nom de marque*) Newton

NI *nom* joint denial

nickel-cadmium *m nom* nickel cadmium

nickel-métal-hydrure *m nom* nickel metal hydride

NI exclusif *nom* exclusive NOR

NI *m* **exclusif** *nom* EXNOR

niveau *nom* level ◇ **niveau de pression acoustique** sound pressure level (SPL)

'...tout signal de niveau compris entre +3 et +25 volts est considéré comme étant au niveau logique' [*Action PC*]

'...pour l'Etat, la mise à nivau des systèmes informatiques des administrations coûtera 25% du budget informatique' [*Le Figaro Economique*]

niveau *m* **cible** *nom* target level

niveau *m* **d'accès** *nom* access level

niveau *m* **d'activité** *nom* activity level

niveau *m* **d'adressage** *nom* addressing level

niveau *m* **de complexité** *nom* complexity measure

niveau *m* **de confiance** *nom* confidence level

niveau *m* **de données** *nom* data level

niveau *m* **de noir** *nom* black level

niveau *m* **d'enregistrement** *nom* recording level

niveau *m* **de pression acoustique** *nom* **1.** sound pressure level **2.** SPL

niveau *m* **de transmission (d'une ligne)** *nom* line level

niveau *m* **d'imbrication** *nom* (*de boucles*) nesting level

niveau *m* **d'interruption** *nom* interrupt level

niveau *m* **logique** *nom* logic level

niveau *m* **maximum de production** *nom* peak output

niveau *m* **utilisateur** *nom* user level

niveaux *mpl* **de gris** *nom* grey scale

niveaux *mpl* **de luminosité** *nom* brightness range

noeud *m nom* node ◇ **ce réseau est relié par fibres optiques avec des noeuds positionnés jusqu'à un kilomètre les uns des autres**

this network has fibre optic connection with nodes up to one kilometre apart ◇ **une arborescence est formée de branches reliées les unes aux autres par des points de liaison ou noeuds** a tree is made of branches that connect together at nodes

noeud *m* **actif** *nom* active node

noeud *m* **d'accès au réseau** *nom* concentrator

noeuds *mpl* **adjacents** *plural noun* adjacent nodes

noir ◇ **noir et blanc** black and white

noir et blanc *adjectif, nom* monochrome

nom *nom* **1.** heading **2.** name **3.** title ◇ **nom** *m* **d'accès** (*dans une base de données*) access name ◇ **nom de fichier** file name ◇ **nom** *m* **de fichier long de plusieurs caractères** long filename ◇ **nom** *ou* **titre d'une disquette** title of disk

nombre *nom* number ◇ **élévation** *f* **d'un nombre à la puissance x** exponentiation ◇ **nombre** *m* **de mots contenus dans un fichier** (*word-processing*) word count ◇ **nombre** *m* **duquel on soustrait un autre nombre** minuend ◇ **nombre** *m* **entier long de plusieurs octets de données** long integer ◇ **nombre hexadécimal équivalent du 15 décimal** F

nombre *m* **aléatoire** *nom* random number

nombre *m* **à soustraire d'un autre** *nom* subtrahend

nombre *m* **à virgule flottante** *nom* floating point number

nombre *m* **binaire** *nom* binary number

nombre *m* **cardinal** *nom* cardinal number

nombre *m* **choisi au hasard** *nom* random number

nombre *m* **de caractères par pouce** *plural noun* characters per inch ■ *nom* pitch

nombre *m* **de caractères par seconde (cps)** *nom* characters per second

nombre *m* **de cycles** *nom* cycle count

nombre *m* **de frappes** *nom* keystroke count

nombre *m* **de lignes par page** *nom* page length

nombre *m* **de puces** *nom* chip count ◇ **le nombre de puces est malheureusement encore trop élevé** it's no good, the chip count is still too high

nombre *m* **entier** *nom* integer

nombre *m* **entier en double précision** *nom* double-precision integer

nombre *m* **hexadécimal du 10 décimal** *symbole* A

nombre *m* **hexadécimal équivalent du 11 décimal** *abrév* B

nombre *m* **maximum d'utilisateurs** *plural noun* maximum users

nombre *m* **négatif** *nom* negative number

nombre *m* **rationnel** *nom* rational number

nombre *m* **réel** *nom* real number

nombres *mpl* **à précision finie** *nom* finite-precision numbers

nombres *mpl* **assignés** *plural noun* assigned numbers

nombres *mpl* **complets** *nom* complementation

nom *m* **d'alias** *nom* alias name

nom *m* **de chaîne** *nom* string name

nom *m* **de compte** *nom* account name ◇ **le nom de compte de John Smith est JSMITH** John Smith's account name is JSMITH

nom *m* **de domaine** *nom* domain name

nom *m* **de domaine complet** *nom* **1.** FQDN **2.** fully qualified domain name

nom *m* **de donnée** *nom* data name ◇ **les difficultés surviennent lorsque le nom de donnée est ambigu** problems occur if an ambiguous data name is chosen

nom *m* **de fichier ambigu** *nom* ambiguous filename

nom *m* **de périphérique** *nom* (*sous forme d'abréviation*) device name

nom *m* **de programme** *nom* program name

nom *m* **de site Web** *nom* host name

nom *m* **de sous-domaine** *nom* subdomain name

nom *m* **de variable** *nom* variable name

nom *m* **de volume** *nom* volume label *ou* volume name

nom *m* **d'ordinateur** *plural noun* computer name

nom *m* **du chemin d'accès** *nom* pathname ◇ **\FILES\SIMON\DOCS\LETTER.DOC est le nom du chemin d'accès au fichier de la lettre** the pathname for the letter file is \FILES\SIMON\DOCS\LETTER.DOC

nom *m* **d'un fichier** *nom* filename ◇ **sous MS-DOS, le nom d'un fichier peut comporter jusqu'à huit caractères suivis d'une extension de trois caractères** in MS-DOS, a filename can be up to eight characters long together with a three character filename extension

nom *m* **d'utilisateur** *nom* user name

nomenclature *f* *nom* nomenclature

nomogramme *m* *nom* nomogram *ou* nomograph

nom *m* **symbolique** *nom* symbolic name

non- *préfixe* non-

non aligné *adjectif* **1.** nonaligned **2.** out of alignment

non altéré *adjectif* uncorrupted

non asservi,-e à l'horloge *adjectif* unclocked

non autorisé *adjectif* **1.** illegal **2.** unauthorised *ou* unauthorized

non bidouillé *adjectif* well-behaved

non classé *adjectif* unsorted ◇ **il a fallu quatre fois plus de temps pour chercher dans le fichier aux données non classées** it took four times as long to search the unsorted file

non *f* **compatibilité** *nom* noncompatibility

non compatible *adjectif* incompatible

non connecté *adjectif* connectionless ■ *adverbe, adjectif* off-line

non corrigé *adjectif* unedited

non disponibilité *nom* outage

non édité *adjectif* unedited

non entrelacé *adjectif* non interlaced

non équipé *adjectif* unpopulated

non formaté *adjectif* unformatted ◇ **il est impossible de copier quoi que ce soit sur une disquette non formatée** it is impossible to copy to an unformatted disk

non intelligent *adjectif* dumb

non justifié *adjectif* unjustified

non justifié à droite *nom* ragged right

non justifié à gauche *nom* ragged left

non linéaire *adjectif* nonlinear

non modulé *adjectif* unmodulated

non protégé *adjectif* unprotected

non-remise *f* **à zéro** *nom* non-return to zero

non renforcé *adjectif* unsupported

non-répudiation *f nom* nonrepudiation

non-retour *m* **à zéro** *nom* non-return to zero ■ *abrév* NRZ

non spécialisé *adjectif* device-independent

non tributaire *adjectif* device-independent

non trié *adjectif* unsorted ◇ **il a fallu quatre fois plus de temps pour chercher dans le fichier aux données non classées** it took four times as long to search the unsorted file

non volatile *adjectif* non-volatile ◇ **mémoire vive non volatile** *ou* **RAM non volatile** *ou* **NVRAM** non-volatile random access memory (NVRAM) ◇ **une bande magnétique constitue une mémoire non volatile** using magnetic tape provides non-volatile memory

normal *adjectif* normal ◇ **la procédure normale préconise une sauvegarde de tout le travail en fin de journée** the normal procedure is for backup copies to be made at the end of each day's work

normalisation *nom* normalisation *ou* normalization

> '...bénificiant d'un numéro et d'un protocole de normalisation de l'ISO (International Standards Organization), il est déjà utilisé par les organisations internationales, certaines administrations et quelques grandes entreprises' [*Informatique & Bureautique (Suisse)*]

normaliser *verbe* **1.** *vt* to normalise *ou* to normalize **2.** *vt* to standardise

norme *nom* standard ◇ **norme** *f* **IEEE 802.2** (*définissant les liens entre données*) IEEE-802.2 ◇ **norme** *f* **IEEE 802.3** (*définissant le système de réseau Ethernet*) IEEE-802.3 ◇ **normes** *fpl* **de protocoles de transmission** protocol standards ◇ **norme** *f* **V21** (*transmission en duplex à 300 bits par seconde en émission et réception*) V.21 ◇ **norme** *f* **V22** (*transmission en semi-duplex à 1200 bits par seconde en émission et réception*) V.22 ◇ **norme** *f* **V29** (*modem à 9600 bits par seconde sur le réseau public commuté ou sur lignes louées*) V.29 ◇ **norme** *f* **V32** (*transmission de données à 9600 bits par seconde*) V.32 ◇ **norme** *f* **V32 BIS** (*transmission de données à 14400 bits par seconde*) V.32bis ◇ **norme** *f* **V42** (*protocole de contrôle et de correction d'erreurs*) V.42 ◇ **norme** *f* **V90** (*débit: 56000 bps ou 56 Kbps*) V.90 ◇ **norme** *f* **XGA de carte graphique couleur pour vidéo sur PC, de IBM** XGA

norme *f* **ACPI** *nom* **1.** ACPI **2.** advanced configuration and power interface

norme *f* **AT** *nom* (*nom de marque*) AT

norme *f* **ATAPI** *nom* **1.** advanced technology attachment packet interface **2.** ATA packet interface

norme *f* **de codage MFM** *nom* **1.** MFM **2.** modified frequency modulation

norme *f* **de conversion ADPCM** *nom* adaptive differential pulse code modulation

norme *f* **de conversion ADPCM** *nom* ADPCM

norme *f* **d'écran VGA** *nom* video graphics array

norme *f* **de cryptage de données** *nom* **1.** data encryption standard **2.** DES

norme *f* **de facto** *nom* de facto standard

norme *f* **de fait** *nom* de facto standard

norme *f* **de télévision couleur PAL** *nom* phase alternation line

norme *f* **de télévision PAL** *nom* PAL

norme *f* **EEMS** *nom* EEMS

norme *f* **EMS** *nom* Lotus-Intel-Microsoft Expanded Memory System

norme *f* **FDDI (pour réseau à fibre optique)** *nom* fibre distributed data interface

norme *f* **FDDI II** *nom* fibre distributed data interface II

norme *f* **Général MIDI** *nom* General MIDI

norme *f* **H.323** *nom* H.323 *ou* H.324

norme *f* **IEEE-488 (d'interface parallèle standard)** *nom* IEEE-488

norme *f* **IEEE 802.4** *nom* (*définissant le bus Token-Ring*) IEEE-802.4

norme *f* **IEEE-802.5** *nom* (*définissant le réseau Token-Ring IBM*) IEEE-802.5

norme *f* **ISO 9660** *nom* **1.** ISO 9660 **2.** Yellow Book

norme *f* **JPEG** *nom* **1.** Joint Photographic Experts Group **2.** JPEG

norme *f* **Livre Blanc** *nom* White Book

norme *f* **Livre Orange** *nom* Orange Book

norme *f* **Livre vert** *nom* Green Book

norme *f* **MJPEG** *nom* **1.** MJPEG **2.** motion JPEG

norme *f* **MPEG** *nom* **1.** motion picture experts group **2.** Moving Pictures Expert Group

norme *f* **MSX** *nom* MSX

norme *f* **PCMCIA (de carte d'extension)** *nom* PCMCIA ◇ **la mémoire additionnelle est stockée sur une carte PCMCIA que j"utilise sur mon (ordinateur) portable** the extra memory is stored on this PCMCIA card and I use it on my laptop

norme *f* **RS-85** *nom* RS-485

norme *f* **RS-232C (pour interface série)** *nom* RS-232C

norme *f* **RS-422** *nom* RS-422

norme *f* **RS-423** *nom* RS-423

normes *fpl plural noun* programming standards

norme *f* **SAA** (*de IBM*) SAA

normes de production *plural noun* production standards

normes *fpl* **pour modems** *plural noun* modem standards

norme *f* **V.22 bis** *nom* (*transmission en duplex à 1200 bits par seconde en émission et réception*) V.22bis

norme *f* **V.42 bis** *nom* (*compression de données avec contrôle d'erreurs V42*) V.42bis

norme *f* **XMS** *nom* extended memory specification

NOS *nom* network operating system

notation *f* **à virgule flottante** *nom* floating point notation

notation *f* **infixée** *nom* infix notation

notation *f* **polonaise (préfixée)** *nom* prefix notation

notation *f* **polonaise inversée** *nom* **1.** postfix notation **2.** reverse Polish notation **3.** suffix notation

notation *f* **préfixée** *nom* prefix notation

notation *f* **suffixée** *nom* **1.** Polish notation **2.** postfix notation ■ *abrév* RPN ■ *nom* suffix notation

note *f nom* **1.** annotation **2.** comment **3.** footnote

notice *f* **d'utilisation** *nom* **1.** operational information **2.** user documentation

notice *f* **d'utilisation d'un logiciel** *nom* software documentation

nouveau *adjectif* new ◇ **ils ont installé un nouveau système informatique** *ou* **un nouvel ordinateur** they have installed a new computer system

nouveau venu *m nom* newbie

nouvelle pagination *f nom* repagination

nouvelle technologie *f nom* new technology

nouvelle version *f* **(d'un progiciel)** *nom* update

nouvelle version *f* **d'un fichier** *nom* file update

nouvelle version *f* **d'un progiciel** *nom* update

Novell™ (*société qui fabrique des systèmes d'exploitation de réseau*) Novell

novice *m nom* newbie

noyau *m* **(du système d'exploitation)** *nom* kernel ◇ **fonctions graphiques GKS** graphics kernel system (GKS)

NT *nom* NT

NTSC *nom* National Television System Committee

nu *adjectif* unpopulated

nuancier *m* **Pantone** (*nom de marque*) Pantone Matching System ■ *abrév* PMS

nul *adjectif* null ◇ **jeu de caractères nuls** null set

nulle *adjectif* null

null modem *nom* null modem

numéral *adjectif* numeric

numération *f nom* notation ◇ **numération décimale** *ou* **à base 10** decimal notation ◇ **num,ration octale** *ou* **... base 8** octal notation

numération *f* **à base** *nom* radix notation

numération *f* **à virgule fixe** *nom* fixed-point notation

numération *f* **binaire** *nom* **1.** binary notation **2.** binary representation

numération *f* **en base 8** *nom* octal *ou* octal notation

numération *f* **hexadécimale** *nom* **1.** hex *ou* hexadecimal notation **2.** sexadecimal

numération *f* **octale** *nom* octal *ou* octal notation

numérique *adjectif* **1.** digital **2.** (*se rapportant à un nombre*) numeric **3.** (*se rapportant à un nombre*) numerical ◇ **affichage numérique** digital readout ◇ **bande audionumérique** digital audio tape (DAT) ◇ **caméra vidéo numérique** digital video camera ◇ **cassette compacte numérique** digital compact cassette (DCC) ◇ **circuit DSP** *ou* **circuit (intégré) de traitement de signaux numériques** *ou* **processeur de signaux numériques** digital signal processor (DSP) ◇ **contrôle numérique** numerical control (NC) *ou* computer numerical control (CNC) ◇ **disque vidéo numérique** *ou* **disque DVD** digital video disc *ou* digital versatile disc (DVD) ◇ **enregistrement numérique** digital recording ◇ **lecture optique de données numériques** digital optical reading (DOR) ◇ **ligne numérique d'abonné** digital subscriber line (DSL) ◇ **multimètre numérique** digital multimeter (DMM) ◇ **signal**

numérique niveau 0 digital signal level 0 (DS-0) ◇ **signal numérique niveau 1** digital signal level 1 (DS-1) ◇ **traitement de signaux numériques** digital signal processing

numérisation *f* **de micro-images** *nom* computer input microfilm

numérisation *f* **d'une onde** *nom* waveform digitisation

numériser *verbe vt* to digitise *ou* to digitize

numériseur *m nom* digitiser *ou* digitizer

numériseur *m* **vidéo** *nom* video digitiser

numéro *nom* number ◇ **chacune des pièces de l'ordinateur possède un numéro de fabrication** each piece of hardware has a production number ◇ **numéro** *m* **de référence d'une ligne d'un programme** program line number ◇ **numéro** *m* **de suite d'une tâche dans la file d'attente** job number ◇ **touches de numérotation** number keys

'...il inscrira également le numéro du central vidéotex de son arrondissement, son numéro personnel d'identification et son mot de passe' [*Informatique & Bureautique (Suisse)*]

numéro *m* **d'accès** *nom* **1.** accession number **2.** access number

numéro *m* **de code confidentiel** *nom* **1.** personal identification number **2.** PID

numéro *m* **de code personnel** *nom* **1.** identity number **2.** personal identification number **3.** PID

numéro *m* **de page** *nom* page number

numéro *m* **de téléphone** *nom* phone number

numéro *m* **de version** *nom* **1.** release number **2.** version number

numéro *m* **d'identification d'un fichier** *nom* handle

numéro *m* **d'instruction** *nom* statement number

numéro *m* **d'ordre** *nom* handle

numéro *m* **d'ordre de fichier** *nom* file handle

numéro *m* **d'une ligne** *nom* (*de programme*) line number

numérotation *f* **sur clavier tonal** *nom* tone dialling

numéroter *verbe vt* to number

numéroteur *m* **téléphonique** *nom* Phone Dialer

O

o *symbole* B

objectif *nom* objective

'...des chercheurs de l'Université d'Edimbourg viennent de faire tenir une caméra vidéo sur une surface de 8 millimètres carrés, avec des objectifs de la taille d'une tête d'épingle' [*Le Point*]

objet *m nom* object ◇ **bibliothèque d'objets** object library

objet *m* **d'action** *nom* action-object

objet *m* **délimité** *nom* enclosed object

objet *m* **disponible** *nom* instance

objet *m* **fractal** *nom* fractal

objet *m* **graphique** *nom* graphic object

objet *m* **incorporé** *nom* embedded object

objet *m* **lié** *nom* linked object

objet *m* **OLE** *nom* OLE object *ou* OLE container object

objet *m* **parent** *nom* parent object

objets *mpl* **d'accès aux données** *nom* DAO ■ *plural noun* data access objects

objet *m* **source** *nom* source object

objet *m* **statique** *nom* static object

obliquité *f nom* skew

obtenir *verbe vt* to obtain ◇ **le filtrage permet d'obtenir un signal très clair** a clear signal is obtained after filtering

octet *symbole* B ■ *nom* **1.** byte **2.** eight-bit byte *ou* eight-bit octet **3.** eight-bit octet **4.** octet ◇ **octets par seconde** bytes per second (Bps)

octet *m* **de caractères** *nom* character byte

octet *m* **de contrôle d'accès** *nom* access control byte

octet *m* **de placement** *nom* postbyte

octet *m* **par seconde** *nom* bytes per second

octets *mpl* **par pouce** *nom* bytes-per-inch

octets *mpl* **par seconde** *nom* Bps

OEM *nom* OEM

off-line *adverbe, adjectif* off-line ◇ **avant de remplacer le papier de l'imprimante, assurez-vous que l'imprimante est hors ligne** *ou* **off-line** before changing the paper in the printer, switch it off-line

offre *f* **groupée** *nom* bundle

offre *f* **promotionnelle** *nom* bundle

offrir ◇ **offrir des logiciels dans le prix d'achat d'un ordinateur** bundle

offset *m nom* offset ◇ **impression (en) offset** offset printing ◇ **lithographie offset** offset lithography

ohm *m nom* ohm ◇ **kilo-ohm** kilo-ohm ◇ **la valeur de cette résistance est de 100 ohms** this resistance has a value of 100 ohms

OK *nom* OK

ombrage *m nom* shading

ombrage *m* **de Gouraud** *nom* Gouraud shading

omettre *verbe vt* to skip ◇ **omettre de faire quelque chose** fail

onde *f nom* **1.** wave **2.** waveform ◇ **onde sonore** sound wave

onde *f* **audio** *nom* waveform audio

onde *f* **carrée** *nom* square wave

onde *f* **porteuse** *nom* **1.** carrier **2.** carrier wave

onde *f* **porteuse de données** *nom* data carrier

ondes *fpl* **sonores** *plural noun* sound waves

onduleur *m nom* **1.** uninterruptible power supply **2.** UPS

on-line *adverbe, adjectif* online

OnNow *nom* OnNow

OpenScript *nom* OpenScript

Open Software Foundation *abrév* OSF

opérande *m nom* operand ◇ **par effet de l'instruction ADD 74, l'opérateur ADD va ajouter l'opérande 74 à l'accumulateur** in the instruction ADD 74, the operator ADD will add the operand 74 to the accumulator

opérande *m* **alphanumérique** *nom* alphanumeric operand

opérande *m* **d'une conjonction** *nom* conjunct

opérande *m* **d'une opération ET** *nom* conjunct

opérande *m* **immédiat** *nom* immediate operand

opérande *m* **littéral** *nom* literal operand

opérande *m* **numérique** *nom* numeric operand

opérateur *m nom* operator ◇ **l'opérateur était assis devant l'écran de son ordinateur** *ou* **à son pupitre** the operator was sitting at his console ◇ **x est l'opérateur de la multiplication** x is the multiplication operator

opérateur, -trice d'ordinateur *nom* computer operator

opérateur, -trice de saisie *nom* keyboarder

opérateur *m* **arithmétique** *nom* arithmetic operator

opérateur *m* **booléen** *nom* Boolean operator

opérateur *m* **central** *nom* centre operator

opérateur *m* **de concaténation** *nom* concatenation operator

opérateur *m* **de dérivation** *nom* pipe

opérateur *m* **de globalisation** *nom* aggregate operator

opérateur *m* **de redirection (sous DOS)** *nom* redirect operator *ou* redirection operator

opérateur *m* **de système** *nom* **1.** sysop **2.** system operator

opérateur *m* **de transfert (de données)** *nom* pipe

opérateur *m* **d'inégalité** *nom* inequality operator

opérateur *m* **logique** *nom* logical operator

opérateur *m* **monadique à un opérande** *nom* **1.** monadic Boolean operator **2.** monadic operator

opérateur *m* **relationnel** *ou* **logique** *nom* relational operator

opération *f nom* **1.** duplex operation **2.** (*activité*) operation ◇ **code (d')opération** *ou* **op-code** operation code (op code) ◇ **lecteur de DVD-RAM** DVD-RAM drive

opération *f* **à deux opérandes** *nom* dyadic operation

opération *f* **arithmétique** *nom* arithmetic operation

opération *f* **au complet** *nom* complete operation

opération *f* **à un opérande** *nom* unary operation

opération *f* **(booléenne) à un opérande** *nom* monadic Boolean operation

opération *f* **binaire** *nom* binary operation

opération *f* **booléenne** *nom* Boolean operation

opération *f* **booléenne dyadique** *nom* dyadic Boolean operation

opération *f* **complémentaire** *nom* complementary operation

opération *f* **de branchement** *nom* jump operation

opération *f* **de fermeture de fichier** *nom* close file

opération *f* **d'équivalence** *nom* equivalence function

opération *f* **de réunion** *nom* disjunction

opération *f* **d'identité** *nom* identity operation

opération *f* **d'union** *nom* **1.** disjunction **2.** either-or operation

opération *f* **dyadique** *nom* dyadic operation

opération *f* **dyadique à deux opérandes** *nom* dyadic Boolean operation

opération *f* **en cycle fixe** *nom* fixed cycle operation

opération *f* **en simple précision** *nom* single length working

opération *f* **en une passe** *nom* single pass operation

opération *f* **en virgule flottante** *nom* floating point operation ■ *abrév* FLOP

opération *f* **ET** *nom* **1.** AND operation **2.** coincidence operation **3.** conjunction

opération *f* **incontrôlable** *nom* runaway

opération *f* **logique** *nom* logic operation

opération *f* **monadique** *nom* **1.** monadic operation **2.** unary operation

opération *f* **(booléenne) monadique** *nom* monadic Boolean operation

opération *f* **monopasse** *nom* single pass operation

opérationnel *adjectif* operational

opération *f* **non autorisée** *nom* illegal operation

opération *f* **NON-OU** *nom* joint denial

opération *f* **non prioritaire** *nom* background operation

opération *f* **OU** *nom* **1.** disjunction **2.** join **3.** union

opération *f* **OU inclusif** *nom* either-or operation

opération *f* **(en) parallèle** *nom* parallel operation

opération *f* **sans adresse** *nom* no-address operation

opérations *fpl* **en virgule flottante par seconde** *nom* FLOPs per second

opération *f* **séquentielle** *nom* **1.** sequential operation **2.** serial operation

opérations *fpl* **numériques ultra-rapides** *nom* number crunching

opération *f* **surveillée** *nom* attended operation

opération *f* **synchronisée** *nom* fixed cycle operation

opposé *m nom* inverse ◇ **l'opposé de 1 est 0** the inverse of 1 is 0

optimal *adjectif* optimum ■ *nom* optimum

optimisation *f nom* **1.** enhancement **2.** image enhancement **3.** optimisation *ou* optimization

optimiser *verbe* **1.** *vt* to optimise *ou* to optimize **2.** *vt* to upgrade ◇ **ils peuvent optimiser l'imprimante** they can upgrade the printer ◇ **les trois modèles offrent des possibilités de mise à niveau sur site** all three models have an on-site upgrade facility

optimiseur *m nom* **1.** enhancer **2.** optimiser *ou* optimizer **3.** optimizer

optimum *(m) adjectif* optimum ■ *nom* optimum

option *f nom* option ◇ **les options disponibles sont décrites dans le menu principal** the options available are described in the main menu ◇ **on trouve habituellement quatre options affichées en haut de l'écran** there are usually four options along the top of the screen

option *f* **carte d'accès distant** *nom* Dial-up Networking

option *f* **de configuration** *nom* setup option

option *f* **Fermer du menu** *nom* close menu option

option *f* **implicite** *nom* default option

option *f* **intrinsèque** *nom* default option

option *f* **multidisque** *nom* multi-disk option

optionnel *adjectif* optional

option *f* **par défaut** *nom* default option

optique *f nom* imaging system ■ *adjectif* optical ◇ **lecteur optique de caractères** optical character reader (OCR) ◇ **lecteur optique de marques** optical mark reader (OMR) ◇ **reconnaissance optique de caractères** optical character recognition (OCR) ◇ **reconnaissance optique de marques** *ou* **de signes** *ou* **de symboles** optical mark recognition (OMR) ◇ **système de communication optoélectronique** *ou* **par fibres optiques** optical communications system ◇ **un lecteur optique utilise un rayon lumineux qui balaye les caractères, les dessins ou les lignes** an optical reader uses a light beam to scan characters, patterns or lines

ordinateur *m nom* **1.** appliance computer **2.** computer **3.** machine **4.** master computer **5.** programmable ◇ **(instruction** *ou* **donnée) en langage machine** *ou* **exploitable par l'ordinateur** machine-readable ◇ **(logiciel) non standard** *ou* **qui ne fonctionne que sur un type d'ordinateur** machine-dependent ◇ **ordinateur** *m* **à mots de longueur variable** variable word length computer ◇ **ordinateur** *m* **dont le programme contient un virus** infected computer ◇ **ordinateur** *m* **infecté par un virus** infected computer ◇ **ordinateur monocarte** *ou* **à carte unique** single board computer (sbc) ◇ **ordinateur** *m* **pour la maison** home computer ◇ **ordinateur** *m* **qu'on tient à la main** palmtop ◇ **(logiciel) propre à la machine** *ou* **sur mesure** *ou* **de constructeur** *ou* **adapté à l'ordinateur** machine-intimate ◇ **(logiciel) standard** *ou* **universel** *ou* **qui fonctionne sur la plupart des ordinateurs** *ou* **indépendant de la machine** machine-independent

ordinateur *m nom (utilisé pour le traitement de l'information)* information processor

ordinateur *m* **à adresse unique** *nom* one-address computer

ordinateur *m* **à carte unique** *nom* **1.** SBC **2.** single board computer

ordinateur *m* **à crayon optique** *nom* pen computer

ordinateur *m* **à jeu d'instructions complexe (CISC)** *nom* **1.** CISC **2.** complex instruction set computer

ordinateur *m* **à jeu d'instructions modifiable** *nom* **1.** WISC **2.** writable instruction set computer

ordinateur *m* **à logique câblée** *nom* fixed program computer

ordinateur *m* **à longueur de mots fixe** *nom* fixed word length

ordinateur *m* **à puce unique** *nom* single chip computer

ordinateur *m* **asynchrone** *nom* asynchronous computer

ordinateur *m* **à usage professionnel** *nom* office computer

ordinateur *m* **à valeurs variables** *nom* incremental computer

ordinateur *m* **central** *nom* **1.** central computer **2.** mainframe *ou* mainframe computer

ordinateur *m* **cible** *nom* target computer

ordinateur-compilateur *m nom* source machine

ordinateur *m* **de bureau** *nom* **1.** business computer **2.** desktop computer *ou* desktop computer system **3.** office computer

ordinateur *m* **de cinquième génération** *nom* fifth generation computer

ordinateur *m* **de contrôle** *nom* control computer

ordinateur *m* **de contrôle de processus** *nom* process control computer

ordinateur *m* **de contrôle des transmissions** *nom* communications computer

ordinateur *m* **dédié** *nom* **1.** applications terminal **2.** application terminal **3.** control computer **4.** dedicated computer

ordinateur *m* **de grande puissance** *nom* supercomputer

ordinateur *m* **de poche** *nom* **1.** hand-held computer *ou* hand-held programmable **2.** notebook computer **3.** palmtop

ordinateur *m* **de première génération** *nom* first generation computer

ordinateur *m* **de quatrième génération** *nom* fourth generation computer

ordinateur *m* **de réseau** *abrév* NC ■ *nom* network computer

ordinateur *m* **de troisième génération** *nom* third generation computer

ordinateur *m* **d'exécution** *nom* target computer

ordinateur *m* **d'exécution de programme objet** *nom* object computer

ordinateur *m* **géant** *nom* supercomputer

ordinateur *m* **hôte** *nom* **1.** central computer **2.** host computer

ordinateur *m* **hybride** *nom* hybrid computer

ordinateur IBM AT (*nom de marque*) IBM AT

ordinateur *m* **imbriqué (dans un autre)** *nom* embedded computer

ordinateur *m* **incrémentiel** *nom* incremental computer

ordinateur *m* **individuel** *nom* **1.** PC **2.** personal computer **3.** single-user system

ordinateur *m* **Mac** (*nom de marque*) Apple Mac *ou* Apple Macintosh computer

ordinateur *m* **Macintosh** (*nom de marque*) Apple Mac *ou* Apple Macintosh computer

ordinateur *m* **maître** *nom* master computer ◇ **l'ordinateur maître contrôle tout le reste** the master computer controls everything else

ordinateur *m* **monocarte** *nom* **1.** SBC **2.** single board computer

ordinateur *m* **monopuce** *nom* single chip computer

ordinateur *m* **multicarte** *nom* multi-board computer

ordinateur *m* **multimédia** *nom* MPC

ordinateur *m* **neuronal** *nom* **1.** neural computer **2.** neurocomputer

ordinateur *m* **non spécialisé** *nom* general purpose computer

ordinateur *m* **numérique** *nom* digital computer

ordinateur *m* **optique** *nom* optical computer

ordinateur *m* **parallèle** *nom* parallel computer

ordinateur *m* **personnel** *nom* **1.** PC **2.** personal computer

ordinateur *m* **principal** *nom* **1.** host computer **2.** mainframe *ou* mainframe computer

ordinateur *m* **sans clavier** *nom* pen computer

ordinateur *m* **satellite** *nom* satellite computer

ordinateurs *mpl* **de deuxième génération** *nom* second generation computers

ordinateur *m* **série** *nom* **1.** sequential computer **2.** serial computer

ordinateurs *mpl* **jumelés** *nom* duplex computer

ordinateur *m* **spécialisé** *nom* **1.** applications terminal **2.** application terminal **3.** dedicated computer

ordinateur *m* **synchrone** *nom* synchronous computer

ordinateur *m* **transportable** *nom* luggable

ordinateur *m* **ultraportatif** *nom* subnotebook

ordinateur *m* **vêtement** *nom* wearable computer

ordinogramme *m* *nom* **1.** flowchart **2.** flow diagram

ordinogramme *m* **de données** *nom* data flowchart

ordinogramme *m* **d'un système** *nom* (*Apple Macintosh folder*) system flowchart

ordinogramme *m* **logique** *nom* logical flowchart

ordonnancement *m* *nom* scheduling

ordonnanceur *m* *nom* scheduler

ordonnée *f* *nom* y-coordinate

ordonner *verbe vt* to order

ordre *m* *nom* **1.** order **2.** sequence ◇ **en** *ou* **par ordre alphabétique** in alphabetical order ◇ **les noms sont classés par ordre alphabétique** the sequence of names is arranged alphabetically ◇ **ordre** *m* **d'interrogation d'appel** polling list

ordre *m* **croissant** *nom* ascending order

ordre *m* **de priorité** *nom* priority sequence

ordre *m* **de priorité des opérateurs** *nom* operator precedence

ordre *m* **de priorité des opérations** *nom* operation priority

ordre *m* **des cahiers** *nom* collating sequence

organigramme *m* **de programme** *nom* program flowchart

organisation *f* *nom* **1.** disk map **2.** organisation *ou* organization

organisation *f* **en pipeline** *nom* pipelining *ou* pipeline memory

organisationnel *adjectif* organisational *ou* organizational

organiser *verbe* **1.** *vt* to organise *ou* to organize **2.** *vt* to structure ◇ **vous organisez d'abord le document pour répondre à vos besoins, puis vous remplissez les blancs** you first structure a document to meet your requirements and then fill in the blanks

organiser en pipeline *verbe* to pipeline

organisme *m* **international de normalisation ISO** *nom* International Standards Organization

orientable *adjectif* tilt and swivel

orientation *f* *nom* orientation

orientation *f* **(paysage ou portrait)** *nom* orientation

orientation *f* **de la page** *nom* page orientation

orienté *adjectif* orientated

orienté objet *adjectif* object-oriented ◇ **ce programme graphique orienté objet vous permet de déplacer les formes très facilement** this object-oriented graphics program lets you move shapes around very easily ◇ **programmation orientée objet** *ou* **POO** object-oriented programming (OOP)

original *m* *nom* master disc ■ *adjectif* original ■ *nom* original ◇ **l'original n'est pas assez con-**

trasté pour être photocopié the original is too faint to photocopy well

original *m* **sauvegardé** *nom* protection master

origine *f nom* origin

orphelin *m nom* orphan

orthogonal *adjectif* orthogonal

OU *m* **exclusif** *nom* **1.** exclusive OR **2.** EXOR

OU *m* **inclusif** *nom* inclusive OR

outil *m nom* tool

outil *m* **d'effacement** *nom* eraser tool

outil *m* **de programmation** *nom* software tool

outil *m* **de recherche Gopher** *nom* Gopher

outil *m* **de sélection** *nom* selection tool

outil *m* **gomme** *f nom* eraser tool

outil *m* **Pipette** *nom* eye-dropper

outils *mpl nom* **1.** toolkit **2.** (*de programmation*) tools

outils *mpl* **complémentaires** *plural noun* assets

outils *mpl* **de diagnostic** *plural noun* diagnostics

outils *mpl* **de diagnostic d'erreurs** *nom* error diagnostics

outils *mpl* **de diagnostic du compilateur** *plural noun* compiler diagnostics ◇ **les outils de diagnostic de compilation bien conçus facilitent le débogage** thorough compiler diagnostics make debugging easy

outils *mpl* **de diagnostic d'un système** *nom* system diagnostics

ouvert *adjectif* open ◇ **boucle ouverte** open loop ◇ **interconnexion de systèmes ouverts (aux normes ISO)** Open Systems Interconnection (OSI) ◇ **vous ne pouvez accéder aux données que si le fichier est ouvert** you cannot access the data unless the file is open

ouverture *f nom* aperture

ouverture *f* **automatique de session** *nom* auto-login *ou* auto-logon

ouverture *f* **automatique d'une session** *nom* automatic log on

ouverture *f* **de session** *nom* **1.** logging in **2.** logging on ■ *verbe* to logon

ouverture *f* **en fondu** *nom* fade in

ouvrir (un fichier) *verbe* to open ◇ **vous ne pouvez pas accéder aux données avant d'avoir ouvert le fichier** you cannot access the data unless the file has been opened

OverDrive (*nom de marque*) OverDrive

overlay *m nom* overlay ◇ **segment superposable** *ou* **segment d'overlay** overlay segment

oxyde *m* **de fer** *nom* ferric oxide *ou* ferrite

P

packaging *m nom* packaging

page *f nom* **1.** leaf **2.** page ◇ **cette imprimante laser peut imprimer huit pages par minute** this laser printer can output eight pages per minute ◇ **cette imprimante matricielle n'est pas une imprimante page, elle n'imprime qu'une ligne à la fois** this dot-matrix printer is not a page printer, it only prints one line at a time ◇ **langage de description de page** page description language (PDL) ◇ **pages** *fpl* **d'un système vidéotex** magazine ◇ **(nombre de) pages par minute (ppm)** (*vitesse d'une imprimante*) pages per minute (ppm)

page *f* **(de mémoire)** *nom* page

page *f* **ASP** *nom* Active Server Page ■ *abrév* ASP

page *f* **d'accès** *nom* gateway page

page *f* **d'accueil** *nom* home page

page *f* **de codes** *nom* code page

page *f* **de destination** *nom* destination page

page *f* **de présentation** *nom* splash screen

page *f* **de routage** *nom* routing page

page *f* **d'index** *nom* index page

page *f* **d'ouverture** *nom* **1.** banner page **2.** start page

page *f* **index** *nom* index page

page *f* **mémoire** *nom* memory page

page *f* **mémoire sans modification** *nom* clean page

pages *fpl* **par minute** *nom* ppm

pages *fpl* **par minute (ppm)** *nom* pages per minute

pagination *f nom* **1.** pagination **2.** paging

pagination *f* **transparente** *nom* transparent paging

paginer *verbe vt* to page

paginer de nouveau *verbe* to repaginate

pair *m nom* peer

paire *f* **torsadée blindée** *abrév* STP

palette *f nom* paint

palette *f* **de couleurs** *nom* **1.** colour palette **2.** palette

palette *f* **de formes prédéfinies** *nom* pattern palette

palette *f* **graphique Paintbrush/Paint™** *nom* Paintbrush/Paint

palette *f* **système** *plural noun* system colours

panier *m nom* bit bucket

panne *f nom* **1.** crash **2.** fault **3.** system crash ◇ **tolérance** *f* **de panne** fault tolerance

panneau *m nom* panel ◇ **la prise est située sur le panneau arrière** the socket is on the back panel

panneau *m* **antérieur** *nom* front panel

panneau *m* **arrière** *nom* back panel

panneau *m* **avant** *nom* front panel

panneau *m* **de commande** *nom* front panel

panneau *m* **de commandes** *nom* control panel

panneau *m* **de commandes d'un système** *nom* system control panel

panneau *m* **de configuration** *nom* control panel

panneau *m* **de contrôle** *nom* control panel

panneau *m* **de raccordement** *nom* patch panel

panneau *m* **d'insonorisation** *nom* acoustic panel

panne *f* **de courant** *nom* power failure

panne *f* **d'électricité** *nom* power failure

panne *f* **de l'ordinateur** *nom* **1.** hard failure **2.** hardware failure

panne *f* **de protection générale** *nom* **1.** general protection fault **2.** GPF

panne *f* **désordonnée** *nom* disorderly close-down

panne *f* **fatale** *nom* catastrophic failure

panne *f* **par échauffement** *nom* burn out

papier *m* **à en-tête** *nom* preprinted stationery

papier *m* **autocopiant** *nom* NCR paper

papier-calque *m nom* detail paper

papier *m* **électrosensible** *nom* electrosensitive paper

papier *m* **en accordéon** *nom* concertina fold

papier *m* **(plié) en accordéon** *nom* fanfold

papier *m* **en continu** *nom* **1.** accordion fold *ou* accordion fanfold **2.** concertina fold **3.** continuous stationery **4.** fanfold **5.** listing paper

papier *m* **en éventail** *nom* concertina fold

papier *m* **(plié) en éventail** *nom* fanfold

papier *m* **(plié) en paravent** *nom* fanfold

papier *m* **listing** *nom* **1.** computer stationery **2.** listing paper

papier *m* **NCR** *nom* NCR paper

papier *m* **peint** *nom* (*fond d'écran du bureau Windows*) wallpaper

papier *m* **plié en accordéon** *nom* accordion fold *ou* accordion fanfold

papier *m* **plié en éventail** *nom* accordion fold *ou* accordion fanfold

papier *m* **plié en paravent** *nom* **1.** accordion fold *ou* accordion fanfold **2.** concertina fold

papier *m* **thermique** *nom* **1.** heat-sensitive paper **2.** thermal paper

papillotement *m nom* **1.** blinking **2.** flicker **3.** jitter ◇ **j'ai mal à la tête à force de regarder cet écran qui tremblote** looking at this screen jitter is giving me a headache

papilloter *verbe vi* to flicker

paquet *m nom* **1.** batch **2.** pack **3.** packet ◇ **assembleur** *or* **désassembleur (de paquets)** packet assembler/disassembler (PAD) ◇ **le terminal à distance est relié à un assembleur** *or* **désassembleur de paquets qui lui permet d'accéder à l'ordinateur hôte** the remote terminal is connected to a PAD device through which it accesses the host computer ◇ **mode de traitement par lots** *ou* **par paquets** (processing data in) batch mode ◇ **système de transmission par paquets** *ou* **PSS** packet switching system (PSS)

paquet *m* **de cartes perforées** *nom* deck

paquet *m* **IP** *nom* IP Datagram

paquet *m* **rapide** *nom* fast packet

paquet *m* **vide (d'information)** *nom* empty slot

par per ■ *preposition* via ◇ **les signaux nous ont été transmis par satellite** the signals have reached us via satellite ◇ **le téléchargement des données sur l'unité centrale peut se faire par l'intermédiaire d'un modem** you can download the data to the CPU via a modem

paragraphe *m nom* paragraph

paragraphe *m* **standard** *nom* template

parallèle *adjectif* parallel ◇ **entrée** *or* **sortie (en) parallèle** parallel input/output (PIO) ◇ **entrée parallèle** *or* **sortie parallèle** parallel input/parallel output (PIPO) ◇ **entrée parallèle** *or* **sortie série** parallel input/serial output (PISO) ◇ **exploitation** *f* **en parallèle** parallel running

paramétrable par l'utilisateur *adjectif* user-definable

paramétrable selon les besoins de l'utilisateur *adjectif* user-definable ◇ **la feuille de style comporte 125 symboles programmables selon les besoins de l'utilisateur** the style sheet contains 125 user-definable symbols

paramétrage *m nom* parameterisation *ou* parameterization

paramètre *m nom* parameter ◇ **la taille du tableau est fixée par ce paramètre** the size of the array is set with this parameter ◇ **le paramètre X définit le nombre de caractères contenus dans une ligne d'écran** the X parameter defines the number of characters displayed across a screen

paramètre *m* **physique** *nom* physical parameter

paramétrer *verbe vt* to set

par année *adverbe* per year

parasite *m nom* **1.** drop in **2.** line noise

parasites *(mpl) nom* noise

parcage *m* **de la tête** *nom* head park

pare-feu *m nom* firewall

parenthèse(s) *plural noun* round brackets

parité *nom* parity ◇ **sans (bit de) parité** no parity

> '...théoriquement, le bit de parité placé en fin des 7 ou 8 bits utiles du caractère, sert à contrôler la qualité de la transmission' [*Action PC*]

parité *f* **de colonnes** *nom* column parity

parité *f* **d'un bloc** *nom* block parity

parité *f* **impaire** *nom* odd parity *ou* odd parity check

par jour *phrase* per day

par l'intermédiaire de *preposition* via

parquer ◇ **en position parquée, la tête du disque ne peut pas ruiner les données si elle touche à la surface du disque** when parked, the disk head will not damage any data if it touches the disk surface ◇ **parquer la tête de lecture du disque** park

par semaine *adverbe* per week

partage *m nom* division

partage *m* **de données** *nom* data sharing

partage *m* **de fichier** *nom* file sharing

partage *m* **de ressources** *nom* resource sharing

partage *m* **des tâches** *nom* load sharing

partage *m* **de temps** *nom* time-sharing

partagiciel *m nom* shareware

participer à une discussion *verbe* to chat

particule *f* **de rayonnement alpha** *nom* alpha-particle

partie *f nom* part

partie *f* **fractionnaire** *nom* fractional part

partie *f* **mantisse** *f nom* fractional part

partition *f nom* **1.** boot partition **2.** boot sector **3.** partition ◇ **j'ai défini deux partitions sur ce disque dur désignées par C: et D:** I defined two partitions on this hard disk – called drive C: and D: ◇ **partition** *f* **privilégiée** (*avec niveau d'accès prioritaire*) privileged account

partition *f* **de traitement par lots** *nom* batch region

partition *f* **d'un disque dur** *nom* disk partition

partition *f* **privée** *nom* private address space

pas *m nom* **1.** pitch **2.** program step **3.** step

pas *m* **d'échantillonnage** *nom* **1.** sample interval **2.** sampling interval

passage *m nom* **1.** crossover **2.** pass

passage *m* **de paramètre** *nom* parameter passing

passage *m* **de tri** *nom* sorting pass

passage *m* **du jeton** *nom* token-passing

passage *m* **graduel** *nom* (*à un nouveau système*) staged change-over

passager *adjectif* transient

passe *f nom* pass

passe *f* **de balayage** *nom* raster scan

passer *verbe vti* to play back

passer d'un système à un autre *verbe* to change over

passerelle *f nom* gateway ◇ **nous avons utilisé une passerelle pour relier le réseau local au réseau étendu** we use a gateway to link the LAN to WAN

passerelle *nom* gateway ◇ **pour envoyer des messages par fax au lieu de les envoyer par le réseau, vous devez installer une passerelle fax** to send messages by fax instead of across the network, you'll need to install a fax gateway

'…et, surtout, il dispose de passerelles qui lui permettent d'être utilisé dans un environnement industriel' [*L'Evénement*]

passerelle *f* **active** *nom* active gateway

passerelle *f* **de courrier électronique** *nom* mail gateway

passerelle *f* **de télécopie** *nom* fax gateway

passerelle *f* **fax** *nom* fax gateway

passer en majuscule *verbe* to shift

pause *f* **accidentelle** *nom* holdup

pavé *m nom* **1.** button **2.** handle **3.** pad

pavé *m* **à effleurement** *nom* touch pad

pavé *m* **clavier** *nom* numeric pad

pavé *m* **numérique** *nom* **1.** keypad **2.** numeric keypad **3.** numeric pad ◇ **utilisez le pavé numérique pour saisir les chiffres** you can use the numeric keypad to enter the figures

pavé *m* **tactile** *nom* touch pad

paysage *m nom* landscape

PC *nom* **1.** PC **2.** personal computer

PC-97 *nom* PC-97

PC-98 *nom* PC-98

PC/AT *nom* (*ordinateur compatible IBM PC, avec processeur Intel 80286*) PC/AT

PC-DOS (version IBM de MS-DOS) *nom* PC-DOS

PC *m* **multimédia** *nom* multimedia PC

PC/XT *nom* (*ordinateur compatible IBM PC, avec processeur Intel 8086*) PC/XT

peindre *verbe vt* to paint

peinture *f nom* paint

pépin *m nom* glitch

perceptible à l'oreille *adjectif* audible

perdre de l'intensité *verbe* to fade

perforation *nom* (*de bande papier*) perforation ◇ **perforations** *fpl* **de marquage du bord d'un disque** disk index holes

perforation *f* **(de la ligne) 11** *nom* x punch

perforation *f* **(de ligne) 12** *nom* y punch

perforation *f* **d'entraînement** *nom* feed hole

perforation *f* **de positionnement** *nom* sectoring hole

perforation *f* **marginale** *nom* feed hole

perforation *f* **numérique** *nom* numeric punch

perforations *fpl* **d'entraînement** *plural noun* sprocket holes

perforations *fpl* **marginales** *plural noun* sprocket holes

perforation *f* **X** *nom* x punch

perforation *f* **Y** *nom* y punch

perforatrice *f nom* perforator

perforatrice *f* **à clavier** *nom* key punch

perforer *verbe vt* to punch

performance *f nom* performance ◇ **(de) haute performance** high performance ◇ **les bancs d'essais consistent à évaluer les performances de plusieurs systèmes ou périphériques en utilisant le même test standard** in benchmarking, the performances of several systems or devices are tested against a standard benchmark ◇ **pour juger de la performance du système** as a measure of the system's performance

période *f nom* **1.** latency **2.** period ◇ **pendant six ans** *ou* **sur une période de six ans** for a six-year period

période *f* **d'accès** *nom* access period

période *f* **de demande maximum** *nom* time of peak demand

période *f* **de référence** *nom* reference time

période *f* **de suppression horizontale** *nom* horizontal blanking period

période *f* **de travail** *nom* session ◇ **clé d'ouverture d'une session** session key

périodique *adjectif* periodic *ou* periodical

périodiquement *adverbe* periodically

périphérique *m nom* **1.** device **2.** external device **3.** input/output unit ■ *adjectif* peripheral ■ *nom* **1.** peripheral **2.** peripheral unit ◇ **adaptateur d'interface de périphérique** peripheral interface adapter (PIA) ◇ **les périphériques, tels que lecteurs de disquettes et imprimantes, qui permettent le transfert de données et sont asservis à un système (central), possèdent des circuits indépendants pour l'exécution de leurs opérations** peripherals such as disk drives or printers allow data transfer and are controlled by a system, but contain independent circuits for their operation ◇ **limité par la vitesse du périphérique** peripheral limited ◇ **proces-**

seur périphérique peripheral processing unit (PPU) ◇ **unité de commande** *ou* **unité de contrôle de périphérique** *ou* **contrôleur de périphérique** peripheral control unit (PCU)

périphérique *m* **d'entrée** *nom* input device

périphérique *m* **d'entrée/sortie** *nom* input/output device

périphérique *m* **lent** *nom* slow peripheral

périphérique *m* **rapide** *nom* fast peripheral

périphériques *mpl nom* peripheral equipment

périphériques *mpl* **reliés en grappe** *nom* cluster

permis *adjectif* legal ■ *nom* licence

permission *f* **d'accès** *nom* access permission

permutation *f nom* **1.** change over **2.** cyclic shift **3.** permutation **4.** ring shift **5.** task swapping ■ *abrév* TAT ◇ **ce code chiffré est très sûr puisqu'il comporte une clé avec un très grand nombre de permutations possibles** this cipher system is very secure since there are so many possible permutations for the key ◇ **permutation** *f* **(de programme)** swap

permutation *f nom* (*de programme*) swapping

permutation *f* **circulaire** *verbe* to cycle shift

permutation *f* **de bits** *nom* **1.** bit rotation **2.** rotate operation

permuter *verbe* **1.** *vt* to exchange **2.** *vt* to shift **3.** *vt* to swap

persistance *f nom* **1.** afterglow **2.** persistence

personnalisation *f nom* personalising *ou* personalizing

personnalisé *adjectif* custom-built

personnaliser *verbe* **1.** *vt* to customise *ou* to customize **2.** *vt* to personalise *ou* to personalize

personne *f* **autorisée** *nom* (*à utiliser un système*) authorised user *ou* authorized user

personnel *m* **informatique** *nom* liveware

perspective *f nom* perspective

perspective *f* **aérienne** *nom* aerial perspective

perspective *f* **fuyante** *nom* vanishing point perspective

perte *f nom* **1.** attenuation **2.** breakup **3.** drop out ◇ **avec un câble trop long, l'atténuation du signal provoquera des erreurs de données** if the cable is too long, the signal attenuation will start to cause data errors ◇ **perte** *f* **de transmission inexplicable** line gremlin

perte *f* **d'insertion** *nom* insertion loss

péta *préfixe* peta

péta-octet *m nom* petabyte

petit modèle *m nom* (*de mémoire Intel de 64Ko*) tiny model

petit programme *m nom* applet

phase *f nom* **1.** phase **2.** stage ◇ **nous n'en sommes qu'à la phase de rodage du système d'exploitation** we are in the first stage of running in the new computer system

phase *f* **de compilation** *nom* compile phase

phase *f* **de lecture d'une instruction** *nom* fetch phase

phase *f* **d'exécution** *nom* **1.** execute phase **2.** execution phase **3.** run phase **4.** target phase

phonème *m nom* phoneme ◇ **les mots 'too' et 'zoo' contiennent le phonème 'oo'** the phoneme 'oo' is present in the words too and zoo

phosphore *m nom* **1.** long persistence phosphor **2.** phosphor

photo *f nom* picture ◇ **voici la photo du nouveau modèle** this picture shows the new design

photo- *préfixe* photo-

PhotoCD™ *nom* PhotoCD

photocomposeuse *f nom* phototypesetter

photographie *f* **en demi-teinte** *nom* continuous tone

photographie *f* **numérisée** *nom* digitised photograph *ou* digitized photograph

photos *fpl plural noun* pix

pic *m nom* peak

PIC *nom* PIC

pico- *abrév* p ■ *préfixe* pico-

picoseconde *f nom* picosecond ■ *abrév* pS

PICT *nom* PICT

pièce *f* **détachée** *nom* spare part

pied *m nom* foot

pied *m* **de page** *nom* footer *ou* footing

piège *m nom* trap

pige *f* **d'alignement** *nom* alignment pin

pile *f nom* **1.** battery backup **2.** heap **3.** re-chargeable battery **4.** stack ◇ **pointeur de pile** stack pointer (SP)

pile *f* **binaire** *nom* heap

pile *f* **de données en mémoire** *nom* cellar

pile *f* **de mémoire virtuelle** *nom* virtual memory stack

pile *f* **de protocoles de communication** *nom* protocol stack

pile *f* **d'instructions d'un programme** *nom* program stack

pile *f* **en file d'attente** *nom* push-up list *ou* push-up stack

pile *f* **en mode FIFO** *nom* push-up list *ou* push-up stack

pile *f* **inversée** *nom* push-down list *ou* push-down stack

pillage *m* **(d'une base de données)** *nom* scavenging

piller une base de données *verbe* to browse

pilotage *m* **à distance** *nom* remote control

pilote *nom* **1.** control **2.** handler ■ *adjectif* pilot ■ *nom* plotter driver ◇ **la société a mis sur pied un projet-pilote pour évaluer le procédé de**

fabrication proposé the company set up a pilot project to see if the proposed manufacturing system was efficient ◇ **le code du gestionnaire de l'unité de disque se trouve dans la bibliothèque** the disk drive handler code is supplied in the library ◇ **l'usine-pilote a été construite pour tester le nouveau procédé de fabrication** the pilot factory has been built to test the new production process

'...les pilotes de périphériques ou 'device drivers' sont des programmes ajoutés au système d'exploitation (DOS) pour piloter des accessoires et des périphériques' [*L'Ordinateur Individuel*]

piloté, -ée par une souris *nom* mouse sensitivity

pilote *m* **de périphérique** *nom* **1.** device handler **2.** driver

pilote *m* **de périphériques** *nom* controller

pilote *m* **de souris** *nom* mouse driver

pilote *m* **d'imprimante** *nom* **1.** printer driver **2.** printer's controller

pinceau *m nom* brush ◇ **le logiciel de dessin vous permet de changer la largeur du pinceau (en pixels) et la couleur qu'il applique** the paint package lets you vary the width of the brush (in pixels) and the colour it produces

piratage *m nom* piracy

piratage *m* **de logiciel** *nom* software piracy

pirate *nom* pirate ◇ **la société tente d'amener les pirates de logiciel devant les tribunaux** the company is trying to take the software pirates to court

'Quatre ans de prison et deux millions de francs d'amende: c'est la peine maximale encourue par le pirate informatique' [*l'Ordinateur Individuel*]

pirate *m* **informatique** *nom* hacker

pirater *verbe vt* to pirate ◇ **il a utilisé une disquette piratée bon marché et a découvert que le programme contenait des bogues** he used a cheap pirated disk and found the program had bugs in it ◇ **les schémas du nouveau système ont été piratés** the designs for the new system were pirated ◇ **une bande piratée** a pirated tape

pirater un système *verbe* to hack

piste *f nom* track ◇ **(nombre de) pistes par pouce** tracks per inch (TPI)

piste *f* **couchée** *nom* magnetic stripe

piste *f* **d'adresses** *nom* address track

piste *f* **de données binaires** *nom* bit track

piste *f* **de parité** *nom* parity track

piste *f* **de référence** *nom* library track

piste *f* **d'horloge** *nom* clock track

piste *f* **d'un disque** *nom* disk track

piste *f* **magnétique (d'une carte magnétique)** *nom* magnetic strip

pistes *fpl* **par pouce** *abrév* TPI ■ *nom* tracks per inch

pitch *m nom* pitch

pixel *nom* **1.** pel **2.** picture element **3.** pixel

'...le pixel correspond à la plus petite unité d'information d'une image numérique' [*Science et Vie Micro*]

'...un pixel est le plus petit élément d'une image. En noir et blanc, c'est un simple point sur l'écran, défini par un bit. En couleur, chaque point correspond à trois faisceaux: un rouge, un vert, un bleu (R,G,B en anglais).' [*Mon PC Multimédia*]

pixélisé *adjectif* pixelated

PL/1 *nom* programming language/1

placage *m* **de texture** *nom* texture mapping

place *f nom* place

placé, -ée entre deux feuilles *adjectif* interleaved

place *f* **d'un chiffre** *nom* digit place *ou* digit position

placer *verbe vt* to queue

plage *f* **normale** *nom* normal range

plan *m nom* **1.** blueprint **2.** plan **3.** plane ◇ **jeu de plans** *ou* **les plans** plans ◇ **plan d'ensemble (d'un étage)** floor plan ◇ **plan des rues** *ou* **plan de la ville** street plan *ou* town plan

plan *m* **binaire** *nom* bit plane

plan *m* **de sauvegarde** *nom* backup plan

plan *m* **d'urgence** *nom* contingency plan

planification *f nom* planning ◇ **planification à courte échéance** short-term planning ◇ **planification à longue échéance** long-term planning

planification *f* **de la séquence d'exécution des tâches** *nom* job scheduling

planifier *verbe vt* to plan

planning *m nom* planning

plan *m* **schématique** *adjectif* schematic

plantage *m nom* **1.** crash **2.** disk crash **3.** lock up

plaque *f* **(présensibilisée) double face pour circuit imprimé** *nom* double-sided printed circuit board

plaque *f* **(présensibilisée) pour circuit imprimé** *nom* board ◇ **(carte de) circuit imprimé** printed circuit board (PCB) ◇ **tableau d'affichage électronique** *ou* **babillard électronique** *ou* **BBS** bulletin board system (BBS)

plaque *f* **présensibilisée pour circuit imprimé** *nom* circuit board

plateau ◇ **plateaux** *mpl* **de disque dur** disk pack

'...un disque dur comporte un ou plusieurs disques rigides empilés les uns sur les autres: les plateaux' [*l'Ordinateur Individuel*]

plateau *m* **(d'un disque dur)** *nom* platter

plate-forme *f nom* platform

plate-forme *f* **de collecte de données** *nom* data collection platform

plate-forme *f* **de matériel** *nom* hardware platform

plate-forme *f* **matérielle** *nom* hardware platform

platine *f* **de disques compacts** *nom* compact disc player

platine *f* **laser** *nom* compact disc player

platine *f* **magnétophone** *nom* tape deck

plein écran *adjectif* full-screen

plein écran *m nom* screenful

PL/M *nom* programming language for microprocessors

plume *f* **pour traceur** *nom* plotter pen

pochette *f nom* sleeve

poignée *f* **(de manipulation)** *nom* handle ◇ **dans ce programme de PAO, on sélectionne d'abord la boîte qu'on veut agrandir pour faire apparaître les poignées, puis on tire une des poignées pour modifier la taille de la boîte** to stretch the box in the DTP program, select it once to display the handles then drag one handle to change its shape

poignée *f* **de sélection** *nom* selection handle

poinçon ◇ **poinçon** *m* **de perforation pour bandes papier** paper tape punch; tape punch

poinçon *m nom* punch

poinçon *m* **de perforation** *nom* perforator

point *nom* **1.** entry point **2.** *US* period ◇ **point** *m* **de contrôle dans un programme de traçage** trace trap ◇ **point** *m* **de début d'enregistrement d'une bande magnétique** tape load-point ◇ **points** *mpl* **de phosphore** phosphor dots ◇ **points** *mpl* **par pouce** dots per inch; d.p.i. ◇ **un moniteur monochrome format A4 avec une définition de 300 points par pouce** a 300 d.p.i. black and white A4 monitor ◇ **un scanner d'image avec définition de 300 ppp** a 300 dpi image scanner

> '...sur des réseaux privés point à point, le codeur-décodeur d'images fonctionne dans une plage de débit comprise entre 9600bps et 384Kbps' [*Informatique & Bureautique (Suisse)*]

point *m* **adressable** *nom* addressable point

point *m* **chaud** *nom* hotspot

point *m* **d'accès** *nom* **1.** access point **2.** port

point *m* **d'accès sans fil** *nom* wireless access point

point *m* **d'accrochage** *nom* hook

point *m* **d'arrêt** *nom* breakpoint ◇ **programmer les points d'arrêt** to set breakpoints

point *m* **d'arrêt variable** *nom* (*de déroulement d'un programme*) regional breakpoint

point *m* **de branchement** *nom* branchpoint

point *m* **de connexion** *nom* terminal ◇ **bloc de raccordement** terminal block

point *m* **de contrôle** *nom* **1.** access point **2.** check point

point *m* **de départ** *nom* starting point

point *m* **d'entrée dans un système** *nom* **1.** backdoor **2.** trapdoor

point *m* **de présence** *nom* point of presence

point *m* **de rentrée** *nom* re-entry point

point *m* **de reprise** *nom* **1.** check point **2.** rerun point

point *m* **de sortie** *nom* exit point

point *m* **de transition** *nom* transition point

point *m* **de vente** *nom* point-of-sale

point de vente *m* **électronique** *nom* **1.** electronic point-of-sale **2.** EPOS

point *m* **de vidage** *nom* dump point

point *m* **de vie** *nom* hit point

point *m* **d'image** *nom* available point

point *m* **d'insertion** *nom* **1.** cursor **2.** insertion point

point *m* **d'insertion (de code)** *nom* hook

point *m* **d'interrogation** *nom* question mark

point *m* **d'interruption** *nom* breakpoint

pointe *f nom* **1.** peak **2.** stylus ◇ **les pointes et les creux** (*d'une onde*) peaks and troughs

pointe *f* **de tension** *nom* **1.** spike **2.** surge **3.** voltage transient

pointeur *nom* pointer ◇ **incrémenter le pointeur jusqu'à l'adresse (d'instruction) suivante** increment the contents of the pointer to the address of the next instruction ◇ **la PAO sur ordinateur individuel est facilitée par l'emploi de la souris et du pointeur** desktop publishing on a PC is greatly helped by the use of a pointer and mouse ◇ **pointeur** *m* **qu'on déplace avec la souris** arrow pointer

pointeur *m* **avant** *nom* forward pointer

pointeur *m* **contrôlé par la souris** *nom* mouse pointer

pointeur *m* **de pile** *abrév* SP ■ *nom* stack pointer

pointeur *m* **de position de données** *nom* data pointer

pointeur *m* **de souris** *nom* mouse pointer

pointeur *m* **d'instruction** *nom* instruction pointer

pointeur *m* **relatif** *nom* relative pointing device

pointeur *m* **retour** *nom* back pointer

point *m* **indicateur de couleur** *nom* bullet

point-virgule *m nom* semicolon

polaire *adjectif* polar ◇ **diagramme polaire** *ou* **en coordonnées polaires** polar diagram ◇ **orbite polaire** polar orbit

polarisé *adjectif* polarised

polarité *f nom* polarity

polarité *f* **électrique** *nom* electrical polarity

polarité *f* **inversée** *nom* reverse polarity

polarité *f* **magnétique** *nom* magnetic polarity

policé *adjectif* well-behaved

police *f* **de caractères** *nom* **1.** character set **2.** face **3.** font **4.** typeface ◇ **police** *f* **de caractères par défaut utilisée pour le corps d'un texte**

body type ◇ **police** *f* **de caractères reconnaissable par lecture optique** optical font ◇ **police** *f* **de caractères reconnaissable par lecture optique** *ou* **par lecteur optique** OCR font ◇ **police** *f* **de caractères utilisable par un terminal** terminal character set

police *f* **de caractères à espacements uniformes** *nom* monospaced font

police *f* **de caractères bitmap** *nom* bitmapped font

police *f* **de caractères de base** *nom* base font

police *f* **de caractères disponible** *nom* alternate character set

police *f* **de caractères intégrée** *nom* built-in font

police *f* **de caractères par défaut** *nom* base font

police *f* **de caractères téléchargeable** *nom* downloadable font

police *f* **de caractères vectorielle** *nom* dynamically redefinable character set

police *f* **d'écran** *nom* screen font ◇ **la police d'écran est affichée à 72 ppp sur le moniteur plutôt qu'à 300 ppp comme pour l'imprimante laser** the screen font is displayed at 72dpi on a monitor, rather than printed at 300dpi on this laser printer

polices *fpl* **de caractères** *plural noun* resident fonts

pollution *f* **électronique** *nom* electronic smog

polygone *m nom* polygon

polyphonie *f nom* polyphony

pompage *m nom* **1.** race **2.** thrashing

pondération *f nom* weighting

pont *m nom* **1.** bridge **2.** bridgeware **3.** bridging product

pont *m* **de routage** *nom* brouter ◇ **le pont de routage permet un routage dynamique entre deux réseaux locaux** the brouter provides dynamic routing and can bridge two local area networks

pont *m* **local** *nom* local bridge

port *nom* port ◇ **port** *m* **parallèle LPT1** LPT1 ◇ **port** *m* **partagé** port sharing

portabilité *f nom* portability

portabilité *f* **d'une formule** *nom* formula portability

portable *m nom* **1.** laptop *ou* laptop computer **2.** portable ■ *adjectif* portable

portable *m* **ultraléger** *nom* microwriter

portail *m nom* portal

portail *m nom* web portal

portail *m* **vertical** *nom* **1.** vertical portal **2.** VORTAL

portatif *adjectif* portable

port *m* **Centronics** *nom* Centronics port

port *m* **d'accès** *nom* dataport

port *m* **d'accès asynchrone** *nom* asynchronous port ◇ **l'utilisation de ports asynchrones ne demande pas un matériel spécialisé** when asynchronous ports are used no special hardware is required

port *m* **de communication** *nom* communications port

port *m* **de sortie** *nom* output port

porte *f nom* **1.** equivalence gate **2.** except gate **3.** EXNOR gate **4.** EXOR gate **5.** gate **6.** logic gate

porte *f* **analogique** *nom* analog gate

porte *f* **de disjonction** *nom* NEQ gate

porte *f* **d'identité** *nom* identity gate *ou* identity element

Porte-documents *m nom* Briefcase utility

portée *f nom* **1.** range **2.** scope

porte *f* **ET** *nom* **1.** AND circuit *ou* AND element **2.** AND gate **3.** coincidence gate *ou* coincidence circuit *ou* coincidence element

porte-monnaie *m* **électronique** *nom* ewallet *ou* e-wallet

porte *f* **NON** *nom* NOT gate

porte *f* **NON-ET** *nom* NAND gate

porte *f* **NON-OU** *nom* NOR gate

port *m* **(d') entrée** *nom* input port

port *m* **(d') entrée/sortie** *nom* **1.** input/output port **2.** I/O port

porte *f* **OU** *nom* OR gate

porte *f* **OU exclusif** *nom* **1.** anticoincidence circuit *ou* anticoincidence function **2.** nonequivalence gate

porteuse *f* **T** *nom* T carrier

port *m* **(d')imprimante** *nom* printer port

port *m* **(de) jeu** *nom* game port

port *m* **parallèle amélioré** *nom* **1.** enhanced parallel port **2.** EPP

port *m* **pour périphérique** *nom* user port

portrait *adjectif* portrait

port *m* **série** *nom* serial port

port *m* **zoom vidéo** *nom* **1.** zoomed video port **2.** ZV Port

pose *f* **d'un enduit** *nom* deposition

positif *adjectif* **1.** affirmative **2.** positive

position *f nom* place

position *f* **binaire** *nom* bit position

position *f* **de départ** *nom* home

position *f* **du signe** *nom* sign position

position *f* **initiale** *nom* home

positionnel *adjectif* positional

positionnement *m* **absolu** *nom* absolute positioning

positionnement *m* **de la tête** *nom* head positioning

positionner *verbe vt* to align

positionner sur repères *verbe* to register

POSIX *nom* portable operating system interface

postage *m nom* posting

poste *nom* station ◇ **poste** *m* **de travail ouvert** open access

poste *m* **à distance** *nom* remote station

poste *m* **autonome** *adjectif* stand-alone *ou* standalone ■ *nom* stand-alone *ou* standalone

poste *m* **de contrôle mixte** *nom* combined station

poste *m* **de travail** *nom* **1.** console **2.** My Computer **3.** operating console **4.** terminal **5.** workstation ◇ **accro de l'informatique** *ou* **fana d'informatique** *ou* **infomaniaque** terminal junky (TJ) ◇ **la console comporte un périphérique d'entrée, soit un clavier, et un périphérique de sortie, soit une imprimante ou un écran** the console consists of input device such as a keyboard, and an output device such as a printer or CRT ◇ **le gestionnaire de système utilise le terminal principal pour relancer le système** the system manager uses the master terminal to restart the system ◇ **le nouveau terminal intelligent comporte un éditeur de texte** the new intelligent terminal has a built-in text editor ◇ **le système comprend un réseau de cinq postes de travail reliés en anneau** the system includes five workstations linked together in a ring network ◇ **mon fils est devenu un véritable infomaniaque** my son has turned into a real terminal junky ◇ **sept postes de travail se partagent une mémoire d'archivage d'une capacité de 1200 Mo** the archive storage has a total capacity of 1200 MB between seven workstations ◇ **tous les messages sont transmis à tous les terminaux puisqu'aucun d'eux ne possède un adressage protégé** all the messages go to all the terminals since none are addressable terminals

poste *m* **de travail multifonction** *nom* multifunction workstation

poste *m* **d'interrogation** *nom* inquiry station

poste *f* **électronique** *nom* mail

poste *m* **éloigné** *nom* remote station

poste *m* **individuel** *adjectif* stand-alone *ou* standalone

poste *m* **informatique de télétransmission** *nom* data station

post-processeur *m nom* (*microprocesseur*) postprocessor

postproduction *f nom* post production

PostScript *m* **encapsulé** *nom* encapsulated PostScript ■ *abrév* EPS

poubelle *f* **à bits** *nom* bit bucket

pouce ◇ **pouces** *mpl* **par seconde (pps)** inches-per-second

pouce(s)/seconde *nom* **1.** inches-per-second **2.** ips

pouces *mpl* **par seconde** *nom* ips

pour *preposition* per ◇ **le taux d'erreur est tombé à douze pour cent** the error rate has fallen to twelve per hundred ◇ **le taux s'élève à vingt-cinq pour mille** the rate is twenty-five per thousand

pour cent *adjectif, adverbe* per cent ◇ **cinquante pour cent de rien est toujours rien** fifty per cent of nothing is still nothing ◇ **dix pour cent** 10 per cent (10%)

pouvoir *m* **de résolution** *nom* resolving power

PowerBook™ (*laptop*) PowerBook

PowerCD (*nom de marque*) PowerCD

PowerPC (*nom de marque*) PowerPC

ppp *abrév* d.p.i. *ou* dpi ◇ **certaines imprimantes (à) laser sont dotées d'une haute définition de 400 ppp** *ou* **400 points par pouce** some laser printers offer high resolution printing: 400 dpi

pratique *adjectif* hands on

pré- *préfixe* pre-

préallocation *f nom* pre-allocation

préamplificateur *m nom* pre-amplifier

précéder *verbe vt* to precede

précis *adjectif* precise ◇ **l'horloge atomique indiquera l'heure précise du début du processus** the atomic clock will give the precise time of starting the process

précision *f nom* **1.** accuracy **2.** precision ◇ **haute précision** high specification

précision *f* **d'un nombre** *nom* precision of a number

préconditionner *verbe vt* to precondition

prédéfini *adjectif* predefined

prédicat *m nom* predicate

prédictif *adjectif* predictive

prééditer *verbe vt* to pre-edit

préfiltration *f nom* pre-filtering

préfixe *m nom* prefix

préformaté *adjectif* preformatted ◇ **disquette préformatée** a preformatted disk

prélever ◇ **prélever un jeton** (*dans un réseau Token-Ring*) capture

première génération *f nom* first generation

premier emplacement *m* **capable** *nom* first fit

première position *nom* load point

premier plan *m nom* foreground

premier terme *m* **d'une addition** *nom* augend

prénumérisation *f nom* prescan

préparation *f* **des données** *nom* data preparation

préparation *f* **d'un index à l'aide d'un ordinateur** *nom* computer indexing

préparer *verbe vt* to arm

préparer un index *verbe* to index ◇ **le livre a été envoyé à l'extérieur pour la préparation de l'index** the book was sent out for indexing ◇ **l'index de ce livre a été très mal fait** the book has been badly indexed

préprocesseur *m nom* preprocessor

préprogrammé *adjectif* preprogrammed

préprogrammer *verbe vt* to preprogram

prérégler *verbe vt* to preset

présélectionner *verbe vt* to preset

présentation-aperçu *f nom* **1.** previewer **2.** print preview

présentation *f* **de page assistée par ordinateur** *plural noun* desktop presentations

présentation *f* **graphique** *plural noun* presentation graphics ■ *nom* (*de nombres ou données*) visualisation *ou* visualization

présentation *f* **graphique sous forme de colonnes** *nom* columnar working

présentation *f* **graphique sous forme de histogrammes** *nom* columnar working

présentation *f* **isométrique** *nom* isometric view

Presentation Manager™ *nom* Presentation Manager

présenter sous forme de mosaïque *verbe* to tessellate

presse-papiers *m nom* clipboard ◇ **copiez le texte dans le presse-papiers, puis collez-le dans le nouveau document** copy the text to the clipboard, then paste it back into a new document

Presse-papiers™ *m nom* clipboard

presseur *m nom* clapper

presseur *m* **de bande** *nom* capstan

prêt *adjectif* ready ◇ **le voyant vert allumé signifie que le système est prêt à accepter le programme suivant** the green light indicates the system is ready for another program

prêt à émettre *nom* clear to send

prêt à fonctionner *adjectif* configured-in

prétraiter des données *verbe* to preprocess

préventif *adjectif* preventative *ou* preventive

prévention *f* **d'erreurs** *nom* error trapping

prévision *f nom* projection

prévisualisation *f nom* page preview

prévisualiser *verbe vt* to preview

prévoir *verbe vt* to project

primaire *adjectif* primary ◇ **couleurs fondamentales** *ou* **primaires** primary colours ◇ **groupe primaire** primary group

primitive *f* **graphique** *nom* display element

principal *adjectif* main ◇ **faisceau principal** main beam ◇ **porteuse principale** main beam ◇ **tableau de distribution** *ou* **répartiteur principal** main distributing frame

priorité *f nom* **1.** precedence **2.** priority

priorité *f* **absolue** *nom* absolute priority

priorité *f* **d'un appareil** *nom* device priority

priorité *f* **d'une tâche** *nom* job priority

priorité *f* **d'un périphérique** *nom* device priority

priorités *fpl* **d'interruption** *plural noun* interrupt priorities

prise *f nom* socket

prise *f* **de courant** *nom* outlet

prise *f* **de force d'insertion nulle** *nom* **1.** zero insertion force socket **2.** ZIF socket

prise *f* **de terre** *nom* **1.** earth **2.** ground ◇ **tous les fils non rattachés doivent être mis à la terre** *ou* **à la masse** all loose wires should be tied to earth

prise *f* **femelle** *nom* female socket

prise *f* **femelle de connecteur** *nom* connector receptacle

prise *f* **mâle de connecteur** *nom* connector plug

prise *f* **péritélévision** *nom* SCART connector

privatif *adjectif* private ◇ **autocommutateur privatif (raccordé au réseau public)** private branch exchange (PBX) ◇ **autocommutateur privatif (raccordé au réseau public) (PABX)** private automatic branch exchange (PABX) ◇ **central téléphonique manuel privatif (raccordé au secteur public)** private manual branch exchange (PMBX) ◇ **central téléphonique privatif (non raccordé au réseau public)** private automatic exchange (PAX) ◇ **port privatif** *ou* **réservé** private dial port ◇ **système téléphonique privatif** private telephone system

privé *adjectif* private ◇ **ligne privée** *ou* **réservée** *ou* **privative** private line

privilège *m nom* privilege

privilège *m* **d'accès** *nom* access privilege

prix *m* **forfait** *m nom* flat rate

prix *m* **forfaitaire** *nom* flat rate

problème *m nom* glitch

procédé *m nom* process

procédé *m* **aléatoire** *nom* random process

procédé *m* **d'assemblage SMT** *nom* **1.** SMT **2.** surface-mount technology

procédé *m* **de liaison et incorporation d'objets** *nom* object linking and embedding

procédé *m* **de traitement d'image** *nom* document image processing

procédé *f* **OLE** *nom* OLE

procédé *m* **OLE** *nom* object linking and embedding 2

procédé *m* **OLE 2** *nom* object linking and embedding 2

procédé *m* **OLE-2** *nom* OLE-2

procédé *m* **planar** *adjectif* (*de production de circuits intégrés*) planar

procédure *nom* **1.** procedure **2.** process ◇ **cette procédure qui sert à classer les fichiers par**

ordre alphabétique peut être sélectionnée depuis le programme principal par la commande SORT this procedure sorts all the files into alphabetic order, you can call it from the main program by the instruction SORT ◇ **la procédure est expliquée dans le manuel d'utilisation** the procedure is given in the manual ◇ **procédure** *f* **de remise en marche après incident** (*d'un système*) recovery procedure ◇ **procédure** *f* **remplacer globalement** global exchange

procédure *f* **de commande** *nom* operator procedure

procédure *f* **de commande à haut niveau** *abrév* **1.** HDLC **2.** HLDLC

procédure *f* **de contrôle d'acheminement** *plural noun* routing overheads ◇ **la vitesse de transmission d'informations est beaucoup moins grande une fois qu'on tient compte du protocole d'acheminement** the information transfer rate is very much less once all routing overheads have been accommodated

procédure *f* **de deuxième génération** *nom* child process *ou* child program

procédure *f* **de file d'attente** *nom* queue discipline

procédure *f* **de sauvegarde** *nom* backup procedure

procédure *f* **de secours** *nom* fall back

procédure *f* **de traitement des erreurs** *nom* **1.** error handling **2.** error management

procédure *f* **d'interpréteur de commandes** *nom* shell script

procédure *f* **fille** *nom* child process *ou* child program

procédure *f* **récursive** *nom* recursive call

processeur *nom* **1.** graphics processor **2.** machine **3.** processor ◇ **mot d'état d'un processeur** processor status word (PSW) ◇ **processeur 32 bits développé par Intel Pentium** (*de Intel Pentium*) Pentium ◇ **processeur** *m* **auxiliaire relié au processeur central** attached processor ◇ **processeur** *m* **de traitement de texte à logique partagée** shared logic text processor ◇ **processeur** *m* **de traitement par lots** batch processor ◇ **processeur** *m* **de traitement par paquets** batch processor ◇ **processeur frontal** front-end processor (FEP) ◇ **saisie au clavier contrôlée par processeur** processor-controlled keying

processeur *m* **à architecture RISC** *nom* **1.** reduced instruction set computer **2.** RISC

processeur *m* **à jeu d'instruction réduit** *nom* RISC

processeur *m* **à jeu d'instructions réduit** *nom* reduced instruction set computer

processeur *m* **à mots variables** *nom* **1.** byte machine **2.** character machine

processeur *m* **asservi** *nom* slave processor

processeur *m* **auxiliaire** *nom* **1.** auxiliary processor **2.** coprocessor **3.** support chip

processeur *m* **auxiliaire spécialisé** *nom* back-end processor

processeur *m* **avec mémoire associative** *nom* associative processor

processeur *m* **à virgule flottante** *nom* **1.** floating point processor **2.** floating point unit ◇ **le processeur à virgule flottante accélère la vitesse de traitement des logiciels graphiques** the floating point processor speeds up the processing of the graphics software

processeur *m* **central** *nom* CPU

processeur *m* **de code commande** *nom* order code processor

processeur *m* **de codes de commande** *nom* OCP

processeur *m* **de console** *nom* **1.** CCP **2.** command console processor

processeur *m* **d'écran** *nom* display processor

processeur *m* **de fichier de commandes** *nom* command file processor

processeur *m* **de fond** *nom* back-end processor

processeur *m* **de langage** *nom* language processor

processeur *m* **d'entrée/sortie** *nom* input/output processor ■ *abrév* IOP

processeur *m* **de réseau** *nom* **1.** communications network processor **2.** network processor

processeur *m* **d'image tramée** *abrév* RIP

processeur *m* **d'instruction** *nom* instruction processor

processeur *m* **d'interface** *nom* interface processor

processeur *m* **double** *nom* dual processor

processeur *m* **en mode caractère** *nom* character machine

processeur *m* **frontal** *nom* **1.** FEP **2.** front-end processor

processeur *m* **K6™** K6

processeur *m* **mathématique pour calcul ultra-rapide** *nom* number cruncher

processeur *m* **périphérique** *nom* peripheral processing unit

processeur *m* **réparti** *nom* distributed processor

processeur *m* **scalaire** *nom* scalar processor

processeurs *mpl* **en tandem** *plural noun* tandem processors

processeur *m* **V20** *nom* V20

processeur *m* **V30** *nom* V30

processeur *m* **vectoriel** *nom* **1.** array processor **2.** vector processor ◇ **le processeur vectoriel permet de faire pivoter le tableau qui contient l'image d'écran à l'aide d'une seule**

commande the array processor allows the array that contains the screen image to be rotated with one simple command

processeur *m* **Z80** *nom* Z80

processus *m nom* process ◇ **le processus compte cinq étapes** there are five stages in the process

processus *m* **coopératif** *nom* cooperative processing

processus *m* **itératif** *nom* iterative process

productif *adjectif* productive

production *f nom* **1.** generation **2.** origination **3.** production ◇ **cycle de production** production run

production *f* **record** *nom* peak output

productique *f* **intégrée** *nom* **1.** CIM **2.** computer-integrated manufacturing

produire *verbe* **1.** *vt* to generate **2.** *vt* to originate **3.** *vt* to produce

produire un courant induit *verbe* to induce

produire une induction *verbe* to induce

produire un label *verbe* to label

produit *m nom* product

produit *m* **de base** *nom* basic product

produit *m* **fini** *nom* **1.** end product **2.** final product

produits *mpl plural noun* consumables

produits *mpl* **fictifs** *nom* vapourware

profil *m nom* **1.** outline **2.** profile

PROFS™ (*système de messagerie électronique*) PROFS

progiciel *nom* **1.** packaged software **2.** software package **3.** software system ◇ **progiciel** *m* **adapté aux besoins de l'utilisateur** middleware

progiciel *m* **d'application** *nom* **1.** application package **2.** applications package

progiciel *m* **personnalisé** *nom* middleware

progiciel *m* **sur mesure** *nom* middleware

programmable *adjectif* **1.** programmable **2.** user-definable ◇ **circuit logique programmable** *ou* **logique câblée programmable** programmable logic array (PLA) *ou* programmable logic device (PLD) ◇ **mémoire morte programmable** *ou* **(mémoire) PROM** programmable read only memory (PROM) ◇ **mémoire programmable** *ou* **(mémoire) PROM** programmable memory (PROM)

programmable par l'utilisateur *adjectif* user-selectable

programmateur *m nom* programmer

programmateur *m* **de mémoire morte** *nom* burner

programmateur *m* **de ROM** *nom* burner

programmation *nom* **1.** coding **2.** programming ◇ **programmation** *f* **avancée des programmes de communications** advanced program to program communications

programmation *f* **automatique** *nom* automatic programming

programmation *f* **avancée des programmes de communications (APPC)** *nom* APPC

programmation *f* **bien conçue** *nom* elegant programming

programmation *f* **d'appels** *nom* call scheduling

programmation *f* **de champ** *nom* field programming

programmation *f* **défensive** *nom* defensive computing

programmation *f* **d'une PROM** *nom* programming

programmation *f* **élégante** *nom* elegant programming

programmation *f* **en langage machine** *nom* machine language programming

programmation *f* **en langage universel** *nom* universal programming

programmation *f* **linéaire** *nom* linear programming

programmation *f* **modulaire** *nom* **1.** modularisation *ou* modularization **2.** modular programming

programmation *f* **neuro-linguistique** *abrév* NLP

programmation *f* **orientée objet** *nom* object-oriented programming

programmation *f* **structurée** *nom* **1.** structured programming **2.** top down programming

programmation *f* **symbolique** *nom* symbolic programming

programmation *f* **visuelle** *nom* visual programming

programmatique *adjectif* programmatic

programme *nom* **1.** kludge *ou* kluge **2.** program ◇ **fichier PIF (fichier d'information d'un programme, sous MS-Windows)** program information file (PIF) ◇ **j'ai omis d'inclure une instruction importante dans le programme de sorte que le programme s'est planté et tous les fichiers ont été effacés contenus sur le disque** I forgot to insert an important instruction which caused a program to crash, erasing all the files on the disk! ◇ **langage de conception de programme** program design language (PDL) ◇ **pour lancer le programme, cliquez deux fois sur l'icône du programme** to run the program, double-click on the program icon ◇ **programme d'assemblage** assembly program ◇ **programme** *m* **d'édition de lettres types** mailmerge ◇ **programme** *m* **de récupération de fichier après une interruption** abend recovery program ◇ **si vous quittez votre feuille de calcul sans la sauvegarder, il vous sera impossible de la récupérer** once you have abandoned your spreadsheet, you cannot retrieve it again ◇ **spéci-**

fications d'un programme program specifications ◇ **technique d'évaluation et de révision de programme** program evaluation and review technique (PERT)

programmé, -ée d'avance *adjectif* preprogrammed

programme *m* **absolu** *nom* absolute program

programme *m* **actif** *nom* active program

programme *m* **activé par commande** *nom* command-driven program

programme *m* **agenda Schedule+™** *nom* **1.** (*Microsoft Windows 95*) schedule **2.** (*Microsoft Windows 95*) Schedule+

programme *m* **agent intelligent** *nom* agent

programme *m* **antivirus** *nom* anti-virus program

programme *m* **assembleur pour macro langage** *nom* macro assembler *ou* macro assembly program

programme *m* **à usage multiple** *nom* general purpose program

programme *m* **auto-relogeable** *nom* self-relocating program

programme *m* **avec documentation en ligne** *nom* self-documenting program

programme *m* **canon** *nom* (*qui tourne sans erreur du premier coup*) blue-ribbon program

programme *m* **convertisseur** *nom* conversion program

programme *m* **d'allocation** *nom* allocation routine

programme *m* **d'assemblage** *nom* **1.** assembler **2.** assembler program

programme *m* **de bibliothèque** *nom* library program ◇ **la fonction racine carrée se trouve déjà dans le programme de bibliothèque** the square root function is already in the library program

programme *m* **débogué** *nom* debugged program

programme *m* **de commande** *nom* master control program

programme *m* **de contrôle** *nom* **1.** checking program **2.** monitor program

programme *m* **de contrôle d'entrée/sortie** *nom* input/output control program

programme *m* **de contrôle de réseau** *nom* network control program

programme *m* **de contrôle de tâche** *nom* job control program

programme *m* **de conversion** *nom* conversion program

programme *m* **de diagnostic** *nom* maintenance routine

programme *m* **d'édition de texte** *nom* text editor ◇ **cet éditeur de texte ne peut lire que les fichiers de moins de 64Ko** the text editor will only read files smaller than 64Kbytes long

programme *m* **de fusionnement de données** *nom* collator

programme *m* **de localisation de panne** *nom* fault location program

programme *m* **de maintenance** *nom* **1.** housekeeping routine **2.** maintenance routine **3.** service program

programme *m* **de prétraitement** *nom* preprocessor

programme *m* **de remise en état automatique** *nom* automatic recovery program

programme *m* **de restauration** *nom* automatic recovery program

programme *m* **de retraitement** *nom* postprocessor

programme *m* **de test** *nom* exerciser

programme *m* **de traçage** *nom* trace program

programme *m* **de traduction** *nom* translator *ou* translator program

programme *m* **de vérification orthographique** *nom* spellchecker *ou* spelling checker ◇ **on va optimiser le programme en ajoutant un traitement de texte et un vérificateur d'orthographe** the program will be upgraded with a word-processor and a spelling checker

programme *m* **déverminé** *nom* debugged program

programme *m* **d'impression désynchronisé** *nom* spooling device

programme *m* **d'insertion directe** *nom* direct-insert routine

programme *m* **d'installation** *nom* **1.** install program **2.** setup program

programme *m* **d'origine** *nom* source program

programme *m* **d' utilisateur** *nom* user's program

programme *m* **écrit par l'utilisateur** *nom* user's program

programme *m* **en chapelet** *nom* thread

programme *m* **en langage machine** *nom* absolute program

programme *m* **en logique câblée** *nom* hardwired program

programme *m* **en mémoire centrale** *nom* core program

programme *m* **enregistré** *nom* stored program

programme *m* **Eudora** (*logiciel*) Eudora

programme *m* **extensible** *nom* open-ended program

programme *m* **informatique** *nom* computer program

programme *m* **interprétatif** *nom* **1.** interpretative program **2.** shell

programme *m* **itératif** *nom* **1.** looping program **2.** loop program

programme *m* **linéaire** *nom* **1.** in-line program **2.** linear program

programme *m* **mémorisé** *nom* stored program

programme *m* **mis en mémoire** *nom* stored program

programme *m* **moniteur** *nom* monitor program

programme *m* **multifonction** *nom* general purpose program

programme *m* **multiphase** *nom* multiphase program

programme *m* **multiposte** *nom* multiuser program

programme *m* **multiutilisateur** *nom* multiuser program

programme *m* **non prioritaire** *nom* background program

programme *m* **objet** *nom* **1.** object program **2.** target program

programme *m* **ouvert** *nom* open-ended program

programme *m* **parent** *nom* parent program

programme *m* **portable** *nom* **1.** portable programs **2.** portable software

programme *m* **prêt à être exécuté** *nom* executable form

programme Print Manager™ (*à Microsoft Windows NT*) Print Manager

programme *m* **prioritaire** *nom* **1.** foreground program **2.** high priority program

programmer *verbe* **1.** *vt* to code **2.** *vt* to set ◇ **nous avons programmé** *ou* **fixé la marge de droite à 80 caractères** we set the right-hand margin at 80 characters ◇ **nous avons programmé** *ou* **fixé la marge de droite pour donner une ligne de 80 caractères** we set the right-hand margin at 80 characters

programmer d'avance *verbe* to preset ◇ **on avait programmé d'avance les nouveaux paramètres de page de l'imprimante** the printer was preset with new page parameters

programmer de nouveau *verbe* to reprogram

programme *m* **ré-entrant** *nom* re-entrant program *ou* re-entrant code *ou* re-entrant routine

programme *m* **relogeable** *nom* relocatable program

programme *m* **résident** *nom* **1.** internally stored program **2.** RAM resident program **3.** terminate and stay resident software **4.** terminate and stay resident program ◇ **en appuyant sur les touches Ctrl-F5, vous activez le programme résident et ouvrez l'agenda de la journée** when you hit Ctrl-F5, you will activate the RAM resident program and it will display your day's diary

programme résident *abrév* TSR

programmer les points d'arrêt *verbe* to set breakpoints

programmer une PROM *verbe* **1.** to blast **2.** to blow

programme *m* **shell** *nom* shell

programme *m* **souche** *nom* stub

programme *m* **source** *nom* source program

programmes *mpl* **sur ROM** *nom* romware

programme *m* **superviseur** *nom* **1.** executive program **2.** supervisor **3.** supervisor program **4.** supervisory program

programme *m* **système** *nom* systems program

programme *m* **translatable** *nom* relocatable program ◇ **le système d'exploitation peut charger et exécuter un programme translatable** *ou* **relogeable sans distinction de la zone d'origine** the operating system can load and run a relocatable program from any area of memory

programme *m* **TSR** *nom* **1.** terminate and stay resident software **2.** terminate and stay resident program

programmeur *m* *nom* **1.** computer programmer **2.** programmer ◇ **analyste-programmeur, -euse** analyst/programmer *ou* programmer/analyst ◇ **le programmeur n'a pas encore terminé le nouveau logiciel** the programmer is still working on the new software

programmeur *m* **d'application** *nom* applications programmer

programmeur *m* **de PROM** *nom* PROM blaster *ou* PROM burner *ou* PROM programmer

programmeur *m* **de systèmes** *nom* systems programmer

programme *m* **(d') utilisateur** *nom* user program

programme *m* **utilitaire de maintenance** *nom* service program

programme *m* **utilitaire de service** *nom* application service element

programme *m* **vedette** *nom* star program

projecteur *m* **multimédia** *nom* data projector

projection *f* *nom* projection

projet *m* *nom* **1.** plan **2.** project ◇ **il projette maintenant d'informatiser le service des ventes** his latest project is computerizing the sales team

projeter *verbe* **1.** *vt* to plan **2.** *vt* to replay

promouvoir *verbe vt* to plug

propagation *f* **d'erreur** *nom* error propagation

propre ◇ **propre à la machine** *ou* **sur mesure** *ou* **de constructeur** *ou* **adapté à l'ordinateur** machine-intimate

propriété *m* **du fichier** *plural noun* file property

propriétés *f* *nom* properties

protection *f nom* file security ◇ **protection** *f* **contre le survoltage** *or* **la surtension** overvoltage protection ◇ **protection** *f* **de la mémoire** memory protect

protection *f* **(par mot de passe)** *nom* interlock

protection *f* **contre la copie** *nom* copy protect

protection *f* **de bloc** *nom* block protection

protection *f* **de cellule** *nom* cell protection

protection de fichiers *f nom* file locking

protection *f* **de page** *nom* page protection

protection *f* **des données** *nom* data protection

protection *f* **des limites** *nom* boundary protection

protection *f* **par mot de passe** *nom* password protection

protégé contre tout arrêt *adjectif* crash-protected ◇ **si vous vous servez d'un disque protégé contre tout arrêt intempestif, vous ne perdrez jamais vos données** if the disk is crash-protected, you will never lose your data

protéger *verbe vt* to shield

protéger contre la copie *verbe* to copy protect ◇ **le programme n'est pas protégé (contre la copie)** the program is not copy protected ◇ **toutes les disquettes sont munies d'un système de protection** *ou* **tous les disques sont protégés contre la copie** all disks are copy protected

protéger contre l'écriture *verbe* (*une disquette, un disque*) to write protect

protocole *nom* protocol ◇ **langage WML (de description de pages WAP)** WAP markup language (WML) ◇ **norme WAP 1.1** WAP 1.1 ◇ **protocole** *m* **CSLIP** (*de compression de données*) CSLIP ◇ **protocole** *m* **d'échange d'informations entre CPU et périphérique** CPU handshaking ◇ **protocole** *m* **de communication** (*entre deux postes*) full handshaking ◇ **protocole** *m* **de contrôle par signal d'arrêt** stop and wait protocol ◇ **protocole** *m* **de gestion de fichier Apple** Apple filing protocol ◇ **protocole** *m* **de gestion de fichier AppleTalk** AppleTalk Filing Protocol ◇ **protocole** *m* **de validation d'échange d'informations** handshake ◇ **protocole** *m* **de validation de transfert de données** handshake ◇ **protocole** *m* **SNMP (de gestion de réseau)** SNMP ◇ **protocole** *m* **standard de contrôle de liaisons** basic mode link control ◇ **protocole** *m* **TCP** *or* **IP (de communication de réseau)** transmission control protocol/interface program ◇ **protocole** *m* **WAP (protocole mondial de communication)** Wireless Application Protocol ◇ **protocole** *m* **X 25** (*de transmission de données par paquets*) X.25 ◇ **protocole** *m* **XMODEM** (*de transmission de fichiers*) XMODEM ◇ **protocole** *m* **XMODEM CRC** XMODEM CRC ◇ **protocole** *m* **XON** *or* **XOFF (de transmission asynchrone)** software flow control ◇ **WMLScript** WAP markup language script (WMLScript)

protocole *m* **AFP** *nom* AFP ■ **1.** Apple filing protocol **2.** AppleTalk Filing Protocol

protocole *m* **à niveau octet** *nom* byte-orientated protocol

protocole *m* **APPC** *nom* advanced program to program communications

protocole *m* **ARP** *nom* **1.** address resolution protocol **2.** ARP

protocole *m* **BGP** *nom* BGP

protocole *m* **caractère par caractère** *nom* byte-orientated protocol

protocole *m* **CLNP** *abrév* CLNP ■ *nom* connectionless network protocol

protocole *m* **CMIP** *nom* **1.** CMIP **2.** common management information protocol

protocole *m* **d'accès à la liaison** *nom* link access protocol

protocole *m* **d'accès de télécommunications** *nom* **1.** basic telecommunications access method **2.** BTAM

protocole *m* **de communication** *nom* **1.** communications protocol **2.** link control procedure **3.** link control protocol

protocole *m* **de communication de réseau Microcom (MNP)** *nom* MNP

protocole *m* **de connexion des modems** *nom* LAP-M

protocole *m* **de contrôle** *nom* audit trail

protocole *m* **de contrôle de protocole** *nom* **1.** TCP **2.** transmission control protocol

protocole *m* **de gestion de fichier AppleTalk** *nom* AFP

protocole *m* **de messagerie IMAP** *nom* **1.** IMAP **2.** Internet message access protocol

protocole *m* **d'émulation telnet** *nom* telnet

protocole *m* **(de communication) de réseau** *nom* network protocol

protocole *m* **de résolution d'adresse** *nom* address resolution protocol

protocole *m* **de routage d'un message** *plural noun* routing overheads

protocole *m* **de routage IS-IS** *nom* IS-IS

protocole *m* **des accès** *nom* **1.** access log **2.** server access log

protocole *m* **de traçage** *nom* audit trail

protocole *m* **de transfert de fichiers** *nom* **1.** file transfer protocol **2.** FTP

protocole *m* **de transmission** *nom* LCP

protocole *m* **de transmission CSMA-CD** *nom* **1.** carrier sense multiple access-collision detection **2.** CSMA-CD

protocole *m* **de transmission en temps réel** *nom* real time transport protocol ■ *abrév* RTP

protocole *m* **de vérification** *nom* audit trail
protocole *m* **d'interfaçage** *nom* high-level data link control
protocole *m* **FTP** *nom* **1.** file transfer protocol **2.** FTP
protocole *m* **HTTP** *nom* **1.** HTTP **2.** hypertext transfer protocol
protocole *m* **ICMP** *nom* **1.** ICMP **2.** Internet control message protocol
protocole *m* **IGMP** *nom* **1.** IGMP **2.** Internet group management protocol
protocole *m* **Internet de multidiffusion** *nom* IP multicast
protocole interréseau (de Novell) (*de Novell*) Internetwork Packet Exchange
protocole *m* **IP** *nom* Internet protocol
protocole *m* **Ipv6** *nom* IPng
protocole *m* **IPX** (*de Novell*) Internetwork Packet Exchange
protocole *m* **LDAP** *nom* **1.** LDAP **2.** lightweight directory access protocol
protocole *m* **Mime** *nom* **1.** MIME **2.** multimedia Internet mail extensions **3.** multipurpose Internet mail extensions
protocole *m* **NetBEUI** *nom* NetBIOS extended user interface
protocole *m* **NetBIOS** *nom* Network Basic Input Output System
protocole *m* **NNTP** *nom* **1.** network news transfer protocol **2.** NNTP
protocole *m* **OSPF** *nom* **1.** open shortest path first **2.** OSPF
protocole *m* **PICS** *nom* PICS
protocole *m* **POP** *nom* post office protocol
protocole *m* **PPP** *nom* **1.** point to point protocol **2.** PPP
protocole *m* **PPTP** *nom* **1.** point-to-point tunneling protocol **2.** POP **3.** PPTP
protocole *m* **RIP** *abrév* RIP ■ *nom* routing information protocol
protocole *m* **SDLC** *nom* **1.** (*de transmission de données en mode synchrone*) SDLC **2.** (*de transmission de données en mode synchrone*) synchronous data link control
protocole *m* **S-HTTP** *nom* **1.** secure hypertext transfer protocol **2.** S-HTTP
protocole *m* **SLIP** *nom* **1.** serial line Internet protocol **2.** SLIP
protocole *m* **SMTP** *nom* **1.** simple mail transfer protocol **2.** (*de messagerie électronique*) SMTP
protocole *m* **SNMP** *nom* simple network management protocol
protocole *m* **SSL** *nom* **1.** secure sockets layer **2.** SSL
protocole *m* **TCP de transmission** *nom* **1.** TCP **2.** transmission control protocol
protocole *m* **TCP/IP (de communication de réseau)** *nom* TCP/IP
protocole *m* **TFTP** *nom* **1.** TFTP **2.** trivial file transfer protocol
protocole *m* **UDP** *nom* **1.** UDP **2.** user datagram protocol
protocole *m* **ViSCA** *nom* ViSCA
protocole *m* **WAP** *nom* WAP
protocole *m* **XMODEM 1K** *nom* XMODEM 1K
protocole *m* **XNS (pour réseau)** (*développé par Xerox*) Xerox Network System
protocole *m* **XON/XOFF** *nom* XON/XOFF
prototypage *m nom* prototyping
prototype *m nom* prototype
provenir (de) *verbe* to derive
PS/2™ (*modèle de PC IBM avec bus d'extension MCA*) PS/2
pseudo- *préfixe* pseudo-
pseudocode *m nom* **1.** P-code **2.** pseudo-code
pseudo-code *m* **binaire** *nom* bytecode
pseudo-instruction *f nom* **1.** P-code **2.** pseudo-instruction
pseudo-opération *f nom* pseudo-operation
pseudostatique *adjectif* pseudo-static
publication *f* **assistée par ordinateur** *nom* **1.** desktop publishing **2.** DTP **3.** electronic publishing
publicité *f* **non sollicitée** *nom* spam ◇ **filtre (pour bloquer les messages non sollicités)** anti-spam
publier *verbe vt* to publish ◇ **cette maison d'édition publie principalement des livres de référence** the company specializes in publishing reference books ◇ **l'institut a publié une liste des statistiques de vente de plusieurs ordinateurs personnels** the institute has published a list of sales figures for different home computers
publier une nouvelle version *verbe* to release
publipostage *m nom* mailmerge
puce *nom* **1.** chip **2.** microchip **3.** microprocessor chip **4.** silicon chip ◇ **ils font des recherches sur les puces de diagnostic destinées au contrôle des ordinateurs équipés de processeurs** they are carrying out research on diagnostic chips to test computers that contain processors

> '...bourrer les armes de puces électroniques ne suffit pas; il faut aussi des programmes pour les faire fonctionner' [*L'Express*]

puce *f* **à ADN** *nom* biochip
puce *f* **antiviolence** *nom* Clipper chip
puce *f* **de diagnostic** *nom* diagnostic chip ◇ **ils font des recherches sur les puces de diagnostic destinées au contrôle des ordinateurs équipés de processeurs** they are carrying out research on diagnostic chips to test computers that contain processors

puce *f* **de synthèse vocale** *nom* speech chip
puce *f* **géante** *nom* jumbo chip
puce *f* **mémoire** *nom* memory chip
puce *f* **RAM** *nom* RAM chip
puissance *f nom* power
puissance *f* **de calcul** *nom* computing power
puissance *f* **d'un ordinateur** *nom* computer power
puissance *f* **fractionnaire** *nom* root

puissance *f* **maximale disponible** *nom* available power

puissance *f* **réelle disponible** *nom* available power

puits *m nom* sink

purger *verbe vt* to purge ◇ **chaque mois, je purge le disque de tous les messages périmés** each month, I purge the disk of all the old email messages

Q

quadr- *préfixe* quadr-
quadrat *m adjectif* quad
quadruple densité *f nom* quad density
quadruplex *m nom* quadruplex
qualifier négativement *verbe* to negate ◇ **la valeur négative** *ou* **l'inverse de 23,4 est –23,4** if you negate 23.4 the result is –23.4
qualité *nom* **1.** data reliability **2.** reliability
'...doté d'une tête à 18 aiguilles, cette imprimante matricielle atteint la vitesse de 600cps (caractères par seconde) en qualité brouillon, et 150cps en qualité courrier' [*Action PC*]
qualité *f* **broadcast** *nom* broadcast quality
qualité *f* **brouillon** *nom* **1.** draft printing **2.** draft quality
qualité *f* **d'archivage** *nom* archival quality
qualité *f* **de service** *nom* quality of service
qualité *m* **de service** *abrév* QOS
qualité *f* **de transmission** *nom* broadcast quality
qualité *f* **d'impression** *nom* print quality ◇ **une imprimante graphique avec une résolution de 600 dpi fournit une bonne qualité d'impression** a desktop printer with a resolution of 600dpi provides good print quality
qualité *f* **d'impression (d'une imprimante)** *nom* printer quality
qualité *f* **listing** *nom* draft quality
qualité *f* **photo** *adjectif* photorealistic
qualité *f* **quasi-courrier** *abrév* NLQ
qualité *f* **vocale** *nom* speech quality
Quantel Quantel
quantifiable *adjectif* quantifiable
quantificateur *m nom* **1.** quantifier **2.** quantiser *ou* quantizer
quantification *f nom* quantisation *ou* quantization
quantification *f* **d'amplitude** *nom* amplitude quantisation
quantification *f* **de niveau quatre** *nom* quaternary level quantization
quantifier *verbe* **1.** *vt* to quantify **2.** *vt* to quantise *ou* to quantize ◇ **il est impossible de quantifier l'effet du nouveau système informatique sur notre production** it is impossible to quantify the effect of the new computer system on our production
quantité *f nom* quantity ◇ **il a acheté une grande quantité de pièces détachées** he bought a large quantity of spare parts
quantité *f* **d'information** *nom* information content
quantum *m nom* quantum
quartet *m nom* nibble
quasi- *préfixe* quasi-
quaternaire *adjectif* quaternary
quatre adresses *f* **plus une** *nom* four-plus-one address
qui a des connaissances en informatique *adjectif* computer-literate
QuickDraw™ (*nom de marque*) QuickDraw
QuickTime™ (*nom de marque*) QuickTime
qui donne satisfaction *adjectif* reliable
qui ne change pas *adjectif* static
qui n'évolue pas *adjectif* static
quintet *m nom* quintet
qui peut être lu *adjectif* readable ◇ **(commande** *ou* **donnée) en langage machine** *ou* **directement exploitable** machine-readable ◇ **le texte électronique est converti en image vidéo qui peut être lue par l'imprimante** the electronic page is converted to a printer-readable video image
qui peut être maîtrisé *adjectif* manageable ◇ **les données devraient être réparties en fichiers plus courts et plus faciles à utiliser** data should be split into manageable files
qui peut être masqué *adjectif* maskable ◇ **interruption obligatoire** *ou* **qui ne peut être invalidée** *ou* **qui ne peut être masquée** non-maskable interrupt (NMI)
qui peut être programmé *adjectif* selectable ◇ **les vitesses (de réception et de transmission) de ce modem sont réglables** this modem has user-selectable baud rates
qui peut être redéfini *adjectif* redefinable
qui peut être sélectionné *adjectif* selectable
qui s'écrit avec un trait d'union *adjectif* hyphenated
quitter *verbe* **1.** *vt* to abandon **2.** *vt* to exit **3.** *vt* to quit ◇ **n'oubliez pas de sauvegarder votre texte avant de quitter le système** do not forget to save your text before you quit the system ◇ **pour ajouter des en-têtes, il faut quitter ce**

programme et entrer dans un autre you have to exit to another editing system to add headlines

qui va contre les règles de la syntaxe *adjectif* illegal

quotient *m nom* quotient

R

raccourci *m nom* shortcut

raccourci *m* **clavier** *nom* **1.** accelerator key **2.** menu shortcut

raccroché *adverbe* on-hook

racine *f nom* root ◇ **la racine carrée de 25 est 5** the square root of 25 is 5 ◇ **sous DOS, le répertoire racine du disque C: est désigné par C:** in DOS, the root directory on drive C: is called C:\

racine *f* **carrée** *nom* square root

racine *f* **de discussion** *nom* comp

rack *m nom* rack ◇ **(carte) montée dans un rack** *ou* **dans une baie avec guide-cartes** rack-mounted

radar *m* **infrarouge** *nom* IrDA

radiateur *m* **à ailette(s)** *nom* heat-sink

radiodiffuser *verbe vt* to broadcast ◇ **il a diffusé les dernières informations à la radio** *ou* **via le réseau étendu** he broadcast the latest news over the radio *ou* over the WAN ◇ **station de radiodiffusion** *ou* **de télédiffusion** broadcasting station

radiofréquence *f nom* **1.** radio frequency **2.** RF *ou* R/F

rafale *f nom* burst ◇ **rafale de signaux couleur** colour burst

rafale *f* **d'erreurs** *nom* error burst

rafraîchir *verbe vt* to refresh ◇ **signal de rafraîchissement de la mémoire** memory refresh signal

rafraîchir l'écran *verbe* to screen refresh

rafraîchir une connexion *verbe* to retrain

RAM ◇ **rafraîchissement** *m* **de la mémoire RAM** RAM refresh

RAM *f* **auto-entretenue** *nom* self-refreshing RAM

RAM *f* **auto-rafraîchie** *nom* self-refreshing RAM

RAM *f* **dynamique** *abrév* DRAM ■ *nom* **1.** dynamic RAM **2.** dynamic random access memory

RAM *f* **non rafraîchie** *nom* SRAM

RAM *f* **statique** *nom* SRAM

RAM *f* **vidéo** *nom* video memory

rang *m nom* row

rangement *m* **en mémoire tampon** *nom* buffering

ranger *verbe vt* to plant

ranger en mémoire *verbe* to store

ranger une donnée en mémoire *verbe* to write ◇ **disque optique WORM (permettant une seule écriture et des lectures multiples)** write once, read many times memory (WORM) ◇ **le temps d'accès est le temps requis pour consulter une donnée en mémoire ou pour ranger une donnée en mémoire** access time is the time taken to read from or write to a location in memory

rapide *adjectif* high-speed ◇ **duplicateur rapide** *ou* **grande vitesse** high-speed duplicator ◇ **interface série version rapide** *ou* **interface HSSI** high-speed serial interface (HSSI)

rappel *m nom* **1.** backspace **2.** callback ■ *abrév* CB ■ *nom* recall

rappeler *verbe* **1.** *vt* to call up **2.** *vt* to quote **3.** *vt* to recall ◇ **dès réception d'une entrée, on appelle la première fonction** after an input is received, the first function is called up ◇ **rappeler de mémoire centrale en mémoire auxiliaire** to roll out ◇ **rappelez le fichier précédent à l'écran** call up the previous file ◇ **veuillez rappeler ce numéro de référence dans votre réponse** in reply please quote this number

rapport *nom* ratio ◇ **le rapport 10 sur 5 est (égal à) 2:1** the ratio of 10 to 5 is 2:1

'…le laboratoire de la FNAC a réalisé des mesures et obtenu un rapport signal/bruit de 76 à 83dB, selon les appareils' [*Science et Vie*]

rapport *m* **de compression** *nom* compression ratio

rapport *m* **de discrimination** *nom* one to zero ratio

rapport *m* **longueur/largeur** *nom* (*d'un pixel*) aspect ratio

rapport *m* **signal/bruit** *nom* signal to noise ratio

rapport *m* **signal sur bruit** *abrév* S/N

rapport *m* **un à zéro** *nom* one to zero ratio

rassembler *verbe* **1.** *vt* to accumulate **2.** *vt* to collect **3.** *vt* to gather ◇ **nous avons rassemblé progressivement un impressionnant fichier d'adresses** we have gradually accumulated a large databank of names and addresses

raster *m nom* raster ◇ **raster (RIP)** *ou* **processeur graphique à balayage de trame** *ou* **processeur d'image matricielle** raster image processor (RIP)

raster *m* **(RIP)** *nom* raster image processor ◇ **une page électronique peut être convertie en image vidéo imprimable à l'aide d'un raster** *ou* **d'un processeur d'image matricielle** an electronic page can be converted to a printer-readable video image by an on-board raster image processor

ratio *m nom* **1.** file activity ratio **2.** ratio

rayer *verbe vt* to delete

rayon *m nom* beam ◇ **le laser émet un mince rayon lumineux** the laser produces a thin beam of light ◇ **l'imprimante utilise un rayon laser pour obtenir une haute résolution graphique** a beam of laser light is used in this printer to produce high-resolution graphics

rayonnement *m nom* beam

rayonnement *m* **ultraviolet** *nom* **1.** ultraviolet light **2.** UV light

rayons *mpl* **ultraviolets** *nom* **1.** ultraviolet light **2.** UV light

rayure *f nom* scratch ◇ **cette rayure rend la lecture du disque impossible** this scratch makes the disk unreadable

RD *abrév* RMDIR

réacheminement *m nom* redirection

réacheminement *m* **d'entrée/sortie** *nom* I/O redirection

réacheminer *verbe* **1.** *vt* to forward **2.** *vt* to redirect **3.** *vt* to re-route ◇ **le dispositif de transfert d'appel sert à réacheminer les appels** the call diverter re-routes a call

réaction *f nom* feedback ◇ **boucle de feedback** *ou* **de réaction** *ou* **de rétroaction** feedback loop

réadressable *adjectif* (*relogeable*) relocatable

réadressage *m nom* relocation

réagir *verbe vi* to react ◇ **réagir à quelque chose** to react to something

Real (*nom de marque*) Real

RealAudio (*nom de marque*) RealAudio

réalisateur *m nom* producer

réaliser un mauvais alignement *verbe* to skew ◇ **cette page est mal alignée** this page is badly skewed

réalité *f* **virtuelle** *nom* **1.** virtual reality **2.** VR ◇ **ce nouveau logiciel de réalité virtuelle peut créer une pièce en trois dimensions dans laquelle vous pouvez vous déplacer** this new virtual reality software can create a three-dimensional room that you can navigate around

RealNames RealNames

réassemblage *m nom* folding

rebond *m nom* (*de contact, de touche*) contact bounce

rebond *m* **d'une touche de clavier** *nom* **1.** bounce **2.** keyboard contact bounce

rebut *m nom* junk ◇ **satellites hors d'usage** *ou* **de rebut (qui tournent dans l'espace)** space junk

recadrage *m nom* reshape handle

recalcul *m* **automatique** *nom* automatic recalculation

recalcul *m* **en arrière-plan** *nom* background recalculation

recalcul *m* **en tâche de fond** *nom* background recalculation

récent *adjectif* new

récepteur *m nom* receiver ■ *abrév* RX ◇ **récepteur radio** radio receiver ◇ **votre signal a été capté très clairement par le récepteur radio** the radio receiver picked up your signal very strongly

récepteur-performateur *m* **transmetteur** *nom* reperforator transmitter

réception ◇ **avis** *m* **de réception de copie discrète** blind copy receipt

recevoir *verbe* **1.** *vt* to obtain **2.** *vt* to receive ■ *abrév vt* RX

rechargement *m* **d'un programme** *nom* **1.** (*après incident*) roll back **2.** (*après incident*) rollback

recharger *verbe* **1.** *vt* to reload **2.** *vt* to replenish ◇ **nous avons rechargé le programme après la panne** we reloaded the program after the crash

recherche *f nom* **1.** block retrieval **2.** hunting **3.** research **4.** retrieval **5.** search ◇ **la société a dépensé des millions de dollars pour la recherche et le développement** the company has spent millions of dollars on R & D ◇ **recherche dichotomique** chop ◇ **recherche et développement** research and development (R & D) ◇ **recherche** *f* **par coupe binaire** chop ◇ **recherche par dichotomie** chop ◇ **recherche** *f* **qui distingue les majuscules des minuscules** *ou* **qui tient compte des majuscules** case sensitive search

recherché *adjectif* sophisticated

recherche *f* **arrière** *nom* backwards search

recherche *f* **binaire** *nom* binary look-up

recherche *f* **booléenne** *nom* Boolean search

recherche *f* **dans tout le texte** *nom* full-text search

recherche *f* **d'erreurs** *nom* error trapping

recherche *f* **de zone** *nom* area search

recherche *f* **dichotomique** *nom* **1.** binary chop **2.** binary search **3.** dichotomising search *ou* dichotomizing search

recherche *f* **documentaire** *nom* **1.** data retrieval **2.** information retrieval ■ *abrév* IR

recherche *f* **documentaire en ligne** *nom* online information retrieval

recherche *f* **en amont** *nom* backwards search

recherche *f* **en chaîne** *nom* chaining search

recherche *f* **et développement** *nom* **1.** R & D **2.** research and development

recherche *f* **et extraction de texte** *nom* text retrieval

recherche *f* **exhaustive** *nom* exhaustive search

recherche *f* **globale** *nom* full-text search

recherche *f* **par coupe binaire** *nom* binary search

recherche *f* **par dichotomie** *nom* **1.** binary chop **2.** binary search **3.** dichotomising search *ou* dichotomizing search

recherche *f* **par mots-clés** *nom* disjunctive search

rechercher *verbe vt* to search

Rechercher (*de Windows 95*) Find

recherche *f* **rétrospective** *nom* retrospective search

recherche *f* **sélective** *nom* area search

recherche *f* **séquentielle** *nom* **1.** linear search **2.** sequential search

recherche *f* **très poussée** *nom* exhaustive search

recommencer *verbe vt* to rerun

recomposer *verbe vt* to rekey

reconfiguration *f nom* reconfiguration

reconfigurer *verbe vt* to reconfigure ◇ **avec ce programme, il est possible de reconfigurer le système selon nos besoins** this program allows us to reconfigure the system to our own requirements ◇ **j'ai reconfiguré la structure des champs du fichier** I reconfigured the field structure in the file

reconnaissable *adjectif* recognisable *ou* recognizable

reconnaissance *nom* **1.** recognition **2.** sense ◇ **reconnaissance** *f* **automatique du débit d'une ligne** auto-baud scanning

reconnaissance *f* **automatique des numéros d'appels** *nom* automatic number identification

reconnaissance *f* **de caractères magnétiques** *nom* **1.** magnetic ink character recognition **2.** MICR

reconnaissance *f* **d'écriture** *nom* handwriting recognition

reconnaissance *f* **de formes** *nom* pattern recognition

reconnaissance *f* **de la parole** *nom* **1.** speech recognition **2.** voice recognition

reconnaissance *f* **optique de caractères** *nom* **1.** character recognition **2.** OCR **3.** OMR **4.** optical character recognition

reconnaissance *f* **optique de marques** *nom* optical mark recognition

reconnaissance *f* **optique de signes** *nom* optical mark recognition

reconnaissance *f* **optique de symboles** *nom* optical mark recognition

reconnaissance *f* **vocale** *nom* **1.** speech recognition **2.** voice recognition

reconnaître *verbe* **1.** *vt* to recognise *ou* to recognize **2.** *vt* to sense ◇ **le programme a pu détecter l'état du connecteur** the condition of the switch was sensed by the program

reconstituer *verbe vt* to reconstitute

reconstitution *f* **de procédure** *nom* backward recovery

recopier *adjectif* master ◇ **ces diapos et photos sont les supports intermédiaires qui doivent être recopiés sur le vidéodisque** those slides and photographs are the intermediate materials to be mastered onto the video disk

recouvrement *m nom* overlap

recouvrir *verbe vt* to overlap

recréer *verbe vt* to regenerate

reculer d'un pas *verbe* to step

récupération *f nom* **1.** document recovery **2.** recovery ◇ **les fichiers perdus peuvent être récupérés à l'aide d'une procédure de récupération de données** the recovery of lost files can be carried out using a recovery procedure

récupération *f* **de fichier à rebours** *nom* backward recovery

récupérer *verbe* **1.** *vt* to backout **2.** *vti* to recover **3.** *vti* to restore **4.** *vti* to retrieve **5.** *vt* to undelete ◇ **par bonheur, nous avons pu récupérer ce fichier** thankfully we could undelete the files ◇ **récupérer et transférer** (*des données dans un registre*) to collect transfer

récursivité *f nom* recursive routine

recycler *verbe vt* to retrain

redéfinir *verbe vt* to redefine ◇ **nous avons redéfini les premiers paramètres** we redefined the initial parameters ◇ **redéfinir la fonction d'une touche** *ou* **reprogrammer une touche** to redefine a key

redémarrage *m nom* restart

redémarrer *verbe vi* to restart

redémarrer à chaud *verbe* to warmboot

redondance *f nom* redundancy

redondant *adjectif* redundant ◇ **les bits de parité des données reçues sont redondants et peuvent être supprimés** the parity bits on the received data are redundant and can be removed

réduction *f* **des performances** *nom* degradation

réduire *verbe* **1.** *vt* to cut **2.** *vt* to minimise *ou* to minimize ◇ **on a demandé à l'auteur de réduire son manuscrit à 250 pages** the author was asked to cut his manuscript to 250 pages

réduire l'échelle *verbe* **1.** to downsize **2.** to scale down ◇ **la réduction d'échelle est très efficace sur le plan des coûts et donne plus de puissance de traitement à l'utilisateur** downsizing is more cost effective and gives more processing power to the end-user

réduire l'espace entre deux caractères *verbe* to kern ◇ **nous avons réduit l'espace entre le T et le o pour les rapprocher** we have kerned 'T' and 'o' so they are closer together

réduire une fenêtre en icône *verbe* to minimise *ou* to minimize

refaire depuis le début *verbe* to redo from start

refaire la pagination *verbe* to repaginate

référençage *m* **d'entrée/sortie** *nom* input/output referencing

référence *f nom* **1.** benchmark **2.** reference ◇ **niveau de référence** reference level

référence *f* **circulaire** *nom* circular reference

référence *f* **explicite** *nom* explicit reference

référencer *verbe vt* to reference

réflectance *f nom* reflectance

réflectance *f* **d'arrière-plan** *nom* background reflectance

réflectance *f* **de fond** *nom* background reflectance

reflets *mpl nom* glare

réflexion *f nom* glare ◇ **la réflexion sur l'écran me fatigue la vue** the glare from the screen makes my eyes hurt

reformatage *m nom* reformatting ◇ **toutes les données contenues sur un disque sont détruites par le reformatage** reformatting destroys all the data on a disk

reformater *verbe vt* to reformat ◇ **évitez de reformater votre disque dur à moins qu'il n'y ait aucune autre solution** do not reformat your hard disk unless you can't do anything else

réfraction *f nom* refraction

régénérateur *m nom* regenerator

régénérer *verbe* **1.** *vt* to refresh **2.** *vt* to regenerate

région *f nom* region ◇ **région** *f* **de la Californie où l'on trouve une forte concentration de sociétés productrices de semi-conducteurs** Silicon Valley

registre *nom* **1.** microprogram counter **2.** register ◇ **accumulateur** *ou* **registre externe** external register ◇ **dans ce micro-ordinateur, la taille du registre de données est de huit bits, alors que celle d'un registre d'adresse est de 16 bits** in this small micro, the data register is eight bits wide, an address register is sixteen bits wide ◇ **registre d'adresse d'instruction** instruction address register (IAR) ◇ **registre d'adresse en mémoire** memory address register (MAR) ◇ **registre** *m* **de contrôle de séquence** sequence register ◇ **registre** *m* **de pagination à accès direct** direct page register ◇ **registre** *m* **des codes condition** (*du processeur central*) condition code register ◇ **registre des mots d'état** program status word register (PSW register) ◇ **registre d'index** index register ◇ **registre d'instruction à suivre** *ou* **à exécuter** sequence control register (SCR)

registre *m* **à bits circulants** *nom* circulating register

registre *m* **à décalage** *nom* shift register

registre *m* **à décalage circulaire** *nom* circulating register

registre *m* **arithmétique** *nom* arithmetic register

registre *m* **auxiliaire de routage d'adresse** *nom* B-line counter

registre *m* **banalisé** *nom* **1.** general register **2.** gpr

registre *m* **compteur** *nom* **1.** program address counter **2.** program counter

registre *m* **couplé** *nom* adjunct register

registre *m* **d'addition** *nom* add register

registre *m* **d'adresse** *nom* **1.** address register **2.** base register

registre *m* **d'adresse courante** *abrév* CAR ■ *nom* current address register

registre *m* **d'adresse de base** *nom* base address register

registre *m* **d'adresse d'instruction** *nom* **1.** IAR **2.** instruction address register

registre *m* **d'adresse en mémoire** *nom* **1.** memory address register **2.** SAR **3.** store address register

registre *m* **d'adresse indexé** *nom* B register

registre *m* **d'adresses de limites** *nom* boundary register

registre *m* **d'affichage** *nom* display register

registre *m* **de base** *nom* base register

registre *m* **de code d'opération** *nom* op register

registre *m* **de commande** *nom* command register

registre *m* **de commande de contrôle** *nom* control register

registre *m* **de contrôle** *nom* check register

registre *m* **de contrôle de séquence** *nom* sequence control register *ou* sequence counter

registre *m* **de décalage** *nom* shift register

registre *m* **de données** *nom* data register

registre *m* **de la prochaine instruction** *nom* next instruction register

registre *m* **de masque** *nom* mask register

registre *m* **de mémoire associative** *nom* associative storage register

registre *m* **de mémoire tampon** *nom* **1.** MBR **2.** memory buffer register

registre *m* **d'entrée** *nom* input register

registre *m* **d'entrée/sortie** *nom* input/output register

registre *m* **des données en mémoire** *nom* **1.** MDR **2.** memory data register **3.** store data register

registre *m* **des drapeaux** *nom* flag register

registre *m* **des entrées** *nom* receiver register

registre *m* **de sortie** *nom* output register

registre *m* **des témoins** *nom* flag register

registre *m* **d'état** *nom* status register

registre *m* **de texte** *nom* text register

registre *m* **d'index** *nom* index register ■ *abrév* IR

registre *m* **d'instruction** *nom* **1.** command register **2.** instruction register ■ *abrév* IR ■ *nom* program register

registre *m* **d'instruction à exécuter** *nom* next instruction register

registre *m* **d'instruction courante** *nom* **1.** CIR **2.** current instruction register

registre *m* **d'opération** *nom* operation register

registre *m* **en mode point** *nom* bit-mapped register

registre *m* **externe** *nom* external register

registre *m* **général** *nom* **1.** general register **2.** gpr

registre *m* **polyvalent** *nom* **1.** general register **2.** gpr

registres *mpl* **appariés** *nom* paired register

registres *mpl* **associés** *nom* paired register

registre *m* **secondaire** *nom* B box

registre *m* **tampon** *nom* buffer register

registre *m* **tampon des entrées** *nom* input buffer register

registre *m* **tampon de sortie** *nom* output buffer register

registre *m* **temporaire** *nom* temporary register

réglable par l'utilisateur *adjectif* user-selectable ◇ **les vitesses (de réception et de transmission) de ce modem sont réglables** this modem has user-selectable baud rates

réglage *m nom* **1.** adjustment **2.** dial ◇ **la luminosité a besoin d'un réglage** the brightness needs adjustment

réglage *m* **d'alignement des angles d'azimut** *nom* azimuth alignment

réglage *m* **d'alignement des têtes d'azimut** *nom* azimuth alignment ◇ **c'est cette petite vis qui sert à régler l'alignement des têtes** *ou* **des angles d'azimut** azimuth alignment is adjusted with this small screw

réglage *m* **du volume automatique** *nom* **1.** automatic volume control **2.** AVC

réglage *m* **précis** *nom* calibration

règle *f nom* **1.** rule **2.** ruler ◇ **il est de règle d'attendre le signal CTS avant de commencer à transmettre** the rule states that you wait for the clear signal before transmitting

règle *f* **de tabulation** *nom* **1.** ruler line **2.** tab rack ◇ **la règle de tabulation indique les marges de gauche et de droite** a tab rack shows you the left and right margins

règle *f* **graduée** *nom* ruler

régler *verbe* **1.** *vt* to calibrate **2.** *vt* to regulate **3.** *vt* to set **4.** *vt* to tune ◇ **régler avec grande précision** *ou* **effectuer un réglage plus fin** to fine tune

régler (avec grande précision) *verbe* to fine-tune ◇ **une mise au point très précise améliore la vitesse de dix pour cent** fine-tuning improved the speed by ten per cent

règles *fpl* **de politesse électronique** *nom* netiquette

règles *fpl* **de transformation** *nom* transformational rules

regroupé *adjectif* ganged

regrouper *verbe* **1.** *vt* to batch **2.** *vt* to gather ◇ **regrouper les différentes parties d'un programme** (*routines, macros, paramètres*) assemble

régulateur *m* **de tension** *nom* voltage regulator

réguler *verbe vt* to regulate

ré-initialisation *f* **(du système) par commande** *nom* soft reset

ré-initialiser *verbe vt* to reset ◇ **réinitialisation** *f* **automatique à la mise sous tension** power-on reset ◇ **réinitialisation** *f* **du système en utilisant le contacteur** hard reset

rejouer une bande *verbe* to replay ◇ **elle a enregistré le programme de télévision sur une bande vidéo et l'a visionné le lendemain soir** she recorded the TV programme on video tape and replayed it the next evening ◇ **il a repassé la bande** *ou* **il a remis la bande** he replayed the tape

relâcher *verbe vt* to release

relais *m nom* relay ◇ **il est protégé par un relais de 5A** it is relay-rated at 5 Amps ◇ **le circuit comporte un relais** there is a relay in the circuit ◇ **relais hertzien** microwave relay

relance *nom* restart

> '...le système est tel que l'utilisateur peut lui-même identifier la panne, autorisant ainsi la relance automatique ou la reconfiguration à distance de l'élément déficient' [*Le Monde informatique*]

relance *f* **automatique** *nom* auto restart

relancer *verbe* **1.** *vt* to reboot **2.** *vt* to restart ◇ **nous avons relancé le système et les fichiers sont réapparus sur l'écran** we rebooted and the files reappeared

relation *f* **booléenne** *nom* Boolean connective

relecture *f nom* replay

relié, -ée à une pile auxiliaire *adjectif* battery-backed

relier *verbe vt* to link ◇ **les deux ordinateurs sont reliés** the two computers are linked

relier à *verbe* **1.** to connect **2.** (*utilisant une interface*) to interface

relier en chaîne *verbe* to daisy-chain

relieur *m nom* binder

relogeable *adjectif* relocatable ◇ **le système d'exploitation peut charger et exécuter un programme translatable** *ou* **relogeable sans distinction de la zone d'origine** the operating system can load and run a relocatable program from any area of memory

relogement *m nom* relocation

relogement *m* **dynamique** *nom* dynamic relocation

relogement *m* **statique** *nom* static relocation

reloger *verbe vt* to relocate

REM *nom* REM

rémanence *f* **de l'image** *nom* image retention

rémanence *f* **d'image** *nom* hangover

rembobiner *verbe vt* to rewind ◇ **le film s'enroule automatiquement sur la bobine** the tape rewinds onto the spool automatically

remettre à zéro *verbe* **1.** to erase **2.** to reset

remettre en bon état *verbe* to restore

remettre en marche *verbe* to restart

remise ◇ **remise** *f* **en marche au point de reprise** fall back recovery

remise *f* **en état** *nom* recovery

remise *f* **en marche** *nom* restart

Remove Directory (pour supprimer un répertoire sous DOS) *abrév* RMDIR

remplacement *m* **des traits d'union** *nom* rehyphenation

remplacer *verbe* **1.** *vt* to overwrite **2.** *vt* to replace **3.** *vt* to supersede ◇ **le nouveau programme, qui remplace le précédent, est beaucoup plus rapide** the new program supersedes the earlier one, and is much faster ◇ **les nouvelles données ont remplacé les anciennes (par superposition d'écriture)** the latest data input has overwritten the old information

remplir *verbe vt* to fill

remplissage *m nom* bit stuffing ◇ **remplissage** *m* (*d'une chaîne de caractères*) padding

remplissage *m* **avec caractères blancs** *nom* **1.** character fill **2.** character stuffing

remplissage *m* **des astérisques** *nom* asterisk fill

remplissage *m* **de zone** *nom* **1.** area fill **2.** region fill

rencontre *f* **matrimoniale assistée par ordinateur** *nom* computer dating

rendement *m nom* throughput

rendement *m* **de phosphorescence** *nom* phosphor efficiency

rendement *m* **effectif** *nom* effective throughput

rendement *m* **estimé** *nom* rated throughput

rendre flou *verbe* to blur ◇ **en tournant le bouton de mise au point l'image devient floue** *ou* **perd de sa netteté** the image becomes blurred when you turn the focus knob

renseignements *mpl nom* documentation

renseigner *verbe vt* to document

rentrée *f nom* re-entry

renumérotation *f nom* renumber

renvoi *m nom* reference mark

renvoi *m* **en bas de page** *nom* footnote

réorganiser *verbe vt* to reorganise *ou* to reorganize ◇ **il faut attendre que la base de données du correcteur orthographique soit réorganisée** wait while the spelling checker database is being reorganized

repagination *f nom* **1.** renumber **2.** repagination ◇ **le système de PAO permet de faire une simple repagination** the dtp package allows simple repagination

repaginer *verbe vt* to repaginate

réparation *f nom* **1.** corrective maintenance **2.** remedial maintenance

réparer *verbe vt* to service ◇ **nous avons fait réviser** *ou* **réparer les lecteurs de disquettes hier et tout fonctionne très bien** the disk drives were serviced yesterday and are working well

repartir *verbe vi* to resume

répartir *verbe vt* to allocate

répartition *f* **des tâches** *nom* job scheduling

repérer *verbe* **1.** *vt* to find **2.** *vt* to locate ◇ **le débogueur a repéré la faute très rapidement** the debugger found the error very quickly

repères *mpl* **de tabulation** *plural noun* tabulation markers

reperforatrice *f nom* reperforator

répertoire *m plural noun* contents ■ *nom* **1.** directory **2.** Fonts Folder **3.** index **4.** repertoire **5.** search directory ◇ **le répertoire entier est inclus dans le manuel** the manual describes the full repertoire

répertoire *m* **courant** *nom* current directory

répertoire *m* **d'adresses** *nom* directory

répertoire *m* **d'adresses électroniques** *plural noun* white pages

répertoire *m* **de caractères** *nom* character repertoire

répertoire *m* **de départ** *nom* root directory

répertoire *m* **de disque** *nom* disk directory

répertoire *m* **de fichiers** *nom* file directory

répertoire *m* **de réseau** *nom* network directory

répertoire *m* **de réseau partagé** *nom* shared network directory

répertoire *m* **hiérarchique** *nom* hierarchical directory

répertoire *m* **parent** *nom* parent directory

répertoire *m* **partagé** *nom* shared directory

répertoire *m* **racine** *nom* root directory

répertoire *m* **typographique** *nom* character repertoire

répertorier *verbe vt* to catalogue ◇ **tous les terminaux sont répertoriés avec (indication de) leur emplacement, leur code** *ou* **signe d'appel et leur table d'attributs** all the terminals are catalogued, with their location, call sign and attribute table

répéteur *m nom* (*relais amplificateur*) repeater ◇ **ce répéteur bon marché ne régénère pas les signaux** this cheap repeater does not regenerate the signals

répétiteur *m nom* (*dispositif qui répète les signaux*) repeater

répétition *f* **automatique** *nom* **1.** automatic repeat **2.** auto repeat

replâtrage *m nom* bug patch

répondeur ◇ **répondeur** *m* **avec message vocal de synthèse** voice answer back

répondeur *m* **téléphonique** *nom* answering machine

répondeur *m* **vocal** *nom* audio response unit

répondre à un appel *verbe* to answer ◇ **le premier modem transmet l'appel tandis que le second y répond** the first modem originates the call and the second answers it

répondre à un message électronique *verbe* to reply

réponse *f nom* hit

réponse *f* **affirmative** *nom* positive response

réponse *f* **automatique** *nom* auto-answer

réponse *f* **cardioïde** *nom* cardioid response

réponse *f* **intrinsèque** *ou* **par défaut** *nom* default response

réponse *f* **positive** *nom* positive response

report *m nom* carry

report *m* **accéléré** *nom* high-speed carry

report *m* **circulaire** *nom* **1.** end about carry **2.** end around carry

report *m* **en boucle** *nom* **1.** end about carry **2.** end around carry

report *m* **en cascade** *nom* cascade carry

reporter *adjectif* master ◇ **ces diapos et photos sont les supports intermédiaires qui doivent être recopiés sur le vidéodisque** those slides and photographs are the intermediate materials to be mastered onto the video disk

report *m* **partiel** *nom* partial carry

report *m* **simultané** *nom* ripple-through carry

reprendre *verbe vt* to resume

reprendre l'exécution *verbe* to rerun

représentation *f* **analogique** *nom* analog representation

représentation *f* **filaire** *nom* **1.** stick model **2.** wire frame model **3.** wire mesh model

représentation *f* **numérique** *nom* digital representation

représentations *f* **graphiques** *nom* graphics

reprise *f nom* part exchange

reprise *f* **après erreur** *nom* error recovery

reprise *f* **après incident** *nom* error recovery

reprise *f* **après interruption de l'alimentation** *nom* cold start

reprise *f* **au point d'arrêt** *nom* warm start

reprise *f* **sur incident** *nom* failure recovery

reprise *f* **sur l'instruction d'arrêt** *nom* warm start

reproduire *verbe* **1.** *vt* to copy **2.** *vt* to reproduce ◇ **il existe un utilitaire résident qui copie les fichiers les plus récents sur un support de sauvegarde toutes les 40 minutes** there is a memory resident utility which copies the latest files onto backing store every 40 minutes

reprogrammable *adjectif* redefinable

reprogrammé *adjectif* redefinable

reprogrammer *verbe* **1.** *vt* to redefine **2.** *vt* to reprogram ◇ **j'ai reprogrammé cette touche pour obtenir un 5** I have redefined this key to display the figure five when pressed ◇ **redéfinir la fonction d'une touche** *ou* **reprogrammer une touche** to redefine a key

requête *f nom* inquiry ◇ **caractère de requête** *ou* **d'interrogation** inquiry character (ENQ)

requête *f* **relationnelle** *nom* relational query

réseau *m nom* **1.** array **2.** network ◇ **carte (interface de) réseau** network interface card (NIC) ◇ **gestionnaire de réseau** network manager ◇ **interface NDIS (de réseau)** network driver interface specification (NDIS) ◇ **réseau de télévision** television network ◇ **réseau étendu** *ou* **à distance** wide area network (WAN) ◇ **réseau local (d'entreprise)** local area network (LAN) ◇ **réseau** *m* **local en bande de base** base band local area network ◇ **réseau** *m* **local sans carte d'extension** (*utilisant les ports séries ou un adaptateur externe*) zero slot LAN ◇ **réseau radiophonique** radio network ◇ **réseau** *m* **synchrone de transmission de données** synchronous data network ◇ **système d'exploitation de réseau** *ou* **NOS** network operating system (NOS)

réseau *m* **à commutation de paquets** *abrév* PSN

réseau *m* **à intégration de service (RIS)** *nom* value-added network ■ *abrév* VAN

réseau *m* **(en anneau) à jeton** *nom* Token Ring network ◇ **les réseaux Token Ring sont très démocratiques et conservent leurs performances en cas d'accroissement de la**

charge Token Ring networks are very democratic and retain performance against increasing load

réseau *m* **APPN** *nom* advanced peer-to-peer networking

réseau *m* **ARCNET** *nom* attached resource computer network

réseau *m* **Arpanet** *nom* **1.** Advanced Research Projects Agency Network **2.** ARPANET

réseau *m* **auxiliaire** *nom* back-end network

réseau *m* **à valeur ajoutée** *nom* value-added network ■ *abrév* VAN

réseau *m* **avec synchronisation despotique** *nom* despotic network

réseau *m* **câblé** *nom* cabling

réseau *m* **client-serveur** *nom* client-server network

Réseau *m* **d'accès direct à l'information pour l'Europe** *abrév* DIANE

réseau *m* **décentralisé** *nom* decentralised computer network *ou* decentralized computer network

réseau *m* **de communication** *nom* communications network

réseau *m* **de commutation de données par paquets** *nom* packet switched data service *ou* packet switched network

réseau *m* **de diffusion** *nom* broadcast network

réseau *m* **de distribution** *nom* distribution network

réseau *m* **d'égal à égal** *nom* peer-to-peer network ◇ **les quatre PCs de notre petit bureau sont reliés en réseau sans serveur dédié** we have linked the four PCs in our small office using a peer-to-peer network

réseau *m* **démocratique** *nom* democratic network

réseau *m* **de neurones** *nom* neural network

réseau *m* **d'entreprise** *nom* enterprise network

réseau *m* **départemental** *nom* departmental LAN

réseau *m* **de service** *nom* departmental LAN

réseau *m* **de transmission de données** *nom* **1.** data communications network **2.** data network

réseau *m* **de type bus** *nom* bus network

réseau *m* **d'ordinateurs** *nom* computer network

réseau *m* **d'ordinateurs hiérarchisé** *nom* hierarchical computer network

réseau *m* **égal à égal avancé** *nom* advanced peer-to-peer networking

réseau *m* **en anneau** *nom* ring topology network

réseau *m* **en bus à jeton** *nom* token bus network

réseau *m* **en étoile** *nom* star network

réseau *m* **en étoile actif** *nom* active star

réseau *m* **étendu** *nom* **1.** WAN **2.** wide area network

réseau *m* **informatique** *nom* **1.** computer network **2.** information network

réseau *m* **informatique centralisé** *nom* centralised computer network *ou* centralized computer network

réseau *m* **informatique hétérogène** *nom* heterogeneous network

réseau *m* **informatique homogène** *nom* homogeneous computer network

réseau *m* **intégralement interconnecté** *nom* plex structure

réseau *m* **isochrone** *nom* isochronous network

réseau *m* **local (d'entreprise)** *nom* LAN *ou* lan

réseau *m* **local d'entreprise** *nom* local area network

réseau *m* **local sans fil** *nom* **1.** wireless LAN **2.** wireless network *ou* wireless LAN

réseau LocalTalk™ (*de réseau AppleTalk*) LocalTalk

réseau *m* **maillé** *nom* mesh network

réseau *m* **neuronal** *nom* neural network

réseau *m* **NSFNET** *nom* NSFnet

réseau *m* **numérique à intégration de services** *nom* integrated services digital network

réseau *m* **numérique à intégration de services (RNIS)** *nom* ISDN

réseau *m* **numérique à intégration de services à large bande** *nom* broadband ISDN

réseau *m* **poste à poste avancé** *nom* advanced peer-to-peer networking

réseau *m* **public de transmission de données** *abrév* PDN ■ *nom* public data network

réseau *m* **réparti** *nom* distributed network

réseau *m* **sans serveur dédié** *nom* peer-to-peer network ◇ **les quatre PCs de notre petit bureau sont reliés en réseau sans serveur dédié** we have linked the four PCs in our small office using a peer-to-peer network

réseau *m* **sans serveur dédié (SSD)** *nom* advanced peer-to-peer networking

réseau *m* **synchrone** *nom* **1.** isochronous network **2.** synchronous network

réseau *m* **téléinformatique** *nom* **1.** data communications network **2.** data network

réseau *m* **Token Ring** *nom* Token Ring network

réseau *m* **très étendu** *nom* long haul network

réseau *m* **universitaire** *nom* campus network

réseau *m* **urbain** *nom* metropolitan area network

réseau *m* **Usenet (d'utilisateurs)** *nom* Usenet

réserve ◇ **de réserve** standby

résident, -e *adjectif* resident ◇ **police (de caractères)** *ou* **fonte résidente** resident font ◇ **programme résident** *ou* **TSR** terminate and stay resident software (TSR)

'...ces produits sont constitués de programmes de communication résidents, qui possèdent toutes les caractéristiques des réseaux, mais sont limités à deux PC' [*Action PC*]

résiduel *adjectif* residual

résine ◇ **résine** *f* **photosensible en positif** positive photoresist

résine *f* **photosensible** *nom* photoresist

résolu *adjectif* manageable ◇ **problèmes de traitement qui peuvent être résolus** processing problems which are still manageable

résolution *nom* **1.** res **2.** (*définition*) resolution ◇ **la plupart des écrans d'ordinateurs individuels ont une résolution de 72 ppp (points par pouce)** the resolution of most personal computer screens is 72 dpi (dots per inch) ◇ **résolution optique** optical resolution

'...la plupart ont une résolution de 300 x 300 points avec un débit de l'ordre de 6 pages/minute, la résolution des meilleurs modèles atteignant les 400 points par pouce' [*L'Ordinateur Individuel*]

résolution *f* **d'adresse** *nom* address resolution

résolution *f* **d'un nombre** *nom* digital resolution

résonance *f nom* resonance

responsable *mf* **de base de données** *nom* database administrator

responsable du service informatique *nom* data processing manager

responsable *mf* **du service informatique** *nom* system manager

resquilleur *m nom* intruder

ressource *f nom* resource

ressource *f* **critique** *nom* critical resource

restauration *f nom* recovery

restauration *f* **par progression** *verbe* to roll forward

restaurer *verbe* **1.** *vt* to backout **2.** *vt* to reconstitute **3.** *vt* to restore

reste *m nom* remainder ◇ **7 divisé par 3 égale 2 reste 1** 7 divided by 3 is equal to 2 remainder 1

restriction *f nom* restriction

résultat *m nom* result

résultat *m* **erroné** *nom* **1.** (*d'une recherche*) false drop **2.** (*d'une recherche*) false retrieval

retapé,-ée *adjectif* kluged

retard *m nom* lag

retenue *f nom* **1.** borrow **2.** carry

réticule *m nom* crosshair

retirer un disque dur *verbe* to unmount

retour *m nom* return

retour *m nom* flyback ◇ **retour de trame** field flyback

retour *m* **à la ligne automatique** *nom* **1.** automatic carriage return **2.** word wrap **3.** wraparound

retour *m* **à l'application quittée** *nom* cold start

retour *m* **arrière** *nom* backspace

retour *m* **chariot** *nom* carriage return ◇ **les opérateurs de saisie trouvent que la touche de retour de chariot est mal placée** the carriage return key is badly placed for touch-typists

retour *m* **de ligne** *nom* line flyback

retourner *verbe vt* to turn

retransmettre *verbe vt* to relay ◇ **tous les messages sont retransmis par l'intermédiaire de ce petit micro** all messages are relayed through this small micro

rétro- *préfixe* retro-

rétroaction *f nom* feedback ◇ **boucle de feedback** *ou* **de réaction** *ou* **de rétroaction** feedback loop ◇ **rétroaction négative** *ou* **feedback négatif** negative feedback

rétroéclairage *m nom* (*d'un écran à cristaux liquides*) backlight

rétro-ingénierie *f nom* reverse engineering

retrouver *verbe* **1.** *vt* to find **2.** *vt* to recover ◇ **il a fallu beaucoup de temps pour trouver la puce défectueuse** it took a lot of time to find the faulty chip

réussir (à faire quelque chose) *verbe* to master

réussite *f nom* hit

réveil *m* **par le réseau** *nom* wake-on-LAN

révéler *verbe vt* to reveal

revendeur *m* **à intégration de service** *nom* value-added reseller ■ *abrév* VAR

revendeur *m* **à valeur ajoutée** *nom* value-added reseller ■ *abrév* VAR

réverbération *f nom* reverb *ou* reverberation

réviser *verbe* **1.** *vt* to edit **2.** *vt* to revise **3.** *vt* to service ◇ **nous avons fait réviser** *ou* **réparer les lecteurs de disquettes hier et tout fonctionne très bien** the disk drives were serviced yesterday and are working well

revoir *verbe vt* to revise

RGB *nom* red, green, blue

rideau *m* **de fumée** *nom* vapourware

RLE *nom* RLE

RNIS à bande *f* **étroite** *nom* narrow band ISDN

robot *m nom* **1.** crawler **2.** robot **3.** web crawler

robot *m* **d'annulation de message** *nom* cancelbot

robot *m* **de shopping** *nom* shopping agent

robotique *f nom* robotics

robot *m* **logiciel** *nom* bot

robuste *adjectif* robust ◇ **ce disque dur n'est pas très robuste** this hard disk is not very robust

robustesse *nom* robustness

'...le principal avantage de Netscape est sa robustesse. Il n'est pas rare de voir Mosaic 'planter' ou donner des résultats aberrants. Ici, les plantages sont presque inexistants' [*PC Magazine*]

roder *verbe vt* to run in

rôle ◇ **à tour de rôle** round robin

ROM *f abrév* ROM

ROM *f* **à fusibles** *nom* fusible read only memory

ROM *f* **amovible** *nom* ROM cartridge ◇ **l'ordinateur portatif n'est pas équipé de lecteur de disquettes mais possède un emplacement** *ou* **un connecteur pour cartouches ROM** the portable computer has no disk drives, but has a slot for ROM cartridges

ROM *f* **annexe** *nom* shadow ROM

ROM *f* **auxiliaire** *nom* sideways ROM

ROM *f* **BIOS** *nom* ROM BIOS

ROM *f* **personnalisée** *nom* custom ROM

rotation *f nom* rotation

rotation *f* **de matrice** *nom* matrix rotation

roue *f* **à picots** *nom* **1.** sprocket **2.** sprocket wheel

rouleau *m* **de papier pour téléimprimeur** *nom* teleprinter roll

routage *m nom* routing

routage *m* **adaptatif** *nom* **1.** distributed adaptive routing **2.** dynamic routing

routage *m* **dynamique** *nom* **1.** adaptive routing **2.** dynamic routing

routage *m* **flexible** *nom* distributed adaptive routing

routage *m* **IGP** *nom* **1.** IGP **2.** interior gateway protocol

routage *m* **inter-domaine sans classes** *nom* CIDR

routage *m* **source** *nom* source routing

routeur *m nom* router

routeur *m nom* router

routine *f nom* routine ◇ **la routine** *ou* **le programme permet d'imprimer le contenu de l'écran** the routine copies the screen display onto a printer ◇ **l'instruction RETOUR à la fin de la routine permet de redonner la main au programme principal** the RETURN instruction at the end of the routine sends control back to the main program

routine *f* **d'assemblage** *nom* assembly routine

routine *f* **de base** *nom* primitive

routine *f* **de bibliothèque** *nom* library routine

routine *f* **de compression (de données)** *nom* packing routine

routine *f* **de diagnostic** *nom* diagnostic routine

routine *f* **de gestion de périphérique** *nom* peripheral software driver

routine *f* **de manipulation de fichier** *nom* file handling routine

routine *f* **de normalisation** *nom* normalisation routine

routine *f* **d'entrée** *nom* input routine

routine *f* **(de traitement) d'erreur** *nom* error routine

routine *f* **d'installation LAP-B** *nom* LAP-B

routine *f* **d'introduction** *nom* input routine

routine *f* **fermée** *nom* closed routine

routine *f* **interactive** *nom* interactive routine

routine *f* **itérative** *nom* **1.** iterate **2.** iterative routine

routine *f* **ouverte** *nom* open routine

routine *f* **primitive** *nom* primitive

routine *f* **principale** *nom* main routine

routine *f* **récursive** *nom* recursion

routines *fpl plural noun* fall back routines

routines *fpl* **d'accès** *plural noun* access method routines

routines *fpl* **de clôture (d'exécution)** *plural noun* end of run routines

routines *fpl* **d'interface** *plural noun* interface routines

routine *f* **sous-programme fermée** *nom* closed routine

routine *f* **sous-routine** *nom* closed routine

ruban *m* **(en tissu)** *nom* fibre ribbon

ruban *m* **à un seul passage** *nom* single-strike ribbon

ruban *m* **carbone** *nom* carbon ribbon

ruban *m* **de raccord** *nom* splicing tape

ruban *m* **d'imprimante** *nom* printer ribbon

ruban *m* **en cartouche** *nom* cartridge ribbon

ruban *m* **non réutilisable** *nom* single-strike ribbon

ruban *m* **perforé** *nom* perforated tape

rubrique *f nom* **1.** heading **2.** headline

rubrique *f* **de déclaration des données** *nom* data division

rupteur *m nom* burster

rupture *f nom* breach

rustine *f nom* **1.** bug patch **2.** patch

RVB (rouge, vert, bleu) *nom* RGB ■ *adjectif* trichromatic

rythme *m nom* clock pulse

rythme *m* **de la production** *nom* **1.** production rate **2.** rate of production

S

sablier *m nom* egg timer

s'abonner (à) *verbe* to subscribe

saisie *f nom* **1.** data input **2.** entering **3.** input ◇ **saisie** *f* **directe sur disque par clavier** key-to-disk ◇ **saisie** *f* **directe sur disquette par clavier** keyboard to disk entry

saisie *f* **(au clavier)** *nom* keyboarding

saisie *f* **au clavier contrôlée par ordinateur** *nom* processor controlled keying

saisie *f* **automatique de données** *nom* automatic data capture

saisie *f* **de données** *nom* **1.** data capture **2.** information input

saisie *f* **de données au clavier** *nom* **1.** manual entry **2.** manual input

saisie *f* **de données par clavier** *nom* **1.** manual entry **2.** manual input

saisie *f* **de données sur clavier** *nom* **1.** manual entry **2.** manual input

saisie *f* **directe de données (au clavier)** *nom* direct data entry

saisie *f* **vocale** *nom* voice data entry *ou* voice data input

saisir *verbe* **1.** *vt* to enter **2.** *vt* to input ◇ **les données ont été saisies** the data has been entered

saisir des données au clavier *verbe* to keyboard ◇ **il était plus économique de faire saisir** *ou* **de faire taper le manuscrit par quelqu'un d'autre** it was cheaper to have the manuscript keyboarded by someone else

saisir des données sur clavier *verbe* to type ◇ **j'ai retapé la commande, mais ça ne marche toujours pas** I typed in the command again, but it still didn't work

sans clignotement *adjectif* flicker-free

sans composant *adjectif* unpopulated

sans correction *adjectif* clean ◇ **épreuve sans correction** clean proof

sans disque *adjectif* diskless

sans erreur *adjectif* clean

sans interligne *adjectif* solid

sans modem *nom* null modem ◇ **ce câble est configuré pour fonctionner sans modem et me permet de relier facilement ces deux ordinateurs** this cable is configured as a null modem, which will allow me to connect these 2 computers together easily

sans papier *adjectif* paperless

sans papillotement *adjectif* flicker-free

sans réserve *adjectif* unconditional

sans signe *adjectif* unsigned

sans vacillement *adjectif* flicker-free

sans valeur à l'entrée, sans valeur à la sortie *nom* GIGO

satellite *nom* satellite ◇ **diffusion par satellite** satellite broadcasting ◇ **liaison (par) satellite** satellite link ◇ **satellite de diffusion directe** direct broadcast satellite (DBS) ◇ **satellite de télécommunication** communications satellite ◇ **satellite météorologique** weather satellite

'...un PC 'satellite' communique avec un PC 'serveur', soit par le port série à une vitesse maximale de 115 200bps, soit par le port parallèle à 50 000bps' [*Action PC*]

s'atténuer *verbe vr* to fade

saturation *f nom* saturation

saturation *f* **de couleur** *nom* colour saturation

saucissonnage *m nom* salami technique

saut *nom* jump instruction ◇ **saut** *f* **de page obligatoire** forced page break

saut *m* **conditionnel** *nom* conditional jump

saut *m* **de ligne** *abrév* LF ■ *nom* **1.** line break **2.** line feed

saut *m* **du papier** *nom* paper throw

sauter *verbe* **1.** *vi* to bomb **2.** *vi* to skip ◇ **l'imprimante a sauté les trois lignes suivantes** the printer skipped the next three lines of text

sautillement *m nom* jitter

saut *m* **rapide** *nom* high-speed skip

sauvegarde *f nom* backup ◇ **de sauvegarde** backup

sauvegarde *f* **automatique** *nom* **1.** automatic backup **2.** auto save

sauvegarde *f* **globale d'un disque dur** *nom* global backup

sauvegarde *f* **globale d'un serveur** *nom* global backup

sauvegarde *f* **globale du réseau** *nom* global backup

sauvegarde *f* **incrémentielle** *nom* incremental backup

sauvegarde *f* **intégrale** *nom* system backup

sauvegarde *f* **programmée** *nom* timed backup

sauvegarder *verbe* **1.** *vt* to back up **2.** *vt* to save ◇ **ce programme permet aux utilisateurs de sauvegarder les fichiers du disque dur en une seule opération** the program enables users to back up hard disk files with a single command ◇ **ce système de traitement de texte fait une sauvegarde toutes les 15 minutes en cas de défaillance** this WP saves the text every 15 minutes in case of a fault ◇ **la comptabilité de la société a été sauvegardée sur disque en cas d'incendie** the company accounts were backed up on disk as a protection against fire damage ◇ **n'oubliez pas de sauvegarder le fichier avant d'éteindre votre appareil** don't forget to save the file before switching off

'...lorsque vous ne désirez plus travailler sur un fichier donné, sauvegardez-le grâce à la commande 'Enregistrer', du même fichier' [*L'Ordinateur Individuel*]

sauvegarder de nouveau *verbe* to resave ◇ **cela permet de sauvegarder le texte de nouveau automatiquement** it automatically resaves the text

sauvegarde *f* **sur bande** *nom* tape backup

scalaire *m nom* scalar ◇ **un scalaire n'a qu'une valeur de grandeur, alors qu'un vecteur possède au moins deux valeurs orientées** a scalar has a single magnitude value, a vector has two or more positional values

scan *m nom* scan ◇ **le scanner a très vite repéré le composant qui surchauffait** the heat scan of the computer quickly showed which component was overheating

ScanDisk *nom* ScanDisk

scannage *m nom* scanning

scanner *verbe vt* to scan ■ *nom* scanner ◇ **l'appareil peut scanner jusqu'à 300 points par pouce** the machine scans at up to 300 dpi resolution

scanner *m nom* page reader

scanner *m* **à plat** *nom* flatbed scanner

scanner *m* **de contrôle d'appel** *nom* communications scanner

scanner *m* **de demande de communication** *nom* communications scanner

scanner *m* **d'image** *nom* image scanner

scanner *m* **d'images** *nom* video scanner

scanner *m* **optique** *nom* optical scanner

scanner *m* **qu'on tient à la main** *nom* handheld scanner

scanner *m* **vidéo** *nom* video scanner

scanneur *m nom* scanner

scanning *m nom* scanning

sceau *m* **électronique** *nom* authenticator

scénarimage *m nom* story board

schéma *nom* **1.** functional diagram **2.** process chart **3.** schema ◇ **schéma** *m* **de base de données standard** canonical schema

schéma *m* **canonique** *nom* canonical schema

schéma *m* **de base de données** *nom* database schema

schéma *m* **de câblage** *nom* cabling diagram

schéma *m* **de circuit câblé** *nom* cabling diagram

schéma *m* **directeur** *nom* outline flowchart

schéma *m* **du point de vue de l'utilisateur** *nom* external schema

schéma *m* **fonctionnel** *nom* block diagram

schmilblick *m nom* gremlin

scintillement *m nom* **1.** flicker **2.** flutter **3.** screen flicker ◇ **le pleurage et les variations de vitesse** *ou* **le scintillement sont des défauts courants des magnétophones bon marché** wow and flutter are common faults on cheap tape recorders

script *m nom* script ◇ **je débute automatiquement la session en utilisant ce script avec mon logiciel de communication** I log in automatically using this script with my communications software

script *m* **CGI** *nom* gateway interface

scripteur *m nom* **1.** script editor **2.** writer

script *m* **WML** *nom* WMLScript

ScriptX *nom* ScriptX

se baser (sur) *verbe* to base

SECAM *nom* Système Electronique Couleur Avec Mémoire

secondaire *adjectif* secondary ■ *préfixe* sub- ◇ **couleur secondaire** secondary colour

second écran *nom* slave tube

second terme *m* **d'une addition** *nom* **1.** addend **2.** augmenter

se connecter *verbe* to log

secours ◇ **de secours** backup ◇ **équipement** *m* **de secours à démarrage semi-automatique** warm standby

secteur *nom* sector

'...sur les disques modernes, chaque secteur renferme 512 octets. Quatre secteurs forment un 'cluster'. Il y a entre 17 et 34 secteurs par piste' [*PC Expert*]

secteur *m* **CD-I** *nom* CD-i sector

secteur *m* **de disque** *nom* disk sector

secteur *m* **de disquette** *nom* floppy disk sector

secteur *m* **défectueux** *nom* **1.** bad sector **2.** defective sector **3.** faulty sector

secteur *m* **réservé** *nom* reserved sector

secteurs *mpl* **contigus** *nom* cluster

section *f nom* part

section *f* **d'entrée** *nom* input section

section *f* **de programme superposable** *nom* overlay ◇ **segment superposable** *ou* **segment d'overlay** overlay segment

sectoriser *verbe vt* to sector ◇ **formatage de secteurs (d'un disque)** (disk) sector formatting

sécurisé *adjectif* secured

sécurité *f* **de l'information** *nom* data security

sécurité *f* **des données** *nom* data security

sécurité *f* **du matériel** *nom* hardware security

sécurité *f* **d'un système** *nom* system security

sécurité *f* **par niveau d'opération** *nom* share level security

se désabonner *verbe* to unsubscribe

segment *m nom* **1.** section **2.** segment

segmentation *f nom* fragmentation ◇ **degré** *m* **de segmentation de la mémoire** granularity

segment *m* **de programme** *nom* program segment

segment *m* **de réseau local** *nom* LAN segment

segmenter *verbe vt* to segment

segment *m* **mémoire de code** *nom* code segment

segments *mpl* **d'overlay** *plural noun* overlay segments

segments *mpl* **superposables** *plural noun* overlay segments

seize bits *adjectif* sixteen-bit

sélecteur *m nom* selector ◇ **canal sélecteur** *ou* **de sélection** selector channel ◇ **tournez le sélecteur** turn the selector control ◇ **voilà o— se trouve le sélecteur d'amplitude** the selector knob for the amplification is located there

sélecteur *m* **de port** *nom* port selector

sélection *f* **de circuit** *nom* chip select ■ *abrév* CS

sélectionner *verbe* **1.** *vt* to enable **2.** *vt* to select ◇ **qui peut être sélectionné** to jumper-selectable

sélectionner par filtrage *verbe* to filter

sélection *f* **par menu** *nom* menu selection

sémantique *f nom* semantics

sémaphore *m nom* semaphore

semi- *préfixe* semi-

semi-compilé *adjectif* semicompiled

semi-conducteur *m nom* **1.** metal oxide semiconductor **2.** semiconductor

semi-conducteur *m* **à effet de champ MOSFET** *nom* MOSFET

semi-conducteur *m* **CMOS** *nom* complementary metal oxide semiconductor

semi-conducteur *m* **MOS** *nom* MOS

sensibilité *f* **aux rayons alpha** *nom* alpha-particle sensitivity

sensibilité *f* **de la souris** *nom* mouse tracking

sensible *adjectif* sensitive ◇ **cet ordinateur est sensible aux moindres variations du courant** the computer is sensitive even to very slight changes in current ◇ **les films photosensibles réagissent à la lumière** light-sensitive films change when exposed to light

séparateur *m nom* **1.** burster **2.** separator

séparateur *m* **(d'information)** *nom* delimiter

séparateur *m* **d'arguments** *nom* argument separator

séparateur *m* **de champs** *nom* **1.** field marker **2.** field separator

séparateur *m* **d'information** *nom* delimiter

séparation *f nom* colour separation

séparation *f* **binaire** *nom* binary split

séparer *verbe vt* to filter

se perdre *verbe* to hang

se planter *verbe* **1.** *vr* to bomb **2.** to crash **3.** to go down ◇ **la tête de lecture du disque a cessé de fonctionner** *ou* **s'est plantée et il se peut que les données soient perdues** the disk head has crashed and the data may have been lost ◇ **le programme s'est planté et nous avons perdu toutes les données** the program bombed, and we lost all the data ◇ **le système peut se planter si vous installez en même temps plusieurs accessoires de bureau ou programmes résidents** the system can bomb if you set up several desk accessories or memory-resident programs at the same time

se produire *verbe* to occur

se propager *verbe* to propagate

septet *m nom* septet

séquence *f nom* **1.** sequence **2.** string ◇ **séquence d'ouverture de session** *ou* **d'identification** the logon sequence

séquence *f* **binaire** *nom* binary sequence

séquence *f* **d'appel** *nom* calling sequence

séquence *f* **d'échappement** *nom* escape sequence

séquence *f* **d'échappement ANSI** *nom* ANSI escape sequence

séquence *f* **de clôture anormale** *nom* abort sequence

séquence *f* **de commande** *nom* control sequence

séquence *f* **de contrôle** *nom* supervisory sequence

séquence *f* **de drapeaux** *nom* flag sequence

séquence *f* **de fin** *nom* abort sequence

séquence *f* **de marqueurs** *nom* flag sequence

séquence *f* **de micro-instructions** *nom* microsequence

séquence *f* **de touches** *nom* accelerator key ◇ **au lieu de sélectionner le menu Fichier puis l'option Enregistrer, utilisez les touches**

d'accélération ALT-S *ou* **le raccourci clavier ALT-S pour sauvegarder votre fichier** instead of selecting the File menu then the Save option, use the accelerator keys Alt and S to do the same thing and save the file

séquence *f* **d'identification** *nom* identity burst

séquence *f* **d'indicateurs** *nom* flag sequence

séquence *f* **d'initialisation** *nom* log in script

séquence *f* **d'instructions d'un microprogramme** *nom* microsequence

séquence *f* **d'interruption prématurée** *nom* abort sequence

séquence *f* **MIDI** *nom* MIDI sequence

séquenceur *m nom* sequencer

séquenceur *m* **d'appels automatique** *nom* ACS

séquenceur *m* **MIDI** *nom* MIDI sequencer

séquentiel *adjectif* **1.** linear **2.** sequential **3.** serial

série *f nom* **1.** series **2.** set ■ *plural noun* SET ◇ **série** *f* **X** (*des protocoles de télétransmission*) X-series

série *f* **(de produits)** *nom* family

série *f* **de programmes** *nom* (*l'un à la suite de l'autre*) suite of programs ◇ **le système de traitement de texte utilise une série de trois programmes: un éditeur de texte, un correcteur d'orthographe et un contrôleur d'impression** the word-processing system uses a suite of three programs, editor, spelling checker and printing controller

série *f* **d'erreurs consécutives** *nom* error burst

série *f* **du cliquage** *nom* clickstream

serrer *verbe vt* to kern

serveur *nom* **1.** file server **2.** host computer **3.** server ◇ **serveur** *m* **de fax** fax server ◇ **serveur Web** Web server

serveur *m* **auxiliaire** *nom* back-end server

serveur *m* **commercial** *nom* commerce server

serveur *m* **de base de données** *nom* database server

serveur *m* **de communication** *nom* communications server

serveur *m* **de communications asynchrone** *nom* asynchronous communication server

serveur *m* **de contrôle des accès** *nom* log on server

serveur *m* **de courrier (électronique)** *nom* mail server

serveur *m* **dédié à l'impression** *nom* dedicated print server

serveur *m* **de fond** *nom* back-end server

serveur *m* **de liste** *nom* listserv *ou* listserver

serveur *m* **de message** *nom* interface message processor

serveur *m* **de noms de domaines** *nom* **1.** domain name server **2.** name server

serveur *m* **de réseau** *nom* network server

serveur *m* **de réseau local (d'entreprise)** *nom* local area network server

serveur *m* **de sauvegarde** *nom* backup server

serveur *m* **de secours** *nom* backup server

serveur *m* **d'impression** *nom* print server

serveur *m* **d'information Internet** *nom* Internet Information Server

serveur *m* **intermédiaire** *nom* proxy server

serveur *m* **non dédié** *nom* non dedicated server

serveur *m* **sécurisé** *nom* secure server

serveur *m* **vidéo** *nom* video server

serveur *m* **Web** *nom* web server

service *m nom* facility ◇ **nous offrons à nos clients un service de traitement de leurs propres disquettes** we offer facilities for processing a customer's own disks

service *m* **après-vente** *nom* customer service department

service *m* **bureau** *nom* service bureau

service *m* **clients** *nom* customer service department

service *m* **d'affectation de noms** *nom* naming services

service *m* **d'appels** *nom* **1.** dialup **2.** dial-up service

service *m* **d'assistance** *nom* **1.** backup **2.** help desk

service *m* **d'attribution de noms** *nom* naming services

service *m* **de gestion de message** *nom* message handling service

service *m* **de maintenance** *nom* maintenance ◇ **service d'assistance technique sur le lieu de travail** *ou* **maintenance sur site** on-site maintenance ◇ **télémaintenance** remote maintenance

service *m* **de messages courts** *nom* short message service ■ *abrév* SMS

service *m* **de recherche et développement** *nom* R & D department

service *m* **de transmission par paquets** *nom* packet switching service

service *m* **d'ordinateur central** *nom* **1.** hosting service provider **2.** host service

service *m* **en ligne** **1.** America Online **2.** (*fournisseur d'information*) Delphi

service *m* **informatique** *nom* computer department ■ *abrév* MIS

service *m* **IRC** *abrév* IRC

service *m* **R et D** *nom* R & D department

services *mpl plural noun* services
services *mpl* **d'annuaire** *nom* directory services
services *mpl* **de communications personnelles** *abrév* PCS ■ *plural noun* personal communications services
services *mpl* **de téléinformatique** *plural noun* teleinformatic services
services *mpl* **informatiques** *plural noun* computer services
services *mpl* **partagés** *plural noun* fractional services
service *m* **T1 partagé** *nom* fractional T-1
service *m* **téléphonique ordinaire** *nom* **1.** plain old telephone service **2.** POTS
service *m* **WINS** Windows Internet Naming Service ■ *nom* WINS
se servir de (quelque chose) *verbe* to use ◇ **la préparation de ces étiquettes se fera beaucoup plus rapidement avec l'ordinateur** if you use the computer for processing the labels, it will be much quicker ◇ **les commerciaux utilisent l'ordinateur trop souvent** the computer is used too often by the sales staff
se spécialiser *verbe* to specialise
session *f nom* **1.** session **2.** terminal session ◇ **clé d'ouverture d'une session** session key
s'étendre *verbe* **1.** *vr* to propagate **2.** *vr* to range
seuil *m nom* threshold ◇ **circuit à seuil** threshold gate ◇ **valeur de seuil** threshold value
sextet *m nom* sextet
shadow RAM *nom* (*UMB*) shadow RAM
shareware *m nom* shareware
Shockwave™ (*nom de marque*) Shockwave
shopping *m* **en ligne** *nom* cybershopping
SID *nom* executive information system
signal *m nom* **1.** command **2.** signal ◇ **ce système est à la disposition des étudiants qui se spécialisent dans la recherche sur les techniques de traitement du signal** the system is used by students doing research on signal processing techniques ◇ **le signal émis par l'ordinateur contenait la réponse** the signal received from the computer contained the answer ◇ **rapport signal *or* bruit** signal to noise ratio (S/N) ◇ **signal** *m* **d'interruption** external interrupt ◇ **signal** *m* **ligne occupée** line busy tone ◇ **signaux** *mpl* **de transmission de données** data signals
signal *m* **analogique** *nom* analog signal
signal *m* **bas actif** *nom* active low
signal *m* **bipolaire** *nom* bipolar signal
signal *m* **CD** *nom* carrier detect
signal *m* **continu** *nom* continuous signal
signal *m* **CTS** *nom* CTS
signal *m* **d'acceptation d'appel** *nom* call accepted signal *ou* call accept signal
signal *m* **d'activation** *nom* enabling signal
signal *m* **d'appel** *nom* calling
signal *m* **d'appel accepté** *nom* call accepted signal *ou* call accept signal
signal *m* **de chrominance** *nom* chrominance signal
signal *m* **de contrôle** *nom* supervisory signal
signal *m* **de contrôle d'appel** *nom* call control signal
signal *m* **de demande de transmission** *nom* **1.** request to send **2.** request to send signal ■ *abrév* RTS
signal *m* **de détection de porteuse** *nom* **1.** carrier detect **2.** data carrier detect
signal *m* **de fin de la transmission** *nom* end of transmission
signal *m* **de fin de report** *nom* carry complete signal
signal *m* **de lecture d'instruction** *nom* fetch signal
signal *m* **de modem prêt à transmettre/recevoir** *nom* DSR
signal *m* **de modulation** *nom* modulating signal
signal *m* **de porteuse** *nom* **1.** carrier signal **2.** carrier signalling
signal *m* **de prêt à recevoir** *nom* data set ready
signal *m* **de prêt à transmettre** *nom* **1.** CTS **2.** data terminal ready
signal *m* **de ré-initialisation** *nom* return to zero signal
signal *m* **de remise à zéro** *nom* return to zero signal
signal *m* **de réponse** *nom* **1.** answer back **2.** answertone
signal *m* **de sélection** *nom* enabling signal
signal *m* **de supervision** *nom* supervisory signal
signal *m* **de synchronisation** *nom* hold ◇ **en veille** on hold
signal *m* **de validation** *nom* enabling signal
signal *m* **de validité d'adresse** *nom* address strobe
signal *m* **d'exécution** *nom* execute signal
signal *m* **d'interdiction de transmission** *nom* inhibiting input
signal *m* **d'interruption** *nom* interrupt signal
signal *m* **d'invalidation de transmission** *nom* inhibiting input
signal *m* **électrique** *nom* input
signal *m* **haut actif** *nom* active high
signalisation *f nom* signalling ◇ **signalisation** *f* **à contrôle programmé en mémoire** stored program signalling
signalisation *f* **monofréquence** *nom* **1.** sf signalling **2.** single frequency signalling

signalisation *f* **par canal banal** *nom* common channel signalling
signalisation *f* **par voie commune** *nom* common channel signalling
signal *m* **modulé** *nom* modulated signal
signal *m* **numérique** *nom* digital signal
signal *m* **numérique de niveau 0** *nom* digital signal level zero
signal *m* **numérique de niveau 1** *nom* digital signal level one
signal *m* **unipolaire** *nom* unipolar signal
signal *m* **vidéo** *nom* video signal
signal *m* **vidéo vertical** *nom* vertical sync signal
signature *f nom* signature ◇ **reconnaissez-vous la signature sur le chèque?** do you recognize the signature on the cheque?
signature *f* **électronique** *nom* electronic signature
signature *f* **numérique** *nom* digital signature
signaux *mpl* **de commande** *plural noun* control signals
signaux *mpl* **de contrôle** *plural noun* control signals
signaux *mpl* **parasites** *nom* garbage
signaux *mpl* **synchrones aux impulsions d'horloge** *plural noun* clocked signals
signe *m nom* mark ◇ **signes de correction (d'épreuves d'imprimerie)** proof correction marks
signe *m* **de l'addition** *nom* plus *ou* plus sign
signe *m* **de la multiplication** *nom* multiplication sign
signe *m* **de la soustraction** *nom* minus *ou* minus sign
signe *m* **de polarité** *nom* sign
signe *m* **de ponctuation** *nom* punctuation mark
signe *m* **du dollar** *nom* dollar sign
signe *m* **et modulo** *nom* sign and modulus
signe *m* **moins** *nom* minus *ou* minus sign
signe *m* **plus** *nom* plus *ou* plus sign
signer *verbe vt* to sign
signet *m nom* bookmark
signe *m* **typographique** *nom* hashmark *ou* hash mark
signe *m* **typographique &#;** *nom* hash
significatif *adjectif* significant
signification *f nom* significance
signifier *verbe* **1.** *vt* to mean **2.** *vt* to signify ◇ **l'envoi du code CR signifie que la ligne saisie est terminée** a carriage return code signifies the end of an input line
silicium *m nom* silicon ◇ **porte (de circuit) au silicium** silicon gate ◇ **silicium sur saphir** silicon on sapphire (SOS) ◇ **transistor au silicium** silicon transistor
simple densité *f abrév* SD
simple précision *nom* single length precision
simple précision *f nom* single precision
simplex *m nom* SPX
simulateur *nom* simulator

> '...d'un côté, l'électronique rend la bataille de plus en plus abstraite – comme dans les simulateurs, le conducteur de char voit sa cible non plus à l'oeil nu, mais sur l'écran' [*L'Express*]

simulateur *m* **de Turing** *nom* Turing machine
simulateur *m* **de vol** *nom* flight simulator
simulation *f nom* simulation ◇ **les techniques de simulation sont devenues très sophistiquées** simulation techniques have reached a high degree of sophistication ◇ **logiciel de simulation** simulation software
simulation *f* **en temps réel** *nom* real-time simulation
simuler *verbe vt* to simulate ◇ **ce logiciel simule les manoeuvres aériennes** *ou* **est un simulateur de vol** this software simulates the action of an aircraft
simultané *adjectif* simultaneous
simultanéité *f nom* simultaneity
s'introduire ◇ **s'introduire sans autorisation dans un système** hack
s'introduire sans autorisation dans un système *verbe* to hack
SIT *nom* **1.** BACS **2.** Bankers Automated Clearing Services
site *m nom* site ◇ **ON-SITE** web site ◇ **site Web** web site
site *m* **d'archives** *nom* archive site
site *m* **de bêta test** *nom* beta site
site *m* **miroir** *nom* mirror site
site *m* **miteux** *nom* cobweb site
site *m* **protégé** *nom* website
site *m* **sécurisé** *nom* **1.** secure site **2.** secure website **3.** website
site *m* **témoin** *nom* beta site
situer *verbe vt* to locate
16 bits (*données*) 16-bit
Smalltalk™ (*langage de programmation*) Smalltalk
SMPTE *nom* **1.** SMPTE **2.** Society for Motion Picture and TV Engineers
société *f* **de services** *nom* bureau ◇ **la société offre, entre autres, des services d'imprimerie et de saisie de données** the company offers a number of bureau services, such as printing and data collection ◇ **nous confions notre correspondance à un bureau de secrétariat local** we farm out the office typing to a local bureau ◇ **nous faisons faire la manipulation de données par une société de services informatiques** our data manipulation is handled by a bureau

société *f* **de services et d'ingénierie informatique (SSII)** *nom* computer bureau
société *f* **spécialisée en logiciels** *nom* software house
socle *m* **de synchronisation** *nom* docking station
solidité *f nom* robustness
solution *f* **de rechange** *nom* workaround
sommaire *m nom* lead in
somme *f nom* sum
sommet *m nom* vertex
sonorité *f nom* timbre
Sony (*société éléctronique innovatrice*) Sony
sophistication *f nom* sophistication ◇ **le degré de sophistication du nouveau progiciel est remarquable** the sophistication of the new package is remarkable
sophistiqué *adjectif* sophisticated
sorcier *m* **dépanneur** *nom* wizard
sortance *f nom* fan-out
sortie *abrév* o/p *ou* O/P ■ *nom* **1.** outlet **2.** output

'...il possède également une sortie vidéo et une sortie audio pour se connecter à un téléviseur' [*Hi-fi Vidéo*]

sortie *f* **de ligne** *nom* line out
sortie *f* **de session** *nom* timeout
sortie *f* **d'imprimante** *nom* **1.** computer listing **2.** computer printout **3.** hard copy **4.** information output **5.** printout
sortie *f* **d'ordinateur sur microfilm** *nom* COM
sortie *f* **numérique** *nom* digital output
sortie *f* **vocale** *nom* voice output
sortir ◇ **je suis sorti du traitement de texte pour vérifier quels étaient les fichiers disponibles sur la disquette, puis je suis retourné dans le programme** I shelled out from the word-processor to check which files were on the floppy, then went back to the program ◇ **sortir du programme en cours pour passer au programme d'exploitation et revenir à l'application** shell out
sortir (de) *verbe* to exit
sortir de *verbe* to originate ◇ **les données viennent** *ou* **sortent du nouvel ordinateur** the data originated from the new computer
soulignage *m nom* **1.** underline **2.** underlining
soulignement *m nom* underline
souligner *verbe* **1.** *vt* to underline **2.** *vt* to underscore
sound *nom* sound
source *f nom* **1.** data source **2.** source
souriant *m nom* emoticon
souris *fpl plural noun* mice ■ *nom* mouse ◇ **(logiciel) contrôlé** *ou* **piloté par une souris** mouse-driven (software) ◇ **souris à molette** scroll mouse *ou* wheel mouse ◇ **souris sans fil** cordless mouse ◇ **tapis souris** *ou* **tapis pour la souris** mouse mat *ou* mouse pad
souris *f* **3 D** *nom* flying mouse
souris *f* **mécanique** *nom* mechanical mouse
souris *f* **optique** *nom* optical mouse
souris *f* **optomécanique** *nom* optomechanical mouse
souris *f* **pour gauchers** *nom* left-handed mouse
souris *f* **série** *nom* serial mouse
sous- *préfixe* sub-
sous-classe *f nom* subclass
sous-domaine *m nom* sub-domain
sous-ensemble *m nom* **1.** bead **2.** subset
sous-menu *m nom* **1.** cascading menu **2.** submenu
sous-programme *m nom* **1.** bead **2.** routine **3.** subprogram **4.** subroutine ◇ **appel d'un sous-programme** subrroutine call
sous-programme *m* **additionnel** *nom* inserted subroutine
sous-programme *m* **à deux niveaux** *nom* two-level subroutine
sous-programme *m* **à virgule flottante** *nom* floating point routine
sous-programme *m* **chaîné** *nom* linked subroutine
sous-programme *m* **de bibliothèque** *nom* library subroutine
sous-programme *m* **direct** *nom* one-level subroutine
sous-programme *m* **dynamique** *nom* dynamic subroutine
sous-programme *m* **fermé** *nom* closed subroutine
sous-programme *m* **ouvert** *nom* open subroutine
sous-programme *m* **paramétrable** *nom* dynamic subroutine
sous-programme *m* **paramétré** *nom* parametric subroutine
sous-programme *m* **paramétrique** *nom* parametric subroutine
sous-programmes *mpl* **mathématiques** *plural noun* mathematical subroutines
sous-programme *m* **standard** *nom* standard subroutine
sous-programme *m* **statique** *nom* static subroutine
sous-répertoire *nom* subdirectory

'...les fichiers MS-DOS d'un utilisateur sont stockés dans un sous-répertoire' [*L'Information professionnelle*]

sous-réseau *m nom* subnet ◇ **adresse de sous-r,seau** subnet address *ou* subnet number
sous-segment *m nom* subsegment

sous-système *m nom* subsystem

sous-titrage *m* **codé pour malentendants** *nom* closed captioning

soustracteur *m* **à trois entrées** *nom* full subtractor

soustracteur *m* **complet** *nom* full subtractor

soustraction *f nom* subtraction

soutenir *verbe vt* to back up ◇ **le document papier soutenait ses arguments en faveur d'un nouveau système** the printout backed up his argument for a new system

special *nom* special purpose

spécialisé *adjectif* dedicated ◇ **ligne téléphonique spécialisée** *ou* **dédiée** dedicated line

spécialiste *m&f nom* specialist

spécialiste *m&f* **en déboguage** *nom* troubleshooter

spécification *f nom* **1.** functional specification **2.** spec **3.** specification

spécification *f* **NDIS** *nom* **1.** NDIS **2.** network driver interface specification

spécifications *f nom* blueprint ■ *plural noun* design parameters

spécifications *fpl* **de mémoire étendue** *nom* XMS

spécifications *fpl* **de présentation des données** *nom* layout

spécifications *fpl* **d'un logiciel** *nom* software specification

spécifications *fpl* **d'un système** *plural noun* system specifications

spécifications *fpl* **relatives à un programme** *nom* program specification

spécifications *fpl* **XMS** *nom* XMS

spécificité *f nom* specificity

spoule *m nom* spooling

sprite *m nom* sprite

SPX (*nom de marque*) SPX

stabilité *f* **de l'image** *nom* image stability

stade *m nom* stage

standard *adjectif* universal ◇ **le standard ST506 a été remplacé par les normes IDE et SCSI** the ST506 standard has now been replaced by IDE and SCSI ◇ **non standard** *ou* **qui ne fonctionne que sur un type d'ordinateur** machine-dependent ◇ **standard CCITT X 400** X.400 ◇ **standard CCITT X 500** (*gestion des noms et des transferts de messages*) X.500 ◇ **standard** *m* **ST506** (*d'interface de disques durs*) ST506 standard ◇ **standard** *ou* **universel** *ou* **qui fonctionne sur la plupart des ordinateurs** *ou* **indépendant de la machine** machine-independent

standard *m* **10Base2** 10Base2

standard *m* **10Base5** 10Base5

standard *m* **10BaseT** 10BaseT

standard *m* **automatique** *nom* automatic call distribution

standard *m* **Corba** *nom* common object request broker architecture

standard *m* **d'affichage MDA** *nom* monochrome display adapter

standard *m* **de bus EISA** *nom* EISA

standard *m* **de cryptage de données** *nom* data encryption standard

standard *m* **de télévision SECAM** *nom* SECAM

standard *m* **FDD** *nom* FDDI

standard *m* **FDD II** *nom* FDDI II

standard GOSIP (de comptabilité) *nom* GOSIP

standard *m* **GOSIP (de comptabilité)** *nom* Government Open Systems Interconnect Profile

standard *m* **IEEE POSIX (de portabilité des services d'un système d'exploitation)** *nom* POSIX

standardiser *verbe vt* to standardise

standard *m* **LAP** *nom* LAP

standard *m* **LLC** *nom* **1.** LLC **2.** logical link control

standard *m* **MCGA** *nom* multicolour graphics adapter

standard *m* **MCGA (d'adaptateur graphique couleur)** *nom* MCGA

standard *m* **MSX** *nom* MSX

standards de production *plural noun* production standards

standard *m* **VT-52** *nom* VT-52

station *f nom* station ◇ **gestion de station SMT** station management (SMT) ◇ **le signal de cette station émettrice** *ou* **de cet émetteur radio est très faible** the signal from this radio station is very weak ◇ **nous essayons de brouiller les signaux émis par cette station** we are trying to jam the signals from that station ◇ **station radio** radio station ◇ **station terrestre** earth station

station *f* **à connexion unique** *nom* single attachment station

station *f* **à double connexion (sur réseau FFDI)** *nom* dual attachment *ou* dual attached station

station *f* **à liaison unique** *nom* single attachment station

station *f* **d'accueil** *nom* docking station *ou* docking unit

station *f* **de travail** *nom* **1.** operating console **2.** workstation ◇ **le système comprend un réseau de cinq postes de travail reliés en anneau** the system includes five workstations linked together in a ring network ◇ **sept postes de travail se partagent une mémoire d'archivage d'une capacité de 1200 Mo** the archive storage has a total capacity of 1200 MB between seven workstations

station *f* **primaire** *nom* primary station

station *f* **secondaire** *nom* secondary station

statique *adjectif* static

statistique *adjectif* statistical ■ *nom* statistics ◇ **multiplexage temporel statistique** *ou* **en fonction des appels** statistical time division multiplexing (STDM)

statistiques *plural noun* statistics

stéganographie *f nom* steganography

stencil *m nom* stencil

stéréo *adjectif* stereo *ou* stereophonic

stéréophonique *adjectif* stereo *ou* stereophonic

stockage *m nom* **1.** data storage **2.** holographic storage **3.** storage

stockage *m* **actif** *nom* active storage

stockage *m* **de données** *nom* information storage

stockage *m* **de données en ligne** *nom* on-line storage

stockage *m* **de données sur support optique** *nom* optical storage

stockage *m* **de fichier** *nom* file storage

stockage *m* **d'instruction** *nom* instruction storage

stockage *m* **et restitution de données** *nom* information storage and retrieval ■ *abrév* ISR

stockage *m* **hors ligne** *nom* off-line storage

stockage *m* **séquentiel** *nom* serial storage

stockage *m* **sur microfilm** *nom* computer output on microfilm

stockage *m* **temporaire** *nom* clipboard ◇ **copiez le texte dans le presse-papiers, puis collez-le dans le nouveau document** copy the text to the clipboard, then paste it back into a new document

stocker *verbe vt* (*dans la mémoire*) to plant

'…sa capacité énorme permet de stocker sur l'une de ses faces une très grande quantité de données' [*Micro Systèmes*]

stocker des données avant traitement *verbe* to prestore

stocker en mémoire cache *verbe* to cache

stopper *verbe vti* to inhibit

streamer *m nom* **1.** streaming tape drive **2.** stringy floppy **3.** tape streamer

structure *f nom* **1.** framework **2.** structure ◇ **on a d'abord établi le cadre** *ou* **la structure du programme** the program framework was designed first

structure *f* **à maillage intégral** *nom* plex structure

structure *f* **cartésienne** *nom* cartesian structure

structure *f* **de contrôle** *nom* control structure

structure *f* **de données** *nom* information structure

structure *f* **de données dynamique** *nom* dynamic data structure

structure *f* **de fichier** *nom* file structure

structure *f* **de réseau** *nom* network structure

structure *f* **des données** *nom* data structure

structure *f* **d'un bus** *nom* bus structure

structure *f* **d'un enregistrement** *nom* record structure

structure *f* **d'un fichier** *nom* file layout

structure *f* **d'un programme** *nom* program structure

structure *f* **en arbres** *nom* forest

structure *f* **imbriquée** *nom* nested structure

structurer *verbe vt* to structure

style *m nom* style

style *m* **de caractère** *nom* type style

style *m* **de trait** *nom* line style

style *m* **d'impression** *nom* print style

stylo *m nom* pen

stylo *m* **électronique** *nom* **1.** electronic stylus **2.** electronic wand

stylo *m* **optique** *nom* **1.** bar code reader **2.** electronic pen **3.** light pen **4.** optical bar reader **5.** optical wand **6.** pen **7.** wand

stylo *m* **optique graphique** *nom* graphics light pen

subdiviser *verbe vt* to partition

substance *f* **résistante** *nom* (*à un produit chimique*) resist

substituer *verbe vt* to substitute

substrat *m nom* substrate

suffixe *m nom* postfix

suite *f nom* continuation page

suite *f* **de programmes** *nom* suite of programs

suivant accord préalable *adjectif* pre-agreed

suivant un ordre séquentiel *adverbe* sequentially

suivi *m nom* deletion tracking

suivi *m* **automatique** *nom* auto trace

suivi *m* **d'activité** *nom* activity trail

suivre *verbe vt* to monitor

Sun Microsystems Sun Microsystems

super- *préfixe* super- ◇ **(standard d'écran) super VGA** *ou* **SVGA** super VGA (SVGA)

superflu *adjectif* redundant

superposer *verbe* **1.** *vt* to overlap **2.** *vt* to piggyback ◇ **superposez ces deux puces pour augmenter la capacité de la mémoire** piggyback those two memory chips to boost the memory capacity

superposer des données *verbe* to overwrite ◇ **les nouvelles données ont remplacé les**

anciennes (par superposition d'écriture) the latest data input has overwritten the old information

superposition *f nom* overlap ◇ **superposition** *f* **d'un accusé de réception au message suivant** piggybacking

super VGA *nom* super VGA

superviseur *adjectif* executive ■ *nom* **1.** runtime system **2.** supervisor

superviseur *m* **(de multiprogrammation)** *nom* scheduler

superviseur *m* **d'entrée/sortie** *nom* input/output executive

supplémentaire *adjectif* **1.** add-in **2.** additional **3.** (*dispositif*) add-on ◇ **peut-on ajouter trois postes** *ou* **stations de travail supplémentaires au réseau?** can we add three additional workstations to the network?

support *m plural noun* media ■ *nom* **1.** medium **2.** support ◇ **il existe différents types de supports de stockage dont les bandes papier, les disques et bandes magnétiques, les cartes et microfiches** data storage mediums such as paper tape, magnetic disk, magnetic tape, card and microfiche are available ◇ **les ordinateurs peuvent stocker des données sur différents types de supports: disques, cartes perforées ou CD-ROM** computers can store data on a variety of media, such as disk, punched card or CD-ROM ◇ **pour transférer le contenu d'une bande magnétique sur une disquette, il vous faut un équipement de conversion de support** to transfer from magnetic tape to floppy disk, you need a media conversion device ◇ **support publicitaire** advertising medium

support *m* **à accès direct** *nom* **1.** DASD **2.** direct access storage device

support *m* **de carte d'extension** *nom* card extender

support *m* **de cartes** *nom* (*de circuits imprimés*) frame

support *m* **de châssis avec guide-cartes** *nom* **1.** card cage **2.** card chassis **3.** card frame **4.** carpal tunnel syndrome

support *m* **de données** *nom* **1.** data carrier **2.** data medium

support *m* **de données d'un fichier** *nom* file storage

support *m* **de mémoire** *nom* storage medium

support *m* **de mémoire de masse** *nom* **1.** bulk storage medium **2.** mass storage device ◇ **un disque dur est un véritable support de mémoire de masse** a hard disk is definitely a mass storage device

support *m* **de stockage de grande capacité** *nom* bulk storage medium

support *m* **de transmission** *nom* transmission medium

support *m* **(magnétique) effaçable** *nom* **1.** erasable memory **2.** erasable storage

supporter *verbe vt* to support ◇ **l'ordinateur principal supporte** *ou* **accepte** *ou* **contrôle six postes de travail** the main computer supports six workstations

support *m* **magnétique** *nom* **1.** magnetic material **2.** magnetic medium

support *m* **magnétique original** *nom* magnetic master

support *m* **magnétique vierge** *nom* empty medium

support *m* **réutilisable** *nom* erasable memory

support *m* **(magnétique) réutilisable** *nom* erasable storage

supports *mpl* **magnétiques** *plural noun* magnetic media

suppression *nom* **1.** blanking **2.** deletion ◇ **suppression** *f* **de signal d'appel parasite** anti-tinkle suppression

suppression *f* **d'écho** *nom* echo cancellation

supprimer *verbe* **1.** *vt* to delete **2.** *vt* to scratch **3.** *vt* to scrub ◇ **le traitement de texte permet de supprimer un fichier complet en appuyant sur cette touche** the word-processor allows us to delete the whole file by pressing this key

supprimer l'effet *verbe* (*d'une commande*) to undo ◇ **vous venez de supprimer un paragraphe, vous pouvez annuler cette action avec l'option 'annuler' (undo) du menu Edition** you've just deleted the paragraph, but you can undo it from the option in the Edit menu

sur- *préfixe* super-

surcharge *f nom* channel overload

surcharge *f* **d'un opérateur** *nom* operator overloading

surcharger *verbe vt* to overload ◇ **l'ordinateur est vraiment surchargé par tout ce travail** the computer is overloaded with that amount of processing

surchauffer *verbe vt* to overheat ◇ **il se peut que le système (sur)chauffe dans une pièce qui n'est pas climatisée** the system may overheat if the room is not air-conditioned

sur commande *adjectif* custom-built

surimposer *verbe vt* to superimpose

sur lequel on peut compter *adjectif* reliable ◇ **les premières versions du logiciel ne donnaient pas satisfaction** the early versions of the software were not completely reliable

surligner *verbe vt* to highlight

surligneur *m nom* **1.** marker **2.** redliner

sur mesure *adjectif* intimate

surperforation *f nom* overpunching

sur place *adjectif* on-site

sur support magnétique *adjectif* soft ◇ **réinitialisation logicielle** *ou* **par logiciel** *ou* **par commande** soft-reset

surtension *f nom* surge
surveillant *m nom* supervisor
surveiller *verbe vt* to monitor
survenir *verbe vi* to occur
suspendre l'exécution *verbe* to abort ◇ **interrompez** *ou* **arrêtez l'exécution du programme, avant qu'il efface d'autres fichiers** abort the program before it erases any more files ◇ **on a interrompu le programme en appuyant sur la touche rouge** the program was aborted by pressing the red button
SVGA *nom* **1.** super VGA **2.** SVGA
S-vidéo *f nom* Y/C video
S-Video *nom* S-Video
SX *nom* SX
symbole *nom* symbol ◇ **ce langage utilise le symbole ? pour la commande d'impression** this language uses the symbol ? to represent the print command ◇ **(code** *ou* **touche de) retour (du) chariot** *ou* **retour à la ligne** carriage return (CR) ◇ **symbole de fin** *f* **de ligne** return ◇ **symbole graphique** graphic symbol
symbole *m* **d'arrêt** *nom* breakpoint symbol
symbole *m* **de branchement** *nom* decision box
symbole *m* **de commentaire** *nom* annotation symbol
symbole *m* **de condition** *nom* decision box
symbole *m* **de décision** *nom* decision box
symbole *m* **de détection** *nom* aiming symbol *ou* aiming field
symbole *m* **d'un ordinogramme** *plural noun* flowchart symbol
symbole *m* **ECMA** *nom* ECMA symbol
symbole *m* **intercalaire** *nom* separator
symbole *m* **logique** *nom* logic symbol
symbolique *adjectif* symbolic
symétrie *f nom* balance
synchro *f nom* synchronisation
synchro *f* **automatique** *nom* autosync
synchrone *adjectif* synchronous ◇ **protocole SDLC (de transmission de données en mode synchrone)** synchronous data link control (SDLC) ◇ **repérage synchrone** synchronous detection
synchronisation *f nom* **1.** sync **2.** synchronisation
synchronisation *f* **de blocs** *nom* block synchronisation
synchronisation *f* **de l'annuaire** *nom* directory synchronisation
synchronisation *f* **de réseau** *nom* network timing
synchroniser *verbe* **1.** *vt* to clock **2.** *vt* to synchronise

'...dès lors, le rôle du programme de gestion de données consiste aussi à synchroniser la lecture des différents blocs texte/image et son' [*Micro Systèmes*]

synchroniseur *m nom* synchroniser
syndicat ◇ **syndicat** *m* **européen des constructeurs d'ordinateurs** ECMA
syntaxe *f nom* grammar ■ *plural noun* language rules ■ *nom* syntax ◇ **qui va contre les règles de la syntaxe** illegal
synthèse *f nom* synthesis
synthèse *f* **additive de couleurs** *nom* additive colour
synthèse *f* **vocale** *nom* **1.** speech synthesis **2.** voice synthesis
synthétiser *verbe vt* to synthesise
synthétiseur *m nom* synthesiser
synthétiseur *m* **de modulations de fréquence** *nom* FM synthesiser
synthétiseur *m* **d'onde** *nom* waveform synthesiser
synthétiseur *m* **vocal** *nom* voice synthesiser
synthétiseur *m* **vocal de la parole** *nom* speech synthesiser
SyQuest (*fabricant de dispositifs de stockage*) SyQuest
systématique *adjectif* unconditional
système *nom* (*informatique*) system ◇ **système** *m* **de définition de couleurs: cyan, magenta, jaune, noir** CMYK ◇ **système** *m* **de gestion des priorités en fonctionnement parallèle** parallel priority system ◇ **système** *m* **de programmation à surcharge de fonctions** function overloading ◇ **système** *m* **de rappel automatique d'un correspondant** auto-redial ◇ **système** *m* **de référence de couleurs Pantone** (*nom de marque*) Pantone Matching System ◇ **système** *m* **de secours prêt à fonctionner** hot standby ◇ **système** *m* **de sécurité** (*en cas de défaillance*) fail safe system ◇ **système** *m* **de sécurité en cas de coupure de courant** fail safe system ◇ **système** *m* **de traitement de texte doté d'une interface de communication** communicating word processor ◇ **système d'exploitation** operating system (op sys) ◇ **système** *m* **d'information pour la direction** executive information system ◇ **système** *m* **moderne de télécommunication avec les mobiles** universal mobile telecommunications system
système *m* **à 64 bits** 64-bit
système *m* **à accès multiple** *nom* **1.** multi-access system **2.** multiple access system
système *m* **à base de connaissances** *nom* knowledge-based system
système *m* **à base de règles** *nom* rule-based system
système *m* **à bus auxiliaire** *nom* dual bus system
système *m* **à bus double** *nom* dual bus system

système *m* **à bus fermé** *nom* closed bus system

système *m* **à bus multiples** *nom* **1.** multibus system *ou* multibus architecture **2.** multiple bus system *ou* multiple bus architecture

système *m* **à courants porteurs** *nom* carrier system

système *m* **à double rang de broches** *nom* DIL

système *m* **à double rang de broches (parallèles)** *nom* dual-in-line package

système *m* **à fichiers répartis** *nom* distributed file system

système *m* **à multiples connexions** *nom* multilink system

système *m* **à plusieurs terminaux** *nom* multi terminal system

système *m* **arborescent** *nom* tree and branch network system

système *m* **à ressources partagées** *nom* shared resources system

système *m* **à transfert de mémoire** *nom* memory switching system

système *m* **auteur** *nom* authoring software *ou* authoring system

système *m* **auto-adaptable** *nom* adaptive system

système *m* **auto-adaptatif** *nom* self-adapting system

système *m* **autonome** *nom* stand-alone system ◇ **les postes ont été reliés en réseau plutôt que d'être utilisés comme postes autonomes** *ou* **comme postes individuels** the workstations have been networked together rather than used as stand-alone systems

système *m* **avec autocontrôle** *nom* self-checking system

système *m* **avec contrôle automatique** *nom* self-checking system

système *m* **avec mémoire de masse** *nom* mass storage system

système *m* **binaire** *nom* binary system

système *m* **britannique équivalent au Minitel™** *nom* viewdata

système *m* **clé en main** *nom* turnkey system

système-conseil *m nom* advisory system

système *m* **d'aide à la décision** *nom* decision support system

système *m* **d'alimentation** *nom* feeder

système *m* **d'appel automatique** *nom* **1.** (*d'un correspondant*) auto-dial **2.** automatic calling unit

système *m* **d'assemblage** *nom* assembly system

système *m* **de base de données** *nom* database system

système *m* **de base de données réparties** *nom* distributed database system

système *m* **décentralisé** *nom* distributed system

système *m* **de chiffrement PGP** *nom* **1.** PGP **2.** pretty good privacy

système *m* **de communication hiérarchisé** *nom* hierarchical communications system

système *m* **de communication optoélectronique** *nom* optical communication system

système *m* **de conduite de processus** *nom* process control system

système *m* **de contrôle** *nom* process control system

système *m* **de contrôle intégré** *nom* built-in check

système *m* **de déboguage interactif** *nom* interactive debugging system

système *m* **de déverminage** *nom* interactive debugging system

système *m* **de fichiers hiérarchisés** *nom* hierarchical filing system

système *m* **de fiducie de la clé** *nom* key escrow

système *m* **de gestion de base de données** *nom* DBMS

système *m* **de gestion de base de données relationnelle** *abrév* RDBMS

système *m* **de gestion de données** *abrév* DMS

système *m* **de gestion de fichiers en réseau** *nom* network file system ■ *abrév* NFS

système *m* **de gestion de l'information** *abrév* IMS ■ *nom* information management system

système *m* **de gestion hiérarchique des fichiers** *nom* HFS

système *m* **de hash code** *nom* hash-code system

système *m* **de lancement de tâches à distance** *nom* **1.** remote job entry **2.** RJE

système *m* **de ligne de commande** *nom* command line operating system

système *m* **de machines-outils à commandes numériques** *nom* **1.** flexible machining system **2.** FMS

système *m* **de mémoire à disque magnétique** *nom* FEDS

système *m* **de messagerie** *nom* computer-based message system

système *m* **de monoprogrammation** *nom* monoprogramming system

système *m* **de noms de domaine** *nom* DNS

système *m* **d'entraînement** *nom* feeder

système *m* **de paiement bancaire par Internet** *nom* bank Internet payment system

système *m* **de rappel automatique** *nom* ring back system

système *m* **de recherche par descripteurs** *nom* aspect system

système *m* **de reconnaissance de caractères CSM** *nom* **1.** (*par identification des caractéristiques combinées*) combined symbol matching **2.** (*par identification des caractéristiques combinées*) CSM

système *m* **de référence** *nom* (*de transfert de message électronique*) reference retrieval system

système *m* **de secours lancé manuellement** *nom* cold standby

système *m* **de stockage par descripteurs** *nom* aspect system

système *m* **de stockage rapide sur disques multiples (RAID)** *nom* **1.** RAID **2.** redundant array of inexpensive disks

système *m* **de thésaurus** *nom* KWAC

système *m* **de traitement de l'image** *nom* image processor

système *m* **de traitement de texte communicant** *abrév* CWP

système *m* **de traitement de texte spécialisé** *nom* dedicated word-processor

système *m* **de traitement par lots** *nom* batch system

système *m* **de traitement par paquets** *nom* batch system

système *m* **de transmission numérique** *nom* digital transmission system

système *m* **d'exploitation** *nom* **1.** executive control program **2.** operating system **3.** OS

système *m* **d'exploitation Apple System** (*nom de marque*) Apple System

système *m* **d'exploitation de disque** *nom* **1.** disk operating system **2.** DOS

système *m* **d'exploitation de réseau** *nom* network operating system ■ *abrév* NOS

système *m* **d'exploitation en temps réel** *nom* real-time operating system

système *m* **d'exploitation intégrée** *nom* computer-integrated system

système *m* **d'exploitation mobile** (*nom de marque*) Windows CE

système *m* **d'exploitation MS-DOS** Microsoft DOS

système *m* **d'exploitation multiprogramme** *nom* concurrent operating system

système *m* **d'exploitation PICK™** *nom* PICK

système *m* **d'exploitation Taligent™** *nom* Taligent

système *m* **d'information de gestion** *abrév* MIS

système *m* **d'information pour la direction** *nom* EIS

système *m* **disjoncteur progressif** *nom* fail soft system

système *m* **Dolby AC-3** Dolby AC-3

système *m* **DOS** *nom* disk operating system

système *m* **duodécimal** *nom* duodecimal number system

système *m* **duplex** *nom* duplex computer

système *m* **dynamique** *nom* adaptive system

système *m* **EDI** *nom* electronic data interchange

système *m* **électronique d'échange de données** *nom* electronic data interchange

système *m* **embarqué** *nom* embedded system

système *m* **en ligne** *nom* online system

système *m* **en temps réel** *nom* real-time system ◇ **dans un système en temps réel, le déplacement de l'image vers la gauche est parfaitement synchronisé au mouvement du manche à balai vers la gauche** in a real-time system, as you move the joystick left, the image on the screen moves left. If there is a pause for processing it is not a true real-time system ◇ **s'il se produit un délai de traitement entre l'action et le résultat, il ne s'agit pas d'un véritable système en temps réel** in a real-time system, as you move the joystick left, the image on the screen moves left. If there is a pause for processing it is not a true real-time system

système *m* **expert** *nom* **1.** expert system **2.** IKBS **3.** intelligent knowledge-based system

système *m* **extensible** *nom* expandable system

système *m* **général de radiocommunication par paquets** *nom* general packet radio service

système *m* **hâtivement bricolé** *nom* kludge *ou* kluge

système *m* **hybride** *nom* hybrid system

système *m* **imbriqué (dans un autre)** *nom* embedded computer

système *m* **indéterminé** *nom* indeterminate system

système *m* **infographique PHIGS** *nom* **1.** PHIGS **2.** programmer's hierarchical interactive graphics standard

système *m* **informatique** *nom* **1.** computer system **2.** information system

système *m* **informatique de 32 bits** *nom* thirty-two bit system *ou* 32-bit system

système *m* **informatique pour bureau** *nom* computer office system

système *m* **intégré** *nom* embedded computer

système *m* **intégré d'information** IIS

système *m* **intelligent à base de connaissances** *nom* **1.** IKBS **2.** intelligent knowledge-based system

système *m* **interactif** *nom* interactive system

système *m* **interbancaire de télécompensation** *nom* **1.** BACS **2.** Bankers Automated Clearing Services

système *m* **intermédiaire** *nom* intermediate system ■ *abrév* IS

système *m* **intermédiaire à système** *m* **intermédiaire** *nom* intermediate system to intermediate system

système *m* **IRC** *nom* Internet relay chat

système *m* **logique partagé** *nom* shared logic system

système *m* **maillé** *nom* multilink system

système *m* **maître/esclave** *nom* master/slave computer system

système *m* **maître/maître** *nom* master/master computer system

système *m* **moderne de télécommunication avec les mobiles** *nom* UMTS

système *m* **mondial de communications mobiles** *nom* **1.** global system for mobile communications **2.** GSM

système *m* **mono-utilisateur** *nom* single-user system

système *m* **multi-accès** *nom* **1.** multi-access system **2.** multiple access system

système *m* **multibus** *nom* **1.** multibus system *ou* multibus architecture **2.** multiple bus system *ou* multiple bus architecture

système *m* **multilecteur (de disques dur)** *nom* drive array

système *m* **multiligne** *nom* multilink system

système *m* **multimédia interactif** *nom* interactive multimedia ◇ **ce logiciel multimédia interactif permet à l'utilisateur de faire de la musique avec un programme de synthétiseur** this interactive multimedia title allows a user to make music with a synthesizer program

système *m* **multipage** *nom* multiple base page

système *m* **multiplex** *nom* carrier system

système *m* **multiposte** *nom* **1.** multi terminal system **2.** multiuser system ◇ **on peut exécuter le programme sur un ordinateur indépendant ou sur un système multiposte** the program runs on a standalone machine or a multi-user system

système *m* **multiprocesseur** *nom* multiprocessing system

système *m* **multitâche préemptif** *nom* preemptive multitasking

système *m* **multi-utilisateur** *nom* **1.** multiuser system **2.** shared resources system

système *m* **numérique** *nom* digital system

système (d'exploitation) OS/2™ OS/2

système *m* **ouvert** *nom* open system

système *m* **(de référence de couleurs) Pantone** *abrév* PMS

système-pilote *m* *nom* pilot system

système *m* **POP 3** *nom* POP 3

système *m* **relié à l'ordinateur** *nom* online system

système *m* **réparti** *nom* distributed system

système *m* **RSA** *nom* Rivest, Shamir, Adleman

système *m* **satellite de base** *nom* basic control system satellite

systèmes *mpl* **de contrôle** *plural noun* control systems

systèmes *mpl* **d'exploitation des entrées/sorties** *nom* (*adapté à chaque ordinateur*) basic input/output operating system

systèmes *mpl* **doubles** *plural noun* dual systems

système *m* **sécurisé** *nom* secure system

système *m* **simple image** *nom* single-system image

système *m* **SMB** *nom* (*de partage de fichiers*) server message block

système *m* **SMB (de partage de fichiers)** *nom* SMB

système *m* **synchrone** *nom* synchronous system

système *m* **transactionnel** *nom* **1.** TDS **2.** transaction-driven system

système *m* **verrouillé** *nom* secure system

système *m* **WAIS** *nom* **1.** WAIS **2.** wide area information server

système *m* **X-Window (d'API)** X-Window System *ou* X-Windows

T

T1 *nom* T1

table *nom* **1.** reference table **2.** table ◇ **table** *f* **d'adresse des secteurs marqués inutilisables** sector map ◇ **table** *f* **de contrôle des paramètres d'écran couleur** video lookup table ◇ **table de référence** *ou* **d'équivalence** lookup table (LUT) ◇ **table des fichiers système** system file table ◇ **table** *f* **d'occupation des pages en mémoire annexe** shadow page table ◇ **tables** *fpl* **d'équivalence** conversion tables ◇ **voici la fonction de cette touche, pour la traduire en ASCII consultez la table d'équivalence** this is the value of the key pressed, use a lookup table to find its ASCII value

tableau *m nom* **1.** array **2.** spreadsheet **3.** table

tableau *m* **à deux dimensions** *nom* two-dimensional array

tableau *m* **à dimensions variables** *nom* flexible array

tableau *m* **alphanumérique** *nom* alphanumeric array

tableau *m* **à trois dimensions** *nom* three-dimensional array

tableau *m* **bidimensionnel** *nom* two-dimensional array

tableau *m* **d'affichage** *nom* **1.** BBS **2.** notice board

tableau *m* **de chaînes de caractères** *nom* string array

tableau *m* **de chiffres** *nom* numeric array

tableau *m* **des indicateurs** *nom* indicator chart

tableau *m* **multidimensionnel** *nom* multidimensional array

tableau *m* **noir électronique** *nom* electronic blackboard

tableau *m* **numérique** *nom* numeric array

tableau *m* **réduit** *nom* sparse array

table *f* **d'allocation de fichier** *nom* file allocation table

table *f* **d'allocation des fichiers** *nom* FAT

table *f* **d'attributs** *nom* image table

table *f* **de Boole** *nom* Boolean operation table

table *f* **de branchements** *nom* branch table

table *f* **de conversion** *nom* LUT

table *f* **de correspondance des adresses** *nom* address mapping

table *f* **de décision** *nom* decision table

table *f* **de fausses couleurs** *nom* CLUT

table *f* **de fonctions** *nom* function table

table *f* **de Karnaugh** *nom* Karnaugh map ◇ **le prototype a fait l'objet d'un contrôle de fiabilité statistique sur la base des tables de Karnaugh** the prototype was checked for hazards with a Karnaugh map

table *f* **de noms** *nom* name table

table *f* **de pages** *nom* page table

table *f* **de priorité des interruptions** *nom* priority interrupt table

table *f* **d'équivalence** *nom* **1.** look-up table **2.** substitution table

table *f* **d'équivalence couleur** *nom* colour look-up table

table *f* **de référence** *nom* look-up table

table *f* **de référence couleur** *nom* colour look-up table

table *f* **de référence de programme** *nom* reference program table

table *f* **de routage** *nom* routing table

table *f* **des adresses hash codées** *nom* hash table

table *f* **des matières** *nom* table of contents

table *f* **de substitution** *nom* substitution table

table *f* **de vérité** *nom* **1.** Boolean operation table **2.** truth table

table *f* **FAT** *nom* FAT

tables *fpl* **de conversation** *plural noun* translation tables

tables *fpl* **de conversion** *plural noun* conversion tables

tables *fpl* **d'équivalence** *plural noun* **1.** conversion tables **2.** translation tables

tables *fpl* **de référence** *plural noun* translation tables

table *f* **symbolique** *nom* symbolic table

tablette ◇ **tablette** *f* **à numériser** (*pour saisie de texte écrit à la main*) writing pad

tablette *f* **à numériser** *nom* **1.** data tablet **2.** digitising pad *ou* digitising tablet *ou* digitizing pad *ou* digitizing tablet **3.** graphics pad **4.** tablet

tablette *f* **graphique** *nom* **1.** digitising pad *ou* digitising tablet *ou* digitizing pad *ou* digitizing tablet **2.** graphics pad **3.** tablet

tablette *f* graphique *ou* à numériser *nom* graphics tablet
tableur *m nom* spreadsheet
tabulateur *m nom* tabulator
tabulation *f nom* tabbing ■ *plural noun* tab settings *ou* tab stops ■ *nom* tabulation ◇ **la tabulation peut être incorporée au programme** tabbing can be done from inside the program
tabulation *f* décimale *nom* decimal tabbing
tabulation *f* verticale *nom* vertical tab
tabuler *verbe* **1.** *vt* to tab **2.** *vt* to tabulate ◇ **en appuyant sur la touche de tabulation en début de ligne, pour se placer à la colonne 10, la liste se trouvait parfaitement alignée** the list was neatly lined up by tabbing to column 10 at the start of each new line
tâche *f nom* **1.** job **2.** task ◇ **commande de tâches à distance** remote job entry (RJE) ◇ **langage contrôle de tâche *ou* de commande de tâche** job control language (JCL) ◇ **la tâche suivante consistera à trier tous les enregistrements** the next job to be processed is to sort all the records ◇ **tâche *f* qui peut être exécutée automatiquement** unattended operation
tâche *f* d'arrière-plan *nom* low-priority work
tâche *f* de fond *nom* **1.** background job **2.** background task
tâche *f* de premier plan *nom* foreground
tâche *f* d'impression *nom* print job
tâche *f* non prioritaire *nom* **1.** background job **2.** background task **3.** low-priority work
tâche *f* prioritaire *nom* foreground
tâches *fpl plural noun* (*d'un ordinateur*) activities
taille *f nom* size ◇ **la taille des caractères a été augmentée pour rendre la lecture plus facile** the size of the print has been increased to make it easier to read ◇ **taille *ou* grandeur *ou* format de la page** page size
taille *f* de caractères *nom* type size
taille *f* de fichier *nom* file size
taille *f* de la mémoire tampon *nom* buffer length
taille *f* de l'échantillon *nom* sample size
taille *f* de l'écran *nom* screen size
taille *f* de l'environnement *nom* environment space
taille *f* de mémoire *nom* storage capacity ◇ **la capacité *ou* la taille de la mémoire est maintenant de 3Mo** total storage capacity is now 3MB
taille *f* de mémoire tampon *nom* buffer size
taille *f* des caractères *nom* point size
taille *f* d'un champ *nom* field length
taille *f* d'une chaîne *nom* string length
taille *f* d'un enregistrement *nom* record length
taille *f* d'un fichier *nom* file extent
taille *f* d'un registre *nom* register length
tambour *m nom* drum
tambour *m* magnétique *nom* magnetic drum
tampon *m* circulaire *nom* circular buffer
tampon *m* d'imprimante *nom* printer buffer
tampon *m* élémentaire *nom* unit buffer
tampon *m* (d') entrée/sortie *nom* input/output buffer
taper (un code) *verbe* to enter
taper au clavier *verbe* to type
tapis *m nom* mat
tapis *m* antistatique *nom* anti-static mat
tarif *m nom* tariff ◇ **il existe un tarif forfaitaire d'utilisation plus un taux *or* minute de temps d'ordinateur** there is a set tariff for logging on, then a rate for every minute of computer time used
tatouage *m* numérique *nom* watermark
taux *m nom* **1.** rate **2.** transfer rate
taux *m* d'activité *nom* activity ratio
taux *m* de clics *nom* click through rate
taux *m* de cliquage *nom* click rate
taux *m* de défaillance *nom* failure rate
taux *m* d'émission *nom* release rate
taux *m* d'erreur *nom* error rate ◇ **le taux d'erreur est inférieur à 1%** the error rate is less than 1%
taux *m* d'erreur de transmission *nom* **1.** BER **2.** bit error rate
taux *m* d'erreur par bloc *nom* block error rate
taux *m* d'erreur résiduel *nom* **1.** ratio **2.** residual error rate ◇ **le taux des bits corrompus par message transmis est moins élevé grâce aux nouvelles technologies** the ratio of corrupt bits per transmitted message is falling with new technology
taux *m* de trame *nom* frame rate
technicien, -ienne *m,f nom* technician ◇ **le nouveau système a été mis en place par les techniciens *ou* ce sont les techniciens qui ont installé le nouveau système** the computer technicians installed the new system ◇ **technicien, -ienne de laboratoire** laboratory technician
technicien/réparateur *m nom* troubleshooter
technique *adjectif* technical ■ *nom* technique ◇ **ce document contient tous les renseignements d'ordre technique concernant le nouvel ordinateur** the document gives all the technical details on the new computer ◇ **la société a mis au point une nouvelle technique de traitement des disquettes clients** the company has developed a new technique for processing customers' disks
technique *f* alpha bêta *nom* alpha beta technique
technique *f* d'évaluation et de révision de programme *nom* PERT

technique *f* **d'évaluation et de révision des programmes** *nom* program evaluation and review technique

techniques *f nom* technology

techniques *fpl* **de l'information** *nom* information technology

technologie *nom* technology ◇ **l'introduction de nouvelles technologies** the introduction of new technology ◇ **technologie** *f* **audiotex** audiotex ◇ **technologie** *f* **de la fibre optique** fibre optics ◇ **technologie de l'information** information technology (IT) ◇ **technologie** *f* **STT** (*d'achat en ligne sécurisé*) secure transaction technology

technologie *f* **ActiveX** (*nom de marque*) ActiveX

technologie *f* **de pointe** *adjectif* high-tech ■ *nom* new technology

technologie *f* **d'interconnexion Fibre Channel** *nom* fibre channel

technologie *f* **du pousser** *nom* push technology

technologie *f* **Indeo™** (*nom de marque*) Indeo

technologie *f* **MMX** (*nom de marque*) MMX

technologie *f* **patrimoniale** *nom* legacy

technologies *fpl* **de l'information** *abrév* IT

technologie *f* **VBX** (*nom de marque*) Visual Basic Extension

technologie *f* **Visual C** (*nom de marque*) Visual C

technologique *adjectif* technological ◇ **la révolution technologique** the technological revolution

teinte *f nom* **1.** hue **2.** hue, saturation and intensity **3.** tint

télé- *préfixe* tele-

télébanque *f nom* home banking

téléchargement *m* **de police de caractères** *nom* automatic font downloading

télécharger *abrév vt* DL ■ *verbe* **1.** *vt* (*des données, des polices de caractères*) to download **2.** *vt* to download **3.** *vt* to upload ◇ **il n'en coûte rien de télécharger, depuis le tableau d'affichage, un logiciel qui n'est pas protégé par un copyright** there is no charge for downloading public domain software from the BBS ◇ **l'utilisateur peut télécharger les données d'un PC sur un gros ordinateur, pour faire la mise à jour des applications** the user can upload PC data to update mainframe applications ◇ **télécharger des données vers un autre ordinateur ou serveur** to upload

télécommande *f nom* remote control

télécommunications *f nom* telecommunications

téléconférence *f nom* **1.** conferencing **2.** (*téléphone*) teleconference **3.** (*téléphone*) teleconferencing

téléconférence *f nom* computer conferencing

télécopie *f nom* **1.** facsimile transmission **2.** fax *ou* FAX ◇ **modem avec fonction télécopie** *ou* **télécopieur-modem** *ou* **fax-modem** *ou* **fax** *or* **modem** fax-modem ◇ **nous enverrons les plans par télécopie** *ou* **par fax** we will send a fax of the design plan ◇ **papier pour télécopieur** fax paper ◇ **transmission par télécopie** fax transmission

téléimprimeur *m nom* **1.** teleprinter **2.** teletypewriter ◇ **opérateur, -trice de téléimprimeur** *ou* **télétypiste** teleprinter operator ◇ **vous pouvez connecter un téléimprimeur sur ce port série modifié** you can drive a teleprinter from this modified serial port

téléinformatique *f nom* data communications

télématique *f nom* telematics

télématique *f* **médicale** *nom* medical telematics

téléphone *m nom* **1.** phone **2.** telephone ◇ **abonné, -ée du téléphone** telephone subscriber ◇ **annuaire des téléphones** *ou* **annuaire téléphonique** telephone book *ou* telephone directory ◇ **annuaire téléphonique** *ou* **des téléphones** phone book ◇ **elle a passé la matinée (à parler) au téléphone** she has been on the phone all morning ◇ **faire un appel** *ou* **téléphoner** *ou* **appeler** to make a telephone call ◇ **faire une commande par téléphone** to place an order by telephone ◇ **il a eu le directeur au téléphone** he spoke to the manager on the phone ◇ **il a une liste de numéros de téléphone dans un petit carnet noir** he keeps a list of phone numbers in a little black book ◇ **le numéro de téléphone figure sur le papier à en-tête de la société** the phone number is on the company notepaper ◇ **numéro de téléphone** telephone number ◇ **parler au téléphone** to be on the phone ◇ **parler au téléphone** *ou* **être en ligne** to be on the telephone ◇ **par téléphone** by telephone ◇ **par téléphone** *ou* **téléphonique** by phone ◇ **pouvez-vous me donner votre numéro de téléphone?** can you give me your phone number?; can you give me your telephone number? ◇ **répéteur de téléphone** telephone repeater ◇ **répondre au téléphone** to answer the phone *ou* to take a phone call ◇ **répondre au téléphone** *ou* **prendre un appel** *ou* **prendre une communication** to answer the telephone *ou* to take a telephone call ◇ **téléphone à carte** card phone ◇ **téléphone cellulaire** cellular telephone ◇ **téléphone de conférence** conference telephone ◇ **téléphone interne** house phone *ou* internal phone; house telephone *ou* internal telephone ◇ **téléphoner** *ou* **appeler** *ou* **faire un appel** *ou* **passer un coup de fil** to make a phone call ◇ **transmission de**

données par téléphone *ou* **sur le réseau commuté** telephone (data carrier)

téléphone *m* **cellulaire** *nom* cellular phone

téléphone *m* **mobile** *nom* mobile phone

téléphonie *f nom* telephony ◇ **convergence téléphonie-informatique (CTI)** computer telephony integration (CTI)

téléphonie *f* **sur Internet** *nom* **1.** Internet telephony **2.** netphone

téléscripteur *m nom* **1.** teleprinter **2.** teletype

téléspectateur *m nom* viewer

Télétex™ *nom* teletext

'...mal connu et, de ce fait, peu aimé, le mode télétex combine cependant des avantages. Il fonctionne à 2400 bits/seconde, une vitesse tout à fait correcte pour transmettre de l'information codée. Les 309 symboles permettent la transmission de documents bien préparés avec un minimum de graphisme' [*Temps Micro*]

télétraitement *m nom* teleprocessing ■ *abrév* TP

télétravail *m nom* telecommuting

télétype *m nom* teleprinter ■ *abrév* TTY

télévision *f abrév* TV

télévision *f nom* television

télévision *f* **à balayage lent** *nom* slow scan TV

télévision *f* **à définition améliorée** *nom* **1.** EDTV **2.** enhanced-definition television **3.** extended-definition television

télévision *f* **à haute définition** *abrév* HDTV ■ *nom* high definition television

télévision *f* **interactive** *nom* interactive TV

télévision *f* **numérique** *nom* digital TV

témoin *nom* **1.** carry flag **2.** flag ◇ **témoin** *m* **lumineux de charge** (*de la batterie*) battery meter

témoin *m* **d'activité** *nom* activity light

témoin *m* **lumineux de charge** *nom* meter – power supply

température *f* **ambiante** *nom* ambient temperature

température *f* **chromatique** *nom* colour temperature

tempo *m nom* tempo ◇ **avec MIDI, le tempo est habituellement de 120bpm** a typical MIDI tempo is 120bpm

temporaire *adjectif* temporary

temps ◇ **temps** *m* **de préparation entre deux tâches** takedown time ◇ **temps** *m* **d'exécution (d'un programme)** run-duration

temps *m* **absolu** *nom* absolute time

temps *m* **CPU** *nom* CPU time

temps *m* **d'accélération** *nom* acceleration time

temps *m* **d'accès** *nom* **1.** access time **2.** positioning time **3.** reaction time **4.** seek time

temps *m* **d'accès à la mémoire** *nom* memory access time

temps *m* **d'accès moyen** *nom* average access time

temps *m* **d'addition** *nom* **1.** addition time **2.** add time

temps *m* **d'adressage** *nom* address access time

temps *m* **d'appels sélectifs** *nom* polling overhead

temps *m* **d'arrêt** *nom* stop time

temps *m* **d'association** *nom* (*d'une adresse*) binding time

temps *m* **d'attente dans la file** *nom* queuing time

temps *m* **de bon fonctionnement** *nom* uptime *ou* up time

temps *m* **de compilation** *nom* compilation time

temps *m* **de connexion** *nom* connect time

temps *m* **d'écriture** *nom* write time

temps *m* **de cycle** *nom* cycle time

temps *m* **de cycle d'instruction** *nom* instruction cycle time

temps *m* **de débit d'un onduleur** *nom* holdup

temps *m* **de décélération** *nom* **1.** deceleration time **2.** stop time

temps *m* **de développement** *nom* (*de mise au point d'un nouveau produit*) development time

temps *m* **de disponibilité** *nom* available time

temps *m* **de latence** *nom* **1.** idle time **2.** latency

temps *m* **de mise en place** *nom* positioning time

temps *m* **de montée** *nom* acceleration time ◇ **il faut inclure le temps de montée dans le temps d'accès** allow for acceleration time in the access time

temps *m* **d'enregistrement** *nom* write time

temps *m* **de réponse** *nom* **1.** acceleration time **2.** answer time **3.** response time

temps *m* **de report** *nom* carry time

temps *m* **de traitement** *nom* run-time *ou* run duration

temps *m* **de transfert** *nom* transfer time

temps *m* **de transfert d'un mot** *nom* word time

temps *m* **d'exécution** *nom* **1.** execution time **2.** (*d'un programme*) run-time *ou* run duration **3.** turnaround time

temps *m* **d'exécution (d'une tâche)** *nom* operating time

temps *m* **d'exécution d'une instruction** *nom* instruction execution time

temps *m* **d'exécution d'une opération** *nom* operation time

temps *m* **d'exécution d'une tâche** *nom* elapsed time

temps *m* **d'instruction** *nom* instruction time

temps *m* **disponible** *nom* available time

temps *m* **d'occupation de la ligne** *nom* holding time

temps *m* **d'ordinateur** *nom* computer time ◇ **tous ces rapports de vente coûtent cher en temps d'ordinateur** running all those sales reports costs a lot in computer time

temps *m* **d'un dispositif de secours** *nom* holdup

temps *m* **d'utilisation de l'unité centrale** *nom* CPU time

temps *m* **d'utilisation du processeur** *nom* CPU time

temps *m* **mort** *nom* **1.** dead time **2.** downtime *ou* down time

temps *m* **partagé** *nom* time-sharing

temps *m* **passé à une tâche** *nom* elapsed time

temps *m* **productif** *nom* **1.** productive time **2.** uptime *ou* up time

temps *m* **réel** *nom* real time ◇ **émission en direct** program shown in real time ◇ **en direct** in real time ◇ **en temps réel** in real time ◇ **exécution (d'un programme) en temps réel** real time execution (RTE) ◇ **un système de navigation doit pouvoir faire le point en temps réel et prendre les mesures nécessaires pour éviter de heurter un écueil** a navigation system needs to be able to process the position of a ship in real time and take suitable action before she hits a rock

tenir un journal *verbe* to log

tension *nom* voltage ◇ **baisse de tension** voltage dip *ou* dip in voltage

> '...cette fonction permet de mesurer la chute de tension d'une fonction de semi-conducteur traversée par une intensité d'environ un milliampère' [*Electronique pratique*]

téra- *préfixe* tera-

téraflops *m nom* teraflop

téraoctet *m nom* terabyte

terminaison *f nom* termination

terminal *nom* **1.** data terminal **2.** station **3.** terminal ◇ **le gestionnaire de système utilise le terminal principal pour relancer le système** the system manager uses the master terminal to restart the system ◇ **terminal** *m* **de mise à jour rapide** bulk update terminal

terminal *m* **(de réseau)** *nom* terminal

terminal *m* **à adressage protégé** *nom* addressable terminal ◇ **tous les messages sont transmis à tous les terminaux puisqu'aucun d'eux ne possède un adressage protégé** all the messages go to all the terminals since none are addressable terminals

terminal *m* **à distance** *nom* remote terminal

terminal *m* **asservi** *nom* slave terminal

terminal *m* **autonome** *nom* stand-alone terminal

terminal *m* **conversationnel** *nom* interactive terminal

terminal *m* **d'application** *nom* job orientated terminal

terminal *m* **d'arrivée** *nom* **1.** receive only **2.** RO

terminal *m* **de CAO** *nom* graphics terminal

terminal *m* **de données prêt** *nom* DTR

terminal *m* **d'entrée de données vidéotex** *nom* IP terminal

terminal *m* **de traitement de données** *nom* data terminal equipment

terminal *m* **de transfert de données** *nom* DTE

terminal *m* **de transfert électronique de fonds** *nom* electronic funds transfer point-of-sale

terminal *m* **de transmission de données** *nom* data terminal equipment

terminal *m* **éloigné** *nom* remote terminal

terminal *m* **entrée/sortie** *nom* **1.** keyboard send/receive **2.** KSR

terminal *m* **graphique** *nom* graphics terminal

terminal *m* **intelligent** *nom* **1.** intelligent terminal **2.** smart terminal ◇ **le nouveau terminal intelligent comporte un éditeur de texte** the new intelligent terminal has a built-in text editor

terminal *m* **interactif** *nom* interactive terminal

terminal *m* **maître** *nom* master terminal

terminal *m* **non intelligent** *nom* dumb terminal

terminal *m* **principal** *nom* **1.** key terminal **2.** master terminal ◇ **le gestionnaire de système utilise le terminal principal pour relancer le système** the system manager uses the master terminal to restart the system

terminal *m* **principal** *ou* **central** *nom* central terminal

terminal *m* **public** *nom* public access terminal

terminal *m* **satellite** *nom* satellite terminal

terminal *m* **spécialisé** *nom* job orientated terminal

terminal *m* **vidéo** *abrév* VDT ■ *nom* video terminal

terminal *m* **virtuel** *nom* virtual terminal

terminateur *m* **de réseau** *nom* terminator ◇ **dispositif de fin de ligne** line terminator

terminateur *m* **SCSI** *nom* terminator

terminer *verbe* **1.** *vt* to close **2.** *vt* to terminate

ternaire *adjectif* ternary

test *m nom* test

test *m* **à chaud** *nom* burn-in

test *m* **assisté par ordinateur** *nom* **1.** CAT **2.** computer-aided testing **3.** computer-assisted testing

test *m* **bêta** *nom* beta test ◇ **cette application a passé le stade des tests alpha et commence la série de tests bêta** the application has passed the alpha tests and is just entering the beta test phase

test *m* **de câble par réflectométrie** *nom* **1.** TDR **2.** time domain reflectometry

test *m* **de diagnostic** *nom* diagnostic test

test *m* **de lecture/écriture aléatoire des mémoires** *nom* leap-frog test

test *m* **de polarité** *nom* polarity test

test *m* **des paramètres** *nom* parameter testing

test *m* **de Turing** *nom* Turing test

test *m* **d'évaluation des performances** *nom* benchmark ◇ **la revue a publié les résultats du banc d'essai** *ou* **du test d'évaluation des performances du nouveau programme** the magazine gave the new program's benchmark test results

test *m* **d'évaluation d'un logiciel** *nom* test run

test *m* **d'homologation** *nom* **1.** acceptance test **2.** acceptance testing

test *m* **(d'évaluation des performances) Dhrystone** *nom* Dhrystone benchmark

testé, -ée dans des conditions réelles *adjectif* field-tested

tester *verbe vt* to test ◇ **l'appareil a été testé à outrance** *ou* **testé sous tous les angles avant la livraison** the device was soak-tested prior to delivery ◇ **tester en continu sur une longue période** soak

tester à chaud *verbe* to burn in

tester à outrance *verbe* to soak ◇ **l'appareil a été testé à outrance** *ou* **testé sous tous les angles avant la livraison** the device was soak-tested prior to delivery

testeur *m nom* **1.** exerciser **2.** test equipment ◇ **l'ingénieur possède un équipement spécialisé pour effectuer les tests sur ce modèle** the engineer has special test equipment for this model

testeur *m* **de câble** *nom* cable tester

test *m* **rétrospectif en parallèle** *nom* retrospective parallel running

test *m* **saut de puce** *nom* leap-frog test

test *m* **saut de puce limité à un seul emplacement** *nom* crippled leapfrog test

tests *mpl* **de saturation** *nom* saturation testing

test *m* **sélectif** *nom* leap-frog test

test *m* **sélectif limité** *nom* crippled leapfrog test

tête *nom* head ◇ **durée** *f* **de vie de la tête** headlife ◇ **tête** *ou* **début d'une page (de papier listing)** head of form (HOF) ◇ **tête** *f* **de lecture** *or* **écriture** read/write head ◇ **tête** *f* **de lecture** *or* **écriture de disquettes** disk head ◇ **tête** *f* **de lecture ou d'écriture de bande magnétique** tape head

tête *f* **d'accès** *nom* access head

tête *f* **de bobine** *nom* head

tête *f* **d'écriture** *nom* **1.** record head **2.** write head

tête *f* **d'effacement** *nom* erase head

tête *f* **de lecture** *nom* playback head ◇ **tête de lecture de bande** tape playback head ◇ **tête de lecture de disque** disk playback head

tête *m* **de lecture** *nom* read head

tête *f* **de lecture désalignée** *nom* nonaligned read head

tête *f* **de lecture/écriture** *nom* **1.** combined head **2.** R/W head

tête *f* **d'enregistrement** *nom* record head

tête *f* **de réseau** *nom* head end

tête *f* **de scanner** *nom* scan head ◇ **ce modèle possède une tête de scanner qui reconnaît** *ou* **identifie 256 couleurs** this model uses a scan head that can distinguish 256 different colours

tête *f* **dichroïque** *nom* dichroic head

tête *f* **d'impression** *nom* printhead ◇ **la tête d'impression a une durée de vie de plus de 400 millions de caractères** the printhead has a print life of over 400 million characters

tête *f* **d'une page** *nom* head of form ■ *abrév* HOF

tête *f* **flottante** *nom* **1.** floating head **2.** flying head

tête *f* **magnétique** *nom* magnetic head

téton *m* **d'alignement** *nom* alignment pin

tétra- *préfixe* quadr-

texel *m nom* texel

texte *m nom* **1.** form overlay **2.** text ◇ **cet éditeur de texte ne peut lire que les fichiers de moins de 64Ko** the text editor will only read files smaller than 64Kbytes long ◇ **(code de) début de texte** start-of-text (SOT *ou* STX) ◇ **logiciel de traitement de texte** text processor *ou* word processor ◇ **machine de traitement de texte** text processor *ou* word processor ◇ **MS-DOS fonctionne habituellement en mode texte** MS-DOS normally operates in a text mode ◇ **on utilise le formatage de texte comme programme de base de PAO** people use the text formatter as a basic desk-top publishing program ◇ **traitement de texte** text processing *ou* word processing

texte *m* **ASCII** *nom* ASCII text

texte *m* **d'écran** *nom* soft copy

texte *m* **d'un message** *nom* message text

texte *m* **en clair** *nom* plaintext ◇ **introduire le texte non chiffré dans la machine à chiffrer** enter the plaintext message into the cipher machine ◇ **le texte du message a été transmis en clair par téléphone** the messages were sent as plaintext by telephone

texte *m* **non chiffré** *nom* plaintext ◇ **introduire le texte non chiffré dans la machine à chiffrer** enter the plaintext message into the cipher machine

texte *m* **non justifié** *nom* ragged text

texture *f nom* texture

théorie *f* **de l'information** *nom* information theory

théorie *f* **des ensembles** *nom* set theory

thésaurus *m nom* thesaurus

32 bits (*données*) 32-bit

3D *adjectif* three-dimensional

3G *nom* 3G

tiers *m nom* third party

tirer *verbe vt* to drag

titre *m nom* **1.** heading **2.** headline **3.** title ◇ **bouton de la barre de titre** title bar button ◇ **nom** *ou* **titre d'une disquette** title of disk ◇ **page de titre** title page

titre *m* **courant** *nom* **1.** header **2.** heading **3.** running head

toile *f* **de fond** *nom* desktop background

tomber en panne *verbe* **1.** to crash **2.** to fail **3.** to go down ◇ **on peut dire que l'ordinateur est en panne si rien ne se produit à la mise sous tension** a computer has failed if you turn on the power supply and nothing happens

tonalité *f nom* **1.** hue **2.** tint

toner *m nom* toner ◇ **pour remettre du toner ou changer la cartouche, voir la marche à suivre dans le manuel d'utilisation** change toner and toner cartridge according to the manual ◇ **si vous avez du toner sur les mains, il faut absolument les laver à l'eau froide** if you get toner on your hands, you can only wash it off with cold water

tonneau *m nom* barrel

Toolbox *nom* **1.** toolbox **2.** Toolbox

topogramme *m* **binaire** *nom* bitmap

topologie *f nom* **1.** ring topology **2.** topology ◇ **le réseau à jeton** *ou* **token ring utilise une topologie en anneau** token ring uses a ring topology ◇ **si le câble d'une station d'un réseau en étoile se casse, les autres stations ne sont pas affectées, ce qui n'est pas le cas dans une topologie en bus** if one workstation cable snaps in a star topology, the rest continue, unlike a bus topology

topologie *f* **en bus** *nom* bus topology ◇ **Ethernet est un réseau qui utilise une architecture en bus** Ethernet is a network that uses the bus topology

topologie *f* **en étoile** *nom* star topology ◇ **si le câble d'une station d'un réseau en étoile se casse, les autres stations ne sont pas affectées, ce qui n'est pas le cas dans une topologie en bus** if one workstation cable snaps in a star topology, the rest continue, unlike a bus topology

topologie *f* **physique** *nom* physical topology

tore *m* **magnétique** *nom* magnetic core

tortue *f nom* turtle

torturer *verbe vt* to soak

total *adjectif* global ◇ **total** *m* **de contrôle** control total ◇ **total** *m* **de vérification pour hash code** hash total

total *m* **de contrôle** *nom* checksum *ou* check total ◇ **les données sont sûrement erronées si le total de contrôle est faux** the data must be corrupted if the checksum is different

total *m* **de vérification** *nom* checksum *ou* check total ◇ **les données sont sûrement erronées si le total de contrôle est faux** the data must be corrupted if the checksum is different

total *m* **par groupe** *nom* batch total

total *m* **par lot** *nom* batch total

touche *f nom* **1.** key **2.** record button ◇ **jeu vertical** *ou* **course d'une touche** key travel ◇ **le clavier comporte 84 touches** there are 84 keys on the keyboard ◇ **pression nécessaire pour actionner une touche** key force ◇ **sans la grille d'aide, je ne saurais jamais quelle touche de fonction je dois utiliser** without the key overlay, I would never remember which function key does what ◇ **touche** *f* **de blocage du pavé numérique** Num Lock key ◇ **touche des majuscules** shift key ◇ **touches de numérotation (d'un téléphone)** number keys

touche *f* **alphanumérique** *nom* alphanumeric key

touche *f* **Alt** *nom* Alt key

touche *f* **Apple** Apple Key

touche *f* **caractère** *nom* character key

touche *f* **CTR** *nom* CTR *ou* CTRL *ou* Ctrl

touche *f* **d'accélération** *nom* **1.** accelerator key **2.** menu shortcut

touche *f* **d'activation** *nom* hot key

touche *f* **d'aide** *nom* help key ◇ **appuyez sur la touche AIDE** *ou* **sur la touche d'aide pour connaître la marche à suivre** hit the HELP key if you want information about what to do next

touche *f* **d'échappement** *nom* **1.** ESC **2.** escape key **3.** Esc key

touche *f* **de commande** *nom* **1.** command key **2.** control ◇ **carte de contrôle** control card ◇ **pour arrêter un programme, appuyez sur Ctrl-C, c'est-à-dire appuyez sur la touche de contrôle et la touche C en même temps** to halt a program, press Ctrl-C – the control key and letter C – at the same time ◇ **pour relancer votre PC, appuyez sur Ctrl-Alt-Del** to reset your PC, press Ctrl-Alt-Del ◇ **signal de contrôle** *ou* **de commande** control signal

touche *f* **de contraste** *nom* contrast

touche *f* **de contrôle** *nom* **1.** control **2.** control key **3.** CTR *ou* CTRL *ou* Ctrl ◇ **pour arrêter un programme, appuyez sur Ctrl-C, c'est-à-dire appuyez sur la touche de contrôle et la touche C en même temps** to halt a program, press Ctrl-C – the control key and letter C – at the same time

touche *f* **(de fonction) d'édition** *nom* edit key ◇ **il y a plusieurs touches d'édition – celle-ci permet de reformater le texte** there are several special edit keys – this one will re-format the text

touche *f* **d'effacement** *nom* DEL key

touche *f* **de fonction** *nom* **1.** dead key **2.** function key ◇ **on peut allouer une étiquette aux touches de fonction** tags can be allocated to function keys

touche *f* **DEL** *nom* DEL key

touche *f* **de retour arrière** *nom* (*du curseur*) backspace key

touche *f* **de retour du chariot** *nom* carriage return key ◇ **retour de chariot** *or* **retour à la ligne** carriage return/line feed (CR/LF)

touche *f* **des majuscules** *nom* case change

touche *f* **de tabulation** *nom* tab key

touche *f* **de tabulation décimale** *nom* decimal tab key

touche *f* **de verrouillage des majuscules** *nom* caps lock

touche *f* **d'impression** *nom* Print Screen key

touche *f* **d'impression (sous DOS)** *nom* Print Screen key

touche *f* **d'interruption** *nom* Break key

touche *f* **d'intervention** *nom* **1.** attention key **2.** dead key

touche *f* **ECHAPPEMENT** *nom* escape key

touche *f* **End** *nom* end key

touche *f* **Enter** *nom* enter key

touche *f* **entrée** *nom* return

touche *f* **fléchée** *nom* arrow key

touche *f* **Home** *nom* home key

touche *f* **Imp Ecran** *nom* PrtSc

touche *f* **Ins** *nom* **1.** insert key **2.** Ins key

touche *f* **Inser** *nom* Ins key

touche *f* **majuscule** *nom* Shift key

touche *f* **Option** *nom* Option key

touche *f* **Page précédente** *abrév* PgUp

touche *f* **Page suivante** *abrév* PgDn

touche *f* **Pause** *nom* pause key

touche *f* **PgDn** *nom* page down key

touche *f* **PgUp** *nom* page up key

touche *f* **Print Screen** *nom* PrtSc

touche *f* **(de fonction) programmable** *nom* programmable key

touche *f* **PrtSc** *nom* PrtSc

touche *f* **raccourci** *nom* **1.** key combination **2.** key shortcut

touche *f* **répétition** *nom* repeat key

touche *f* **Scroll lock** *nom* Scroll Lock key

touches *fpl* **de contrôle du curseur** *plural noun* cursor control keys ■ *nom* cursor pad

touche *f* **secondaire** *nom* alternate key

touches *fpl* **fléchées** *plural noun* cursor control keys ■ *nom* cursor pad

touches *fpl* **programmables** *plural noun* soft keys

touche *f* **Tab** *nom* tab key

tourner *verbe* **1.** *vt* to rotate **2.** *vt* to turn

traçage *m* **d'activité** *nom* activity trail

traçage *m* **d'un programme** *nom* trace

tracé *m nom* (*courbe*) plot

tracé *m* **d'un circuit** *nom* circuit design

tracé *m* **filaire** *nom* ray tracing

tracer une courbe *verbe* to plot

traceur *m nom* **1.** drum plotter **2.** pen recorder **3.** plotter

traceur *m* **à plat** *nom* flatbed plotter

traceur *m* **à plumes** *nom* pen plotter

traceur *m* **de courbes** *nom* **1.** graph plotter **2.** x-y plotter

traceur *m* **de graphiques** *nom* x-y plotter

traceur *m* **incrémentiel** *nom* incremental plotter

traceur *m* **numérique** *nom* digital plotter

traducteur *m nom* translator *ou* translator program

traducteur *m* **(de langage)** *nom* language translator

traduction *f* **assistée par ordinateur** *nom* machine translation

traduction *f* **d'adresses de réseau** *nom* **1.** NAT **2.** network address translation

traduire *verbe* **1.** *vt* to interpret **2.** *vt* to translate

trafic *m nom* traffic ◇ **notre réseau Ethernet commence à ralentir lorsque le trafic atteint 60 pour cent de la bande passante** our Ethernet network begins to slow down if the traffic reaches 60 per cent of the bandwidth

train *m* **de bits** *nom* bit stream

train *m* **d'impulsions** *nom* **1.** pulse stream **2.** pulse train

traînée *f nom* hangover

traîner *verbe vt* to drag

train *m* **secondaire** *nom* IP

trait *m nom* **1.** bar **2.** check mark **3.** line **4.** stroke ◇ **trait d'union** *m* **d'écran qui ne s'imprime pas** soft hyphen

trait *m nom* (*sous un mot ou une ligne de texte*) underline

trait d'union *m* **qui n'apparaît pas à l'écran** *nom* discretionary hyphen

trait d'union *m* **qui ne s'imprime pas** *nom* discretionary hyphen

traitement *nom* processing ◇ **le temps d'ordinateur requis pour le traitement d'une page de texte varie en fonction de la complexité du document** page processing time depends on the complexity of a given page ◇ **traitement** *m* **de contrôle de bloc à l'entrée** block input processing ◇ **traitement** *m* **de données sur cartes perforées par tabulatrice** tabulating ◇ **traitement** *m* **par lots en mode séquentiel** sequential batch processing

traitement *m* **aléatoire** *nom* (*des données*) random processing

traitement *m* **automatique de données** *nom* **1.** ADP **2.** automatic calling unit **3.** automatic data processing

traitement *m* **centralisé de l'information** *nom* centralised data processing *ou* centralized data processing

traitement *m* **décentralisé des données** *nom* decentralised data processing *ou* decentralized data processing

traitement *m* **de document** *nom* document processing

traitement de données *abrév* dp *ou* DP

traitement *m* **de données** *nom* information processing

traitement *m* **de données immédiat** *nom* demand processing

traitement *m* **de données intégré** *abrév* IDP ■ *nom* integrated data processing

traitement *m* **de données sur demande** *nom* demand processing

traitement *m* **de fichier** *nom* file processing

traitement *m* **de l'image** *nom* **1.** image editing **2.** image processing **3.** picture processing

traitement *f* **de l'information** *abrév* dp *ou* DP

traitement *m* **de l'information** *nom* **1.** EDP **2.** information processing

traitement *m* **de l'information sans l'aide d'un ordinateur** *nom* manual data processing

traitement *m* **de liste** *nom* list processing

traitement *m* **de mouvements** *abrév* TP ■ *nom* transaction processing

traitement *m* **de pile de tâches** *nom* stack job processing

traitement *m* **de requête** *nom* query processing

traitement *m* **des erreurs** *nom* exception handling

traitement *m* **de signaux numériques** *nom* digital signal processing

traitement *m* **de tâche** *nom* job processing

traitement de texte *plural noun* text-editing facilities

traitement *m* **de texte** *nom* **1.** document processing **2.** text processing **3.** word-processing ■ *abrév* WP

traitement *m* **direct** *nom* (*des données*) random processing

traitement *m* **du bit** *nom* bit handling

traitement *m* **du langage naturel** *nom* natural language processing

traitement *m* **du signal** *nom* signal processing ◇ **ce système est à la disposition des étudiants qui se spécialisent dans la recherche sur les techniques de traitement du signal** the system is used by students doing research on signal processing techniques

traitement *m* **électronique de données** *nom* EDP

traitement *m* **électronique de l'information** *nom* electronic data processing

traitement *m* **en différé** *nom* off-line processing

traitement *m* **en ligne** *nom* online processing

traitement *m* **en série** *nom* serial processing

traitement *m* **en temps réel** *nom* real-time processing

traitement *m* **frontal** *nom* foregrounding

traitement *m* **hors ligne** *nom* off-line processing

traitement *m* **immédiat** *nom* immediate processing

traitement *m* **informatique** *nom* EDP

traitement *m* **informatique de l'image** *nom* computer image processing

traitement *m* **interactif** *nom* interactive processing

traitement *m* **linéaire** *nom* input/output request

traitement *m* **multitâche en temps réel** *nom* real-time multi-tasking

traitement *m* **non prioritaire** *nom* background processing

traitement *m* **numérique de la lumière** *nom* **1.** digital light processing **2.** DLP

traitement *m* **off-line** *nom* off-line processing

traitement *m* **(en) parallèle** *nom* parallel processing

traitement *m* **par lots** *nom* batch processing

traitement *m* **par paquets** *nom* batch processing

traitement *m* **séquentiel** *nom* sequential processing

traitement *m* **simultané** *nom* simultaneous processing

traitement *m* **transactionnel en ligne** *nom* online transaction processing

traiter (des données, etc.) *verbe* to process ◇ **le traitement des données sera assez long** processing all the information will take a long time ◇ **nous avons traité les données** we processed the new data

traiter (des instructions) en pipeline *verbe* to pipeline
trait *m* **oblique** *nom* slash
trame *f nom* frame
trame *f* **d'alerte** *nom* beacon frame
trame *f* **de page** *nom* page frame
trame *f* **d'initialisation** *nom* (*de réseau sous protocole FDDI*) claim frame
tranche *f* **de silicium** *nom* **1.** silicon wafer **2.** wafer
tranche *f* **de temps** *nom* time slice
tranche *f* **horaire** *nom* time slice
tranche *f* **vide** *nom* empty slot
transaction *f nom* transaction ◇ **système transactionnel** transaction-driven system (TDS) ◇ **traitement de mouvements** *ou* **de transactions** transaction processing (TP)
transaction *f* **de données** *nom* data transaction
transcrire *verbe vt* to transcribe
transducteur *m nom* transducer ◇ **un transducteur de pression transforme un signal physique de pression en signal électrique** a pressure transducer converts physical pressure signals into electrical signals
transférer *verbe* **1.** *vt* to dump **2.** *vt* to offload **3.** *vt* to output **4.** *vt* to transfer ◇ **les résultats comptables ont été transférés sur le disque de sauvegarde** the account results were dumped to the backup disk ◇ **toutes les opérations de traitement ont été transférées sur l'ordinateur principal** all processing activities have been transferred to the mainframe
transférer des données *verbe* (*d'un petit ordinateur à un plus gros*) to upload
transfert *nom* **1.** change over **2.** transfer ◇ **transfert** *m* **de programme avec l'aide d'un pont** bridging
transfert, accès et gestion de fichiers *nom* file transfer access and management
transfert branchement *m nom* conditional transfer
transfert *m* **conditionnel** *nom* conditional transfer
transfert *m* **de bits par blocs** *nom* bit block transfer
transfert *m* **de contrôle** *nom* control transfer
transfert *m* **de données** *nom* data migration
transfert *m* **de données asynchrone** *nom* asynchronous data transfer
transfert *m* **de fichier** *nom* file transfer
transfert *m* **direct** *nom* **1.** direct change-over **2.** direct transfer
transfert *m* **d'un bloc** *nom* block transfer
transfert *m* **d'un paragraphe** *nom* block transfer
transfert *m* **électronique de fonds** *nom* electronic funds transfer
transfert *m* **magnétique** *nom* magnetic transfer
transfert *m* **(en) parallèle** *nom* parallel transfer
transfert *m* **radial (de données/programmes)** *nom* radial transfer
transferts *mpl* **de page incontrôlés** *nom* (*entre la mémoire et le disque*) thrashing
transfert *m* **sur demande** *nom* (*d'une mémoire à une autre*) demand staging
transfert *m* **sur disque** *nom* dump
transfert *m* **sur support magnétique** *nom* dump
transformateur *m* **de protection** *nom* isolation transformer
transformateur *m* **d'isolement** *nom* isolation transformer
transformation *f* **sérielle** *nom* tweening
transformer *verbe vt* to transform
transistor *m nom* transistor ◇ **logique transistor résistance (LTR)** transistor-resistor logic (TRL) ◇ **logique transistor transistor (LTT)** transistor-transistor logic (TTL)
transistor *m* **à effet de champ (TEC)** *nom* **1.** FET **2.** field effect transistor
transistor *m* **à effet de champ à semiconducteur à oxyde métallique** *nom* metal oxide semiconductor field effect transistor
transistor *m* **à jonction** *nom* junction transistor
transistor *m* **bipolaire** *nom* **1.** bipolar transistor **2.** junction transistor
transistor *m* **de type pnp** *nom* pnp transistor
transistorisé *adjectif* solid-state ◇ **laser transistorisé** *ou* **à semi-conducteur** solid-state laser
transistor *m* **(de type) npn** *nom* npn transistor
transistor *m* **unipolaire** *nom* unipolar transistor
translatable *adjectif* relocatable
translater *verbe vt* to relocate
translation *f nom* **1.** program relocation **2.** relocation
translation *f* **dynamique** *nom* dynamic relocation
translation *f* **statique** *nom* static relocation
transmetteur *nom* transmitter ◇ **transmetteur** *m* **de données sur bande perforée** tape transmitter
transmettre *verbe* **1.** *vt* to channel **2.** *vt* to conduct **3.** *vt* to forward **4.** *vt* to output **5.** *vt* to transmit
transmettre un signal *verbe* to signal ◇ **signale au réseau que nous sommes occupés**

ou **envoie un signal au réseau pour prévenir que nous sommes occupés** signal to the network that we are busy

transmission *nom* **1.** (*des caractéristiques d'un objet ou d'une classe*) inheritance **2.** networking **3.** transmission ◇ **erreur de transmission** transmission error ◇ **fenêtre de transmission** transmission window ◇ **protocole TCP (de contrôle de transmission)** transmission control protocol (TCP) ◇ **protocole TCP** *or* **IP (de transmission de données)** transmission control protocol/internet protocol (TCP/IP) ◇ **transmission bidirectionnelle** bidirectional transmission ◇ **transmission** *f* **de signaux dans la bande passante** in-band signalling ◇ **transmission** *f* **de signaux par courant continu** DC signalling ◇ **transmission** *f* **en bande de base** baseband signalling

transmission *f* **analogique** *nom* analog transmission

transmission *f* **asymétrique** *nom* asymmetric transmission

transmission *f* **asynchrone** *nom* asynchronous transmission

transmission *f* **aval** *nom* downstream

transmission *f* **bidirectionnelle** *nom* bi-directional transmission

transmission *f* **confidentielle** *nom* blind carbon copy

transmission *f* **de données** *nom* data transmission

transmission *f* **de données en parallèle** *nom* parallel data transmission

transmission *f* **de signaux en binaire** *nom* binary signalling

transmission *f* **de signaux numériques** *nom* digital signalling

transmission *f* **d'image** *nom* picture transmission

transmission *f* **d'octets en série** *nom* byte serial transmission

transmission *f* **électronique** *nom* electronic traffic

transmission *f* **en aveugle** *nom* blind dialling

transmission *f* **en modulation de tension** *nom* baseband signalling

transmission *f* **en série** *nom* **1.** serial input/output **2.** serial transmission ■ *abrév* SIO

transmission *f* **isochrone** *nom* isochronous transmission

transmission *f* **neutre** *nom* neutral transmission

transmission *f* **(en) parallèle** *nom* parallel transmission

transmission *f* **parallèle bit par bit** *nom* bit parallel

transmission *f* **par fibres optiques** *nom* optical transmission

transmission *f* **par système optoélectronique** *nom* optical transmission

transmission *f* **sans contrôle de retour** *nom* free wheeling

transmission *f* **sans décrochage** *nom* blind dialling

transmission *f* **série de données** *nom* **1.** serial data communications **2.** serial data transmission

transmission *f* **simplex** *nom* simplex

transmission *f* **simplex** *m nom* single operation

transmission *f* **simultanée** *nom* simultaneous transmission

transmission *f* **synchrone** *nom* **1.** isochronous transmission **2.** synchronous transmission

transmission *f* **unidirectionnelle** *nom* **1.** simplex **2.** single operation **3.** SPX

transparence *f nom* **1.** back projection **2.** transparency

transparent *adjectif* transparent ◇ **interruptions transparentes** transparent interrupts

transparent,-e *adjectif* transparent

transphaseur *m nom* transphasor

transportable *adjectif* transportable ◇ **un ordinateur transportable n'est pas aussi petit** *ou* **aussi léger qu'un portable** a transportable computer is not as small as a portable

travail *m nom* **1.** job **2.** work ◇ **flux** *m* **de travaux** workflow ◇ **qui permet le travail de groupe** workgroup enabled

travail *m* **à la chaîne** *nom* in-line processing

travail *m* **en attente** *nom* backlog

travail *m* **en retard** *nom* backlog ◇ **la file d'attente trop courte ne suffisait pas à la série de tâches à traiter** the queue was too short for the backlog of tasks waiting to be processed ◇ **les programmeurs ne réussissent pas à venir à bout de toute la programmation en retard** the programmers can't deal with the backlog of programming work

travail *m* **en souffrance** *nom* backlog

tremblotement *m nom* jitter

très *préfixe* ultra-

très important *adjectif* prime ◇ **heures de grande écoute** *ou* **d'écoute maximale** prime time ◇ **nous commençons à diffuser des spots publicitaires aux heures de grande écoute** we are putting out a series of prime-time commercials

tri *nom* weighting ◇ **tri** *m* **et fusion** merge sort

'...entrez le nom du champ sur lequel doit porter le tri; définissez ensuite l'ordre du tri, croissant (A à Z) ou décroissant (Z à A). Validez la définition' [*L'Ordinateur Individuel*]

triade *f nom* triad

tributaire du type d'unité *adjectif* device-dependent

tri *m* **de fichiers** *verbe* to file sort

tri *m* **de paires** *nom* bubble sort

tridimensionnel *adjectif* three-dimensional

tri *m* **en arborescence** *nom* tree selection sort

tri *m* **en mémoire interne** *nom* internal sort

tri *m* **enveloppe** *nom* shell sort

trier *verbe* **1.** *vt* to cull **2.** *vt* to sort ■ *nom vt* sort

trier/fusionner *nom vt* sort/merge

trier par clé(s) *verbe* to order

tri *m* **par échange** *nom* exchange selection

tri *m* **par permutation de bulles** *nom* bubble sort

triplet *m* **de points lumineux** *nom* (*rouge, vert, bleu*) phosphor triad

tri *m* **rapide** *nom* quicksort

tri *m* **sélectif** *nom* selective sort

tri *m* **sur disque** *nom* external sort

tri *m* **sur support externe** *nom* external sort

troisième *f* **génération** *nom* third generation

troncature *f nom* **1.** rounding **2.** truncation

tronquer *verbe vt* to truncate ◇ **3,5678 tronqué** *ou* **arrondi par défaut à 3,56** 3.5678 truncated to 3.56

trou *m* **laser** *nom* ablation

trousse de développement logiciel (*nom de marque*) Windows SDK

trousse *f* **de développement logiciel multimédia** *nom* multimedia developer's kit

trouvaille *f nom* hit

trouver *verbe* **1.** *vt* to diagnose **2.** *vt* to find **3.** *vt* to locate ◇ **il a fallu beaucoup de temps pour trouver la puce défectueuse** it took a lot of time to find the faulty chip ◇ **l'ordinateur se trouve dans l'édifice principal** the computer is located in the main office building

Tseng Labs (*société fabricante de jeux de circuits*) Tseng Labs

TSL *abrév* HLS

TSR *nom* RAM resident program ■ *abrév* TSR

tube *m nom* conduit

tube *m* **à mémoire** *nom* cathode ray tube storage

tube *m* **cathodique** *nom* **1.** CRT **2.** television tube

tunnellisation *f nom* tunnelling

tuyau *m nom* conduit

24/96 24/96

2D (*image graphique*) 2D

type *m nom* access category

type *m* **de caractères** *nom* **1.** face **2.** typeface

type *m* **de données** *nom* data type

type *m* **de fichier** *nom* file type

type *m* **de liaison (de IBM)** *nom* Type cable

type *m* **de pinceau** *nom* brush style ◇ **pour couvrir une grande surface, j'utilise un pinceau large et à bout carré** to fill in a big area, I select a wide, square brush style

typographe *m nom* typesetter ◇ **le texte est prêt à être envoyé au typographe** the text is ready to be sent to the typesetter

U

Ultimedia™ *(de IBM)* Ultimedia

ultra- *préfixe* ultra- ◇ **ultra-haute fréquence (UHF)** ultra-high frequency (UHF)

Ultra ATA *nom* Ultra ATA

ultra-haute fréquence *nom* **1.** UHF **2.** ultra high frequency

ultrarapide *adjectif* high-speed

ultrasensible *adjectif* high-speed

une adresse *f* **plus une** *nom* one-plus-one address

un graphe (par points numérisés) *verbe* to plot

uni- *préfixe* uni-

uniformiser *verbe vt* to normalise *ou* to normalize

union *f nom* union

unipolaire *adjectif* unipolar

unité *nom (appareil ou système)* unit ◇ **unité arithmétique et logique** arithmetic and logic unit (ALU) ◇ **unité centrale (de traitement)** *ou* **processeur central** central processing unit (CPU) ◇ **unité** *f* **de bande magnétique en continu** streaming tape drive ◇ **unité** *f* **de disque avec tête de lecture chercheuse** movable head disk ◇ **unité** *f* **de sauvegarde rapide sur bande magnétique** stringy floppy ◇ **unité** *f* **de sauvegarde rapide sur bande magnétique en continu** streaming tape drive

unité *f* **arithmétique et logique (UAL)** *nom* **1.** arithmetic logic unit **2.** arithmetic unit

unité *f* **à virgule flottante** *abrév* FPU

unité centrale ◇ **limité par l'unité centrale** CPU bound

unité *f* **centrale** *nom* **1.** *(de traitement)* central processing unit *ou* central processor **2.** CPU

unité *f* **centrale à microprocesseur** *abrév* MPU

unité *f* **centrale de calcul** *nom (d'un processeur en tranches)* central processing element

unité *f* **comprenant des disques fixes et des disques amovibles** *nom* fixed and exchangeable disk storage

unité *f* **d'accès** *nom* access unit

unité *f* **d'accès multiposte** *nom* multistation access unit

unité *f* **d'accès multistation** *abrév* MAU

unité *f* **d'allocation** *nom* allocation unit

unité *f* **d'appel automatique** *nom* automatic call distribution

unité *f* **de bureau** *nom* desktop unit

unité *f* **de commande de périphérique** *nom* **1.** PCU **2.** peripheral control unit

unité *f* **de commande d'un système** *nom* system unit

unité *f* **de contrôle** *nom* control unit ■ *abrév* CU ■ *nom* system unit

unité *f* **de contrôle de périphérique** *nom* **1.** PCU **2.** peripheral control unit

unité *f* **de contrôle de périphériques disposés en grappe** *nom* cluster controller

unité *f* **de disque** *nom* magnetic disk unit

unité *f* **de disque(s)** *nom* disk unit

unité *f* **de disque/disquette** *nom* disk drive

unité *f* **de disque dur** *nom* **1.** hard disk drive **2.** hard drive

unité *f* **de disque dur d'un réseau** *nom* network drive

unité *f* **de disquette** *nom* magnetic disk unit

unité *f* **de disquette(s)** *nom* **1.** floppy disk drive **2.** floppy disk unit

unité *f* **de disquettes (de) demi-hauteur** *nom* half-height drive

unité *f* **de formatage vertical** *nom* vertical format unit ■ *abrév* VFU

unité *f* **de gestion de la mémoire** *nom* MMU

unité *f* **de gestion de la mémoire paginée** *nom* paged-memory management unit

unité *f* **de synchronisation** *nom* synchroniser

unité *f* **de traitement périphérique** *abrév* PPU

unité *f* **de visu** *nom* display unit

unité *f* **de visualisation** *nom* display unit

unité *f* **logique** *nom* logical unit

unité *f* **physique** *nom* physical record

univers *m nom* world

universel *adjectif* universal ◇ **canal universel de transmission par blocs** universal block channel (UBC) ◇ **dispositif universel** universal device (UART, USRT, USART) ◇ **émetteur** *or* **récepteur asynchrone universel** universal asynchronous receiver/transmitter (UART) ◇ **émetteur** *or* **récepteur synchrone asyn-**

chrone universel universal synchronous asynchronous receiver-transmitter (USART) ◇ **émetteur** *or* **récepteur synchrone universel** universal synchronous receiver/transmitter (USRT)

UNIX *nom* UNIX

UNIX BSD *nom* Berkeley UNIX

un pour cent *nom* percentage point

usine *f* **de montage** *nom* assembly plant

usurpation *f* **d'adresse IP** *nom* IP spoofing

usurper une adresse IP *verbe* to spoof

utilisant des disquettes *adjectif* disk-based

utilisant un disque dur *adjectif* disk-based

utilisateur *m nom* user ◇ **agent (d')utilisateur** user agent (UA) ◇ **j'ai trouvé la solution au problème en me renseignant auprès des autres utilisateurs rencontrés à la réunion des membres du groupe** I found how to solve the problem by asking people at the user group meeting ◇ **la feuille de style comporte 125 symboles programmables selon les besoins de l'utilisateur** the style sheet contains 125 user-definable symbols ◇ **l'utilisateur peut sélectionner une résolution d'écran de 640 x 300, 240 ou 200 pixels** the video resolution of 640 by 300, 240 or 200 pixels is user-selectable ◇ **protocole UDP (d'échange de données utilisateur)** user datagram protocol (UDP)

utilisateur, -trice (final) *nom* end user ◇ **la société cherche à créer un ordinateur adapté aux besoins de l'utilisateur** the company is creating a computer with a specific end user in mind

utilisateur *m* **avancé** *nom* power user

utilisateur *m* **ayant un droit d'accès** *nom* accessor

utilisateur *m* **distant** *nom* remote client

utilisateur *m* **intermédiaire** *nom* mid-user

utilisation *f* **d'adresses abrégées** *nom* abbreviated addressing

utilisation *f* **de double mémoire tampon** *nom* double buffering

utilisation *f* **de mémoire tampon** *nom* buffering

utilisation *f* **d'une seconde source de composants** *nom* second sourcing

utiliser *verbe vt* to use ◇ **les commerciaux utilisent l'ordinateur trop souvent** the computer is used too often by the sales staff

utiliser un cache *verbe* to cache

utilitaire *nom* **1.** EDLIN **2.** utility program ◇ **utilitaire** *m* **de récupération** (*pour disque dur*) disk doctor ◇ **utilitaire** *m* **de suivi de version** version control ◇ **utilitaire** *m* **FDISK** FDISK ◇ **utilitaire** *m* **System Monitor** (*de contrôle de performances*) System Monitor

utilitaire *m* **antivirus** *nom* **1.** anti-virus program **2.** vaccine

utilitaire *m* **Chooser™** (*de Apple Macintosh*) Chooser™

utilitaire *m* **d'application** *nom* applet

utilitaire *m* **de connexion UUCP** *abrév* UUCP

utilitaire *m* **de plan** *nom* outliner

utilitaire *m* **de requête** *nom* query facility

utilitaire *m* **de routage TCP-IP traceroute** *nom* traceroute

utilitaire *m* **de sauvegarde** *nom* backup utility

utilitaire *m* **de stockage de dessin** *nom* (*Apple Macintosh utility*) scrapbook ◇ **nous conservons le logo dans l'album (de croquis)** we store our logo in the scrapbook

utilitaire *m* **de transfert de fichiers** *nom* file transfer utility

utilitaire *m* **de vérification de grammaire** *nom* grammar checker

utilitaire *m* **d'interrogation** *nom* query facility

utilitaire *m* **PING** *nom* **1.** packet Internet groper **2.** PING

utilitaires *mpl nom* toolkit

utilitaire *m* **UNIX démon** *nom* daemon

utilitaire *m* **UUCP** *nom* UNIX-to-UNIX copy

Uuencodage *m nom* Uuencoding

V

V *abrév* V

vacillement *m nom* flicker

vaciller *verbe vi* to flicker ◇ **l'image sur l'écran vacille lors de la mise sous tension de l'imprimante** the image flickers when the printer is switched on

valeur *f nom* value

valeur *f* **absolue** *nom* (*d'un nombre*) absolute value ◇ **la valeur absolue de –62,34 est 62,34** the absolute value of –62.34 is 62.34

valeur *f* **binaire** *nom* truth value

valeur *f* **booléenne** *nom* **1.** Boolean value **2.** truth value

valeur *f* **dans un tableau** *nom* array element

valeur *f* **de départ** *nom* seed

valeur *f* **d'un hash code** *nom* hash value

valeur *f* **implicite** *nom* default value ◇ **la largeur implicite** *ou* **par défaut d'un écran est de 80** screen width has a default value of 80

valeur *f* **initiale** *nom* initial value

valeur *f* **intrinsèque** *nom* default value

valeur *f* **prédéterminée** *nom* default value

valeur *f* **relative** *nom* offset value *ou* offset word

validation *nom* validation ◇ **validation** *f* **de données transmises** data strobe ◇ **validation** *f* **de ligne** line input

validation *f* **à deux phases** *nom* two-phase commit

validation *f* **de données** *nom* **1.** data validation **2.** data vetting

validation *f* **de fichier** *nom* file validation

valide *adjectif* **1.** legal **2.** valid

validé *adjectif* selectable

valider *verbe* **1.** *vt* to arm **2.** *vt* to enable **3.** *vt* to select **4.** *vt* to strobe **5.** *vt* to validate ◇ **valider** *ou* **activer un circuit intégré** chip select (CS) ◇ **valider qc à l'aide d'un commutateur à bascule** to toggle

validité *f nom* validity

valise *f nom* suitcase

vanter *verbe vt* to plug

variable *adjectif* variable ■ *nom* variable ◇ **variable** *f* **de type chaîne de caractères** string type

'...pendant longtemps le traitement du signal s'est essentiellement intéressé aux signaux dépendant d'une seule variable (le temps)' [*Traitement du signal*]

variable *f* **binaire** *nom* binary variable

variable *f* **booléenne** *nom* **1.** Boolean data type **2.** Boolean variable

variable *f* **caractérisée par un indice** *nom* subscripted variable

variable *f* **commune** *nom* global variable

variable *f* **de chaîne** *nom* string variable

variable *f* **d'environnement** *nom* environment variable

variable *f* **de référence d'une cellule** *nom* cell reference variable

variable *f* **de type non précisé** *nom* variable data type

variable *f* **factice** *nom* dummy variable

variable *f* **générale** *nom* global variable

variable *f* **globale** *nom* global variable

variable *f* **indicée** *nom* subscripted variable

variable *f* **locale** *nom* local variable

variable *f* **scalaire** *nom* scalar variable

variable *f* **système** *nom* system variable

variation *f* **de vitesse** *nom* flutter ◇ **le pleurage et les variations de vitesse** *ou* **le scintillement sont des défauts courants des magnétophones bon marché** wow and flutter are common faults on cheap tape recorders

varier *verbe vti* to range

vecteur *m nom* vector

vecteur *m* **de retard** *nom* delay vector

vectoriel *adjectif* scalable

véhiculer *verbe vt* to channel

vendeur *m nom* vendor

venir de *verbe* to originate

ver *m nom* WORM

vérificateur *m* **d'orthographe** *nom* spell-checker *ou* spelling checker

vérificateur *m* **grammatical** *nom* grammar checker

vérification *f nom* **1.** loop check **2.** verification ◇ **vérification** *f* **de validité des données** validity check ◇ **vérification** *f* **du bon fonctionnement d'un programme** program verification ◇ **vérification et validation** *ou* **contrôle et validation** verification and validation (V & V)

vérification *f* **arithmétique** *nom* arithmetic check

vérification *f* **automatique** *nom* auto verify

vérification *f* **de données** *nom* data vetting

vérification *f* **et validation** *nom* **1.** V & V **2.** verification and validation

vérificatrice *f nom* verifier

vérifier *verbe* **1.** *vt* to monitor **2.** *vt* to verify

vérifier l'orthographe *verbe* to spellcheck

vérin *m nom* actuator

véroler *verbe vt* to corrupt

Veronica (*outil de recherche documentaire sur le Web*) Veronica

verrouillage *m nom* interlock

verrouillage *m* **d'enregistrement** *nom* record locking

verrouillage *m* **de protection** *nom* advisory lock

verrouiller *verbe* **1.** *vt* to interlock **2.** *vt* to latch **3.** *vt* to lock ◇ **verrouiller (l'accès à) un fichier** locking a file

version *nom* **1.** build **2.** release **3.** version ◇ **la dernière version du logiciel comprend une routine graphique améliorée** the latest version of the software includes an improved graphics routine ◇ **la nouvelle version du logiciel porte le numéro 5** the latest software is release 5 ◇ **version** *f* **périmée d'un produit qui ne supporte pas certaines fonctions** back-level

version *f* **avancée** *nom* advanced version

version *f* **bêta** *nom* **1.** beta version **2.** betaware

version *f* **de démonstration d'un logiciel** *nom* demonstration software

version *f* **dépassée** *nom* back-level

version *f* **de sauvegarde** *nom* backup version

version *f* **étendue de NetBIOS** *nom* NetBEUI

version *f* **évoluée** *nom* advanced version

version *f* **exécutable** *nom* run-time version

version *f* **run-time** *nom* run-time version

version *f* **XT** *nom* (*basée sur le processeur Inter 8088*) XT

vertical *adjectif* vertical ◇ **contrôle par redondance verticale** vertical redundancy check (VRC) ◇ **unité de formatage vertical** vertical format unit (VFU)

verticale *f nom* y-direction

verticalement *adverbe* vertically ◇ **signal avec polarisation verticale** *ou* **signal polarisé verticalement** vertically polarized signal

veuve *f nom* widow

VHS *nom* video home system

via *preposition* via

vidage *m nom* **1.** deposit **2.** dump **3.** storage dump

vidage *m* **au format** *nom* formatted dump

vidage *m* **binaire** *nom* binary dump

vidage *m* **de contrôle** *nom* check point dump

vidage *m* **d'écran sur imprimante** *nom* screen dump

vidage *m* **de fichier** *nom* file purge

vidage *m* **de mémoire sur imprimante** *nom* memory dump

vidage *m* **de mouvements** *nom* change dump

vidage *m* **de sauvegarde** *nom* rescue dump

vidage *m* **dynamique** *nom* dynamic dump

vidage *m* **et reprise** *nom* dump and restart

vidage *m* **hexadécimal** *nom* hex dump

vidage *m* **instantané sur imprimante** *nom* snapshot dump

vidage *m* **irréversible** *nom* disaster dump

vidage *m* **sélectif** *nom* selective dump

vidage *m* **statique** *nom* static dump

vidage *m* **sur disque** *nom* dump

vidage *m* **sur imprimante** *nom* dump

VidCap *nom* VidCap

vidéo *f nom* video ◇ **bande vidéo** videotape ◇ **caméra vidéo** video camera ◇ **caméra vidéo de vision nocturne** infrared video camera ◇ **caméra vidéo numérique** digital video camera ◇ **carte vidéo** video card ◇ **certains instructeurs utilisent une caméra vidéo de vision nocturne pour suivre leurs élèves** some instructors monitor their trainees with infrared video cameras ◇ **déconcentrateur pour transmission vidéo** video expander ◇ **films d'épouvante** *ou* **d'horreur sur vidéocassettes** *ou* **sur bandes vidéo** video nasties ◇ **image vidéo** video frame; video image ◇ **mémoire vidéo à accès aléatoire (VRAM)** video random access memory (VRAM) ◇ **normes vidéo** video standards ◇ **port vidéo** video port ◇ **réducteur (de largeur de bande) vidéo** video compressor ◇ **système vidéo** video player ◇ **une image vidéo imprimable peut être transmise sur une imprimante laser classique par le port vidéo** a printer-readable video image can be sent to a basic laser printer through a video port ◇ **vidéocassette** video cassette ◇ **vidéophone** video phone ◇ **vidéothèque** video library

vidéo *f* **active** *nom* active video *ou* active video signal

vidéo *f* **composite** *nom* composite video

vidéo *f* **comprimé** *nom* compressed video

vidéoconférence *f nom* video conferencing

vidéodisque *nom* videodisc

> '...il assure l'acquisition, le traitement et le stockage sur vidéodisque' [*01 Informatique*]

Video Electronics Standards Association *abrév* VESA ■ *nom* Video Electronics Standards Association

vidéo *f* **en temps réel** *nom* **1.** real-time video **2.** RTV

vidéo *f* **entrelacée** *nom* interlaced video

Video for Windows (*nom de marque*) Video for Windows

vidéographie *f* **interactive** *nom* **1.** interactive video **2.** interactive videotext **3.** videotext *ou* videotex

vidéo *f* **interactive** *nom* interactive video

vidéo *f* **inverse** *nom* inverse video

vidéo *f* **inversée** *nom* reverse video

vidéo *f* **numérique interactive** *nom* DV-I

vidéo *f* **numérisée** *nom* digital video

vidéo *f* **numérisée interactive** *nom* digital video interactive

vidéotex *m nom* videotext *ou* videotex

vidéotique *f nom* DTV

vider *verbe* **1.** *vt* to clear **2.** *vt* to dump **3.** *vt* to flush **4.** *vt* to purge ◇ **vider (le contenu d'une mémoire)** to deposit ◇ **vider la mémoire tampon** to flush buffers ◇ **vider le registre de données** to clear the data register ◇ **vider une zone de mémoire** to clear an area of memory

vider l'écran *verbe* to zap ◇ **il a tapé CONTROL Z pour vider l'écran** he pressed CONTROL Z and zapped all the text

vie *f* **artificielle** *nom* artificial life

vierge *adjectif* (*disquette ou bande*) virgin

vignette *f nom* bullet

vignette *f* **réduite** *nom* thumbnail

viral *adjectif* viral

virement *m* **électronique de fonds** *nom* electronic funds transfer

virer *verbe vt* to junk ◇ **virer** *ou* **effacer un fichier** to junk a file

virgule *f nom* **1.** comma **2.** radix point

virgule *f* **binaire** *nom* binary point

virtualisation *f* **du stockage** *abrév* VS

virtuel *adjectif* virtual ◇ **réalité virtuelle** virtual reality (VR)

virus *m nom* virus ◇ **si vous avez un virus dans votre PC, vos données sont en danger** if your PC is infected with a virus, your data is at risk

virus *m* **informatique** *nom* computer virus

visioconférence *f nom* video teleconferencing

vision *f* **d'utilisateur** *nom* external schema

visionner *verbe* **1.** *vt* to browse **2.** *vt* to play back **3.** *vt* to replay **4.** *vt* to view ◇ **après avoir enregistré la musique, appuyez sur ce bouton-ci pour faire jouer la bande et vous assurer de la bonne qualité du son enregistré** after you have recorded the music, press this button to play back the tape and hear what it sounds like ◇ **elle a enregistré le programme de télévision sur une bande vidéo et l'a visionné le lendemain soir** she recorded the TV programme on video tape and replayed it the next evening

visite *f nom* hit

Visual Basic™ (*outil de programmation*) Visual Basic

visualisation *f nom* **1.** display **2.** visualisation *ou* visualization

visualisation *f* **de contrôle d'entrée** *nom* marching display

visualisé *adjectif* on-screen

visualiser *verbe* **1.** *vt* to picture **2.** *vt* to view ◇ **essayez de visualiser l'implantation avant de commencer à dessiner** try to picture the layout before starting to draw it in ◇ **l'utilisateur paie un droit pour visualiser le tableau d'affichage** the user has to pay a charge for viewing pages on a bulletin board

visualiser (avant impression) *verbe* to preview

visuel *adjectif* visual

vital *adjectif* mission-critical

vitesse *nom* **1.** rate **2.** scan rate ◇ **la vitesse d'exécution des commandes de ce processeur est plus grande qu'avec l'ancienne version** the processor's instruction execution rate is better than the older version ◇ **vitesse** *f* **de défilement** (*d'une bande magnétique*) playback speed

> '...trois vitesses caractérisent les graveurs – elles s'expriment en multiple de la vitesse des lecteurs de CD pour les chaînes hi-fi. Ainsi un modèle 12x10x32 est censé graver les CD-R, écrire les CD-RW et lire les CD-ROM 12, 10 et 32 fois plus vite qu'un lecteur audio' [*l'Ordinateur Individuel*]

vitesse *f* **angulaire constante** *nom* **1.** CAV **2.** constant angular velocity

vitesse *f* **de balayage** *nom* scanning speed

vitesse *f* **de calcul par ordinateur** *nom* computing speed

vitesse *f* **de lecture** *nom* read rate

vitesse *f* **de recherche effective** *nom* effective search speed

vitesse *f* **de sortie de l'information** *nom* information rate

vitesse *f* **de traitement de données** *nom* data rate

vitesse *f* **de transmission** *nom* **1.** baud rate **2.** transmission rate

vitesse *f* **de transmission de données** *nom* data rate

vitesse *f* **linéaire constante** *nom* **1.** CLV **2.** constant linear velocity

vitesse *f* **maximale** *nom* maximum transmission rate

vitesse *f* **moyenne** *nom* medium speed

vitesse *f* **unique** *nom* single speed

vocabulaire *m* **contrôlé** *nom* controlled vocabulary

voie *nom* **1.** channel **2.** transmission channel ◇ **groupement de voies** channel group ◇ **voie** *f* **de liaison d'un bus d'adresses** bus address lines ◇

voie *f* **de retour du réseau local** backward LAN channel
voie *f* **analogique** *nom* analog channel
voie *f* **d'accès direct à la mémoire** *nom* direct memory access channel
voie *f* **d'acheminement** *nom* feeder
voie *f* **de déroutement** *nom* alternate route
voie *f* **de lecture/écriture** *nom* read/write channel
voie *f* **d'entrée/sortie** *nom* I/O channel
voie *f* **de retour** *nom* backward channel
voie *f* **de transmission de signaux** *nom* feeder ◇ **câble d'acheminement des signaux** *ou* **câble antenne-circuit** feeder cable
voie *f* **de transmission d'informations** *nom* information bearer channel
voie *f* **double** *nom* dual channel
voie *f* **logique** *nom* logical channel
voie *f* **spécialisée** *nom* dedicated channel
voile *m nom* **1.** fogging **2.** haze
voir ◇ **ce que vous voyez est ce que vous obtenez** What-You-See-Is-What-You-Get ◇ **ce que vous voyez est tout ce que vous obtenez** What-You-See-Is-All-You-Get
voix *f* **numérisée** *ou* **de synthèse** *nom* digital speech
voix *f* **sur IP** *nom* **1.** voice over Internet protocol **2.** VoIP
voix *f* **synthétisée** *nom* synthesised voice
volatilité *f nom* volatility
volet ◇ **volet** *m* **de protection en écriture** write-protect tab
volt *m nom* volt
voltage *m nom* voltage
volume *m nom* **1.** level **2.** volume ◇ **baissez le volume (du son)** turn the sound level down
volume *m nom* volume
vouloir dire *verbe* **1.** to mean **2.** to signify
voxel *m nom* voxel
voyant *m* **d'alarme** *nom* warning light
voyant *m* **lumineux** *nom* indicator light
VRAI *adjectif* true

WXYZ

watt *m nom* watt

WAVE *f nom* WAVE

Web *m abrév* W3 ■ *nom* web ■ *abrév* www ◇ **vous avez créé votre site, vous désirez maintenant le télécharger sur le Web** once you've created your site, you'll want to upload it to a Web server

WebBot *m* (*nom de marque*) WebBot

Webcaméra *f nom* web cam

Web designer *m nom* web designer

Webémission *f nom* webcast

Webmestre *m nom* webmaster

webtélé (*nom de marque*) WebTV

Windows MS-Windows

Windows™ (de Microsoft) (*interface graphique d'utilisateur*) Windows ◇ **Démarrer** Start button ◇ **Windows 98™** (*software de système d'exploitation*) Windows 98 ◇ **Windows for Workgroups™** Windows for Workgroups™ ◇ **(système d'exploitation) Windows NT™** Windows NT™

Windows 3.1 (*nom de marque*) Windows 3.1

Windows 3.1x (*nom de marque*) Windows 3.1x

Windows 3.11 Windows 3.11

Windows 95 (*nom de marque*) Windows 95

Windows 2000 (*nom de marque*) Windows 2000

Windows API (*nom de marque*) Windows API

Windows Explorer (*nom de marque*) Windows Explorer

Windows for Workgroups (*nom de marque*) Windows for Workgroups

Windows GDI (*nom de marque*) Windows GDI

Windows ME (*nom de marque*) Windows ME

Windows NT (*nom de marque*) Windows NT

Windows XP (*nom de marque*) Windows XP

WordPad (*utilitaire*) WordPad

World Wide Web *m nom* World Wide Web

X2 *nom* X2

XP *abrév* XP

YMCK *nom* (*définition de couleurs basée sur: jaune, magenta, cyan, noir*) YMCK

YMODEM *nom* YMODEM

> 'YMODEM apporte relativement peu d'améliorations techniques à XMODEM-1K; c'est principalement en autorisant le transfert de plusieurs fichiers en une seule session qu'il innove, de même qu'en transmettant leur nom et leurs principaux attributs (dans des blocs numérotés 0)' [*PC Expert*]

zéro *m nom* zero ◇ **en Grande-Bretagne, l'indicatif des appels internationaux est zéro zéro (00)** in Britain, the code for international calls is zero zero (00)

zéro *m* **barré d'un trait (oblique/transversal)** *nom* slashed zero

zéro *m* **de tête** *nom* leading zero

zettaoctet *m nom* zettabyte

ZMODEM *nom* ZMODEM

> 'ZMODEM transmet toutes les informations – les commandes et les données – sous forme de paquets précédés d'un en-tête et suivis d'un délimiteur de fin' [*PC Expert*]

zonage *m nom* fielding

zone *f nom* **1.** area **2.** region **3.** zone ◇ **graphique à zone sensible** *ou* **à zone active** hot zone graphic ◇ **graphisme à zone sensible** *ou* **cliquable** hot zone graphic ◇ **l'image de la trompette est une zone active qui produira un son lorsqu'on la sélectionne avec le pointeur** the image of the trumpet is a hotspot and will play a sound when you move the pointer over it ◇ **zone** *f* **de mémoire des programmes non résidents** transient area ◇ **zone** *f* **sur laquelle on peut cliquer** hotspot; hot zone

zone *f* **active** *nom* **1.** active area **2.** active region **3.** hotspot

zone *f* **cliquable** *nom* active region

zone *f* **commune de la mémoire** *nom* common storage area

zone *f* **d'affichage** *nom* image area

zone *f* **de balayage** *nom* scan area

zone *f* **de chaîne** *nom* string area

zone *f* **de code** *nom* code area

zone *f* **de connexions** *nom* terminal area

zone *f* **de détection** *nom* aiming symbol *ou* aiming field

zone *f* **de discussion** *nom* chat room

zone *f* **de données** *nom* data area

zone *f* **de liste déroulante** *nom* list box

zone *f* **de mémoire haute** *abrév* HMA

zone *f* **de mémoire supérieure** *nom* high memory area

zone *f* **de notification** *nom* system tray

zone *f* **d'entrée (de données)** *nom* input area

zone *f* **de parcage** *nom* (*de la tête de lecture*) landing zone

zone *f* **de pixels active** *nom* active pixel region

zone *f* **de recherche** *nom* seek area

zone *f* **de sauvegarde** *nom* save area

zone *f* **de segment de recouvrement** *nom* overlay region

zone *f* **de stockage de l'image** *nom* image storage space

zone *f* **de texte** *nom* soft zone

zone *f* **de traitement par lots** *nom* batch region

zone *f* **de travail** *nom* work area

zone *f* **de travail (en mémoire)** *nom* memory workspace

zone *f* **d'instruction** *nom* (*dans une mémoire*) instruction area

zone *f* **d'overlay** *nom* overlay region

zone *f* **pour programme utilisateur** *nom* user area

zone *f* **protégée** *nom* isolated location

zone *f* **(d'image) sélectionnée** *nom* marquee

zone *f* **sensible/active** *nom* hot zone

zone *f* **sortie (de la mémoire)** *nom* output area *ou* output block

zone *f* **utilisateur** *nom* user area

zoom *m nom* zooming

zoomer *verbe vi* to zoom

ENGLISH-FRENCH
ANGLAIS-FRANÇAIS

A

A[1] /eɪ/ *symbol* nombre *m* hexadécimal du 10 décimal

A[2] /eɪ/ *abbr* (*ampere*) A

A: (*first disk drive on an operating system*) A:

Å *abbr* (*angstrom*) A (anström)

AAL *abbr* (*ATM adaptation layer*) couche *f* d'adaptation ATM

abandon /ə'bændən/ *verb* quitter *vt*; abandonner *vt* ◇ **once you have abandoned your spreadsheet, you cannot retrieve it again** si vous quittez votre feuille de calcul sans la sauvegarder, il vous sera impossible de la récupérer

abb. add. *abbr* (*abbreviated addressing*) adressage *m* abrégé; adressage *m* simplifié

abbreviated address /əˌbriːvieɪtid ə'dres/ *noun* adresse *f* abrégée

abbreviated addressing /əˌbriːvieɪtid ə 'dresɪŋ/ *noun* utilisation *f* d'adresses abrégées

abbreviated installation /əˌbriːvieɪtid ˌɪnstə'leɪʃ(ə)n/ *noun* installation *f* simplifiée

abbreviation /əˌbriːvi'eɪʃ(ə)n/ *noun* abréviation *f* ◇ **within the text, the abbreviation 'proc' is used instead of processor** dans le texte, on a remplacé le terme processeur par l'abréviation 'proc'

abend /'æbend/ *noun* (*end of a program*) fin *f* anormale; interruption *f* anormale; interruption *f* prématurée; arrêt *m* anormal ◇ **an interrupt from a faulty printer caused an abend** une commande *or* un signal d'interruption venant d'une imprimante défectueuse a provoqué une fin anormale de traitement ◇ **if a fault occurs, data loss will be minimized due to the improved abend recovery program** en cas de panne, la perte de données sera minimale grâce au nouveau programme de récupération des fichiers suite à une interruption anormale

abend code /'æbend kəʊd/ *noun* code *m* de fin anormale; code *m* d'interruption

abend recovery program /ˌæbend rɪ 'kʌv(ə)ri ˌprəʊgræm/ *noun* programme *m* de récupération de fichier après une interruption ◇ **once you have abandoned your spreadsheet, you cannot retrieve it again** si vous quittez votre feuille de calcul sans la sauvegarder, il vous sera impossible de la récupérer

aberration /ˌæbə'reɪʃ(ə)n/ *noun* **1.** (*of light beam or image, etc.*) aberration *f* **2.** (*of TV picture – caused by corrupt signal or incorrect adjustment*) déformation *f*

ablation /ə'bleɪʃ(ə)n/ *noun* (*method of writing data to an optical storage device*) brûlage *m* laser; trou *m* laser

abnormal end /æbˌnɔːm(ə)l 'end/ *noun* (*end of a program*) fin *f* anormale; fin *f* prématurée; interruption *f* anormale; interruption *f* prématurée

abnormal termination /æbˌnɔːm(ə)l ˌtɜːmɪ 'neɪʃ(ə)n/ *noun* fin *f* anormale

abort /ə'bɔːt/ *verb* (*to interrupt a process*) faire avorter; abandonner prématurément; interrompre *vt*; arrêter *vt*; suspendre l'exécution ◇ **abort the program before it erases any more files** interrompez *or* arrêtez l'exécution du programme, avant qu'il efface d'autres fichiers ◇ **the program was aborted by pressing the red button** on a interrompu le programme en appuyant sur la touche rouge

aborted connection /əˌbɔːtɪd kə'nekʃ(ə)n/ *noun* connexion *f* avortée

abort sequence /ə'bɔːt ˌsiːkwəns/ *noun* (*indication of transmission failure*) séquence *f* de clôture anormale; séquence *f* de fin; séquence *f* d'interruption prématurée

About... /ə'baʊt/ (*menu selection that tells you who developed the program and gives copyright information*) A propos de...

ABR /ˌeɪ biː 'ɑː/ *noun* débit *m* binaire disponible

AB roll /ˌeɪ 'biː ˌrəʊl/ *noun* (*two video or music segments that are synchronised*) fondu *m* enchaîné

ABS /ˌeɪ biː 'es/ *noun* ABS; fonction *f* valeur absolue

absolute address /ˌæbsəluːt ə'dres/ *noun* **1.** adresse *f* absolue **2.** adresse *f* machine; adresse *f* réelle

absolute addressing /ˌæbsəluːt ə'dresɪŋ/ *noun* adressage *m* absolu

absolute assembler /ˌæbsəluːt ə'semblə/ *noun* assembleur *m* absolu

absolute cell reference /ˌæbsəluːt sel 'ref(ə)rəns/ *noun* adresse *f* absolue de la cellule

absolute code /'æbsəluːt kəʊd/ *noun* code *m* binaire absolu

absolute coordinates /ˌæbsəluːt kəʊ 'ɔːdɪnətz/ *plural noun* coordonnées *fpl* absolues

absolute device /ˌæbsəluːt dɪˈvaɪs/ *noun* dispositif *m* de pointage absolu

absolute error /ˌæbsəluːt ˈerə/ *noun* erreur *f* absolue

absolute expression /ˌæbsəluːt ɪk ˈspreʃ(ə)n/ *noun* expression *f* absolue

absolute instruction /ˌæbsəluːt ɪn ˈstrʌkʃən/ *noun* instruction *f* absolue; code *m* absolu

absolute loader /ˈæbsəluːt ˌləʊdə/ *noun* chargeur *m* absolu

absolute maximum rating /ˌæbsəluːt ˈmæksɪməm ˌreɪtɪŋ/ *noun* capacité *f* théorique absolue

absolute positioning /ˌæbsəluːt pə ˈzɪʃ(ə)nɪŋ/ *noun* positionnement *m* absolu

absolute priority /ˌæbsəluːt praɪˈɒrɪti/ *noun* priorité *f* absolue

absolute program /ˌæbsəluːt ˈprəʊgræm/ *noun* programme *m* absolu; programme *m* en langage machine

absolute time /ˈæbsəluːt taɪm/ *noun* temps *m* absolu

absolute value /ˌæbsəluːt ˈvæljuː/ *noun* valeur *f* absolue ◇ **the absolute value of –62.34 is 62.34** la valeur absolue de –62,34 est 62,34

absorb /əbˈzɔːb/ *verb* absorber *vt*

absorptance /əbˈzɔːptəns/ *noun* absorptance *f*; indice *m* d'absorption

absorption /əbˈzɔːpʃən/ *noun* absorption *f*

abstract data type /ˌbstrækt ˈdeɪtə ˌtaɪp/ *noun* (*general data type that can store any kind of information*) données *fpl* de type général ◇ **the stack is a structure of abstract data types, it can store any type of data** la pile est une structure de données de type général, elle peut stocker des données de tous types

A-bus /eɪ bʌs/ *noun* (*main internal bus*) bus *m* principal; bus *m* A

accelerated graphics port /əkˌseləreɪtɪd ˈgræfɪks ˌpɔːt/ *noun* graphique *m* accéléré

acceleration time /əkˌseləˈreɪʃ(ə)n taɪm/ *noun* **1.** (*to spin a disk at correct speed*) temps *m* d'accélération; temps *m* de montée **2.** (*time between access instruction and data transfer*) temps *m* de réponse ◇ **allow for acceleration time in the access time** il faut inclure le temps de montée dans le temps d'accès

accelerator board /əkˈseləˌreɪtə bɔːd/, **accelerator card** /əkˈseləˌreɪtə kɑːd/ *noun* carte *f* accélératrice; carte *f* d'accélération

accelerator key /əkˈseləˌreɪtə kiː/ *noun* (*may also be a combination of keys that carry out a function*) touche *f* d'accélération; raccourci *m* clavier; séquence *f* de touches ◇ **instead of selecting the File menu then the Save option, use the accelerator keys Alt and S to do the same thing and save the file** au lieu de sélectionner le menu Fichier puis l'option Enregistrer, utilisez les touches d'accélération ALT-S *or* le raccourci clavier ALT-S pour sauvegarder votre fichier

accept /əkˈsept/ *verb* (*to establish a session or connection*) accepter *vt* ◇ **he accepted the quoted price for printing** il a accepté le devis de l'imprimeur ◇ **he did not accept the programming job he was offered** il n'a pas accepté *or* il a refusé le poste de programmeur qu'on lui offrait

acceptance sampling /əkˈseptəns ˌsɑːmplɪŋ/ *noun* échantillonnage *m* de qualité

acceptance test /əkˈseptəns test/ *noun* test *m* d'homologation

acceptance testing /əkˌseptəns ˈtestɪŋ/ *noun* test *m* d'homologation

access /ˈækses/ *noun* **1.** (*ability to use something*) accès *m* **2.** (*being allowed to use a computer*) accès *m* ■ *verb* (*call up data stored on a computer*) accéder à; avoir accès à ◇ **after he was discovered hacking, he was barred access to the system** après avoir découvert qu'il faisait du piratage, on lui a interdit l'accès au système ◇ **direct access storage device (DASD)** support *m* à accès direct ◇ **he has access to numerous sensitive files** il a accès à de nombreux fichiers confidentiels ◇ **she accessed the employee's file stored on the computer** elle a accédé au fichier (informatique) de l'employé stocké sur l'ordinateur ◇ **the instantaneous access of the RAM disk was welcome** l'accès instantané au disque RAM a été bien accueilli ◇ **to bar access to a system** interdire (à quelqu'un) l'accès à un système ◇ **to have access to a file of data** avoir accès à un fichier informatique ◇ **to have access to something** avoir accès à quelque chose

access arm /ˈækses ɑːm/ *noun* (*device in a disk drive*) bras *m* de lecture/écriture

access authority /ˈækses ɔːˌθɒrəti/ *noun* autorisation *f* d'accès

access-barred /ˌækses ˈbɑːd/ *adjective* accès *m* non autorisé; interdit

access category /ˈækses ˌkætəg(ə)ri/ *noun* type *m*

access channel control /ˌækses ˌtʃæn(ə)l kənˈtrəʊl/ *noun* contrôle *m* des canaux d'accès

access charge /ˈækses tʃɑːdʒ/ *noun* frais *mpl* d'accès au système

access code /ˈækses kəʊd/ *noun* code *m* d'accès; mot *m* de passe

access control /ˈækses kənˌtrəʊl/ *noun* contrôle *m* d'accès

access control byte /ˌækses kənˈtrəʊl baɪt/ *noun* octet *m* de contrôle d'accès

access controller /ˈækses kənˌtrəʊlə/ *noun* contrôleur *m* d'accès

access control list /ˌækses kənˈtrəʊl lɪst/ *noun* liste *f* de contrôle d'accès

access head /ˈækses hed/ *noun* tête *f* d'accès

access hole /'ækses həʊl/ *noun* fenêtre *f* d'accès

accession number /ək'seʃ(ə)n ˌnʌmbə/ *noun* (*number in a record*) numéro *m* d'accès

access level /'ækses ˌlev(ə)l/ *noun* niveau *m* d'accès

access line /'ækses laɪn/ *noun* ligne *f* d'accès

access log /'ækses lɒg/ *noun* protocole *m* des accès

access mechanism /'ækses ˌmekənɪz(ə)m/ *noun* mécanisme *m* d'accès

access method /'ækses ˌmeθəd/ *noun* méthode *f* d'accès

access method routines /'ækses ˌmeθəd ruːˌtiːnz/ *plural noun* routines *fpl* d'accès

access name /'ækses neɪm/ *noun* nom *m* d'accès

access number /'ækses ˌnʌmbə/ *noun* numéro *m* d'accès

accessor /'æksesə/ *noun* (*person who accesses data*) utilisateur *m* ayant un droit d'accès

accessory /ək'sesəri/ *noun* accessoire *m* ◇ **the printer comes with several accessories, such as a soundproof hood** plusieurs accessoires, dont un capot d'insonorisation, sont fournis avec l'imprimante ◇ **this popular home computer has a large range of accessories** il existe de nombreux accessoires pour cet ordinateur individuel très populaire

access path /'ækses pɑːθ/ *noun* chemin *m* d'accès

access path journalling /ˌækses ˌpɑːθ 'dʒɜːnəlɪŋ/ *noun* enregistrement *m* des chemins d'accès

access period /'ækses ˌpɪəriəd/ *noun* période *f* d'accès

access permission /'ækses pəˌmɪʃ(ə)n/ *noun* permission *f* d'accès

access point /'ækses pɔɪnt/ *noun* (*test point to check signals or data*) point *m* d'accès; point *m* de contrôle

access privilege /'ækses ˌprɪvɪlɪdʒ/ *noun* privilège *m* d'accès

access provider /'ækses prəˌvaɪdə/ *noun* fournisseur *m* de services Internet

access rights /'ækses raɪts/ *plural noun* droits *mpl* d'accès

access time /'ækses ˌtaɪm/ *noun* **1.** (*time needed between request and data being shown*) temps *m* d'accès **2.** (*time needed to find a file, etc.*) temps *m* d'accès

access unit /'ækses ˌjuːnɪt/ *noun* unité *f* d'accès

accidental /ˌæksɪ'dent(ə)l/ *adjective* accidentel *or* -elle

accordion fold /ə'kɔːdiən fəʊld/, **accordion fanfold** *noun* (*printing*) papier *m* plié en accordéon; papier *m* plié en éventail; papier *m* plié en paravent; papier *m* en continu

account /ə'kaʊnt/ *noun* (*record of a user's name, password and rights*) compte *m* ■ *verb* (*logging how much time and resources each user uses*) comptabiliser *vt* ◇ **if you are a new user, you will have to ask the supervisor to create an account for you** si vous êtes un nouvel utilisateur, vous devez demander à l'administrateur de vous ouvrir un compte

accounting package /ə'kaʊntɪŋ ˌpækɪdʒ/ *noun* logiciel *m* de comptabilité

account name /ə'kaʊnt neɪm/ *noun* nom *m* de compte ◇ **John Smith's account name is JSMITH** le nom de compte de John Smith est JSMITH

accounts package /ə'kaʊnts ˌpækɪdʒ/ *noun* logiciel *m* de comptabilité

accumulate /ə'kjuːmjʊleɪt/ *verb* accumuler *vt*; rassembler *vt* ◇ **we have gradually accumulated a large databank of names and addresses** nous avons rassemblé progressivement un impressionnant fichier d'adresses

accumulator /ə'kjuːmjʊleɪtə/, **accumulator register** /ˌeɪ siː 'siː/ *noun* accumulateur *m*; ACC ◇ **store the two bytes of data in registers A and B and execute the add instruction – the answer will be in the accumulator** stockez les 2 octets de données dans les registres A et B et exécutez l'instruction 'add' – vous obtiendrez le résultat dans l'accumulateur

accumulator address /ə'kjuːmjʊleɪtə ə ˌdres/ *noun* adresse *f* d'accumulateur

accumulator shift instruction /ə ˌkjuːmjʊleɪtə 'ʃɪft ɪnˌstrʌkʃən/ *noun* commande *f* de décalage dans le registre

accuracy /'ækjʊrəsi/ *noun* **1.** (*extent to which something is correct*) précision *f* **2.** (*extent to which someone avoids errors*) précision *f* **3.** (*number of bits used to define number*) exactitude *f*

accuracy control character /ˌækjʊrəsi kən 'trəʊl ˌkærɪktə/ *noun* caractère *m* de contrôle de précision

ACD /ˌeɪ siː 'diː/ *noun* distribution *f* automatique d'appels

achromatic colour /ˌeɪkrəʊmætɪk 'kʌlə/ *noun* couleur *f* achromatique

ACIA /ˌeɪ siː aɪ 'eɪ/ *noun* interface *f* pour communication asynchrone

ACK /ˌeɪ siː 'keɪ/ *noun* accusé *m* de réception positif

Ackerman's function /'ækəmənz ˌfʌŋkʃən/ *noun* fonction *f* d'Ackerman

acknowledge /ək'nɒlɪdʒ/ *noun* (*signal that message has been received*) caractère *m* d' accusé de réception ■ *verb* **1.** (*to confirm receipt of letter or message*) accuser réception; envoyer un accusé de réception **2.** (*to send signal confirming *receipt*) accuser réception; envoyer un accusé de réception

acknowledge character /ək,nɒlɪdʒ 'kærɪktə/ *noun* caractère *m* d'accusé de réception

acknowledged mail /ək,nɒlɪdʒd 'meɪl/ *noun* (*signals to the sender when an electronic mail message has been read*) message *m* avec accusé de réception

ACL /,eɪ siː 'el/ *noun* liste *f* des droits d'accès

acoustic /ə'kuːstɪk/ *adjective* acoustique

acoustic coupler /ə,kuːstɪk 'kʌplə/ *noun* coupleur *m* acoustique

acoustic delay line /ə,kuːstɪk dɪ'leɪ laɪn/ *noun* ligne *f* à retard acoustique

acoustic hood /ə'kuːstɪk hʊd/ *noun* (*soundproof cover*) hotte *f*

acoustic memory /ə,kuːstɪk 'mem(ə)ri/ *noun* mémoire *f* acoustique

acoustic panel /ə,kuːstɪk 'pæn(ə)l/ *noun* panneau *m* d'insonorisation

acoustic store /ə'kuːstɪk stɔː/ *noun* mémoire *f* acoustique

ACPI /,eɪ siː piː 'aɪ/ *noun* norme *f* ACPI

acquisition /,ækwɪ'zɪʃ(ə)n/ *noun* acquisition *f*

Acrobat (*file format developed by Adobe Systems*) Acrobat

ACS /,eɪ siː 'es/ *noun* séquenceur *m* d'appels automatique

action /'ækʃən/ *noun* (*in SAA CUA front-end: user event, such as pressing a key*) action *f* ◇ **action field** (*photography*) champ *m* (d'action)

action bar /'ækʃən bɑː/ *noun* barre *f* de menu

action bar pull-down /'ækʃən bɑː pʊl/ *noun* déroulement *m* du menu

action code /'ækʃən kəʊd/ *noun* code *m* action

action cycle /,ækʃən 'saɪk(ə)l/ *noun* cycle *m* fonctionnel

action list /'ækʃən lɪst/ *noun* liste *f* d'actions

ActionMedia /,ækʃən'miːdiə/ (*trade name for a digital video system developed by Intel*) ActionMedia

action message /,ækʃən 'mesɪdʒ/ *noun* message *m* d'intervention

action-object /,ækʃən əb'dʒekt/ *noun* objet *m* d'action

activate /'æktɪ,veɪt/ *verb* **1.** (*to start*) activer *vt*; mettre en marche **2.** (*to make available*) activer *vt*; mettre en marche ◇ **pressing CR activates the printer** en appuyant sur la touche CR, on met l'imprimante en marche

active /'æktɪv/ *adjective* actif *or* -ive; en cours d'utilisation

active application /,æktɪv ,æplɪ'keɪʃ(ə)n/ *noun* application *f* active

active area /,æktɪv 'eəriə/ *noun* zone *f* active

active cell /'æktɪv sel/ *noun* cellule *f* de travail

active code page /,æktɪv 'kəʊd ,peɪdʒ/ *noun* code *m* page en vigueur

active database /,æktɪv 'deɪtəbeɪs/ *noun* base *f* de données active

active device /,æktɪv dɪ'vaɪs/ *noun* dispositif *m* électronique actif; dispositif *m* électronique armé

active file /,æktɪv 'faɪl/ *noun* fichier *m* actif

active gateway /,æktɪv 'geɪtweɪ/ *noun* passerelle *f* active

active high /'æktɪv haɪ/ *noun* signal *m* haut actif

active hub /,æktɪv 'hʌb/ *noun* concentrateur *m*; hub *m* actif

active line /,æktɪv 'laɪn/ *noun* ligne *f* active

active link /,æktɪv 'lɪŋk/ *noun* connexion *f* active; liaison *f* active

active low /,æktɪv 'ləʊ/ *noun* signal *m* bas actif

active matrix display /,æktɪv ,meɪtrɪks dɪs 'pleɪ/ *noun* écran *m* à matrice active

active menu /,æktɪv 'menjuː/ *noun* menu *m* actif

active node /,æktɪv 'nəʊd/ *noun* noeud *m* actif

active pixel region /,æktɪv 'pɪks(ə)l ,riːdʒən/ *noun* zone *f* de pixels active

active printer /,æktɪv 'prɪntə/ *noun* imprimante *f* active

active program /,æktɪv 'prəʊgræm/ *noun* programme *m* actif

active record /,æktɪv 'rekɔːd/ *noun* enregistrement *m* actif

active region /,æktɪv 'riːdʒ(ə)n/ *noun* zone *f* active; zone *f* cliquable

Active Server Page /,æktɪv 'sɜːvə peɪdʒ/ *noun* page *f* ASP

active star /'æktɪv stɑː/ *noun* réseau *m* en étoile actif

active state /,æktɪv 'steɪt/ *noun* mode *m* actif

active storage /,æktɪv 'stɔːrɪdʒ/ *noun* stockage *m* actif

active streaming format /,æktɪv 'striːmɪŋ ,fɔːmæt/ *noun* format *m* ASF

active video /,æktɪv 'vɪdiəʊ/, **active video signal** /,æktɪv 'vɪdiəʊ ,sɪgn(ə)l/ *noun* vidéo *f* active

ActiveVRML /,æktɪv viː ɑː em 'el/ *noun* langage *m* VRML

active window /,æktɪv 'wɪndəʊ/ *noun* fenêtre *f* active

ActiveX /,æktɪv 'eks/ (*trade name for a programming language*) technologie *f* ActiveX

activities /æk'tɪvɪtiz/ *plural noun* tâches *fpl*

activity level /æk,tɪvəti 'lev(ə)l/ *noun* niveau *m* d'activité

activity light /æk'tɪvəti laɪt/ *noun* (*small light or LED*) lampe *f* témoin; témoin *m* d'activité

activity loading /æk,tɪvəti 'ləʊdɪŋ/ *noun* chargement *m* en fonction du taux d'activité

activity ratio /æk,tɪvəti 'reɪʃiəʊ/ *noun* taux *m* d'activité

activity trail /æk'tɪvəti treɪl/ *noun* enregistrement *m* d'activité; suivi *m* d'activité; traçage *m* d'activité

actual address /,æktʃuəl ə'dres/ *noun* adresse *f* absolue; adresse *f* réelle

actual code /'æktʃuəl kəʊd/ *noun* code *m* absolu; code *m* machine

actual data transfer rate /,æktʃuəl ,deɪtə 'trænsfɜː ,reɪt/ *noun* débit *m* réel de transfert de données

actual instruction /,æktʃuəl ɪn'strʌkʃən/ *noun* instruction *f* absolue

actuator /'æktʃʊeɪtə/ *noun* (*mechanical device controlled by an external signal*) bras *m* de lecture; (*mechanical device*) vérin *m*

ACU /,eɪ siː 'juː/ *noun* dispositif *m* d'appel automatique

ad *abbr* (*Andorra*) Andorre

A/D *abbr* (*analog to digital*) analogique/numérique

ADA /,eɪ diː 'eɪ/ *noun* langage *m* ADA

adapt /ə'dæpt/ *verb* adapter *vt* ◇ **can this computer be adapted to take 5.25 inch disks?** peut-on adapter cet ordinateur pour les disquettes 5,25 pouces?

adaptation /,ædæp'teɪʃ(ə)n/ *noun* adaptation *f* ◇ **the adaptation of the eye to respond to different levels of brightness** l'adaptation de l'oeil pour répondre à différents niveaux de luminosité *or* de brillance

adapter /ə'dæptə/, **adaptor** /ə'dæptə/ *noun* (*connector*) adaptateur *m* ◇ **the cable adapter allows attachment of the scanner to the SCSI interface** l'adaptateur du câble permet de relier le scanner à une interface SCSI ◇ **the cable to connect the scanner to the adapter is included in the package** le câble de liaison entre le scanner et l'adaptateur est compris

adapter card /ə'dæptə kɑːd/ *noun* carte *f* adaptateur

adapter plug /ə'dæptə plʌg/ *noun* adaptateur *m*

adaptive channel allocation /ə,dæptɪv 'tʃæn(ə)l ælə,keɪʃ(ə)n/ *noun* allocation *f* dynamique de canal

adaptive compression /ə,dæptɪv kəm 'preʃ(ə)n/ *noun* encodage *m* adaptif

adaptive differential pulse code modulation /ə,dæptɪv dɪfə,renʃ(ə)l 'pʌls kəʊd mɒdju,leɪʃ(ə)n/ *noun* modulation *f* différentielle dynamique par impulsions et codage; norme *f* de conversion ADPCM

adaptive packet assembly /ə,dæptɪv 'pækɪt ə,sembli/ *noun* assemblage *m* adaptatif de paquets; groupage *m* adaptatif de données

adaptive routing /ə,dæptɪv 'ruːtɪŋ/ *noun* acheminement *m* dynamique; routage *m* dynamique

adaptive system /ə,dæptɪv 'sɪstəm/ *noun* (*system that can alter its responses and processes*) système *m* auto-adaptable; système *m* dynamique

adaptor /ə'dæptə/ *noun* adaptateur *m*

ADC /,eɪ diː 'siː/ *noun* convertisseur *m* analogique-numérique

add /æd/ *verb* **1.** (*figures*) additionner *vt* **2.** (*parts or text*) ajouter *vt* ◇ **adding or deleting material from the text is easy using function keys** avec les touches de fonction, il est facile d'ajouter ou de supprimer du texte ◇ **in the spreadsheet each column should be added to make a subtotal** l'addition de chacune des colonnes du tableau donne un sous-total ◇ **the software house has added a new management package to its range of products** les producteurs de logiciels ont ajouté un nouveau progiciel de gestion à leur gamme de produits

addend /'ædend/ *noun* cumulateur *m*; second terme *m* d'une addition

adder /'ædə/ *noun* additionneur *m*

adder-subtractor /,ædə səb'træktə/ *noun* additionneur-soustracteur *m*

add file /'æd faɪl/ *noun* fichier *m* avec ajouts

add-in /'æd ɪn/ *noun, adjective* (*supplementary device*) dispositif *m* supplémentaire; dispositif *m* additionnel ■ *adjective* (*additional*) additionnel; supplémentaire ◇ **add-in card** carte additionnelle *or* carte d'extension

addition /ə'dɪʃ(ə)n/ *noun* (*in arithmetic*) addition *f*

additional /ə'dɪʃ(ə)nəl/ *adjective* additionnel *or* -elle; supplémentaire ◇ **can we add three additional workstations to the network?** peut-on ajouter trois postes *or* stations de travail supplémentaires au réseau?

addition record /ə,dɪʃ(ə)n 'rekɔːd/ *noun* enregistrement *m*; fichier *m* de mise à jour

addition time /ə'dɪʃ(ə)n taɪm/ *noun* (*time to carry out an addition operation*) temps *m* d'addition

addition without carry /ə,dɪʃ(ə)n wɪð,aʊt 'kæri/ *noun* addition *f* sans retenue

additive colour /,ædətɪv 'kʌlə/ *noun* synthèse *f* additive de couleurs

add-on /'æd ɒn/ *adjective* (*added to a computer system*) complément *m*; supplémentaire; additionnel *or* -elle ■ *noun* (*additional software or hardware*) dispositif *m* additif; dispositif *m* additionnel; dispositif *m* supplémentaire; complément *m*

add on board /'æd ɒn bɔːd/ *noun* carte *f* d'extension

add register /æd 'redʒɪstə/ *noun* registre *m* d'addition

address /ə'dres/ *noun* **1.** (*number allowing a central processing unit to reference a physical location in a storage*) adresse *f* **2.** (*unique number that identifies a device on a network*) adresse *f* ■ *verb* (*to enter location data into an address bus*) accéder à une adresse ◇ **address list** liste *f* d'adresses ◇ **address resolution protocol (ARP)** (*used to link one IP address to a low-level physical address*) protocole *m* de résolution d'adresse *or* protocole ARP ◇ **address window** (*on the screen*) zone *f* d'adresse ◇ **each separate memory word has its own unique address** chaque mot mémoire distinct a sa propre et unique adresse ◇ **this is the address at which the data starts** c'est l'adresse à laquelle les données commencent ◇ **we keep an address list of two thousand businesses in Europe** notre fichier contient les adresses de deux mille sociétés en Europe

addressability /əˌdresə'bɪlɪti/ *noun* (*of pixels*) capacité *f* d'adressage

addressable /ə'dresəb(ə)l/ *adjective* adressable ◇ **with the new operating system, all of the 5MB of RAM is addressable** dans le nouveau système d'exploitation, la totalité des 5Mo de RAM installée est adressable

addressable cursor /əˌdresəb(ə)l 'kɜːsə/ *noun* curseur *m* adressable

addressable point /əˌdresəb(ə)l 'pɔɪnt/ *noun* point *m* adressable

addressable terminal /əˌdresəb(ə)l 'tɜːmɪn(ə)l/ *noun* terminal *m* à adressage protégé ◇ **all the messages go to all the terminals since none are addressable terminals** tous les messages sont transmis à tous les terminaux puisqu'aucun d'eux ne possède un adressage protégé

address access time /əˌdres 'ækses taɪm/ *noun* temps *m* d'adressage

address base /ə'dres beɪs/ *noun* base *f* d'adressage

address book /ə'dres bʊk/ *noun* **1.** carnet *m* d'adresses **2.** livre *m* d'adresses

address bus /ə'dres bʌs/ *noun* (*physical connection that carries address data*) bus *m* d'adresses

address code /ə'dres kəʊd/ *noun* code *m* adresse

address computation /əˌdres ˌkɒmpjʊ'teɪʃ(ə)n/ *noun* calcul *m* d'une adresse

address decoder /ə'dres diːˌkəʊdə/ *noun* décodeur *m* d'adresses

address field /ə'dres fiːld/ *noun* champ *m* d'adresse

address format /ə'dres ˌfɔːmæt/ *noun* format *m* d'adresse

address highway /ə'dres ˌhaɪweɪ/ *noun* bus *m* d'adresses

addressing /ə'dresɪŋ/ *noun* (*accessing a location in memory*) adressage *m*

addressing capacity /ə'dresɪŋ kəˌpæsɪti/ *noun* (*memory*) capacité *f* d'adressage; capacité *f* de mémoire; disponibilité *f* d'adressage; disponibilité *f* de mémoire

addressing level /ə'dresɪŋ ˌlev(ə)l/ *noun* niveau *m* d'adressage

addressing method /ə'dresɪŋ ˌmeθəd/ *noun* méthode *f* d'adressage

addressing mode /ə'dresɪŋ məʊd/ *noun* mode *m* d'adressage

address mapping /ə'dres ˌmæpɪŋ/ *noun* table *f* de correspondance des adresses

address mark /ə'dres mɑːk/ *noun* marque *f* de début d'adresse

address mask /ə'dres mɑːsk/ *noun* masque *m* de sous-réseau

address modification /əˌdres ˌmɒdɪfɪ'keɪʃ(ə)n/ *noun* modification *f* d'adresse

address register /ə'dres ˌredʒɪstə/ *noun* registre *m* d'adresse

address resolution /ə'dres ˌrezəluːʃ(ə)n/ *noun* résolution *f* d'adresse

address resolution protocol /əˌdres ˌrezə'luːʃ(ə)n ˌprəʊtəkɒl/ *noun* protocole *m* ARP; protocole *m* de résolution d'adresse

address space /ə'dres speɪs/ *noun* espace *m* adresse

address strobe /ə'dres strəʊb/ *noun* (*signal*) signal *m* de validité d'adresse

address track /ə'dres træk/ *noun* piste *f* d'adresses

address translation /əˌdres træns'leɪʃ(ə)n/ *noun* adresse *f* calculée

address word /ə'dres wɜːd/ *noun* mot *m* adresse ◇ **a larger address word increases the amount of memory a computer can address** plus le mot adresse est long, plus la mémoire adressable de l'ordinateur augmente

add time /'æd taɪm/ *noun* temps *m* d'addition

adjacent domains /əˌdʒeɪs(ə)nt dəʊ'meɪnz/ *plural noun* domaines *mpl* adjacents

adjacent nodes /ə'dʒeɪs(ə)nt nəʊdz/ *plural noun* noeuds *mpl* adjacents

adjunct register /ˌædʒʌŋkt 'redʒɪstə/ *noun* (*where the top 16 bits are used for control information and the bottom 16 bits are available for use by a program*) registre *m* couplé

adjustment /ə'dʒʌstmənt/ *noun* (*minor change made to improve a system*) ajustement *m*; réglage *m*; mise *f* au point; modification *f* ◇ **I think the joystick needs adjustment as it sometimes gets stuck** il faudrait vérifier la manette de commande qui reste parfois coincée ◇ **the brightness needs adjustment** la luminosité a besoin d'un réglage

AdLib™ /æd'lɪb/ *noun* (*type of sound card for the PC with basic sound playback and MIDI functions*) carte *f* son AdLib™

administrator /əd'mɪnɪstreɪtə/ *noun* (*person who is responsible for looking after a network*) administrateur *m*

Adobe Acrobat /əˌdəʊbi 'ækrəbæt/ (*trade name for a piece of software that converts documents and formatted pages into a file format that can be viewed on almost any computer platform or Internet browser*) Adobe Acrobat

Adobe Systems /əˌdəʊbi 'sɪstəmz/ Adobe

Adobe Type Manager /əˌdəʊbi taɪp 'mænɪdʒə/ (*trade name for a standard for describing scalable fonts*) ATM; gestionnaire *m* de police Adobe

ADP /ˌeɪ diː 'piː/ *noun* traitement *m* automatique de données

ADPCM /ˌeɪ diː piː siː 'em/ *noun* modulation *f* différentielle dynamique par impulsions et codage; norme *f* de conversion ADPCM

ADSL /ˌeɪ diː es 'el/ *noun* ligne *f* d'abonné numérique à débit asymétrique

advanced configuration and power interface /ədˌvɑːnst kənˌfɪgjəˌreɪʃ(ə)n ən ˌpaʊə 'ɪntəfeɪs/ *noun* norme *f* ACPI

advanced peer-to-peer networking /əd ˌvɑːnst ˌpɪə tə ˌpɪə 'netwɜːkɪŋ/ *noun* (*extension to the IBM SNA protocol*) réseau *m* APPN; réseau *m* égal à égal avancé; réseau *m* poste à poste avancé; réseau *m* sans serveur dédié (SSD)

advanced program to program communications /ədˌvɑːnst ˌprəʊgræm tə ˌprəʊgræm kəˌmjuːnɪ'keɪʃ(ə)nz/ *noun* (*set of protocols for peer-to-peer communication*) programmation *f* avancée des programmes de communications; protocole *m* APPC

Advanced Research Projects Agency Network /ədˌvɑːnst ˌriːsɜːtʃ ˌprɒdʒekts ˌeɪdʒ(ə)nsi 'netwɜːk/ *noun* réseau *m* Arpanet

advanced run-length limited /ədˌvɑːnst 'rʌn leŋθ ˌlɪmɪtɪd/ *noun* encodage *m* ARLL

advanced technology attachment packet interface /ədˌvɑːnst tekˌnɒlədʒi ə ˌtætʃmənt ˌpækɪt 'ɪntəfeɪs/ *noun* norme *f* ATAPI

advanced version /ədˌvɑːnst 'vɜːʃ(ə)n/ *noun* version *f* avancée; version *f* évoluée

advisory lock /əd'vaɪz(ə)ri lɒk/ *noun* (*lock placed on a region of a file*) verrouillage *m* de protection

advisory system /ədˌvaɪz(ə)ri 'sɪstəm/ *noun* (*expert system that provides advice to a user*) système-conseil *m*

aerial perspective /ˌeəriəl pə'spektɪv/ *noun* perspective *f* aérienne

AFAIK *abbr* (*as far as I know*) pour autant que je sache

affiliate marketing /ə'fɪliət ˌmɑːkɪtɪŋ/ *noun* marketing *m* d'affiliation

affirmative /ə'fɜːmətɪv/ *adjective* affirmatif *or* -ive; positif *or* -ive

affirmative acknowledgement /əˌfɜːmətɪv ək'nɒlɪdʒmənt/ *noun* accusé *m* de réception positif; confirmation *f* positive

AFIPS *abbr* (*American Federation of Information Processing Societies*) AFIPS

AFP /ˌeɪ ef 'piː/ *noun* protocole *m* de gestion de fichier AppleTalk; protocole *m* AFP

afterglow /'ɑːftəgləʊ/ *noun* persistance *f*

after-image /ˌɑːftə 'ɪmɪdʒ/ *noun* (*copy of a block of data that has been modified*) copie *f* corrigée

AGC /ˌeɪ dʒiː 'siː/ *noun* contrôle *m* de gain automatique

agent /'eɪdʒənt/ *noun* **1.** (*program or software that runs on a workstation in a network*) agent *m*; programme *m* agent intelligent **2.** (*series of commands or actions carried out automatically*) agent *m*

aggregate /'ægrɪgət/ *noun* agrégat *m*

aggregate bandwidth /ˌægrɪgət 'bændwɪdθ/ *noun* largeur *f* de bande agréée; largeur *f* de bande autorisée

aggregate function /ˌægrɪgət 'fʌŋkʃən/ *noun* fonction *f* d'agrégation; fonction *f* de globalisation

aggregate line speed /ˌægrɪgət 'laɪn ˌspiːd/ *noun* débit *m* théorique

aggregate operator /ˌægrɪgət 'ɒpəreɪtə/ *noun* opérateur *m* de globalisation

AGP /ˌeɪ dʒiː 'piː/ *noun* bus *m* AGP

AI /ˌeɪ 'aɪ/ *noun* intelligence *f* artificielle

aiming symbol /ˌeɪmɪŋ 'sɪmbəl/, **aiming field** /fiːld/ *noun* (*defines the area in which a light-pen can be detected*) symbole *m* de détection; zone *f* de détection

airbrush /'eəˌbrʌʃ/ *noun* (*painting tool that creates a diffuse pattern of dots*) aérographe *m* ◇ **we used the airbrush tool to create the cloud effects in this image** nous avons utilisé l'aérographe pour créer un effet de nuage dans cette image

air gap /'eə gæp/ *noun* entrefer *m*

AIX AIX

A law /'ə lɔː/ *noun* loi *f* A

alert /ə'lɜːt/ *noun* (*warning message*) message *m* d'alerte

alert box /ə'lɜːt bɒks/ *noun* message *m* d'alerte

alert condition /əˌlɜːt kən'dɪʃ(ə)n/ *noun* condition *f* d'alerte

algebra /'ældʒɪbrə/ *noun* algèbre *f*

algebraic language /ˌældʒɪbreɪɪk 'læŋgwɪdʒ/ *noun* (*context-free language*) langage *m* documentaire; langage *m* algébrique

ALGOL /'ælgɒl/ *noun* langage *m* algorithmique; ALGOL *m*

algorithm /'ælgərɪð(ə)m/ *noun* algorithme *m*

'...image processing algorithms are step by step procedures for performing image processing operations' [*Byte*]

'...the steps are: acquiring a digitized image, developing an algorithm to process it, processing the image, modifying the algorithm until you are satisfied with the result' [*Byte*]

algorithmic /ˌælgəˈrɪðmɪk/ *adjective* algorithmique

algorithmic language /ˌælgərɪðmɪk ˈlæŋgwɪdʒ/ *noun* langage *m* algorithmique

alias /ˈeɪliəs/ *noun* (*name given to a file, port, device, etc.*) alias *m* ◇ **the operating system uses the alias COM1 to represent the serial port address 3FCh** le système d'exploitation utilise l'alias COM1 pour désigner le port série à l'adresse 3FCh

aliasing /ˈeɪliəsɪŋ/ *noun* (*jagged edges along diagonal or curved lines on a computer screen*) crénelage *m*; effet *m* d'escalier

alias name /ˈeɪliəs neɪm/ *noun* nom *m* d'alias

alien /ˈeɪliən/ *adjective* étranger *or* -ère

alien disk /ˈeɪliən dɪsk/ *noun* disquette *f* non compatible

alien disk reader /ˌeɪliən ˈdɪsk ˌriːdə/ *noun* lecteur *m* de disquettes non compatibles; lecteur *m* multidisques

align /əˈlaɪn/ *verb* **1.** (*to make sure that characters are spaced and levelled correctly*) aligner *vt*; justifier le texte **2.** (*to arrange numbers into a column with all figured lines up against the left or right hand*) positionner *vt*; aligner *vt* **3.** (*to position read/write head*) aligner *vt*; positionner *vt*

aligner /əˈlaɪnə/ *noun* (*on printer*) dispositif *m* d'alignement; dispositif *m* de cadrage; dispositif *m* de positionnement

aligning edge /əˈlaɪnɪŋ edʒ/ *noun* (*of optical character recognition system*) bord *m* d'alignement; bord *m* de référence

alignment /əˈlaɪnmənt/ *noun* alignement *m*

alignment pin /əˈlaɪnmənt pɪn/ *noun* (*device to check alignment*) pige *f* d'alignement; téton *m* d'alignement

allocate /ˈæləˌkeɪt/ *verb* (*to divide something between users*) allouer *vt*; répartir *vt*; attribuer *vt*; affecter *vt* ◇ **the operating system allocated most of main memory to the spreadsheet program** le système d'exploitation a alloué *or* attribué presque toute la mémoire principale au tableur

allocation /ˌæləˈkeɪʃ(ə)n/ *noun* (*dividing something in various ways*) allocation *f*; attribution *f* ◇ **band allocation** attribution de bandes de fréquences *or* de longueurs d'ondes ◇ **the new band allocation means we will have more channels** la nouvelle attribution de bandes de fréquences permettra d'avoir un plus grand nombre de canaux de transmission

allocation routine /ˌæləˈkeɪʃ(ə)n ruːˌtiːn/ *noun* programme *m* d'allocation

allocation unit /ˌæləˈkeɪʃ(ə)n ˌjuːnɪt/ *noun* unité *f* d'allocation

all points addressable mode /ˌɔːl ˌpɔɪnts əˈdresəb(ə)l ˌməʊd/ *noun* (*graphics mode in which each pixel can be individually addressed*) mode *m* d'adressage à matrice active

alpha /ˈælfə/ *noun* (*alpha test – first test of a computer product*) alpha test *m* ◇ **alpha stage** stade alpha ◇ **the new software is still in an alpha product stage** le nouveau logiciel en est au stade alpha

ALPHA /ˈælfə/ *noun* ALPHA™

alpha beta technique /ˌælfə ˈbiːtə tekˌniːk/ *noun* (*technique used in artificial intelligence*) technique *f* alpha bêta

alphabetic character set /ˌælfəbetɪk ˈkærɪktə ˌset/ *noun* lettres *fpl* de l'alphabet

alphabetic string /ˌælfəbetɪk ˈstrɪŋ/ *noun* chaîne *f* de caractères alphabétiques

alphabetise /ˈælfəbetaɪz/, **alphabetize** *verb* classer par ordre alphabétique

alpha channel /ˈælfə ˌtʃæn(ə)l/ *noun* (*top eight bits that define the properties of a pixel*) canal *m* alpha

alphageometric /ˌælfədʒiːəʊˈmetrɪk/ *adjective* alphagéométrique

alphameric /ˌælfəˈmerɪk/ *adjective US* alphanumérique

alphamosaic /ˌælfəməʊˈzeɪɪk/ *adjective* alphamosaïque

alphanumeric /ˌælfənjʊˈmerɪk/ *adjective* alphanumérique

alphanumeric array /ˌælfənjʊmerɪk əˈreɪ/ *noun* tableau *m* alphanumérique

alphanumeric characters /ˌælfənjʊmerɪk ˈkærɪktəz/ *plural noun* caractères *mpl* alphanumériques

alphanumeric data /ˌælfənjʊmerɪk ˈdeɪtə/ *noun* données *fpl* alphanumériques

alphanumeric display /ˌælfənjʊmerɪk dɪˈspleɪ/ *noun* affichage *m* alphanumérique

alphanumeric key /ˌælfənjʊmerɪk ˈkiː/ *noun* touche *f* alphanumérique

alphanumeric keyboard /ˌælfənjʊmerɪk ˈkiːbɔːd/ *noun* clavier *m* alphanumérique

alphanumeric operand /ˌælfənjʊmerɪk ˈɒpərænd/ *noun* opérande *m* alphanumérique

alphanumerics /ˌælfənjʊˈmerɪks/ *plural noun* caractères *mpl* alphanumériques

alphanumeric string /ˌælfənjʊmerɪk ˈstrɪŋ/ *noun* chaîne *f* de caractères alphanumériques

alpha-particle /ˈælfə ˌpɑːtɪk(ə)l/ *noun* particule *f* de rayonnement alpha

alpha-particle sensitivity /ˌælfə ˌpɑːtɪk(ə)l ˌsensəˈtɪvəti/ *noun* sensibilité *f* aux rayons alpha

alphaphotographic /ˌælfəfəʊtəʊˈgræfɪk/ *adjective* alphaphotographique

alphasort /ˌælfəˈsɔːt/ *verb* classer des données en ordre alphabétique; classer des données par ordre alphabétique

alpha test /ˈælfə test/ *noun* (*first test of a computer product*) alpha *m* test

alternate /ˈɒltəneɪt/ *verb* alterner *vi*

alternate character set /ɔːlˌtɜːnət ˈkærɪktə ˌset/ *noun* (*second set of characters*) jeu *m* de caractères disponible; police *f* de caractères disponible

alternate key /ɔːlˈtɜːnət kiː/ *noun* touche *f* secondaire

alternate mode /ɔːlˈtɜːnət məʊd/ *noun* mode *m* alterné

alternate route /ɔːlˈtɜːnət ruːt/ *noun* (*backup path*) déviation *f*; voie *f* de déroutement

alternating current /ˌɔːltəneɪtɪŋ ˈkʌrənt/ *noun* courant *m* alternatif (CA)

alternation /ˌɔːltəˈneɪʃ(ə)n/ *noun* alternance *f*

alternative denial /ɔːlˌtɜːnətɪv dɪˈnaɪəl/ *noun* fonction *f* NON-ET

Alt key /ˈɔːlt kiː/ *noun* touche *f* Alt

always on /ˈɔːlweɪz ɒn/ *adjective* connecté, -ée en permanence

AM *abbr* (*amplitude modulation*) modulation *f* d'amplitude

ambient /ˈæmbiənt/ *adjective* ambiant *or* -e

ambient noise /ˌæmbiənt ˈnɔɪz/ *noun* bruit *m* ambiant; bruit *m* de fond ◇ **ambient noise level** niveau *m* de bruit de fond *or* de bruit ambiant

ambient temperature /ˌæmbiənt ˈtemprɪtʃə/ *noun* température *f* ambiante

ambiguity /ˌæmbɪˈgjuːɪti/ *noun* ambiguïté *f*

ambiguity error /ˌæmbɪˈgjuːɪti ˌerə/ *noun* erreur *f* d'ambiguïté

ambiguous /æmˈbɪgjuəs/ *adjective* ambigu; équivoque

ambiguous filename /æmˌbɪgjuəs ˈfaɪlneɪm/ *noun* nom *m* de fichier ambigu

amendment record /əˌmen(d)mənt ˈrekɔːd/ *noun* enregistrement *m* des détails; enregistrement *m* des mouvements; enregistrement *m* des modifications

American National Standards Institute /əˌmerɪkən ˌnæʃ(ə)nəl ˈstændədz ˌɪnstɪtjuːt/ *noun* (*American equivalent of*) association *f* française de normalisation (AFNOR)

American Standard Code for Information Interchange /əˌmerɪkən ˌstændəd kəʊd fər ˌɪnfəmeɪʃ(ə)n ˈɪntətʃeɪndʒ/ *noun* ASCII

America Online /əˌmerɪkə ˈɒnlaɪn/ (*largest Internet service provider in the world*) America Online; service *m* en ligne

amp /æmp/ *noun* ampère *m* (A)

ampere /ˈæmpeə/ *noun* ampère *m* (A)

amplification /ˌæmplɪfɪˈkeɪʃ(ə)n/ *noun* amplification *f* ◇ **increase the amplification of the input signal** augmentez l'amplification *or* le gain du signal d'entrée ◇ **the amplification is so high, the signal is distorting** l'amplification est si grande qu'elle cause une distorsion du signal

amplifier /ˈæmplɪˌfaɪə/ *noun* amplificateur *m* ◇ **amplifier class** classe *f* d'amplificateur ◇ **audio amplifier** amplificateur audio *or* (d')audiofréquence ◇ **low noise amplifier** amplificateur à faible bruit

amplify /ˈæmplɪˌfaɪ/ *verb* amplifier *vt* ◇ **amplified telephone** téléphone *m* amplifié *or* à écoute amplifiée ◇ **the received signal needs to be amplified before it can be processed** le signal reçu doit être amplifié avant d'être traité

amplitude /ˈæmplɪˌtjuːd/ *noun* amplitude *f* ◇ **amplitude distortion** distorsion *f* d'amplitude ◇ **amplitude modulation (AM)** modulation *f* d'amplitude (MA)

amplitude modulation /ˈæmplɪtjuːd mɒdjuˌleɪʃ(ə)n/ *noun* modulation *f* d'amplitude

amplitude quantisation /ˌæmplɪtjuːd ˌkwɒntaɪˈzeɪʃ(ə)n/ *noun* quantification *f* d'amplitude

analog /ˈænəlɒg/, **analogue** /ˈæn(ə)lɒg/ *noun* analogue *m*; appareil *m* analogique ◇ **analog device** appareil analogique *or* dispositif analogique ◇ **analog multimeter (AMM)** multimètre *m* analogique

analog channel /ˌænəlɒg ˈtʃæn(ə)l/ *noun* voie *f* analogique

analog computer /ˌænəlɒg kəmˈpjuːtə/ *noun* calculateur *m* analogique

analog data /ˌænəlɒg ˈdeɪtə/ *noun* données *fpl* analogiques

analog display /ˌænəlɒg dɪˈspleɪ/ *noun* écran *m* analogique

analog gate /ˈænəlɒg geɪt/ *noun* circuit *m* analogique; porte *f* analogique

analog input card /ˌænəlɒg ˈɪnpʊt ˌkɑːd/ *noun* carte *f* d'entrée analogique

analog line /ˌænəlɒg ˈlaɪn/ *noun* ligne *f* analogique; ligne *f* commutée

analog loopback /ˌænəlɒg ˈluːpbæk/ *noun* boucle *f* analogique ◇ **analog loopback with selftest** boucle analogique avec autotest

analog monitor /ˌænəlɒg ˈmɒnɪtə/ *noun* moniteur *m* analogique

analog output card /ˌænəlɒg ˌaʊtˈpʊt ˌkɑːd/ *noun* carte *f* de sortie analogique

analog recording /ˌænəlɒg rɪˈkɔːdɪŋ/ *noun* enregistrement *m* analogique

analog representation /ˌænəlɒg ˌreprɪzenˈteɪʃ(ə)n/ *noun* représentation *f* analogique

analog signal /ˌænəlɒg ˈsɪgn(ə)l/ *noun* signal *m* analogique

analog to digital /ˌænəlɒg tə ˈdɪdʒɪt(ə)l/ *adjective* analogique à digital; analogique-numérique

analog to digital converter /ˌænəlɒg tə ˌdɪdʒɪt(ə)l kən'vɜːtə/ *noun* convertisseur *m* analogique-numérique

analog transmission /ˌænəlɒg trænz 'mɪʃ(ə)n/ *noun* transmission *f* analogique

analyser /'ænəlaɪzə/ *noun* analyseur *m*

analyst /'ænəlɪst/ *noun* analyste *m&f*

analytical engine /ˌænəlɪtɪk(ə)l 'endʒɪn/ *noun* machine *f* de Babbage

anamorphic /ˌænə'mɔːfɪk/ *adjective* anamorphosé *or* -ée

ancestral file /ænˌsestrəl 'faɪl/ *noun* fichier *m* ancêtre

anchor cell /'æŋkə sel/ *noun* (*cell that defines the start of a range of cells*) cellule *f* d'ancrage

ancillary equipment /ænˌsɪləri ɪ'kwɪpmənt/ *noun* (*useful, but not essential, accessories*) accessoires *mpl*; matériels *mpl* annexes

AND /ænd/ *noun* circuit *m* ET; porte *f* ET

AND circuit /ænd 'sɜːkɪt/, **AND element** /ænd 'elɪmənt/ *noun* circuit *m* ET; porte *f* ET

AND function /'ænd ˌfʌŋkʃən/ *noun* ET; fonction *f* d'intersection

AND gate /'ænd geɪt/ *noun* (*electronic gate*) circuit *m* ET; porte *f* ET

AND operation /'ænd ˌɒpəreɪʃ(ə)n/ *noun* conjonction *f* logique; intersection *f* logique; opération *f* ET

anechoic chamber /ˌænekəʊɪk 'tʃeɪmbə/ *noun* chambre *f* blanche; chambre *f* sans écho; chambre *f* sourde

angle /'æŋgəl/ *noun* (*measure of the change in direction*) angle *m*

angstrom /'æŋstrɒm/ *noun* angström *m*

ANI /ˌeɪ en 'aɪ/ *noun* identification *f* automatique des numéros d'appel

animated GIF /ˌænɪˌmeɪtɪd ˌdʒiː aɪ 'ef/ *noun* fichier *m* GIF animé

animation /ˌænɪ'meɪʃ(ə)n/ *noun* animation *f*

animation software /ˌænɪ'meɪʃ(ə)n ˌsɒftweə/ *noun* logiciel *m* d'animation

annotation /ˌænə'teɪʃ(ə)n/ *noun* (*comment or note*) annotation *f*; commentaire *m*; note *f*

annotation symbol /ˌænəʊ'teɪʃ(ə)n ˌsɪmb(ə)l/ *noun* symbole *m* de commentaire

announce /ə'naʊns/ *verb* annoncer *vt*

annunciator /ə'nʌnsieɪtə/ *noun* (*of signal, etc.*) annonciateur *m*

anode /'ænəʊd/ *noun* anode *f*

anonymiser /ə'nɒnɪmaɪzə/, **anonymizer** *noun* anonymiseur *m*

anonymous FTP /əˌnɒnɪməs ef tiː 'piː/ *noun* FTP *m* anonyme

ANSI /'ænsi/ ANSI

ANSI C /ˌænsi 'siː/ *noun* C ANSI

ANSI driver /'ænsi ˌdraɪvə/ *noun* logiciel *m* de commande ANSI

ANSI escape sequence /ˌænsi ɪ'skeɪp ˌsiːkwəns/ *noun* séquence *f* d'échappement ANSI

ANSI keyboard /ˌænsi 'kiːbɔːd/ *noun* clavier *m* ANSI

ANSI screen control /ˌænsi 'skriːn kən ˌtrəʊl/ *noun* contrôle *m* d'écran ANSI

answer /'ɑːnsə/ *verb* (*replying a call*) répondre à un appel ◇ **the first modem originates the call and the second answers it** le premier modem transmet l'appel tandis que le second y répond

answer back /'ɑːnsə bæk/ *noun* signal *m* de réponse

answering machine /'ɑːns(ə)rɪŋ məˌʃiːn/ *noun* répondeur *m* téléphonique

answer mode /'ɑːnsə məʊd/ *noun* mode *m* réponse

answer modem /'ɑːnsə ˌməʊdem/ *noun* modem *m* de retour de réponse

answer/originate, answer/originate device *noun* (*device, such as a modem, that can receive or send data*) dispositif *m* de retour/d'appel

answer time /'ɑːnsə taɪm/ *noun* temps *m* de réponse

answertone /'ɑːnsətəʊn/ *noun* (*tone an answering modem emits before the carrier is exchanged*) signal *m* de réponse

anthropomorphic software /ˌænθrəpəmɔːfɪk 'sɒftweə/ *noun* (*software that appears to react to what a user says*) logiciel *m* anthropomorphique

anti-aliasing /ˌænti 'eɪliəsɪŋ/ *noun* **1.** (*in graphics*) anti-crénelage *m*; lissage *m* de courbes **2.** (*of sound signals*) anti-repliement *m*

anticoincidence circuit /ˌæntikəʊ'ɪnsɪdəns ˌsɜːkɪt/, **anticoincidence function** *noun* circuit *m* OU exclusif; fonction *f* OU exclusif; porte *f* OU exclusif

anti-static mat /ˌænti ˌstætɪk 'mæt/ *noun* tapis *m* antistatique

anti-tinkle suppression /ˌænti 'tɪŋk(ə)l sə ˌpreʃ(ə)n/ *noun* suppression *f* de signal d'appel parasite

anti-virus program /ˌænti 'vaɪrəs ˌprəʊgræm/ *noun* programme *m* antivirus; utilitaire *m* antivirus

anti-virus software /ˌænti 'vaɪrəs ˌsɒftweə/ *noun* logiciel *m*

Apache™ HTTPD /əˌpætʃi ˌeɪtʃ tiː tiː piː 'diː/ *noun* (*web server software product*) Apache™ HTTP

APC *abbr* (*asynchronous procedure call*) appel *m* de procédure asynchrone

aperture /'æpətʃə/ *noun* ouverture *f*

aperture mask /'æpətʃə mɑːsk/ *noun* masque *m* de séparation

API /ˌeɪ piː 'aɪ/ *noun* interface *f* de programmation

APL /ˌeɪ piː 'el/ *noun* langage *m* de programmation APL

APPC /ˌeɪ piː piː 'siː/ *noun* programmation *f* avancée des programmes de communications (APPC)

append /ə'pend/ *verb* (*file or data*) annexer *vt*; (*to attach*) joindre *vt*; (*to add*) ajouter *vt* ◇ **if you enter the DOS command COPY A+B, the file B will be appended to the end of file A** (*add a file or data to the end of an existing file*) si vous tapez la commande DOS 'COPY A+B', vous annexé le fichier B au fichier A *or* vous ajoutez le fichier B à la suite du fichier A

Apple Computer Corporation /ˌæp(ə)l kəm'pjuːtə ˌkɔːpəreɪʃ(ə)n/ (*company that has developed a range of personal computers, including Apple Mac*) Apple Computer Corporation

'Apple Computer has fleshed out details of a migration path to the PowerPC RISC architecture for its 7 million Apple Macintosh users. Developments in the pipeline include PowerPC versions of the AppleTalk Remote Access networking protocol.' [*Computing*]

Apple Desktop Bus /ˌæp(ə)l ˌdesktɒp 'bʌs/ (*trade name for a serial bus built into Apple Macs*) bus *m* Apple Desktop

Apple file exchange /ˌæp(ə)l 'faɪl ɪks ˌtʃeɪndʒ/ (*program on an Apple Macintosh computer allowing it to read disks from a PC*) AFX

Apple filing protocol /ˌæp(ə)l 'faɪlɪŋ ˌprəʊtəkɒl/ (*trade name for a method of storing files on a network server*) protocole *m* AFP; protocole *m* de gestion de fichier Apple

Apple Key /'æp(ə)l kiː/ (*key on the keyboard of an Apple Macintosh that provides a short cut to a menu selection*) touche *f* Apple

Apple Mac /'æp(ə)l mæk/, **Apple Macintosh computer** /ˌæp(ə)l ˌmækɪntɒʃ kəm'pjuːtə/ (*trade name for any of a range of personal computers developed by Apple Computer Corporation*) ordinateur *m* Mac; ordinateur *m* Macintosh

AppleScript /'æp(ə)lskrɪpt/ AppleScript

Appleshare /'æp(ə)lʃeə/ (*trade name for software that allows Apple Macs to share files and printers using a file server*) Appleshare

Apple System /ˌæp(ə)l 'sɪstəm/ système *m* d'exploitation Apple System

applet /'æplət/ *noun* **1.** (*utility application program*) utilitaire *m* d'application **2.** (*small program to enhance a web page*) applet *m*; miniprogramme *m*; petit programme *m*

AppleTalk™ /'æp(ə)ltɑːk/ (*trade name for a communications protocol developed by the Apple Computer Corporation*) AppleTalk™

AppleTalk Filing Protocol /ˌæp(ə)ltɑːk 'faɪlɪŋ ˌprəʊtəkɒl/ protocole *m* AFP; protocole *m* de gestion de fichier AppleTalk

appliance computer /əˌplaɪəns kəm'pjuːtə/ *noun* ordinateur *m*

application /ˌæplɪ'keɪʃ(ə)n/ *noun* (*task which a computer performs or problem that a computer solves*) application *f* ◇ **application programming interface (API)** (*standard program functions that allow any programmer to interface a program with another application*) interface *f* de programmation d'application *or* API ◇ **application specific integrated circuit (ASIC)** circuit *m* intégré spécialisé *or* sur mesure *or* circuit spécifique à une application (ASIC)

application developer /ˌæplɪkeɪʃ(ə)n dɪ 'veləpə/ *noun* développeur *m* d'application

application file /ˌæplɪ'keɪʃ(ə)n faɪl/ *noun* fichier *m* d'application

application form /ˌæplɪ'keɪʃ(ə)n ˌfɔːm/ *noun* formulaire *m*

application generator /ˌæplɪ'keɪʃ(ə)n ˌdʒenəreɪtə/ *noun* générateur *m* d'application

application icon /ˌæplɪ'keɪʃ(ə)n ˌaɪkɒn/ *noun* icône *f* d'application

application layer /ˌæplɪ'keɪʃ(ə)n ˌleɪə/ *noun* couche *f* application

application orientated language /ˌæplɪkeɪʃ(ə)n ˌɔːriənteɪtɪd 'læŋgwɪdʒ/ *noun* langage *m* d'application

application package /ˌæplɪ'keɪʃ(ə)n ˌpækɪdʒ/ *noun* progiciel *m* d'application

application program /ˌæplɪ'keɪʃ(ə)n ˌprəʊgræm/ *noun* logiciel *m* ◇ **the multi-window editor is used to create and edit applications programs** l'éditeur multifenêtre est utilisé pour créer et éditer les programmes d'application

application programming interface /ˌæplɪkeɪʃ(ə)n 'prəʊgræmɪŋ ˌɪntəfeɪs/ *noun* interface *f* API; interface *f* de programmation d'application

application service element /ˌæplɪkeɪʃ(ə)n 'sɜːvɪs ˌelɪmənt/ *noun* programme *m* utilitaire de service

application service provider /ˌæplɪkeɪʃ(ə)n 'sɜːvɪs prəˌvaɪdə/ *noun* fournisseur *m* de services applicatifs

application software /ˌæplɪkeɪʃ(ə)n 'sɒftweə/ *noun* logiciel *m* d'application

applications package /ˌæplɪ'keɪʃ(ə)nz ˌpækɪdʒ/ *noun* progiciel *m* d'application

application specific integrated circuits /ˌæplɪkeɪʃ(ə)n spəˌsɪfɪk ˌɪntɪgreɪtɪd 'sɜːkɪts/ *noun* circuit *m* intégré spécialisé; circuit *m* intégré sur mesure; circuit *m* spécifique à une application

applications programmer /ˌæplɪ'keɪʃ(ə)nz ˌprəʊgræmə/ *noun* programmeur *m* d'application

applications software /ˌæplɪ'keɪʃ(ə)nz ˌsɒftweə/ *noun* logiciel d'application *or* progiciel *m*

applications terminal /ˌæplɪ'keɪʃ(ə)nz ˌtɜːmɪn(ə)l/ *noun* ordinateur *m* dédié *or* spécialisé; ordinateur *m* dédié; ordinateur *m* spécialisé

application terminal /ˌæplɪ'keɪʃ(ə)n ˌtɜːmɪn(ə)l/ *noun* ordinateur *m* dédié; ordinateur *m* spécialisé

application window /ˌæplɪ'keɪʃ(ə)n ˌwɪndəʊ/ *noun* fenêtre *f* d'application

approximation error /əˌprɒksɪ'meɪʃ(ə)n ˌerə/ *noun* erreur *f* d'arrondi

A programming language /ˌeɪ 'prəʊgræmɪŋ ˌlæŋgwɪdʒ/ *noun* langage *m* de programmation APL

APT /ˌeɪ piː 'tiː/ *noun* langage *m* de commande numérique

Arabic figures /ˌærəbɪk 'fɪgəz/ *plural noun* chiffres *mpl* arabes

Arabic numbers /ˌærəbɪk 'nʌmbəz/, **Arabic figures** /ˌærəbɪk 'fɪgəz/, **Arabic numerals** /ˌærəbɪk 'njuːmərəl/ *noun* chiffres *mpl* arabes

Archie /'ɑːtʃiː/ *noun* (*system of servers that catalogue the public files available on the internet*) Archie

architecture /'ɑːkɪtektʃə/ *noun* architecture *f* ◇ **the onion skin architecture of this computer is made up of a kernel at the centre, an operating system, a low-level language and then the user's programs** l'architecture en pelure d'oignon de cet ordinateur consiste en un noyau central, une couche système d'exploitation, une couche langage de bas niveau et enfin une couche programmes (d') utilisateur

> 'Software giant Microsoft is also interested in using Xerox' Glyph technology as part of its Microsoft At Work architecture that seeks to unite office computers with fax machines and copiers.' [*Computing*]

archival quality /'ɑːkaɪv(ə)l ˌkwɒləti/ *noun* qualité *f* d'archivage

archive /'ɑːkaɪv/ *noun* archives *f* ■ *verb* archiver *vt*

archive attribute /ˌɑːkaɪv ə'trɪbjuːt/, **archive bit** /'ɑːkaɪv bɪt/ *noun* (*attribute attached to a file*) attribut *m* d'archivage; bit *m* d'archivage; drapeau *m* d'archivage

archived copy /ˌɑːkaɪvd 'kɒpi/ *noun* copie *f* archivée; copie *f* d'archives

archive file /'ɑːkaɪv faɪl/ *noun* fichier *m* archives

archive flag /'ɑːkaɪv flæg/ *noun* (*attribute attached to a file*) drapeau *m* d'archivage

archive site /'ɑːkaɪv saɪt/ *noun* site *m* d'archives

archive storage /ˌɑːkaɪv 'stɔːrɪdʒ/ *noun* mémoire *f* d'archivage

area /'eəriə/ *noun* (*section of memory*) zone *f*

area fill /'eəriə fɪl/ *noun* remplissage *m* de zone

area graph /'eəriə grɑːf/ *noun* graphe *m* à aires

area search /'eəriə sɜːtʃ/ *noun* recherche *f* de zone; recherche *f* sélective

arg /ɑːg/ *noun* argument *m*

argument /'ɑːgjʊmənt/ *noun* argument *m*

argument separator /'ɑːgjʊmənt ˌsepəreɪtə/ *noun* séparateur *m* d'arguments

arithmetic capability /ˌærɪθmetɪk ˌkeɪpə'bɪlɪti/ *noun* capacité *f* de calcul arithmétique

arithmetic check /ə'rɪθmətɪk tʃek/ *noun* vérification *f* arithmétique

arithmetic functions /əˌrɪθmətɪk 'fʌŋkʃənz/ *plural noun* fonctions *fpl* arithmétiques

arithmetic instruction /ˌærɪθmetɪk ɪn'strʌkʃən/ *noun* instruction *f* arithmétique

arithmetic logic unit /ˌærɪθmetɪk 'lɒdʒɪk ˌjuːnɪt/ *noun* unité *f* arithmétique et logique (UAL)

arithmetic operation /ˌærɪθmetɪk ˌɒpə'reɪʃ(ə)n/ *noun* opération *f* arithmétique

arithmetic operator /ˌærɪθmetɪk 'ɒpəreɪtə/ *noun* opérateur *m* arithmétique

arithmetic register /ˌærɪθmetɪk 'redʒɪstə/ *noun* registre *m* arithmétique

arithmetic shift /ˌærɪθmetɪk 'ʃɪft/ *noun* décalage *m* arithmétique

arithmetic unit /ˌærɪθmetɪk 'juːnɪt/ *noun* unité *f* arithmétique et logique (UAL)

arm /ɑːm/ *verb* (*to prepare*) préparer *vt*; armer *vt*; (*to activate*) valider *vt*; activer *vt*

armed interrupt /ɑːmd 'ɪntərʌpt/ *noun* interruption *f* validée; interruption *f* activée

ARP /ˌeɪ ɑː 'piː/ *noun* protocole *m* ARP

ARPANET /'ɑːpənet/ *noun* réseau *m* Arpanet

ARQ /ˌeɪ ɑː 'kjuː/ *noun* demande *f* de répétition automatique; correcteur *m* d'erreurs ARQ

array /ə'reɪ/ *noun* (*of figures or data*) tableau *m*; (*antennae or circuits*) réseau *m*

array bounds /ə'reɪ baʊndz/ *plural noun* bornes *fpl* d'un tableau

array dimension /ə'reɪ daɪˌmenʃ(ə)n/ *noun* dimension *f* d'un tableau

array element /ə'reɪ ˌelɪmənt/ *noun* élément *m* dans un tableau; valeur *f* dans un tableau

array processor /ə'reɪ ˌprəʊsesə/ *noun* (*computer for fast applications*) processeur *m* vectoriel ◇ **the array processor allows the array that contains the screen image to be rotated with one simple command** le processeur vectoriel permet de faire pivoter le tableau qui contient l'image d'écran à l'aide d'une seule commande

arrow key /'ærəʊ kiː/ *noun* touche *f* fléchée

arrow pointer /ˌærəʊ 'pɔɪntə/ *noun* (*small arrow on-screen that you can move using the mouse*) pointeur *m* qu'on déplace avec la souris

artefact /'ɑːtɪfækt/, **artifact** *noun* artefact *m*

article /'ɑːtɪk(ə)l/ *noun* (*of newspaper or magazine*) article *m* ◇ **he wrote an article about the user group for the local newspaper** il a écrit, pour le journal local, un article concernant le groupe d'utilisateurs

artifact /'ɑːtɪfækt/ *noun* artefact *m*

artificial intelligence /ˌɑːtɪfɪʃ(ə)l ɪn ˈtelɪdʒ(ə)ns/ *noun* intelligence *f* artificielle

artificial life /ˌɑːtɪfɪʃ(ə)l ˈlaɪf/ *noun* vie *f* artificielle

artwork /ˈɑːtˌwɜːk/ *noun* (*graphical work or images which are to be printed*) maquette *f* ◇ **the artwork has been sent for filming** la maquette a été envoyée au flashage

ascend /əˈsend/ *verb* (*increase*) monter *vi*; augmenter *vt*

ascender /əˈsendə/ *noun* (*of a character*) hampe *m*

ascending order /əˌsendɪŋ ˈɔːdə/ *noun* ordre *m* croissant

ASCII /ˈæskiː/ *noun* ASCII

ASCII character /ˈæski ˌkærɪktə/ *noun* caractère *m* ASCII

ASCII file /ˈæski faɪl/ *noun* fichier *m* ASCII

ASCII keyboard /ˌæski ˈkiːbɔːd/ *noun* clavier *m* ASCII

ASCII text /ˈæski tekst/ *noun* texte *m* ASCII

ASCIIZ string /ˌæskiː ˈzed ˌstrɪŋ/ *noun* chaîne *f* de caractères ASCIIZ

ASF /ˌeɪ es ˈef/ *noun* format *m* ASF

ASIC /ˌeɪ es aɪ ˈsiː/ *plural noun* circuits *mpl* intégrés à application spécifique

ASP *abbr* **1.** (*Active Server Page*) page *f* ASP **2.** (*application service provider*) fournisseur *m* de services applicatifs

aspect ratio /ˌæspekt ˈreɪʃiəʊ/ *noun* rapport *m* longueur/largeur

aspect system /ˌæspekt ˈsɪstəm/ *noun* système *m* de recherche par descripteurs; système *m* de stockage par descripteurs

ASR /ˌeɪ es ˈɑː/ *noun* émetteur-récepteur *m*

ASR keyboard /ˌeɪ es ɑː ˈkiːbɔːd/ *noun* clavier *m* émetteur/récepteur; clavier *m* de téléscripteur

assemble /əˈsemb(ə)l/ *verb* **1.** (*to put together*) assembler *vt*; monter *vt* **2.** (*to translate assembly code into machine code*) assembler *vt* **3.** (*to insert something into a program*) assembler un programme; regrouper les différentes parties d'un programme ◇ **syntax errors spotted whilst the source program is being assembled** des erreurs de syntaxe repérées au cours de l'assemblage du programmme source ◇ **the parts for the disk drive are made in Japan and assembled in France** les pièces de l'unité de disque sont fabriquées au Japon, mais l'assemblage se fait en France ◇ **there is a short wait during which time the program is assembled into object code** il y a un certain délai pendant lequel s'effectue l'assemblage en code objet du programme

assembler /əˈsemblə/ *noun* assembleur *m*; programme *m* d'assemblage

assembler error messages /əˌsemblə ˈerə ˌmesɪdʒ/ *plural noun* message *m* d'erreur de l'assembleur

assembler language /əˈsemblə ˌlæŋgwɪdʒ/ *noun* langage *m* d'assemblage

assembler program /əˈsemblə ˌprəʊgræm/ *noun* (*assembly program*) assembleur *m*; programme *m* d'assemblage

assembly /əˈsemblɪ/ *noun* (*putting together*) assemblage *m*; montage *m* ◇ **there are no assembly instructions to show you how to put the computer together** il n'y a pas de notice de montage pour aider à la mise en place de l'ordinateur

assembly code /əˈsembli kəʊd/ *noun* code *m* d'assemblage

assembly language /əˈsembli ˌlæŋgwɪdʒ/ *noun* langage *m* d'assemblage

assembly listing /əˈsembli ˌlɪstɪŋ/ *noun* (*display of an assembler*) liste *f* d'un programme d'assemblage

assembly plant /əˈsembli plɑːnt/ *noun* usine *f* de montage

assembly routine /əˈsembli ruːˌtiːn/ *noun* routine *f* d'assemblage

assembly system /əˈsemblɪ ˌsɪstəm/ *noun* système *m* d'assemblage

assembly time /əˈsembli taɪm/ *noun* (*for the translation of a program*) durée *f* d'assemblage

assertion /əˈsɜːʃ(ə)n/ *noun* (*program statement of a fact or rule*) assertion *f*; (*fact that is true or defined as being true*) affirmation *f*; assertion *f*

assets /ˈæsets/ *plural noun* atouts *mpl*; avantages *mpl*; (*separate data elements, such as video or audio, that are used in a multimedia application*) outils *mpl* complémentaires; fonctions *fpl* complémentaires

assign /əˈsaɪn/ *verb* **1.** (*to allocate task*) assigner à; affecter à; allouer *vt* **2.** (*to set a variable*) définir *vt* **3.** (*to allocate part of memory*) allouer *vt*; assigner *vt*; affecter une zone de mémoire à une tâche ◇ **assigned frequency** fréquence *f* assignée *or* allouée ◇ **two PCs have been assigned to outputting the labels** deux PC ont été affectés à la préparation des étiquettes

assigned numbers /əˌsaɪnd ˈnʌmbəz/ *plural noun* nombres *mpl* assignés

assignment /əˈsaɪnmənt/ *noun* affectation *f*

assignment compatible /əˌsaɪnmənt kəm ˈpætəb(ə)l/ *adjective* compatibilité *f* d'affectation

assignment conversion /əˌsaɪnmənt kən ˈvɜːʃ(ə)n/ *noun* conversion *f* d'affectation

assignment statement /əˌsaɪnmənt ˈsteɪtmənt/ *noun* déclaration *f* d'affectation; instruction *f* d'affectation

associated document /əˌsəʊsieɪtɪd ˈdɒkjʊmənt/**, associated file** /faɪl/ *noun* (*document or file linked to its originating application*) document *m* associé; fichier *m* associé

associative addressing /əˌsəʊsiətɪv əˈdresɪŋ/ *noun* adressage *m* associatif

associative memory /əˌsəʊsiətɪv ˈmem(ə)ri/ *noun* mémoire *f* associative

associative processor /əˌsəʊsiətɪv ˈprəʊsesə/ *noun* processeur *m* avec mémoire associative

associative storage /əˌsəʊsiətɪv ˈstɔːrɪdʒ/ *noun* mémoire *f* associative

associative storage register /əˌsəʊsiətɪv ˈstɔːrɪdʒ ˌredʒɪstə/ *noun* registre *m* de mémoire associative

asterisk /ˈæstərɪsk/ *noun* **1.** (*multiplication symbol*) astérisque *m*; étoile *f* **2.** (*wildcard symbol*) astérisque *m*

asterisk fill /ˈæst(ə)rɪsk fɪl/ *noun* remplissage *m* des astérisques

asymmetric compression /ˌæsɪˌmetrɪk kəmˈpreʃ(ə)n/ *noun* compression *f* asymétrique

Asymmetric Digital Subscriber Line /ˌæsɪˌmetrɪk ˌdɪdʒɪt(ə)l səbˈskraɪbə ˌlaɪn/ *noun* ligne *f* d'abonné numérique à débit asymétrique

asymmetric transmission /eɪsɪˌmetrɪk trænzˈmɪʃ(ə)n/ *noun* (*data transmission used in high-speed modems*) transmission *f* asymétrique

asymmetric video compression /eɪsɪˌmetrɪk ˈvɪdiəʊ kəmˌpreʃ(ə)n/ *noun* (*using a powerful computer to compress video*) compression *f* vidéo asymétrique

async /eɪˈsɪŋk/ *adjective informal* asynchrone

asynchronous /əˈsɪŋkrənəs/ *adjective* asynchrone ◇ **asynchronous balanced mode (ABM)** mode *m* asynchrone équilibré ◇ **asynchronous balanced mode extended (ABME)** mode asynchrone équilibré étendu ◇ **asynchronous communications device interface (ACDI)** interface *f* pour communication asynchrone ◇ **asynchronous communications interface adapter (ACIA)** interface *f* pour communication asynchrone ◇ **asynchronous communications server (ACS)** serveur *m* de communication asynchrone ◇ **asynchronous procedure call (APC)** appel *m* de procédure asynchrone ◇ **asynchronous transfer mode (ATM)** (*method of transferring data very rapidly; CCITT and ANSI standard defining cell relay transmission*) mode *m* de transfert asynchrone *or* mode ATM; commutation *f* temporelle asynchrone

asynchronous access /eɪˌsɪŋkrənəs ˈækses/ *noun* accès *m* asynchrone

asynchronous cache /eɪˌsɪŋkrənəs ˈkæʃ/ *noun* mémoire *f* cache asynchrone

asynchronous communication /eɪ ˌsɪŋkrənəs kəˌmjuːnɪˈkeɪʃ(ə)n/ *noun* communication *f* asynchrone

asynchronous communication server /eɪˌsɪŋkrənəs kəˌmjuːnɪˈkeɪʃ(ə)n ˌsɜːvə/ *noun* serveur *m* de communications asynchrone

asynchronous communications interface adapter /əˌsɪŋkrənəs kəˌmjuːnɪkeɪʃ(ə)nz ˈɪntəfeɪs əˌdæptə/ *noun* interface *f* pour communication asynchrone

asynchronous computer /eɪˌsɪŋkrənəs kəmˈpjuːtə/ *noun* ordinateur *m* asynchrone

asynchronous data transfer /eɪˌsɪŋkrənəs ˌdeɪtə ˈtrænsfɜː/ *noun* transfert *m* de données asynchrone

asynchronous mode /eɪˈsɪŋkrənəs məʊd/ *noun* mode *m* asynchrone

asynchronous port /eɪˌsɪŋkrənəs ˈpɔːt/ *noun* (*connection*) port *m* d'accès asynchrone ◇ **when asynchronous ports are used no special hardware is required** l'utilisation de ports asynchrones ne demande pas un matériel spécialisé

asynchronous procedure call /eɪ ˌsɪŋkrənəs prəˈsiːdʒə ˌkɔːl/ *noun* appel *m* de procédure asynchrone

asynchronous transfer mode /eɪ ˌsɪŋkrənəs ˈtrænsfɜː ˌməʊd/ *noun* mode *m* de transfert asynchrone

asynchronous transmission /eɪˌsɪŋkrənəs trænzˈmɪʃ(ə)n/ *noun* transmission *f* asynchrone

AT /ˌeɪ ˈtiː/ *noun* (*standard of PC*) norme *f* AT

ATA Fast /ˌeɪ tiː ˌeɪ ˈfɑːst/ *noun* ATA Fast

ATA packet interface /ˌeɪ tiː ˌeɪ ˈpækɪt ˌɪntəfeɪs/ *noun* norme *f* ATAPI

ATAPI *abbr* (*advanced technology attachment packet interface*) ATAPI

AT-bus /ət bʌs/ *noun* bus *m* AT

ATC /ˌeɪ tiː ˈsiː/ *noun* autorisation *f* de copier; autorisation *f* de dupliquer

AT command set /ˌeɪ tiː kəˈmɑːnd set/ *noun* jeu *m* de commandes AT

ATD /ˌeɪ tiː ˈdiː/ *noun* (*standard command for compatible modems used to dial a telephone number*) ATD

ATE /ˌeɪ tiː ˈiː/ *noun* équipement *m* de vérification automatique (EVA)

Athlon XP /ˈæθlɒn eks ˌpiː/ (*trade name for a 32-bit processor, developed by AMD*) Athlon XP

AT-keyboard /ət ˈkiːˌbɔːd/ *noun* clavier *m* AT

ATM[1] /ˌeɪ tiː ˈem/ *noun* mode *m* de transfert asynchrone

ATM[2] /ˌeɪ tiː ˈem/ *noun* guichet *m* automatique bancaire

ATM adaptation layer /ˌeɪ tiː ˌem ˌædæpˈteɪʃ(ə)n ˌleɪə/ *noun* couche *f* d'adaptation ATM

ATM cell format /ˌeɪ tiː ˈem sel/ *noun* format *m* de cellule ATM

ATM layers /ˌeɪ tiː ˌem ˈleɪəs/ *noun* couches *f*

AT mode /ˌeɪ ˈtiː ˌməʊd/ *noun* mode *m* AT

A to D /eɪ tə diː/ *adjective* analogique/numérique

A to D converter /ˈə tə, tʊ diː/ *noun* convertisseur *m* analogique-numérique

atom /'ætəm/ *noun* **1.** (*smallest particle of an element*) atome *m* **2.** (*value or string that cannot be reduced to a simpler form*) donnée *f* absolue; atome *m*

atomic /ə'tɒmɪk/ *adjective* (*referring to atoms; operation that returns data to its original state if it is stopped during processing*) atomique

ATSC /ˌeɪ tiː es 'siː/ *noun* Comité *m* pour l'avancement des systèmes télévisés

attached processor /əˌtætʃt 'prəʊsesə/ *noun* processeur *m* auxiliaire relié au processeur central

attached resource computer network /əˌtætʃt rɪˌzɔːs kəm'pjuːtə ˌnetwɜːk/ *noun* réseau *m* ARCNET; ARCnet

attachment /ə'tætʃmənt/ *noun* (*named file with an electronic mail message*) fichier *m* annexé; fichier *m* joint; fichier *m* en annexe

attack /ə'tæk/ *noun* (*start of a sound*) attaque *f* ◇ **attack envelope** enveloppe *f* d'attaque

attended operation /əˌtendɪd ˌɒpə'reɪʃ(ə)n/ *noun* opération *f* surveillée

attention code /ə'tenʃən kəʊd/ *noun* (*the characters AT used within the Hayes AT command set to tell a modem that a command follows*) code *m* AT

attention interruption /əˌtenʃ(ə)n ˌɪntə 'rʌpʃən/ *noun* interruption *f* d'intervention

attention key /ə'tenʃ(ə)n kiː/ *noun* touche *f* d'intervention

attenuation /əˌtenju'eɪʃ(ə)n/ *noun* **1.** (*reduction of a signal*) atténuation *f*; affaiblissement *m*; perte *f* **2.** (*difference in power*) atténuation *f* ◇ **if the cable is too long, the signal attenuation will start to cause data errors** avec un câble trop long, l'atténuation du signal provoquera des erreurs de données

attribute /'ætrɪbjuːt/ *noun* **1.** (*characteristic*) attribut *m*; caractéristique *f* **2.** (*control data*) attribut *m* ◇ **this attribute controls the colour of the screen** cet attribut contrôle la couleur de l'écran

auctioneering device /ˌɔːkʃə'nɪərɪŋ dɪ ˌvaɪs/ *noun* filtre *m* de sélection du signal maximal

audible /'ɔːdɪb(ə)l/ *adjective* (*signal*) audible; perceptible à l'oreille

audio /'ɔːdiəʊ/ *adjective* audio

audio board /'ɔːdiəʊ bɔːd/ *noun* carte *f* son

audio file /'ɔːdiəʊ faɪl/ *noun* fichier *m* audio

audio range /'ɔːdiəʊ reɪndʒ/ *noun* (*frequency range*) gamme *f* des audiofréquences; limites *fpl* de la bande des audiofréquences

audio response unit /ˌɔːdiəʊ rɪ'spɒns ˌjuːnɪt/ *noun* répondeur *m* vocal

audiotex /'ɔːdiəʊteks/ *noun* (*interactive voice response over the telephone*) technologie *f* audiotex

audio/video interleaved /ˌɔːdiəʊ ˌvɪdiəʊ ˌɪntə'liːvd/ *noun* format *m* vidéo AVI (de Microsoft)

audit /'ɔːdɪt/ *noun* (*noting tasks carried out by a computer*) audit *m* informatique ■ *verb* (*examine the state of a system and check that it is still working properly*) faire un audit

audit trail /'ɔːdɪt treɪl/ *noun* (*record of details of the use made of a system*) protocole *m* de traçage; (*record of details of the use of a system*) protocole *m* de contrôle; protocole *m* de vérification

augend /'ɔːgend/ *noun* (*in an addition: the number to which another number is added*) premier terme *m* d'une addition

augmented addressing /ɔːgˌmentɪd ə 'dresɪŋ/ *noun* adressage *m* augmenté

augmenter /ˌɔːg'mentə/ *noun* (*value added to another*) cumulateur *m*; second terme *m* d'une addition

AUI connector /ˌeɪ juː 'aɪ kəˌnektə/ *noun* (*connector used to connect Ethernet cable to a network adapter*) connecteur *m* AUI

authentication of messages /ɔː ˌθentɪkeɪʃ(ə)n əv 'mesɪdʒɪz/ *noun* authentification *f* de messages

authenticator /ɔː'θentɪkeɪtə/ *noun* sceau *m* électronique

author /'ɔːθə/ *noun* (*person who wrote a program*) auteur *m* ■ *verb* créer *vt*

> 'The authoring system is a software product that integrates text and fractally compressed images, using any wordprocessor line editor, to create an electronic book with hypertext links between different pages.' [*Computing*]

authoring language /ˌɔːθərɪŋ 'læŋgwɪdʒ/ *noun* langage *m* auteur

authoring software /ˌɔːθərɪŋ 'sɒftweə/, **authoring system** /ˌɔːθərɪŋ 'sɪstəm/ *noun* **1.** (*multimedia software*) système *m* auteur **2.** (*webpage design software*) logiciel *m* auteur

authorisation /ˌɔːθəraɪ'zeɪʃ(ə)n/, **authorization** *noun* **1.** autorisation *f* **2.** (*to access a system*) autorisation *f*

authorisation code /ˌɔːθəraɪ'zeɪʃ(ə)n kəʊd/ *noun* code *m* d'accès; mot *m* de passe

authorisation to copy /ˌɔːθəraɪzeɪʃ(ə)n tə 'kɒpɪ/ *noun* autorisation *f* de copier; autorisation *f* de dupliquer

authorised user /ˌɔːθəˌraɪzd 'juːzə/, **authorized user** *noun* personne *f* autorisée

authority file /ɔː'θɒrɪti faɪl/, **authority list** /ɔː 'θɒrɪti lɪst/ *noun* fichier *m* de référence; liste *f* de référence

auto advance /ˌɔːtəʊ əd'vɑːns/ *noun* alimentation *f* automatique du papier; entraînement *m* automatique du papier

auto-answer /ˌɔːtəʊ 'ɑːnsə/ *noun* autoréponse *f*; réponse *f* automatique

auto-baud scanning /'ɔːtəʊ bɔːd/, **auto-baud sensing** /'ɔːtəʊ bɔːd/ *noun* (*modem*) reconnaissance *f* automatique du débit d'une ligne

auto-boot /'ɔːtəʊ buːt/ *noun* amorçage *m* automatique; lancement *m* automatique

auto-dial /ˌɔːtəʊ 'daɪəl/ *noun* système *m* d'appel automatique

AUTOEXEC.BAT /ˌɔːtəʊɪg'zek bæt/ *noun* (*batch file which contains commands that are executed when the computer is first switched on*) autoexec.bat

autoflow /'ɔːtəʊfləʊ/ *noun* habillage *m* automatique

auto-login /ˌɔːtəʊ 'lɒgɪn/, **auto-logon** /ˌɔːtəʊ 'lɒgɒn/ *noun* ouverture *f* automatique de session

automated teller machine /ˌɔːtəmeɪtɪd 'telə məˌʃiːn/ *noun* guichet *m* automatique bancaire

automatically programmed tools /ˌɔːtəmætɪkli ˌprəʊgræmd 'tuːlz/ *plural noun* langage *m* de commande numérique

automatic backup /ˌɔːtəmætɪk 'bækʌp/ *noun* sauvegarde *f* automatique

automatic call distribution /ˌɔːtəmætɪk 'kɔːl ˌdɪstrɪbjuːʃ(ə)n/ *noun* distribution *f* automatique des appels; standard *m* automatique; unité *f* d'appel automatique

automatic calling unit /ˌɔːtəmætɪk 'kɔːlɪŋ ˌjuːnɪt/ *noun* système *m* d'appel automatique; traitement *m* automatique de données

automatic carriage return /ˌɔːtəmætɪk 'kærɪdʒ rɪˌtɜːn/ *noun* retour *m* à la ligne automatique

automatic checking /ˌɔːtəmætɪk 'tʃekɪŋ/ *noun* autotest *m*

automatic data capture /ˌɔːtəmætɪk 'deɪtə ˌkæptʃə/ *noun* saisie *f* automatique de données

automatic data processing /ˌɔːtəmætɪk 'deɪtə ˌprəʊsesɪŋ/ *noun* traitement *m* automatique de données

automatic decimal adjustment /ˌɔːtəmætɪk 'desɪm(ə)l əˌdʒʌstmənt/ *noun* (*process of lining up all the decimal points in a column of figures*) alignement *m* automatique des virgules

automatic error correction /ˌɔːtəmætɪk 'erə kəˌrekʃ(ə)n/ *noun* correction *f* automatique d'erreurs

automatic error detection /ˌɔːtəmætɪk 'erə dɪˌtekʃ(ə)n/ *noun* détection *f* automatique d'erreurs

automatic font downloading /ˌɔːtəmætɪk 'fɒnt daʊnˌləʊdɪŋ/ *noun* téléchargement *m* de police de caractères

automatic frequency switching /ˌɔːtəmætɪk 'friːkwənsi ˌswɪtʃɪŋ/ *noun* adaptation *f* automatique de la fréquence vidéo; adaptation *f* automatique du mode vidéo

automatic gain /ˌɔːtəmætɪk 'geɪn/ *noun* gain *m* automatique

automatic gain control /ˌɔːtəmætɪk ˌgeɪn kən'trəʊl/ *noun* contrôle *m* de gain automatique

automatic hyphenation /ˌɔːtəmætɪk ˌhaɪfə 'naɪʃ(ə)n/ *noun* coupure *f* automatique des mots

automatic letter writing /ˌɔːtəmætɪk 'letə ˌraɪtɪŋ/ *noun* composition *f* automatique de lettres types

automatic loader /ˌɔːtəmætɪk 'ləʊdə/ *noun* chargeur *m* automatique

automatic log on /ˌɔːtəmætɪk 'lɒg ˌɒn/ *noun* ouverture *f* automatique d'une session

automatic mailing list /ˌɔːtəmætɪk 'meɪlɪŋ ˌlɪst/ *noun* liste *f* de diffusion

automatic mode /ˌɔːtə'mætɪk məʊd/ *noun* adaptation *f* automatique de la fréquence vidéo; adaptation *f* automatique du mode vidéo

automatic number identification /ˌɔːtəmætɪk 'nʌmbə aɪˌdentɪfɪkeɪʃ(ə)n/ *noun* reconnaissance *f* automatique des numéros d'appels

automatic power off /ˌɔːtəmætɪk ˌpaʊə 'ɒf/ *noun* dispositif *m* d'arrêt; dispositif *m* de mise hors tension automatique

automatic programming /ˌɔːtəmætɪk 'prəʊgræmɪŋ/ *noun* programmation *f* automatique

automatic recalculation /ˌɔːtəmætɪk riː ˌkælkju'leɪʃ(ə)n/ *noun* recalcul *m* automatique

automatic recovery program /ˌɔːtəmætɪk rɪ'kʌv(ə)ri ˌprəʊgræm/ *noun* programme *m* de restauration; programme *m* de remise en état automatique

automatic repeat /ˌɔːtəmætɪk rɪ'piːt/ *noun* répétition *f* automatique

automatic repeat request /ˌɔːtəmætɪk rɪ 'piːt rɪˌkwest/ *noun* correction *f* d'erreurs ARQ; demande *f* de répétition automatique

automatic send/receive /ˌɔːtəmætɪk ˌsend rɪ'siːv/ *noun* émission-réception *f*

automatic sequencing /ˌɔːtəmætɪk 'siːkwənsɪŋ/ *noun* fonctionnement *m* itératif automatique

automatic speed matching /ˌɔːtəmætɪk 'spiːd ˌmætʃɪŋ/ *noun* accord *m* automatique des vitesses de transmission

automatic test equipment /ˌɔːtəmætɪk 'test ɪˌkwɪpmənt/ *noun* équipement *m* de vérification automatique (EVA)

automatic volume control /ˌɔːtəmætɪk 'vɒljuːm kənˌtrəʊl/ *noun* réglage *m* du volume automatique

auto-redial /ˌɔːtəʊ 'riːdaɪəl/ *noun* système *m* de rappel automatique d'un correspondant

auto repeat /ˌɔːtəʊ rɪ'piːt/ *noun* répétition *f* automatique

autoresponder /ˌɔːtəʊrɪˈspɒndə/ *noun* autorépondeur *m*

auto restart /ˌɔːtəʊ ˈriːstɑːt/ *noun* relance *f* automatique

auto save /ˈɔːtəʊ seɪv/ *noun* sauvegarde *f* automatique

auto scan /ˈɔːtəʊ skæn/ *noun* autobalayage *m*

auto start /ˈɔːtəʊ stɑːt/ *noun* (*facility to load a program automatically*) démarrage *m* automatique; lancement *m* automatique; mise *f* en route automatique

auto stop /ˈɔːtəʊ stɒp/ *noun* arrêt *m* automatique

autosync /ˈɔːtəʊsɪŋk/ *noun* (*of modem*) conversion *f* automatique asynchrone/synchrone; synchro *f* automatique

auto trace /ˈɔːtəʊ treɪs/ *noun* suivi *m* automatique

auto verify /ˌɔːtəʊ ˈverɪfaɪ/ *noun* vérification *f* automatique

A/UX (*trade name for a version of the Unix operating system for the Apple Mac range of computers*) A/UX

auxiliary /ɔːgˈzɪliəri/ *noun* auxiliaire *(m&f)*

auxiliary device /ɔːgˌzɪliəri dɪˈvaɪs/ *noun* dispositif *m* auxiliaire

auxiliary equipment /ɔːgˌzɪliəri ɪ ˈkwɪpmənt/ *noun* (*backup equipment*) matériel *m* de secours

auxiliary memory /ɔːgˌzɪliəri ˈmem(ə)ri/ *noun* mémoire *f* auxiliaire

auxiliary processor /ɔːgˌzɪliəri ˈprəʊsesə/ *noun* processeur *m* auxiliaire

auxiliary storage /ɔːgˌzɪliəri ˈstɔːrɪdʒ/, **auxiliary store** /ɔːgˈzɪliəri stɔː/ *noun* mémoire *f* auxiliaire

auxilliary audio device /ɔːgˌzɪliəri ˈɔːdiəʊ dɪˌvaɪs/ *noun* dispositif *m* audio auxiliaire

available bit rate /əˌveɪləb(ə)l ˈbɪt ˌreɪt/ *noun* débit *m* binaire disponible

available list /əˈveɪləb(ə)l lɪst/ *noun* liste *f* des ressources disponibles

available point /əˈveɪləb(ə)l pɔɪnt/ *noun* élément *m* d'image; point *m* d'image

available power /əˌveɪləb(ə)l ˈpaʊə/ *noun* puissance *f* maximale disponible; puissance *f* réelle disponible

available time /əˈveɪləb(ə)l taɪm/ *noun* temps *m* de disponibilité; temps *m* disponible

avalanche /ˈævəlɑːntʃ/ *noun* (*one action starting a number of other actions*) avalanche *f* ◇ **avalanche photodiode (APD)** photodiode *f* à avalanche

avatar /ˈævətɑː/ *noun* **1.** (*graphical image*) avatar *m* **2.** (*superuser account in UNIX*) avatar *m*

AVC /ˌeɪ viː ˈsiː/ *noun* réglage *m* du volume automatique

average access time /ˌæv(ə)rɪdʒ ˈækses ˌtaɪm/ *noun* temps *m* d'accès moyen

average delay /ˌæv(ə)rɪdʒ dɪˈleɪ/ *noun* (*time taken to access a communication network*) délai *m* moyen

AVI /ˌeɪ viː ˈaɪ/ *noun* format *m* AVI

axis /ˈæksɪs/ *noun* **1.** (*around which something turns*) axe *m* **2.** (*on a graph*) axe *m*

azerty keyboard /əˌzɜːti ˈkiːbɔːd/ *noun* clavier *m* AZERTY

azimuth /ˈæzɪməθ/ *noun* azimut *m*

azimuth alignment /ˌæzɪməθ əˈlaɪnmənt/ *noun* (*horizontal angle of a tape head*) réglage *m* d'alignement des angles d'azimut; réglage *m* d'alignement des têtes d'azimut ◇ **azimuth alignment is adjusted with this small screw** c'est cette petite vis qui sert à régler l'alignement des têtes *or* des angles d'azimut

B

b *abbr* (*one bit*) (*bit*) b; bit

B¹ *abbr* (*one byte*) (*byte*) nombre *m* hexadécimal équivalent du 11 décimal; B

B² *symbol* (*hexadecimal number equivalent to decimal 11*) o; octet; B

B: B:

B2B /ˌbiː tə ˈbiː/ *adjective* entreprise à entreprise

B2C /ˌbiː tə ˈsiː/ *adjective* achat *m* grand public

babble /ˈbæb(ə)l/ *noun* diaphonie *f*; bruit *m* de fond

BABT /ˌbiː eɪ biː ˈtiː/ *noun* (*organisation that tests and certifies telecommunications equipment*) commission *f* qui approuve et certifie les matériels de télécommunication avant leur mise en service dans le Royaume-Uni ◇ **if you design a new modem, you must have BABT approval before you can sell it** si vous développez un nouveau modem, vous devrez obtenir l'approbation du BABT avant de le commercialiser

BABT approval /ˌbiː eɪ biː ˌtiː əˈpruːvəl/ *noun* approbation *f* du BABT

backbone /ˈbækˌbəʊn/ *noun* (*high-speed, high-capacity connection path*) arête *f* dorsale; épine *f* dorsale

backbone ring /ˈbækˌbəʊn rɪŋ/ *noun* anneau *m* collecteur; backbone *m*

backdoor /ˈbækˌdɔː/ *noun* point *m* d'entrée dans un système

back-end network /ˌbæk end ˈnetwɜːk/ *noun* (*connection between a mainframe computer and a high-speed mass storage device*) réseau *m* auxiliaire

back-end processor /ˌbæk end ˈprəʊsesə/ *noun* (*special purpose auxiliary processor*) processeur *m* de fond; processeur *m* auxiliaire spécialisé

back-end server /ˌbæk end ˈsɜːvə/ *noun* (*computer that carries out tasks requested by client workstations*) serveur *m* de fond; serveur *m* auxiliaire

background /ˈbækgraʊnd/ *noun* **1.** (*part of a picture*) arrière-plan *m*; fond *m* **2.** arrière-plan *m* ◇ **black text on a white background is less stressful for the eyes** un texte en noir sur fond blanc est moins fatigant pour la vue ◇ **the modem is sensitive to background noise** le modem est sensible au bruit de fond ◇ **the new graphics processor chip can handle background, foreground and sprite movement independently** le nouveau processeur graphique permet de manipuler indépendamment les images d'arrière-plan et d'avant-plan ainsi que les plans-objets

background colour /ˌbækgraʊnd ˈkʌlə/ *noun* fond *m*

background communication /ˌbækgraʊnd kəˌmjuːnɪˈkeɪʃ(ə)n/ *noun* communication *f* en arrière-plan; communication *f* non prioritaire

background image /ˌbækgraʊnd ˈɪmɪdʒ/ *noun* image *f* en arrière-plan

background job /ˈbækgraʊnd dʒɒb/ *noun* tâche *f* de fond; tâche *f* non prioritaire

background noise /ˌbækgraʊnd ˈnɔɪz/ *noun* bruit *m* de fond ◇ **the other machines around this device will produce a lot of background noise** les autres appareils placés autour de cet équipement produiront un fort bruit de fond

background operation /ˌbækgraʊnd ˌɒpəˈreɪʃ(ə)n/ *noun* opération *f* non prioritaire

background printing /ˌbækgraʊnd ˈprɪntɪŋ/ *noun* (*printing done while a computer processes another task*) impression *f* en arrière-plan

background processing /ˌbækgraʊnd ˈprəʊsesɪŋ/ *noun* (*low priority job*) traitement *m* non prioritaire

background program /ˌbækgraʊnd ˈprəʊgræm/ *noun* (*low-priority computer program*) programme *m* non prioritaire

background recalculation /ˌbækgraʊnd riː ˌkælkjuˈleɪʃ(ə)n/ *noun* recalcul *m* en arrière-plan; recalcul *m* en tâche de fond

background reflectance /ˌbækgraʊnd rɪˈflektəns/ *noun* réflectance *f* d'arrière-plan; réflectance *f* de fond

background task /ˈbækgraʊnd tɑːsk/ *noun* tâche *f* de fond; tâche *f* non prioritaire

backing /ˈbækɪŋ/ *noun* auxiliaire *mf*

backing memory /ˌbækɪŋ ˈmem(ə)ri/ *noun* mémoire *f* auxiliaire

backing storage /ˈbækɪŋ ˌstɔːrɪdʒ/ *noun* mémoire *f* de masse; mémoire *f* auxiliaire

backing store /ˈbækɪŋ stɔː/, **backing storage** /ˈbækɪŋ ˌstɔːrɪdʒ/, **backing memory** /ˌbækɪŋ ˈmem(ə)ri/ *noun* mémoire *f* auxiliaire; mémoire *f* de masse ◇ **by adding another disk drive, I will increase the backing store capa-**

bilities je vais augmenter la capacité de mémoire auxiliaire en ajoutant un deuxième lecteur de disquettes

back-level /bæk 'lev(ə)l/ *noun* (*earlier release of a product*) version *f* dépassée; version *f* périmée d'un produit qui ne supporte pas certaines fonctions

backlight /'bæklaɪt/ *noun* (*light behind a LCD*) rétroéclairage *m*

backlit display /ˌbæklɪt dɪ'spleɪ/ *noun* écran *m* à cristaux liquides rétroéclairé

backlog /'bækˌlɒg/ *noun* travail *m* en retard; (*work or tasks to be done*) travail *m* en attente; travail *m* en souffrance ◇ **the programmers can't deal with the backlog of programming work** les programmeurs ne réussissent pas à venir à bout de toute la programmation en retard ◇ **the queue was too short for the backlog of tasks waiting to be processed** la file d'attente trop courte ne suffisait pas à la série de tâches à traiter

back office /ˌbæk 'ɒfɪs/ *noun* arrière-guichet *m*

backout /ˌbæk'aʊt/ *verb* (*to restore a file to its original condition*) restaurer *vt*; récupérer *vt*

back panel /bæk 'pæn(ə)l/ *noun* (*at the rear of a computer*) panneau *m* arrière

backplane /'bækpleɪn/ *noun* fond *m* de panier

back pointer /bæk 'pɔɪntə/ *noun* pointeur *m* retour

back projection /bæk prə'dʒekʃ(ə)n/ *noun* (*cinema*) transparence *f*

backslash /'bækslæʃ/ *noun* (*ASCII character 92: the sign *) antislash *m*; barre *f* oblique inverse (\\)

backspace /'bækˌspeɪs/ *noun* (*of cursor*) retour *m* arrière; rappel *m*

backspace character /'bækspeɪs ˌkærɪktə/ *noun* caractère *m* de rappel du curseur; caractère *m* de retour arrière

backspace key /'bækˌspeɪs kiː/ *noun* touche *f* de retour arrière

backtab /'bæktæb/ *verb* (*move the cursor back to the previous field*) aller à rebours; faire une tabulation arrière

backtrack /'bæktræk/ *verb* aller à rebours; faire marche arrière

back up /'bæk ʌp/ *verb* **1.** (*to support or help*) soutenir *vt*; étayer *vt* **2.** (*to make a copy of a file or data or disk*) sauvegarder *vt*; faire une copie de sauvegarde ◇ **he brought along a file of documents to back up his claim** il a apporté tout un dossier pour étayer sa réclamation ◇ **the company accounts were backed up on disk as a protection against fire damage** la comptabilité de la société a été sauvegardée sur disque en cas d'incendie ◇ **the printout backed up his argument for a new system** le document papier soutenait ses arguments en faveur d'un nouveau système ◇ **the program enables users to back up hard disk files with a single command** ce programme permet aux utilisateurs de sauvegarder les fichiers du disque dur en une seule opération

backup /'bækʌp/ *noun* **1.** (*support*) assistance *f*; (*technical support*) service *m* d'assistance **2.** (*copy for security*) copie *f* de sauvegarde **3.** (*process of making a copy*) sauvegarde *f* ■ *adjective, noun* (*which helps*) de secours; auxiliaire; (*of a file*) de sauvegarde

'...the previous version is retained, but its extension is changed to .BAK indicating that it's a back-up' [*Personal Computer World*]

BACKUP *noun* (*MS-DOS command*) BACKUP ◇ **the company accounts were backed up on disk as a protection against fire damage** la comptabilité de la société a été sauvegardée sur disque en cas d'incendie ◇ **the program enables users to back up hard disk files with a single command** ce programme permet aux utilisateurs de sauvegarder les fichiers du disque dur en une seule opération

backup copy /'bækʌp ˌkɒpi/ *noun* copie *f* de sauvegarde

backup disk /'bækʌp dɪsk/ *noun* disque *m* de sauvegarde; disquette *f* de sauvegarde

backup domain controller /ˌbækʌp dəʊ'meɪn kənˌtrəʊlə/ *noun* contrôleur *m* de sauvegarde par domaine

backup file /'bækʌp faɪl/ *noun* fichier *m* de sauvegarde

backup path /'bækʌp pɑːθ/ *noun* chemin *m* de sauvegarde

backup plan /'bækʌp plæn/ *noun* plan *m* de sauvegarde

backup procedure /ˌbækʌp prə'siːdʒə/ *noun* procédure *f* de sauvegarde

backup server /ˌbækʌp 'sɜːvə/ *noun* serveur *m* de sauvegarde; serveur *m* de secours

backup utility /ˌbækʌp juː'tɪlɪti/ *noun* utilitaire *m* de sauvegarde

backup version /ˌbækʌp 'vɜːʃ(ə)n/ *noun* copie *f* de sauvegarde; version *f* de sauvegarde

Backus-Naur-Form /ˌbækəs 'naʊə ˌfɔːm/ *noun* (*programming language*) convention *f* BNF; métalangage *m* BNF

backward chaining /'bækwəd tʃeɪnɪŋ/ *noun* chaînage *m* arrière; chaînage *m* en amont

backward channel /ˌbækwəd 'tʃæn(ə)l/ *noun* canal *m* de retour; voie *f* de retour

backward error correction /ˌbækwəd 'erə kəˌrekʃ(ə)n/ *noun* correction *f* d'erreurs par retransmission

backward LAN channel /ˌbækwəd 'læn ˌtʃæn(ə)l/ *noun* voie *f* de retour du réseau local

backward mode /'bækwəd məʊd/ *noun* mode *m* à marche arrière; mode *m* à rebours

backward recovery /ˌbækwəd rɪ'kʌv(ə)ri/ *noun* reconstitution *f* de procédure; récupération *f* de fichier à rebours

backwards compatible /ˌbækwədz kəm ˈpætəb(ə)l/ *adjective* de compatibilité ascendante

backwards search /ˌbækwədz ˈsɜːtʃ/ *noun* recherche *f* arrière; recherche *f* en amont

backwards supervision /ˌbækwədz ˌsuːpə ˈvɪʒ(ə)n/ *noun* contrôle *m* par le récepteur

BACS /bæks/ *noun* système *m* interbancaire de télécompensation; SIT

bad break /ˌbæd ˈbreɪk/ *noun* (*wrong way of splitting a word*) coupe *f* impropre; mauvaise coupe *f*

badge reader /bædʒ ˈriːdə/ *noun* lecteur *m* de badges ◇ **a badge reader makes sure that only authorized personnel can gain access to a computer room** le lecteur de badges garantit que seules les personnes autorisées ont accès à la salle des ordinateurs

bad sector /bæd ˈsektə/ *noun* secteur *m* défectueux; mauvais secteur *m*

baffle /ˈbæf(ə)l/ *noun* (*sound absorber and deflector*) enceinte *f* acoustique

bag /bæg/ *noun* (*of elements*) éléments *mpl* en vrac

BAK file extension /ˌbæk faɪl ɪgˈstenʃ(ə)n/ *noun* (*standard extension used in MS-DOS systems to signify a backup*) extension *f* BAK

balance /ˈbæləns/ *noun* (*of text and graphics*) équilibre *m*; symétrie *f* ◇ **the DTP package allows the user to see if the overall page balance is correct** le logiciel de PAO permet à l'utilisateur de juger du bon équilibre *or* de la bonne disposition d'une page

balanced circuit /ˌbælənst ˈsɜːkɪt/ *noun* circuit *m* équilibré

balanced error /ˌbælənst ˈerə/ *noun* erreur *f* à valeur moyenne nulle; erreur *f* équilibrée

balanced line /ˈbælənst laɪn/ *noun* ligne *f* équilibrée

balanced routing /ˈbælənst raʊtɪŋ/ *noun* équilibrage *m* des lignes de transmission

balun /ˈbælən/ *noun* (*transformer*) équilibreur *m* d'impédance

band /bænd/ *noun* **1.** (*of frequencies*) bande *f* **2.** (*on magnetic disk*) bande *f* multipiste ◇ **do not use a base band modem with a normal phone line** n'utilisez jamais un modem en bande de base sur une ligne téléphonique normale ◇ **two-band telephone** téléphone *m* bibande

bandpass filter /ˈbændpɑːs ˌfɪltə/ *noun* filtre *m* passe-bande

bandwidth /ˈbændwɪdθ/ *noun* **1.** (*range of frequencies*) bande *f* passante **2.** (*amount of data that can be transmitted*) bande *f* passante; largeur *f* de bande de fréquence; capacité *f* de transfert ◇ **telephone bandwidth is 3100Hz** bande passante; la largeur de bande d'un téléphone est de 3100Hz L/ (c) ◇ **this fibre-optic cable has a greater bandwidth than the old copper cable and so it can carry data at higher speeds** la bande passante de câble à fibres optiques est plus étendue que celle des anciens câbles en cuivre et peut transmettre les données à des vitesses plus grandes

bandwidth on demand /ˌbændˌwɪdθ ɒn dɪ ˈmɑːnd/ *noun* largeur *f* de bande à la demande

bank /bæŋk/ *noun* (*collection of similar devices*) banque *f*; groupe *m*; bloc *m* ◇ **a bank of minicomputers process all the raw data** un groupe de mini-ordinateurs traite toutes les données brutes

Bankers Automated Clearing Services /ˌbæŋkəz ˌɔːtəmeɪtɪd ˈklɪərɪŋ ˌsɜːvɪsɪz/ *noun* (*system to transfer money between banks*) système *m* interbancaire de télécompensation; SIT

bank Internet payment system /ˌbæŋk ˌɪntənet ˈpeɪmənt ˌsɪstəm/ *noun* système *m* de paiement bancaire par Internet

bank switching /ˈbæŋk ˌswɪtʃɪŋ/ *noun* changement *m* de banque de mémoire; changement *m* de bloc de mémoire

banner /ˈbænə/, **banner advertisement** /ˌbænə ədˈvɜːtɪsmənt/, **banner ad** /ˈbænə æd/ *noun* bandeau *m* publicitaire

banner page /ˈbænə peɪdʒ/ *noun* page *f* d'ouverture

bar /bɑː/ *noun* (*thick line*) barre *f*; ligne *f*; trait *m*; (*printing rule*) filet *m* ◇ **menu bar** (*on the screen*) barre de menu

bar chart /ˈbɑː tʃɑːt/ *noun* diagramme *m* en bâtons

bar code /ˈbɑː kəʊd/ *noun* code-barre *m*

bar code reader /ˈbɑː kəʊd ˌriːdə/ *noun* lecteur *m* optique de codes-barres; stylo *m* optique

bare board /ˈbeə bɔːd/ *noun* (*circuit board with no components*) carte *f* nue; carte *f* d'extension sans mémoires; carte *f* mémoire sans composants

bar graph /ˈbɑː grɑːf/ *noun* graphique *m* à barres

barrel /ˈbærəl/ *noun* tonneau *m*; baril *m*; borne *f* de raccordement

base /beɪs/ *noun* **1.** (*lowest position*) base *f* **2.** (*collection of files*) base *f* **3.** (*initial position*) base *f* **4.** (*notation referring to a number system*) base *f* **5.** (*class in C++*) base *f* ■ *verb* **1.** (*to calculate from*) se baser (sur) **2.** (*to set something up somewhere*) localiser *vt*

base 2 /ˈbeɪs tuː/ *noun* base *f* 2; base *f* binaire

base 8 /ˈbeɪs eɪt/ *noun* base *f* 8; base *f* octale

base 10 /ˌbeɪs ˈten/ *noun* base *f* 10; base *f* décimale

base 16 /ˌbeɪs sɪksˈtiːn/ *noun* base *f* 16; base *f* hexadécimale

base address /beɪs əˈdres/ *noun* adresse *f* de base

base address register /ˌbeɪs əˈdres ˌredʒɪstə/ *noun* registre *m* d'adresse de base

baseband /'beɪsbænd/, **base band** *noun* **1.** (*frequency range of a signal*) bande *f* de base **2.** (*digital signals without modulation*) bande *f* de base **3.** (*information modulated*) bande *f* de base ◇ **baseband local area network** réseau *m* local en bande de base ◇ **base band local area networks can support a maximum cable length of around 300m** les réseaux locaux en bande de base peuvent avoir des longueurs de câbles d'environ 300m au maximum

base band local area network /ˌbeɪs bænd ˌləʊk(ə)l ˌeəriə 'netwɜːk/ *noun* réseau *m* local en bande de base

base band modem /ˌbeɪs bænd 'məʊdem/ *noun* modem *m* en bande de base ◇ **do not use a base band modem with a normal phone line** n'utilisez jamais un modem en bande de base sur une ligne téléphonique normale

baseband signalling /ˌbeɪsbænd 'sɪgnəlɪŋ/ *noun* transmission *f* en bande de base; transmission *f* en modulation de tension

base font /'beɪs fɒnt/ *noun* police *f* de caractères de base; police *f* de caractères par défaut

base language /beɪs 'læŋgwɪdʒ/ *noun* langage *m* d'assemblage

base line /'beɪs laɪn/ *noun* ligne *f* de base

base memory /beɪs 'mem(ə)ri/, **base RAM** /beɪs ræm/ *noun* mémoire *f* conventionnelle; mémoire *f* de base

base register /beɪs 'redʒɪstə/ *noun* (*register that contains the start of a program*) registre *m* d'adresse; registre *m* de base

base station /beɪs 'steɪʃ(ə)n/ *noun* base *f* de transmission; centrale *f* de transmission

BASIC /'beɪsɪk/ *noun* langage *m* de haut niveau BASIC; langage *m* de base; langage *m* fondamental; langage *m* standard ◇ **basic control system satellite (BCS)** satellite *m* de système de contrôle de base ◇ **basic direct access method (BDAM)** (*method of directly updating or retrieving*) méthode *f* d'accès direct de base ◇ **basic operating system (BOS)** système *m* d'exploitation de base ◇ **basic rate access (BRA)** (*basic ISDN service that provides two data channels*) débit de base (d'un RNIS) ◇ **basic sequential access method (BSAM)** (*method of storing or retrieving blocks of data in a continuous sequence*) méthode d'accès séquentiel de base

basic code /'beɪsɪk kəʊd/ *noun* code *m* de base; code *m* élémentaire

basic controller /ˌbeɪsɪk kən'trəʊlə/ *noun* contrôleur *m* de base

basic control system satellite /ˌbeɪsɪk kən ˌtrəʊl ˌsɪstəm 'sætəlaɪt/ *noun* système *m* satellite de base

basic direct access method /ˌbeɪsɪk ˌdaɪrekt 'ækses ˌmeθəd/ *noun* méthode *f* d'accès direct de base

basic exchange format /ˌbeɪsɪk ɪks'tʃeɪndʒ ˌfɔːmæt/ *noun* format *m* d'échange format

basic input/output operating system /ˌbeɪsɪk ˌɪnpʊt ˌaʊtpʊt 'ɒpəreɪtɪŋ ˌsɪstəm/ *noun* systèmes *mpl* d'exploitation des entrées/sorties

basic instruction /ˌbeɪsɪk ɪn'strʌkʃən/ *noun* instruction *f* de base; instruction *f* primitive

basic mode link control /ˌbeɪsɪk məʊd 'lɪŋk kənˌtrəʊl/ *noun* protocole *m* standard de contrôle de liaisons

basic product /ˌbeɪsɪk 'prɒdʌkt/ *noun* produit *m* de base

basic rate access /ˌbeɪsɪk reɪt 'ækses/ *noun* accès *m* au débit primaire

basic rate interface /ˌbeɪsɪk reɪt 'ɪntəfeɪs/ *noun* accès *m* de base

basic sequential access method /ˌbeɪsɪk sɪˌkwenʃ(ə)l ˌækses 'meθəd/ *noun* méthode *f* d'accès séquentiel de base

basic telecommunications access method /ˌbeɪsɪk ˌtelikəmjuːnɪkeɪʃ(ə)nz 'ækses ˌmeθəd/ *noun* méthode *f* BTAM; protocole *m* d'accès de télécommunications

BAT /bæt/ *noun* BAT

batch /bætʃ/ *noun* **1.** (*documents processed at same time*) paquet *m*; lot *m* **2.** (*tasks or data processed as single unit*) paquet *m*; lot *m* ■ *verb* (*to put data or tasks together*) regrouper *vt* ◇ **(processing data in) batch mode** mode de traitement par lots *or* par paquets

batched communication /ˌbætʃ kəˌmjuːnɪ 'keɪʃ(ə)n/ *noun* communications *fpl* groupées

batch file /'bætʃ faɪl/ *noun* fichier *m* de commandes ◇ **this batch file is used to save time and effort when carrying out a routine task** ce fichier de commandes (de traitement par lots) est utilisé pour économiser du temps et des efforts lorsqu'on effectue une tâche de routine

batch mode *noun* mode *m* de traitement par lots; mode *m* de traitement par paquets

batch processing /'bætʃ ˌprəʊsesɪŋ/ *noun* traitement *m* par lots; (*of computer system*) traitement *m* par paquets

batch processor /'bætʃ ˌprəʊsesə/ *noun* processeur *m* de traitement par paquets; processeur *m* de traitement par lots

batch region /bætʃ 'riːdʒ(ə)n/ *noun* partition *f* de traitement par lots; zone *f* de traitement par lots

batch system /bætʃ 'sɪstəm/ *noun* système *m* de traitement par lots; système *m* de traitement par paquets

batch total /bætʃ 'təʊt(ə)l/ *noun* total *m* par groupe; total *m* par lot

BAT file extension /ˌbæt faɪl ɪk'stenʃən/ *noun* (*file extension used in MS-DOS systems to signify a batch file*) extension *f* BAT

battery-backed /'bæt(ə)ri bækd/ *adjective* (*volatile storage devices*) équipé, -ée d'une pile auxiliaire; relié, -ée à une pile auxiliaire; à une pile de secours ◇ **battery-backed CMOS memory**

replaces a disk drive in this portable dans ce portable, le lecteur de disquettes est remplacé par une mémoire CMOS dont le fonctionnement est assuré par une pile auxiliaire ◇ **the RAM disk card has the option to be battery-backed** la carte RAM peut être équipée, en option, d'une pile de secours

battery backup /ˌbæt(ə)ri 'bækʌp/ *noun* (*battery to provide power to volatile storage devices*) pile *f*; alimentation *f* auxiliaire

battery charging /'bæt(ə)ri ˌtʃɑːdʒɪŋ/ *noun* charge *f* d'une pile

battery meter /ˌbæt(ə)ri 'miːtə/ *noun* témoin *m* lumineux de charge

baud /bɔːd/ *noun* baud *m*

baud rate /'bɔːd reɪt/ *noun* débit *m* de transmission; vitesse *f* de transmission

baud rate generator /ˌbɔːd ˌreɪt 'dʒenəreɪtə/ *noun* adaptateur *m* de vitesse de transmission

bay /beɪ/ *noun* (*space where a disk drive is fitted*) baie *f*; emplacement *m* de lecteur de disque

B box /'biː bɒks/ *noun* registre *m* secondaire

BBS /ˌbiː biː 'es/ *noun* messagerie *f*; tableau *m* d'affichage

BCD /ˌbiː siː 'diː/ *noun* décimal *m* codé binaire (DCB)

BCD adder /ˌbiː siː ˌdiː 'ædə/ *noun* additionneur *m* binaire; additionneur *m* DCB

BCH code /ˌbiː ˌsiː'eɪtʃ kəʊd/ *noun* code *m* BCH

BCPL /ˌbiː siː piː 'el/ *noun* langage *m* de haut niveau BCPL

beacon /'biːkən/ *verb* (*signal transmitted by a device that is malfunctioning*) alerteur *m* d'évènement; alerteur *m* d'incident

beacon frame /'biːkən freɪm/ *noun* (*frame that is sent after a network break has occurred*) trame *f* d'alerte

bead /biːd/ *noun* (*small section of a program*) module *m*; sous-ensemble *m*; sous-programme *m*; fonction *f*

beam /biːm/ *noun* rayon *m*; rayonnement *m*; faisceau *m* ◇ **a beam of laser light is used in this printer to produce high-resolution graphics** l'imprimante utilise un rayon laser pour obtenir une haute résolution graphique ◇ **a magnetic field is used for beam deflection in a CRT** dans un tube à rayons cathodiques, la déflexion du faisceau est effectuée par un champ magnétique ◇ **beam diversity** dédoublement *m* du faisceau ◇ **beam width** largeur *f* d'un faisceau *or* d'un lobe ◇ **the laser produces a thin beam of light** le laser émet un mince rayon lumineux

beam deflection /biːm dɪ'flekʃ(ə)n/ *noun* déflexion *f* de rayon; déviation *f* de rayon ◇ **a magnetic field is used for beam deflection in a CRT** dans un tube à rayons cathodiques, la déflexion du faisceau est effectuée par un champ magnétique

BEC *abbr* (*bus extension card*) fiche *f* complémentaire de bus

beginner's all-purpose symbolic instruction code /bɪˌɡɪnəz ɔːl ˌpɜːpəs sɪm ˌbɒlɪk ɪn'strʌkʃən ˌkəʊd/ *noun* langage *m* de haut niveau BASIC

beginning of file /bɪˌɡɪnɪŋ əv 'faɪl/ *noun* début *m* de fichier

beginning of information mark /bɪˌɡɪnɪŋ əv ˌɪnfə'meɪʃ(ə)n ˌmɑːk/ *noun* marque *f* de début d'enregistrement

beginning of tape marker /bɪˌɡɪnɪŋ əv 'teɪp ˌmɑːkə/ *noun* marque *f* de début de bande

bell character /bel 'kærɪktə/, **BEL** *noun* caractère *m* d'alarme

Bell-compatible modem /ˌbel kəm ˌpætɪb(ə)l 'məʊdem/ *noun* (*modem that operates according to standards set by AT&T*) modem *m* compatible Bell

bells and whistles /ˌbelz ənd 'wɪs(ə)lz/ *plural noun* (*advanced features*) choix *m*

benchmark /'bentʃmɑːk/ *noun* **1.** (*important point in an index which can be used for comparison*) référence *f* **2.** (*to test performance*) banc *m* d'essai; essai *m* comparatif; test *m* d'évaluation des performances ◇ **the magazine gave the new program's benchmark test results** la revue a publié les résultats du banc d'essai *or* du test d'évaluation des performances du nouveau programme

benchmarking /'bentʃmɑːkɪŋ/ *noun* évaluation *f* des performances

benchmark problem /ˌbentʃmɑːk 'prɒbləm/ *noun* épreuves *fpl* pour évaluation des performances

BER /ˌbiː iː 'ɑː/ *noun* taux *m* d'erreur de transmission

Berkeley UNIX /ˌbɜːkli 'juːnɪks/ *noun* UNIX BSD

bespoke software /bɪˌspəʊk 'sɒftweə/ *noun* (*software that has been written especially for a customer*) logiciel *m* sur mesure; logiciel *m* adapté aux exigences du client

best fit /best 'fɪt/ *noun* meilleur choix *m*; meilleure affectation *f* en mémoire

beta site /'biːtə saɪt/ *noun* (*company that tests new software before it is released*) site *m* de bêta test; site *m* témoin

beta software /'biːtə ˌsɒf(t)weə/ *noun* (*software that has not finished all its testing*) logiciel *m* en version bêta

beta test /'biːtə ˌtest/ *noun* (*second stage of tests performed on new software*) test *m* bêta ◇ **the application has passed the alpha tests and is just entering the beta test phase** cette application a passé le stade des tests alpha et commence la série de tests bêta

'The client was so eager to get his hands on the product that the managing director bypassed internal testing and decided to let it go straight out to beta test.' [*Computing*]

beta version /'biːtə ˌvɜːʒn/ *noun* (*version of software that is almost ready to be released*) version *f* bêta

betaware /'biːtəweə/ *noun* version *f* bêta

bezel /'bez(ə)l/ *noun* (*front cover of a computer's casing*) façade *f*

Bézier curve /'bezieɪ kɜːv/ *noun* (*geometric curve*) courbe *f* de Bézier

BGP /ˌbiː dʒiː 'piː/ *noun* protocole *m* BGP

biased exponent /ˌbaɪəst ɪk'spəʊnənt/ *noun* exposant *m*

bid /bɪd/ *verb* (*of a computer*) demander la ligne ◇ **the terminal had to bid three times before there was a gap in transmissions on the network** le terminal a dû demander trois fois la ligne avant d'obtenir un créneau sur le réseau

bi-directional bus /ˌbaɪ daɪˌrekʃ(ə)n(ə)l 'bʌs/ *noun* bus *m* bidirectionnel

bi-directional printer /ˌbaɪ daɪˌrekʃ(ə)n(ə)l 'prɪntə/ *noun* imprimante *f* bidirectionnelle

bi-directional transmission /ˌbaɪ daɪ ˌrekʃ(ə)n(ə)l trænz'mɪʃ(ə)n/ *noun* transmission *f* bidirectionnelle

Big Blue /bɪg 'bluː/ *noun informal* la société *f* IBM

bilinear filtering /baɪˌlɪniə 'fɪltərɪŋ/ *noun* filtrage *m* bilinéaire

billion /'bɪljən/ *noun* (*one thousand million or one million million*) million *m* de millions; milliard *m*

BIM /ˌbiː aɪ 'em/ *noun* marque *f* de début d'enregistrement

bin /bɪn/ *noun* (*of printer*) bac *m* à feuilles; bac *m* à papier ◇ **lower bin** bac inférieur ◇ **recycle bin** (*icon in Windows*) corbeille *f* ◇ **upper bin** bac supérieur

binary /'baɪnəri/ *adjective* binaire ■ *noun* bit *m*; chiffre *m* binaire; élément *m* binaire ◇ **binary number** nombre *m* binaire ◇ **binary synchronous communications (BSC)** communication *f* synchrone binaire ◇ **binary tree (btree)** arbre *m* binaire ◇ **in a four bit word, the binary scale is 1,2,4,8** dans un mot à quatre bits, l'échelle binaire est 1,2,4,8 ◇ **the program instructions are stored in the binary file** les instructions du programme sont stockées dans le fichier binaire ◇ **your letter is a text file, not a binary file** votre lettre est un fichier texte et non pas un fichier binaire

binary adder /ˌbaɪnəri 'ædə/ *noun* additionneur *m* binaire

binary arithmetic /ˌbaɪnəri ə'rɪθmətɪk/ *noun* calcul *m* binaire

binary bit /'baɪnəri bɪt/ *noun* élément *m* binaire; bit *m*

binary cell /'baɪnəri sel/ *noun* cellule *f* binaire

binary chop /'baɪnəri tʃɒp/ *noun* recherche *f* (par coupe) binaire; recherche *f* dichotomique; recherche *f* par dichotomie

binary code /'baɪnəri kəʊd/ *noun* code *m* binaire

binary coded characters /ˌbaɪnəri ˌkəʊdɪd 'kærɪktəz/ *plural noun* caractères *mpl* codés binaires

binary coded decimal /ˌbaɪnəri ˌkəʊdɪd 'desɪm(ə)l/ *noun* décimal *m* codé binaire

binary counter /ˌbaɪnəri 'kaʊntə/ *noun* compteur *m* binaire

binary digit /ˌbaɪnəri 'dɪdʒɪt/ *noun* bit *m*; chiffre *m* binaire; élément *m* binaire

binary dump /'baɪnəri dʌmp/ *noun* vidage *m* binaire

binary encoding /ˌbaɪnəri ɪn'kəʊdɪŋ/ *noun* (*representation of characters with bits*) codage *m* binaire

binary exponent /ˌbaɪnəri ɪk'spəʊnənt/ *noun* exposant *m* binaire

binary field /'baɪnəri fiːld/ *noun* champ *m* binaire

binary file /'baɪnəri faɪl/ *noun* fichier *m* binaire ◇ **your letter is a text file, not a binary file** votre lettre est un fichier texte et non pas un fichier binaire

binary fraction /ˌbaɪnəri 'frækʃən/ *noun* fraction *f* binaire ◇ **the binary fraction 0.011 is equal to one quarter plus one eighth (i.e. three eighths)** la fraction binaire 0,011 est égale à un quart plus un huitième (ou trois huitièmes)

binary half adder /ˌbaɪnəri 'hɑːf ˌædə/ *noun* demi-additionneur *m* binaire

binary large object /ˌbaɪnəri lɑːdʒ 'ɒbdʒekt/ *noun* grands objets *mpl* binaires

binary loader /ˌbaɪnəri 'ləʊdə/ *noun* chargeur *m* binaire

binary look-up /'baɪnəri lʊk/ *noun* recherche *f* binaire

binary mantissa /ˌbaɪnəri mæn'tɪsə/ *noun* mantisse *f* binaire

binary notation /ˌbaɪnəri nəʊ'teɪʃ(ə)n/ *noun* numération *f* binaire

binary number /ˌbaɪnəri 'nʌmbə/ *noun* nombre *m* binaire

binary operation /ˌbaɪnəri ˌɒpə'reɪʃ(ə)n/ *noun* opération *f* binaire

binary point /'baɪnəri pɔɪnt/ *noun* virgule *f* binaire

binary representation /ˌbaɪnəri ˌreprɪzen 'teɪʃ(ə)n/ *noun* numération *f* binaire

binary scale /'baɪnəri skeɪl/ *noun* échelle *f* binaire ◇ **in a four bit word, the binary scale is 1,2,4,8** dans un mot à quatre bits, l'échelle binaire est 1,2,4,8

binary search /'baɪnəri sɜːtʃ/ *noun* recherche *f* par coupe binaire; recherche *f* dichotomique; recherche *f* par dichotomie

binary sequence /ˌbaɪnəri 'siːkwəns/ *noun* séquence *f* binaire

binary signalling /ˌbaɪnəri 'sɪgnəlɪŋ/ *noun* transmission *f* de signaux en binaire

binary split /'baɪnəri splɪt/ *noun* séparation *f* binaire

binary synchronous communications /ˌbaɪnəri ˌsɪŋkrənəs kəˌmjuːnɪ'keɪʃ(ə)nz/ *noun* communication *f* synchrone binaire

binary system /'baɪnəri ˌsɪstəm/ *noun* système *m* binaire

binary-to-decimal conversion /ˌbaɪnəri tə, tʊ 'desɪm(ə)l/ *noun* conversion *f* binaire-décimale

binary tree /'baɪnəri triː/ *noun* arbre *m* binaire

binary variable /ˌbaɪnəri 'veəriəb(ə)l/ *noun* variable *f* binaire

binaural sound /baɪn'ɔːrl saʊnd/ *noun* binauralité *f*

bind /baɪnd/ *verb* (*to link*) établir des liens; (*address*) associer *vt*

BIND /ˌbiː aɪ en 'diː/ *noun* BIND

binder /'baɪndə/ *noun* (*of books*) relieur *m or* -euse *f*; (*program that converts object code into a form that can be executed*) éditeur *m* de liens

Bindery /'baɪndəri/ *noun* (*database used in a Novell NetWare network operating system*) fichier *m*; (*special database used in a Novell NetWare network operating system*) atelier *m* de reliure; (*database used in a Novell NetWare network operating system*) bibliothèque *f* de liens

binding offset /ˌbaɪndɪŋ 'ɒfset/ *noun* marge *f* de reliure; marge *f* d'agrafage

binding time /'baɪndɪŋ taɪm/ *noun* temps *m* d'association

BinHex /bɪn'heks/ *noun* BinHex

biochip /'baɪəʊtʃɪp/ *noun* puce *f* à ADN

biocomputer /'baɪəʊkəmˌpjuːtə/ *noun* bio-ordinateur *m*

BIOS /'baɪɒs/ *noun* BIOS *m*

bipolar /baɪ'pəʊlə/ *adjective* bipolaire ◇ **bipolar junction transistor (BJT)** transistor *m* à jonction bipolaire

bipolar coding /ˌbaɪpəʊlə 'kɒdɪŋ/ *noun* codage *m* bipolaire

bipolar signal /ˌbaɪpəʊlə 'sɪgn(ə)l/ *noun* signal *m* bipolaire

bipolar transistor /ˌbaɪpəʊlə træn'zɪstə/ *noun* transistor *m* bipolaire

biquinary code /baɪˌkwɪnəri 'kəʊd/ *noun* code *m* biquinaire

bistable /baɪ'steɪb(ə)l/ *adjective* bistable

bit /bɪt/ *noun* **1.** (*binary digit*) bit *m*; élément *m* binaire; chiffre *m* binaire **2.** (*smallest unit of data*) bit *m* ◇ **bits per inch (bpi)** (nombre de) bits par pouce ◇ **bits per pixel (BPP)** (*number of bits assigned to store the colour of each pixel*) bits par pixel ◇ **bits per second (bps)** (nombre de) bits par seconde (bps) ◇ **least significant bit (LSB)** bit de poids (le plus) faible ◇ **most significant bit (MSB)** bit de poids (le plus) fort *or* bit significatif ◇ **significant bit** bit significatif ◇ **testing bit six of a byte containing an ASCII character is bit significant and determines if the ASCII character is upper or lower case** la recherche du sixième bit d'un octet contenant un caractère ASCII détermine si le bit significatif indique un caractère en majuscule ou en minuscule ◇ **their transmission rate is 60,000 bits per second (bps) through a parallel connection** leur débit est de 60 000 bits par seconde sur une liaison parallèle

bit addressing /bɪt ə'dresɪŋ/ *noun* adressage *m* binaire

bit blit /'bɪt blɪt/ *noun* déplacement *m* de bit

bit block /'bɪt blɒk/ *noun* bloc *m* de bits

bit block transfer /ˌbɪt blɒk 'trænsfɜː/ *noun* transfert *m* de bits par blocs

bit bucket /bɪt 'bʌkɪt/ *noun* panier *m*; poubelle *f* à bits

bit density /bɪt 'densəti/ *noun* densité *f* binaire

bit error rate /ˌbɪt 'erə ˌreɪt/ *noun* taux *m* d'erreur de transmission

bit flipping /bɪt 'flɪpɪŋ/ *noun* inversion *f* binaire

bit handling /bɪt 'hændlɪŋ/ *noun* traitement *m* du bit

bit image /bɪt 'ɪmɪdʒ/ *noun* image *f* binaire

bit interleaving /'bɪt ɪntəˌliːvɪŋ/ *noun* entrelaçage *m* binaire

bit manipulation /bɪt məˌnɪpjʊ'leɪʃ(ə)n/ *noun* manipulation *f* binaire

bitmap /'bɪtmæp/ *noun* **1.** (*of an image*) topogramme *m* binaire **2.** (*of a binary representation*) topogramme *m* binaire **3.** (*file format*) bitmap *m*

> '...microcomputers invariably use raster-scan cathode ray tube displays, and frequently use a bit-map to store graphic images' [*Soft*]

bit-map /bɪt mæp/, **bitmap** /'bɪtmæp/ *verb* exécuter qc en mode points

> '...the expansion cards fit into the PC's expansion slot and convert bit-mapped screen images to video signals' [*Publish*]

bit-mapped font /ˌbɪt mæpt 'fɒnt/ *noun* police *f* de caractères bitmap

bit-mapped graphics /ˌbɪt mæpt 'græfɪks/ *plural noun* infographie *f* à adressage binaire; infographie *f* par points

bit-mapped register /ˌbɪt mæpt 'redʒɪstə/ *noun* registre *m* en mode point

BitNet /'bɪtnet/ *noun* BitNet *m*

bit parallel /bɪt 'pærəlel/ *noun* transmission *f* parallèle bit par bit

bit pattern /bɪt 'pæt(ə)n^{n}/ *noun* arrangement *m* binaire

bit plane /'bɪt pleɪn/ *noun* couche *f* binaire; plan *m* binaire

bit position /bɪt pə'zɪʃ(ə)n/ *noun* position *f* binaire

bit rate /'bɪt reɪt/ *noun* débit *m* binaire

bit rotation /bɪt rəʊ'teɪʃ(ə)n/ *noun* permutation *f* de bits

bit-significant /ˌbɪt sɪg'nɪfɪkənt/ *adjective* à bit significatif

bit-slice architecture /ˌbɪt slaɪs 'ɑːkɪtektʃə/, **bit-slice design** /ˌbɪt slaɪs dɪ'zaɪn/ *noun* architecture *f* en tranches ◇ **the bit slice design uses four 4-bit word processors to construct a 16-bit processor** le processeur en tranches utilise quatre processeurs à 4 bits pour réaliser un processeur à 16 bits

bit-slice microprocessor /ˌbɪt slaɪs 'maɪkrəʊprəʊsesə/, **bit-slice processor** /ˌbɪt slaɪs 'prəʊsesə/ *noun* microprocesseur *m* en tranches

bits per inch /ˌbɪts pɜː 'ɪntʃ/ *noun* bits *mpl* par pouce

bits per pixel /ˌbɪts pɜː 'pɪks(ə)l/ *noun* bits *mpl* par pixel

bits per second /ˌbɪts pɜː 'sekənd/ *noun* bits *mpl* par seconde ◇ **their transmission rate is 60,000 bits per second (bps) through a parallel connection** leur débit est de 60 000 bits par seconde sur une liaison parallèle

bit stream /'bɪt striːm/ *noun* flot *m* de bits; train *m* de bits

bit stuffing /bɪt 'stʌfɪŋ/ *noun* remplissage *m*

bit track /'bɪt træk/ *noun* piste *f* de données binaires

bitwise /'bɪtwaɪz/ *adverb* au niveau binaire

BIX /ˌbiː aɪ 'eks/ *noun* (*commercial online system*) BIX

black and white /ˌblæk ən 'waɪt/ *noun* (*of an image*) noir et blanc; image *f* monochrome

black box /blæk 'bɒks/ *noun* boîte *f* noire

black level /blæk 'lev(ə)l/ *noun* niveau *m* de noir

black matrix /blæk 'meɪtrɪks/ *noun* matrice *f* à fond noir

black writer /blæk 'raɪtə/ *noun* imprimante *f* à définition des noirs

blank cell /blæŋk 'sel/ *noun* cellule *f* vide

blank character /blæŋk 'kærɪktə/ *noun* caractère *m* d'espace

blank disk /blæŋk 'dɪsk/ *noun* disque *m* vierge

blanking /'blæŋkɪŋ/ *noun* (*loss of signal*) suppression *f*; inhibition *f* du signal ◇ **blanking pulse** impulsion *f* d'inhibition du signal ◇ **line blanking interval** délai de retour de ligne

blanking interval /'blæŋkɪŋ ˌɪntəvəl/ *noun* délai *m* de retour de ligne

blank instruction /blæŋk ɪn'strʌkʃən/ *noun* instruction *f* de remplissage

blank string /blæŋk 'strɪŋ/ *noun* chaîne *f* vide

blank tape /blæŋk 'teɪp/ *noun* bande *f* vierge

blast /blɑːst/ *verb* **1.** (*in relation to PROM*) brûler une PROM; programmer une PROM **2.** (*in relation to memory or resources*) libérer une partie de la mémoire; désallouer *vt*

blast-through alphanumerics /ˌblɑːst θruː ˌælfənjuː'merɪks/ *plural noun* (*characters which can be displayed on a videotext terminal when it is in graphics mode*) caractères *mpl* alphanumériques acceptés

bleed /bliːd/ *noun* **1.** (*line that runs off the edge of the paper*) bavure *f* **2.** (*badly adjusted colour monitor*) écran *m* brouillé

blessed folder /ˌblesɪd 'fəʊldə/ *noun* (*the System Folder that contains files loaded when the Macintosh is switched on*) dossier *m* préférentiel

blind /blaɪnd/ *adjective* aveugle

blind carbon copy /ˌblaɪnd ˌkɑːbən 'kɒpɪ/ *noun* transmission *f* confidentielle

blind copy receipt /blaɪnd ˌkɒpɪ rɪ'siːt/ *noun* (*in electronic mail, method of sending a message to several users whose identities are not known*) avis *m* de réception de copie discrète

blind dialling /ˌblaɪnd 'daɪəlɪŋ/ *noun* transmission *f* en aveugle; transmission *f* sans décrochage

blind keyboard /ˌblaɪnd 'kiːbɔːd/ *noun* clavier *m* aveugle

B-line counter /ˌbiː laɪn 'kaʊntə/ *noun* registre *m* auxiliaire de routage d'adresse

blinking /'blɪŋkɪŋ/ *noun* clignotement *m*; papillotement *m*

blit /blɪt/ *verb* (*to move a block of bits from one memory location to another*) effectuer un déplacement de bit en mémoire

blitter /'blɪtə/ *noun* (*component designed to process or move a bit-mapped image*) coprocesseur *m* graphique

bloatware /'bləʊtweə/ *noun* inflagiciel *m*

blob /blɒb/ *noun* grands objets *mpl* binaires

block /blɒk/ *noun* **1.** (*records treated as single unit*) bloc *m* **2.** (*wide printed bar*) bloc *m*

block capitals /ˌblɒk 'kæpɪt(ə)lz/ *plural noun* majuscules *fpl*

block character check /ˌblɒk 'kærɪktə tʃek/ *noun* contrôle *m* de bloc de caractères

block code /blɒk 'kəʊd/ *noun* code *m* de contrôle de bloc

block-copy /ˌblɒk 'kɒpi/ *verb* **1.** (*to copy data in a block*) effectuer une copie de bloc; faire une copie de bloc **2.** (*to copy text in a block*) effectuer une copie de bloc; faire une copie de bloc

block cursor /blɒk 'kɜːsə/ *noun* curseur *m* en pavé

block-delete /ˌblɒk dɪ'liːt/ *verb* effectuer une suppression de bloc

block device /blɒk dɪˈvaɪs/ *noun* manipulateur *m* de bloc

block diagram /blɒk ˈdaɪəˌɡræm/ *noun* (*illustration of how the main components in a system are connected*) bloc-diagramme *m*; schéma *m* fonctionnel

block error rate /blɒk ˈerə reɪt/ *noun* taux *m* d'erreur par bloc

block gap /blɒk ˈɡæp/ *noun* espace *m* interbloc; espace *m* entre blocs

block header /blɒk ˈhedə/ *noun* en-tête *m* de bloc

block ignore character /ˌblɒk ɪɡˈnɔː ˌkærɪktə/ *noun* caractère *m* de rejet de bloc

blocking factor /blɒkɪŋ ˈfæktə/ *noun* (*records in a block*) facteur *m* de bloc

block input processing /ˌblɒk ˈɪnpʊt ˌprəʊsesɪŋ/ *noun* traitement *m* de contrôle de bloc à l'entrée

block length /blɒk ˈleŋθ/ *noun* (*data*) longueur *f*

block letters /ˌblɒk ˈletəz/ *plural noun* majuscules *fpl*

block list /ˈblɒk lɪst/ *noun* fichier *m* d'enregistrement des blocs

block mark /ˈblɒk mɑːk/ *noun* marque *f* de sélection d'un bloc

block marker /ˈblɒk ˌmɑːkə/ *plural noun* marqueur *m* de bloc

block move /ˈblɒk muːv/ *noun* déplacement *m* de bloc

block operation /blɒk ˌɒpəˈreɪʃ(ə)n/ *noun* manipulation *f* de blocs

block parity /blɒk ˈpærəti/ *noun* parité *f* d'un bloc

block protection /blɒk prəˈtekʃən/ *noun* protection *f* de bloc

block retrieval /blɒk rɪˈtriːv(ə)l/ *noun* recherche *f*

block synchronisation /ˌblɒk ˌsɪŋkrənaɪ ˈzeɪʃ(ə)n/ *noun* synchronisation *f* de blocs

block transfer /blɒk ˈtrænsfɜː/ *noun* (*data transfer*) transfert *m* d'un bloc; transfert *m* d'un paragraphe

blog /blɒɡ/ *verb* effectuer un blogue ■ *noun* blogue *m*

blogger /ˈblɒɡə/ *noun* blogueur *m*

blogging *noun* blogage *m*

> 'Over the past year, blogging has grown, in both importance and size. The original hardcore blogging community is still there, and still vociferous. But every month, thousands of others are trying their hand at this unique publishing form.' [*The Guardian*]

blogosphere /ˈblɒɡəˌsfɪə/ *noun informal* blogosphère *f*

bloop /bluːp/ *verb* démagnétiser *vt*

blow /bləʊ/ *verb* (*burn*) programmer une PROM

Blue Book Ethernet /ˌbluː bʊk ˈiːθənet/ *noun* Blue Book Ethernet

blueprint /ˈbluːˌprɪnt/ *noun* (*set of specifications or design*) spécifications *f*; plan *m*; épure *f*

blue-ribbon program /ˌbluː ˈrɪbən ˌprəʊɡræm/ *noun informal* programme *m* canon

Bluetooth /ˈbluːtuːθ/ (*trade name for a short-range radio communications system*) Bluetooth

blur /blɜː/ *noun* flou *m* ■ *verb* rendre flou ◇ **the image becomes blurred when you turn the focus knob** en tournant le bouton de mise au point l'image devient floue *or* perd de sa netteté

BMP /ˌbiː em ˈpiː/ *noun* (*extension to a filename that indicates that the file contains a bit-mapped image*) extension *f* BMP ◇ **this paint package lets you import BMP files** ce logiciel de peinture permet l'importation de fichiers BMP

bn *abbr* (*billion*) milliard *m*

BNC connector /ˌbiː en ˈsiː kəˌnektə/ *noun* (*cylindrical metal connector with a copper core*) connecteur *m* BNC coaxial

BNC T-piece connector /ˌbiː en ˌsiː ˈtiː piːs kəˌnektə/ *noun* (*T-shaped metal connector*) connecteur *m* en T BNC

BNF /ˌbiː en ˈef/ *noun* forme *f* de Backus-Naur

board /bɔːd/ *noun* (*for printed circuit*) carte *f*; plaque *f* (présensibilisée) pour circuit imprimé ◇ **bulletin board system (BBS)** tableau *m* d'affichage électronique *or* babillard *m* électronique *or* BBS ◇ **printed circuit board (PCB)** (carte de) circuit *m* imprimé

body /ˈbɒdi/ *noun* **1.** (*main section of text or program*) corps *m* d'un texte **2.** (*main section of text or program*) corps *m* d'un programme ◇ **body size** dimension *f* (en points) du corps d'un texte; corps (d'un caractère)

body type /ˈbɒdi taɪp/ *noun* police *f* de caractères par défaut utilisée pour le corps d'un texte

boilerplate /ˈbɔɪləpleɪt/ *noun* document *m* monté; document *m* créé à partir de paragraphes standard

boilerplating /ˈbɔɪləpleɪtɪŋ/ *noun* montage *m* d'un document à partir de paragraphes standard

bold face /ˈbəʊld feɪs/ *noun* caractères *mpl* gras

bomb /bɒm/ *noun* (*routine designed to crash the system*) bombe *f* ■ *verb informal* (*to fail*) sauter *vi*; se planter *vr* ◇ **the program bombed, and we lost all the data** le programme s'est planté et nous avons perdu toutes les données ◇ **the system can bomb if you set up several desk accessories or memory-resident programs at the same time** le système peut se planter si vous installez en même temps plusieurs accessoires de bureau ou programmes résidents

book /bʊk/ *noun* livre *m* ◇ **the book is available in paperback and hard cover** ce livre existe en édition brochée et en édition cartonnée ◇ **they**

can print books of up to 96 pages ils peuvent imprimer des livres qui ont jusqu'à 96 pages

bookmark /'bʊkmɑːk/ *noun* (*coding*) marque *f* qui permet de retrouver facilement une partie du programme; signet *m*

Boolean algebra /ˌbuːliən 'ældʒɪbrə/ *noun* algèbre *f* booléenne; algèbre *f* de Boole

Boolean connective /ˌbuːliən kə'nektɪv/ *noun* relation *f* booléenne

Boolean data type /ˌbuːliən 'deɪtə ˌtaɪp/ *noun* variable *f* booléenne

Boolean logic /ˌbuːliən 'lɒdʒɪk/ *noun* algèbre *f* booléen; algèbre *f* de Boole

Boolean operation /ˌbuːliən ˌɒpə'reɪʃ(ə)n/ *noun* opération *f* booléenne

Boolean operation table /ˌbuːliən ˌɒpə'reɪʃ(ə)n ˌteɪb(ə)l/ *noun* table *f* de Boole; table *f* de vérité

Boolean operator /ˌbuːliən 'ɒpəreɪtə/ *noun* opérateur *m* booléen

Boolean search /ˌbuːliən 'sɜːtʃ/ *noun* recherche *f* booléenne

Boolean value /ˌbuːliən 'væljuː/ *noun* valeur *f* booléenne

Boolean variable /ˌbuːliən 'veəriəb(ə)l/ *noun* variable *f* booléenne

boot /buːt/ *verb* lancer un système; amorcer un système ◇ **after you switch on the computer, insert the boot disk** après avoir mis l'ordinateur en route, insérez la disquette de lancement *or* d'amorçage

bootable /'buːtəb(ə)l/ *adjective* de démarrage

boot block /'buːt blɒk/ *noun* bloc *m*

boot disk /'buːt dɪsk/ *noun* disque *m* d'amorçage; disque *m* de lancement; disquette *f* d'amorçage ◇ **after you switch on the computer, insert the boot disk** après avoir mis l'ordinateur en route, insérez la disquette de lancement *or* d'amorçage

booting /'buːtɪŋ/ *noun* lancement *m*; amorçage *m*

bootleg /'buːtˌleg/ *noun* copie *f* illégale; copie *f* piratée

boot partition /buːt pɑː'tɪʃ(ə)n/ *noun* partition *f*

boot record /'buːt ˌrekɔːd/ *noun* bloc *m*

boot sector /buːt 'sektə/ *noun* partition *f*

bootstrap, bootstrap loader *noun* amorce *f*

bootstrap memory /'buːtstræp ˌmem(ə)ri/ *noun* mémoire *f* de lancement

boot up /buːt 'ʌp/ *noun* (*booting – of system*) lancement *m*; amorçage *m*

border /'bɔːdə/ *noun* **1.** (*area around printed or displayed text*) bordure *f*; cadre *m* **2.** (*line*) bordure *f*; cadre *m*; encadrement *m*

borrow /'bɒrəʊ/ *noun* retenue *f*

Bose-Chandhuri-Hocquenghem code *noun* code *m* BCH

bot¹ /bɒt/, **BOT** *abbr* (*beginning of tape*) marque *f* de début de bande

bot² /bɒt/ *noun* robot *m* logiciel

BOT marker /'bɒt ˌmɑːkə/ *noun* marque *f* de début de bande

bottom up method /ˌbɒtəm ʌp 'meθəd/, **bottom up programming** /'prəʊgræmɪŋ/ *noun* conception *f* ascendante d'un programme

bounce /baʊns/ *noun* **1.** (*of key*) rebond *m* d'une touche de clavier **2.** (*of an email*) message *m* retourné

boundary /'baʊnd(ə)ri/ *noun* limite *f*

boundary protection /ˌbaʊnd(ə)ri prə'tekʃən/ *noun* protection *f* des limites

boundary punctuation /ˌbaʊnd(ə)ri ˌpʌŋktʃu'eɪʃ(ə)n/ *noun* marquage *m* de limites d'un fichier

boundary register /ˌbaʊnd(ə)ri 'redʒɪstə/ *noun* registre *m* d'adresses de limites

bounding box /'baʊndɪŋ bɒks/ *noun* (*rectangle that determines the shape and position of an image*) cadre *m*

Boyce-Codd normal form /ˌbɔɪs kɒd 'nɔːməl ˌfɔːm/ *noun* format *m* normal Boyce-Codd; format *m* BCNF

bozo bit /'bəʊzəʊ bɪt/ *noun* (*in an Apple Macintosh system*) bit *m* de protection; bozo *m*

BPI, bpi *noun* bits *mpl* par pouce

BPP /ˌbiː piː 'piː/ *noun* bits *mpl* par pixel

bps /ˌbiː piː 'es/ *noun* bits *mpl* par seconde

Bps /ˌbiː piː 'es/ *noun* octets *mpl* par seconde

bps rate /ˌbiː piː 'es reɪt/ *noun* bits *mpl* par seconde; bps par seconde

bps rate adjust /ˌbiː piː ˌes reɪt ə'dʒʌst/ *noun* débit *m* corrigé en bps

BRA /ˌbiː ɑː 'eɪ/ *noun* débit *m* de base (d'un RNIS)

braces /'breɪsɪz/ *plural noun* (*curly bracket characters { }*) accolades *fpl*

bracket /'brækɪt/ *noun* accolade *f*

branch /brɑːntʃ/ *noun* **1.** (*path or jump from one instruction to another*) branche *f*; branchement *m* **2.** (*link to network*) branchement *m* ■ *verb* (*to jump section in program*) brancher *vt* ◇ **the faulty station is on this branch** le poste défectueux est connecté sur ce branchement

branch cable /brɑːntʃ 'keɪb(ə)l/ *noun* câble *m* de dérivation

branch instruction /brɑːntʃ ɪn'strʌkʃən/ *noun* instruction *f* de branchement; instruction *f* de saut

branchpoint /'brɑːntʃpɔɪnt/ *noun* point *m* de branchement

branch table /'brɑːntʃ ˌteɪb(ə)l/ *noun* table *f* de branchements

breach /briːtʃ/ *noun* rupture *f*

breadboard /'bredbɔːd/ *noun* (*device that allows prototype electronic circuits to be constructed easily*) carte *f* de montage sans soudure

break /breɪk/ *noun* (*of program execution*) interruption *f* ◇ **I stopped the problem by pressing Ctrl-Break** j'ai résolu le problème en appuyant sur les touches CTRL et Interruption

Break key /'breɪk kiː/ *noun* touche *f* d'interruption

breakout box /'breɪkaʊt bɒks/ *noun* (*device that displays the status of lines within an interface*) contrôleur *m* d'interface

breakpoint /'breɪkpɔɪnt/ *noun* (*control point*) point *m* d'arrêt; point *m* d'interruption ◇ **to set breakpoints** programmer les points d'arrêt

breakpoint halt /'breɪkpɔɪnt ˌhɔːlt/ *noun* instruction *f* d'arrêt

breakpoint instruction /'breɪkpɔɪnt ɪn ˌstrʌkʃən/ *noun* instruction *f* d'arrêt

breakpoint symbol /'breɪkpɔɪnt ˌsɪmb(ə)l/ *noun* symbole *m* d'arrêt

breakup /'breɪkʌp/ *noun* (*usually in video*) coupure *f*; perte *f*; distorsion *f* d'un signal

B register /biː 'redʒɪstə/ *noun* registre *m* d'adresse indexé

bricks-and-mortar /ˌbrɪks ən 'mɔːtə/ *adjective* clic et mortier

bridge /brɪdʒ/ *verb* (*transfer programs*) établir un pont; établir une transition ■ *noun* **1.** (*communications equipment between two networks*) gestionnaire *m* de transition; pont *m* **2.** (*matching computer equipment to prevent power problems*) pont *m* **3.** (*hardware or software allowing old system to be used on new system*) interface *f* de transition; logiciel *m* de transition; pont *m*

> 'Lotus Development and IMRS are jointly developing a bridge linking their respective spreadsheet and client server reporting tools. It will allow users of IMRS' Hyperion reporting tool to manipulate live data from Lotus Improv.' [*Computing*]

bridgeware /'brɪdʒweə/ *noun* (*hardware or software used to facilitate the transfer between computers*) pont *m*; équipement *m* de transition; logiciel *m* de transition

bridging /'brɪdʒɪŋ/ *noun* (*communications equipment*) mise en place d'une dérivation; transfert *m* de programme avec l'aide d'un pont

bridging product /'brɪdʒɪŋ ˌprɒdʌkt/ *noun* pont *m*

Briefcase utility /'briːfkeɪs juːˌtɪlɪti/ *noun* (*Windows utility*) Porte-documents *m*

brightness /'braɪtnəs/ *noun* luminosité *f*; brillance *f* ◇ **a control knob allows you to adjust brightness and contrast** un bouton vous permet de régler la luminosité et les contrastes

brightness range /'braɪtnəs reɪndʒ/ *noun* niveaux *mpl* de luminosité

brilliant /'brɪljənt/ *adjective* brillant *or* -e ◇ **he used brillant white for the highlights** il utilise un blanc brillant pour les mises en valeur ◇ **the background colour is a brilliant red** le fond est d'un rouge brillant

bring up /ˌbrɪŋ 'ʌp/ *verb* (*start a computer system*) mettre en marche; faire monter

British Standards Institute /ˌbrɪtɪʃ 'stændədz ˌɪnstɪtjuːt/ *noun* (*British equivalent of*) association *f* française de normalisation (AFNOR)

broadband /'brɔːdbænd/ *noun* (*wideband – transmission method that combines several channels of data onto a carrier signal*) large bande ◇ **broadband radio** radio à large bande

broadband ISDN /ˌbrɔːdbænd ˌaɪ es diː 'en/ *noun* réseau *m* numérique à intégration de services à large bande

broadcast /'brɔːdkɑːst/ *noun* (*data transmission to many receivers*) diffusion *f* ■ *verb* radiodiffuser *vt* ◇ **broadcasting station** station *f* de radiodiffusion *or* de télédiffusion ◇ **he broadcast the latest news over the radio** *or* **over the WAN** il a diffusé les dernières informations à la radio *or* via le réseau étendu

broadcast message /ˌbrɔːdkɑːst 'mesɪdʒ/ *noun* message *m* diffusé

broadcast network /ˌbrɔːdkɑːst 'netwɜːk/ *noun* réseau *m* de diffusion

broadcast quality /ˌbrɔːdkɑːst 'kwɒlɪti/ *noun* qualité *f* de transmission; qualité *f* broadcast

brouter /'bruːtə/ *noun* (*device that combines the functions of a router and bridge*) pont *m* de routage ◇ **the brouter provides dynamic routing and can bridge two local area networks** le pont de routage permet un routage dynamique entre deux réseaux locaux

brown-out /'braʊn aʊt/ *noun* (*electricity*) baisse *f*; chute *f* de tension

browse /braʊz/ *verb* **1.** (*to view data on online system*) visionner *vt* **2.** (*to search database material without permission*) consulter une base de données sans autorisation; piller une base de données

browser /'braʊzə/ *noun* (*software program that is used to navigate through WWW pages*) navigateur *m*; logiciel *m* de navigation ◇ **browser window** fenêtre *f* du navigateur

browsing /'braʊzɪŋ/ *noun* navigation *f*

brush /brʌʃ/ *noun* (*tool in paint package software that draws pixels on screen*) pinceau *m*; brosse *f* ◇ **the paint package lets you vary the width of the brush (in pixels) and the colour it produces** le logiciel de dessin vous permet de changer la largeur du pinceau (en pixels) et la couleur qu'il applique

brush style /'brʌʃ staɪl/ *noun* (*width and shape of brush tool*) type *m* de pinceau ◇ **to fill in a big area, I select a wide, square brush style**

pour couvrir une grande surface, j'utilise un pinceau large et à bout carré

brute force method /ˌbruːt fɔːs 'meθəd/ *noun* méthode *f* brutale

BS *abbr* (*backspace*) (*backspace*) caractère *m* retour arrière

BSAM *abbr* (*basic sequential access method*) méthode *f* d'accès séquentiel de base

BSC /ˌbiː es 'siː/ *noun* communication *f* synchrone binaire

BSI /ˌbiː es 'aɪ/ *abbr* (*British Standards Institute*) Association *f* française de normalisation (AFNOR)

BTAM /ˌbiː tiː eɪ 'em/ *noun* protocole *m* d'accès de télécommunications

btree /'biː triː/ *noun* arbre *m* binaire

bubble-help /'bʌb(ə)l help/ *noun* (*single line that appears on screen to describe what you are pointing at*) bulle *f*; légende *f*

bubble jet printer /ˌbʌb(ə)l dʒet 'prɪntə/ *noun* imprimante *f* à bulle d'encre

bubble memory /ˌbʌb(ə)l 'mem(ə)ri/ *noun* (*method of storing binary data*) mémoire *f* à bulles magnétiques

bubble memory cassette /ˌbʌb(ə)l 'mem(ə)ri kəˌset/ *noun* cassette *f* mémoire à bulles magnétiques

bubble sort /'bʌb(ə)l sɔːt/ *noun* (*sorting method*) tri *m* par permutation de bulles; tri *m* de paires

bucket /'bʌkɪt/ *noun* emplacement *m* de rangement

buffer /'bʌfə/ *noun* **1.** (*circuit*) circuit *m* tampon **2.** (*temporary storage area for data*) mémoire *f* tampon ■ *verb* (*to use temporary memory*) utiliser une mémoire tampon

buffered input/output /ˌbʌfəd ˌɪnpʊt 'aʊtpʊt/ *noun* entrée/sortie *f* utilisant une mémoire tampon

buffered memory /ˌbʌfəd 'mem(ə)ri/ *noun* mémoire *f* avec tampon

buffering /'bʌfərɪŋ/ *noun* utilisation *f* de mémoire tampon; rangement *m* en mémoire tampon

buffer length /'bʌfə leŋθ/ *noun* taille *f* de la mémoire tampon

buffer register /ˌbʌfə 'redʒɪstə/ *noun* registre *m* tampon

buffer size /'bʌfə saɪz/ *noun* taille *f* de mémoire tampon

bug /bʌg/ *noun* (*in software*) bogue *m&f*; bug *m*

buggy /'bʌgi/ *noun* (*small computer-controlled vehicle*) chariot *m* piloté par ordinateur

bug patch /'bʌg pætʃ/ *noun* **1.** (*temporary correction to program*) rustine *f*; replâtrage *m* **2.** (*correction to software*) rustine *f*; replâtrage *m*

build /bɪld/ *noun* (*particular version of a program*) mouture *f*; version *f* ◇ **this is the latest build of the new software** c'est la dernière mouture du nouveau logiciel

building block /'bɪldɪŋ blɒk/ *noun* (*self-contained unit to form a system*) élément *m*; module *m*

built-in /ˌbɪlt 'ɪn/ *adjective* intégré *or* -ée; incorporé *or* -ée ◇ **the built-in adapter card makes it fully IBM compatible** la carte adaptateur intégrée rend l'appareil compatible IBM ◇ **the computer has a built-in hard disk** l'ordinateur est équipé d'un disque dur intégré

built-in check /ˌbɪlt ɪn 'tʃek/ *noun* système *m* de contrôle intégré

built-in font /ˌbɪlt ɪn 'fɒnt/ *noun* police *f* de caractères intégrée

built-in function /ˌbɪlt ɪn 'fʌŋkʃ(ə)n/ *noun* fonction *f* incorporée

built-in message /ˌbɪlt ɪn 'mesɪdʒ/ *noun* message *m* intégré

bulk erase /bʌlk ɪ'reɪz/ *verb* effacer en masse

bulk storage medium /ˌbʌlk 'stɔːrɪdʒ ˌmiːdiəm/ *noun* support *m* de mémoire de masse; support *m* de stockage de grande capacité

bulk update terminal /ˌbʌlk 'ʌpdeɪt ˌtɜːmɪn(ə)l/ *noun* terminal *m* de mise à jour rapide

bullet /'bʊlɪt/ *noun* (*of colour print*) vignette *f*; point *m* indicateur de couleur; (*filled circle or square in front of a line of text*) marqueur *m* d'énumération

> 'For a bullet chart use four to six bullet points and no more than six to eight words each' [*Computing*]

bulleted *adjective* avec un marqueur d'énumération

bulletin board /'bʊlɪtɪn bɔːd/, **bulletin board system** /ˌbʊltɪn bɔːd 'sɪstəm/ *noun* messagerie *f*

bundle /'bʌnd(ə)l/ *noun* **1.** (*of optic fibres*) faisceau *m* de fibres optiques **2.** (*package containing a computer with software or accessories*) offre *f* groupée; offre *f* promotionnelle ■ *verb* (*market a computer together with a range of software at a special price*) faire une offre groupée; offrir des logiciels dans le prix d'achat d'un ordinateur

bundled software /ˌbʌnd(ə)ld 'sɒftweə/ *noun* logiciel *m* inclus à l'achat d'un ordinateur

bureau /'bjʊərəʊ/ *noun* bureau *m*; société *f* de services ◇ **our data manipulation is handled by a bureau** nous faisons faire la manipulation de données par une société de services informatiques ◇ **the company offers a number of bureau services, such as printing and data collection** la société offre, entre autres, des services d'imprimerie et de saisie de données ◇ **we farm out the office typing to a local bureau** nous confions notre correspondance à un bureau de secrétariat local

> 'IMC has a colour output bureau that puts images onto the uncommon CD-ROM XA format.' [*Computing*]

burn /bɜːn/ *verb* **1.** programmer une PROM **2.** graver *vt*

burner /'bɜːnə/ *noun* programmateur *m* de mémoire morte; programmateur *m* de ROM

burn in /bɜːn 'ɪn/ *verb* **1.** (*for electronic components*) tester à chaud; (*television or monitor screen*) faire un brûlage d'écran **2.** (*PROM chip*) graver *vt*

burn-in /'bɜːn ɪn/ *noun* (*for electronic components*) déverminage *m*; test *m* à chaud

burn out /ˌbɜːn 'aʊt/ *noun* (*electronic circuit or device*) panne *f* par échauffement

burst /bɜːst/ *noun* (*of signals*) rafale *f* ◇ **colour burst** (*TV*) rafale de signaux couleur

burster /'bɜːstə/ *noun* (*for paper*) rupteur *m*; séparateur *m*; éclateur *m* de feuilles

burst mode /'bɜːst məʊd/ *noun* mode *m* rafale

bursty /'bɜːsti/ *adjective* en paquets

bus /bʌs/ *noun* **1.** (*communication link*) bus *m* **2.** (*central information source*) carte *f* connecteur; bus *m* central ◇ **Ethernet is a network that uses the bus topology; token ring uses a ring topology** Ethernet est un réseau qui utilise une topologie en bus ◇ **input *or* output data bus (I *or* O bus)** bus d'entrée/sortie

bus address lines /ˌbʌs ə'dres ˌlaɪnz/ *plural noun* voie *f* de liaison d'un bus d'adresses

bus arbitration /bʌs ˌɑːbɪ'treɪʃ(ə)n/ *noun* arbitrage *m* bus; gestion *f* bus

> 'The slot controller detects when a new board is inserted, it activates power up and assigns a bus arbitration and card slot ID to the board.' [*Computing*]

bus bar /'bʌs bɑː/ *noun* barre *f* omnibus

bus board /'bʌs bɔːd/ *noun* (*PCB containing conducting paths*) carte *f* bus

bus clock /'bʌs klɒk/ *noun* horloge *f* du bus

bus clock speed /ˌbʌs klɒk 'spiːd/ *noun* fréquence *f* d'horloge du bus

bus control lines /ˌbʌs kən'trəʊl ˌlaɪnz/ *plural noun* lignes *fpl* de contrôle

bus data lines /ˌbʌs 'deɪtə ˌlaɪnz/ *plural noun* lignes de transmission de données ◇ **Ethernet is a network that uses the bus topology; token ring uses a ring topology** Ethernet est un réseau qui utilise une topologie en bus

bus driver /bʌs 'draɪvə/ *noun* circuit *m* de commande du bus

bus extender /ˌbʌs iks'tendə/, **bus extension card** /bʌs ɪk'stenʃən kɑːd/ *noun* carte *f* d'extension de bus

business computer /'bɪznɪs kəmˌpjuːtə/ *noun* (*computer for business tasks*) ordinateur *m* de bureau

business package /'bɪznɪs ˌpækɪdʒ/ *noun* logiciel *m* de comptabilité-gestion; logiciel *m* de bureautique

business system /'bɪznɪs ˌsɪstəm/ *noun* logiciel *m* de comptabilité-gestion; logiciel *m* de bureautique

bus master /bʌs 'mɑːstə/ *noun* maître *m* d'un bus ◇ **the bus master network adapter provides much faster data throughput than the old adapter** l'adaptateur maître du bus du réseau a un débit de transfert beaucoup plus élevé que l'ancien

bus master adapter /ˌbʌs ˌmɑːstə ə'dæptə/ *noun* adaptateur *m* maître

bus network /bʌs 'netwɜːk/ *noun* réseau *m* de type bus

bus slave /'bʌs sleɪv/ *noun* asservi à un bus; esclave *m* d'un bus

bus structure /bʌs 'strʌktʃə/ *noun* structure *f* d'un bus

bus topology /ˌbʌs tə'pɒlədʒi/ *noun* topologie *f* en bus ◇ **Ethernet is a network that uses the bus topology** Ethernet est un réseau qui utilise une architecture en bus

busy /'bɪzi/ *adjective* (*machine*) en service

button /'bʌt(ə)n/ *noun* **1.** (*switch that carries out an action*) bouton *m* **2.** (*square shape that can be selected by a pointer*) bouton *m*; pavé *m* ◇ **there are two buttons at the bottom of the status line, select the left button to cancel the operation or the right to continue** il y a deux boutons au bas de la ligne d'état, sélectionnez le bouton de gauche pour annuler l'opération et le bouton de droite pour continuer ◇ **use the mouse to move the cursor to the icon and start the application by pressing the mouse button** utilisez la souris pour placer le curseur sur l'icône et démarrez l'application en appuyant sur le bouton de la souris

button bar /'bʌt(ə)n bɑː/ *noun* barre *f* d'outils

bypass /'baɪˌpɑːs/ *noun* (*alternative route*) dérivation *f* ◇ **there is an automatic bypass around any faulty equipment** il y a dérivation automatique lorsqu'une des machines tombe en panne

byte /baɪt/ *noun* octet *m* ◇ **bytes per second (Bps)** octets par seconde

byte address /'baɪt əˌdres/ *plural noun* adresse *f* d'octets

bytecode /'baɪtkəʊd/ *noun* pseudo-code *m* binaire

byte machine /baɪt mə'ʃiːn/ *noun* processeur *m* à mots variables

byte manipulation /baɪt məˌnɪpjʊ'leɪʃ(ə)n/ *noun* manipulation *f* d'octets

byte mode /'baɪt məʊd/ *noun* mode *m* octet

byte-orientated protocol /ˌbaɪt ˌɔːriənteɪtɪd 'prəʊtəkɒl/ *noun* protocole *m* à niveau octet; protocole *m* caractère par caractère

byte serial transmission /ˌbaɪt ˌsɪəriəl trænz'mɪʃ(ə)n/ *noun* transmission *f* d'octets en série

bytes-per-inch /baɪtz pə/ *noun* octets *mpl* par pouce

bytes per second /ˌbaɪts pɜː ˈsekənd/ *noun* octet *m* par seconde

C

C *noun* (*high level programming language providing object oriented programming functions*) langage *m* C

C++ /ˌsiː plʌs ˈplʌs/ *noun* langage *m* de programmation orienté objets C++

CA *abbr* (*certificate authority*) autorité *f* de certification

cable /ˈkeɪb(ə)l/ *noun* câble *m* ◇ **audio cable** câble audio ◇ **cable télévision** *or* **cable TV** télévision câblée *or* le câble ◇ **video cable** câble vidéo

cable connector /ˌkeɪb(ə)l kəˈnektə/ *noun* connecteur *m* de câble

cable matcher /ˈkeɪb(ə)l ˌmætʃə/ *noun* accordeur *m* d'impédance

cable modem /ˌkeɪb(ə)l ˈməʊdem/ *noun* modem *m* câble

cable plant /ˈkeɪb(ə)l plɑːnt/ *noun* câblage *m*

cable tester /ˌkeɪb(ə)l ˈtestə/ *noun* testeur *m* de câble

cabling /ˈkeɪblɪŋ/ *noun* (*cable as a material*) câblage *m*; câbles *mpl*; réseau *m* câblé ◇ **using high-quality cabling will allow the user to achieve very high data transfer rates** les câbles de haute qualité vont permettre à l'utilisateur d'obtenir un taux de transfert de données très élevé

'It has won a £500,000 contract to supply a structured voice and data cabling system to the bank and its stockbrocking subsidiary.' [*Computing*]

cabling diagram /ˈkeɪb(ə)lɪŋ ˌdaɪəgræm/ *noun* schéma *m* de câblage; schéma *m* de circuit câblé

cache /kæʃ/ *noun* (*section of memory*) antémémoire *m*; cache *f*; mémoire *f* cache ■ *verb* stocker en mémoire cache; utiliser un cache

cache controller /kæʃ kənˈtrəʊlə/ *noun* contrôleur *m* de cache

cache hit /ˈkæʃ hɪt/ *noun* données *fpl* extraites directement de la mémoire cache

cache memory /ˈkæʃ ˌmem(ə)ri/ *noun* (*cache*) mémoire *f* cache; cache *m*

CAD /kæd/ *noun* conception *f* assistée par ordinateur; CAO *f* ◇ **all our engineers design on CAD workstations** tous nos ingénieurs travaillent sur des stations de CAO

'John Smith of CAD supplier CAD/CAM Limited has moved into sales with responsibilities for the North of England. He was previously a technical support specialist.' [*Computing*]

caddy /ˈkædi/ *noun* boîtier *m*

CAE /ˌsiː eɪ ˈiː/ *noun* ingénierie *f* assistée par ordinateur

CAI /ˌsiː eɪ ˈaɪ/ *noun* enseignement *m* assisté par ordinateur

CAL /ˌsiː eɪ ˈel/ *noun* formation *f* assistée par ordinateur

calculated field /ˈkælkjʊˌleɪtɪd fiːlⁿd/ *noun* (*field that contains the results of calculations*) champ *m* calculé

Calculator /ˈkælkjʊˌleɪtə/ (*software utility that is part of Microsoft Windows*) calculatrice *f* ◇ **he worked out the discount on his calculator** il a calculé la remise sur sa calculatrice ◇ **my pocket calculator needs a new battery** j'ai besoin d'une pile pour ma calculatrice de poche

calendar program /ˌkælɪndə ˈprəʊgræm/ *noun* (*software diary utility*) logiciel *m* de calendrier

calibrate /ˈkælɪbreɪt/ *verb* (*to adjust a monitor or joystick so that it is responding correctly*) mettre au point; régler *vt*

calibration /ˌkæləˈbreɪʃ(ə)n/ *noun* mise *f* au point; réglage *m* précis

call /kɔːl/ *verb* **1.** (*to transfer control to a separate program or routine from a main program*) appeler un programme **2.** (*computer*) appeler un programme

call accepted signal /kɔːl əkˈseptɪd/, **call accept signal** /kɔːl əkˈsept/ *noun* signal *m* d'acceptation d'appel; signal *m* d'appel accepté

callback /ˈkɔːlbæk/ *noun* (*security system*) rappel *m*

call back modem /ˈkɔːl bæk ˌməʊdem/ *noun* modem *m* avec fonction rappel

call control signal /ˈkɔːl kənˌtrəʊl ˌsɪgn(ə)l/ *noun* signal *m* de contrôle d'appel

call discrimination /kɔːl dɪˌskrɪmɪˈneɪʃ(ə)n/ *noun* discrimination *f* d'appels

call duration /kɔːl djʊˈreɪʃ(ə)n/ *noun* durée *f* d'un appel

called party /kɔːld ˈpɑːti/ *noun* correspondant *m or* -e *f*

caller /ˈkɔːlə/ *noun* personne *f* qui fait un appel téléphonique; personne *f* qui demande une communication

calling /'kɔːlɪŋ/ *noun* (*signal to request attention, sent from a terminal or device to the main computer*) signal *m* d'appel

calling sequence /ˌkɔːlɪŋ 'siːkwəns/ *noun* séquence *f* d'appel

call instruction /kɔːl ɪn'strʌkʃən/ *noun* instruction *f* d'appel

call logger /kɔːl 'lɒgə/ *noun* enregistreur *m* d'appels

call scheduling /'kɔːl ˌʃedjuːlɪŋ/ *noun* programmation *f* d'appels

call up /ˌkɔːl 'ʌp/ *verb* (*to ask for information from a backing store to be displayed*) appeler *vt*; rappeler *vt*; afficher à l'écran ◇ **after an input is received, the first function is called up** dès réception d'une entrée, on appelle la première fonction ◇ **all the customers addresses were called up** on a affiché à l'écran les adresses des clients ◇ **call up the previous file** rappelez le fichier précédent à l'écran

CAM /ˌsiː eɪ 'em/ *noun* fabrication *f* assistée par ordinateur ■ *abbr* (*content addressable memory*) fabrication *f* assistée par ordinateur

Cambridge ring /ˌkeɪmbridʒ 'rɪŋ/ *noun* anneau *m* de Cambridge

campus environment /ˌkæmpəs ɪn 'vaɪrənmənt/ *noun* environnement *m* universitaire

campus network /ˌkæmpəs 'netwɜːk/ *noun* réseau *m* universitaire

cancel /'kænsəl/ *verb* annuler *vt* ◇ **cancel character (CAN)** caractère *m* d'annulation

cancelbot /'kæns(ə)lbɒt/ *noun* robot *m* d'annulation de message

cancel character /ˌkæns(ə)l 'kærɪktə/ *noun* caractère *m* d'annulation ◇ **the software automatically sends a cancel character after any error** le logiciel émet automatiquement un caractère d'annulation suite à une erreur

cancellation /ˌkænsə'leɪʃ(ə)n/ *noun* annulation *f*

canonical schema /kəˌnɒnɪkl 'skiːmə/ *noun* schéma *m* canonique; schéma *m* de base de données standard

capability list /ˌkeɪpə'bɪləti lɪst/ *noun* liste *f* des fonctions; liste *f* des possibilités

capacitance /kæ'pæsɪtəns/ *noun* capacitance *f*

capacitative /kə'pæsɪtətɪv/, **capacititive** *adjective* capacitatif *or* -ive

capacitor /kə'pæsɪtə/ *noun* condensateur *m*; capacité *f* ◇ **capacitor microphone** microphone *m* à condensateur ◇ **ceramic capacitor** condensateur céramique ◇ **electrolytic capacitor** condensateur électrolytique ◇ **non-electrolytic capacitor** condensateur non électrolytique ◇ **variable capacitor** condensateur variable *or* capacité variable

capacitor storage /kəˌpæsɪtə 'stɔːrɪdʒ/ *noun* mémoire *f* à condensateur; mémoire *f* capacitive

capacity /kə'pæsɪti/ *noun* (*space*) capacité *f*

capitalisation /ˌkæpɪt(ə)laɪ'zeɪʃ(ə)n/, **capitalization** *noun* (*word-processor function that converts text into capitals*) mise *f* en majuscule

capitals /'kæpɪt(ə)lz/, **caps** *plural noun* majuscules *fpl*

caps lock /'kæps lɒk/ *noun* touche *f* de verrouillage des majuscules

capstan /'kæpstən/ *noun* (*of tape player*) cabestan *m*; presseur *m* de bande

caption /'kæpʃən/ *noun* légende *f* ◇ **the captions are printed in italics** les légendes sont (imprimées) en italique

capture /'kæptʃə/ *verb* **1.** (*of data*) capturer *vt* **2.** (*remove a token from the network*) prélever un jeton ◇ **scanners usually capture images at a resolution of 300 dots per inch (dpi)** un scanner peut habituellement capturer des images à une résolution de 300 points par pouce (ppp) ◇ **the software allows captured images to be edited** le logiciel permet d'éditer les images capturées

CAR *abbr* (*current address register*) registre *m* d'adresse courante

carbon copy /ˌkɑːbən 'kɒpi/ *noun* copie *f* carbone; double *m*

carbon ribbon /ˌkɑːbən 'rɪbən/ *noun* ruban *m* carbone

card /kɑːd/ *noun* (*circuit card*) carte *f* de circuit imprimé

> 'A smart card carries an encryption chip, which codifies your ID and password prior to their being transmitted across a network.' [*Computing*]

CardBus /'kɑːdbʌs/ CardBus

card cage /'kɑːd keɪdʒ/ *noun* support *m* de châssis avec guide-cartes; châssis *m* avec guide-cartes

card chassis /kɑːd 'ʃæsi/ *noun* support *m* de châssis avec guide-cartes

card edge connector /ˌkɑːd edʒ kə'nektə/ *noun* connecteur *m* de carte

card extender /'kɑːd ikˌstendə/ *noun* support *m* de carte d'extension

card frame /'kɑːd freɪm/ *noun* support *m* de châssis avec guide-cartes; châssis *m* avec guide-cartes

cardinal number /ˌkɑːdɪn(ə)l 'nʌmbə/ *noun* (*positive integer*) nombre *m* cardinal

cardioid microphone /ˌkɑːdiɔɪd 'maɪkrəfəun/ *noun* microphone *m* cardioïde

cardioid response /ˌkɑːdiɔɪd rɪ'spɒns/ *noun* réponse *f* cardioïde

card reader /kɑːd 'riːdə/ *noun* lecteur *m* de cartes

caret /'kærət/ *noun* (*symbol of the Control key*) caret *m*

carpal tunnel syndrome /ˌkɑːp(ə)l 'tʌn(ə)l ˌsɪndrəʊm/ *noun* support *m* de châssis avec guide-cartes

carriage /'kærɪdʒ/ *noun* (*of printer*) chariot *m* ◇ **carriage return (CR)** retour *m* de chariot ◇ **carriage return *or* line feed (CR *or* LF)** retour *m* de chariot/retour à la ligne ◇ **the carriage return key is badly placed for touch-typists** les opérateurs de saisie trouvent que la touche de retour de chariot est mal placée

carriage control /'kærɪdʒ kənˌtrəʊl/ *noun* commande *f* de chariot ◇ **carriage control codes can be used to move the paper forward two lines between each line of text** les codes de commande de chariot peuvent être utilisés pour faire avancer le papier de deux interlignes

carriage return /ˌkærɪdʒ rɪ'tɜːn/ *noun* retour *m* chariot ◇ **the carriage return key is badly placed for touch-typists** les opérateurs de saisie trouvent que la touche de retour de chariot est mal placée

carriage return key /ˌkærɪdʒ rɪ'tɜːn ˌkiː/ *noun* touche *f* de retour du chariot ◇ **carriage return *or* line feed (CR *or* LF)** retour *m* de chariot/retour à la ligne

carrier /'kæriə/ *noun* (*high frequency waveform*) onde *f* porteuse

carrier detect /ˌkæriə dɪ'tekt/ *noun* signal *m* CD; signal *m* de détection de porteuse

carrier frequency /ˌkæriə 'friːkwənsi/ *noun* fréquence *f* de porteuse

carrier sense multiple access-collision detection /ˌkæriə sens ˌmʌltip(ə)l ˌækses kə'lɪʒ(ə)n dɪˌtekʃ(ə)n/ *noun* méthode *f* d'accès à test de porteuse et détection de collision; protocole *m* de transmission CSMA-CD

carrier signal /ˌkæriə 'sɪgn(ə)l/ *noun* signal *m* de porteuse

carrier signalling /'kæriə ˌsɪgnəlɪŋ/ *noun* signal *m* de porteuse

carrier system /ˌkæriə 'sɪstəm/ *noun* (*analog or digital*) système *m* multiplex; (*analog*) système *m* à courants porteurs

carrier wave /'kæriə weɪv/ *noun* onde *f* porteuse

carry /'kæri/ *noun* (*maths*) retenue *f*; report *m*

carry bit /'kæri bɪt/ *noun* balise *f*; bit *m* de report

carry complete signal /ˌkæri kəm'pliːt ˌsɪgn(ə)l/ *noun* signal *m* de fin de report

carry flag /'kæri flæg/ *noun* témoin *m*; indicateur *m* de retenue

carry look ahead /ˌkæri lʊk ə'hed/ *noun* additionneur *m* à retenue automatique

carry time /'kæri taɪm/ *noun* temps *m* de report

cartesian coordinates /kɑːˌtiːziən kəʊ'ɔːdɪnəts/ *plural noun* coordonnées *fpl* cartésiennes

cartesian structure /kɑːˌtiːziən 'strʌktʃə/ *noun* structure *f* cartésienne

cartridge /'kɑːtrɪdʒ/ *noun* cartouche *f*

cartridge drive /'kɑːtrɪdʒ draɪv/ *noun* lecteur *m* de cartouches

cartridge fonts /'kɑːtrɪdʒ fɒntz/ *plural noun* cartouche *f* de police de caractères

cartridge ribbon /ˌkɑːtrɪdʒ 'rɪbən/ *noun* ruban *m* en cartouche

cascade carry /kæˌskeɪd 'kæri/ *noun* report *m* en cascade

cascade connection /kæˌskeɪd kə'nekʃ(ə)n/ *noun* connexion *f* montée en cascade

cascade control /kæˌskeɪd kən'trəʊl/ *noun* contrôle *m* en cascade

cascading menu /kæˌskeɪdɪŋ 'menjuː/ *noun* sous-menu *m*

cascading style sheet /kæˌskeɪdɪŋ 'staɪl ˌʃiːt/ *noun* CSS

cascading windows /kæˌskeɪdɪŋ 'wɪndəʊz/ *plural noun* fenêtres *fpl* en cascade

case /keɪs/ *noun* (*programming command*) commande *f* CASE; commande *f* de branchement conditionnel

case branch /'keɪs brɑːntʃ/ *noun* branchement *m* conditionnel

case change /'keɪs tʃeɪndʒ/ *noun* touche *f* des majuscules

case sensitive /keɪs 'sensətɪv/ *adjective* qui distingue les majuscules des minuscules

case sensitive search /ˌkeɪs ˌsensətɪv 'sɜːtʃ/ *noun* recherche *f* qui distingue les majuscules des minuscules *or* qui tient compte des majuscules; recherche *f* qui tient compte des majuscules

cassette /kə'set/ *noun* cassette *f* ◇ **video cassette** vidéocassette *f* ◇ **you must back up the information from the computer onto a cassette** il faut copier vos données sur une cassette de sauvegarde

cassette recorder /kə'set rɪˌkɔːdə/ *noun* magnétophone *m* à cassette

cassette tape /kə'set teɪp/ *noun* (*reel of magnetic tape*) bande *f* magnétique; cassette *f*

cast /kɑːst/ *noun* (*in a programming language, instruction that converts data*) commande *f* de conversion CAST ◇ **to convert the variable from an integer to a character type, use the cast command** pour convertir une variable de type nombre entier en une variable de type caractère, utilisez la commande CAST

CAT /kæt/ *noun* **1.** (*computer-aided training or computer-assisted training*) apprentissage *m* assisté par ordinateur **2.** (*computer-aided testing or computer-assisted testing*) test *m* assisté par ordinateur

catalogue /'kæt(ə)lɒg/ *noun* catalogue *m* ■ *verb* cataloguer *vt*; répertorier *vt* ◇ **all the terminals are catalogued, with their location, call**

sign and attribute table tous les terminaux sont répertoriés avec (indication de) leur emplacement, leur code *or* signe d'appel et leur table d'attributs

catastrophe /kə'tæstrəfi/ *noun* catastrophe *f*

catastrophic error /ˌkætəstrɒfɪk 'erə/ *noun* erreur *f* catastrophique; erreur *f* fatale

catastrophic failure /ˌkætəstrɒfɪk 'feɪljə/ *noun* panne *f* fatale

Category 1 /ˌkætəg(ə)ri 'wʌn/ *noun* catégorie *f* 1

Category 2 /ˌkætəg(ə)ri 'tuː/ *noun* catégorie *f* 2

Category 3 /ˌkætəg(ə)ri 'θriː/ *noun* catégorie *f* 3

Category 4 /ˌkætəg(ə)ri 'fɔː/ *noun* catégorie *f* 4

Category 5 /ˌkætəg(ə)ri 'faɪv/ *noun* catégorie *f* 5

catena /kə'tiːnə/ *noun* **1.** (*items in a chained list*) caractères *mpl* dans une chaîne; chaîne *f* de caractères **2.** (*character chain*) caractères *mpl* dans une chaîne; chaîne *f* de caractères

catenate /'kætəneɪt/ *verb* enchaîner *vt*; lier *vt*; concaténer *vt*; faire une concaténation

cathode ray tube /ˌkæθəʊd 'reɪ tjuːb/ *noun* écran *m* à tube cathodique

cathode ray tube storage /ˌkæθəʊd reɪ ˌtjuːb 'stɔːrɪdʒ/ *noun* tube *m* à mémoire

CAV /ˌsiː eɪ 'viː/ *noun* vitesse *f* angulaire constante

CB *abbr* (*call back*) rappel

CBI /n/ *abbr* (*computer-based instruction*) enseignement *m* assisté par ordinateur

CBL /ˌsiː biː 'el/ *noun* formation *f* assistée par ordinateur

CBMS /ˌsiː biː em 'es/ *noun* messagerie *f* électronique

CBR *abbr* (*constant bit rate*) débit *m* binaire constant

CBT /ˌsiː biː 'tiː/ *noun* apprentissage *m* assisté par ordinateur

cc /ˌsiː 'siː/ *noun* cc

CCD *abbr* (*charge-coupled device*) dispositif *m* à couple de charge; CCD

CCD memory /ˌsiː siː diː 'mem(ə)ri/ *noun* mémoire *f* CCD; mémoire *f* à couplage de charge

CCITT /ˌsiː siː aɪ tiː 'tiː/ *noun* Comité *m* Consultatif International Télégraphique et Téléphonique

CCP /ˌsiː siː 'piː/ *noun* processeur *m* de console

CD[1] /siː'diː/ *noun* (*instruction in MS-DOS and UNIX*) cd *m* ◇ **type in CD DOCS to move into the DOCS subdirectory** tapez CD DOCS pour entrer dans le sous-répertoire DOCS

CD[2] /siː'diː/ *abbr* (*compact disc*) disque *m* compact; disque *m* CD

CD-audio /ˌsiː ˌdiː 'ɔːdiəʊ/ *noun* disque *m* compact audionumérique; CD-audio *m*

CD caddy /ˌsiː 'diː ˌkædi/ *noun* boîtier *m* pour CD; boîte *f* de cristal pour CD

CD-E /ˌsiː 'diː iː/ *noun* (*format that allows data to be saved to and erased from a compact disc*) cd *m* effaçable; CD-E *m*

CD-i /ˌsiː diː 'aɪ/ *noun* (*standards that combine sound, data, video and text onto a CD*) disque *m* compact interactif; cd *m* interactif

CD-I /ˌsiː 'diː aɪ/ *noun* (*standards that combine sound, data, video and text onto a CD*) disque *m* compact interactif; cd *m* interactif; CD-I *m*

CD-i digital audio /ˌsiː diː aɪ ˌdɪdʒɪt(ə)l 'ɔːdiəʊ/ *noun* format *m* audionumérique CD-I

CD-i digital imaging /ˌsiː diː aɪ ˌdɪdʒɪt(ə)l 'ɪmɪdʒɪŋ/ *plural noun* imagerie *f* numérique CD-I

CD-i sector /ˌsiː diː 'aɪ ˌsektə/ *noun* secteur *m* CD-I

CD Player /ˌsiː 'diː ˌpleɪə/ *noun* lecteur *m* CD

CD quality /ˌsiː 'diː ˌkwɒlɪti/ *adjective* (*recording*) de qualité CD

CD-R /ˌsiː diː 'ɑː/ *noun* (*technology that allows a user to write data to and read from a CD-R disc*) cd *m* enregistrable; cd *m* inscriptible; CD-R *m* ◇ **a CD-R disc can be played in any standard CD-ROM drive but needs a special CD-R drive to write data to the disc** un lecteur de CD-Rom standard peut lire un CD-R mais il faut un graveur pour inscrire des données sur le CD-R

C: drive /'siː draɪv/ *noun* lecteur *m* C:

CD-ROM /ˌsiː diː 'rɒm/ *noun* (*disc drive*) disque *m* compact à lecture seule; disque *m* compact non réinscriptible; disque *m* CD-ROM; CD-ROM *m*

> ''Customers' images will be captured, digitised, and stored on optical disk or CD-ROM, and produced if queries arise about responsibility for ATM transactions.'' [*Computing*]

CD-ROM drive /ˌsiː 'diː rɒm/ *noun* lecteur *m* de CD-ROM; lecteur *m* de CD

CD-ROM Extended Architecture /ˌsiː ˌdiː rɒm ɪkˌstendɪd 'ɑːkɪtektʃə/ *noun* architecture *f* étendue multimédia; CD-ROM/XA *m*

CD-ROM mode 1 /ˌsiː 'diː rɒm məʊd/ *noun* CD-ROM *m* mode 1

CD-ROM mode 2 /ˌsiː 'diː rɒm məʊd/ *noun* CD-ROM *m* mode 2

CD-ROM player /ˌsiː 'diː rɒm/ *noun* lecteur *m* de CD-ROM

CD-ROM Re-Writable /ˌsiː 'diː rɒm reɪ/ *noun* CD-ROM *m* réinscriptible

CD-ROM/XA *abbr* (*CD-ROM Extended Architecture*) architecture *f* étendue multimédia; CD-ROM à architecture étendue

CDRTOS /ˌsiː diː ɑː tiː əʊ 'es/ *noun* (*operating system*) CDRTOS

CD-RW /ˌsiː diː ɑː 'dʌb(ə)ljuː/ *noun* disque *m* compact réinscriptible; CD *m* réinscriptible; CD-RW *m*

CD-video /ˌsiː diː 'vɪdiəʊ/ *noun* CD-vidéo *m*

CD-WO /ˌsiː ˌdʌb(ə)l juː 'əʊ/ *noun* (*CD-ROM disc and drive technology that allows a user to write data to the disc once only*) disque *m* compact non réinscriptible; cd *m* non réinscriptible; CD-WO *m*

cell /sel/ *noun* **1.** (*single function in a spreadsheet*) cellule *f* **2.** (*single memory location*) cellule *f* **3.** (*in transmission system*) cellule *f*

cell address /sel ə'dres/ *noun* adresse *f* de cellule

cellar /'selə/ *noun* pile *f* de données en mémoire

cell definition /sel ˌdefə'nɪʃ(ə)n/ *noun* définition *f* de cellule

cell format /sel 'fɔːmæt/ *noun* format *m* de cellule ◇ **the cell format is right-aligned and emboldened** le format de cette cellule est justification à droite et caractères gras

Cello /'tʃeləʊ/ *noun* Cello *m*

cell protection /sel prə'tekʃən/ *noun* protection *f* de cellule

cell reference variable /ˌsel ˌref(ə)rəns 'veəriəb(ə)l/ *noun* variable *f* de référence d'une cellule

cell relay /sel 'riːˌleɪ/ *noun* commutation *f* de cellules

cellular phone /ˌseljʊlə 'fəʊn/ *noun* téléphone *m* cellulaire

central computer /ˌsentrəl kəm'pjuːtə/ *noun* ordinateur *m* central; ordinateur *m* hôte

centralised computer network /ˌsentrəˌlaɪzd kəm'pjuːtə/, **centralized computer network** *noun* réseau *m* informatique centralisé

centralised data processing /ˌsentrəˌlaɪzd 'deɪtə/, **centralized data processing** *noun* traitement *m* centralisé de l'information

central memory /ˌsentrəl 'mem(ə)ri/ *noun* mémoire *f* principale

central processing element /ˌsentrəl 'prəʊsesɪŋ ˌelɪmənt/ *noun* unité *f* centrale de calcul

central processing unit /ˌsentrəl ˌprəʊsesɪŋ 'juːnɪt/, **central processor** /ˌsentrəl ˌprəʊ'sesə/ *noun* unité *f* centrale

central terminal /ˌsentrəl 'tɜːmɪn(ə)l/ *noun* terminal *m* principal *or* central

centre /'sentə/ *verb* **1.** (*to align read/write head*) centrer *vt*; aligner *vt*; ajuster *vt* **2.** (*in text or on screen*) centrer *vt* ◇ **which key do you press to centre the heading?** sur quelle touche faut-il appuyer pour centrer l'en-tête?

centre operator /ˌsentə 'ɒpəreɪtə/ *noun* opérateur *m* central

Centronics interface /sen'trɒnɪks ˌɪntəfeɪs/ *noun* interface *f* parallèle de type Centronics

Centronics port /sen'trɒnɪks ˌpɔːt/ *noun* port *m* Centronics

CERN /sɜːn/ *noun* (*research laboratory in Switzerland where the world wide web was originally invented*) Centre *f* Européen pour la Recherche Nucléaire

certificate /sə'tɪfɪkət/ *noun* certificat *m*

certificate authority /sə'tɪfɪkət ɔːˌθɒrɪti/ *noun* autorité *f* de certification

certificate of approval /səˌtɪfɪkət əv ə 'pruːv(ə)l/ *noun* certificat *m* d'homologation

CF *abbr* (*compact Flash*) CF (Compact Flash)

chain /tʃeɪn/ *noun* **1.** (*linked data or files*) chaîne *f* **2.** (*sequential instructions*) chaîne *f* ■ *verb* (*to link files or data*) enchaîner *vt* ◇ **more than 1,000 articles or chapters can be chained together when printing** plus de 1000 articles ou chapitres peuvent être enchaînés à l'impression ◇ **to daisy-chain** (*hardware*) relier en série *or* en chaîne *or* en cascade

chain code /'tʃeɪn kəʊd/ *noun* (*series of words*) code *m* en chaîne; code *m* chaîné

chained file /ˌtʃeɪnd 'faɪl/ *noun* fichier *m* chaîné

chained list /'tʃeɪnd lɪst/ *noun* (*list containing data and an address*) liste *f* chaînée; liste *f* concaténée

chained record /tʃeɪnd 'rekɔːd/ *noun* enregistrement *m*

chaining /'tʃeɪnɪŋ/ *noun* enchaînement *m*; chaînage *m*

chaining search /'tʃeɪnɪŋ sɜːtʃ/ *noun* recherche *f* en chaîne

chain list /'tʃeɪn lɪst/ *noun* liste *f* en chaîne

chain printer /tʃeɪn 'prɪntə/ *noun* imprimante *f* à chaîne

change /tʃeɪndʒ/ *noun* modification *f*

change directory /'tʃeɪndʒ daɪˌrekt(ə)ri/ *noun* commande *f* CD

change dump /'tʃeɪndʒ dʌmp/ *noun* vidage *m* de mouvements

change file /'tʃeɪndʒ faɪl/ *noun* fichier *m* de mouvements; fichier *m* de mise à jour

change over /ˌtʃeɪndʒ 'əʊvə/ *noun* permutation *f*; transfert *m* ■ *verb* passer d'un système à un autre

changer /'tʃeɪndʒə/ *noun* changeur *m* ◇ **record changer** changeur (de disques) automatique

change record /tʃeɪndʒ 'rekɔːd/ *noun* enregistrement *m* de mouvements; enregistrement *m* de modifications

change tape /ˌtʃeɪndʒ 'teɪp/ *noun* bande *f* de mouvements

channel /'tʃæn(ə)l/ *noun* (*physical connection*) canal *m*; voie *f* ■ *verb* (*signals or data*) acheminer *vt*; véhiculer *vt*; transmettre *vt* ◇ **channel group** groupement *m* de voies

channel adapter /'tʃæn(ə)l əˌdæptə/ *noun* interface *f*

channel bank /'tʃæn(ə)l bæŋk/ *noun* banque *f* de canaux

channel capacity /ˈtʃæn(ə)l kəˌpæsɪti/ *noun* capacité *f*; débit *m* d'une voie de transmission

channel command /ˈtʃæn(ə)l kəˌmɑːnd/ *noun* commande *f* de canal

channel isolation /ˌtʃæn(ə)l ˌaɪsəˈleɪʃ(ə)n/ *noun* isolation *f* de canaux

channelling /ˈtʃænəlɪŋ/ *noun* (*protective pipes*) conduite *f*; canalisation *f*

channel overload /ˈtʃæn(ə)l ˌəʊvələʊd/ *noun* (*transmission of data*) surcharge *f*

channel queue /ˈtʃæn(ə)l kjuː/ *noun* file *f* d'attente

channel-to-channel connection /ˌtʃæn(ə)l tə ˌtʃæn(ə)l kəˈnekʃ(ə)n/ *noun* liaison *f* directe entre canaux

chapter /ˈtʃæptə/ *noun* (*of program*) module *m*

char /tʃɑː/ *noun* (*in programming*) char *m*

character /ˈkærɪktə/ *noun* caractère *m* ◇ **a daisy-wheel printer is a character printer** l'imprimante à marguerite imprime un caractère à la fois ◇ **character orientated (computer)** (ordinateur) à mode caractère ◇ **character skew** oblique *f* (d'un caractère) ◇ **characters per inch (cpi)** (nombre de) caractères par pouce ◇ **the ASCII code is the most frequently used character coding system** le code ASCII est le code de caractères le plus fréquemment utilisé ◇ **you can select 10 or 12 cpi with the green button** le bouton vert vous permet de sélectionner 10 ou 12 caractères par pouce

character assembly /ˈkærɪktə əˌsembli/ *noun* (*designing characters with pixels*) assemblage *m*

character-based /ˈkærɪktə ˌbeɪst/ *adjective* à base de caractères

character block /ˈkærɪktə blɒk/ *noun* bloc *m* de caractères

character byte /ˈkærɪktə baɪt/ *noun* octet *m* de caractères

character check /ˈkærɪktə tʃek/ *noun* contrôle *m* de caractère

character code /ˈkærɪktə kəʊd/ *noun* code *m* de caractères

character density /ˈkærɪktə ˌdensɪti/ *noun* densité *f* de caractère

character display /ˈkærɪktə dɪˌspleɪ/ *noun* affichage *m* de texte; affichage *m* de caractères

character fill /ˈkærɪktə fɪl/ *noun* remplissage *m* avec caractères blancs

character generator /ˈkærɪktə ˌdʒenəreɪtə/ *noun* générateur *m* de caractères ◇ **the ROM used as a character generator can be changed to provide different fonts** on peut utiliser une ROM comme générateur de caractères pour obtenir les différentes polices

character interleaving /ˌkærɪktə ˌɪntəˈliːvɪŋ/ *noun* entrelaçage *m* de caractères

characteristic /ˌkærɪktəˈrɪstɪk/ *noun* **1.** (*maths*) exposant *m*; caractéristique *f* **2.** (*properties of component*) caractéristique *f* ◇ **the floating point number 1.345 x 10³, has a characteristic of 3** la valeur de l'exposant du nombre à virgule flottante 1,345 x 10³ est 3

characteristic overflow /ˌkærɪktərɪstɪk ˈəʊvəfləʊ/ *noun* dépassement *m* de capacité de la caractéristique

character key /ˈkærɪktə kiː/ *noun* touche *f* caractère

character machine /ˈkærɪktə məˌʃiːn/ *noun* processeur *m* en mode caractère; processeur *m* à mots variables

character matrix /ˈkærɪktə ˌmeɪtrɪks/ *noun* matrice *f* de caractères

character mode /ˈkærɪktə məʊd/ *noun* mode *m* caractère

character-orientated /ˈkærɪktə ˌɔːriənteɪtɪd/ *adjective* à mode caractère

character printer /ˈkærɪktə ˌprɪntə/ *noun* imprimante *f* caractère (par caractère)

character recognition /ˌkærɪktə ˌrekəgˈnɪʃ(ə)n/ *noun* reconnaissance *f* optique de caractères

character repertoire /ˌkærɪktə ˌrepəˈtwɑː/ *noun* (*list of characters*) répertoire *m* de caractères; répertoire *m* typographique

character representation /ˌkærɪktə ˌreprɪzenˈteɪʃ(ə)n/ *noun* expression *f* binaire d'un caractère

character rounding /ˈkærɪktə ˌraʊndɪŋ/ *noun* arrondissement *m* de caractère

character set /ˈkærɪktə set/ *noun* (*printing*) police *f* de caractères; (*codes*) jeu *m* de caractères; (*typeface*) fonte *f*

characters per inch /ˌkærɪktəz pɜːr ˈɪntʃ/ *plural noun* nombre *m* de caractères par pouce

characters per second /ˌkærɪktəz pə ˈsekənd/ *noun* nombre *m* de caractères par seconde (cps)

character string /ˈkærɪktə strɪŋ/ *noun* chaîne *f* de caractères

'This explains a multitude of the database's problems – three-letter months are treated like character strings instead of as dates.' [*Computing*]

character stuffing /ˈkærɪktə ˌstʌfɪŋ/ *noun* (*addition of blank characters to a file*) remplissage *m* avec caractères blancs

charge /tʃɑːdʒ/ *noun* **1.** (*of electricity*) charge *f* **2.** (*of electrons*) charge *f* ■ *verb* (*to supply device with electric charge*) charger *vt*

charge-coupled device /ˌtʃɑːdʒ ˌkʌp(ə)ld dɪˈvaɪs/ *noun* dispositif *m* CCD; dispositif *m* à couplage de charge

charge-coupled device memory /tʃɑːdʒ ˌkʌp(ə)ld dɪˈvaɪs/ *noun* mémoire *f* à couplage de charge; mémoire *f* CCD

chart /tʃɑːt/ *noun* diagramme *m*; graphique *m*; courbe *f* ◇ **chart recorder** enregistreur *m* graphique

chassis /'ʃæsi/ *noun* châssis *m*

chat /tʃæt/ *verb* (*on the Internet*) dialoguer *vt*; participer à une discussion

chat group /'tʃæt gruːp/ *noun* forum *m* de discussion

chat room /'tʃæt ruːm/ *noun* (*on the Internet*) zone *f* de discussion

CHCP /ˌsiː aɪtʃ siː 'piː/ *noun* (*in MS-DOS OS/2: system command that selects which code page to use*) commande *f* CHCP

CHDIR /ˌsiː aɪtʃ diː aɪ 'ɑː/ *abbr* (*change directory*) commande *f* CHDIR (de changement de répertoire)

cheapernet /'tʃiːpənet/ *noun informal* (*informal: thin-Ethernet*) Ethernet *m* câble fin (et bon marché)

check bit /'tʃek bɪt/ *noun* (*one bit of a binary word*) bit *m* de contrôle

check box /'tʃek bɒks/ *noun* case *f* à cocher

check character /tʃek 'kærɪktə/ *noun* caractère *m* de contrôle

check digit /'tʃek ˌdɪdʒɪt/ *noun* chiffre *m*

checkerboarding /'tʃekəˌbɔːdɪŋ/ *noun* utilisation *f* incomplète de la mémoire

check indicator /tʃek 'ɪndɪˌkeɪtə/ *noun* indicateur *m* de contrôle

checking program /tʃekɪŋ 'prəʊgræm/ *noun* programme *m* de contrôle

check key /'tʃek kiː/ *noun* clé *f* de contrôle

check mark /'tʃek mɑːk/ *noun* trait *m*

check number /tʃek 'nʌmbə/ *noun* chiffre *m*

check point /'tʃek pɔɪnt/ *noun* point *m* de contrôle; point *m* de reprise

check point dump /ˌtʃek pɔɪnt 'dʌmp/ *noun* vidage *m* de contrôle

check register /tʃek 'redʒɪstə/ *noun* registre *m* de contrôle

checksum /tʃek 'təʊt(ə)l/, **check total** *noun* (*program that checks data*) total *m* de vérification; total *m* de contrôle ◇ **the data must be corrupted if the checksum is different** les données sont sûrement erronées si le total de contrôle est faux

child process /tʃaɪld prəʊ'ses/, **child program** /tʃaɪld 'prəʊgræm/ *noun* (*routine or program*) procédure *f* de deuxième génération; procédure *f* fille

child window /tʃaɪld 'wɪndəʊ/ *noun* fenêtre *f* fille

chip /tʃɪp/ *noun* (*device used in transistors, resistors and capacitors*) puce *f*; composant *m*; circuit *m* intégré ◇ **they are carrying out research on diagnostic chips to test computers that contain processors** ils font des recherches sur les puces de diagnostic destinées au contrôle des ordinateurs équipés de processeurs

chip architecture /tʃɪp 'ɑːkɪˌtektʃə/ *noun* architecture *f* d'un circuit intégré

chip card /ˌtʃɪp 'kɑːd/ *noun* carte *f* à puce; carte *f* à mémoire

chip count /ˌtʃɪp 'kaʊnt/ *noun* nombre *m* de puces ◇ **it's no good, the chip count is still too high** le nombre de puces est malheureusement encore trop élevé

'Where the display is provided by an LCD system, high levels of performance must be achieved with the lowest cost, smallest chip count and lowest power consumption.' [*Computing*]

chip select /ˌtʃɪp sɪ'lekt/ *noun* sélection *f* de circuit

chip select line /ˌtʃɪp sɪ'lekt ˌlaɪn/ *noun* ligne *f* de sélection d'un circuit intégré; ligne *f* de validation d'un circuit intégré

chip set /ˌtʃɪp 'set/ *noun* jeu *m* de composants; jeu *m* de circuits; chipset *m*

CHKDSK /'tʃekdɪsk/ *noun* (*in MS-DOS: system command that checks the status of a disk drive*) commande *f* CHKDSK (de contrôle de lecteur de disque)

choke /tʃəʊk/ *noun* inducteur *m*; bobine *f* d'induction

Chooser™ /'tʃuːzə/ (*Apple Macintosh operating system*) utilitaire *m* Chooser™

chop /tʃɒp/ recherche *f* par coupe binaire; recherche dichotomique; recherche par dichotomie

chord keying /'kɔːd kiːɪŋ/ *noun* action *f* d'appuyer sur deux touches en même temps

chroma /'krəʊmə/ *noun* chrominance *f*; chroma *f* ◇ **chroma control** (*TV*) contrôle *m* chromatique ◇ **chroma detector** détecteur *m* chromatique

chroma key /'krəʊmə kiː/ *noun* incrustation *f* couleur

chrominance /'krəʊmɪnəns/ *noun* chrominance *f*; chroma *f*

chrominance signal /'krəʊmɪnəns ˌsɪgn(ə)l/ *noun* signal *m* de chrominance

CIDR /ˌsiː aɪ diː 'ɑː/ *noun* routage *m* inter-domaine sans classes

CIE /ˌsiː aɪ 'iː/ *noun* CIE

CIM /ˌsiː aɪ 'em/ *noun* **1.** (*computer input microfilm*) entrée *f* à partir de microfilm; entrée *f* par lecture de microfilm **2.** (*computer-integrated manufacturing*) productique *f* intégrée

cine-oriented /'sɪni ˌɔːrientɪd/ *adjective* image *f* orientée en film

cipher /'saɪfə/ *noun* code *m* chiffré; écriture *f* chiffrée; (*system, method*) codage *m*; chiffrage *m*; cryptage *m* ◇ **public key cipher** cryptage *or* code chiffré à clé publique

cipher key /'saɪfə kiː/ *noun* clé *f* de codage; clé *f* de chiffrage; clé *f* de cryptage

cipher system /'saɪfə ˌsɪstəm/ *noun* code *m* chiffré

ciphertext /'saɪfətekst/ *noun* message *m* chiffré; message *m* crypté

CIR /ˌsiː aɪ 'ɑː/ *noun* registre *m* d'instruction courante

circuit /'sɜːkɪt/ *noun* (*electric*) circuit *m* ◇ **circuit grade** caractéristique *f* d'un circuit ◇ **circuit noise level** niveau *m* de bruit d'un circuit ◇ **circuit switched digital circuitry** circuits numériques commutés ◇ **circuit switched network** réseau *m* à commutation de circuits ◇ **printed circuit board (PCB)** (*with circuit printed*) (carte de) circuit imprimé (CI)

circuit analyser /'sɜːkɪt ˌænəlaɪzə/ *noun* analyseur *m* de circuit

circuit board /'sɜːkɪt bɔːd/ *noun* carte *f* de circuit imprimé; plaque *f* présensibilisée pour circuit imprimé

'The biggest shock was to open up the PC and find the motherboard smothered in patch wires (usually a sign that a design fault in the printed circuit board was rectified at the last minute).' [*Computing*]

circuit capacity /'sɜːkɪt kəˌpæsɪti/ *noun* capacité *f* d'un circuit

circuit card /'sɜːkɪt kɑːd/ *noun* carte *f* de circuit imprimé

circuit design /'sɜːkɪt dɪˌzaɪn/ *noun* tracé *m* d'un circuit

circuit diagram /'sɜːkɪt ˌdaɪəgræm/ *noun* diagramme *m* d'un circuit ◇ **the CAD program will plot the circuit diagram rapidly** le programme de CAO peut tracer le circuit très rapidement

circuit switching /'sɜːkɪt ˌswɪtʃɪŋ/ *noun* commutation *f* de circuit

circular buffer /ˌsɜːkjʊlə 'bʌfə/ *noun* tampon *m* circulaire

circular file /'sɜːkjʊlə faɪl/ *noun* fichier *m* en boucle

circularity /ˌsɜːkjʊ'lærɪti/ *noun* circularité *f*

circular list /'sɜːkjʊlə lɪst/ *noun* liste *f* en boucle

circular reference /ˌsɜːkjʊlə 'ref(ə)rəns/ *noun* référence *f* circulaire

circular shift /'sɜːkjʊlə ʃɪft/ *noun* décalage *m* circulaire

circulate /'sɜːkjʊˌleɪt/ *verb* (*to go in circle*) décrire un cercle; (*to send information to*) circuler *vi*

circulating register /ˌsɜːkjuleɪtɪŋ 'redʒɪstə/ *noun* registre *m* à décalage circulaire; registre *m* à bits circulants

circulating storage /ˌsɜːkjuleɪtɪŋ 'stɔːrɪdʒ/ *noun* mémoire *f* circulante; mémoire *f* dynamique

CISC /ˌsiː aɪ es 'siː/ *noun* ordinateur *m* à jeu d'instructions complexe (CISC)

CIT *abbr* (*computer-integrated telephony*) couplage *m* de la téléphonie et de l'informatique

cladding /'klædɪŋ/ *noun* (*surrounding a conducting core*) gaine *f* ◇ **if the cladding is chipped, the fibre-optic cable will not function well** la fibre optique sera moins performante si sa gaine est endommagée

claim frame /'kleɪm freɪm/ *noun* (*FDDI protocol network: frame used to determine which station will initialise the network*) trame *f* d'initialisation

clamper /'klæmpə/ *noun* circuit *m* de calage

clapper /'klæpə/ *noun* (*on printer*) presseur *m*

class /klɑːs/ *noun* (*definition of what a software routine will do*) classe *f*

class interval /klɑːs 'ɪntəv(ə)l/ *noun* intervalle *m* de classe

clean /kliːn/ *adjective* (*containing no errors*) sans erreur; sans correction ■ *verb* nettoyer *vt* ◇ **clean proof** épreuve *f* sans correction

clean copy /kliːn 'kɒpi/ *noun* (*text that does not need changing*) copie *f* finale

clean machine /kliːn mə'ʃiːn/ *noun* (*computer that contains only the minimum of ROM-based code*) machine *f* nue

clean page /'kliːn peɪdʒ/ *noun* page *f* mémoire sans modification

clean room /'kliːn ruːm/ *noun* chambre *f* stérile

clear /klɪə/ *verb* **1.** (*to wipe out*) vider *vt*; effacer *vt* **2.** (*release a communications link*) libérer la ligne lorsque la transmission est terminée ◇ **to clear an area of memory** vider une zone de mémoire ◇ **to clear the data register** vider le registre de données ◇ **type CLS to clear the screen** tapez CLS pour effacer *or* faire disparaître ce qu'il y a sur l'écran

clearance /'klɪərəns/ *noun* autorisation *f* ◇ **you do not have the required clearance for this processor** vous n'avez pas l'autorisation d'accéder à ce processeur

Clearing House Interbank Payment System /ˌklɪərɪŋ haʊs ˌɪntəbæŋk 'peɪmənts ˌsɪstəm/ *noun* CHIPS

clear to send /ˌklɪə tə 'send/ *noun* prêt à émettre

click /klɪk/ *noun* (*pressing a key or button especially of a mouse*) clic *m* ■ *verb* (*to press a key or button or mouse*) cliquer *vi*; effectuer un clic; faire un clic ◇ **click (on) Search** cliquer sur Rechercher ◇ **to click on the left button (of the mouse)** *or* **to left click** cliquer sur le bouton gauche (de la souris) *or* effectuer un clic gauche ◇ **to click on the right button (of the mouse)** *or* **to right click** cliquer sur le bouton droit (de la souris) *or* effectuer un clic droit ◇ **to double-click** (*two press-release actions on a mouse button*) double-cliquer ◇ **use the mouse to enlarge a frame by clicking inside its border and dragging to the position wanted** utilisez la souris pour agrandir le cadre: cliquez à l'intérieur des limites du cadre et glissez jusqu'à la position voulue ◇ **you move through text and graphics with a click of the button** un clic (sur la souris) vous permet de vous déplacer dans les textes et graphiques

click rate /'klɪk reɪt/ *noun* taux *m* de cliquage

clicks-and-mortar /ˌklɪks ən ˈmɔːtə/ *noun* clic *m* et mortier

clickstream /ˈklɪkstriːm/ *noun* série *f* du cliquage

'...the only way of achieving it would be to monitor the clickstreams of every single UK user of the net.' [*The Guardian*]

click through /ˈklɪk θruː/ *noun* clic *m* publicitaire

click through rate /ˈklɪk θruː ˌreɪt/ *noun* taux *m* de clics

client /ˈklaɪənt/ *noun* (*in a network, a workstation connected to a network*) client *m*

client application /ˌklaɪənt ˌæplɪˈkeɪʃ(ə)n/ *noun* application *f* client

client-server architecture /ˌklaɪənt ˌsɜːvə ˈɑːkɪtektʃə/ *noun* (*in a network*) architecture *f* client-serveur

client-server network /ˌklaɪənt ˈsɜːvə ˌnetwɜːk/ *noun* réseau *m* client-serveur

client-side /ˈklaɪənt saɪd/ *adjective* de côté client ◇ **client side application** (*that runs on the client's computer*) application client

clip /klɪp/ *verb* (*short piece of live film*) extraire un clip ◇ **there was a clip of the disaster on the news** un clip de l'accident a été passé aux informations

clip-art /klɪp ɑːt/ *noun* clip-art *m*; image *f* de bibliothèque

clipboard /ˈklɪpˌbɔːd/ *noun* (*temporary storage area for data*) stockage *m* temporaire; presse-papiers *m*; (*utility that temporarily stores any type of data*) Presse-papiers™ *m* ◇ **copy the text to the clipboard, then paste it back into a new document** copiez le texte dans le presse-papiers, puis collez-le dans le nouveau document

Clipper chip /ˈklɪpə tʃɪp/ *noun* puce *f* antiviolence

CLNP *abbr* (*connectionless network protocol*) protocole *m* CLNP

clock /klɒk/ *noun* (*used to synchronize equipment*) horloge *f* ■ *verb* synchroniser *vt*

clock cycle /klɒk ˈsaɪk(ə)l/ *noun* cycle *m* d'horloge

clock doubler /ˈklɒk ˌdʌb(ə)lə/ *noun* doubleur *m* d'horloge ◇ **the new CPU from Intel has an optional clock doubler that will double performance** le nouveau processeur d'Intel a un doubleur d'horloge en option qui permet de doubler ses performances

clocked signals /klɒkd ˈsɪgn(ə)lz/ *plural noun* signaux *mpl* synchrones aux impulsions d'horloge

clock frequency /klɒk ˈfriːkwənsi/ *noun* fréquence *f* d'horloge

clock pulse /ˈklɒk pʌls/ *noun* impulsion *f* d'horloge; rythme *m*

clock rate /ˈklɒk reɪt/ *noun* fréquence *f* d'horloge

clock speed /ˈklɒk spiːd/ *noun* fréquence *f* d'horloge

clock track /ˈklɒk træk/ *noun* piste *f* d'horloge

clone /kləʊn/ *noun* clone *m* ◇ **higher performance clones are available for all the models in our range** il existe des clones de tous nos modèles et tous sont plus performants ◇ **they have copied our new personal computer and brought out a cheaper clone** ils ont copié notre nouveau modèle d'ordinateur et commercialisé un clone qui se vend beaucoup moins cher

'On the desktop, the IBM/Motorola/Apple triumvirate is planning to energise a worldwide clone industry based on the PowerPC chip.' [*Computing*]

close /kləʊz/ *verb* (*to shut down*) arrêter *vt*; fermer *vt*; terminer *vt*

CLOSE /kləʊz/ *noun* (*in a programming language*) commande *f* CLOSE

closed bus system /ˌkləʊzd ˈbʌs ˌsɪstəm/ *noun* système *m* à bus fermé

closed captioning /ˌkləʊzd ˈkæpʃənɪŋ/ *noun* sous-titrage *m* codé pour malentendants

closed loop /ˌkləʊzd ˈluːp/ *noun* boucle *f* fermée

closed routine /kləʊzd ruːˈtiːn/ *noun* routine *f* fermée; routine *f* sous-routine; routine *f* sous-programme fermée

closed subroutine /kləʊzd ˈsʌbruːˌtiːn/ *noun* sous-programme *m* fermé

closed user group /ˌkləʊzd ˌjuːzə ˈgruːp/ *noun* groupe *m* fermé d'usagers

close file /ˈkləʊs faɪl/ *noun* opération *f* de fermeture de fichier

close menu option /ˌkləʊz ˈmenjuː ˌɒpʃ(ə)n/ *noun* option *f* Fermer du menu

CLS /ˌsiː el ˈes/ *noun* (*in MS-DOS*) CLS

cluster /ˈklʌstə/ *noun* **1.** (*sectors on a hard disk*) secteurs *mpl* contigus; cluster *m* **2.** (*of terminals*) grappe *f*; périphériques *mpl* reliés en grappe

cluster controller /ˈklʌstə kənˌtrəʊlə/ *noun* unité *f* de contrôle de périphériques disposés en grappe

clustering /ˈklʌstərɪŋ/ *noun* liaison *f* en grappe de plusieurs périphériques

'...these include IBM networking and clustering hardware and software' [*Personal Computer World*]

CLUT /ˌsiː el juː ˈtiː/ *noun* table *f* de fausses couleurs

CLV /ˌsiː el ˈviː/ *noun* vitesse *f* linéaire constante

CM /ˌsiː ˈem/ *noun* mémoire *f* centrale; mémoire *f* principale

CMI *abbr* (*computer-managed instruction*) gestion *f* informatique de l'apprentissage

CMIP /ˌsiː em aɪ ˈpiː/ *noun* protocole *m* CMIP

CMIS /ˌsiː em aɪ ˈes/ *noun* CMIS

CML *abbr* (*computer-managed learning*) apprentissage *m* géré par ordinateur

CMOS /ˌsiː em əʊ ˈpiː/ *noun* CMOS

‘Similarly, customers who do not rush to acquire CMOS companion processors for their mainframes will be rewarded with lower prices when they finally do migrate.’ [*Computergram*]

CMOT /ˌsiː em əʊ ˈtiː/ *noun* (*using of CMIP and CMIS network management protocols to manage gateways*) gestionnaire *m* de passerelle CMOT

CMYK /ˌsiː em waɪ ˈkeɪ/ *noun* (*method of describing a colour*) système *m* de définition de couleurs: cyan, magenta, jaune, noir

CNC /ˌsiː en ˈsiː/ *noun* commandes *fpl* numériques de machines-outils

coalesce /ˌkəʊəˈles/ *verb* (*to merge files*) combiner *vt*; fusionner *vti*; fondre *vt*

co-axial cable /kəʊks/, **coax** *noun* câble *m* coaxial

COBOL /ˈkəʊbɒl/ *noun* langage *m* COBOL

cobweb site /ˈkɒbweb saɪt/ *noun* site *m* miteux

code /kəʊd/ *noun* (*sequence of computer instructions*) code *m* ■ *verb* (*to write a program in a programming language*) coder *vt*; programmer *vt*

{Unrecovered Error: TEMP84BC1661-D61D-49BB-9286-EBF043998A0F post code US zip code TEMP6136AC8B-358E-479A-ADC4-E27700D180E1 TEMPC587051B-C851-4A94-AD1C-84219CD47EC3 code postal}

code area /kəʊd ˈeəriə/ *noun* zone *f* de code

code bit /ˈkəʊd bɪt/ *noun* bit *m* de code

CODEC /ˈkəʊdek/ *noun* codeur/décodeur *m*

code conversion /kəʊd kənˈvɜːʃ(ə)n/ *noun* conversion *f* de code

code element /kəʊd ˈelɪmənt/ *noun* élément *m* d’un code

code group /ˈkəʊd gruːp/ *noun* groupe *m* code

code line /ˈkəʊd laɪn/ *noun* ligne *f* de code

code page /ˈkəʊd peɪdʒ/ *noun* page *f* de codes

coder /ˈkəʊdə/ *noun* codeur *m*

coder/decoder /ˌkəʊdə diːˈkəʊdə/ *noun* codec *m*

code segment /kəʊd ˈsegmənt/ *noun* segment *m* mémoire de code

coding /ˈkəʊdɪŋ/ *noun* codage *m*; programmation *f*

coding form /ˈkɒdɪŋ fɔːm/ *noun* feuille *f*

coding sheet /ˈkɒdɪŋ ʃiːt/ *noun* feuille *f*

coincidence circuit /kəʊˌɪnsɪd(ə)ns ˈsɜːkɪt/, **coincidence element** /ˈelɪmənt/ *noun* circuit *m* à coïncidence

coincidence function /kəʊˈɪnsɪd(ə)ns ˌfʌŋkʃən/ *noun* fonction *f* d’intersection

coincidence gate /kəʊˈɪnsɪd(ə)ns geɪt/, **coincidence circuit** /kəʊˌɪnsɪd(ə)ns ˈsɜːkɪt/, **coincidence element** /kəʊˌɪnsɪd(ə)ns ˈelɪmənt/ *noun* (*electronic circuit*) circuit *m* ET; porte *f* ET

coincidence operation /kəʊˈɪnsɪd(ə)ns ˌɒpəreɪʃ(ə)n/ *noun* opération *f* ET; intersection *f* logique; conjonction *f* logique

COL *abbr* (*computer-oriented language*) langage *m* de bas niveau

cold boot /ˌkəʊld ˈbuːt/ *noun* démarrage *m* à froid; mise *f* en route

coldboot /ˈkəʊldbuːt/ *verb* démarrer à froid; mettre en route

cold fault /ˈkəʊld fɔːlt/ *noun* erreur *f* au démarrage

cold standby /kəʊld ˈstændbaɪ/ *noun* (*backup system*) système *m* de secours lancé manuellement

cold start /ˌkəʊld ˈstɑːt/ *noun* (*running a program from its original start point*) reprise *f* après interruption de l’alimentation; (*switching on a computer*) mise *f* en route; (*computer or program*) démarrage *m* à froid; retour *m* à l’application quittée

collating sequence /kəˈleɪtɪŋ ˌsiːkwəns/ *noun* ordre *m* des cahiers

collator /kəˈleɪtə/ *noun* **1.** (*of data*) programme *m* de fusionnement de données **2.** (*of punched cards*) interclasseuse *f*; (*for signatures of books*) assembleuse *f*

collect /kəˈlekt/ *verb* (*data*) rassembler *vt*

collect transfer /kəˌlekt trænsˈfɜː/ *verb* récupérer et transférer

collision /kəˈlɪʒ(ə)n/ *noun* (*of two signals*) collision *f*

collision detection /kəˈlɪʒ(ə)n dɪˌtekʃ(ə)n/ *noun* détection *f* de collision

co-location /kəʊ ləʊˈkeɪʃ(ə)n/ *noun* colocalisation *f*

colour balance /ˈkʌlə ˌbæləns/ *noun* équilibre *m* des couleurs

colour bits /ˈkʌlə bɪts/ *plural noun* bits *mpl* de description de couleur

colour cell /ˈkʌlə sel/ *noun* cellule *f* de contrôle des couleurs

colour depth /ˈkʌlə depθ/ *noun* intensité *f* de la couleur

colour display /ˌkʌlə dɪˈspleɪ/ *noun* affichage *m* couleur

colour look-up table /ˌkʌlə ˈlʊk ʌp ˌteɪb(ə)l/ *noun* table *f* de référence couleur; table *f* d’équivalence couleur

colour monitor /ˌkʌlə ˈmɒnɪtə/ *noun* moniteur *m* couleur

colour palette /ˌkʌlə ˈpælət/ *noun* palette *f* de couleurs

colour printer /ˌkʌlə ˈprɪntə/ *noun* imprimante *f* couleur

colour saturation /ˌkʌlə ˌsætʃəˈreɪʃ(ə)n/ *noun* saturation *f* de couleur

colour separation /ˌkʌlə ˌsepə'reɪʃ(ə)n/ *noun* (*colour printing*) séparation *f*

colour temperature /'kʌlə ˌtemprɪtʃə/ *noun* température *f* chromatique

column /'kɒləm/ *noun* colonne *f* ◇ **an 80-column printer is included in the price** le prix comprend une imprimante 80 colonnes ◇ **put the total at the bottom of the column** écrivez le total au bas de la colonne ◇ **to add up a column of figures** additionner une colonne de chiffres

columnar graph /kəˌlʌmnə 'grɑːf/ *noun* (*graph on which values are shown as vertical or horizontal bars*) diagramme *m* en bâtons; histogramme *m* en colonnes

columnar working /kəˌlʌmnə 'wɜːkɪŋ/ *noun* présentation *f* graphique sous forme de colonnes; présentation *f* graphique sous forme de histogrammes

column balance /'kɒləm ˌbæləns/ *noun* équilibrage *m* des colonnes

column guide /'kɒləm gaɪd/ *noun* guide *m*

column indicator /'kɒləm ˌɪndɪkeɪtə/ *noun* indicateur *m* de colonne

column parity /ˌkɒləm 'pærɪti/ *noun* parité *f* de colonnes

com /kɒm/ *suffix* extension *f* COM

COM /ˌsiː əʊ 'em/ *noun* **1.** (*component object model*) modèle *m* COM **2.** (*computer output on microfilm*) sortie *f* d'ordinateur sur microfilm

COM1 /ˌkɒm 'wʌn/ *noun* (*first serial port in a PC*) COM1

COMAL /'kəʊbæl/ *noun* langage *m* de programmation structurée COMAL

comb filter /kəʊm 'fɪltə/ *noun* filtre-peigne *m*

combinational circuit /ˌkɒmbɪneɪʃən(ə)l 'sɜːkɪt/ *noun* circuit *m* combinatoire

combinational logic /ˌkɒmbɪneɪʃən(ə)l 'lɒdʒɪk/ *noun* logique *f* combinatoire

combined head /kəm'baɪnd hed/ *noun* tête *f* de lecture/écriture

combined station /kəmˌbaɪnd 'steɪʃ(ə)n/ *noun* poste *m* de contrôle mixte

combined symbol matching /kəmˌbaɪnd 'sɪmbəl ˌmætʃɪŋ/ *noun* système *m* de reconnaissance de caractères CSM

combo box /'kɒmbəʊ bɒks/ *noun* (*box that displays a number of different input and output objects*) boîte *f* de listes

COM file /'kɒm faɪl/ *noun* (*three-letter extension to a file name*) fichier *m* COM; fichier *m* binaire exécutable ◇ **to start the program, type the name of the COM file at the MS-DOS prompt** pour démarrer le programme, tapez le nom du fichier COM à l'invite MS-DOS

comic-strip oriented /ˌkɒmɪk strɪp 'ɔːrientɪd/ *adjective* mode *m* bande dessinée

comma /'kɒmə/ *noun* (*typography*) virgule *f*

comma-delimited file /ˌkɒmə diːˌlɪmɪtd 'faɪl/ *noun* fichier *m* délimité par virgule ◇ **all databases can import and export to a comma-delimited file format** à partir de toutes bases de données on peut soit importer des données d'un fichier délimité par virgule, soit en exporter vers le fichier

command /kə'mɑːnd/ *noun* **1.** (*electrical pulse or signal*) commande *f*; instruction *f*; signal *m* **2.** (*word recognized by a computer*) commande *f*; instruction *f* ◇ **interrupt command** commande d'interruption (de programme) ◇ **the command to execute the program is RUN** RUN est la commande d'exécution du programme ◇ **type the command 'DIR' to get the list of files** tapez la commande DIR pour obtenir la liste des fichiers ◇ **use the command 'DIR' to view the files on disk, add the command line argument 'A:' to view the files on drive A:** utilisez la commande DIR pour afficher la liste des fichiers du disque et ajoutez l'argument de ligne A: pour les fichiers du disque A:

command chain /kə'mɑːnd tʃeɪn/ *noun* chaîne *f* de commandes

command code /kə'mɑːnd kəʊd/ *noun* code *m* d'opération

COMMAND.COM /kə'mɑːnd kɒm/ *noun* (*program file that contains the command interpreter*) fichier *m* COMMAND.COM

command console processor /kə'mɑːnd ˌkɒnsəʊl ˌprəʊsesə/ *noun* processeur *m* de console

command control language /kəˌmɑːnd kən'trəʊl ˌlæŋgwɪdʒ/ *noun* langage *m* de contrôle

command-driven program /kəˌmɑːnd ˌdrɪv(ə)n 'prəʊgræm/ *noun* programme *m* activé par commande

command file /kə'mɑːnd faɪl/ *noun* fichier *m* de commandes

command file processor /kə'mɑːnd faɪl ˌprəʊsesə/ *noun* processeur *m* de fichier de commandes

command interface /kə'mɑːnd ˌɪntəfeɪs/ *noun* interface *f* de commande; interface *f* de contrôle

command interpreter /kə'mɑːnd ɪn ˌtɜːprɪtə/ *noun* interpréteur *m* de commandes

command key /kə'mɑːnd kiː/ *noun* touche *f* de commande

command language /kə'mɑːnd ˌlæŋgwɪdʒ/ *noun* langage *m* de commande

command line /kə'mɑːnd laɪn/ *noun* **1.** (*of a program line*) ligne *f* de commande (d'un programme) **2.** (*of a prompt*) ligne *f* de commande

> 'This gives Unix a friendly face instead of the terrifyingly complex command-line prompts that make most users reach for their manuals.' [*Computing*]

command line argument /kəˌmaːnd laɪn 'aːgjʊmənt/ *noun* argument *m* de ligne de commande

command line interface /kəˌmaːnd laɪn 'ɪntəfeɪs/ *noun* interface *f* de ligne de commande

command line operating system /kə ˌmaːnd laɪn 'ɒpəreɪtɪŋ ˌsɪstəm/ *noun* système *m* de ligne de commande

command message /kə'maːnd ˌmesɪdʒ/ *noun* message *m* d'ordre

command mode /kə'maːnd məʊd/ *noun* mode *m* commande

command prompt /kə'maːnd prɒmpt/ *noun* invite *f*

command register /kə'maːnd ˌredʒɪstə/ *noun* registre *m* de commande; registre *m* d'instruction

command state /kə'maːnd steɪt/ *noun* état *m* commande

command window /kə'maːnd ˌwɪndəʊ/ *noun* fenêtre *f* de commande ◇ **the command window is a single line at the bottom of the screen** la fenêtre de commande est une seule ligne au bas de l'écran

comment /'kɒment/ *noun* (*note in a program*) note *f*; explication *f*; commentaire *m* ◇ **BASIC allows comments to be written after a REM instruction** en BASIC il est possible d'inclure des commentaires à la suite de l'instruction REM

comment field /'kɒment fiːld/ *noun* champ *m* bloc-notes

comment out /'kɒment aʊt/ *noun* mise *f* en commentaire

commerce /'kɒmɜːs/ commerce *m* électronique

commerce server /'kɒmɜːs ˌsɜːvə/ *noun* serveur *m* commercial

commercial Internet exchange /kə ˌmɜːʃ(ə)l 'ɪntənet ɪksˌtʃeɪndʒ/ *noun* couplage *m* de la téléphonie et de l'informatique

common algorithmic language /ˌkɒmən ˌælgərɪðmɪk 'læŋgwɪdʒ/ *noun* langage *m* (de programmation structurée) COMAL

common business orientated language /ˌkɒmən ˌbɪznɪs ˌɔːriənteɪtɪd 'læŋgwɪdʒ/ *noun* COBOL

common carrier /ˌkɒmən 'kæriə/ *noun* (*network*) ligne *f* banalisée; (*information*) entreprise *m* de diffusion d'informations grand public; (*private company that supplies data*) canal *m* banal

common channel signalling /ˌkɒmən 'tʃæn(ə)l ˌsɪgn(ə)lɪŋ/ *noun* signalisation *f* par canal banal; signalisation *f* par voie commune

common gateway interface /ˌkɒmən 'geɪtweɪ ˌɪntəfeɪs/ *noun* CGI

common hardware /ˌkɒmən 'haːdweə/ *noun* matériel *m* commun

common language /ˌkɒmən 'læŋgwɪdʒ/ *noun* langage *m* commun

common management information protocol /ˌkɒmən ˌmænɪdʒmənt ˌɪnfə'meɪʃ(ə)n ˌprəʊtəkɒl/ *noun* protocole *m* CMIP

common object request broker architecture /ˌkɒmən əbˌdʒekt rɪˌkwest ˌbrəʊkə 'aːkɪtektʃə/ *noun* standard *m* Corba

common ordinary business-oriented language /ˌkɒmən ˌɔːd(ə)n(ə)ri ˌbɪznɪs ˌɔːriəntɪd 'læŋgwɪdʒ/ *noun* COBOL

common software /ˌkɒmən 'sɒftweə/ *noun* (*routine used by any program*) logiciel *m* commun; logiciel *m* de réseau; logiciel *m* partagé

common storage area /ˌkɒmən 'stɔːrɪdʒ ˌeəriə/ *noun* zone *f* commune de la mémoire

communicating word processor /kə ˌmjuːnɪkeɪtɪŋ 'wɜːd ˌprəʊsesə/ *noun* système *m* de traitement de texte doté d'une interface de communication

communications buffer /kəˌmjuːnɪ 'keɪʃ(ə)nz ˌbʌfə/ *noun* mémoire *f* tampon de transmission de données

communications channel /kəˌmjuːnɪ 'keɪʃ(ə)nz ˌtʃæn(ə)l/ *noun* canal *m* de transmission

communications computer /kəˌmjuːnɪ 'keɪʃ(ə)nz kəmˌpjuːtə/ *noun* ordinateur *m* de contrôle des transmissions

communications control unit /kə ˌmjuːnɪkeɪʃ(ə)nz kən'trəʊl ˌjuːnɪt/ *noun* contrôleur *m* de communication

communications executive /kəˌmjuːnɪ 'keɪʃ(ə)nz ɪgˌzekjʊtɪv/ *noun* gestionnaire *m* de transmission

communications interface adapter /kə ˌmjuːnɪkeɪʃ(ə)nz 'ɪntəfeɪs əˌdæptə/ *noun* adaptateur *m* d'interface de communication

communications link /kəˌmjuːnɪ'keɪʃ(ə)nz lɪŋk/ *noun* liaison *f*

communications link control /kə ˌmjuːnɪkeɪʃ(ə)nz lɪŋk kən'trəʊl/ *noun* contrôle *m* de ligne de communication; contrôle *m* de ligne de transmission

communications network /kəˌmjuːnɪ 'keɪʃ(ə)nz ˌnetwɜːk/ *noun* (*transfer of data*) réseau *m* de communication

communications network processor /kə ˌmjuːnɪkeɪʃ(ə)nz ˌnetwɜːk 'prəʊsesə/ *noun* processeur *m* de réseau

communications package /kəˌmjuːnɪ 'keɪʃ(ə)nz ˌpækɪdʒ/ *noun* logiciel *m*

communications port /kəˌmjuːnɪ'keɪʃ(ə)nz pɔːt/ *noun* port *m* de communication

communications protocol /kəˌmjuːnɪ 'keɪʃ(ə)nz ˌprəʊtəʊkɒl/ *noun* protocole *m* de communication

communications scanner /kəˌmjuːnɪ 'keɪʃ(ə)nz ˌskænə/ *noun* (*monitoring equipment*) scanner *m* de contrôle d'appel; scanner *m* de demande de communication

communications server /kə,mju:nɪ 'keɪʃ(ə)nz ,sɜːvə/ *noun* serveur *m* de communication

communications software /kə,mju:nɪ 'keɪʃ(ə)nz ,sɒftweə/ *noun* logiciel *m* de communication

community /kə'mju:nɪti/ *noun* communauté *f* virtuelle

comp /kɒmp/ *noun* racine *f* de discussion

compact code /'kɒmpækt kəʊd/ *noun* code *m* compacté

compact disc /,kɒmpækt 'dɪsk/ *noun* disque *m* compact

compact disc-digital audio /,kɒmpækt ,dɪsk ,dɪdʒɪt(ə)l 'ɔːdiəʊ/ *noun* CD *m* audio

compact disc erasable /,kɒmpækt ,dɪsk ɪ 'reɪzəb(ə)l/ *noun* CD *m* réinscriptible

compact disc-interactive /,kɒmpækt dɪsk ,ɪntər'æktɪv/ *noun* CD *m* interactif

compact disc player /,kɒmpækt 'dɪsk ,pleɪə/ *noun* platine *f* laser; platine *f* de disques compacts

compact disc ROM /,kɒmpækt ,dɪsk 'rɒm/ *noun* disque *m* compact à lecture seule

compact Flash /kəm,pækt 'flæʃ/ *noun* compact Flash

compacting algorithm /,kɒmpæktɪŋ 'ælgə ,rɪð(ə)m/ *noun* algorithme *m* de compression

compact model /'kɒmpækt ,mɒd(ə)l/ *noun* modèle *m* compact

companding /kɒm'pændɪŋ/ *noun* compression-extension *f*

COMPAQ /'kɒmpæk/ (*US personal computer company*) Compaq™

comparator /kəm'pærətə/ *noun* comparateur *m*

compatibility /kəm,pætɪ'bɪlɪti/ *noun* (*ability of two devices to function together*) compatibilité *f* ◇ **OS *or* 2 has a compatibility box to allow it to run DOS applications** OS/2 possède une fenêtre de compatibilité qui permet de faire tourner les applications sous DOS

'The manufacturer claims that this card does not require special drivers on the host machine... and therefore has fewer compatibility problems.' [*Computing*]

compatibility box /kəm,pætə'bɪlɪti bɒks/ *noun* fenêtre *f* de compatibilité

compatible /kəm'pætɪb(ə)l/ *adjective* compatible ■ *noun* compatible *m*

'...this was the only piece of software I found that wouldn't work, but it does show that there is no such thing as a totally compatible PC clone' [*Personal Computer World*]

compilation /,kɒmpɪ'leɪʃ(ə)n/ *noun* compilation *f*

'This utility divides the compilation of software into pieces and performs the compile in parallel across available machines on the network.' [*Computergram*]

compilation error /,kɒmpɪ'leɪʃ(ə)n ,erə/ *noun* erreur *f* de compilation ◇ **compilation errors result in the job being aborted** les erreurs de compilation provoquent l'interruption inopinée de la tâche

compilation time /,kɒmpɪ'leɪʃ(ə)n taɪm/ *noun* temps *m* de compilation; durée *f* de compilation

compile /kəm'paɪl/ *verb* compiler *vt* ◇ **compiled BASIC programs run much faster than the interpreter version** les programmes BASIC compilés sont plus rapides que la version interpréteur ◇ **compiling takes a long time with this old version** il faut beaucoup de temps pour faire la compilation avec cette ancienne version du programme ◇ **debug your program, then compile it** déboguez votre programme avant de le compiler

compile and go /kəm,paɪl ən 'gəʊ/ *noun* compilation *f* et exécution

compile phase /kəm'paɪl feɪz/ *noun* phase *f* de compilation

compiler /kəm,paɪlə 'prəʊgræm/, **compiler program** *noun* compilateur *m*

compiler diagnostics /kəm,paɪlə ,daɪəg 'nɒstɪks/ *plural noun* outils *mpl* de diagnostic du compilateur ◇ **thorough compiler diagnostics make debugging easy** les outils de diagnostic de compilation bien conçus facilitent le débogage

compiler language /kəm'paɪlə ,læŋgwɪdʒ/ *noun* langage *m* de compilation

complement /'kɒmplɪment/ *noun* **1.** (*inversion of binary digit*) complément *m* **2.** (*result of subtraction*) complément *m* ■ *verb* (*to invert a binary digit*) calculer un complément ◇ **the complement is found by changing the 1s to 0s and 0s to 1s** on trouve les compléments en remplaçant les 1 par des 0 et les 0 par des 1

complementary metal oxide semiconductor /,kɒmplɪment(ə)ri ,met(ə)l ,ɒksaɪd 'semikən,dʌktə/ *noun* semi-conducteur *m* CMOS

complementary operation /,kɒmplɪment(ə)ri ,ɒpə'reɪʃ(ə)n/ *noun* opération *f* complémentaire

complementation /,kɒmplɪmən'teɪʃ(ə)n/ *noun* nombres *mpl* complets

complemented /'kɒmplɪməntɪd/ *adjective* complémenté *or* -ée

complete operation /kəm,pliːt ,ɒpə 'reɪʃ(ə)n/ *noun* opération *f* au complet

completion /kəm'pliːʃ(ə)n/ *noun* fin *f*; achèvement *m*

complex instruction set computer /,kɒmpleks ɪn,strʌkʃən ,set kəm'pjuːtə/ *noun* ordinateur *m* à jeu d'instructions complexe (CISC)

complexity measure /kəm'pleksɪti ,meʒə/ *noun* niveau *m* de complexité

compliant /kəm'plaɪənt/ *adjective* compatible

component density /kəm,pəʊnənt 'densɪti/ *noun* densité *f* des composants

component error /kəm'pəʊnənt ,erə/ *noun* erreur *f* imputable à un composant défectueux

composite circuit /,kɒmpəzɪt 'sɜːkɪt/ *noun* circuit *m* composite

composite display /,kɒmpəzɪt dɪ'spleɪ/ *noun* affichage *m* composite

composite video /,kɒmpəzɪt 'vɪdiəʊ/ *noun* vidéo *f* composite

compound /'kɒmpaʊnd/ *adjective* composé *or* -ée

compound document /'kɒmpaʊnd ,dɒkjʊmənt/ *noun* document *m* composite

compound file /'kɒmpaʊnd faɪl/ *noun* fichier *m* composite

compound logical element /,kɒmpaʊnd ,lɒdʒɪk(ə)l 'elɪmənt/ *noun* élément *m* logique composé; élément *m* logique multiple

compound statement /,kɒmpaʊnd 'steɪtmənt/ *noun* instruction *f* composée ◇ **the debugger cannot handle compound statements** le débogueur ne peut agir sur les instructions composées

compressed video /,kɒmprest 'vɪdiəʊ/ *noun* vidéo *f* comprimé

compression /kəm'preʃ(ə)n/ *noun* compression *f*

compression ratio /kəm'preʃ(ə)n ,reɪʃiəʊ/ *noun* rapport *m* de compression

CompuServe /'kɒmpjuːsɜːv/ (*one of the largest US-based online information services*) CompuServe™

computer /kəm'pjuːtə/ *noun* ordinateur *m*; (*calculating machine*) calculateur *m* ◇ **single board computer (sbc)** ordinateur monocarte *or* à carte unique

computer-aided /kəm,pjuːtə 'eɪdɪd/ *adjective* assisté,-ée par ordinateur

computer-aided design /kəm,pjuːtər ,eɪdɪd dɪ'zaɪn/ *noun* conception *f* assistée par ordinateur

computer-aided engineering /kəm,pjuːtər ,eɪdɪd ,endʒɪ'nɪərɪŋ/ *noun* ingénierie *f* assistée par ordinateur

computer-aided instruction /kəm,pjuːtər ,eɪdɪd ɪn'strʌkʃən/ *noun* enseignement *m* assisté par ordinateur

computer-aided learning /kəm,pjuːtər ,eɪdɪd 'lɜːnɪŋ/ *noun* formation *f* assistée par ordinateur

computer-aided manufacture /kəm ,pjuːtər ,eɪdɪd ,mænjʊ'fæktʃə/ *noun* fabrication *f* assistée par ordinateur

computer-aided testing /kəm,pjuːtər ,eɪdɪd 'testɪŋ/ *noun* test *m* assisté par ordinateur

computer-aided training /kəm,pjuːtər ,eɪdɪd 'treɪnɪŋ/ *noun* apprentissage *m* assisté par ordinateur

computer animation /kəm,pjuːtə ,ænɪ'meɪʃ(ə)n/ *noun* animation *f* sur ordinateur

computer applications /kəm,pjuːtə ,æplɪ'keɪʃ(ə)nz/ *plural noun* applications *fpl* informatiques

computer architecture /kəm,pjuːtə 'ɑːkɪtektʃə/ *noun* **1.** architecture *f* d'un système **2.** architecture *f* d'ordinateur

computer-assisted /kəm,pjuːtər ə'sɪstɪd/ *adjective* assisté par ordinateur

computer-assisted design /kəm,pjuːtər ə ,sɪstɪd dɪ'zaɪn/ *noun* conception *f* assistée par ordinateur

computer-assisted engineering /kəm ,pjuːtər ə,sɪstɪd ,endʒɪ'nɪərɪŋ/ *noun* ingénierie *f* assistée par ordinateur

computer-assisted instruction /kəm ,pjuːtər ə,sɪstɪd ɪn'strʌkʃən/ *noun* enseignement *m* assisté par ordinateur

computer-assisted learning /kəm,pjuːtər ə,sɪstɪd 'lɜːnɪŋ/ *noun* enseignement *m* assisté par ordinateur

computer-assisted manufacture /kəm ,pjuːtər ə,sɪstɪd ,mænjʊ'fæktʃə/ *noun* fabrication *f* assistée par ordinateur

computer-assisted testing /kəm,pjuːtər ə ,sɪstɪd 'testɪŋ/ *noun* test *m* assisté par ordinateur

computer-assisted training /kəm,pjuːtər ə,sɪstɪd 'treɪnɪŋ/ *noun* formation *f* assistée par ordinateur

computer-based learning /kəm,pjuːtə beɪst 'lɜːnɪŋ/ *noun* enseignement *m* assisté par ordinateur

computer-based message system /kəm ,pjuːtə beɪst 'mesɪdʒ ,sɪstəm/ *noun* système *m* de messagerie

computer-based training /kəm,pjuːtə beɪst 'treɪnɪŋ/ *noun* apprentissage *m* assistée par ordinateur

computer bureau /kəm'pjuːtə ,bjʊərəʊ/ *noun* société *f* de services et d'ingénierie informatique (SSII)

computer code /kəm'pjuːtə kəʊd/ *noun* code *m* d'instruction

computer conferencing /kəm,pjuːtə 'kɒnf(ə)rənsɪŋ/ *noun* (*use of computers and terminals to communicate*) téléconférence *f*

computer crime /kəm'pjuːtə kraɪm/ *noun* fraude *f* informatique

computer dating /kəm,pjuːtə 'deɪtɪŋ/ *noun* rencontre *f* matrimoniale assistée par ordinateur

computer department /kəm'pjuːtə dɪ ,pɑːtmənt/ *noun* service *m* informatique

computer engineer /kəm,pjuːtə ,endʒɪ'nɪə/ *noun* ingénieur *m* informaticien

computer error /kəmˌpjuːtər 'erə/ *noun* erreur *f* due à l'ordinateur

computer file /kəm'pjuːtə faɪl/ *noun* fichier *m* informatique; fichier *m* d'ordinateur

computer fraud /kəm'pjuːtə frɔːd/ *noun* fraude *f* informatique

computer game /kəm'pjuːtə geɪm/ *noun* (*game played on a computer*) jeu *m* électronique

computer-generated /kəmˌpjuːtə 'dʒenəreɪtɪd/ *adjective* conçu,-e par ordinateur; créé, -ée par ordinateur ◇ **computer-generated graphics** images conçues sur ordinateur *or* images de synthèse *or* graphismes *mpl*

computer generation /kəmˌpjuːtə ˌdʒenə'reɪʃ(ə)n/ *noun* génération *f* d'ordinateurs

computer graphics /kəmˌpjuːtə 'græfɪks/ *plural noun* (*information displayed graphically*) infographie *fpl*

computer graphics metafile /kəmˌpjuːtə ˌgræfɪks 'metəfaɪl/ *noun* CGM

computer illiterate /kəmˌpjuːtə ɪ'lɪtərət/ *adjective* qui ne possède aucune connaissance informatique; qui ne comprend pas le jargon informatique

computer image processing /kəmˌpjuːtə 'ɪmɪdʒ ˌprəʊsesɪŋ/ *noun* traitement *m* informatique de l'image

computer-independent language /kəm ˌpjuːtə ˌɪndɪpendənt 'læŋgwɪdʒ/ *noun* langage *m* commun

computer indexing /kəmˌpjuːtə 'ɪndeksɪŋ/ *noun* indexation *f* sur ordinateur; préparation *f* d'un index à l'aide d'un ordinateur

computer input microfilm /kəmˌpjuːtə ˌɪnpʊt 'maɪkrəʊfɪlm/ *noun* numérisation *f* de micro-images

computer-integrated manufacturing /kəmˌpjuːtə ˌɪntɪgreɪtɪd ˌmænjʊ'fæktʃərɪŋ/ *noun* productique *f* intégrée

computer-integrated system /kəmˌpjuːtə ˌɪntɪgreɪtɪd 'sɪstəm/ *noun* système *m* d'exploitation intégrée

computer-integrated telephony /kəm ˌpjuːtə ˌɪntɪgreɪtɪd tə'lefəni/ *noun* couplage *m* de la téléphonie et de l'informatique

computerisation /kəmˌpjʊtəraɪ'zeɪʃ(ə)n/, **computerization** *noun* informatisation *f*

computerise /kəm'pjuːtəraɪz/, **computerize** *verb* informatiser *vt*

computer language /kəm'pjuːtə ˌlæŋgwɪdʒ/ *noun* langage *m* informatique

computer listing /kəmˌpjuːtə 'lɪstɪŋ/ *noun* (*printout of a list of items*) sortie *f* d'imprimante; listing *m*

computer literacy /kəmˌpjuːtə 'lɪt(ə)rəsi/ *noun* connaissances *fpl* en informatique

computer-literate /kəmˌpjuːtə 'lɪt(ə)rət/ *adjective* qui a des connaissances en informatique

computer logic /kəmˌpjuːtə 'lɒdʒɪk/ *noun* logique *f* des ordinateurs; logique *f* informatique

computer-managed instruction /kəm ˌpjuːtə ˌmænɪdʒd ɪn'strʌkʃən/ *noun* gestion *f* informatique de l'apprentissage

computer-managed learning /kəmˌpjuːtə ˌmænɪdʒd 'lɜːnɪŋ/ *noun* apprentissage *m* géré par ordinateur

computer manager /kəm'pjuːtə ˌmænɪdʒə/ *noun* directeur, -trice *m,f* du service informatique

computer name /kəm'pjuːtə neɪm/ *plural noun* nom *m* d'ordinateur

computer network /kəmˌpjuːtə 'netwɜːk/ *noun* (*shared use of computers, terminals and peripherals*) réseau *m* informatique; réseau *m* d'ordinateurs

computer numerical control /kəmˌpjuːtə njuːˌmerɪk(ə)l kən'trəʊl/ *noun* commande *f* numérique par calculateur

computer office system /kəmˌpjuːtər 'ɒfɪs ˌsɪstəm/ *noun* système *m* informatique pour bureau

computer operator /kəm'pjuːtər ˌɒpəreɪtə/ *noun* opérateur, -trice d'ordinateur

computer organisation /kəm'pjuːtər ˌɔːgənaɪzeɪʃ(ə)n/, **computer organization** *noun* architecture *f* d'un système; architecture *f* d'un ordinateur

computer output /kəmˌpjuːtər 'aʊtpʊt/ *noun* (*data processed by a computer*) données *fpl* de sortie

computer output on microfilm /kəm ˌpjuːtər ˌaʊtpʊt ɒn 'maɪkrəʊfɪlm/ *noun* stockage *m* sur microfilm

computer power /kəm'pjuːtə ˌpaʊə/ *noun* puissance *f* d'un ordinateur

computer printer /kəmˌpjuːtə 'prɪntə/ *noun* imprimante *f* d'ordinateur

computer printout /kəmˌpjuːtə 'prɪntaʊt/ *noun* (*printed information*) sortie *f* d'imprimante

computer program /kəm'pjuːtə ˌprəʊgræm/ *noun* programme *m* informatique

computer programmer /kəmˌpjuːtə 'prəʊgræmə/ *noun* programmeur *m or* -euse *f*

computer-readable /kəmˌpjuːtə 'riːdəb(ə)l/ *adjective* en langage machine

computer run /kəm'pjuːtə rʌn/ *noun* exécution *f* d'un programme

computer science /kəmˌpjuːtə 'saɪəns/ *noun* l'informatique *f*

computer services /kəmˌpjuːtə 'sɜːvɪsɪz/ *plural noun* services *mpl* informatiques

computer stationery /kəmˌpjuːtə 'steɪʃ(ə)n(ə)ri/ *noun* (*computer printer*) papier *m* listing

computer system /kəm'pjuːtə ˌsɪstəm/ *noun* système *m* informatique

computer-telephony integration /kəm ˌpjuːtə təˌlefəni ˌɪntɪ'greɪʃ(ə)n/ *noun* couplage *m* de la téléphonie et de l'informatique

computer time /kəm'pjuːtə taɪm/ *noun* temps *m* d'ordinateur ◇ **running all those sales reports costs a lot in computer time** tous ces rapports de vente coûtent cher en temps d'ordinateur

computer virus /kəm'pjuːtə ˌvaɪrəs/ *noun* virus *m* informatique

computer word /kəm'pjuːtə wɜːd/ *noun* mot *m*

computing /kəm'pjuːtɪŋ/ *noun* informatique *f*

computing power /kəm'pjuːtɪŋ ˌpaʊə/ *noun* puissance *f* de calcul

computing speed /kəm'pjuːtɪŋ spiːd/ *noun* vitesse *f* de calcul par ordinateur

CON /kɒn/ *noun* (*in IBM-PC compatible systems: name used to identify the console*) CON; console *f*

concatenate /kən'kætəneɪt/ *verb* enchaîner *vt*; chaîner *vt*; concaténer *vt*

concatenated data set /kənˌkætəneɪtɪd 'deɪtə ˌset/ *noun* concaténation *f*

concatenation operator /kənˌkætə 'neɪʃ(ə)n ˌɒpəreɪtə/ *noun* opérateur *m* de concaténation

conceal /kən'siːl/ *verb* (*to hide information or graphics*) cacher *vt*; (*information or graphics*) dissimuler *vt*; (*to hide information or graphics*) masquer *vt* ◇ **the hidden lines are concealed from view with this algorithm** les lignes qui n'apparaissent pas sont masquées par cet algorithme

concentrate /'kɒnsəntreɪt/ *verb* (*light ray*) concentrer *vt*; (*line or circuit or data*) condenser *vt*; compresser *vt*; compacter *vt*; comprimer *vt* ◇ **the concentrated data was transmitted cheaply** les données compressées *or* comprimées ont pu être transmises à peu de frais ◇ **to concentrate a beam of light on a lens** concentrer un rayon lumineux sur une lentille

concentrator /'kɒnsəntreɪtə/ *noun* **1.** (*in a Token-Ring network*) concentrateur *m* **2.** (*in an FDDI network*) noeud *m* d'accès au réseau **3.** (*in an 10Base-T Ethernet network*) concentrateur *m* 10base-T **4.** (*in general networking*) concentrateur *m* de réseau

conceptual model /kənˌseptʃuəl 'mɒd(ə)l/ *noun* (*description of a database*) modèle *m* conceptuel

concertina fold /ˌkɒnsə'tiːnə fəʊld/ *noun* papier *m* plié en paravent; papier *m* en accordéon; papier *m* en éventail; papier *m* en continu

concurrency /kən'kʌrənsi/ *noun* accès *m* simultané

concurrent operating system /kənˌkʌrənt 'ɒpəreɪtɪŋ ˌsɪstəm/ *noun* système *m* d'exploitation multiprogramme

concurrent processing /kənˌkʌrənt 'prəʊsesɪŋ/ *noun* multitraitement *m*

concurrent programming /kənˌkʌrənt 'prəʊgræmɪŋ/ *noun* multiprogrammation *f*

condition /kən'dɪʃ(ə)n/ *noun* **1.** (*state of device etc*) condition *f*; état *m* **2.** (*requirement for action*) condition *f vt* ■ *verb* (*to modify data*) adapter *vt*; conditionner *vt* ◇ **condition the raw data to a standard format** adaptez les données brutes à un format standard

conditional /kən'dɪʃ(ə)n(ə)l/ *adjective* **1.** conditionnel *or* -elle **2.** (*of a process*) conditionnel *or* -elle

conditional branch /kənˌdɪʃ(ə)n(ə)l 'brɑːntʃ/ *noun* branchement *m* conditionnel

conditional breakpoint /kənˌdɪʃ(ə)nəl 'breɪkpɔɪnt/ *noun* arrêt *m* conditionnel

conditional jump /kən'dɪʃ(ə)nəl dʒʌmp/ *noun* branchement *m* conditionnel; saut *m* conditionnel

conditional statement /kənˌdɪʃ(ə)nəl 'steɪtmənt/ *noun* commande *f* conditionnelle; instruction *f* conditionnelle

conditional transfer /kənˌdɪʃ(ə)nəl 'trænsfɜː/ *noun* transfert branchement *m*; transfert *m* conditionnel

condition code /kən'dɪʃ(ə)n kəʊd/ *noun* indicateur *m* d'état

condition code register /kənˌdɪʃ(ə)n 'kəʊd ˌredʒɪstə/ *noun* registre *m* des codes condition

conduct /kən'dʌkt/ *verb* conduire *vt*; transmettre *vt* ◇ **copper conducts well** le cuivre est bon conducteur (d'électricité) ◇ **to conduct electricity** conduire l'électricité

conduction /kən'dʌkʃən/ *noun* conductibilité *f*; conduction *f* ◇ **the conduction of electricity by gold contacts** conduction (d'électricité) par broches de contact (en) or

conductive /kən'dʌktɪv/ *adjective* conductible

conductor /kən'dʌktə/ *noun* conducteur *m* ◇ **copper is a good conductor of electricity** le cuivre est un bon conducteur

conduit /'kɒndjuɪt/ *noun* (*protective pipe*) conduite *f*; tube *m*; tuyau *m*; canalisation *f* ◇ **the cables from each terminal are channelled to the computer centre by metal conduit** les câbles de liaison de tous les terminaux sont acheminés par conduite métallique *or* par canalisation métallique *or* sous gaine métallique jusqu'au centre informatique

conferencing /'kɒnf(ə)rənsɪŋ/ *noun* (*connection by modem*) téléconférence *f*

> 'Small organisations and individuals find it convenient to use online services, offering email, conferencing and information services.' [*Computing*]

confidence level /'kɒnfɪd(ə)ns ˌlev(ə)l/ *noun* (*statistics*) niveau *m* de confiance

CONFIG.SYS /kən'fɪɡ sɪs/ *noun* (*configuration text file*) CONFIG.SYS ◇ **if you add a new adapter card to your PC you will have to add a new command to the CONFIG.SYS file** si vous installez une nouvelle carte adaptateur sur votre PC, il faudra ajouter une nouvelle commande dans le fichier CONFIG.SYS

configuration /kən,fɪɡjə'reɪʃ(ə)n/ *noun* configuration *f*

'He said only Banyan Vines had the network configuration and administration capabilities required for implementing an international business plan based on client-server computing.' [*Computing*]

configuration file /kən,fɪɡjə'reɪʃ(ə)n faɪl/ *noun* fichier *m* de configuration

configuration state /kən,fɪɡjə'reɪʃ(ə)n steɪt/ *noun* état *m* de configuration

configure /kən'fɪɡə/ *verb* configurer *vt* ◇ **this terminal has been configured to display graphics** ce terminal est configuré pour l'affichage de graphiques ◇ **you only have to configure the PC once – when you first buy it** il suffit de configurer l'ordinateur individuel une seule fois, à l'achat

configured-in /kən'fɪɡəd ɪn/ *adjective* (*ready to use*) configuré *or* -ée; avec configuration validée; prêt à fonctionner; disponible

configured-off /kən'fɪɡəd ɒf/, **configured-out** /kən'fɪɡəd aʊt/ *adjective* avec configuration invalidée; indisponible

congestion /kən'dʒestʃən/ *noun* (*of system*) encombrement *m*

conjunct /'kɒndʒʌŋkt/ *noun* (*in an logical function*) opérande *m* d'une opération ET; opérande *m* d'une conjonction

conjunction /kən'dʒʌŋkʃən/ *noun* (*logical function*) conjonction *f*; opération *f* ET; intersection *f*

connect /kə'nekt/ *verb* (*to link circuits or communication networks*) connecter à; relier à; brancher sur

connect charge /kə'nekt tʃɑːdʒ/ *noun* coût *m* de connexion

connectionless /kə'nekʃənləs/ *adjective* non connecté *or* -ée

connectionless network protocol /kə,nekʃənləs 'netwɜːk ,prəʊtəkɒl/ *noun* protocole *m* CLNP

connection-oriented /kə'nekʃ(ə)n ,ɔːrientɪd/ *adjective* avec connexion

connective /kə'nektɪv/ *noun* (*symbol between two operands*) connectif *m*

connectivity /,kɒnek'tɪvɪti/ *noun* (*ability of a device to connect with other devices*) connectivité *f*; liaison *f*

connector /kə'nektə/ *noun* connecteur *m* ◇ **the connector at the end of the cable will fit any standard serial port** le connecteur attaché au câble s'adapte sur tout port série standard

connector plug /kə'nektə plʌɡ/ *noun* prise *f* mâle de connecteur

connector receptacle /kə'nektə rɪ,septək(ə)l/ *noun* prise *f* femelle de connecteur

connect state /kə'nekt steɪt/ *noun* état *m* connecté

connect time /kə'nekt taɪm/ *noun* temps *m* de connexion

conscious error /,kɒnʃəs 'erə/ *noun* erreur *f* consciente

consistency check /kən'sɪstənsi tʃek/ *noun* (*to make sure that data or items conform*) contrôle *m* de cohérence

console /'kɒnsəʊl/ *noun* (*unit connected to a computer system*) console *f*; poste *m* de travail ◇ **the console consists of input device such as a keyboard, and an output device such as a printer or CRT** la console comporte un périphérique d'entrée, soit un clavier, et un périphérique de sortie, soit une imprimante ou un écran

constant /'kɒnstənt/ *noun* (*as opposed to a variable*) constante *f* ■ *adjective* (*which does not change*) constant *or* -e; fixe ◇ **constant angular velocity (CAV)** (*disk technology*) vitesse angulaire constante ◇ **constant bit rate (CBR)** (*data transfer service that is part of ATM*) débit binaire constant ◇ **constant linear velocity (CLV)** vitesse linéaire constante ◇ **constant velocity** vitesse constante ◇ **the disk drive motor spins at a constant velocity** le moteur du lecteur de disque tourne à une vitesse constante

constant angular velocity /,kɒnstənt ,æŋɡjʊlə və'lɒsɪti/ *noun* vitesse *f* angulaire constante

constant bit rate /,kɒnstənt 'bɪt ,reɪt/ *noun* débit *m* binaire constant

constant length field /,kɒnstənt leŋθ 'fiːld/ *noun* champ *m* de taille fixe

constant linear velocity /,kɒnstənt ,lɪniə və'lɒsɪti/ *noun* vitesse *f* linéaire constante

constant ratio code /,kɒnstənt 'reɪʃiəʊ ,kəʊd/ *noun* code *m* à rapport constant; code *m* à rapport de bits fixe

constrain /kən'streɪn/ *verb* contraindre *vt*

consumables /kən'sjuːməb(ə)lz/ *plural noun* produits *mpl*; articles *mpl* de consommation; consommables *mpl* ◇ **put all the printer leads and paper under the heading 'consumables'** il faut inclure les câbles pour imprimantes et le papier sous la rubrique 'consommables'

contact /'kɒntækt/ *noun* (*section of a switch or connector*) contact *m*; connexion *f* ■ *verb* contacter *vt* ◇ **contact negative** (*photography*) (film) négatif *m* contact ◇ **contact print** épreuve *f* de contact ◇ **the circuit is not working be-**

cause the contact is dirty** le circuit ne fonctionne pas parce que la connexion est encrassée

contact bounce /'kɒntækt baʊns/ *noun* rebond *m*

contact card /'kɒntækt kɑːd/ *noun* carte *f* intelligente par contact

content /'kɒntent/ *noun* (*ideas*) contenu *m*

content-addressable /ˌkɒntent ə 'dresəb(ə)l/ *adjective* adressable par le contenu

content-addressable addressing /ˌkɒntent əˌdresəb(ə)l ə'dresɪŋ/ *noun* adressage *m* associatif

content-addressable file /ˌkɒntent ə ˌdresəb(ə)l 'faɪl/ *noun* fichier *m*

content-addressable memory /ˌkɒntent ə ˌdresəb(ə)l 'mem(ə)ri/, **content-addressable storage** /əˌsəʊsiətɪv 'stɔːrɪdʒ/ *noun* mémoire *f* adressable par son contenu

contention /kən'tenʃən/ *noun* contention *f*

contention bus /kən'tenʃ(ə)n bʌs/ *noun* bus *m* d'arbitrage

contention delay /kən'tenʃ(ə)n dɪˌleɪ/ *noun* délai *m*

content provider /'kɒntent prəˌvaɪdə/ *noun* fournisseur *m* d'information

contents /'kɒntents/ *plural noun* liste *fpl*; répertoire *m*

context /'kɒntekst/ *noun* contexte *m* ◇ **the example shows how the word is used in context** l'exemple démontre l'emploi du mot dans son contexte

context-sensitive /ˌkɒntekst 'sensɪtɪv/ *adjective* (*relating to the particular context*) en fonction du contexte

context-sensitive help /ˌkɒntekst ˌsensɪtɪv 'help/ *noun* aide *f* en ligne liée au contexte

context-switching /'kɒntekst ˌswɪtʃɪŋ/ *noun* basculement *m*; changement *m* d'application

contiguous file /kənˌtɪgjʊəs 'faɪl/ *noun* fichier *m* contigu

contiguous graphics /kənˌtɪgjʊəs 'græfɪks/ *plural noun* graphiques *mpl* contigus

contingency plan /kən'tɪndʒənsi plæn/ *noun* plan *m* d'urgence

continuation page /kənˌtɪnjʊ'eɪʃ(ə)n peɪdʒ/ *noun* suite *f*

continuity /ˌkɒntɪ'njuːɪti/ *noun* (*conduction path*) continuité *f*

continuous data stream /kənˌtɪnjʊəs 'deɪtə ˌstriːm/ *noun* flux *m* continu; ininterrompu de données

continuous feed /kənˌtɪnjuəs 'fiːd/ *noun* alimentation *f* du papier en continu

continuous labels /kənˌtɪnjʊəs 'leɪb(ə)lz/ *plural noun* étiquettes *fpl* en continu

continuous loop /kənˌtɪnjʊəs 'luːp/ *noun* boucle *f* sans fin

continuous signal /kənˌtɪnjʊəs 'sɪgn(ə)l/ *noun* signal *m* continu

continuous stationery /kənˌtɪnjʊəs 'steɪʃ(ə)n(ə)ri/ *noun* papier *m* en continu

continuous tone /kən'tɪnjʊəs təʊn/ *noun* photographie *f* en demi-teinte

contouring /'kɒntʊərɪŋ/ *noun* contournage *m*

contrast /'kɒntrɑːst/ *noun* **1.** (*differences in colours*) contraste *m* **2.** (*knob or key*) bouton *m*; touche *f* de contraste ◇ **the control allows you to adjust brightness and contrast** ce bouton vous permet de régler la luminosité et le contraste

contrast enhancement filter /ˌkɒntrɑːst ɪn 'hɑːnsmənt ˌfɪltə/ *noun* filtre *m* d'amélioration du contraste

control /kən'trəʊl/ *noun* **1.** (*section of computer or device that carries out instructions*) contrôle *m*; pilote *m* **2.** (*conditional statement in a program*) contrôle *m*; pilote *m* **3.** (*key sending control character*) touche *f* de contrôle; touche *f* de commande **4.** (*data or key that controls*) données *fpl* de contrôle; touche *f* de commande; touche *f* de contrôle ◇ **control card** carte *f* de contrôle ◇ **control signal** signal *m* de contrôle *or* de commande ◇ **control unit (CU)** unité de contrôle (de processus) ◇ **to halt a program, press Ctrl-C – the control key and letter C – at the same time** pour arrêter un programme, appuyez sur Ctrl-C, c'est-à-dire appuyez sur la touche de contrôle et la touche C en même temps ◇ **to reset your PC, press Ctrl-Alt-Del** pour relancer votre PC, appuyez sur Ctrl-Alt-Del

control block /kən'trəʊl blɒk/ *noun* bloc *m* de données de contrôle

control bus /kən'trəʊl bʌs/ *noun* bus *m* de commande

control character /kən'trəʊl ˌkærɪktə/ *noun* caractère *m* de contrôle

> '...there are seven print control characters which can be placed in a document' [*Personal Computer World*]

control computer /kən'trəʊl kəmˌpjuːtə/ *noun* ordinateur *m* dédié; ordinateur *m* de contrôle

control cycle /kən'trəʊl ˌsaɪk(ə)l/ *noun* cycle *m* de contrôle

control data /kən'trəʊl ˌdeɪtə/ *noun* données *fpl* de commande; données *fpl* de contrôle

control-driven /kən'trəʊl ˌdrɪv(ə)n/ *adjective* commandé par les codes CTRL; asservi aux codes CTRL

control field /kən'trəʊl fiːld/ *noun* champ *m* de contrôle

control group /kən'trəʊl gruːp/ *noun* groupe *m* témoin; groupe *m* de contrôle

control instruction /kən'trəʊl ɪnˌstrʌkʃən/ *noun* instruction *f* de contrôle ◇ **the next control instruction will switch to italics** la prochaine instruction de contrôle vous donnera les italiques

control key /kən'trəʊl kiː/ *noun* touche *f* de contrôle; Ctrl

control language /kən'trəʊl ˌlæŋgwɪdʒ/ *noun* langage *m* de commande

controlled vocabulary /kənˌtrəʊld vəʊ 'kæbjʊləri/ *noun* vocabulaire *m* contrôlé

controller /kən'trəʊlə/ *noun* contrôleur *m*; pilote *m* de périphériques

'...a printer's controller is the brains of the machine. It translates the signals coming from your computer into printing instructions that result in a hard copy of your electronic document' [*Publish*]

control memory /kən'trəʊl ˌmem(ə)ri/ *noun* mémoire *f* fixe; mémoire *f* de commande

control menu /kən'trəʊl ˌmenjuː/ *noun* menu *m* de contrôle de commandes

control mode /kən'trəʊl məʊd/ *noun* (*state of a device*) mode *m* de contrôle

control panel /kən'trəʊl ˌpæn(ə)l/ *noun* **1.** panneau *m* de configuration **2.** panneau *m* de contrôle; panneau *m* de commandes

control register /kən'trəʊl ˌredʒɪstə/ *noun* (*storage location*) registre *m* de commande de contrôle

control ROM /kənˌtrəʊl 'rɒm/ *noun* mémoire *f* de commande

control sequence /kən'trəʊl ˌsiːkwəns/ *noun* séquence *f* de commande

control signals /kən'trəʊl ˌsɪgn(ə)lz/ *plural noun* signaux *mpl* de contrôle; signaux *mpl* de commande

control statement /kən'trəʊl ˌsteɪtmənt/ *noun* **1.** instruction *f* **2.** instruction *f* de commande

control structure /kən'trəʊl ˌstrʌktʃə/ *noun* structure *f* de contrôle

control systems /kən'trəʊl ˌsɪstəmz/ *plural noun* systèmes *mpl* de contrôle

control token /kən'trəʊl ˌtəʊkən/ *noun* jeton *m* de contrôle

control total /kən'trəʊl ˌtəʊt(ə)l/ *noun* total *m* de contrôle

control transfer /kən'trəʊl ˌtrænsfɜː/ *noun* transfert *m* de contrôle

control unit /kən'trəʊl ˌjuːnɪt/ *noun* unité *f* de contrôle

control word /kən'trəʊl wɜːd/ *noun* mot *m* de contrôle; mot *m* de commande

convention /kən'venʃən/ *noun* convention *f*

conventional memory /kənˌvenʃ(ə)n(ə)l 'mem(ə)ri/ *noun* mémoire *f* conventionnelle; mémoire *f* RAM

convergence /kən'vɜːdʒəns/ *noun* convergence *f*

conversation /ˌkɒnvə'seɪʃ(ə)n/ *noun* dialogue *m*

conversational mode /ˌkɒnvə'seɪʃ(ə)n(ə)l məʊd/ *noun* mode *m* conversationnel; mode *m* dialogué; mode *m* interactif

converse /kən'vɜːs/ *verb* dialoguer (avec)

conversion /kən'vɜːʃ(ə)n/ *noun* conversion *f*

conversion equipment /kən'vɜːʃ(ə)n ɪ ˌkwɪpmənt/ *noun* convertisseur *m*

conversion program /kən'vɜːʃ(ə)n ˌprəʊgræm/ *noun* **1.** (*of programs*) convertisseur *m* **2.** (*of formatting, etc.*) programme *m* convertisseur; programme *m* de conversion

conversion tables /kən'vɜːʃ(ə)n ˌteɪb(ə)lz/ *plural noun* **1.** (*of source codes*) tables *fpl* d'équivalence; tables *fpl* de conversion **2.** (*of stored results*) tables *fpl* d'équivalence; tables *fpl* de conversion

converter /kən'vɜːtə/ *noun* convertisseur *m*

convertibility /kənˌvɜːtə'bɪləti/ *noun* convertibilité *f*

convertible /kən'vɜːtəb(ə)l/ *adjective* convertible

convertor /kən'vɜːtə/ *noun* convertisseur *m*

cookie /'kʊki/ *noun* (*data supplied by a remote internet site and stored on the user's hard disk*) cookie *m*; fichier *m* cookie

cookie file /'kʊki faɪl/ *noun* fichier *m* de témoins

cooperative processing /kəʊˌɒp(ə)rətɪv 'prəʊsesɪŋ/ *noun* (*system in which computers in a distributed network can execute a part of a program*) processus *m* coopératif

coordinate graph /kəʊ'ɔːdɪnət grɑːf/ *noun* graphe *m* exprimé en coordonnées

coordinates /kəʊ'ɔːdɪnəts/ *plural noun* coordonnées *fpl*

coordination /kəʊˌɔːdɪ'neɪʃ(ə)n/ *noun* coordination *f*

coprocessor /kəʊ'prəʊsesə/ *noun* co-processeur *m*; processeur *m* auxiliaire

'Inmos is hiring designers to create highly integrated transputers and co-processors for diverse computer and telecoms systems.' [*Computing*]

copy /'kɒpɪ/ *verb* (*file*) copier *vt*; (*document*) reproduire *vt* ◇ **there is a memory resident utility which copies the latest files onto backing store every 40 minutes** il existe un utilitaire résident qui copie les fichiers les plus récents sur un support de sauvegarde toutes les 40 minutes

COPY /'kɒpi/ *noun* copie *f*; double *m*

copy protect /ˌkɒpi prə'tekt/ *noun* protection *f* contre la copie ■ *verb* protéger contre la copie ◇ **all disks are copy protected** toutes les disquettes sont munies d'un système de protection *or* tous les disques sont protégés contre la copie ◇ **the program is not copy protected** le programme n'est pas protégé (contre la copie)

copy protection /'kɒpi prəˌtekʃən/ *noun* (*preventing copies from being made*) codage *m* anticopie; dispositif *m* de protection contre la copie ◇ **a hard disk may crash because of faulty copy protection** il arrive qu'une protection anticopie défectueuse entraîne la détérioration du disque dur ◇ **the new program will come without copy protection** le nouveau programme ne sera pas protégé contre la copie

CORAL /'kɒpi/ *noun* langage *m* d'application temps réel CORAL

core /kɔː/ *noun* (*of cable*) âme *f*; coeur *m*

core memory /kɔː 'mem(ə)ri/ *noun* mémoire *f* centrale

core program /kɔː 'prəʊgræm/ *noun* programme *m* en mémoire centrale

coresident /kəʊ'rezɪd(ə)nt/ *adjective* (*program*) co-résident *or* -e

core store /'kɔː stɔː/ *noun* mémoire *f* centrale

corona /kə'rəʊnə/ *noun* (*electric discharge that charges toner*) charge *f* statique

corona wire /kə'rəʊnə ˌwaɪə/ *noun* fil *m* de charge statique

coroutine /'kəʊruːˌtiːn/ *noun* module *m* d'accompagnement; coroutine *f*

corrective maintenance /kəˌrektɪv 'meɪntənəns/ *noun* maintenance *f* corrective; dépannage *m*; réparation *f*

corrupt /kə'rʌpt/ *adjective* corrompu *or* -e; erroné *or* -ée ■ *verb* (*to introduce errors into something*) corrompre *vt*; détériorer *vt*; altérer *vt*; *informal* véroler *vt* ◇ **power loss during disk access can corrupt the data** une baisse de tension durant l'accès au disque peut altérer *or* corrompre les données

corruption /kə'rʌpʃən/ *noun* (*faulty data*) corruption *f*; détérioration *f*

cost analysis /'kɒst əˌnæləsɪs/ *noun* étude *f* des coûts

counter /'kaʊntə/ *noun* compteur *m*

counter-rotating ring /ˌkaʊntə rəʊˌeɪtɪŋ 'rɪŋ/ *noun* anneau *m* de contre-rotation

country file /'kʌntri faɪl/ *noun* (*file in an operating system that defines parameters*) fichier *m* localisation

coupler /'kʌplə/ *noun* coupleur *m*

Courier /'kʊriə/ *noun* (*typeface*) Courier

courseware /'kɔːsweə/ *noun* didacticiel *m*

cpi /ˌsiː piː 'aɪ/ *noun* caractères *mpl* par pouce ◇ **you can select 10 or 12 cpi with the green button** le bouton vert vous permet de sélectionner 10 ou 12 caractères par pouce

CPM *abbr* (*critical path method*) méthode *f* du chemin critique

cps /ˌsiː piː 'es/ *noun* caractères *mpl* par seconde

CPU /ˌsiː piː 'juː/ *noun* unité *f* centrale; processeur *m* central

CPU bound /ˌsiː piː 'juː baʊnd/ *adjective* limité par l'unité centrale

CPU clock /ˌsiː piː 'juː klɒk/ *noun* horloge *f* du processeur central

CPU clock speed /ˌsiː piː 'juː klɒk/ *noun* fréquence *f* d'horloge du processeur central

CPU cycle /ˌsiː piː ˌjuː 'saɪk(ə)l/ *noun* cycle *m* de l'unité centrale; cycle *m* d'horloge; cycle *m* CPU

CPU elements /ˌsiː piː ˌjuː 'elɪmənts/ *plural noun* éléments *mpl* de l'unité centrale; éléments *mpl* CPU

CPU handshaking /ˌsiː piː juː 'hændʃeɪkɪŋ/ *noun* protocole *m* d'échange d'informations entre CPU et périphérique

CPU time /ˌsiː piː 'juː taɪm/ *noun* (*time to process instructions*) temps *m* d'utilisation de l'unité centrale; temps *m* d'utilisation du processeur; temps *m* CPU

crash /kræʃ/ *noun* (*program failure*) crash *m*; (*failure*) défaillance *f*; panne *f*; plantage *m* ■ *verb* (*of hardware or disk or software*) tomber en panne; se planter; cesser de fonctionner ◇ **the disk head has crashed and the data may have been lost** la tête de lecture du disque a cessé de fonctionner *or* s'est plantée et il se peut que les données soient perdues

crash-protected /kræʃ prə'tektɪd/ *adjective* protégé contre tout arrêt ◇ **if the disk is crash-protected, you will never lose your data** si vous vous servez d'un disque protégé contre tout arrêt intempestif, vous ne perdrez jamais vos données

crawler /'krɔːlə/ *noun* robot *m*

CRC *abbr* (*cyclic redundancy check*) contrôle *m* par redondance cyclique

crippled leapfrog test /ˌkrɪp(ə)ld 'liːpfrɒg ˌtest/ *noun* (*standard leapfrog test*) test *m* sélectif limité; test *m* saut de puce limité à un seul emplacement

critical error /ˌkrɪtɪk(ə)l 'erə/ *noun* erreur *f* critique

critical fusion frequency /ˌkrɪtɪk(ə)l 'fjuːʒ(ə)n ˌfriːkwənsi/ *noun* fréquence *f* critique de fusion

critical path analysis /ˌkrɪtɪk(ə)l 'pɑːθ ə ˌnæləsɪs/ *noun* analyse *f* du chemin critique ◇ **critical path method (CPM)** méthode *f* du chemin critique

> 'Surprisingly, critical path analysis and project management, frequently the next career step for engineers, did not seem to warrant a mention.' [*Computing*]

critical path method /ˌkrɪtɪk(ə)l 'pɑːθ ˌmeθəd/ *noun* méthode *f* du chemin critique

critical resource /ˌkrɪtɪk(ə)l rɪ'zɔːs/ *noun* ressource *f* critique

crop /krɒp/ *verb* **1.** (*reduce the size of an image*) découper *vt*; cadrer *vt* **2.** (*cut a rectangular section of image*) cadrer *vt*; découper *vt*

crop mark /'krɒp mɑːk/ *noun* (*printed marks that show the edge of a page*) marque *f* de cadrage

cross-assembler /krɒs ə'semblə/ *noun* assembleur *m* croisé; cross-assembleur *m*

cross-compiler /krɒs kəm'paɪlə/ *noun* (*assembler that compiles programs*) compilateur *m* croisé

crosshair /'krɒsheə/ *noun* réticule *m*

cross-linked files /ˌkrɒs lɪŋkt 'faɪlz/ *plural noun* (*error in which two files claim to be using the same cluster on disk*) fichiers *mpl* mélangés; interférence *f* de fichiers

crossover /'krɒsˌəʊvə/ *noun* (*change from one system to another*) changement *m*; passage *m*

cross-platform /ˌkrɒs 'plætfɔːm/ *adjective* multiplate-forme

cross-post /ˌkrɒs 'pəʊst/ *verb* envoyer un message croisé

cross-reference generator /ˌkrɒs 'ref(ə)rəns ˌdʒenəreɪtə/ *noun* générateur *m* de renvois

crosstalk /'krɒstɑːk/ *noun* diaphonie *f* ◇ **the crosstalk was so bad, the signal was unreadable** il y avait une telle diaphonie que le signal était illisible

CRT /ˌsiː ɑː 'tiː/ *noun* tube *m* cathodique

crunch /krʌntʃ/ *verb* calculer à toute vitesse

cruncher, crunching *noun* calcul *m* ultra-rapide

cryogenic memory /ˌkraɪəʊdʒenɪk 'mem(ə)ri/ *noun* mémoire *f* cryogénique; mémoire *f* à supraconducteur

cryptanalysis /ˌkrɪptə'næləsɪs/ *noun* analyse *f* cryptographique

cryptographic /ˌkrɪptə'græfɪk/ *adjective* cryptographique

cryptographic algorithm /ˌkrɪptəgræfɪk 'ælgərɪð(ə)m/ *noun* algorithme *m* de chiffrement; algorithme *m* de cryptage

cryptographic key /ˌkrɪptəgræfɪk 'kiː/ *noun* clé *f* de cryptage; clé *f* de chiffrage

cryptography /ˌkrɪp'tɒgrəfi/ *noun* cryptographie *f*

crystal /'krɪstəl/ *noun* cristal *m*

crystal shutter printer /ˌkrɪst(ə)l ˌʃʌtə 'prɪntə/ *noun* imprimante *f* à transfert LCD

CS *abbr* (*chip select*) sélection *f* de circuit

CSLIP *noun* (*version of the SLIP protocol that compresses data before it is transmitted*) protocole *m* CSLIP

CSM /ˌsiː es 'em/ *noun* système *m* de reconnaissance de caractères CSM

CSMA-CD /ˌsiː es em siː 'diː/ *noun* méthode *f* d'accès à test de porteuse et détection de collision; protocole *m* de transmission CSMA-CD

CSS *abbr* (*cascading style sheet*) CSS

CTI /ˌsiː tiː 'aɪ/ *noun* couplage *m* de la téléphonie et de l'informatique

CTR /kən'trəʊl/, **CTRL, Ctrl** *noun* (*control key*) touche *f* CTR; CTRL; Ctrl; touche *f* de contrôle

CTS /ˌsiː tiː 'es/ *noun* signal *m* CTS; signal *m* de prêt à transmettre

CU *abbr* (*control unit*) unité *f* de contrôle

cue /kjuː/ *noun* message *m* d'invitation; invite *f*

CUG /ˌsiː juː 'dʒiː/ *noun* groupe *m* fermé d'utilisateurs

cull /kʌl/ *verb* trier *vt*

cumulative trauma disorder /ˌkjuːmjʊlətɪv 'trɔːmə dɪsˌɔːdə/ *noun* microtraumatismes *mpl* répétés

curly brackets /'kɜːli 'brækɪtz/, **curly braces** /ˌkɜːli 'breɪsɪz/ *plural noun* accolades *fpl*

current address /ˌkʌrənt ə'dres/ *noun* adresse *f* courante

current address register /ˌkʌrənt ə'dres ˌredʒɪstə/ *noun* registre *m* d'adresse courante

current directory /ˌkʌrənt daɪ'rekt(ə)ri/ *noun* répertoire *m* courant

current drive /ˌkʌrənt 'draɪv/ *noun* lecteur *m* de disque courant

current instruction register /ˌkʌrənt ɪn 'strʌkʃən ˌredʒɪstə/ *noun* registre *m* d'instruction courante

cursor /'kɜːsə/ *noun* curseur *m*; point *m* d'insertion

> 'Probably the most exciting technology demonstrated was ScreenCam, which allows users to combine voice, cursor movement and on-screen activities into a movie which can be replayed.' [*Computing*]

> '...further quick cursor movements are available for editing by combining one of the arrow keys with the control function' [*Personal Computer World*]

cursor control keys /'kɜːsə kənˌtrəʊl kiːz/ *plural noun* touches *fpl* de contrôle du curseur; touches *fpl* fléchées

cursor home /'kɜːsə həʊm/ *noun* coin *m* gauche supérieur de l'écran

cursor pad /'kɜːsə pæd/ *noun* touches *fpl* de contrôle du curseur; touches *fpl* fléchées

custom-built /'kʌstəm bɪlt/ *adjective* personnalisé *or* -ée; fait, -e sur mesure; sur commande

customer engineering /ˌkʌstəmə ˌendʒɪ 'nɪərɪŋ/ *noun* maintenance *f* du parc clients

customer service department /ˌkʌstəmə 'sɜːvɪs dɪˌpɑːtmənt/ *noun* service *m* après-vente; service *m* clients

customise /'kʌstəmaɪz/, **customize** *verb* (*to modify something so that it meets customers' requirements*) fabriquer sur commande; personnaliser *vt*

custom ROM /ˌkʌstəm 'rɒm/ *noun* ROM *f* personnalisée

cut /kʌt/ *noun* **1.** (*process of deletion*) coupure *f* **2.** (*piece removed*) coupure *f* ■ *verb* (*to remove sections of text*) couper *vt*; réduire *vt* ◇ **the author was asked to cut his manuscript to 250 pages** on a demandé à l'auteur de réduire son manuscrit à 250 pages ◇ **the editors have asked for cuts in the first chapter** les éditeurs ont demandé de faire des coupures au premier chapitre *or* de réduire le premier chapitre

cut and paste /ˌkʌt ən 'peɪst/ *noun* couper et coller

cut sheet feeder /ˌkʌt 'ʃiːt ˌfiːdə/ *noun* (*printing*) alimentation *f* feuille à feuille

CWP *abbr* (*communicating word processor*) système *m* de traitement de texte communicant

cXML /ˌsiː eks em 'el/ *noun* cXML

cyber- /saɪbə/ *prefix* cyber-

cybercafé /'saɪbəˌkæfeɪ/ *noun* (*internet*) cybercafé *m*

cybernetics /ˌsaɪbə'netɪks/ *noun* cybernétique *f*

cybershopping /'saɪbəˌʃɒpɪŋ/ *noun* shopping *m* en ligne

cyberspace /'saɪbəspeɪs/ *noun* cyberespace *m*

cybersquatting /'saɪbəˌskwɒtɪŋ/ *noun* cybersquattage *m*

cyberterrorism /'saɪbəˌterərɪz(ə)m/ *noun* cyberterrorisme *m*

> 'There were some instances of war-related hacking over the past few weeks, but nothing that would be considered cyberterrorism.' [*The Guardian*]

cycle /'saɪk(ə)l/ *noun* cycle *m*

cycle availability /ˌsaɪk(ə)l əˌveɪlə'bɪlɪti/ *noun* disponibilité *f* dans le cycle

cycle count /'saɪk(ə)l kaʊnt/ *noun* nombre *m* de cycles

cycle index /'saɪk(ə)l ˌɪndeks/ *noun* index *m* de cycle

cycle shift /'saɪk(ə)l ʃɪft/ *verb* permutation *f* circulaire

cycle stealing /'saɪk(ə)l ˌstiːlɪŋ/ *noun* vol *m* de cycle

cycle time /'saɪk(ə)l taɪm/ *noun* temps *m* de cycle

cyclic /'sɪklɪk, 'saɪklɪk/ *adjective* cyclique; circulaire ◇ **cyclic redundancy check (CRC)** contrôle de redondance cyclique

cyclic access /ˌsaɪklɪk 'ækses/ *noun* accès *m* cyclique

cyclic check /ˌsaɪklɪk 'tʃek/ *noun* contrôle *m* cyclique

cyclic code /ˌsaɪklɪk 'kəʊd/ *noun* code *m* binaire réfléchi; code *m* de Gray

cyclic decimal code /ˌsaɪklɪk 'desɪm(ə)l kəʊd/ *noun* code *m* décimal réfléchi

cyclic redundancy check /ˌsɪklɪk rɪ 'dʌndənsi ˌtʃek/ *noun* contrôle *m* par redondance cyclique

cyclic shift /ˌsaɪklɪk 'ʃɪft/ *noun* permutation *f*

cylinder /'sɪlɪndə/ *noun* **1.** (*group of tracks on a disk*) cylindre *m* **2.** (*tracks on a multidisk device*) cylindre *m*

cypher /'saɪfə/ *noun* chiffre *m*

D

DA *abbr* (*desk accessory*) accessoire *m* de bureau

DAC /ˌdiː eɪ ˈsiː/ *noun* convertisseur *m* numérique-analogique

d/a converter /ˌdiː tʊ eɪ kənˈvɜːtə/ *noun* convertisseur *m* numérique-analogique

daemon /ˈdiːmən/ *noun* (*utility program in a UNIX system*) utilitaire *m* UNIX démon; daemon *m*

daisy chain /ˈdeɪzi tʃeɪn/ *noun* chaîne *f*

daisy-chain /ˈdeɪzi tʃeɪn/ *verb* relier en chaîne

'…you can often daisy-chain cards or plug them into expansion boxes' [*Byte*]

daisy chain bus /ˌdeɪzi tʃeɪn ˈbʌs/ *noun* (*communication bus*) bus *m* série; bus *m* de chaîne

daisy-chaining /ˈdeɪzi tʃeɪnɪŋ/ *noun* (*of hardware*) connexion *f* en chaîne ◇ **daisy-chaining saves a lot of cable** la connexion en chaîne réduit le câblage

daisy chain interrupt /ˌdeɪzi tʃeɪn ˈɪntərʌpt/ *noun* interruption *f* en chaîne

daisy chain recursion /ˌdeɪzi tʃeɪn rɪ ˈkɜːʒ(ə)n/ *noun* boucle *f* de récurrence

DAL *abbr* (*data access language*) langage *m* d'accès

DAMA *abbr* (*demand assigned multiple access*) accès *m* multiple asservi à la demande

DAO /ˌdiː eɪ ˈəʊ/ *noun* objets *mpl* d'accès aux données

DASD /ˌdiː eɪ es ˈdiː/ *noun* mémoire *f* à accès direct; support *m* à accès direct

DAT /ˌdiː eɪ ˈtiː/ *noun* (*system of recording sound as digital information on DAT tape*) enregistrement *m* sur bande audionumérique ◇ **DAT produces a very high quality sound** l'enregistrement sur bande audionumérique produit un son de très haute qualité ◇ **DAT tape** bande *f* audionumérique *or* bande audio

data /ˈdeɪtə/ *noun* données *fpl*

data access language /ˌdeɪtə ˈækses ˌlæŋgwɪdʒ/ *noun* langage *m* d'accès

data access management /ˌdeɪtə ˈækses ˌmænɪdʒmənt/ *noun* gestion *f* d'accès aux données

data access objects /ˌdeɪtə ˈækses ˌɒbjekts/ *plural noun* objets *mpl* d'accès aux données

data acquisition /ˈdeɪtə ækwɪˌzɪʃ(ə)n/ *noun* acquisition *f* de données

data adapter unit /ˌdeɪtə əˈdæptə ˌjuːnɪt/ *noun* (*device that interfaces a CPU*) adaptateur *m* de canal de transmission de données

data administrator /ˌdeɪtə ədˈmɪnɪstreɪtə/ *noun* (*database management system*) gestionnaire *m* de données

data aggregate /ˈdeɪtə ˌægrɪgət/ *noun* (*collection of related data items*) agrégat *m* de données; données *fpl* agrégées; données *fpl* structurées

data analysis /ˌdeɪtə əˈnæləsɪs/ *noun* analyse *f* de données

data area /ˈdeɪtə ˌeəriə/ *noun* zone *f* de données

databank /ˈdeɪtəbæŋk/ *noun* banque *f* de données

database /ˈdeɪtəbeɪs/ *noun* base *f* de données ◇ **database administrator (DBA)** (*person*) responsable *m&f* de base de données

'This information could include hypertext references to information held within a computer database, or spreadsheet formulae.' [*Computing*]

database administrator /ˌdeɪtəbeɪs əd ˈmɪnɪstreɪtə/ *noun* responsable *mf* de base de données

database engine /ˈdeɪtəbeɪs ˌendʒɪn/ *noun* moteur *m* de base de données

database language /ˈdeɪtəbeɪs ˌlæŋgwɪdʒ/ *noun* langage *m* de base de données

database machine /ˌdeɪtəbeɪs məˈʃiːn/ *noun* machine *f* dédiée au traitement de bases de données

database management system /ˌdeɪtəbeɪs ˈmænɪdʒmənt ˌsɪstəm/, **database manager** /ˌdeɪtəbeɪs ˈmænɪdʒə/ *noun* gestion *f* de base de données

database mapping /ˈdeɪtəbeɪs ˌmæpɪŋ/ *noun* (*database management system*) configuration *f* d'une base de données

database schema /ˌdeɪtəbeɪs ˈskiːmə/ *noun* schéma *m* de base de données

database server /ˌdeɪtəbeɪs ˈsɜːvə/ *noun* serveur *m* de base de données

database system /ˈdeɪtəbeɪs ˌsɪstəm/ *noun* système *m* de base de données

data block /ˈdeɪtə blɒk/ *noun* bloc *m* de données

data break /ˈdeɪtə breɪk/ *noun* interruption *f* de traitement pour transfert de données

data buffer /ˈdeɪtə ˌbʌfə/ *noun* mémoire *f* tampon de données

data bus /ˈdeɪtə bʌs/ *noun* (*bus carrying data*) bus *m* de données

data bus connector /ˌdeɪtə ˈbʌs kəˌnektə/ *noun* connecteur *m* DB; connecteur *m* en D

data capture /ˈdeɪtə ˌkæptʃə/ *noun* (*obtaining data into a computer system*) saisie *f* de données

data carrier /ˈdeɪtə ˌkæriə/ *noun* **1.** support *m* de données **2.** onde *f* porteuse de données

data carrier detect /ˌdeɪtə ˌkæriə dɪˈtekt/ *noun* détecteur *m* d'onde porteuse; signal *m* de détection de porteuse

data cartridge /ˈdeɪtə ˌkɑːtrɪdʒ/ *noun* (*cartridge that contains data*) cartouche *f* de données

data cassette /ˈdeɪtə kəˌset/ *noun* cassette *f* informatique

data chaining /ˈdeɪtə ˌtʃeɪnɪŋ/ *noun* (*data storage*) liaison *f* de données en chaîne; chaînage *m* de données

data channel /ˈdeɪtə ˌtʃæn(ə)l/ *noun* canal *m* de transmission de données

data check /ˈdeɪtə tʃek/ *noun* brève interruption *f* de transmission de données

data circuit /ˈdeɪtə ˌsɜːkɪt/ *noun* circuit *m* de données

data cleaning /ˈdeɪtə ˌkliːnɪŋ/ *noun* (*data storage*) nettoyage *m* de données; correction *f* d'erreurs

data collection /ˈdeɪtə kəˌlekʃən/ *noun* (*data storage*) collecte *f* de données

data collection platform /ˌdeɪtə kəˈlekʃən ˌplætfɔːm/ *noun* (*station that transmits collected data*) plate-forme *f* de collecte de données

data communications /ˌdeɪtə kəˌmjuːnɪ ˈkeɪʃ(ə)nz/ *noun* (*transmission and reception of data*) téléinformatique *f*

data communications buffer /ˌdeɪtə kə ˌmjuːnɪˈkeɪʃ(ə)nz ˌbʌfə/ *noun* mémoire *f* tampon de transmission de données

data communications equipment /ˌdeɪtə kəˌmjuːnɪˈkeɪʃ(ə)nz ɪˌkwɪpmənt/ *noun* équipement *m* de transmission de données

data communications network /ˌdeɪtə kə ˌmjuːnɪˈkeɪʃ(ə)nz ˌnetwɜːk/ *noun* réseau *m* téléinformatique; réseau *m* de transmission de données

data compacting /ˈdeɪtə ˌkɒmpæktɪŋ/ *noun* (*reducing data storage*) compression *f* de données

data compression /ˌdeɪtə kəmˈpreʃ(ə)n/ *noun* (*reducing size of data*) compression *f* de données

data concentrator /ˈdeɪtə ˌkɒns(ə)ntreɪtə/ *noun* concentrateur *m* de données

data connection /ˌdeɪtə kəˈnekʃ(ə)n/ *noun* connexion *f* pour transmission de données

data control /ˈdeɪtə kənˌtrəʊl/ *noun* contrôle *m* de données

data corruption /ˈdeɪtə kəˌrʌpʃ(ə)n/ *noun* (*introduction of errors into data*) corruption *f* de données; détérioration *f* de données; altération *f* de données ◇ **acoustic couplers suffer from data corruption more than the direct connect form of modem** les coupleurs acoustiques sont plus susceptibles aux détériorations de données que les modems branchés directement sur la ligne ◇ **data corruption on the disk has made one file unreadable** la corruption de données sur la disquette a rendu un des fichiers impossible à lire

data delimiter /ˈdeɪtə diːˌlɪmɪtə/ *noun* délimiteur *m* de données

data description language /ˌdeɪtə dɪ ˈskrɪpʃən ˌlæŋgwɪdʒ/ *noun* langage *m* de définition de données

data dictionary/directory /ˌdeɪtə ˌdɪkʃən(ə)ri daɪˈrekt(ə)ri/ *noun* dictionnaire/répertoire *m* de données

data division /ˈdeɪtə dɪˌvɪʒ(ə)n/ *noun* rubrique *f* de déclaration des données

data-driven /ˈdeɪtə ˌdrɪv(ə)n/ *adjective* activé, -ée par reconnaissance des données

data element /ˈdeɪtə ˌelɪmənt/ *noun* élément *m* de données

data element chain /ˌdeɪtə ˈelɪmənt ˌtʃeɪn/ *noun* chaîne *f* d'éléments de données

data encryption /ˈdeɪtə ɪnˌkrɪpʃ(ə)n/ *noun* (*process of encrypting data using a cipher system*) chiffrage *m*

data encryption standard /ˌdeɪtə ɪn ˈkrɪpʃən ˌstændəd/ *noun* norme *f* de cryptage de données; standard *m* de cryptage de données

data entry /ˌdeɪtə ˈentri/ *noun* (*entering data into a system*) entrée *f*

data error /ˈdeɪtə ˌerə/ *noun* erreur *f* de données

data field /ˈdeɪtə fiːld/ *noun* champ *m* de données

data file /ˈdeɪtə faɪl/ *noun* fichier *m* de données

data flow /ˈdeɪtə fləʊ/ *noun* flux *m* de données

data flowchart /ˌdeɪtə ˈfləʊtʃɑːt/ *noun* ordinogramme *m* de données

data flow diagram /ˈdeɪtə fləʊ ˌdaɪəgræm/ *noun* diagramme *m* de flux de données

data format /ˈdeɪtə ˌfɔːmæt/ *noun* format *m* de données

data glove /ˈdeɪtə glʌv/ *noun* gant *m* de données; gant *m* électronique; dataglove *m*

datagram /ˈdeɪtəgræm/ *noun* datagramme *m*

data hierarchy /ˌdeɪtə ˈhaɪərɑːki/ *noun* hiérarchie *f* des données

data highway /ˌdeɪtə 'haɪweɪ/ *noun* (*transfer of data*) bus *m* de transfert de données

data independence /ˌdeɪtə ˌɪndɪ'pendəns/ *noun* autonomie *f* des données

data input /ˌdeɪtə 'ɪnpʊt/ *noun* saisie *f*

data input bus /ˌdeɪtə 'ɪnpʊt ˌbʌs/ *noun* bus *m* d'entrée

data integrity /ˌdeɪtə ɪn'tegrɪti/ *noun* intégrité *f* des données

data interchange format /ˌdeɪtə 'ɪntətʃeɪndʒ ˌfɔːmæt/ *noun* format *m* DIF

data item /'deɪtə ˌaɪtəm/ *noun* élément *m* de données

data jack /'deɪtə dʒæk/ *noun* fiche *f* téléphone pour modem

data level /'deɪtə ˌlev(ə)l/ *noun* niveau *m* de données

data link /'deɪtə lɪŋk/ *noun* liaison *f* de données

data link control /ˌdeɪtə lɪŋk kən'trəʊl/ *noun* contrôle *m* de liaison de données

data link layer /'deɪtə lɪŋk ˌleɪə/ *noun* (*data transmission*) couche *f* de liaison de données

data logging /'deɪtə ˌlɒgɪŋ/ *noun* (*automatic data collection*) enregistrement *m* de données

data management /'deɪtə ˌmænɪdʒmənt/ *noun* gestion *f* de données

data manipulation language /ˌdeɪtə məˌnɪpjʊ'leɪʃ(ə)n ˌlæŋgwɪdʒ/ *noun* langage *m* de manipulation de données

data medium /'deɪtə ˌmiːdiəm/ *noun* support *m* de données

data migration /ˌdeɪtə maɪ'greɪʃ(ə)n/ *noun* (*data transfer*) migration *f* de données; transfert *m* de données

data mining /'deɪtə ˌmaɪnɪŋ/ *noun* exploration *f* de données

'Both companies specialise in decision support, statistical analysis and data mining.' [*The Guardian*]

data name /'deɪtə neɪm/ *noun* nom *m* de donnée ◇ **problems occur if an ambiguous data name is chosen** les difficultés surviennent lorsque le nom de donnée est ambigu

data network /'deɪtə ˌnetwɜːk/ *noun* réseau *m* téléinformatique; réseau *m* de transmission de données

data origination /'deɪtə əˌrɪdʒɪneɪʃ(ə)n/ *noun* génération *f*

data path /'deɪtə pɑːθ/ *noun* (*data transfer*) chemin *m*

dataplex /'deɪtəpleks/ *noun* multiplexage *m*

data pointer /'deɪtə ˌpɔɪntə/ *noun* (*data storage*) pointeur *m* de position de données

dataport /'deɪtəpɔːt/ *noun* port *m* d'accès

data preparation /ˌdeɪtə ˌprepə'reɪʃ(ə)n/ *noun* préparation *f* des données

data processing /ˌdeɪtə 'prəʊsesɪŋ/ *noun* informatique *f*

data processing manager /ˌdeɪtə 'prəʊsesɪŋ ˌmænɪdʒə/ *noun* chef *m* du service informatique; responsable du service informatique; directeur, -trice du service informatique

data projector /'deɪtə prəˌdʒektə/ *noun* projecteur *m* multimédia

data protection /'deɪtə prəˌtekʃən/ *noun* (*data storage*) protection *f* des données

Data Protection Act /ˌdeɪtə prə'tekʃən ˌækt/ *noun* loi *f* Informatique et Libertés

data rate /'deɪtə reɪt/ *noun* vitesse *f* de traitement de données; vitesse *f* de transmission de données

data record /'deɪtə ˌrekɔːd/ *noun* enregistrement *m* de données

data reduction /ˌdeɪtə rɪ'dʌkʃən/ *noun* compression *f* de données

data register /'deɪtə ˌredʒɪstə/ *noun* registre *m* de données

data reliability /'deɪtə rɪˌlaɪəbɪlɪti/ *noun* qualité *f*

data retrieval /ˌdeɪtə rɪ'triːv(ə)l/ *noun* recherche *f* documentaire

data routing /'deɪtə ˌruːtɪŋ/ *noun* acheminement *m*

data security /'deɪtə sɪˌkjʊərɪti/ *noun* sécurité *f* des données; sécurité *f* de l'information

dataset /'deɪtəset/ *noun US* modem *m* ◇ **dataset ready (DSR)** (*RS232C signal*) (signal de modem) prêt à transmettre/recevoir

data set ready /ˌdeɪtə set 'redi/ *noun* signal *m* de prêt à recevoir

data sharing /'deɪtə ˌʃeərɪŋ/ *noun* partage *m* de données

data signalling rate /ˌdeɪtə 'sɪgn(ə)lɪŋ ˌreɪt/ *noun* débit *m* binaire de transmission de données

data signals /'deɪtə ˌsɪgn(ə)lz/ *plural noun* signaux *mpl* de transmission de données

data sink /'deɪtə sɪŋk/ *noun* (*device which receives data*) collecteur *m* de données

data source /'deɪtə sɔːs/ *noun* source *f*

data station /'deɪtə ˌsteɪʃ(ə)n/ *noun* poste *m* informatique de télétransmission

data storage /'deɪtə ˌstɔːrɪdʒ/ *noun* (*medium for holding information*) stockage *m*; mise *f* en mémoire de données; mémoire *f* de données

data stream /'deɪtə striːm/ *noun* flot *m* de données

data strobe /'deɪtə strəʊb/ *noun* validation *f* de données transmises

data structure /'deɪtə ˌstrʌktʃə/ *noun* structure *f* des données

data switching exchange /ˌdeɪtə 'swɪtʃɪŋ ɪksˌtʃeɪndʒ/ *noun* centre *m* de commutation des données

data tablet /'deɪtə ˌtæblət/ *noun* tablette *f* à numériser

data terminal /'deɪtə ˌtɜːmɪn(ə)l/ *noun* terminal *m*

data terminal equipment /'deɪtə ˌtɜːmɪn(ə)l ɪˌkwɪpmənt/ *noun* terminal *m* de traitement de données; terminal *m* de transmission de données

data terminal ready /ˌdeɪtə ˌtɜːmɪn(ə)l 'redi/ *noun* signal *m* de prêt à transmettre

data transaction /'deɪtə trænˌzækʃən/ *noun* transaction *f* de données

data transfer rate /ˌdeɪtə 'trænsfɜː ˌreɪt/ *noun* débit *m*

data translation /'deɪtə trænsˌleɪʃ(ə)n/ *noun* conversion *f* de données

data transmission /'deɪtə trænzˌmɪʃ(ə)n/ *noun* transmission *f* de données

data type /'deɪtə taɪp/ *noun* type *m* de données

data validation /'deɪtə ˌvælɪdeɪʃ(ə)n/ *noun* validation *f* de données

data vetting /'deɪtə ˌvetɪŋ/ *noun* validation *f* de données; vérification *f* de données

data warehouse /'deɪtə ˌweəhaʊs/ *noun* entrepôt *m* de données

data word /'deɪtə wɜːd/ *noun* mot *m* de données

data word length /ˌdeɪtə 'wɜːd ˌleŋθ/ *noun* longueur *f* d'un mot

DAT drive /'dæt draɪv/ *noun* (*to record and retrieve data*) lecteur *m* de bandes audionumériques ◇ **we use a DAT drive as the backup device for our network** la sauvegarde du réseau est assurée par un lecteur de bandes audio(numériques)

date /deɪt/ *noun* date *f* ◇ **I have received your message of yesterday's date** j'ai bien reçu votre message en date d'hier ◇ **the date of creation for the file was the 10th of June** la date de création de ce fichier est le 10 juin

date-time /ˌdeɪt 'taɪm/ *noun* date *f* et heure

daughter board /'dɔːtə bɔːd/ *noun* carte *f* fille

daylight saving time /ˌdeɪlaɪt 'seɪvɪŋ ˌtaɪm/ *noun* heure *f* avancée

dB *abbr* (*decibel*) décibel *m*

DBA /ˌdiː biː 'eɪ/ *noun* administrateur *m* de base de données

DB connector /ˌdiː biː kə'nektə/ *noun* (*D-shape connector*) connecteur *m* DB; connecteur *m* en D

DBMS /ˌdiː biː em 'es/ *noun* système *m* de gestion de base de données

DC *abbr* (*direct current*) courant *m* continu

DCA /ˌdiː siː 'eɪ/ *noun* architecture *f* de description de document; DCA

DCC /ˌdiː siː 'siː/ *noun* cassette *f* compacte numérique

DCD /ˌdiː siː 'diː/ *noun* détecteur *m* d'onde porteuse

DCE *abbr* (*data communications equipment*) équipement *m* de transmission de données

DCOM /'diː kɒm/ *noun* modèle *m* DCOM

DC signalling /ˌdiː siː 'sɪgn(ə)lɪŋ/ *noun* transmission *f* de signaux par courant continu

DD *abbr* (*double density*) double densité *f*

DDC /ˌdiː diː 'siː/ *noun* commande *f* numérique directe

DDE /ˌdiː diː 'iː/ *noun* **1.** (*direct data entry*) entrée *f* directe de données **2.** (*dynamic data exchange*) échange *m* dynamique de données

DDL /ˌdiː diː 'el/ *noun* langage *m* de description de données ◇ **many of DDL's advantages come from the fact that it is a second generation language** plusieurs des avantages d'un langage de description de données vient du fait qu'il s'agit d'un langage de deuxième génération

DDP /ˌdiː diː 'piː/ *noun* informatique *f* répartie

dead /ded/ *adjective* (*out of order*) hors service; (*unusable*) inutilisable; (*not responding*) mort *or* -e

deaden /'ded(ə)n/ *verb* (*sound*) assourdir *vt*; étouffer *vt*; amortir *vt*; (*sound or colour*) atténuer *vt*; (*colour*) adoucir *vt* ◇ **acoustic hoods are used to deaden the noise of printers** les capots *or* les hottes d'insonorisation servent à amortir *or* atténuer le bruit des imprimantes

dead halt /'ded hɔːlt/ *noun* arrêt *m* total

dead key /'ded kiː/ *noun* touche *f* de fonction; touche *f* d'intervention

deadlock /'dedˌlɒk/, **deadly embrace** /'dedli ɪm'breɪs/ *noun* impasse *f*

deadstart /'dedstɑːt/ *verb* démarrer à froid; mettre en route

dead time /'ded taɪm/ *noun* temps *m* mort

deal /diːl/ *noun* (*business agreement*) accord *m*; marché *m*; contrat *m* ◇ **they agreed a package deal, which involves the development of software, customizing hardware and training of staff** il se sont mis d'accord sur un contrat global comprenant le développement d'un logiciel, la personnalisation du matériel et la formation du personnel

deallocate /diː'æləkeɪt/ *verb* libérer *vt*; désaffecter *vt*; désallouer *vt* ◇ **when a reset button is pressed all resources are deallocated** lorsque vous appuyez sur la touche *or* le bouton de ré-initialisation, toutes les ressources sont désallouées

debit /'debɪt/ *noun* (*in informatics*) débit *m* binaire

deblock /diː'blɒk/ *verb* éclater *vi*; dégrouper les éléments d' un bloc

de-bounce /diː 'baʊns/ *noun* antirebond *m*

de-bounce circuit /diː 'baʊns ˌsɜːkɪt/ *noun* circuit *m* antirebond

debug /diː'bʌg/ *verb* déboguer *vt*; déverminer *vt*; mettre au point ◇ **debugging takes up more time than construction** il faut plus de temps pour déboguer un programme que pour en créer un ◇ **they spent weeks debugging the system** ils ont mis des semaines à déboguer le système

'Further questions, such as how you debug an application built from multi- sourced software to run on multisourced hardware, must be resolved at this stage.' [*Computing*]

DEBUG /diː'bʌg/ *noun* (*software utility in MS-DOS*) DEBUG

debugged program /ˌdiːbʌgd 'prəʊgræm/ *noun* programme *m* débogué; programme *m* déverminé

debugger /diː'bʌgə/ *noun* (*identification of errors in a program*) logiciel *m* de déboguage; débogueur *m*

decade /'dekeɪd/ *noun* dizaine *f*; décade *f*

decay /dɪ'keɪ/ *noun* (*signal fading away*) extinction *f*; amortissement *m* ◇ **decay time** (*of signal*) délai *m* d'amortissement d'un signal ◇ **with a short decay, it sounds very sharp** un amortissement court donne un son très aigu

deceleration time /diːˌselə'reɪʃ(ə)n ˌtaɪm/ *noun* (*time taken for an access arm to come to a stop*) temps *m* de décélération

decentralised computer network /diː ˌsentrəˌlaɪzd kəm'pjuːtə/, **decentralized computer network** *noun* réseau *m* décentralisé

decentralised data processing /diːˌsentrə ˌlaɪzd 'deɪtə/, **decentralized data processing** *noun* traitement *m* décentralisé des données

decibel /'desɪbel/ *noun* décibel *m* (dB)

deciding factor /dɪˌsaɪdɪŋ 'fæktə/ *noun* facteur *m* décisif; argument *m* décisif

decimal tabbing /ˌdesɪm(ə)l 'tæbɪŋ/ *noun* tabulation *f* décimale

decimal tab key /ˌdesɪm(ə)l 'tæb ˌkiː/ *noun* touche *f* de tabulation décimale

decimal-to-binary conversion /ˌdesɪm(ə)l tə ˌbaɪnəri kən'vɜːʃ(ə)n/ *noun* conversion *f* décimale-binaire

decipher /dɪ'saɪfə/ *verb* déchiffrer *vt*

decision box /dɪ'sɪʒ(ə)n bɒks/ *noun* symbole *m* de décision; symbole *m* de branchement; symbole *m* de condition

decision circuit /dɪ'sɪʒ(ə)n ˌsɜːkɪt/ *noun* circuit *m* de décision

decision instruction /dɪ'sɪʒ(ə)n ɪn ˌstrʌkʃən/ *noun* instruction *f* de décision

decision support system /dɪˌsɪʒ(ə)n sə 'pɔːt ˌsɪstəm/ *noun* système *m* d'aide à la décision

decision table /dɪ'sɪʒ(ə)n ˌteɪb(ə)l/ *noun* table *f* de décision

decision tree /dɪ'sɪʒ(ə)n triː/ *noun* arbre *m* de décision

deck /dek/ *noun* paquet *m* de cartes perforées

declaration /ˌdeklə'reɪʃ(ə)n/ *noun* déclaration *f*

declarative language /dɪˌklærətɪv 'læŋgwɪdʒ/ *noun* langage *m* déclaratif

declarative statement /dɪˌklærətɪv 'steɪtmənt/ *noun* déclaration *f*

declare /dɪ'kleə/ *verb* déclarer *vt*; faire une déclaration ◇ **he declared at the start of the program that X was equal to nine** au début du programme X a été déclaré égal à 9

decode /diː'kəʊd/ *verb* décoder *vt*; désembrouiller *vt*

decoder /diː'kəʊdə/ *noun* décodeur *m*

decode unit /diː'kəʊd ˌjuːnɪt/ *noun* décodeur *m*

decollate /ˌdiːkə'leɪt/ *verb* (*continuous stationery*) déliasser *vt*

decollator /ˌdiːkə'leɪtə/ *noun* déliasseuse *f*

decompilation /diːˌkɒmpɪ'leɪʃ(ə)n/ *noun* décompilation *f* ◇ **incremental compilation and decompilation** compilation et décompilation incrémentielles

decompiler /ˌdiːkəm'paɪlə/ *noun* décompilateur *m*

decompress /ˌdiːkəm'pres/ *verb* décompresser *vt*

decompression /ˌdiːkəm'preʃ(ə)n/ *noun* (*expanding a compressed image or data file*) décompression *f*

decrement /'dekrɪmənt/ *verb* décrémenter *vt* ◇ **the register contents were decremented until they reached zero** le contenu du registre a été décrémenté à zéro

decrypt /diː'krɪpt/ *verb* déchiffrer *vt*; décrypter *vt*

decryption /diː'krɪpʃ(ə)n/ *noun* déchiffrage *m*; décryptage *m* ◇ **decryption is done using hardware to increase speed** le décryptage *or* le déchiffrage se fait à l'aide de l'ordinateur pour assurer une plus grande rapidité

dedicated /'dedɪkeɪtɪd/ *adjective* (*reserved for a particular use*) dédié *or* -ée; spécialisé *or* -ée ◇ **dedicated line** ligne téléphonique spécialisée *or* dédiée ◇ **there's only one dedicated graphics workstation in this network** il n'y a qu'un poste dédié *or* réservé aux graphiques sur ce réseau

'The PBX is changing from a dedicated proprietary hardware product into an open application software development platform.' [*Computing*]

dedicated channel /ˌdedɪkeɪtɪd 'tʃæn(ə)l/ *noun* voie *f* spécialisée; canal *m* dédié

dedicated computer /ˌdedɪkeɪtɪd kəm 'pjuːtə/ *noun* ordinateur *m* dédié; ordinateur *m* spécialisé

dedicated line /ˌdedɪkeɪtɪd 'laɪn/ *noun* ligne *f* téléphonique spécialisée; ligne *f* téléphonique dédiée

dedicated logic /ˌdedɪkeɪtɪd 'lɒdʒɪk/ *noun* fonction *f* logique dédiée; fonction *f* logique spécialisée ◇ **dedicated logic cuts down the chip count** la logique dédiée réduit le nombre de puces

dedicated print server /ˌdedɪkeɪtɪd ˈprɪnt ˌsɜːvə/ *noun* serveur *m* dédié à l'impression

dedicated word-processor /ˌdedɪkeɪtɪd ˈwɜːd ˌprəʊsesə/ *noun* système *m* de traitement de texte spécialisé

de facto standard /deɪ ˌfæktəʊ ˈstændəd/ *noun* (*system which has become a standard*) norme *f* de fait; norme *f* de facto

default /dɪˈfɔːlt/ *adjective* défaut *m* ◇ **by default** par défaut *or* implicite *or* intrinsèque *or* prédéterminé, -ée ◇ **the operating system allows the user to select the default drive** le système d'exploitation permet à l'utilisateur de choisir le lecteur par défaut

default drive /dɪˈfɔːlt draɪv/ *noun* lecteur *m* implicite; lecteur *m* par défaut ◇ **the operating system allows the user to select the default drive** le système d'exploitation permet à l'utilisateur de choisir le lecteur par défaut

default option /dɪˌfɔːlt ˈɒpʃən/ *noun* option *f* implicite; option *f* intrinsèque; option *f* par défaut

default printer /dɪˌfɔːlt ˈprɪntə/ *noun* imprimante *f* par défaut *or* implicite

default rate /dɪˌfɔːlt ˈreɪt/ *noun* débit *m* par défaut

default response /dɪˌfɔːlt rɪˈspɒns/ *noun* réponse *f* intrinsèque *or* par défaut

default value /dɪˌfɔːlt ˈvæljuː/ *noun* valeur *f* implicite; valeur *f* intrinsèque; valeur *f* prédéterminée ◇ **screen width has a default value of 80** la largeur implicite *or* par défaut d'un écran est de 80

'The default values of columns cannot be set in the database schema, so different applications can trash the database.' [*Computing*]

defective sector /dɪˌfektɪv ˈsektə/ *noun* secteur *m* défectueux

defensive computing /dɪˌfensɪv kəm ˈpjuːtɪŋ/ *noun* informatique *f* défensive; programmation *f* défensive

deferred addressing /dɪˌfɜːd əˈdresɪŋ/ *noun* adressage *m* indirect

deferred mode /dɪˈfɜːd məʊd/ *noun* mode *m* différé

deferred printing /dɪˌfɜːd ˈprɪntɪŋ/ *noun* impression *f* en différé

define /dɪˈfaɪn/ *verb* définir *vt* ◇ **all the variables were defined at initialization** toutes les variables ont été définies lors de l'initialisation

definition /ˌdefɪˈnɪʃ(ə)n/ *noun* **1.** (*of a screen*) définition *f* **2.** (*of a value*) définition *f*

deflect /dɪˈflekt/ *verb* (*object or beam*) dévier *vt*

deflection /dɪˈflekʃ(ə)n/ *noun* déviation *f*; déflexion *f*

deflection yokes /dɪˈflekʃ(ə)n jəʊkz/ *plural noun* déflecteurs *mpl*

DEFRAG /ˈdiːfræg/ *noun* (*defragmentation utility in MS-DOS*) DEFRAG

defragmentation /ˌdiːfrægmenˈteɪʃ(ə)n/ *noun* (*reorganisation of files on disk*) défragmentation *f*

defragmentation utility /ˌdiːfrægmen ˈteɪʃ(ə)n juːˌtɪlɪti/ *noun* défragmenteur *m*

degauss /diːˈgaʊs/ *verb* démagnétiser *vt* ◇ **the R *or* W heads have to be degaussed each week to ensure optimum performance** il faut démagnétiser les têtes de lecture/écriture une fois par semaine pour obtenir une performance optimale

degausser /diːˈgaʊsə/ *noun* effaceur *m* magnétique

degradation /ˌdegrəˈdeɪʃ(ə)n/ *noun* **1.** (*loss of picture quality*) dégradation *f* **2.** (*of computers*) dégradation *f*; réduction *f* des performances

dejagging /diːˈdʒægɪŋ/ *noun* anticrénelage *m*

DEL /del/ *noun* (*MS-DOS command*) commande *f* DEL; commande *f* effacer; commande *f* supprimer ◇ **to delete all files with the extension BAK, use the command DEL *or* .BAK** pour effacer tous les fichiers avec l'extension BAK, entrez la commande DEL *or* .BAK ◇ **to remove a word from the screen, press the DEL key repeatedly** pour effacer un mot à l'écran, appuyez plusieurs fois de suite sur la touche DEL *or* sur la touche Suppr

delay line /dɪˈleɪ laɪn/ *noun* ligne *f* à retard

delay line store /dɪˈleɪ laɪn ˌstɔː/ *noun* mémoire *f* à ligne à retard

delay vector /dɪˈleɪ ˌvektə/ *noun* vecteur *m* de retard

delete /dɪˈliːt/ *verb* **1.** (*word in text*) rayer *vt*; effacer *vt*; supprimer *vt* **2.** (*text or data from a storage device*) effacer *vt*; détruire *vt*; supprimer *vt* ◇ **the word-processor allows us to delete the whole file by pressing this key** le traitement de texte permet de supprimer un fichier complet en appuyant sur cette touche

delete character /dɪˌliːt ˈkærɪktə/ *noun* caractère *m* de suppression; caractère *m* d'effacement

deletion /dɪˈliːʃ(ə)n/ *noun* **1.** (*cutting text*) coupure *f*; (*erasing text*) effacement *m*; (*cutting or erasing text*) suppression *f* **2.** (*removal from storage device*) suppression *f* **3.** (*text cut*) suppression *f* ◇ **the editors asked the author to make several deletions in the last chapter** les éditeurs ont demandé à l'auteur de faire plusieurs coupures dans le dernier chapitre

deletion record /dɪˈliːʃ(ə)n ˌrekɔːd/ *noun* enregistrement *m* des suppressions

deletion tracking /dɪˈliːʃ(ə)n ˌtrækɪŋ/ *noun* suivi *m*

delimit /diːˈlɪmɪt/ *verb* délimiter *vt*

delimited-field file /diːˌlɪmɪtd fiːld ˈfaɪl/ *noun* fichier *m* à champs délimités

delimiter /diːˈlɪmɪtə/ *noun* **1.** (*symbol for start or end of data, etc.*) délimiteur *m*; séparateur *m* (d'information) **2.** (*boundary between instruction and argument*) séparateur *m* d'information

DEL key /'del kiː/ *noun* touche *f* d'effacement; touche *f* DEL

Delphi /'delfiː/ (*commercial online information provider*) service *m* en ligne

delta clock /'deltə klɒk/ *noun* horloge *f* à relance automatique; horloge *f* delta

demagnetise, demagnetize *verb* démagnétiser *vt*

demagnetiser, demagnetizer *noun* effaceur *m* magnétique

demand assigned multiple access /dɪ ˌmɑːnd əˌsaɪnd ˌmʌltɪp(ə)l 'ækses/ *noun* accès *m* multiple asservi à la demande

demand fetching /dɪ'mɑːnd ˌfetʃɪŋ/ *noun* accès *m* sur demande à la mémoire paginée

demand paging /dɪ'mɑːnd ˌpeɪdʒɪŋ/ *noun* appel *m* de page sur demande

demand processing /dɪ'mɑːnd ˌprəʊsesɪŋ/ *noun* traitement *m* de données sur demande; traitement *m* de données immédiat

demand protocol architecture /dɪˌmɑːnd ˌprəʊtəkɒl 'ɑːkɪtektʃə/ *noun* architecture *f* DPA

demand reading/writing /dɪˌmɑːnd ˌriːdɪŋ 'raɪtɪŋ/ *noun* (*direct data transfer*) lecture-écriture *f* sur demande; lecture-écriture *f* directe

demand staging /dɪ'mɑːnd ˌsteɪdʒɪŋ/ *noun* transfert *m* sur demande

demarcation /ˌdiːmɑː'keɪʃ(ə)n/ *noun* démarcation *f*

democratic network /ˌdeməkrætɪk 'netwɜːk/ *noun* réseau *m* démocratique

demodulation /diːˌmɒdju'leɪʃ(ə)n/ *noun* démodulation *f*

demonstration software /ˌdemənstreɪʃ(ə)n 'sɒftweə/ *noun* (*software that only shows the functions of a computer*) démo *f*; logiciel *m* de démonstration; version *f* de démonstration d'un logiciel

demultiplex /diː'mʌltɪpleks/ *verb* démultiplexeur *vt*

demultiplexor /diː'mʌltɪpleksə/ *noun* démultiplexeur *m*

denial /dɪ'naɪəl/ *noun* déni *m*; négation *f*

denial-of-service attack /dɪˌnaɪəl əv 'sɜːvɪs əˌtæk/ *noun* attaque *f* par saturation

dense index /dens 'ɪndeks/ *noun* index *m* complet

dense list /'dens lɪst/ *noun* liste *f* complète

density /'densɪti/ *noun* (*amount of light that a negative blocks*) densité *f*

> '...diode lasers with shorter wavelengths will make doubling of the bit and track densities possible' [*Byte*]

departmental LAN /ˌdiːpɑːt'ment(ə)l læn/ *noun* réseau *m* de service; réseau *m* départemental

dependent /dɪ'pendənt/ *adjective* dépendant *or* -e ◇ **a process which is dependent on the result of another process** procédé dépendant des résultats *or* relié aux résultats d'un autre procédé

deposit /dɪ'pɒzɪt/ *noun* (*to print out the content of memory*) vidage *m* ■ *verb* (*to write data into a register or storage location*) enregistrer *vt*; mettre en registre; mettre en mémoire auxiliaire; vider (le contenu d'une mémoire)

deposition /ˌdepə'zɪʃ(ə)n/ *noun* (*on semiconductor*) enduction *f*; dépôt *m*; pose *f* d'un enduit

depth cueing /'depθ ˌkjuːɪŋ/ *noun* estompage *m* en fonction de l'éloignement

derivation graph /ˌderɪ'veɪʃ(ə)n grɑːf/ *noun* graphe *m* de relation

derive /dɪ'raɪv/ *verb* provenir (de); dériver (de)

DES /ˌdiː iː 'es/ *noun* norme *f* de cryptage de données

descender /dɪ'sendə/ *noun* (*of the letters 'q' or 'p'*) jambage *m* (descendant)

de-scramble /diː 'skræmb(ə)l/ *verb* (*coded message*) déchiffrer *vt*; désembrouiller *vt*

de-scrambler /diː 'skræmblə/ *noun* désembrouilleur *m*; décodeur *m*

description list /dɪ'skrɪpʃən lɪst/ *noun* liste *f* descriptive

descriptor /dɪ'skrɪptə/ *noun* descripteur *m*; mot-clé *m*

deselect /ˌdiːsɪ'lekt/ *verb* déselectionner *vt*

design parameters /dɪ'zaɪn pəˌræmɪtəz/ *plural noun* spécifications *fpl*

desk accessory /'desk əkˌsesəri/ *noun* (*Apple Macintosh utility that enhances the system*) accessoire *m* de bureau

desk check /'desk tʃek/ *noun* (*dry run of a program*) essai *m* à blanc

desktop /'desktɒp/ *adjective* de bureau ■ *noun* (*workspace that is a graphical representation of a real-life desktop*) bureau *m*

desktop background /ˌdesktɒp 'bækgraʊnd/ *noun* toile *f* de fond

desktop computer /ˌdesktɒp kəm'pjuːtə/, **desktop computer system** /ˌdesktɒp kəm 'pjuːtə ˌsɪstəm/ *noun* ordinateur *m* de bureau

desktop file /ˌdesktɒp 'faɪl/ *noun* fichier *m* bureau

desktop presentations /ˌdesktɒp ˌprez(ə)n 'teɪʃ(ə)nz/ *plural noun* présentation *f* de page assistée par ordinateur

desktop publishing /ˌdesktɒp 'pʌblɪʃɪŋ/ *noun* publication *f* assistée par ordinateur; édition *f* électronique

> '...desktop publishing or the ability to produce high-quality publications using a minicomputer, essentially boils down to combining words and images on pages' [*Byte*]

Desktop taskbar /ˌdesktɒp 'tɑːskbɑː/ *noun* barre *f* des tâches

desktop unit /ˌdesktɒp 'juːnɪt/ *noun* unité *f* de bureau

despatch /dɪ'spætʃ/ *noun* expédition *f*

despool /diː'spuːl/ *verb* imprimer la file d'attente

despotic network /dɪˌspɒtɪk 'netwɜːk/ *noun* réseau *m* avec synchronisation despotique

destination address /ˌdestɪneɪʃ(ə)n ə'dres/ *noun* adresse *f* de destination

destination page /ˌdestɪ'neɪʃ(ə)n peɪdʒ/ *noun* page *f* de destination

destructive addition /dɪˌstrʌktɪv ə'dɪʃ(ə)n/ *noun* addition *f* destructive

destructive cursor /dɪˌstrʌktɪv 'kɜːsə/ *noun* curseur *m* destructif

destructive read /dɪ'strʌktɪv riːd/ *noun* lecture *f* destructive

destructive readout /dɪˌstrʌktɪv 'riːdaʊt/ *noun* affichage *m* destructif

detail file /'diːteɪl faɪl/ *noun* fichier *m* (de) mouvements

detail paper /'diːteɪl ˌpeɪpə/ *noun* papier-calque *m*

detected error /dɪˌtektɪd 'erə/ *noun* erreur *f* notifiée; erreur *f* détectée

deterministic /dɪˌtɜːmɪ'nɪstɪk/ *adjective* déterministe

Deutsche Industrienorm /ˌdɔɪtʃə 'ɪndʊstriː ˌnɔːm/ *noun* DIN

developer /dɪ'veləpə/ *noun* (*person*) concepteur *m*

development software /dɪ'veləpmənt ˌsɒftweə/ *noun* logiciel *m* de développement

development time /dɪ'veləpmənt taɪm/ *noun* temps *m* de développement

device /dɪ'vaɪs/ *noun* (*machine linked to a computer*) dispositif *m*; appareil *m*; (*linked to a computer*) périphérique *m*

> 'Users in remote locations can share ideas on the Liveboard through the use of a wireless pen-input device and network connections.' [*Computing*]

device address /dɪ'vaɪs əˌdres/ *noun* adresse *f* de contrôleur de périphérique

device character control /dɪˌvaɪs ˌkærɪktə kəŋ'trəʊl/ *noun* contrôle *m* de périphérique par caractère

device code /dɪ'vaɪs kəʊd/ *noun* code *m* d'identification de périphérique

device control character /dɪˌvaɪs kən'trəʊl ˌkærɪktə/ *noun* (*code transmitted to a device*) caractère *m* de contrôle de périphérique

device-dependent /dɪˌvaɪs dɪ'pendənt/ *adjective* tributaire du type d'unité

device driver /dɪ'vaɪs ˌdraɪvə/ *noun* (*driver*) logiciel *m* de commande de périphérique

device flag /dɪ'vaɪs flæg/ *noun* (*indication of a device's state*) marqueur *m*

device handler /dɪˌvaɪs 'hændlə/ *noun* logiciel *m* de commande de périphérique; gestionnaire *m* de périphérique; pilote *m* de périphérique

device-independent /dɪˌvaɪs ˌɪndɪ'pendənt/ *adjective* indépendant *or* -e; non tributaire; non spécialisé *or* -ée

device name /dɪ'vaɪs neɪm/ *noun* nom *m* de périphérique

device priority /dɪ'vaɪs praɪˌɒrɪti/ *noun* priorité *f* d'un périphérique; priorité *f* d'un appareil

device queue /dɪ'vaɪs kjuː/ *noun* file *f* d'attente (de périphériques)

device status word /dɪˌvaɪs 'steɪtəs ˌwɜːd/ *noun* indicateur *m* d'état

devise /dɪ'vaɪz/ *verb* concevoir *vt*

Dhrystone benchmark /ˌdraɪstəʊn 'bentʃmɑːk/ *noun* (*benchmarking system*) test *m* (d'évaluation des performances) Dhrystone; benchmark *m* Dhrystone

diagnose /'daɪəgnəʊz/ *verb* diagnostiquer *vt*; trouver *vt*

diagnosis /ˌdaɪəg'nəʊsɪs/ *noun* diagnostic *m*

diagnostic aid /ˌdaɪəgnɒstɪk 'eɪd/ *noun* aide *f* au diagnostic

diagnostic chip /ˌdaɪəgnɒstɪk 'tʃɪp/ *noun* puce *f* de diagnostic ◇ **they are carrying out research on diagnostic chips to test computers that contain processors** ils font des recherches sur les puces de diagnostic destinées au contrôle des ordinateurs équipés de processeurs

diagnostic message /ˌdaɪəgnɒstɪk 'mesɪdʒ/ *noun* message *m* de diagnostic

diagnostic program /ˌdaɪəgnɒstɪk 'prəʊgræm/ *noun* logiciel *m* de diagnostic

diagnostic routine /ˌdaɪəgnɒstɪk ruː'tiːn/ *noun* routine *f* de diagnostic

diagnostics /ˌdaɪəg'nɒstɪks/ *plural noun* outils *mpl* de diagnostic

diagnostic test /ˌdaɪəgnɒstɪk 'test/ *noun* test *m* de diagnostic

dial /'daɪəl/ *noun* (*used to select or validate*) bouton *m*; réglage *m*; (*on telephone or clock*) cadran *m* ◇ **density dial** bouton de densité ◇ **dial pulse** impulsion *f* de cadran ◇ **if the text fades, turn the density dial on the printer to full black** si l'impression est trop pâle, réglez le bouton de densité (d'impression) sur le noir ◇ **to tune into the radio station, turn the dial** pour obtenir la station de radio, tournez ce bouton

> 'Customers will be able to choose a wide variety of telephony products, from basic auto-dial programs to call-centre applications.' [*Computing*]

dialect /'daɪəlekt/ *noun* dialecte *m*

dial-in modem /ˌdaɪəl ɪn 'məʊdem/ *noun* (*auto-answer modem*) modem *m* à appel automatique

dial modifier /'daɪəl ˌmɒdɪfaɪə/ *noun* modificateur *m* de numéro

dialog /'daɪəlɒg/ *noun US* dialogue *m*

dialog box /'daɪəlɒg bɒks/ *noun* boîte *f* de dialogue

dialogue /'daɪəlɒg/, **dialog** *noun* dialogue *m* ◇ **dialogue box** (*on-screen message*) fenêtre *f* de dialogue

dialup *noun* service *m* d'appels

dial-up access /ˌdaɪəl ʌp 'ækses/ *noun* accès *m* par ligne commutée

dial-up connection /ˌdaɪəl ʌp kə'nekʃ(ə)n/ *noun* connexion *f* par ligne commutée

Dial-up Networking /ˌdaɪəl ʌp 'netwɜːkɪŋ/ *noun* option *f* carte d'accès distant

dial-up service /ˌdaɪəl ʌp 'sɜːvɪs/ *noun* service *m* d'appels

DIANE /daɪ'æn/ *abbr* (*direct information access network for Europe*) Réseau *m* d'accès direct à l'information pour l'Europe

diaphragm /'daɪəfræm/ *noun* (*photography*) diaphragme *m*

DIB /ˌdiː aɪ 'biː/ *noun* bus *m* d'entrée

dibit /'dɪbɪt/ *noun* (*two binary bits*) dibit *m*; groupe *m* de 2 chiffres binaires

dichotomising search /daɪ'kɒtəmaɪzɪŋ ˌsɜːtʃ/, **dichotomizing search** *noun* recherche *f* dichotomique; recherche *f* par dichotomie

dichroic /daɪ'krəʊɪk/ *adjective* dichroïque

dichroic filter /daɪˌkrəʊɪk 'fɪltə/ *noun* filtre *m* dichroïque

dichroic head /daɪˌkrəʊɪk 'hed/ *noun* tête *f* dichroïque

dictionary /'dɪkʃən(ə)ri/ *noun* **1.** (*data management structure*) dictionnaire *m* **2.** (*spell checker*) dictionnaire *m*

dielectric /ˌdaɪɪ'lektrɪk/ *adjective* diélectrique

differential pulse coded modulation /ˌdɪfərenʃəl ˌpʌls ˌkəʊdɪd ˌmɒdjʊ'leɪʃ(ə)n/ *noun* modulation *f* par impulsions et codages (MIC)

DIF file /'dɪf faɪl/ *noun* fichier *m* DIF

diffusion /dɪ'fjuːʒ(ə)n/ *noun* diffusion *f*; dopage *m* par diffusion

digit /'dɪdʒɪt/ *noun* chiffre *m* ◇ **a phone number with eight digits** *or* **an eight-digit phone number** un numéro de téléphone de huit chiffres ◇ **the decimal digit 8** le chiffre décimal 8 *or* la décimale 8 ◇ **the decimal number system uses the digits 0123456789** la base de numération décimale utilise les chiffres 0123456789

digital /'dɪdʒɪt(ə)l/ *adjective* numérique; digital *or* -e ◇ **digital audio tape (DAT)** bande *f* audionumérique ◇ **digital compact cassette (DCC)** cassette compacte numérique ◇ **digital multimeter (DMM)** multimètre *m* numérique ◇ **digital optical reading (DOR)** lecture *f* optique de données numériques ◇ **digital readout** affichage *m* numérique ◇ **digital recording** enregistrement *m* numérique ◇ **digital signal level 0 (DS-0)** (*capable of transmitting information in 8-bit frames at a rate of 8,000 frames per second*) signal numérique niveau 0 ◇ **digital signal level 1 (DS-1)** (*standard that defines the way data is formatted and transmitted over a T-1 line*) signal numérique niveau 1 ◇ **digital signal processing** traitement *m* de signaux numériques ◇ **digital signal processor (DSP)** (*IC used to manipulate digital signals*) circuit *m* DSP *or* circuit (intégré) de traitement de signaux numériques *or* processeur de signaux numériques ◇ **digital subscriber line (DSL)** ligne *f* numérique d'abonné ◇ **digital video camera** (*Webcam*) caméra *f* vidéo numérique ◇ **digital video disc** *or* **digital versatile disc (DVD)** disque *m* vidéo numérique *or* disque DVD

'Xerox Parc's LCD breakthrough promises the digital equivalent of paper, by producing thin, low-cost flat displays with a 600dpi resolution.' [*Computing*]

digital audio tape /ˌdɪdʒɪt(ə)l 'ɔːdiəʊ ˌteɪp/ *noun* enregistrement *m* sur bande audionumérique

digital camera /ˌdɪdʒɪt(ə)l 'kæm(ə)rə/ *noun* appareil photo *m* numérique

digital cash /ˌdɪdʒɪt(ə)l 'kæʃ/ *noun* monnaie *f* électronique

digital cassette /ˌdɪdʒɪt(ə)l kə'set/ *noun* cassette *f* numérique

digital certificate /ˌdɪdʒɪt(ə)l sə'tɪfɪkət/ *noun* certificat *m*

digital channel /ˌdɪdʒɪt(ə)l 'tʃæn(ə)l/ *noun* canal *m* numérique

digital circuit /ˌdɪdʒɪt(ə)l 'sɜːkɪt/ *noun* circuit *m* numérique

digital clock /ˌdɪdʒɪt(ə)l 'klɒk/ *noun* horloge *f* numérique

digital compact cassette /ˌdɪdʒɪt(ə)l ˌkɒmpækt kə'set/ *noun* cassette *f* compacte numérique

digital computer /ˌdɪdʒɪt(ə)l kəm'pjuːtə/ *noun* ordinateur *m* numérique

digital data /ˌdɪdʒɪt(ə)l 'deɪtə/ *noun* données *fpl* numériques; données *fpl* numérisées

digital display /ˌdɪdʒɪt(ə)l dɪ'spleɪ/ *noun* (*video display unit*) écran *m* numérique

digital light processing /ˌdɪdʒɪt(ə)l 'laɪt ˌprəʊsesɪŋ/ *noun* traitement *m* numérique de la lumière

digital logic /ˌdɪdʒɪt(ə)l 'lɒdʒɪk/ *noun* logique *f* numérique

digital monitor /ˌdɪdʒɪt(ə)l 'mɒnɪtə/ *noun* moniteur *m* numérique; écran *m* numérique

digital optical recording /ˌdɪdʒɪt(ə)l ˌɒptɪk(ə)l rɪ'kɔːdɪŋ/ *noun* DOR

digital output /ˌdɪdʒɪt(ə)l 'aʊtpʊt/ *noun* sortie *f* numérique

digital plotter /ˌdɪdʒɪt(ə)l ˈplɒtə/ *noun* traceur *m* numérique

digital read-out /ˌdɪdʒɪt(ə)l ˈriːdaʊt/ *noun* lecture *f* numérique

digital representation /ˌdɪdʒɪt(ə)l ˌreprɪzenˈteɪʃ(ə)n/ *noun* représentation *f* numérique

digital resolution /ˌdɪdʒɪt(ə)l ˌrezəˈluːʃ(ə)n/ *noun* résolution *f* d'un nombre

digital signal /ˌdɪdʒɪt(ə)l ˈsɪgn(ə)l/ *noun* signal *m* numérique

digital signal level one /ˌdɪdʒɪt(ə)l ˌsɪgn(ə)l ˌlev(ə)l ˈwʌn/ *noun* signal *m* numérique de niveau 1

digital signal level zero /ˌdɪdʒɪt(ə)l ˌsɪgn(ə)l ˌlev(ə)l ˈzɪərəʊ/ *noun* signal *m* numérique de niveau 0

digital signalling /ˌdɪdʒɪt(ə)l ˈsɪgnəlɪŋ/ *noun* transmission *f* de signaux numériques

digital signal processing /ˌdɪdʒɪt(ə)l ˈsɪgn(ə)l ˌprəʊsesɪŋ/ *noun* traitement *m* de signaux numériques

digital signature /ˌdɪdʒɪt(ə)l ˈsɪgnətʃə/ *noun* signature *f* numérique

digital speech /ˌdɪdʒɪt(ə)l ˈspiːtʃ/ *noun* voix *f* numérisée *or* de synthèse

digital subscriber line /ˌdɪdʒɪt(ə)l səbˈskraɪbə ˌlaɪn/ *noun* ligne *f* d'abonné numérique

digital switching /ˌdɪdʒɪt(ə)l ˈswɪtʃɪŋ/ *noun* commutation *f* numérique

digital system /ˌdɪdʒɪt(ə)l ˈsɪstəm/ *noun* système *m* numérique

digital to analog converter /ˌdɪdʒɪt(ə)l tə ˌænəlɒg kənˈvɜːtə/ *noun* convertisseur *m* numérique-analogique

digital transmission system /ˌdɪdʒɪt(ə)l trænzˈmɪʃ(ə)n ˌsɪstəm/ *noun* système *m* de transmission numérique

digital TV /ˌdɪdʒɪt(ə)l tiːˈviː/ *noun* télévision *f* numérique

digital versatile disc /ˌdɪdʒɪt(ə)l ˌvɜːsətaɪl ˈdɪsk/ *noun* DVD *m*

digital video /ˌdɪdʒɪt(ə)l ˈvɪdiəʊ/ *noun* vidéo *f* numérisée

digital videodisc /ˌdɪdʒɪt(ə)l ˈvɪdiəʊdɪsk/ *noun* DVD *m* vidéo

digital video interactive /ˌdɪdʒɪt(ə)l ˌvɪdiəʊ ˌɪntərˈæktɪv/ *noun* vidéo *f* numérisée interactive

digitise /ˈdɪdʒɪˌtaɪz/, **digitize** *verb* numériser *vt*

> 'The contract covers fibre optic cable and Synchronous Digital Hierarchy transmission equipment to be used to digitize the telecommunications network.' [*Computergram*]

digitised photograph /ˌdɪdʒɪˌtaɪzd ˌfəʊtəˈgrɑːf/, **digitized photograph** *noun* photographie *f* numérisée

digitiser, digitizer *noun* convertisseur *m* analogique-numérique; numériseur *m*

digitising pad /ˈdɪdʒɪtaɪzɪŋ ˌpæd/, **digitising tablet, digitizing pad, digitizing tablet** *noun* tablette *f* graphique; tablette *f* à numériser

digit place /ˈdɪdʒɪt pleɪs/, **digit position** /ˌdɪdʒɪt pəˈzɪʃ(ə)n/ *noun* place *f* d'un chiffre

DIL /ˌdiː aɪ ˈel/ *noun* système *m* à double rang de broches

dimension /daɪˈmenʃən/ *noun* dimension *f*

dimensioning /daɪˈmenʃənɪŋ/ *noun* calcul *m* des dimensions ◇ **array dimensioning occurs at this line** le calcul des dimensions du tableau se fait à ce niveau-ci

diminished radix complement /dɪˌmɪnɪʃt ˈreɪdɪks ˌkɒmpleks/ *noun* complément *m* restreint

DIMM /ˌdiː aɪ em ˈem/ *noun* module *m* de mémoire à double rangée de connexions

DIN /ˌdiː aɪ ˈen/ *noun* (*German industry standards organisation*) DIN

Dingbat™ /ˈdɪŋbæt/ *noun* (*font*) caractères *mpl* Dingbat™; caractères *mpl* spéciaux ◇ **to insert a copyright symbol, use the Dingbat font** pour insérer une marque de copyright, utilisez les caractères spéciaux *or* Dingbat

diode /ˈdaɪəʊd/ *noun* diode *f* ◇ **light-emitting diode (LED)** diode électroluminescente

DIP switch /ˈdɪp swɪtʃ/ *noun* commutateur *m* DIP; commutateur *m* à bascule

DIR /ˌdiː aɪ ˈɑː/ *noun* (*MS-DOS system command*) commande *f* DIR

direct /daɪˈrekt/ *adjective, adverb* **1.** (*straight*) direct **2.** (*without interruption*) directement; en direct **3.** (*with no processing*) direct ◇ **to dial direct** appeler *or* téléphoner en direct ◇ **you can dial New York direct from London if you want** vous pouvez appeler New York en direct depuis Londres

direct access /ˌdaɪrekt ˈækses/ *noun* accès *m* direct

direct access storage device /daɪˌrekt ˌækses ˈstɔːrɪdʒ dɪˌvaɪs/ *noun* mémoire *f* à accès direct; support *m* à accès direct

direct addressing /ˌdaɪrekt əˈdresɪŋ/ *noun* adressage *m* direct

direct cable connection /ˌdaɪrekt ˈkeɪb(ə)l kəˌneks(ə)n/ *noun* liaison *f* directe par câble

direct change-over /daɪˈrekt tʃeɪndʒ/ *noun* transfert *m* direct

direct code /daɪˈrekt kəʊd/ *noun* code *m* direct

direct coding /daɪˈrekt kɒdɪŋ/ *noun* codage *m* direct

direct connect /ˌdaɪrekt kəˈnekt/ *adjective* avec connexion directe

direct connection /daɪˌrekt kəˈnekʃən/ *noun* connexion *f* directe

direct current /dɪˌrekt ˈkʌrənt/ *noun* courant *m* continu

direct data entry /daɪˌrekt ˌdeɪtə 'entri/ *noun* saisie *f* directe de données (au clavier); entrée *f* directe de données

direct digital control /daɪˌrekt ˌdɪdʒɪt(ə)l kən'trəʊl/ *noun* commande *f* numérique directe

directed scan /daɪ'rektd skæn/ *noun* balayage *m* dirigé

direct image /ˌdaɪrekt 'ɪmɪdʒ/ *noun* image *f* directe

direct information access network for Europe /daɪˌrekt ˌɪnfəmeɪʃ(ə)n ˌækses ˌnetwɜːk fə 'jʊərəp/ *noun* DIANE

direct-insert routine /ˌdaɪrekt ɪn'sɜːt ruːˌtiːn/ *noun* programme *m* d'insertion directe

direct instruction /ˌdaɪrekt ɪn'strʌkʃən/ *noun* instruction *f* directe

directive /daɪ'rektɪv/ *noun* directive *f*

'...directives are very useful for selecting parts of the code for particular purposes' [*Personal Computer World*]

directive statement /daɪˌrektɪv 'steɪtmənt/ *noun* instruction *f* directive

direct memory access /daɪˌrekt 'mem(ə)ri ˌækses/ *noun* accès *m* direct à la mémoire

direct memory access channel /daɪˌrekt ˌmem(ə)ri 'ækses ˌtʃæn(ə)l/ *noun* voie *f* d'accès direct à la mémoire

direct mode /daɪ'rekt məʊd/ *noun* mode *m* direct

Director /daɪ'rektə/ Director

directory /daɪ'rekt(ə)ri/ *noun* **1.** annuaire *m*; répertoire *m* d'adresses **2.** répertoire *m*

directory services /daɪ'rekt(ə)ri ˌsɜːvɪsɪz/ *noun* services *mpl* d'annuaire

directory synchronisation /daɪˌrekt(ə)ri ˌsɪŋkrənaɪ'zeɪʃ(ə)n/ *noun* synchronisation *f* de l'annuaire

direct page register /daɪˌrekt 'peɪdʒ ˌredʒɪstə/ *noun* registre *m* de pagination à accès direct

direct reference address /ˌdaɪrekt ˌref(ə)rəns ə'dres/ *noun* adresse *f* de référence directe

DirectSound /ˌdaɪrekt'saʊnd/ DirectSound

direct transfer /ˌdaɪrekt 'trænsfɜː/ *noun* transfert *m* direct

dirty bit /'dɜːti bɪt/ *noun* (*flag bit indicating the loading of programs*) bit *m* marqué

disable interrupt /dɪsˌeɪb(ə)l 'ɪntərʌpt/ *noun* commande *f* d'invalidation d'interruption

disarm /dɪs'ɑːm/ *verb* invalider *vt*; désactiver *vt*

disarmed state /dɪs'ɑːmd steɪt/ *noun* état *m* désactivé

disassemble /ˌdɪsə'semb(ə)l/ *verb* (*translation of machine instructions*) désassembler *vt*

disassembler /ˌdɪsə'semblə/ *noun* désassembleur *m*

disaster dump /dɪ'zɑːstə dʌmp/ *noun* vidage *m* irréversible

disc /dɪsk/ *noun* disque *m* compact

disconnect /ˌdɪskə'nekt/ *verb* débrancher *vt*; déconnecter *vt* ◇ **do not forget to disconnect the cable before moving the printer** n'oubliez pas de débrancher (le câble de) l'imprimante avant de la changer de place

discrete /dɪ'skriːt/ *adjective* (*in small individual units*) discret *or* -ète ◇ **a data word is made up of discrete bits** le mot de données est formé de bits discrets

discrete multi-tone /dɪˌskriːt 'mʌlti ˌtəʊn/ *noun* multitonalité *f* discrète

discretionary hyphen *noun* trait d'union *m* qui ne s'imprime pas; trait d'union *m* qui n'apparaît pas à l'écran

discrimination instruction /dɪˌskrɪmɪˌneɪʃ(ə)n ɪn'strʌkʃən/ *noun* instruction *f* (d'opération) conditionnelle

discussion group /dɪ'skʌʃ(ə)n gruːp/ *noun* groupe *m*; forum *m* de discussion

disjunction /dɪs'dʒʌŋkʃ(ə)n/ *noun* (*logical function*) disjonction *f*; opération *f* OU; opération *f* de réunion; opération *f* d'union

disjunctive search /dɪsˌdʒʌnktɪv 'sɜːtʃ/ *noun* recherche *f* par mots-clés

disk /dɪsk/ *noun* (*record or computer hard disk*) disque *m*

disk access /dɪsk 'ækses/ *noun* accès *m* au disque

disk access management /ˌdɪsk ˌækses 'mænɪdʒmənt/ *noun* gestion *f* d'accès au disque

disk-based /'dɪsk beɪsd/ *adjective* utilisant un disque dur; utilisant des disquettes

disk cache /'dɪsk kæʃ/ *noun* mémoire *f* cache d'un disque

disk cartridge /dɪsk 'kɑːtrɪdʒ/ *noun* cartouche *f* de disque dur; disque *m* dur amovible

disk compression /dɪsk kəm'preʃ(ə)n/ *noun* compression *f* de disque

disk compression software /ˌdɪsk kəm'preʃ(ə)n ˌsɒftweə/ *noun* logiciel *m* de compression de disque

disk controller /dɪsk kən'trəʊlə/ *noun* contrôleur *m* de disque; contrôleur *m* de disquettes

disk-controller card /'dɪsk kənˌtrəʊlə ˌkɑːd/ *noun* carte *f* contrôleur de disques; carte *f* contrôleur de disquettes

disk crash /'dɪsk kræʃ/ *noun* (*faulty disk*) plantage *m*

disk directory /dɪsk də'rekt(ə)ri/ *noun* répertoire *m* de disque

disk doctor /dɪsk 'dɒktə/ *noun* utilitaire *m* de récupération

disk drive /'dɪsk draɪv/ *noun* lecteur *m* de disque/disquette; unité *f* de disque/disquette

disk duplexing /ˈdɪsk ˌdjuːpleksɪŋ/ *noun* copie *f* miroir

diskette /dɪˈsket/ *noun* disquette *f*; disque *m* souple

disk file /ˈdɪsk faɪl/ *noun* (*data stored on disk*) fichier *m* sur disque; fichier *m* sur disquette

disk formatting /ˈdɪsk ˌfɔːmætɪŋ/ *noun* (*setting up of a blank disk*) formatage *m* de disque *f*; formatage *m* de disquette *f*

disk head /ˈdɪsk hed/ *noun* tête *f* de lecture/écriture de disquettes

disk index holes /ˌdɪsk ˈɪndeks ˌhəʊlz/ *plural noun* perforations *fpl* de marquage du bord d'un disque

diskless /ˈdɪskləs/ *adjective* sans disque

disk map /ˈdɪsk mæp/ *noun* organisation *f*

disk memory /dɪsk ˈmem(ə)ri/ *noun* (*memory on disk*) mémoire *f* sur disque

disk mirroring /ˈdɪsk ˌmɪrərɪŋ/ *noun* copie *f* miroir; duplication *f* de données sur un disque miroir; mirroring *m*

disk operating system /ˌdɪsk ˈɒpəreɪtɪŋ ˌsɪstəm/ *noun* système *m* d'exploitation de disque; système *m* DOS

disk pack /ˈdɪsk pæk/ *noun* (*disks on a single hub*) plateaux *mpl* de disque dur

disk partition /dɪsk pɑːˈtɪʃ(ə)n/ *noun* partition *f* d'un disque dur

disk sector /dɪsk ˈsektə/ *noun* secteur *m* de disque

disk sector formatting /ˌdɪsk ˌsektə ˈfɔːmætɪŋ/ *noun* formatage *m* de secteur de disque

disk storage /dɪsk ˈstɔːrɪdʒ/ *noun* (*using disks for storage*) mémoire *f* sur disque

disk track /ˈdɪsk træk/ *noun* piste *f* d'un disque

disk unit /dɪsk ˈjuːnɪt/ *noun* unité *f* de disque(s); lecteur *m* de disque(s)

disorderly close-down /dɪsˈɔːdəli kləʊs/ *noun* panne *f* désordonnée; arrêt *m* désordonné

dispatch /dɪˈspætʃ/, **despatch** /dɪˈspætʃ/ *noun* envoi *m*

dispersion /dɪˈspɜːʃ(ə)n/ *noun* (*of beam*) dispersion *f*

displacement /dɪsˈpleɪsmənt/ *noun* déplacement *m*

display /dɪˈspleɪ/ *noun* (*of information or images*) affichage *m*; visualisation *f*, écran *m*

display adapter /dɪˈspleɪ əˌdæptə/ *noun* adaptateur *m* d'écran

display attribute /dɪˈspleɪ ˌætrɪbjuːt/ *noun* attribut *m* d'écran

display character /dɪˈspleɪ ˌkærɪktə/ *noun* caractère *m* d'écran

display character generator /dɪˈspleɪ ˌkærɪktə ˌdʒenəreɪtə/ *noun* générateur *m* de caractères d'écran

display colour /dɪˈspleɪ ˌkʌlə/ *noun* couleur *f* d'affichage

display controller /dɪˈspleɪ kənˌtrəʊlə/ *noun* (*device used for displaying dot-matrix patterns*) contrôleur *m* d'écran; contrôleur *m* d'affichage

display cycle /dɪˈspleɪ ˌsaɪk(ə)l/ *noun* cycle *m* d'affichage

display element /dɪˈspleɪ ˌelɪmənt/ *noun* **1.** élément *m* d'image (sur l'écran) **2.** primitive *f* graphique

display format /dɪˈspleɪ ˌfɔːmæt/ *noun* format *m* d'affichage; format *m* d'écran

display highlights /dɪˈspleɪ ˌhaɪlaɪts/ *plural noun* mots *mpl*

display line /dɪˈspleɪ laɪn/ *noun* ligne *f* d'écran

display mode /dɪˈspleɪ məʊd/ *noun* mode *m* affichage; mode *m* visualisation

Display PostScript™ /dɪˌspleɪ ˈpəʊstskrɪpt/ (*trade name for an extension of PostScript*) Display PostScript™; affichage *m* PostScript™

display processor /dɪˈspleɪ ˌprəʊsesə/ *noun* (*to make data suitable for a display controller*) processeur *m* d'écran

display register /dɪˈspleɪ ˌredʒɪstə/ *noun* registre *m* d'affichage

display resolution /dɪˌspleɪ ˌrezəˈluːʃ(ə)n/ *noun* définition *f* de l'écran

display screen /dɪˈspleɪ skriːn/ *noun* écran *m* de visualisation

display scrolling /dɪˈspleɪ ˌskrəʊlɪŋ/ *noun* défilement *m* (du texte sur l'écran)

display space /dɪˈspleɪ speɪs/ *noun* espace *m* d'affichage

display unit /dɪˈspleɪ ˌjuːnɪt/ *noun* unité *f* de visualisation; unité *f* de visu; écran *m* de visualisation

dissolve /dɪˈzɒlv/ *noun* (*in presentation graphics software or multimedia: to fade out one image and fade in the next*) fondu *m* enchaîné

distort /dɪˈstɔːt/ *verb* déformer *vt*

distortion /dɪˈstɔːʃ(ə)n/ *noun* (*unwanted differences in a signal*) déformation *f*; distorsion *f*; aberration *f*; altération *f* ◇ **image distortion** déformation *or* distorsion *or* aberration de l'image

distribute /dɪˈstrɪbjuːt/ *verb* distribuer *vt*; faire circuler

distributed adaptive routing /dɪˌstrɪbjʊtɪd əˌdæptɪv ˈruːtɪŋ/ *noun* routage *m* adaptatif; routage *m* flexible

distributed database system /dɪ ˌstrɪbjʊtɪd ˈdeɪtəbeɪs ˌsɪstəm/ *noun* système *m* de base de données réparties

distributed data processing /dɪˌstrɪbjʊtɪd ˈdeɪtə ˌprəʊsesɪŋ/ *noun* informatique *f* répartie

distributed file system /dɪˌstrɪbjʊtɪd ˈfaɪl ˌsɪstəm/ *noun* système *m* à fichiers répartis

distributed intelligence /dɪˌstrɪbjʊtɪd ɪn ˈtelɪdʒ(ə)ns/ *noun* intelligence *f* répartie

distributed network /dɪˌstrɪbjʊtɪd 'netwɜːk/ *noun* réseau *m* réparti

distributed processing /dɪˌstrɪbjʊtɪd 'prəʊsesɪŋ/ *noun* informatique *f* répartie

distributed processor /dɪˌstrɪbjʊtɪd 'prəʊsesə/ *noun* processeur *m* réparti

distributed system /dɪˌstrɪbjʊtɪd 'sɪstəm/ *noun* système *m* décentralisé; système *m* réparti

distribution /ˌdɪstrɪ'bjuːʃ(ə)n/ *noun* distribution *f* ◇ **distribution point** centre *m* de distribution

distribution network /ˌdɪstrɪ'bjuːʃ(ə)n ˌnetwɜːk/ *noun* réseau *m* de distribution

dither /'dɪðə/ *verb* (*to create a curve or line that looks smoother by adding shaded pixels*) adoucir *vt*

divide /dɪ'vaɪd/ *verb* diviser *vt* ◇ **to divide a number by four** diviser un nombre par quatre ◇ **twenty-one divided by three gives seven** vingt-et-un divisé par trois égale sept

dividend /'dɪvɪdend/ *noun* dividende *m*

division /dɪ'vɪʒ(ə)n/ *noun* division *f*; partage *m*; (*of word*) coupe *f* (d'un mot)

divisor /dɪ'vaɪzə/ *noun* diviseur *m*

DL *abbr* (*download*) télécharger *vt*

DLL /ˌdiː el 'el/ *noun* bibliothèque *f* dynamique des liens; DLL ◇ **the word-processor calls a spell-check program that is stored as a DLL** le traitement de texte appelle le vérificateur d'orthographe stocké dans la bibliothèque DLL

DLL file /ˌdiː el 'el ˌfaɪl/ *noun* fichier *m* DLL

DLP /ˌdiː el 'piː/ *noun* traitement *m* numérique de la lumière

DMA /ˌdiː em 'eɪ/ *noun* (*interface IC that controls high-speed data transfer*) accès *m* direct à la mémoire; DMA

'A 32-bit DMA controller, 16-bit video I/O ports and I/O filters complete the chip.' [*Computing*]

DMA controller /ˌdiː em 'eɪ kənˌtrəʊlə/ *noun* contrôleur *m* DMA

DMA cycle stealing /ˌdiː em eɪ 'saɪk(ə)l ˌstiːlɪŋ/ *noun* accès *m* direct à la mémoire par vol de cycle

DML *abbr* (*data manipulation language*) langage *m* de manipulation de données

DMS *abbr* (*data management system*) système *m* de gestion de données

DMT /ˌdiː em 'tiː/ *noun* multitonalité *f* discrète

DNS /ˌdiː en 'es/ *noun* système *m* de noms de domaine

dock /dɒk/ *verb* brancher un ordinateur portatif sur une station d'accueil

docking station[1] /'dɒkɪŋ ˌsteɪʃ(ə)n/ *noun* socle *m* de synchronisation

docking station[2] /'dɒkɪŋ ˌsteɪʃ(ə)n/, **docking unit** /'dɒkɪŋ ˌjuːnɪt/ *noun* station *f* d'accueil

document *noun* /'dɒkjʊmənt/ document *m* ■ *verb* /'dɒkjʊˌment/ documenter *vt*; donner les renseignements appropriés; renseigner *vt*

document assembly /'dɒkjʊmənt əˌsembli/ *noun* fusion *f*

documentation /ˌdɒkjʊmen'teɪʃ(ə)n/ *noun* (*information, notes, etc.*) documentation *f*; renseignements *mpl*

document content architecture /ˌdɒkjʊmənt 'kɒntent ˌɑːkɪtektʃə/ *noun* architecture *f* du contenu des documents

document image management /ˌdɒkjʊmənt ˌɪmɪdʒ 'mænɪdʒmənt/ *noun* imagerie *f* documentaire

document image processing /ˌdɒkjʊmənt 'ɪmɪdʒ ˌprəʊsesɪŋ/ *noun* procédé *m* de traitement d'image

document interchange architecture/document content architecture /ˌdɒkjʊmənt ˌɪntətʃeɪndʒ ˌɑːkɪtektʃə ˌdɒkjʊmənt 'kɒntent ˌɑːkɪtektʃə/ *noun* architecture *f* d'échange de documents

document merge /'dɒkjʊmənt mɜːdʒ/ *noun* fusion *f*

document processing /ˌdɒkjʊmənt 'prəʊsesɪŋ/ *noun* traitement *m* de texte; traitement *m* de document

document reader /'dɒkjʊmənt ˌriːdə/ *noun* lecteur *m* de documents

document recovery /ˌdɒkjʊmənt rɪ 'kʌv(ə)ri/ *noun* récupération *f*

Dolby /'dɒlbi/ Dolby

Dolby AC-3 /ˌdɒlbi eɪ esiː 'θriː/ système *m* Dolby AC-3

Dolby Digital™ /ˌdɒlbi 'dɪdʒɪt(ə)l/ (*trade name for a multichannel audio compression and transmission system*) Dolby Digital™

Dolby system™ /'dɒlbi ˌsɪstəm/ (*trade name for a system for reducing background noise for recordings*) Dolby system™

dollar sign /'dɒlə saɪn/ *noun* signe *m* du dollar

DOM /ˌdiː əʊ 'em/ *noun* modèle *m* DOM

domain /dəʊ'meɪn/ *noun* (*scope*) domaine *m*

domain name /dəʊ'meɪn neɪm/ *noun* nom *m* de domaine

domain name registration /dəʊˌmeɪn neɪm ˌredʒɪ'streɪʃ(ə)n/ *noun* enregistrement *m* de nom de domaine

domain name server /dəʊˌmeɪn neɪm 'sɜːvə/ *noun* serveur *m* de noms de domaines

domain name system /dəʊ'meɪn neɪm ˌsɪstəm/ *noun* base *f* de données des adresses et des domaines (dans Internet); DNS

dongle /'dɒŋgl/ *noun* circuit *m* crypté; clé *f* électronique

do-nothing instruction /ˌdəʊ 'nʌθɪŋ ɪn ˌstrʌkʃən/ *noun* instruction *f* sans effet; instruction *f* ineffective

dopant /ˈdəʊpənt/ *noun* dopant *m*

doped /ˈdəʊpt/ *adjective* dopé *or* -ée; enduit, -e d'un dopant

DOR /ˌdiː əʊ ˈɑː/ *noun* lecture *f* optique de données numériques

DOS /dɒs/ *noun* système *m* d'exploitation de disque; DOS ◇ **boot up the DOS after you switch on the PC** lancez le (système) DOS après la mise en route de l'ordinateur

DOS prompt /ˈdɒs prɒmpt/ *noun* invite *f* DOS

dot address /ˈdɒt əˌdres/ *noun* adresse *f* IP

dot addressable /ˈdɒt əˌdresəb(ə)l/ *adjective* adressable au niveau du pixel

dot command /dɒt kəˈmɑːnd/ *noun* commande *f* point

dot matrix /ˌdɒt ˈmeɪtrɪks/ *noun* matrice *f* de points

dot-matrix printer /ˌdɒt ˈmeɪtrɪks ˌprɪntə/ *noun* (*a printer whose output is made up of characters formed by a series of closely spaced dots*) imprimante *f* matricielle

dot pitch /ˈdɒt pɪtʃ/ *noun* espacement *m* des pixels

dot prompt /ˈdɒt prɒmpt/ *noun* invite *f* point

dots per inch /ˌdɒtz pɜːr ˈɪntʃ/ *plural noun* points *mpl* par pouce; ppp

double buffering /ˌdʌb(ə)l ˈbʌfərɪŋ/ *noun* (*use of two buffers*) utilisation *f* de double mémoire tampon

double-click /ˌdʌb(ə)l ˈklɪk/ *noun* (*to click twice on the mouse*) double-clic *m* ■ *verb* (*two clicks on the mouse*) faire un double-clic ◇ **move the pointer to the icon then start the program with a double-click** déplacer le pointeur sur l'icône puis démarrez le programme avec un double-clic

double density /ˌdʌb(ə)l ˈdensəti/ *noun* double *m* densité

double density disk /ˌdʌb(ə)l ˌdensɪti ˈdɪsk/ *noun* disquette *f* double densité

double ended queue /ˌdʌb(ə)l ˌendɪd ˈkjuː/ *noun* file *f* d'attente à deux entrées; file *f* d'attente à deux extrémités

double-length arithmetic /ˌdʌb(ə)l ˌleŋθ ə ˈrɪθmətɪk/ *noun* calcul *m* en double précision

double precision /ˌdʌb(ə)l prɪˈsɪʒ(ə)n/ *noun* double *m* précision

double-precision arithmetic /ˌdʌb(ə)l prɪ ˌsɪʒ(ə)n əˈrɪθmətɪk/ *noun* calcul *m* en double précision

double-precision integer /ˌdʌb(ə)l prɪ ˌsɪʒ(ə)n ˈɪntɪdʒə/ *noun* nombre *m* entier en double précision

double-sided disk /ˌdʌb(ə)l ˌsaɪdɪd ˈdɪsk/ *noun* disquette *f* (à) double face

double-sided disk drive /ˌdʌb(ə)l ˌsaɪdɪd ˈdɪsk ˌdraɪv/ *noun* lecteur *m* de disquettes à double face

double-sided printed circuit board /ˌdʌb(ə)l ˌsaɪdɪd ˌprɪntɪd ˈsɜːkɪt ˌbɔːd/ *noun* plaque *f* (présensibilisée) double face pour circuit imprimé

DoubleSpace /ˌdʌb(ə)lˈspeɪs/ (*software program that is part of MS-DOS 6*) DoubleSpace

double speed /ˌdʌb(ə)l ˈspiːd/ *noun* double *m* vitesse

double-speed drive /ˌdʌb(ə)l spiːd ˈdraɪv/ *noun* lecteur *m* à double vitesse

double strike /ˈdʌb(ə)l straɪk/ *noun* double *m* frappe

doublet /ˈdʌblət/ *noun* doublet *m*; dyade *f*

double word /ˈdʌb(ə)l wɜːd/ *noun* mot *m* double; mot *m* long

down /daʊn/ *adjective, adverb* (*not working*) en panne ◇ **the computer system went down twice during the afternoon** l'ordinateur est tombé en panne deux fois au cours de l'après-midi

download /ˌdaʊnˈləʊd/ *verb* **1.** (*to load a program or retrieve a section of data*) télécharger *vt* **2.** (*to load data from a CPU to a small computer*) télécharger *vt* **3.** (*to send print font data stored on disk to a printer, etc.*) télécharger *vt* ◇ **there is no charge for downloading public domain software from the BBS** il n'en coûte rien de télécharger, depuis le tableau d'affichage, un logiciel qui n'est pas protégé par un copyright

'The cards will also download the latest version of the network drivers from the server.' [*Computing*]

downloadable font /ˌdaʊnləʊdəb(ə)l ˈfɒnt/ *noun* police *f* de caractères téléchargeable

downsize /ˈdaʊnsaɪz/ *verb* (*change from a central mainframe to a network*) réduire l'échelle ◇ **downsizing is more cost effective and gives more processing power to the end-user** la réduction d'échelle est très efficace sur le plan des coûts et donne plus de puissance de traitement à l'utilisateur

downstream /ˈdaʊnstriːm/ *noun* transmission *f* aval

downtime /ˈdaʊn taɪm/, **down time** *noun* temps *m* mort

downward compatibility /ˌdaʊnwəd kəm ˌpætəˈbɪlɪti/ *noun* compatibilité *f* avec un système de niveau inférieur

downward compatible /ˌdaʊnwəd kəm ˈpætɪb(ə)l/ *adjective* compatible avec un système de niveau inférieur

dp, DP *abbr* (*data processing*) traitement *f* de l'information; traitement de données

DPA /ˌdiː piː ˈeɪ/ *noun* architecture *f* DPA

DPCM /ˌdiː piː siː ˈem/ *noun* modulation *f* MIC à détection différentielle

d.p.i. /ˌdiː piː ˈaɪ/, **dpi** *abbr* (*dots per inch*) points *mpl* par pouce; ppp ◇ **a 300 d.p.i. black and white A4 monitor** un moniteur monochrome format A4 avec une définition de 300 points par pouce ◇ **a 300 dpi image scanner** un scanner d'image avec définition de 300 ppp ◇ **some laser printers offer high resolution printing: 400 dpi** certaines imprimantes (à) laser sont dotées d'une haute définition de 400 ppp *or* 400 points par pouce

DPM /ˌdiː piː 'em/ *abbr* (*data processing manager*) chef *m* du service informatique

draft printing /drɑːft 'prɪntɪŋ/ *noun* qualité *f* brouillon

draft quality /drɑːft 'kwɒlɪti/ *noun* qualité *f* brouillon; qualité *f* listing

drag /dræg/ *verb* (*a mouse*) déplacer *vt*; glisser *vi*; traîner *vt*; (*a handle*) tirer *vt* ◇ **you can enlarge a frame by clicking inside its border and dragging to the position wanted** pour agrandir un cadre, vous cliquez à l'intérieur de ses limites et vous glissez jusqu'à la position voulue

'...press the mouse button and drag the mouse: this produces a dotted rectangle on the screen; you can easily enlarge the frame by dragging from any of the eight black rectangles round the border, showing that it is selected' [*Desktop Publishing*]

drag and click /ˌdræg ən 'klɪk/ *verb* glisser et cliquer

drag and drop /ˌdræg ən 'drɒp/ *verb* glisser et déposer ◇ **drag and drop the document icon onto the word-processor icon and the system will start the program and load the document** traînez l'icône document jusque sur l'icône traitement de texte puis lâchez le bouton de la souris, le système démarrera le programme et chargera le document

drag image /dræg 'ɪmɪdʒ/ *noun* curseur *m* d'entraînement; icône *f* d'entraînement

DRAM /'diː ræm/ *abbr* (*dynamic random access memory*) RAM *f* dynamique

drawing program /'drɔːɪŋ ˌprəʊgræm/ *noun* logiciel *m* de dessin

drive /draɪv/ *noun* lecteur *m*

drive array /draɪv ə'reɪ/ *noun* système *m* multilecteur (de disques dur)

drive bay /'draɪv beɪ/ *noun* baie *f*; emplacement *m* (de lecteur de disque)

drive designator /'draɪv ˌdezɪgneɪtə/ *noun* lettre *f* d'identification du lecteur; lettre *f* de l'unité de disque

drive letter /draɪv 'letə/, **drive designator** /'draɪv ˌdezɪgneɪtə/ *noun* lettre *f* d'identification du lecteur; lettre *f* de l'unité de disque

driver /'draɪvə/ *noun* (*device driver or device handler*) logiciel *m* de commande de périphérique; gestionnaire *m* de périphérique; pilote *m* de périphérique

DRO /ˌdiː ɑːr 'əʊ/ *noun* lecture *f* destructive

drop cable /drɒp 'keɪb(ə)l/ *noun* (*cable that links an adapter to the main network cable*) câble *m* de dérivation; câble *m* de branchement

drop dead halt /ˌdrɒp ded 'hɔːlt/ *noun* arrêt *m* total

drop-down list box /ˌdrɒp daʊn 'lɪst/ *noun* (*list of options for an entry*) liste *f* déroulante; boîte *f* de liste

drop-down menu /ˌdrɒp daʊn 'menjuː/ *noun* (*menu that appears below a menu title*) menu *m* déroulant

drop in /ˌdrɒp 'ɪn/ *noun* (*on disk or tape*) parasite *m*; crasse *f*

drop out /ˌdrɒp 'aʊt/ *noun* (*of signal*) perte *f*; (*data storage*) défaut *m* (de magnétisation)

drum /drʌm/ *noun* cylindre *m*; tambour *m*

drum plotter /'drʌm ˌplɒtə/ *noun* traceur *m*

dry contact /draɪ 'kɒntækt/ *noun* contact *m* intermittent; contact *m* sec

dry run /ˌdraɪ 'rʌn/ *noun* essai *m* à blanc

DSL /ˌdiː es 'el/ *noun* ligne *f* d'abonné numérique

DSP /ˌdiː es 'piː/ *noun* circuit *m* DSP; circuit *m* de numérisation des signaux

DSR /ˌdiː es 'ɑː/ *noun* signal *m* de modem prêt à transmettre/recevoir

DTE /ˌdiː tiː 'iː/ *noun* terminal *m* de transfert de données

DTMF /ˌdiː tiː em 'ef/ *noun* appel *m* à tonalité multifréquence

D to A converter /ˌdiː tʊ ˌeɪ kən'vɜːtə/ *noun* convertisseur *m* numérique-analogique

DTP /ˌdiː tiː 'piː/ *noun* publication *f* assistée par ordinateur

DTR /ˌdiː tiː 'ɑː/ *noun* terminal *m* de données prêt

DTV /ˌdiː tiː 'viː/ *noun* vidéotique *f*

D-type connector /ˌdiː taɪp kə'nektə/ *noun* (*connector shaped like the letter D*) connecteur *m* en D; connecteur *m* de type D ◇ **the serial port on a PC uses a 9-pin D-type connector** le port série du PC utilise un connecteur à neuf broches de type D

dual /'djuːəl/ *adjective* double ◇ **dual attachment station** *or* **dual attached station (DAS)** (*FDDI system station*) station *f* à double connexion (sur réseau FDDI)

dual attachment /'djuːəl ə'tætʃmənt/, **dual attached station** /ˌdjuːəl əˌtætʃt 'steɪʃ(ə)n/ *noun* station *f* à double connexion (sur réseau FFDI)

dual bus system /ˌdjuːəl 'bʌs ˌsɪstəm/ *noun* système *m* à bus auxiliaire; système *m* à bus double

dual channel /ˌdjuːəl 'tʃæn(ə)l/ *noun* voie *f* double

dual clocking /'djuːəl klɒkɪŋ/ *noun* double *m* chronométrie; décalage *m* de fréquence

dual column /ˌdjuːəl 'kɒləm/ *noun* colonne *f* double

dual in-line memory module /ˌdjuːəl ˌɪn laɪn 'mem(ə)ri ˌmɒdjuːl/ *noun* module *m* de mémoire à double rangée de connexion

dual-in-line package /ˌdjuːəl ɪn laɪn ˈpækɪdʒ/ *noun* système *m* à double rang de broches (parallèles)

dual port memory /ˌdjuːəl pɔːt ˈmem(ə)ri/ *noun* mémoire *f* à double accès

dual processor /ˌdjuːəl ˈprəusesə/ *noun* processeur *m* double

dual-scan display /ˌdjuːəl skæn dɪˈspleɪ/ *noun* écran *m* à matrice passive à double balayage

dual systems /ˌdjuːəl ˈsɪstəmz/ *plural noun* systèmes *mpl* doubles

dual tone multi-frequency /ˌdjuːəl təun ˌmʌlti ˈfriːkwənsi/ *noun* appel *m* à tonalité multifréquence

dub /dʌb/ *verb* doubler (un film)

duct /dʌkt/ *noun* conduit *m*; conduite *f*; canalisation *f*

dumb /dʌm/ *adjective* non intelligent *or* -e

dumb terminal /dʌm ˈtɜːmɪn(ə)l/ *noun* terminal *m* non intelligent

dummy /ˈdʌmi/ *noun* maquette *f*

dummy instruction /ˈdʌmi ɪnˌstrʌkʃən/ *noun* (*blank instruction*) instruction *f* de remplissage

dummy variable /ˌdʌmi ˈveəriəb(ə)l/ *noun* variable *f* factice

dump /dʌmp/ *noun* **1.** (*data copied*) analyse *f* (de) mémoire **2.** (*transferring of data*) vidage *m*; vidage *m* sur disque; transfert *m* sur disque; transfert *m* sur support magnétique **3.** *US* (*printout of data*) vidage *m* sur imprimante ■ *verb* (*to transfer data*) copier *vt*; transférer *vt*; vider *vt* ◇ **the account results were dumped to the backup disk** les résultats comptables ont été transférés sur le disque de sauvegarde

dump and restart /ˌdʌmp ən ˈriːstɑːt/ *noun* vidage *m* et reprise

dump point /ˈdʌmp pɔɪnt/ *noun* point *m* de vidage

duodecimal number system /djuːəu ˌdesɪm(ə)l ˈnʌmbə ˌsɪstəm/ *noun* système *m* duodécimal

duplex /ˈdjuːpleks/ *noun* (*transmission of two signals*) duplex *m*

duplex circuit /ˈdjuːpleks ˌsɜːkɪt/ *noun* circuit *m* duplex

duplex computer /ˈdjuːpleks kəmˌpjuːtə/ *noun* système *m* duplex; ordinateurs *mpl* jumelés

duplexing /ˈdjuːpleksɪŋ/ *noun* copie *f* miroir; duplication *f* de données sur un disque miroir; mirroring *m*

duplex operation /ˌdjuːpleks ˌɒpəˈreɪʃ(ə)n/ *noun* opération *f* ◇ **DVD-RAM drive** lecteur de DVD-RAM

duty-rated /ˈdjuːti rætd/ *adjective* évalué en cycles possibles par unité de temps

DVD /ˌdiː viː ˈdiː/ *noun* disque *m* vidéo numérique; disque *m* DVD ◇ **DVD drive** lecteur de DVD ◇ **DVD player** (*standalone that plugs into a TV set*) lecteur de DVD ◇ **DVD-ROM drive** lecteur de DVD-ROM ◇ **DVD writer** graveur *m* de DVD

DVD-A /ˌdiː viː ˈdiː eɪ/ *noun* DVD *m* audio

DVD-R /ˌdiː viː ˈdiː ɑː/ *abbr* (*DVD-Recordable*) DVD *m* inscriptible

DVD-RAM /ˌdiː viː ˈdiː ræm/ *noun* DVD-RAM *m*

DVD-Recordable /ˌdiː viː diː rɪˈkɔːdəb(ə)l/ *noun* DVD *m* inscriptible

DVD-ROM /ˌdiː viː ˈdiː rɒm/ *noun* DVD-ROM *m* ◇ **DVD-ROM drive** lecteur de DVD-ROM

DVD+RW /ˌdiː viː diː plʌs ɑː ˈdʌb(ə)l juː/ *noun* DVD+RW *m*; DVD *m* réinscriptible

DVD-video /ˌdiː viː ˌdiː ˈvɪdiəu/ *noun* DVD-vidéo *m*

DVE /ˌdiː viː ˈiː/ *noun* générateur *m* d'effets vidéo

DV-I /ˌdiː viː ˈaɪ/ *noun* vidéo *f* numérique interactive

Dvorak keyboard /ˌdvɔːræk ˈkiːbɔːd/ *noun* (*special keyboard layout*) clavier *m* DVORAK

DX /diː eks/ *suffix* DX

dyad /ˈdaɪæd/ *noun* dyade *f*

dyadic Boolean operation /daɪˌædɪk ˌbuːliən ˌɒpəˈreɪʃ(ə)n/ *noun* opération *f* booléenne dyadique; opération *f* dyadique à deux opérandes

dyadic operation /daɪˌædɪk ˌɒpəˈreɪʃ(ə)n/ *noun* opération *f* dyadique; opération *f* à deux opérandes

dye-polymer recording /ˌdaɪ ˈpɒlɪmə rɪ ˌkɔːdɪŋ/ *noun* (*optical disk recording method*) enregistrement *m* sur couche polymérisée

dye-sublimation printer /daɪ sʌblɪ ˌmeɪʃ(ə)n ˈprɪntə/ *noun* (*high-quality colour printer*) imprimante *f* à sublimation thermique ◇ **the new dye-sublimation printer can produce colour images at a resolution of 300dpi** la nouvelle imprimante à sublimation thermique peut fournir une image couleur avec une définition de 300 ppp

dynamic /daɪˈnæmɪk/ *adjective* dynamique ◇ **dynamic microphone** microphone *m* dynamique ◇ **dynamic range** amplitude *f* dynamique

dynamic allocation /daɪˌnæmɪk ˌæləˈkeɪʃ(ə)n/ *noun* allocation *f* dynamique

dynamically redefinable character set /daɪˌnæmɪkli riːdɪˌfaɪnəb(ə)l ˈkærɪktə ˌset/ *noun* police *f* de caractères vectorielle

dynamic buffer /daɪˌnæmɪk ˈbʌfə/ *noun* mémoire *f* tampon dynamique

dynamic data exchange /daɪˌnæmɪk ˈdeɪtə ɪksˌtʃeɪndʒ/ *noun* DDE; échange *m* dynamique des données

dynamic data structure /daɪˌnæmɪk 'deɪtə ˌstrʌktʃə/ *noun* (*transferring of data*) structure *f* de données dynamique

dynamic dump /daɪˌnæmɪk 'dʌmp/ *noun* vidage *m* dynamique

dynamic host configuration protocol /daɪˌnæmɪk həʊst kənˌfɪgjʊ'reɪʃ(ə)n ˌprəʊtəkɒl/ *noun* DHCP

dynamic link library /daɪˌnæmɪk 'lɪŋk ˌlaɪbrəri/ *noun* (*Microsoft Windows and OS/2 library of utility programs*) bibliothèque *f* dynamique de liens; bibliothèque *f* DLL

dynamic memory /daɪˌnæmɪk 'mem(ə)ri/ *noun* (*dynamic storage*) mémoire *f* dynamique

dynamic multiplexing /daɪˌnæmɪk 'mʌltɪpleksɪŋ/ *noun* multiplexage *m* dynamique

dynamic RAM /daɪˌnæmɪk 'ræm/ *noun* RAM *f* dynamique; mémoire *f* vive dynamique

dynamic random access memory /daɪ ˌnæmɪk ˌrændəm ˌækses 'mem(ə)ri/ *noun* RAM *f* dynamique; mémoire vive *f* dynamique

dynamic relocation /daɪˌnæmɪk ˌriːləʊ 'keɪʃ(ə)n/ *noun* relogement *m* dynamique; translation *f* dynamique; déplacement *m* dynamique

dynamic relocation program /daɪˌnæmɪk ˌriːləʊ'keɪʃ(ə)n ˌprəʊgræm/ *noun* déplacement *m* dynamique

dynamic routing /daɪˌnæmɪk 'ruːtɪŋ/ *noun* routage *m* dynamique; routage *m* adaptatif

dynamic stop /daɪˌnæmɪk 'stɒp/ *noun* arrêt *m* dynamique

dynamic storage /daɪˌnæmɪk 'stɔːrɪdʒ/ *noun* mémoire *f* dynamique

dynamic storage allocation /daɪˌnæmɪk 'stɔːrɪdʒ ˌæləkeɪʃ(ə)n/ *noun* allocation *f* dynamique de la mémoire

dynamic subroutine /daɪˌnæmɪk 'sʌbruːtiːn/ *noun* sous-programme *m* dynamique; sous-programme *m* paramétrable

dynamic update /daɪ'næmɪk ˌʌpdeɪt/ *noun* mise *f* à jour dynamique

E

EAPROM /ˌiː eɪ ˈpiː ˌrɒm/ *noun* mémoire *f* EAPROM

early token release /ˌɜːli ˈtəʊkən rɪˌliːs/ *noun* (*Token-Ring or FDDI network system*) libération *f* anticipée du jeton

EAROM /ˌiː ˈeɪ ˌrɒm/ *noun* mémoire *f* EAROM; mémoire *f* ROM programmable et effaçable électriquement

earth /ɜːθ/ *noun* (*connection representing zero potential*) prise *f* de terre ■ *verb* (*to connect an electrical device to earth*) mettre à la terre ◇ **all appliances must be earthed** tous les appareils doivent être mis à la terre ◇ **all loose wires should be tied to earth** tous les fils non rattachés doivent être mis à la terre *or* à la masse

earth wire /ɜːθ ˈwaɪə/ *noun* fil *m* de terre; fil *m* de mise à la masse

EBCDIC /ˌiː biː siː diː aɪ ˈsiː/ *noun* code *m* EBCDIC; code *m* binaire à 8 bits

EBNF /ˌiː biː en ˈef/ *noun* métalangage *m* BNF étendu

ebook /ˈiːbʊk/ *noun* (*electronic book*) livre *m* électronique

EBR /ˌiː biː ˈɑː/ *noun* enregistrement *m* par faisceau électronumérique (sur microfilm)

e-business /ˈiː ˌbɪznəs/ *noun* affaires *fpl* électroniques

echo /ˈekəʊ/ *noun* écho *m* ■ *verb* faire écho ◇ **echo chamber** chambre *f* à écho ◇ **echo suppressor** suppresseur *m* d'écho *or* dispositif *m* anti-écho

echo cancellation /ˈekəʊ ˌkænsəleɪʃ(ə)n/ *noun* suppression *f* d'écho

echo check /ˈekəʊ tʃek/ *noun* contrôle *m* par écho

ECL /ˌiː siː ˈel/ *noun* logique *f* ECL

ECMA *abbr* (*European Computer Manufacturers Association*) syndicat *m* européen des constructeurs d'ordinateurs

ECMA symbol /ˌiː siː em ˈeɪ ˌsɪmbəl/ *noun* symbole *m* ECMA

e-commerce /ˈiː ˌkɒmɜːs/ *noun* commerce *m* électronique; e-commerce *m*

EDAC /ˌiː diː eɪ ˈsiː/ *noun* détection *f* et correction d'erreurs

edge /edʒ/ *noun* **1.** (*of flat object or signal or clock pulse*) bordure *f*; bord *m*; limite *f* **2.** bord *m*; bordure *f*; limite *f*

edge board /ˈedʒ bɔːd/ *noun* carte *f* à connecteur

edge card /ˈedʒ kɑːd/ *noun* carte *f* à connecteur

edge connector /edʒ kəˈnektə/ *noun* connecteur *m* de carte

> 'Connections to the target board are made via IC test clips or the edge connector.' [*Electronics Today*]

edge detection /edʒ dɪˈtekʃ(ə)n/ *noun* détection *f* de bordures

edge notched card /ˌedʒ nɒtʃt ˈkɑːd/ *noun* carte *f* à encoches marginales

edge-triggered /edʒ ˈtrɪɡəd/ *adjective* déclenché par bascule de front d'impulsion

EDI /ˌiː diː ˈaɪ/ *noun* échange *m* de données informatisé

edit /ˈedɪt/ *verb* (*to format*) éditer *vt*; (*to correct text*) corriger *vt*; réviser *vt* ◇ **there are several special edit keys – this one will re-format the text** il y a plusieurs touches d'édition – celle-ci permet de reformater le texte

edit command /ˈedɪt kəˌmɑːnd/ *plural noun* commande *f* d'édition

edit decision list /ˌedɪt dɪˈsɪʒ(ə)n ˌlɪst/ *noun* liste *f* des décisions de montage

editing run /ˈedɪtɪŋ rʌn/ *noun* exécution *f* d'un programme d'édition

editing term /ˈedɪtɪŋ tɜːm/ *noun* commande *f* et instruction d'édition

edit key /ˈedɪt kiː/ *noun* touche *f* (de fonction) d'édition ◇ **there are several special edit keys – this one will re-format the text** il y a plusieurs touches d'édition – celle-ci permet de reformater le texte

editor /ˈedɪtə/ *noun* (*person who edits films or books*) éditeur *m or* -trice *f* ◇ **linkage editor** éditeur de liens

> 'The Smartbook authoring system is a software product that integrates text and fractally compressed images, using any wordprocessor line editor.' [*Computing*]

> '...while it has many formatting facilities, it does not include an editor with which to create the template for the report' [*Personal Computer World*]

editor program /ˈedɪtə ˌprəʊɡræm/ *noun* éditeur *m*

edit window /ˈedɪt ˌwɪndəʊ/ *noun* fenêtre *f* d'édition

EDLIN /ˌiː diː el aɪ 'en/ *noun* (*MS-DOS system utility*) utilitaire *m*; éditeur *m* EDLIN; edlin

EDO memory /ˌiː diː əʊ 'mem(ə)ri/ *noun* mémoire *f* vive à sortie de données étendue

EDP /ˌiː diː 'piː/ *noun* traitement *m* électronique de données; traitement *m* de l'information; traitement *m* informatique

EDP capability /ˌiː diː piː ˌkeɪpə'bɪlɪti/ *noun* capacité *f* de traitement de données

EDTV /ˌiː diː tiː 'viː/ *noun* télévision *f* à définition améliorée

edu *suffix* (*appears at the end of an internet domain name: educational organization*) edu (= établissement éducatif)

edutainment /ˌedjʊ'teɪnmənt/ *noun* ludo-éducatif *m*

EEMS /ˌiː iː em 'es/ *noun* norme *f* EEMS

EEPROM *abbr* (*electrically erasable programmable read-only memory*) mémoire *f* EEPROM; mémoire *f* ROM programmable et effaçable électriquement

EEROM *abbr* (*electrically erasable read-only memory*) mémoire *f* EEROM; mémoire *f* ROM effaçable électriquement

effective address /ɪˌfektɪv ə'dres/ *noun* adresse *f* effective

effective instruction /ɪˌfektɪv ɪn'strʌkʃən/ *noun* instruction *f* effective

effective search speed /ɪˌfektɪv 'sɜːtʃ ˌspiːd/ *noun* vitesse *f* de recherche effective

effective throughput /ɪˌfektɪv 'θruːpʊt/ *noun* rendement *m* effectif

EFT /ˌiː ef 'tiː/ *noun* dispositif *m* transfert électronique de fonds

egg timer /'eg ˌtaɪmə/ *noun* sablier *m*

EIA interface /ˌiː ˌaɪ ˌeɪ ˌɪntə'feɪs/ *noun* interface *f* aux normes EIA

eight-bit /eɪt bɪt/, **8-bit** /eɪt bɪt/ *adjective* huit bits

eight-bit byte /eɪt bɪt/, **eight-bit octet** /ˌeɪt bɪt ɒk'tet/ *noun* octet *m*

eight-bit octet /ˌeɪt bɪt ɒk'tet/ *noun* octet *m*

8-bit sample /ˌeɪt bɪt 'stændəd/ *noun* échantillon *m* à 8 bits

eight-inch disk /eɪt ɪntʃ dɪsk/, **8-inch disk** *noun* disquette *f* de huit pouces

eight-inch drive /eɪt ɪntʃ draɪv/, **8-inch drive** *noun* lecteur *m* de disquettes de huit pouces

eighty-column screen /ˌeɪti 'kɒləm skriːn/, **80-column screen** *noun* (*screen that displays 80 characters horizontally*) écran *m* de quatre-vingts colonnes

eighty-track disk /'eɪti træk dɪsk/, **80-track disk** *noun* disque *m* de quatre-vingts pistes

EIS /ˌiː aɪ 'es/ *noun* système *m* d'information pour la direction

EISA /ˌiː aɪ es 'eɪ/ *noun* standard *m* de bus EISA

either-or operation /ˌaɪðə 'ɔː ˌɒpəreɪʃ(ə)n/ *noun* (*logical function*) opération *f* OU inclusif; opération *f* d'union

either-way operation /ˌaɪðə 'weɪ ˌɒpəreɪʃ(ə)n/ *noun* mode *m* de transmission bidirectionnelle à l'alternat

elapsed time /ɪˌlæpst 'taɪm/ *noun* temps *m* passé à une tâche; temps *m* d'exécution d'une tâche

elastic banding /ɪ'læstɪk bændɪŋ/ *noun* (*defining the limits of an image on a screen*) recadrage *m* d'une image sur l'écran

elastic buffer /ɪˌlæstɪk 'bʌfə/ *noun* mémoire *f* tampon de capacité

electrically alterable programmable read-only memory /ɪˌlektrɪkli ˌɔːltərəʙ(ə)l ˌprəʊgræməb(ə)l ˌriːd ˌəʊnli 'mem(ə)ri/ *noun* mémoire *f* EAPROM; mémoire *f* ROM programmable, modifiable électriquement

electrically alterable read-only memory /ɪˌlektrɪkli ˌɔːltərəʙ(ə)l ˌriːd ˌəʊnli 'mem(ə)ri/ *noun* mémoire *f* EAPROM; mémoire *f* ROM programmable, modifiable électriquement

electrically erasable programmable read-only memory /ɪˌlektrɪkli ɪˌreɪzəb(ə)l ˌprəʊgræməb(ə)l ˌriːd ˌəʊnli 'mem(ə)ri/ *noun* mémoire *f* EEPROM; mémoire *f* ROM programmable et effaçable électriquement

electrically erasable read-only memory /ɪˌlektrɪkli ɪˌreɪzəb(ə)l ˌriːd ˌəʊnli 'mem(ə)ri/ *noun* mémoire *f* EEROM; mémoire *f* ROM effaçable électriquement

electrical polarity /ɪˌlektrɪk(ə)l pəʊ'lærɪti/ *noun* polarité *f* électrique

electric charge /ɪ'lektrɪk tʃɑːdʒ/ *noun* charge *f* électrique

electric current /ɪˌlektrɪk 'kʌrənt/ *noun* courant *m* électrique

electricity /ɪˌlek'trɪsɪti/ *noun* électricité *f* ◇ **electricity prices are an important factor in the production costs** les frais d'électricité constituent un élément important des coûts de production

electrographic printer /ɪˌlektrəʊgræfɪk 'prɪntə/ *noun* imprimante *f* électrostatique

electroluminescence /ˌelektrəʊˌluːmɪ 'nes(ə)ns/ *noun* électroluminescence *f*

electroluminescent /ˌelektrəʊˌluːmɪ 'nes(ə)nt/ *adjective* électroluminescent *or* -e ◇ **the screen coating is electroluminescent** l'écran est recouvert d'une couche électroluminescente

electroluminescent display /ɪ ˌlektrəʊluːmɪnesənt dɪ'spleɪ/ *noun* affichage *m* électroluminescent; écran *m* électroluminescent

electroluminescing /ˌelektrəʊˌluːmɪ'nesɪŋ/ *adjective* électroluminescent *or* -e

electromagnetic /ɪˌlektrəʊmæg'netɪk/ *adjective* électromagnétique ◇ **electromagnetic in-**

terference (EMI) interférence *f* électromagnétique ◇ **electromagnetic spectrum** spectre *m* électromagnétique

electromagnetic interference /ɪˌlektrəʊmægnetɪk ˌɪntə'fɪərəns/ *noun* interférence *f* électromagnétique

electron beam /ɪ'lekˌtrɒn biːm/ *noun* faisceau *m* d'électrons; faisceau *m* électronique

electron beam recording /ɪˌlektrɒn ˌbiːm rɪ 'kɔːdɪŋ/ *noun* enregistrement *m* par faisceau électronique

electron gun /ɪ'lekˌtrɒn gʌn/ *noun* canon *m* à électrons

electronic agenda /ˌelektrɒnɪk ə'dʒendə/ *noun* agenda *m* électronique

electronic blackboard /ˌelektrɒnɪk 'blækbɔːd/ *noun* tableau *m* noir électronique

electronic book /ˌelektrɒnɪk 'bʊk/ *noun* livre *m* électronique

electronic commerce /ˌelektrɒnɪk 'kɒmɜːs/ *noun* commerce *m* électronique *or* e-commerce

electronic data interchange /ˌelektrɒnɪk 'deɪtə ˌɪntətʃeɪndʒ/ *noun* système *m* électronique d'échange de données; système *m* EDI

electronic data processing /ˌelektrɒnɪk 'deɪtə ˌprəʊsesɪŋ/ *noun* traitement *m* électronique de l'information

electronic data processing capability /ˌelektrɒnɪk ˌdeɪtə ˌprəʊsesɪŋ ˌkeɪpə'bɪlɪti/ *noun* facilité *f* de traitement électronique de données

electronic digital computer /ˌelektrɒnɪk ˌdɪdʒɪt(ə)l kəm'pjuːtə/ *noun* calculateur *m*

electronic filing /ˌelektrɒnɪk 'faɪlɪŋ/ *noun* (*storage of documents*) archivage *m* sur ordinateur

electronic funds transfer /ˌelektrɒnɪk 'fʌndz ˌtrænsfɜː/ *noun* transfert *m* électronique de fonds; virement *m* électronique de fonds

electronic funds transfer point-of-sale /ˌelektrɒnɪk ˌfʌndz ˌtrænsfɜː ˌpɔɪnt əv 'seɪl/ *noun* terminal *m* de transfert électronique de fonds

electronic mail /ˌelɪktrɒnɪk 'meɪl/ *noun* messagerie *f* électronique

electronic mailbox /ˌelektrɒnɪk 'meɪlbɒks/ *noun* boîte *f* aux lettres électronique

electronic pen /ˌelektrɒnɪk 'pen/ *noun* stylo *m* optique

electronic point-of-sale /ˌelektrɒnɪk ˌpɔɪnt əv 'seɪl/ *noun* point de vente *m* électronique

electronic publishing /ˌelektrɒnɪk 'pʌblɪʃɪŋ/ *noun* édition *f* électronique; publication *f* assistée par ordinateur

electronic pulse /ˌelektrɒnɪk 'pʌls/ *noun* impulsion *f* électronique

electronics /ˌelek'trɒnɪks/ *noun* (*science*) électronique *f*

electronic shopping /ˌelektrɒnɪk 'ʃɒpɪŋ/ *noun* achats *mpl* sur Internet; achats *mpl* en ligne

electronic signature /ˌelektrɒnɪk 'sɪgnɪtʃə/ *noun* signature *f* électronique

electronics industry association interface /ˌelektrɒnɪks ˌɪndəstri əˌsəʊsieɪʃ(ə)n 'ɪntəfeɪs/ *noun* interface *f* aux normes EIA

electronic smog /ˌelektrɒnɪk 'smɒg/ *noun* pollution *f* électronique

electronic stylus /ˌelektrɒnɪk 'staɪləs/ *noun* stylo *m* électronique

electronic traffic /ˌelektrɒnɪk 'træfɪk/ *noun* transmission *f* électronique

electronic wand /ˌelektrɒnɪk 'wɒnd/ *noun* stylo *m* électronique

electrophotographic /ˌelektrəʊˌfəʊtə 'græfɪk/ *adjective* électrophotographique

electrosensitive paper /ɪˌlektrəʊsensɪtɪv 'peɪpə/ *noun* papier *m* électrosensible

electrosensitive printing /ɪˌlektrəʊsensɪtɪv 'prɪntɪŋ/ *noun* impression *f* thermique

electrostatic /ɪlektrəʊ'stætɪk/ *adjective* électrostatique ◇ **electrostatic speaker** haut-parleur *m* électrostatique

electrostatic printer /ɪˌlektrəʊstætɪk 'prɪntə/ *noun* imprimante *f* électrostatique

electrostatic screen /ɪˌlektrəʊstætɪk 'skriːn/ *noun* écran *m* électrostatique

electrostatic storage /ɪˌlektrəʊstætɪk 'stɔːrɪdʒ/ *noun* mémoire *f* électrostatique

electrothermal printer /ɪˌlektrəʊθɜːməl 'prɪntə/ *noun* imprimante *f* thermique

elegant programming /ˌelɪgənt ˌprəʊ 'græmɪŋ/ *noun* programmation *f* bien conçue; programmation *f* élégante

element /'elɪmənt/ *noun* **1.** (*small part of an object*) élément *m*; composant *m* **2.** (*cell*) élément *m*; cellule *f*

elementary /ˌelɪ'ment(ə)ri/ *adjective* (*made of many similar small sections or objects*) élémentaire ◇ **elementary cable section** section *f* élémentaire de câble

elevator /'elɪveɪtə/ *noun* (*small square indicator displayed within a scroll bar*) ascenseur *m*

elimination factor /ɪˌlɪmɪ'neɪʃ(ə)n ˌfæktə/ *noun* facteur *m* d'élimination

else rule /'els ruːl/ *noun* (*program logical rule*) instruction *f* ELSE; instruction *f* sinon ◇ **IF X=20 THEN PRINT 'X is 20' ELSE PRINT 'X not 20'** si X=20 imprimer 'X égale 20' sinon imprimer 'X différent de 20'

EM /ˌiː 'em/ *abbr* (*end of medium*) code *m* de fin de support (de données)

email /'iː meɪl/, **e-mail** *noun* (*system*) courrier *m* électronique; messagerie *f* électronique; e-mail *m*; (*message*) courrier *m*; message *m* électronique; mail *m*; courriel *m*

embedded code /ɪmˌbedɪd 'kəʊd/ *noun* code *m* d'instruction imbriqué

embedded command /ɪmˌbedɪd kə'mɑːnd/ *noun* commande *f* imbriquée

embedded computer /ɪmˌbedɪd kəm 'pjuːtə/ *noun* **1.** système *m* intégré **2.** ordinateur *m* imbriqué (dans un autre); système *m* imbriqué (dans un autre)

embedded object /ɪmˌbedɪd əb'dʒekt/ *noun* (*feature of Windows OLE*) objet *m* incorporé

embedded system /ɪmˌbedɪd 'sɪstəm/ *noun* système *m* embarqué

embedding /ɪm'bedɪŋ/ *noun* intégration *f*; inclusion *f*

EMI /ˌiː em 'aɪ/ *noun* interférence *f* électromagnétique

emitter-coupled logic /ɪˌmɪtə ˌkʌp(ə)ld 'lɒdʒɪk/ *noun* logique *f* ECL

EMM /ˌiː em 'em/ *noun* gestionnaire *m* de mémoire étendue; gestionnaire *m* de mémoire paginée

emoticon /ɪ'məʊtɪkɒn/ *noun* (*combination of colons, hyphens and parentheses, etc., which becomes a 'smiley' to show feelings*) émoticône *m*; émoticon *m*; souriant *m*

> 'Smileys, or emoticons, have been around for a long time: the simplest ones, such as :-), can indicate in a tense-sounding email or text message that you are not feeling as angry as you may appear.' [*The Guardian*]

emphasis /'emfəsɪs/ *noun* mise en évidence

empty medium /ˌempti 'miːdiəm/ *noun* (*blank storage medium*) support *m* magnétique vierge

empty slot /'empti slɒt/ *noun* **1.** (*for card*) connecteur *m*; (*in transmission*) paquet *m* vide (d'information); (*for card*) créneau *m* inutilisé **2.** tranche *f* vide

EMS /ˌiː em 'es/ *noun* mémoire *f* étendue EMS

emulate /'emjʊˌleɪt/ *verb* émuler *vt* ◇ **laser printer which emulates a wide range of office printers** une imprimante laser qui peut émuler une série d'autres imprimantes de bureau

> '...some application programs do not have the right drivers for a laser printer, so look out for laser printers which are able to emulate the more popular office printers' [*Publish*]

emulation /ˌemjʊ'leɪʃ(ə)n/ *noun* émulation *f*

emulation facility /ˌemju'leɪʃ(ə)n fəˌsɪlɪti/ *noun* capacité *f* d'émulation

> '...full communications error checking built into the software ensures reliable file transfers and a terminal emulation facility enables a user's terminal to be used as if it were a terminal to the remote computer' [*Byte*]

emulator /'emjʊleɪtə/ *noun* émulateur *m*

> '...for an authentic retro coding experience, download an emulator and turn your computer into a virtual BBC Micro.' [*The Guardian*]

emulsion laser storage /ɪˌmʌlʃ(ə)n 'leɪzə ˌstɔːrɪdʒ/ *noun* mémoire *f* laser sur couche haute définition

enable /ɪn'eɪb(ə)l/ *verb* (*to use an electronic signal to start a process*) sélectionner *vt*; activer *vt*; valider *vt*

enabled /ɪn'eɪb(ə)ld/ *adjective* activé *or* -ée

enabling signal /ɪn'eɪblɪŋ ˌsɪgn(ə)l/ *noun* (*signal that starts a process*) signal *m* de sélection; signal *m* de validation; signal *m* d'activation

encapsulated /ɪn'kæpsjʊleɪtɪd/ *adjective* (*contained in something else*) encapsulé *or* -ée

encapsulated PostScript /ɪnˌkæpsjʊleɪtɪd 'pəʊstskrɪpt/ *noun* PostScript *m* encapsulé; EPS

encapsulated PostScript file /ɪn ˌkæpsjʊleɪtɪd 'pəʊstskrɪpt ˌfaɪl/ *noun* fichier *m* PostScript encapsulé; EPSF

encapsulation /ɪn'kæpsjʊleɪʃ(ə)n/ *noun* (*system of sending a frame of data in another frame*) encapsulation *f*

encipher /ɪn'saɪfə/ *verb* chiffrer *vt*; crypter *vt* ◇ **our competitors cannot understand our files – they have all been enciphered** nos concurrents ne peuvent lire nos fichiers qui sont en langage chiffré

enclosed object /ɪnˌkləʊzd əb'dʒekt/ *noun* objet *m* délimité; image *f* circonscrite

encode /ɪn'kəʊd/ *verb* encoder *vt*; coder *vt*

encoder /ɪn'kəʊdə/ *noun* encodeur *m* ◇ **colour encoder** encodeur de couleurs

encoding /ɪn'kəʊdɪŋ/ *noun* encodage *m*; codage *m*

encoding format /ɪn'kəʊdɪŋ ˌfɔːmæt/ *noun* format *m* d'encodage

encrypt /ɪn'krɪpt/ *verb* (*to encode plaintext*) chiffrer *vt*; crypter *vt* ◇ **the encrypted text can be sent along ordinary telephone lines, and no one will be able to understand it** le message chiffré *or* crypté peut être transmis par téléphone sans que personne ne puisse le lire

encryption /ɪn'krɪpʃən/ *noun* (*encoding of plaintext*) chiffrage *m*; chiffrement *m*; cryptage *m* ◇ **data encryption standard (DES)** standard *m* de cryptage de données

end /end/ *noun* fin *f* (de fichier)

end about carry /ˌend ə'baʊt ˌkæri/ *noun* report *m* circulaire; report *m* en boucle

end about shift /ˌend ə'baʊt ˌʃɪft/ *noun* décalage *m* circulaire

end around carry /ˌend ə'raʊnd ˌkæri/ *noun* report *m* circulaire; report *m* en boucle

end key /'end kiː/ *noun* touche *f* End

endless loop /'endləs luːp/ *noun* (*repetition of information or instructions*) boucle *f* sans fin; boucle *f* continue; boucle *f* infinie

end of address /ˌend əv ə'dres/ *noun* code *m* de fin d'adresse

end of block /ˌend əv 'blɒk/ *noun* code *m* de fin de bloc

end of data /ˌend əv 'deɪtə/ *noun* code *m* de fin de données

end of document /ˌend əv 'dɒkjʊmənt/ *noun* fin *f* de document; fin *f* de fichier

end of file /ˌend əv 'faɪl/ *noun* code *m* de fin de document

end of job /ˌend əv 'dʒɒb/ *noun* code *m* de fin de tâche

end of line /ˌend əv 'laɪn/ *noun* code *m* de fin de ligne

end of medium /ˌend əv 'miːdiəm/ *noun* code *m* de fin de support (de données)

end of message /ˌend əv 'mesɪdʒ/ *noun* code *m* de fin de message

end of record /ˌend əv 'rekɔːd/ *noun* code *m* de fin d'enregistrement

end of run routines /ˌend əv 'rʌn ruːˌtiːnz/ *plural noun* routines *fpl* de clôture (d'exécution)

end of tape /ˌend əv 'teɪp/ *noun* code *m* de fin de la bande (magnétique)

end of text /ˌend əv 'tekst/ *noun* code *m* de fin de texte

end of transmission /ˌend əv trænz 'mɪʃ(ə)n/ *noun* code *m* de fin de la transmission; signal *m* de fin de la transmission

end product /ˌend 'prɒdʌkt/ *noun* produit *m* fini

end user /ˌend 'juːzə/ *noun* utilisateur, -trice (final) ◇ **the company is creating a computer with a specific end user in mind** la société cherche à créer un ordinateur adapté aux besoins de l'utilisateur

Energy Star /'enədʒi stɑː/ *noun* Energy Star

engine /'endʒɪn/ *noun* (*part of a software package that carries out a particular function*) moteur *m*

enhanced-definition television /ɪnˌhɑːnst ˌdefɪnɪʃ(ə)n ˌtelɪ'vɪʒ(ə)n/ *noun* télévision *f* à définition améliorée

enhanced dot matrix /ɪnˌhɑːnst ˌdɒt 'meɪtrɪks/ *noun* matrice *f* d'impression à haute définition

enhanced expanded memory specification /ɪnˌhɑːnst ɪkˌspændɪd 'mem(ə)ri ˌspesɪfɪkeɪʃ(ə)n/ *noun* gestion *f* avancée de la mémoire étendue

enhanced keyboard /ɪnˌhɑːnst 'kiːbɔːd/ *noun* clavier *m* étendu

enhanced parallel port /ɪnˌhɑːnst 'pærəlel ˌpɔːt/ *noun* port *m* parallèle amélioré

enhanced small device interface /ɪn ˌhɑːnst smɔːl dɪ'vaɪs ˌɪntəfeɪs/ *noun* interface *f* ESDI

enhancement /ɪn'hɑːnsmənt/ *noun* (*add-on facility*) optimisation *f*; amélioration *f*

enhancer /ɪn'hɑːnsə/ *noun* optimiseur *m*

ENQ *abbr* (*enquiry*) demande *f*

enquiry /ɪn'kwaɪri/ *noun* **1.** demande *f* **2.** interrogation *f*

enquiry character /ɪn'kwaɪri ˌkærɪktə/ *noun* caractère *m* de requête

enter /'entə/ *verb* (*data or code*) entrer *vi*; saisir *vt*; introduire (des données); taper (un code) ◇ **the data has been entered** les données ont été saisies ◇ **to enter a name on a list** entrer *or* inscrire un nom sur une liste

entering /'entərɪŋ/ *noun* (*action*) entrée *f*; saisie *f*; introduction *f* (de données)

enter key /'entə kiː/ *noun* touche *f* Enter

enterprise network /'entəpraɪz ˌnetwɜːk/ *noun* (*network connecting all the workstations in a company*) réseau *m* d'entreprise

enterprise software /'entəpraɪz ˌsɒftweə/ *noun* logiciel *m* de l'entreprise

entity /'entɪti/ *noun* entité *f*

entry /'entri/ *noun* (*single record*) entrée *f*

entry condition /'entri kənˌdɪʃ(ə)n/ *noun* condition *f* d'entrée

entry instruction /ˌentri ɪn'strʌkʃən/ *noun* instruction *f* d'entrée

entry point /'entri pɔɪnt/ *noun* point *m*

entry time /'entri taɪm/ *noun* heure *f* d'entrée

enumerated type /ɪ'njuːməreɪtd taɪp/ *noun* classement *m* énumératif

envelope /'envələʊp/ *noun* **1.** (*for sending letters*) enveloppe *f* **2.** (*variation of amplitude of signal or sound*) enveloppe *f* **3.** (*transmitted packet of data containing error-detection and control information*) enveloppe *f*; (*in e-mail*) enveloppe *f* ◇ **attack envelope** enveloppe d'attaque (d'un signal) ◇ **envelope delay** (temps de) propagation *f* d'une enveloppe ◇ **envelope detection** détection *f* d'enveloppe

envelope feeder /'envələʊp ˌfiːdə/ *noun* bac *m* d'alimentation pour enveloppes

envelope printer /'envələʊp ˌprɪntə/ *noun* imprimante *f* d'enveloppes

environment /ɪn'vaɪrənmənt/ *noun* **1.** (*condition in a computer system of all registers and memory locations*) environnement *m* **2.** environnement *m*

environment space /ɪn'vaɪrənmənt speɪs/ *noun* taille *f* de l'environnement

environment variable /ɪn'vaɪrənmənt ˌveəriəb(ə)l/ *noun* variable *f* d'environnement

EOA *abbr* (*end of address*) code *m* de fin d'adresse

EOB *abbr* (*end of block*) code *m* de fin de bloc

EOD /ˌiː əʊ 'diː/ *abbr* (*end of data*) code *m* de fin de données

EOF *abbr* (*end of file*) code *m* de fin de fichier

EOJ *abbr* (*end of job*) code *m* de fin de tâche

EOL *abbr* (*end of line*) code *m* de fin de ligne

EOM *abbr* (*end of message*) code *m* de fin de message

EOR *abbr* (*end of record*) code *m* de fin d'enregistrement

EOT *abbr* **1.** (*end of text*) code *m* de fin de texte **2.** (*end of transmission*) code *m* de fin de transmission

EPOS /'iːpɒs/ *noun* point de vente *m* électronique

EPP /ˌiː piː 'piː/ *noun* port *m* parallèle amélioré

EPROM /ˌiː 'piː ˌrɒm/ *abbr* (*erasable programmable read-only memory*) mémoire *f* EPROM; mémoire *f* ROM programmable électriquement; mémoire *f* ROM programmable et effaçable

EPS *abbr* (*encapsulated PostScript*) PostScript *m* encapsulé; EPS

EPSF *abbr* (*encapsulated PostScript file*) fichier *m* Postscript encapsulé; EPSF

equality /ɪ'kwɒlɪti/ *noun* égalité *f*

equipment failure /ɪ'kwɪpmənt ˌfeɪljə/ *noun* défaillance *f* du matériel; défaillance *f* de l'ordinateur

equivalence /ɪ'kwɪvələns/ *noun* (*logical operation*) équivalence *f*

equivalence function /ɪ'kwɪvələns 'fʌŋkʃən/ *noun* **1.** fonction *f* **2.** fonction *f* d'équivalence; opération *f* d'équivalence; équivalence *f* logique

equivalence gate /ɪ'kwɪvələns geɪt/ *noun* porte *f*

erasable memory /ɪˌreɪzəb(ə)l 'mem(ə)ri/ *noun* support *m* (magnétique) effaçable; support *m* réutilisable

erasable programmable read-only memory /ɪˌreɪzəb(ə)l ˌprəʊgræməb(ə)l ˌriːd ˌəʊnli 'mem(ə)ri/ *noun* (*memory chip which can be programmed and erased*) mémoire *f* EPROM; mémoire *f* ROM programmable et effaçable

erasable read-only memory /ɪˌreɪzəb(ə)l ˌriːd ˌəʊnli 'mem(ə)ri/ *noun* mémoire *f* EROM; mémoire *f* ROM effaçable

erasable storage /ɪˌreɪzəb(ə)l 'stɔːrɪdʒ/ *noun* **1.** support *m* (magnétique) effaçable; support *m* (magnétique) réutilisable **2.** mémoire *f* temporaire

erase /ɪ'reɪz/ *verb* **1.** (*to set all the digits in a storage area to zero*) effacer *vt*; (*of memory*) remettre à zéro **2.** (*data*) effacer *vt*; détruire *vt*

erase character /ɪ'reɪz ˌkærɪktə/ *noun* caractère *m* d'effacement

erase head /ɪ'reɪz hed/ *noun* tête *f* d'effacement

eraser /ɪ'reɪzə/ *noun* (*device that removes the contents of something*) dispositif *m* d'effacement; méthode *f* d'effacement

eraser tool /ɪ'reɪzə tuːl/ *noun* outil *m* d'effacement; outil *m* gomme *f*

EROM /'iː rɒm/ *noun* mémoire *f* ROM effaçable

error /'erə/ *noun* **1.** (*due to a human operator*) erreur *f*; faute *f*; anomalie *f* **2.** (*caused by hardware or software fault*) anomalie *f*; erreur *f*; faute *f* **3.** (*in a program*) erreur *f* ◇ **a wrinkled or torn page may be the cause of scanning errors** un pli ou une déchirure dans une page peut être la cause d'une erreur de balayage *or* d'un balayage incorrect ◇ **diagnostic (error) message** message *m* de diagnostic d'erreur ◇ **error correcting codes** codes de correction d'erreurs ◇ **error detecting codes** codes *mpl* de détection d'erreurs ◇ **error detection and correction (EDAC)** détection et correction d'erreurs ◇ **error interrupt** (signal d')interruption *f* sur (une) erreur *or* sur (un) incident ◇ **he made an error in calculating the total** il a fait une erreur de total ◇ **in error** *or* **by error** par erreur ◇ **the error rate is less than 1%** le taux d'erreur est inférieur à 1% ◇ **the secretary must have made a typing error** la secrétaire doit avoir fait une faute de frappe

'...syntax errors, like omitting a bracket, will produce an error message from the compiler' [*Personal Computer World*]

error ambiguity /ˌerə ˌæmbɪ'gjuːɪti/ *noun* incertitude *f* causée par une erreur

error box /'erə bɒks/ *noun* message *m* d'erreur

error burst /'erə bɜːst/ *noun* (*group of errors*) rafale *f* d'erreurs; série *f* d'erreurs consécutives

error checking code /'erə ˌtʃekɪŋ ˌkəʊd/ *noun* code *m* de détection et correction d'erreurs

error code /'erə kəʊd/ *noun* code *m* (indicateur) d'erreur

error condition /'erə kənˌdɪʃ(ə)n/ *noun* condition *f* d'erreur

error control /'erə kənˌtrəʊl/ *noun* contrôle *m* d'erreurs

error correcting code /'erə kəˌrektɪŋ ˌkəʊd/ *noun* code *m* correcteur (d'erreur)

error correction /'erə kəˌrekʃ(ə)n/ *noun* correction *f* d'erreurs

error detecting code /'erə dɪˌtektɪŋ ˌkəʊd/ *noun* code *m* détecteur d'erreur

error detection /'erə dɪˌtekʃ(ə)n/ *noun* détection *f* d'erreurs

error detection and correction /ˌerə dɪ ˌtekʃən ən kə'rekʃən/ *noun* détection et correction d'erreurs

error diagnosis /'erə ˌdaɪəgnəʊsɪs/ *noun* diagnostic *m* d'erreurs

error diagnostics /'erə ˌdaɪəgnɒstɪks/ *noun* outils *mpl* de diagnostic d'erreurs

error handler /'erə ˌhændlə/ *noun* gestionnaire *m* d'erreurs

error handling /'erə ˌhændlɪŋ/ *noun* procédure *f* de traitement des erreurs; gestion *f* des erreurs

error interrupt /'erə ˌɪntərʌpt/ *plural noun* interruption *f* sur une erreur; interruption *f* sur un incident

error logging /'erə ˌlɒɡɪŋ/ *noun* enregistrement *m* automatique des erreurs ◇ **features of the program include error logging** ce programme permet l'enregistrement (automatique) des erreurs

error management /'erə ˌmænɪdʒmənt/ *noun* procédure *f* de traitement des erreurs; gestion *f* des erreurs

error message /'erə ˌmesɪdʒ/ *noun* message *m* d'erreur

error propagation /'erə ˌprɒpəɡeɪʃ(ə)n/ *noun* propagation *f* d'erreur

error rate /'erə reɪt/ *noun* taux *m* d'erreur ◇ **the error rate is less than 1%** le taux d'erreur est inférieur à 1%

error recovery /'erə rɪˌkʌv(ə)ri/ *noun* reprise *f* après erreur; reprise *f* après incident

error routine /'erə ruːˌtiːn/ *noun* routine *f* (de traitement) d'erreur

error trapping /'erə ˌtræpɪŋ/ *noun* (*process of detecting and correcting errors*) détection *f* d'erreurs; recherche *f* d'erreurs; prévention *f* d'erreurs

ESC /ɪ'skeɪp/ *noun* **1.** code *m* échappement **2.** touche *f* d'échappement

escape character /ɪ'skeɪp ˌkærɪktə/ *noun* caractère *m* d'échappement

escape code /ɪ'skeɪp kəʊd/ *noun* code *m* échappement

escape key /ɪ'skeɪp kiː/ *noun* touche *f* d'échappement; touche *f* ECHAPPEMENT

escapement /ɪ'skeɪpmənt/ *noun* (*of paper in a printer*) échappement *m*

escape sequence /ɪ'skeɪp ˌsiːkwəns/ *noun* séquence *f* d'échappement

Esc key /ɪ'skeɪp kiː/ *noun* touche *f* d'échappement

ESDI /ˌiː es diː 'aɪ/ *noun* interface *f* ESDI

Ethernet /'iːθənet/ *noun* (*network*) Ethernet *m*

EtherTalk /'iːθətɑːk/ (*Apple Macintosh variation of Ethernet*) EtherTalk

ETX *abbr* (*end of text*) fin *f* de texte

Eudora /juː'dɔːrə/ programme *m* Eudora

even parity /ˌiːv(ə)n 'pærɪti/, **even parity check** /ˌiːv(ə)n 'pærɪti tʃek/ *noun* contrôle *m* de parité paire

event /ɪ'vent/ *noun* événement *m*

event-driven /ɪ'vent ˌdrɪv(ə)n/ *adjective* activé *or* -ée; actionné, -ée par événement

> 'Forthcoming language extensions will include object-oriented features, including classes with full inheritance, as well as event-driven programming.' [*Computing*]

event handler /ɪ'vent ˌhændlə/ *noun* gestionnaire *m* ◇ **if a user clicks a mouse button this generates a message which can be acted upon by the event handler** l'utilisateur qui clique sur le bouton de la souris lance un message qui est pris en charge par le gestionnaire d'événements

ewallet /'iːˌwɒlət/, **e-wallet** /iː 'wɒlɪt/ *noun* porte-monnaie *m* électronique

except gate /ɪk'sept ɡeɪt/ *noun* porte *f*

exception /ɪk'sepʃən/ *noun* exception *f* ◇ **exception report** rapport *m* d'exceptions *or* d'anomalies

exception dictionary /ɪk'sepʃ(ə)n ˌdɪkʃən(ə)ri/ *noun* (*for word-processing and photocomposition*) liste *f*

exception handling /ɪk'sepʃ(ə)n ˌhændlɪŋ/ *noun* traitement *m* des erreurs

excess-3 code /ˌekses 'θriː kəʊd/ *noun* code *m* (binaire) plus 3

exchange /ɪks'tʃeɪndʒ/ *noun* (*telephone equipment*) central *m* téléphonique ■ *verb* **1.** (*to give one thing in place of another*) faire un échange; échanger *vt* **2.** (*to swap data between two locations*) échanger *vt*; permuter *vt*; basculer (des données)

exchangeable /ɪks'tʃeɪndʒəb(ə)l/ *adjective* (*returnable*) échangeable; (*moveable*) amovible ◇ **exchangeable disk storage (EDS)** disque *m* dur amovible

exchangeable disk storage /ɪks ˌtʃeɪndʒəb(ə)l dɪsk 'stɔːrɪdʒ/ *noun* disque *m* dur amovible

exchange selection /ɪks'tʃeɪndʒ sɪˌlekʃən/ *noun* tri *m* par échange

exclusion /ɪk'skluːʒ(ə)n/ *noun* (*restriction of access to a telephone line*) exclusion *f*

exclusive NOR /ɪkˌskluːsɪv 'nɔː/ *noun* NI exclusif

exclusive OR /ɪkˌskluːsɪv 'ɔː/ *noun* (*logical function*) OU *m* exclusif

exe /'eksi/ *noun* (*three-letter extension to a filename*) EXE

executable file /'eksɪˌkjuːtəb(ə)l faɪl/ *noun* (*file containing a program*) fichier *m* exécutable

executable form /'eksɪˌkjuːtəb(ə)l fɔːm/ *noun* programme *m* prêt à être exécuté

execute /'eksɪˌkjuːt/ *verb* (*computer program*) exécuter *vt*

execute cycle /'eksɪkjuːt ˌsaɪk(ə)l/ *noun* cycle *m* d'exécution

execute mode /'eksɪkjuːt məʊd/ *noun* mode *m* d'exécution

execute phase /'eksɪkjuːt feɪz/ *noun* phase *f* d'exécution

execute signal /'eksɪkjuːt ˌsɪɡn(ə)l/ *noun* signal *m* d'exécution

execute statement /'eksɪkjuːt ˌsteɪtmənt/ *noun* déclaration *f*

execute time /'eksɪkjuːt taɪm/ *noun* durée *f*

execution /ˌeksɪ'kjuːʃ(ə)n/ *noun* (*carrying out of a computer program*) exécution *f*

execution address /ˌeksɪ'kjuːʃ(ə)n əˌdres/ *noun* adresse *f* d'exécution

execution cycle /ˌeksɪ'kjuːʃ(ə)n ˌsaɪk(ə)l/ *noun* cycle *m* d'exécution

execution error /ˌeksɪ'kjuːʃ(ə)n ˌerə/ *noun* erreur *f* d'exécution

execution phase /ˌeksɪ'kjuːʃ(ə)n ˌfeɪz/ *noun* phase *f* d'exécution

execution time /ˌeksɪ'kjuːʃ(ə)n ˌtaɪm/ *noun* temps *m* d'exécution

executive /ɪg'zekjʊtɪv/ *adjective* (*refers to the operating system of a computer*) superviseur

executive control program /ɪgˌzekjʊtɪv kən'trəʊl ˌprəʊgræm/ *noun* système *m* d'exploitation

executive information system /ɪg ˌzekjʊtɪv ɪnfə'meɪʃ(ə)n ˌsɪstəm/ *noun* SID; système *m* d'information pour la direction

executive instruction /ɪgˌzekjʊtɪv ɪn 'strʌkʃən/ *noun* instruction *f* de superviseur

executive program /ɪgˌzekjʊtɪv 'prəʊgræm/ *noun* programme *m* superviseur

exerciser /'eksəsaɪzə/ *noun* (*tester for a device*) testeur *m*; programme *m* de test

exhaustive search /ɪg'zɔːstɪv sɜːtʃ/ *noun* recherche *f* exhaustive; recherche *f* très poussée

exit /'egzɪt/ *verb* sortir (de); (*to stop program execution*) abandonner *vt*; (*to leave a program*) quitter *vt* ◇ **you have to exit to another editing system to add headlines** pour ajouter des en-têtes, il faut quitter ce programme et entrer dans un autre

EXIT /'eksɪt/ *noun* (*MS-DOS system command*) EXIT

exit point /'eksɪt pɔɪnt/ *noun* point *m* de sortie

exjunction /'ɛksˌdʒʌŋkʃən/ *noun* (*logical function*) disjonction *f*

EXNOR /ˌeks 'nɔː/ *noun* (*logical function*) NI *m* exclusif

EXNOR gate /ˌeks 'nɔː ˌgeɪt/ *noun* porte *f*

EXOR /ˌeks 'ɔː/ *noun* (*logical function*) OU *m* exclusif

EXOR gate /ˌeks 'ɔː ˌgeɪt/ *noun* porte *f*

expandable system /ɪkˌspændəb(ə)l 'sɪstəm/ *noun* système *m* extensible

expanded memory /ɪkˌspændɪd 'mem(ə)ri/ *noun* (*IBM PC standard*) mémoire *f* étendue

expanded memory board /ɪkˌspændɪd 'mem(ə)ri ˌbɔːd/ *noun* carte *f* d'extension de mémoire

expanded memory manager /ɪkˌspændɪd 'mem(ə)ri ˌmænɪdʒə/ *noun* gestionnaire *m* de mémoire étendue; gestionnaire *m* de mémoire paginée

expanded memory system /ɪkˌspændɪd 'mem(ə)ri ˌsɪstəm/ *noun* mémoire *f* étendue EMS

expansion /ɪk'spænʃən/ *noun* expansion *f*; extension *f*

expansion board /ɪk'spænʃən bɔːd/ *noun* carte *f* d'extension

expansion box /ɪk'spænʃ(ə)n bɒks/ *noun* boîtier *m* pour cartes d'extension

> '...it can be attached to most kinds of printer, and, if that is not enough, an expansion box can be fitted to the bus connector' [*Personal Computer World*]

expansion bus /ɪk'spænʃ(ə)n bʌs/ *noun* (*data and address lines leading to a connector*) bus *m* d'expansion; bus *m* d'extension

expansion card /ɪk'spænʃ(ə)n kɑːd/ *noun* carte *f* d'extension

expansion slot /ɪk'spænʃ(ə)n slɒt/ *noun* (*connector*) créneau *m* ◇ **insert the board in the free expansion slot** enfichez la carte d'extension dans l'emplacement libre

expert system /'ekspɜːt ˌsɪstəm/ *noun* système *m* expert

explicit address /ɪkˌsplɪsɪt ə'dres/ *noun* adresse *f* explicite

explicit reference /ɪkˌsplɪsɪt 'ref(ə)rəns/ *noun* référence *f* explicite

Explorer™ /ɪk'splɔːrə/ (*Windows 95 program that lets you manage all the files stored on a disk*) navigateur *m* Explorer™ (de Microsoft)

exponentiation /ˌekspəˌnenʃi'eɪʃ(ə)n/ *noun* élévation *f* d'un nombre à la puissance x

export /ɪk'spɔːt/ *verb* (*save data*) exporter *vt* ◇ **to use this data with dBASE, you will have to export it as a DBF file** pour utiliser ces données avec dBase, il faut les exporter sous la forme d'un fichier de format dBase

expression /ɪk'spreʃ(ə)n/ *noun* **1.** (*mathematical formula*) expression *f*; formule *f* **2.** (*definition of a variable in a program*) expression *f*

extended arithmetic element /ɪkˌstendɪd ˌærɪθmetɪk 'elɪmənt/ *noun* élément *m* arithmétique étendu

extended Backus-Naur-Form /ɪkˌstendɪd ˌbiː en 'ef/, **extended BNF** *noun* métalangage *m* BNF étendu; BNF étendu

extended binary coded decimal interchange code /ɪkˌstendɪd ˌbaɪnəri ˌkəʊdɪd ˌdesɪm(ə)l 'ɪntətʃeɪndʒ ˌkəʊd/ *noun* (*numerical system*) code *m* EBCDIC; code *m* binaire à 8 bits

extended character set /ɪkˌstendɪd 'kærɪktə ˌset/ *noun* jeu *m* étendu de caractères

extended-definition television /ɪkˌstendɪd ˌdefɪnɪʃ(ə)n ˌtelɪ'vɪʒ(ə)n/ *noun* télévision *f* à définition améliorée

extended graphics array /ɪkˌstendɪd 'græfɪks əˌreɪ/ *noun* carte *f* graphique étendue

extended memory /ɪkˌstendɪd 'mem(ə)ri/ *noun* mémoire *f* d'extension; mémoire *f* étendue

extended memory manager /ɪkˌstendɪd ˈmem(ə)ri ˌmænɪdʒə/ *noun* gestionnaire *m* de mémoire étendue

extended memory specification /ɪk ˌstendɪd ˈmem(ə)ri ˌspesɪfɪkeɪʃ(ə)n/ *noun* norme *f* XMS

extending serial file /ɪkˌstendɪŋ ˈsɪəriəl ˌfaɪl/ *noun* fichier *m* série extensible

extensible hypertext markup language /ɪkˌstensɪb(ə)l ˌhaɪpətekst ˈmɑːkʌp ˌlæŋgwɪdʒ/ *noun* langage *m* XHMTL

extensible language /ɪkˌstensɪb(ə)l ˈlæŋgwɪdʒ/ *noun* langage *m* extensible; langage *m* adaptable

extensible markup language /ɪk ˌstensɪb(ə)l ˈmɑːkʌp ˌlæŋgwɪdʒ/ *noun* langage *m* XML

extension memory /ɪkˈstenʃən ˌmem(ə)ri/ *noun* mémoire *f* d'extension

external arithmetic /ɪkˌstɜːn(ə)l əˈrɪθmətɪk/ *noun* arithmétique *f* externe

external clock /ɪkˈstɜːn(ə)l klɒk/ *noun* horloge *f* externe; horloge *f* extérieure

external data file /ɪkˌstɜːn(ə)l ˈdeɪtə ˌfaɪl/ *noun* fichier *m* de données externe

external device /ɪkˌstɜːn(ə)l dɪˈvaɪs/ *noun* **1.** dispositif *m* externe **2.** dispositif *m* externe; périphérique *m*

external disk drive /ɪkˌstɜːn(ə)l ˈdɪsk ˌdraɪv/ *noun* lecteur *m* externe

external interrupt /ɪkˌstɜːn(ə)l ˈɪntərʌpt/ *noun* signal *m* d'interruption; d'appel émis par un périphérique

external label /ɪkˌstɜːn(ə)l ˈleɪb(ə)l/ *noun* (*of a device or disk*) étiquette *f* extérieure

external memory /ɪkˌstɜːn(ə)l ˈmem(ə)ri/ *noun* mémoire *f* externe

external modem /ɪkˌstɜːn(ə)l ˈməʊdem/ *noun* modem *m* externe

external register /ɪkˌstɜːn(ə)l ˈredʒɪstə/ *noun* registre *m* externe

external schema /ɪkˌstɜːn(ə)l ˈskiːmə/ *noun* (*user's view of data or program*) vision *f* d'utilisateur; schéma *m* du point de vue de l'utilisateur

external sort /ɪkˌstɜːn(ə)l ˈsɔːt/ *noun* tri *m* sur disque; tri *m* sur support externe

external storage /ɪkˌstɜːn(ə)l ˈstɔːrɪdʒ/, **external store** /ɪkˌstɜːn(ə)l ˈstɔː/ *noun* mémoire *f* externe

extracode /ˈekstrəkəʊd/ *noun* (*routines within the operating system that emulate a hardware system*) extracode *m*

extract /ɪkˈstrækt/ *verb* extraire *vt* ◇ **we can extract the files required for typesetting** nous pouvons extraire les dossiers qui doivent aller à la composition

extract instruction /ekˈstrækt ɪnˌstrʌkʃən/ *noun* instruction *f* d'extraction

extractor /ɪkˈstræktə/ *noun* extracteur *m*

extranet /ˈekstrənet/ *noun* extranet *m*

eye-dropper /aɪ ˈdrɒpə/ *noun* outil *m* Pipette

e-zine /ˈiː ziːn/ *noun* magazine *m* électronique

F

F *symbol* (*hexadecimal number equivalent to decimal 15*) nombre hexadécimal équivalent du 15 décimal

face /feɪs/ *noun* fonte *f*; modèle *m* de caractères; police *f* de caractères; type *m* de caractères

faceted code /ˈfæsɪtd kəʊd/ *noun* code *m* à facettes

facility /fəˈsɪlɪti/ *noun* **1.** (*means or mechanism by which a task can be executed*) facilité *f*; service *m* **2.** (*communications path*) dispositif *m* d'accès ◇ **we offer facilities for processing a customer's own disks** nous offrons à nos clients un service de traitement de leurs propres disquettes

facsimile character generator /fækˌsɪmɪli ˈkærɪktə ˌdʒenəreɪtə/ *noun* générateur *m* de caractères fac-similés

facsimile copy /fækˌsɪmɪli ˈkɒpi/ *noun* **1.** fac-similé *m* **2.** fac-similé *m*

facsimile transmission /fækˈsɪmɪlɪ trænz ˌmɪʃ(ə)n/ *noun* télécopie *f*; fax *m*

factor /ˈfæktə/ *noun* (*number*) facteur *m*

factorial /fækˈtɔːriəl/ *noun* factorielle *f* ◇ **4 factorial (written 4!) or 1x2x3x4 equals 24** la factorielle de 4 (qui s'écrit 4!) ou 1x2x3x4 est 24

factorise /ˈfæktəraɪz/, **factorize** *verb* (*numbers*) factoriser *vt*; mettre en facteur

fade /feɪd/ *verb* (*radio or electrical signal*) faiblir *vi*; baisser *vt*; perdre de l'intensité; s'atténuer *vr*

fade in /ˌfeɪd ˈɪn/ *noun* ouverture *f* en fondu

fade out /ˌfeɪd ˈaʊt/ *noun* (*of an image*) fermeture *f* en fondu ■ *verb* faire disparaître progressivement; faire un fondu

fail /feɪlⁿ/ *verb* **1.** (*machine*) ne pas faire quelque chose; (*not to do something*) omettre de faire quelque chose **2.** (*of machine*) tomber en panne ◇ **a computer has failed if you turn on the power supply and nothing happens** on peut dire que l'ordinateur est en panne si rien ne se produit à la mise sous tension ◇ **the company failed to carry out routine maintenance of its equipment** la société ne s'est pas souciée d'effectuer la maintenance de routine de son matériel ◇ **the prototype disk drive failed its first test** le premier essai du prototype de lecteur de disquettes a été un échec

fail safe system /fˈeɪl seɪf ˌsɪstəm/ *noun* système *m* de sécurité; système *m* de sécurité en cas de coupure de courant

'The DTI is publishing a new code of best practice which covers hardware reliability and fail-safe software systems.' [*Computing*]

fail soft system /ˈfeɪl sɒft ˌsɪstəm/ *noun* système *m* disjoncteur progressif

failure logging /ˈfeɪljə ˌlɒgɪŋ/ *noun* enregistrement *m* (automatique) des états d'incidents

failure rate /ˈfeɪljə reɪt/ *noun* taux *m* de défaillance

failure recovery /ˈfeɪljə rɪˌkʌv(ə)ri/ *noun* (*resuming a process*) reprise *f* sur incident

fall back /ˌfɔːl ˈbæk/ *noun* procédure *f* de secours

fall back recovery /ˌfɔːl bæk rɪˈkʌv(ə)ri/ *noun* (*resuming a program*) remise *f* en marche au point de reprise

fall back routines /ˈfɔːl bæk ruːˌtiːnz/ *plural noun* (*when a system or machine has failed*) routines *fpl*

false /fɔːls/ *adjective* **1.** (*not true or wrong*) faux; fausse; incorrect *or* -e; erroné *or* -ée **2.** (*logic*) faux; fausse

false code /ˌfɔːls ˈkəʊd/ *noun* code *m* erroné

false drop /ˌfɔːls ˈdrɒp/ *noun* résultat *m* erroné

false error /fɔːls ˈerə/ *noun* fausse erreur *f*

false retrieval /ˌfɔːls rɪˈtriːv(ə)l/ *noun* résultat *m* erroné

FAM *abbr* (*fast access memory*) mémoire *f* rapide

family /ˈfæm(ə)li/ *noun* **1.** (*range of typefaces*) famille *f* **2.** (*range of machines*) famille *f*; gamme *f*; série *f* (de produits)

fanfold /ˈfænfəʊld/ *noun* papier *m* (plié) en accordéon; papier *m* (plié) en éventail; papier *m* (plié) en paravent; papier *m* en continu

fan-in /fæn ɪn/ *noun* entrance *f*

fanning strip /ˈfænɪŋ strɪp/ *noun* tresse *f* de mise à la masse

fan-out /ˈfæn aʊt/ *noun* (*maximum number of outputs*) sortance *f*

FAQ /fæk, ˌef eɪ ˈkjuː/ *noun* foire *f* aux questions

Faraday cage /ˈfærədeɪ keɪdʒ/ *noun* cage *f* de Faraday

fast access memory /ˌfɑːst ˌækses ˈmem(ə)ri/ *noun* mémoire *f* à accès rapide

fast core /ˈfɑːst kɔː/ *noun* mémoire *f* centrale rapide

fast line /'fɑːst laɪn/ *noun* ligne *f* de transmission rapide

fast packet /fɑːst 'pækɪt/ *noun* paquet *m* rapide

fast peripheral /fɑːst pə'rɪf(ə)rəl/ *noun* périphérique *m* rapide

Fast-SCSI /fɑːst 'skʌzi/ *noun* interface *f* Fast-SCSI

fast time-scale /'fɑːst taɪm/ *noun* (*operation*) base *f* de temps réduite

FAT /ˌef eɪ 'tiː/ *noun* table *f* d'allocation des fichiers; table *f* FAT

fatal error /ˌfeɪt(ə)l 'erə/ *noun* erreur *f* fatale

FatBits /'fætbɪts/ mode *m* loupe

father file /'fɑːðə faɪl/ *noun* fichier *m* père

fault /fɔːlt/ *noun* (*defect*) défaut *m*; (*mistake*) faute *f*; erreur *f*; (*stoppage*) panne *f*; incident *m*; défaillance *f* ◇ **the technical staff are trying to correct a programming fault** les techniciens essayent de corriger une erreur de programmation ◇ **we think there is a basic fault in the product design** nous estimons qu'il y a une erreur fondamentale dans la conception du produit

fault detection /fɔːlt dɪ'tekʃ(ə)n/ *noun* localisation *f* (automatique) de panne

fault diagnosis /fɔːlt ˌdaɪəg'nəʊsɪs/ *noun* diagnostic *m* de localisation de panne; diagnostic *m* de localisation de défaillance

fault location program /ˌfɔːlt ləʊ'keɪʃ(ə)n ˌprəʊgræm/ *noun* programme *m* de localisation de panne

fault management /fɔːlt 'mænɪdʒmənt/ *noun* gestion *f* de défaillance

fault time /ˌfɔːlt 'taɪm/ *noun* durée *f* d'une panne

fault tolerance /fɔːlt 'tɒlərəns/ *noun* tolérance *f* de panne

fault-tolerant /fɔːlt 'tɒlərənt/ *adjective* à tolérance de panne

fault trace /ˌfɔːlt 'treɪs/ *noun* enregistrement *m*

faulty sector /ˌfɔːlti 'sektə/ *noun* secteur *m* défectueux

fax /fæks/, **FAX** *noun* **1.** *informal* (*method of sending images digitally*) télécopie *f*; fax *m* **2.** (*copy of document sent digitally*) télécopie *f*; fax *m* ■ *verb* (*to send message by fax*) envoyer par télécopie; envoyer par fax; faxer *vt* ◇ **fax-modem** (*modem that can be used to send and receive faxes*) modem *m* avec fonction télécopie *or* télécopieur-modem *or* fax-modem *or* fax/modem ◇ **fax paper** papier pour télécopieur ◇ **fax transmission** transmission par télécopie ◇ **I've faxed the documents to our New York office** j'ai faxé les documents *or* j'ai envoyé les documents par télécopie à notre bureau de New York ◇ **the fax machine is next to the telephone switchboard** notre fax est tout à côté du standard téléphonique ◇ **we will send a fax of the design plan** nous vous enverrons les plans par télécopie *or* par fax

fax card /fæks kɑːd/, **fax adapter** /fæks ə 'dæptə/, **fax board** /fæks bɔːd/ *noun* carte *f* fax

fax gateway /fæks 'geɪtweɪ/ *noun* passerelle *f* fax; passerelle *f* de télécopie

fax modem /fæks 'məʊˌdem/ *noun* modem *m* télécopieur

fax server /fæks 'sɜːvə/ *noun* serveur *m* de fax

fd, FD *abbr* (*floppy disk*) disque *m* souple; disquette *f*

FDC /ˌef diː 'siː/ *noun* contrôleur *m* de disquettes

FDD *abbr* (*floppy disk drive*) lecteur *m* de disquette

FDDI /ˌef diː diː 'aɪ/ *noun* standard *m* FDD

FDDI II /ˌef diː diː aɪ 'tuː/ *noun* standard *m* FDD II

FDISK /'ef dɪsk/ *noun* (*MS-DOS system utility*) utilitaire *m* FDISK

FDM /ˌef diː 'em/ *noun* multiplexage *m* (par répartition) en fréquence ◇ **using FDM we can transmit 100 telephone calls along one main cable** le multiplexage en fréquence permet de transférer 100 appels téléphoniques sur un seul câble

fdx, FDX *abbr* (*full duplex*) bidirectionnel *m* simultané

feasibility /ˌfiːzə'bɪlɪti/ *noun* faisabilité *f*

feasibility study /ˌfiːzə'bɪlɪti ˌstʌdi/ *noun* étude *f* de faisabilité

FED *abbr* (*field emission display*) écran *m* à micropointes

FEDS /ˌef iː diː 'es/ *noun* système *m* de mémoire à disque magnétique

feed /fiːd/ *noun* (*printer or photocopier*) entraînement *m*; alimentation *f*

feedback /'fiːdbæk/ *noun* feedback *m*; rétroaction *f*; (*information which can be used to modify something*) action *m* en retour; réaction *f* ◇ **feedback loop** boucle *f* de feedback *or* de réaction *or* de rétroaction ◇ **negative feedback** rétroaction négative *or* feedback négatif

feedback control /'fiːdbæk kənˌtrəʊl/ *noun* contrôle *m* par retour

feeder /'fiːdə/ *noun* **1.** (*channel*) voie *f* d'acheminement; voie *f* de transmission de signaux **2.** (*for paper*) système *m* d'alimentation; système *m* d'entraînement ◇ **feeder cable** câble *m* d'acheminement des signaux *or* câble antenne-circuit

feed hole /'fiːd həʊl/ *noun* (*printing*) perforation *f* d'entraînement; perforation *f* marginale

female /'fiːmeɪl/ *adjective* femelle

female connector /ˌfiːmeɪl kə'nektə/ *noun* connecteur *m* femelle

female socket /ˌfiːmeɪl 'sɒkɪt/ *noun* prise *f* femelle

femto- /femtəʊ/ *prefix* femto-

femtosecond /'femtəʊˌsekənd/ *noun* femtoseconde *f*

FEP /ˌef iː 'piː/ *noun* processeur *m* frontal

ferric oxide /ˌferɪk 'ɒksaɪd/, **ferrite** /'feraɪt/ *noun* oxyde *m* de fer

ferrite /'feraɪt/ *noun* ferrite *f*

ferromagnetic material /ˌferəʊmægnetɪk mə'tɪəriəl/ *noun* matériau *m* ferromagnétique

FET /ˌef iː 'tiː/ *noun* transistor *m* à effet de champ (TEC)

fetch /fetʃ/ *noun* lecture *f* d'instruction

fetch cycle /fetʃ 'saɪk(ə)l/ *noun* (*series of events that retrieve the next instruction*) cycle *m* de lecture d'une instruction

fetch-execute cycle /ˌfetʃ 'eksɪkjuːt ˌsaɪk(ə)l/ *noun* cycle *m* de lecture/exécution

fetch instruction /fetʃ ɪn'strʌkʃən/ *noun* instruction *f* de lecture d'une instruction

fetch phase /'fetʃ feɪz/ *noun* (*section of the fetch-execute cycle*) phase *f* de lecture d'une instruction

fetch-protect /ˌfetʃ prə'tekt/ *verb* établir une protection des accès mémoire

fetch signal /fetʃ 'sɪgn(ə)l/ *noun* signal *m* de lecture d'instruction

FF *abbr* **1.** (*flip-flop*) commutateur *m* à bascule **2.** (*form feed*) alimenter en papier

fibre /'faɪbə/ *noun* (*very thin glass or plastic strand that can carry data in the form of light signals*) fibre *f*

fibre channel /'faɪbə ˌtʃæn(ə)l/ *noun* technologie *f* d'interconnexion Fibre Channel

fibre connector /'faɪbə kəˌnektə/ *noun* connecteur *m* de fibres optiques

fibre distributed data interface /ˌfaɪbə dɪ ˌstrɪbjʊtɪd 'deɪtə ˌɪntəfeɪs/ *noun* norme *f* FDDI (pour réseau à fibre optique)

fibre distributed data interface II /ˌfaɪbə dɪ ˌstrɪbjʊtɪd ˌdeɪtə ˌɪntəfeɪs 'tuː/ *noun* norme *f* FDDI II

fibre Ethernet /ˌfaɪbə 'iːθənet/ *noun* fibre *f* Ethernet

fibre optic cable /'faɪbə 'ɒptɪk/, **fibre optic connection** /ˌfaɪbə ˌɒptɪk kə'nekʃən/ *noun* (*material for data transfer*) câble *m* à fibres optiques; liaison *f* à fibres optiques; câble *m* optique ◇ **fibre optic connections enable nodes up to one kilometre apart to be used** les câbles à fibres optiques permettent de placer les noeuds jusqu'à un kilomètre l'un de l'autre

fibre optics /ˌfaɪbə 'ɒptɪks/ *plural noun* (*used for transmission of light signals*) technologie *f* de la fibre optique

fibre ribbon /ˌfaɪbə 'rɪbən/ *noun* ruban *m* (en tissu)

field /fiːld/ *noun* **1.** (*area of force*) champ *m* **2.** (*in a record*) champ *m* ◇ **field effect transistor (FET)** transistor *m* à effet de champ (TEC) ◇ **field strength** intensité *f* de champ ◇ **the employee record has a field for age** le dossier 'employés' possède un champ 'âge'

field effect transistor /ˌfiːld ɪˌfekt træn 'zɪstə/ *noun* transistor *m* à effet de champ (TEC)

field emission display /ˌfiːld ɪ'mɪʃ(ə)n dɪ ˌspleɪ/ *noun* écran *m* à micropointes

field engineer /fiːlⁿd ˌendʒɪ'nɪə/ *noun* (*person who carries maintenance work off-site*) ingénieur *m* d'entretien; ingénieur *m* d'après-vente; ingénieur *m* de maintenance sur site

fielding /'fiːldɪŋ/ *noun* zonage *m*

field label /fiːld 'leɪb(ə)l/ *noun* label *m*

field length /'fiːld leŋθ/ *noun* (*number of characters*) taille *f* d'un champ

field marker /fiːld 'mɑːkə/ *noun* séparateur *m* de champs

field name /'fiːld neɪm/ *noun* label *m*

field programmable device /ˌfiːld ˌprəʊgræməb(ə)l dɪ'vaɪs/ *noun* dispositif *m* à champ programmable

field programming /fiːlⁿd 'prəʊˌgræmɪŋ/ *noun* programmation *f* de champ

field separator /'fiːld ˌsepəreɪtə/ *noun* séparateur *m* de champs

field-tested /'fiːld ˌtestɪd/ *adjective* testé, -ée dans des conditions réelles

FIF /ˌef aɪ 'ef/ *noun* format *m* FIF

FIFO /'faɪfəʊ/ *noun* méthode *f* du premier entré premier sorti (FIFO)

FIFO memory /ˌfaɪfəʊ 'mem(ə)ri/ *noun* mémoire *f* qui fonctionne sur le principe du premier entré premier sorti

FIFO queue /'faɪfəʊ kjuː/ *noun* file *f* d'attente qui fonctionne sur le principe 'premier entré premier sorti'

fifth generation computer /ˌfɪfθ ˌdʒenəreɪʃ(ə)n kəm'pjuːtə/ *noun* ordinateur *m* de cinquième génération

figures shift /'fɪgəs ʃɪft/ *noun* **1.** inversion *f* chiffres **2.** commutation *f* du clavier

file /faɪl/ *noun* (*documents*) dossier *m* ■ *verb* classer des documents ◇ **to place (something) on file** insérer (un document) au dossier

> 'The first problem was solved by configuring a Windows swap file, which I hadn't done before because my 4Mb 486 had never been overloaded.' [*Computing*]

> '...the lost file, while inaccessible without a file-recovery utility, remains on disk until new information writes over it' [*Publish*]

file activity ratio /ˌfaɪl æk'tɪvɪti ˌreɪʃiəʊ/ *noun* ratio *m*

file allocation table /ˌfaɪl ˌælə'keɪʃ(ə)n ˌteɪb(ə)l/ *noun* table *f* d'allocation de fichier

file attribute /'faɪl ˌætrɪbjuːt/ *plural noun* attribut *m* de fichier

file cleanup /'faɪl ˌkliːnʌp/ *noun* nettoyage de fichiers *m*

file collating /ˈfaɪl kəˌleɪtɪŋ/ *noun* fusion *f*

file conversion /ˈfaɪl kənˌvɜːʃ(ə)n/ *noun* conversion *f* de fichier

file copy /ˈfaɪl ˌkɒpi/ *noun* copie *f* pour archivage

file creation /ˈfaɪl kriˌeɪʃ(ə)n/ *noun* création *f* de fichier

file defragmentation /ˈfaɪl ˌdiːfrægmenteɪʃ(ə)n/ *noun* défragmentation *f* de fichier

file deletion /ˈfaɪl dɪˌliːʃ(ə)n/ *noun* annulation *f*

file descriptor /ˈfaɪl dɪˌskrɪptə/ *noun* descripteur *m* de fichier

file directory /ˈfaɪl daɪˌrekt(ə)ri/ *noun* répertoire *m* de fichiers

file extent /ˈfaɪl ɪkˌstent/ *noun* taille *f* d'un fichier

file format /ˈfaɪl ˌfɔːmæt/ *noun* format *m* de fichier

file fragmentation /ˈfaɪl ˌfrægmənteɪʃ(ə)n/ *noun* fragmentation *f* de fichier

file gap /ˈfaɪl gæp/ *noun* espace *m* neutre

file handle /ˈfaɪl ˌhænd(ə)l/ *noun* numéro *m* d'ordre de fichier

file handling routine /ˈfaɪl ˌhændlɪŋ ruːˌtiːn/ *noun* routine *f* de manipulation de fichier

file header /ˈfaɪl ˌhedə/ *noun* en-tête *m* de fichier

file identification /ˈfaɪl aɪˌdentɪfɪkeɪʃ(ə)n/ *noun* identification *f* de fichier

file index /ˈfaɪl ˌɪndeks/ *noun* index *m* des fichiers

file interrogation /ˈfaɪl ɪnˌterəgeɪʃ(ə)n/ *noun* interrogation *f* de fichier

file label /ˈfaɪl ˌleɪb(ə)l/ *noun* label *m*

file layout /ˈfaɪl ˌleɪaʊt/ *noun* structure *f* d'un fichier

file length /ˈfaɪl leŋθ/ *noun* longueur *f* d'un fichier; dimension *f* d'un fichier

file locking /ˈfaɪl ˌlɒkɪŋ/ *noun* protection de fichiers *f*

file maintenance /ˈfaɪl ˌmeɪntənəns/ *noun* (*updating files*) maintenance *f* de fichier

file management /ˈfaɪl ˌmænɪdʒmənt/, **file management system** /ˈfaɪl ˌmænɪdʒmənt ˌsɪstəm/ *noun* gestion *f* de fichiers

file manager /ˈfaɪl ˌmænɪdʒə/ *noun* (*section of a disk operating system*) gestionnaire *m* de fichier

file merger /ˈfaɪl ˌmɜːdʒə/ *noun* fusion *f* de fichiers

filename /ˈfaɪlneɪm/ *noun* nom *m* d'un fichier ◇ **in MS-DOS, a filename can be up to eight characters long together with a three character filename extension** sous MS-DOS, le nom d'un fichier peut comporter jusqu'à huit caractères suivis d'une extension de trois caractères

'...when the filename is entered at the prompt, the operating system looks in the file and executes any instructions stored there' [*PC User*]

filename extension /ˈfaɪlneɪm ɪkˌstenʃ(ə)n/ *noun* extension *f* du nom du fichier ◇ **the filename extension SYS indicates that this is a system file** l'extension SYS ajoutée au nom du fichier indique qu'il s'agit d'un fichier système

file organisation /ˈfaɪl ˌɔːgənaɪzeɪʃ(ə)n/ *noun* disposition *f* de fichier

file processing /ˈfaɪl ˌprəʊsesɪŋ/ *noun* traitement *m* de fichier

file property /ˈfaɪl ˌprɒpəti/ *plural noun* propriété *m* du fichier

file protection /ˌfaɪl prəˈtekʃən/ *noun* logiciel *m* de protection; dispositif *m* de protection

file protect tab /ˌfaɪl prəˈtekt ˌtæb/ *noun* dispositif *m* de protection d'écriture

file purge /ˈfaɪl pɜːdʒ/ *noun* vidage *m* de fichier

file queue /ˈfaɪl kjuː/ *noun* fichiers *mpl* dans une file d'attente

file-recovery utility /ˌfaɪl rɪˈkʌv(ə)ri juː ˌtɪlɪti/ *noun* logiciel *m* de récupération de fichiers ◇ **a lost file cannot be found without a file-recovery utility** il est impossible de retrouver un fichier perdu sans l'aide d'un logiciel de récupération de fichiers

file security /ˈfaɪl sɪˌkjʊərɪti/ *noun* protection *f*

file server /ˈfaɪl ˌsɜːvə/ *noun* serveur *m*

file set /ˈfaɪl set/ *noun* groupe *m* de fichiers (connexes)

file sharing /ˈfaɪl ˌʃeərɪŋ/ *noun* partage *m* de fichier

file size /ˈfaɪl saɪz/ *noun* taille *f* de fichier

file sort /ˈfaɪl sɔːt/ *verb* tri *m* de fichiers

file storage /ˈfaɪl ˌstɔːrɪdʒ/ *noun* (*storage medium*) support *m* de données d'un fichier; (*memory*) mémoire *f* contenant des fichiers; (*action*) mise *f* en mémoire; (*data storage*) stockage *m* de fichier

file store /ˈfaɪl stɔː/ *noun* fichiers *mpl* en mémoire

file structure /ˈfaɪl ˌstrʌktʃə/ *noun* structure *f* de fichier

file transfer /ˈfaɪl ˌtrænsfɜː/ *noun* transfert *m* de fichier

file transfer access and management /ˌfaɪl ˌtrænsfɜː ˌækses ən ˈmænɪdʒmənt/ *noun* transfert, accès et gestion de fichiers; méthode *f* FTAM

file transfer protocol /ˌfaɪl ˈtrænsfɜː ˌprəʊtəkɒl/ *noun* protocole *m* de transfert de fichiers; protocole *m* FTP

file transfer utility /ˌfaɪl ˈtrænsfɜː juːˌtɪlɪti/ *noun* utilitaire *m* de transfert de fichiers

file type /ˈfaɪl taɪp/ *noun* type *m* de fichier

file update /'faɪl ˌʌpdeɪt/ *noun* **1.** (*corrected version*) nouvelle version *f* d'un fichier; (*action*) mise à jour *f* d'un fichier **2.** mise à jour *f* d'un fichier

file validation /'faɪl ˌvælɪdeɪʃ(ə)n/ *noun* validation *f* de fichier

filing system /'faɪlɪŋ ˌsɪstəm/ *noun* **1.** (*way of putting documents in order*) méthode *f* de classement; méthode *f* d'archivage **2.** (*software*) logiciel *m* d'archivage

fill /fɪl/ *verb* **1.** (*to put characters into gaps*) remplir *vt* **2.** (*to draw*) combler *vt*

fill character /fɪl 'kærɪktə/ *noun* caractère *m* de remplissage

film recorder /fɪlm rɪ'kɔːdə/ *noun* imageur *m*

filter /'fɪltə/ *noun* **1.** (*electronic circuit*) filtre *m* **2.** (*for selecting bits*) masque *m* ■ *verb* **1.** (*to select various bits*) séparer *vt*; éliminer *vt*; sélectionner par filtrage; (*to remove unwanted elements*) filtrer *vt* **2.** (*to remove unwanted elements*) filtrer *vt* ◇ **high pass filter** filtre passe-haut ◇ **low pass filter** filtre passe-bas

final product /ˌfaɪn(ə)l 'prɒdʌkt/ *noun* produit *m* fini

find /faɪnd/ *verb* (*command*) trouver *vt*; retrouver *vt*; repérer *vt* ■ *noun* chercher ◇ **it took a lot of time to find the faulty chip** il a fallu beaucoup de temps pour trouver la puce défectueuse ◇ **the debugger found the error very quickly** le débogueur a repéré la faute très rapidement

Find /faɪnd/ Rechercher

find and replace /ˌfaɪnd ən rɪ'pleɪs/ *noun* chercher et remplacer

Finder /'faɪndə/ (*Apple Macintosh graphical user interface*) Finder™

fine-tune /ˌfaɪn 'tjuːn/ *verb* (*to carry out small adjustments*) mettre au point; régler (avec grande précision) ◇ **fine-tuning improved the speed by ten per cent** une mise au point très précise améliore la vitesse de dix pour cent

finger /'fɪŋgə/ *noun* (*on the internet, a software program that will retrieve information about a user*) identificateur *m* de l'utilisateur d'un site

finite-precision numbers /ˌfaɪnaɪt prɪ ˌsɪʒ(ə)n 'nʌmbəz/ *noun* nombres *mpl* à précision finie

firewall /'faɪəwɔːl/ *noun* (*hardware or software security system between a server or intranet and the public internet*) coupe-feu *m*; pare-feu *m* ◇ **we have installed a firewall in our intranet to prevent hackers accessing company data via the internet link** nous avons mis en place un coupe-feu sur notre intranet pour empêcher l'accès non autorisé aux données de la société par l'intermédiaire de l'Internet

Firewire /'faɪəwaɪə/ (*trade name for a high-speed serial interface developed by the Apple Computer Corporation*) Firewire

firmware /'fɜːmweə/ *noun* (*data or program stored in a hardware memory chip*) logiciel *m* (de) système sur puce; logiciel *m* microprogrammé; firmware *m*

firmware monitor /'fɜːmweə ˌmɒnɪtə/ *noun* moniteur *m* intégré

first fit /'fɜːst fɪt/ *noun* premier emplacement *m* capable

first generation /ˌfɜːst dʒenə'reɪʃ(ə)n/ *noun* première génération *f*

first generation computer /ˌfɜːst ˌdʒenəreɪʃ(ə)n kəɰ'pjuːtə/ *noun* ordinateur *m* de première génération

first generation image /ˌfɜːst ˌdʒenəreɪʃ(ə)n 'ɪmɪdʒ/ *noun* image *f* originale; image *f* de première génération

first in first out /ˌfɜːst ɪn ˌfɜːst 'aʊt/ *noun* (*storage read/write method*) méthode *f* du premier entré premier sorti

first-level address /ˌfɜːst ˌlev(ə)l ə'dres/ *noun* adresse *f* de premier niveau; adresse *f* réelle

fit /fɪt/ *verb* (*calculate a curve*) ajuster *vt*

fixed and exchangeable disk storage /ˌfɪkst ən ɪksˌtʃeɪndʒəb(ə)l 'dɪsk ˌstɔːrɪdʒ/ *noun* unité *f* comprenant des disques fixes et des disques amovibles

fixed cycle operation /ˌfɪkst ˌsaɪk(ə)l ˌɒprə 'reɪʃ(ə)n/ *noun* **1.** opération *f* en cycle fixe **2.** opération *f* synchronisée; opération *f* en cycle fixe

fixed data /fɪkst 'deɪtə/ *noun* données *fpl* constantes; données *fpl* permanentes

fixed disk /ˌfɪkst 'dɪsk/ *noun* (*disk which cannot be removed*) disque *m* fixe

fixed disk storage /ˌfɪkst dɪsk 'stɔːrɪdʒ/ *noun* disque *m* dur fixe

fixed field /ˌfɪkst 'fiːld/ *noun* champ *m* de taille fixe

fixed-field file /ˌfɪkst fiːld 'faɪl/ *noun* fichier *m* de champ de taille constante; fichier *m* de champ de taille fixe

fixed-frequency monitor /ˌfɪkst ˌfriːkwənsi 'mɒnɪtə/ *noun* moniteur *m* à fréquence fixe

fixed head disk /ˌfɪkst hed 'dɪsk/, **fixed head disk drive** /ˌfɪkst hed 'dɪsk ˌdraɪv/ *noun* (*separate immovable read/write head*) lecteur *m* (de disque) à tête de lecture fixe

fixed-length field /ˌfɪkst leŋθ 'fiːld/ *noun* champ *m* de longueur fixe; champ *m* de longueur déterminée

fixed-length record /ˌfɪkst leŋθ 'rekɔːd/ *noun* enregistrement *m* de longueur fixe

fixed-length word /ˌfɪkst leŋθ 'wɜːd/ *noun* (*preset number of bits*) mot *m* de longueur fixe

fixed-point arithmetic /ˌfɪkst pɔɪnt ə 'rɪθmətɪk/ *noun* arithmétique *f* à virgule fixe

fixed-point notation /ˌfɪkst pɔɪnt nəʊ 'teɪʃ(ə)n/ *noun* numération *f* à virgule fixe

fixed program computer /ˌfɪkst ˌprəʊɡræm kəmˈpjuːtə/ *noun* ordinateur *m* à logique câblée

fixed routing /ˌfɪkst ˈraʊtɪŋ/ *noun* acheminement *m* présélectionné

fixed word length /ˌfɪkst ˈwɜːd ˌleŋθ/ *noun* ordinateur *m* à longueur de mots fixe

flag /flæɡ/ *noun* **1.** (*for block or field*) balise *f*; marqueur *m*; drapeau *m*; (*for status*) indicateur *m*; témoin *m*; drapeau *m* **2.** (*showing status of register*) drapeau *m*; indicateur *m*; témoin *m* ■ *verb* (*to indicate status*) baliser *vt*

flag bit /ˈflæɡ bɪt/ *noun* bit *m* indicateur *or* indicateur binaire

flag code /ˈflæɡ kəʊd/ *noun* code *m* balise

flag event /flæɡ ɪˈvent/ *noun* (*a process or condition that sets a flag*) fonction *f*

flagging /ˈflæɡɪŋ/ *noun* (*putting an indicator*) balisage *m*; marquage *m*; mise *f* en place d'un drapeau

flag register /flæɡ ˈredʒɪstə/ *noun* registre *m* des témoins; registre *m* des drapeaux

flag sequence /flæɡ ˈsiːkwəns/ *noun* séquence *f* de marqueurs; séquence *f* d'indicateurs; séquence *f* de drapeaux

flame /fleɪm/ *verb* (*on the internet – to send a rude or angry message to a user*) envoyer un message d'un ton (particulièrement) agressif

flash /flæʃ/ *verb* faire clignoter

flash A/D /ˌflæʃ eɪ ˈdiː/ *noun* convertisseur *m* analogique-numérique parallèle

flashing character /flæʃɪŋ ˈkærɪktə/ *noun* caractère *m* clignotant

flash memory /flæʃ ˈmem(ə)ri/ *noun* mémoire *f* flash

flash ROM /ˈflæʃ rɒm/ *noun* mémoire *f* flash

flat address space /ˌflæt əˈdres ˌspeɪs/ *noun* espace *m* d'adressage simple

flatbed /ˈflætˌbed/ *adjective* (*printer or scanner*) à plat; de type 'flatbed'

flatbed plotter /ˌflætbed ˈplɒtə/ *noun* traceur *m* à plat

flatbed scanner /ˌflætbed ˈskænə/ *noun* scanner *m* à plat

flat file /ˈflæt faɪl/ *noun* fichier *m* plat; fichier *m* bidimensionnel

flat file database /ˌflæt faɪl ˈdeɪtəbeɪs/ *noun* base *f* de données linéaire

flat pack /ˈflæt pæk/ *noun* boîtier *m* plat

flat panel /ˌflæt ˈpæn(ə)l/ *noun* écran *m* plat

flat rate /ˌflæt ˈreɪt/ *noun* prix *m* forfaitaire; prix *m* forfait *m*

flat screen /ˈflæt skriːn/ *noun* écran *m* plat

flexible array /ˌfleksəb(ə)l əˈreɪ/ *noun* tableau *m* à dimensions variables

flexible disk /ˈfleksəb(ə)l dɪsk/ *noun* disque *m* souple; disquette *f*

flexible disk cartridge /ˌfleksəb(ə)l ˈdɪsk ˌkɑːtrɪdʒ/ *noun* cartouche *f* de disquette

flexible machining system /ˌfleksɪb(ə)l məˈʃiːnɪŋ ˌsɪstəm/ *noun* système *m* de machines-outils à commandes numériques

flexible manufacturing system /ˌfleksɪb(ə)l ˌmænjʊˈfæktʃərɪŋ ˌsɪstəm/ *noun* atelier *m* flexible

flicker /ˈflɪkə/ *noun* (*variation of brightness*) scintillement *m*; vacillement *m*; papillotement *m* ■ *verb* clignoter *vi*; vaciller *vi*; papilloter *vi* ◇ **the image flickers when the printer is switched on** l'image sur l'écran vacille lors de la mise sous tension de l'imprimante

flicker-free /ˈflɪkə friː/ *adjective* (*display*) sans vacillement; sans clignotement; sans papillotement

'A CRT (cathode ray tube) monitor paints the screen from top to bottom, and is usually considered 'flicker free' if it refreshes the image 75 times a second, or more' [*The Guardian*]

flight simulator /ˈflaɪt ˌsɪmjʊleɪtə/ *noun* simulateur *m* de vol

flip-flop /flɪp flɒp/ *noun* (*electronic circuit or chip*) commutateur *m* à bascule ◇ **D-flip-flop** commutateur à bascule de type D

flippy /ˈflɪpi/ *noun* disquette *f* réversible

float /fləʊt/ *noun* décalage *m*; déplacement *m*

float factor /fləʊt ˈfæktə/ *noun* facteur *m* de déplacement

floating /ˈfləʊtɪŋ/ *adjective* **1.** flottant *or* -e **2.** flottant ◇ **floating accent** accent flottant ◇ **floating point** virgule flottante ◇ **floating point notation** notation à virgule flottante ◇ **floating point operation (FLOP)** opération en virgule flottante ◇ **floating voltage** courant *m* flottant ◇ **the floating point processor speeds up the processing of the graphics software** le processeur à virgule flottante accélère la vitesse de traitement des logiciels graphiques ◇ **this model includes a built-in floating point processor** ce modèle est livré avec un processeur à virgule flottante installé

floating address /ˌfləʊtɪŋ əˈdres/ *noun* adresse *f* relative

floating head /ˈfləʊtɪŋ hed/ *noun* tête *f* flottante

floating point arithmetic /ˌfləʊtɪŋ pɔɪnt əˈrɪθmətɪk/ *noun* calcul *m* en virgule flottante ◇ **the fixed number 56.47 in floating-point arithmetic would be 0.5647 and a power of 2** dans un calcul en virgule flottante, le nombre 56,47 serait écrit 0,5647 puissance 2

floating point notation /ˌfləʊtɪŋ pɔɪnt nəʊˈteɪʃ(ə)n/ *noun* notation *f* à virgule flottante

floating point number /ˌfləʊtɪŋ pɔɪnt ˈnʌmbə/ *noun* nombre *m* à virgule flottante

floating point operation /ˌfləʊtɪŋ pɔɪnt ˌɒpəˈreɪʃ(ə)n/ *noun* opération *f* en virgule flottante

floating point processor /ˌfləʊtɪŋ pɔɪnt ˈprəʊsesə/ *noun* processeur *m* à virgule flottante ◇ **the floating point processor speeds up the processing of the graphics software** le processeur à virgule flottante accélère la vitesse de traitement des logiciels graphiques

floating point routine /ˌfləʊtɪŋ pɔɪnt ruːˈtiːn/ *noun* sous-programme *m* à virgule flottante

floating point unit /ˌfləʊtɪŋ pɔɪnt ˈjuːnɪt/ *noun* processeur *m* à virgule flottante

floating symbolic address /ˌfləʊtɪŋ sɪmˌbɒlɪk əˈdres/ *noun* adresse *f* symbolique; adresse *f* relative

float relocate /fləʊt ˌriːləʊˈkeɪt/ *noun* réadressage *m* par déplacement en ajoutant une adresse origine à une adresse relative

FLOP /flɒp/ *abbr* (*floating point operation*) opération *f* en virgule flottante

floppy disk /ˌflɒpi ˈdɪsk/, **floppy** /ˈflɒpi/ *noun* disque *m* souple; disquette *f*

floppy disk controller /ˌflɒpi ˈdɪsk kənˌtrəʊlə/ *noun* contrôleur *m* de disquettes

floppy disk drive /ˌflɒpi ˈdɪsk ˌdraɪv/ *noun* (*of a computer*) lecteur *m* de disquette(s); unité *f* de disquette(s)

floppy disk sector /ˌflɒpi ˈdɪsk ˌsektə/ *noun* secteur *m* de disquette

floppy disk unit /ˌflɒpi ˈdɪsk ˌjuːnɪt/ *noun* lecteur *m* de disquette(s); unité *f* de disquette(s)

FLOPs per second /ˌflɒps pɜː ˈsekənd/ *noun* opérations *fpl* en virgule flottante par seconde

flowchart /ˈfləʊtʃɑːt/ *noun* (*graphic description of a process*) diagramme *m* d'opérations; ordinogramme *m* ■ *verb* faire *m* un ordinogramme

flowchart stencil /ˈfləʊtʃɑːt ˌstens(ə)l/ *noun* grille *f*

flowchart symbol /ˈfləʊtʃɑːt ˌsɪmb(ə)l/ *plural noun* symbole *m* d'un ordinogramme

flowchart template /ˈfləʊtʃɑːt ˌtempleɪt/ *noun* grille *f*

flow control /fləʊ kənˈtrəʊl/ *noun* contrôle *m* du flux (de données)

flow diagram /ˈfləʊ ˌdaɪəgræm/ *noun* ordinogramme *m*

flow direction /fləʊ daɪˈrekʃən/ *noun* direction *f* du flux

flowline /ˈfləʊlaɪn/ *noun* ligne *f* de jonction des symboles d'un ordinogramme

flow text /ˌfləʊ ˈtekst/ *verb* injecter du texte

flush /flʌʃ/ *verb* (*levelled*) vider *vt* ■ *adjective* au même niveau; de niveau ◇ **the cover is trimmed flush with the pages** la couverture est rognée de niveau avec les pages

flush buffers /flʌʃ ˈbʌfəz/ *phrase* vider la mémoire tampon

flutter /ˈflʌtə/ *noun* variation *f* de vitesse; scintillement *m* ◇ **wow and flutter are common faults on cheap tape recorders** le pleurage et les variations de vitesse *or* le scintillement sont des défauts courants des magnétophones bon marché

flyback /ˈflaɪbæk/ *noun* retour *m* ◇ **field flyback** retour de trame

flying head /ˈflaɪɪŋ hed/ *noun* (*floating head*) tête *f* flottante

flying mouse /ˌflaɪɪŋ ˈmaʊs/ *noun* souris *f* 3 D

FM /ˌef ˈem/ *verb* modulation *f* de fréquence

FMS /ˌef em ˈes/ *noun* **1.** système *m* de machines-outils à commandes numériques **2.** atelier *m* flexible

FM synthesiser /ˌef em ˈsɪnθəˌsaɪzə/ *noun* synthétiseur *m* de modulations de fréquence

focus /ˈfəʊkəs/ *noun* foyer *m* ■ *verb* mettre au point

fogging /ˈfɒgɪŋ/ *noun* voile *m*

folder /ˈfəʊldə/ *noun* (*Apple Macintosh, e-mail, Windows group of files*) chemise *f*; classeur *m*; (*with documents*) dossier *m*; (*Apple Macintosh group of files*) dossier *m*

folding /ˈfəʊldɪŋ/ *noun* (*hashing method*) folding *m*; réassemblage *m*

font /fɒnt/ *noun* fonte *f*; police *f* de caractères

> 'Word Assistant is designed to help wordprocessing users produce better- looking documents. It has style templates and forms providing 25 TrueType fonts, 100 clip-art images and two font utility programs.' [*Computing*]

> '...laser printers store fonts in several ways: as resident, cartridge and downloadable fonts' [*Desktop Publishing Today*]

font card /ˈfɒnt kɑːd/ *noun* carte *f* de police de caractères

font change /ˈfɒnt tʃeɪndʒ/ *noun* changement *m* de police de caractères

Font/DA Mover /ˌfɒnt ˌdiː eɪ ˈmuːvə/ *noun* gestionnaire *m* de polices et d'accessoires de bureau

font disk /ˈfɒnt dɪsk/ *noun* disquette *f* de fontes; disquette *f* de polices de caractères

Fonts Folder /ˈfɒnts ˌfəʊldə/ *noun* répertoire *m*

foot /fʊt/ *noun* (*bottom part*) pied *m*; base *f*; bas *m* ◇ **he signed his name at the foot of the letter** il a signé au bas de la lettre

footer /ˈfʊtə/, **footing** /ˈfʊtɪŋ/ *noun* (*message at the bottom of pages*) pied *m* de page

footnote /ˈfʊtˌnəʊt/ *noun* note *f*; renvoi *m* en bas de page

footprint /ˈfʊtˌprɪnt/ *noun* **1.** (*area covered by a beam*) empreinte *f* **2.** (*desk space*) encombrement *m*

> '...signals from satellites in orbit 36,000km above the earth don't care very much whether you are close to an exchange or not....as long as you have a dish within their footprint.' [*The Guardian*]

forbidden character /fəˈbɪd(ə)n ˈkærɪktə/, **forbidden combination** /fəˌbɪd(ə)n ˌkɒmbɪ 'neɪʃ(ə)n/ *noun* caractère *m* interdit; chaîne *f* de caractères interdite

forced page break /ˌfɔːst 'peɪdʒ ˌbreɪk/ *noun* saut *f* de page obligatoire

foreground /'fɔːgraʊnd/ *noun* **1.** (*front part*) premier plan *m* **2.** (*high priority task*) tâche *f* de premier plan; tâche *f* prioritaire

'This brighter – but still anti-glare – type of screen is especially useful for people using colourful graphic applications, where both the background and foreground are visually important.' [*Computing*]

foreground colour /ˌfɔːgraʊnd 'kʌlə/ *noun* couleur *f* de premier plan

foregrounding /'fɔːgraʊndɪŋ/ *noun* traitement *m* frontal

foreground mode /'fɔːgraʊnd məʊd/ *plural noun* mode *m* avant-plan

foreground processing memory /ˌfɔːgraʊnd 'prəʊsesɪŋ ˌmem(ə)ri/ *noun* mémoire *f* de traitement frontal

foreground program /ˌfɔːgraʊnd 'prəʊgræm/ *noun* programme *m* prioritaire

forest /'fɒrɪst/ *noun* structure *f* en arbres

form /fɔːm/ *noun* **1.** (*preprinted document*) formulaire *m*; bordereau *m*; (*preset computer layout for addresses, etc.*) masque *m* de saisie; format *m* d'écran de saisie **2.** (*plate or block of type*) forme *f* d'impression **3.** (*size and shape of a device*) encombrement *m* ◇ **it's been easy to train the operators to use the new software since its display looks like the existing printed forms** il a été facile de former les opérateurs à l'utilisation de ce nouveau logiciel, parce que les formats d'écran ressemblent aux rapports d'impression existants

format /'fɔːmæt/ *noun* **1.** (*of book*) format *m* **2.** (*of text*) format *m* ■ *verb* (*to arrange text*) formater *vt*; mettre en forme ◇ **style sheets are used to format documents** on utilise des feuilles de style pour formater les documents *or* mettre les documents en forme ◇ **the printer can deal with all formats up to quarto** l'imprimante peut accommoder tous les formats jusqu'au quarto

'As an increasing amount of information within businesses is generated in wordprocessed format, text retrieval tools are becoming a highly attractive pragmatic solution.' [*Computing*]

formatted dump /ˌfɔːmætɪd 'dʌmp/ *noun* vidage *m* au format

formatter /'fɔːmætə/ *noun* (*piece of hardware or software*) matériel *m*; logiciel *m* de formatage

form factor /fɔːm 'fæktə/ *noun* facteur *m* de forme

form feed /'fɔːm fiːd/ *verb* alimenter en papier

form flash /ˌfɔːm 'flæʃ/ *noun* en-tête *m* préétabli (gardé en mémoire)

form handling equipment /ˌfɔːm 'hændlɪŋ ɪˌkwɪpmənt/ *noun* équipement *m* de traitement de formulaires

form letter /'fɔːm ˌletə/ *noun* (*standard letter*) lettre *f* type; lettre *f* standard

form mode /'fɔːm məʊd/ *noun* (*display method on a data entry terminal*) mode *m* masque

form overlay /fɔːm ˌəʊvə'leɪ/ *noun* (*printing*) texte *m*

form stop /ˌfɔːm 'stɒp/ *noun* (*sensor on a printer*) arrêt *m* pour manque de papier

formula /'fɔːmjʊlə/ *noun* formule *f* ◇ **formula translator (FORTRAN)** traducteur *m* de formule *or* langage *m* FORTRAN

formula portability /ˌfɔːmjʊlə ˌpɔːtə'bɪlɪti/ *noun* portabilité *f* d'une formule

formula translator /'fɔːmjələ trænsˌleɪtə/ *noun* FORTRAN

for-next loop /ˌfɔː 'nekst ˌluːp/ *noun* boucle *f* conditionnelle FOR...NEXT ◇ **for X=1 to 5: print X: next X – this will print out 1 2 3 4 5** pour X=1 à 5: imprimer X: calculer la valeur suivante de X – le résultat imprimé sera 1 2 3 4 5

FORTH /fɔːθ/ *noun* langage *m* FORTH

FORTRAN /'fɔːtræn/ *noun* langage *m* FORTRAN

forum /'fɔːrəm/ *noun* forum *m*

forward /'fɔːwəd/ *verb* **1.** (*to send an email message that you have received on to another user*) transmettre *vt*; (*a letter or a call*) faire suivre; réacheminer *vt* **2.** transmettre *vt*

forward error correction /ˌfɔːwəd 'erə kəˌrekʃ(ə)n/ *noun* correction *f* d'erreur en cours de transmission

forward pointer /ˌfɔːwəd 'pɔɪntə/ *noun* pointeur *m* avant

FOSDIC /ˌef əʊ es diː aɪ 'siː/ *noun* lecteur *m* optique de microfilms pour entrée de données sur ordinateur

four-address instruction /ˌfɔː əˌdres ɪn 'strʌkʃən/ *noun* instruction *f* à quatre adresses

fourcc /ˌfɔː siː 'siː/, **four-character code** /ˌfɔː ˌkærɪktə 'kəʊd/ *noun* code *m* à quatre caractères

4GL *abbr* (*fourth-generation language*) langage *m* de quatrième génération

four-plus-one address /'fɔː plʌs ˌwʌn/ *noun* quatre adresses *f* plus une

fourth generation computer /ˌfɔːθ ˌdʒenəreɪʃ(ə)n kəm'pjuːtə/ *noun* ordinateur *m* de quatrième génération

fourth generation language /ˌfɔːθ ˌdʒenəreɪʃ(ə)n 'læŋgwɪdʒ/ *noun* langage *m* de quatrième génération

fps *noun* images *fpl* par seconde; images/seconde

FPU *abbr* (*floating point unit*) unité *f* à virgule flottante

FQDN /ˌef kjuː diː 'en/ *noun* nom *m* de domaine complet

fractal /'frækt(ə)l/ *noun* (*shape that repeats itself*) fractale *f*; objet *m* fractal

fractal compression /ˌfrækt(ə)l kəm ˈpreʃ(ə)n/ *noun* compression *f* fractale (d'images)

fractal image format /ˌfrækt(ə)l ˈɪmɪdʒ ˌfɔːmæt/ *noun* format *m* FIF

fraction /ˈfrækʃən/ *noun* **1.** fraction *f* **2.** fraction *f*

fractional part /ˈfrækʃənəl pɑːt/ *noun* partie *f* fractionnaire; partie *f* mantisse *f*

fractional services /ˌfrækʃənəl ˈsɜːvɪsɪz/ *plural noun* (*parts of a bandwidth*) services *mpl* partagés

fractional T-1 /ˈfrækʃənəl tiː/ *noun* service *m* T1 partagé

fragment /ˈfrægmənt/ *noun* fragment *m*

fragmentation /ˌfrægmənˈteɪʃ(ə)n/ *noun* **1.** (*memory allocation to a number of files*) fragmentation *f*; segmentation *f*; fractionnement *m*; (*files stored across non-contiguous sectors*) fragmentation *f* **2.** (*of files on a disk*) fragmentation *f*

frame /freɪm/ *noun* **1.** (*on magnetic tape*) trame *f* **2.** (*of transmitted data*) bloc *m* **3.** (*one image*) image *f* complète **4.** (*in HTML webpage*) image *f* **5.** (*communications information*) image *f* **6.** (*for printed circuit boards*) support *m* de cartes; châssis *m* avec guide-cartes; baie *f* (pour cartes) ◇ **frame flyback** saut *m* d'image ◇ **frame frequency** fréquence *f* de l'image ◇ **frame store** mémoire *f* image ◇ **in the UK the frame frequency is 25 fps** la télévision britannique utilise une fréquence de 25 images par seconde *or* 25 images/seconde ◇ **the frame store can be used to display weather satellite pictures** la mémoire image peut servir à l'affichage des images météorologiques transmises par satellite ◇ **the image processor allows you to store a video frame in a built-in 8-bit frame store** le processeur d'images permet le stockage d'une image vidéo dans une mémoire image intégrée de 8 bits ◇ **video frame** image vidéo ◇ **with the image processor you can freeze a video frame** le processeur d'images permet de figer une image *or* de faire un arrêt sur image

frame-based animation % /freɪm beɪsd ˌænɪˈmeɪʃ(ə)n/ *noun* animation *f* image par image

frame buffer /freɪm ˈbʌfə/ *noun* mémoire *f* tampon d'image

frame error /freɪm ˈerə/ *noun* erreur *f* de trame

frame grabber /ˈfreɪm ˌgræbə/ *noun* (*high speed digital sampling circuit*) capteur *m* d'image vidéo

> '...the frame grabber is distinguished by its ability to acquire a TV image in a single frame interval' [*Electronics & Wireless World*]

frame rate /ˈfreɪm reɪt/ *noun* taux *m* de trame

frame relay /freɪm rɪˈleɪ/ *noun* (*communications protocol*) échange *m* de trames

frames per second /ˌfreɪmz pə ˈsekənd/ *noun* image *f* par seconde

framework /ˈfreɪmwɜːk/ *noun* cadre *m*; structure *f* ◇ **the program framework was designed first** on a d'abord établi le cadre *or* la structure du programme

free /friː/ *adjective* (*available for use*) libre ■ *noun* (*of bytes*) libre ■ *verb* (*to clear space in memory*) libérer *vt* ◇ **free indexing** indexage *m* libre ◇ **free line** ligne *f* libre

freedom of information /ˌfriːdəm əv ɪnfəˈmeɪʃ(ə)n/ *noun* liberté d'accès à l'information

free form database /ˌfriː fɔːm ˈdeɪtəbeɪs/ *noun* base *f* de données à structure de champs libre

free running mode /ˌfriː ˈrʌnɪŋ ˌməʊd/ *noun* mode *m* multi-utilisateur

free WAIS /ˌfriː ˌdʌb(ə)l juː eɪ aɪ ˈes/ *noun* accès *m* gratuit au système WAIS

freeware /ˈfriːweə/ *noun* (*software in the public domain*) logiciel *m* gratuit

free wheeling /ˈfriː wiːlɪŋ/ *noun* transmission *f* sans contrôle de retour

freeze /friːz/ *verb* figer *vt* ◇ **the image processor will freeze a single TV frame** le processeur d'image peut figer une image de télévision ◇ **to freeze (frame)** figer une image *or* faire un arrêt sur image

freeze frame /ˈfriːz freɪm/ *noun* image *f* figée

frequency /ˈfriːkwənsi/ *noun* fréquence *f* ◇ **frequency changer** convertisseur *m* de fréquence ◇ **frequency divider** diviseur *m* de fréquence ◇ **frequency domain** domaine *m* fréquentiel *or* de fréquence ◇ **frequency modulation (FM)** modulation *f* de fréquence (MF) ◇ **frequency range** gamme *f* de fréquences ◇ **frequency response** réponse *f* en fréquence ◇ **frequency shift keying (FSK)** (système) de modulation *f* par déplacement *or* décalage de fréquence ◇ **frequency variation** variation *f* de fréquence ◇ **the main clock frequency is 10MHz** la principale fréquence d'horloge est de 10MHz

frequency division multiplexing /ˌfriːkwənsi dɪˌvɪʒ(ə)n ˈmʌltɪˌpleksɪŋ/ *noun* multiplexage *m* (par répartition) en fréquence

frequency modulation /ˌfriːkwənsi mɒdjuˈleɪʃ(ə)n/ *noun* modulation *f* de fréquence

frequently asked questions /ˌfriːkwənt(ə)li ɑːskd ˈkwestʃənz/ *plural noun* foire *f* aux questions

friendly front end /ˌfrendli ˌfrʌnt ˈend/ *noun* (*display that is easy to use and understand*) interface *f* utilisateur conviviale

front end /ˌfrʌnt ˈend/ *adjective* (*program that is seen by an end user*) interface *f* utilisateur

front-end processor /ˌfrʌnt end ˈprəʊsesə/ *noun* processeur *m* frontal

front panel /frʌnt ˈpæn(ə)l/ *noun* panneau *m* avant; panneau *m* antérieur; panneau *m* de commande

FTAM /ˌef tiː eɪ ˈem/ *noun* méthode *f* de gestion, accès et transfert de fichiers; méthode *f* FTAM

FTP /ˌef tiː ˈpiː/ *noun* protocole *m* de transfert de fichiers; protocole *m* FTP

full adder /ˌfʊl ˈædə/ *noun* additionneur *m* à trois entrées; additionneur *m* complet

full duplex /ˌfʊl ˈdjuːpleks/ *noun* bidirectionnel *m* simultané

full handshaking /ˌfʊl ˈhændʃeɪkɪŋ/ *noun* protocole *m* de communication

full-motion video /ˌfʊl ˌməʊʃ(ə)n ˈvɪdiəʊ/ *noun* fréquence *f* d'images

full-motion video adapter /ˌfʊl ˌməʊʃ(ə)n ˈvɪdiəʊ əˌdæptə/ *noun* carte *f* vidéo pleine animation; carte *f* vidéo à grand débit

full path /ˌfʊl ˈpɑːθ/ *noun* chemin *m* complet

full-screen /fʊl skriːn/ *adjective* plein écran

full-size display /ˌfʊl saɪz dɪsˈpleɪ/ *noun* écran *m* pleine page

full subtractor /ˌfʊl səbˈtræktə/ *noun* soustracteur *m* complet; soustracteur *m* à trois entrées

full-text search /ˌfʊl tekst ˈsɜːtʃ/ *noun* recherche *f* globale; recherche *f* dans tout le texte

fully formed character /ˌfʊli fɔːmd ˈkærɪktə/ *plural noun* caractère *m* complet

fully-populated /ˌfʊli ˈpɒpjʊˌleɪtɪd/ *adjective* **1.** (*PCB with components in all free sockets*) carte complètement garnie (de composants); (*all the options fitted into a computer*) avec toutes les options **2.** carte *f* entièrement équipée

fully qualified domain name /ˌfʊli ˌkwɒlɪfaɪd dəʊˈmeɪn ˌneɪm/ *noun* nom *m* de domaine complet

function /ˈfʌŋkʃən/ *noun* **1.** (*mathematical formula*) fonction *f* **2.** (*computer program instructions*) fonction *f* **3.** (*special feature on a computer*) fonction *f* ◇ **the word-processor had a spelling-checker function but no built-in text-editing function** cette machine de traitement de texte possédait une fonction correction orthographique *or* possédait un correcteur orthographique mais n'était pas équipée d'éditeur intégré

functional diagram /ˌfʌŋkʃ(ə)nəl ˈdaɪəgræm/ *noun* schéma *m*; diagramme *m* fonctionnel

functional specification /ˌfʌŋkʃ(ə)nəl ˌspesɪfɪˈkeɪʃ(ə)n/ *noun* spécification *f*

functional unit /ˌfʌŋkʃən(ə)l ˈjuːnɪt/ *noun* appareil *m* en bon état de marche

function call /ˈfʌŋkʃən kɔːl/ *noun* appel *m* de fonction

function code /ˈfʌŋkʃən kəʊd/ *noun* code *m* de fonction

function key /ˈfʌŋkʃən kiː/ *noun* touche *f* de fonction ◇ **tags can be allocated to function keys** on peut allouer une étiquette aux touches de fonction

function library /ˈfʌŋkʃən ˌlaɪbrəri/ *noun* bibliothèque *f* de fonctions

function overloading /ˈfʌŋkʃ(ə)n ˌəʊvələʊdɪŋ/ *noun* système *m* de programmation à surcharge de fonctions

function table /ˈfʌŋkʃən ˌteɪb(ə)l/ *noun* table *f* de fonctions

fusible link /ˌfjuːzɪb(ə)l ˈlɪŋk/ *noun* élément *m* fusible

fusible read only memory /ˌfjuːzɪb(ə)l riːd ˌəʊnli ˈmem(ə)ri/ *noun* ROM *f* à fusibles; mémoire *f* morte à fusibles

fuzzy logic /ˌfʌzi ˈlɒdʒɪk/, **fuzzy theory** /ˌfʌzi ˈθɪəri/ *noun* logique *f* floue

FYI /ˌef waɪ ˈaɪ/ *noun* à titre d'information

G

gain /geɪn/ *noun* **1.** (*increase*) gain *m* **2.** (*in signal amplitude*) gain *m* ◇ **gain control** contrôle *m* de gain

gallium arsenide /ˌgæliəm 'ɑːs(ə)naɪd/ *noun* arséniure *m* de gallium

game cartridge /'geɪm ˌkɑːtrɪdʒ/ *noun* cartouche *f* de jeu

game console /'geɪm ˌkɒnsəʊl/ *noun* console *f* de jeu

gamepad /'geɪmpæd/ *noun* manette *f* de jeu

game port /'geɪm pɔːt/ *noun* port *m* (de) jeu

games console /'geɪmz ˌkɒnsəʊl/ *noun* console *f* de jeu

gaming gear /'geɪmɪŋ gɪə/ *noun* (*joystick, foot pedal, etc.*) accessoires *mpl* de jeux

ganged /gæŋd/ *adjective* (*mechanically linked*) regroupé *or* -ée; monté, -ée en série

ganged switch /ˌgæŋd 'swɪtʃ/ *noun* (*series of switches*) regroupement *m* de commutateurs; commutateurs *mpl* en série; commutateurs *mpl* chaînés

gap /gæp/ *noun* **1.** (*between recorded data*) espace *m*; intervalle *m* **2.** (*space*) entrefer *m*

gap character /gæp 'kærɪktə/ *noun* caractère *m* de remplissage

gap digit /gæp 'dɪdʒɪt/ *noun* chiffre *m* de remplissage

gap loss /ˌgæp 'lɒs/ *noun* atténuation *f* de signal par perte d'alignement

garbage /'gɑːbɪdʒ/ *noun* **1.** (*radio interference*) signaux *mpl* parasites; brouillage *m*; interférences *fpl* radio **2.** (*information no longer required*) informations *fpl* sans intérêt; informations *fpl* de rebut ◇ **garbage in garbage out (GIGO)** à données erronées, résultats erronés *or* des données douteuses produisent des résultats douteux

garbage collection /'gɑːbɪdʒ kəˌlekʃən/ *noun* nettoyage *m* de mémoire

garbage in garbage out /ˌgɑːbɪdʒ ɪn ˌgɑːbɪdʒ 'aʊt/ *noun* à données erronées, résultats erronés; des données douteuses produisent des résultats douteux

gas discharge display /gæs dɪsˌtʃɑːdʒ dɪ'spleɪ/, **gas plasma display** /gæs ˌplæzmə dɪ'spleɪ/ *noun* affichage *m*; écran *m* à plasma

gate /geɪt/ *noun* **1.** (*logical electronic switch*) porte *f* **2.** (*connection pin of a FET device*) connecteur *m*

gate array /geɪt ə'reɪ/ *noun* circuit *m* logique complexe

gate circuit /geɪt 'sɜːkɪt/ *noun* circuit *m* logique

gate delay /geɪt dɪ'leɪ/ *noun* délai *m*

gateway /'geɪtweɪ/ *noun* **1.** (*device or software that links two dissimilar networks*) passerelle *f* **2.** (*electronic mail software*) passerelle *f* **3.** (*allowing access to network*) passerelle *f* ◇ **to send messages by fax instead of across the network, you'll need to install a fax gateway** pour envoyer des messages par fax au lieu de les envoyer par le réseau, vous devez installer une passerelle fax ◇ **we use a gateway to link the LAN to WAN** nous avons utilisé une passerelle pour relier le réseau local au réseau étendu

gateway interface /'geɪtweɪ ˌɪntəfeɪs/ *noun* script *m* CGI

gateway page /'geɪtweɪ peɪdʒ/ *noun* page *f* d'accès

gather /'gæðə/ *verb* regrouper *vt*; rassembler *vt*

gather write /'gæðə raɪt/ *verb* grouper *vt*; agglomérer (des données)

Gb *abbr* (*gigabyte*) giga-octet (Go) *m*

gender changer /'dʒendə ˌtʃeɪndʒə/ *noun informal* (*for connectors*) changeur *m* de genre ◇ **you can interconnect all these peripherals with just two cables and a gender changer** il est possible de relier tous ces périphériques en utilisant seulement deux câbles et un changeur de genre

General MIDI /ˌdʒen(ə)rəl 'mɪdi/ *noun* norme *f* Général MIDI

general packet radio service /ˌdʒen(ə)rəl ˌpækɪt 'reɪdiəʊ ˌsɜːvɪs/ *noun* système *m* général de radiocommunication par paquets

general protection fault /ˌdʒen(ə)rəl prə'tekʃən ˌfɔːlt/ *noun* panne *f* de protection générale

general purpose computer /ˌdʒen(ə)rəl ˌpɜːpəs kəm'pjuːtə/ *noun* ordinateur *m* non spécialisé

general purpose interface adapter /ˌdʒen(ə)rəl ˌpɜːpəs 'ɪntəfeɪs əˌdæptə/ *noun* carte *f* réseau universelle; carte *f* réseau banalisée

general purpose interface bus /ˌdʒen(ə)rəl ˌpɜːpəs 'ɪntəfeɪs ˌbʌs/ *noun* bus *m* d'interface universel; bus *m* d'interface banalisé

general purpose program /ˌdʒen(ə)rəl ˌpɜːpəs ˈprəʊgræm/ *noun* programme *m* à usage multiple; programme *m* multifonction

general register /ˌdʒen(ə)rəl ˈredʒɪstə/ *noun* registre *m* général; registre *m* banalisé; registre *m* polyvalent

generate /ˈdʒenəˌreɪt/ *verb* (*codes or programs*) produire *vt*; générer *vt*; créer *vt* ◇ **to generate an image from digitally recorded data** créer une image à partir de données numériques

generated address /ˌdʒenəreɪtɪd əˈdres/ *noun* adresse *f* générée; adresse *f* calculée

generated error /ˌdʒenəreɪtɪd ˈerə/ *noun* erreur *f* générée (par des arrondis)

generation /ˌdʒenəˈreɪʃ(ə)n/ *noun* **1.** (*producing data*) production *f*; création *f* **2.** (*age of the technology*) génération *f* **3.** (*of file*) génération *f* ◇ **the computer is used in the generation of graphic images** on utilise l'ordinateur pour créer des images *or* pour la création d'images (de synthèse) ◇ **the father file is a first generation backup** le fichier père est un fichier de sauvegarde de première génération

generator /ˈdʒenəˌreɪtə/ *noun* (*program*) générateur *m* de programmes

generic /dʒəˈnerɪk/ *adjective* générique

geometry /dʒiˈɒmətri/ *noun* géométrie *f*

get /get/ *noun* instruction *f* 'GET'; instruction *f* 'chercher'

ghost /gəʊst/ *noun* image *f* fantôme

ghost cursor /gəʊst ˈkɜːsə/ *noun* curseur *m* secondaire

GHz *abbr* (*gigahertz*) gigahertz *m*

GIF /gɪf/ (*trade name for a graphics file format*) GIF

GIF file /ˌdʒiː aɪ ˈef faɪl/ *noun* (*graphics file format*) fichier *m* (graphique) GIF

giga- /gɪgə/ *prefix* **1.** (*meaning one thousand million*) giga- **2.** giga-; G

gigabit /ˈgɪgəbɪt/ *noun* gigabit *m*

gigabyte /ˈgɪgəbaɪt/ *noun* giga-octet (Go)

gigaflop /ˈgɪgəflɒp/ *noun* (*one thousand million floating-point operations per second*) gigaflop *m*; GFLOPS

gigahertz /ˈgɪgəhɜːts/ *noun* gigahertz *m*

GIGO /ˈgaɪgəʊ/ *noun* sans valeur à l'entrée, sans valeur à la sortie

GINO /ˌdʒiː aɪ en ˈəʊ/ *noun* entrée/sortie *f* graphique

GKS /ˌdʒiː keɪ ˈes/ *noun* fonctions *fpl* graphiques GKS

glare /gleə/ *noun* reflets *mpl*; réflexion *f* ◇ **the glare from the screen makes my eyes hurt** la réflexion sur l'écran me fatigue la vue

glare filter /gleə ˈfɪltə/ *noun* filtre *m* antireflets

glitch /glɪtʃ/ *noun informal* pépin *m*; problème *m*; défaillance *f*

'The programmer was upgrading a verification system at Visa's UK data centre when his work triggered a software glitch causing hundreds of valid cards to be rejected for several hours.' [*Computing*]

global /ˈgləʊb(ə)l/ *adjective* global *or* -e; total *or* -e

'In an attempt to bring order to an electronic Tower of Babel, pharmaceutical giant Rhone-Poulenc has assembled an X.400-based global messaging network and a patchwork directory system that will be used until a single email system is deployed worldwide.' [*Computing*]

global backup /ˌgləʊb(ə)l ˈbækʌp/ *noun* **1.** sauvegarde *f* globale du réseau **2.** sauvegarde *f* globale du réseau; sauvegarde *f* globale d'un disque dur; sauvegarde *f* globale d'un serveur

global exchange /ˌgləʊb(ə)l ɪksˈtʃeɪndʒ/ *noun* procédure *f* remplacer globalement; procédure *f* dans tout le texte

global knowledge /ˌgləʊb(ə)l ˈnɒlɪdʒ/ *noun* connaissance *f* globale; connaissance *f* exhaustive

global memory /ˌgləʊb(ə)l ˈmem(ə)ri/ *noun* mémoire *f* commune

global search and replace /ˌgləʊb(ə)l ˌsɜːtʃ ən rɪˈpleɪs/ *noun* chercher et remplacer globalement; chercher et remplacer dans tout le texte

global system for mobile communications /ˌgləʊb(ə)l ˌsɪstəm fə ˌməʊbaɪl kəˌmjuːnɪˈkeɪʃ(ə)nz/ *noun* système *m* mondial de communications mobiles

global variable /ˌgləʊb(ə)l ˈveəriəb(ə)l/ *noun* variable *f* globale; variable *f* commune; variable *f* générale

glyph /glɪf/ *noun* glyphe *m*

goal /gəʊl/ *noun* but *m* (visé ou atteint)

go down /ˌgəʊ ˈdaʊn/ *verb* se planter; tomber en panne

gold contact /ˌgəʊld ˈkɒntækt/ *noun* contact *m* en or

Google /ˈguːg(ə)l/ (*trade name for a popular Internet search engine*) Google

Gopher /ˈgəʊfə/ *noun* (*system that allows a user to find information and files stored on the Internet*) outil *m* de recherche Gopher

GOSIP /ˈgɒsɪp/ *noun* standard GOSIP (de comptabilité)

GOSUB /ˈgəʊsʌb/ *noun* (*programming command to execute a routine*) commande *f* GOSUB

GOTO /ˈgəʊtuː/ *noun* (*command which instructs a jump*) instruction *f* GOTO; instruction *f* de saut; instruction *f* de branchement

Gouraud shading /ˈguːrəʊ ˌʃeɪdɪŋ/ *noun* lissage *m*; ombrage *m* de Gouraud

Government Open Systems Interconnect Profile /ˌgʌv(ə)nmənt ˌəʊpən ˌsɪstəm ˈɪntəkənekt ˌprəʊfaɪl/ *noun* standard *m* GOSIP (de comptabilité)

GPF /ˌdʒiː piː 'ef/ *noun* panne *f* de protection générale

GPIB /ˌdʒiː piː aɪ 'biː/ *noun* bus *m* d'interface universel; bus *m* d'interface banalisé

gpr /ˌdʒiː piː 'ɑː/ *noun* registre *m* banalisé; registre *m* général; registre *m* polyvalent

grabber /'græbə/ *noun* capteur *m* d'images

graceful degradation /ˌgreɪsf(ə)l ˌdegrə 'deɪʃ(ə)n/ *noun* (*process of allowing some parts of a system to continue to function after a part has broken down*) dégradation *f* limitée; dégradation *f* douce; dégradation *f* progressive

gradient /'greɪdiənt/ *noun* dégradé *m*

grammar /'græmə/ *noun* (*rules for language use*) syntaxe *f*; grammaire *f*

grammar checker /'græmə ˌtʃekə/ *noun* vérificateur *m* grammatical; utilitaire *m* de vérification de grammaire

grammatical error /grəˌmætɪk(ə)l 'erə/ *noun* faute *f* de syntaxe

grandfather cycle /'grænfɑːðə ˌsaɪk(ə)l/ *noun* cycle *m* de rotation des fichiers de sauvegarde

grandfather file /'grænfɑːðə faɪl/ *noun* (*when followed by two other files: father and son*) fichier *m* grand-père; fichier *m* de première génération

granularity /ˌgrænjʊ'lærɪti/ *noun* (*size of memory segments*) granularité *f*; modularité *f* de la mémoire; degré *m* de segmentation de la mémoire

graphic /'græfɪk/ *adjective* graphique ◇ **graphic images** représentations *fpl* graphiques

graphical input output /ˌgræfɪkl ˌɪnpʊt 'aʊtpʊt/ *noun* GINO

graphical user interface /ˌgræfɪkl 'juːzə ˌɪntəfeɪs/ *noun* (*interface between an operating system and the user*) interface *f* graphique d'utilisateur; GUI

graphic data /'græfɪk ˌdeɪtə/ *noun* données *fpl* graphiques

graphic display /'græfɪk dɪˌpleɪ/ *noun* affichage *m* graphique

graphic display resolution /'græfɪk dɪ ˌspleɪ ˌrezəluːʃ(ə)n/ *noun* définition *f* de l'affichage graphique

graphic language /'græfɪk ˌlæŋgwɪdʒ/ *noun* langage *m* graphique ◇ **this graphic language can plot lines, circles and graphs with a single command** ce langage graphique permet de tracer lignes, cercles et graphes en une seule opération

graphic object /ˌgræfɪk 'ɒbdʒekt/ *noun* objet *m* graphique

graphics /'græfɪks/ *noun* représentations *f* graphiques; graphismes *mpl* ◇ **graphics output such as bar charts, pie charts, etc.** les graphismes tels que diagrammes en bâtons, diagrammes circulaires, etc.

graphics accelerator /'græfɪks ək ˌseləreɪtə/ *noun* accélérateur *m* graphique

graphics adapter /'græfɪks əˌdæptə/ *noun* (*electronic device to display graphics*) adaptateur *m* graphique; carte *f* graphique

graphics character /'græfɪks ˌkærɪktə/ *noun* caractère *m* graphique

graphics coprocessor /'græfɪks kəʊ ˌprəʊsesə/ *noun* coprocesseur *m* graphique

graphics file /'græfɪks faɪl/ *noun* fichier *m* graphique

graphics file format /'græfɪks faɪl ˌfɔːmæt/ *noun* format *m* de fichier graphique

graphics interface format /ˌgræfɪks 'ɪntəfeɪs ˌfɔːmæt/ *noun* format *m* GIF

graphics kernel system /ˌgræfɪks 'kɜːn(ə)l ˌsɪstəm/ *noun* fonctions *fpl* graphiques

graphics library /'græfɪks ˌlaɪbr(ə)ri/ *noun* bibliothèque *f* graphique; bibliothèque *f* de graphismes

graphics light pen /ˌgræfɪks 'laɪt ˌpen/ *noun* stylo *m* optique graphique

graphics mode /'græfɪks məʊd/ *noun* mode *m* graphique

graphics pad /'græfɪks pæd/ *noun* tablette *f* graphique; tablette *f* à numériser

graphics primitive /ˌgræfɪks 'prɪmɪtɪv/ *noun* forme *f* primitive; forme *f* de base

graphics printer /'græfɪks ˌprɪntə/ *noun* imprimante *f* graphique

graphics processor /'græfɪks ˌprəʊsesə/ *noun* processeur *m*

graphics software /'græfɪks ˌsɒftweə/ *noun* (*routines which perform standard graphics commands*) logiciel *m* (de création) graphique

graphics tablet /'græfɪks ˌtæblət/ *noun* tablette *f* graphique *or* à numériser

graphics terminal /'græfɪks ˌtɜːmɪn(ə)l/ *noun* terminal *m* graphique; terminal *m* de CAO

graphics VDU /ˌgræfɪks ˌviː diː 'juː/ *noun* écran *m* (à affichage) graphique

graph plotter /'grɑːf ˌplɒtə/ *noun* traceur *m* de courbes

Gray code /'greɪ kəʊd/ *noun* code *m* de Gray

greeked /griːkd/ *adjective* (*font with a point size too small to display*) en faux texte; en texte muet; en bolo-bolo

Green Book /griːn 'bʊk/ *noun* norme *f* Livre vert

gremlin /'gremlɪn/ *noun informal* (*unexplained fault in a system*) schmilblick *m*; erreur *f* inexplicable

grey scale /'greɪ skeɪl/ *noun* (*shades of grey on a monochrome monitor*) niveaux *mpl* de gris; (*used to measure the correct exposure when filming*) échelle *f* de gris

grid /grɪd/ *noun* **1.** (*when drawing*) grille *f* **2.** (*matrix*) grille *f*

grid snap /ˈgrɪd snæp/ *noun* ancrage *m* (du pointage)

ground /graʊnd/ *noun* (*electrical connection to earth or GND*) prise *f* de terre

group /gruːp/ *noun* **1.** (*set of computer records*) groupe *m* **2.** (*in telegraphic communications*) groupe *m* de caractères; groupe *m* de mots **3.** (*collection of icons in a GUI*) groupe *m* d'icônes; groupe *m* de programmes **4.** (*collection of users*) groupe *m* (d'utilisateurs) ■ *verb* (*bring together*) grouper *vt*

Group 3 /ˌgruːp ˈθriː/ *noun* groupe *m* 3

group icon /gruːp ˈaɪkɒn/ *noun* icône *f* de groupe

group mark /gruːp mɑːk/, **group marker** /gruːp ˈmɑːkə/ *noun* marqueur *m* de groupe

group poll /ˈgruːp pəʊl/ *noun* appel *m* sélectif de groupe

groupware /ˈgruːpweə/ *noun* (*software written to be used by a group*) logiciel *m* de groupe (de travail)

GSM /ˌdʒiː es ˈem/ *noun* système *m* mondial de communications mobiles

guard band /ˈgɑːd bænd/ *noun* (*section of magnetic tape*) bande *f* de fréquence intercalaire; bande *f* de protection

guard bit /ˈgɑːd bɪt/ *noun* bit *m* de protection

GUI /ˈguːi/ *noun* GUI

guide bar /ˈgaɪd bɑː/ *noun* ligne *f* de référence; ligne *f* guide

gulp /gʌlp/ *noun* multiplet *m*; groupe *m* d'octets

gun /gʌn/ *noun* canon *m* à électrons

gutter /ˈgʌtə/ *noun* (*inner margin between two facing pages of a book*) marge *f* intérieure

H

H *abbr* (*hex*) hexadécimal

H.323, H.324 *noun* norme *f* H.323

hack /hæk/ *verb* **1.** (*to gain access to a computer system for criminal purposes*) pirater un système; faire du piratage informatique; s'introduire sans autorisation dans un système **2.** (*to gain access to a computer system for criminal purposes*) faire du piratage informatique; pirater un système; (*for criminal purposes*) s'introduire sans autorisation dans un système

hacker /ˈhækə/ *noun* (*person who breaks into a computer system for criminal purposes*) pirate *m* informatique

> 'The two were also charged with offences under the Computer Misuse Act and found guilty of the very actions upon which every hacker is intent.' [*Computing*]

hairline rule /ˈheəˌlaɪn ruːl/ *noun* (*in DTP system: very thin line*) filet *m* ultrafin

half adder /hɑːf ˈædə/ *noun* additionneur *m* à deux entrées; demi-additionneur *m*

half card /ˌhɑːf ˈkɑːd/ *noun* carte *f* demi-longueur; demi-carte *f*

half-duplex modem /ˌhɑːf ˌdjuːpleks ˈməʊdem/ *noun* modem *m* half duplex

half-height drive /ˌhɑːf haɪt ˈdraɪv/ *noun* unité *f* de disquettes (de) demi-hauteur

half-intensity /hɑːf ɪnˈtensɪti/ *adjective* demi-intensité *fpl*

halftone /ˌhɑːfˈtəʊn/ *noun* demi-teinte *f*

half word /ˌhɑːf ˈwɜːd/ *noun* demi-mot *m*

Hall effect /hɔːl ɪˈfekt/ *noun* effet *m* Hall ◇ **Hall effect switch** commutateur *m* à effet (de champ) Hall

halt /hɔːlt/ *noun* arrêt *m*

halt condition /hɔːlt kənˈdɪʃ(ə)n/ *noun* condition *f* d'arrêt

halt instruction /hɔːlt ɪnˈstrʌkʃən/ *noun* instruction *f* d'arrêt

Hamming code /ˈhæmɪŋ kəʊd/ *noun* code *m*; codage *m* de Hamming

Hamming distance /ˈhæmɪŋ ˌdɪstəns/ *noun* distance *f* entre signaux; distance *f* de Hamming

hand /hænd/ *noun* main *f* ◇ **hands-free telephone** (*mobile phone*) téléphone *m* mains-libres ◇ **hand viewer** petite visionneuse *f* (qu'on tient à la main)

hand-held computer /ˌhænd held kəmˈpjuːtə/, **hand-held programmable** /ˌhænd held ˈprəʊgræməb(ə)l/ *noun* ordinateur *m* de poche

hand-held scanner /ˌhænd held ˈskænə/ *noun* scanner *m* qu'on tient à la main

handle /ˈhænd(ə)l/ *noun* **1.** (*number to identify an active file*) numéro *m* d'ordre; numéro *m* d'identification d'un fichier **2.** (*small square to change a shape*) poignée *f* (de manipulation); pavé *m* ◇ **to stretch the box in the DTP program, select it once to display the handles then drag one handle to change its shape** dans ce programme de PAO, on sélectionne d'abord la boîte qu'on veut agrandir pour faire apparaître les poignées, puis on tire une des poignées pour modifier la taille de la boîte

handler /ˈhændlə/ *noun* (*driver*) logiciel *m* de commande; gestionnaire *m*; pilote *m* ◇ **the disk drive handler code is supplied in the library** le code du gestionnaire de l'unité de disque se trouve dans la bibliothèque

handshake /ˈhæn(d)ˌʃeɪk/, **handshaking** *noun* (*between transmitter and receptor*) protocole *m* de validation de transfert de données; protocole *m* de validation d'échange d'informations

handshake I/O control /ˌhæn(d)ʃeɪk aɪ ˈəʊ kənˌtrəʊl/ *noun* contrôle *m* de mise en communication

hands off /ˌhændz ˈɒf/ *adjective* (*training*) théorique accès à l'ordinateur; (*automatic*) automatique; (*automatic working system*) sans intervention manuelle; sans accès à l'ordinateur

hands on /ˌhændz ˈɒn/ *adjective* (*manual*) manuel; (*training*) pratique

handwriting recognition /ˈhændraɪtɪŋ ˌrekəgnɪʃ(ə)n/ *noun* (*of software – that recognises handwritten text*) reconnaissance *f* d'écriture

hang /hæŋ/ *verb* (*to stop responding*) se perdre; être accroché dans une boucle

hangover /ˈhæŋəʊvə/ *noun* (*on a TV screen*) traînée *f*; rémanence *f* d'image

hangup /ˈhæŋʌp/ *noun* arrêt *m* inattendu

hard /hɑːd/ *adjective* (*solid*) dur; (*not programmable*) fermé

hardboot /ˈhɑːdbuːt/ *verb* démarrer à froid; mettre en route

hard card /ˌhɑːd 'kɑːd/ *noun* carte *f* de disque dur

hard copy /ˌhɑːd 'kɒpi/ *noun* (*printed document or copy of information*) sortie *f* d'imprimante

hard copy interface /ˌhɑːd 'kɒpi ˌɪntəfeɪs/ *noun* interface *f* d'imprimante

hard disk /ˌhɑːd 'dɪsk/ *noun* disque *m* dur

hard disk drive /ˌhɑːd 'dɪsk ˌdraɪv/ *noun* (*to store and retrieve data*) unité *f* de disque dur; disque *m* dur

hard drive /'hɑːd draɪv/ *noun* unité *f* de disque dur; disque *m* dur ◇ **a 6.4GB hard drive** (unité de) disque dur de 6,4 Go

hard error /hɑːd 'erə/ *noun* erreur *f*

hard failure /hɑːd 'feɪljə/ *noun* défaillance *f* du matériel; panne *f* de l'ordinateur

hard reset /hɑːd ˌriː'set/ *noun* réinitialisation *f* du système en utilisant le contacteur

hard return /hɑːd rɪ'tɜːn/ *noun* fin *f* de paragraphe

hardware /'hɑːdˌweə/ *noun* (*physical components of a computer*) matériel *m* informatique

'Seuqent's Platform division will focus on hardware and software manufacture, procurement and marketing, with the Enterprise division concentrating on services and client-server implementation.' [*Computing*]

hardware compatibility /ˌhɑːdweə kəm ˌpætə'bɪlɪti/ *noun* compatibilité *f* du matériel

hardware configuration /ˌhɑːdweə kən ˌfɪgjə'reɪʃ(ə)n/ *noun* configuration *f* du matériel

hardware dependent /ˌhɑːdweə dɪ 'pendənt/ *adjective* dépendant, -e du matériel

hardware failure /'hɑːdweə ˌfeɪljə/ *noun* défaillance *f* du matériel; panne *f* de l'ordinateur

hardware interrupt /'hɑːdweə ˌɪntərʌpt/ *noun* interruption *f* provenant d'une machine

hardware platform /'hɑːdweə ˌplætfɔːm/ *noun* plate-forme *f* matérielle; plate-forme *f* de matériel

hardware reliability /ˌhɑːdweə rɪˌlaɪə'bɪlɪti/ *noun* fiabilité *f*

hardware reset /ˌhɑːdweə 'riːset/ *noun* interrupteur *m* de reprise

hardware security /ˌhɑːdweə sɪ'kjʊərɪti/ *noun* sécurité *f* du matériel

hardwired connection /ˌhɑːdwaɪəd kə 'nekʃ(ə)n/ *noun* câblage *m* permanent; connexion *f* fixe

hardwired logic /ˌhɑːdwaɪəd 'lɒdʒɪk/ *noun* logique *f* câblée

hardwired program /ˌhɑːdwaɪəd 'prəʊgræm/ *noun* programme *m* en logique câblée

harmonics /hɑː'mɒnɪks/ *noun* harmonique *f*

hartley /'hɑːtli/ *noun* (*unit of information equal to 3.32 bits*) hartley *m*

hash /hæʃ/ *noun* signe *m* typographique &#; ■ *verb* générer un hash code

hash code /ˌhæʃ 'kəʊd/ *noun* hash code *m*

hash-code system /'hæʃ kəʊd ˌsɪstəm/ *noun* système *m* de hash code

hash index /hæʃ 'ɪndeks/ *noun* index *m* hash code

hashing function /hæʃɪŋ 'fʌŋkʃən/ *noun* algorithme *m*

hashmark /'hæʃmɑːk/, **hash mark** /'hæʃ mɑːk/ *noun* (*printed sign &#;*) signe *m* typographique

hash table /hæʃ 'teɪb(ə)l/ *noun* table *f* des adresses hash codées

hash total /hæʃ 'təʊt(ə)l/ *noun* (*total of a number of hashed entries*) total *m* de vérification pour hash code

hash value /hæʃ 'væljuː/ *noun* valeur *f* d'un hash code

Hayes AT command set /ˌheɪz eɪ tiː kə 'mɑːnd set/ *noun* jeu *m* de commandes Hayes AT

Hayes-compatible /ˌheɪz kəm'pætɪb(ə)l/ *adjective* compatible Hayes

Hayes Corporation /'heɪz ˌkɔːpəreɪʃ(ə)n/ (*modem manufacturer*) Hayes Corporation™

hazard /'hæzəd/ *noun* erreur *f*; défaut *m* d'horloge

hazard-free implementation /ˌhæzəd friː ˌɪmplɪmen'teɪʃ(ə)n/ *noun* application *f* qui tolère toutes les erreurs possibles

haze /heɪz/ *noun* voile *m*

HD /ˌeɪtʃ 'diː/ *noun* half duplex; bidirectionnel à l'alternat

HDD *abbr* (*hard disk drive*) lecteur *m* de disque dur

HDLC *abbr* (*high-level data link control*) procédure *f* de commande à haut niveau

HDTV *abbr* (*high definition television*) télévision *f* à haute définition

HDX *abbr* (*half duplex*) bidirectionnel à l'alternat

head /hed/ *noun* **1.** (*device*) début *m* de fichier **2.** (*of book or page*) tête *f* **3.** (*of book or page*) tête *f* de bobine; amorce *f* **4.** (*of film or tape*) tête *f* ■ *verb* (*to be the first item in a list*) être en tête de liste ◇ **head of form (HOF)** tête *or* début *m* d'une page (de papier listing) ◇ **the queue was headed by my file** mon fichier était en tête de la file d'attente

head alignment /hed ə'laɪnmənt/ *noun* alignement *m* de la tête de lecture

head cleaning disk /'hed ˌkliːnɪŋ dɪsk/ *noun* disquette *f* de nettoyage des têtes

head crash /'hed kræʃ/ *noun* crash *m* du disque dur causé par la tête de lecture; choc *m* de la tête de lecture contre le disque; atterrissage *m* de la tête de lecture

head demagnetiser /'hed diːˌmægnətaɪzə/ *noun* démagnétiseur *m* de tête

head end /'hed end/ *noun* tête *f* de réseau

header /'hedə/ *noun* **1.** (*in a local area network*) bloc *m* d'identification **2.** (*at top of a list of data*) en-tête *m* de fichier **3.** (*at top of page*) en-tête *m*; titre *m* courant

header block /'hedə blɒk/ *noun* bloc *m* d'identification

header card /'hedə kɑːd/ *noun* carte *f* en-tête

header label /'hedə ˌleɪb(ə)l/ *noun* label *m* d'identification

head gap /'hed gæp/ *noun* entrefer *m*

heading /'hedɪŋ/ *noun* **1.** (*name or title of document or file*) en-tête *m*; titre *m*; rubrique *f*; (*title of document or file*) nom *m* **2.** (*at the top of each page*) titre *m* courant

headlife /'hedlaɪf/ *noun* durée *f* de vie de la tête

headline /'hedlaɪn/ *noun* en-tête *m*; titre *m*; rubrique *f*

head of form /ˌhed əv 'fɔːm/ *noun* tête *f* d'une page; début *m* d'une page

head park /'hed pɑːk/ *noun* mise *f* en position de transport de la tête; parcage *m* de la tête

head positioning /hed pə'zɪʃ(ə)nɪŋ/ *noun* positionnement *m* de la tête

head wheel /'hed wiːl/ *noun* molette *f* de pressage; galet *m* presseur

heap /hiːp/ *noun* **1.** (*temporary storage area*) pile *f* binaire **2.** (*binary tree*) pile *f*

heat-sensitive paper /ˌhiːt ˌsensɪtɪv 'peɪpə/ *noun* papier *m* thermique

heat-sink /hiːt sɪŋk/ *noun* dissipateur *m* thermique; radiateur *m* à ailette(s)

helical scan /ˌhelɪk(ə)l 'skæn/ *noun* lecture *f* hélicoïdale

help /help/ *noun* (*function*) aide *f* ◇ **context sensitive help** (*help message*) aide *f* en ligne *or* aide contextuelle

help desk /'help desk/ *noun* service *m* d'assistance

help key /'help kiː/ *noun* touche *f* d'aide ◇ **hit the HELP key if you want information about what to do next** appuyez sur la touche AIDE *or* sur la touche d'aide pour connaître la marche à suivre

help screen /'help skriːn/ *noun* écran *m* d'aide

hertz /hɜːts/ *noun* (*unit of frequency*) hertz *m*

heterogeneous multiplexing /ˌhetərəʊdʒiːniəs 'mʌltɪˌpleksɪŋ/ *noun* multiplexage *m* hétérogène

heterogeneous network /ˌhetərəʊdʒiːniəs 'netwɜːk/ *noun* réseau *m* informatique hétérogène

heuristic /hjʊə'rɪstɪk/ *adjective* heuristique ◇ **a heuristic program learns from its previous actions and decisions** un programme heuristique exploite ses actions et décisions antérieures

Hewlett Packard /ˌhewlət 'pækɑːd/ (*manufacturer of computers, etc.*) Hewlett Packard™ ◇ **Hewlett Packard Interface Bus (HPIB)** (*standard method of interfacing peripheral devices*) bus *m* d'interface HP ◇ **Hewlett Packard Printer Control Language (HP-PCL)** (*standard set of commands*) langage *m* de contrôle d'imprimante HP *or* langage HP-PCL

Hewlett Packard Graphics Language /ˌhewlət ˌpækɑːd 'græfɪks ˌlæŋgwɪdʒ/ (*standard set of commands used to describe graphics*) langage *m* graphique Hewlett Packard

Hewlett Packard Interface Bus /ˌhewlət ˌpækɑːd 'ɪntəfeɪs bʌs/ (*standard method of interfacing peripheral devices*) bus *m* d'interface HP

Hewlett Packard LaserJet /ˌhewlət ˌpækɑːd 'leɪzədʒet/ (*trade name for a laser printer that uses its PCL language to describe a page*) imprimante *f* graphique HP LaserJet

Hewlett Packard Printer Control Language /ˌhewlət ˌpækɑːd ˌprɪntə kən'trəʊl ˌlæŋgwɪdʒ/ (*standard set of commands that allows a software application to control a laser printer's functions*) langage *m* de contrôle d'imprimante HP; langage *m* HP-PCL

hex /heksəˌdesɪm(ə)l nəʊ'teɪʃ(ə)n/, **hexadecimal notation** *noun* numération *f* hexadécimale

hex dump /'heks dʌmp/ *noun* vidage *m* hexadécimal

hex keypad /heks 'kiːˌpæd/ *noun* clavier *m* hexadécimal

HFS /ˌeɪtʃ ef 'es/ *noun* système *m* de gestion hiérarchique des fichiers

hidden files /'hɪd(ə)n faɪlz/ *plural noun* fichiers *mpl* cachés

hidden line algorithm /ˌhɪd(ə)n laɪn 'ælgərɪð(ə)m/ *noun* algorithme *m* d'effacement de lignes cachées

hidden line removal /ˌhɪd(ə)n 'laɪn rɪ ˌmuːvəl/ *noun* effacement *m* des lignes cachées

hidden lines /'hɪd(ə)n laɪnz/ *plural noun* lignes cachées

hierarchical /haɪə'rɑːkɪk(ə)l/ *adjective* hiérarchique; hiérarchisé

hierarchical communications system /ˌhaɪərɑːkɪk(ə)l kəˌmjuːnɪ'keɪʃ(ə)nz ˌsɪstəm/ *noun* système *m* de communication hiérarchisé

hierarchical computer network /ˌhaɪərɑːkɪk(ə)l kəm'pjuːtə ˌnetwɜːk/ *noun* réseau *m* d'ordinateurs hiérarchisé

hierarchical database /ˌhaɪərɑːkɪk(ə)l 'deɪtəbeɪs/ *noun* base *f* de données hiérarchisées

hierarchical directory /ˌhaɪərɑːkɪk(ə)l daɪ 'rekt(ə)ri/ *noun* répertoire *m* hiérarchique

hierarchical filing system /ˌhaɪərɑːkɪk(ə)l 'faɪlɪŋ ˌsɪstəm/ *noun* système *m* de fichiers hiérarchisés

hierarchical routing /ˌhaɪərɑːkɪk(ə)l 'ruːtɪŋ/ *noun* acheminement *m*

hierarchy /'haɪərɑːki/ *noun* hiérarchie *f*

high definition television /ˌhaɪ ˌdefɪnɪʃ(ə)n ˈtelɪˌvɪʒ(ə)n/ *noun* télévision *f* à haute définition

high density storage /ˌhaɪ ˌdensɪ ˈstɔːrɪdʒti/ *noun* mémoire *f*

high-end /ˈhaɪ end/ *adjective* haut de gamme

high fidelity /haɪ fɪˈdeləti/ *noun* haute *f* fidélité; hi-fi *f*

high-level data link control /haɪ ˌlev(ə)l ˌdeɪtə lɪŋk kənˈtrəʊl/ *noun* contrôle *m* de liaison de données de haut niveau; protocole *m* d'interfaçage

high-level data link control station /ˌhaɪ ˌlev(ə)l ˌdeɪtə lɪŋk kənˈtrəʊl ˌsteɪʃ(ə)n/ *noun* équipement *m* interfacé HDLC

high-level language /ˌhaɪ ˌlev(ə)l ˈlæŋgwɪdʒ/, **high-level programming language** /haɪ ˌlev(ə)l ˌprəʊgræmɪŋ ˈlæŋgwɪdʒ/ *noun* langage *m* de programmation évolué; langage *m* de haut niveau

highlight /ˈhaɪlaɪt/ *noun* caractères *mpl* mis en évidence; mots *mpl* mis en évidence ■ *verb* (*underscore*) surligner *vt*; (*on screen*) mettre en évidence; mettre en surbrillance

highlight bar /ˈhaɪˌlaɪt bɑː/ *noun* barre *f* de sélection

high memory /haɪ ˈmem(ə)ri/ *noun* mémoire *f* haute

high memory area /ˌhaɪ ˈmem(ə)ri ˌeəriə/ *noun* zone *f* de mémoire supérieure

high order /haɪ ˈɔːdə/ *noun* chiffre *m* de poids fort

high performance filing system /ˌhaɪ pə ˌfɔːməns ˈfaɪlɪŋ ˌsɪstəm/ *noun* gestionnaire *m* de fichiers HPFS

high priority program /ˌhaɪ praɪˌɒrɪti ˈprəʊgræm/ *noun* programme *m* prioritaire

high-resolution /haɪ ˌrezəˈluːʃ(ə)n/, **high-res** /haɪ rez/ *noun* haute définition *f*; haute résolution *f*

high resolution graphics /ˌhaɪ ˌrezəluːʃ(ə)n ˈgræfɪks/ *noun* graphiques *mpl* haute définition

High Sierra /ˌhaɪ siˈerə/ *noun* High Sierra

high-spec /haɪ spek/ *plural noun* de haute précision; de haute technologie

high specification /haɪ ˌspesɪfɪˈkeɪʃ(ə)n/ *noun* haute précision; haute technologie

high-speed /ˈhaɪ spiːd/ *adjective* rapide; ultrarapide; de grande vitesse; (*film*) ultrasensible ◇ **high-speed duplicator** duplicateur *m* rapide *or* grande vitesse ◇ **high-speed serial interface (HSSI)** (*serial link that can transfer data at data rates up to 52Mbits/second*) interface *f* série version rapide *or* interface HSSI

high-speed carry /ˌhaɪ spiːd ˈkæri/ *noun* report *m* accéléré

high-speed serial interface /haɪ spiːd ˌsɪəriəl ˈɪntəfeɪs/ *noun* interface *f* HSSI

high-speed skip /ˌhaɪ spiːd ˈskɪp/ *noun* (*printing*) saut *m* rapide

high-tech /haɪ ˈtek/ *adjective* (*advanced*) technologie *f* de pointe; haute technologie *f*

high technology /haɪ tekˈnɒlədʒi/ *noun* haute technologie *f*

highway /ˈhaɪweɪ/ *noun* (*bus*) bus *m*

hill climbing /hɪl ˈklaɪmɪŋ/ *noun* (*in an expert system*) escalade *f*; méthode *f* ascendante

hi-res /haɪ reɪz/ *noun* haute *f* résolution

histogram /ˈhɪstəgræm/ *noun* histogramme *m*

history /ˈhɪst(ə)ri/ *noun* historique *m*

hit /hɪt/ *noun* (*successful search*) réussite *f*; trouvaille *f*; réponse *f*; (*of Web page*) contact *m*; consultation *f*; visite *f* ■ *verb* (*to press a key*) appuyer (sur une touche) ◇ **hit on the line** (*noise*) courte perturbation sur la ligne ◇ **there are three hits for this search key** cette clé (de recherche) produit trois contacts ◇ **there was a hit after just a few seconds** il n'a fallu que quelques secondes pour trouver la réponse *or* pour obtenir les données

hit point /ˈhɪt pɔɪnt/ *noun* point *m* de vie

HLDLC *abbr* (*high-level data link control*) procédure *f* de commande à haut niveau

HLL *abbr* (*high-level language*) langage *m* évolué

HLS *abbr* (*hue, lightness, saturation*) TSL

HMA *abbr* (*high memory area*) zone *f* de mémoire haute

HMI *abbr* (*human-machine interface*) interface *f* homme machine

HOF *abbr* (*head of form*) tête *f* d'une page; début *m* d'une page

hold /həʊld/ *noun* (*TV*) signal *m* de synchronisation; (*oscilloscope*) commande *f* de stabilisation du signal ■ *verb* (*in memory*) garder *vt* ◇ **on hold** (*mobile phone*) en veille

holding loop /ˈhəʊldɪŋ luːp/ *noun* boucle *f* de maintien

holding time /ˈhəʊldɪŋ taɪm/ *noun* temps *m* d'occupation de la ligne

holdup /ˈhɒldʌp/ *noun* **1.** (*period over which power will be supplied by a UPS*) temps *m* de débit d'un onduleur; temps *m* d'un dispositif de secours; (*pause in a program*) décrochage *m* **2.** (*pause in a program*) pause *f* accidentelle

hologram /ˈhɒləˌgræm/ *noun* hologramme *m*

holographic image /ˌhɒləgræfɪk ˈɪmɪdʒ/ *noun* hologramme *m*

holographic storage /ˌhɒləgræfɪk ˈstɔːrɪdʒ/ *noun* stockage *m*

home /həʊm/ *noun* (*starting point for printing on a screen*) position *f* initiale; position *f* de départ

home banking /ˌhəʊm ˈbæŋkɪŋ/ *noun* télébanque *f*

home computer /həʊm kəm'pjuːtə/ *noun* (*computer designed for home use*) ordinateur *m* pour la maison

home key /'həʊm kiː/ *noun* touche *f* Home

home page /'həʊm peɪdʒ/ *noun* (*opening page of a Web site*) page *f* d'accueil

home record /həʊm 'rekɔːd/ *noun* début *m* d'enregistrement

homogeneous computer network /ˌhəʊməʊdʒiːniəs kəm'pjuːtə ˌnetwɜːk/ *noun* réseau *m* informatique homogène

homogeneous multiplexing /ˌhəʊməʊdʒiːniəs 'mʌltɪˌpleksɪŋ/ *noun* (*switching multiplexer system*) multiplexage *m* homogène

hood /hʊd/ *noun* capot *m*

hook /hʊk/ *noun* (*point where a programmer can insert test code or debugging code*) point *m* d'insertion (de code); point *m* d'accrochage

hop /hɒp/ *noun* (*transmission*) bond *m*

hopper /'hɒpə/ *noun* chargeur *m* de cartes perforées

horizontal axis /ˌhɒrɪzɒnt(ə)l 'æksɪs/ *noun* axe *m* des abscisses

horizontal blanking period /ˌhɒrɪzɒnt(ə)l 'blæŋkɪŋ ˌpɪəriəd/ *noun* période *f* de suppression horizontale

horizontal check /ˌhɒrɪzɒnt(ə)l 'tʃek/ *noun* contrôle *m* horizontal

horizontal scrollbar /ˌhɒrɪzɒnt(ə)l 'skrəʊlbɑː/ *noun* barre *f* de défilement horizontal

horizontal scrolling /ˌhɒrɪzɒnt(ə)l 'skrəʊlɪŋ/ *noun* défilement *m* horizontal

horizontal wraparound /ˌhɒrɪzɒnt(ə)l 'ræpəˌraʊnd/ *noun* (*movement of cursor*) enroulement *m*

host /həʊst/ *noun, adjective* hôte *m*

> '...you select fonts manually or through commands sent from the host computer along with the text' [*Byte*]

host adapter /həʊst ə'dæptə/ *noun* adaptateur *m* de l'ordinateur hôte ◇ **the cable to connect the scanner to the host adapter is included** le câble qui relie le scanner et l'adaptateur de l'ordinateur hôte est fourni

host address /'həʊst əˌdres/ *noun* adresse *f* de site

host computer /həʊst kəm'pjuːtə/ *noun* **1.** (*main controlling computer*) ordinateur *m* principal; ordinateur *m* hôte **2.** (*used to write and debug software*) serveur *m* **3.** (*in a network*) serveur *m*

> '...you select fonts manually or through commands sent from the host computer along with the text' [*Byte*]

hosting service provider /'həʊstɪŋ ˌsɜːvɪs prəˌvaɪdə/ *noun* service *m* d'ordinateur central

host name /'həʊst ˌneɪm/ *noun* nom *m* de site Web

host number /'həʊst ˌnʌmbə/ *noun* adresse *f* Internet; adresse *f* de site

host service /'həʊst ˌsɜːvɪs/ *noun* service *m* d'ordinateur central

hot /hɒt/ *adjective* chaud

hot chassis /hɒt 'ʃæsi/ *noun* châssis *m* sous tension

hot fix /ˌhɒt 'fɪks/ *noun* (*repairing*) correction *f*

hot key /'hɒt kiː/ *noun* (*key which starts a process*) touche *f* d'activation

hot link /ˌhɒt 'lɪŋk/ *noun* (*command within a hypertext program*) lien *m* actif; lien *m* hypertexte

hot plugging /'hɒt ˌplʌgɪŋ/ *noun* connexion *f* à chaud

hotspot /'hɒtspɒt/ *noun* point *m* chaud; (*area or image*) zone *f* active; zone *f* sur laquelle on peut cliquer ◇ **the image of the trumpet is a hotspot and will play a sound when you move the pointer over it** l'image de la trompette est une zone active qui produira un son lorsqu'on la sélectionne avec le pointeur

hot standby /hɒt 'stændbaɪ/ *noun* (*piece of hardware used as backup*) système *m* de secours prêt à fonctionner

hot swapping /'hɒt ˌswɒpɪŋ/ *noun* connexion *f* à chaud

hotword /'hɒtwɜːd/ *noun* mot *m* actif; lien *m* hypertexte

hot zone /'hɒt zəʊn/ *noun* zone *f* sensible/active; zone *f* sur laquelle on peut cliquer ◇ **hot zone graphic** graphisme à zone sensible *or* cliquable; graphique à zone sensible *or* à zone active

housekeeping /'haʊsˌkiːpɪŋ/ *noun* maintenance *f* courante

housekeeping routine /'haʊskiːpɪŋ ruːˌtiːn/ *noun* programme *m* de maintenance

housing /'haʊzɪŋ/ *noun* boîtier *m* ◇ **the computer housing was damaged when it fell on the floor** quand on a laissé tomber l'ordinateur, son boîtier s'est abîmé

howler /'haʊlə/ *noun* (*sound device*) avertisseur *m* (sonore)

HP *abbr* (*Hewlett Packard*) HP

HPFS /ˌeɪtʃ piː ef 'es/ *noun* gestionnaire *m* de fichiers HPFS

HPGL *abbr* (*Hewlett Packard Graphics Language*) langage *m* graphique Hewlett Packard

HPIB *abbr* (*Hewlett Packard Interface Bus*) bus *m* d'interface Hewlett Packard

HP-PCL /ˌeɪtʃ ˌpiː ˌpiː siː 'el/ *abbr* (*Hewlett Packard Printer Control Language*) langage *m* de commande d'imprimante

HRG /ˌeɪtʃ ɑː 'dʒiː/ *noun* graphiques *mpl* haute définition ◇ **the HRG board can control up to 300 pixels per inch** la carte graphique haute définition contrôle jusqu'à 300 pixels par pouce

HSSI /ˌeɪtʃ es es 'aɪ/ *noun* interface *f* HSSI

HSV *abbr* (*hue, saturation and value*) HSV

HTML /ˌeɪtʃ tiː em ˈel/ *noun* langage *m* HTML

HTTP /ˌeɪtʃ tiː tiː ˈpiː/ *noun* protocole *m* HTTP

hub /hʌb/ *noun* (*central ring in a star-topology network*) concentrateur *m*; hub *m*

hue /hjuː/ *noun* **1.** teinte *f* **2.** tonalité *f*

hue, saturation and intensity /ˌhjuː ˌsætʃəreɪʃ(ə)n ənd ɪnˈtensɪti/ *noun* teinte *f*

Huffman code /ˈhʌfmən kəʊd/ *noun* (*data compression code*) code *m* de Huffman

human-computer interface /ˌhjuːmən kəm ˌpjuːtə ˈɪntəfeɪs/ *noun* interface *f* utilisateur/machine; interface *f* homme/machine

human-machine interface /ˌhjuːmən mə ˌʃiːn ˈɪntəfeɪs/ *noun* interface *f* utilisateur/machine; interface *f* homme/machine

hunting /ˈhʌntɪŋ/ *noun* recherche *f*

hybrid circuit /ˌhaɪbrɪd ˈsɜːkɪt/ *noun* (*connection of electronic components*) circuit *m* hybride; circuit *m* mixte; circuit *m* composite

hybrid computer /ˌhaɪbrɪd kəmˈpjuːtə/ *noun* ordinateur *m* hybride

hybrid interface /ˌhaɪbrɪd ˈɪntəfeɪs/ *noun* interface *f* hybride

hybrid system /ˌhaɪbrɪd ˈsɪstəm/ *noun* système *m* hybride

HyperCard /ˈhaɪpəkɑːd/ (*database system*) HyperCard™

hyperlink /ˈhaɪpəlɪŋk/ *noun* (*word or image or button in a Web page or multimedia title that moves the user to another page when clicked*) lien *m* hypertexte

hypermedia /ˈhaɪpəmiːdiə/ *noun* (*hypertext document*) hypermédia *m*

HyperTalk /ˈhaɪpətɔːk/ (*programming language*) HyperTalk™

HyperTerminal /ˈhaɪpəˌtɜːmɪn(ə)l/ *noun* HyperTerminal

hypertext /ˈhaɪpətekst/ *noun* **1.** (*system of organising information*) hypertexte *m* **2.** (*linking one word or image to another page*) hypertexte *m* ◇ **hypertext document** document *m* hypertexte ◇ **in this hypertext page, click once on the word ‘computer’ and it will tell you what a computer is** dans cette page hypertexte, cliquez sur le mot ‘ordinateur’ et vous obtiendrez la définition du mot ‘ordinateur’

hypertext markup language /ˌhaɪpətekst ˈmɑːkʌp ˌlæŋgwɪdʒ/ *noun* langage *m* HTML

hypertext transfer protocol /ˌhaɪpətekst ˈtrænsfɜː ˌprəʊtəkɒl/ *noun* protocole *m* HTTP

hyphenated /ˈhaɪfəneɪtɪd/ *adjective* qui s’écrit avec un trait d’union

hyphenate justify /ˌhaɪfəneɪt ˈdʒʌstɪfaɪ/ *verb* couper un mot et justifier

hyphenation /ˌhaɪfəˈneɪʃ(ə)n/ *noun* coupe *f* d’un mot

hyphenation and justification /haɪfə ˌnaɪʃ(ə)n ən ˌdʒʌstɪfɪˈkeɪʃ(ə)n/ *noun* coupe *f* de mot (en bout de ligne) et justification *f* ◇ **an American hyphenation and justification program will not work with British English spellings** un programme de coupe de mots et justification établi aux Etats-Unis ne peut être utilisé pour un texte en anglais britannique

Hz *abbr* (*hertz*) hertz *m*

I

IAM /ˌaɪ eɪ 'em/ *noun* mémoire *f* à accès intermédiaire

IANA *abbr* (*Internet Assigned Numbers Authority*) IANA *f*

IAR /ˌaɪ eɪ 'ɑː/ *abbr* (*instruction address register*) registre *m* d'adresse d'instruction

IAS /ˌaɪ eɪ 'es/ *noun* mémoire *f* interne à accès immédiat

I-beam /aɪ biːm/ *noun* (*cursor shaped like 'I'*) curseur *m* (en) bâton; curseur *m* en I

IBG *abbr* (*interblock gap*) espace *m* interbloc

IBM /ˌaɪ biː 'em/ (*largest computer company in the world*) IBM

IBM AT /ˌaɪ biː em eɪ 'tiː/ (*trade name for a personal computer based on the Intel 80286 16-bit processor*) ordinateur IBM AT

IBM AT keyboard /ˌaɪ biː em eɪ ˌtiː 'kiːbɔːd/ (*keyboard layout that features 12 function keys in a row along the top of the keyboard, with a separate numeric keypad*) clavier IBM AT

IBM-compatible /ˌaɪ biː em kəm'pætɪb(ə)l/ *adjective* compatible IBM

IBM PC /ˌaɪ biː em piː 'siː/ (*trade name for a personal computer based on the Intel 8088 8-bit processor*) IBM PC

IBM PC keyboard /ˌaɪ biː em piː ˌsiː 'kiːbɔːd/ (*keyboard layout that features 10 function keys arranged to the left of the main keys, with no separate numeric keypad*) clavier IBM PC

IBM PS/2 /ˌaɪ biː ˌem 'pɜːs(ə)nəl/, **IBM Personal System/2** (*trade name for a range of personal computers*) IBM PS/2

IBM XT /ˌaɪ biː em eks 'tiː/ (*trade name for a personal computer based on the IBM PC*) IBM-XT

IC *abbr* (*integrated circuit*) circuit *m* intégré

icand /'ɪkænd/ *noun* multiplicande *m*

ICMP /ˌaɪ ciː em 'piː/ *noun* protocole *m* ICMP

icon /'aɪkɒn/, **ikon** *noun* icône *f* ◇ **click twice over the wordprocessor icon – the picture of the typewriter** cliquez deux fois sur l'icône Machine à écrire pour accéder au traitement de texte ◇ **the icon for the graphics program is a small picture of a palette** l'icône du programme graphique à la forme d'une petite palette

'Despite (or because of?) the swap file, loading was slow and the hourglass icon of the mouse pointer frequently returned to the arrow symbol well before loading was complete.' [*Computing*]

ICQ (*pronounced 'I-seek-you'*) logiciel ICQ (pour messagerie instantanée)

ID *abbr* **1.** (*identification*) identification *f* **2.** (*identifier*) identificateur *m*; caractère *m* d'identification

ID code /ˌaɪ'diː kəʊd/ *noun* code *m* personnel; code *m* d'identification

IDE /ˌaɪ diː 'iː/ *noun* contrôleur *m* de disque IDE

identification /aɪˌdentɪfɪ'keɪʃ(ə)n/ *noun* identification *f*

identification character /aɪˌdentɪfɪ 'keɪʃ(ə)n ˌkærɪktə/ *noun* caractère *m* d'identification

identification division /aɪˌdentɪfɪ'keɪʃ(ə)n dɪˌvɪʒ(ə)n/ *noun* division *f* avec paramètres d'identification

identifier /aɪ'dentɪfaɪə/ *noun* (*set of characters used to distinguish between different blocks of data or files*) identificateur *m*; caractère *m* d'identification

identifier word /aɪ'dentɪfaɪə wɜːd/ *noun* identificateur *m*; mot *m* d'identification

identity burst /aɪ'dentɪti bɜːst/ *noun* séquence *f* d'identification

identity gate /aɪ'dentɪti geɪt/, **identity element** /aɪ'dentɪti ˌelɪmənt/ *noun* porte *f* d'identité

identity number /aɪ'dentɪti ˌnʌmbə/ *noun* numéro *m* de code personnel

identity operation /aɪˌdentɪti ˌɒpə'reɪʃ(ə)n/ *noun* opération *f* d'identité

idle /'aɪd(ə)l/ *adjective* (*machine*) au repos

idle character /ˌaɪd(ə)l 'kærɪktə/ *noun* caractère *m* nul

idle time /'aɪd(ə)l taɪm/ *noun* (*of a device*) temps *m* de latence

IDP *abbr* (*integrated data processing*) traitement *m* de données intégré

IEC connector /ˌaɪ iː 'siː kəˌnektə/ *noun* (*standard for a three-pin connector*) connecteur *m* IEC

IEE *abbr* (*Institution of Electrical Engineers*) IEE

IEEE *abbr* (*Institute of Electrical and Electronic Engineers*) IEEE

IEEE-488 *noun* norme *f* IEEE-488 (d'interface parallèle standard)

IEEE-802.2 *noun* norme *f* IEEE 802.2

IEEE-802.3 *noun* norme *f* IEEE 802.3

IEEE-802.4 *noun* norme *f* IEEE 802.4

IEEE-802.5 *noun* norme *f* IEEE-802.5

IEEE bus *noun* bus *m* IEEE

ier multiplicateur *m*

IETF /ˌaɪ iː tiː 'ef/ *noun* groupe *m* de travail IETF

IF statement /ɪf 'steɪtmənt/ *noun* instruction *f* IF; instruction *f* SI

IF-THEN-ELSE /ɪf ðen/ *noun* instruction *f* IF-THEN-ELSE (de branchement conditionnel)

IGMP /ˌaɪ dʒiː em 'piː/ *noun* protocole *m* IGMP

ignore character /ɪg'nɔː ˌkærɪktə/ *noun* caractère *m* de remplissage

IGP /ˌaɪ dʒiː 'piː/ *noun* routage *m* IGP

IH *abbr* (*interrupt handler*) gestionnaire *m* d'interruptions

IIL *abbr* (*integrated injection logic*) logique *f* intégrée à injection; logique *f* ILL; logique *f* I2L

IIS système *m* intégré d'information

IKBS /ˌaɪ keɪ biː 'em/ *noun* système *m* intelligent à base de connaissances; système *m* expert

ikon /'aɪkɒn/ *noun* icône *f*

illegal /ɪ'liːg(ə)l/ *adjective* **1.** (*against the law*) illégal; (*against the rules*) non autorisé *or* -ée; qui va contre les règles de la syntaxe **2.** invalide; qui va contre les règles de la syntaxe

illegal character /ɪˌliːg(ə)l 'kærɪktə/ *noun* caractère *m* non autorisé

illegal instruction /ɪˌliːg(ə)l ɪn'strʌkʃən/ *noun* instruction *f* non autorisée

illegal operation /ɪˌliːg(ə)l ˌɒpə'reɪʃ(ə)n/ *noun* opération *f* non autorisée

IM *abbr* (*instant messaging*) messagerie *f* instantanée

iMac /ˌaɪ 'mæk/ iMac

image /'ɪmɪdʒ/ *noun* **1.** (*of an area of memory*) image *f* **2.** (*picture*) image *f* ◇ **image carrier** porteuse *f* d'image *or* de signal vidéo ◇ **image distortion** distorsion *f* de l'image

image area /'ɪmɪdʒ ˌeəriə/ *noun* (*region of microfilm or display screen*) zone *f* d'affichage

image buffer /'ɪmɪdʒ ˌbʌfə/ *noun* mémoire *f* tampon de l'image

image compression /'ɪmɪdʒ kəmˌpreʃ(ə)n/ *noun* compression *f* d'image

image degradation /'ɪmɪdʒ ˌdegrədeɪʃ(ə)n/ *noun* dégradation *f* de l'image

image editing /'ɪmɪdʒ ˌedɪtɪŋ/ *noun* traitement *m* de l'image

image editor /'ɪmɪdʒ ˌedɪtə/ *noun* éditeur *m* d'images

image enhancement /'ɪmɪdʒ ɪnˌhɑːnsmənt/ *noun* optimisation *f*

imagemap /'ɪmɪdʒmæp/ *noun* image *f* cliquable

image processing /'ɪmɪdʒ ˌprəʊsesɪŋ/ *noun* traitement *m* de l'image

image processing software /'ɪmɪdʒ ˌprəʊsesɪŋ ˌsɒftweə/ *noun* logiciel *m* de traitement de l'image

image processor /'ɪmɪdʒ ˌprəʊsesə/ *noun* (*electronic or computer system used for image processing*) système *m* de traitement de l'image; analyseur *m* d'image

'The Max FX also acts as a server to a growing number of printers, including a Varityper 5300 with emerald raster image processor and a Canon CLC 500 colour photocopier.' [*Computing*]

image retention /'ɪmɪdʒ rɪˌtenʃən/ *noun* rémanence *f* de l'image

image scanner /'ɪmɪdʒ ˌskænə/ *noun* scanner *m* d'image

image sensor /'ɪmɪdʒ ˌsensə/ *noun* capteur *m* d'image

image setter /'ɪmɪdʒ ˌsetə/ *noun* imageuse *f* film

image stability /'ɪmɪdʒ stəˌbɪlɪti/ *noun* stabilité *f* de l'image

image storage space /ˌɪmɪdʒ 'stɔːrɪdʒ ˌspeɪs/ *noun* espace *m* mémoire de l'image; zone *f* de stockage de l'image

image table /'ɪmɪdʒ ˌteɪb(ə)l/ *noun* table *f* d'attributs

imaging /'ɪmɪdʒɪŋ/ *noun* imagerie *f* médicale; imagerie *f* de synthèse

imaging system /ˌɪmɪdʒɪŋ 'sɪstəm/ *noun* optique *f*

IMAP /'aɪmæp/ *noun* protocole *m* de messagerie IMAP

immediate access store /ɪˌmiːdiət ˌækses 'stɔː/ *noun* mémoire *f* interne à accès immédiat

immediate address /ɪˌmiːdiət ə'dres/ *noun* adresse *f* immédiate; adresse *f* directe

immediate addressing /ɪˌmiːdiət ə'dresɪŋ/ *noun* adressage *m* immédiat

immediate instruction /ɪˌmiːdiət ɪn 'strʌkʃən/ *noun* instruction *f* immédiate

immediate mode /ɪ'miːdiət məʊd/ *noun* mode *m* immédiat

immediate operand /ɪ'miːdiət ˌɒpərænd/ *noun* opérande *m* immédiat

immediate processing /ɪˌmiːdiət 'prəʊsesɪŋ/ *noun* traitement *m* immédiat

impedance /ɪm'piːd(ə)ns/ *noun* impédance *f* ◇ **impedance matching** accord *m* d'impédance ◇ **impedance matching between a transmitter and a receiver minimizes power losses to transmitted signals** l'accord d'impédance entre un émetteur et un récepteur réduit au minimum la perte de puissance des signaux transmis ◇ **impedance mismatch** désaccord *m* d'impédance

implication /ˌɪmplɪ'keɪʃ(ə)n/ *noun* (*logical operation*) implication *f*

implied addressing /ɪmˌplaɪd ə'dresɪŋ/ *noun* adressage *m* implicite

import /ɪm'pɔːt/ *verb* **1.** (*to bring something in from outside a system*) importer *vt* **2.** (*to convert a file to default format*) importer *vt* ◇ **you can import images from the CAD package into the DTP program** il est possible d'importer des images d'un logiciel CAO dans un programme de PAO

'At the moment, Acrobat supports only the sending and viewing of documents. There are legal implications associated with allowing users to edit documents in the style of the original application, without having the tool itself on their desks, and there is no import facility back into applications.' [*Computing*]

impulse /'ɪmpʌls/ *noun* impulsion *f*; excitation *f*

impulsive noise /ɪm'pʌlsɪv nɔɪz/ *noun* (*interference on a signal*) bruit *m*

IMS *abbr* (*information management system*) système *m* de gestion de l'information

inactive window /ɪnˌæktɪv 'wɪndəʊ/ *noun* fenêtre *f* inactive

in-band signalling /ˌɪn bænd 'sɪgn(ə)lɪŋ/ *noun* (*data transmission*) transmission *f* de signaux dans la bande passante

InBox /'ɪnbɒks/ *noun* (*Windows messaging system*) Boîte *f* de réception

inbuilt /'ɪnbɪlt/ *adjective* intégré ◇ **this software has inbuilt error correction** ce logiciel possède un système de correction d'erreurs intégré

inches-per-second /ˌɪntʃɪz pɜː 'sekənd/ *noun* pouces *mpl* par seconde (pps); pouce(s)/seconde

in-circuit emulator /ˌɪn ˌsɜːkɪt 'emjʊleɪtə/ *noun* émulateur *m* intégré au circuit ◇ **this in-circuit emulator is used to test the floppy disk controller by emulating a disk drive** cet émulateur intégré au circuit sert à tester le contrôleur de la disquette, en simulant le fonctionnement d'un lecteur de disquettes

inclusion /ɪn'kluːʒ(ə)n/ *noun* inclusion *f*

inclusive OR /ɪn'kluːsɪv ɔː/ *noun* OU *m* inclusif

incoming message /ˌɪnkʌmɪŋ 'mesɪdʒ/ *noun* message *m* reçu

incoming traffic /ˌɪnkʌmɪŋ 'træfɪk/ *noun* (*data received*) messages *mpl* reçus; données *fpl* reçues

incompatible /ˌɪnkəm'pætɪb(ə)l/ *adjective* incompatible; non compatible ◇ **they tried to link the two systems, but found they were incompatible** en essayant de relier les deux systèmes, ils ont trouvé qu'ils étaient incompatibles

increment /'ɪŋkrɪmənt/ *noun* **1.** (*addition of a number*) incrémentation *f*; augmentation *f* **2.** (*number added*) incrément *m* ■ *verb* **1.** (*to increase a number*) augmenter *vt*; incrémenter *vt* **2.** (*to move forward*) avancer d'un pas ◇ **increase the increment to three** augmentez l'incrément à trois ◇ **the counter is incremented each time an instruction is executed** le compteur est incrémenté à chaque instruction exécutée

incremental backup /ˌɪŋkrɪment(ə)l 'bækʌp/ *noun* sauvegarde *f* incrémentielle

incremental computer /ˌɪŋkrɪment(ə)l kəm 'pjuːtə/ *noun* ordinateur *m* à valeurs variables; ordinateur *m* incrémentiel

incremental data /ˌɪŋkrɪment(ə)l 'deɪtə/ *noun* données *fpl* incrémentielles

incremental plotter /ɪŋkrɪment(ə)l 'plɒtə/ *noun* traceur *m* incrémentiel

indent *noun* /'ɪndent/ alinéa *m* ■ *verb* /ɪn'dent/ faire un alinéa ◇ **the first line of the paragraph is indented two spaces** comptez deux espaces pour l'alinéa du premier paragraphe

indentation /ˌɪnden'teɪʃ(ə)n/ *noun* alinéa *m*

Indeo /'ɪndiəʊ/ (*video software technology*) technologie *f* Indeo™

indeterminate system /ˌɪndɪtɜːmɪnət 'sɪstəm/ *noun* système *m* indéterminé

index /'ɪndeks/ *noun* **1.** (*in a computer memory*) index *m*; (*list*) répertoire *m* **2.** (*of book*) index *m*; (*guide mark on film or microfilm*) indice *m* de position; (*computer address*) adresse *f* indexée ■ *verb* (*to mark with an index*) indexer *vt*; (*a book*) préparer un index ◇ **the book has been badly indexed** l'index de ce livre a été très mal fait ◇ **the book was sent out for indexing** le livre a été envoyé à l'extérieur pour la préparation de l'index

index build /'ɪndeks bɪld/ *noun* indexation *f*

indexed address /ˌɪndeksd ə'dres/ *noun* adresse *f* indexée

indexed addressing /ˌɪndeksd ə'dresɪŋ/ *noun* (*addressing mode*) adressage *m* indexée

indexed file /'ɪndeksd faɪl/ *noun* fichier *m* indexé

indexed instruction /ˌɪndeksd ɪn'strʌkʃən/ *noun* instruction *f* indexée

indexed sequential access method /ˌɪndeks sɪˌkwensəl 'ækses ˌmeθəd/ *noun* méthode *f* d'accès séquentiel indexé

indexed sequential storage /ˌɪndeksd sɪ ˌkwenʃ(ə)l 'stɔːrɪdʒ/ *noun* mémoire *f* séquentielle indexée

index.html /ˌɪndeks dɒt ˌeɪtʃ tiː em 'el/ *noun* index.html

indexing /'ɪndeksɪŋ/ *noun* **1.** (*in a computer*) indexation *f* **2.** (*list of records*) classement *m*; indexation *f*

index key /'ɪndeks kiː/ *noun* clé *f* d'index

index letter /'ɪndeks ˌletə/ *noun* indicatif *m* littéral

index number /'ɪndeks ˌnʌmbə/ *noun* indicatif *m* numérique

index page /ˈɪndeks peɪdʒ/ *noun* **1.** page *f* index **2.** page *f* d'index

index register /ˈɪndeks ˌredʒɪstə/ *noun* registre *m* d'index

index value word /ˌɪndeks ˌvæljuː ˈwɜːd/ *noun* mot *m* d'index

indicator /ˈɪndɪˌkeɪtə/ *noun* indicateur *m*

indicator chart /ˈɪndɪˌkeɪtə tʃɑːt/ *noun* tableau *m* des indicateurs

indicator flag /ˈɪndɪˌkeɪtə flæg/ *noun* (*register or single bit*) indicateur *m*; balise *f*

indicator light /ˈɪndɪˌkeɪtə laɪt/ *noun* voyant *m* lumineux

indirect address /ˌɪndaɪrekt əˈdres/ *noun* adresse *f* relative

indirect addressing /ˌɪndaɪrekt əˈdresɪŋ/ *noun* adressage *m* indirect

induce /ɪnˈdjuːs/ *verb* **1.** (*electricity*) induire *vt*; produire un courant induit; produire une induction; (*mathematics*) induire *vt* **2.** induire *vt*

induced failure /ɪnˌdjuːsd ˈfeɪljə/ *noun* (*failure due to external effects*) défaillance *f* provoquée par une cause externe; défaillance *f* induite

induced interference /ɪnˌdjuːsd ˌɪntəˈfɪərəns/ *noun* (*electrical noise on a signal*) interférence *f* induite par une autre machine

inductance /ɪnˈdʌktəns/ *noun* inductance *f*

induction /ɪnˈdʌkʃən/ *noun* **1.** (*in electricity*) induction *f* **2.** (*in mathematics*) induction *f* ◇ **induction coil** bobine *f* d'induction

inductive coordination /ɪnˌdʌktɪv kəʊˌɔːdɪˈneɪʃ(ə)n/ *noun* coordination *f* inductive

inductor /ɪnˈdʌktə/ *noun* inducteur *m*; bobine *f* d'induction

Industry Standard Architecture /ˌɪndəstri ˌstændəd ˈɑːkɪˌtektʃə/ *noun* (*standard for 16-bit expansion bus*) architecture *f* (de bus) ISA

inequality operator /ˌɪnɪˈkwɒlɪti ˌɒpəreɪtə/ *noun* (*symbol indicating that two variables are not equal*) opérateur *m* d'inégalité

inequivalence /ˌɪnɪˈkwɪvələns/ *noun* (*logical function*) exclusion *f* réciproque

infect /ɪnˈfekt/ *verb* infecter *vt*

infected computer /ɪnˌfektɪd kəmˈpjuːtə/ *noun* (*computer with a virus*) ordinateur *m* infecté par un virus; (*computer with a virus program*) ordinateur *m* dont le programme contient un virus

inference /ˈɪnf(ə)rəns/ *noun* **1.** (*operation*) inférence *f*; déduction *f* **2.** (*result*) déduction *f*; inférence *f*

inference control /ˈɪnf(ə)rəns kənˌtrəʊl/ *noun* contrôle *m* d'inférence

inference engine /ˈɪnf(ə)rəns ˈendʒɪn/, **inference machine** /ˌɪnf(ə)rəns məˈʃiːn/ *noun* moteur *m* d'inférence

inferior figure /ɪnˌfɪəriə ˈfɪgə/ *noun* (*smaller number printed slightly below normal characters*) indice *m*

INF file /ˌaɪ en ˈef faɪl/ *noun* fichier *m* INF

infinite loop /ˈɪnfɪnət luːp/ *noun* boucle *f* sans fin

infinity /ɪnˈfɪnɪti/ *noun* **1.** (*quantity*) infini *m* **2.** (*distance*) infini *m*

infix notation /ɪnˌfɪks nəʊˈteɪʃ(ə)n/ *noun* notation *f* infixée

informatics /ˌɪnfɔːˈmætɪks/ *noun* informatique *f*

information /ˌɪnfəˈmeɪʃ(ə)n/ *noun* (*data*) information *f*; données *f* ◇ **information networks** réseaux *mpl* d'information *or* réseaux informatiques ◇ **information provider (IP)** source *f* d'information; service *m* (fournisseur) d'information *or* agence d'information ◇ **information retrieval (IR)** restitution *f* de données ◇ **information storage and retrieval (ISR)** stockage et restitution de données ◇ **information technology (IT)** technologies *fpl* de l'information

information bearer channel /ˌɪnfəmeɪʃ(ə)n ˈbeərə ˌtʃæn(ə)l/ *noun* voie *f* de transmission d'informations

information content /ˌɪnfəˈmeɪʃ(ə)n ˌkɒntent/ *noun* quantité *f* d'information

information flow control /ˌɪnfəˈmeɪʃ(ə)n fləʊ kənˌtrəʊl/ *noun* contrôle *m* de flux d'informations

information input /ˌɪnfəˈmeɪʃ(ə)n ˌɪnpʊt/ *noun* saisie *f* de données

information line /ˌɪnfəˈmeɪʃ(ə)n laɪn/ *noun* ligne *f* d'état; ligne *f* d'information

information management system /ˌɪnfəmeɪʃ(ə)n ˈmænɪdʒmənt ˌsɪstəm/ *noun* système *m* de gestion de l'information

information network /ˌɪnfəˈmeɪʃ(ə)n ˌnetwɜːk/ *noun* réseau *m* informatique

information output /ˌɪnfəmeɪʃ(ə)n ˈaʊtpʊt/ *noun* (*on screen*) affichage *m* de données; (*on printer*) sortie *f* d'imprimante

information processing /ˌɪnfəmeɪʃ(ə)n ˈprəʊsesɪŋ/ *noun* traitement *m* de données; traitement *m* de l'information

information processor /ˌɪnfəmeɪʃ(ə)n ˈprəʊsesə/ *noun* ordinateur *m*

information provider /ˌɪnfəˈmeɪʃ(ə)n prəˌvaɪdə/ *noun* (*company or user who provides information*) fournisseur *m* d'informations

information rate /ˌɪnfəˈmeɪʃ(ə)n reɪt/ *noun* vitesse *f* de sortie de l'information

information retrieval /ˌɪnfəmeɪʃ(ə)n rɪˈtriːv(ə)l/ *noun* recherche *f* documentaire

information retrieval centre /ˌɪnfəmeɪʃ(ə)n rɪˈtriːv(ə)l ˌsentə/ *noun* centre *m* de recherche documentaire; centre *m* serveur; banque *f* de données

information storage /ˌɪnfəmeɪʃ(ə)n ˈstɔːrɪdʒ/ *noun* (*data storage*) stockage *m* de données

information storage and retrieval /ˌɪnfəmeɪʃ(ə)n ˌstɔːrɪdʒ ən rɪˈtriːv(ə)l/ *noun* stockage *m* et restitution de données

information structure /ˌɪnfəˈmeɪʃ(ə)n ˌstrʌktʃə/ *noun* structure *f* de données

information system /ˌɪnfəˈmeɪʃ(ə)n ˌsɪstəm/ *noun* système *m* informatique

information technology /ˌɪnfəmeɪʃ(ə)n tek ˈnɒlədʒi/ *noun* informatique *f*; techniques *fpl* de l'information

information theory /ˌɪnfəˈmeɪʃ(ə)n ˌθɪəri/ *noun* théorie *f* de l'information

information transfer channel /ˌɪnfəmeɪʃ(ə)n ˈtrænsfɜː ˌtʃæn(ə)l/ *noun* canal de transfert d'information *m*

infrared /ˌɪnfrəˈred/ *noun* infrarouge *m*

infra-red link /ˌɪnfrə red ˈlɪŋk/ *noun* liaison *f* infrarouge

infrastructure /ˈɪnfrəˌstrʌktʃə/ *noun* infrastructure *f*

inherent addressing /ɪnˌhɪərənt əˈdresɪŋ/ *noun* adressage *m* inhérent; adressage *m* particulier

inherit /ɪnˈherɪt/ *verb* (*acquire the characteristics of another data type*) hériter *vt*

inheritance /ɪnˈherɪt(ə)ns/ *noun* (*passing the characteristics of one data type to another*) héritage *m*; transmission *f*

inherited error /ɪnˌherɪtɪd ˈerə/ *noun* erreur *f* transmise; erreur *f* héritée

inhibit /ɪnˈhɪbɪt/ *verb* (*process or circuit or gate*) inhiber *vt*; arrêter *vt*; stopper *vti*

inhibiting input /ɪnˌhɪbɪtɪŋ ˈɪnpʊt/ *noun* signal *m* d'invalidation de transmission; signal *m* d'interdiction de transmission

INI file /ˌaɪ en ˈaɪ faɪl/ *noun* fichier *m* INI

initial address /ɪˌnɪʃ(ə)l əˈdres/ *noun* adresse *f* de lancement; adresse *f* initiale

initial condition /ɪˌnɪʃ(ə)l kənˈdɪʃ(ə)n/ *noun* condition *f* initiale

initial error /ɪˌnɪʃ(ə)l ˈerə/ *noun* erreur *f* au départ

initial instructions /ɪˌnɪʃ(ə)l ɪnˈstrʌkʃənz/ *plural noun* instructions *fpl* de lancement; instructions *fpl* instructions initiales

initialisation, initialization *noun* initialisation *f*

initialisation string /ɪˌnɪʃ(ə)laɪˈzeɪʃ(ə)n ˌstrɪŋ/, **initialization string** *noun* chaîne *f* d'initialisation

initialise /ɪˈnɪʃəˌlaɪz/, **initialize** *verb* initialiser *vt*

initial program header /ɪˌnɪʃ(ə)l ˈprəʊgræm ˌhedə/ *noun* lanceur *m* de programme de chargement

initial program loader /ɪˌnɪʃ(ə)l ˈprəʊgræm ˌləʊdə/ *noun* chargeur *m* de programme de lancement

initial value /ɪˌnɪʃ(ə)l ˈvæljuː/ *noun* valeur *f* initiale

ink /ɪŋk/ *verb* imprégner d'encre; couvrir d'encre

ink cartridge /ɪŋk ˈkɑːtrɪdʒ/ *noun* cartouche *f* d'encre

ink-jet printer /ˈɪnk dʒet ˌprɪntə/ *noun* imprimante *f* à jet d'encre ◇ **colour ink-jet technology and thermal transfer technology compete with each other** les technologies du jet d'encre couleur et du transfert thermique sont concurrentielles

> '…ink-jet printers work by squirting a fine stream of ink onto the paper' [*Personal Computer World*]

inlay card /ɪnˈleɪ kɑːd/ *noun* (*inside tape or disk box*) étiquette *f* interne

in-line /ɪn laɪn/ *adjective* avec broches disposées en ligne ■ *noun* (*connection pins arranged in one or two rows*) avec broches disposées en ligne

in-line processing /ˌɪn laɪn ˈprəʊsesɪŋ/ *noun* travail *m* à la chaîne

in-line program /ˌɪn laɪn ˈpeəʊgræm/ *noun* programme *m* linéaire

inner loop /ˈɪnə luːp/ *noun* boucle *f* intérieure

input /ˈɪnpʊt/ *verb* (*to transfer data*) entrer *vi*; introduire *vt*; saisir *vt* ■ *noun* **1.** (*introducing or adding data to a system*) entrée *f*; introduction *f*; saisie *f* **2.** (*data*) données *fpl* d'entrée; données *fpl* saisies **3.** (*electrical signals*) signal *m* électrique

> 'In fact, the non-Qwerty format of the Maltron keyboard did cause a few gasps when it was first shown to the staff, but within a month all the Maltron users had regained normal input speeds.' [*Computing*]

input area /ˈɪnpʊt ˌeəriə/ *noun* zone *f* d'entrée (de données)

input block /ˈɪnpʊt blɒk/ *noun* bloc *m* d'entrée

input-bound /ˈɪnpʊt ˌbaʊnd/ *adjective* (ordinateur) limité par le débit d'entrée des données; limité par les entrées

input buffer register /ˌɪnpʊt ˈbʌfə ˌredʒɪstə/ *noun* registre *m* tampon des entrées

input device /ˈɪnpʊt dɪˌvaɪs/ *noun* périphérique *m* d'entrée

input lead /ˈɪnpʊt liːd/ *noun* câble *m* d'entrée

input-limited /ˌɪnpʊt ˈlɪmɪtɪd/ *adjective* limité par la vitesse d'entrée des données

input mode /ˈɪnpʊt məʊd/ *noun* (*of data*) mode *m* (d') entrée

input/output /ˌɪnpʊt ˈaʊtpʊt/ *noun* **1.** entrée/sortie *f* **2.** entrée/sortie *f*

input/output buffer /ˌɪnpʊt ˈaʊtpʊt ˌbʌfə/ *noun* tampon *m* (d') entrée/sortie

input/output bus /ˌɪnpʊt ˈaʊtpʊt bʌs/ *noun* bus *m* (d') entrée/sortie

input/output channel /ˌɪnpʊt ˈaʊtpʊt ˌtʃæn(ə)l/ *noun* canal *m*

input/output controller /ˌɪnpʊt ˈaʊtpʊt kən ˌtrəʊlə/ *noun* contrôleur *m* d'entrée/sortie

input/output control program /ˌɪnpʊt 'aʊtpʊt kənˌtrəʊl/ *noun* programme *m* de contrôle d'entrée/sortie

input/output device /ˌɪnpʊt 'aʊtpʊt dɪˌvaɪs/ *noun* périphérique *m* d'entrée/sortie

input/output executive /ˌɪnpʊt 'aʊtpʊt ɪg ˌzekjʊtɪv/ *noun* superviseur *m* d'entrée/sortie

input/output instruction /ˌɪnpʊt 'aʊtpʊt ɪn ˌstrʌkʃən/ *noun* instruction *f* d'entrée/sortie

input/output interface /ˌɪnpʊt 'aʊtpʊt ɪntə ˌfeɪs/ *noun* interface *f* d'entrée/sortie

input/output interrupt /ˌɪnpʊt 'aʊtpʊt ɪntə ˌrʌpt/ *noun* interruption *f* d'entrée/sortie

input/output library /ˌɪnpʊt 'aʊtpʊt ˌlaɪbrəri/ *noun* bibliothèque *f* de programmes d'entrée/sortie

input/output port /ˌɪnpʊt 'aʊtpʊt ˌpɔːt/ *noun* port *m* (d') entrée/sortie

input/output processor /ˌɪnpʊt 'aʊtpʊt ˌprəʊsesə/ *noun* processeur *m* d'entrée/sortie

input/output referencing /ˌɪnpʊt 'aʊtpʊt ˌref(ə)rənsɪŋ/ *noun* référençage *m* d'entrée/sortie

input/output register /ˌɪnpʊt 'aʊtpʊt ˌredʒɪstə/ *noun* registre *m* d'entrée/sortie

input/output request /ˌɪnpʊt 'aʊtpʊt rɪ ˌkwest/ *noun* traitement *m* linéaire

input/output status word /ˌɪnpʊt ˌaʊtpʊt 'steɪtəs wɜːd/ *noun* mot *m* d'état d'entrée/sortie

input/output unit /ˌɪnpʊt 'aʊtpʊt ˌjuːnɪt/ *noun* périphérique *m*

input port /'ɪnpʊt pɔːt/ *noun* port *m* (d') entrée

input register /'ɪnpʊt ˌredʒɪstə/ *noun* registre *m* d'entrée

input routine /'ɪnpʊt ruːˌtiːn/ *noun* routine *f* d'entrée; routine *f* d'introduction

input section /'ɪnpʊt ˌsekʃ(ə)n/ *noun* section *f* d'entrée

input statement /'ɪnpʊt ˌsteɪtmənt/ *noun* déclaration *f*

input storage /'ɪnpʊt ˌstɔːrɪdʒ/ *noun* mémoire *f* d'entrée

input work queue /ˌɪnpʊt 'wɜːk ˌkjuː/ *noun* file *f* d'attente des données d'entrée

inquiry /ɪn'kwaɪəri/ *noun* demande *f*; requête *f*; interrogation *f* ◇ **inquiry character (ENQ)** caractère *m* de requête *or* d'interrogation ◇ **inquiry *or* response (function)** (fonction) interrogation/réponse *or* demande/réponse

inquiry character /ɪn'kwaɪəri ˌkærɪktə/ *noun* caractère *m* de requête; caractère *m* d'interrogation

inquiry/response /ɪnˌkwaɪəri rɪ'spɒns/ *noun* fonction *f* demande/réponse; fonction *f* interrogation/réponse

inquiry station /ɪn'kwaɪri ˌsteɪʃ(ə)n/ *noun* poste *m* d'interrogation

insert /ɪn'sɜːt/ *verb* (*to add new text*) ajouter *vt*

inserted subroutine /ˌɪnsɜːtɪd 'sʌbruːtiːn/ *noun* sous-programme *m* additionnel

insertion loss /ɪn'sɜːʃ(ə)n lɒs/ *noun* (*attenuation to a signal*) perte *f* d'insertion; affaiblissement *m* d'insertion

insertion point /ɪn'sɜːʃ(ə)n pɔɪnt/ *noun* (*cursor*) point *m* d'insertion; curseur *m*

insert key /ɪn'sɜːt kiː/ *noun* touche *f* Ins

insert mode /'ɪnsɜːt məʊd/ *noun* (*mode for correcting and editing documents*) mode *m* insertion

Ins key /'ɪns kiː/ *noun* (*insert key – key that switches into insert mode*) touche *f* Ins; touche *f* Inser; insertion *f* (sur un clavier français)

install /ɪn'stɔːl/ *verb* **1.** mettre en place; installer *vt* **2.** mettre en place ◇ **the system is easy to install and simple to use** ce système est facile à mettre en place et à utiliser

installable device driver /ɪnˌstɔːləb(ə)l dɪ 'vaɪs ˌdraɪvə/ *noun* (*device driver loaded into memory*) gestionnaire *m* de périphérique installable

installation /ˌɪnstə'leɪʃ(ə)n/ *noun* **1.** (*equipment*) matériel *m* informatique; équipement *m* informatique **2.** (*setting up*) mise *f* en place; installation *f* ◇ **the installation of the equipment took only a few hours** il n'a fallu que quelques heures pour mettre l'équipement en place

installation manual /ˌɪnstə'leɪʃ(ə)n ˌmænjʊəl/ *noun* manuel *m* d'installation

install program /'ɪnstɔːl ˌprəʊgræm/ *noun* programme *m* d'installation

instance /'ɪnstəns/ *noun* (*duplicate object that has been created*) objet *m* disponible; instance *f*

instantaneous access /ˌɪnstənteɪniəs 'ækses/ *noun* accès *m* instantané

instant messaging /ˌɪnstənt 'mesɪdʒɪŋ/ *noun* messagerie *f* instantanée

instruction /ɪn'strʌkʃən/ *noun* instruction *f* ◇ **instruction address register (IAR)** registre *m* d'adresse d'instruction ◇ **instruction register (IR)** registre d'instruction ◇ **jump instruction** instruction de branchement *or* de saut ◇ **macro instruction** macro-instruction *f* ◇ **the instruction PRINT is used in this BASIC dialect as an operand to display the following data** l'instruction PRINT est un opérande employé dans cette version BASIC pour l'affichage des données suivantes ◇ **three-address-instruction** instruction à trois adresses ◇ **two-address-instruction** instruction à deux adresses

> 'A Taos kernel, typically 15Kb in size, resides at each processing node to 'translate', non-native instructions – on the fly when needed. This kernel contains the only code which has to be written in the processor's native instruction set.' [*Computing*]

instruction address /ɪn'strʌkʃən əˌdres/ *noun* adresse *f* d'instruction

instruction address register /ɪnˌstrʌkʃən əˈdres ˌredʒɪstə/ *noun* registre *m* d'adresse d'instruction

instruction area /ɪnˈstrʌkʃən ˌeəriə/ *noun* zone *f* d'instruction

instruction cache /ɪnˈstrʌkʃən kæʃ/ *noun* cache *m* d'instructions; antémémoire *m* d'instructions

instruction character /ɪnˈstrʌkʃən ˌkærɪktə/ *noun* caractère *m* d'instruction

instruction codes /ɪnˈstrʌkʃən kəʊdz/ *plural noun* codes d'instruction

instruction counter /ɪnˈstrʌkʃən ˌkaʊntə/ *noun* compteur *m* d'instruction

instruction cycle /ɪnˈstrʌkʃən ˌsaɪk(ə)l/ *noun* cycle *m* d'instruction

instruction cycle time /ɪnˌstrʌkʃən ˈsaɪk(ə)l ˌtaɪm/ *noun* temps *m* de cycle d'instruction

instruction decoder /ɪnˈstrʌkʃən diːˌkəʊdə/ *noun* décodeur *m* d'instructions

instruction execution time /ɪnˌstrʌkʃən ˌeksɪˈkjuːʃ(ə)n ˌtaɪm/ *noun* temps *m* d'exécution d'une instruction

instruction format /ɪnˈstrʌkʃən ˌfɔːmæt/ *noun* format *m* d'instruction

instruction manual /ɪnˈstrʌkʃən ˌmænjuəl/ *noun* manuel *m* d'utilisation

instruction modification /ɪnˌstrʌkʃən ˌmɒdɪfɪˈkeɪʃ(ə)n/ *noun* modification *f* d'une instruction

instruction pipelining /ɪnˈstrʌkʃən ˌpaɪplaɪnɪŋ/ *noun* mode *m* d'exécution d'instructions en pipeline

instruction pointer /ɪnˈstrʌkʃən ˌpɔɪntə/ *noun* pointeur *m* d'instruction

instruction processor /ɪnˈstrʌkʃən ˌprəʊsesə/ *noun* processeur *m* d'instruction

instruction register /ɪnˈstrʌkʃən ˌredʒɪstə/ *noun* registre *m* d'instruction

instruction repertoire /ɪnˈstrʌkʃən ˌrepətwɑː/, **instruction set** /set/ *noun* jeu *m* d'instructions

instruction storage /ɪnˈstrʌkʃən ˌstɔːrɪdʒ/ *noun* (*area*) mémoire *f* d'instruction; (*storing*) mise *f* en mémoire; (*memory*) stockage *m* d'instruction

instruction time /ɪnˈstrʌkʃən taɪm/ *noun* temps *m* d'instruction

instruction word /ɪnˈstrʌkʃən wɜːd/ *noun* mot *m* instruction ◇ **the manufacturers of this CPU have decided that JMP will be the instruction word to call the jump function** les fabricants du CPU ont décidé que l'instruction JMP servirait à indiquer un branchement *or* un saut

instrument /ˈɪnstrʊmənt/ *noun* instrument *m*

integer /ˈɪntɪdʒə/ *noun* nombre *m* entier

integral /ɪntɪgrəl, ɪnˈtegəl/ *adjective* (*device*) intégré ◇ **the integral disk drives and modem reduce desk space** puisque les lecteurs de disquettes et le modem sont intégrés, l'encombrement est réduit

integrated /ˈɪntɪˌgreɪtɪd/ *adjective* intégré -ée

integrated circuit /ˌɪntɪgreɪtɪd ˈsɜːkɪt/ *noun* circuit *m* intégré

integrated database /ˌɪntɪgreɪtɪd ˈdeɪtəbeɪs/ *noun* base *f* de données intégrée

integrated data processing /ˌɪntɪgreɪtɪd ˈdeɪtə ˌprəʊsesɪŋ/ *noun* traitement *m* de données intégré

integrated device electronics /ˌɪntɪ ˌgreɪtɪd dɪˌvaɪs ˌelekˈtrɒnɪks/, **integrated drive electronics** /ˌɪntɪˌgreɪtɪd draɪv ˌelekˈtrɒnɪks/ *noun* contrôleur *m* de disque IDE

integrated emulator /ˌɪntɪgreɪtɪd ˈemjʊleɪtə/ *noun* émulateur *m* intégré

integrated injection logic /ˌɪntɪgreɪtɪd ɪnˈdʒekʃən ˌlɒdʒɪk/ *noun* logique *f* intégrée à injection; logique *f* ILL; logique *f* I2L

integrated modem /ˌɪntɪgreɪtɪd ˈməʊdem/ *noun* modem *m* intégré

integrated office /ˌɪntɪgreɪtɪd ˈɒfɪs/ *noun* bureautique *f* intégrée

integrated services digital network /ˌɪntɪgreɪtɪd ˌsɜːvɪsɪz ˌdɪdʒɪt(ə)l ˈnetwɜːk/ *noun* réseau *m* numérique à intégration de services

integrated software /ˌɪntɪgreɪtɪd ˈsɒftweə/ *noun* logiciel *m* intégré

integration /ˌɪntɪˈgreɪʃ(ə)n/ *noun* intégration *f* ◇ **large scale integration (LSI)** intégration à grande échelle ◇ **medium scale integration (MSI)** intégration à moyenne échelle ◇ **small scale integration (SSI)** intégration à petite échelle ◇ **ultra large scale integration (ULSI)** intégration à ultra grande échelle ◇ **very large scale integration (VLSI)** intégration à très grande échelle

integrity /ɪnˈtegrɪti/ *noun* intégrité *f* ◇ **integrity of a file** intégrité d'un fichier

Intel /ˈɪntel/ (*company which developed the first microprocessor*) Intel™

Intel 8086 (*trade name for a microprocessor that uses a 16-bit data bus and can address up to 1Mb of RAM*) Intel 8086

Intel 8088 (*trade name for a microprocessor that uses a 16-bit data bus internally, but uses an 8-bit data bus externally*) Intel 8088

Intel 80286 (*trade name for a microprocessor that uses a 16-bit data bus and can address up to 16Mb of RAM*) Intel 80286

Intel 80386 (*trade name for a microprocessor that uses a 32-bit data bus and can address up to 4Gb of RAM*) Intel 80386

Intel 80486 (*trade name for a microprocessor that uses a 32-bit data bus and can address up to 64Gb of RAM*) Intel 80486

Intel Indeo /ˌɪntel 'ɪndiəʊ/ (*trade name for software technology that allows a computer to store and play back compressed video sequences*) Intel Indeo

intelligence /ɪn'telɪdʒəns/ *noun* (*of person or machine*) intelligence *f* ◇ **business intelligence (BI)** intelligence économique

intelligent /ɪn'telɪdʒənt/ *adjective* (*program or machine*) intelligent

intelligent device /ɪnˌtelɪdʒ(ə)nt dɪ'vaɪs/ *noun* machine *f* intelligente

intelligent knowledge-based system /ɪn ˌtelɪdʒ(ə)nt ˌnɒlɪdʒ beɪsd 'sɪstəm/ *noun* système *m* intelligent à base de connaissances; système *m* expert

intelligent spacer /ɪnˌtelɪdʒ(ə)nt 'speɪsə/ *noun* gestionnaire *m* d'espacement intelligent

intelligent terminal /ɪnˌtelɪdʒ(ə)nt 'tɜːmɪn(ə)l/ *noun* terminal *m* intelligent ◇ **the new intelligent terminal has a built-in text editor** le nouveau terminal intelligent comporte un éditeur de texte

intelligent tutoring system /ɪnˌtelɪdʒ(ə)nt 'tjuːtərɪŋ ˌsɪstəm/ *noun* formation *f* assistée par système expert

intelligent wiring hub /ɪnˌtelɪdʒ(ə)nt 'waɪərɪŋ hʌb/ *noun* boîtier *m* de câblage intelligent

Intel MMX /ˌɪntel em em 'eks/ (*trade name for a range of processors*) Intel MMX

Intel Pentium /ˌɪntel 'pentiəm/ (*trade name for a range of advanced microprocessors*) Intel Pentium

Intel Pentium Pro /ˌɪntel ˌpentiəm 'prəʊ/ (*trade name for a 32-bit processor*) Intel Pentium Pro

intensity /ɪn'tensɪti/ *noun* (*of signal or light or sound*) intensité *f*

interactive /ˌɪntər'æktɪv/ *adjective* (*system or software*) interactif; (*mode*) dialogué; conversationnel ◇ **this interactive multimedia title allows a user to make music with a synthesizer program** ce logiciel multimédia interactif permet à l'utilisateur de faire de la musique avec un programme de synthétiseur

> 'Oracle today details its interactive information superhighway aims, endorsed by 17 industry partners. The lynchpin to the announcement will be software based on the Oracle Media Server, a multimedia database designed to run on massively parallel computers.' [*Computing*]

interactive debugging system /ˌɪntəræktɪv diː'bʌgɪŋ ˌsɪstəm/ *noun* système *m* de déverminage; système *m* de déboguage interactif

interactive graphics /ˌɪntəræktɪv 'græfɪks/ *plural noun* (*display system*) graphiques *mpl* interactifs; infographie *f* interactive ◇ **the space invaders machine has great interactive graphics, the player controls the position of his spaceship with the joystick** le jeu (électronique) 'les envahisseurs de l'espace' présente d'excellents graphiques interactifs

interactive keyboard /ˌɪntəræktɪv 'kiːbɔːd/ *noun* clavier *m* interactif

interactive media /ˌɪntəræktɪv 'miːdiə/ *plural noun* média interactif

interactive mode /ˌɪntər'æktɪv ˌməʊd/ *noun* mode *m* interactif; mode *m* dialogué; mode *m* conversationnel

interactive multimedia /ˌɪntəræktɪv ˌmʌlti 'miːdiə/ *noun* système *m* multimédia interactif ◇ **this interactive multimedia title allows a user to make music with a synthesizer program** ce logiciel multimédia interactif permet à l'utilisateur de faire de la musique avec un programme de synthétiseur

interactive processing /ˌɪntəræktɪv 'prəʊsesɪŋ/ *noun* traitement *m* interactif

interactive routine /ˌɪntəræktɪv ruː'tiːn/ *noun* routine *f* interactive

interactive system /ˌɪntəræktɪv 'sɪstəm/ *noun* système *m* interactif

interactive terminal /ˌɪntəræktɪv 'tɜːmɪn(ə)l/ *noun* terminal *m* interactif; terminal *m* conversationnel

interactive TV /ˌɪntəræktɪv tiː 'viː/ *noun* télévision *f* interactive

interactive video /ˌɪntəræktɪv 'vɪdiəʊ/ *noun* vidéo *f* interactive; vidéographie *f* interactive

interactive videotext /ˌɪntəræktɪv 'vɪdiəʊtekst/ *noun* dialogue *m* vidéotex; vidéographie *f* interactive

interactivity /ˌɪntəræk'tɪvɪti/ *noun* interactivité *f*

> '...interactivity is a buzzword you've been hearing a lot lately. Resign yourself to it because you're going to be hearing a lot more of it' [*Music Technology*]

interblock /'ɪntəblɒk/ *adjective* entre blocs; interbloc ◇ **interblock gap (IBG)** espace *m* interbloc

interblock gap /'ɪntəblɒk gæp/ *noun* (*blank magnetic tape*) espace *m* interbloc

intercharacter spacing /ɪntəˌkærəktə 'speɪsɪŋ/ *noun* (*DTP*) espacement *m* proportionnel de caractères

interconnection /ˌɪntəkə'nekʃən/ *noun* (*connecting material*) interconnexion *f*; liaison *f* (entre plusieurs machines/dispositifs)

interface /'ɪntəfeɪs/ *noun* **1.** (*point at which one computer system ends and another begins*) interface *f* **2.** (*linking device in communications system*) interface *f* **3.** (*section of a program which allows transmission of data to another program*) interface *f* ■ *verb* (*to connect incom-*

patible devices) interfacer avec; relier à ◇ **general purpose interface adapter (GPIA)** interface universelle *or* interface GPIA ◇ **general purpose interface bus (GPIB)** bus d'interface universelle *or* bus GPIB ◇ **interface adapter** adaptateur d'interface ◇ **serial interface** interface série

'The original release of ODBC only included a driver for Microsoft's own SQL Server database. Microsoft has subsequently published the ODBC application program interface enabling third-party vendors to create drivers for other databases and tools.' [*Computing*]

interface card /'ɪntəfeɪs kɑːd/ *noun* carte *f* d'interface

interface message processor /ˌɪntəfeɪs 'mesɪdʒ ˌprəʊsesə/ *noun* serveur *m* de message

interface processor /'ɪntəfeɪs ˌprəʊsesə/ *noun* processeur *m* d'interface

interface routines /'ɪntəfeɪs ruːˌtiːnz/ *plural noun* routines *fpl* d'interface

interfacing /'ɪntəfeɪsɪŋ/ *noun* (*hardware or software*) interface *f*

interfere /ˌɪntə'fɪə/ ◇ **to interfere with something** interférer; nuire (à)

interference /ˌɪntə'fɪərəns/ *noun* (*unwanted addition of signal*) brouillage *m*; (*effect seen when two signals are added*) interférence *f* ◇ **constructive interference** interférence constructive ◇ **destructive interference** interférence destructive ◇ **interference fading** atténuation *f* (du signal) due à l'interférence ◇ **interference immunity** tolérance *f* à l'interférence ◇ **interference pattern** empreinte *f* d'interférence

interframe coding /ˌɪntəfreɪm 'kəʊdɪŋ/ *noun* codage *m* indépendant

interior gateway protocol /ɪnˌtɪəriə ˌgeɪtweɪ ˌprəʊtəʊ'kɒl/ *noun* routage *m* IGP

interior label /ɪnˌtɪəriə 'leɪb(ə)l/ *noun* label *m* d'identification; label *m* interne

interlace /ˌɪntə'leɪs/ *verb* entrelacer

interlaced scanning /ˌɪntəleɪsd 'skænɪŋ/ *noun* balayage *m* entrelacé

interlaced video /ˌɪntəleɪsd 'vɪdiəʊ/ *noun* vidéo *f* entrelacée

interleave /ˌɪntər'liːv/ *noun* imbrication *f*

interleaved /ˌɪntər'liːvd/ *adjective* (*sheets of paper*) interfolié -ée; placé, -ée entre deux feuilles; intercalé; (*sections of programs*) imbriqué,-ée

interleaved memory /ˌɪntərliːvd 'mem(ə)ri/ *noun* mémoire *f* imbriquée

interleave factor /ˌɪntərˌliːv 'fæktə/ *noun* (*ratio of sectors skipped between access operations*) facteur *m* d'imbrication

interleaving /ˌɪntər'liːvɪŋ/ *noun* **1.** (*putting blank paper between printed sheets*) interfoliage *m* **2.** (*dealing with processes alternately*) entrelacement *m*; emboîtement *m*

interlock /ˌɪntə'lɒk/ *noun* (*security device*) verrouillage *m*; protection *f* (par mot de passe) ■ *verb* verrouiller *vt*

interlude /'ɪntəˌluːd/ *noun* (*routine*) interlude *m*

intermediate access memory /ˌɪntəmiːdiət ˌækses 'mem(ə)ri/ *noun* mémoire *f* à accès intermédiaire

intermediate code /ˌɪntəmiːdiət 'kəʊd/ *noun* code *m* intermédiaire

intermediate file /ˌɪntəmiːdiət 'faɪl/ *noun* fichier *m* intermédiaire

intermediate storage /ˌɪntəmiːdiət 'stɔːrɪdʒ/ *noun* (*temporary area of memory*) mémoire *f* intermédiaire

intermediate system /ˌɪntəmiːdiət 'sɪstəm/ *noun* système *m* intermédiaire

intermediate system to intermediate system /ˌɪntəmiːdiət ˌsɪstəm tə ˌɪntəmiːdiət 'sɪstəm/ *noun* système *m* intermédiaire à système *m* intermédiaire

intermittent error /ˌɪntəmɪt(ə)nt 'erə/ *noun* erreur *f* intermittente

internal arithmetic /ɪnˌtɜːn(ə)l ə'rɪθmətɪk/ *noun* arithmétique *f* interne

internal character code /ɪnˌtɜːn(ə)l 'kærɪktə ˌkəʊd/ *noun* code *m* de caractères interne

internal command /ɪnˌtɜːn(ə)l kə'mɑːnd/ *noun* commande *f* interne

internal format /ɪnˌtɜːn(ə)l 'fɔːmæt/ *noun* format *m* interne

internal hard disk /ɪnˌtɜːn(ə)l 'hɑːd ˌdɪsk/ *noun* disque *m* dur interne

internal language /ɪnˌtɜːn(ə)l 'læŋgwɪdʒ/ *noun* langage *m* interne; langage *m* machine

internally stored program /ɪnˌtɜːn(ə)li stɔːd 'prəʊgræm/ *noun* programme *m* résident

internal memory /ɪnˌtɜːn(ə)l 'mem(ə)ri/ *noun* mémoire *f* interne

internal modem /ɪnˌtɜːn(ə)l ˌməʊ'dem/ *noun* (*modem that transfers information to the processor through the bus*) carte *f* modem

internal sort /ɪn'tɜːn(ə)l sɔːt/ *noun* tri *m* en mémoire interne

internal store /ɪnˌtɜːn(ə)l 'stɔː/ *noun* mémoire *f* interne

International Business Machines /ˌɪntənæʃ(ə)nəl 'bɪznəs məˌʃiːnz/ IBM

International Standards Organization /ˌɪntənæʃ(ə)nəl 'stændədz ˌɔːgənaɪzeɪʃ(ə)n/ *noun* organisme *m* international de normalisation ISO

International Standards Organization Open System Interconnection /ˌɪntənæʃ(ə)nəl ˌstændədz ˌɔːgənaɪzeɪʃ(ə)n ˌəʊpən ˌsɪstəm ˌɪntəkə'nekʃ(ə)n/ *noun* architecture *f* ISO/OSI

Internet /ˈɪntənet/ *noun* (*wide area network formed of local area networks*) Internet *m*

Internet address /ˈɪntənet əˌdres/ *noun* adresse *f* Internet; adresse *f* de site internet

Internet Assigned Numbers Authority /ˌɪntənet əˌsaɪnd ˈnʌmbəz ɔːˌθɒrɪti/ *noun* IANA

Internet banking /ˌɪntənet ˈbæŋkɪŋ/ *noun* banque *f* virtuelle

'...most banks now offer reasonable telephone and Internet banking facilities.' [*The Guardian*]

Internet café /ˈɪntənet ˌkæfeɪ/ *noun* café *m* Internet

Internet control message protocol /ˌɪntənet kənˌtrəʊl ˈmesɪdʒ ˌprəʊtəkɒl/ *noun* protocole *m* ICMP

Internet engineering task force /ˌɪntənet ˌendʒɪnɪərɪŋ ˈtɑːsk ˌfɔːs/ *noun* groupe *m* de travail IETF

Internet Explorer /ˌɪntənet ɪkˈsplɔːrə/ *noun* navigateur *m* Web

Internet group management protocol /ˌɪntənet gruːp ˈmænɪdʒmənt ˌprəʊtəkɒl/ *noun* protocole *m* IGMP

Internet Information Server /ˌɪntənet ˌɪnfə ˈmeɪʃ(ə)n ˌsɜːvə/ *noun* serveur *m* d'information Internet

Internet message access protocol /ˌɪntənet ˈmesɪdʒ ˌækses ˌprəʊtəkɒl/ *noun* protocole *m* de messagerie IMAP

Internet number /ˈɪntənet ˌnʌmbə/ *noun* adresse *f* Internet; adresse *f* de site internet

Internet protocol /ˌɪntənet ˈprəʊtəkɒl/ *noun* (*transmission of data over a network*) protocole *m* IP

Internet protocol address /ˌɪntənet ˌprəʊtəkɒl əˈdres/ *noun* adresse *f* IP

Internet relay chat /ˌɪntənet ˌriːleɪ ˈtʃæt/ *noun* système *m* IRC

Internet service provider /ˌɪntənet ˈsɜːvɪs prəˌvaɪdə/ *noun* fournisseur *m* de service internet

Internet telephony /ˌɪntənet təˈlefəni/ *noun* téléphonie *f* sur Internet

Internetwork /ˌɪntəˈnetwɜːk/ *noun* (*number of networks connected together*) interréseau *m*

Internetwork Packet Exchange /ˌɪntənetwɜːk ˈpækɪt ɪksˌtʃeɪndʒ/ (*network protocol developed by Novell*) protocole *m* IPX; protocole interréseau (de Novell)

interoperability /ˌɪntəˌɒpərəˈbɪlɪti/ *noun* (*the ability of two devices or computers to exchange information*) interopérabilité *f*

interpolation /ɪnˌtɜːpəˈleɪʃ(ə)n/ *noun* interpolation *f*

interpret /ɪnˈtɜːprɪt/ *verb* interpréter *vt*; traduire *vt*

interpretative /ɪnˈtɜːrprɪtətɪv/ *adjective* interprétatif

interpretative code /ɪnˌtɜːrprɪtətɪv ˈkəʊd/ *noun* code *m* interprétatif

interpretative program /ɪnˌtɜːrprɪtətɪv ˈprəʊgræm/ *noun* programme *m* interprétatif

interpreted language /ɪnˌtɜːprɪtd ˈlæŋgwɪdʒ/ *noun* langage *m* interprété

interpreter /ɪnˈtɜːprɪtə/ *noun* (*software*) interpréteur *m*

interrecord gap /ˌɪntərekɔːd ˈgæp/ *noun* espace *m* interbloc

interrogate /ɪnˈterəgeɪt/ *verb* interroger *vt*

interrupt /ˌɪntəˈrʌpt/ *noun* **1.** (*stopping of a transmission*) interruption *f* **2.** (*signal*) interruption *f* ◇ **interrupt handler (IH)** gestionnaire *m* d'interruption ◇ **interrupt request (IRQ)** demande *f* d'interruption ◇ **non-maskable interrupt (NMI)** interruption obligatoire *or* qui ne peut être invalidée *or* qui ne peut être masquée

interrupt-driven /ˈɪntərʌpt ˌdrɪv(ə)n/ *adjective* déclenché, -ée par interruption

interrupt handler /ˈɪntərʌpt ˌhændlə/ *noun* gestionnaire *m* d'interruption

interrupt level /ˈɪntərʌpt ˌlev(ə)l/ *noun* niveau *m* d'interruption

interrupt line /ˈɪntərʌpt laɪn/ *noun* ligne *f* d'interruption ◇ **this printer port design uses an interrupt line to let the CPU know it is ready to receive data** ce modèle de connecteur d'imprimante utilise une ligne d'interruption pour avertir l'unité centrale qu'il est prêt à recevoir des données

interrupt mask /ˈɪntərʌpt mɑːsk/ *noun* (*computer programming*) masque *m* d'interruption

interrupt priorities /ˈɪntərʌpt praɪˌɒrɪtiz/ *plural noun* priorités *fpl* d'interruption

interrupt request /ˈɪntərʌpt rɪˌkwest/ *noun* demande *f* d'interruption

interrupt servicing /ˈɪntərʌpt ˌsɜːvɪsɪŋ/ *noun* contrôle *m* et exécution d'interruption

interrupt signal /ˈɪntərʌpt ˌsɪgn(ə)l/ *noun* signal *m* d'interruption

interrupt stacking /ˈɪntərʌpt ˌstækɪŋ/ *noun* constitution *f* de pile d'interruptions

intersection /ˈɪntəˌsekʃən/ *noun* intersection *f*

interval /ˈɪntəv(ə)l/ *noun* intervalle *m*; délai *m* ◇ **there was an interval between pressing the key and the starting of the printout** il y a eu un intervalle entre le moment où on a appuyé sur la touche et la mise en marche de l'imprimante

interword spacing /ɪntəˌwɜːd ˈspeɪsɪŋ/ *noun* espacement *m* entre les mots

intimate /ˈɪntɪmət/ *adjective* (*software*) sur mesure; de constructeur; adapté à un ordinateur

intra /ˈɪntrə/, **intra frame** /ˈɪntrə freɪm/ *noun* intra-image *f*

intraframe coding /ˌɪntrəfreɪm ˈkəʊdɪŋ/ *noun* compression *f* spatiale

intranet /'ɪntrənet/ *noun* (*private network of computers within a company*) Intranet *m*

intruder /ɪn'truːdə/ *noun* (*person who is not authorized to use a computer*) intrus *m*; resquilleur *m*

inverse /ˌɪn'vɜːs/ *noun* contraire *m*; inverse *m*; opposé *m* ◇ **the inverse of 1 is 0** l'opposé de 1 est 0 ◇ **the inverse of true is false** le contraire de vrai est faux

inverse video /ˌɪnvɜːs 'vɪdiəʊ/ *noun* vidéo *f* inverse

inversion /ɪn'vɜːʃ(ə)n/ *noun* **1.** (*of numbers*) inversion *f* **2.** (*of signal or device*) inversion *f* ◇ **the inversion of a binary digit takes place in one's complement** il y a inversion du chiffre binaire dans le complément à un

invert /ˌɪn'vɜːt/ *verb* inverser *vt*

inverted backbone /ɪnˌvɜːtɪd 'bækbəʊn/ *noun* dorsale *f* inversée

inverted commas /ɪnˌvɜːtɪd 'kɒməz/ *plural noun* guillemets

inverted file /ɪnˌvɜːtɪd 'faɪl/ *noun* fichier *m* inversé

inverter /ɪn'vɜːtə/ *noun* **1.** (*logical gate*) inverseur *m* **2.** (*circuit*) inverseur *m* de courant

invisible /ɪn'vɪzɪb(ə)l/ *adjective* invisible; qui n'apparaît pas sur le texte imprimé

invitation /ˌɪnvɪ'teɪʃ(ə)n/ *noun* invitation *f* ◇ **invitation to send (ITS)** (signal d') invitation à transmettre

invitation to send /ˌɪnvɪteɪʃ(ə)n tə 'send/ *noun* invitation *f* à émettre

invoke /ɪn'vəʊk/ *verb* (*a program*) appeler *vt*

'…when an error is detected, the editor may be invoked and positioned at the statement in error' [*Personal Computer World*]

I/O /ˌaɪ 'əʊ/ *noun* entrée(s)/sortie(s) *f(pl)*

I/O address /ˌaɪ 'əʊ əˌdres/ *noun* adresse *f* des ports d'entrée/sortie

I/O bound /ˌaɪ əʊ 'baʊnd/ *adjective* limité par le débit d'entrée/sortie; avec contrainte de vitesse d'entrée/sortie

I/O buffer /ˌaɪ 'əʊ ˌbʌfə/ *noun* (*temporary storage area*) mémoire *f* tampon d'entrée/sortie

I/O bus /ˌaɪ 'əʊ ˌbʌs/ *noun* (*for transmission of data and control signals*) bus *m* (d') entrée/sortie

I/O channel /ˌaɪ 'əʊ ˌtʃæn(ə)l/ *noun* (*data transfer*) canal *m* d'entrée/sortie; voie *f* d'entrée/sortie

I/O device /ˌaɪ 'əʊ dɪˌvaɪs/ *noun* (*peripheral for inputting and outputting data*) appareil *m* d'entrée/sortie

I/O file /ˌaɪ 'əʊ ˌfaɪl/ *noun* fichier *m* (d') entrée/sortie

I/O instruction /ˌaɪ 'əʊ ˌɪnstrʌkʃ(ə)n/ *noun* instruction *f* (d') entrée/sortie

I/O mapping /ˌaɪ əʊ 'mæpɪŋ/ *noun* (*assigning a special address to I/O port*) configuration *f* d'entrée/sortie

IOP *abbr* (*input/output processor*) processeur *m* d'entrée/sortie

I/O port /ˌaɪ 'əʊ ˌpɔːt/ *noun* port *m* (d') entrée/sortie

I/O redirection /ˌaɪ əʊ ˌriːdaɪ'rekʃ(ə)n/ *noun* réacheminement *m* d'entrée/sortie

IORQ *abbr* (*input/output request*) demande *f* d'entrée/sortie

IP /ˌaɪ 'piː/ *noun* train *m* secondaire

i/p, I/P *abbr* (*input*) entrée *f*

IP address /aɪ 'piː əˌdres/ *noun* adresse *f* Internet

IP Datagram /ˌaɪ piː 'deɪtəgræm/ *noun* paquet *m* IP

IPL *abbr* (*initial program loader*) amorce *f*

IP multicast /ˌaɪ piː 'mʌltikɑːst/ *noun* protocole *m* Internet de multidiffusion

IPng /ˌaɪ piː en 'dʒiː/ *noun* protocole *m* Ipv6

ips /ˌaɪ piː 'es/ *noun* pouces *mpl* par seconde; pouce(s)/seconde

Ipsec /ˌaɪ ˌpiː sɪ'kjʊərəti/, **IP Security** *noun* association *f* de sécurité

IP spoofing /ˌaɪ ˌpiː 'spuːfɪŋ/ *noun* usurpation *f* d'adresse IP

IP terminal /ˌaɪ ˌpiː 'tɜːmɪn(ə)l/ *noun* terminal *m* d'entrée de données vidéotex

IR *abbr* **1.** (*information retrieval*) recherche *f* documentaire **2.** (*index register*) registre *m* d'index **3.** (*instruction register*) registre *m* d'instruction

IRC *abbr* (*Internet relay chat*) service *m* IRC

IrDA /ˌaɪ ɑː diː 'eɪ/ *noun* radar *m* infrarouge

IRQ /ˌaɪ ɑː 'kjuː/ *noun* IRQ

IS *abbr* (*intermediate system*) système *m* intermédiaire

ISAM *abbr* (*indexed sequential access method*) méthode *f* d'accès séquentiel indexé

ISDN /ˌaɪ es diː 'en/ *noun* réseau *m* numérique à intégration de services (RNIS)

IS-IS /ɪz ɪz/ *noun* protocole *m* de routage IS-IS

ISO *abbr* (*International Standards Organization*) ISO

ISO 9660 *noun* norme *f* ISO 9660

isochronous network /aɪˌsɒkrən(ə)s 'netwɜːk/ *noun* réseau *m* isochrone; réseau *m* synchrone

isochronous transmission /aɪˌsɒkrən(ə)s trænz'mɪʃ(ə)n/ *noun* transmission *f* isochrone; transmission *f* synchrone

isolate /'aɪsəˌleɪt/ *verb* (*to separate or to insulate*) isoler *vt*

isolated location /ˌaɪsəleɪtɪd ləʊ'keɪʃ(ə)n/ *noun* zone *f* protégée

isolation transformer /ˌaɪsəˌleɪʃ(ə)n træns ˈfɔːmə/ *noun* transformateur *m* de protection; transformateur *m* d'isolement

isolator /ˈaɪsəleɪtə/ *noun* (*device or material which isolates*) isolateur *m*

isometric view /ˌaɪsəʊˈmetrɪk vjuː/ *noun* (*in graphics – a drawing that shows all three dimensions of an object in equal proportion*) présentation *f* isométrique

ISO/OSI model /ˌaɪ es əʊ əʊ es ˈaɪ ˌmɒd(ə)l/ *noun* modèle *m* de référence OSI

ISP /ˌaɪ es ˈpiː/ *noun* fournisseur *m* de services Internet

ISR *abbr* (*information storage and retrieval*) stockage *m* et restitution de données

IT *abbr* (*information technology*) technologies *fpl* de l'information

italic /ɪˈtælɪk/ *noun* italique *(m)* ◇ **all the footnotes are printed in italics** les notes de bas de page sont toutes en italique ◇ **hit CTRL I to print the text in italics** tapez CTRL I pour imprimer les italiques ◇ **the headline is printed in italic and underlined** le titre est en italique souligné

item size /ˈaɪtəm saɪz/ *noun* dimension *f* d'une unité d'information; dimension *f* d'un item

iterate /ˈɪtəreɪt/ *noun* routine *f* itérative

iteration /ˌɪtəˈreɪʃ(ə)n/ *noun* itération *f*

iterative process /ˌɪtərətɪv ˈprəʊses/ *noun* processus *m* itératif

iterative routine /ˌɪtərətɪv ruːˈtiːn/ *noun* routine *f* itérative

ITS *abbr* (*invitation to send*) invitation *f* à émettre

J

jabber /ˈdʒæbə/ *noun* (*continuous random signal*) bruit *m* parasite

jack /dʒæk/, **jack plug** /dʒæk plʌg/ *noun* fiche *f*; jack *m*

jaggies /ˈdʒægiːz/ *plural noun* (*jagged edges*) crénelage *m*; effet *m* d'escalier

Java /ˈdʒɑːvə/ (*programming language and program definition developed by Sun Microsystems used to create small applications called 'applets'*) Java™

Java Beans /ˈdʒɑːvə biːnz/ (*trade name for a software system developed by Sun Microsystems*) modèle *m* de composant JavaBeans

Java Database Connectivity /ˌdʒɑːvə ˌdeɪtəbeɪs ˌkɒnekˈtɪvɪti/ (*trade name for a set of standard functions*) connectivité JDBC

JavaScript /ˈdʒɑːvəskrɪpt/ (*set of programming commands that can be included within a normal Web page that is written using HTML commands*) JavaScript™

JCL /ˌdʒaɪ siː ˈel/ *noun* langage *m* de commande de tâche

JDBC *abbr* (*Java Database Connectivity*) connectivité *f* JDBC

jitter /ˈdʒɪtə/ *noun* **1.** (*in a facsimile transmission*) tremblotement *m*; sautillement *m*; papillotement *m* **2.** (*image or screen*) gigue *f* ◇ **looking at this screen jitter is giving me a headache** j'ai mal à la tête à force de regarder cet écran qui tremblote

JK-flip-flop /ˌdʒeɪ keɪ ˈflɪp flɒp/ *noun* bascule *f* de type JK

job /dʒɒb/ *noun* tâche *f*; travail *m* ◇ **job control language (JCL)** langage *m* contrôle de tâche *or* de commande de tâche ◇ **remote job entry (RJE)** commande *f* de tâches à distance ◇ **the next job to be processed is to sort all the records** la tâche suivante consistera à trier tous les enregistrements

job control file /ˈdʒɒb kənˌtrəʊl faɪl/ *noun* fichier *m* de contrôle de tâche

job control language /ˌdʒɒb kənˈtrəʊl ˌlæŋgwɪdʒ/ *noun* langage *m* de commande de tâche

job control program /ˈdʒɒb kənˌtrəʊl ˌprəʊgræm/ *noun* programme *m* de contrôle de tâche

job file /ˈdʒɒb ˌfaɪl/ *noun* fichier *m* de travaux; fichier *m* de tâches à exécuter

job mix /ˈdʒɒb ˌmɪks/ *noun* ensemble *m* des travaux en cours d'exécution; ensemble *m* des tâches en cours d'exécution

job number /dʒɒb ˈnʌmbə/ *noun* numéro *m* de suite d'une tâche dans la file d'attente

job orientated language /ˌdʒɒb ˌɔːriənteɪtɪd ˈlæŋgwɪdʒ/ *noun* langage *m* d'application

job orientated terminal /ˌdʒɒb ˌɔːriənteɪtɪd ˈtɜːmɪn(ə)l/ *noun* terminal *m* d'application; terminal *m* spécialisé

job priority /dʒɒb praɪˈɒrɪti/ *noun* priorité *f* d'une tâche

job processing /dʒɒb ˌprəˈsesɪŋ/ *noun* traitement *m* de tâche

job queue /ˈdʒɒb ˌkjuː/ *noun* file *f* d'attente

job scheduling /ˈdʒɒb ˌʃedjuːlɪŋ/ *noun* (*arranging the order of jobs to be processed*) planification *f* de la séquence d'exécution des tâches; répartition *f* des tâches

job statement control /ˈdʒɒb ˌsteɪtmənt kənˌtrəʊl/ *noun* contrôle *m* d'exécution des tâches

job step /ˈdʒɒb ˌstep/ *noun* étape *f* d'un travail

job stream /ˈdʒɒb ˌstriːm/ *noun* (*job queue*) file *f* d'attente

join /dʒɔɪn/ *verb* (*to combine pieces of information*) assembler *vt*; fusionner *vti* ■ *noun* (*logical function*) fonction *f* d'union; opération *f* OU

joint denial /dʒɔɪnt dɪˈnaɪəl/ *noun* (*logical function*) négation *f* connexe; opération *f* NON-OU; NI

Joint Photographic Experts Group /ˌdʒɔɪnt fəʊtəˌgræfɪks ˈekspɜːts gruːp/ *noun* norme *f* JPEG

journal /ˈdʒɜːn(ə)l/ *noun* **1.** (*record of communications*) journal *m* **2.** (*list of changes to a file*) journal *m*; liste *f* des modifications ◇ **learned journal** revue *f* spécialisée *or* revue savante ◇ **the modified records were added to the master file and noted in the journal** les enregistrements modifiés ont été ajoutés au fichier maître et inscrits au journal des modifications

journal file /ˈdʒɜːn(ə)l faɪl/ *noun* fichier *m* chronologique; fichier-journal *m*

joystick /'dʒɔɪˌstɪk/ *noun* (*device that allows a user to move a cursor*) manette *f* de jeu; manche *m* à balai; joystick *m*

joystick port /'dʒɔɪˌstɪk pɔːt/ *noun* (*socket and interfacing circuit*) connecteur *m* ◇ **a joystick port is provided with the home computer** l'ordinateur familial possède un port (pour manette de) jeu

JPEG /'dʒeɪ peg/ *noun* norme *f* JPEG

JPEG++ /ˌdʒaɪ peg plʌs 'plʌs/ *noun* JPEG++

JScript /'dʒaɪskrɪpt/ (*trade name for a version of JavaScript developed by Microsoft*) Java Script

jukebox /'dʒuːkˌbɒks/ *noun* (*CD-ROM drive that can hold several CD-ROM discs and select the correct disc when required*) juke-box *m*

Julian date /'dʒuːliən deɪt/ *noun* date *f* ordinale

jumbo chip /'dʒʌmbəʊ tʃɪp/ *noun* puce *f* géante; circuit *m* à très haut niveau d'intégration

jump /dʒʌmp/ *noun* instruction *f* de branchement; instruction *f* de saut ■ *verb* effectuer un branchement

jumper /'dʒʌmpə/ *noun* (*on circuit board*) cavalier *m*; connecteur *m* mâle à deux broches ◇ **the printer's typeface is jumper-selectable** sur cette imprimante, la police de caractères peut être sélectionnée par cavalier

jumper-selectable /ˌdʒʌmpə sɪ'lektəb(ə)l/ *adjective* qui peut être sélectionné; validé par cavalier ◇ **the printer's typeface is jumper-selectable** sur cette imprimante, la police de caractères peut être sélectionnée par cavalier

jump instruction /'dʒʌmp ɪnˌstrʌkʃən/ *noun* branchement *m*; saut *m*

jump on zero /ˌdʒʌmp ɒn 'zɪərəʊ/ *noun* branchement *m* conditionnel à zéro ◇ **the jump on zero instruction tests the zero flag** l'instruction de branchement conditionnel à zéro teste l'indicateur zéro

jump operation /dʒʌmp ˌɒpə'reɪʃ(ə)n/ *noun* opération *f* de branchement

junction /'dʒʌŋkʃən/ *noun* (*connection*) jonction *f*

junction box /'dʒʌŋkʃən bɒks/ *noun* (*connection of wires*) boîte *f* de jonction

junction transistor /ˌdʒʌŋkʃən træn'zɪstə/ *noun* transistor *m* bipolaire; transistor *m* à jonction

junk /dʒʌŋk/ *noun* camelote *f*; rebut *m* ■ *verb* virer *vt*; éjecter *vt*; mettre à la poubelle ◇ **space junk** satellites *mpl* hors d'usage *or* de rebut (qui tournent dans l'espace) ◇ **to junk a file** virer *or* effacer un fichier

justification /ˌdʒʌstɪfɪ'keɪʃ(ə)n/ *noun* justification *f* ◇ **an American hyphenation and justification program will not work with British English spellings** un programme de coupe de mots et justification établi aux Etats- Unis ne peut être utilisé pour un texte en anglais britannique

justify /'dʒʌstɪˌfaɪ/ *verb* **1.** (*changes of characters in a document*) justifier *vt* **2.** (*computer register*) justifier (la pile)

justify inhibit /'dʒʌstɪfaɪ ɪnˌhɪbɪt/ *noun* instruction *f* d'invalider la justification

K

K *symbol* (*represents 1,024 or 2^{10}*) K; kilo

K6 (*64-bit processor developed by AMD Corporation*) processeur *m* K6™

K56flex K56flex

Karnaugh map /ˈkɑːnəʊ mæp/ *noun* table *f* de Karnaugh ◇ **the prototype was checked for hazards with a Karnaugh map** le prototype a fait l'objet d'un contrôle de fiabilité statistique sur la base des tables de Karnaugh

KB, Kb *abbr* (*kilobyte*) kilobit *m*; kilo-octet *m*

Kbit /ˈkeɪ bɪt/ *abbr* (*kilobit*) kilobit *m*

Kbps /ˌkeɪ biː piː ˈes/ *noun* kilobit *m* par seconde

Kbyte /ˈkeɪ baɪt/ *abbr* (*kilobyte*) kilo-octet *m*

Kermit /ˈkɜːmɪt/ *noun* (*file transfer protocol*) Kermit

kern /kɜːn/ *verb* (*adjust space between letters*) serrer *vt*; réduire l'espace entre deux caractères ◇ **we have kerned 'T' and 'o' so they are closer together** nous avons réduit l'espace entre le T et le o pour les rapprocher

kernel /ˈkɜːn(ə)l/ *noun* (*essential instruction routines*) noyau *m* (du système d'exploitation) ◇ **graphics kernel system (GKS)** fonctions *fpl* graphiques GKS

key /kiː/ *noun* **1.** (*on a keyboard*) touche *f* **2.** (*important object*) clé *f*; clef *f* **3.** (*numbers to encrypt or decrypt a message*) clé *f* d'un code **4.** (*identification code*) clé *f* (d'identification); clé *f* de recherche; mot-clé *m* ■ *verb* (*to activate a key*) actionner une touche ◇ **key force** pression *f* nécessaire pour actionner une touche ◇ **key management** gestion *f* de clé ◇ **key travel** jeu vertical *or* course *f* d'une touche ◇ **number keys** (*on a phone*) touches de numérotation (d'un téléphone) ◇ **shift key** touche des majuscules ◇ **there are 84 keys on the keyboard** le clavier comporte 84 touches ◇ **type this key into the machine, that will decode the last message** tapez la clé et vous pourrez décoder le dernier message ◇ **we selected all the records with the word DISK in their keys** nous avons sélectionné les enregistrements en utilisant le mot DISK comme clé de recherche ◇ **without the key overlay, I would never remember which function key does what** sans la grille d'aide, je ne saurais jamais quelle touche de fonction je dois utiliser

keyboard /ˈkiːbɔːd/ *noun* clavier *m* ■ *verb* saisir des données au clavier ◇ **AZERTY keyboard** clavier AZERTY (utilisé surtout dans les pays francophones) *or* clavier français accentué ◇ **it was cheaper to have the manuscript keyboarded by someone else** il était plus économique de faire saisir *or* de faire taper le manuscrit par quelqu'un d'autre ◇ **keyboard scan** (*method of control*) contrôle *m* de clavier *or* d'utilisation de touches par scanning ◇ **keyboard send *or* receive (KSR)** terminal *m* entrée/sortie *or* émetteur/récepteur à clavier ◇ **touch-sensitive keyboard** clavier tactile *or* à effleurement

'…the main QWERTY typing area is in the centre of the keyboard with the 10 function keys on the left' [*Personal Computer World*]

keyboard contact bounce /ˌkiːbɔːd ˌkɒntækt ˈbaʊns/ *noun* rebond *m* d'une touche de clavier

keyboard encoder /ˈkiːbɔːd ɪnˌkəʊdə/ *noun* encodeur *m* des touches

keyboarder /ˈkiːbɔːdə/ *noun* claviste *m&f*; opérateur, -trice de saisie

keyboarding /ˈkiːbɔːdɪŋ/ *noun* saisie *f* (au clavier)

keyboard layout /ˈkiːbɔːd ˌleɪaʊt/ *noun* disposition *f*

keyboard overlay /ˈkiːbɔːd ˌəʊvəleɪ/ *noun* grille *f* d'aide de clavier; mémento *m* de fonction des touches de clavier

keyboard send/receive /ˌkiːbɔːd send rɪ ˈsiːv/ *noun* terminal *m* entrée/sortie; émetteur/récepteur *m* à clavier

keyboard to disk entry /ˌkiːbɔːd tə ˈdɪsk ˌentri/ *noun* saisie *f* directe sur disquette par clavier

key click /ˈkiː klɪk/ *noun* clic *m* témoin de touche

key combination /ˈkiː ˌkɒmbɪneɪʃ(ə)n/ *noun* touche *f* raccourci

keyed sequential access method /ˌkiːd sɪ ˌkwenʃəl ˈækses ˌmeθəd/ *noun* méthode *f* d'accès séquentiel indexé multiclé(s)

key escrow /ˌkiː ˈeskrəʊ/ *noun* système *m* de fiducie de la clé

key feature /ˌkiː ˈfiːtʃə/ *noun* caractéristique *f* principale

key field /ˌkiː ˈfiːld/ *noun* champ *m* clé

key matrix /ˌkiː 'meɪtrɪks/ *noun* (*keyboard*) implantation *f* des touches sur un clavier

key number /'kiː ˌnʌmbə/ *noun* code *m* numérique d'une touche

key overlay /ˌkiː 'əʊvəleɪ/ *noun* grille *f* d'aide de clavier; mémento *m* de fonction des touches de clavier ◇ **without the key overlay, I would never remember which function key does what** sans la grille d'aide, je ne saurais jamais quelle touche de fonction je dois utiliser

keypad /'kiːˌpæd/ *noun* clavier *m* auxiliaire; pavé *m* numérique

'...it uses a six button keypad to select the devices and functions' [*Byte*]

key punch /'kiː pʌntʃ/ *noun* perforatrice *f* à clavier

key rollover /ˌkiː 'rəʊləʊvə/ *noun* clavier *m* à mémoire tampon; clavier *m* rapide

key shortcut /ˌkiː 'ʃɔːtkʌt/ *noun* touche *f* raccourci

key strip /'kiː strɪp/ *noun* marquage *m* mnémotechnique

keystroke /'kiːstrəʊk/ *noun* frappe *f* ◇ **he keyboards at a rate of 3500 keystrokes per hour** il peut saisir un texte au rythme de 3500 frappes/heure ◇ **keystroke rate** vitesse *f* de frappe ◇ **keystrokes per hour** (nombre de) frappes par heure *or* frappes/heure

keystroke count /'kiːstrəʊk ˌkaʊnt/ *noun* nombre *m* de frappes

keystroke verification /ˌkiːstrəʊk ˌverɪfɪ 'keɪʃ(ə)n/ *noun* contrôle *m* de la frappe des touches

key terminal /ˌkiː 'tɜːmɪn(ə)l/ *noun* terminal *m* principal

key-to-disk /ˌkiː tə 'dɪsk/ *noun* saisie *f* directe sur disque par clavier

keyword /'kiːwɜːd/ *noun* (*command word*) commande *f*; (*important word in a title or text or subject*) mot *m* principal; mot-clé *m* ◇ **computer is a keyword in IT** le mot computer est un mot-clé en informatique ◇ **keyword and context (KWAC)** (*library system*) mot-clé et contexte ◇ **keyword in context (KWIC)** mot-clé en contexte ◇ **keyword out of context (KWOC)** mot-clé hors contexte

KHz *abbr* (*kilohertz*) kilohertz *m*

kill /kɪl/ *verb* (*file or program*) détruire *vt*; effacer *vt*

kilo /'kɪləʊ/ *prefix* **1.** (*1,024 units, equal to* 2^{10}) kilo *m* **2.** kilo

kilobaud /'kɪləbɔːd/ *noun* kilobaud *m*

kilobit /'kɪləbɪt/ *noun* kilobit *m*

kilo bits per second /ˌkiːləʊ bɪts pɜː 'sekənd/ *noun* kilobits *mpl* par seconde

kilobyte /'kɪləʊˌbaɪt/ *noun* kilo-octet *m*

kilohertz /'kɪləhɜːts/ *noun* kilohertz *m*

kilo instructions per second /ˌkɪləʊ ɪn ˌstrʌkʃənz pɜː 'sekənd/ *noun* millier *m* d'instructions par seconde

kiloword /'kɪləwɜːd/ *noun* kilo-mot *m*

kiosk /'kiːɒsk/ *noun* (*information*) borne *f* interactive

KIPS /ˌkeɪ aɪ piː 'es/ *noun* millier *m* d'instructions par seconde

Klamath /'klæmæθ/ (*code name for the low-cost version of the Intel Pentium Pro processor*) Klamath™

kludge, kluge *noun informal* bricolage *m*; (*software or hardware*) programme *m*; système *m* hâtivement bricolé

kluged /kluːdʒd/ *adjective* bricolé,-ée; retapé,-ée

knob /nɒb/ *noun* bouton *m* ◇ **the brightness can be regulated by turning a knob at the back of the monitor** pour ajuster la luminosité de l'écran, tourner le bouton placé à l'arrière du moniteur ◇ **turn the on *or* off knob** tourner le bouton marche/arrêt

knowledge base /'nɒlɪdʒ beɪs/ *noun* base *f* de connaissances

knowledge-based system /ˌnɒlɪdʒ beɪst 'sɪstəm/ *noun* système *m* à base de connaissances

knowledge engineering /'nɒlɪdʒ ˌendʒɪnɪərɪŋ/ *noun* ingénierie *f* de la connaissance

knowledge industry /'nɒlɪdʒ ˌɪndəstri/ *noun* industrie *f* de matière grise

KSAM /ˌkeɪ es eɪ 'em/ *noun* méthode *f* d'accès séquentiel indexé multiclé(s)

KSR /ˌkeɪ es 'ɑː/ *noun* terminal *m* entrée/sortie; émetteur/récepteur *m* à clavier

KW *abbr* **1.** (*kilowatt*) kilowatt *m* **2.** (*kiloword*) K-mot *m*

KWAC /kwæk/ *noun* système *m* de thésaurus; mot-clé *m* et contexte

KWIC /kwɪk/ *noun* mot-clé *m* en contexte

KWOC /kwɒk/ *noun* mot-clé *m* hors contexte

L

L1 cache /ˌel ˈwʌn ˌkæʃ/ *noun* mémoire *f* cache premier niveau; mémoire *f* cache de niveau 1

L2 cache /ˌel ˈtuː ˌkæʃ/ *noun* mémoire *f* cache second niveau; mémoire *f* de niveau 2

label /ˈleɪb(ə)l/ *noun* **1.** (*word or other symbol used to identify a routine or statement*) étiquette *f*; label *m*; (*character or characters used to identify data*) identificateur *m* **2.** (*character or characters used to identify data*) étiquette *f*; label *m*; (*for quality*) label *m* de qualité ■ *verb* (*to put a label on a product*) étiqueter *vt*; (*to put a label on a program*) produire un label ◇ **BASIC uses many program labels such as line numbers** les programmes en langage BASIC contiennent plusieurs labels dont la numérotation des lignes

label field /ˈleɪb(ə)l fiːld/ *noun* champ *m* label

labelling /ˈleɪb(ə)lɪŋ/ *noun* (*putting a label on a product*) étiquetage *m*; (*printing labels*) impression *f* d'étiquettes

label printer /ˈleɪb(ə)l ˌprɪntə/ *noun* imprimante *f* d'étiquettes

lag /læg/ *noun* (*of signal*) retard *m*; décalage *m* ◇ **time lag is noticeable on international phone calls** le décalage est perceptible sur les lignes téléphoniques internationales

lambda calculus /ˌlæmdə ˈkælkjʊləs/ *noun* lambda-calcul *m*

LAN, lan *noun* réseau *m* local (d'entreprise)

> 'The opportunities to delete and destroy data are far greater on our LAN than in the days when we had a mainframe. PC people are culturally different from mainframe people. You really don't think about security problems when you can physically lock your system up in a closet.' [*Computing*]

landing zone /ˈlændɪŋ zəʊn/ *noun* (*area of a hard disk which does not carry data*) zone *f* de parcage

landline /ˈlæn(d)ˌlaɪn/ *noun* (*communications link via cable*) câble *m*; liaison *f*; (*cable*) ligne *f* terrestre

landscape /ˈlændskeɪp/ *noun* (*page where the longest edge is horizontal*) paysage *m*

language /ˈlæŋgwɪdʒ/ *noun* (*spoken or written*) langue *f*; (*for computers*) langage *m* ◇ **foreign language** langue étrangère ◇ **he speaks several European languages** il parle plusieurs langues européennes ◇ **high-level language (HLL)** langage de haut niveau *or* langage évolué ◇ **low-level language (LLL)** langage de bas niveau *or* langage peu évolué ◇ **query language (QL)** langage de requête *or* d'interrogation

language assembler /ˈlæŋgwɪdʒ əˌsemblə/ *noun* assembleur *m*

language compiler /ˈlæŋgwɪdʒ kəmˌpaɪlə/ *noun* (*encoding of a source program*) compilateur *m* d'un langage évolué

language interpreter /ˈlæŋgwɪdʒ ɪn ˌtɜːprɪtə/ *noun* interpréteur *m*

language processor /ˌlæŋgwɪdʒ ˌprəʊsesə/ *noun* processeur *m* de langage

language rules /ˈlæŋgwɪdʒ ruːlz/ *plural noun* syntaxe *fpl*

language support environment /ˌlæŋgwɪdʒ səˈpɔːt ɪnˌvaɪərənmənt/ *noun* aides *mpl* à la programmation dans un langage déterminé

language translation /ˈlæŋgwɪdʒ træns ˌleɪʃ(ə)n/ *noun* traduction *f* d'un langage en un autre langage

language translator /ˈlæŋgwɪdʒ træns ˌleɪtə/ *noun* traducteur *m* (de langage)

LAN Manager /ˈlæn ˌmænɪdʒə/ (*Microsoft network operating system*) LAN Manager™

LAN segment /læn ˈsegmənt/ *noun* segment *m* de réseau local

LAN server /læn ˈsɜːvə/ *noun* (*IBM network operating system*) LAN Server™

LAN Server /ˈlæn ˌsɜːvə/ (*IBM network operating system*) LAN Server™

lap /læp/ *noun* (*overlap*) chevauchement *m*

LAP /ˌel eɪ ˈpiː/ *noun* (*CCITT standard protocol*) standard *m* LAP

LAP-B /læp biː/ *noun* routine *f* d'installation LAP-B

LAP-M /læp em/ *noun* protocole *m* de connexion des modems

laptop /ˈlæptɒp/, **laptop computer** /ˌlæptɒp kəmˈpjuːtə/ *noun* portable *m*; laptop *m*

> 'Michael Business Systems has provided research company BMRB with 240 Toshiba laptop computers in a deal valued at £300,000. The deal includes a three-year maintenance contract.' [*Computing*]

large model /lɑːdʒ ˈmɒd(ə)l/ *noun* (*memory model in an Intel processor*) grand modèle *m* (de mémoire des processeurs INTEL)

large-scale /'lɑːdʒ skeɪl/ *adjective* à grande échelle

large-scale computer /ˌlɑːdʒ skeɪl kəm'pjuːtə/ *noun* gros ordinateur *m*

large-scale integration /ˌlɑːdʒ skeɪl ˌɪntɪ'greɪʃ(ə)n/ *noun* intégration *f* à grande échelle

laser /'leɪzə/ *noun* (*Light Amplification by Stimulated Emission of Radiation*) laser *m* ◇ **laser beam communications** communication *f* par rayon laser ◇ **laser beam recording (LBR)** enregistrement *m* par rayon laser

laser disc /'leɪzə dɪsk/ *noun* disque *m* laser

laser emulsion storage /ˌleɪzə ɪˌmʌlʃ(ə)n 'stɔːrɪdʒ/ *noun* mémoire *f* (à) laser sur couche haute définition

LaserJet /'leɪzədʒet/ (*Hewlett Packard laser printer*) LaserJet

laser printer /'leɪzə ˌprɪntə/ *noun* imprimante *f* à laser

LaserWriter /'leɪzəraɪtə/ (*Apple laser printer*) imprimante *f* Apple LaserWriter™

last in first out /ˌlɑːst ɪn ˌfɜːst 'aʊt/ *adjective* méthode *f* du dernier entré premier sorti; méthode *f* LIFO

last in last out /ˌlɑst ɪn lɑːst 'aʊt/ *adjective* dernier entré, dernier sorti

latch /lætʃ/ *verb* (*electronic component that maintains an output value*) verrouiller *vt*

latency /'leɪt(ə)nsi/ *noun* période *f*; temps *m* de latence

launch /lɔːntʃ/ *noun* (*of new product*) lancement *m*; (*satellite*) mise *f* en orbite ■ *verb* **1.** (*new product*) lancer *vt* **2.** (*start a program*) lancer *vt* ◇ **the launch date for the network will be September** le lancement du réseau aura lieu en septembre ◇ **the launch of the new PC has been put back six months** le lancement du nouvel ordinateur individuel se fera avec six mois de retard ◇ **the new PC was launched at the Personal Computer Show** on a lancé le nouvel ordinateur personnel au Salon de l'Informatique ◇ **you launch the word-processor by double-clicking on this icon** on lance le traitement de texte avec un double clic sur cette icône

layer /'leɪə/ *noun* (*division of space*) couche *f*

layered /'leɪəd/ *adjective* disposé en couches *or*, -ée

layout /'leɪaʊt/ *noun* **1.** (*outline or design*) mise *f* en page(s) **2.** (*distribution*) spécifications *fpl* de présentation des données ◇ **the design team is working on the layouts for the new magazine** les designers travaillent à la mise en pages de la nouvelle revue

LCD /ˌel siː 'diː/ *noun* (*display that uses liquid crystals*) écran *m* à cristaux liquides; affichage *m* à cristaux liquides

LCD screen /ˌel siː 'diː skriːn/ *noun* écran *m* à cristaux liquides; affichage *m* à cristaux liquides

LCD shutter printer /ˌel siː ˌdiː 'ʃʌtə/ *noun* imprimante *f* à transfert LCD

LCP /ˌel siː 'piː/ *noun* protocole *m* de transmission

LDAP /'el dæp/ *noun* protocole *m* LDAP

lead /liːd/ *noun* (*wire*) câble *m*; fil *m* conducteur

leader /'liːdə/ *noun* (*beginning of the reel*) amorce *f*

leader record /'liːdə ˌrekɔːd/ *noun* enregistrement *m* de tête

lead in /'liːd ɪn/ *noun* sommaire *m*

leading /'liːdɪŋ/ *noun* (*space in printing*) interligne *m*; (*action*) interlignage *m*

leading edge /'liːdɪŋ edʒ/ *noun* (*of punched card*) bord *m* d'introduction; bord *m* avant

leading zero /ˌliːdɪŋ 'zɪərəʊ/ *noun* zéro *m* de tête

leaf /liːf/ *noun* (*final node in data tree*) feuille *f* (de papier); (*of book*) page *f*; (*final node in data tree*) élément *m* final d'une arborescence

leap-frog test /'liːp frɒg ˌtest/ *noun* test *m* sélectif; test *m* de lecture/écriture aléatoire des mémoires; test *m* saut de puce

learning curve /'lɜːnɪŋ kɜːv/ *noun* (*graph of how someone can acquire knowledge*) courbe *f* d'apprentissage

lease /liːs/ *noun* bail *m* (de location) ■ *verb* louer *vt* ◇ **the company has a policy of only using leased equipment** la société a pour politique de louer son matériel ◇ **the company leases all its computers** la société loue tous ses ordinateurs

leased line /'liːsd ˌlaɪn/ *noun* (*communication channel*) ligne *f* louée; ligne *f* de location

least cost design /ˌliːst kɒst dɪ'zaɪn/ *noun* conception *f* économique; design *m* économique

least recently used algorithm /ˌliːst ˌriːs(ə)ntli juːzd 'ælgəˌrɪð(ə)m/ *noun* algorithme *m* d'ancienneté; algorithme *m* de la page la moins récemment utilisée

least significant bit /ˌliːst sɪgˌnɪfɪkənt 'bɪt/ *noun* bit *m* de poids faible; bit *m* le moins significatif

least significant digit /ˌliːst sɪgˌnɪfɪkənt 'dɪdʒɪt/ *noun* chiffre *m* le moins significatif; chiffre *m* de poids faible ◇ **least significant bit (LSB)** bit *m* le moins significatif *or* de poids faible

LED /ˌel iː 'diː/ *noun* diode *f* électroluminescente

LED printer /ˌel iː ˌdiː 'prɪntə/ *noun* imprimante *f* à diodes

left-click /left klɪk/ *verb* cliquer à l'aide du bouton gauche (de la souris)

left-handed mouse /ˌeft ˌhændɪd 'maʊs/ *noun* (*configuration of a mouse so that the function of the two buttons are reversed*) souris *f* pour gauchers

left justification /left ˌdʒʌstɪfɪ'keɪʃ(ə)n/ *noun* justification *f* à gauche

left justify /left 'dʒʌstɪˌfaɪ/ *verb* (*printing or binary number*) justifier à gauche

left shift /ˌleft 'ʃɪft/ *noun* décalage *m* à gauche; glissement *m* à gauche

leg /leg/ *noun* branchement *m*

legacy /'legəsi/ *noun* technologie *f* patrimoniale

legal /'liːg(ə)l/ *adjective* (*acceptable*) légal *or* -e; (*valid*) valide; (*permitted*) permis *or* -e; (*authorised*) autorisé *or* -ée

length /leŋθ/ *noun* longueur *f*

length of filename /ˌleŋθ əv 'faɪlneɪm/ *noun* longueur *f* du nom d'un fichier

letter bomb /'letə bɒm/ *noun* lettre *f* piégée

level /'lev(ə)l/ *noun* (*of electrical signal*) niveau *m*; (*of sound*) volume *m* ◇ **sound pressure level (SPL)** niveau de pression acoustique ◇ **turn the sound level down** baissez le volume (du son)

lexical analysis /ˌleksɪk(ə)l ə'næləsɪs/ *noun* analyse *f* lexicale

LF *abbr* (*line feed*) saut *m* de ligne

library /'laɪbrəri/ *noun* **1.** (*of files, books, etc.*) bibliothèque *f* **2.** (*of programs*) bibliothèque *f* **3.** (*of computer routines*) bibliothèque *f* ◇ **look up the bibliographical details in the library catalogue** consultez le catalogue de la bibliothèque pour obtenir les renseignements bibliographiques ◇ **the editors have checked all the references in the local library** les éditeurs ont vérifié toutes les références à la bibliothèque locale

library function /'laɪbrəri ˌfʌŋkʃən/ *noun* fonction *f* bibliothèque

library program /'laɪbrəri ˌprəʊgræm/ *noun* programme *m* de bibliothèque ◇ **the square root function is already in the library program** la fonction racine carrée se trouve déjà dans le programme de bibliothèque

library routine /'laɪbrəri ruːˌtiːn/ *noun* routine *f* de bibliothèque

library subroutine /ˌlaɪbrəri 'sʌbruːtiːn/ *noun* sous-programme *m* de bibliothèque

library track /'laɪbrəri træk/ *noun* piste *f* de référence

licence /'laɪs(ə)ns/ *noun* permis *m*; licence *f* ◇ **this software is manufactured under licence** ce logiciel est fabriqué sous licence

licence agreement /'laɪs(ə)ns əˌgriːmənt/ *noun* licence *f* d'utilisation d'un logiciel

lifetime /'laɪftaɪm/ *noun* (*time during which a device is useful*) durée *f* de vie ◇ **this new computer has a four-year lifetime** ce nouvel ordinateur a une durée de vie de quatre ans

LIFO /'laɪfəʊ/ *adjective* méthode *f* du dernier entré premier sorti; méthode *f* LIFO

lifter /'lɪftə/ *noun* écarteur *m* de bande

light /laɪt/ *noun* lumière *f* ◇ **coherent light** lumière cohérente *or* monochrome ◇ **light conduit** conducteur *m* de lumière ◇ **the VDU should not be placed under a bright light** il faut éviter de placer l'écran sous une lumière trop forte ◇ **ultraviolet light (UV light)** lumière ultra-violette *or* rayonnement ultra-violet ◇ **visible light** lumière visible

light-emitting diode /ˌlaɪt ɪˌmɪtɪŋ 'daɪəʊd/ *noun* diode *f* électroluminescente

light pen /'laɪt pen/ *noun* stylo *m* optique

lightweight /'laɪtweɪt/ *adjective* léger *or* -ère ◇ **a lightweight computer which can easily fit into a suitcase** un ordinateur léger qui tient facilement dans une valise

lightweight directory access protocol /ˌlaɪtweɪt daɪ'rekt(ə)ri ˌækses ˌprəʊtəkɒl/ *noun* protocole *m* LDAP

LILO /'laɪləʊ/ *adjective* dernier entré, dernier sorti

limited distance modem /ˌlɪmɪtɪd ˌdɪstəns 'məʊdem/ *noun* modem *m* pour réseau local; modem *m* à distance de transmission limitée

limiter /'lɪmɪtə/ *noun* (*electricity*) limitateur *m*

limiting resolution /ˌlɪmɪtɪŋ ˌrezə'luːʃ(ə)n/ *noun* définition *f* maximum

limits /'lɪmɪts/ *noun* (*for numbers in a computer*) limites *f*

line /laɪn/ *noun* **1.** (*cable*) ligne *f*; liaison *f* **2.** (*thin mark*) ligne *f*; trait *m*; (*printing*) filet *m* **3.** (*on screen*) ligne *f* **4.** (*of text*) ligne *f* (de texte) **5.** (*characters received as a single input*) ligne *f* **6.** (*row of commands*) ligne *f* de programme ◇ **line blanking interval** délai *m* de retour de ligne ◇ **line extender** (*in cable TV*) unité *f* d'extension d'une ligne ◇ **line impedance** impédance *f* de ligne ◇ **line load** charge *f* d'une ligne ◇ **line terminator** (*connection*) dispositif *m* de fin de ligne ◇ **line transient** courant *m* transitoire d'une ligne ◇ **the printer has difficulty in reproducing very fine lines** l'imprimante ne réussit pas très bien à imprimer les lignes très fines

> '...straight lines are drawn by clicking the points on the screen where you would like the line to start and finish' [*Personal Computer World*]

line adapter /laɪn ə'dæptə/ *noun* équilibreur *m* de ligne; équilibreur *m* d'impédance

line analyser /'laɪn ˌænəlaɪzə/ *noun* analyseur *m* de ligne

linear /'lɪniə/ *adjective* linéaire; séquentiel *or* -elle ◇ **linear array** (*antenna*) antenne *f* linéaire ◇ **linear function** fonction *f* linéaire ◇ **linear integrated circuit** circuit *m* intégré linéaire ◇ **the expression Y = 10 + 5X – 3W is a linear function** l'expression Y = 10 + 5X – 3W est une fonction linéaire ◇ **the expression Y = (10 + 5X²) is not a linear function** l'expression Y = (10 + 5X²) n'est pas une fonction linéaire

linear frame buffer /ˌlɪniə freɪm 'bʌfə/ *noun* mémoire *f* d'image linéaire

linearity /ˌlɪni'ærɪti/ *noun* linéarité *f*

linear list /'lɪniə lɪst/ *noun* liste *f* séquentielle

linear program /ˌlɪniə ˈprəʊgræm/ *noun* programme *m* linéaire

linear programming /ˌlɪniə ˈprəʊgræmɪŋ/ *noun* programmation *f* linéaire

linear search /ˌlɪniə ˈsɜːtʃ/ *noun* recherche *f* séquentielle

line break *noun* saut *m* de ligne

line busy tone /ˌlaɪn ˈbɪzi ˌtəʊn/ *noun* signal *m* ligne occupée

line communications /laɪn kəˌmjuːnɪˈkeɪʃ(ə)ns/ *plural noun* communication *f* par câble

line conditioning /laɪn kənˈdɪʃ(ə)nɪŋ/ *noun* maintenance *f* de ligne

line control /laɪn kənˈtrəʊl/ *noun* (*communication channel*) commandes *f*

line drawing /ˈlaɪn ˌdrɔːɪŋ/ *noun* dessin *m* au trait ◇ **the book is illustrated with line drawings and halftones** on trouve dans ce livre des dessins (au trait) et des illustrations en demi-teinte

line driver /laɪn ˈdraɪvə/ *noun* amplificateur *m* de ligne; amplificateur *m* de signal

line editor /laɪn ˈedɪtə/ *noun* (*or source program*) éditeur *m* ligne à ligne

line feed /ˈlaɪn fiːd/ *noun* saut *m* de ligne; interlignage *m*

line flyback /ˈlaɪn ˌflaɪbæk/ *noun* retour *m* de ligne

line frequency /laɪn ˈfriːkwənsi/ *noun* fréquence *f* (de balayage) de lignes

line gremlin /laɪn ˈgremlɪn/ *noun* perte *f* de transmission inexplicable

line in /ˈlaɪn ɪn/ *noun* entrée *f* de ligne

line input /ˌlaɪn ˈɪnpʊt/ *noun* validation *f* de ligne

line length /ˈlaɪn leŋθ/ *noun* (*horizontal display of characters*) longueur *f* d'une ligne

line level /laɪn ˈlev(ə)l/ *noun* niveau *m* de transmission (d'une ligne)

line noise /ˈlaɪn nɔɪz/ *noun* parasite *m*

line number /laɪn ˈnʌmbə/ *noun* numéro *m* d'une ligne

line out /ˈlaɪn aʊt/ *noun* sortie *f* de ligne

> '...while pixel editing is handy for line art, most desktop scanners have trouble producing the shades of grey or half-tones found in black and white photography' [*Publish*]

line printer /ˈlaɪn ˌprɪntə/ *noun* imprimante *f* ligne à ligne

line spacing /laɪn ˈspeɪsɪŋ/ *noun* interligne *m* ◇ **we use a local bridge to link the two LANs in the office** nous utilisons un pont local pour connecter les deux réseaux (locaux) du bureau

line speed /ˈlaɪn spiːd/ *noun* débit *m* d'une ligne

lines per minute /ˌlaɪnz pɜː ˈmɪnət/ *noun* lignes *fpl* par minute

line style /ˈlaɪn staɪl/ *noun* style *m* de trait

line width /ˈlaɪn, wɪdθ/ *noun* longueur *f* de ligne (en caractères)

Lingo /ˈlɪŋgəʊ/ Lingo

link /lɪŋk/ *noun* **1.** (*communication path*) liaison *f* **2.** (*software routine*) lien *m* ■ *verb* (*with interface*) relier *vt*; connecter *vt*; interfacer ◇ **satellite link** liaison *or* transmission *f* par satellite ◇ **the two computers are linked** les deux ordinateurs sont reliés ◇ **to transmit faster, you can use the direct link with the mainframe** pour une transmission plus rapide, vous pouvez utiliser la liaison directe avec le gros ordinateur

link access protocol /ˌlɪŋk ˈækses ˌprəʊtəkɒl/ *noun* protocole *m* d'accès à la liaison

linkage /ˈlɪŋkɪdʒ/ *noun* (*connection*) liaison *f*; (*of two devices*) couplage *m*; (*for program*) création *f* de liens ◇ **linkage editor** éditeur *m* de liens

linkage editing /ˈlɪŋkɪdʒ ˌedɪtɪŋ/ *noun* (*combining separate programs together*) mise *f* en place de liens (à l'aide d'un éditeur de liens)

linkage software /ˈlɪŋkɪdʒ ˌsɒftweə/ *noun* générateur *m* de liens ◇ **graphics and text are joined without linkage software** les graphiques et le texte sont assemblés sans l'aide d'un générateur de liens

link control procedure /ˌlɪŋk kənˈtrəʊl prəˌsiːdʒə/ *noun* protocole *m* de communication

link control protocol /ˌlɪŋk kənˈtrəʊl ˌprəʊtəkɒl/ *noun* protocole *m* de communication

linked list /ˌlɪŋkd ˈlɪst/ *noun* liste *f* chaînée; liste *f* concaténée

linked object /lɪŋkd ˈɒbdʒekt/ *noun* objet *m* lié

linked subroutine /ˌlɪŋkɪd ˌsʌbruːˈtiːn/ *noun* sous-programme *m* chaîné

linking /ˈlɪŋkɪŋ/ *noun* (*merging of small programs*) liaison *f*; enchaînement *m*; assemblage *m*

linking loader /ˈlɪŋkɪŋ ˌləʊdə/ *noun* chargeur/éditeur *m* de liens

link trials /lɪŋk ˈtraɪəlz/ *plural noun* tests *mpl* de contrôle de liens

Linux /ˈlɪnəks/ (*trade name for a version of the UNIX operating system originally developed by Linus Torvalds*) logiciel *m* libre

LIPS /lɪps/ *noun* interférences *fpl* logiques par seconde; LIPS

liquid crystal display /ˌlɪkwɪd ˌkrɪst(ə)l dɪsˈpleɪ/ *noun* (*for watches, calculators and digital displays*) écran *m* à cristaux liquides; affichage *m* à cristaux liquides

liquid crystal display shutter printer /ˌlɪkwɪd ˌkrɪstəl dɪˌspleɪ ˈʃʌtə ˌprɪntə/ *noun* imprimante *f* à transfert LCD

LISP /lɪsp/ *noun* langage *m* LISP

list /lɪst/ *noun* liste *f* ■ *verb* (*to print or display information*) lister *vt*; éditer sous forme de liste ◇ **to list a program** lister (les lignes d'instruction d') un programme

list box /ˈlɪst ˌbɒks/ *noun* zone *f* de liste déroulante

listing /ˈlɪstɪŋ/ *noun* listage *m*; listing *m* ◇ **a program listing** listage *or* listing d'un programme

listing paper /ˈlɪstɪŋ ˌpeɪpə/ *noun* papier *m* listing; papier *m* en continu

list processing /ˈlɪst ˌprəʊsesɪŋ/ *noun* **1.** langage *m* LISP **2.** langage *m* LISP; traitement *m* de liste

listserv /ˈlɪstˌsɜːv/, **listserver** /ˈlɪstsɜːvə/ *noun* gestionnaire *m* de liste de diffusion; serveur *m* de liste

listserver /ˈlɪstsɜːvə/ *noun* gestionnaire *m* de liste de diffusion

literal /ˈlɪt(ə)rəl/ *noun* **1.** (*operand*) littéral *m* **2.** (*printing error*) coquille *f*

literal operand /ˈlɪt(ə)rəl ˌɒpərænd/ *noun* opérande *m* littéral

lithium-Ion battery /ˌlɪθiəm ˈaɪən ˌbæt(ə)ri/ *noun* batterie *f* au lithium-ion

Live3D /ˌlaɪv θriː ˈdiː/ *noun* langage *m* VRML

liveware /ˈlaɪvweə/ *noun* personnel *m* informatique

LLC /ˌel el ˈsiː/ *noun* standard *m* LLC

LLL *abbr* (*low-level language*) langage *m* de bas niveau

load /ləʊd/ *verb* **1.** (*file or program*) charger *vt* **2.** (*disk or cartridge, etc.*) mettre en place; insérer *vt*; introduire *vt*; charger *vt* ◇ **load lower bin** introduire le bac inférieur ◇ **to scatter load** faire un chargement dispersé *or* éclaté

> '...this windowing system is particularly handy when you want to load or save a file or change directories' [*Byte*]

load and go /ˌləʊd ən ˈgəʊ/ *noun* chargement *m* et exécution

load and run /ˌləʊd ən ˈrʌn/ *noun* chargement *m* et exécution

loader /ˈləʊdə/ *noun* (*program*) chargeur *m* ◇ **initial program loader (IPL)** chargeur de programme de lancement

load high /ˈləʊd ˌhaɪ/ *verb* commande LOAD HIGH; LH *vt*

loading /ˈləʊdɪŋ/ *noun* (*of file*) chargement *m* ◇ **loading can be a long process** le chargement (d'un programme) peut être assez long à effectuer

load point /ˈləʊd pɔɪnt/ *noun* (*start of a recording section*) première position

load sharing /ˈləʊd ˌʃeərɪŋ/ *noun* partage *m* des tâches

local /ˈləʊk(ə)l/ *adjective* **1.** (*used in a certain section of a computer program*) local *or* -e **2.** (*system with limited access*) local *or* -e; localisé *or* -ée **3.** (*device that is physically attached and close to the controlling computer*) local *or* -e ◇ **the fastest expansion cards fit into this local bus connector** les cartes d'extension les plus rapides se placent dans ce connecteur local bus

local area network /ˌləʊk(ə)l ˌeəriə ˈnetwɜːk/ *noun* réseau *m* local d'entreprise

local area network server /ˌləʊk(ə)l ˌeəriə ˈnetwɜːk ˌsɜːvə/ *noun* serveur *m* de réseau local (d'entreprise)

local bridge /ˈləʊk(ə)l brɪdʒ/ *noun* pont *m* local

local bus /ˌləʊk(ə)l ˈbʌs/ *noun* bus *m* local ◇ **the fastest expansion cards fit into this local bus connector** les cartes d'extension les plus rapides se placent dans ce connecteur local bus

local declaration /ˌləʊk(ə)l ˌdekləˈreɪʃ(ə)n/ *noun* déclaration *f* d'une variable locale

local drive /ˈləʊk(ə)l draɪv/ *noun* lecteur *m* de disquette local; lecteur *m* de disquette non partagé

local format storage /ˌləʊk(ə)l ˌfɔːmæt ˈstɔːrɪdʒ/ *noun* mémoire *f* de format courant

local memory /ˌləʊk(ə)l ˈmem(ə)ri/ *noun* mémoire *f* locale

local mode /ˈləʊk(ə)l məʊd/ *noun* mode *m* local

local printer /ˌləʊk(ə)l ˈprɪntə/ *noun* imprimante *f* locale; imprimante *f* non partagée

LocalTalk /ˈləʊkəltɔːk/ (*cabling system in AppleTalk network*) réseau LocalTalk™

local variable /ˌləʊk(ə)l ˈveəriəb(ə)l/ *noun* variable *f* locale

locate /ləʊˈkeɪt/ *verb* **1.** (*place*) trouver *vt*; repérer *vt*; localiser *vt*; situer *vt* **2.** (*find*) trouver *vt* ◇ **have you managed to locate the programming fault?** avez-vous réussi à localiser l'erreur de programmation? ◇ **the computer is located in the main office building** l'ordinateur se trouve dans l'édifice principal

location /ləʊˈkeɪʃ(ə)n/ *noun* (*absolute address*) emplacement *m* (de mémoire) ◇ **location shots** les extérieurs *mpl* (d'un film) ◇ **on location** (*filming*) (prise de vue) en extérieur ◇ **the programme was shot on location in Spain** les extérieurs pour ce programme ont été tournés en Espagne

lock /lɒk/ *verb* (*system or file*) verrouiller *vt* ◇ **locking a file** verrouiller (l'accès à) un fichier

lockout /ˈlɒkaʊt/ *noun* (*over a network*) lockout *m*

lock up /ˌlɒk ˈʌp/ *noun* (*of computer*) blocage *m*; accrochage *m*; plantage *m*

log /lɒg/ *noun* (*computer science*) enregistrement *m*; entrée *f* dans un journal de bord ■ *verb* **1.** (*telecommunications*) enregistrer *vt*; tenir un journal **2.** (*start using device*) se connecter ◇ **to log calls** (*telephone*) enregistrer les appels

log file /ˈlɒg faɪl/ *noun* fichier *m* journal

logger /ˈlɒgə/ *noun* enregistreur *m* (chronologique)

logging /ˈlɒgɪŋ/ *noun* (*recording data*) enregistrement *m* ◇ **call logging** enregistrement d'appels ◇ **features of the program include error**

logging ce programme permet l'enregistrement (automatique) des erreurs

logging in /ˈlɒgɪŋ ɪn/ *noun* ouverture *f* de session

logging off /ˈlɒgɪŋ ɒf/ *noun* clôture *f* de session

logging on /ˈlɒgɪŋ ɒn/ *noun* ouverture *f* de session

logging out /ˈlɒgɪŋ aʊt/ *noun* fermeture *f* de session

logic /ˈlɒdʒɪk/ *noun* **1.** (*mathematical treatment*) logique *f* **2.** (*for deducing results from binary data*) logique *f* binaire **3.** (*components of a computer system*) logique *f* ◇ **logic array** circuit *m* logique en réseau ◇ **programmable logic array (PLA)** circuit logique en réseau programmable *or* logique câblée programmable ◇ **uncommitted logic array (ULA)** circuit logique en réseau non connecté

logical /ˈlɒdʒɪk(ə)l/ *adjective* logique ◇ **logical inferences per second (LIPS)** (*standard for the measurement of processing power of an inference engine*) (nombre d') inférences logiques par seconde *or* LIPS ◇ **logical reasoning can be simulated by an artificial intelligence machine** le raisonnement logique peut être simulé par une machine intelligente *or* un système expert

logical channel /ˌlɒdʒɪk(ə)l ˈtʃæn(ə)l/ *noun* voie *f* logique

logical chart /ˈlɒdʒɪk(ə)l tʃɑːt/ *noun* diagramme *m* logique

logical comparison /ˌlɒdʒɪk(ə)l kəm ˈpærɪs(ə)n/ *noun* comparaison *f* logique

logical decision /ˌlɒdʒɪk(ə)l dɪˈsɪʒ(ə)n/ *noun* décision *f* logique

logical drive /ˈlɒdʒɪk(ə)l draɪv/ *noun* lecteur *m* ◇ **the logical drive F: actually stores data on part of the server's disk drive** l'unité de disque logique F: stocke des données sur une section de l'unité de disque du serveur

logical error /ˌlɒdʒɪk(ə)l ˈerə/ *noun* erreur *f* logique

logical expression /ˌlɒdʒɪk(ə)l ɪkˈspreʃ(ə)n/ *noun* expression *f* logique

logical flowchart /ˈlɒdʒɪk(ə)l ˌfləʊtʃɑːt/ *noun* ordinogramme *m* logique

logical high /ˈlɒdʒɪk(ə)l haɪ/ *adjective* état *m* logique haut

logical inferences per second /ˌlɒdʒɪk(ə)l ˌɪnf(ə)rənsɪz pɜː ˈsekənd/ *noun* interférences *fpl* logiques par seconde; LIPS

logical link control /ˌlɒdʒɪk(ə)l ˈlɪŋk kən ˌtrəʊl/ *noun* standard *m* LLC

logical low /ˈlɒdʒɪk(ə)l ləʊ/ *adjective* état *m* logique bas

logical operator /ˌlɒdʒɪk(ə)l ˌɒpəˈreɪtə/ *noun* opérateur *m* logique

logical record /ˌlɒdʒɪk(ə)l ˈrekɔːd/ *noun* enregistrement *m*

logical ring /ˈlɒdʒɪk(ə)l rɪŋ/ *noun* anneau *m*

logical shift /ˈlɒdʒɪk(ə)l ʃɪft/ *noun* (*data movement*) décalage *m* logique

logical unit /ˌlɒdʒɪk(ə)l ˈjuːnɪt/ *noun* unité *f* logique

logic board /ˈlɒdʒɪk bɔːd/ *noun* carte *f* logique

logic bomb /ˈlɒdʒɪk bɒm/ *noun* bombe *f* logique

logic card /ˈlɒdʒɪk kɑːd/ *noun* carte *f* logique

logic circuit /ˈlɒdʒɪk ˌsɜːkɪt/ *noun* circuit *m* logique

logic element /ˈlɒdʒɪk ˌelɪmənt/ *noun* élément *m* logique

logic flowchart /ˈlɒdʒɪk ˌfləʊtʃɑːt/ *noun* diagramme *m* logique

logic gate /ˈlɒdʒɪk geɪt/ *noun* porte *f*

logic level /ˈlɒdʒɪk ˌlev(ə)l/ *noun* niveau *m* logique

logic map /ˈlɒdʒɪk mæp/ *noun* (*in a logic circuit*) configuration *f* logique

logic operation /ˈlɒdʒɪk ˌɒpəreɪʃ(ə)n/ *noun* opération *f* logique

logic-seeking /ˈlɒdʒɪk ˌsiːkɪŋ/ *adjective* à recherche logique

logic state /ˈlɒdʒɪk steɪt/ *noun* état *m* logique

logic state analyser /ˈlɒdʒɪk steɪt ˌænəlaɪzə/ *noun* analyseur *m* d'état de logique

logic symbol /ˈlɒdʒɪk ˌsɪmbəl/ *noun* symbole *m* logique

log in script /ˈlɒg ɪn ˌskrɪpt/ *noun* instructions *fpl* d'initialisation; séquence *f* d'initialisation

logo /ˈləʊgəʊ/ *noun* logotype *m*; (*high level programming language*) langage *m* LOGO; logo *m*

LOGO /ˈləʊgəʊ/ *noun* logotype *m*; (*high level programming language*) langage *m* LOGO; logo *m*

logoff /lɒgˈɒf/ *verb* fermeture *f* de session

logon /lɒgˈɒn/ *verb* ouverture *f* de session

log on server /lˈɒg ɒn ˌsɜːvə/ *noun* serveur *m* de contrôle des accès

logout /ˈlɒgaʊt/ *noun* fermeture *f* de session

long filename /lɒŋ ˈfaɪlˌneɪm/ *noun* (*feature of Windows 95 that lets a user give files a long name – up to 254 characters long*) nom *m* de fichier long de plusieurs caractères

long haul network /ˌlɒŋ hɔːl ˈnetwɜːk/ *noun* (*communications network*) réseau *m* très étendu

long integer /lɒŋ ˈɪntɪdʒə/ *noun* (*integer represented by several bytes of data*) nombre *m* entier long de plusieurs octets de données

longitudinal redundancy check /ˌlɒŋgɪtjuːdɪn(ə)l rɪˈdʌndənsi ˌtʃek/ *noun* contrôle *m* par redondance longitudinale

longitudinal time code /ˌlɒŋgɪtjuːdɪn(ə)l ˈtaɪm kəʊd/ *noun* code *m* temporel longitudinal

long persistence phosphor /lɒŋ pə ˌsɪstəns ˈfɒsfə/ *noun* (*television screen coating*) phosphore *m*; couche *f* phosphorée à grande persistance ◇ **slow scan rate monitors need long persistence phosphor to prevent the image flickering** les écrans à faible fréquence de balayage ont besoin de phosphore à longue persistance pour éviter l'instabilité de l'image

look-ahead /'lʊk əˌhed/ *noun* lecture *f* anticipée

look-up /'lʊk ʌp/ *noun* consultation *f* de table

look-up table /'lʊk ʌp ˌteɪb(ə)l/ *noun* table *f* de référence; table *f* d'équivalence

'...a lookup table changes a pixel's value based on the values in a table' [*Byte*]

loop /luːp/ *noun* (*instruction in a computer program*) boucle *f* ◇ **loop film** film *m* en boucle ◇ **loop network** réseau en anneau *or* en boucle

loopback /'luːpbæk/ *noun* (*diagnostic test*) boucle *f* de rétroaction; boucle *f* de correction

loopback test /'luːpbæk test/ *noun* essai *m* en boucle

loop body /luːp 'bɒdi/ *noun* corps *m* de la boucle

loop check /'luːp ˌtʃek/ *noun* vérification *f*

loop counter /luːp 'kaʊntə/ *noun* compteur *m* de boucles

looping program /luːpɪŋ 'prəʊgræm/ *noun* programme *m* itératif; boucle *f* d'itération; boucle *f* de fond; boucle *f* de programme

loop program /luːp 'prəʊgræm/ *noun* programme *m* itératif; boucle *f* d'itération; boucle *f* de programme; boucle *f* de fond

lo-res /ləʊ riːs/ *noun* faible résolution *f*

lossless compression /ˌlɒsləs kəm 'preʃ(ə)nn/ *noun* (*image compression techniques that can reduce the number of bits used for each pixel in an image, without losing any information or quality*) compression *f* d'image sans perte de qualité

lossy compression /'ˌlɒsi kəmˌpreʃ(ə)n/ *noun* (*image compression techniques that can reduce the number of bits used for each pixel in an image, but in doing so lose information*) compression *f* d'image avec perte de qualité

lost cluster /lɒst 'klʌstə/ *noun* cluster *m* perdu; grappe *f* de données perdues

Lotus /'ləʊtəs/ (*software company*) Lotus™

Lotus-Intel-Microsoft Expanded Memory System /ˌləʊtəs ˌɪntel ˌmaɪkrəsɒft ɪks ˌpændɪd 'mem(ə)ri ˌsɪstəm/ *noun* norme *f* EMS

loudspeaker /ˌlaʊd'spiːkə/ *noun* (*system*) haut-parleur *m*; enceinte *f* acoustique

low-end /ˌləʊ 'end/ *adjective* (*hardware that is not very powerful or sophisticated*) bas *m* de gamme

lower case /ˌləʊə 'keɪs/ *noun* minuscule *f*; bas *m* de casse

low-level format /ˌləʊ 'lev(ə)l ˌfɔːmæt/ *noun* (*defines the pattern of tracks on a disk*) formatage *m* de bas niveau

low-level language /ˌləʊ ˌlev(ə)l 'læŋgwɪdʒ/ *noun* (*programming language similar to assembler*) langage *m* de bas niveau; LLL

low memory /ˌləʊ 'mem(ə)ri/ *noun* (*memory locations in a PC*) mémoire *f* basse

low-order digit /ˌləʊ ˌɔːdə 'dɪdʒɪt/ *noun* chiffre *m* de poids faible; chiffre *m* le moins significatif ◇ **the number 234156 has a low-order digit of 6** 6 est le chiffre le moins significatif du nombre 234156

low-priority work /ˌləʊ praɪˌɒrɪti 'wɜːk/ *noun* tâche *f* non prioritaire; tâche *f* d'arrière-plan

low resolution /ˌləʊ ˌrezə'luːʃ(ə)n/ *noun* basse *f* définition

low-resolution graphics /ləʊ ˌrezəˌluːʃ(ə)n 'græfɪks/, **low-res graphics** /ləʊ rez 'græfɪks/ *plural noun* graphiques *mpl* de basse définition; de basse résolution

low-speed communications /ˌləʊ spiːd kə ˌmjuːnɪ'keɪʃ(ə)nz/ *plural noun* communication *f* à faible débit

LPM *abbr* (*lines per minute*) ligne *f* par minute

LPT1 /ˌel piː tiː 'wʌnː/ *noun* (*first parallel printer port*) port *m* parallèle LPT1

LRU *abbr* (*least recently used algorithm*) algorithme *m* d'ancienneté

LSB /ˌel es 'biː/ *noun* bit *m* le moins significatif; bit *m* de poids faible

LSD /ˌel es 'diː/ *noun* chiffre *m* le moins significatif; chiffre *m* de poids faible

LSI /ˌel es 'aɪ/ *noun* intégration *f* à grande échelle

LTC /ˌel tiː 'siː/ *noun* code *m* temporel longitudinal

luggable /'lʌgəb(ə)l/ *noun* ordinateur *m* transportable

luminance /'luːmɪn(ə)ns/ *noun* luminance *f* ◇ **luminance signal** signal *m* de luminance

lurk /lɜːk/ *verb* badauder *vi*

LUT /ˌel juː 'tiː/ *noun* table *f* de conversion

'...an image processing system can have three LUTs that map the image memory to the display device' [*Byte*]

M

mA /ˌem 'eɪ/ *noun* milliampère *m* (mA)

Mac /mæk/ *noun* Mac *m*

MAC /ˌem eɪ 'siː/ *noun* code *m* d'identification de message ■ *abbr* (*media access control*) contrôle *m* d'accès au support

MacBinary /mæk'baɪnəri/ (*file storage and transfer system*) MacBinary™

machine /mə'ʃiːn/ *noun* **1.** machine *f* **2.** (*processors and computers*) ordinateur *m*; processeur *m*; machine *f* ◇ **machine-dependent** (*software*) (logiciel) non standard *or* qui ne fonctionne que sur un type d'ordinateur ◇ **machine-independent** (*software*) (logiciel) standard *or* universel *or* qui fonctionne sur la plupart des ordinateurs *or* indépendant de la machine ◇ **machine-intimate** (logiciel) propre à la machine *or* sur mesure *or* de constructeur *or* adapté à l'ordinateur ◇ **machine proof** (*proof sheets of a book*) épreuve *f* de machine ◇ **machine-readable** (*command or data*) (instruction *or* donnée) en langage machine *or* exploitable par l'ordinateur ◇ **the disk stores data in machine-readable form** le disque garde en mémoire des données en langage machine *or* sous une forme exploitable par l'ordinateur

machine address /mə'ʃiːn əˌdres/ *noun* adresse *f* absolue

machine check /mə'ʃiːn tʃek/ *noun* arrêt *m* dû à une défaillance de l'appareil

machine code /mə'ʃiːn kəʊd/ *noun* code *m* d'instruction; code *m* en langage machine

machine code format /mə'ʃiːn kəʊd ˌfɔːmæt/ *noun* (*format for machine code instructions*) format *m* de code machine

machine code instruction /mə'ʃiːn kəʊd ɪn ˌstrʌkʃən/ *noun* instruction *f* en code; instruction *f* en langage machine

machine cycle /mə'ʃiːn ˌsaɪk(ə)l/ *noun* cycle *m* de machine

machine-dependent /məˌʃiːn dɪ'pendənt/ *adjective* (*unable to be used on hardware or software*) non standard *or* qui ne fonctionne que sur un type d'ordinateur

machine equation /mə'ʃiːn ɪˌkweɪʒ(ə)n/ *noun* (*formula*) équation *f* machine

machine error /mə'ʃiːn ˌerə/ *noun* erreur *f* (causée par la) machine

machine-independent /məˌʃiːn ˌɪndɪ 'pendənt/ *adjective* (*that can be run on any computer system*) standard *or* universel *or* qui fonctionne sur la plupart des ordinateurs *or* indépendant de la machine

machine-independent language /məˌʃiːn ˌɪndɪpendənt 'læŋgwɪdʒ/ *noun* (*programming language*) langage *m* standard; langage *m* universel

machine instruction /mə'ʃiːn ɪnˌstrʌkʃən/ *noun* instruction *f* en langage machine

machine intelligence /mə'ʃiːn ɪn ˌtelɪdʒ(ə)ns/ *noun* intelligence *f* artificielle

machine-intimate /məˌʃiːn 'ɪntɪmət/ *adjective* (*that operates closely with the hardware*) propre à la machine *or* sur mesure *or* de constructeur *or* adapté à l'ordinateur

machine language /mə'ʃiːn ˌlæŋgwɪdʒ/ *noun* **1.** langage *m* machine **2.** langage *m* machine

machine language programming /məˌʃiːn ˌlæŋgwɪdʒ 'prəʊgræmɪŋ/ *noun* programmation *f* en langage machine

machine readable /məˌʃiːn 'riːdəb(ə)l/ *adjective* en langage machine; exploitable par l'ordinateur ◇ **the disk stores data in machine-readable form** le disque garde en mémoire des données en langage machine *or* sous une forme exploitable par l'ordinateur

machine-readable code /məˌʃiːn ˌriːdəb(ə)l 'kəʊd/ *noun* code *m* assimilable par machine

machine run /mə'ʃiːn rʌn/ *noun* exécution *f* d'un programme

machine translation /məˌʃiːn træns 'leɪʃ(ə)n/ *noun* (*texts and commands*) traduction *f* assistée par ordinateur

machine word /mə'ʃiːn wɜːd/ *noun* mot *m* machine

Macintosh /'mækɪntɒʃ/ (*trade name for a range of personal computers designed by Apple Corporation*) Macintosh

macro /mækrəʊ/ *noun* macro-instruction *f*; macro *f* ◇ **macro assembler** *or* **assembly program** macro-assembleur *m*; assembleur pour macrolangage ◇ **macro instruction** macro-instruction *f*; macro *f*

macro- /mækrəʊ/ *prefix* macro(-)

macro assembler /'mækrəʊ əˌsemblə/, **macro assembly program** /ˌmækrəʊ ə'semblə ˌprəʊgræm/ *noun* (*program able to decode macro instructions*) assembleur *m* macro; programme *m* assembleur pour macro langage

macro call /ˈmækrəʊ kɔːl/ *noun* macro-instruction *f*

macro code /ˈmækrəʊ kəʊd/ *noun* (*program writing*) macrocode *m*

macro command /ˈmækrəʊ kəˌmɑːnd/ *noun* (*macro code*) macrocommande *f*

macro definition /ˈmækrəʊ ˌdefənɪʃ(ə)n/ *noun* macrodéfinition *f*

macroelement /ˈmækrəʊˌelɪmənt/ *noun* (*data items treated as one element*) macro-élément *m*

macro expansion /ˈmækrəʊ ɪkˌspænʃ(ə)n/ *noun* (*process*) macro-expansion *f*

macro flowchart /ˈmækrəʊ ˌfləʊtʃɑːt/ *noun* macro-ordinogramme *m*

macroinstruction /ˈmækrəʊˌɪnstrʌkʃən/ *noun* macro-instruction *f*

macro language /ˈmækrəʊ ˌlæŋgwɪdʒ/ *noun* macrolangage *m*

'Microsoft has released a developer's kit for its Word 6.0 for Windows wordprocessing package. The 900-page kit explains how to use the WordBasic macro language supplied with the software.' [*Computing*]

macro library /ˈmækrəʊ ˌlaɪbrəri/ *noun* (*routines to ease program writing*) bibliothèque *f* de macros

macro programming /ˌmækrəʊ ˌprəʊgræmɪŋ/ *noun* (*writing a program using macro instructions*) macroprogrammation *f*

macro virus /ˈmækrəʊ ˌvaɪrəs/ *noun* macrovirus *m*

magazine /ˌmægəˈziːn/ *noun* (*pages of videotext system*) pages *fpl* d'un système vidéotex

magnet /ˈmægnɪt/ *noun* aimant *m*

magnetic /mægˈnetɪk/ *adjective* magnétique; aimanté *or* -ée ◇ **magnetic focusing** (*of beam of electrons*) mise *f* au point magnétique ◇ **magnetic ink character recognition (MICR)** reconnaissance *f* de caractères magnétiques *or* en encre magnétique ◇ **magnetic storm** orage *m* magnétique

magnetic bubble memory /mægˌnetɪk ˈbʌb(ə)l ˌmem(ə)ri/ *noun* mémoire *f* à bulles magnétiques

magnetic card /mægˌnetɪk ˈkɑːd/ *noun* carte *f* magnétique

magnetic card reader /mægˌnetɪk ˈkɑːd ˌriːdə/ *noun* lecteur *m* de cartes magnétiques

magnetic cartridge /mægˌnetɪk ˈkɑːtrɪdʒ/ *noun* cartouche *f* de bande magnétique

magnetic cassette /mægˌnetɪk kəˈset/ *noun* cassette *f* de bande magnétique

magnetic cell /mægˈnetɪk sel/ *noun* cellule *f* magnétique

magnetic core /mægˈnetɪk kɔː/ *noun* tore *m* magnétique

magnetic disk /mægˈnetɪk dɪsk/ *noun* disque *m* magnétique

magnetic disk unit /mægˌnetɪk ˈdɪsk ˌjuːnɪt/ *noun* unité *f* de disque; unité *f* de disquette

magnetic drum /mægˈnetɪk drʌm/ *noun* (*cylindrical magnetic storage device*) tambour *m* magnétique

magnetic encoding /mægˌnetɪk ɪnˈkəʊdɪŋ/ *noun* encodage *m* magnétique

magnetic field /mægˌnetɪk ˈfiːld/ *noun* champ *m* magnétique

magnetic flux /mægˈnetɪk flʌks/ *noun* (*measure of magnetic field strength*) flux *m* magnétique

magnetic head /mægˈnetɪk hed/ *noun* tête *f* magnétique

magnetic ink /mægˌnetɪk ˈɪŋk/ *noun* (*printing ink that contains a magnetic material*) encre *f* magnétique

magnetic ink character recognition /mægˌnetɪk ɪŋk ˌkærɪktə ˌrekəgˈnɪʃ(ə)n/ *noun* reconnaissance *f* de caractères magnétiques

magnetic master /mægˌnetɪk ˈmɑːstə/ *noun* (*original version of a recorded tape or disk*) support *m* magnétique original; bande *f* originale; disque *m* original

magnetic material /mægˌnetɪk məˈtɪəriəl/ *noun* support *m* magnétique

magnetic media /mægˌnetɪk ˈmiːdiə/ *plural noun* supports *mpl* magnétiques

magnetic medium /mægˌnetɪk ˈmiːdiəm/ *noun* support *m* magnétique

magnetic memory /mægˌnetɪk ˈmem(ə)ri/ *noun* mémoire *f* magnétique

magnetic polarity /mægˌnetɪk pəʊˈlærɪti/ *noun* polarité *f* magnétique

magnetic recording /mægˌnetɪk rɪˈkɔːdɪŋ/ *noun* enregistrement *m* sur support magnétique

magnetic screen /mægˈnetɪk skriːn/ *noun* écran *m* magnétique

magnetic storage /mægˌnetɪk ˈstɔːrɪdʒ/ *noun* mémoire *f* magnétique

magnetic strip /mægˌnetɪk ˈstrɪp/ *noun* (*data recording*) piste *f* magnétique (d'une carte magnétique)

magnetic stripe /mægˌnetɪk ˈstraɪp/ *noun* piste *f* couchée

magnetic strip reader /mægˌnetɪk ˈstrɪp ˌriːdə/ *noun* lecteur *m* de cartes magnétiques

magnetic tape /mægˈnetɪk teɪp/ *noun* bande *f* magnétique

magnetic tape cartridge /mægˌnetɪk teɪp ˈkɑːtrɪdʒ/ *noun* cartouche *f*

magnetic tape cassette /mægˌnetɪk teɪp kəˈset/ *noun* cartouche *f* de bande magnétique

magnetic tape encoder /mægˌnetɪk teɪp en ˈkəʊdə/ *noun* (*data writing*) encodeur *m* de bandes magnétiques

magnetic tape reader /mægˌnetɪk teɪp ˈriːdə/ *noun* lecteur *m* de bandes magnétiques

magnetic tape recorder /mæɡˌnetɪk 'teɪp rɪ ˌkɔːdə/ *noun* (*data writing*) enregistreur *m* de bandes

magnetic tape transport /mæɡˌnetɪk teɪp 'trænspɔːt/ *noun* dérouleur *m*

magnetic transfer /mæɡˌnetɪk 'trænsfɜː/ *noun* (*copying of signals*) transfert *m* magnétique

magnetise /'mæɡnəˌtaɪz/, **magnetize** *verb* magnétiser *vt*

magneto-optical disc /mæɡˌniːtəʊ ˌɒptɪk(ə)l 'dɪsk/ *noun* (*optical disc*) disque *m* magnéto-optique; disque *m* optique

magneto-optical recording /mæɡˌniːtəʊ ˌɒptɪk(ə)l rɪ'kɔːdɪŋ/ *noun* enregistrement *m* sur disque magnéto-optique; enregistrement *m* sur disque magnétique

magnitude /'mæɡnɪtjuːd/ *noun* (*of a signal*) amplitude *f*; grandeur *f* ◇ **signal magnitude** amplitude d'un signal

mag tape /'mæɡ teɪp/ *noun informal* bande *f* magnétique

mail /meɪl/ *noun* courrier *m* électronique; messagerie *f* électronique; poste *f* électronique

mailbox /'meɪlbɒks/, **mail box** /'meɪl bɒks/ *noun* (*electronic*) boîte *f* aux messages électroniques

mail-enabled /meɪl ɪn'eɪb(ə)ld/ *adjective* (*application that has access to an electronic mail system*) avec fonction courrier; messagerie (électronique)

mail gateway /'meɪl ˌɡeɪtweɪ/ *noun* passerelle *f* de courrier électronique

mailing /'meɪlɪŋ/ *noun* (*e-mail*) envoi *m* par la poste; (*post or e-mail*) mailing *m* ◇ **direct mailing** publipostage *m*; publicité *f* directe *or* mailing *m* ◇ **his name is on our mailing list** son nom figure sur notre fichier d'adresses ◇ **mailing piece** prospectus *m* envoyé par la poste ◇ **mailing shot** envoi *m* de prospectus publicitaires ◇ **the mailing of publicity material** l'envoi (par la poste) de prospectus publicitaires ◇ **to build up a mailing list** établir un fichier d'adresses

mailing list /'meɪlɪŋ lɪst/ *noun* (*list of e-mail addresses*) fichier *m* d'adresses ◇ **his name is on our mailing list** son nom figure sur notre fichier d'adresses

mailmerge /'meɪlmɜːdʒ/ *noun* publipostage *m*; programme *m* d'édition de lettres types

> 'Spreadsheet views for data and graphical forms for data entry have been added to the Q&A database, with the traditional reporting, mailmerge, and labels improved through Windows facilities.' [*Computing*]

mail server /meɪl 'sɜːvə/ *noun* serveur *m* de courrier (électronique)

main /meɪn/ *adjective* principal *or* -e ◇ **main beam** (*of antenna transmission*) faisceau principal; porteuse principale ◇ **main distributing frame** tableau de distribution *or* répartiteur principal

main body /ˌmeɪn 'bɒdi/ *noun* corps *m* principal (d'un programme)

main clock /'meɪn klɒk/ *noun* (*clock signal*) horloge *f* centrale

main entry /meɪn 'entri/ *noun* entrée *f* principale

mainframe /'meɪnfreɪm kəmˌpjuːtə/, **mainframe computer** /ˌmeɪnfreɪm kəm'pjuːtə/ *noun* gros ordinateur *m*; ordinateur *m* central; ordinateur *m* principal

mainframe access /'meɪnfreɪm ˌækses/ *noun* accès *m* à l'ordinateur principal (par l'intermédiaire d'un micro)

main index /meɪn 'ɪndeks/ *noun* index *m* général; index *m* principal

main loop /ˌmeɪn 'luːp/ *noun* boucle *f* principale (d'un programme)

main memory /meɪn 'mem(ə)ri/ *noun* mémoire *f* principale; mémoire *f* centrale

main menu /meɪn 'menjuː/ *noun* menu *m* principal

main routine /meɪn ruː'tiːn/ *noun* routine *f* principale

main storage /meɪn 'stɔːrɪdʒ/ *noun* mémoire *f* principale; mémoire *f* centrale

maintain /meɪn'teɪn/ *verb* (*system*) entretenir *vt* ◇ **well maintained** bien entretenu, -e

maintainability /ˌmeɪnteɪnə'bɪlɪti/ *noun* (*repairs*) maintenabilité *f*

maintenance /'meɪntənəns/ *noun* **1.** (*of machine*) maintenance *f*; entretien *m*; service *m* de maintenance **2.** (*of database, website*) entretien *m*; maintenance *f* ◇ **on-site maintenance** service *m* d'assistance technique sur le lieu de travail *or* maintenance sur site ◇ **remote maintenance** télémaintenance *f*

maintenance contract /'meɪntənəns ˌkɒntrækt/ *noun* contrat *m* de maintenance

maintenance release /'meɪntənəns rɪˌliːs/ *noun* (*program revision*) mise *f* à jour corrective ◇ **the maintenance release of the database program, version 2.01, corrects the problem with the margins** la mise à jour corrective de ce programme de base de données, version 2.01, corrige le problème des marges

maintenance routine /'meɪntənəns ruːˌtiːn/ *noun* programme *m* de diagnostic; programme *m* de maintenance

major cycle /ˌmeɪdʒə 'saɪk(ə)l/ *noun* cycle *m* principal

majordomo /ˌmeɪdʒə'dəʊməʊ/ *noun* gestionnaire *m* de liste de diffusion

make directory /ˌmeɪk daɪ'rekt(ə)ri/ *noun* commande *f* MD (de création de répertoire)

male connector /meɪl kə'nektə/ *noun* connecteur *m* mâle

malfunction /mæl'fʌŋkʃən/ *noun* (*of hardware or software*) défaillance *f*; dysfonctionnement *m* ■ *verb* mal fonctionner; être en dérangement ◇ **some of the keys on the keyboard have started to malfunction** quelques-unes des touches du clavier ne fonctionnent déjà plus très bien ◇ **the data was lost due to a software malfunction** les données ont été perdues par suite d'une défaillance du logiciel

malfunctioning /mæl'fʌŋkʃənɪŋ/ *adjective* mauvais fonctionnement; dysfonctionnement *m*

malfunction routine /mæl'fʌŋkʃən ruːˌtiːn/ *noun* (*software routine that detects faults*) diagnostic *m* de dysfonctionnement

manageable /'mænɪdʒəb(ə)l/ *adjective* qui peut être maîtrisé *or* -ée; résolu *or* -e ◇ **data should be split into manageable files** les données devraient être réparties en fichiers plus courts et plus faciles à utiliser ◇ **processing problems which are still manageable** problèmes de traitement qui peuvent être résolus

management information service /ˌmænɪdʒmənt ˌɪnfə'meɪʃ(ə)n ˌsɜːvɪs/ *noun* logiciel *m* de gestion

management information system /ˌmænɪdʒmənt ˌɪnfə'meɪʃ(ə)n ˌsɪstəm/ *noun* (*software for managers*) logiciel *m* de gestion

manager /'mænɪdʒə/ *noun* (*software*) gestionnaire *m*

Manchester coding /'mæntʃestə ˌkɒdɪŋ/ *noun* (*method of encoding data*) encodage *m* Manchester

Mandlebrot set /'mænd(ə)lbrɒt set/ *noun* (*mathematical equation*) équation *f* de Mandlebrot

manipulate /mə'nɪpjʊˌleɪt/ *verb* manipuler *vt* ◇ **an image processor that captures, displays and manipulates video images** un processeur d'images qui peut capturer, afficher et manipuler les images vidéo

manipulation /məˌnɪpjʊ'leɪʃ(ə)n/ *noun* manipulation *f* (de données/d'images) ◇ **a high-speed database management program allows the manipulation of very large amounts of data** un gestionnaire de base de données ultra-rapide permet la manipulation d'une très grande quantité de données

man machine interface /ˌmæn məˌʃiːn 'ɪntəfeɪs/ *noun* interface *f* homme/machine

mantissa /mæn'tɪsə/ *noun* (*numbers*) mantisse *f* ◇ **the mantissa of the number 45.897 is 0.897** la mantisse du nombre 45,897 est 0,897

manual /'mænjuəl/ *noun* (*book or booklet*) manuel *m* (d'utilisation)

manual data processing /ˌmænjʊəl 'deɪtə ˌprəʊsesɪŋ/ *noun* traitement *m* de l'information sans l'aide d'un ordinateur

manual entry /ˌmænjʊəl 'entri/ *noun* saisie *f* de données par clavier; saisie *f* de données au clavier; saisie *f* de données sur clavier

manual input /ˌmænjʊəl 'ɪnpʊt/ *noun* saisie *f* de données par clavier; saisie *f* de données au clavier; saisie *f* de données sur clavier

manually /'mænjʊəli/ *adverb* manuellement; à la main ◇ **the paper has to be fed into the printer manually** l'alimentation en papier de l'imprimante se fait manuellement

map /mæp/ *noun* (*internal layout of computer's memory or communication regions*) configuration *f*

MAPI /ˌem eɪ piː 'aɪ/ *noun* interface *f* de programmation d'applications de messagerie

marching display /mɑːtʃɪŋ dɪ'spleɪ/ *noun* visualisation *f* de contrôle d'entrée

margin /'mɑːdʒɪn/ *noun* **1.** (*blank space*) marge *f* **2.** (*extra time or space*) marge *f* ◇ **the left margin and right margin are the two sections of blank paper on either side of the page** les marges de droite et de gauche sont les espaces blancs de chaque côté d'une page ◇ **to set a margin** fixer *or* paramétrer une marge ◇ **when typing the contract leave wide margins** lorsque vous taperez le contrat, n'oubliez pas de laisser des marges très larges

margin of error /ˌmɑːdʒɪn əv 'erə/ *noun* marge *f* d'erreur

mark /mɑːk/ *noun* **1.** (*sign*) marque *f*; signe *m* **2.** (*signal*) marque *f* logique ■ *verb* marquer *vt*; indiquer *vt* ◇ **marking interval** intervalle de marquage ◇ **proof correction marks** signes *mpl* de correction (d'épreuves d'imprimerie)

mark block /ˌmɑːk 'blɒk/ *verb* marquer un bloc

marker /'mɑːkə/ *noun* (*writing or signalling tool*) marqueur *m*; surligneur *m* ◇ **marker pen** marqueur *m*; surligneur *m*

mark sense /ˌmɑːk 'sens/ *verb* (*to write detectable characters*) marquer en encre magnétique

mark sense device /ˌmɑːk 'sens dɪˌvaɪs/ *noun* lecteur *m* de marques magnétiques

mark sense reader /ˌmɑːk 'sens ˌriːdə/ *noun* lecteur *m* de cartes magnétiques

mark sensing card /'mɑːk ˌsensɪŋ kɑːd/ *noun* carte *f* à coder en encre magnétique

mark space /ˌmɑːk 'speɪs/ *noun* marque *f* espace

markup /'mɑːkʌp/ *noun* annotation *f* typographique

markup language /'mɑːkʌp ˌlæŋgwɪdʒ/ *noun* langage *m* de balisage

marquee /mɑː'kiː/ *noun* **1.** (*in a graphics application*) zone *f* (d'image) sélectionnée **2.** (*in a website*) bannière *f*

mask /mɑːsk/ *noun* **1.** (*circuit layout stencil*) masque *m* **2.** (*photographic*) masque *m* ■ *verb* (*pattern of binary digits*) masquer *vt* ◇ **a mask or stencil is used to transfer the transistor design onto silicon** on se sert d'un masque ou d'un stencil pour reproduire le tracé du circuit du transistor sur le silicium

maskable /'mɑːskəb(ə)l/ *adjective* qui peut être masqué *or* -ée ◇ **non-maskable interrupt (NMI)** interruption obligatoire *or* qui ne peut être invalidée *or* qui ne peut être masquée

maskable interrupt /ˌmɑːskəb(ə)l 'ɪntərʌpt/ *noun* (*interrupt which can be activated by using an interrupt mask*) interruption *f* qui peut être invalidée; interruption *f* qui peut être masquée

mask bit /'mɑːsk bɪt/ *noun* (*one bit in a mask*) bit *m* masque

masked ROM /'mɑːskt rɒm/ *noun* mémoire *f* morte masquée

masking /'mɑːskɪŋ/ *noun* masquage *m*

mask register /mɑːsk 'redʒɪstə/ *noun* registre *m* de masque

mass production /mæs prə'dʌkʃən/ *noun* fabrication *f* en série ◇ **mass production of monitors** *or* **of calculators** fabrication en série de moniteurs *or* de calculatrices

mass storage /mæs 'stɔːrɪdʒ/ *noun* mémoire *f* de masse; mémoire *f* de grande capacité

mass storage device /ˌmæs 'stɔːrɪdʒ dɪ ˌvaɪs/ *noun* support *m* de mémoire de masse ◇ **a hard disk is definitely a mass storage device** un disque dur est un véritable support de mémoire de masse

mass storage system /ˌmæs 'stɔːrɪdʒ ˌsɪstəm/ *noun* (*data storage system*) système *m* avec mémoire de masse

master /'mɑːstə/ *adjective* **1.** (*person or device*) maître *m* **2.** (*copy*) reporter; copier; recopier ■ *verb* (*learn*) apprendre (quelque chose); réussir (à faire quelque chose) ◇ **master control program (MCP)** programme *m* de commande de l'ordinateur maître ◇ **those slides and photographs are the intermediate materials to be mastered onto the video disk** ces diapos et photos sont les supports intermédiaires qui doivent être recopiés sur le vidéodisque

master card /'mɑːstə kɑːd/ *noun* carte *f* maîtresse

master clock /'mɑːstə klɒk/ *noun* horloge *f* maîtresse; horloge *f* principale

master computer /'mɑːstə kəmˌpjuːtə/ *noun* (*computer that controls the other processors*) ordinateur *m* maître; ordinateur *m* ◇ **the master computer controls everything else** l'ordinateur maître contrôle tout le reste

master control program /ˌmɑːstə kən'trəʊl ˌprəʊgræm/ *noun* programme *m* de commande

master data /ˌmɑːstə 'deɪtə/ *noun* (*reference data*) données *fpl* permanentes; données *fpl* de base

master disc /'mɑːstə dɪsk/ *noun* original *m*

master disk /'mɑːstə dɪsk/ *noun* disque *m* d'exploitation

master file /'mɑːstə faɪl/ *noun* fichier *m* principal; fichier *m* maître; fichier *m* permanent

mastering /'mɑːstərɪŋ/ *noun* (*process to convert finished data to a master disc*) matriçage *m*

master/master computer system /ˌmɑːstə 'mɑːstə kəmˌpjuːtə ˌsɪstəm/ *noun* système *m* maître/maître

master program file /ˌmɑːstə 'prəʊgræm ˌfaɪl/ *noun* fichier *m* de programme maître

master/slave computer system /ˌmɑːstə 'sleɪv kəmˌpjuːtə ˌsɪstəm/ *noun* système *m* maître/esclave

master tape /'mɑːstə teɪp/ *noun* bande *f* originale

master terminal /ˌmɑːstə 'tɜːmɪn(ə)l/ *noun* terminal *m* principal; terminal *m* maître ◇ **the system manager uses the master terminal to restart the system** le gestionnaire de système utilise le terminal principal pour relancer le système

mat /mæt/ *noun* (*border displayed around an image*) tapis *m*

match /mætʃ/ *verb* **1.** (*in pairs*) assortir *vt* **2.** (*to set a register*) accorder *vt*; équilibrer *vt* ◇ **impedance matching** accord *m* d'impédance ◇ **matched load** charge accordée *or* équilibrée

material /mə'tɪəriəl/ *noun* (*substance to make a finished product*) matériau *m* ◇ **gold is the ideal material for electrical connections** l'or est le matériau idéal pour la fabrication des connecteurs électriques ◇ **materials control** contrôle d'approvisionnement en matériaux ◇ **synthetic materials** matériaux synthétiques

math /mæθ/ *noun US informal* maths *f*

mathematical /ˌmæθə'mætɪk(ə)l/ *adjective* mathématique ◇ **mathematical subroutine** sous-programme mathématique ◇ **mathetical model** modèle mathématique

mathematical model /ˌmæθəmætɪk(ə)l 'mɒd(ə)l/ *noun* modèle *m* mathématique

mathematical subroutines /ˌmæθəmætɪk(ə)l 'sʌbruːtiːnz/ *plural noun* sous-programmes *mpl* mathématiques

mathematics /ˌmæθə'mætɪks/ *noun* mathématiques *f*

maths /mæθs/ *noun informal* (*mathematics*) maths *f*

maths chip /'mæθs ˌtʃɪp/ *noun* coprocesseur *m* mathématique

maths coprocessor /'mæθs kəʊˌprəʊsesə/ *noun* coprocesseur *m* mathématique

matrix /'meɪtrɪks/ *noun* **1.** (*array of numbers*) matrice *f* **2.** (*array of connections*) matrice *f* de relation **3.** (*printing*) matrice *f* graphique

matrix printer /'meɪtrɪks ˌprɪntə/ *noun* imprimante *f* matricielle

matrix rotation /'meɪtrɪks rəʊˌteɪʃ(ə)n/ *noun* (*process of swapping the rows with the columns in an array*) rotation *f* de matrice

matte /mæt/ *noun* cache *m*; gobo *m*

matter /ˈmætə/ *noun* (*main section of text*) corps *m* du texte ◇ **printed matter** imprimé *m* ◇ **publicity matter** imprimé *or* matériel *m* publicitaire

MAU *abbr* (*multistation access unit*) unité *f* d'accès multistation

maximise /ˈmæksɪmaɪz/, **maximize** *verb* (*expand an application icon*) agrandir au plein écran

maximum /ˈmæksɪməm/ *noun* maximum *m* ■ *adjective* maximum; maximal *or* -e ◇ **maximum reading** (*of signal*) amplitude maximum enregistrée ◇ **maximum usable frequency** fréquence *f* maximum *or* maximale utilisable

maximum capacity /ˌmæksɪməm kəˈpæsɪti/ *noun* capacité *f* maximale

maximum transmission rate /ˌmæksɪməm trænzˈmɪʃ(ə)n ˌreɪt/ *noun* vitesse *f* maximale; débit *m* maximal de transmission

maximum users /ˌmæksɪməm ˈjuːzəz/ *plural noun* nombre *m* maximum d'utilisateurs

MB *abbr* (*megabyte*) mégaoctet *m*

Mbps *abbr* (*megabits per second*) mégabits *mpl* par seconde

MBR /ˌem biː ˈɑː/ *noun* registre *m* de mémoire tampon

Mbyte /ˈem baɪt/ *abbr* (*megabyte*) mégaoctet *m*

MCA /ˌem siː ˈeɪ/ (*trade name for the expansion bus within IBM's PS/2 range of personal computers*) MCA

MCA chipset /ˌem siː eɪ ˈtʃɪpset/ *noun* jeu *m* de composants MCA

MCGA /ˌem siː dʒiː ˈeɪ/ *noun* carte *f* MCGA; standard *m* MCGA (d'adaptateur graphique couleur)

MCP /ˌem siː ˈpiː ˌdʒɔɪnt/ *abbr* (*master control program*) macroprogramme *m* de régulation

MD /ˌem ˈdiː/ *noun* commande *f* MD (de création de répertoire)

MDA /ˌem diː ˈeɪ/ *noun* carte *f* d'affichage monochrome

MDR /ˌem diː ˈɑː/ *noun* registre *m* des données en mémoire

mean /miːn/ *noun, adjective* moyenne *f* ■ *verb* signifier *vt*; vouloir dire

mean time between failures /ˌmiːn taɪm bɪˌtwiːn ˈfeɪljəz/ *noun* durée *f* moyenne de bon fonctionnement; durée *f* moyenne de temps de bon fonctionnement entre les défaillances

mean time to failure /ˌmiːn taɪm tə ˈfeɪljə/ *noun* durée *f* moyenne de bon fonctionnement

mean time to repair /ˌmiːn ˈtaɪm tə, tʊ/ *noun* moyenne *f* de temps requis pour réparation

measure /ˈmeʒə/ *noun* **1.** (*way of calculating size*) mesure *f* **2.** (*width of a printed line*) largeur *f* d'une ligne **3.** (*action*) mesure *f* ■ *verb* **1.** (*to find out size, etc.*) mesurer *vt* **2.** (*to have certain size, etc.*) mesurer *vt* ◇ **tape measure** mètre *m* (à ruban) ◇ **to take measures to prevent something happening** prendre des mesures pour éviter quelque chose

measurement /ˈmeʒəmənt/ *noun* évaluation *f*

measurements /ˈmeʒəmənts/ *plural noun* dimensions *fpl*

mechanical /mɪˈkænɪk(ə)l/ *adjective* mécanique

mechanical mouse /mɪˈkænɪk(ə)l maʊs/ *noun* souris *f* mécanique

mechanism /ˈmekəˌnɪz(ə)m/ *noun* mécanisme *m* ◇ **the drive mechanism appears to be faulty** le mécanisme du lecteur ne semble pas fonctionner très bien ◇ **the printer mechanism is very simple** l'imprimante possède un mécanisme très simple

media /ˈmiːdiə/ *plural noun* **1.** (*means of communicating information to the public*) media; média *m* **2.** (*physical material that can be used to store data*) média *m*; support *m* ◇ **computers can store data on a variety of media, such as disk, punched card or CD-ROM** les ordinateurs peuvent stocker des données sur différents types de supports: disques, cartes perforées ou CD-ROM ◇ **media analysis** *or* **media research** analyse *f* des médias ◇ **media coverage** couverture *f* médiatique ◇ **the media** les médias ◇ **the product attracted a lot of interest in the media** *or* **a lot of media interest** le produit a beaucoup fait parler de lui dans les medias *or* a suscité un grand intérêt médiatique ◇ **to transfer from magnetic tape to floppy disk, you need a media conversion device** pour transférer le contenu d'une bande magnétique sur une disquette, il vous faut un équipement de conversion de support ◇ **we got good media coverage for the launch of the new model** nous avons eu une bonne couverture médiatique pour le lancement du nouveau modèle

media access control /ˌmiːdiə ˈækses kənˌtrəʊl/ *noun* contrôle *m* d'accès au support

media control interface /ˌmiːdiə kənˌtrəʊl ˈɪntəfeɪs/ *noun* interface *f* de commande de média

media conversion /ˌmiːdjə kənˈvɜːʃ(ə)n/ *noun* conversion *f* de support

media error /ˌmiːdjə ˈerə/ *noun* erreur *f* causée par le support

Media Player /ˈmiːdiə ˌpleɪə/ (*trade name for a Windows utility program*) Media Player

MediaServer /ˈmiːdiəˌsɜːvə/ (*trade name for a system developed by Netscape to provide audio and video delivery over the Internet*) MediaServer

medical telematics /ˌmedɪk(ə)l ˌtelɪˈmætɪks/ *noun* télématique *f* médicale

medium /ˈmiːdiəm/ *adjective* (*middle or average*) moyen *or* -enne ■ *noun* **1.** (*for data storage*) moyen *m*; support *m* **2.** (*for transmitting information*) support *m* ◇ **advertising medium** support *m* publicitaire ◇ **a medium-sized computer**

system un système informatique de taille moyenne ◇ **data storage mediums such as paper tape, magnetic disk, magnetic tape, card and microfiche are available** il existe différents types de supports de stockage dont les bandes papier, les disques et bandes magnétiques, les cartes et microfiches

medium model /ˌmiːdiəm ˈmɒd(ə)l/ *noun* modèle *m* moyen

medium scale integration /ˌmiːdiəm skeɪl ˌɪntɪˈgreɪʃ(ə)n/ *noun* intégration *f* à moyenne échelle

medium speed /ˈmiːdiəm spiːd/ *noun* vitesse *f* moyenne; débit *m* moyen (de transmission)

meet /miːt/ *noun* (*logical function*) conjonction *f*

meg /meg/ *noun informal* (*megabyte*) méga *m*; méga-octet *m* ◇ **this computer has a ninety-meg hard disk** l'ordinateur a un disque de quatre-vingt-dix mégas

mega- /megə/ *prefix* **1.** (*used only in computing and electronic related applications*) méga- **2.** méga-

megabit /ˈmegəbɪt/ *noun* mégabit *m* (Mb)

megabits per second /ˌmegəbɪts pɜː ˈsekənd/ *noun* mégabits *mpl* par seconde

megabyte /ˈmegəbaɪt/ *noun* (*storage capacity of hard disk drives or RAM*) méga-octet *m* (Mo)

'Doing this reduced a bitmap of my desktop from 2.25 megabytes to a 58K GIF' [*The Guardian*]

mega floating point instructions per second /ˌmegə ˌfləʊtɪŋ pɔɪnt ɪnˌstrʌkʃənz pɜː sɪˈkɒnd/ *noun* mégaflops *m*

megaflop /ˈmegəflɒp/ *noun* mégaflops *m*; million *m* d'opérations en virgule flottante par seconde

megahertz /ˈmegəˌhɜːts/ *noun* mégahertz *m*; MHz

megapixel display /megəˌpɪks(ə)l dɪˈspleɪ/ *noun* écran *m* avec définition supérieure à 1024x1024 pixels

Megastream /ˈmegəstriːm/ (*data link provided by British Telecom*) connexion *f* Megastream™

member /ˈmembə/ *noun* élément *m* (d'un champ)

membrane keyboard /ˌmembreɪn ˈkiːbɔːd/ *noun* (*keyboard using a thin plastic sheet*) clavier *m* à membrane

memo field /ˈmeməʊ fiːld/ *noun* (*field in a database*) champ *m* mémo

memorise /ˈmeməˌraɪz/, **memorize** *verb* mémoriser *vt*; mettre en mémoire

memory /ˈmem(ə)ri/ *noun* mémoire *f* ◇ **charge coupled device (CCD) memory** (dispositif) mémoire à couplage de charge ◇ **content-addressable memory** mémoire adressable par son contenu ◇ **fast access memory (FAM)** mémoire à accès rapide ◇ **magnetic tape is a high capacity serial memory** la bande magnétique constitue une mémoire séquentielle d'une grande capacité ◇ **memory address register (MAR)** registre *m* d'adresse en mémoire ◇ **memory buffer register (MBR)** registre de mémoire tampon ◇ **memory data register (MDR)** registre des données en mémoire ◇ **memory location** emplacement *m* de mémoire ◇ **memory management unit (MMU)** (*electronic logic circuits*) unité *f* de gestion de la mémoire ◇ **paged memory** mémoire paginée ◇ **random access memory (RAM)** mémoire vive *or* mémoire RAM ◇ **read only memory (ROM)** mémoire morte *or* mémoire ROM

'The lower-power design, together with an additional 8Kb of on-board cache memory, will increase the chip's performance to 75 million instructions per second.' [*Computing*]

'...when a program is loaded into memory, some is used for the code, some for the permanent data, and some is reserved for the stack which grows and shrinks for function calls and local data' [*Personal Computer World*]

memory access time /ˌmem(ə)ri ˈækses ˌtaɪm/ *noun* temps *m* d'accès à la mémoire

memory address register /ˌmem(ə)ri ə ˈdres ˌredʒɪstə/ *noun* registre *m* d'adresse en mémoire

memory allocation /ˈmem(ə)ri ˌæləkeɪʃ(ə)n/ *noun* allocation *f* de mémoire

memory backup capacitor /ˌmem(ə)ri ˈbækʌp kəˌpæsɪtə/ *noun* alimentation *f* de secours de la mémoire

memory bank /ˈmem(ə)ri bæŋk/ *noun* (*small storage devices connected together*) banque *f* de mémoire ◇ **an add-on card has a 128KB memory bank made up of 16 chips** une carte d'extension possède une banque de mémoire de 128Ko constituée de 16 puces

memory board /ˈmem(ə)ri bɔːd/ *noun* carte *f* mémoire

memory buffer register /ˈmem(ə)ri ˌbʌfə ˌredʒɪstə/ *noun* registre *m* de mémoire tampon

memory bus /ˈmem(ə)ri bʌs/ *noun* bus *m* de mémoire

memory capacity /ˈmem(ə)ri kəˌpæsɪti/ *noun* capacité *f* de mémoire

memory cell /ˈmem(ə)ri sel/ *noun* cellule *f* de mémoire

memory chip /ˈmem(ə)ri tʃɪp/ *noun* puce *f* mémoire

memory cycle /ˈmem(ə)ri ˌsaɪk(ə)l/ *noun* cycle *m* de mémoire

memory data register /ˌmem(ə)ri ˈdeɪtə ˌredʒɪstə/ *noun* registre *m* des données en mémoire

memory diagnostic /ˈmem(ə)ri ˌdaɪəgnɒstɪk/ *noun* logiciel *m* de diagnostic de la mémoire

memory dump /ˈmem(ə)ri dʌmp/ *noun* (*printout of the contents of a memory*) listage *m* de mémoire; vidage *m* de mémoire sur imprimante

memory edit /ˈmem(ə)ri ˌedɪt/ *verb* changement *m* d'adresse en mémoire

memory effect /ˈmem(ə)ri ɪˌfekt/ *noun* effet *m* de mémoire

memory expansion /ˈmem(ə)ri ɪk ˌspænʃ(ə)n/ *noun* extension *f* de la mémoire

memory hierarchy /ˌmem(ə)ri ˌhaɪərɑːki/ *noun* hiérarchie *f* des mémoires

memory-intensive software /ˌmem(ə)ri ɪn ˌtensɪv ˈsɒftweə/ *noun* (*software that uses large amounts of RAM or disk storage*) logiciel *m* qui est grand consommateur de mémoire

memory management /ˈmem(ə)ri ˌmænɪdʒmənt/ *noun* gestion *f* de mémoire

memory management unit /ˈmem(ə)ri ˌmænɪdʒmənt ˌjuːnɪt/ *noun* gestion *f* de mémoire

memory map /ˈmem(ə)ri mæp/ *noun* configuration *f* de la mémoire

memory-mapped /ˈmem(ə)ri ˌmæpt/ *adjective* configuré en mémoire ◇ **a memory-mapped screen has an address allocated to each pixel, allowing direct access to the screen by the CPU** chaque pixel de cet écran configuré en mémoire a une adresse allouée, ce qui permet au processeur d'y accéder directement

memory-mapped input/output /ˌmem(ə)ri ˌmæpt ˌɪnpʊt ˈaʊtpʊt/ *noun* entrée/sortie *f* configurée en mémoire

memory-mapped I/O /ˌmem(ə)ri ˌmæpt aɪ ˈəʊ/ *noun* entrée/sortie *f* configurée en mémoire

memory model /ˈmem(ə)ri ˌmɒd(ə)l/ *noun* modèle *m* de (gestion des accès à la) mémoire

memory page /ˈmem(ə)ri peɪdʒ/ *noun* page *f* mémoire

memory protect /ˈmem(ə)ri prəˌtekt/ *noun* protection *f* de la mémoire

memory-resident software /ˌmem(ə)ri ˌrezɪd(ə)nt ˈsɒftweə/ *noun* logiciel *m* résident

memory switching system /ˈmem(ə)ri ˌswɪtʃɪŋ ˌsɪstəm/ *noun* système *m* à transfert de mémoire

memory workspace /ˈmem(ə)ri ˌwɜːkspeɪs/ *noun* zone *f* de travail (en mémoire)

menu /ˈmenjuː/ *noun* menu *m* ◇ **drop down menu** menu déroulant ◇ **menu bar** (*list of options available in a GUI*) barre *f* de menu

menu-driven software /ˌmenjuː ˌdrɪv(ə)n ˈsɒftweə/ *noun* logiciel *m* avec menu; logiciel *m* à base de menu

menu item /ˈmenjuː ˌaɪtəm/ *noun* (*choice in a menu*) élément *m* de menu

menu selection /ˈmenjuː sɪˌlekʃən/ *noun* sélection *f* par menu

menu shortcut /ˌmenjuː ˈʃɔːtkʌt/ *noun* raccourci *m* clavier; touche *f* d'accélération

merchant account /ˈmɜːtʃənt əˌkaʊnt/ *noun* compte *m* d'affaires

mercury delay line /ˌmɜːkjʊri dɪˈleɪ ˌlaɪn/ *noun* (*old method of storing data*) ligne *f* à retard au mercure

merge /mɜːdʒ/ *verb* (*to combine two data files*) fusionner *vti*; intégrer *vt*; combiner *vt* ◇ **the system automatically merges text and illustrations into the document** le système assure l'intégration automatique du texte et des illustrations dans le document

merge sort /ˌmɜːdʒ ˈsɔːt/ *noun* tri *m* et fusion

mesh /meʃ/ *noun* maille *f*

mesh network /meʃ ˈnetwɜːk/ *noun* (*network connection*) réseau *m* maillé

message /ˈmesɪdʒ/ *noun* **1.** (*piece of information sent*) message *m* **2.** (*detailed amount of information*) message *m* ◇ **message authentication code (MAC)** code d'authentification de message ◇ **message numbering** numérotation *f* des messages ◇ **message switching** commutation *f* de message ◇ **text message** (*written message by phone*) message (écrit) *or* mail *m*

message authentication code /ˌmesɪdʒ ɔːˌθentɪˈkeɪʃ(ə)n kəʊd/ *noun* code *m* d'authentification de message

message board /ˈmesɪdʒ bɔːd/ *noun* messagerie *f*

message box /ˈmesɪdʒ bɒks/ *noun* (*small window on screen*) boîte *f* de message

message code authentication /ˌmesɪdʒ kəʊd ɔːˌθentɪˈkeɪʃ(ə)n/ *noun* code *m* d'identification de message

message format /ˈmesɪdʒ ˌfɔːmæt/ *noun* format *m* de message

message handling service /ˌmesɪdʒ ˈhændlɪŋ ˌsɜːvɪs/ *noun* service *m* de gestion de message

message header /ˈmesɪdʒ ˌhedə/ *noun* (*sequence of data*) en-tête *m* de message

message routing /ˈmesɪdʒ raʊtɪŋ/ *noun* acheminement *m* des messages

message slot /ˈmesɪdʒ slɒt/ *noun* (*number of bits that can hold a message*) créneau *m* pour message

message text /ˈmesɪdʒ tekst/ *noun* texte *m* d'un message

message transfer agent /ˌmesɪdʒ ˈtrænsfɜː ˌeɪdʒənt/ *noun* agent *m* de transfert de messages

messaging /ˈmesɪdʒɪŋ/ *noun* (*sending messages by phone*) messagerie *f*; envoi *m* de messages; envoi *m* de mails ◇ **photo messaging** envoi de photos (par téléphone) ◇ **text messaging** messagerie *f*; envoi de messages (écrits) *or* de mails

metabit /ˈmetəbɪt/ *noun* métabit *m*

metacompilation /ˌmetəkɒmpɪˈleɪʃ(ə)n/ *noun* métacompilation *f*

metacompiler /ˈmetəkɒmˌpaɪlə/ *noun* (*compiler that is used to create another compiler*) métacompilateur *m*

metafile /'metəfaɪl/ *noun* **1.** (*file that contains other files*) métafichier *m* **2.** (*file with data about other files*) métafichier *m* ◇ **the operating system uses a metafile to hold data that defines where each file is stored on disk** le système d'exploitation utilise un métafichier où sont rangées les données qui définissent l'emplacement de chaque fichier sur le disque

metalanguage /'metəˌlæŋgwɪdʒ/ *noun* métalangage *m*

metal oxide semiconductor /ˌmet(ə)l ˌɒksaɪd 'semikənˌdʌktə/ *noun* semi-conducteur *m*; MOS

metal oxide semiconductor field effect transistor /ˌmet(ə)l ˌɒksaɪd ˌsemikəndʌktə fiːld ɪˌfekt træn'zɪstə/ *noun* transistor *m* à effet de champ à semi-conducteur à oxyde métallique

meter – power supply /ˌmiːtə 'pauə səˌplaɪ/ *noun* jauge *f* de charge; témoin *m* lumineux de charge

metropolitan area network /ˌmetrəpɒlɪt(ə)n ˌeəriə 'netwɜːk/ *noun* (*network extending over a limited area*) réseau *m* urbain

MFLOPS /'em flɒps/ *noun* (*measure of computing speed*) million *m* d'opérations en virgule flottante par seconde

MFM /ˌem ef 'em/ *noun* norme *f* de codage MFM

MHS /ˌem eɪtʃ 'es/ *noun* messagerie *f* X400

mice /maɪs/ *plural noun* souris *fpl*

MICR /ˌem aɪ siː 'ɑː/ *noun* reconnaissance *f* de caractères magnétiques

micro /'maɪkrəʊ/ *noun* (*one millionth*) micro *m*

micro- /maɪkrəʊ/ *prefix* **1.** (*one millionth*) micro- **2.** (*very small*) micro-

microcassette /'maɪkrəʊkəˌset/ *noun* (*very small cassette used in pocket dictating equipment*) microcassette *f*

Micro Channel Architecture /ˌmaɪkrəʊ ˌtʃæn(ə)l 'ɑːkɪtektʃə/ architecture *f* MCA

Micro Channel Architecture chipset /ˌmaɪkrəʊ ˌtʃæn(ə)l ˌɑːkɪtektʃə 'tʃɪpset/ jeu *m* de composants MCA

Micro Channel Bus /ˌmaɪkrəʊ ˌtʃæn(ə)l 'bʌs/ (*32-bit expansion bus defined by IBM*) bus *m* Micro-Channel; bus *m* MCA

microchip /'maɪkrəʊˌtʃɪp/ *noun* puce *f*

microcircuit /'maɪkrəʊˌkɜːkɪt/ *noun* (*complex integrated circuit*) microcircuit *m*

microcode /'maɪkrəʊkəʊd/ *noun* microcode *m*; micro-instruction *f*

Microcom Networking Protocol /ˌmaɪkrəkɒm 'netwɜːkɪŋ ˌprəʊtəkɒl/ (*error detection and correction system*) MCA

microcomputer /'maɪkrəʊkəmˌpjuːtə/ *noun* micro-ordinateur *m*; micro *m*

microcomputer architecture /ˌmaɪkrəʊkəmpjuːtə 'ɑːkɪtektʃə/ *noun* architecture *f* de micro-ordinateur

microcomputer backplane /ˌmaɪkrəʊkəmpjuːtə 'bækpleɪn/ *noun* (*main printed circuit board of a system*) fond *m* de panier d'un micro-ordinateur

microcomputer bus /'maɪkrəʊkəmˌpjuːtə ˌbʌs/ *noun* (*set of the main data, address and control buses*) bus *m* d'un micro-ordinateur

microcomputer development kit /ˌmaɪkrəʊkəmpjuːtə dɪ'veləpmənt ˌkɪt/ *noun* kit *m* d'extension de micro-ordinateur

microcontroller /'maɪkrəʊkənˌtrəʊlə/ *noun* micro-ordinateur *m* de contrôle; micro-ordinateur *m* de commande

microcycle /'maɪkrəʊˌsaɪk(ə)l/ *noun* microcycle *m*

microdevice /'maɪkrəʊdɪˌvaɪs/ *noun* (*very small device*) dispositif *m*; (*microprocessor*) composant *m* de très petite dimension; microprocesseur *m*

microelectronics /ˌmaɪkrəʊɪlek'trɒnɪks/ *noun* microélectronique *f*

microfloppy /'maɪkrəʊˌflɒpi/ *noun* (*usually refers to 3.5 inch disks*) disquette *f* 3,5"

microinstruction /'maɪkrəʊɪnˌstrʌkʃən/ *noun* micro-instruction *f*

micrometre /'maɪkrəʊˌmiːtə/ *noun* (*one millionth of a metre – formerly called 'micron'*) micromètre *m*; *formerly* micron *m*

micron /'maɪkrɒn/ *noun* (*now called: micrometre*) micromètre *m*; *formerly* micron *m*

microphone /'maɪkrəfəʊn/ *noun* microphone *m*; micro *m* ◇ **dynamic microphone** micro(phone) dynamique ◇ **moving coil microphone** micro(phone) à aimant mobile

microprocessor /'maɪkrəʊˌprəʊsesə/ *noun* microprocesseur *m* ◇ **microprocessor unit (MPU)** microprocesseur ◇ **the bit-slice microprocessor uses four 4-bit processors to make a 16-bit word processor** le microprocesseur en tranches utilise quatre processeurs à 4 bits pour réaliser un microprocesseur à 16 bits

microprocessor addressing capabilities /ˌmaɪkrəʊprəʊsesə ə'dresɪŋ ˌkeɪpəbɪlɪtiz/ *noun* (*highest address*) capacité *f*

microprocessor architecture /'maɪkrəʊprəʊsesə ˌɑːkɪtektʃə/ *noun* architecture *f* d'un microprocesseur

microprocessor chip /'maɪkrəʊˌprəʊsesə tʃɪp/ *noun* puce *f*

microprocessor timing /'maɪkrəʊ ˌprəʊsesə ˌtaɪmɪŋ/ *noun* fréquence *f* d'horloge du processeur

microprocessor unit /'maɪkrəʊˌprəʊsesə ˌjuːnɪt/ *noun* microprocesseur *m*

microprogram /'maɪkrəʊˌprəʊgræm/ *noun* microprogramme *m*

microprogram assembly language /ˌmaɪkrəʊprəʊgræm ə'sembli ˌlæŋgwɪdʒ/ *noun* langage *m* d'assemblage pour microprogramme

microprogram counter /'maɪkrəʊ ˌprəʊgræm ˌkaʊntə/ *noun* (*register*) registre *m*

microprogram instruction set /ˌmaɪkrəʊprəʊgræm ɪn'strʌkʃən ˌset/ *noun* (*register*) jeu *m* d'instructions d'un microprogramme

microprogramming /'maɪkrəʊ ˌprəʊgræmɪŋ/ *noun* microprogrammation *f*

microprogram store /'maɪkrəʊˌprəʊgræm ˌstɔː/ *noun* mémoire *f* qui contient un microprogramme

microsecond /'maɪkrəʊˌsekənd/ *noun* microseconde *f*

microsequence /'maɪkrəʊˌsiːkwəns/ *noun* séquence *f* de micro-instructions; séquence *f* d'instructions d'un microprogramme

Microsoft /'maɪkrəsɒft/ (*developer and publisher of software*) Microsoft™

Microsoft DOS /ˌmaɪkrəsɒft 'dɒs/ système *m* d'exploitation MS-DOS

Microsoft Exchange /ˌmaɪkrəsɒft ɪks 'tʃeɪndʒ/ (*program included with Windows 95*) Microsoft Exchange

Microsoft Exchange Server /ˌmaɪkrəsɒft ɪks'tʃeɪndʒ ˌsɜːvə/ Microsoft Exchange Server

Microsoft Fax /ˌmaɪkrəsɒft 'fæks/ Microsoft Fax

Microsoft Internet Explorer /ˌmaɪkrəsɒft ˌɪntənet ɪks'plɔːrə/ Microsoft Internet Explorer

Microsoft Network /ˌmaɪkrəsɒft 'netwɜːk/ Microsoft Network

Microsoft Outlook /ˌmaɪkrəsɒft 'aʊtlʊk/ (*trade name for an application that provides a range of features including managing email, contacts and diary appointments*) Microsoft Outlook

Microsoft Outlook Express /ˌmaɪkrəsɒft ˌaʊtlʊk ɪk'spres/ (*trade name for a free version of Outlook*) Microsoft Outlook Express

Microsoft Windows /ˌmaɪkrəsɒft 'wɪndəʊz/ Microsoft Windows

microwriter /'maɪkrəʊˌraɪtə/ *noun* (*portable keyboard and display, used for keyboarding when travelling*) portable *m* ultraléger

middleware /'mɪd(ə)lweə/ *noun* (*system software that has been customised*) progiciel *m* adapté aux besoins de l'utilisateur; progiciel *m* personnalisé; progiciel *m* sur mesure

MIDI /'mɪdi/ *noun* MIDI

MIDI channel /'mɪdi ˌtʃæn(ə)l/ *noun* canal *m* MIDI

MIDI connector /'mɪdi kəˌnektə/ *noun* connecteur *m* MIDI

MIDI device /'mɪdi ðiˌvaɪs/ *noun* dispositif *m* MIDI

MIDI file /'mɪdi faɪl/ *noun* fichier *m* MIDI

MIDI interface card /ˌmɪdi 'ɪntəfeɪs kɑːd/ *noun* carte *f* (d') interface MIDI

MIDI mapping /'mɪdi ˌmæpɪŋ/ *noun* configuration *f* MIDI

MIDI sequence /'mɪdi ˌsiːkwəns/ *noun* séquence *f* MIDI

MIDI sequencer /ˌmɪdi 'siːkwənsə/ *noun* séquenceur *m* MIDI

MIDI time code /ˌmɪdi 'taɪm kəʊd/ *noun* code *m* temporel MIDI

mid-user /mɪd 'juːzə/ *noun* utilisateur *m* intermédiaire

migrate /maɪ'greɪt/ *verb* migrer *vi*

migration /maɪ'greɪʃ(ə)n/ *noun* (*moving users from one hardware platform to another*) migration *f*

milk disk /'mɪlk dɪsk/ *noun* (*disk used to transfer data from a small machine onto a larger computer*) disque *m* à traiter; disque *m* relais

milking machine /'mɪlkɪŋ məˌʃiːn/ *noun* concentrateur *m* de données; capteur *m* de données à traiter

millennium bug /mɪ'leniəm bʌg/ *noun* bogue *m&f* de l'an 2000

milli- /mɪlɪ/ *prefix* (*one thousandth*) milli-

milliampere /ˌmɪli'æmpeə/ *noun* milliampère *m* (mA)

million instructions per second /ˌmɪljən ɪnˌstrʌkʃənz pɜː sɪ'kɒnd/ *noun* million *m* d'instructions par seconde

millisecond /'mɪlɪˌsekənd/ *noun* milliseconde *f*

MIMD /ˌem aɪ em 'diː/ *noun* architecture *f* MIMD; architecture *f* multiflux d'instruction – multiflux de données

MIME /ˌem aɪ em 'iː/ *noun* protocole *m* Mime

mini /'mɪni/ *noun* mini-ordinateur *m*

mini- /mɪni/ *prefix* (*small*) mini *m*

miniaturisation, miniaturization *noun* miniaturisation *f*

minicomputer /'mɪnikəmˌpjuːtə/ *noun* (*small computer*) mini-ordinateur *m*; mini *m*

minidisk /'mɪnidɪsk/ *noun* disquette *f* 3,25; disquette *f* de 3,5 pouces

minifloppy /'mɪniˌflɒpi/ *noun* (*disk*) disquette *f* 5,25 pouces; disquette *f* de 5,25 pouces

minimal latency coding /ˌmɪnɪməl 'leɪtənsi ˌkəʊdɪŋ/ *noun* code *m* optimum

minimal tree /'mɪnɪm(ə)l triː/ *noun* arborescence *f* optimale

minimise /'mɪnɪmaɪz/, **minimize** *verb* **1.** minimiser *vt*; réduire *vt* **2.** (*to shrink an application window*) réduire une fenêtre en icône

miniwinny /ˈmɪniˌwɪni/ *noun informal* minidisque *m* dur (de type Winchester)

minmax /ˈmɪnimæks/ *noun* méthode *f* mini/maxi

minuend /ˈmɪnjuːend/ *noun* nombre *m* duquel on soustrait un autre nombre

minus /ˈmaɪnəs/, **minus sign** /ˈmaɪnəs saɪn/ *noun* signe *m* moins; signe *m* de la soustraction

MIP mapping /ˌem aɪ piː ˈmæpɪŋ/ *noun* configuration *f* MIP

MIPS /mɪps/ *noun* million *m* d'instructions par seconde

'ICL has staked its claim to the massively parallel market with the launch of the Goldrush MegaServer, providing up to 16,000 Unix MIPS of processing power.' [*Computing*]

mirror /ˈmɪrə/ *verb* **1.** copier à l'identique **2.** (*make an identical copy*) copier à l'identique

'Network-attached storage systems which aim to make it easy to mirror data between units' [*The Guardian*]

mirror site /ˈmɪrə saɪt/ *noun* centre *m* miroir; site *m* miroir

MIS *abbr* **1.** (*management information service*) service *m* informatique **2.** (*management information system*) système *m* d'information de gestion

MISD /ˌem aɪ es ˈdiː/ *noun* architecture *f* MISD; architecture *f* multiflux d'instruction – monoflux de données

mission-critical /ˌmɪʃ(ə)n ˈkrɪtɪk(ə)l/ *adjective* (*on which a company depends*) critique; vital *or* -e; crucial, -e

MJPEG /ˌem ˈdʒeɪ peg/ *noun* norme *f* MJPEG

MKDIR *abbr* (*make directory*) commande *f* MD (de création de répertoire)

MMI /ˌem em ˈaɪ/ *noun* interface *f* homme/machine; interface *f* utilisateur/machine

MMU /ˌem em ˈjuː/ *noun* unité *f* de gestion de la mémoire

MMX (*trade name for an enhanced Intel processor chip*) technologie *f* MMX

mnemonic /nɪˈmɒnɪk/ *noun* (*shortened form of a word or function*) mnémonique *m*

MNP /ˌem en ˈpiː/ *noun* protocole *m* de communication de réseau Microcom (MNP)

mobile phone /ˌməʊbaɪl ˈfəʊn/ *noun* téléphone *m* mobile

mock-up /ˈmɒk ʌp/ *noun* maquette *f*

modal /ˈməʊd(ə)l/ *adjective* modal *or* -e

mode /məʊd/ *noun* **1.** (*way of doing something*) mode *m* **2.** (*method of operating computer*) mode *m* ◇ **bit-map mode** mode point *or* mode bit-map ◇ **when you want to type in text, press this function key which will put the terminal in its alphanumeric mode** pour saisir un texte, appuyer d'abord sur cette touche de fonction qui met le terminal en mode alphanumérique

'The approach being established by the Jedec committee provides for burst mode data transfer clocked at up to 100MHz.' [*Computing*]

Mode 1 /ˈməʊd wʌn/ *noun* Mode 1

Mode 2 /ˈməʊd tuː/ *noun* Mode 2

model /ˈmɒd(ə)l/ *noun* **1.** (*small-size copy*) maquette *f*; modèle *m* réduit **2.** (*version*) modèle *m* ■ *adjective* (*perfect*) modèle ■ *verb* (*to make a model*) modéliser *vt* ◇ **he showed us a model of the new computer centre building** il nous a fait voir la maquette du nouveau centre informatique ◇ **the new model B has taken the place of model A** le nouveau modèle B remplace le modèle A ◇ **this is the latest model** voici notre dernier modèle

modelling /ˈmɒd(ə)lɪŋ/ *noun* création *f* de modèles de programmes

modem /ˈməʊˌdem/, **MODEM** *noun* (*modulator/demodulator*) modem *m*

'AST Research has bundled together a notebook PC with a third-party PCMCIA fax modem technology for a limited-period special offer.' [*Computing*]

modem eliminator /ˌməʊdem ɪˈlɪmɪneɪtə/ *noun* câble *m* de liaison directe; câble *m* de connexion série

modem standards /ˈməʊdem ˌstændədz/ *plural noun* normes *fpl* pour modems

moderate /ˈmɒd(ə)rət/ *verb* agir en tant que modérateur

moderated list /ˌmɒd(ə)rətɪd ˈlɪst/, **moderated mailing list** /ˌmɒd(ə)rətd ˈmeɪlɪŋ lɪst/ *noun* (*mailing list checked and approved*) liste *f* approuvée

moderator /ˈmɒdəˌreɪtə/ *noun* modérateur *f*

modification /ˌmɒdɪfɪˈkeɪʃ(ə)n/ *noun* modification *f*; changement *m* ◇ **the modifications to the system allow it to be run as part of a LAN** les modifications apportées au système permettent de l'utiliser sur un réseau local d'entreprise

modification loop /ˌmɒdɪfɪˈkeɪʃ(ə)n luːp/ *noun* (*set of instructions within a loop*) boucle *f* de modification

modified frequency modulation /ˌmɒdɪfaɪd ˈfriːkwənsi ˌmɒdjʊleɪʃ(ə)n/ *noun* (*method of storing data on magnetic media*) norme *f* de codage MFM

modifier /ˈmɒdɪˌfaɪə/ *noun* modificateur *m*

modify /ˈmɒdɪˌfaɪ/ *verb* modifier *vt* ◇ **the keyboard was modified for European users** le clavier a été modifié pour le marché européen ◇ **the software will have to be modified to run on a small PC** il faudra modifier le logiciel pour pouvoir l'utiliser sur un PC ◇ **we are running a modified version of the mail-merge system** nous utilisons une version modifiée du programme d'édition de lettres types *or* de publipostage

Modula-2 /ˌmɒdjulə 'tuː/ *noun* (*high-level programming language derived from Pascal*) langage *m* Modula-2

modular /'mɒdjʊlə/ *adjective* modulaire

modularisation, modularization *noun* programmation *f* modulaire

modularity /ˌmɒdjʊ'lærɪti/ *noun* modularité *f* ◇ **the modularity of the software or hardware allows the system to be changed** la modularité du logiciel ou du matériel permet de modifier le système

modular programming /ˌmɒdjʊlə 'prəʊgræmɪŋ/ *noun* programmation *f* modulaire

modulate /'mɒdjʊˌleɪt/ *verb* moduler *vt*

modulated signal /ˌmɒdjʊleɪtɪd 'sɪgn(ə)l/ *noun* signal *m* modulé

modulating signal /'mɒdjuleɪtɪŋ ˌsɪgn(ə)l/ *noun* signal *m* de modulation

modulator /'mɒdjʊleɪtə/ *noun* modulateur *m* ◇ **modulator** *or* **demodulator (modem)** modulateur-démodulateur *or* modem *m*

modulator/demodulator /ˌmɒdjʊleɪtə diː 'mɒdjʊleɪtə/ *noun* modem *m*

module /'mɒdjuːl/ *noun* **1.** (*section of program*) module *m* **2.** (*piece of hardware*) module *m* ◇ **a multifunction analog interface module includes analog to digital and digital to analog converters** un module d'interface analogique multifonction contient un convertisseur analogique-numérique et un convertisseur numérique-analogique

modulo arithmetic /'mɒdjuləʊ əˌrɪθmətɪk/ *noun* arithmétique *f* à modulo

modulo-N /ˌmɒdjuləʊ 'en/ *noun* modulo-n *m*

modulo-N check /ˌmɒdjuləʊ 'en tʃek/ *noun* contrôle *m* par modulo-n

modulus /'mɒdjʊləs/ *noun* modulo *m*

moiré effect /'mwɑːreɪ ɪˌfekt/ *noun* effet *m* de moiré

momentary switch /'məʊmənt(ə)ri swɪtʃ/ *noun* (*switch*) interrupteur *m* temporaire

monadic Boolean operation /mɒˌnædɪk ˌbuːliən ˌɒpə'reɪʃ(ə)n/ *noun* opération *f* (booléenne) à un opérande; opération *f* (booléenne) monadique

monadic Boolean operator /mɒˌnædɪk ˌbuːliən 'ɒpəreɪtə/ *noun* opérateur *m* monadique à un opérande

monadic operation /mɒˌnædɪk ˌɒpə 'reɪʃ(ə)n/ *noun* opération *f* monadique

monadic operator /mɒˌnædɪk 'ɒpəreɪtə/ *noun* opérateur *m* monadique à un opérande

monitor /'mɒnɪtə/ *noun* **1.** (*VDU*) moniteur *m*; écran *m* (de visualisation) **2.** (*system that watches for faults*) dispositif *m* de contrôle ■ *verb* **1.** (*to check*) vérifier *vt*; contrôler *vt*; surveiller *vt*; suivre *vt* **2.** (*to supervise*) vérifier *vt*; contrôler *vt*; surveiller *vt*; suivre *vt* ◇ **he is monitoring the progress of the trainee programmers** il contrôle *or* suit le progrès des programmeurs débutants ◇ **multi-scan** *or* **multi-sync monitor** écran multistandard ◇ **the machine monitors each signal as it is sent out** l'appareil contrôle chaque signal de sortie

monitor program /'mɒnɪtə ˌprəʊgræm/ *noun* (*computer program*) programme *m* de contrôle; programme *m* moniteur

monitor unit /'mɒnɪtə ˌjuːnɪt/ *noun* moniteur *m*

mono- /mɒnəʊ/ *prefix* mono

monoaural /ˌmɒnəʊ'ɔːrəl/ *adjective* monaural *or* -e

monochrome /'mɒnəkrəʊm/ *adjective, noun* monochrome; noir et blanc ◇ **monochrome display adapter (MDA)** (*video adapter standard*) adaptateur (monochrome) MDA *or* carte MDA

monochrome display adapter /ˌmɒnəkrəʊm dɪ'spleɪ əˌdæptə/ *noun* standard *m* d'affichage MDA

monochrome monitor /ˌmɒnəkrəʊm 'mɒnɪtə/ *noun* (*computer monitor that displays in black or white*) écran *m* monochrome

monolithic driver /mɒnəˌlɪθɪk 'draɪvə/ *noun* lecteur *m* monolithique

monomode fibre /'mɒnəʊməʊd ˌfaɪbə/ *noun* fibre *f* optique monomode

monoprogramming system /'mɒnəʊ ˌprəʊgræmɪŋ ˌsɪstəm/ *noun* système *m* de monoprogrammation

monospaced /'mɒnəʊspeɪst/ *adjective* à espacement constant

monospaced font /ˌmɒnəʊspeɪst 'fɒnt/ *noun* (*font in which each character has the same width*) police *f* de caractères à espacements uniformes

Monte Carlo method /ˌmɒnti 'kɑːləʊ ˌmeθəd/ *noun* méthode *f* de Monte Carlo

MOO *noun* environnement *m* MOO

morphing /'mɔːfɪŋ/ *noun* (*in multimedia and games*) morphage *m*

MOS /ˌem əʊ 'es/ *noun* semi-conducteur *m* MOS

mosaic /məʊ'zeɪɪk/ *noun* mosaïque *f*

Mosaic /məʊ'zeɪɪk/ (*trade name for a popular browser software used to view webpages on the Internet*) mosaïque *f*

MOSFET /'mɒsfet/ *noun* semi-conducteur *m* à effet de champ MOSFET

MOS memory /ˌem əʊ es 'mem(ə)ri/ *noun* mémoire *f* MOS

most significant bit /ˌməʊst sɪgˌnɪfɪkənt 'bɪt/ *noun* bit *m* de poids fort; bit *m* le plus significatif ◇ **the most significant bit in an eight bit binary word represents 128 in decimal notation** le bit le plus significatif dans un mot de huit bits représente 128 en numération décimale

most significant digit /məʊst sɪgˌnɪfɪkənt 'dɪdʒɪt/, **most significant character** /məʊst sɪgˌnɪfɪkənt ˈkærɪktə/ *noun* chiffre *m* de poids fort; chiffre *m* le plus significatif

motherboard /ˈmʌðəbɔːd/ *noun* carte *f* mère

motion JPEG /ˌməʊʃ(ə)n ˈdʒeɪ ˌpeg/ *noun* norme *f* MJPEG

motion picture experts group /ˌməʊʃ(ə)n ˌpɪktʃə ˈekspɜːts gruːp/ *noun* norme *f* MPEG

Motorola /ˌməʊtəˈrəʊlə/ (*manufacturer of electronic components*) Motorola™

mount /maʊnt/ *verb* **1.** (*fix onto base*) monter *vt*; fixer *vt* **2.** (*insert a disk in a disk drive*) monter un disque ◇ **the chips are mounted in sockets on the PCB** les puces sont montées dans des prises de la carte de circuit imprimé

mouse /maʊs/ *noun* souris *f* ◇ **cordless mouse** souris sans fil ◇ **mouse-driven (software)** (logiciel) contrôlé *or* piloté par une souris ◇ **mouse mat** *or* **mouse pad** tapis *m* souris *or* tapis pour la souris ◇ **scroll mouse** *or* **wheel mouse** souris à molette

> 'This project has now borne fruit, with the announcement last week of Windots, a project which allows users to 'see' Windows screens in a Braille form of Ascii. Other areas of research include a sound system which allows a sound to 'move', mirroring the movement of a mouse.' [*Computing*]

mouse acceleration /maʊs əkˌseləˈreɪʃ(ə)n/ *noun* accélération *f* de la souris

mouse-driven /maʊs ˈdrɪv(ə)n/ *adjective* contrôlé, -ée par une souris

mouse driver /maʊs ˈdraɪvə/ *noun* pilote *m* de souris

mouse pointer /maʊs ˈpɔɪntə/ *noun* (*small arrow displayed on screen*) pointeur *m* de souris; pointeur *m* contrôlé par la souris

mouse sensitivity /maʊs ˌsensəˈtɪvəti/ *noun* piloté, -ée par une souris

mouse tracking /maʊs ˈtrækɪŋ/ *noun* sensibilité *f* de la souris

M out of N code /ˌem aʊt əv ˈen ˌkəʊd/ *noun* code *m* N dont M

movable /ˈmuːvəb(ə)l/ *adjective* (*which can be moved*) mobile; (*which can be removed*) amovible

movable head disk /ˌmuːvəb(ə)l hed ˈdɪsk/ *noun* unité *f* de disque avec tête de lecture chercheuse

move /muːv/ *verb* (*to change the position*) déplacer *vt*; changer de place

move block /ˈmuːv ˌblɒk/ *noun* instruction *f* de déplacer un bloc

movement /ˈmuːvmənt/ *noun* mouvement *m*

movement file /ˈmuːvmənt faɪl/ *noun* fichier *m* de mouvements *or* de modifications *or* de mise à jour

Moving Pictures Expert Group /ˌmuːvɪŋ ˌpɪktʃəs ˈekspɜːt ˌgruːp/ *noun* norme *f* MPEG

MP3 /ˌem piː ˈθriː/ *noun* MP3

MPC /ˌem piː ˈsiː/ *noun* ordinateur *m* multimédia

MPEG /ˈem peg/ *noun* groupe *m* MPEG

MPEG audio level 3 /ˌem peg ˌɔːdiəʊ ˌlev(ə)l ˈθriː/ *noun* MP3

MPPP /ˌem piː piː ˈpiː/ *noun* liens *mpl* multiples PPP

MPS *abbr* (*microprocessor system*) multiprocesseur *m*

MPU *abbr* (*microprocessor unit*) unité *f* centrale à microprocesseur

MS *abbr* (*Microsoft*) MS

msb /ˌem es ˈbiː/, **MSB** *noun* bit *m* de poids fort

MSD /ˌem es ˈdiː/ *noun* chiffre *m* de poids fort

MS-DOS /ˌem es ˈdɒs/ (*trade name for an operating system for the IBM PC range of personal computers*) MS-DOS

MSI *abbr* (*medium scale integration*) intégration *f* à moyenne échelle

MSN (*trade name for an Internet portal*) MSN

MS-Windows /ˌem es ˈwɪndəʊz/ Windows

MSX /ˌem es ˈeks/ *noun* norme *f* MSX; standard *m* MSX

MTA /ˌem tiː ˈeɪ/ *noun* agent *m* de transfert de messages

MTBF /ˌem tiː biː ˈef/ *noun* durée *f* moyenne de bon fonctionnement; moyenne *f* de temps de bon fonctionnement entre les défaillances (MTBF)

MTF /ˌem tiː ˈef/ *noun* durée *f* moyenne de bon fonctionnement

MTTR /ˌem tiː tiː ˈɑː/ *noun* durée *f* moyenne de rétablissement

multi- /mʌlti/ *prefix* (*many or more than one*) multi-

multi-access system /ˌmʌltɪ ˌækses ˈsɪstəm/ *noun* (*system that allows access to multi-users*) système *m* à accès multiple; système *m* multi-accès

multi-address /ˌmʌltɪ əˈdres/, **multi-address instruction** /ˌmʌltɪ əˌdres ɪnˈstrʌkʃən/ *noun* (*instruction with more than one address*) instruction *f* multiadresse

multi-board computer /ˌmʌltɪ bɔːd kəm ˈpjuːtə/ *noun* ordinateur *m* multicarte

multibus system /ˌmʌltɪbʌs ˈsɪstəm/, **multibus architecture** /ˌmʌltɪbʌs ˈɑːkɪtektʃə/ *noun* système *m* multibus; système *m* à bus multiples

multicast /ˈmʌltikɑːst/ *verb* faire une multidiffusion

multichannel /ˌmʌltiˈtʃæn(ə)l/ *adjective* multivoie

multicolour /ˌmʌltiˈkʌlə/ *adjective* multicolore

multicolour graphics adapter /ˌmʌltikʌlə ˈgræfɪks əˌdæptə/ *noun* carte *f* MCGA; standard *m* MCGA

multidimensional /ˌmʌltidaɪˈmenʃən(ə)l/ *adjective* multidimensionnel *or* -elle

multidimensional array /ˌmʌltɪdaɪmenʃ(ə)n(ə)l əˈreɪ/ *noun* (*arrays arranged in parallel*) tableau *m* multidimensionnel

multidimensional language /ˌmʌltɪdaɪmenʃ(ə)n(ə)l ˈlæŋgwɪdʒ/ *noun* langage *m* multidimensionnel; langage *m* multiniveau

multi-disk /ˌmʌltɪ ˈdɪsk/ *adjective* multidisque

multi-disk option /ˈmʌltɪ dɪsk ˌɒpʃ(ə)n/ *noun* option *f* multidisque

multi-disk reader /ˌmʌltɪ dɪsk ˈriːdə/ *noun* lecteur *m* multidisque

multidrop circuit /ˈmʌltɪdrɒp ˌsɜːkɪt/ *noun* circuit *m* multipoint

MultiFinder /ˈmʌltifaɪndə/ *noun* (*Apple Macintosh Finder that supports multitasking*) MultiFinder™

multifrequency monitor /ˌmʌltifriːkwənsi ˈmɒnɪtə/ *noun* écran *m* multisynchrone; écran *m* multisync

multifunction, multifunctional *adjective* multifonction *f* ◇ **a multifunction analog interface module includes analog to digital and digital to analog converters** un module d'interface analogique multifonction contient un convertisseur analogique-numérique et un convertisseur numérique-analogique

multifunction card /ˌmʌltɪfʌnkʃ(ə)n ˈkɑːd/ *noun* carte *f* d'extension multifonction

multifunction workstation /ˌmʌltɪfʌnkʃ(ə)n ˈwɜːkˌsteɪʃ(ə)n/ *noun* poste *m* de travail multifonction

multilayer /ˌmʌltiˈleɪə/ *adjective* multicouche; à couches multiples

multilevel /ˌmʌltiˈlev(ə)l/ *adjective* multiniveau; à plusieurs niveaux

multiline *adjective* multiligne *f*

multi-link point to point protocol /ˌmʌlti lɪŋk ˌpɔɪnt tə ˌpɔɪnt ˈpəʊtəkɒl/ *noun* liens *mpl* multiples PPP

multilink system /ˈmʌltɪlɪŋk ˌsɪstəm/ *noun* système *m* multiligne; système *m* à multiples connexions; système *m* maillé

multimedia /ˌmʌltiˈmiːdiə/ *adjective* (*combination of sound, graphics, text, etc.*) multimédia ◇ **multimedia file** fichier *m* multimédia ◇ **multimedia mail** message multimédia ◇ **multimedia terminal** console *f* multimédia

> 'The Oracle Media Server is a multimedia database designed to run on massively parallel computers, running hundreds of transactions per second and managing multiple data types, such as video, audio and text.' [*Computing*]

multimedia card /ˌmʌltimiːdiə ˈkɑːd/ *noun* carte *f* multimédia

multimedia developer's kit /ˌmʌltimiːdiə dɪˈveləpəz kɪt/ *noun* trousse *f* de développement logiciel multimédia

multimedia extensions /ˌmʌltimiːdiə ɪk ˈstenʃ(ə)nz/ *plural noun* extensions *fpl* multimédia

multimedia Internet mail extensions /ˌmʌltimiːdiə ˌɪntənet ˈmeɪl ɪkˌstenʃ(ə)nz/ *noun* protocole *m* Mime

multimedia PC /ˌmʌltimiːdiə ˌpiː ˈsiː/ *noun* PC *m* multimédia

multimedia-ready /ˌmʌltimiːdiə ˈredi/ *adjective* avec configuration multimédia

multimode fibre /ˌmʌltɪməʊd ˈfaɪbə/ *noun* fibre *f* optique multimode

multipass overlap /ˌmʌltɪpɑːs ˈəʊvəlæp/ *noun* impression *f* à passages multiples

multiphase program /ˌmʌltɪfeɪz ˈprəʊgræm/ *noun* programme *m* multiphase

multi platform /ˌmʌltɪ ˈplætˌfɔːm/ *adjective* multiplate-forme

multiple /ˈmʌltɪp(ə)l/ *adjective* multiple

multiple access system /ˌmʌltɪp(ə)l ˈækses ˌsɪstəm/ *noun* système *m* à accès multiple; système *m* multi-accès

multiple address code /ˌmʌltɪp(ə)l əˈdres ˌkəʊd/ *noun* code *m* multiadresse

multiple base page /ˌmʌltɪp(ə)l beɪs ˈpeɪdʒ/ *noun* système *m* multipage

multiple bus architecture /ˌmʌltɪp(ə)l bʌs ˈɑːkɪtektʃə/ *noun* architecture *f* à bus multiples

multiple bus system /ˌmʌltɪp(ə)l bʌs ˈsɪstəm/, **multiple bus architecture** /ˌmʌltɪp(ə)l bʌs ˈɑːkɪtektʃə/ *noun* système *m* multibus; système *m* à bus multiples

multiple instruction stream-multiple data stream /ˌmʌltɪp(ə)l ɪnˌstrʌkʃən ˌstriːm ˌmʌltɪp(ə)l ˈdeɪtə ˌstriːm/ *noun* architecture *f* multiflux d'instruction – multiflux de données; architecture *f* MIMD; architecture *f* MISD

multiple instruction stream-single data stream /ˌmʌltɪp(ə)l ɪnˌstrʌkʃən ˌstriːm ˌsɪŋg(ə)l ˈdeɪtə ˌstriːm/ *noun* (*architecture of a parallel computer*) architecture *f* multiflux d'instruction – monoflux de données

multiple line *adjective* multiligne *f*

multiplex /ˈmʌltɪpleks/ *verb* multiplexer *vt*

multiplexed bus /ˌmʌltɪpleksd ˈbʌs/ *noun* bus *m* multiplexé

multiplexor /ˈmʌltɪpleksə/ *noun* multiplexeur *m*

multiplicand /ˌmʌltiplɪˈkænd/ *noun* multiplicande *m*

multiplication /ˌmʌltɪplɪˈkeɪʃ(ə)n/ *noun* multiplication *f* ◇ **multiplication sign (x)** signe *m* de la multiplication ◇ **the multiplication of 5 and 3 equals 15** la multiplication de 5 par 3 donne 15 comme résultat

multiplication sign /ˌmʌltɪplɪˈkeɪʃ(ə)n saɪn/ *noun* signe *m* de la multiplication

multiplier /ˈmʌltɪplaɪə/ *noun* multiplicateur *m*

multiply /ˈmʌltɪˌplaɪ/ *verb* (*perform the multiplication of a number by another number*) multiplier *vt*

multipoint /ˈmʌltipɔɪnt/ *adjective* multipoint

multiprecision /ˌmʌltiprɪˈsɪʒ(ə)n/ *noun* multiple précision

multiprocessing system /ˌmʌltɪˈprəʊsesɪŋ ˌsɪstəm/ *noun* système *m* multiprocesseur

multiprocessor /ˈmʌltiˌprəʊsesə/ *noun* multiprocesseur *m*

multiprocessor interleaving /ˌmʌltɪprəʊsesə ˌɪntəˈliːvɪŋ/ *noun* (*use of more than one bit of data*) multiprogrammation *f*

multi-programming system /ˌmʌltɪ ˈprəʊgræmɪŋ ˌsɪstəm/ *noun* multiprogrammation *f*

multipurpose Internet mail extensions /ˌmʌltipɜːpəs ˌɪntənet ˈmeɪl ɪkˌstenʃ(ə)nz/ *noun* protocole *m* Mime

multi-scan monitor /ˌmʌltɪ skæn ˈmɒnɪtə/ *noun* (*can lock onto the scanning frequency of any type of graphics card*) moniteur *m* multistandard

multi statement line /ˌmʌltɪ ˌsteɪtmənt ˈlaɪn/ *noun* ligne *f* multi-instruction

multistation access unit /ˌmʌltisteɪʃ(ə)n ˈækses ˌjuːnɪt/ *noun* unité *f* d'accès multiposte

multisync monitor /mʌltɪˌsɪŋk ˈmɒnɪtə/ *noun* écran *m* multisynchrone; moniteur *m* multibalayage

multitasking /ˈmʌltiˌtɑːskɪŋ/ *noun* multitâche *f* ■ *adjective* multi-tâche

> 'X is the underlying technology which allows Unix applications to run under a multi-user, multitasking GUI. It has been adopted as the standard for the Common Open Software Environment, proposed recently by top Unix vendors including Digital, IBM and Sun.' [*Computing*]

multi terminal system /ˌmʌltɪ ˌtɜːmɪn(ə)l ˈsɪstəm/ *noun* système *m* à plusieurs terminaux; système *m* multiposte

multithread /ˈmʌltiθred/ *noun* configuration *f* d'un programme à plusieurs branches

multiuser domain /ˌmʌltijuːzə dəˈmeɪn/ *noun* environnement *m* MUD

multiuser domain, object-oriented /ˌmʌltijuːzə dəˌmeɪn ˌɒbdʒekt ˈɔːrientɪd/ *noun* environnement *m* MOO

multiuser dungeon /ˌmʌltijuːzə ˈdʌndʒən/ *noun* environnement *m* MUD

multiuser program /ˌmʌltijuːzə ˈprəgræm/ *noun* programme *m* multiutilisateur; programme *m* multiposte

multiuser system /ˌmʌltijuːzə ˈsɪstəm/ *noun* système *m* multi-utilisateur; système *m* multiposte ◇ **the program runs on a standalone machine or a multi-user system** on peut exécuter le programme sur un ordinateur indépendant ou sur un système multiposte

multi-window editor /ˌmʌlti ˌwɪndəʊ ˈedɪtə/ *noun* logiciel *m* multifenêtre

musical instrument digital interface /ˌmjuːzɪk(ə)l ˌɪnstrʊmənt ˌdɪdʒɪt(ə)l ˈɪntəfeɪs/ *noun* (*interface that connects electronic instruments*) interface *f* numérique pour instruments de musique; interface *f* MIDI ◇ **MIDI interface (card)** interface *f* MIDI

music chip /ˈmjuːzɪk tʃɪp/ *noun* circuit *m* intégré générateur de son ◇ **music synthesizer** synthétiseur *m* de son

MUX /ˌem juː ˈeks/ *noun* multiplexeur *m*

My Computer /ˌmaɪ kəmˈpjuːtə/ *noun* (*icon that is normally in the upper left-hand corner of the screen on a computer running Windows 95*) poste *m* de travail

N

NAK *abbr* (*negative acknowledgement*) accusé *m* de réception négatif

name /neɪm/ *noun* (*to identify an address*) nom *m* ◇ **file name** nom de fichier

name registration /neɪm ˌredʒɪ'streɪʃ(ə)n/ *noun* enregistrement *m* de nom de domaine

name server /neɪm 'sɜːvə/ *noun* serveur *m* de noms de domaines

namespace /'neɪmspeɪs/ *noun* espace *m* de nommage

name table /neɪm 'teɪb(ə)l/ *noun* table *f* de noms

naming services /'neɪmɪŋ ˌsɜːvɪsɪz/ *noun* service *m* d'affectation de noms; service *m* d'attribution de noms

NAND function /'nænd ˌfʌŋkʃ(ə)n/ *noun* fonction *f* NON-ET; fonction *f* NAND

NAND gate /'nænd geɪt/ *noun* (*electronic circuit*) porte *f* NON-ET; circuit *m* NON-ET

nano- /nænəʊ/ *prefix* (*one thousand millionth or one billionth*) nano-

nanocircuit /'nænəʊˌsɜːkɪt/ *noun* circuit *m* électronique

nanosecond /'nænəʊˌsekənd/ *noun* nanoseconde *f*

nanosecond circuit /'nænəʊˌsekənd ˌsɜːkɪt/ *noun* circuit *m* à délai de réponse de l'ordre de la nanoseconde

Napster /'næpstə/ (*trade name for software that allows users to share files*) Napster

narrative /'nærətɪv/ *noun* (*explanatory notes*) commentaire *m*

narrative statement /'nærətɪv ˌsteɪtmənt/ *noun* (*program*) instruction *f* de procédure

narrow band ISDN /ˌnærəʊ bænd ˌaɪ es diː 'en/ *noun* RNIS à bande *f* étroite

narrowcast /'nærəʊkɑːst/ *verb* faire une multidiffusion

NAT /ˌen eɪ 'tiː/ *noun* traduction *f* d'adresses de réseau

National Television System Committee /ˌnæʃ(ə)nəl ˌtelɪ'vɪʒ(ə)n ˌsɪstəm kəˌmɪti/ *noun* NTSC

native /'neɪtɪv/ *adjective* natif; -ive

native compiler /ˌneɪtɪv kəm'paɪlə/ *noun* compilateur *m* natif; compilateur *m* originel

native file format /ˌneɪtɪv 'faɪl ˌfɔːmæt/ *noun* format *m* de fichier natif

native format /ˌneɪtɪv 'fɔːmæt/ *noun* format *m* initial

native language /ˌneɪtɪv 'læŋgwɪdʒ/ *noun* langage *m* natif; langage *m* de constructeur

natural binary coded decimal /ˌnætʃ(ə)rəl ˌbaɪnəri ˌkəʊdɪd 'desɪm(ə)l/ *noun* décimal *m* codé binaire naturel

natural language /ˌnætʃ(ə)rəl 'læŋgwɪdʒ/ *noun* langage *m* naturel

natural language processing /ˌnætʃ(ə)rəl 'læŋgwɪdʒ ˌprəʊsesɪŋ/ *noun* traitement *m* du langage naturel

navigable /'nævɪgəb(ə)l/ *adjective* navigable

navigation /ˌnævɪ'geɪʃ(ə)n/ *noun* (*moving around a multimedia title using hotspots, buttons and a user interface*) navigation *f*

NC *abbr* **1.** (*network computer*) ordinateur *m* de réseau **2.** (*numerical control*) commande *f* numérique

NCR paper /ˌen siː 'ɑː ˌpeɪpə/ *noun* (*special type of carbonless paper*) papier *m* NCR; papier *m* autocopiant

NCSA /ˌen siː es 'eɪ/ *noun* ICSA

NDIS /ˌen diː eɪ 'es/ *noun* spécification *f* NDIS

NDR /ˌen diː 'ɑː/ *noun* lecture *f* non destructive

negate /nɪ'geɪt/ *verb* (*to reverse the sign of a number*) inverser *vt*; affecter d'un signe négatif; qualifier négativement ◇ **if you negate 23.4 the result is –23.4** la valeur négative *or* l'inverse de 23,4 est –23,4

negation /nɪ'geɪʃ(ə)n/ *noun* (*reversing the sign of a number*) négation *f*; inversion *f*

negative /'negətɪv/ *adjective* (*meaning 'no'*) négatif; -ive ◇ **negative acknowledgement (NAK** *or* **NACK)** (*indicates signal incorrectly or incompletely received*) accusé *m* de réception négatif (NACK) ◇ **negative feedback** rétroaction négative *or* feedback négatif

negative acknowledgement /ˌnegətɪv ək 'nɒlɪdʒmənt/ *noun* accusé *m* de réception négatif

negative number /ˌnegətɪv 'nʌmbə/ *noun* nombre *m* négatif

negative-true logic /ˌnegətɪv 'truː ˌlɒdʒɪk/ *noun* logique *f* négative

neither-nor function /ˌnaɪðə ˈnɔːr ˌfʌŋkʃ(ə)n/ *noun* (*logical function*) fonction *f* NON-OU; fonction *f* NI

NEQ *abbr* (*nonequivalence function*) fonction *f* de disjonction

NEQ function /ˈnek ˌfʌŋkʃ(ə)n/ *noun* fonction *f* de disjonction

NEQ gate /ˈnek geɪt/ *noun* porte *f* de disjonction

nerd /nɜːd/ *noun slang* (*slang for a person obsessed with computers*) accro *m* de l'informatique

nest /nest/ *verb* **1.** (*to insert subroutine*) imbriquer *vt*; emboîter *vt* **2.** (*to use routine*) imbriquer *vt*; emboîter *vt*

nested loop /ˌnestd ˈluːp/ *noun* (*program*) boucle *f* imbriquée; boucle *f* emboîtée

nested macro call /ˌnestɪd ˈmækrəʊ ˌkɔːl/ *noun* appel *m* de macro imbriqué

nested structure /nestd ˈstrʌktʃə/ *noun* structure *f* imbriquée

nesting level /nestɪŋ ˈlev(ə)l/ *noun* niveau *m* d'imbrication

nesting store /ˌnestɪŋ ˈstɔː/ *noun* mémoire *f* à liste permutée

NetBEUI /ˈnet bjuːi/ *noun* version *f* étendue de NetBIOS

NetBIOS /ˈnet ˌbaɪɒs/ *noun* NetBIOS *m*

NetBIOS extended user interface /ˌnet baɪɒs ɪkˌstendɪd ˈjuːzə ˌɪntəfeɪs/ *noun* protocole *m* NetBEUI

netiquette /ˈnetɪket/ *noun* nétiquette *f*; règles *fpl* de politesse électronique

netphone /ˈnetfəʊn/ *noun* téléphonie *f* sur Internet

NetScape /ˈnetskeɪp/ NetScape

Netscape Navigator /ˌnetskeɪp ˈnævɪgeɪtə/ (*trade name for one of the most popular web browsers*) Netscape Navigator

NetShow /ˈnetshəʊ/ NetShow

NetView /ˈnetvjuː/ (*network management architecture developed by IBM*) NetView™

NetWare /ˈnetweə/ (*proprietary network operating system, developed by Novell*) NetWare™

NetWare Loadable Module /ˌnetweə ˌləʊdəb(ə)l ˈmɒdjuːl/ (*trade name for an application that can run under the NetWare operating system*) module *m* chargeable Netware

network /ˈnetwɜːk/ *noun* réseau *m* ■ *verb* (*to link points together in a network*) disposer *vt*; configurer en réseau ◇ **local area network (LAN)** réseau local (d'entreprise) ◇ **network driver interface specification (NDIS)** (*standard command interface between network driver software and network adapter card – defined by Microsoft*) interface *f* NDIS (de réseau) ◇ **networked TV programme** programme *m* transmis sur (tout) un réseau de télévision ◇ **network interface card (NIC)** (*board that connects a computer to a network*) carte *f* (interface de) réseau ◇ **network manager** gestionnaire *m* de réseau ◇ **network operating system (NOS)** (*operating system running on a server computer*) système d'exploitation de réseau *or* NOS ◇ **radio network** réseau radiophonique ◇ **television network** réseau de télévision ◇ **the workstations have been networked together rather than used as standalone systems** les postes de travail ont été reliés en réseau plutôt que d'être utilisés indépendamment ◇ **they run a system of networked micros** ils exploitent un réseau de micros ◇ **wide area network (WAN)** réseau étendu *or* à distance

> 'Asante Technologies has expanded its range of Ethernet-to-LocalTalk converters with the release of AsantePrint 8, which connects up to eight LocalTalk printers, or other LocalTalk devices, to a high-speed Ethernet network.' [*Computing*]

network adapter /ˈnetwɜːk əˌdæptə/ *noun* carte *f* réseau

network address /ˈnetwɜːk əˌdres/ *noun* adresse *f* de réseau

network address translation /ˌnetwɜːk ə ˌdres træns'leɪʃ(ə)n/ *noun* traduction *f* d'adresses de réseau

network administrator /ˌnetwɜːk əd ˈmɪnɪstreɪtə/ *noun* administrateur *m* de réseau

network alert /ˌnetwɜːk əˈlɜːt/ *noun* alerte *f* réseau

network analysis /ˈnetwɜːk əˌnæləsɪs/ *noun* analyse *f* de réseau

network architecture /ˌnetwɜːk ˈɑːkɪtektʃə/ *noun* architecture *f* d'un réseau

Network Basic Input Output System /ˌnetwɜːk ˌbeɪsɪk ˌɪnpʊt ˈaʊtpʊt ˌsɪstəm/ *noun* protocole *m* NetBIOS

network calendar program /ˌnetwɜːk ˈkælɪndə ˌprəʊgræm/ *noun* logiciel *m* de calendrier de groupe

network computer /ˌnetwɜːk kəmˈpjuːtə/ *noun* ordinateur *m* de réseau

network controller /ˌnetwɜːk kənˈtrəʊlə/ *noun* contrôleur *m* de réseau

network control program /ˌnetwɜːk kən ˈtrəʊl ˌprəʊgræm/ *noun* programme *m* de contrôle de réseau

network database /ˌnetwɜːk ˈdeɪtəbeɪs/ *noun* base *f* de données de réseau

network device driver /ˌnetˌwɜːk dɪˈvaɪs ˌdraɪvə/ *noun* gestionnaire *m* de périphérique de réseau

network diagram /ˌnetwɜːk ˈdaɪəgræm/ *noun* diagramme *m* de réseau

network directory /ˌnetwɜːk daɪˈrekt(ə)ri/ *noun* répertoire *m* de réseau

network drive /ˈnetwɜːk draɪv/ *noun* disque *m* serveur; unité *f* de disque dur d'un réseau

network driver interface specification /ˌnetwɜːk ˌdraɪvə ˈɪntəfeɪs ˌspesɪfɪkeɪʃ(ə)n/ *noun* spécification *f* NDIS

network file system /ˌnetwɜːk ˈfaɪl ˌsɪstəm/ *noun* système *m* de gestion de fichiers en réseau

network hardware /ˌnetwɜːk ˈhɑːdweə/ *noun* matériel *m*

networking /ˈnetwɜːkɪŋ/ *noun* **1.** (*TV or radio*) transmission *f*; diffusion *f* sur tout un réseau **2.** (*organization of a computer network*) configuration *f* de réseau; (*interconnecting computers*) mise *f* en réseau ◇ **this computer firm is a UK networking specialist** cette société informatique est une société britannique spécialisée en réseaux

networking hardware /ˌnetwɜːkɪŋ ˈhɑːdweə/ *noun* matériel *m*

networking software /ˌnetwɜːkɪŋ ˈsɒftweə/ *noun* logiciel *m* de réseau; logiciel *m* pour réseau

networking specialist /ˈnetwɜːkɪŋ ˌspeʃəlɪst/ *noun* expert *m*

network interface card /ˌnetwɜːk ˈɪntəfeɪs ˌkɑːd/ *noun* carte *f* interface de réseau

network-intrinsic application /ˌnetwɜːk ɪn ˈtrɪnsɪk ˌæplɪkeɪʃ(ə)n/ *noun* application *f* propre au réseau

network layer /ˈnetwɜːk ˌleɪə/ *noun* couche *f* réseau

network management /ˌnetwɜːk ˈmænɪdʒmənt/ *noun* (*organisation of a network*) gestion *f* de réseau

network news transfer protocol /ˌnetwɜːk njuːz ˈtrænsfɜː ˌprəʊtəkɒl/ *noun* protocole *m* NNTP

network operating system /ˌnetwɜːk ˈɒpəreɪtɪŋ ˌsɪstəm/ *noun* système *m* d'exploitation de réseau; NOS

network printer /ˌnetwɜːk ˈprɪntə/ *noun* imprimante *f* de réseau

network processor /ˌnetwɜːk ˈprəʊsesə/ *noun* processeur *m* de réseau

network protocol /ˌnetwɜːk ˈprəʊtəkɒl/ *noun* protocole *m* (de communication) de réseau

network redundancy /ˌnetwɜːk rɪ ˈdʌndənsi/ *noun* (*organisation of a network*) liaisons *fpl* redondantes

network server /ˌnetwɜːk ˈsɜːvə/ *noun* serveur *m* de réseau

network software /ˌnetwɜːk ˈsɒftweə/ *noun* logiciel *m* de réseau

network structure /ˌnetwɜːk ˈstrʌktʃə/ *noun* structure *f* de réseau

network timing /ˌnetwɜːk ˈtaɪmɪŋ/ *noun* synchronisation *f* de réseau

network topology /ˌnetwɜːk təˈpɒlədʒi/ *noun* configuration *f* de réseau

neural computer /ˌnjʊərəl kəmˈpjuːtə/ *noun* ordinateur *m* neuronal

neural network /ˌnjʊərəl ˈnetwɜːk/ *noun* (*system running an artificial intelligence*) réseau *m* de neurones; réseau *m* neuronal

neurocomputer /ˈnjʊərəʊkəmˌpjuːtə/ *noun* ordinateur *m* neuronal

neutral /ˈnjuːtrəl/ *adjective* neutre

neutral transmission /ˌnjuːtrəl trænz ˈmɪʃ(ə)n/ *noun* transmission *f* neutre

new /njuː/ *adjective* (*recent*) nouveau *or* -elle; récent *or* -e ◇ **they have installed a new computer system** ils ont installé un nouveau système informatique *or* un nouvel ordinateur

newbie /ˈnjuːbi/ *noun slang* (*user*) novice *m*; débutant *m*; nouveau venu *m*

new line character /ˌnjuː ˈlaɪn ˌkærɪktə/ *noun* caractère *m* indiquant d'aller à la ligne; caractère *m* de retour à la ligne

newsgroup /ˈnjuːzˌgruːp/ *noun* (*feature of the Internet that provides free-for-all discussion forums*) forum *m*; groupe *m* de discussion

news reader /ˈnjuːz ˌriːdə/ *noun* lecteur *m* de nouvelles

newswire /ˈnjuːzwaɪə/ *noun* fil *m* de presse

new technology /ˌnjuː tekˈnɒlədʒi/ *noun* (*electronic instruments*) nouvelle technologie *f*; technologie *f* de pointe

Newton /ˈnjuːtən/ Newton

next instruction register /ˌnekst ɪn ˈstrʌkʃən ˌredʒɪstə/ *noun* (*register in a CPU*) registre *m* d'instruction à exécuter; registre *m* de la prochaine instruction

nexus /ˈneksəs/ *noun* connexion *f*

NFS *abbr* (*network file system*) système *m* de gestion de fichiers en réseau

nibble /ˈnɪb(ə)l/ *noun* (*half the length of a standard byte*) quartet *m*

NIC /ˌen aɪ ˈsiː/ *noun* carte *f* (interface de) réseau

NiCad /ˈnaɪkæd/ *noun* batterie *f* au nickel-cadmium

nickel cadmium /ˌnɪk(ə)l ˈkædmiəm/ *noun* nickel-cadmium *m*

nickel metal hydride /ˌnɪk(ə)l ˌmet(ə)l ˈhaɪdraɪd/ *noun* nickel-métal-hydrure *m*

nil pointer /nɪl ˈpɔɪntə/ *noun* marqueur *m* de fin de liste

NiMH /ˌen aɪ em ˈeɪtʃ/ *noun* batterie *f* au nickel-méta-hydrure

nine's complement /ˈnaɪnz ˌkɒmplɪmənt/ *noun* complément *m* à neuf

n-key rollover /ˌen kiː ˈrəʊləʊvə/ *noun* (*using a buffer to provide key stroke storage*) mémoire *f* tampon (de clavier) chronologique à n positions

n-level logic /ˌen ˌlev(ə)l ˈlɒdʒɪk/ *noun* logique *f* à n niveau(x)

NLP *abbr* (*neurolinguistic programming*) programmation *f* neuro-linguistique

NLQ *abbr* (*near-letter-quality*) qualité *f* quasi-courrier

NMI *abbr* (*non maskable interrupt*) interruption *f* non masquable

NNTP /ˌen en tiː 'piː/ *noun* protocole *m* NNTP

no-address operation /ˌnəʊ ə'dres ˌɒpəreɪʃ(ə)n/ *noun* (*instruction with no address*) opération *f* sans adresse

node /nəʊd/ *noun* noeud *m* ◇ **a tree is made of branches that connect together at nodes** une arborescence est formée de branches reliées les unes aux autres par des points de liaison ou noeuds ◇ **this network has fibre optic connection with nodes up to one kilometre apart** ce réseau est relié par fibres optiques avec des noeuds positionnés jusqu'à un kilomètre les uns des autres

no-drop image /ˌnəʊ 'drɒp ˌɪmɪdʒ/ *noun* (*in a GUI – icon image displayed during a drag and drop operation when the pointer is over an object that cannot be the destination object*) icône *f* non compatible; icône *f* non ciblée

noise /nɔɪz/ *noun* bruit *m*; parasites *(mpl)*; brouillage *m* ◇ **noise margin** marge *f* de bruit *or* limite *f* de tolérance au bruit ◇ **noise temperature** température *f* de bruit ◇ **thermal noise** bruit thermique

noise immunity /nɔɪz ɪ'mjuːnəti/ *noun* insensibilité *f*

noisy mode /'nɔɪzi məʊd/ *noun* (*floating point arithmetic system*) mode *m* bruyant

nomenclature /nəʊ'meŋklətʃə/ *noun* nomenclature *f*

nomogram /'nɒməgræm/, **nomograph** /'nɒməgrɑːf/ *noun* nomogramme *m*

non- /nɒn/ *prefix* non-

nonaligned /ˌnɒnə'laɪnd/ *adjective* désaligné; non aligné *or* -ée

nonaligned read head /nɒnəˌlaɪnd 'riːd hed/ *noun* tête *f* de lecture désalignée

non arithmetic shift /ˌnɒn ˌærɪθmetɪk 'ʃɪft/ *noun* décalage *m* logique

non breaking space /ˌnɒn ˌbreɪkɪŋ 'speɪs/ *noun* (*space character that prevents two words being separated*) espace *m* sans rupture

noncompatibility /ˌnɒnkəmˌpætɪ'bɪlɪti/ *noun* incompatibilité *f*; non *f* compatibilité

non dedicated server /ˌnɒn ˌdedɪkeɪtɪd 'sɜːvə/ *noun* (*computer that runs a network operating system in the background*) serveur *m* non dédié

non destructive cursor /ˌnɒn dɪˌstrʌktɪv 'kɜːsə/ *noun* curseur *m* non destructif ◇ **non-destructive readout (NDR)** lecture *f* non destructive ◇ **the screen quickly becomes unreadable when using a non-destructive cursor** l'écran devient rapidement illisible lorsqu'on utilise le curseur non destructif

non destructive readout /ˌnɒn dɪˌstrʌktɪv 'riːdaʊt/ *noun* lecture *f* non-destructive

non destructive test /ˌnɒn dɪˌstrʌktɪv 'test/ *noun* essai *m* non destructif

nonequivalence function /ˌnɒnɪ'kwɪvələns ˌfʌŋkʃən/ *noun* fonction *f* de disjonction

nonequivalence gate /ˌnɒnɪ'kwɪvələns geɪt/ *noun* (*electronic circuit*) porte *f* OU exclusif; circuit *m* OU exclusif

nonerasable storage /nɒnɪˌreɪzəb(ə)l 'stɔːrɪdʒ/ *noun* (*storage medium*) mémoire *f* permanente; mémoire *f* qui ne peut être effacée; mémoire *f* ineffaçable ◇ **paper tape is a nonerasable storage** une bande papier perforée est une mémoire qui ne peut être effacée

non impact printer /ˌnɒn ɪmˌpækt 'prɪntə/ *noun* imprimante *f* sans impact

non interlaced /ˌnɒn 'ɪntəleɪsd/ *adjective* (*system in which the picture electron beam scans each line of the display once*) non entrelacé *or* -ée

nonlinear /nɒn'lɪniə/ *adjective* non linéaire

non maskable interrupt /ˌnɒn ˌmɑːskəb(ə)l 'ɪntərʌpt/ *noun* interruption *f* obligatoire; interruption *f* qui ne peut être invalidée; interruption *f* qui ne peut être masquée

non operable instruction /ˌnɒn ˌɒp(ə)rəb(ə)l ɪn'strʌkʃən/ *noun* instruction *f* factice; instruction *f* nulle; instruction *f* de remplissage

nonprinting code /ˌnɒnprɪntɪŋ 'kəʊd/ *plural noun* code *m* de paramétrage; code *m* paramétrique

non-procedural language /nɒn prə ˌsiːdʒ(ə)rəl 'læŋgwɪdʒ/ *noun* langage *m* non procédural

nonrepudiation /ˌnɒnrɪˌpjuːdi'eɪʃ(ə)n/ *noun* non-répudiation *f*

non-return to zero /ˌnɒn rɪˌtɜːn tə'zɪərəʊ/ *noun* non-retour *m* à zéro; non-remise *f* à zéro

non scrollable /ˌnɒn 'skrəʊləb(ə)l/ *adjective* qu'on ne peut pas faire défiler sur l'écran

non-volatile /nɒn 'vɒləˌtaɪl/ *adjective* (*retains data even when the power has been switched off*) non volatile ◇ **non-volatile random access memory (NVRAM)** mémoire vive non volatile *or* RAM non volatile *or* NVRAM ◇ **using magnetic tape provides non-volatile memory** une bande magnétique constitue une mémoire non volatile

'100 sets of test results can be stored in non-volatile memory for later hard-copy printout.' [*Computing*]

non volatile memory /ˌnɒn ˌvɒlətaɪl 'mem(ə)ri/ *noun* mémoire *f* non-volatile ◇ **bubble memory is a non-volatile storage** la mémoire à bulles est une mémoire non volatile

non-volatile random access memory /ˌnɒn ˌvɒlətaɪl ˌrændəm ˌækses 'mem(ə)ri/ *noun* mémoire *f* vive non-volatile

non volatile storage /ˌnɒn ˌvɒlətaɪl 'stɔːrɪdʒ/, **nonvolatile store** *noun* mémoire *f* non volatile

no-op instruction /nəʊ ɒp/, **no op** *noun* instruction *f* vide; instruction *f* factice; instruction *f* de remplissage

no parity /nəʊ 'pærəti/ *noun* (*data transmission which does not use a parity bit*) sans (bit de) parité

NOR function /nɔːr 'fʌŋkʃən/ *noun* (*logical function*) fonction *f* NON-OU; fonction *f* NI

NOR gate /'nɔːr geɪt/ *noun* (*electric circuit*) porte *f* NON-OU

normal /'nɔːm(ə)l/ *adjective* normal *or* -e ◇ **the normal procedure is for backup copies to be made at the end of each day's work** la procédure normale préconise une sauvegarde de tout le travail en fin de journée

normal form /'nɔːm(ə)l fɔːm/ *noun* forme *f* normale

normal format /'nɔːm(ə)l ˌfɔːmæt/ *noun* format *m* normal; format *m* standard

normalisation /ˌnɔːməlaɪ'zeɪʃ(ə)n/, **normalization** *noun* formatage *m*; normalisation *f*

normalisation routine /ˌnɔːməlaɪ'zeɪʃ(ə)n ruːˌtiːn/ *noun* routine *f* de normalisation

normalise /'nɔːməˌlaɪz/, **normalize** *verb* **1.** (*to convert data*) normaliser *vt* **2.** (*to convert characters*) mettre en mode majuscule or minuscule; uniformiser *vt* **3.** (*to store and represent numbers*) formater *vt*; normaliser *vt*

normalised form /'nɔːməlaɪzd fɔːm/ *noun* forme *f* normalisée

normal range /'nɔːm(ə)l reɪndʒ/ *noun* gamme *f* normale; fourchette *f* normale; plage *f* normale

NOS *abbr* (*network operating system*) système *m* d'exploitation de réseau

NOT-AND /nɒt ən/ *noun* fonction *f* NON-ET; NAND

notation /nəʊ'teɪʃ(ə)n/ *noun* (*numbers*) numération *f* ◇ **decimal notation** numération décimale *or* à base 10 ◇ **octal notation** num,ration octale *or* … base 8

notched /nɒtʃd/ *adjective* carte *f* à encoches marginales

notebook computer /ˌnəʊtbʊk kəm'pjuːtə/ *noun* (*very small portable computer – normally smaller than a laptop computer*) ordinateur *m* de poche

notepad /'nəʊtˌpæd/ *noun* bloc-notes *m*

NOT function /nɒt 'fʌŋkʃən/ *noun* (*logical inverse function*) fonction *f* NON; fonction *f* complément

NOT gate /'nɒt geɪt/ *noun* porte *f* NON; circuit *m* NON

notice board /'nəʊtɪs bɔːd/ *noun* tableau *m* d'affichage

notification message /ˌnəʊtɪfɪ'keɪʃ(ə)n ˌmesɪdʒ/ *noun* message *m* d'avertissement

notify handler /'nəʊtɪfaɪ ˌhændlə/ *noun* gestionnaire *m* de message d'avertissement

Novell /nəʊ'vel/ (*company that produces network software*) Novell™

n-plus-one address instruction /en plʌs wʌn ə'dres/ *noun* instruction *f* à n adresse(s) plus une

n-plus-one instruction /'en plʌs wʌn/ *noun* instruction *f* à n adresse(s) plus une

npn transistor /ˌen piː 'en trænˌzɪstə/ *noun* transistor *m* (de type) npn

NRZ *abbr* (*non return to zero*) non-retour *m* à zéro

NSFnet /ˌen es 'ef net/ *noun* réseau *m* NSFNET

NT /ˌen 'tiː/ *noun* NT

NTSC /ˌen tiː es 'siː/ *noun* Comité *m* National de Normalisation de la Télévision

n-type material /en taɪp mə'tɪəriəl/, **n-type semiconductor** /en taɪp/ *noun* matériau *m* semi-conducteur de type N

NuBus /'njuːbʌs/ *noun* (*high-speed expansion bus*) NuBus™, extension de bus à 96 connecteurs utilisé par les Macintosh de Apple

NUL character /'nʌl ˌkærɪktə/ *noun* caractère *m* de remplissage; caractère *m* nul

null /nʌl/ *adjective* (*nothing*) nul; nulle ◇ **null set** (*that only contains zeros*) jeu *m* de caractères nuls

null character /'nʌl ˌkærɪktə/ *noun* caractère *m* nul; caractère *m* de remplissage

null instruction /nʌl ɪn'strʌkʃən/ *noun* instruction *f* de remplissage; instruction *f* nulle

null list /ˌnʌl 'lɪst/ *noun* liste *f* vide

null modem /nʌl 'məʊˌdem/ *noun* (*connection*) circuit *m* de liaison directe; câble *m* de liaison directe; sans modem; null modem ◇ **this cable is configured as a null modem, which will allow me to connect these 2 computers together easily** ce câble est configuré pour fonctionner sans modem et me permet de relier facilement ces deux ordinateurs

null set /ˌnʌl 'set/ *noun* jeu *m* de caractères nuls

null string /ˌnʌl 'strɪŋ/ *noun* chaîne *f* vide

null terminated string /ˌnʌl ˌtɜːmɪneɪtɪd 'strɪŋ/ *noun* chaîne *f* de caractères qui se termine par le caractère nul

number /'nʌmbə/ *noun* **1.** (*representation of quantities*) nombre *m* **2.** (*written figure*) chiffre *m*; numéro *m* ■ *verb* **1.** (*a document*) numéroter *vt* **2.** (*items on a list*) numéroter *vt* ◇ **each piece of hardware has a production number** chacune des pièces de l'ordinateur possède un numéro de fabrication ◇ **number keys** (*of a telephone, etc.*) touches *fpl* de numérotation

number cruncher /'nʌmbə ˌkrʌntʃə/ *noun* (*calculations*) processeur *m* mathématique pour calcul ultra-rapide

number crunching /'nʌmbə krʌntʃɪŋ/ *noun* calcul *m* ultra-rapide; opérations *fpl* numériques ultra-rapides

number range /'nʌmbə reɪndʒ/ *noun* gamme *f* de valeurs

numeral /'njuːm(ə)rəl/ *noun* chiffre *m*

numeric /njuː'merɪk/ *adjective* **1.** numérique; numéral *or* -e **2.** numérique

numerical /njuː'merɪk(ə)l/ *adjective* (*referring to numbers*) numérique ◇ **numerical control (NC)** *or* **computer numerical control (CNC)** contrôle *m* numérique

numerical analysis /njuːˌmerɪk(ə)l ə 'næləsɪs/ *noun* analyse *f* numérique

numerical control /njuːˌmerɪk(ə)l kən'trəʊl/ *noun* commande *f* numérique; contrôle *m* numérique

numeric array /njuːˌmerɪk ə'reɪ/ *noun* (*array containing numbers*) tableau *m* numérique; tableau *m* de chiffres

numeric character /njuːˌmerɪk 'kærɪktə/ *noun* lettre *f* numérale; caractère *m* à valeur numérique

numeric keypad /njuːˌmerɪk 'kiːpæd/ *noun* pavé *m* numérique ◇ **you can use the numeric keypad to enter the figures** utilisez le pavé numérique pour saisir les chiffres

numeric operand /njuːˌmerɪk 'ɒpərænd/ *noun* opérande *m* numérique

numeric pad /njuːˌmerɪk 'pæd/ *noun* pavé *m* numérique; pavé *m* clavier

numeric punch /njuːˌmerɪk 'pʌntʃ/ *noun* perforation *f* numérique

numeric string /njuːˌmerɪk 'strɪŋ/ *noun* chaîne *f* de caractères numériques

Num Lock key /'nʌm lɒk kiː/ *noun* (*key on a keyboard*) touche *f* de blocage du pavé numérique

NVRAM /ˌen viː 'ræm/ *noun* mémoire *f* vive non volatile

nybble /'nɪb(ə)l/, **nibble** *noun informal* (*half the length of a standard byte*) demi-octet *m*

O

OA *abbr* (*office automation*) bureautique *f*

object /'ɒbdʒekt/ *noun* **1.** (*data that makes a particular image*) objet *m* **2.** (*variable in expert system*) objet *m* **3.** (*data in a statement*) objet *m* ◇ **object library** bibliothèque *f* d'objets

object architecture /ˌɒbdʒekt 'ɑːkɪtektʃə/ *noun* architecture *f* orientée vers l'objet

object code /əb'dʒekt kəʊd/ *noun* **1.** code *m* objet **2.** code *m* exécutable

object computer /ˌɒbdʒekt kəm'pjuːtə/ *noun* ordinateur *m* d'exécution de programme objet

object deck /əb'dʒekt dek/ *noun* jeu *m* (de cartes) objet

object file /əb'dʒekt faɪl/ *noun* fichier *m* objet

objective /əb'dʒektɪv/ *noun* (*aim*) but *m*; objectif *m*

object language /ˌɒbdʒekt 'læŋgwɪdʒ/ *noun* langage *m* objet

object linking and embedding /ˌɒbdʒekt ˌlɪŋkɪŋ ənd ɪm'bedɪŋ/ *noun* procédé *m* de liaison et incorporation d'objets

object linking and embedding 2 /ˌɒbdʒekt ˌlɪŋkɪŋ ənd ɪmˌbedɪŋ 'tuː/ *noun* procédé *m* OLE; procédé *m* OLE 2

object-orientated architecture /ˌɒbdʒekt ˌɔːriənteɪtɪd 'ɑːkɪtektʃə/ *noun* architecture *f* orientée vers l'objet

object-oriented /ˌɒbdʒekt 'ɔːrientɪd/ *adjective* (*that uses objects*) orienté objet *or* ée ◇ **object-oriented programming (OOP)** (*method of programming, in which each element of the program is treated as an object*) programmation orientée objet *or* POO ◇ **this object-oriented graphics program lets you move shapes around very easily** ce programme graphique orienté objet vous permet de déplacer les formes très facilement

object-oriented graphics /ˌɒbdʒekt ˌɔːrientɪd 'græfɪks/ *plural noun* graphique *m* orienté objet

object-oriented language /ˌɒbdʒekt ˌɔːrientɪd 'læŋgwɪdʒ/ *noun* langage *m* orienté objet

object-oriented programming /ˌɒbdʒekt ˌɔːrientɪd 'prəʊgræmɪŋ/ *noun* programmation *f* orientée objet

Object Packager /'ɒbdʒekt ˌpækɪdʒə/ *noun* gestionnaire *m* d'icônes-objets

object program /'ɒbdʒekt ˌprəʊgræm/ *noun* programme *m* objet

Object Request Broker /əbˌdʒekt rɪ'kwest ˌbrəʊkə/ *noun* gestionnaire *m* ORB

obtain /əb'teɪn/ *verb* obtenir *vt*; recevoir *vt* ◇ **a clear signal is obtained after filtering** le filtrage permet d'obtenir un signal très clair

OCCAM /'ɒkəm/ *noun* langage *m* (de programmation) OCCAM

occur /ə'kɜː/ *verb* se produire; avoir lieu; survenir *vi*

OCP /ˌəʊ siː 'piː/ *noun* processeur *m* de codes de commande

OCR /ˌəʊ siː 'ɑː/ *noun* **1.** reconnaissance *f* optique de caractères **2.** lecteur *m* optique de caractères

> 'In 1986, Calera Recognition Systems introduced the first neural-network-based OCR system that could read complex pages containing any mixture of non-decorative fonts without manual training.' [*Computing*]

OCR font /ˌəʊ siː 'ɑː fɒnt/ *noun* police *f* de caractères reconnaissable par lecture optique *or* par lecteur optique

octal /'ɒkt(ə)l/, **octal notation** /ˌɒkt(ə)l nəʊ 'teɪʃ(ə)n/ *noun* numération *f* octale; numération *f* en base 8

octal digit /ˌɒkt(ə)l 'dɪdʒɪt/ *noun* chiffre *m* octal

octal scale /'ɒkt(ə)l skeɪl/ *noun* base *f* 8

octet /ɒk'tet/ *noun* (*group of eight bits*) octet *m*

OCX /ˌəʊ siː 'eks/ *noun* composant *m* OCX

ODBC *noun* interface *f* ODBC

odd-even check /ˌɒd 'iːv(ə)n ˌtʃek/ *noun* contrôle *m* de parité paire-impaire

odd parity /ˌɒd 'pærɪti/, **odd parity check** /ˌɒd 'pærɪti tʃek/ *noun* parité *f* impaire

ODI interface ODI

OEM /ˌəʊ iː 'em/ *noun* OEM; constructeur *m* de matériel informatique

off-hook /ɒf hʊk/ *adverb* (*a modem goes off-hook to answer a call and remains off-hook whilst connected*) en mode décroché

office automation /ˌɒfɪs ˌɔːtə'meɪʃ(ə)n/ *noun* bureautique *f*

office computer /ˌɒfɪs kəm'pjuːtə/ *noun* ordinateur *m* de bureau; ordinateur *m* à usage professionnel

off-line /ɒf laɪn/ *adverb, adjective* **1.** (*peripheral, processing, etc.*) hors ligne; hors connexion; off-line; autonome; en différé **2.** (*connection*) autonome; non connecté *or* -ée ◇ **before changing the paper in the printer, switch it off-line** avant de remplacer le papier de l'imprimante, assurez-vous que l'imprimante est hors ligne *or* off-line

off-line editing /ˌɒf laɪn 'edɪtɪŋ/ *noun* montage *m* en différé

off-line printing /ˌɒf laɪn 'prɪntɪŋ/ *noun* impression *f* hors ligne; impression *f* en différé; impression *f* par imprimante autonome

off-line processing /ˌɒf laɪn 'prəʊsesɪŋ/ *noun* traitement *m* hors ligne; traitement *m* off-line; traitement *m* en différé

off-line storage /ˌɒf laɪn 'stɔːrɪdʒ/ *noun* stockage *m* hors ligne

offload /ɒf'ləʊd/ *verb* transférer *vt*

off-screen buffer /ˌɒf skriːn 'bʌfə/ *noun* mémoire *f* tampon hors champ

off-screen image /ˌɒf skriːn 'ɪmɪdʒ/ *noun* image *f* hors champ

offset /'ɒfset/ *noun* (*printing*) offset *m* ◇ **offset lithography** lithographie *f* offset ◇ **offset printing** impression *f* (en) offset

offset value /ˌɒfˌset 'væljuː/, **offset word** /ˌɒf 'set wɜːd/ *noun* (*indexed address*) valeur *f* relative; adresse *f* relative

ohm /əʊm/ *noun* ohm *m* ◇ **kilo-ohm** (*one thousand ohms*) kilo-ohm *m* ◇ **this resistance has a value of 100 ohms** la valeur de cette résistance est de 100 ohms

OK /ˌəʊ 'keɪ/ *noun* (*prompt meaning 'ready'*) OK

OK button /əʊ'keɪ ˌbʌt(ə)n/ *noun* bouton *m* OK

OLE /ˌəʊ el 'iː/ *noun* procédé *f* OLE

OLE-2 /ˌəʊ el iː 'tuː/ *noun* procédé *m* OLE-2

OLE object /ˌəʊ el ˌiː 'ɒbdʒekt/, **OLE container object** /ˌəʊ el ˌiː kən'teɪnə ˌɒbdʒekt/ *noun* objet *m* OLE

omission factor /əʊ'mɪʃ(ə)n ˌfæktə/ *noun* facteur *m* d'omission; facteur *m* de silence

OMR /ˌəʊ em 'ɑː/ *noun* **1.** lecteur *m* optique de caractères **2.** reconnaissance *f* optique de caractères

on-board /ɒn bɔːd/ *adjective* (*on main PCB*) intégré, -ée au circuit; monté, -ée sur carte de circuit

> '...the electronic page is converted to a printer-readable video image by the on-board raster image processor the key intelligence features of these laser printers are emulation modes and on-board memory' [*Byte*]

on chip /ˌɒn 'tʃɪp/ *noun* intégré, -ée à une puce ◇ **the processor uses on-chip bootstrap software to allow programs to be loaded rapidly** le processeur utilise un logiciel de lancement intégré à la puce, pour permettre le chargement rapide des programmes

on-chip /ɒn tʃɪp/ *adjective* intégré, -ée à une puce ◇ **the processor uses on-chip bootstrap software to allow programs to be loaded rapidly** le processeur utilise un logiciel de lancement intégré à la puce, pour permettre le chargement rapide des programmes

on-chip cache /ˌɒn tʃɪp 'kæʃ/ *noun* mémoire *f* cache intégrée à une puce

one-address computer /ˌwʌn əˌdres kəm 'pjuːtə/ *noun* ordinateur *m* à adresse unique

one-address instruction /ˌwʌn əˌdres ɪn 'strʌkʃən/ *noun* instruction *f* à adresse unique; instruction *f* à adresse directe

one element /wʌn 'elɪmənt/ *noun* (*logical function*) constante *f*

one for one /ˌwʌn fə 'wʌn/ *noun* (*programming language*) un pour un

one-level address /ˌwʌn ˌlev(ə)l ə'dres/ *noun* adresse *f* directe; adresse *f* à un niveau

one-level code /ˌwʌn ˌlev(ə)l 'kəʊd/ *noun* code *m* à un niveau

one-level store /ˌwʌn ˌlev(ə)l 'stɔː/ *noun* mémoire *f* à un niveau

one-level subroutine /ˌwʌn ˌlev(ə)l 'sʌbruːtiːn/ *noun* sous-programme *m* direct

one-pass assembler /ˌwʌn pɑːs ə'semblə/ *noun* assembleur *m* une passe ◇ **this new one-pass assembler is very quick in operation** ce nouvel assembleur une passe travaille très vite

one-plus-one address /'wʌn plʌs wʌn/ *noun* une adresse *f* plus une

one's complement /'wʌnz ˌkɒmplɪment/ *noun* complément *m* à 1 ◇ **the one's complement of 10011 is 01100** le complément à 1 de 10011 est 01100

one-time pad /ˌwʌn 'taɪm pæd/ *noun* (*for coding system*) clé *f* à usage unique

one to zero ratio /wʌn tə, tʊ 'zɪərəʊ/ *noun* rapport *m* de discrimination; rapport *m* un à zéro

on-hook /ɒn hʊk/ *adverb* (*modem*) raccroché

onion skin architecture /'ʌnjən skɪn ˌɑːkɪtektʃə/ *noun* (*computer design*) architecture *f* en pelure d'oignon ◇ **the onion skin architecture of this computer is made up of a kernel at the centre, an operating system, a low-level language and then the user's program** cet ordinateur possède une architecture en pelure d'oignon comprenant un noyau central, un système d'exploitation, un langage de bas niveau et le programme utilisateur

onion skin language /'ʌnjən skɪn ˌlæŋgwɪdʒ/ *noun* langage *m* en pelure d'oignon

online /ɒn'laɪn/ *adverb, adjective* (*connection*) en ligne; on-line

online database /ˌɒnlaɪn ˈdeɪtəbeɪs/ *noun* base *f* de données en ligne

online editing /ɒnˌlaɪn ˈedɪtɪŋ/ *noun* montage *m* en différé

online help /ˌɒnlaɪn ˈhelp/ *noun* aide *f* en ligne

online information retrieval /ˌɒnlaɪn ˌɪnfəˈmeɪʃ(ə)n rɪˌtriːvəl/ *noun* recherche *f* documentaire en ligne

online processing /ˌɒnlaɪn ˈprəʊsesɪŋ/ *noun* traitement *m* en ligne

online storage /ˌɒnlaɪn ˈstɔːrɪdʒ/ *noun* stockage *m* de données en ligne

online system /ˌɒnlaɪn ˈsɪtsəm/ *noun* système *m* en ligne; système *m* relié à l'ordinateur

online transaction processing /ˌɒnlaɪn trænˈzækʃən ˌprəʊsesɪŋ/ *noun* traitement *m* transactionnel en ligne

OnNow /ˌɒnˈnaʊ/ *noun* OnNow

on-screen /ɒn skriːn/ *adjective* (*displayed on a screen*) affiché, -ée à l'écran; visualisé *or* -ée

on-site /ɒn saɪt/ *adjective* sur place

on the fly /ˌɒn ðə ˈflaɪ/ *adverb* (*without stopping the run*) à la volée

o/p, O/P *abbr* (*output*) sortie *f*

op code /ˈɒp kəʊd/ *noun* code *m* opération

open /ˈəʊpən/ *adjective* **1.** (*file*) ouvert *or* -e **2.** (*not closed*) ouvert *or* -e ■ *verb* (*file*) ouvrir (un fichier) ◇ **open loop** boucle ouverte ◇ **Open Systems Interconnection (OSI)** interconnexion *f* de systèmes ouverts (aux normes ISO) ◇ **you cannot access the data unless the file has been opened** vous ne pouvez pas accéder aux données avant d'avoir ouvert le fichier ◇ **you cannot access the data unless the file is open** vous ne pouvez accéder aux données que si le fichier est ouvert

open access /ˌəʊpən ˈækses/ *noun* (*workstation*) poste *m* de travail ouvert; poste *m* à accès illimité; poste *m* banalisé

open architecture /ˌəʊpən ˈɑːkɪtektʃə/ *noun* architecture *f* ouverte

open code /ˈəʊpən kəʊd/ *noun* code *m* ouvert

open database connectivity /ˌəʊpən ˌdeɪtəbeɪs ˌkɒnekˈtɪvɪti/ *noun* interface *f* ODBC

open datalink interface /ˌəʊpən ˈdeɪtəlɪŋk ˌɪntəfeɪs/ *noun* interface *f* ODI

open-ended program /ˌəʊpən ˌendɪd ˈprəʊgræm/ *noun* programme *m* extensible; programme *m* ouvert

open file /ˈəʊpən faɪl/ *noun* fichier *m* ouvert

open reel /ˈəʊpən riːl/ *noun* bobine *f* ouverte ◇ **open reel tape** bande *f* sur bobine ouverte

open routine /ˌəʊpən ruːˈtiːn/ *noun* routine *f* ouverte

OpenScript /ˈəʊpənskrɪpt/ *noun* OpenScript

open shortest path first /ˌəʊpən ˌʃɔːtəst pɑːθ ˈɸɜːʃθ/ *noun* protocole *m* OSPF

open source *adjective* code *m* source libre

'In yet another initiative, aimed at cutting the up-front costs of big IT projects, the OGC is tipping towards a preference for open source software.' [*The Guardian*]

open subroutine /ˌəʊpən ˈsʌbruːtiːn/ *noun* sous-programme *m* ouvert

open system /ˈəʊpən ˌsɪstəm/ *noun* système *m* ouvert

open system interconnection /ˌəʊpən ˌsɪstəm ˌɪntəkəˈnekʃ(ə)n/ *noun* interconnexion *f* de systèmes ouverts (aux normes ISO)

operand /ˈɒpərænd/ *noun* opérande *m* ◇ **in the instruction ADD 74, the operator ADD will add the operand 74 to the accumulator** par effet de l'instruction ADD 74, l'opérateur ADD va ajouter l'opérande 74 à l'accumulateur

operand field /ˈɒpərænd fiːld/ *noun* champ *m* d'opérande; champ *m* d'adresse

operate /ˈɒpəreɪt/ *verb* (*machine*) faire fonctionner; mettre en marche ◇ **do you know how to operate the telephone switchboard?** savez-vous comment fonctionne le standard téléphonique?

operating code /ˈɒpəreɪtɪŋ kəʊd/ *noun* code *m* d'exploitation

operating console /ˈɒpəreɪtɪŋ ˌkɒnsəʊl/ *noun* poste *m* de travail; station *f* de travail

operating instructions /ˈɒpəreɪtɪŋ ɪnˌstrʌkʃənz/ *plural noun* commandes *fpl*

operating system /ˈɒpəreɪtɪŋ ˌsɪstəm/ *noun* système *m* d'exploitation

operating time /ˈɒpəreɪtɪŋ taɪm/ *noun* temps *m* d'exécution (d'une tâche)

operation /ˌɒpəˈreɪʃ(ə)n/ *noun* **1.** (*working of machine*) opération *f* **2.** (*series of actions*) opération *f* **3.** (*mathematical process*) opération *f* ◇ **operation code (op code)** code *m* (d')opération *or* op-code

operational /ˌɒpəˈreɪʃ(ə)nəl/ *adjective* opérationnel *or* -elle

operational information /ˌɒpəˌreɪʃ(ə)nəl ˌɪnfəˈmeɪʃ(ə)n/ *noun* notice *f* d'utilisation

operation code /ˌɒpəˈreɪʃ(ə)n kəʊd/ *noun* code *m* d'opération

operation cycle /ˌɒpəˈreɪʃ(ə)n ˌsaɪk(ə)l/ *noun* cycle *m* d'opération

operation decoder /ˌɒpəˈreɪʃ(ə)n diːˌkəʊdə/ *noun* décodeur *m* d'instruction

operation field /ˌɒpəˈreɪʃ(ə)n ˌfiːld/ *noun* champ *m* d'opération

operation priority /ˌɒpəreɪʃ(ə)n praɪˈɒrɪti/ *noun* ordre *m* de priorité des opérations

operation register /ˌɒpəˈreɪʃ(ə)n ˌredʒɪstə/ *noun* registre *m* d'opération

operations manual /ˌɒpəˌreɪʃ(ə)nz ˈmænjʊəl/ *noun* manuel *m* d'utilisation

operation time /ˌɒpəˈreɪʃ(ə)n taɪm/ *noun* temps *m* d'exécution d'une opération

operation trial /ˌɒpəˈreɪʃ(ə)n ˌtraɪəl/ *noun* essai *m*

operator /ˈɒpəˌreɪtə/ *noun* **1.** (*person*) opérateur *m* **2.** (*character or symbol or word that defines a function or operation*) opérateur *m* ◇ **the operator was sitting at his console** l'opérateur était assis devant l'écran de son ordinateur *or* à son pupitre ◇ **x is the multiplication operator** x est l'opérateur de la multiplication

operator overloading /ˌɒpəreɪtə ˈəʊvələʊdɪŋ/ *noun* surcharge *f* d'un opérateur

operator precedence /ˌɒpəreɪtə ˈpresɪdəns/ *noun* (*mathematical operations*) ordre *m* de priorité des opérateurs

operator procedure /ˈɒpəreɪtə prəˌsiːdʒə/ *noun* procédure *f* de commande

operator's console /ˈɒpəreɪtəz ˌkɒnsəʊl/ *noun* console *f*

op register /ɒp ˈredʒɪstə/ *noun* registre *m* de code d'opération

optical /ˈɒptɪk(ə)l/ *adjective* (*referring to or making use of light*) optique ◇ **an optical reader uses a light beam to scan characters, patterns or lines** un lecteur optique utilise un rayon lumineux qui balaye les caractères, les dessins ou les lignes ◇ **optical character reader (OCR)** lecteur optique de caractères ◇ **optical character recognition (OCR)** reconnaissance *f* optique de caractères ◇ **optical communications system** système de communication optoélectronique *or* par fibres optiques ◇ **optical mark reader (OMR)** lecteur optique de marques ◇ **optical mark recognition (OMR)** reconnaissance *f* optique de marques *or* de signes *or* de symboles

optical bar reader /ˌɒptɪk(ə)l ˈbɑː ˌriːdə/ *noun* lecteur *m* optique de codes barres; stylo *m* optique

optical character reader /ˌɒptɪk(ə)l ˈkærɪktə ˌriːdə/ *noun* lecteur *m* optique de caractères

optical character recognition /ˌɒptɪk(ə)l ˌkærɪktə ˌrekəgˈnɪʃ(ə)n/ *noun* reconnaissance *f* optique de caractères

optical communication system /ˌɒptɪk(ə)l kəˌmjuːnɪˈkeɪʃ(ə)n ˌsɪstəm/ *noun* système *m* de communication optoélectronique

optical computer /ˌɒptɪk(ə)l kəmˈpjuːtə/ *noun* ordinateur *m* optique

optical data link /ˌɒptɪk(ə)l ˈdeɪtə ˌlɪŋk/ *noun* liaison *f* optique pour transmission de données

optical disk /ˈɒptɪk(ə)l dɪsk/ *noun* disque *m* optique

optical fibre /ˌɒptɪk(ə)l ˈfaɪbə/ *noun* fibre *f* optique

optical font /ˈɒptɪk(ə)l fɒnt/ *noun* police *f* de caractères reconnaissable par lecture optique; police *f* de caractères reconnaissable par lecteur optique

optical mark reader /ˌɒptɪk(ə)l ˈmɑːk ˌriːdə/ *noun* lecteur *m* optique de marques

optical mark recognition /ˌɒptɪk(ə)l mɑːk ˌrekəgˈnɪʃ(ə)n/ *noun* (*optical reading*) reconnaissance *f* optique de marques; reconnaissance *f* optique de signes; reconnaissance *f* optique de symboles

optical memory /ˌɒptɪk(ə)l ˈmem(ə)ri/ *noun* mémoire *f* optique

optical mouse /ˈɒptɪk(ə)l maʊs/ *noun* (*optical device*) souris *f* optique

optical scanner /ˌɒptɪk(ə)l ˈskænə/ *noun* (*piece of equipment that converts an image into electrical signals*) scanner *m* optique

optical storage /ˌɒptɪk(ə)l ˈstɔːrɪdʒ/ *noun* (*place*) mémoire *f* optique; (*action*) stockage *m* de données sur support optique

optical transmission /ˌɒptɪk(ə)l trænz ˈmɪʃ(ə)n/ *noun* transmission *f* par système optoélectronique; transmission *f* par fibres optiques

optical wand /ˈɒptɪk(ə)l wɒnd/ *noun* lecteur *m* optique de codes barres; stylo *m* optique

optic fibre /ˌɒptɪk ˈfaɪbə/ *noun* fibre *f* optique

optimisation, optimization *noun* optimisation *f*

optimise /ˈɒptɪmaɪz/, **optimize** *verb* optimiser *vt*

optimised code /ˈɒptɪˌmaɪzd kəʊd/, **optimized code** *noun* code *m* accéléré; code *m* amélioré; code *m* optimisé

optimiser /ˈɒptɪmaɪzə/, **optimizer** *noun* optimiseur *m*

optimising compiler /ˌɒptɪmaɪzɪŋ kəm ˈpaɪlə/ *noun* compilateur *m* d'optimisation

optimizer /ˈɒptɪmaɪzə/ *noun* (*program*) optimiseur *m*

optimum /ˈɒptɪməm/ *adjective* (*best possible*) optimum *(m)*; optimal *or* -e ■ *noun* optimal *or* -e; optimum *m*

optimum code /ˈɒptɪməm kəʊd/ *noun* (*coding system*) code *m* optimum

opt-in mailing list /ˌɒpt ɪn ˈmeɪlɪŋ lɪst/ *noun* liste *f* d'inclusion

option /ˈɒpʃən/ *noun* option *f* ◇ **the options available are described in the main menu** les options disponibles sont décrites dans le menu principal ◇ **there are usually four options along the top of the screen** on trouve habituellement quatre options affichées en haut de l'écran

optional /ˈɒpʃ(ə)n(ə)l/ *adjective* optionnel *or* -elle

Option key /ˈɒpʃ(ə)n kiː/ *noun* touche *f* Option

optomechanical mouse /ˌɒptəʊmɪ ˌkænɪk(ə)l ˈmaʊs/ *noun* souris *f* optomécanique

OR /ˌəʊ ˈɑː/ *noun* fonction *f* OU; fonction *f* OR

Orange Book /ˈɒrɪndʒ bʊk/ *noun* norme *f* Livre Orange

ORB *abbr* (*Object Request Broker*) gestionnaire *m* ORB

order /'ɔːdə/ *noun* **1.** (*instruction*) commande *f*; instruction *f* **2.** (*disposition*) ordre *m* ■ *verb* **1.** (*to instruct*) donner une instruction **2.** (*to put in order*) ordonner *vt*; classer *vt*; trier par clé(s) ◇ **in alphabetical order** en *or* par ordre alphabétique ◇ **order code processor (OCP)** (*in a multiprocessor system*) processeur *m* de codes de commande

order code /'ɔːdə kəʊd/ *noun* code *m* de commande; code *m* d'opération

order code processor /'ɔːdə kəʊd ˌprəʊsesə/ *noun* processeur *m* de code commande

ordered list /'ɔːdəd lɪst/ *noun* liste *f* ordonnée

OR function /ɔː 'fʌŋkʃən/ *noun* (*logical function*) fonction *f* OU; fonction *f* OR

organisation /ˌɔːgənaɪ'zeɪʃ(ə)n/, **organization** *noun* (*way of arranging*) organisation *f*

organisational /ˌɔːgənaɪ'zeɪʃ(ə)n(ə)l/, **organizational** *adjective* organisationnel *or* -elle

organise /'ɔːgəˌnaɪz/, **organize** *verb* organiser *vt*

OR gate /'ɔː geɪt/ *noun* (*electronic circuit*) porte *f* OU; circuit *m* OU

orientated /'ɔːriənteɪtɪd/ *adjective* orienté

orientation /ˌɔːriən'teɪʃ(ə)n/ *noun* **1.** (*direction of a page*) orientation *f* (paysage ou portrait) **2.** orientation *f*

origin /'ɒrɪdʒɪn/ *noun* **1.** (*position on a screen*) origine *f* **2.** (*location in memory*) adresse *f* origine

original /ə'rɪdʒən(ə)l/ *adjective* original *or* -e ■ *noun* (*document*) original *m* ◇ **the original is too faint to photocopy well** l'original n'est pas assez contrasté pour être photocopié

original equipment manufacturer /ə ˌrɪdʒən(ə)l ɪˌkwɪpmənt ˌmænjʊ'fæktʃərə/ *noun* assembleur *m*

originate /ə'rɪdʒɪneɪt/ *verb* (*to start*) produire *vt*; créer *vt*; (*to come from*) venir de; sortir de ◇ **the data originated from the new computer** les données viennent *or* sortent du nouvel ordinateur

originate modem /ə'rɪdʒəneɪt ˌməʊdem/ *noun* modem *m* demandeur

origination /əˌrɪdʒɪ'neɪʃ(ə)n/ *noun* création *f*; production *f* ◇ **the origination of the artwork will take several weeks** la création de la maquette demandera plusieurs semaines

OROM /'əʊ rɒm/ *abbr* (*optical read-only memory*) disque *m* OROM

orphan /'ɔːf(ə)n/ *noun* (*first line of a paragraph at the bottom of a page*) orphelin *m*

orthogonal /ˌɔː'θɒgənəl/ *adjective* orthogonal *or* -e

OS /ˌəʊ 'es/ *noun* système *m* d'exploitation

OS/2 (*multitasking operating system for PCs*) système (d'exploitation) OS/2™

OSF *abbr* (*Open Software Foundation*) Open Software Foundation

OSI /ˌəʊ es 'aɪ/ *noun* interconnexion *f* de systèmes ouverts (aux normes ISO)

OSPF /ˌəʊ es piː 'ef/ *noun* protocole *m* OSPF

outage /'aʊtɪdʒ/ *noun* (*of machine*) non disponibilité; interruption *f* de service (d'un appareil)

outlet /'aʊtlet/ *noun* (*electrical*) sortie *f*; prise *f* de courant

outline /'aʊtlaɪn/ *noun* (*main features*) profil *m*; esquisse *f*

outline flowchart /'aʊt(ə)laɪn ˌfləʊtʃɑːt/ *noun* schéma *m* directeur

outline font /'aʊt(ə)laɪn fɒnt/ *noun* modèle *m* de fonte de caractères

outliner /'aʊtlaɪnə/ *noun* (*program used to help a user order sections of a list*) utilitaire *m* de plan; description *f* de projet

out of alignment /ˌaʊt əv ə'laɪnmənt/ *adjective* non aligné

out of control /ˌaʊt əv kən'trəʊl/ *adjective* hors de contrôle

out of date /ˌaʊt əv 'deɪt/ *adjective* démodé *or* -ée; dépassé

out of range /ˌaʊt əv 'reɪndʒ/ *adjective* hors de portée; inaccessible; qui dépasse la capacité de qc

output /'aʊtpʊt/ *noun* **1.** (*data*) sortie *f* **2.** (*action*) sortie *f* ■ *verb* (*data*) transférer *vt*; transmettre *vt*

output area /'aʊtpʊt ˌeəriə/, **output block** /'aʊtpʊt blɒk/ *noun* zone *f* sortie (de la mémoire)

output-bound /'aʊtpʊt ˌbaʊnd/ *adjective* limité par le débit des données; avec contrainte de vitesse de sortie des données

output buffer register /ˌaʊtpʊt ˌbʌfə 'redʒɪstə/ *noun* registre *m* tampon de sortie

output bureau /'aʊtpʊt ˌbjʊərəʊ/ *noun* flasheur *m*; imprimeur *m*

output device /'aʊtpʊt dɪˌvaɪs/ *noun* (*device which allows information to be displayed*) appareil *m* dispositif de sortie

output file /'aʊtpʊt faɪl/ *noun* fichier *m* de sortie

output formatter /'aʊtpʊt ˌfɔːmætə/ *noun* formateur *m* de données de sortie

output-limited /ˌaʊtpʊt 'lɪmɪtɪd/ *adjective* limité par le débit des données; avec contrainte de vitesse de sortie des données

output mode /'aʊtpʊt məʊd/ *noun* mode *m* sortie

output port /'aʊtpʊt pɔːt/ *noun* port *m* de sortie

output register /'aʊtpʊt ˌredʒɪstə/ *noun* registre *m* de sortie

output stream /'aʊtpʊt striːm/ *noun* flux *m* de données de sortie

outsource /'aʊt,sɔːs/ *verb* (*to employ another company to manage and support a network for your company*) externaliser *vt*

OverDrive /'əʊvədraɪv/ OverDrive

overflow /'əʊvəfləʊ/ *noun* dépassement *m* de capacité

overflow bit /,əʊvə'fləʊ bɪt/ *noun* drapeau *m* de dépassement de capacité

overflow check /,əʊvə'fləʊ tʃek/ *noun* contrôle *m* de dépassement de capacité

overflow flag /'əʊvəfləʊ flæg/ *noun* (*single bit in a word set to 1*) drapeau *m* de dépassement de capacité

overhead /'əʊvəhed/ *noun* (*extra code*) code *m*; élément *m* de structure ◇ **the line numbers in a BASIC program are an overhead** les numéros de lignes sont des éléments de structure en BASIC

overhead bit /,əʊvər'hed bɪt/ *noun* bit *m* supplémentaire

overheat /,əʊvə'hiːt/ *verb* chauffer *vt*; surchauffer *vt* ◇ **the system may overheat if the room is not air-conditioned** il se peut que le système (sur)chauffe dans une pièce qui n'est pas climatisée

overlap /,əʊvə'læp/ *noun* (*data*) chevauchement *m*; recouvrement *m*; superposition *f* ■ *verb* recouvrir *vt*; superposer *vt*

overlay /'əʊvəleɪ/ *noun* (*small section of a program*) section *f* de programme superposable; overlay *m*; fichier *m* OVL ◇ **overlay segment** (*short sections of a long program*) segment *m* superposable *or* segment d'overlay

'Many packages also boast useful drawing and overlay facilities which enable the user to annotate specific maps.' [*Computing*]

overlay card /'əʊvəleɪ kɑːd/ *noun* carte *f* overlay

overlay manager /'əʊvəleɪ ,mænɪdʒə/ *noun* gestionnaire *m* de segment de recouvrement

overlay region /'əʊvəleɪ ,riːdʒ(ə)n/ *noun* zone *f* de segment de recouvrement; zone *f* d'overlay

overlay segments /'əʊvəleɪ ,segmənts/ *plural noun* segments *mpl* superposables; segments *mpl* d'overlay

overload /,əʊvə'ləʊd/ *verb* surcharger *vt* ◇ **the computer is overloaded with that amount of processing** l'ordinateur est vraiment surchargé par tout ce travail

overpunching /,əʊvə'pʌntʃɪŋ/ *noun* surperforation *f*

overrun /,əʊvə'rʌn/ *noun* engorgement *m*

overscan /'əʊvəskæn/ *noun* **1.** balayage *m* en dehors des limites **2.** balayage *m* hors champ

over-voltage protection /,əʊvə 'vəʊltɪdʒ prə,tekʃ(ə)n/ *noun* protection *f* contre le survoltage/la surtension

overwrite /,əʊvə'raɪt/ *verb* (*data*) superposer des données; faire une superposition d'écriture et détruire les données en mémoire; remplacer *vt*; effacer *vt*; détruire des données par superposition d'écriture ◇ **the latest data input has overwritten the old information** les nouvelles données ont remplacé les anciennes (par superposition d'écriture)

P

p *abbr* (*pico-*) pico-

pack /pæk/ *noun* (*punched cards*) paquet *m* ■ *verb* (*goods*) emballer *vt*; conditionner *vt* ◇ **the diskettes are packed in plastic wrappers** les disquettes sont présentées sous emballage plastique

package deal /ˌpækɪdʒ ˈdiːl/ *noun* (*agreement*) contrat *m* global; contrat *m* forfait ◇ **they agreed a package deal, which involves the development of software, customizing hardware and training of staff** il se sont mis d'accord sur un contrat global comprenant le développement d'un logiciel, la personnalisation du matériel et la formation du personnel

packaged software /ˌpækɪdʒd ˈsɒftweə/ *noun* progiciel *m*

packaging /ˈpækɪdʒɪŋ/ *noun* (*creating books for publishers*) packaging *m*

packed decimal /pækt ˈdesɪm(ə)l/ *noun* décimale *f* condensée

packed format /pækt ˈfɔːmæt/ *noun* format *m* condensé

packet /ˈpækɪt/ *noun* (*group of bits*) paquet *m* ◇ **packet assembler *or* disassembler (PAD)** assembleur/désassembleur *m* (de paquets) ◇ **packet switching system (PSS)** système *m* de transmission par paquets *or* PSS ◇ **the remote terminal is connected to a PAD device through which it accesses the host computer** le terminal à distance est relié à un assembleur/désassembleur de paquets qui lui permet d'accéder à l'ordinateur hôte

packet assembler/disassembler /ˌpækɪt ə ˌsembləˌdɪsəˈsemblə/ *noun* assembleur/désassembleur *m* (de paquets)

packet Internet groper /ˌpækɪt ˌɪntənet ˈgrəʊpə/ *noun* utilitaire *m* PING

packet scheduler /ˈpækɪt ˌʃedjuːlə/ *noun* gestionnaire *m* de paquets;;;;

packet-switched /ˈpækɪt ˌswɪtʃd/ *adjective* commutation *f* par paquets

packet switched data service /ˈpækɪt swɪtʃd ˈdeɪtə/, **packet switched network** /ˌpækɪt ˌswɪtʃɪd ˈnetwɜːk/ *noun* réseau *m* de commutation de données par paquets

packet switching /ˈpækɪt swɪtʃɪŋ/ *noun* commutation *f* de paquets

'The network is based on Northern Telecom DPN data switches over which it will offer X.25 packet switching, IBM SNA, and frame-relay transmission.' [*Computing*]

packet switching service /ˈpækɪt ˌswɪtʃɪŋ ˌsɜːvɪs/ *noun* service *m* de transmission par paquets

packing /ˈpækɪŋ/ *noun* (*data*) compression *f*; condensation *f*; compactage *m*

packing density /ˈpækɪŋ ˌdensɪti/ *noun* densité *f* de données

packing routine /ˈpækɪŋ ruːˌtiːn/ *noun* routine *f* de compression (de données)

pad /pæd/ *noun* (*of keys*) clavier *m*; pavé *m*

PAD *abbr* (*packet assembler/disassembler*) assembleur-désassembleur *m* de paquets

pad character /pæd ˈkærɪktə/ *noun* caractère *m* de remplissage

padding /ˈpædɪŋ/ *noun* (*characters added to fill out*) remplissage *m*

paddle /ˈpæd(ə)l/ *noun* manette *f* ◇ **games paddle** manette de jeu

page /peɪdʒ/ *noun* **1.** (*sheet of paper*) page *f* **2.** (*side of a printed sheet or text held on a computer screen*) page *f* **3.** (*section of main store*) page *f* (de mémoire) **4.** (*section of a main program*) page *f* ■ *verb* **1.** (*to divide computer store into sections*) paginer *vt*; (*to make a text into page*) mettre en page; (*to put numbers onto pages*) folioter *vt* **2.** (*to put numbers onto pages*) paginer *vt* ◇ **page description language (PDL)** langage *m* de description de page ◇ **pages per minute (ppm)** (*speed of printer*) (nombre de) pages par minute (ppm) ◇ **this dot-matrix printer is not a page printer, it only prints one line at a time** cette imprimante matricielle n'est pas une imprimante page, elle n'imprime qu'une ligne à la fois ◇ **this laser printer can output eight pages per minute** cette imprimante laser peut imprimer huit pages par minute

page addressing /peɪdʒ əˈdresɪŋ/ *noun* adressage *m* de page

page boundary /peɪdʒ ˈbaʊnd(ə)ri/ *noun* limite *f* de page

page break /ˌpeɪdʒ ˈbreɪk/ *noun* **1.** (*marker*) caractère *m* de fin de page; (*point at which a page ends*) fin *f* de page **2.** caractère *m* de fin de page

paged address /ˌpeɪdʒd əˈdres/ *noun* adresse *f* paginée

page description language /ˌpeɪdʒ dɪ ˈskrɪpʃən ˌlæŋgwɪdʒ/ *noun* langage *m* de description de page

page description programming language /peɪdʒ dɪˌskrɪpʃ(ə)n ˈprəʊgræmɪŋ ˌlæŋgwɪdʒ/ *noun* langage *m* de programmation de description de page

page display /peɪdʒ dɪˈspleɪ/ *noun* affichage *m* d'une page

paged-memory management unit /ˌpeɪdʒd ˌmem(ə)ri ˈmænɪdʒmənt ˌjuːnɪt/ *noun* unité *f* de gestion de la mémoire paginée

paged-memory scheme /ˌpeɪdʒd ˈmem(ə)ri ˌskiːm/ *noun* méthode *f* de pagination

page down key /ˌpeɪdʒ ˈdaʊn ˌkiː/ *noun* touche *f* PgDn

page frame /ˌpeɪdʒ ˈfreɪm/ *noun* trame *f* de page

page image buffer /ˌpeɪdʒ ˈɪmɪdʒ ˌbʌfə/ *noun* mémoire *f* image de page

page layout /peɪdʒ ˈleɪaʊt/ *noun* (*formatting*) mise *f* en page(s) ◇ **computerized page layout** présentation assistée par ordinateur (PréAO)

page length /ˌpeɪdʒ ˈleŋθ/ *noun* longueur *f* de page; nombre *m* de lignes par page

page makeup /ˌpeɪdʒ ˈmeɪkʌp/ *noun* mise *f* en pages

page-mode RAM /ˌpeɪdʒ məʊd ˈræm/ *noun* mémoire *f* RAM en mode page

page number /peɪdʒ ˈnʌmbə/ *noun* numéro *m* de page

page orientation /peɪdʒ ˌɔːriənˈteɪʃ(ə)n/ *noun* orientation *f* de la page

page preview /peɪdʒ ˈpriːˌvjuː/ *noun* aperçu *m* avant impression; prévisualisation *f*

page printer /peɪdʒ ˈprɪntə/ *noun* imprimante *f* par page ◇ **this dot-matrix printer is not a page printer, it only prints one line at a time** cette imprimante matricielle n'est pas une imprimante page, elle n'imprime qu'une ligne à la fois

page protection /peɪdʒ prəˈtekʃən/ *noun* protection *f* de page

page reader /peɪdʒ ˈriːdə/ *noun* scanner *m*

page setup /ˈpeɪdʒ ˌsetʌp/ *noun* mise *f* en page

pages per minute /ˌpeɪdʒɪz pɜː ˈmɪnət/ *noun* pages *fpl* par minute (ppm)

page table /peɪdʒ ˈteɪb(ə)l/ *noun* table *f* de pages

page up key /ˌpeɪdʒ ˈʌp ˌkiː/ *noun* touche *f* PgUp

page width /ˌpeɪdʒ ˈ, wɪdθ/ *noun* largeur *f* de page (en caractères)

pagination /ˌpædʒɪˈneɪʃ(ə)n/ *noun* **1.** (*numbering pages*) pagination *f* **2.** (*dividing into pages*) mise *f* en pages

paging /ˈpeɪdʒɪŋ/ *noun* (*technique that splits main memory*) pagination *f*

paging algorithm /ˈpeɪdʒɪŋ ˌælgərɪð(ə)m/ *noun* algorithme *m* de pagination

paint /peɪnt/ *noun* (*in a graphics program*) peinture *f*; palette *f* ■ *verb* (*in a graphics program*) peindre *vt*; colorier *vt*

Paintbrush/Paint /ˌpaɪntbrʌʃ ˈpeɪnt/ *noun* (*application supplied with Microsoft Windows 3.1x and Windows 95*) palette *f* graphique Paintbrush/Paint™

paint program /ˈpeɪnt ˌprəʊgræm/ *noun* logiciel *m* de dessin; logiciel *m* de peinture ◇ **I drew a rough of our new logo with this paint program** j'ai fait une esquisse de notre nouveau logo en utilisant cette palette graphique

paired register /ˌpeəd ˈredʒɪstə/ *noun* registres *mpl* appariés; registres *mpl* associés

PAL /ˌpiː eɪ ˈel/ *noun* norme *f* de télévision PAL

palette /ˈpælət/ *noun* palette *f* de couleurs

palmtop /ˈpɑːmtɒp/ *noun* (*very small PC*) ordinateur *m* de poche; ordinateur *m* qu'on tient à la main

pan /pæn/ *verb* (*move a viewing window horizontally*) afficher une image par déplacement horizontal

panel /ˈpæn(ə)l/ *noun* (*flat section of a casing*) panneau *m* ◇ **the socket is on the back panel** la prise est située sur le panneau arrière

Pantone Matching System /ˌpæntəʊn ˈmætʃɪŋ ˌsɪstəm/ nuancier *m* Pantone; système *m* de référence de couleurs Pantone

paper-fed /ˈpeɪpə fed/ *adjective* avec alimentation automatique de papier

paper feed /ˈpeɪpə fiːd/ *noun* (*printer*) alimentation *f* du papier; entraînement *m* du papier

paperless /ˈpeɪpələs/ *adjective* sans papier

paperless office /ˌpeɪpələs ˈɒfɪs/ *noun* bureau *m* sans papier; bureau *m* électronique

> 'Indeed, the concept of the paperless office may have been a direct attack on Xerox and its close ties to the paper document. Yet, as we all know, the paperless office has so far been an empty promise.' [*Computing*]

paper tape /ˈpeɪpə teɪp/ *noun* bande *f* papier

paper tape feed /ˌpeɪpə ˈteɪp ˌfiːd/ *noun* entraînement *m* de la bande papier

paper tape punch /ˌpeɪpə ˈteɪp ˌpʌntʃ/ *noun* poinçon *m* de perforation pour bandes papier

paper tape reader /ˌpeɪpə ˈteɪp ˌriːdə/ *noun* lecteur *m* de bandes perforées

paper throw /ˈpeɪpə θrəʊ/ *noun* saut *m* du papier

paper tray /ˈpeɪpə treɪ/ *noun* bac *m* à papier

paper-white monitor /ˌpeɪpə ˈwaɪt ˌmɒnɪtə/ *noun* (*displays black text on a white background*) écran *m* avec texte en noir sur fond blanc

paragraph /ˈpærəgrɑːf/ *noun* **1.** (*in a document*) paragraphe *m* **2.** (*in a memory map*) bloc *m* paragraphe

paragraph marker /ˈpærəgrɑːf ˌmɑːkə/ *noun* (*nonprinting character*) marqueur *m* de paragraphe

parallel /ˈpærəlel/ *adjective* **1.** (*processors*) parallèle **2.** (*bits of words*) parallèle ◇ **parallel input *or* output (PIO)** entrée/sortie *f* (en) parallèle ◇ **parallel input *or* parallel output (PIPO)** entrée parallèle/sortie parallèle ◇ **parallel input *or* serial output (PISO)** entrée parallèle/sortie série

parallel access /ˌpærəlel ˈækses/ *noun* (*data transfer*) accès *m* parallèle

parallel adder /ˌpærəlel ˈædə/ *noun* additionneur *m* parallèle

parallel broadcast /ˌpærəlel ˈbrɔːdkɑːst/ *noun* diffusion *f* parallèle

parallel computer /ˌpærəlel kəmˈpjuːtə/ *noun* ordinateur *m* parallèle

parallel connection /ˌpærəlel kəˈnekʃ(ə)n/ *noun* connexion *f* parallèle ◇ **their average transmission rate is 60,000 bps through parallel connection** leur débit de transmission est de 60 000 bits par seconde en connexion parallèle

parallel data transmission /ˌpærəlel ˈdeɪtə trænzˌmɪʃ(ə)n/ *noun* transmission *f* de données en parallèle

parallel input/output /ˌpærəlel ˌɪnpʊt ˈaʊtpʊt/ *noun* entrée/sortie *f* (en) parallèle

parallel input/output chip /ˌpærəlel ˌɪnpʊt ˈaʊtpʊt ˌtʃɪp/ *noun* circuit *m* intégré d'entrée/sortie en parallèle

parallel input/parallel output /ˌpærəlel ˌɪnpʊt ˌpærəlel ˈaʊtpʊt/ *noun* entrée *f* parallèle/sortie parallèle

parallel input/serial output /ˌpærəlel ˌɪnpʊt ˌsɪəriəl ˈaʊtpʊt/ *noun* entrée *f* parallèle/sortie série

parallel interface /ˌpærəlel ˈɪntəfeɪs/ *noun* interface *f* parallèle

parallel operation /ˌpærəlel ˌɒpəˈreɪʃ(ə)n/ *noun* opération *f* (en) parallèle

parallel port /ˈpærəlel pɔːt/ *noun* interface *f* parallèle

parallel printer /ˌpærəlel ˈprɪntə/ *noun* imprimante *f* qui fonctionne sur port parallèle

'The Wheelwriter 7000 offers 172Kb of document storage and mail-merge capabilities: it can be connected to a PC using the parallel printer port.' [*Computing*]

parallel priority system /ˌpærəlel praɪˈɒrɪti ˌsɪstəm/ *noun* système *m* de gestion des priorités en fonctionnement parallèle

parallel processing /ˌpærəlel ˈprəʊsesɪŋ/ *noun* traitement *m* (en) parallèle

parallel running /ˌpærəlel ˈrʌnɪŋ/ *noun* (*running of a new and old system*) exploitation *f* en parallèle

parallel search storage /ˌpærəlel ˈsɜːtʃ ˌstɔːrɪdʒ/ *noun* mémoire *f* associative

parallel transfer /ˌpærəlel ˈtrænsfɜː/ *noun* transfert *m* (en) parallèle

parallel transmission /ˌpærəlel trænz ˈmɪʃ(ə)n/ *noun* (*data transfer*) transmission *f* (en) parallèle

parameter /pəˈræmɪtə/ *noun* paramètre *m* ◇ **the size of the array is set with this parameter** la taille du tableau est fixée par ce paramètre ◇ **the X parameter defines the number of characters displayed across a screen** le paramètre X définit le nombre de caractères contenus dans une ligne d'écran

parameter-driven software /pəˌræmɪtə ˌdrɪv(ə)n ˈsɒftweə/ *noun* (*with values fixed*) logiciel *m* paramétré; (*with values not yet fixed*) logiciel *m* paramétrable; logiciel *m* paramétrique

parameterisation /pəˌræmɪtəraɪˈzeɪʃ(ə)n/, **parameterization** *noun* paramétrage *m*

parameter passing /pəˈræmɪtə ˌpɑːsɪŋ/ *noun* passage *m* de paramètre

parameter testing /pəˈræmɪtə ˌtestɪŋ/ *noun* test *m* des paramètres

parameter word /pəˈræmɪtə wɜːd/ *noun* mot-paramètre *m*

parametric equaliser /ˌpærəmetrɪk ˈiːkwəlaɪzə/ *noun* égalisateur *m* paramétrique

parametric subroutine /ˌpærəmetrɪk ˈsʌbruːtiːn/ *noun* sous-programme *m* paramétré; sous-programme *m* paramétrique

parent directory /ˈpeərənt daɪˌrekt(ə)ri/ *noun* (*directory above a sub-directory*) répertoire *m* parent

parent folder /ˈpeərənt ˌfəʊldə/ *noun* (*in a Macintosh system, a folder that contains other folders*) fichier *m* parent

parent object /ˈpeərənt ˌɒbdʒekt/ *noun* objet *m* parent

parent program /ˈpeərənt ˌprəʊgræm/ *noun* (*program that starts another program*) programme *m* parent

parity /ˈpærɪti/ *noun* parité *f*

'The difference between them is that RAID level one offers mirroring, whereas level five stripes records in parity across the disks in the system.' [*Computing*]

parity bit /ˈpærɪti bɪt/ *noun* bit *m* de parité

parity check /ˈpærɪti tʃek/ *noun* contrôle *m* de parité

parity flag /ˈpærɪti flæg/ *noun* indicateur *m* de contrôle de parité

parity interrupt /ˈpærɪti ˌɪntərʌpt/ *noun* interruption *f* (de contrôle) de parité

parity track /ˈpærɪti træk/ *noun* piste *f* de parité

park /pɑːk/ *verb* (*move the read/write head over a point on the disk where no data is stored*) parquer la tête de lecture du disque ◇ **when parked, the disk head will not damage any data if it touches the disk surface** en position parquée, la tête du disque ne peut pas ruiner les données si elle touche à la surface du disque

parse /pɑːz/ *verb* (*break down high-level language code into its parts*) faire l'analyse grammaticale; (*language*) faire l'analyse syntaxique

parser /'pɑːzə/ *noun* analyseur *m*

part /pɑːt/ *noun* (*section of something*) section *f*; partie *f*

part exchange /ˌpɑːt ɪks'tʃeɪndʒ/ *noun* reprise *f*

partial carry /ˌpɑːʃ(ə)l 'kæri/ *noun* report *m* partiel

partial RAM /'pɑːʃ(ə)l ræm/ *noun* mémoire *f* RAM partielle; mémoire *f* RAM incomplète

partition /pɑː'tɪʃ(ə)n/ *noun* **1.** (*divider*) division *f*; (*area of hard disk treated as a logical drive*) partition *f* **2.** (*area of hard disk treated as a logical drive*) partition *f* ■ *verb* **1.** (*to divide a hard disk into logical drives*) subdiviser *vt*; (*divide a hard disk into logical drives*) effectuer une partition **2.** (*divide a file or block*) découper *vt*; subdiviser *vt* ◇ **I defined two partitions on this hard disk – called drive C: and D:** j'ai défini deux partitions sur ce disque dur désignées par C: et D:

partitioned file /pɑː'tɪʃ(ə)nd faɪl/ *noun* fichier *m* subdivisé

part page display /ˌpɑːt peɪdʒ dɪ'spleɪ/ *noun* affichage *m* réduit; affichage *m* d'une partie de page

PASCAL /'pæskæl/ *noun* (*programming language*) langage *m* PASCAL

pass /pɑːs/ *noun* passe *f*; passage *m* ■ *verb* (*of magnetic tape*) faire défiler

password /'pɑːsˌwɜːd/ *noun* (*access to a system*) mot *m* de passe ◇ **password-protected** protégé, -ée par mot de passe ◇ **the user has to key in the password before he can access the database** l'utilisateur doit d'abord taper le mot de passe pour avoir accès à la base de données

'...the system's security features let you divide the disk into up to 256 password-protected sections' [*Byte*]

password protection /ˌpɑːswɜːd prə'tekʃ(ə)n/ *noun* protection *f* par mot de passe

paste /peɪst/ *verb* (*insert text that has been cut*) coller *vt* ◇ **cut-and-paste** (*taking text from one point and inserting it at another*) couper/coller ◇ **now that I have cut this paragraph from the end of the document, I can paste it in here** après avoir coupé ce paragraphe à la fin du document, je peux le coller ici

Paste Special /ˌpeɪst 'speʃ(ə)l/ *noun* Collage *m* spécial

patch /pætʃ/ *noun* (*temporary correction made to a program; small correction made to software by the user on the instruction of the publisher*) modification *f*; correction *f* provisoire; rustine *f*

patch cord /'pætʃ kɔːd/ *noun* câble *m* de raccordement

patch panel /pætʃ 'pæn(ə)l/ *noun* panneau *m* de raccordement

path /pɑːθ/ *noun* **1.** (*possible route or sequence of events or instructions*) chemin *m*; filière *f* **2.** (*route from one point in a network to another*) chemin *m* **3.** (*in the DOS system: list of subdirectories*) chemin *m* d'accès (DOS)

pathname /ˌpɑːθ'neɪm/ *noun* (*location of a file with a listing of the subdirectories*) nom *m* du chemin d'accès ◇ **the pathname for the letter file is \FILES\SIMON\DOCS\LETTER.DOC** \FILES\SIMON\DOCS\LETTER.DOC est le nom du chemin d'accès au fichier de la lettre

pattern /'pæt(ə)n/ *noun* (*shapes or lines*) motif *m*; forme *f*; dessin *m*

patterned /'pæt(ə)nd/ *adjective* avec motifs; avec dessins

pattern palette /'pæt(ə)n ˌpælət/ *noun* palette *f* de formes prédéfinies

pattern recognition /ˌpæt(ə)n ˌrekəg'nɪʃ(ə)n/ *noun* reconnaissance *f* de formes

pause key /'pɔːz kiː/ *noun* (*key that stops a process*) touche *f* Pause

payment gateway /'peɪmənt ˌgeɪtweɪ/ *noun* centre *m* terminal de paiement

PBX *abbr* (*private branch exchange*) autocommutateur *m* privé

PC¹ /ˌpiː 'siː/ *noun* (*personal computer*) ordinateur *m* personnel; ordinateur *m* individuel; PC

PC² /ˌpiː 'siː/ *abbr* **1.** (*printed circuit*) circuit *m* imprimé **2.** (*program counter*) compteur *m* de programme

PC-97 *noun* PC-97

PC-98 *noun* PC-98

PC/AT /ˌpiː siː eɪ 'tiː/ *noun* (*IBM PC compatible computer*) PC/AT

PC/AT keyboard /ˌpiː siː eɪ tiː 'kiːbɔːd/ *noun* clavier *m* PC/AT

PCB *abbr* (*printed circuit board*) carte *f* de circuit imprimé

PC Card /ˌpiː 'siː kɑːd/ *noun* carte *f* PC

PC-compatible /ˌpiː ˌsiː kəm'pætəb(ə)l/ *adjective* compatible PC

PC-DOS /ˌpiː siː 'dɒs/ *noun* (*version of MS-DOS sold by IBM*) PC-DOS (version IBM de MS-DOS)

p-channel metal oxide semiconductor /piː ˌtʃæn(ə)l ˌmet(ə)l ˌɒksaɪd ˌsemikən'dʌktə/ *noun* MOS à canal P

PCI /ˌpiː siː 'eɪ/ *noun* bus *m* local PCI

PCL /ˌpiː siː 'el/ *noun* langage *m* PCL; jeu *m* de commandes de contrôle d'imprimante

PCM /ˌpiː siː 'em/ *noun* **1.** fabricant *m* de produits à connecteurs compatibles **2.** modulation *f* par impulsions et codage (MIC)

PCMCIA /ˌpiː siː em siː aɪ 'eɪ/ *noun* (*specification for add-in expansion cards*) norme *f* PCMCIA (de carte d'extension) ◇ **the extra memory**

is stored on this PCMCIA card and I use it on my laptop la mémoire additionnelle est stockée sur une carte PCMCIA que j''utilise sur mon (ordinateur) portable

PCMCIA card /ˌpiː siː ˌem ˌsiː aɪ ˈeɪ kɑːd/ *noun* carte *f* PCMCIA

PCMCIA connector /ˌpiː siː ˌem ˌsiː aɪ ˌeɪ kə ˈnektə/ *noun* connecteur *m* PCMCIA

PCMCIA slot /ˌpiː siː ˌem ˌsiː aɪ ˈeɪ slɒt/ *noun* emplacement *m* pour carte PCMCIA

P-code /piː kəʊd/ *noun* pseudocode *m*; pseudo-instruction *f*

PCS *abbr* (*personal communications services*) services *mpl* de communications personnelles

PCU /ˌpiː siː ˈjuː/ *noun* unité *f* de commande de périphérique; unité *f* de contrôle de périphérique; contrôleur *m* de périphérique

PCX file /ˌpiː siː eks ˈfaɪl/ *noun* (*method of storing a bitmap graphic image file on disk*) fichier *m* PCX

PC/XT /ˌpiː siː eks ˈtiː/ *noun* (*IBM PC compatible computer*) PC/XT

PC/XT keyboard /ˌpiː siː eks tiː ˈkiːbɔːd/ *noun* clavier *m* PC/XT

PD *abbr* (*public domain*) domaine *m* public

PDA /ˌpiː diː ˈeɪ/ *noun* assistant *m* personnel de communication (APC)

PDF /ˌpiː diː ˈef/ *noun* format *m* PDF

PDL *abbr* **1.** (*page description language*) langage *m* de description de page **2.** (*program design language*) langage *m* de conception de programme

PDN *abbr* (*public data network*) réseau *m* public de transmission de données

peak /piːk/ *noun* **1.** (*highest point*) pic *m*; crête *f*; pointe *f* **2.** (*maximum value*) crête *f*; pic *m*; pointe *f* ■ *verb* (*to reach highest point*) atteindre un niveau maximum ◇ **keep the peak power below 60 watts or the amplifier will overheat** veillez à ce que la tension de crête ne dépasse pas 60 watts sinon l'amplificateur surchauffera ◇ **peaks and troughs** (*of waveform*) les pointes et les creux ◇ **the power peaked at 1,200 volts** la tension a atteint le niveau maximum de 1200 volts

peak output /ˌpiːk ˈaʊtpʊt/ *noun* niveau *m* maximum de production; production *f* record

peak period /ˈpiːk ˌpɪəriəd/ *noun* heure(s) *f(pl)* de pointe

peek /piːk/ *noun* instruction *f* PEEK ◇ **you need the instruction PEEK 1452 here to examine the contents of memory location 1452** vous devez utiliser l'instruction PEEK 1452 pour examiner le contenu de la mémoire à l'emplacement 1452

peer /pɪə/ *noun* (*any two similar devices*) égal *m*; pair *m*

peer-to-peer network /ˌpɪə tə ˈpɪə/ *noun* (*local area network*) réseau *m* d'égal à égal; réseau *m* sans serveur dédié ◇ **we have linked the four PCs in our small office using a peer-to-peer network** les quatre PCs de notre petit bureau sont reliés en réseau sans serveur dédié

pel /pel/ *noun* pixel *m*

pen /pen/ *noun* **1.** (*computer writing device*) stylo *m* **2.** stylo *m* optique

pen computer /pen kəmˈpjuːtə/ *noun* ordinateur *m* à crayon optique; ordinateur *m* sans clavier

pen plotter /ˈpen ˌplɒtə/ *noun* traceur *m* à plumes

pen recorder /pen rɪˈkɔːdə/ *noun* traceur *m*

Pentium /ˈpentiəm/ processeur 32 bits développé par Intel Pentium ◇ **Intel Pentium™** (*processor*) le processeur Intel Pentium™

per /pɜː, pə/ (*at a rate of*) par ■ *preposition* (*out of*) pour ◇ **the error rate has fallen to twelve per hundred** le taux d'erreur est tombé à douze pour cent ◇ **the rate is twenty-five per thousand** le taux s'élève à vingt-cinq pour mille

per cent /pə ˈsent/ *adjective, adverb* pour cent ◇ **10 per cent (10%)** dix pour cent ◇ **fifty per cent of nothing is still nothing** cinquante pour cent de rien est toujours rien

percentage point /pəˈsentɪdʒ pɔɪnt/ *noun* un pour cent

percentile /pəˈsenˌtaɪl/ *noun* centile *m*

per day /pə ˈdeɪ/ *phrase* par jour

perforated tape /ˈpɜːfəˌreɪtɪd teɪp/ *noun* bande *f* perforée; ruban *m* perforé

perforation /ˌpɜːfəˈreɪʃ(ə)n/ *noun* (*stationery*) perforation *f*

perforator /ˈpɜːfəreɪtə/ *noun* (*machine*) poinçon *m* de perforation; perforatrice *f*

perform /pəˈfɔːm/ *verb* (*machine*) marcher *vi*; fonctionner *vt*

performance /pəˈfɔːməns/ *noun* performance *f* ◇ **as a measure of the system's performance** pour juger de la performance du système ◇ **high performance** (de) haute performance ◇ **in benchmarking, the performances of several systems or devices are tested against a standard benchmark** les bancs d'essais consistent à évaluer les performances de plusieurs systèmes ou périphériques en utilisant le même test standard

per hour /ˌpər ˈaʊə/ *adverb* à l'heure; de l'heure

period /ˈpɪəriəd/ *noun* **1.** (*length of time*) période *f* **2.** (*typography*) point *m* ◇ **for a six-year period** pendant six ans *or* sur une période de six ans

periodic /ˌpɪəriˈɒdɪk/, **periodical** /ˌpɪəri ˈɒdɪk(ə)l/ *adjective* (*from time to time*) périodique; de temps en temps

periodically /ˌpɪəriˈɒdɪkli/ *adverb* périodiquement; de temps en temps

peripheral /pəˈrɪf(ə)rəl/ *adjective* **1.** (*not essential*) périphérique **2.** (*attached to something else*) périphérique *m* ■ *noun* **1.** (*hardware*) périphérique *m* **2.** (*communication device*) périphérique *m* ◇ **peripheral control unit (PCU)**

unité *f* de commande *or* unité de contrôle de périphérique *or* contrôleur *m* de périphérique ◇ **peripheral interface adapter (PIA)** adaptateur *m* d'interface de périphérique ◇ **peripheral processing unit (PPU)** processeur *m* périphérique ◇ **peripherals such as disk drives or printers allow data transfer and are controlled by a system, but contain independent circuits for their operation** les périphériques, tels que lecteurs de disquettes et imprimantes, qui permettent le transfert de données et sont asservis à un système (central), possèdent des circuits indépendants pour l'exécution de leurs opérations

peripheral component interconnect /pəˌrɪf(ə)rəl kəmˌpəʊnənt 'ɪntəkənekt/ *noun* bus *m* local PCI

peripheral control unit /pəˌrɪf(ə)rəl kən 'trəʊl ˌjuːnɪt/ *noun* unité *f* de commande de périphérique; unité *f* de contrôle de périphérique; contrôleur *m* de périphérique

peripheral driver /pəˌrɪf(ə)rəl 'draɪvə/ *noun* gestionnaire *m*

peripheral equipment /pəˌrɪf(ə)rəl ɪ 'kwɪpmənt/ *noun* **1.** (*piece of equipment*) appareil *m* périphérique; (*all equipment*) périphériques *mpl* **2.** périphériques *mpl*

peripheral interface adapter /pəˌrɪf(ə)rəl 'ɪntəfeɪs əˌdæptə/ *noun* contrôleur *m* d'interface de périphérique

peripheral limited /pəˌrɪf(ə)rəl 'lɪmɪtɪd/ *noun* limité par la vitesse du périphérique

peripheral memory /pəˌrɪf(ə)rəl 'mem(ə)ri/ *noun* mémoire *f* (de) périphérique

peripheral processing unit /pəˌrɪf(ə)rəl 'prəʊsesɪŋ ˌjuːnɪt/ *noun* processeur *m* périphérique

peripheral software driver /pəˌrɪf(ə)rəl 'sɒftweə ˌdraɪvə/ *noun* routine *f* de gestion de périphérique

peripheral transfer /pəˌrɪf(ə)rəl 'trænsfɜː/ *noun* échange *m* d'informations entre unité centrale et périphérique; échange *m* de données entre unité centrale et périphérique

peripheral unit /pəˌrɪf(ə)rəl 'juːnɪt/ *noun* **1.** périphérique *m* **2.** périphérique *m*

Perl /pɜːl/ *noun* langage *m* Perl

permanent dynamic memory /ˌpɜːmənənt daɪˌnæmɪk 'mem(ə)ri/ *noun* mémoire *f* dynamique permanente

permanent error /ˌpɜːmənənt 'erə/ *noun* erreur *f* permanente

permanent file /'pɜːmənənt faɪl/ *noun* fichier *m* permanent

permanent memory /ˌpɜːmənənt 'mem(ə)ri/ *noun* mémoire *f* permanente

permanent swap file /ˌpɜːmənənt 'swɒp ˌfaɪl/ *noun* fichier *m* d'échange permanent

permission /pə'mɪʃ(ə)n/ *noun* (*authorization to access*) autorisation *f* d'accès

permutation /ˌpɜːmjʊ'teɪʃ(ə)n/ *noun* permutation *f* ◇ **this cipher system is very secure since there are so many possible permutations for the key** ce code chiffré est très sûr puisqu'il comporte une clé avec un très grand nombre de permutations possibles

persistence /pə'sɪstəns/ *noun* persistance *f*

personal communications services /ˌpɜːs(ə)n(ə)l kəˌmjuːnɪ'keɪʃ(ə)nz ˌsɜːvɪsɪz/ *plural noun* services *mpl* de communications personnelles

personal computer /ˌpɜːs(ə)n(ə)l kəm 'pjuːtə/ *noun* ordinateur *m* individuel; ordinateur *m* personnel; PC

personal digital assistant /ˌpɜːs(ə)n(ə)l ˌdɪdʒɪt(ə)l ə'sɪstənt/ *noun* assistant *m* numérique personnel

personal identification device /ˌpɜːs(ə)n(ə)l aɪˌdentɪfɪ'keɪʃ(ə)n dɪˌvaɪs/ *noun* dispositif *m* électronique d'identification; carte *f* magnétique

personal identification number /ˌpɜːs(ə)n(ə)l aɪˌdentɪfɪ'keɪʃ(ə)n ˌnʌmbə/ *noun* numéro *m* de code confidentiel; numéro *m* de code personnel

personal information manager /ˌpɜːs(ə)n(ə)l ˌɪnfə'meɪʃ(ə)n ˌmænɪdʒə/ *noun* gestionnaire *m* personnel d'information (GPI)

personalise /'pɜːs(ə)nəlaɪz/, **personalize** *verb* personnaliser *vt*

personalising, personalizing *noun* personnalisation *f*

perspective /pə'spektɪv/ *noun* perspective *f*

PERT /pɜːt/ *noun* technique *f* d'évaluation et de révision de programme

per week /pə 'wiːk/ *adverb* par semaine

per year /pə 'jɪə/ *adverb* par année

peta /petə/ *prefix* (*one quadrillion (250)*) péta

petabyte /'petəbaɪt/ *noun* (*one quadrillion bytes*) péta-octet *m*

PgDn /ˌpeɪdʒ 'daʊn/ *abbr* (*page down key*) touche *f* Page suivante

PGP /ˌpiː dʒiː 'piː/ *noun* système *m* de chiffrement PGP

PgUp /ˌpeɪdʒ 'ʌp/ *abbr* (*page up key*) touche *f* Page précédente

phantom ROM /'fæntəm rɒm/ *noun* (*duplicate area of read-only memory*) mémoire *f* ROM fantôme

phase /feɪz/ *noun* (*part of a larger process*) phase *f*

phase alternation line /ˌfeɪz ˌɔːltə'neɪʃ(ə)n ˌlaɪn/ *noun* norme *f* de télévision couleur PAL

phased change-over /ˌfeɪzd 'tʃeɪndʒ/ *noun* changement *m* graduel; changement *m* progressif

PHIGS /fɪgz/ *noun* système *m* infographique PHIGS

phone /fəʊn/ *noun* téléphone *m* ◇ **by phone** par téléphone *or* téléphonique ◇ **can you give me your phone number?** pouvez-vous me donner votre numéro de téléphone? ◇ **card phone** téléphone à carte ◇ **he keeps a list of phone numbers in a little black book** il a une liste de numéros de téléphone dans un petit carnet noir ◇ **he spoke to the manager on the phone** il a eu le directeur au téléphone ◇ **house phone** *or* **internal phone** téléphone interne ◇ **phone book** annuaire *m* téléphonique *or* des téléphones ◇ **she has been on the phone all morning** elle a passé la matinée (à parler) au téléphone ◇ **the phone number is on the company notepaper** le numéro de téléphone figure sur le papier à en-tête de la société ◇ **to answer the phone** *or* **to take a phone call** répondre au téléphone ◇ **to be on the phone** parler au téléphone ◇ **to make a phone call** téléphoner *or* appeler *or* faire un appel *or* passer un coup de fil

Phone Dialer /ˈfəʊn ˌdaɪələ/ *noun* (*utility supplied with Windows 95*) numéroteur *m* téléphonique

phoneme /ˈfəʊniːm/ *noun* phonème *m* ◇ **the phoneme 'oo' is present in the words too and zoo** les mots 'too' et 'zoo' contiennent le phonème 'oo'

phone number /ˈfəʊn ˌnʌmbə/ *noun* numéro *m* de téléphone

phosphor /ˈfɒsfə/ *noun* phosphore *m*

phosphor coating /ˈfɒsfə ˌkəʊtɪŋ/ *noun* couche *f* de phosphore

phosphor dots /ˈfɒsfə dɒtz/ *plural noun* points *mpl* de phosphore

phosphor efficiency /ˈfɒsfə ɪˌfɪʃ(ə)nsi/ *noun* rendement *m* de phosphorescence

phosphor triad /ˈfɒsfə ˌtraɪæd/ *noun* triplet *m* de points lumineux

photo- /fəʊtəʊ/ *prefix* photo-

PhotoCD /ˈfəʊtəʊ siː ˌdiː/ *noun* (*standard developed to store 35mm photographic slides or negatives in digital format on a CD-ROM*) disque *m* compact photo; CD-Photo *m*; PhotoCD™

photodigital memory /fəʊtəʊˌdɪdʒɪt(ə)l ˈmem(ə)ri/ *noun* mémoire *f* optonumérique

photorealistic /ˌfəʊtəʊriəˈlɪstɪk/ *adjective* (*of computer image – that has almost the same quality and clarity as a photograph*) qualité *f* photo

photoresist /ˌfəʊtəʊrɪˈzɪst/ *noun* résine *f* photosensible

phototypesetter /ˌfəʊtəʊˈtaɪpsetə/ *noun* (*machine*) photocomposeuse *f*

physical address /ˌfɪzɪk(ə)l əˈdres/ *noun* adresse *f* physique

physical database /ˌfɪzɪk(ə)l ˈdeɪtəbeɪs/ *noun* base *f* de données physique

physical layer /ˌfɪzɪk(ə)l ˈleɪə/ *noun* couche *f* physique

physical memory /ˌfɪzɪk(ə)l ˈmem(ə)ri/ *noun* mémoire *f* physique

physical parameter /ˌfɪzɪk(ə)l pəˈræmɪtə/ *noun* paramètre *m* physique; donnée *f* descriptive

physical record /ˌfɪzɪk(ə)l ˈrekɔːd/ *noun* **1.** (*unit of data that can be transmitted*) unité *f* physique **2.** (*all the information for one record*) enregistrement *m* physique

physical topology /ˌfɪzɪk(ə)l təˈpɒlədʒi/ *noun* topologie *f* physique

PIA /ˌpiː aɪ ˈeɪ/ *noun* interface *f* d'adaptation périphérique

PIC /ˌpiː aɪ ˈsiː/ *noun* PIC

PICK /pɪk/ *noun* (*operating system*) système *m* d'exploitation PICK™

pickup reel /ˈpɪkʌp riːl/ *noun* bobine *f* réceptrice; bobine *f* d'enroulement

pico- /piːkəʊ/ *prefix* (*one million millionth*) pico-

picosecond /ˈpiːkəʊˌsekənd/ *noun* picoseconde *f*

PICS /pɪks/ *noun* (*file format to import PICT files on a Macintosh*) protocole *m* PICS

PICT /pɪkt/ *noun* (*Apple Macintosh graphics file format*) PICT

picture /ˈpɪktʃə/ *noun* (*drawing*) dessin *m*; (*book*) illustration *f*; (*TV or book*) image *f*; (*photograph*) photo *f* ■ *verb* imaginer *vt*; visualiser *vt* ◇ **picture image compression (PIC)** (*image compression algorithm used in Intel's DVI video system*) (algorithme de compression d'image) PIC ◇ **this picture shows the new design** voici la photo du nouveau modèle ◇ **try to picture the layout before starting to draw it in** essayez de visualiser l'implantation avant de commencer à dessiner

picture beam /ˈpɪktʃə biːm/ *noun* faisceau *m* d'image

picture element /ˈpɪktʃə ˌelɪmənt/ *noun* pixel *m*

picture processing /ˌpɪktʃə ˌprəˈsesɪŋ/ *noun* traitement *m* de l'image

picture transmission /ˈpɪktʃə trænz ˌmɪʃ(ə)n/ *noun* transmission *f* d'image

PID /ˌpiː aɪ ˈdiː/ *noun* numéro *m* de code confidentiel; numéro *m* de code personnel

pie chart /ˈpaɪ tʃɑːt/ *noun* (*diagram*) diagramme *m* circulaire; diagramme *m* à secteurs; diagramme *m* en camembert ◇ **the memory allocation is shown on this pie chart** l'attribution de mémoire est indiquée sur ce diagramme circulaire

PIF /ˌpiː aɪ ˈef/ *noun* fichier *m* PIF

piggyback /ˈpɪgibæk/ *verb* (*to connect two integrated circuits in parallel*) superposer *vt* ◇ **piggyback those two memory chips to boost the memory capacity** superposez ces deux puces pour augmenter la capacité de la mémoire

piggyback entry /ˈpɪgibæk ˌentri/ *noun* accès *m* à un système par personne non autorisée utilisant un mot de passe valide; accès *m* par usurpation de mot de passe

piggybacking /ˈpɪgibækɪŋ/ *noun* (*messages*) superposition *f* d'un accusé de réception au message suivant

pilot /ˈpaɪlət/ *adjective* (*used as a test*) pilote *m* ■ *verb* faire l'essai ◇ **the company set up a pilot project to see if the proposed manufacturing system was efficient** la société a mis sur pied un projet-pilote pour évaluer le procédé de fabrication proposé ◇ **the pilot factory has been built to test the new production process** l'usine-pilote a été construite pour tester le nouveau procédé de fabrication ◇ **they are piloting the new system** ils font l'essai du nouveau système

PILOT /ˈpaɪlət/ *noun* (*programming language*) langage *m* PILOT

pilot system /ˈpaɪlət ˌsɪstəm/ *noun* système-pilote *m*

PIM /ˌpiː aɪ ˈem/ *noun* gestionnaire *m* personnel d'information (GPI)

pin /pɪn/ *noun* **1.** (*short piece of wire attached to an IC*) broche *f* **2.** (*part of a plug*) broche *f* ◇ **use a three-pin plug to connect the printer to the mains** il faut une fiche à trois broches pour connecter *or* brancher le système sur le secteur

PIN /pɪn/ *noun* (*short piece of wire attached to an IC*) contact *m*

pinchwheel /ˈpɪntʃwiːl/ *noun* molette *f* de serrage

pin-compatible /ˌpɪn kəmˈpætɪb(ə)l/ *adjective* compatible à l'enfichage

pincushion distortion /ˌpɪnkʊʃ(ə)n dɪˈstɔːʃ(ə)n/ *noun* distorsion *f* en oreiller; distorsion *f* en coussinet; distorsion *f* en barillet

pinfeed /ˈpɪnfiːd/ *noun* entraînement *m* (du papier) par picots

PING /pɪŋ/ *noun* (*software utility that will test all the nodes on a network or internet*) utilitaire *m* PING

pinout /ˈpɪnaʊt/ *noun* (*position of pins on an IC*) disposition *f* des broches; configuration *f* d'un connecteur

PIO /ˌpiː aɪ ˈəʊ/ *noun* entrée *f* parallèle/sortie parallèle

pipe /paɪp/ *noun* (*symbol that tells the operating system to send output*) opérateur *m* de transfert (de données); opérateur *m* de dérivation

pipeline /ˈpaɪplaɪn/ *verb* **1.** (*to schedule inputs*) faire du pipeline; organiser en pipeline **2.** exécuter (des instructions) en pipeline; traiter (des instructions) en pipeline

pipelining /ˌpaɪpˌlaɪn ˈmem(ə)ri/, **pipeline memory** *noun* (*scheduling inputs*) organisation *f* en pipeline

PIPO /ˌpiː aɪ piː ˈəʊ/ *noun* entrée/sortie *f* (en) parallèle

piracy /ˈpaɪrəsi/ *noun* piratage *m*

pirate /ˈpaɪrət/ *noun* (*person who copies and sells patented invention or a copyright work*) pirate *m* ■ *verb* pirater *vt* ◇ **a pirated tape** une bande piratée ◇ **he used a cheap pirated disk and found the program had bugs in it** il a utilisé une disquette piratée bon marché et a découvert que le programme contenait des bogues ◇ **the company is trying to take the software pirates to court** la société tente d'amener les pirates de logiciel devant les tribunaux ◇ **the designs for the new system were pirated** les schémas du nouveau système ont été piratés

pirate copy /ˌpaɪrət ˈkɒpi/ *noun* (*illegal copy*) copie *f* pirate; copie *f* piratée; copie *f* illégale

pirate software /ˌpaɪrət ˈsɒftweə/ *noun* logiciel *m* piraté

PISO /ˌpiː aɪ es ˈəʊ/ *noun* entrée *f* parallèle/sortie série

pit /pɪt/ *noun* creux *m*

pitch /pɪtʃ/ *noun* (*horizontal spacing*) espacement *m*; pas *m*; pitch *m*; (*of characters*) densité *f* de caractères; nombre *m* de caractères par pouce

pix /pɪks/ *plural noun* (*images*) images *fpl*; (*photos*) illustrations *fpl*; photos *fpl*

pixel /ˈpɪksəl/ *noun* pixel *m*

> '...adding 40 to each pixel brightens the image and can improve the display's appearance' [*Byte*]

pixelated /ˈpɪksəleɪtɪd/ *adjective* pixélisé *or* -e

PLA /ˌpiː el ˈeɪ/ *noun* circuit *m* logique programmable

place /pleɪs/ *noun* (*numbers*) place *f*; position *f*

plain old telephone service /ˌpleɪn əʊld ˈtelɪfəʊn ˌsɜːvɪs/ *noun* service *m* téléphonique ordinaire

plaintext /ˌpleɪnˈtekst/ *noun* texte *m* en clair; texte *m* non chiffré ◇ **enter the plaintext message into the cipher machine** introduire le texte non chiffré dans la machine à chiffrer ◇ **the messages were sent as plaintext by telephone** le texte du message a été transmis en clair par téléphone

plan /plæn/ *noun* **1.** (*objective*) plan *m*; projet *m* **2.** (*drawing*) plan *m* ■ *verb* (*to organise*) planifier *vt*; projeter *vt* ◇ **floor plan** plan d'ensemble (d'un étage) ◇ **plans** jeu *m* de plans *or* les plans ◇ **street plan** *or* **town plan** plan des rues *or* plan de la ville

PLAN /plæn/ *noun* (*low-level programming language*) langage *m* PLAN

planar /ˈpleɪnə/ *adjective* (*method of producing ICs*) procédé *m* planar ■ *noun* (*graphical images arranged on the same plane*) graphe *m* planar

plane /pleɪn/ *noun* (*in a graphics image*) plan *m*

planner /ˈplænə/ *noun* (*software*) agenda *m* ◇ **wall planner** agenda *m* mural

planning /'plænɪŋ/ *noun* planification *f*; planning *m* ◇ **long-term planning** planification à longue échéance ◇ **short-term planning** planification à courte échéance

plant /plɑːnt/ *verb* (*in memory*) ranger *vt*; implanter *vt*; stocker *vt*

plasma display /'plæzmə dɪˌspleɪ/ *noun* affichage *m* (au) plasma

platform /'plætˌfɔːm/ *noun* (*standard type of hardware*) plate-forme *f*; environnement *m* ◇ **this software will only work on the IBM PC platform** ce logiciel ne fonctionne que dans un environnement IBM

platform independence /ˌplætfɔːm ˌɪndɪ'pendəns/ *noun* indépendance *f* de l'environnement de travail

platter /'plætə/ *noun* (*one disk in a hard disk drive*) plateau *m* (d'un disque dur); disque *m* simple

play back /ˌpleɪ 'bæk/ *verb* (*film, etc.*) passer *vti*; visionner *vt* ◇ **after you have recorded the music, press this button to play back the tape and hear what it sounds like** après avoir enregistré la musique, appuyez sur ce bouton-ci pour faire jouer la bande et vous assurer de la bonne qualité du son enregistré

playback head /'pleɪˌbæk hed/ *noun* tête *f* de lecture ◇ **disk playback head** tête de lecture de disque ◇ **tape playback head** tête de lecture de bande

playback speed /'pleɪˌbæk spiːd/ *noun* vitesse *f* de défilement

PLD *abbr* (*programmable logic device*) circuit *m* logique programmable

plex database /'pleks ˌdeɪtəbeɪs/ *noun* base *f* de données relationnelle

plex structure /'pleks ˌstrʌktʃə/ *noun* structure *f* à maillage intégral; réseau *m* intégralement interconnecté

PL/M /ˌpiː el 'em/ *noun* langage *m* de programmation PL/M

plot /plɒt/ *noun* (*graph or map*) graphe *m*; courbe *f*; tracé *m* ■ *verb* tracer une courbe; un graphe (par points numérisés)

plotter /'plɒtə/ *noun* traceur *m*

plotter driver /'plɒtə ˌdraɪvə/ *noun* pilote *m*

plotter pen /'plɒtə pen/ *noun* plume *f* pour traceur

plotting mode /'plɒtɪŋ məʊd/ *noun* mode *m* graphe

plug /plʌg/ *noun* (*connector*) fiche *f* ■ *verb* (*to publicize*) promouvoir *vt*; vanter *vt* ◇ **the printer is supplied with a plug** la fiche est fournie avec l'imprimante

plug and play /ˌplʌg ən 'pleɪ/ *noun* (*facility whereby users plug a new adapter card into their PC and do not have to configure it or set any switches*) carte *f* PNP; (*part of the Windows 95 system – where the user plugs a new adapter card into their PC they do not have to configure it or set any switches*) carte *f* Plug and Play™

plug-compatible /plʌg kəm'pætəb(ə)l/ *adjective* à connecteur compatible; directement *m* enfichable

plug-compatible manufacturer /ˌplʌg kəm ˌpætɪb(ə)l ˌmænjʊ'fæktʃərə/ *noun* fabricant *m* de produits (à connecteurs) compatibles

plug-in /'plʌg ɪn/ *noun* (*software to enhance a Web browser*) logiciel *m* d'extension/d'optimisation (de navigateur)

plug-in unit /'plʌg ɪn ˌjuːnɪt/ *noun* extension *f* enfichable

plus /plʌs/, **plus sign** /'plʌs saɪn/ *noun* signe *m* plus; signe *m* de l'addition

PMOS /'piː mɒs/ *noun* MOS canal P

PMS /ˌpiː em 'es/ *abbr* (*Pantone Matching System*) système *m* (de référence de couleurs) Pantone; nuancier *m* Pantone

pnp transistor /ˌpiː en 'piː trænˌzɪstə/ *noun* transistor *m* de type pnp

pointer /'pɔɪntə/ *noun* **1.** (*in a computer program*) pointeur *m* **2.** (*graphical symbol*) pointeur *m* ◇ **desktop publishing on a PC is greatly helped by the use of a pointer and mouse** la PAO sur ordinateur individuel est facilitée par l'emploi de la souris et du pointeur ◇ **increment the contents of the pointer to the address of the next instruction** incrémenter le pointeur jusqu'à l'adresse (d'instruction) suivante

pointer file /'pɔɪntə faɪl/ *noun* fichier *m* de pointeurs

pointing device /'pɔɪntɪŋ dɪˌvaɪs/ *noun* (*device that controls the position of a cursor*) dispositif *m* de pointage

point of presence /ˌpɔɪnt əv 'prezəns/ *noun* point *m* de présence

point-of-sale /ˌpɔɪnt əv 'seɪl/ *noun* point *m* de vente

point size /ˌpɔɪnt 'saɪz/ *noun* taille *f* des caractères

point to point /'pɔɪnt tə, tʊ/ *noun* liaison *f* point à point

point to point protocol /ˌpɔɪnt tə ˌpɔɪnt 'prəʊtəkɒl/ *noun* protocole *m* PPP

point-to-point tunneling protocol /pɔɪnt tə, tʊ pɔɪnt ˌ'tʌn(ə)lɪŋ/ *noun* protocole *m* PPTP

poke /pəʊk/ *noun* instruction *f* POKE (d'insertion)

POL *abbr* (*problem-orientated language*) langage *m* d'application

polar /'pəʊlə/ *adjective* polaire ◇ **polar diagram** diagramme *m* polaire *or* en coordonnées polaires ◇ **polar orbit** orbite *f* polaire

polar coordinates /ˌpəʊlə kəʊ'ɔːdɪnəts/ *noun* coordonnées *fpl* polaires

polarised /'pəʊləraɪzd/ *adjective* polarisé

polarised edge connector /ˌpəʊləraɪzd 'edʒ kəˌnektə/ *noun* connecteur *m* à enfichage dirigé; connecteur *m* à un seul bord d'enfichage

polarised plug /ˌpəʊləraɪzd 'plʌg/ *noun* connecteur *m* à une seule position d'enfichage

polarity /pəʊ'lærəti/ *noun* polarité *f*

polarity test /pəʊ'lærəti test/ *noun* test *m* de polarité

Polish notation /ˌpəʊlɪʃ nəʊ'teɪʃ(ə)n/ *noun* notation *f* suffixée

poll /pəʊl/ *verb* (*of computer*) appeler *vt*; interroger *vt*; inviter à émettre

polled interrupt /ˌpəʊld 'ɪntərʌpt/ *noun* interruption *f* d'appel

polling /'pəʊlɪŋ/ *noun* (*from controlling computer to terminal*) interrogation *f*; appel *m* sélectif; invitation *f* à émettre

polling characters /ˌpəʊlɪŋ 'kærɪktəz/ *plural noun* caractères *mpl* d'appel sélectif

polling interval /'pəʊlɪŋ ˌɪntəv(ə)l/ *noun* intervalle *m* d'appels

polling list /'pəʊlɪŋ lɪst/ *noun* ordre *m* d'interrogation d'appel

polling overhead /'pəʊlɪŋ ˌəʊvəhed/ *noun* temps *m* d'appels sélectifs

polygon /'pɒlɪgən/ *noun* (*graphics shape with three or more sides*) polygone *m*

polynomial code /ˌpɒli'nəʊmiəl kəʊd/ *noun* code *m* polynomial

polyphony /pə'lɪfəni/ *noun* polyphonie *f*

pop /pɒp/ *verb* faire apparaître

POP /pɒp/ *noun* protocole *m* PPTP

POP 2 /'pɒp tuː/ *noun* langage *m* POP 2

POP 3 /ˌpɒp 'θriː/ *noun* (*system used to transfer electronic mail messages between a user's computer and a server located at an ISP*) système *m* POP 3

pop-down menu /ˌpɒp daʊn 'menjuː/ *noun* menu *m* déroulant; fenêtre *f* de menu

populate /'pɒpjʊleɪt/ *verb* (*fill the sockets on a printed circuit board with components*) habiller *vt*; garnir une carte

pop-up menu /ˌpɒp ʌp 'menjuː/ *noun* fenêtre *f* de menu

pop-up window /ˌpɒp ʌp 'wɪndəʊ/ *noun* fenêtre *f* de message

> '...you can use a mouse to access pop-up menus and a keyboard for word processing' [*Byte*]

port /pɔːt/ *noun* (*data transfer*) port *m*; point *m* d'accès

portability /ˌpɔːtə'bɪlɪti/ *noun* (*of program*) portabilité *f*

> '...although portability between machines is there in theory, in practice it just isn't that simple' [*Personal Computer World*]

portable /'pɔːtəb(ə)l/ *noun* (*computer*) portable *m* ■ *adjective* (*machine*) portable; portatif *or* -ive

portable document format /ˌpɔːtəb(ə)l 'dɒkjʊmənt ˌfɔːmæt/ *noun* format *m* PDF

portable operating system interface /ˌpɔːtəb(ə)l 'ɒpəreɪtɪŋ ˌsɪstəm ˌɪntəfeɪs/ *noun* POSIX

portable programs /ˌpɔːtəb(ə)l 'prəʊgræmz/ *noun* programme *m* portable

portable software /ˌpɔːtəb(ə)l 'sɒftweə/ *noun* programme *m* portable

portal /'pɔːt(ə)l/ *noun* portail *m*

portrait /'pɔːtrɪt/ *adjective* (*page or piece of paper where the longest edge is vertical*) portrait

port replicator /'pɔːt ˌreplɪkeɪtə/ *noun* duplicateur *m* de port

port selector /pɔːt sɪ'lektə/ *noun* sélecteur *m* de port

port sharing /pɔːt 'ʃeərɪŋ/ *noun* port *m* partagé; partage *m* de port

positional /pə'zɪʃ(ə)nəl/ *adjective* positionnel *or* -elle

positioning time /pə'zɪʃ(ə)nɪŋ taɪm/ *noun* temps *m* de mise en place; temps *m* d'accès

positive /'pɒzɪtɪv/ *adjective* **1.** (*meaning 'yes'*) affirmatif; -ive **2.** (*image*) épreuve positive **3.** (*electrical*) positif

positive display /ˌpɒzɪtɪv dɪ'spleɪ/ *noun* affichage *m* noir sur fond blanc

positive logic /ˌpɒzɪtɪv 'lɒdʒɪk/ *noun* logique *f* positive

positive photoresist /ˌpɒzɪtɪv ˌfəʊtəʊrɪ'zɪst/ *noun* résine *f* photosensible en positif

positive presentation /ˌpɒzɪtɪv ˌprez(ə)n'teɪʃ(ə)n/ *noun* affichage *m* en positif

positive response /ˌpɒzɪtɪv rɪ'spɒns/ *noun* réponse *f* affirmative; réponse *f* positive

positive terminal /ˌpɒzɪtɪv 'tɜːmɪn(ə)l/ *noun* borne *f* positive

POSIX /'pɒsɪks/ *noun* standard *m* IEEE POSIX (de portabilité des services d'un système d'exploitation)

post /pəʊst/ *verb* (*to enter data*) enregistrer *vt*

postbyte /'pəʊstbaɪt/ *noun* octet *m* de placement

post-editing /pəʊst ˌ'edɪtɪŋ/ *noun* (*editing and modifying text*) édition *f* après compilation; édition *f* après calculs

postfix /'pəʊstfɪks/ *noun* suffixe *m*

postfix notation /ˌpəʊstfɪks nəʊ'teɪʃ(ə)n/ *noun* (*mathematical operations*) notation *f* suffixée; notation *f* polonaise inversée

post-formatted /ˌpəʊst 'fɔːmætɪd/ *adjective* mis en forme à l'impression

posting /'pəʊstɪŋ/ *noun* postage *m*

postmaster /'pəʊstmɑːstə/ *noun* maître *m* de poste

post mortem /pəʊst 'mɔːtəm/ *noun* autopsie *f*

post office /'pəʊst ˌɒfɪs/ *noun* bureau *m* de poste

post office protocol /pəʊst 'ɒfɪs/ *noun* protocole *m* POP

postprocessor /ˌpəʊst'prəʊsesə/ *noun* **1.** (*microprocessor*) post-processeur *m* **2.** (*program*) programme *m* de retraitement

post production /ˌpəʊst prə'dʌkʃən/ *noun* postproduction *f*

PostScript /'pəʊstskrɪpt/ (*standard page description language developed by Adobe Systems*) PostScript™ ◇ **if you do a lot of DTP work, you will benefit from a PostScript printer** si vous utilisez beaucoup la PAO, vous tirerez profit d'une imprimante PostScript

potential difference /pəˌtenʃəl 'dɪf(ə)rəns/ *noun* différence *f* de potentiel

POTS /pɒts/ *noun* service *m* téléphonique ordinaire

power /'paʊə/ *noun* **1.** (*unit of energy*) énergie *f*; alimentation *f*; puissance *f* **2.** (*mathematical term*) puissance *f* ■ *verb* (*to provide electrical energy to a device*) alimenter (en courant électrique) ◇ **power LED** voyant *m* d'alimentation ◇ **power-saving mode** mode *m* économie d'énergie ◇ **the monitor is powered from a supply in the main PC** l'écran est alimenté par le transformateur du PC principal ◇ **which is powered (by)** (appareil) qui marche *or* qui fonctionne (à l'électricité, etc.)

PowerBook /'paʊəbʊk/ (*laptop version of a Macintosh*) PowerBook™

PowerCD /'paʊə siː ˌdiː/ PowerCD

power down /'paʊə daʊn/ *verb* mettre hors tension

power dump /'paʊə dʌmp/ *verb* coupure *f* de courant; coupure *f* d'alimentation de l'ordinateur

power failure /'paʊə ˌfeɪljə/ *noun* (*loss of electric power supply*) coupure *f* de courant; panne *f* d'électricité; panne *f* de courant

power loss /'paʊə lɒs/ *noun* chute *f* de tension

power management /'paʊə ˌmænɪdʒmənt/ *noun* gestion *f* de l'utilisation de l'énergie; gestion *f* de l'alimentation

power monitor /'paʊə ˌmɒnɪtə/ *noun* contrôle *m* de l'alimentation

power-on reset /ˌpaʊə 'ɒn ˌriːset/ *noun* réinitialisation *f* automatique à la mise sous tension

power on self test /ˌpaʊə ɒn ˌself 'test/ *noun* autotest *m* à la mise sous tension

power pack /'paʊə pæk/ *noun* (*for a circuit*) bloc *m* d'alimentation

PowerPC /'paʊə piː ˌsiː/ PowerPC

power supply /ˌpaʊə sə'plaɪ/ *noun* alimentation *f* ◇ **power supply unit (PSU)** bloc d'alimentation

power transient /ˌpaʊə 'trænziənt/ *noun* courant *m* transitoire

power up /'paʊə ʌp/ *verb* mettre sous tension; mettre en marche; allumer *vt*

power user /'paʊə ˌjuːzə/ *noun* utilisateur *m* avancé

ppm /ˌpiː piː 'em/ *noun* pages *fpl* par minute

PPP /ˌpiː piː 'piː/ *noun* protocole *m* PPP

PPTP /ˌpiː piː tiː 'piː/ *noun* protocole *m* PPTP

PPU *abbr* (*peripheral processing unit*) unité *f* de traitement périphérique

pre- /priː/ *prefix* (*before*) pré-; d'avance

pre-agreed /pri ə'griːd/ *adjective* accepté, -ée d'avance; suivant accord préalable

pre-allocation /pri ˌælə'keɪʃ(ə)n/ *noun* préallocation *f*

pre-amplifier /pri 'æmplɪˌfaɪə/ *noun* préamplificateur *m*

precede /prɪ'siːd/ *verb* précéder *vt*

precedence /'presɪd(ə)ns/ *noun* priorité *f*

precise /prɪ'saɪs/ *adjective* précis *or* -e; exact *or* -e ◇ **the atomic clock will give the precise time of starting the process** l'horloge atomique indiquera l'heure précise du début du processus

precision /prɪ'sɪʒ(ə)n/ *noun* précision *f*; exactitude *f*

precision of a number /prɪˌsɪʒ(ə)n əv ə 'nʌmbə/ *noun* précision *f* d'un nombre

precompiled code /prikəmˌpaɪld 'kəʊd/ *noun* code *m* précompilé

precondition /ˌpriːkən'dɪʃ(ə)n/ *verb* préconditionner *vt*

predefined /ˌpriːdɪ'faɪnd/ *adjective* défini, -e d'avance; prédéfini *or* -e

predicate /'predɪkət/ *noun* prédicat *m*

predictive /prɪ'dɪktɪv/ *adjective* prédictif *or* -ive

pre-edit /pri 'edɪt/ *verb* prééditer *vt*

preemptive multitasking /priˌemptɪv 'mʌltitɑːskɪŋ/ *noun* système *m* multitâche préemptif; multitâche *f* en temps partagé

pre-fetch /priː 'fetʃ/ *verb* appel *m* d'instruction anticipé

pre-filtering /priː'fɪltərɪŋ/ *noun* préfiltration *f*

prefix /'priːˌfɪks/ *noun* (*code*) préfixe *m*

prefix notation /'priːfɪks nəʊˌteɪʃ(ə)n/ *noun* (*mathematical operations*) notation *f* préfixée; notation *f* polonaise (préfixée)

preformatted /priː'fɔːmætɪd/ *adjective* formaté, -ée d'avance; préformaté *or* -ée ◇ **a preformatted disk** disquette *f* préformatée

preprinted stationery /priˌprɪntɪd 'steɪʃ(ə)n(ə)ri/ *noun* (*computer stationery*) papier *m* à en-tête

preprocess /priː'prəʊses/ *verb* prétraiter des données

preprocessor /priːˈprəʊsesə/ *noun* **1.** (*software*) programme *m* de prétraitement **2.** (*small computer*) préprocesseur *m*

'...the C preprocessor is in the first stage of converting a written program into machine instructions the preprocessor can be directed to read in another file before completion, perhaps because the same information is needed in each module of the program' [*Personal Computer World*]

preprogram /priːˈprəʊgræm/ *verb* préprogrammer *vt*

preprogrammed /priːˈprəʊgræmd/ *adjective* programmé, -ée d'avance; préprogrammé *or* -ée

prescan /ˈpriːskæn/ *noun* prénumérisation *f*

presentation graphics /ˌprez(ə)nteɪʃ(ə)n ˈgræfɪks/ *plural noun* (*used to represent business information*) diagramme(s) *m(pl)*; présentation *f* graphique

presentation layer /ˌprez(ə)nˈteɪʃ(ə)n ˌleɪə/ *noun* (*network layer*) couche *f* présentation

Presentation Manager /ˌprez(ə)nˈteɪʃ(ə)n ˌmænɪdʒə/ *noun* (*graphical user interface*) Presentation Manager™

presentation software /ˌprez(ə)nteɪʃ(ə)n ˈsɒftweə/ *noun* logiciel *m* de présentation (de document)

preset /ˌpriːˈset/ *verb* (*to set something in advance*) établir *vt*; fixer *vt*; programmer d'avance; prérégler *vt*; présélectionner *vt* ◇ **the printer was preset with new page parameters** on avait programmé d'avance les nouveaux paramètres de page de l'imprimante

prestore /priːˈstɔː/ *verb* stocker des données avant traitement

presumptive address /prɪˌzʌmptɪv əˈdres/ *noun* adresse *f* de base; adresse *f* origine; adresse *f* primitive

presumptive instruction /prɪˌzʌmptɪv ɪn ˈstrʌkʃən/ *noun* instruction *f* de base; instruction *f* primitive; instruction *f* d'origine

pretty good privacy /ˌprɪti gʊd ˈprɪvəsi/ *noun* système *m* de chiffrement PGP

preventative /prɪˈventətɪv/, **preventive** /prɪ ˈventɪv/ *adjective* préventif *or* -ive

preventive maintenance /prɪˌventɪv ˈmeɪntənəns/ *noun* (*of a system*) maintenance *f* préventive

preview /ˈpriːˌvjuː/ *verb* visualiser (avant impression); prévisualiser *vt*

previewer /ˈpriːvjuːə/ *noun* (*before printing*) aperçu *m* avant impression; présentation-aperçu *f* ◇ **the built-in previewer allows the user to check for mistakes** la fonction intégrée 'aperçu avant impression' permet à l'utilisateur de vérifier s'il s'est glissé des erreurs

PRI /ˌpiː ɑː ˈaɪ/ *noun* accès *m* primaire

primary /ˈpraɪməri/ *adjective* primaire; élémentaire; fondamental *or* -e ◇ **primary colours** (*(i) red, green, blue; (ii) magenta, cyan, yellow*) couleurs *fpl* fondamentales *or* primaires ◇ **primary group** (*12 voice channels*) groupe *m* primaire

primary channel /ˌpraɪməri ˈtʃæn(ə)l/ *noun* canal *m* principal

primary key /ˈpraɪməri kiː/ *noun* clé *f* primaire *or* principale

primary memory /ˌpraɪməri ˈmem(ə)ri/ *noun* mémoire *f* centrale; mémoire *f* à accès direct

primary rate interface /ˌpraɪməri reɪt ˈɪntəfeɪs/ *noun* accès *m* primaire

primary station /ˌpraɪməri ˈsteɪʃ(ə)n/ *noun* station *f* primaire

primary storage /ˌpraɪməri ˈstɔːrɪdʒ/ *noun* mémoire *f* principale

prime /praɪm/ *adjective* (*very important*) très important *or* -e; essentiel *or* -elle ◇ **prime time** (*TV*) heures *fpl* de grande écoute *or* d'écoute maximale ◇ **we are putting out a series of prime-time commercials** nous commençons à diffuser des spots publicitaires aux heures de grande écoute

prime attribute /ˌpraɪm əˈtrɪbjuːt/ *noun* caractéristique *f* essentielle

primer /ˈpraɪmə/ *noun* guide *m* élémentaire; manuel *m* d'utilisation élémentaire

primitive /ˈprɪmɪtɪv/ *noun* (*in programming*) routine *f* primitive; instruction *f* de base; (*in graphics*) forme *f* primitive; routine *f* de base

print /prɪnt/ *noun* (*characters on paper*) impression *f* ■ *verb* (*to put characters in ink*) imprimer *vt* ◇ **a desktop printer with a resolution of 600dpi provides good print quality** une imprimante graphique avec une résolution de 600 dpi fournit une bonne qualité d'impression ◇ **the printer prints at 60 characters per second** cette imprimante a un débit de 60 caractères/seconde

print control character /prɪnt kənˈtrəʊl/, **print control code** *noun* caractère *m* de contrôle d'impression; code *m* de contrôle d'impression

printed circuit /ˌprɪntɪd ˈsɜːkɪt/, **printed circuit board** *noun* circuit *m* imprimé

printer /ˈprɪntə/ *noun* **1.** (*device*) imprimante *f* **2.** (*company*) imprimeur *m* ◇ **bubble-jet printer** (*produces characters by sending a stream of tiny drops of ink*) imprimante à bulle d'encre ◇ **duplex printer** imprimante recto/verso ◇ **printer control language (PCL)** (*standard set of commands*) langage PCL *or* jeu de commandes de contrôle d'imprimante PCL ◇ **printer-readable** imprimable *or* qui peut être lu, -e *or* accepté, -ée par l'imprimante ◇ **the book will be sent to the printer next week** on doit envoyer le livre chez l'imprimeur la semaine prochaine

printer buffer /ˈprɪntə ˌbʌfə/ *noun* tampon *m* d'imprimante

printer control characters /ˌprɪntə kən ˈtrəʊl ˌkærɪktəz/ *noun* caractères *mpl* de contrôle d'impression

printer control language /ˌprɪntə kən'trəʊl ˌlæŋgwɪdʒ/ *noun* langage *m* PCL; jeu *m* de commandes de contrôle d'imprimante PCL

printer driver /'prɪntə ˌdraɪvə/ *noun* gestionnaire *m* d'imprimante; pilote *m* d'imprimante

printer emulation /'prɪntə emjuˌleɪʃ(ə)n/ *noun* émulation *f* d'imprimante ◇ **this printer emulation allows my NEC printer to emulate an Epsom** cette émulation permet à mon imprimante NEC d'émuler une imprimante Epsom

printer-plotter /'prɪntə ˌplɒtə/ *noun* imprimante *f* graphique

printer port /'prɪntə pɔːt/ *noun* port *m* (d')imprimante

printer quality /'prɪntə ˌkwɒlɪti/ *noun* (*printing*) qualité *f* d'impression (d'une imprimante)

printer ribbon /'prɪntə ˌrɪbən/ *noun* ruban *m* d'imprimante

printer's controller /ˌprɪntəz kən'trəʊlə/ *noun* contrôleur *m* d'imprimante; pilote *m* d'imprimante

print format /prɪnt 'fɔːmæt/ *noun* format *m* d'impression

print formatter /'prɪnt ˌfɔːmætə/ *noun* logiciel *m* de formatage d'impression

print hammer /prɪnt 'hæmə/ *noun* marteau *m* d'impression

printhead /'prɪnthed/ *noun* tête *f* d'impression ◇ **the printhead has a print life of over 400 million characters** la tête d'impression a une durée de vie de plus de 400 millions de caractères

printing /'prɪntɪŋ/ *noun* (*action*) impression *f*

print job /'prɪnt dʒɒb/ *noun* tâche *f* d'impression

print life /ˌprɪnt 'laɪf/ *noun* durée *f* de vie d'une imprimante; durée *f* de vie d'un dispositif d'impression

Print Manager /'prɪnt ˌmænɪdʒə/ (*software utility that is part of Microsoft Windows*) programme Print Manager™

print modifiers /prɪnt 'mɒdɪˌfaɪəs/ *plural noun* modificateurs *mpl*

printout /'prɪntˌaʊt/ *noun* (*final printed page*) sortie *f* d'imprimante; listing *m* ◇ **the sales director asked for a printout of the agents' commissions** le directeur des ventes a demandé un listing des commissions d'agents

print pause /ˌprɪnt 'pɔːz/ *noun* arrêt *m* de l'impression

print preview /prɪnt 'priːˌvjuː/ *noun* aperçu *m* avant impression; présentation-aperçu *f*

print quality /prɪnt 'kwɒlɪti/ *noun* qualité *f* d'impression ◇ **a desktop printer with a resolution of 600dpi provides good print quality** une imprimante graphique avec une résolution de 600 dpi fournit une bonne qualité d'impression

print queue /ˌprɪnt 'kjuː/ *noun* file *f* d'attente à l'impression

Print Screen key /ˌprɪnt 'skriːn ˌkiː/ *noun* (*special key in the top right-hand side of the keyboard – under DOS*) touche *f* d'impression (sous DOS); (*under DOS*) touche *f* d'impression

print server /prɪnt 'sɜːvə/ *noun* serveur *m* d'impression

print spooling /ˌprɪnt 'spuːlɪŋ/ *noun* impression *f* en différé; impression *f* en arrière-plan; impression *f* par spouling

print style /ˌprɪnt 'staɪl/ *noun* style *m* d'impression

printwheel /'prɪntwiːl/ *noun* marguerite *f*

priority /praɪ'ɒrɪti/ *noun* priorité *f*

priority interrupt /praɪˌɒrɪti 'ɪntərʌpt/ *noun* interruption *f* prioritaire

priority interrupt table /praɪˌɒrɪti 'ɪntərʌpt ˌteɪb(ə)l/ *noun* table *f* de priorité des interruptions

priority scheduler /praɪ'ɒrɪti ˌʃedjuːlə/ *noun* gestionnaire *m* de priorités

priority sequence /praɪ'ɒrɪti ˌsiːkwəns/ *noun* ordre *m* de priorité

privacy /'prɪvəsi/ *noun* confidentialité *f* ◇ **privacy transformation** cryptage *m* de l'information pour en assurer la confidentialité

privacy of data /ˌprɪvəsi əv 'deɪtə/ *noun* confidentialité *f* des données

privacy of information /ˌprɪvəsi əv ˌɪnfə'meɪʃ(ə)n/ *noun* confidentialité *f* de l'information

privacy statement /'prɪvəsi ˌsteɪtmənt/ *noun* déclaration *f* de confidentialité

private /'praɪvət/ *adjective* privé *or* -e; privatif; -ive ◇ **private automatic branch exchange (PABX)** autocommutateur privatif (raccordé au réseau public) (PABX) ◇ **private automatic exchange (PAX)** central téléphonique privatif (non raccordé au réseau public) ◇ **private branch exchange (PBX)** autocommutateur privatif (raccordé au réseau public) ◇ **private dial port** port privatif *or* réservé ◇ **private line** ligne *f* privée *or* réservée *or* privative ◇ **private manual branch exchange (PMBX)** central téléphonique manuel privatif (raccordé au secteur public) ◇ **private telephone system** système *m* téléphonique privatif

private address space /ˌpraɪvət ə'dres ˌspeɪs/ *noun* partition *f* privée; espace *m* mémoire réservé à l'usage d'un utilisateur

private branch exchange /ˌpraɪvət 'brɑːntʃ ɪksˌtʃeɪndʒ/ *noun* autocommutateur *m* privatif (raccordé au réseau public)

privilege /'prɪvɪlɪdʒ/ *noun* privilège *m*

privileged account /ˌprɪvəlɪdʒd ə'kaʊnt/ *noun* partition *f* privilégiée

privileged instructions /ˌprɪvəlɪdʒd ɪn'strʌkʃənz/ *plural noun* instructions privilégiées

privileged mode /'prɪvəlɪdʒd məʊd/ *noun* mode *m* protégé

PRN /ˌpiː ɑː 'en/ *noun* (*represents the standard printer port in MS-DOS*) PRN

problem /'prɒbləm/ *noun* (*fault*) mauvais fonctionnement *m*; dysfonctionnement *m*; défaillance *f*

problem definition /'prɒbləm ˌdefənɪʃ(ə)n/ *noun* exposé *m* d'un problème

problem diagnosis /'prɒbləm ˌdaɪəgnəʊsɪs/ *noun* diagnostic *m* (de cause) de défaillance

problem-orientated language /ˌprɒbləm ˌɔːriənteɪtɪd 'læŋgwɪdʒ/ *noun* langage *m* de résolution de problème; langage *m* adapté au problème

procedural /prə'siːdʒərəl/ *adjective* à base de procédure

procedural language /prəˌsiːdʒ(ə)rəl 'læŋgwɪdʒ/ *noun* langage *m* de procédure

procedure /prə'siːdʒə/ *noun* **1.** (*instruction code*) procédure *f* **2.** (*route used*) procédure *f*; méthode *f*; marche *f* à suivre ◇ **the procedure is given in the manual** la procédure est expliquée dans le manuel d'utilisation ◇ **this procedure sorts all the files into alphabetic order, you can call it from the main program by the instruction SORT** cette procédure qui sert à classer les fichiers par ordre alphabétique peut être sélectionnée depuis le programme principal par la commande SORT ◇ **you should use this procedure to retrieve lost files** voici la marche à suivre pour retrouver des fichiers perdus

procedure declaration /prə'siːdʒə ˌdekləreɪʃ(ə)n/ *noun* déclaration *f* de procédure

procedure-orientated language /prə ˌsiːdʒə ˌɔːriənteɪtɪd 'læŋgwɪdʒ/ *noun* langage *m* de procédure; langage *m* adapté à la procédure

process /prəʊ'ses/ *noun* (*number of tasks that must be performed to achieve a goal*) processus *m*; procédure *f*; procédé *m* ■ *verb* traiter (des données, etc.); effectuer un traitement ◇ **processing all the information will take a long time** le traitement des données sera assez long ◇ **there are five stages in the process** le processus compte cinq étapes ◇ **we processed the new data** nous avons traité les données

process bound /'prəʊses baʊnd/ *noun* limité par le traitement *or* avec contrainte de vitesse du traitement

process chart /'prəʊses tʃɑːt/ *noun* (*diagram*) schéma *m*

process control /'prəʊses kənˌtrəʊl/ *noun* commande *f*

process control computer /ˌprəʊses kən ˌtrəʊl kəm'pjuːtə/ *noun* ordinateur *m* de contrôle de processus

process control system /ˌprəʊses kən 'trəʊl ˌsɪstəm/ *noun* système *m* de contrôle; système *m* de conduite de processus

processing /'prəʊsesɪŋ/ *noun* traitement *m* ◇ **page processing time depends on the complexity of a given page** le temps d'ordinateur requis pour le traitement d'une page de texte varie en fonction de la complexité du document

processor /'prəʊˌsesə/ *noun* processeur *m* ◇ **front-end processor (FEP)** processeur frontal ◇ **processor-controlled keying** saisie *f* au clavier contrôlée par processeur ◇ **processor status word (PSW)** mot *m* d'état d'un processeur

processor controlled keying /ˌprəʊsesə kənˌtrəʊld 'kiːɪŋ/ *noun* saisie *f* au clavier contrôlée par ordinateur

processor interrupt /ˌprəʊsesə 'ɪntərʌpt/ *noun* interruption *f* du processeur; interruption *f* du traitement

processor-limited /ˌprəʊsesə 'lɪmɪtɪd/ *adjective* dépendant de la vitesse du processeur *or* -e; avec contrainte de vitesse du processeur

processor status word /ˌprəʊsesə 'steɪtəs ˌwɜːd/ *noun* mot *m* d'état d'un processeur

produce /prə'djuːs/ *verb* produire *vt*

producer /prə'djuːsə/ *noun* (*TV or film*) réalisateur *m*

producing capacity /prə'djuːsɪŋ kəˌpæsəti/ *noun* capacité *f* de production

product /'prɒdʌkt/ *noun* **1.** (*item*) produit *m* **2.** (*manufactured item for sale*) produit *m* **3.** (*result of multiplication*) produit *m*

product design /'prɒdʌkt dɪˌzaɪn/ *noun* conception *f* de produits

product engineer /ˌprɒdʌkt ˌendʒɪ'nɪə/ *noun* ingénieur *m* de produit

production /prə'dʌkʃən/ *noun* (*making or manufacturing*) production *f*; fabrication *f* ◇ **production run** cycle *m* de production

production control /prə'dʌkʃən kənˌtrəʊl/ *noun* contrôle *m* de la production

production rate /prə'dʌkʃ(ə)n reɪt/ *noun* rythme *m* de la production

production standards /prə'dʌkʃən ˌstændədz/ *plural noun* normes de production; standards de production

productive /prə'dʌktɪv/ *adjective* productif; -ive

productive time /prəˌdʌktɪv 'taɪm/ *noun* temps *m* productif

product line /'prɒdʌkt laɪn/, **product range** /'prɒdʌkt reɪndʒ/ *noun* ligne *f* de produits; gamme *f* de produits

product range /'prɒdʌkt reɪndʒ/ *noun* ligne *f* de produits; gamme *f* de produits

profile /'prəʊfaɪl/ *noun* (*feature of Windows 95 that stores the settings for different users on one PC*) profil *m*

PROFS /prɒfs/ (*electronic mail system*) PROFS™

program /'prəʊgræm/ *noun* (*software*) programme *m* ■ *verb* écrire un programme ◇ **assembly program** programme d'assemblage ◇ **I forgot to insert an important instruction which caused a program to crash, erasing all the files on the disk!** j'ai omis d'inclure une instruction importante dans le programme de sorte que le programme s'est planté et tous les fichiers ont été effacés contenus sur le disque ◇ **program design language (PDL)** langage *m* de conception de programme ◇ **program evaluation and review technique (PERT)** technique *f* d'évaluation et de révision de programme ◇ **program information file (PIF)** (*Microsoft Windows: file that contains environment settings*) fichier PIF (fichier d'information d'un programme, sous MS-Windows) ◇ **program specifications** spécifications *fpl* d'un programme ◇ **to run the program, double-click on the program icon** pour lancer le programme, cliquez deux fois sur l'icône du programme

program address counter /ˌprəʊgræm əˈdres ˌkaʊntə/ *noun* compteur *m* d'inscription; registre *m* compteur

program branch /ˈprəʊgræm brɑːntʃ/ *noun* branchement *m* d'un programme

program cards /ˈprəʊgræm kɑːdz/ *plural noun* cartes *fpl* programme

program coding sheet /ˌprəʊgræm ˈkəʊdɪŋ ˌʃiːt/ *noun* formulaire *m* de programmation

program compatibility /ˌprəʊgræm kəm ˌpætəˈbɪlɪti/ *noun* compatibilité *f* de logiciel

program compilation /ˌprəʊgræm ˌkɒmpəˈleɪʃ(ə)n/ *noun* compilation *f* de programme

program counter /ˈprəʊgræm ˌkaʊntə/ *noun* compteur *m* d'instruction; registre *m* compteur

program crash /ˈprəʊgræm kræʃ/ *noun* défaillance *f*

program design language /ˌprəʊgræm dɪˈzaɪn ˌlæŋgwɪdʒ/ *noun* langage *m* de conception de programme

program development /ˈprəʊgræm dɪ ˌveləpmənt/ *noun* développement *m* d'un programme

program development system /ˌprəʊgræm dɪˈveləpmənt ˌsɪstəm/ *noun* environnement *m* de développement de programme

program documentation /ˌprəʊgræm ˌdɒkjʊmenˈteɪʃ(ə)n/ *noun* documentation *f* relative à l'utilisation d'un programme

program editor /ˈprəʊgræm ˌedɪtə/ *noun* éditeur *m* de programme

program evaluation and review technique /ˌprəʊgræm ɪˌvæljueɪʃ(ə)n ən rɪˈvjuː tekˌniːk/ *noun* technique *f* d'évaluation et de révision des programmes; méthode *f* PERT

program execution /ˌprəʊgræm ˌeksɪˈkjuːʃ(ə)n/ *noun* exécution *f* d'un programme

program file /ˈprəʊgræm faɪl/ *noun* fichier *m* programme

program flowchart /ˌprəʊgræm ˈfləʊtʃɑːt/ *noun* organigramme *m* de programme

program generation /ˌprəʊgræm ˌdʒenəˈreɪʃ(ə)n/ *noun* création *f* de programme

program generator /ˈprəʊgræm ˌdʒenəreɪtə/ *noun* générateur *m* de programme

program group /ˈprəʊgræm gruːp/ *noun* groupe *m* de programmes

program icon /ˈprəʊgræm ˌaɪkɒn/ *noun* icône *f* de programme

program information file /ˌprəʊgræm ˌɪnfəˈmeɪʃ(ə)n ˌfaɪl/ *noun* fichier *m* PIF

program instruction /ˈprəʊgræm ɪn ˌstrʌkʃən/ *noun* instruction *f*

program item /ˈprəʊgræm ˌaɪtəm/ *noun* élément *m* de programme

program library /ˈprəʊgræm ˌlaɪbrəri/ *noun* bibliothèque *f* de programmes; bibliothèque *f* de logiciels

program line /ˈprəʊgræm laɪn/ *noun* ligne *f* d'instruction d'un programme

program line number /ˌprəʊgræm ˈlaɪn ˌnʌmbə/ *noun* numéro *m* de référence d'une ligne d'un programme

program listing /ˈprəʊgræm ˌlɪstɪŋ/ *noun* listing *m*

programmable /ˈprəʊgræməb(ə)l/ *adjective* (*device*) programmable ■ *noun* ordinateur *m* ◇ **programmable logic array (PLA)** *or* **programmable logic device (PLD)** circuit *m* logique programmable *or* logique câblée programmable ◇ **programmable memory (PROM)** mémoire *f* programmable *or* (mémoire) PROM ◇ **programmable read only memory (PROM)** mémoire morte programmable *or* (mémoire) PROM

programmable calculator /ˌprəʊgræməb(ə)l ˈkælkjʊleɪtə/ *noun* calculatrice *f* programmable

programmable clock /ˌprəʊgræməb(ə)l ˈklɒk/ *noun* horloge *f* programmable

programmable interrupt controller /ˌprəʊgræməb(ə)l ˈɪntərʌpt kənˌtrəʊlə/ *noun* contrôleur *m* d'interruption programmable

programmable key /ˌprəʊgræməb(ə)l ˈkiː/ *noun* touche *f* (de fonction) programmable

programmable logic array /ˌprəʊgræməb(ə)l ˌlɒdʒɪk əˈreɪ/ *noun* circuit *m* logique programmable

programmable logic device /ˌprəʊgræməb(ə)l ˈlɒdʒɪk dɪˌvaɪs/ *noun* circuit *m* logique programmable

programmable memory /ˌprəʊgræməb(ə)l ˈmem(ə)ri/ *noun* mémoire *f* programmable

programmable read only memory /ˌprəʊgræməb(ə)l riːd ˌəʊnli ˈmem(ə)ri/ *noun* mémoire *f* morte programmable; mémoire *f* PROM

program maintenance /ˈprəʊgræm ˌmeɪntənəns/ *noun* maintenance *f* d'un programme

Program Manager /ˌprəʊgræm ˈmænɪdʒə/ *noun* Gestionnaire *m* de programmes

programmatic /ˌprəʊgrəˈmætɪk/ *adjective* programmatique

programmed halt /'prəʊgræmd hɔːlt/ *noun* arrêt *m* programmé

programmed learning /ˌprəʊgræmd 'lɜːnɪŋ/ *noun* formation *f* à l'aide de didacticiel

programmer /'prəʊˌgræmə/ *noun* **1.** (*person*) programmeur *mf or* -euse **2.** (*device*) programmateur *m* ◇ **analyst** *or* **programmer** *or* **programmer** *or* **analyst** analyste-programmeur, -euse ◇ **the programmer is still working on the new software** le programmeur n'a pas encore terminé le nouveau logiciel

programmer's hierarchical interactive graphics standard /ˌprəʊgræməz haɪəˌrɑːkɪk(ə)l ɪntərˌæktɪv 'græfɪks ˌstændəd/ *noun* système *m* infographique PHIGS

programming /'prəʊgræmɪŋ/ *noun* **1.** (*writing programs*) programmation *f* **2.** (*writing data*) programmation *f* d'une PROM

programming in logic /ˌprəʊgræmɪŋ ɪn 'lɒdʒɪk/ *noun* langage *m* PROLOG

programming language /'prəʊgræmɪŋ ˌlæŋgwɪdʒ/ *noun* langage *m* de programmation

programming language/1 /ˌprəʊgræmɪŋ ˌlæŋgwɪdʒ 'wʌn/ *noun* PL/1

programming language for microprocessors /ˌprəʊgræmɪŋ ˌlæŋgwɪdʒ fə 'maɪkrəɪ ˌprəʊsesəz/ *noun* PL/M

programming standards /'prəʊgræmɪŋ ˌstændədz/ *plural noun* normes *fpl*

program name /'prəʊgræm neɪm/ *noun* nom *m* de programme

program origin /ˌprəʊgræm 'ɒrɪdʒɪn/ *noun* adresse *f* origine

program register /'prəʊgræm ˌredʒɪstə/ *noun* registre *m* d'instruction

program relocation /ˌprəʊgræm ˌriːləʊ'keɪʃ(ə)n/ *noun* (*moving a program*) translation *f*

program report generator /ˌprəʊgræm rɪ'pɔːt ˌdʒenəreɪtə/ *noun* générateur *m* d'application

program run /'prəʊgræm rʌn/ *noun* exécution *f* d'un programme

program segment /'prəʊgræm ˌsegmənt/ *noun* segment *m* de programme

Programs menu /'prəʊgræmz ˌmenjuː/ *noun* menu *m* Programmes

program specification /ˌprəʊgræm ˌspesɪfɪ'keɪʃ(ə)n/ *noun* spécifications *fpl* relatives à un programme

program stack /'prəʊgræm stæk/ *noun* pile *f* d'instructions d'un programme

program statement /'prəʊgræm ˌsteɪtmənt/ *noun* instruction *f*

program status word /ˌprəʊgræm 'steɪtəs ˌwɜːd/ *noun* mot *m* d'état du programme

program status word register /ˌprəʊgræm 'steɪtəs wɜːd ˌredʒɪstə/ *noun* mot *m* d'état du programme

program step /'prəʊgræm step/ *noun* pas *m*

program storage /ˌprəʊgræm 'stɔːrɪdʒ/ *noun* mémoire *f* (de) programme

program structure /ˌprəʊgræm 'strʌktʃə/ *noun* structure *f* d'un programme

program testing /'prəʊgræm ˌtestɪŋ/ *noun* essai *m*

program trading /'prəʊgræm ˌtreɪdɪŋ/ *noun* négociation *f* informatisée

program verification /ˌprəʊgræm ˌverɪfɪ'keɪʃ(ə)n/ *noun* vérification *f* du bon fonctionnement d'un programme

progressive scanning /prəʊˌgresɪv 'skænɪŋ/ *noun* balayage *m* progressif

project *noun* /'prɒdʒekt/ projet *m* ■ *verb* /prə'dʒekt/ (*to forecast*) prévoir *vt* ◇ **his latest project is computerizing the sales team** il projette maintenant d'informatiser le service des ventes

projection /prə'dʒekʃən/ *noun* (*of sales, etc.*) prévision *f*; projection *f*

PROLOG /'prəʊlɒg/ *noun* langage *m* PROLOG

PROM /prɒm/ *noun* **1.** mémoire *f* morte programmable **2.** mémoire *f* morte programmable

PROM blaster /'bɜːnə/, **PROM burner, PROM programmer** /'prəʊˌgræmə/ *noun* programmeur *m* de PROM

prompt /prɒmpt/ *noun* message *m* d'invitation à faire qc; invite *f* ◇ **MS-DOS normally displays the command prompt C:\> to indicate that it is ready to process instructions typed in by a user** MS-DOS affiche normalement l'invite (de commande) C:\> pour indiquer qu'il est prêt à traiter les commandes entrées par l'utilisateur ◇ **the prompt READY indicates that the system is available to receive instructions** le message READY signifie que le système est prêt à recevoir des instructions

propagate /'prɒpəˌgeɪt/ *verb* (*to spread*) se propager; s'étendre *vr*

propagated error /ˌprɒpəgeɪtɪd 'erə/ *noun* erreur *f* propagée

propagating error /'prɒpəgeɪtɪŋ ˌerə/ *noun* erreur *f* qui se propage

propagation delay /ˌprɒpə'geɪʃ(ə)n dɪˌleɪ/ *noun* délai *m* de propagation ◇ **propagation delay in the transmission path causes signal distortion** le délai de propagation dans une voie de communication produit une distorsion du signal

propagation time /ˌprɒpə'geɪʃ(ə)n ˌtaɪm/ *noun* délai *m*

properties /'prɒpətiz/ *noun* (*in Windows 95 – attributes of a file or object*) propriétés *f*; (*of a file or object*) attributs *mpl*

proportionally spaced /prəˌpɔːʃ(ə)nəli 'speɪst/ *adjective* d'espacement proportionnel

proprietary file format /prəˌpraɪət(ə)ri 'faɪl ˌfɔːmæt/ *noun* (*data storing method devised by* *a company*) format *m* de fichier (de) propriétaire; format *m* de fichier (de) constructeur ◇ **you cannot read this spreadsheet file because my software saves it in a proprietary file format** vous ne pouvez pas lire ce fichier de tableur parce que mon logiciel le sauvegarde en format (de) constructeur

protected field /prə'tektɪd fiːld/ *noun* champ *m* protégé

protected location /prə,tektɪd ləʊ'keɪʃ(ə)n/ *noun* emplacement *m* protégé

protected mode /prə'tektɪd məʊd/ *noun* mode *m* protégé

protected storage /prə,tektɪd 'stɔːrɪdʒ/ *noun* mémoire *f* protégée

protection key /prə'tekʃən kiː/ *noun* clé *f* de protection

protection master /prə'tekʃən ,mɑːstə/ *noun* original *m* sauvegardé; copie *f* d'original

protocol /'prəʊtəkɒl/ *noun* protocole *m*

protocol stack /'prəʊtəʊkɒl stæk/ *noun* pile *f* de protocoles de communication

protocol standards /'prəʊtəʊkɒl ,stændədz/ *plural noun* normes *fpl* de protocoles de transmission

prototype /'prəʊtə,taɪp/ *noun* prototype *m*

prototyping /'prəʊtətaɪpɪŋ/ *noun* fabrication *f* de prototype; prototypage *m*

proxy agent /'prɒksi ,eɪdʒənt/ *noun* agent *m* mandataire

proxy server /,prɒksi 'sɜːvə/ *noun* serveur *m* intermédiaire

PrtSc /,prɪnt 'skriːn/ *noun* (*key that sends the contents of the screen to the printer*) touche *f* PrtSc; touche *f* Print Screen; touche *f* Imp Ecran

pS /,piː 'es/ *abbr* (*picosecond*) picoseconde *f*

PS/2 (*IBM PC computers*) PS/2™

pseudo- /sjuːdəʊ/ *prefix* pseudo-

pseudo-code /'sjuːdəʊ kəʊd/ *noun* pseudocode *m*

pseudo-digital /,sjuːdəʊ 'dɪdʒɪt(ə)l/ *adjective* analogique modulé

pseudo-instruction /,sjuːdəʊ ɪn'strʌkʃən/ *noun* pseudo-instruction *f*

pseudo-operation /,sjuːdəʊ ,ɒpə'reɪʃ(ə)n/ *noun* pseudo-opération *f*

pseudo-random /,sjuːdəʊ 'rændəm/ *noun* coïncidence *f* inexacte

pseudo-random number generator /,sjuːdəʊ ,rændəm 'nʌmbə ,dʒenəreɪtə/ *noun* générateur *m* de nombres pseudo-aléatoires

pseudo-static /,sjuːdəʊ 'stætɪk/ *adjective* pseudostatique

PSN *abbr* (*packet switched network*) réseau *m* à commutation de paquets

PSU /,piː es 'juː/ *noun* bloc *m* d'alimentation

PTR *abbr* (*paper tape reader*) lecteur *m* de ruban de papier

public access terminal /,pʌblɪk ,ækses 'tɜːmɪn(ə)l/ *noun* terminal *m* public

public data network /,pʌblɪk ,deɪtə 'netwɜːk/ *noun* réseau *m* public de transmission de données

public domain /,pʌblɪk dəʊ'meɪn/ *noun* domaine *m* public

public key cipher system /,pʌblɪk kiː 'saɪfə ,sɪstəm/ *noun* cryptage *m* à clé public

public key encryption /,pʌblɪk kiː ɪn 'krɪpʃ(ə)n/ *noun* cryptage *m* à clé publique

publish /'pʌblɪʃ/ *verb* publier *vt* ◇ **the company specializes in publishing reference books** cette maison d'édition publie principalement des livres de référence ◇ **the institute has published a list of sales figures for different home computers** l'institut a publié une liste des statistiques de vente de plusieurs ordinateurs personnels

pull /pʊl/ *verb* (*to remove data from a stack*) extraire *vt*

pull-down menu /'pʊl daʊn ,menjuː/ *noun* menu *m* déroulant ◇ **the pull-down menu is viewed by clicking on the menu bar at the top of the screen** on affiche le menu déroulant en cliquant sur la barre de menu au sommet de l'écran

pulse /pʌls/ *noun* impulsion *f* ■ *verb* émettre des impulsions ◇ **pulse amplitude modulation (PAM)** modulation *f* d'impulsions en amplitude (MIA) ◇ **pulse code modulation (PCM)** modulation par impulsions et codage (MIC) ◇ **pulse duration modulation (PDM)** modulation d'impulsions en durée (MID) ◇ **pulse generator** générateur *m* d'impulsions ◇ **pulse modulation** modulation d'impulsion ◇ **pulse position modulation (PPM)** modulation d'impulsions en position (MIP) ◇ **pulse width modulation (PWM)** modulation d'impulsions en largeur *or* en durée (MIL *or* MID)

pulse-code modulation /,pʌls kəʊd ,mɒdjʊ'leɪʃ(ə)n/ *noun* modulation *f* par impulsions et codage (MIC)

pulse-dialling /'pʌls ,daɪəlɪŋ/ *noun* (*telephone dialling that sends a series of pulses*) composition *f* de numéro d'appel par impulsion; composition *f* au cadran (rotatif) ◇ **pulse-dialling takes longer to dial than the newer tone-dialling system** composer un numéro au cadran prend plus de temps que le nouveau système à touches

pulse stream /,pʌls 'striːm/ *noun* train *m* d'impulsions

pulse train /'pʌls treɪn/ *noun* train *m* d'impulsions

punch /pʌntʃ/ *noun* poinçon *m* ■ *verb* perforer *vt*

punch card /'pʌntʃ kɑːd/ *noun* (*punched card*) carte *f* perforée

punch-down block /ˌpʌntʃ daʊn 'blɒk/ *noun* (*device used to connect UTP cable*) bloc *m* d'enfichage

punched card /ˌpʌntʃt 'kɑːd/ *noun* (*punched card*) carte *f* perforée

punched card reader /ˌpʌntʃd 'kɑːd ˌriːdə/ *noun* lecteur *m* de cartes perforées

punched code /ˌpʌntʃd 'kəʊd/ *noun* code *m* de perforation

punched tag /ˌpʌntʃd 'tæg/ *noun* étiquette *f* perforée

punched tape[1] /ˌpʌntʃd 'teɪp/, **punched paper tape** /ˌpʌntʃɪd 'peɪpə teɪp/ *noun* bande *f* papier perforée

punched tape[2] /ˌpʌntʃd 'teɪp/ *noun* bande *f* perforée; bande *f* papier

punctuation mark /ˌpʌŋktʃu'eɪʃ(ə)n mɑːk/ *noun* signe *m* de ponctuation

pure code /ˌpjʊə 'kəʊd/ *noun* code *m* pur

purge /pɜːdʒ/ *verb* (*remove unnecessary data from a file*) vider *vt*; purger *vt* ◇ **each month, I purge the disk of all the old email messages** chaque mois, je purge le disque de tous les messages périmés

pushbutton /'pʊʃbʌt(ə)n/ *adjective* à *m* bouton-poussoir; (*on telephone*) à *f* touches

push-down list /ˌpʊʃdaʊn 'lɪst/, **push-down stack** /pʊʃ daʊn/ *noun* pile *f* inversée; en mode LIFO

push instruction /pʊʃ ɪn'strʌkʃən/, **push operation** /pʊʃ ˌɒpə'reɪʃ(ə)n/ *noun* **non-synchronous sound, non-sync sound** instruction *f* d'entrée dans la pile

push technology /'pʊʃ tekˌnɒlədʒi/ *noun* technologie *f* du pousser

push-up list /pʊʃ ʌp lɪst/, **push-up stack** /stæk/ *noun* pile *f* en file d'attente; pile *f* en mode FIFO

put /pʊt/ *verb* (*to place data onto a stack*) introduire *vt*; mettre des données dans la pile

Q

QAM *abbr* (*quadrature amplitude modulation*) modulation *f* d'amplitude en quadrature

QBE /ˌkjuː biː 'iː/ *noun* langage *m* QBE; langage *m* de requête

QISAM *noun* méthode *f* d'accès séquentiel indexé en file

QL *abbr* (*query language*) langage *m* d'interrogation

QOS *abbr* (*quality of service*) qualité *m* de service

QSAM /ˌkjuː es eɪ 'em/ *noun* méthode *f* d'accès séquentiel en file

quad /kwɒd/ *adjective* (*sheet of paper*) quadrat *m*

quadbit /'kwɒdbɪt/ *noun* (*four bits used by modems to increase transmission rates*) mot *m* de quatre bits

quad density /kwɒd 'densəti/ *noun* quadruple densité *f*

quadding /'kwɒdɪŋ/ *noun* (*insertion of spaces*) insertion *f* d'espaces

quadr- /kwɒdr/ *prefix* (*meaning four*) quadr-; tétra-

quadrature amplitude modulation /ˌkwɒdtrətʃə 'æmplɪtjuːd mɒdjuˌleɪʃ(ə)n/ *noun* (*data encoding method*) modulation *f* d'amplitude en quadrature (MAQ)

quadrature encoding /'kwɒdtrətʃə ɪn ˌkəʊdɪŋ/ *noun* (*determines the direction of a mouse*) encodage *m* en quadrature

quadruplex /'kwɒdrʊpleks/ *noun* (*four signals*) quadruplex *m*

quad-speed drive /ˌkwɒd spiːd 'draɪv/ *noun* lecteur *m* de disque quadruple vitesse

quality control /'kwɒlɪti kənˌtrəʊl/ *noun* contrôle *m* de qualité

quality of service /ˌkwɒlɪti əv 'sɜːvɪs/ *noun* qualité *f* de service

Quantel /'kwɒntel/ Quantel

quantifiable /'kwɒntɪfaɪəb(ə)l/ *adjective* quantifiable

quantifier /'kwɒntɪˌfaɪə/ *noun* quantificateur *m*

quantify /'kwɒntɪˌfaɪ/ *verb* quantifier *vt* ◇ **it is impossible to quantify the effect of the new computer system on our production** il est impossible de quantifier l'effet du nouveau système informatique sur notre production

quantisation, quantization *noun* quantification *f*

quantisation error /ˌkwɒn'teɪʃ(ə)n ˌerə/ *noun* erreur *f* de quantification

quantise, quantize *verb* (*to estimate*) quantifier *vt*

quantiser, quantizer *noun* quantificateur *m*

quantising noise /ˌkwɒntaɪzɪŋ 'nɔɪz/ *noun* bruits *mpl* de quantification

quantity /'kwɒntɪti/ *noun* (*amount*) quantité *f* ■ *adjective* (*large amount*) en grande quantité ◇ **he bought a large quantity of spare parts** il a acheté une grande quantité de pièces détachées

quantum /'kwɒntəm/ *noun* (*in communications: packet of data*) quantum *m*

quartz clock /ˌkwɔːts 'klɒk/, **quartz crystal clock** /ˌkwɔːts ˌkrɪstəl 'klɒk/ *noun* horloge *f* à quartz

quasi- /kweɪzaɪ/ *prefix* quasi-

quasi-instruction /ˌkweɪzaɪ ɪn'strʌkʃən/ *noun* label *m*

quaternary /'kwɔːtɜːnəri/ *adjective* quaternaire

quaternary level quantization /kwə ˌtɜːnəri ˌlev(ə)l ˌkwɒntaɪ'zeɪʃ(ə)n/ *noun* quantification *f* de niveau quatre

query by example /ˌkwɪəri baɪ ɪg'zɑːmpəl/ *noun* langage *m* QBE; langage *m* de requête

query facility /'kwɪəri fəˌsɪlɪti/ *noun* utilitaire *m* de requête; utilitaire *m* d'interrogation

query language /'kwɪəri ˌlæŋgwɪdʒ/ *noun* langage *m* de requête

query message /'kwɪəri ˌmesɪdʒ/ *noun* message *m* d'interrogation

query processing /'kwɪəri ˌprəʊsesɪŋ/ *noun* traitement *m* de requête

query window /'kwɪəri ˌwɪndəʊ/ *noun* fenêtre *f* d'interrogation

question mark /'kweʃtʃən mɑːk/ *noun* (*the character ?*) point *m* d'interrogation; (*often used as a wildcard*) joker *m*

queue /kjuː/ *noun* (*of data*) file *f* d'attente ■ *verb* placer *vt* ◇ **output devices such as laser printers are connected on-line with an automatic file queue** les périphériques tels que les imprimantes laser sont reliés en ligne et les fichiers sont gérés par un système de file d'attente automatique

queued access method /ˌkjuːd 'ækses ˌmeθəd/ *noun* méthode *f* de gestion de la file d'attente

queued indexed sequential access method /ˌkjuːd ˌɪndeksd sɪˌkwenʃəl 'ækses ˌmeθəd/ *noun* méthode *f* d'accès séquentiel indexé en file

queue discipline /kjuː 'dɪsəˌplɪn/ *noun* procédure *f* de file d'attente

queued sequential access method /ˌkjuːd sɪˌkwenʃəl 'ækses ˌmeθəd/ *noun* méthode *f* d'accès séquentiel en file

queue management /kjuː 'mænɪdʒmənt/, **queue manager** /kjuː 'mænɪdʒə/ *noun* gestion *f* de file d'attente ◇ **this is a new software spooler with built-in queue management** il s'agit d'un nouveau logiciel de spouling avec gestionnaire de file d'attente intégré

queuing time /'kjuːɪŋ taɪm/ *noun* temps *m* d'attente dans la file

QuickDraw /'kwɪkdrɔː/ (*Apple Macintosh graphics routines*) QuickDraw™

quicksort /'kwɪksɔːt/ *noun* tri *m* rapide

QuickTime /'kwɪktaɪm/ (*Apple Macintosh graphics routines*) QuickTime™

quiescent /kwi'es(ə)nt/ *adjective* (*process or circuit or device*) à l'état de repos; au repos

quintet /kwɪn'tet/ *noun* (*five bits*) quintet *m*

quit /kwɪt/ *verb* (*system or program*) quitter *vt*; abandonner *vt* ◇ **do not forget to save your text before you quit the system** n'oubliez pas de sauvegarder votre texte avant de quitter le système

quotation /kwəʊ'teɪʃ(ə)n/ *noun* (*text borrowed from another text*) citation *f*

quotation marks /kwəʊ'teɪʃ(ə)n mɑːks/ *noun* (*inverted commas*) guillemets *mpl*

quote /kwəʊt/ *verb* citer *vt*; mentionner *vt*; rappeler *vt* ◇ **he quoted figures from the newspaper report** il a cité des chiffres mentionnés dans le journal ◇ **in reply please quote this number** veuillez rappeler ce numéro de référence dans votre réponse ◇ **when making a complaint please quote the batch number printed on the computer case** en cas de réclamation, mentionnez toujours le numéro de lot qui apparaît sur le boîtier de l'ordinateur

quotes /kwəʊts/ *plural noun informal* guillemets *mpl*

quotient /'kwəʊʃ(ə)nt/ *noun* quotient *m*

quoting /'kwəʊtɪŋ/ *noun* action *f* d'inclure le message d'origine

QWERTY keyboard /ˌkwɜːti 'kiːbɔːd/ *noun* (*standard English language key layout*) clavier *m* QWERTY

R

race /reɪs/ *noun* (*error condition in digital circuit*) pompage *m*

rack /ræk/ *noun* (*for electronic circuit boards and peripheral devices*) rack *m*; baie *f* avec guide-cartes ◇ **rack-mounted** (carte) montée dans un rack *or* dans une baie avec guide-cartes

rack mounted /ræk 'maʊntɪd/ *adjective* monté, -ée sur supports

radial transfer /ˌreɪdiəl 'trænsfɜː/ *noun* (*data transfer*) transfert *m* radial (de données/programmes)

radio button /'reɪdiəʊ ˌbʌt(ə)n/ *noun* (*in a GUI: circle displayed beside an option*) bouton *m* radio

radio frequency /'reɪdiəʊ ˌfriːkwənsi/ *noun* fréquence *f* radio; radiofréquence *f*

radix /'reɪdɪks/ *noun* (*of a number system*) base *f* de numération ◇ **the hexadecimal number has a radix of 16** le nombre hexadécimal est à base 16

radix complement /'reɪdɪks ˌkɒmplɪmənt/ *noun* complément *m* à la base

radix notation /'reɪdɪks nəʊˌteɪʃ(ə)n/ *noun* numération *f* à base

radix point /'reɪdɪks pɔɪnt/ *noun* virgule *f*

ragged left /'rægɪd left/ *noun* non justifié à gauche

ragged right /'rægɪd raɪt/ *noun* non justifié à droite

ragged text /'rægɪd tekst/ *noun* texte *m* non justifié

RAID /reɪd/ *noun* système *m* de stockage rapide sur disques multiples (RAID)

> 'A Japanese investor group led by system distributor Technography has pumped $4.2 million (#2.8 million) into US disk manufacturer Storage Computer to help with the development costs of RAID 7 hard disk technology.' [*Computing*]

RAM /ræm/ *noun* (*memory*) mémoire *f* vive; mémoire *f* RAM; mémoire *f* à accès direct; mémoire *f* aléatoire ◇ **you can increase the printer's memory by plugging in another RAM cartridge** vous pouvez augmenter la mémoire de l'imprimante en enfichant une cartouche RAM supplémentaire

> 'The HP Enterprise Desktops have hard-disk capacities of between 260Mb and 1Gb, with RAM ranging from 16Mb up to 128Mb.' [*Computing*]

> '...fast memory is RAM that does not have to share bus access with the chip that manages the video display' [*Byte*]

RAM cache /'ræm kæʃ/ *noun* mémoire *f* cache; antémémoire *f*

RAM card /'ræm kɑːd/ *noun* carte *f* RAM

RAM cartridge /ræm 'kɑːtrɪdʒ/ *noun* cartouche *f* RAM ◇ **you can increase the printer's memory by plugging in another RAM cartridge** vous pouvez augmenter la mémoire de l'imprimante en enfichant une cartouche RAM supplémentaire

RAM chip /'ræm tʃɪp/ *noun* puce *f* RAM

RAMDAC /'ræmdæk/ *noun* DAC RAM

RAM disk /'ræm dɪsk/ *noun* disque *m* RAM; disque *m* mémoire

RAM loader /'ræm ˌləʊdə/ *noun* chargeur *m*

RAM refresh /ræm rɪ'freʃ/ *noun* rafraîchissement *m* de la mémoire RAM

RAM refresh rate /ˌræm rɪ'freʃ ˌreɪt/ *noun* fréquence *f* de rafraîchissement de la mémoire RAM

RAM resident program /ˌræm ˌrezɪd(ə)nt 'prəʊgræm/ *noun* programme *m* résident; TSR ◇ **when you hit Ctrl-F5, you will activate the RAM resident program and it will display your day's diary** en appuyant sur les touches Ctrl-F5, vous activez le programme résident et ouvrez l'agenda de la journée

R & D /ˌɑːr ən 'diː/ *noun* recherche *f* et développement

R & D department /ˌɑːr ən 'diː dɪˌpɑːtmənt/ *noun* service *m* de recherche et développement; service *m* R et D

random access /ˌrændəm 'ækses/ *noun* (*memory locations*) accès *m* aléatoire; accès *m* direct; accès *m* sélectif

random access device /ˌrændəm 'ækses dɪˌvaɪs/ *noun* mémoire *f* à accès aléatoire; mémoire *f* à accès direct

random access digital to analog converter /ˌrændəm ˌækses ˌdɪdʒɪt(ə)l tə ˌænəlɒg kən'vɜːtə/ *noun* convertisseur *m* numérique-analogique à accès aléatoire

random access files /ˌrændəm 'ækses ˌfaɪlz/ *noun* fichiers *mpl* à accès aléatoire

random access memory /ˌrændəm 'ækses ˌmem(ə)ri/ *noun* (*memory*) mémoire *f* vive; mémoire *f* à accès aléatoire; mémoire *f* RAM

random access storage /ˌrændəm 'ækses ˌstɔːrɪdʒ/ *noun* mémoire *f* à accès aléatoire; mémoire *f* à accès direct; mémoire *f* à accès sélectif

random number /ˌrændəm 'nʌmbə/ *noun* nombre *m* aléatoire; nombre *m* choisi au hasard

random number generation /ˌrændəm 'nʌmbə ˌdʒenəreɪʃ(ə)n/ *noun* génération *f* de nombres aléatoires

random number generator /ˌrændəm 'nʌmbə ˌdʒenəreɪtə/ *noun* générateur *m* de nombres aléatoires

random process /ˌrændəm 'prəʊses/ *noun* (*system*) procédé *m* aléatoire

random processing /ˌrændəm 'prəʊsesɪŋ/ *noun* traitement *m* aléatoire; traitement *m* direct

range /reɪndʒ/ *noun* **1.** (*reach*) portée *f*; étendue *f* **2.** (*set of values*) gamme *f*; fourchette *f* ■ *verb* **1.** (*to vary*) varier *vti*; s'étendre *vr*; aller (de ... à) **2.** (*text*) aligner *vt*; justifier *vt* ◇ **frequency range** gamme de fréquences ◇ **the company's products range from a cheap lapheld micro to a multistation mainframe** la gamme des produits de la société va du micro portatif au gros ordinateur multiposte ◇ **the telephone channel can accept signals in the frequency range 300 – 3400Hz** la transmission par téléphone accepte des signaux dans la gamme de fréquences 300 à 3400 Hz

range left /'reɪndʒ left/ *noun* aligner à gauche

rank /ræŋk/ *verb* classer par rang; classer par ordre d'importance

rapid access /ˌræpɪd 'ækses/ *noun* accès *m* rapide

rapid access memory /ˌræpɪd ˌækses 'mem(ə)ri/ *noun* mémoire *f* à accès rapide

raster /'ræstə/ *noun* raster *m* ◇ **raster image processor (RIP)** raster (RIP) *or* processeur *m* graphique à balayage de trame *or* processeur d'image matricielle

raster graphics /'ræstə ˌgræfɪks/ *plural noun* infographie *fpl*

raster image processor /ˌræstə 'ɪmɪdʒ ˌprəʊsesə/ *noun* raster *m* (RIP); graphisme *m* par balayage de trame ◇ **an electronic page can be converted to a printer-readable video image by an on-board raster image processor** une page électronique peut être convertie en image vidéo imprimable à l'aide d'un raster *or* d'un processeur d'image matricielle

raster scan /'ræstə skæn/ *noun* passe *f* de balayage

rate /reɪt/ *noun* (*ratio*) taux *m*; (*speed*) vitesse *f* ◇ **the processor's instruction execution rate is better than the older version** la vitesse d'exécution des commandes de ce processeur est plus grande qu'avec l'ancienne version

rated throughput /ˌreɪtɪd 'θruːpʊt/ *noun* (*maximum throughput of a device*) rendement *m* estimé

rate of production /ˌreɪt əv prə'dʌkʃən/ *noun* rythme *m* de la production

ratio /'reɪʃiəʊ/ *noun* (*proportion*) ratio *m*; (*coefficient*) rapport *m*; (*proportion*) taux *m* d'erreur résiduel ◇ **the ratio of 10 to 5 is 2:1** le rapport 10 sur 5 est (égal à) 2:1 ◇ **the ratio of corrupt bits per transmitted message is falling with new technology** le taux des bits corrompus par message transmis est moins élevé grâce aux nouvelles technologies

rational number /ˌræʃ(ə)nəl 'nʌmbə/ *noun* nombre *m* rationnel

raw data /ˌrɔː 'deɪtə/ *noun* **1.** (*not in computer system*) données *fpl* brutes **2.** (*needing to be processed*) données *fpl* brutes **3.** (*unprocessed*) données *fpl* non traitées

raw mode /ˌrɔː 'məʊd/ *noun* mode *m* brut; mode *m* direct

ray tracing /reɪ 'treɪsɪŋ/ *noun* tracé *m* filaire

RD /ˌɑː 'diː/ *noun* commande *f* RD

RDBMS *abbr* (*relational database management system*) système *m* de gestion de base de données relationnelle

react /ri'ækt/ *verb* réagir *vi* ◇ **to react to something** réagir à quelque chose

reaction time /ri'ækʃən taɪm/ *noun* temps *m* d'accès

reactive mode /ri'æktɪv məʊd/ *noun* mode *m* réactif

read /riːd/ *verb* **1.** (*to retrieve data*) extraire *vt*; lire *vt* **2.** (*scan printed data*) lire *vt* ◇ **this instruction reads the first record of a file** cette instruction va lire le premier enregistrement du fichier

readable /'riːdəb(ə)l/ *adjective* qui peut être lu *or* -e ◇ **machine-readable** (*command or data*) (commande *or* donnée) en langage machine *or* directement exploitable ◇ **the electronic page is converted to a printer-readable video image** le texte électronique est converti en image vidéo qui peut être lue par l'imprimante

read back check /'riːd bæk ˌtʃek/ *noun* contrôle *m* par relecture

read cycle /riːd 'saɪk(ə)l/ *noun* cycle *m* de lecture

reader /'riːdə/ *noun* (*device*) lecteur *m*

reader level /'riːdə ˌlev(ə)l/ *noun* mode *m* lecture

read error /riːd 'erə/ *noun* erreur *f* de lecture

read head /ˌriːd 'hed/ *noun* tête *m* de lecture

read in /ˌriːd 'ɪn/ *verb* (*data transfer*) enregistrer *vt*; entrer *vi*; introduire *vt*

reading /'riːdɪŋ/ *noun* lecture *f* ◇ **optical reading** lecture optique

readme file /'riːdmi faɪl/ *noun* fichier *m* Lisez-moi

read only /'riːd ˌəʊnli/ *noun* mémoire *f* à lecture seule

read only attribute /ˌriːd 'əʊnli ˌætrɪbjuːt/ *noun* attribut *m* lecture seule

read only memory /ˌriːd ˌəʊnli 'mem(ə)ri/ *noun* mémoire *f* morte; mémoire *f* ROM

readout /'riːdaʊt/ *noun* affichage *m* ◇ **the clock has a digital readout** cette horloge a un affichage numérique

readout device /'riːdaʊt dɪˌvaɪs/ *noun* dispositif *m* d'affichage; dispositif *m* écran

read rate /ˌriːd 'reɪt/ *noun* vitesse *f* de lecture

read/write channel /ˌriːd 'raɪt ˌtʃæn(ə)l/ *noun* voie *f* de lecture/écriture

read/write cycle /ˌriːd 'raɪt ˌsaɪk(ə)l/ *noun* cycle *m* de lecture/écriture

read/write head /ˌriːd 'raɪt hed/ *noun* tête *f* de lecture/écriture

read/write memory /ˌriːd ˌraɪt 'mem(ə)ri/ *noun* mémoire *f* lecture/écriture

ready /'redi/ *adjective* prêt *or* -e ◇ **the green light indicates the system is ready for another program** le voyant vert allumé signifie que le système est prêt à accepter le programme suivant

ready state /'redi steɪt/ *noun* état *m* prêt

Real /rɪəl/ (*trade name for a system used to transmit sound and video over the Internet*) Real

real address /rɪəl ə'dres/ *noun* adresse *f* absolue; adresse *f* réelle; adresse *f* machine

RealAudio /ˌrɪəl'ɔːdiəʊ/ (*trade name for a system used to transmit sound over the Internet*) RealAudio

real memory /rɪəl 'mem(ə)ri/ *noun* mémoire *f* réelle

RealNames /ˌrɪəl'neɪmz/ RealNames

real number /rɪəl 'nʌmbə/ *noun* nombre *m* réel

real time /'rɪəl taɪm/ *noun* temps *m* réel ◇ **a navigation system needs to be able to process the position of a ship in real time and take suitable action before she hits a rock** un système de navigation doit pouvoir faire le point en temps réel et prendre les mesures nécessaires pour éviter de heurter un écueil ◇ **in real time** en temps réel; en direct ◇ **program shown in real time** émission *f* en direct ◇ **real time execution (RTE)** exécution *f* (d'un programme) en temps réel

'Quotron provides real-time quotes, news and analysis on equity securities through a network of 40,000 terminals to US brokers and investors.' [*Computing*]

'…define a real-time system as any system which is expected to interact with its environment within certain timing constraints' [*British Telecom Technology Journal*]

real-time animation /ˌrɪəl taɪm ˌænɪ'meɪʃ(ə)n/ *noun* animation *f* en temps réel

real-time authorisation /ˌrɪəl taɪm ˌɔːθəraɪ'zeɪʃ(ə)n/, **real-time authentication** /ˌrɪəl taɪm ˌɔːθentɪ'keɪʃ(ə)n/ *noun* autorisation *f* en temps réel

real-time clock /ˌrɪəl taɪm 'klɒk/ *noun* horloge *f* en temps réel

real-time input /ˌrɪəl taɪm 'ɪnpʊt/ *noun* entrée *f* en temps réel

real-time multi-tasking /ˌrɪəl taɪm 'mʌlti ˌtɑːskɪŋ/ *noun* traitement *m* multitâche en temps réel

real-time operating system /ˌrɪəl taɪm 'ɒpəreɪtɪŋ ˌsɪstəm/ *noun* système *m* d'exploitation en temps réel

real-time processing /ˌrɪəl taɪm 'prəʊsesɪŋ/ *noun* traitement *m* en temps réel

real-time simulation /ˌrɪəl taɪm ˌsɪmjʊ'leɪʃ(ə)n/ *noun* simulation *f* en temps réel

real-time system /'rɪəl taɪm ˌsɪstəm/ *noun* système *m* en temps réel ◇ **in a real-time system, as you move the joystick left, the image on the screen moves left. If there is a pause for processing it is not a true real-time system** dans un système en temps réel, le déplacement de l'image vers la gauche est parfaitement synchronisé au mouvement du manche à balai vers la gauche; s'il se produit un délai de traitement entre l'action et le résultat, il ne s'agit pas d'un véritable système en temps réel

real time transport protocol /ˌrɪəl taɪm 'trænspɔːt ˌprəʊtəkɒl/ *noun* protocole *m* de transmission en temps réel

real-time video /ˌrɪəl taɪm 'vɪdiəʊ/ *noun* vidéo *f* en temps réel

reboot /riː'buːt/ *verb* relancer *vt* ◇ **we rebooted and the files reappeared** nous avons relancé le système et les fichiers sont réapparus sur l'écran

recall /rɪ'kɔːl/ *noun* rappel *m* ■ *verb* rappeler *vt*

receipt notification /rɪ'siːt ˌnəʊtɪfɪkeɪʃ(ə)n/ *noun* (*use in email applications to confirm that the recipient has received the message*) avis *m* de réception; (*of electronic mail applications – to confirm that the recipient has received the message*) accusé *m* de réception

receive /rɪ'siːv/ *verb* recevoir *vt*

receive only /rɪˌsiːv 'əʊnli/ *noun* terminal *m* d'arrivée

receiver /rɪ'siːvə/ *noun* récepteur *m* ◇ **radio receiver** récepteur radio ◇ **the radio receiver picked up your signal very strongly** votre signal a été capté très clairement par le récepteur radio

receiver register /rɪ'siːvə ˌredʒɪstə/ *noun* registre *m* des entrées

re-chargeable battery /riː ˌtʃɑːdʒəb(ə)l 'bæt(ə)ri/ *noun* pile *f*

recode /riː'kəʊd/ *verb* modifier les codes d'un programme

recognisable /'rekəgnaɪzəb(ə)l/, **recognizable** *adjective* reconnaissable

recognise /'rekəg,naɪz/, **recognize** *verb* reconnaître *vt*

recognition /,rekəg'nɪʃ(ə)n/ *noun* reconnaissance *f*

recognition logic /,rekəg'nɪʃ(ə)n ,lɒdʒɪk/ *noun* logique *f* de reconnaissance

recompile /,riːkəm'paɪl/ *verb* effectuer une nouvelle compilation

reconfiguration /,riːkənfɪgə'reɪʃ(ə)n/ *noun* reconfiguration *f*

reconfigure /,riːkən'fɪgə/ *verb* reconfigurer *vt* ◇ **I reconfigured the field structure in the file** j'ai reconfiguré la structure des champs du fichier ◇ **this program allows us to reconfigure the system to our own requirements** avec ce programme, il est possible de reconfigurer le système selon nos besoins

reconstitute /riː'kɒnstɪtjuːt/ *verb* (*after crash or corruption*) reconstituer *vt*; restaurer *vt*

record *noun* /'rekɔːd/ (*items of data*) article *m*; enregistrement *m* ■ *verb* /rɪ'kɔːd/ (*disk*) enregistrer *vt* ◇ **record changer** changeur *m* de disques automatique ◇ **records management** programme de gestion d'enregistrements *or* de fichiers ◇ **this record contains all their personal details** cet enregistrement contient toutes leurs coordonnées ◇ **your record contains several fields that have been grouped together under the one heading** votre article *or* enregistrement contient divers champs regroupés sous une même rubrique

recordable CD /rɪ,kɔːdəb(ə)l siː 'diː/ *noun* disque *m* compact enregistrable; disque *m* inscriptible

record button /rɪ'kɔːd ,bʌt(ə)n/ *noun* touche *f*

record count /'rekɔːd kaʊnt/ *noun* articles *mpl* dans un fichier; enregistrements *mpl* dans un fichier

recorder /rɪ'kɔːdə/ *noun* (*equipment*) enregistreur *m*

record format /'rekɔːd ,fɔːmæt/ *noun* format *m* d'enregistrements

record gap /'rekɔːd gæp/ *noun* intervalle *m* blanc entre deux enregistrements

record head /re'kɔːd ,hed/ *noun* tête *f* d'écriture; tête *f* d'enregistrement

recording /rɪ'kɔːdɪŋ/ *noun* (*process of storing signals, etc.*) enregistrement *m*

recording density /rɪ'kɔːdɪŋ ,densɪti/ *noun* densité *f* d'enregistrement

recording level /rɪ'kɔːdɪŋ ,lev(ə)l/ *noun* niveau *m* d'enregistrement

record layout /,rekɔːd 'leɪaʊt/ *noun* format *m*

record length /'rekɔːd leŋθ/ *noun* (*total number of characters*) longueur *f* d'un enregistrement; taille *f* d'un enregistrement

record locking /'rekɔːd lɒkɪŋ/ *noun* verrouillage *m* d'enregistrement

recordset /'rekɔːdset/ *noun* enregistrements *mpl* sélectionnés

records manager /'rekɔːdz ,mænɪdʒə/ *noun* (*program which maintains records*) gestionnaire *m* d'enregistrements

record structure /'rekɔːd ,strʌktʃə/ *noun* structure *f* d'un enregistrement

recover /rɪ'kʌvə/ *verb* retrouver *vt*; récupérer *vti*

recoverable error /rɪ,kʌv(ə)rəb(ə)l 'erə/ *noun* erreur *f* récupérable; erreur *f* réparable

recovery /rɪ'kʌv(ə)ri/ *noun* **1.** (*return to normal*) restauration *f*; remise *f* en état **2.** (*getting back something*) récupération *f* ◇ **the recovery of lost files can be carried out using a recovery procedure** les fichiers perdus peuvent être récupérés à l'aide d'une procédure de récupération de données

recovery procedure /rɪ'kʌv(ə)ri prə,siːdʒə/ *noun* procédure *f* de remise en marche après incident

recursion /rɪ'kɜːʒ(ə)n/ *noun* routine *f* récursive

recursive call /rɪ,kɜːsɪv 'kɔːl/ *noun* appel *m* récursif; procédure *f* récursive

recursive routine /rɪ,kɜːsɪv 'ruːtiːn/ *noun* récursivité *f*

Recycle Bin /riː'saɪk(ə)l bɪn/ *noun* (*icon displayed on a Desktop in the form of a wastepaper bin*) bac *m* de recyclage; (*icon displayed on the Windows 95 Desktop – like a wastepaper bin*) corbeille *f* ◇ **if you want to delete a file or folder, drag it onto the Recycle Bin icon or press the Delete key** pour détruire un fichier ou un dossier, traînez-le jusqu'à l'icône 'corbeille' ou encore appuyez sur la touche 'supprimer'

red, green, blue /,red griːn 'bluː/ *noun* RGB; rouge, vert, bleu

red book audio /,red bʊk 'ɔːdiəʊ/ *noun* CD *m* audio

redefinable /,riːdɪ'faɪnəb(ə)l/ *adjective* qui peut être redéfini *or* -e; reprogrammé *or* -ée; reprogrammable

redefine /,riːdɪ'faɪn/ *verb* (*to change the function or value*) redéfinir *vt*; définir de nouveau; reprogrammer *vt*; établir de nouveaux paramètres ◇ **I have redefined this key to display the figure five when pressed** j'ai reprogrammé cette touche pour obtenir un 5 ◇ **to redefine a key** redéfinir la fonction d'une touche *or* reprogrammer une touche ◇ **we redefined the initial parameters** nous avons redéfini les premiers paramètres

'…one especially useful command lets you redefine the printer's character-translation table' [*Byte*]

redirect /,riːdaɪ'rekt/ *verb* **1.** (*a message*) réacheminer *vt* **2.** (*to treat the output of one pro-*

gram as input for another program) réacheminer *vt*

redirection /ˌriːdaɪ'rekʃən/ *noun* (*message*) réacheminement *m*

redirect operator /ˌriːdaɪˌrekt ˌɒpə'reɪtə/, **redirection operator** /ˌriːdaɪˌrekʃən 'ɒpəreɪtə/ *noun* opérateur *m* de redirection (sous DOS); caractère *m* de redirection

redliner /'redlaɪnə/ *noun* (*highlights text in a different colour*) surligneur *m*

redo from start /ˌriːduː frəm 'stɑːt/ *verb* refaire depuis le début

reduce /rɪ'djuːs/ *verb* (*to convert data into a more compact form*) comprimer *vt*

reduced instruction set computer /rɪ ˌdjuːst ɪnˌstrʌkʃən set kəm'pjuːtə/ *noun* processeur *m* à jeu d'instructions réduit; processeur *m* à architecture RISC

redundancy /rɪ'dʌndənsi/ *noun* redondance *f*

redundancy checking /rɪ'dʌndənsi tʃekɪŋ/ *noun* contrôle *m* par redondance

redundant /rɪ'dʌndənt/ *adjective* (*data that can be removed without losing any information*) en trop; superflu *or* -e; redondant *or* -e; de redondance ◇ **the parity bits on the received data are redundant and can be removed** les bits de parité des données reçues sont redondants et peuvent être supprimés

redundant array of inexpensive disks /rɪ ˌdʌndənt əˌreɪ əv ˌɪnɪkspensɪv 'dɪsks/ *noun* système *m* de stockage rapide sur disques multiples (RAID)

redundant character /rɪˌdʌndənt 'kærɪktə/ *noun* caractère *m* de redondance

redundant code /rɪ'dʌndənt kəʊd/ *noun* code *m* de redondance

reel to reel /ˌriːl tə 'riːl/ *noun* copie *f* de bobine à bobine

reel to reel recorder /ˌriːl tə riːl rɪ'kɔːdə/ *noun* enregistreur *m* bobine à bobine

re-entrant program /riː ˌentrənt 'prəʊgræm/, **re-entrant code** /kəʊd/, **re-entrant routine** /ruː'tiːn/ *noun* programme *m* réentrant

re-entry /reɪ 'entri/ *noun* rentrée *f*

re-entry point /ˌriː 'entri ˌpɔɪnt/ *noun* (*point in a program or routine*) point *m* de rentrée

reference /'ref(ə)rəns/ *noun* **1.** (*value used as a starting point*) référence *f* **2.** (*mentioning something*) référence *f* ■ *verb* (*to access location*) référencer *vt* ◇ **reference level** (*of signal*) niveau *m* de référence

reference address /'ref(ə)rəns əˌdres/ *noun* adresse *f* de référence

reference file /'ref(ə)rəns faɪl/ *noun* fichier *m* de référence

reference instruction /'ref(ə)rəns ɪn ˌstrʌkʃən/ *noun* instruction *f* de base

reference list /'ref(ə)rəns lɪst/ *noun* liste *f* de référence

reference mark /'ref(ə)rəns mɑːk/ *noun* renvoi *m*

reference program table /ˌref(ə)rəns 'prəʊgræm ˌteɪb(ə)l/ *noun* table *f* de référence de programme

reference retrieval system /ˌref(ə)rəns rɪ 'triːv(ə)l ˌsɪstəm/ *noun* système *m* de référence

reference table /'ref(ə)rəns ˌteɪb(ə)l/ *noun* table *f*

reference time /'ref(ə)rəns taɪm/ *noun* période *f* de référence

reflectance /rɪ'flektəns/ *noun* réflectance *f*

reflected code /rɪ'flektd kəʊd/ *noun* code *m* réfléchi

reformat /ˌriː'fɔːmæt/ *verb* reformater *vt* ◇ **do not reformat your hard disk unless you can't do anything else** évitez de reformater votre disque dur à moins qu'il n'y ait aucune autre solution

reformatting /riː'fɔːmætɪŋ/ *noun* reformatage *m* ◇ **reformatting destroys all the data on a disk** toutes les données contenues sur un disque sont détruites par le reformatage

refraction /rɪ'frækʃən/ *noun* réfraction *f*

refresh /rɪ'freʃ/ *verb* (*to update a memory*) rafraîchir *vt*; régénérer *vt*; entretenir *vt* ◇ **memory refresh signal** signal *m* de rafraîchissement de la mémoire

refresh cycle /rɪ'freʃ ˌsaɪk(ə)l/ *noun* cycle *m*

refresh rate /rɪ'freʃ reɪt/ *noun* fréquence *f* de rafraîchissement

> 'Philips autoscan colour monitor, the 4CM6099, has SVGA refresh rates of 72Hz (800 x 600) and EVGA refresh rates of 70Hz (1,024 x 768).' [*Computing*]

regenerate /rɪ'dʒenəˌreɪt/ *verb* **1.** recréer *vt* **2.** (*to process distorted signals*) recréer *vt*; régénérer *vt*

regenerative memory /rɪˌdʒenərətɪv 'mem(ə)ri/ *noun* mémoire *f* qui demande à être rafraîchie ◇ **dynamic RAM is regenerative memory – it needs to be refreshed every 250ns** une RAM dynamique demande à être rafraîchie toutes les 250ns ◇ **the CRT display can be thought of as regenerative memory, it requires regular refresh picture scans to prevent flicker** l'écran peut être comparé à une mémoire qui demande à être rafraîchie, il doit être balayé régulièrement pour éviter de présenter des images instables

regenerative reading /rɪˌdʒenərətɪv 'riːdɪŋ/ *noun* lecture *f* régénératrice

regenerator /riː'dʒenəreɪtə/ *noun* (*device that regenerates a received signal*) régénérateur *m*; amplificateur *m* de signal

region /'riːdʒən/ *noun* (*area of memory or program*) zone *f*; région *f*

regional breakpoint /ˌriːdʒ(ə)nəl ˈbreɪkpɔɪnt/ *noun* point *m* d'arrêt variable

region fill /ˈriːdʒ(ə)n fɪl/ *noun* remplissage *m* de zone

register /ˈredʒɪstə/ *noun* **1.** (*for data*) registre *m* **2.** (*reserved memory location*) registre *m* ■ *verb* (*to react*) inscrire *vt*; (*to superimpose two images*) faire coïncider; positionner sur repères ◇ **external register** accumulateur *or* registre externe ◇ **index register** registre d'index ◇ **instruction address register (IAR)** registre d'adresse d'instruction ◇ **in this small micro, the data register is eight bits wide, an address register is sixteen bits wide** dans ce micro-ordinateur, la taille du registre de données est de huit bits, alors que celle d'un registre d'adresse est de 16 bits ◇ **memory address register (MAR)** registre d'adresse en mémoire ◇ **program status word register (PSW register)** registre des mots d'état ◇ **sequence control register (SCR)** registre d'instruction à suivre *or* à exécuter

register addressing /ˌredʒɪstə əˈdresɪŋ/ *noun* adressage *m* de registre

register file /ˈredʒɪstə faɪl/ *noun* fichier *m* des registres

register length /ˈredʒɪstə leŋθ/ *noun* (*number of bits*) dimension *f* d'un registre; taille *f* d'un registre

register map /ˈredʒɪstə mæp/ *noun* configuration *f* de registre; contenu *m* de registre

Registry /ˈredʒɪstri/ *noun* (*database that forms the basis of Windows*) base *f* de registre

regulate /ˈregjʊleɪt/ *verb* (*process*) contrôler *vt*; ajuster *vt*; régler *vt*; réguler *vt*

regulated power supply /ˌregjʊleɪtɪd ˈpaʊə səˌplaɪ/ *noun* courant *m* régulé; courant *m* contrôlé

rehyphenation /riːˌhaɪfəˈneɪʃ(ə)n/ *noun* remplacement *m* des traits d'union

rejection error /rɪˈdʒekʃən ˌerə/ *noun* erreur *f* de rejet; erreur *f* de refus

rekey /riːˈkiː/ *verb* recomposer *vt*

relational database /rɪˌleɪʃ(ə)n(ə)l ˈdeɪtəbeɪs/, **relational database management system** /rɪˌleɪʃn(ə)l ˌdeɪtəbeɪs ˌmænɪdʒmənt ˈsɪstəm/ *noun* base *f* de données relationnelle

relational operator /rɪˌleɪʃ(ə)n(ə)l ˈɒpəreɪtə/ *noun* opérateur *m* relationnel *or* logique

relational query /rɪˌleɪʃ(ə)n(ə)l ˈkwɪəri/ *noun* requête *f* relationnelle

relative address /ˌrelətɪv əˈdres/ *noun* adresse *f* relative

relative coding /ˈrelətɪv kɒdɪŋ/ *noun* codage *m* relatif

relative coordinates /ˌrelətɪv kəʊˈɔːdɪnəts/ *plural noun* coordonnées *Fpl* relatives

relative data /ˌrelətɪv ˈdeɪtə/ *noun* données *fpl* relatives

relative error /ˌrelətɪv ˈerə/ *noun* erreur *f* relative

relative pointing device /ˌrelətɪv ˈpɔɪntɪŋ dɪˌvaɪs/ *noun* dispositif *m* de pointage relatif; pointeur *m* relatif

relative-time clock /ˌrelətɪv taɪm ˈklɒk/ *noun* horloge *f* relative

relay /ˈriːleɪ/ *noun* (*switch*) relais *m* ■ *verb* retransmettre *vt* ◇ **all messages are relayed through this small micro** tous les messages sont retransmis par l'intermédiaire de ce petit micro ◇ **it is relay-rated at 5 Amps** il est protégé par un relais de 5A ◇ **microwave relay** relais hertzien ◇ **there is a relay in the circuit** le circuit comporte un relais

release /rɪˈliːs/ *noun* (*version of a product*) version *f* ■ *verb* **1.** (*new product*) mettre un nouveau produit sur le marché; lancer qc sur le marché; commercialiser *vt*; (*a new software version*) publier une nouvelle version; mise *f* à jour **2.** (*of software: relinquish control*) relâcher *vt*; libérer *vt* ◇ **the latest software is release 5** la nouvelle version du logiciel porte le numéro 5

release number /rɪˈliːs ˌnʌmbə/ *noun* numéro *m* de version

release rate /rɪˈliːs reɪt/ *noun* taux *m* d'émission

reliability /rɪˌlaɪəˈbɪlɪti/ *noun* fiabilité *f*; qualité *f* ◇ **it has an excellent reliability record** il est reconnu pour sa fiabilité ◇ **the product has passed its reliability tests** ce produit a réussi tous les tests de fiabilité

reliable /rɪˈlaɪəb(ə)l/ *adjective* fiable; sur lequel on peut compter; auquel on peut se fier; qui donne satisfaction ◇ **the early versions of the software were not completely reliable** les premières versions du logiciel ne donnaient pas satisfaction

reliable connection /rɪˌlaɪəb(ə)l kəˈnekʃən/ *noun* connexion *f* fiable

reload /riːˈləʊd/ *verb* recharger *vt* ◇ **we reloaded the program after the crash** nous avons rechargé le programme après la panne

relocatable /ˌriːləʊˈkeɪtəb(ə)l/ *adjective* (*to another area of memory*) translatable; relogeable; réadressable ◇ **the operating system can load and run a relocatable program from any area of memory** le système d'exploitation peut charger et exécuter un programme translatable *or* relogeable sans distinction de la zone d'origine

relocatable program /ˌriːləʊkeɪtəb(ə)l ˈprəʊgræm/ *noun* programme *m* relogeable; programme *m* translatable ◇ **the operating system can load and run a relocatable program from any area of memory** le système d'exploitation peut charger et exécuter un programme translatable *or* relogeable sans distinction de la zone d'origine

relocate /ˌriːləʊˈkeɪt/ *verb* (*to move data*) reloger *vt*; déplacer *vt*; translater *vt*; changer d'adresse

◇ **the data is relocated during execution** cette donnée est déplacée au cours de l'éxécution

relocation /ˌriːləʊˈkeɪʃ(ə)n/ *noun* (*memory*) translation *f*; relogement *m*; déplacement *m*; réadressage *m*

relocation constant /ˌriːləʊˈkeɪʃ(ə)n ˌkɒnstənt/ *noun* constante *f* de réadressage

REM /rem/ *noun* déclaration *f* de remarque; REM

remainder /rɪˈmeɪndə/ *noun* (*in division*) reste *m* ◇ **7 divided by 3 is equal to 2 remainder 1** 7 divisé par 3 égale 2 reste 1

remark /rɪˈmɑːk/ *noun* (*statement ignored by the interpreter*) déclaration *f* de remarque

remedial maintenance /rɪˌmiːdiəl ˈmeɪntənəns/ *noun* (*repair*) maintenance *f* curative; maintenance *f* corrective; réparation *f*

remote /rɪˈməʊt/ *adjective* éloigné *or* -ée; à distance ◇ **remote job entry (RJE)** (système de) lancement *m* de tâches à distance ◇ **remote procedure call (RPC)** (*communication between two programs running on two connected computers*) appel *m* de procédure à distance *or* appel RPC ◇ **users can print reports on remote printers** les utilisateurs peuvent imprimer leurs rapports sur des imprimantes à distance

remote access /rɪˌməʊt ˈækses/ *noun* accès *m* à distance

remote client /rɪˌməʊt ˈklaɪənt/ *noun* utilisateur *m* distant

remote console /rɪˌməʊt ˈkɒnsəʊl/ *noun* console *f*

remote control /rɪˌməʊt kənˈtrəʊl/ *noun* (*of TV set*) télécommande *f*; (*allows a user to control a computer from a distance*) contrôle *m* à distance; (*control of a system from a distance*) pilotage *m* à distance

remote control software /rɪˌməʊt kənˈtrəʊl ˌsɒftweə/ *noun* logiciel *m* de prise de contrôle à distance; logiciel *m* de pilotage à distance ◇ **this remote control software will work with Windows and lets me operate my office PC from home over a modem link** ce logiciel de prise de contrôle à distance travaille sous Windows et me permet d'utiliser de chez moi le PC de mon bureau relié par modem

remote device /rɪˌməʊt dɪˈvaɪs/ *noun* console *f*

remote job entry /rɪˌməʊt dʒɒb ˈentri/ *noun* système *m* de lancement de tâches à distance

remote procedure call /rɪˌməʊt prəˈsiːdʒə ˌkɔːl/ *noun* appel *m* de procédure à distance; appel *m* RPC

remote station /rɪˌməʊt ˈsteɪʃ(ə)n/ *noun* poste *m* à distance; poste *m* éloigné

remote terminal /rɪˌməʊt ˈtɜːmɪn(ə)l/ *noun* terminal *m* à distance; terminal *m* éloigné

removable /rɪˈmuːvəb(ə)l/ *adjective* amovible ◇ **a removable hard disk** un disque dur amovible

removable Winchester disk /rɪˌmuːvəb(ə)l ˈɹɪntʃestə/ *noun* disque *m* Winchester amovible

remove directory /rɪˌmuːv daɪˈrekt(ə)ri/ *noun* commande *f* RD

REN /ren/ *noun* indice *m* d'équivalence de la sonnerie

rename /riːˈneɪm/ *verb* changer le nom ◇ **save the file and rename it CLIENT** sauvegarder le fichier mais changez-en le nom et appelez-le CLIENT

renumber /ˈriːnʌmbə/ *noun* (*line, etc.*) renumérotation *f*; (*page*) repagination *f*

reorganise /riːˈɔːgənaɪz/, **reorganize** *verb* réorganiser *vt* ◇ **wait while the spelling checker database is being reorganized** il faut attendre que la base de données du correcteur orthographique soit réorganisée

repaginate /riːˈpædʒɪneɪt/ *verb* (*to number pages*) repaginer *vt*; paginer de nouveau; refaire la pagination; (*to change the lengths of pages*) faire une nouvelle mise en pages ◇ **the text was repaginated with a new line width** la mise en page a été refaite avec une nouvelle largeur de ligne

repagination /riːˌpædʒɪˈneɪʃ(ə)n/ *noun* (*numbering*) repagination *f*; nouvelle pagination *f* ◇ **the dtp package allows simple repagination** le système de PAO permet de faire une simple repagination

repeat counter /rɪˌpiːt ˈkaʊntə/ *noun* compteur *m* de répétitions

repeater /rɪˈpiːtə/ *noun* (*device that repeats a signal*) répétiteur *m*; (*device that amplifies or regenerates a received signal*) répéteur *m*; amplificateur *m* intermédiaire ◇ **this cheap repeater does not regenerate the signals** ce répéteur bon marché ne régénère pas les signaux

repeating group /rɪˈpiːtɪŋ gruːp/ *noun* groupe *m* à répétition; groupe *m* de données qui se répètent de façon périodique

repeat key /rɪˈpiːt kiː/ *noun* touche *f* répétition

repeat rate /rɪˈpiːt reɪt/ *noun* cadence *f* de répétition d'un caractère

reperforator /riːˈpɜːfəreɪtə/ *noun* reperforatrice *f*

reperforator transmitter /riːˈpɜːfəreɪtə trænzˌmɪtə/ *noun* récepteur-performateur *m* transmetteur

repertoire /ˈrepəˌtwɑː/ *noun* répertoire *m* ◇ **the manual describes the full repertoire** le répertoire entier est inclus dans le manuel

repetitive letter /rɪˌpetətɪv ˈletə/ *noun* lettre *f* standard; lettre *f* type

repetitive strain injury /rɪˌpetɪtɪv ˈstreɪn ˌɪndʒəri/, **repetitive stress injury** /rɪˌpetɪtɪv stres 'ɪndʒəri/ *noun* micro-traumatismes *mpl* répétés

replace /rɪ'pleɪs/ *verb* **1.** (*instruction*) remplacer *vt* **2.** remplacer *vt*

replace mode /rɪ'pleɪs məʊd/ *noun* mode *m* remplacement

replay *noun* /'riːpleɪ/ (*data or music*) relecture *f* ■ *verb* /riː'pleɪ/ (*something which has been recorded*) faire jouer (une bande nouvellement enregistrée); rejouer une bande; faire passer; projeter *vt*; visionner *vt* ◇ **he replayed the tape** il a repassé la bande *or* il a remis la bande ◇ **she recorded the TV programme on video tape and replayed it the next evening** elle a enregistré le programme de télévision sur une bande vidéo et l'a visionné le lendemain soir

replenish /rɪ'plenɪʃ/ *verb* (*a battery*) recharger *vt*

replication /ˌreplɪ'keɪʃ(ə)n/ *noun* **1.** (*copying a record*) duplication *f*; (*copy*) double *m*; copie *f* **2.** duplication *f*

reply /rɪ'plaɪ/ *verb* (*to a letter or e-mail*) répondre à un message électronique

report generator /rɪˌpɔːt 'dʒenəreɪtə/ *noun* (*software*) générateur *m* de rapport

report program generator /rɪ'pɔːt ˌprəʊgræm ˌdʒenəreɪtə/ *noun* générateur *m* de programme d'édition de rapport

reproduce /ˌriːprə'djuːs/ *verb* reproduire *vt*

reprogram /riː'prəʊgræm/ *verb* reprogrammer *vt*; programmer de nouveau

request for comment /rɪˌkwest fə 'kɒment/ *noun* document *m* RFC

request to send /rɪˌkwest tə 'send/ *noun* signal *m* de demande de transmission

request to send signal /rɪˌkwest tə 'send ˌsɪgn(ə)l/ *noun* signal *m* de demande de transmission

requirements /rɪ'kwaɪəmənts/ *plural noun* besoins *mpl*; exigences *f*

re-route /riː ruːt/ *verb* (*to send something by a different route*) réacheminer *vt* ◇ **the call diverter re-routes a call** le dispositif de transfert d'appel sert à réacheminer les appels

rerun /ˌriː'rʌn/ *verb* (*to redo a program or printing job*) recommencer *vt*; reprendre l'exécution

rerun point /'riːˌrʌn pɔɪnt/ *noun* point *m* de reprise

res /rez/ *noun* résolution *f*

resave /riː'seɪv/ *verb* sauvegarder de nouveau ◇ **it automatically resaves the text** cela permet de sauvegarder le texte de nouveau automatiquement

rescue dump /'reskjuː dʌmp/ *noun* vidage *m* de sauvegarde

research /rɪ'sɜːtʃ/ *noun* recherche *f* ◇ **research and development (R & D)** recherche et développement ◇ **the company has spent millions of dollars on R & D** la société a dépensé des millions de dollars pour la recherche et le développement

research and development /rɪˌsɜːtʃ ən dɪ 'veləpmənt/ *noun* recherche *f* et développement

reserved character /rɪˌzɜːvd 'kærɪktə/ *noun* (*special character used by the operating system*) caractère *m* réservé

reserved sector /rɪˌzɜːvd 'sektə/ *noun* secteur *m* réservé

reserved word /rɪ'zɜːvd wɜːd/ *noun* mot *m* réservé

reset /ˌriː'set/ *verb* **1.** ré-initialiser *vt* **2.** (*register or counter*) remettre à zéro

reset button /ˌriːˌset 'bʌt(ə)n/, **reset key** /ˌriː 'set kiː/ *noun* bouton *m* de ré-initialisation

reshape handle /'riːʃeɪp ˌhænd(ə)l/ *noun* recadrage *m*

resident /'rezɪd(ə)nt/ *adjective* (*data or program*) résident *or* -e ◇ **resident font** (*font data always present in a printer*) police (de caractères) *or* fonte résidente ◇ **terminate and stay resident software (TSR)** (*program started from the command line*) programme résident *or* TSR

resident engineer /ˌrezɪd(ə)nt ˌendʒɪ'nɪə/ *noun* ingénieur *m* de l'entreprise

resident fonts /ˌrezɪd(ə)nt 'fɒntz/ *plural noun* polices *fpl* de caractères; fontes *fpl* résidentes

resident software /ˌrezɪd(ə)nt 'sɒftweə/ *noun* logiciel *m* résident

residual /rɪ'zɪdjuəl/ *adjective* résiduel *or* -elle

residual error rate /rɪˌzɪdjuəl 'erə ˌreɪt/ *noun* taux *m* d'erreur résiduel

residue check /'rezɪˌdjuː tʃek/ *noun* contrôle *m* sur reste

resist /rɪ'zɪst/ *noun* (*substance not affected by etching chemicals*) substance *f* résistante

resolution /ˌrezə'luːʃ(ə)n/ *noun* (*number of pixels*) définition *f*; résolution *f* ◇ **high resolution (hi-res)** haute définition ◇ **image resolution** (*of web camera*) définition de l'image ◇ **optical resolution** (*of scanner*) résolution optique ◇ **the high resolution screen can display 640 by 450 pixels** avec un écran haute définition on obtient un affichage de 640 par 450 pixels ◇ **the resolution of most personal computer screens is 72 dpi (dots per inch)** la plupart des écrans d'ordinateurs individuels ont une résolution de 72 ppp (points par pouce)

> 'Group IV fax devices can send a grey or colour A4 page in about four seconds, at a maximum resolution of 15.7 lines per millimetre over an Integrated Services Digital Network circuit.' [*Computing*]

resolving power /rɪ'zɒlvɪŋ ˌpaʊə/ *noun* (*of an optical system*) pouvoir *m* de résolution

resonance /'rez(ə)nəns/ *noun* résonance *f*

resource /rɪ'zɔːs/ *noun* ressource *f*

resource allocation /rɪ'zɔːs ˌæləkeɪʃ(ə)n/ *noun* allocation *f* de ressources

resource fork /rɪ'zɔːs fɔːk/ *noun* fourche *f* de ressources

resource sharing /rɪ'zɔːs ˌʃeərɪŋ/ *noun* (*in a network*) partage *m* de ressources

response frame /rɪ'spɒns freɪm/ *noun* cadre-réponse *m*

response position /rɪ'spɒns pəˌzɪʃ(ə)n/ *noun* emplacement *m*

response time /rɪ'spɒns taɪm/ *noun* temps *m* de réponse

restart /rɪ'stɑːt/ *verb* redémarrer *vi*; relancer *vt*; remettre en marche ■ *noun* remise *f* en marche; redémarrage *m*; relance *f*

restore /rɪ'stɔː/ *verb* restaurer *vt*; remettre en bon état; récupérer *vti*

'...first you have to restore the directory that contains the list of deleted files' [*Personal Computer World*]

restrict /rɪ'strɪkt/ *verb* **1.** limiter l'accès; limiter l'utilisation de qc; imposer une contrainte à quelque chose **2.** limiter l'accès; limiter l'utilisation de qc ◇ **the document is restricted, and cannot be placed on open access** ce document de diffusion restreinte ne doit pas être rendu public

restriction /rɪ'strɪkʃ(ə)n/ *noun* (*data flow or access*) restriction *f*; limite *f* limite *fr* l'utilisation (de quelque chose); contrainte *f*

result /rɪ'zʌlt/ *noun* résultat *m*

result code /rɪ'zʌlt kəʊd/ *noun* (*indicates the state of a modem*) code *m* résultat

resume /rɪ'zjuːm/ *verb* (*to restart*) continuer *vt*; repartir *vi*; reprendre *vt*

retrain /ˌriː'treɪn/ *verb* (*re-establish a better quality connection*) recycler *vt*; rafraîchir une connexion

retrieval /rɪ'triːv(ə)l/ *noun* recherche *f*; extraction *f*

retrieve /rɪ'triːv/ *verb* extraire *vt*; récupérer *vti* ◇ **these are the records retrieved in that search** voici les informations extraites au cours de cette recherche ◇ **this command will retrieve all names beginning with S** on utilise cette commande pour extraire la liste de tous les noms qui commencent par S

retro- /retrəʊ/ *prefix* rétro-

retrofit /'retrəʊˌfɪt/ *noun* dispositif *m* d'actualisation

retrospective parallel running /ˌretrəʊspektɪv 'pærəlel ˌrʌnɪŋ/ *noun* test *m* rétrospectif en parallèle

retrospective search /ˌretrəʊspektɪv 'sɜːtʃ/ *noun* recherche *f* rétrospective

return /rɪ'tɜːn/ *noun* **1.** (*instruction*) retour *m* **2.** (*key on a keyboard*) touche *f* entrée **3.** (*at end of line*) symbole de fin *f* de ligne ◇ **carriage return (CR)** (*code or key*) (code *or* touche de) retour (du) chariot *or* retour à la ligne

return address /rɪ'tɜːn əˌdres/ *noun* adresse *f* de retour

return to zero signal /rɪˌtɜːn tə 'zɪərəʊ ˌsɪgn(ə)l/ *noun* signal *m* de remise à zéro; signal *m* de ré-initialisation

reveal /rɪ'viːl/ *verb* révéler *vt*; mettre à jour; faire apparaître

reverb, reverberation *noun* réverbération *f*

reverse /rɪ'vɜːs/ *adjective* (*opposite to usual*) inversé *or* -ée ■ *verb* **1.** (*with movement*) faire marche arrière; inverser *vt* **2.** (*of data*) inverser *vt* ◇ **normal notation: (x-y) + z, but using RPN: xy – z+** alors que la notation conventionnelle s'écrit: (x-y) + z, la notation polonaise inversée s'écrit: xy – z+ ◇ **reverse Polish notation (RPN)** notation *f* polonaise inversée ◇ **three plus four, minus two is written in RPN as 3 4 + 2 – = 5** suivant la notation polonaise inversée, trois plus quatre moins deux s'écrit 3 4 + 2 – = 5

'...the options are listed on the left side of the screen, with active options shown at the top left in reverse video' [*PC User*]

reverse channel /rɪˌvɜːs 'tʃæn(ə)l/ *noun* canal *m* de retour

reverse characters /rɪˌvɜːs 'kærɪktəz/ *plural noun* caractères *mpl* inversés

reverse engineering /rɪˌvɜːs ˌendʒɪ'nɪərɪŋ/ *noun* rétro-ingénierie *f*

reverse index /rɪˌvɜːs 'ɪndeks/ *noun* index *m* inversé

reverse interrupt /rɪˌvɜːs 'ɪntərʌpt/ *noun* interruption *f* d'inversion

reverse polarity /rɪˌvɜːs pəʊ'lærɪti/ *noun* (*in an electric or electronic circuit*) polarité *f* inversée

reverse Polish notation /rɪˌvɜːs ˌpəʊlɪʃ nəʊ'teɪʃ(ə)n/ *noun* notation *f* polonaise inversée

reverse video /rɪˌvɜːs 'vɪdiəʊ/ *noun* vidéo *f* inversée

revert command /rɪ'vɜːt kəˌmɑːnd/ *noun* commande *f* de retour à la situation de départ

revise /rɪ'vaɪz/ *verb* (*document or file*) revoir *vt*; réviser *vt*

rewind /ˌriː'waɪnd/ *verb* rembobiner *vt* ◇ **the tape rewinds onto the spool automatically** le film s'enroule automatiquement sur la bobine

RF, R/F *noun* (*electromagnetic spectrum*) fréquence *f* radio; radiofréquence *f*

RFC /ˌɑː ef 'siː/ *noun* document *m* RFC

RF shielding /ˌɑː ef 'ʃiːldɪŋ/ *noun* blindage *m*

RGB /ˌɑː dʒiː 'biː/ *noun* (*producing colours by mixing three primary colours red, green and blue*) RVB (rouge, vert, bleu)

RGB display /ˌɑː dʒiː ˌbiː dɪ'spleɪ/, **RGB monitor** /'mɒnɪtə/ *noun* écran *m* RVB

ribbon cable /'rɪbən ˌkeɪb(ə)l/ *noun* câble *m* ruban; câble *m* plat; nappe *f*

rich text /ˌrɪtʃ 'tekst/ *noun* format *m* RTF

rich text format /ˌrɪtʃ 'tekst ˌfɔːmæt/ *noun* (*way of storing a document with all the commands for page, type, font and formatting*) format *m* RTF

RIFF /rɪf/ *noun* format *m* RIFF

RIFF file /'rɪf faɪl/ *noun* fichier *m* RIFF

right-click /ˌraɪt 'klɪk/ *verb* cliquer sur le bouton droit de la souris

right-click menu /ˌraɪt 'klɪk ˌmenjuː/ *noun* (*small pop-up menu that appears when you click on the right button of a two-button mouse*) menu *m* contextuel

right-hand button /ˌraɪt hænd 'bʌt(ə)n/ *noun* bouton *m* droit

right justification /raɪt ˌdʒʌstɪfɪ'keɪʃ(ə)n/ *noun* justification *f* à droite

right justify /raɪt 'dʒʌstɪˌfaɪ/ *verb* (*printing*) justifier à droite

right shift /ˌraɪt 'ʃɪft/ *noun* (*maths*) effectuer un décalage vers la droite

rightsizing /'raɪt ˌsaɪzɪŋ/ *noun* (*changing a company's IT structure to a new hardware platform*) mise *f* à la bonne échelle d'un système informatique

rigid disk /'rɪdʒɪd dɪsk/ *noun* disque *m* dur

ring /rɪŋ/ *noun* **1.** (*data list whose last entry points back to the first entry*) liste *f* circulaire **2.** (*network topology*) anneau *m*

ring back system /'rɪŋ bæk ˌsɪstəm/ *noun* système *m* de rappel automatique

ringer equivalence number /ˌrɪŋər ɪ 'kwɪvələns ˌnʌmbə/ *noun* indice *m* d'équivalence de la sonnerie

ring shift /ˌrɪŋ 'ʃɪft/ *noun* (*data movement*) permutation *f*; décalage *m* circulaire

ring topology /'rɪŋ təˌpɒlədʒi/ *noun* topologie *f* ◇ **token ring uses a ring topology** le réseau à jeton *or* token ring utilise une topologie en anneau

ring topology network /rɪŋ təˌpɒlədʒi 'netwɜːk/ *noun* réseau *m* en anneau

RIP *abbr* **1.** (*raster image processor*) processeur *m* d'image tramée **2.** (*routing information protocol*) protocole *m* RIP

ripple-through carry /'rɪp(ə)l θruː ˌkæri/ *noun* (*mathematical operations*) report *m* simultané

ripple-through effect /'rɪp(ə)l θruː ɪˌfekt/ *noun* (*changes in a spreadsheet when the value in one cell is changed*) effet *m* de cascade; mise *f* à jour en cascade

RISC /ˌɑː aɪ es 'siː/ *noun* processeur *m* à jeu d'instruction réduit; processeur *m* à architecture RISC

Rivest, Shamir, Adleman /ˌrɪvest ʃəˌmɪə 'æd(ə)lmən/ *noun* système *m* RSA

RJ-11 /ˌɑː dʒeɪ ɪ'lev(ə)n/ *noun* (*standard four-wire modular connector*) connecteur *m* RJ11

RJ-45 /ˌɑː dʒeɪ ˌfɔːti 'faɪv/ *noun* (*modular connector*) connecteur *m* de réseau RJ45

RJE /ˌɑː dʒeɪ 'iː/ *noun* système *m* de lancement de tâches à distance

RLE /ˌɑː el 'iː/ *noun* RLE

RLL encoding /ˌɑː el el ɪn'kəʊdɪŋ/ *noun* encodage *m* RLE

rm /ˌɑː 'em/ *noun* (*UNIX command*) commande *f* rm

RMDIR *abbr* (*remove directory*) RD; Remove Directory (pour supprimer un répertoire sous DOS)

RO /ˌɑː 'əʊ/ *noun* terminal *m* d'arrivée

roam /rəʊm/ *verb* (*in wireless communications*) se déplacer sans quitter le secteur

robot /'rəʊˌbɒt/ *noun* robot *m*

robotics /rəʊ'bɒtɪks/ *noun* robotique *f*

robust /rəʊ'bʌst/ *adjective* (*system*) robuste ◇ **this hard disk is not very robust** ce disque dur n'est pas très robuste

robustness /rəʊ'bʌstnəs/ *noun* (*strength of a casing*) robustesse *f*; solidité *f*

rogue indicator /rəʊg 'ɪndɪˌkeɪtə/ *noun* indicateur *m* de contrôle spécial

rogue value /ˌrəʊg 'væljuː/ *noun* (*terminator*) indicateur *m*; marqueur *m* de fin de liste

role indicator /rəʊl 'ɪndɪˌkeɪtə/ *noun* indicateur *m* de fonction

roll back /'rəʊl bæk/ *noun* rechargement *m* d'un programme

rollback *noun* rechargement *m* d'un programme

roll forward /rəʊl 'fɔːwəd/ *verb* restauration *f* par progression

roll in /ˌrəʊl 'ɪn/ *verb* déplacer de mémoire auxiliaire en mémoire centrale

roll out /ˌrəʊl 'aʊt/ *verb* rappeler de mémoire centrale en mémoire auxiliaire

rollover /'rəʊləʊvə/ *noun* mémoire *f* tampon de clavier

roll scroll /'rəʊl skrəʊl/ *noun* faire défiler un texte ligne à ligne sur l'écran ■ *verb* faire défiler ligne à ligne sur l'écran

ROM /rɒm/ *abbr* (*read only memory*) mémoire *f* fixe; ROM *f*

Roman numerals /ˌrəʊmən 'njuːmərəlz/ *plural noun* (*figures written I, II, III, IV, etc.*) chiffres *mpl* romains

ROM BIOS /rɒm 'baɪɒs/ *noun* ROM *f* BIOS

ROM cartridge /rɒm 'kɑːtrɪdʒ/ *noun* cartouche *f* ROM; ROM *f* amovible ◇ **the portable computer has no disk drives, but has a slot for ROM cartridges** l'ordinateur portatif n'est pas équipé de lecteur de disquettes mais possède un emplacement *or* un connecteur pour cartouches ROM

romware /'rɒmweə/ *noun* programmes *mpl* sur ROM

root /ruːt/ *noun* **1.** (*in a data tree structure*) racine *f* **2.** (*fractional power of a number*) puissance *f* fractionnaire; racine *f* ◇ **in DOS, the root directory on drive C: is called C:** sous DOS, le répertoire racine du disque C: est désigné par C:\ ◇ **the square root of 25 is 5** la racine carrée de 25 est 5

root directory /ruːt də'rekt(ə)ri/ *noun* répertoire *m* racine; répertoire *m* de départ

rotate /rəʊ'teɪt/ *verb* tourner *vt*

rotate operation /rəʊ'teɪt ˌɒpəreɪʃ(ə)n/ *noun* permutation *f* de bits

rotation /rəʊ'teɪʃ(ə)n/ *noun* rotation *f*

rough copy /ˌrʌf 'kɒpi/ *noun* brouillon *m*

round brackets /raʊnd 'brækɪts/ *plural noun* parenthèse(s)

rounding /'raʊndɪŋ/ *noun* **1.** (*of a number*) arrondi *m* au plus près; troncature *f* **2.** (*giving a smoother look*) arrondissement *m*

rounding error /'raʊndɪŋ ˌerə/, **round-off error** /'raʊnd ɒf ˌerə/ *noun* erreur *f* d'arrondi; erreur *f* de troncature

round robin /raʊnd 'rɒbɪn/ *noun* à tour de rôle

route /ruːt/ *noun* (*of message*) chemin *m*; cheminement *m*; itinéraire *m* ◇ **the route taken was not the most direct since a lot of nodes were busy** le chemin choisi ne s'est pas révélé le plus direct puisque de nombreux noeuds étaient occupés

router /'ruːtɪd/ *noun* **1.** (*communications device that receives data packets*) gestionnaire *m* de routage; (*LAN: device that connects two or more LANs*) routeur *m*; dispositif *m* de routage **2.** dispositif *m* de routage; routeur *m*

routine /ruː'tiːn/ *noun* (*set of instructions to carry out a task*) sous-programme *m*; routine *f* ◇ **the RETURN instruction at the end of the routine sends control back to the main program** l'instruction RETOUR à la fin de la routine permet de redonner la main au programme principal ◇ **the routine copies the screen display onto a printer** la routine *or* le programme permet d'imprimer le contenu de l'écran

> 'Hewlett-Packard has announced software which aims to reduce PC-network downtime and cut support costs by automating housekeeping routines such as issuing alerts about potential problems.' [*Computing*]

routing /'ruːtɪŋ/ *noun* (*network*) acheminement *m*; routage *m* ◇ **routing information protcol (RIP)** protocole RIP (d'acheminement de l'information)

routing information protocol /'ruːtɪŋ ˌɪnfəmeɪʃ(ə)n ˌprəʊtəkɒl/ *noun* protocole *m* RIP

routing overheads /ˌraʊtɪŋ 'əʊvəhedz/ *plural noun* (*protocol used when routing messages*) procédure *f* de contrôle d'acheminement; protocole *m* de routage d'un message ◇ **the information transfer rate is very much less once all routing overheads have been accommodated** la vitesse de transmission d'informations est beaucoup moins grande une fois qu'on tient compte du protocole d'acheminement

routing page /ˌraʊtɪŋ 'peɪdʒ/ *noun* page *f* de routage

routing table /raʊtɪŋ 'teɪb(ə)l/ *noun* table *f* de routage

row /raʊ/ *noun* **1.** (*of characters*) ligne *f*; (*of perforations*) rang *m* **2.** (*in an array or matrix*) ligne *f* d'un tableau; ligne *f* d'une matrice ◇ **each entry is separated by a row of dots** une ligne pointillée sépare les entrées les unes des autres

RPC /ˌɑː piː 'siː/ *noun* appel *m* de procédure à distance; appel *m* RPC

RPG *abbr* (*report program generator*) générateur *m* de rapport

RPN *abbr* (*reverse Polish notation*) notation *f* suffixée

RS-232C *noun* (*EIA approved standard used in serial data transmission, covering voltage and control signals*) norme *f* RS-232C (pour interface série)

RS-422 *noun* (*EIA approved standards*) norme *f* RS-422

RS-423 *noun* (*EIA approved standards*) norme *f* RS-423

RS-485 *noun* norme *f* RS-85

RSA *noun* code *m* de cryptage RSA

RSI *abbr* (*repetitive strain injury*) micro-traumatismes *mpl* répétés

RTF *abbr* (*rich text format*) format *m* RTF

RTFM *abbr* (*common abbreviation used in messages to mean 'read the manual'*) consultez donc le manuel!

RTP *abbr* (*real time transport protocol*) protocole *m* de transmission en temps réel

RTS *abbr* (*request to send signal*) signal *m* de demande de transmission

RTV /ˌɑː tiː 'viː/ *noun* vidéo *f* en temps réel

rub out /ˌrʌb 'aʊt/ *verb* effacer *vt*

rule /ruːl/ *noun* **1.** (*set of conditions*) règle *f* **2.** (*thin line*) filet *m* ◇ **the rule states that you wait for the clear signal before transmitting** il est de règle d'attendre le signal CTS avant de commencer à transmettre

rule-based system /ˌruːl beɪst 'sɪstəm/ *noun* système *m* à base de règles

ruler /'ruːlə/ *noun* (*bar on screen that is a unit of measurement*) règle *f* graduée; règle *f*

ruler line /'ruːlə laɪn/ *noun* règle *f* de tabulation

run /rʌn/ *noun* exécution *f* ■ *verb* (*a device*) fonctionner *vi*; (*a program*) être en marche; (*program, device*) exécuter *vt* ◇ **do not interrupt the spelling checker while it is running** n'arrêtez pas la vérification de l'orthographe en cours de route ◇ **the computer has been running ten hours a day** l'ordinateur fonctionne jusqu'à dix heures par jour ◇ **the new package runs on our**

PC le nouveau progiciel peut être utilisé sur notre PC

run around /rʌn ə'raʊnd/ *verb* (*to fit text around an image*) faire l'habillage d'une illustration

runaway /'rʌnə,weɪ/ *noun* opération *f* incontrôlable

Run command /'rʌn kə,mɑːnd/ *noun* commande *f* d'exécution; commande *f* Run

run-duration /'rʌn djʊ,reɪʃ(ə)n/ *noun, adjective* durée *f* d'exécution (d'un programme); temps *m* d'exécution (d'un programme)

run in /'rʌn ɪn/ *verb* roder *vt*

run indicator /rʌn 'ɪndɪ,keɪtə/ *noun* indicateur *m*

run-length limited encoding /,rʌn leŋθ ,lɪmɪtɪd en'kəʊdɪŋ/ *noun* encodage *m* RLL

running head /'rʌnɪŋ hed/ *noun* (*title line*) titre *m* courant

run on /,rʌn 'ɒn/ *verb* (*text*) composer à la suite; laisser courir le texte ◇ **the line can run on to the next without any space** le texte peut courir sans alinéa

run phase /'rʌn feɪz/ *noun* phase *f* d'exécution

run-time /rʌn taɪm/, **run duration** /rʌn djʊ 'reɪʃ(ə)n/ *noun* **1.** (*length of time a program takes to run*) durée *f* d'exécution **2.** (*time when a computer is executing a program*) temps *m* de traitement; temps *m* d'exécution

run-time error /'rʌn taɪm ,erə/ *noun* erreur *f* à l'exécution

run-time library /'rʌn taɪm ,laɪbrəri/ *noun* bibliothèque *f* des routines d'applications

run-time licence /'rʌn taɪm ,laɪs(ə)ns/ *noun* licence *f* d'utilisation

run-time system /'rʌn taɪm ,sɪstəm/ *noun* superviseur *m*

run-time version /'rʌn taɪm ,vɜːʒ(ə)n/ *noun* **1.** version *f* exécutable **2.** version *f* run-time

R/W *abbr* (*read/write*) lecture/écriture *f*

R/W cycle /,ɑː 'dʌb(ə)l juː ,saɪ(ə)l/ *noun* cycle *m* de lecture/écriture

R/W head /,ɑː 'dʌb(ə)l juː ,hed/ *noun* tête *f* de lecture/écriture

RX *abbr* **1.** (*receive*) recevoir *vt* **2.** (*receiver*) récepteur *m*

S

S100 bus, S-100 bus *noun* bus *m* (de type) S-100

SAA (*trade name for a standard developed by IBM which defines the look and feel of an application*) norme *f* SAA; architecture *f* de système d'application

safe format /seɪf 'fɔːmæt/ *noun* (*format operation that does not destroy the existing data*) formatage *m* non destructif

safety margin /'seɪfti ˌmɑːdʒɪn/ *noun* marge *f* de sécurité

safety measures /'seɪfti ˌmeʒəz/ *plural noun* mesures *f* de sécurité

safety net /'seɪfti net/ *noun* (*software or hardware device*) dispositif *m* de sécurité; dispositif *m* de secours; dispositif *m* auxiliaire ◇ **if there is a power failure, we have a safety net in the form of a UPS** en cas de panne d'électricité, nous avons un onduleur qui peut prendre la relève

sag /sæg/ *noun* (*short drop in the voltage level from a power supply*) légère chute *f* de tension

salami technique /sə'lɑːmi tekˌniːk/ *noun* (*computer fraud involving many separate small transactions that are difficult to detect and trace*) multiples fraudes *f* de peu de valeur; saucissonnage *m*

SAM /ˌes eɪ 'em/ *noun* mémoire *f* à accès séquentiel

sample /'sɑːmpəl/ *noun* échantillon *m* ■ *verb* échantillonner *vt* ◇ **the sample at three seconds showed an increase** la prise d'échantillon toutes les trois secondes a révélé une augmentation

sample and hold circuit /ˌsɑːmpəl ən 'həʊld ˌsɜːkɪt/ *noun* échantillonneur-bloqueur *m*

sample interval /'sɑːmpəl ˌɪntəv(ə)l/ *noun* pas *m* d'échantillonnage

sampler /'sɑːmplə/ *noun* (*electronic circuit*) échantillonneur *m*

sample rate /'sɑːmpəl reɪt/ *noun* fréquence *f* d'échantillonnage

sample size /'sɑːmpəl saɪz/ *noun* taille *f* de l'échantillon

sampling interval /'sɑːmplɪŋ ˌɪntəv(ə)l/ *noun* pas *m* d'échantillonnage

sampling rate /'sɑːmplɪŋ reɪt/ *noun* fréquence *f* d'échantillonnage

SAR /ˌes eɪ 'ɑː/ *noun* registre *m* d'adresse en mémoire

satellite /'sætəˌlaɪt/ *noun* (*device*) satellite *m* ◇ **communications satellite** satellite de télécommunication ◇ **direct broadcast satellite (DBS)** satellite de diffusion directe ◇ **satellite broadcasting** diffusion *f* par satellite ◇ **satellite link** liaison *f* (par) satellite ◇ **weather satellite** satellite météorologique

satellite computer /ˌsætəlaɪt kəm'pjuːtə/ *noun* ordinateur *m* satellite

satellite terminal /'sætəlaɪt ˌtɜːmɪn(ə)l/ *noun* terminal *m* satellite

saturated colour /ˌsætʃəreɪtɪd 'kʌlə/ *noun* couleur *f* intense

saturation /ˌsætʃə'reɪʃ(ə)n/ *noun* (*magnetic*) saturation *f*

saturation noise /ˌsætʃə'reɪʃ(ə)n nɔɪz/ *noun* bruit *m* de saturation

saturation testing /ˌsætʃə'reɪʃ(ə)n ˌtestɪŋ/ *noun* tests *mpl* de saturation

save /seɪv/ *verb* (*to store data*) sauvegarder *vt* ◇ **don't forget to save the file before switching off** n'oubliez pas de sauvegarder le fichier avant d'éteindre votre appareil ◇ **this WP saves the text every 15 minutes in case of a fault** ce système de traitement de texte fait une sauvegarde toutes les 15 minutes en cas de défaillance

save area /seɪv 'eəriə/ *noun* zone *f* de sauvegarde

save as /'seɪv əz/ *verb* enregistrer sous

SBC /ˌes biː 'siː/ *noun* ordinateur *m* à carte unique; ordinateur *m* monocarte

scalable /'skeɪləb(ə)l/ *adjective* **1.** à échelle variable **2.** vectoriel *or* -elle; à échelle variable

scalable software /ˌskeɪləb(ə)l 'sɒftweə/ *noun* (*groupware application*) logiciel *m* à échelle variable

scalar /'skeɪlə/ *noun* (*variable*) scalaire *m* ◇ **a scalar has a single magnitude value, a vector has two or more positional values** un scalaire n'a qu'une valeur de grandeur, alors qu'un vecteur possède au moins deux valeurs orientées

scalar data /'skeɪlə ˌdeɪtə/ *noun* données *fpl* scalaires

scalar processor /ˌskeɪlə 'prəʊsesə/ *noun* processeur *m* scalaire

Scalar Processor Architecture /ˌskeɪlə ˈprəʊsesə ˌɑːkɪtektʃə/ (*RISC processor designed by Sun Microsystems*) architecture *f* de processeur scalaire; architecture *f* SPARC

scalar value /ˈskeɪlə ˌvæljuː/ *noun* grandeur *f* scalaire

scalar variable /ˌskeɪlə ˈveəriəb(ə)l/ *noun* variable *f* scalaire

scale /skeɪl/ *noun* échelle *f* ◇ **large scale integration (LSI)** (*of circuit with 500 – 10,000 components*) intégration *f* à grande échelle ◇ **medium scale integration (MSI)** (*10 – 500 components*) intégration à moyenne échelle ◇ **small scale integration (SSI)** (*1 – 10 components*) intégration à petite échelle ◇ **super large scale integration (SLSI)** (*with several microprocessors*) intégration à super grande échelle ◇ **very large scale integration (VLSI)** (*10,000 – 100,000 components*) intégration à très grande échelle

scale down /ˌskeɪl ˈdaʊn/ *verb* réduire l'échelle

scale up /ˌskeɪl ˈʌp/ *verb* augmenter l'échelle

scan /skæn/ *noun* (*examination of an image*) balayage *m*; scan *m* ■ *verb* (*to check electronically*) scanner *vt*; (*to sweep*) faire un balayage; (*to check electronically*) faire un scanning; faire un scannage; lire *vt*; (*to look closely at something*) examiner (quelque chose) attentivement ◇ **a facsimile machine scans the picture and converts this to digital form before transmission** le fax balaye l'image et la numérise avant transmission ◇ **he scanned the map for Teddington** il a cherché Teddington sur la carte ◇ **the heat scan of the computer quickly showed which component was overheating** le scanner a très vite repéré le composant qui surchauffait ◇ **the machine scans at up to 300 dpi resolution** l'appareil peut scanner jusqu'à 300 points par pouce ◇ **the scan revealed which records were now out of date** un balayage a fait apparaître les données périmées

scan area /skæn ˈeəriə/ *noun* zone *f* de balayage

scan code /ˌskæn ˈkəʊd/ *noun* code *m* d'identification de touche

ScanDisk /ˈskændɪsk/ *noun* (*/MS-DOS and Windows utility*) ScanDisk

scan head /ˈskæn hed/ *noun* tête *f* de scanner ◇ **this model uses a scan head that can distinguish 256 different colours** ce modèle possède une tête de scanner qui reconnaît *or* identifie 256 couleurs

scan length /ˌskæn ˈleŋθ/ *noun* étendue *f* de la zone de balayage

scan line /ˌskæn ˈlaɪn/ *noun* ligne *f* de balayage

scanner /ˈskænə/ *noun* scanner *m*; scanneur *m*

> 'Ricoh's Fax 300L Computer Link is connected to a PC via a RS232C serial interface, and enables users to send faxes from within Dos and Windows applications without printing a hard copy: It can also act as a scanner for graphics, and a printer for documents.' [*Computing*]

scanner memory /ˈskænə ˌmem(ə)ri/ *noun* mémoire *f* d'images optiques

scanning /ˈskænɪŋ/ *noun* (*data*) scanning *m*; scannage *m*; balayage *m*; lecture *f* par balayage ◇ **its scanning speed is 9.9 seconds for an 8.5 inch by 11 inch document** il faut au scanner 9,9 secondes pour lire un document de 8,5 x 11 pouces ◇ **raster scanning** balayage de trame ◇ **scanning device** dispositif *m* de lecture par balayage; scanner *m*; scanneur *m* ◇ **scanning radio receiver** récepteur *m* à recherche de signal ◇ **throughput is 1.3 inches per second scanning speed** la vitesse de lecture par balayage est de 1,3 pouces par seconde

scanning error /ˈskænɪŋ ˌerə/ *noun* (*error introduced while scanning*) erreur *f* de balayage

scanning line /ˈskænɪŋ laɪn/ *noun* ligne *f* de balayage

scanning rate /ˈskænɪŋ reɪt/ *noun* fréquence *f* de balayage

scanning resolution /ˈskænɪŋ rezəˌluːʃ(ə)n/ *noun* définition *f* de balayage

scanning software /ˈskænɪŋ ˌsɒf(t)weə/ *noun* logiciel *m* de scanning; logiciel *m* de saisie par balayage

scanning speed /ˈskænɪŋ spiːd/ *noun* vitesse *f* de balayage

scan rate /ˌskæn ˈreɪt/ *noun* vitesse *f*

SCART connector /ˈskɑːt kəˌnektə/ *noun* prise *f* péritélévision

scatter-load /ˈskætə ləʊd/ *verb* faire un chargement éclaté

scatter-read /ˈskætə riːd/ *verb* faire une lecture sélective

scavenging /ˈskævɪndʒɪŋ/ *noun* (*searching through and access database material without permission*) pillage *m* (d'une base de données)

schedule /ˈʃedjuːl/ *noun* (*order in which tasks are to be done*) programme *m* agenda Schedule+™

Schedule+ /ˌʃedjuːlˈplʌs/ *noun* programme *m* agenda Schedule+™

scheduled circuits /ˌʃedʒuːld ˈsɜːkɪtz/ *noun* lignes *fpl* spécialisées

scheduler /ˈʃedjuːlə/ *noun* **1.** (*computer program which organizes the use of a CPU*) superviseur *m* (de multiprogrammation); gestionnaire *m* de tâches **2.** (*utility software used to help organize meetings*) logiciel *m* d'agenda; (*utility software used to help organize meetings, etc.*) logiciel *m* de plan de travail; ordonnanceur *m*

scheduling /ˈʃedjuːlɪŋ/ *noun* (*share of CPU*) détermination *f* de l'ordre de priorité; constitution *f* de file d'attente; (*of production*) ordonnancement *m* ◇ **programme scheduling** établissement *m* d'un horaire de programme de télévision *or* radio

schema /'skiːmə/ *noun* (*graphical description*) graphique *m*; schéma *m*; diagramme *m*

schematic /ski'mætɪk/ *adjective* plan *m* schématique

scissor /'sɪzə/ *verb* **1.** (*to define and then cut out text or graphics*) couper *vt* **2.** couper *vt*

scope /skəʊp/ *noun* portée *f*

SCR *abbr* (*sequence control register*) compteur *m* ordinal

scramble /'skræmb(ə)l/ *verb* (*message*) embrouiller *vt*

scrambler /'skræmblə/ *noun* (*device that codes a data stream in pseudorandom form*) embrouilleur *m*

scrapbook /'skræpˌbʊk/ *noun* (*Apple Macintosh utility*) utilitaire *m* de stockage de dessin; album *m* de croquis ◇ **we store our logo in the scrapbook** nous conservons le logo dans l'album (de croquis)

scratch /skrætʃ/ *noun* (*mark on disk or film*) rayure *f*; éraflure *f*; égratignure *f*; défaut *m* de surface ■ *verb* supprimer *vt* ◇ **this scratch makes the disk unreadable** cette rayure rend la lecture du disque impossible

scratch file /'skrætʃ faɪl/ *noun* (*work file*) fichier *m* de travail; fichier *m* de manoeuvre

scratchpad /'skrætʃpæd/ *noun* (*workspace for temporary storage of data*) bloc-notes *m*

> 'Mathcad is described as an easy-to-use 'handy scratch pad for quick number crunching', which is positioned as an alternative to popular spreadsheets.' [*Computing*]

scratchpad memory /'skrætʃpæd ˌmem(ə)ri/ *noun* (*cache memory*) mémoire *f* 'bloc-notes'

scratch tape /'skrætʃ teɪp/ *noun* bande *f* de travail

screen /skriːn/ *noun* (*display device*) écran *m* ◇ **screen image** image d'écran

screen angle /skriːn 'æŋg(ə)l/ *noun* angle *m* d'écran

screen attribute /skriːn 'ætrɪˌbjuːt/ *noun* attribut *m* d'écran

screen border /skriːn 'bɔːdə/ *noun* bordure *f* d'écran

screen buffer /skriːn 'bʌfə/ *noun* mémoire *f* tampon d'écran

screen burn /'skriːn bɜːn/ *noun* brûlage *m* d'écran

screen capture /skriːn 'kæptʃə/ *verb* capture *f* d'écran

screen cleaning kit /'skriːn ˌkliːnɪŋ ˌkɪt/ *noun* kit *m* de nettoyage pour écran

screen dump /'skriːn ˌdʌmp/ *noun* vidage *m* d'écran sur imprimante

screen editor /skriːn 'edɪtə/ *noun* éditeur *m* d'écran

screen flicker /skriːn 'flɪkə/ *noun* scintillement *m*

screen font /ˌskriːn 'fɒnt/ *noun* police *f* d'écran ◇ **the screen font is displayed at 72dpi on a monitor, rather than printed at 300dpi on this laser printer** la police d'écran est affichée à 72 ppp sur le moniteur plutôt qu'à 300 ppp comme pour l'imprimante laser

screen format /skriːn 'fɔːmæt/ *noun* format *m* d'écran

screenful /'skriːnfʊl/ *noun* plein écran *m*

screen grab /ˌskriːn 'græb/ *noun* capture *f* d'écran

screen memory /skriːn 'mem(ə)ri/ *noun* mémoire *f* écran

screen notepad /skriːn 'nəʊtˌpæd/ *noun* bloc-notes *m* d'écran; fenêtre *f* bloc-notes

screen refresh /skriːn rɪ'freʃ/ *verb* rafraîchir l'écran

screen saver /skriːn 'seɪvə/ *noun* économiseur *m* d'écran

screen shot /ˌskriːn 'ʃɒt/ *noun* capture *f* d'écran

screen size /ˌskriːn 'saɪz/ *noun* **1.** dimension *f* de l'écran **2.** taille *f* de l'écran

script /skrɪpt/ *noun* (*instructions which carry out a function*) script *m* ◇ **I log in automatically using this script with my communications software** je débute automatiquement la session en utilisant ce script avec mon logiciel de communication

script editor /skrɪpt 'edɪtə/ *noun* scripteur *m*

scripting language /skrɪptɪŋ 'læŋgwɪdʒ/ *noun* langage *m* de script ◇ **this communications software has a scripting language that lets me dial and log in automatically** ce logiciel de communication possède un langage de script qui me permet de composer le numéro d'appel et de débuter la session automatiquement

ScriptX /ˌskrɪpt'eks/ *noun* (*multimedia applications*) ScriptX

scroll /skrəʊl/ *verb* faire défiler ◇ **the marker is in the middle of the scroll bar so I know I am in the middle of the document** l'ascenseur est situé au milieu de la barre de défilement

scroll arrows /skrəʊl 'ærəʊz/ *plural noun* flèches *fpl* de défilement

scroll bar /'skrəʊl bɑː/ *noun* barre *f* de défilement ◇ **the marker is in the middle of the scroll bar so I know I am in the middle of the document** je sais ainsi que je suis au milieu du document

Scroll Lock key /'skrəʊl lɒk ˌkiː/ *noun* touche *f* Scroll lock

scroll mode /ˌskrəʊl 'məʊd/ *noun* mode *m* défilement

scrub /skrʌb/ *verb* (*information or data*) effacer *vt*; supprimer *vt*; détruire *vt* ◇ **scrub all files with**

the .BAK extension détruisez tous les fichiers avec l'extension .BAK

SCSI /ˌes siː es 'aɪ/ *noun* interface *f* SCSI

'...the system uses SCSI for connecting to the host and ESDI for interconnecting among drives within a multidrive system' [*Byte*]

SCSI-2 /'skʌzi tuː/ *noun* interface *f* SCSI-2

'The Tricord ES4000 is an entry-level superserver machine, with 525Mb of SCSI-2 fixed disk, 64Mb of ECC memory, and support for Raid levels 0, 1 and 10.' [*Computing*]

SD *abbr* (*single density*) simple densité *f*

SDLC /ˌes diː el 'siː/ *noun* protocole *m* SDLC

SDR /ˌes diː 'ɑː/ *noun* enregistreur *m* cumulatif d'erreurs par unité d'entrée/sortie

SDRAM /ˌes 'diː ˌræm/ *noun* mémoire *f* vive dynamique synchrone

seamless integration /ˌsiːmləs ˌɪntɪ 'greɪʃ(ə)n/ *noun* (*including a new device or software without any problems*) intégration *f* parfaite; intégration *f* sans hiatus

search /sɜːtʃ/ *noun* recherche *f* ■ *verb* (*look for an item of data*) rechercher *vt*; faire une recherche

'...a linear search of 1,000 items takes 500 comparisons to find the target, and 1,000 to report that it isn't present. A binary search of the same set of items takes roughly ten divisions either to find or not to find the target' [*Personal Computer World*]

searchable *adjective* de recherche

search and replace /ˌsɜːtʃ ənd rɪ'pleɪs/ *noun* chercher et remplacer

search directory /'sɜːtʃ daɪˌrekt(ə)ri/ *noun* répertoire *m*

search engine /'sɜːtʃ ˌendʒɪn/ *noun* **1.** (*software that carries out a search of a database*) moteur *m* de recherche **2.** moteur *m* de recherche

searching storage /'sɜːtʃɪŋ ˌstɔːrɪdʒ/ *noun* mémoire *f* associative; mémoire *f* adressable par le contenu

search key /'sɜːtʃ kiː/ *noun* clé *f* de recherche

search memory /sɜːtʃ 'mem(ə)ri/ *noun* mémoire *f* adressable par le contenu

SECAM /ˌes iː siː eɪ 'em/ *noun* (*'Système Électronique Couleur Avec Mémoire'*) standard *m* de télévision SECAM

secondary /'sekənd(ə)ri/ *adjective* secondaire ◇ **secondary colour** (*from two primary colours*) couleur *f* secondaire

secondary channel /ˌsekənd(ə)ri 'tʃæn(ə)l/ *noun* canal *m*

secondary memory /ˌsekənd(ə)ri 'mem(ə)ri/ *noun* mémoire *f* auxiliaire

secondary service provider /ˌsekənd(ə)ri 'sɜːvɪs prəˌvaɪdə/ *noun* fournisseur *m* d'accès secondaire

secondary station /ˌsekənd(ə)ri 'steɪʃ(ə)n/ *noun* station *f* secondaire

secondary storage /ˌsekənd(ə)ri 'stɔːrɪdʒ/ *noun* mémoire *f* auxiliaire

second generation computers /ˌsekənd ˌdʒenəreɪʃ(ə)n kəm'pjuːtə/ *noun* ordinateurs *mpl* de deuxième génération

second hand /ˌsekənd 'hænd/ *adjective* d'occasion

second-level addressing /ˌsekənd ˌlev(ə)l ə'dresɪŋ/ *noun* adressage *m* indirect

second sourcing /ˌsekənd 'sɔːsɪŋ/ *noun* utilisation *f* d'une seconde source de composants

second user /ˌsekənd 'juːzə/ *adjective* d'occasion

section /'sekʃən/ *noun* (*of main program*) segment *m*

sector /'sektə/ *noun* (*on magnetic disk*) secteur *m* ■ *verb* (*disk*) diviser en secteur; sectoriser *vt* ◇ **(disk) sector formatting** formatage *m* de secteurs (d'un disque)

sectoring hole /'sektərɪŋ həʊl/ *noun* perforation *f* de positionnement

sector interleave /ˌsektə 'ɪntəliːv/ *noun* entrelacement *m* de secteurs

sector map /'sektə mæp/ *noun* table *f* d'adresse des secteurs marqués inutilisables

secured /sɪ'kjʊəd/ *adjective* (*file*) sécurisé

secure hypertext transfer protocol /sɪ ˌkjʊə ˌhaɪpətekst 'trænsfɜː ˌprəʊtəkɒl/ *noun* protocole *m* S-HTTP

secure server /sɪˌkjʊə 'sɜːvə/ *noun* serveur *m* sécurisé

secure site /sɪˌkjʊə 'saɪt/ *noun* site *m* sécurisé

secure sockets layer /sɪˌkjʊə 'sɒkɪts ˌleɪə/ *noun* protocole *m* SSL

secure system /sɪˌkjʊə 'sɪstəm/ *noun* système *m* sécurisé; système *m* verrouillé

secure transaction technology /sɪˌkjʊə træn'zækʃən tekˌnɒlədʒi/ *noun* (*system developed by Microsoft*) technologie *f* STT

secure website /sɪˌkjʊə 'websaɪt/ *noun* site *m* sécurisé

security backup /sɪ'kjʊərɪti ˌbækʌp/ *noun* copie *f* de sauvegarde

security check /sɪ'kjʊərɪti tʃek/ *noun* contrôle *m* de sécurité

seed /siːd/ *noun* (*starting value when generating random numbers*) valeur *f* de départ; amorce *f* théorique

seek area /siːk 'eəriə/ *noun* zone *f* de recherche

seek time /ˌsiːk 'taɪm/ *noun* temps *m* d'accès

segment /'segmənt/ *noun* (*section of a main program*) segment *m* ■ *verb* (*a long program*) segmenter *vt*; diviser *vt*

'...you can also write in smaller program segments. This simplifies debugging and testing' [*Personal Computer World*]

segmented address space /segˌmentɪd ə 'dres ˌspeɪs/ *noun* espace *m* d'adresse segmenté

select /sɪ'lekt/ *verb* (*to find and retrieve specific information from a database*) sélectionner *vt*;

valider *vt*; activer *vt* ◇ **chip select (CS)** (*line or signal*) valider *or* activer un circuit intégré

selectable /sɪ'lektəb(ə)l/ *adjective* qui peut être sélectionné; validé; qui peut être programmé ◇ **this modem has user-selectable baud rates** les vitesses (de réception et de transmission) de ce modem sont réglables

selectable attributes /sɪˌlektəb(ə)l 'ætrɪbjuːtz/ *plural noun* attributs *mpl* programmables

selection handle /sɪ'lekʃən ˌhænd(ə)l/ *noun* poignée *f* de sélection

selection tool /sɪ'lekʃən tuːl/ *noun* outil *m* de sélection

selective dump /sɪ'lektɪv dʌmp/ *noun* vidage *m* sélectif

selective sort /sɪ'lektɪv sɔːt/ *noun* tri *m* sélectif

selector /sɪ'lektə/ *noun* sélecteur *m* ◇ **selector channel** canal *m* sélecteur *or* de sélection ◇ **the selector knob for the amplification is located there** voilà o— se trouve le sélecteur d'amplitude ◇ **turn the selector control** tournez le sélecteur

self- /self/ *prefix* (*referring to oneself*) auto-

self-adapting system /ˌself əˌdæptɪŋ 'sɪstəm/ *noun* système *m* auto-adaptatif

self-checking code /ˌself ˌtʃekɪŋ 'kəʊd/ *noun* (*character coding system*) code *m* détecteur d'erreur

self-checking system /ˌself ˌtʃekɪŋ 'sɪstəm/ *noun* système *m* avec autocontrôle; système *m* avec contrôle automatique

self-correcting /ˌselfkə'rektɪŋ/ *adjective* autocorrecteur

self-correcting codes % /self kəˌrektɪŋ 'kəʊdz/ *plural noun* codes *mpl* (auto)correcteurs

self-diagnostic /self ˌdaɪəg'nɒstɪk/ *noun* autodiagnostic *m*

self-documenting program /ˌself ˌdɒkjʊmentɪŋ 'prəʊgræm/ *noun* programme *m* avec documentation en ligne

self extracting archive /ˌself ɪkˌstræktɪŋ 'ɑːkaɪv/ *noun* fichier *m* auto-extractible

self-refreshing RAM /ˌself rɪˌfreʃɪŋ 'ræm/ *noun* RAM *f* auto-rafraîchie; RAM *f* auto-entretenue

self-relocating program /self riːləʊˌkeɪtɪŋ 'prəʊgræm/ *noun* programme *m* auto-relogeable

self-resetting loop /ˌself riːˌsetɪŋ 'luːp/ *noun* boucle *f* avec retour automatique à zéro; boucle *f* avec retour automatique aux paramètres de départ

self-restoring loop /ˌself rɪˌstɔːrɪŋ 'luːp/ *noun* boucle *f* avec retour automatique à zéro; boucle *f* avec retour automatique aux paramètres de départ

semantic error /səˌmæntɪk 'erə/ *noun* erreur *f* sémantique

semantics /sɪ'mæntɪks/ *noun* sémantique *f*

semaphore /'seməˌfɔː/ *noun* (*flags*) sémaphore *m*

semi- /semi/ *prefix* semi-; demi-

semicolon /ˌsemi'kəʊlɒn/ *noun* point-virgule *m*

semicompiled /ˌsemikəɰ'paɪld/ *adjective* semi-compilé

semiconductor /ˌsemikən'dʌktə/ *noun* semi-conducteur *m*

semiconductor device /ˌsemikəndʌktə dɪ'vaɪs/ *noun* dispositif *m* à semi-conducteur

semiconductor memory /ˌsemikəndʌktə 'mem(ə)ri/ *noun* mémoire *f* à semi-conducteur

semi-processed data /ˌsemi ˌprəʊsesd 'deɪtə/ *noun* données *fpl* partiellement traitées

sender /'sendə/ *noun* (*person*) émetteur *m*

send-only device /ˌsend 'əʊnli dɪˌvaɪs/ *noun* émetteur *m*

sense /sens/ *verb* détecter *vt*; lire *vt*; identifier *vt*; reconnaître *vt* ■ *noun* détection *f*; lecture *f*; reconnaissance *f* ◇ **the condition of the switch was sensed by the program** le programme a pu détecter l'état du connecteur

sense recovery time /ˌsens rɪ'kʌv(ə)ri ˌtaɪm/ *noun* délai *m* de conversion

sense switch /'sens swɪtʃ/ *noun* détecteur *m*

sensitive /'sensɪtɪv/ *adjective* sensible ◇ **light-sensitive films change when exposed to light** les films photosensibles réagissent à la lumière ◇ **the computer is sensitive even to very slight changes in current** cet ordinateur est sensible aux moindres variations du courant

sensor /'sensə/ *noun* capteur *m* ◇ **the process is monitored by a bank of sensors** le processus est contrôlé par une batterie de capteurs ◇ **the sensor's output varies with temperature** le signal de sortie du capteur varie suivant la température

sentinel /'sentɪn(ə)l/ *noun* **1.** (*marker or pointer*) drapeau *m*; marqueur *m* **2.** drapeau *m*; marqueur *m*

separate channel signalling /ˌsep(ə)rət ˌtʃæn(ə)l 'sɪgn(ə)lɪŋ/ *noun* émission *f* de signaux par canaux indépendants

separated graphics /ˌsepəreɪtɪd 'græfɪks/ *plural noun* caractères graphiques espacés; caractères graphiques séparés

separator /'sepəˌreɪtə/ *noun* (*symbol or code in a program*) séparateur *m*; symbole *m* intercalaire

septet /sep'tet/ *noun* (*word made up of seven bits*) septet *m*

sequence /'siːkwəns/ *noun* séquence *f*; ordre *m* ◇ **the logon sequence** séquence d'ouverture de session *or* d'identification ◇ **the sequence of names is arranged alphabetically** les noms sont classés par ordre alphabétique

sequence check /'siːkwəns tʃek/ *noun* contrôle *m* de séquence

sequence control register /ˌsiːkwəns kən ˌtrəʊl 'redʒɪstə/, **sequence counter** /ˌsiːkwəns 'kaʊntə/ *noun* registre *m* de contrôle de séquence

sequencer /'siːkwənsə/ *noun* séquenceur *m*

sequence register /'siːkwəns ˌredʒɪstə/ *noun* registre *m* de contrôle de séquence

sequential /sɪ'kwenʃ(ə)l/ *adjective* séquentiel *or* -elle

sequential access /sɪˌkwenʃ(ə)l 'ækses/ *noun* accès *m* séquentiel ◇ **queued indexed sequential access method (QISAM)** méthode *f* d'accès séquentiel indexé en file ◇ **queued sequential access method (QSAM)** méthode d'accès séquentiel en file

sequential access storage /sɪˌkwenʃ(ə)l 'ækses ˌstɔːrɪdʒ/ *noun* mémoire *f* à accès séquentiel

sequential batch processing /sɪ ˌkwenʃ(ə)l 'bætʃ ˌprəʊsesɪŋ/ *noun* traitement *m* par lots en mode séquentiel

sequential computer /sɪˌkwenʃ(ə)l kəm 'pjuːtə/ *noun* ordinateur *m* série

sequential file /sɪ'kwenʃ(ə)l faɪl/ *noun* fichier *m* à accès séquentiel

sequential logic /sɪˌkwenʃ(ə)l 'lɒdʒɪk/ *noun* logique *f* séquentielle ◇ **if the input sequence to the sequential logic circuit is 1101 the output will always be zero (0)** si l'entrée dans le circuit séquentiel logique est 1101, la sortie sera toujours zéro (0)

sequentially /sɪ'kwenʃəli/ *adverb* en série; suivant un ordre séquentiel

sequential mode /sɪ'kwenʃ(ə)l məʊd/ *noun* (*in a program*) mode *m* séquentiel

sequential operation /sɪˌkwenʃ(ə)l ˌɒpə 'reɪʃ(ə)n/ *noun* opération *f* séquentielle

sequential processing /sɪˌkwenʃ(ə)l 'prəʊsesɪŋ/ *noun* traitement *m* séquentiel

sequential search /sɪˌkwenʃ(ə)l 'sɜːtʃ/ *noun* recherche *f* séquentielle

serial /'sɪəriəl/ *adjective* séquentiel *or* -elle; en série ◇ **serial input *or* output (SIO)** entrée/sortie *f* (en) série

serial access /ˌsɪəriəl 'ækses/ *noun* (*item accessed by reading through all the data*) accès *m* séquentiel

serial-access memory /ˌsɪəriəl ˌækses 'mem(ə)ri/ *noun* mémoire *f* à accès séquentiel

serial adder /ˌsɪəriəl 'ædə/ *noun* additionneur *m* séquentiel

serial computer /ˌsɪəriəl kəm'pjuːtə/ *noun* ordinateur *m* série

serial data communications /ˌsɪəriəl ˌdeɪtə kəˌmjuːnɪ'keɪʃ(ə)nz/ *noun* transmission *f* série de données

serial data transmission /ˌsɪəriəl 'deɪtə trænzˌmɪʃ(ə)n/ *noun* transmission *f* série de données

serial file /ˌsɪəriəl 'faɪl/ *noun* fichier *m* à accès séquentiel

serial input/output /ˌsɪəriəl ˌɪnpʊt 'aʊtpʊt/ *noun* transmission *f* en série; entrée/sortie *f* en série

serial input/parallel output /ˌsɪəriəl ˌɪnpʊt ˌpærəlel 'aʊtpʊt/ *noun* entrée *f* série/sortie parallèle

serial input/serial output /ˌsɪəriəl ˌɪnpʊt ˌsɪəriəl 'aʊtpʊt/ *noun* entrée *f* série/sortie série

serial line Internet protocol /ˌsɪəriəl laɪn 'ɪntənet ˌprəʊtəkɒl/ *noun* protocole *m* SLIP

serially /'sɪəriəli/ *adverb* en série

serial memory /ˌsɪəriəl 'mem(ə)ri/ *noun* (*storage whose locations can only be accessed in a serial way*) mémoire *f* séquentielle ◇ **magnetic tape is a high capacity serial memory** la bande magnétique constitue une mémoire séquentielle d'une grande capacité

serial mouse /ˌsɪəriəl 'maʊs/ *noun* (*mouse that connects to the serial port of a PC*) souris *f* série

serial operation /ˌsɪəriəl ˌɒpə'reɪʃ(ə)n/ *noun* opération *f* séquentielle

serial port /'sɪəriəl pɔːt/ *noun* port *m* série

serial printer /ˌsɪəriəl 'prɪntə/ *noun* imprimante *f* série

serial processing /ˌsɪəriəl 'prəʊsesɪŋ/ *noun* (*connection/disconnection*) traitement *m* en série

serial storage /ˌsɪəriəl 'stɔːrɪdʒ/ *noun* (*place*) mémoire *f* à accès séquentiel; (*action*) stockage *m* séquentiel

serial to parallel converter /ˌsɪəriəl tə ˌpærəlel kən'vɜːtə/ *noun* convertisseur *m* série/parallèle

serial transmission /ˌsɪəriəl trænz'mɪʃ(ə)n/ *noun* transmission *f* en série; entrée/sortie *f* en série

series /'sɪəriːz/ *noun* série *f*

series circuit /'sɪəriːz ˌsɜːkɪt/ *noun* circuit *m* disposé en série; montage *m* en série

server /'sɜːvə/ *noun* (*dedicated computer or peripheral*) serveur *m* ◇ **Web server** serveur Web

> 'Sequent Computer Systems' Platform division will focus on hardware and software manufacture, procurement and marketing, with the Enterprise division concentrating on services and server implementation.' [*Computing*]

server access log /ˌsɜːvə 'ækses lɒg/ *noun* protocole *m* des accès

server-based application /ˌsɜːvə beɪst ˌæplɪ'keɪʃ(ə)n/ *noun* application *f* partagée *or* sur serveur

server farm /'sɜːvə fɑːm/ *noun* batterie *f* de serveurs

server message block /ˌsɜːvə 'mesɪdʒ blɒk/ *noun* système *m* SMB

service /'sɜːvɪs/ *verb* (*system*) réviser *vt*; réparer *vt* ■ *noun* (*data transmission*) contrôle *m* ◇ **the disk drives were serviced yesterday and are working well** nous avons fait réviser *or* réparer les lecteurs de disquettes hier et tout fonctionne très bien

service bit /'sɜːvɪs bɪt/ *noun* bit *m* de contrôle

service bureau /'sɜːvɪs ˌbjʊərəʊ/ *noun* service *m* bureau

service contract /'sɜːvɪs ˌkɒntrækt/ *noun* contrat *m* de maintenance

service program /'sɜːvɪs ˌprəʊgræm/ *noun* programme *m* de maintenance; programme *m* utilitaire de maintenance

service provider /'sɜːvɪs prəˌvaɪdə/ *noun* fournisseur *m* d'accès à l'Internet (FAI)

services /'sɜːvɪsɪz/ *plural noun* **1.** (*functions provided by a device*) services *mpl*; fonctions *fpl* de service **2.** services

session /'seʃ(ə)n/ *noun* (*time when a program is running*) session *f*; période *f* de travail ◇ **session key** clé d'ouverture d'une session

session layer /'seʃ(ə)n ˌleɪə/ *noun* (*connection/disconnection*) couche *f* session

set /set/ *noun* (*number of related data items*) ensemble *m*; jeu *m*; série *f* ■ *verb* **1.** (*to define a value*) fixer *vt*; programmer *vt*; paramétrer *vt*; régler *vt* **2.** (*to give a bit the value of 1*) charger *vt*; affecter *vt* **3.** (*to compose a text into typeset characters*) composer *vt* ◇ **the text is set in 12 point Times Roman** le texte est (composé) en Times romain corps 12 ◇ **we set the right-hand margin at 80 characters** nous avons programmé *or* fixé la marge de droite à 80 caractères; nous avons programmé *or* fixé la marge de droite pour donner une ligne de 80 caractères

SET /set/ *plural noun* ensemble *m*; jeu *m*; série *f*

set breakpoints /set 'breɪkpɔɪnts/ *verb* programmer les points d'arrêt

set theory /set 'θɪəri/ *noun* théorie *f* des ensembles

set up /'set ʌp/ *verb* (*to install or configure*) installer *vt*; configurer *vt*; définir *vt*; (*to initialize or start*) initialiser *vt*; mettre en route ◇ **set-up option** (*choices*) option *f* de configuration ◇ **set-up time** (*between signal and start*) délai *m* de configuration *or* d'installation ◇ **the new computer worked well as soon as the engineer had set it up** dès qu'il a été configuré par l'ingénieur, le nouvel ordinateur a bien fonctionné

setup option /'setʌp ˌɒpʃ(ə)n/ *noun* option *f* de configuration

setup program /'setʌp ˌprəʊgræm/ *noun* programme *m* d'installation

setup time /'setʌp taɪm/ *noun* délai *m* de configuration; délai *m* d'installation

sexadecimal /ˌseksə'desɪməl/ *noun* numération *f* hexadécimale

sex changer /'seks ˌtʃeɪndʒə/ *noun* (*device for changing a connection*) changeur *m* de genre; adaptateur *m* mâle/femelle; adaptateur *m* femelle/mâle

sextet /ˌseks'tet/ *noun* (*byte made up of six bits*) sextet *m*

sf signalling /ˌes ef 'sɪgn(ə)lɪŋ/ *noun* signalisation *f* monofréquence

SGML /ˌes dʒiː em'el/ *noun* langage *m* de balisage SGML

shading /'ʃeɪdɪŋ/ *noun* ombrage *m*

shadowmask /'ʃædəʊmɑːsk/ *noun* (*separates three-colour picture beams*) masque *m* filtre

shadow memory /ˌʃædəʊ 'mem(ə)ri/, **shadow page** /'ʃædəʊ peɪdʒ/ *noun* mémoire *f* annexe

shadow page table /'ʃædəʊ peɪdʒ ˌteɪb(ə)l/ *noun* table *f* d'occupation des pages en mémoire annexe

shadow RAM /'ʃædəʊ ræm/ *noun* shadow RAM; mémoire *f* haute

shadow ROM /'ʃædəʊ rɒm/ *noun* (*read-only shadow memory*) ROM *f* annexe

Shannon's Law /'ʃænənz lɔː/ *noun* loi *f* de Shannon

shared access /ʃeəd 'ækses/ *noun* accès *m* partagé

shared bus /ˌʃeəd 'bʌs/ *noun* bus *m* partagé

shared directory /ʃeəd də'rekt(ə)ri/ *noun* répertoire *m* partagé

shared file /ˌʃeəd 'faɪl/ *noun* fichier *m* partagé; fichier *m* commun

shared folder /ʃeəd 'fəʊldə/ *noun* dossier *m* commun; dossier *m* partagé

shared logic system /ˌʃeəd 'lɒdʒɪk ˌsɪstəm/ *noun* système *m* logique partagé

shared logic text processor /ˌʃeəd ˌlɒdʒɪk 'tekst ˌprəʊsesə/ *noun* processeur *m* de traitement de texte à logique partagée

shared memory /ʃeəd 'mem(ə)ri/ *noun* mémoire *f* partagée

shared network directory /ˌʃeəd 'netwɜːk daɪˌrekt(ə)ri/ *noun* répertoire *m* de réseau partagé

shared resources system /ˌʃeəd rɪ'zɔːsɪz ˌsɪstəm/ *noun* système *m* à ressources partagées; système *m* multi-utilisateur

share-level access /ˌʃeə ˌlev(ə)l 'ækses/ *noun* accès *m* par niveau d'opération

share level security /ˌʃeə ˌlev(ə)l sɪ 'kjʊərɪti/ *noun* sécurité *f* par niveau d'opération

shareware /'ʃeəˌweə/ *noun* partagiciel *m*; shareware *m*

'Bulletin board users know the dangers of 'flaming' (receiving hostile comments following a naive or ridiculous assertion) and of being seen 'troughing' (grabbing every bit of shareware on the network).' [*Computing*]

sheet /ʃiːt/ *noun* feuille *f* ◇ **(single) sheet feed** (*paper feed system*) alimentation *f* feuille à feuille

sheet feed /'ʃiːt fiːd/ *noun* alimentation *f* feuille à feuille

shell /ʃel/ *noun* (*software operating between the user and the system*) programme *m* shell; programme *m* interprétatif; interpréteur *m* de commande

shell out /ˌʃel 'aʊt/ *verb* (*to exit to the operating system*) sortir du programme en cours pour passer au programme d'exploitation et revenir à l'application ◇ **I shelled out from the wordprocessor to check which files were on the floppy, then went back to the program** je suis sorti du traitement de texte pour vérifier quels étaient les fichiers disponibles sur la disquette, puis je suis retourné dans le programme

shell script /ˌʃel 'skrɪpt/ *noun* procédure *f* d'interpréteur de commandes

shell sort /ˌʃel 'sɔːt/ *noun* tri *m* enveloppe

shield /ʃiːld/ *noun* écran *m*; blindage *m* ■ *verb* protéger *vt*; blinder *vt* ◇ **shielded twisted pair (STP) cable** (*two insulated copper wires twisted around each other, wrapped in an insulating layer*) câble *m* en paires torsadées blindé ◇ **unshielded twisted pair (UTP) cable** (*two insulated copper wires twisted around each other*) câble en paires torsadées non blindé *or* sans blindage

shielded cable /ˌʃiːldɪd 'keɪb(ə)l/ *noun* câble *m* blindé

shielded twisted pair cable /ˌʃiːldɪd ˌtwɪstɪd 'peə ˌkeɪb(ə)l/ *noun* câble *m* en paires torsadées blindé

shift /ʃɪft/ *verb* **1.** (*to move*) déplacer *vt*; décaler *vt*; permuter *vt* **2.** (*to change from one character set to another, allowing other characters (such as capitals) to be used*) passer en majuscule

shift character /ʃɪft 'kærɪktə/ *noun* caractère *m* de déplacement

shift code /ˌʃɪft 'kəʊd/ *noun* code *m* de déplacement

shift instruction /ʃɪft ɪn'strʌkʃən/ *noun* instruction *f* de décalage

Shift key /'ʃɪft kiː/ *noun* touche *f* majuscule

shift left /'ʃɪft ˌleft/ *noun* faire un décalage vers la gauche

shift register /ʃɪft 'redʒɪstə/ *noun* registre *m* à décalage; registre *m* de décalage

shift right /'ʃɪft ˌraɪt/ *noun* décalage *m* vers la droite

Shockwave /'ʃɒkweɪv/ (*system developed by Macromedia that allows Web browsers to display complex multimedia effects*) Shockwave™

shopping agent /'ʃɒpɪŋ ˌeɪdʒənt/ *noun* robot *m* de shopping

shopping basket /'ʃɒpɪŋ ˌbɑːskɪt/, **shopping cart** /'ʃɒpɪŋ kɑːt/ *noun* caddie *m* en ligne

short card /ˌʃɔːt 'kɑːd/ *noun* carte *f* de taille réduite; carte *f* courte

shortcut /'ʃɔːtˌkʌt/ *noun* raccourci *m*

short haul modem /ˌʃɔːt hɔːl 'məʊdem/ *noun* modem *m* de courte portée

short message service /ˌʃɔːt 'mesɪdʒ ˌsɜːvɪs/ *noun* service *m* de messages courts

shout /ʃaʊt/ *verb* (*term of abuse – typing a message or electronic mail in capital letters*) être en colère; exprimer son mécontentement en écrivant un message en majuscules

S-HTTP /es ˌeɪtʃ tiː tiː 'piː/ *noun* protocole *m* S-HTTP

shut down /ˌʃʌt 'daʊn/ *verb* arrêter *vt*; fermer *vt*; éteindre *vt*

shut-off mechanism /'ʃʌt ɒf ˌmekənɪz(ə)m/ *noun* mécanisme *m* d'arrêt

sideways ROM /'saɪdweɪz rɒm/ *noun* ROM *f* auxiliaire; mémoire *f* morte auxiliaire

SIG /sɪg/ *noun* groupe *m* d'intérêt particulier

sign /saɪn/ *noun* signe *m* de polarité ■ *verb* signer *vt*

signal /'sɪgn(ə)l/ *noun* **1.** (*waveform*) signal *m* **2.** (*short message*) signal *m* ■ *verb* (*to send a message*) émettre un signal; transmettre un signal ◇ **signal to noise ratio (S *or* N)** (*difference between the power of the signal and the noise on the line*) rapport signal/bruit ◇ **signal to the network that we are busy** signale au réseau que nous sommes occupés *or* envoie un signal au réseau pour prévenir que nous sommes occupés ◇ **the signal received from the computer contained the answer** le signal émis par l'ordinateur contenait la réponse ◇ **the system is used by students doing research on signal processing techniques** ce système est à la disposition des étudiants qui se spécialisent dans la recherche sur les techniques de traitement du signal

signal conditioning /'sɪgn(ə)l kən ˌdɪʃ(ə)nɪŋ/ *noun* mise *f* en forme de signaux; conversion *f* de signaux

signal conversion /'sɪgn(ə)l kənˌvɜːʃ(ə)n/ *noun* conversion *f* de signaux

signal distance /'sɪgn(ə)l ˌdɪstəns/ *noun* distance *f* entre signaux; distance *f* de Hamming

signal element /'sɪgn(ə)l ˌelɪmənt/ *noun* élément *m* d'un signal ◇ **the signal element in this system is a short voltage pulse, indicating a binary one** l'élément signal de ce système est une courte impulsion de tension qui représente un 1 binaire

signalling /'sɪgn(ə)lɪŋ/ *noun* signalisation *f*

signal processing /'sɪgn(ə)l ˌprəʊsesɪŋ/ *noun* traitement *m* du signal ◇ **the system is used by students doing research on signal processing techniques** ce système est à la disposition des étudiants qui se spécialisent dans la recherche sur les techniques de traitement du signal

signal to noise ratio /ˌsɪgn(ə)l tə 'nɔɪz ˌreɪʃiəʊ/ *noun* rapport *m* signal/bruit

sign and modulus /ˌsaɪn ən 'mɒdjʊləs/ *noun* signe *m* et modulo

signature /'sɪgnɪtʃə/ *noun* (*name*) signature *f*; (*authentication code*) code *m* personnel; code *m* confidentiel ◇ **do you recognize the signature on the cheque?** reconnaissez-vous la signature sur le chèque?

signature file /'sɪgnɪtʃə faɪl/ *noun* fichier *m* signature

sign bit /ˌsaɪn 'bɪt/ *noun* bit *m* de signe

sign digit /saɪn 'dɪdʒɪt/ *noun* chiffre *m* indicateur de signe

signed field /ˌsaɪnd 'fiːld/ *noun* champ *m* de signe

significance /sɪg'nɪfɪkəns/ *noun* (*special meaning*) signification *f*

significant /sɪg'nɪfɪkənt/ *adjective* significatif; important *or* -e

significant digit codes /sɪgˌnɪfɪkənt 'dɪdʒɪt ˌkəʊdz/ *plural noun* codes *mpl* significatifs; codes *mpl* à chiffres significatifs

signify /'sɪgnɪˌfaɪ/ *verb* (*to mean*) signifier *vt*; vouloir dire ◇ **a carriage return code signifies the end of an input line** l'envoi du code CR signifie que la ligne saisie est terminée

sign indicator /saɪn 'ɪndɪˌkeɪtə/ *noun* bit *m* de signe; indicateur *m* de signe

sign position /saɪn pə'zɪʃ(ə)n/ *noun* position *f* du signe

silicon /'sɪlɪkən/ *noun* silicium *m* ◇ **silicon gate** porte *f* (de circuit) au silicium ◇ **silicon on sapphire (SOS)** silicium sur saphir ◇ **silicon transistor** transistor *m* au silicium

silicon chip /'sɪlɪkən tʃɪp/ *noun* (*small piece of silicon*) puce *f*

silicon disk /'sɪlɪkən dɪsk/ *noun* disque *m* RAM; disque *m* virtuel

silicon foundry /'sɪlɪkən ˌfaʊndri/ *noun* fonderie *f* de silicium

Silicon Valley /ˌsɪlɪkən 'væli/ *noun* région *f* de la Californie où l'on trouve une forte concentration de sociétés productrices de semi-conducteurs

silicon wafer /ˌsɪlɪkən 'weɪfə/ *noun* tranche *f* de silicium

SIMD /ˌes aɪ em 'diː/ *noun* architecture *f* SIMD; flux *m* simple d'instructions, flux multiple de données

SIMM /ˌes aɪ em 'em/ *noun* barette *f* de mémoire de type SIMM

simple device /ˌsɪmp(ə)l dɪ'vaɪs/ *noun* appareil *m* simple

simple mail transfer protocol /ˌsɪmpəl meɪl 'trænsfɜː ˌprəʊtəkɒl/ *noun* protocole *m* SMTP

simple network management protocol /ˌsɪmpəl ˌnetwɜːk 'mænɪdʒmənt ˌprəʊtəkɒl/ *noun* (*network management system*) protocole *m* SNMP

simple to use /'sɪmp(ə)l tə, tʊ/ *adjective* d'utilisation facile

simplex /'sɪmpleks/ *noun* (*transmission in one direction*) transmission *f* simplex; transmission *f* unidirectionnelle

simulate /'sɪmjʊˌleɪt/ *verb* simuler *vt* ◇ **this software simulates the action of an aircraft** ce logiciel simule les manoeuvres aériennes *or* est un simulateur de vol

simulation /ˌsɪmjʊ'leɪʃ(ə)n/ *noun* simulation *f* ◇ **simulation software** logiciel *m* de simulation ◇ **simulation techniques have reached a high degree of sophistication** les techniques de simulation sont devenues très sophistiquées

simulator /'sɪmjʊˌleɪtə/ *noun* simulateur *m*

simultaneity /ˌsɪm(ə)ltə'niːəti/ *noun* simultanéité *f*

simultaneous /ˌsɪm(ə)l'teɪniəs/ *adjective* simultané *or* -ée

simultaneous processing /ˌsɪm(ə)lteɪniəs 'prəʊsesɪŋ/ *noun* traitement *m* simultané

simultaneous transmission /ˌsɪm(ə)lteɪniəs trænz'mɪʃ(ə)n/ *noun* transmission *f* simultanée

single address code /ˌsɪŋg(ə)l ə'dres ˌkəʊd/ *noun* code *m* d'instruction à adresse unique; code *m* d'instruction à adresse directe

single address instruction /ˌsɪŋg(ə)l ə ˌdres ɪn'strʌkʃən/ *noun* instruction *f* à adresse unique

single address message /ˌsɪŋg(ə)l ə'dres ˌmesɪdʒ/ *noun* message *m* à une seule adresse

single attachment station /ˌsɪŋg(ə)l ə ˌtætʃmənt 'steɪʃ(ə)n/ *noun* station *f* à connexion unique; station *f* à liaison unique

single board computer /ˌsɪŋg(ə)l bɔːd kəm 'pjuːtə/ *noun* ordinateur *m* à carte unique; ordinateur *m* monocarte

single-board microcomputer /ˌsɪŋg(ə)l bɔːd 'maɪkrəʊkəmˌpjuːtə/ *noun* microordinateur *m* à carte unique; microordinateur *m* monocarte

single chip computer /ˌsɪŋg(ə)l tʃɪp kəm 'pjuːtə/ *noun* (*complete simple computer*) ordinateur *m* monopuce; ordinateur *m* à puce unique

single-chip microcontroller /ˌsɪŋg(ə)l tʃɪp 'maɪkrəkənˌtrəʊlə/ *noun* micro-ordinateur *m* de contrôle à puce unique

single density disk /ˌsɪŋg(ə)l ˌdensɪti 'dɪsk/ *noun* disquette *f* à simple densité

single frequency signalling /ˌsɪŋg(ə)l 'friːkwənsi ˌsɪgn(ə)lɪŋ/ *noun* signalisation *f* monofréquence

single function software /ˌsɪŋg(ə)l ˈfʌŋkʃən ˌsɒftweə/ *noun* logiciel *m* d'application spécialisée

single in-line memory module /ˌsɪŋg(ə)l ɪn laɪn ˈmem(ə)ri ˌmɒdjuːl/ *noun* batterie *f* de mémoire de type SIMM

single in-line package /ˌsɪŋg(ə)l ɪn laɪn ˈpækɪdʒ/ *noun* composant *m* de type SIP; barrette *f* de type SIP

single instruction stream multiple data stream /ˌsɪŋg(ə)l ɪnˌstrʌkʃən striːm ˌmʌltɪp(ə)l ˈdeɪtə ˌstriːm/ *noun* architecture *f* SIMD; flux *m* simple d'instructions, flux multiple de données

single instruction stream single data stream /ˌsɪŋg(ə)l ɪnˌstrʌkʃən striːm ˌsɪŋg(ə)l ˈdeɪtə striːm/ *noun* architecture *f* SISD; flux *m* simple d'instructions, flux simple de données

single key response /ˌsɪŋg(ə)l ˈkiː rɪˌspɒns/ *noun* activé par une seule touche

single length precision /ˌsɪŋg(ə)l leŋθ prɪ ˈsɪʒ(ə)n/ *noun* simple précision

single length working /ˌsɪŋg(ə)l leŋθ ˈwɜːkɪŋ/ *noun* opération *f* en simple précision

single line display /ˌsɪŋg(ə)l laɪn dɪsˈpleɪ/ *noun* écran *m* d'une ligne

single mode fibre /ˌsɪŋg(ə)l məʊd ˈfaɪbə/ *noun* fibre *f* optique monomodale

single operand instruction /ˌsɪŋg(ə)l ˌɒpərænd ɪnˈstrʌkʃən/ *noun* instruction *f* à un opérande

single operation /ˌsɪŋg(ə)l ˌɒpəˈreɪʃ(ə)n/ *noun* transmission *f* unidirectionnelle; transmission *f* simplex *m*

single-pass assembler /ˌsɪŋg(ə)l pɑːs ə ˈsemblə/ *noun* (*object code produced in one run*) assembleur *m* une passe

single pass operation /ˌsɪŋg(ə)l pɑːs ˌɒpə ˈreɪʃ(ə)n/ *noun* opération *f* en une passe; opération *f* monopasse

single precision /ˌsɪŋg(ə)l prɪˈsɪʒ(ə)n/ *noun* simple précision *f*

single quotes /ˈsɪŋg(ə)l kwəʊtz/ *plural noun* guillemets simples

single sheet feed /ˌsɪŋg(ə)l ʃiːt ˈfiːd/ *noun* alimentation *f*

single-sided disk /ˌsɪŋg(ə)l ˌsaɪdɪd ˈdɪsk/ *noun* disquette *f* simple face

single speed /ˈsɪŋg(ə)l spiːd/ *noun* vitesse *f* unique

single step /ˈsɪŋg(ə)l step/ *adjective* (*for debugging*) exécution *f* pas à pas

single-strike ribbon /ˌsɪŋg(ə)l straɪk ˈrɪbən/ *noun* ruban *m* à un seul passage; ruban *m* non réutilisable

single-system image /ˌsɪŋg(ə)l ˌsɪstəm ˈɪmɪdʒ/ *noun* système *m* simple image

single-user system /ˌsɪŋg(ə)l ˌjuːzə ˈsɪstəm/ *noun* système *m* mono-utilisateur; ordinateur *m* individuel

sink /sɪŋk/ *noun* (*end of line*) puits *m*; collecteur *m* de données ◇ **heat sink** (*conducts heat away from component*) dissipateur *m* thermique *or* radiateur *m* à ailette(s)

sink tree /ˌsɪŋk ˈtriː/ *noun* arborescence *f* en puits

SIO *abbr* (*serial input/output*) transmission *f* en série; entrée/sortie *f* en série

SIP *abbr* (*single in-line package*) boîtier *m* à simple rangée de connexions

SIPO *abbr* (*serial input/parallel output*) entrée *f* série/sortie parallèle

SISD /ˌes aɪ es ˈdiː/ *noun* architecture *f* SISD; flux *m* simple d'instructions, flux simple de données

SISO *abbr* (*serial input/serial output*) entrée série/sortie série

site /saɪt/ *noun* emplacement *m*; site *m* ◇ **web site** (*collection of web pages that are linked*) site Web; ON-SITE

site licence /saɪt ˈlaɪs(ə)ns/ *noun* licence *f* de site ◇ **we have negotiated a good deal for the site licence for our 1200 employees in our HQ** nous avons négocié longtemps pour obtenir une licence de site pour les 1200 employés du siège

site poll /ˌsaɪt ˈpəʊl/ *verb* appel *m* à émettre à tous les terminaux d'un site

16-bit /ˈsɪkstiːn bɪt/ (*data that is transferred sixteen bits at a time along sixteen parallel conductors*) 16 bits

sixteen-bit /ˌsɪksˈtiːn bɪt/ *adjective* seize bits

16-bit sample /ˌsɪkstiːn bɪt ˈsɑːmp(ə)l/ *noun* échantillon *m* à 16 bits

64-bit /ˌsɪksti ˈfɔː bɪt/ système *m* à 64 bits

size /saɪz/ *noun* dimension *f*; taille *f*; grandeur *f* ■ *verb* dimensionner *vt* ◇ **page size** taille *or* grandeur *or* format *m* de la page ◇ **the size of the print has been increased to make it easier to read** la taille des caractères a été augmentée pour rendre la lecture plus facile

skeletal code /ˈskelɪt(ə)l kəʊd/ *noun* (*incomplete program*) code *m* incomplet; code *m* de base; code *m* support; code *m* paramétrable

skew /skjuː/ *noun* (*amount by which something is not correctly aligned*) inclinaison *f*; obliquité *f*; défaut *m* d'alignement ■ *verb* (*align incorrectly*) réaliser un mauvais alignement ◇ **this page is badly skewed** cette page est mal alignée

skin /skɪn/ *noun* habillage *m* ■ *verb* habiller *vt*

skip /skɪp/ *verb* (*omit*) sauter *vi*; omettre *vt* ◇ **the printer skipped the next three lines of text** l'imprimante a sauté les trois lignes suivantes

skip capability /skɪp ˌkeɪpəˈbɪləti/ *noun* capacité *f* de saut

skip instruction /skɪp ɪn'strʌkʃən/ *noun* instruction *f* de saut

slash /slæʃ/ *noun* (*oblique stroke /*) trait *m* oblique; barre *f* oblique

slashed zero /slæʃd 'zɪərəʊ/ *noun* (*used to distinguish a zero from the letter O*) zéro *m* barré d'un trait (oblique/transversal)

slave /sleɪv/ *noun* esclave *m*

slave cache /ˌsleɪv 'kæʃ/ *noun* mémoire *f* auxiliaire

slave processor /sleɪv 'prəʊˌsesə/ *noun* processeur *m* asservi

slave store /'sleɪv stɔː/ *noun* mémoire *f* auxiliaire

slave terminal /sleɪv 'tɜːmɪn(ə)l/ *noun* terminal *m* asservi

slave tube /ˌsleɪv 'tjuːb/ *noun* écran *m* asservi; second écran

sleep /sliːp/ *noun* en attente

sleeve /sliːv/ *noun* pochette *f*

slew /sluː/ *noun* (*of paper in a printer*) avance *f* rapide de papier

slide /slaɪd/ *noun* diapositive *f* ◇ **slide projector** projecteur *m* de diapositives *or* de diapos

slide show /'slaɪd ʃəʊ/ *noun* diaporama *m*

SLIP /slɪp/ *noun* protocole *m* SLIP

slot /slɒt/ *verb* glisser *vi*; insérer dans une fente ou dans une ouverture ◇ **the disk slots into one of the floppy drive apertures** la disquette s'insère *or* se glisse dans l'une des deux fentes du lecteur de disquettes

slow peripheral /sləʊ pə'rɪf(ə)rəl/ *noun* périphérique *m* lent

slow scan TV /ˌsləʊ skæn tiː 'viː/ *noun* télévision *f* à balayage lent

small computer systems interface /ˌsmɔːl kəmˌpjuːtə 'sɪstəmz ˌɪntəfeɪs/ *noun* interface *f* SCSI

small-scale /'smɔːl skeɪl/ *adjective* à petite échelle

small scale integration /ˌsmɔːl skeɪl ˌɪntɪ'greɪʃ(ə)n/ *noun* intégration *f* à petite échelle f

Smalltalk /'smɔːltɔːk/ (*programming language developed by Xerox*) Smalltalk™

smart card /'smɑːt kɑːd/ *noun* carte *f* à mémoire; carte *f* à puce; carte *f* magnétique

smart terminal /smɑːt 'tɜːmɪn(ə)l/ *noun* terminal *m* intelligent

smart wiring hub /ˌsmɑːt 'waɪərɪŋ ˌhʌb/ *noun* concentrateur *m*

SMB /ˌes em 'biː/ *noun* système *m* SMB (de partage de fichiers)

smiley /'smaɪli/ *noun* binette *f*

smooth scroll /ˌsmuːð 'skrəʊl/ *verb* faire défiler un texte point par point

SMPTE /ˌes em piː tiː 'iː/ *noun* SMPTE

SMPTE time code /ˌes em piː tiː iː 'taɪm ˌkəʊd/ *noun* code *m* horaire de la SMPTE

SMS *abbr* (*short message service*) service *m* de messages courts

SMT /ˌes em 'tiː/ *noun* procédé *m* d'assemblage SMT

SMTP /ˌes em tiː 'piː/ *noun* protocole *m* SMTP

S/N *abbr* (*signal to noise ratio*) rapport *m* signal sur bruit

SNA /ˌes en 'eɪ/ *noun* architecture *f* de réseau; architecture *f* SNA

snail mail /'sneɪl meɪl/ *noun* (*informal – refers to the normal slow postal delivery*) courrier *m* postal

snapshot /'snæpˌʃɒt/ *noun* instantané *m*

snapshot dump /'snæpˌʃɒt dʌmp/ *noun* vidage *m* instantané sur imprimante

sniffer /'snɪfə/ *noun* analyseur *m* de réseau

SNMP *abbr* (*simple network management protocol*) protocole *m* SNMP (de gestion de réseau)

SNOBOL /'snəʊbɒl/ *noun* langage *m* SNOBOL

snow /snəʊ/ *noun* (*TV image distortion*) neige *f* sur l'écran

soak /səʊk/ *verb* tester à outrance; tester en continu sur une longue période; torturer *vt* ◇ **the device was soak-tested prior to delivery** l'appareil a été testé à outrance *or* testé sous tous les angles avant la livraison

Society for Motion Picture and TV Engineers /səˌsaɪəti fə ˌməʊʃ(ə)n ˌpɪktʃə ən ˌtiː 'viː/ *noun* SMPTE

socket /'sɒkɪt/ *noun* prise *f*; douille *f*

socket driver /'sɒkɪt ˌdraɪvə/ *noun* bibliothèque *f* Winsock

soft /sɒft/ *adjective* **1.** (*material that loses magnetic effects*) doux; douce **2.** (*data not permanently stored*) sur support magnétique; effaçables ◇ **soft-reset** (*instruction*) ré-initialisation *f* logicielle *or* par logiciel *or* par commande

soft copy /sɒft 'kɒpi/ *noun* texte *m* d'écran

soft error /sɒft 'erə/ *noun* erreur *f* de logiciel

soft-fail /sɒft feɪl/ *adjective* à panne douce; à panne partielle

soft font /ˌsɒft 'fɒnt/ *noun* fonte *f* logicielle; fonte *f* téléchargeable; fonte *f* non résidente

soft goods /'sɒft gʊdz/ *plural noun* logiciels *mpl* téléchargés à la vente

soft hyphen /sɒft 'haɪf(ə)n/ *noun* trait d'union *m* d'écran qui ne s'imprime pas

soft keyboard /sɒft 'kiːˌbɔːd/ *noun* clavier *m* à touches programmables

soft keys /ˌsɒft 'kiːz/ *plural noun* (*keys which can be changed via a program*) touches *fpl* programmables

soft reset /sɒft ˌriː'set/ *noun* ré-initialisation *f* (du système) par commande

soft-sectored disk /ˌsɒft ˌsektəd 'dɪsk/ *noun* disque *m* formaté par logiciel; disque *m* sectorisé par logiciel

software /'sɒftweə/ *noun* (*program or group of programs*) logiciel *m* ◇ **applications software** logiciel d'application *or* progiciel *m* ◇ **software quality assurance (SQA)** assurance *f* qualité d'un logiciel ◇ **software writer** concepteur *m* de logiciel

software compatible /ˌsɒftweə kəm 'pætɪb(ə)l/ *adjective* compatible avec des logiciels écrits pour d'autres systèmes; compatible logiciels

software developer /'sɒftweə dɪˌveləpə/ *noun* (*person or company which writes software*) concepteur *m* de logiciel; développeur *m* de logiciel

software development /'sɒftweə dɪ ˌveləpmənt/ *noun* développement *m* d'un logiciel

software documentation /ˌsɒftweə ˌdɒkjʊmen'teɪʃ(ə)n/ *noun* notice *f* d'utilisation d'un logiciel

software engineer /'sɒftweə ˌendʒɪnɪə/ *noun* ingénieur *m* logiciel; ingénieur *m* programmeur

software engineering /'sɒftweə ˌendʒɪnɪərɪŋ/ *noun* génie *m* logiciel

software flow control /'sɒftweə fləʊ kən ˌtrəʊl/ *noun* protocole *m* XON/XOFF (de transmission asynchrone)

software house /'sɒftweə haʊs/ *noun* société *f* spécialisée en logiciels

software interrupt /ˌsɒftweə 'ɪntərʌpt/ *noun* interruption *f* générée par logiciel

software library /'sɒftweə ˌlaɪbrəri/ *noun* bibliothèque *f* de programmes; bibliothèque *f* de logiciels

software licence /'sɒftweə ˌlaɪs(ə)ns/ *noun* autorisation *f* de copie (d'un logiciel)

software life cycle /ˌsɒftweə 'laɪf ˌsaɪk(ə)l/ *noun* cycle *m* de vie d'un logiciel

software maintenance /'sɒftweə ˌmeɪntənəns/ *noun* maintenance *f*

software modem /'sɒftweə ˌməʊdem/ *noun* modem *m* logiciel

software package /'sɒftweə ˌpækɪdʒ/ *noun* progiciel *m*

software piracy /'sɒftweə ˌpaɪrəsi/ *noun* piratage *m* de logiciel

software quality assurance /ˌsɒftweə ˌkwɒlɪti ə'ʃʊərəns/ *noun* assurance *f* qualité dans le domaine du génie logiciel

software reliability /ˌsɒftweə rɪˌlaɪəbɪlɪti/ *noun* fiabilité *f* d'un logiciel

software specification /ˌsɒftweə ˌspesɪfɪ 'keɪʃ(ə)n/ *noun* spécifications *fpl* d'un logiciel; définition *f* et standards de qualité d'un logiciel

software system /'sɒftweə ˌsɪstəm/ *noun* progiciel *m*

software tool /'sɒftweə tuːl/ *noun* outil *m* de programmation

soft zone /ˌsɒft 'zəʊn/ *noun* zone *f* de texte

solid /'sɒlɪd/ *adjective* (*printed text*) sans interligne

solid error /ˌsɒlɪd 'erə/ *noun* erreur *f* persistante; erreur *f* permanente

solid font printer /ˌsɒlɪd fɒnt 'prɪntə/ *noun* imprimante *f* à caractères pleins

solid-state /'sɒlɪd steɪt/ *adjective* transistorisé; à semi-conducteur ◇ **solid-state laser** laser *m* transistorisé *or* à semi-conducteur

solid-state device /ˌsɒlɪd steɪt dɪ'vaɪs/ *noun* dispositif *m* à semi-conducteur

solid state disk /ˌsɒlɪd steɪt 'dɪsk/ *noun* disque *m* transistorisé

solid-state memory device /ˌsɒlɪd steɪt 'mem(ə)ri dɪˌvaɪs/ *noun* mémoire *f* transistorisée; mémoire *f* à semi-conducteur

son file /'sʌn faɪl/ *noun* fichier *m* fils; fichier *m* de troisième génération

Sony /'səʊni/ (*leading electronics innovator*) Sony

sophisticated /sə'fɪstɪkeɪtɪd/ *adjective* sophistiqué; évolué; recherché; avancé ◇ **a sophisticated desktop publishing program** un programme de PAO évolué *or* avancé

sophistication /səˌfɪstɪ'keɪʃ(ə)n/ *noun* sophistication *f*; avance *f* technologique ◇ **the sophistication of the new package is remarkable** le degré de sophistication du nouveau progiciel est remarquable

sort /sɔːt/ *verb* trier *vt*; classer *vt* ■ *noun* classer; trier ◇ **to sort addresses into alphabetical order** classer les adresses en *or* par ordre alphabétique

sorting pass /ˌsɔːtɪŋ 'pɑːs/ *noun* passage *m* de tri

sortkey /'sɔːtkiː/, **sort field** /'sɔːt fiːld/ *noun* clé *f* de tri; champ *m* de tri ◇ **the orders were sorted according to dates by assigning the date field as the sortkey** les commandes ont été triées suivant leur date en designant le champ date comme clé de tri

sort/merge /ˌsɔːt 'mɜːdʒ/ *noun* trier/fusionner

SOT *abbr* (*start of text*) début *m* de texte

sound /saʊnd/ *noun* sound

sound bandwidth /saʊnd 'bændˌwɪdθ/ *noun* largeur *f* de bande audio

Sound Blaster /'saʊnd ˌblɑːstə/ (*trade name for a type of sound card for PC compatibles developed by Creative Labs*) carte *f* audio Sound Blaster™

sound capture /saʊnd 'kæptʃə/ *noun* capture *f* de son

sound card /ˌsaʊnd 'kɑːd/ *noun* carte *f* audio; carte *f* son

sound chip /ˌsaʊnd 'tʃɪp/ *noun* générateur *m* de son

sound file /ˌsaʊnd 'faɪl/ *noun* fichier *m* audio; fichier *m* son

sound hood /ˌsaʊnd 'hʊd/ *noun* hotte *f*

sound pressure level /ˌsaʊnd 'preʃə ˌlev(ə)l/ *noun* niveau *m* de pression acoustique

Sound Recorder /'saʊnd rɪˌkɔːdə/ (*utility included with Microsoft Windows that allows a user to play back digitised sound files*) enregistreur *m* de sons

sound waves /ˌsaʊnd 'weɪvz/ *plural noun* ondes *fpl* sonores

source /sɔːs/ *noun* (*point where a signal enters a network*) source *f*; (*terminal on an FET device*) borne *f* d'entrée

source address filtering /'sɔːs əˌdres ˌfɪltərɪŋ/ *noun* filtrage *m* des adresses sources

source book /ˌsɔːs 'bʊk/ *noun* fichiers *mpl* sources

source code /ˌsɔːs 'kəʊd/ *noun* code *m* source

source deck /ˌsɔːs 'dek/ *noun* jeu *m* original

source document /sɔːs 'dɒkjʊˌment/ *noun* document *m* original; document *m* d'origine

source editor /sɔːs 'edɪtə/ *noun* éditeur *m* de programme source

source file /ˌsɔːs 'faɪl/ *noun* fichier *m* source

source language /sɔːs 'læŋgwɪdʒ/ *noun* **1.** (*language in which a program is originally written*) langue *f* source **2.** (*language of a program prior to translation*) langue *f* source

source listing /sɔːs 'lɪstɪŋ/ *noun* (*text in its original form*) listage *m*; liste *f* du texte source; (*of source program*) listage *m* d'un programme source

source machine /sɔːs mə'ʃiːn/ *noun* (*computer which can compile source code*) ordinateur-compilateur *m*

source object /sɔːs 'ɒbdʒekt/ *noun* objet *m* source

source pack /'sɔːs pæk/ *noun* jeu *m* original

source program /sɔːs 'prəʊgræm/ *noun* programme *m* source; programme *m* d'origine

source routing /ˌsɔːs 'raʊtɪŋ/ *noun* routage *m* source

SP *abbr* (*stack pointer*) pointeur *m* de pile

space /speɪs/ *noun* (*gap between characters or lines*) espace *m*; espacement *m* ■ *verb* espacer *vt*

space bar /'speɪs bɑː/ *noun* barre *f* d'espacement

space character /speɪs 'kærɪktə/ *noun* (*character code which prints a space*) caractère *m* d'espacement; caractère *m* espace; caractère *m* blanc

spacer /'speɪsə/ *noun* gestionnaire *m* d'espaces

spacing /'speɪsɪŋ/ *noun* espaces *mpl* ◇ **the spacing on some lines is very uneven** il y a quelques lignes o— les espaces sont très inégaux

spam /spæm/ *noun slang* (*junk mail through your e-mail*) publicité *f* non sollicitée; message *m* publicitaire sans intérêt ◇ **anti-spam** (*feature of some e-mail programs that will automatically delete any unwanted message received*) filtre *m* (pour bloquer les messages non sollicités)

span /spæn/ *noun* fourchette *f*

spanning tree /'spænɪŋ triː/ *noun* (*creating a logical topology*) arborescence *f*

SPARC /spɑːk/ *noun* architecture *f* de processeur scalaire; architecture *f* SPARC

spare part /ˌspeə 'pɑːt/ *noun* pièce *f* détachée

spark printer /spɑːk 'prɪntə/ *noun* imprimante *f* thermique à étincelle

sparse array /spɑːs ə'reɪ/ *noun* tableau *m* réduit; matrice *f* réduite

spec /spek/ *noun informal* spécification *f*

special character /ˌspeʃ(ə)l 'kærɪktə/ *noun* caractère *m* spécial

special interest group /ˌspeʃ(ə)l 'ɪntrəst ˌgruːp/ *noun* groupe *m* d'intérêt spécial

specialise /'speʃəlaɪz/ *verb* être expert; être spécialiste; se spécialiser

specialist /'speʃəlɪst/ *noun* expert *m*; spécialiste *m&f*

special purpose /ˌspeʃ(ə)l 'pɜːpəs/ *noun* spécial *or* -e; dédié *or* -ée

special sort /'speʃ(ə)l sɔːt/ *noun* caractère *m* spécial

specific address /spəˌsɪfɪk ə'dres/ *noun* adresse *f* spécifique

specification /ˌspesɪfɪ'keɪʃ(ə)n/ *noun* spécification *f*

specific code /spə'sɪfɪk kəʊd/ *noun* code *m* binaire absolu; code *m* spécifique

specific coding /spə'sɪfɪk kɒdɪŋ/ *noun* codage *m* spécifique; codage *m* binaire à adresse absolue

specificity /ˌspesɪ'fɪsəti/ *noun* spécificité *f*

speech chip /ˌspiːtʃ 'tʃɪp/ *noun* puce *f* de synthèse vocale

speech quality /spiːtʃ 'kwɒlɪti/ *noun* qualité *f* vocale

speech recognition /spiːtʃ ˌrekəg'nɪʃ(ə)n/ *noun* reconnaissance *f* vocale; reconnaissance *f* de la parole

speech synthesis /spiːtʃ 'sɪnθəsɪs/ *noun* synthèse *f* vocale

speech synthesiser /'spiːtʃ ˌsɪnθəsaɪzə/ *noun* synthétiseur *m* vocal de la parole

speed of loop /ˌspiːd əv 'luˑ'/ *noun* fréquence *f* de boucle

spellcheck /'speltʃek/ *verb* vérifier l'orthographe; faire une vérification orthographique

spellchecker /'speltʃekə/, **spelling checker** /ˌspelɪŋ 'tʃekə/ *noun* vérificateur *m* d'orthographe; programme *m* de vérification orthographique ◇ **the program will be upgraded with a word-processor and a spelling checker** on va optimiser le programme en ajoutant un traitement de texte et un vérificateur d'orthographe

spider /'spaɪdə/ *noun* (*search program*) araignée *f*

spike /spaɪk/ *noun* (*of voltage pulse*) pointe *f* de tension

spillage /'spɪlɪdʒ/ *noun* débordement *m*; excès *m*

spindle /'spɪnd(ə)l/ *noun* (*for disk*) axe *m*

spindling /'spɪndlɪŋ/ *noun* (*turning a disk by hand*) mouvement *m* de rotation (transmis manuellement)

SPL /ˌes piː 'el/ *noun* niveau *m* de pression acoustique

splash screen /'splæʃ skriːn/ *noun* fenêtre *f* splash; page *f* de présentation

splice /splaɪs/ *verb* (*to join ends of tape or film*) coller *vt*; faire un raccord ◇ **splicing block** colleuse *f* de film *or* de bande ◇ **you can use glue or splicing tape to splice the ends** utilisez de la colle ou du ruban gommé pour raccorder les extrémités (du film)

splicing tape /'splaɪsɪŋ teɪp/ *noun* ruban *m* de raccord

split baud rate /ˌsplɪt 'bɔːd ˌreɪt/ *noun* modem *m* à deux vitesses ◇ **the viewdata modem uses a 1200 *or* 75 split baud rate** le modem viewdata reçoit à 1200 bauds et transmet à 75

split screen /'splɪt skriːn/ *noun* écran *m* divisé; écran *m* partagé ◇ **we use split screen mode to show the text being worked on and another text from memory for comparison** nous utilisons le mode d'écran partagé pour comparer le texte en cours de travail à un texte de référence conservé en mémoire

spoof /spuːf/ *verb* usurper une adresse IP

spool /spuːl/ *noun* (*for tape or ribbon*) bobine *f* ■ *verb* (*to transfer data*) faire un spoule

spooler *noun* (*for storage*) dispositif *m* mémoire pour spoule

spooling /'spuːlɪŋ/ *noun* spoule *m*

spooling device /'spuːlɪŋ dɪˌvaɪs/ *noun* programme *m* d'impression désynchronisé

sporadic fault /spə'rædɪk fɔːlt/ *noun* erreur *f* sporadique

spreadsheet /'spredˌʃiːt/ *noun* **1.** (*program*) tableur *m*; (*printout*) tableau *m* **2.** tableur *m*

sprite /spraɪt/ *noun* (*in computer graphics*) esprit *m*; sprite *m*

sprocket *noun* roue *f* à picots

sprocket feed /'sprɒkɪt fiːd/ *noun* entraînement *m* par picots

sprocket holes /'sprɒkɪt həʊlz/ *plural noun* perforations *fpl* d'entraînement; perforations *fpl* marginales

sprocket wheel /'sprɒkɪt wiːl/ *noun* roue *f* à picots

SPX /ˌes piː 'eks/ SPX ■ *noun* simplex *m*; transmission *f* unidirectionnelle

spyware /'spaɪweə/ *noun* logiciel *m* espion

SQA *abbr* (*software quality assurance*) assurance *f* qualité logiciel

SQL /ˌes kjuː 'el/ *noun* langage *m* SQL; langage *m* de requête

square brackets /skweə 'brækɪts/ *plural noun* crochet(s)

square measure /ˌskweə 'meʒə/ *noun* mesure *f* de surface

square root /skweə 'ruːt/ *noun* racine *f* carrée

square wave /ˌskweə 'weɪv/ *noun* onde *f* carrée

SRAM /'es ræm/ *noun* RAM *f* statique; RAM *f* non rafraîchie

SSD *abbr* (*single-sided disk*) disquette *f* à simple face

SSI *abbr* (*small scale integration*) intégration *f* à petite échelle

SSL /ˌes es 'el/ *noun* protocole *m* SSL

ST506 standard /ˌes tiː ˌfaɪv əʊ 'sɪks ˌstændəd/ *noun* (*old disk interface standard*) standard *m* ST506 ◇ **the ST506 standard has now been replaced by IDE and SCSI** le standard ST506 a été remplacé par les normes IDE et SCSI

stable state /'steɪb(ə)l steɪt/ *noun* état *m* stable

stack /stæk/ *noun* pile *f* ◇ **stack pointer (SP)** pointeur *m* de pile

stackable hub /ˌstækəb(ə)l 'hʌb/ *noun* concentrateur *m* empilable

stack address /stæk ə'dres/ *noun* adresse *f* de pile

stack base /'stæk beɪs/ *noun* base *f* de la pile

stacked job control /ˌstækt 'dʒɒb kənˌtrəʊl/ *noun* contrôle *m* de travaux groupés en pile

stack job processing /ˌstæk dʒɒb 'prəʊsesɪŋ/ *noun* traitement *m* de pile de tâches

stack overflow /stæk ˌəʊvə'fləʊ/ *noun* espace *m* disponible insuffisant

stack pointer /'stæk ˌpɔɪntə/ *noun* pointeur *m* de pile

stackware /'stækweə/ *noun* (*Apple applications*) application *f* pour le système Apple Macintosh HyperCard stackware

stage /steɪdʒ/ *noun* (*one of several points in a process*) étape *f*; phase *f*; stade *m* ◇ **we are in the first stage of running in the new computer system** nous n'en sommes qu'à la phase de rodage du système d'exploitation

staged /steɪdʒd/ *adjective* graduel *or* -elle; effectuéé -ée par étapes; effectuéé -ée par paliers

staged change-over /ˌstægd 'tʃeɪndʒ/ *noun* passage *m* graduel

stand-alone /stænd ə'ləʊn/, **standalone** *adjective* poste *m* autonome; poste *m* individuel ■ *noun* poste *m* autonome

stand-alone system /'stænd əˌləʊn ˌsɪstəm/ *noun* système *m* autonome ◇ **the workstations have been networked together rather than used as stand-alone systems** les postes ont été reliés en réseau plutôt que d'être utilisés comme postes autonomes *or* comme postes individuels

stand-alone terminal /'stænd əˌləʊn ˌtɜːmɪn(ə)l/ *noun* terminal *m* autonome

standard /'stændəd/ *noun* (*normal or usual*) norme *f*

standard colours /ˌstændəd 'kʌləz/ *plural noun* couleurs *fpl* normalisées

standard document /ˌstændəd 'dɒkjʊmənt/, **standard form** /'stændəd fɔːm/ *noun* document *m*

standard function /ˌstændəd 'fʌŋkʃən/ *noun* fonction *f* standard

Standard Generalized Markup Language /ˌstændəd ˌdʒen(ə)rəlaɪzd 'mɑːkʌp ˌlæŋgwɪdʒ/ *noun* langage *m* de balisage SGML

standard interface /ˌstændəd 'ɪntəfeɪs/ *noun* (*interface which conforms to pre-defined standards*) interface *f* standard

standardise /'stændədaɪz/ *verb* normaliser *vt*; standardiser *vt*

standard letter /ˌstændəd 'letə/ *noun* lettre *f* type; lettre *f* standard

standard memory /ˌstændəd 'mem(ə)ri/ *noun* mémoire *f* conventionnelle

standard paragraph /ˌstændəd 'pærəgrɑːf/ *noun* document *m*

standards converter /'stændədz kənˌvɜːtə/ *noun* convertisseur *m* de normes

standard subroutine /ˌstændəd 'sʌbruːtiːn/ *noun* sous-programme *m* standard

standard text /ˌstændəd 'tekst/ *noun* document *m*

standby /'stændbaɪ/ *adjective* (*device or program*) de réserve; auxiliaire ■ *noun* dispositif *m* de secours; de réserve; auxiliaire *(m&f)*

standby equipment /'stændbaɪ ɪ ˌkwɪpmənt/ *noun* (*secondary system*) équipement *m*

star network /'stɑː ˌnetwɜːk/ *noun* réseau *m* en étoile

star program /stɑː 'prəʊgræm/ *noun* programme *m* vedette

start /stɑːt/ *noun* (*of file*) début *m*; (*of machine*) démarrage *m*; mise *f* en route ◇ **start of text (SOT** *or* **STX)** (code de) début de texte

start bit /'stɑːt ˌbɪt/ *noun* bit *m*

Start button /'stɑːt ˌbʌt(ə)n/ *noun* (*button that is normally in the bottom left-hand corner of a Windows 95 Desktop screen*) Démarrer

start element /'stɑːt ˌelɪmənt/ *noun* bit *m*

starting point /'stɑːtɪŋ pɔɪnt/ *noun* point *m* de départ

start of header /ˌstɑːt əv 'hedə/ *noun* début *m* d'en-tête

start of text /ˌstɑːt əv 'tekst/ *noun* début *m* de texte

star topology /'stɑː təˌpɒlədʒi/ *noun* configuration *f* en étoile; topologie *f* en étoile ◇ **if one workstation cable snaps in a star topology, the rest continue, unlike a bus topology** si le câble d'une station d'un réseau en étoile se casse, les autres stations ne sont pas affectées, ce qui n'est pas le cas dans une topologie en bus

start page /'stɑːt peɪdʒ/ *noun* page *f* d'ouverture

startup disk /'stɑːtʌp dɪsk/ *noun* (*disk which holds the operating system and system configuration files*) disquette *f* système

startup screen /'stɑːtʌp skriːn/ *noun* écran *m* de démarrage

statement /'steɪtmənt/ *noun* **1.** instruction *f* **2.** (*instruction in a source language*) instruction *f* ◇ **multi-statement line** ligne multi-instruction

statement number /'steɪtmənt ˌnʌmbə/ *noun* numéro *m* d'instruction

state-of-the-art /ˌsteɪt əv ði 'ɑːt/ *adjective* (*technology, etc.*) de pointe; avancé *or* -ée

'...the main PCB is decidedly non-state-of-the-art' [*Personal Computer World*]

static /'stætɪk/ *adjective* **1.** (*not dynamic*) statique; qui n'évolue pas; qui ne change pas **2.** (*charge*) statique

static dump /'stætɪk dʌmp/ *noun* vidage *m* statique

static electricity /ˌstætɪk ɪlek'trɪsɪti/ *noun* électricité *f* statique

static memory /ˌstætɪk 'mem(ə)ri/ *noun* (*nonvolatile memory*) mémoire *f* statique

static object /ˌstætɪk 'ɒbdʒekt/ *noun* objet *m* statique

static RAM /ˌstætɪk 'ræm/ *noun* mémoire *f* RAM statique

static relocation /ˌstætɪk ˌriːləʊ'keɪʃ(ə)n/ *noun* relogement *m* statique; translation *f* statique; déplacement *m* statique

static storage /ˌstætɪk 'stɔːrɪdʒ/ *noun* mémoire *f* statique

static subroutine /ˌstætɪk 'sʌbruːtiːn/ *noun* sous-programme *m* statique

station /'steɪʃ(ə)n/ *noun* (*point in a network or communications system*) station *f*; poste *m*; terminal *m*; console *f* ◇ **earth station** station *f* terrestre ◇ **play station** *or* **playstation** console de jeu ◇ **radio station** station radio ◇ **station management (SMT)** (*software and hardware within* *the FDDI specification*) gestion *f* de station SMT ◇ **the signal from this radio station is very weak** le signal de cette station émettrice *or* de cet émetteur radio est très faible ◇ **we are trying to jam the signals from that station** nous essayons de brouiller les signaux émis par cette station

station management /ˌsteɪʃ(ə)n ˈmænɪdʒmənt/ *noun* gestion *f* de travail SMT

statistical /stəˈtɪstɪk(ə)l/ *adjective* statistique ◇ **statistical time division multiplexing (STDM)** multiplexage temporel statistique *or* en fonction des appels

statistics /stəˈtɪstɪks/ *noun* (*science*) statistique *f* ■ *plural noun* statistiques

status bar /ˈsteɪtəs bɑː/ *noun* barre *f* d'état

status bit /ˈsteɪtəs bɪt/ *noun* bit *m* d'état

status line /ˈsteɪtəs laɪn/ *noun* ligne *f* d'état

status poll /ˈsteɪtəs pəʊl/ *noun* appel de contrôle *m* d'état

status register /ˈsteɪtəs ˌredʒɪstə/ *noun* registre *m* d'état

ST connector /ˌes tiː kəˈnektə/ *noun* (*connector used to terminate optical fibres*) connecteur *m* ST

steady state /ˈstedi steɪt/ *noun* état *m* stationnaire

steganography /ˌstegəˈnɒgrəfi/ *noun* stéganographie *f*

stencil /ˈstens(ə)l/ *noun* (*for duplicating*) stencil *m*

step /step/ *noun* (*single unit*) étape *f*; pas *m* ■ *verb* (*to move forwards*) faire un pas; avancer d'un pas; (*to move backwards*) reculer d'un pas

step frame /step freɪm/ *verb* capturer des images vidéo une à une

stepper motor, stepping motor *noun* moteur *m* à pas

step through /step θruː/ *noun* (*function of a debugger that allows to execute a program one instruction at a time to see where the fault lies*) déroulement *m* d'un programme avec arrêt sur chaque instruction; exécution *f* d'un programme une instruction à la fois

stereo /ˈsteriəʊ/, **stereophonic** /ˌsteriəˈfɒnɪk/ *adjective* stéréo; stéréophonique

stickiness /ˈstɪkinəs/ *noun* attractivité *f*

stick model /stɪk ˈmɒd(ə)l/ *noun* représentation *f* filaire

sticky /ˈstɪki/ *adjective* attractif

still /stɪl/ *noun* image *f* fixe

stochastic model /stəˈkæstɪk ˌmɒd(ə)l/ *noun* modèle *m* stochastique

stop and wait protocol /ˌstɒp ən ˈweɪt ˌprəʊtəkɒl/ *noun* protocole *m* de contrôle par signal d'arrêt

stop bit /stɒp bɪt/ *noun* bit *m* d'arrêt; élément *m* d'arrêt

stop code /stɒp kəʊd/ *noun* code *m* d'arrêt

stop element /stɒp ˈelɪmənt/ *noun* bit *m* d'arrêt; élément *m* d'arrêt

stop instruction /stɒp ɪnˈstrʌkʃən/ *noun* instruction *f* d'arrêt

stop list /stɒp lɪst/ *noun* (*list of words which are not to be used*) liste *f* d'interdictions

stop time /stɒp taɪm/ *noun* (*disk*) temps *m* d'arrêt; temps *m* de décélération

storage /ˈstɔːrɪdʒ/ *noun* (*place*) mémoire *f*; (*action*) stockage *m*; mise *f* en mémoire ◇ **storage size** taille *f* de la mémoire ◇ **volatile storage** mémoire volatile

storage allocation /ˈstɔːrɪdʒ ˌæləkeɪʃ(ə)n/ *noun* allocation *f* de mémoire

storage capacity /ˈstɔːrɪdʒ kəˌpæsɪti/ *noun* (*data storage*) capacité *f* de mémoire; taille *f* de mémoire ◇ **total storage capacity is now 3MB** la capacité *or* la taille de la mémoire est maintenant de 3Mo

storage density /ˈstɔːrɪdʒ ˌdensɪti/ *noun* densité *f* de mémoire

storage device /ˈstɔːrɪdʒ dɪˌvaɪs/ *noun* dispositif *m* mémoire; dispositif *m* de stockage

storage disk /ˈstɔːrɪdʒ dɪsk/ *noun* (*data storage*) disquette *f*

storage dump /ˈstɔːrɪdʒ dʌmp/ *noun* vidage *m*

storage medium /ˈstɔːrɪdʒ ˌmiːdiəm/ *noun* support *m* de mémoire

storage tube /ˈstɔːrɪdʒ tjuːb/ *noun* écran *m*

store /stɔː/ *noun* mémoire *f* ■ *verb* (*to save data*) mettre en mémoire; ranger en mémoire ◇ **store address register (SAR)** registre *m* d'adresse en mémoire ◇ **store data register (SDR)** registre des données en mémoire

store address register /ˌstɔː əˈdres ˌredʒɪstə/ *noun* registre *m* d'adresse en mémoire

store and forward /ˌstɔː ən ˈfɔəwəd/ *noun* envoi *m* différé

store cell /ˈstɔː sel/ *noun* cellule *f* de mémoire

store data register /ˌstɔː ˈdeɪtə ˌredʒɪstə/ *noun* registre *m* des données en mémoire

stored program /stɔːd ˈprəʊgræm/ *noun* programme *m* mis en mémoire; programme *m* mémorisé; programme *m* enregistré

stored program signalling /ˌstɔːd ˌprəʊgræm ˈsɪgn(ə)lɪŋ/ *noun* signalisation *f* à contrôle programmé en mémoire

store location /stɔː ləʊˈkeɪʃ(ə)n/ *noun* emplacement *m* de mémoire

story board /ˈstɔːri bɔːd/ *noun* scénarimage *m*

STP *abbr* (*shielded twisted pair*) paire *f* torsadée blindée

straight-line coding /ˌstreɪt laɪn ɪnˈkəʊdɪŋ/ *noun* codage *m* en ligne directe

stream /striːm/ *noun* flux *m* continu; flot *m*

streaming audio /ˌstriːmɪŋ ˈɔːdiəʊ/ *noun* lecture *f* audio en transit

streaming data /ˌstriːmɪŋ 'deɪtə/, **streaming protocol** *noun* données *fpl* de transmission en continu

streaming tape drive /ˌstriːmɪŋ 'teɪp ˌdraɪv/ *noun* unité *f* de bande magnétique en continu; streamer *m*; unité *f* de sauvegarde rapide sur bande magnétique en continu

streaming video /ˌstriːmɪŋ 'vɪdiəʊ/ *noun* contenu *m* vidéo sur Internet

strikethrough *noun* biffure *f*

string /strɪŋ/ *noun* (*series of characters*) chaîne *f*; séquence *f* ◇ **string orientated symbolic language (SNOBOL)** langage *m* SNOBOL (de traitement et de manipulation de chaîne)

string area /strɪŋ 'eəriə/ *noun* zone *f* de chaîne

string array /strɪŋ ə'reɪ/ *noun* tableau *m* de chaînes de caractères

string concatenation /strɪŋ kənˌkætə'neɪʃ(ə)n/ *noun* concaténation *f* de chaînes

string function /strɪŋ 'fʌŋkʃən/ *noun* fonction *f* de chaîne

string length /strɪŋ leŋθ/ *noun* taille *f* d'une chaîne

string name /strɪŋ neɪm/ *noun* nom *m* de chaîne

string orientated symbolic language /ˌstrɪŋ ˌɔːriənteɪtɪd sɪmˌbɒlɪk 'læŋgwɪdʒ/ *noun* langage *m* SNOBOL

string type /strɪŋ taɪp/ *noun* variable *f* de type chaîne de caractères

string variable /strɪŋ 'veəriəb(ə)l/ *noun* variable *f* de chaîne

stringy floppy /ˌstrɪŋi 'flɒpi/ *noun* unité *f* de sauvegarde rapide sur bande magnétique; streamer *m*

strip /strɪp/ *verb* dépouiller *vt*

strip window /strɪp 'wɪndəʊ/ *noun* fenêtre *f* d'une ligne

strobe /strəʊb/ *verb* émettre une impulsion; échantillonner *vt*; valider *vt*; émettre un signal ■ *noun* (*pulse of an electric circuit*) impulsion *f* électrique

stroke /strəʊk/ *noun* **1.** frappe *f* **2.** trait *m*

structure /'strʌktʃə/ *noun* structure *f* ■ *verb* structurer *vt*; organiser *vt* ◇ **you first structure a document to meet your requirements and then fill in the blanks** vous organisez d'abord le document pour répondre à vos besoins, puis vous remplissez les blancs

structured cabling /ˌstrʌktʃəd 'keɪb(ə)lɪŋ/ *noun* câblage *m* structuré

structured design /ˌstrʌktʃəd dɪ'zaɪn/ *noun* modèle *m* structuré

structured programming /ˌstrʌktʃəd 'prəʊgræmɪŋ/ *noun* programmation *f* structurée

structured query language /ˌstrʌktʃəd 'kwɪəri ˌlæŋgwɪdʒ/ *noun* langage *m* SQL; langage *m* de requête

structured wiring /ˌstrʌktʃəd 'waɪərɪŋ/ *noun* câblage *m* structuré

stub /stʌb/ *noun* (*short program routine*) programme *m* souche

stuck beacon /stʌk 'biːkən/ *noun* (*error where a station continuously transmits beacon frames*) alerteur *m* bloqué

STX *abbr* (*start of text*) début *m* de texte

style /staɪl/ *noun* (*formatting*) style *m*

style sheet /staɪl ʃiːt/ *noun* feuille *f* de style

stylus /'staɪləs/ *noun* (*for audio record*) pointe *f*; diamant *m* de lecture; (*for video disk*) lecteur *m*

stylus printer /'staɪləs ˌprɪntə/ *noun* imprimante *f* matricielle; imprimante *f* à aiguilles

sub- /sʌb/ *prefix* sous-; secondaire

subaddress /'sʌbəˌdres/ *noun* adresse *f* secondaire

subclass /'sʌbklɑːs/ *noun* sous-classe *f*

subdirectory /'sʌbdɪˌrekt(ə)ri/ *noun* sous-répertoire *m*

> '...if you delete a file and then delete the subdirectory where it was located, you cannot restore the file because the directory does not exist' [*Personal Computer World*]

sub-domain /sʌb dəʊ'meɪn/ *noun* sous-domaine *m*

subdomain name /ˌsʌbdə'meɪn ˌneɪm/ *noun* nom *m* de sous-domaine

subject line /'sʌbdʒɪkt laɪn/ *noun* ligne *f* objet

submenu /'sʌbmenjuː/ *noun* (*secondary menu displayed as a choice from a menu*) sous-menu *m*

submit button /səbˌmɪt 'bʌt(ə)n/ *noun* bouton *m* Soumettre

subnet /'sʌbnet/ *noun* sous-réseau *m* ◇ **subnet address** *or* **subnet number** adresse *f* de sous-r,seau

subnet address /'sʌbnet əˌdres/, **subnet number** /'sʌbnet ˌnʌmbə/ *noun* adresse *f* de sous-réseau

subnet mask /'sʌbnet mɑːsk/ *noun* masque *m* de sous-réseau

subnotebook /sʌb'nəʊtbʊk/ *noun* ordinateur *m* ultraportatif

subprogram /'sʌbprəʊgræm/ *noun* sous-programme *m*

subroutine /'sʌbruːˌtiːn/ *noun* sous-programme *m* ◇ **subrroutine call** appel *m* d'un sous-programme

subroutine call /'sʌbruːˌtiːn kɔːl/ *noun* appel *m* d'un sous-programme

subscribe /səb'skraɪb/ *verb* s'abonner (à)

subscriber /səb'skraɪbə/ *noun* **1.** (*telephone or service*) abonné *mf or* -ée *or* -ée **2.** abonné *mf or* -ée

subscript /'sʌbskrɪpt/ *noun* indice *m*

subscripted variable /ˌsʌbskrɪptɪd 'veəriəb(ə)l/ *noun* variable *f* indicée; variable *f* caractérisée par un indice

subsegment /'sʌbsegmənt/ *noun* sous-segment *m*

subset /'sʌbˌset/ *noun* sous-ensemble *m*

substitute /'sʌbstɪtjuːt/ *verb* substituer *vt*

substitute character /ˌsʌbstɪtjuːt 'kærɪktə/ *noun* (*character displayed if a received character is not recognised*) caractère *m* de substitution

substitution error /ˌsʌbstɪ'tjuːʃ(ə)n ˌerə/ *noun* erreur *f* de substitution

substitution table /ˌsʌbstɪ'tjuːʃ(ə)n ˌteɪb(ə)l/ *noun* table *f* de substitution; table *f* d'équivalence

substrate /'sʌbstreɪt/ *noun* (*base material*) substrat *m*

subsystem /'sʌbsɪstəm/ *noun* (*smaller part of a large system*) sous-système *m*

subtraction /səb'trækʃən/ *noun* soustraction *f*

subtrahend /'sʌbtrəhend/ *noun* nombre *m* à soustraire d'un autre; diminuteur *m*

sub-woofer /sʌb 'wʊfə/ *noun* caisson *m* de basse

suffix notation /ˌsʌfɪks nəʊ'teɪʃ(ə)n/ *noun* (*postfix notation*) notation *f* suffixée; notation *f* polonaise inversée

suitcase /'suːtkeɪs/ *noun* (*Apple Macintosh icon which contains a screen font*) valise *f*; icône *f* de police de caractères

suite of programs /ˌswiːt əv 'prəʊgræmz/ *noun* **1.** (*which run one after the other*) suite *f* de programmes; série *f* de programmes **2.** (*used for a particular task*) série *f* de programmes; suite *f* de programmes ◇ **the word-processing system uses a suite of three programs, editor, spelling checker and printing controller** le système de traitement de texte utilise une série de trois programmes: un éditeur de texte, un correcteur d'orthographe et un contrôleur d'impression

sum /sɒm/ *noun* somme *f*; addition *f*

summation check /sʌ'meɪʃ(ə)n tʃek/ *noun* contrôle *m* par totalisation

Sun Microsystems /ˌsʌn 'maɪkrəʊsɪstəmz/ Sun Microsystems

super- /suːpə/ *prefix* super-; sur- ◇ **super VGA (SVGA)** (*enhancement to the standard VGA graphics system*) (standard d'écran) super VGA *or* SVGA

supercomputer /ˌsuːpəkəm'pjuːtə/ *noun* (*for high speed mathematical tasks*) ordinateur *m* géant; ordinateur *m* de grande puissance

superimpose /ˌsuːpərɪm'pəʊz/ *verb* surimposer *vt*

superior number /sʊˌpɪəriə 'nʌmbə/ *noun* exposant *m*; chiffre *m* en exposant

superscript /'suːpəˌskrɪpt/ *noun* exposant *m*

supersede /ˌsuːpə'siːd/ *verb* remplacer *vt* ◇ **the new program supersedes the earlier one, and is much faster** le nouveau programme, qui remplace le précédent, est beaucoup plus rapide

super VGA /ˌsuːpə viː dʒiː 'eɪ/ *noun* super VGA; SVGA

supervisor /'suːpəˌvaɪzə/ *noun* **1.** (*person*) surveillant *m or* -e; contrôleur *m or* -euse; superviseur *m*; (*program*) programme *m* superviseur **2.** (*program*) programme *m* superviseur

supervisor program /'suːpəvaɪzə ˌprəʊgræm/ *noun* programme *m* superviseur

supervisory /'suːpəvaɪzəri/ *adjective* de supervision; de surveillance; de contrôle

supervisory instruction /ˌsuːpəvaɪzəri ɪn'strʌkʃən/ *noun* instruction *f* de surveillance

supervisory program /ˌsuːpəvaɪzəri 'prəʊgræm/ *noun* programme *m* superviseur

supervisory sequence /'suːpəvaɪzəri ˌsiːkwəns/ *noun* séquence *f* de contrôle

supervisory signal /ˌsuːpəvaɪzəri 'sɪgn(ə)l/ *noun* signal *m* de contrôle; signal *m* de supervision

supplier /sə'plaɪə/ *noun* fournisseur *m* ◇ **a supplier of computer parts** un fournisseur de pièces pour ordinateurs ◇ **a supplier of disk drives** *or* **a disk drive supplier** un fournisseur d'unités de disques *or* de lecteurs de disquettes ◇ **our Japanese suppliers have set up a warehouse in England** nos fournisseurs japonais ont ouvert un entrepôt en Angleterre

supply /sə'plaɪ/ *noun* fourniture *f*; approvisionnement *m* ■ *verb* fournir *vt*; approvisionner *vt* ◇ **the computer was supplied by a recognized dealer** l'ordinateur vient de chez un fournisseur connu ◇ **they have signed a contract to supply on-line information** ils ont signé un contrat pour fournir des informations en ligne ◇ **they signed a contract for the supply of computer stationery** ils ont signé un contrat pour la fourniture de papier pour imprimante

support /sə'pɔːt/ *verb* supporter *vt* ■ *noun* (*providing help*) support *m* ◇ **the main computer supports six workstations** l'ordinateur principal supporte *or* accepte *or* contrôle six postes de travail

support chip /sə'pɔːt tʃɪp/ *noun* processeur *m* auxiliaire

suppressor /sə'presə/ *noun* dispositif *m* antiparasite

surf /sɜːf/ *verb* naviguer *vt*

surface-mount technology /ˌsɜːfɪs maʊnt tek'nɒlədʒi/ *noun* (*manufacturing circuit boards*) procédé *m* d'assemblage SMT

surge /sɜːdʒ/ *noun* (*electrical*) surtension *f*; pointe *f* de tension

surge protector /sɜːdʒ prə'tektə/ *noun* limiteur *m* de tension

SVGA /ˌes viː dʒiː 'eɪ/ *noun* SVGA

S-Video /ˌes 'vɪdiəʊ/ *noun* S-Video

swap /swɒp/ *noun* basculement *m* (de programme); permutation *f* (de programme) ■ *verb* permuter *vt*; basculer *vi*; échanger *vt*; changer de place

swap file /swɒp faɪl/ *noun* (*file stored on the hard disk used as a temporary storage area for data held in RAM, to provide virtual memory*) copie *f* de fichier

swapping /'swɒpɪŋ/ *noun* basculement *m*; permutation *f*

swim /swɪm/ *noun* flottement *m*

switch /swɪtʃ/ *noun* **1.** (*additional character*) commutateur *m* **2.** (*point in a computer program*) aiguillage *m*; bifurcation *f* logique **3.** (*device*) commutateur *m* ■ *verb* (*connect two lines*) connecter *vt* ◇ **add the switch '*or* W' to the DOS command DIR and the directory listing will be displayed across the screen** ajoutez le commutateur '/W' à la commande DIR (sous DOS) pour afficher le répertoire sur toute la largeur de l'écran ◇ **switch train** série *f* de commutateurs *or* commutateurs en série

switched network backup /ˌswɪtʃ 'netwɜːk ˌbækʌp/ *noun* commutation *f* de secours

switching /'swɪtʃɪŋ/ *noun* commutation *f*; connexion *f*

switching centre /swɪtʃɪŋ 'sentə/ *noun* centre *m* de commutation

switching circuit /swɪtʃɪŋ 'sɜːkɪt/ *noun* circuit *m* de commutation

SX /ˌes 'eks/ *noun* (*processor chip*) SX

symbol /'sɪmbəl/ *noun* symbole *m* ◇ **graphic symbol** symbole graphique ◇ **this language uses the symbol ? to represent the print command** ce langage utilise le symbole ? pour la commande d'impression

symbolic /sɪm'bɒlɪk/ *adjective* symbolique

symbolic address /sɪmˌbɒlɪk ə'dres/ *noun* adresse *f* symbolique

symbolic code /sɪmˌbɒlɪk 'kəʊd/ *noun* code *m* symbolique

symbolic-coding format /sɪmˌbɒlɪk 'kəʊdɪŋ ˌfɔːmæt/ *noun* format *m* de langage symbolique

symbolic debugger /sɪmˌbɒlɪk diː'bʌgə/ *noun* débogueur *m* symbolique

symbolic instruction /sɪmˌbɒlɪk ɪn 'strʌkʃən/ *noun* code *m* symbolique

symbolic language /sɪmˌbɒlɪk 'læŋgwɪdʒ/ *noun* langage *m* symbolique

symbolic logic /sɪmˌbɒlɪk 'lɒdʒɪk/ *noun* logique *f* symbolique

symbolic name /sɪmˌbɒlɪk 'neɪm/ *noun* nom *m* symbolique

symbolic programming /sɪmˌbɒlɪk 'prəʊgræmɪŋ/ *noun* programmation *f* symbolique

symbolic table /sɪmˌbɒlɪk 'teɪb(ə)l/ *noun* table *f* symbolique

symmetrical compression /sɪˌmetrɪk(ə)l kəm'preʃ(ə)n/ *noun* compression *f* symétrique

symmetric difference /sɪˌmetrɪk 'dɪfrəns/ *noun* (*logical function*) exclusion *f* réciproque

sync /sɪŋk/ *noun informal* synchronisation *f*

sync bit /sɪŋk bɪt/ *noun* bit *m* de synchro

sync character /sɪŋk 'kærɪktə/ *noun* caractère *m* de synchro

synchronisation /ˌsɪŋkrənaɪ'zeɪʃ(ə)n/ *noun* synchro *f*; synchronisation *f*

synchronisation pulses /ˌsɪŋkrənaɪ 'zeɪʃ(ə)n ˌpʌlsɪz/ *plural noun* impulsions *fpl* de synchronisation

synchronise /'sɪŋkrəˌnaɪz/ *verb* synchroniser *vt*

synchronised dynamic RAM /ˌsɪŋkrənaɪzd daɪˌnæmɪk 'ræm/ *noun* mémoire *f* vive dynamique synchronisée

synchroniser /'sɪŋkrənaɪzə/ *noun* synchroniseur *m*; unité *f* de synchronisation

synchronous /'sɪŋkrənəs/ *adjective* (*which runs in sync*) synchrone ◇ **synchronous data link control (SDLC)** (*data transmission protocol*) protocole *m* SDLC (de transmission de données en mode synchrone) ◇ **synchronous detection** repérage *m* synchrone

synchronous cache /'sɪŋkrənəs kæʃ/ *noun* mémoire *f* cache synchrone

synchronous computer /ˌsɪŋkrənəs kəm 'pjuːtə/ *noun* ordinateur *m* synchrone

synchronous data link control /ˌsɪŋkrənəs 'deɪtə lɪŋk kənˌtrəʊl/ *noun* protocole *m* SDLC

synchronous data network /ˌsɪŋkrənəs 'deɪtə ˌnetwɜːk/ *noun* réseau *m* synchrone de transmission de données

synchronous DRAM /'sɪŋkrənəs dræm/ *noun* DRAM synchrone

synchronous idle character /ˌsɪŋkrənəs ˌaɪd(ə)l 'kærɪktə/ *noun* caractère *m* de synchronisation

synchronous mode /'sɪŋkrənəs məʊd/ *noun* mode *m* synchrone

synchronous network /ˌsɪŋkrənəs 'netwɜːk/ *noun* réseau *m* synchrone

synchronous system /ˌsɪŋkrənəs 'sɪstəm/ *noun* système *m* synchrone

synchronous transmission /ˌsɪŋkrənəs trænz'mɪʃ(ə)n/ *noun* transmission *f* synchrone

sync pulses /sɪŋk 'pʌlsɪz/ *plural noun* impulsions *fpl* de synchronisation

syntactic error /sɪnˌtæktɪk 'erə/ *noun* faute *f* de syntaxe

syntax /'sɪntæks/ *noun* syntaxe *f*

syntax analysis /'sɪntæks əˌnæləsɪs/ *noun* analyse *f* syntaxique

syntax error /ˈsɪntæks ˌerə/ *noun* faute *f* de syntaxe

synthesis /ˈsɪnθəsɪs/ *noun* synthèse *f*

synthesise /ˈsɪnθəsaɪz/ *verb* synthétiser *vt*

'...despite the fact that speech can now be synthesized with very acceptable quality, all it conveys is linguistic information' [*Personal Computer World*]

synthesised voice /ˌsɪnθəsaɪzd ˈvɔɪs/ *noun* voix *f* synthétisée

synthesiser /ˈsɪnθəsaɪzə/ *noun* synthétiseur *m*

synthetic address /sɪnˌθetɪk əˈdres/ *noun* adresse *f* calculée

synthetic language /sɪnˌθetɪk ˈlæŋgwɪdʒ/ *noun* langage *m* de synthèse

SyQuest /ˈsaɪkwest/ SyQuest

sysgen /ˈsɪsdʒen/ *noun* génération *f* d'un système

sysop /ˈsɪsˌɒp/ *noun* opérateur *m* de système

system /ˈsɪstəm/ *noun* système *m* ◇ **operating system (op sys)** système d'exploitation

system administrator /ˌsɪstəm ədˈmɪnɪstreɪtə/ *noun* administrateur *m* de réseau

system attribute /ˌsɪstəm ˈætrɪbjuːt/ *noun* attribut *m* système

system backup /ˌsɪstəm ˈbækʌp/ *noun* sauvegarde *f* intégrale

system board /ˈsɪstəm bɔːd/ *noun* carte *f* mère

system check /ˈsɪstəm tʃek/ *noun* diagnostic *m*

system clock /ˈsɪstəm klɒk/ *noun* horloge *f* de synchronisation d'un système

system colours /ˌsɪstəm ˈkʌləz/ *plural noun* palette *f* système

system console /ˌsɪstəm ˈkɒnsəʊl/ *noun* console *f* système

system control panel /ˌsɪstəm kənˈtrəʊl ˌpæn(ə)l/ *noun* panneau *m* de commandes d'un système

system crash /ˈsɪstəm kræʃ/ *noun* panne *f*

system design /ˌsɪstəm dɪˈzaɪn/ *noun* conception *f*

system diagnostics /ˌsɪstəm ˌdaɪəgˈnɒstɪks/ *noun* outils *mpl* de diagnostic d'un système

system disk /ˈsɪstəm dɪsk/ *noun* disquette *f* système; disquette *f* d'exploitation

Système Electronique Couleur Avec Mémoire *noun* SECAM

system firmware /ˌsɪstəm ˈfɜːmweə/ *noun* firmware *m*

system flowchart /ˈsɪstəm ˌfləʊtʃɑːt/ *noun* ordinogramme *m* d'un système

system folder /ˈsɪstəm ˌfəʊldə/ *noun* dossier *m* système

system generation /ˌsɪstəm ˌdʒenəˈreɪʃ(ə)n/ *noun* génération *f* d'un système

system library /ˌsɪstəm ˈlaɪbrəri/ *noun* bibliothèque *f* d'un système

system life cycle /ˌsɪstəm ˈlaɪf ˌsaɪk(ə)l/ *noun* durée *f* de vie d'un système

system log /ˈsɪstəm lɒg/ *noun* journal *m* de bord d'un système

system manager /ˌsɪstəm ˈmænɪdʒə/ *noun* chef *m* du service informatique; directeur, -trice *mf* du service informatique; responsable *mf* du service informatique

System Monitor /ˈsɪstəm ˌmɒnɪtə/ *noun* (*Windows 95 utility*) utilitaire *m* System Monitor

system operator /ˌsɪstəm ˈɒpəreɪtə/ *noun* opérateur *m* de système

system prompt /ˈsɪstəm prɒmpt/ *noun* invite *f* du système

systems analysis /ˈsɪstəmz əˌnæləsɪs/ *noun* analyse *f* de systèmes

systems analyst /ˈsɪstəmz ˌænəlɪst/ *noun* informaticien, -ienne analyste

Systems Application Architecture /ˌsɪstəmz ˌæplɪkeɪʃ(ə)n ˈɑːkɪtektʃə/ *noun* (*standard which defines the look and feel of an application*) architecture *f* de système d'application

system security /ˌsɪstəm sɪˈkjʊərɪti/ *noun* sécurité *f* d'un système

systems integration /ˌsɪstəmz ˌɪntɪˈgreɪʃ(ə)n/ *noun* intégration *f* de systèmes

Systems Network Architecture /ˌsɪstəmz ˈnetwɜːk ˌɑːkɪtektʃə/ *noun* (*design methods developed by IBM*) architecture *f* de réseau SNA

system software /ˌsɪstəm ˈsɒftweə/ *noun* logiciel *m* système

system specifications /ˌsɪstəm ˌspesɪfɪˈkeɪʃ(ə)nz/ *plural noun* spécifications *fpl* d'un système

systems program /ˈsɪstəmz ˌprəʊgræm/ *noun* programme *m* système

systems programmer /ˌsɪstəmz ˈprəʊgræmə/ *noun* programmeur *m* de systèmes

system support /ˌsɪstəm səˈpɔːt/ *noun* assistance *f* technique pour un système

system tray /ˈsɪstəm treɪ/ *noun* zone *f* de notification

system unit /ˈsɪstəm ˌjuːnɪt/ *noun* unité *f* de contrôle; unité *f* de commande d'un système

system variable /ˌsɪstəm ˈveəriəb(ə)l/ *noun* variable *f* système

T

T1 /ˌtiː ˈwʌn/ *noun* T1

T1 committee /ˌtiː ˈwʌn kəˌmɪti/ *noun* (*ANSI committee which sets digital communications standards*) commission *f* (ANSI) T1

T1 link /ˌtiː ˈwʌn ˌlɪŋk/ *noun* (*in the USA – long distance data transmission link*) liaison *f* T1

T2 link /ˌtiː ˈtuː ˌlɪŋk/ *noun* liaison *f* T2

T3 link /ˌtiː ˈθriː ˌlɪŋk/ *noun* liaison *f* T3

tab /tæb/ *verb* (*to tabulate or to arrange text in columns*) tabuler *vt*; disposer en tableau ◇ **a tab rack shows you the left and right margins** la règle de tabulation indique les marges de gauche et de droite ◇ **the list was neatly lined up by tabbing to column 10 at the start of each new line** en appuyant sur la touche de tabulation en début de ligne, pour se placer à la colonne 10, la liste se trouvait parfaitement alignée

tabbing /ˈtæbɪŋ/ *noun* tabulation *f* ◇ **tabbing can be done from inside the program** la tabulation peut être incorporée au programme

tabbing order /ˈtæbɪŋ ˌɔːdə/ *noun* commande *f* de tabulation

tab character /tæb ˈkærɪktə/ *noun* (*ASCII character 09hex*) caractère *m* tab

tab key /ˈtæb kiː/ *noun* (*key on a keyboard*) touche *f* de tabulation; touche *f* Tab

table /ˈteɪb(ə)l/ *noun* **1.** table *f*; tableau *m* **2.** tableau *m* ◇ **lookup table (LUT)** table de référence *or* d'équivalence ◇ **system file table** (*in DOS*) table des fichiers système ◇ **this is the value of the key pressed, use a lookup table to find its ASCII value** voici la fonction de cette touche, pour la traduire en ASCII consultez la table d'équivalence

table lookup /ˈteɪb(ə)l ˌlʊkʌp/ *noun* (*process of using one known value to select one entry in a table*) consultation *f* d'une table de référence

table of contents /ˌteɪb(ə)l əv ˈkɒntents/ *noun* table *f* des matières

tablet /ˈtæblət/ *noun* (*graphics pad or flat device*) tablette *f* graphique; tablette *f* à numériser

tab memory /tæb ˈmem(ə)ri/ *noun* mémoire *f* de tabulation

tab rack /tæb ræk/ *noun* règle *f* de tabulation ◇ **a tab rack shows you the left and right margins** la règle de tabulation indique les marges de gauche et de droite

tab settings /tæb ˈsetɪŋz/, **tab stops** /tæb stɒpz/ *plural noun* tabulation *fpl*

tabulate /ˈtæbjʊˌleɪt/ *verb* (*to arrange text in columns*) tabuler *vt*; disposer en tableau

tabulating /ˈtæbjʊleɪtɪŋ/ *noun* (*punched cards*) traitement *m* de données sur cartes perforées par tabulatrice

tabulation /ˌtæbjʊˈleɪʃ(ə)n/ *noun* tabulation *f*

tabulation markers /ˌtæbjuˈleɪʃ(ə)n ˌmɑːkəz/ *plural noun* repères *mpl* de tabulation

tabulation stops /ˌtæbjuˈleɪʃ(ə)n stɒpz/ *plural noun* arrêts *mpl* de tabulation

tabulator /ˈtæbjʊleɪtə/ *noun* (*on typewriters, etc.*) tabulateur *m*

tactile keyboard /ˌtæktaɪl ˈkiːbɔːd/ *noun* clavier *m* tactile; clavier *m* sensitif; clavier *m* à effleurement

tag /tæg/ *noun* **1.** (*section of computer instruction*) étiquette *f*; (*in machine language*) adresse *f* symbolique **2.** (*of file or item of data*) étiquette *f* ◇ **each file has a three letter tag for rapid identification** chaque fichier peut être identifié rapidement par son étiquette de trois lettres

tag image file format /ˌtæg ˌɪmɪdʒ ˈfaɪl ˌfɔːmæt/ *noun* (*file format used to store graphic images*) format *m* de fichier image; format *m* TIFF

tail /teɪl/ *noun* **1.** (*data which is the end of a list*) fin *f* de liste **2.** (*code which signals the end of a message*) fin *f* de message

takedown /ˈteɪkdaʊn/ *verb* désinstaller *vt*; démonter *vt*

takedown time /ˈteɪkdaʊn taɪm/ *noun* temps *m* de préparation entre deux tâches

take-up reel /ˈteɪk ʌp ˌriːl/ *noun* bobine *f* réceptrice; bobine *f* de réception; bobine *f* d'enroulement

Taligent /ˈtælɪdʒənt/ *noun* (*operating system developed by IBM and Apple*) système *m* d'exploitation Taligent™

tandem processors /ˌtændəm ˈprəʊsesəz/ *plural noun* processeurs *mpl* en tandem

tape backup /teɪp ˈbækʌp/ *noun* sauvegarde *f* sur bande

tape cable /teɪp ˈkeɪb(ə)l/ *noun* câble *m* plat; câble *m* ruban

tape cartridge /teɪp 'kɑːtrɪdʒ/ *noun* (*cassette box containing magnetic tape*) cartouche *f* de bande

tape cassette /teɪp kə'set/ *noun* cassette *f*

tape code /teɪp kəʊd/ *noun* code *m* de perforation; code *m* de marquage

tape deck /'teɪp dek/ *noun* (*device which plays back and records data*) platine *f* magnétophone

tape drive /teɪp draɪv/ *noun* (*mechanism which controls magnetic tape movement over the tape heads*) lecteur *m*

tape format /teɪp 'fɔːmæt/ *noun* format *m* de bande

tape guide /teɪp gaɪd/ *noun* guide-bande *m*

tape head /teɪp hed/ *noun* (*mechanism which controls magnetic tape movement over the tape heads*) tête *f* de lecture ou d'écriture de bande magnétique

tape header /teɪp 'hedə/ *noun* (*identification information*) en-tête *m*

tape label /teɪp 'leɪb(ə)l/ *noun* label *m*

tape library /teɪp 'laɪbrəri/ *noun* bibliothèque *f* de bandes; bandothèque *f*

tape loadpoint /'teɪp ˌləʊdpɔɪnt/ *noun* point *m* de début d'enregistrement d'une bande magnétique

tape punch /teɪp pʌntʃ/ *noun* poinçon *m* de perforation pour bandes papier

tape reader /teɪp 'riːdə/ *noun* lecteur *m* de bandes magnétiques

tape streamer /teɪp 'striːmə/ *noun* streamer *m*

tape to card converter /teɪp tə, tʊ kɑːd/ *noun* convertisseur *m* bande magnétique/carte perforée

tape trailer /teɪp 'treɪlə/ *noun* label *m* de fin de bande

tape transmitter /teɪp trænz'mɪtə/ *noun* transmetteur *m* de données sur bande perforée

tape transport /teɪp 'trænspɔːt/ *noun* dérouleur *m*

TAPI *abbr* (*telephony application programming interface*) interface *f* de programmation d'application téléphonique

Targa /'tɑːgə/ *noun* **1.** (*graphics file format*) format *m* de fichier graphique Targa™ **2.** (*graphics adapter*) adaptateur *m* graphique couleur haute définition Targa™

target computer /ˌtɑːgɪt kəm'pjuːtə/ *noun* ordinateur *m* cible; ordinateur *m* d'exécution

target disk /'tɑːgɪt dɪsk/ *noun* disque *m* cible

target language /'tɑːgɪt ˌlæŋgwɪdʒ/ *noun* (*computing*) langage *m* objet; (*translation*) langue *f* d'arrivée

target level /'tɑːgɪt ˌlev(ə)l/ *noun* niveau *m* cible

target phase /'tɑːgɪt feɪz/ *noun* phase *f* d'exécution

target program /ˌtɑːgɪt 'prəʊgræm/ *noun* programme *m* objet

tariff /'tærɪf/ *noun* (*charge*) tarif *m* ◇ **there is a set tariff for logging on, then a rate for every minute of computer time used** il existe un tarif forfaitaire d'utilisation plus un taux/minute de temps d'ordinateur

task /tɑːsk/ *noun* tâche *f*

taskbar /'tɑːskˌbɑː/ *noun* (*normally runs along the bottom of the screen in Windows 95*) barre *f* des tâches

task management /tɑːsk 'mænɪdʒmənt/ *noun* gestion *f* de tâches

task queue /tɑːsk kjuː/ *noun* file *f* d'attente des tâches à exécuter

task swapping /'tɑːsk ˌswɒpɪŋ/ *noun* (*exchanging one program in memory for another*) permutation *f*

TAT *abbr* (*turnaround time*) permutation *f*

T carrier /'tiː ˌkæriə/ *noun* (*US standard for digital data transmission lines*) porteuse *f* T

T-commerce /ˌtiː 'kɒmɜːs/ *noun* commerce *m* effectué aux moyens de télévision interactive

T connector /tiː kə'nektə/ *noun* (*coaxial connector shaped like a 'T'*) connecteur *m* en T

TCP /ˌtiː siː 'piː/ *noun* protocole *m* de contrôle de protocole; protocole *m* TCP de transmission

TCP/IP /ˌtiː siː piː aɪ 'piː/ *noun* protocole *m* TCP/IP (de communication de réseau)

TDM /ˌtiː diː 'em/ *noun* multiplexage *m* temporel; multiplexage *m* par répartition dans le temps (MRT)

TDR /ˌtiː diː 'ɑː/ *noun* test *m* de câble par réflectométrie

TDS /ˌtiː diː 'es/ *noun* système *m* transactionnel

technical /'teknɪk(ə)l/ *adjective* technique ◇ **the document gives all the technical details on the new computer** ce document contient tous les renseignements d'ordre technique concernant le nouvel ordinateur

technical support /ˌteknɪk(ə)l sə'pɔːt/ *noun* assistance *f* technique

technician /tek'nɪʃ(ə)n/ *noun* technicien, -ienne *m,f* ◇ **laboratory technician** technicien, -ienne de laboratoire ◇ **the computer technicians installed the new system** le nouveau système a été mis en place par les techniciens *or* ce sont les techniciens qui ont installé le nouveau système

technique /tek'niːk/ *noun* technique *f*; méthode *f* ◇ **the company has developed a new technique for processing customers' disks** la société a mis au point une nouvelle technique de traitement des disquettes clients

technological /ˌteknə'lɒdʒɪk(ə)l/ *adjective* technologique ◇ **the technological revolution** la révolution technologique

technology /tek'nɒlədʒi/ *noun* technologie *f*; techniques *f* ◇ **information technology (IT)**

technologie de l'information ◇ **the introduction of new technology** l'introduction *f* de nouvelles technologies

tele- /teli/ *prefix* (*referring to TV or long distance*) télé-

telecommunications /ˌtelikəˌmjuːnɪ 'keɪʃ(ə)nz/ *noun* (*passing and receiving messages over a distance*) télécommunications *f*

telecommuting /'telikəmjuːtɪŋ/ *noun* (*working on a computer from home*) télétravail *m*

teleconference /'teliˌkɒnf(ə)rəns/ *noun* téléconférence *f*

teleconferencing /'teliˌkɒnf(ə)rənsɪŋ/ *noun* (*linking video, audio and computer signals as if in a conference room*) téléconférence *f*

teleinformatic services /teliɪnˌfɔːmətɪk 'sɜːvɪsɪz/ *plural noun* services *mpl* de téléinformatique

telematics /ˌtelɪ'mætɪks/ *noun* télématique *f*

telephone /'telɪfəʊn/ *noun* téléphone *m* ◇ **by telephone** par téléphone ◇ **can you give me your telephone number?** pouvez-vous me donner votre numéro de téléphone? ◇ **cellular telephone** téléphone cellulaire ◇ **conference telephone** téléphone de conférence ◇ **house telephone** *or* **internal telephone** téléphone interne ◇ **telephone (data carrier)** transmission de données par téléphone *or* sur le réseau commuté ◇ **telephone book** *or* **telephone directory** annuaire *m* des téléphones *or* annuaire téléphonique ◇ **telephone number** numéro *m* de téléphone ◇ **telephone repeater** répéteur *m* de téléphone ◇ **telephone subscriber** abonné, -ée du téléphone ◇ **to answer the telephone** *or* **to take a telephone call** répondre au téléphone *or* prendre un appel *or* prendre une communication ◇ **to be on the telephone** parler au téléphone *or* être en ligne ◇ **to make a telephone call** faire un appel *or* téléphoner *or* appeler ◇ **to place an order by telephone** faire une commmande par téléphone

telephone line /'telɪfəʊn laɪn/ *noun* ligne *f* téléphonique

telephony /tə'lefəni/ *noun* téléphonie *f* ◇ **computer telephony integration (CTI)** convergence téléphonie-informatique (CTI)

telephony application programming interface /təˌlefəni ˌæplɪkeɪʃ(ə)n 'prəʊgræmɪŋ ˌɪntəfeɪs/ *noun* interface *f* de programmation d'application téléphonique

telephony services application programming interface /təˌlefəni ˌsɜːvɪsɪz ˌæplɪkeɪʃ(ə)n 'prəʊgræmɪŋ ˌɪntəfeɪs/ *noun* interface *f* de programmation d'application de services téléphoniques

teleprinter /'teliˌprɪntə/ *noun* téléimprimeur *m*; téléscripteur *m*; télétype *m* ◇ **teleprinter operator** opérateur, -trice de téléimprimeur *or* télétypiste *m&f* ◇ **you can drive a teleprinter from this modified serial port** vous pouvez connecter un téléimprimeur sur ce port série modifié

teleprinter interface /'teliprɪntə ˌɪntəfeɪs/ *noun* interface *f* téléimprimeur

teleprinter roll /'teliprɪntə ˌrəʊl/ *noun* rouleau *m* de papier pour téléimprimeur

teleprocessing /'teliˌprəʊsesɪŋ/ *noun* (*processing of data at a distance*) télétraitement *m*

telesoftware /'teliˌsɒftweə/ *noun* logiciel *m* téléchargé

teletext /'teliˌtekst/ *noun* (*over television*) Télétex™ *m*

teletype /'telitaɪp/ *noun* téléscripteur *m*

teletypewriter /ˌtelɪ'taɪpraɪtə/ *noun* téléimprimeur *m*

television /ˌtelɪ'vɪʒ(ə)n/ *noun* (*device or set*) télévision *f*

television monitor /ˌtelɪ'vɪʒ(ə)n ˌmɒnɪtə/ *noun* moniteur *m* de télévision

television receiver/monitor /ˌtelɪvɪʒ(ə)n rɪ ˌsiːvə 'mɒnɪtə/ *noun* moniteur/téléviseur *m*

television scan /'telɪˌvɪʒ(ə)n skæn/ *noun* balayage *m* d'écran

television tube /'telɪˌvɪʒ(ə)n tjuːb/ *noun* tube *m* cathodique

telnet /'telnet/ *noun* (*TCP/IP protocol*) protocole *m* d'émulation telnet

template /'temˌpleɪt/ *noun* **1.** (*cut-out shape*) gabarit *m* **2.** (*standard letter*) lettre *f* type; (*standard paragraph*) paragraphe *m* standard

template command /'templeɪt kəˌmɑːnd/ *noun* commande *f* de formatage

tempo /'tempəʊ/ *noun* **1.** (*in MIDI or music – the speed at which the notes are played*) tempo *m* **2.** (*in a multimedia title – the speed at which frames are displayed*) cadence *f*; fréquence *f* ◇ **a typical MIDI tempo is 120bpm** avec MIDI, le tempo est habituellement de 120bpm

temporary *adjective* temporaire

temporary register /ˌtemp(ə)rəri 'redʒɪstə/ *noun* registre *m* temporaire

temporary storage /ˌtemp(ə)rəri 'stɔːrɪdʒ/ *noun* (*storage which is not permanent*) mémoire *f* temporaire

temporary swap file /ˌtemp(ə)rəri 'swɒp ˌfaɪl/ *noun* fichier *m* d'échange temporaire

10Base2 /ˌten beɪs 'tuː/ (*IEEE standard specifications*) standard *m* 10Base2

10Base5 /ˌten beɪs 'faɪv/ (*IEEE standard specification*) standard *m* 10Base5

10BaseT /ˌten beɪs 'tiː/ (*IEEE standard specification*) standard *m* 10BaseT

ten's complement /'tenz ˌkɒmplɪmənt/ *noun* complément *m* à dix

tera- /terə/ *prefix* téra-

terabyte /'terəˌbaɪt/ *noun* (*one thousand gigabytes or one million megabytes*) téraoctet *m*

teraflop /'terəflɒp/ *noun* téraflops *m*

terminal /'tɜːmɪn(ə)l/ *noun* **1.** (*display unit and keyboard*) terminal *m*; poste *m* de travail **2.** (*electrical connection point*) borne *f*; point *m* de connexion; borne *f* de raccordement **3.** (*point in a network where a message can be transmitted and received*) terminal *m* (de réseau) ■ *adjective* (*transmission*) fatal *or* -e ◇ **all the messages go to all the terminals since none are addressable terminals** tous les messages sont transmis à tous les terminaux puisqu'aucun d'eux ne possède un adressage protégé ◇ **my son has turned into a real terminal junky** mon fils est devenu un véritable infomaniaque ◇ **terminal block** bloc *m* de raccordement ◇ **terminal junky (TJ)** accro *m&f* de l'informatique *or* fana *m&f* d'informatique *or* infomaniaque *m&f* ◇ **the new intelligent terminal has a built-in text editor** le nouveau terminal intelligent comporte un éditeur de texte ◇ **the system manager uses the master terminal to restart the system** le gestionnaire de système utilise le terminal principal pour relancer le système

terminal adapter /'tɜːmɪn(ə)l əˌdæptə/ *noun* adaptateur *m* de terminal

terminal area /'tɜːmɪn(ə)l ˌeəriə/ *noun* zone *f* de connexions

terminal character set /ˌtɜːmɪn(ə)l 'kærɪktə ˌset/ *noun* police *f* de caractères utilisable par un terminal

terminal controller /'tɜːmɪn(ə)l kənˌtrəʊlə/ *noun* contrôleur *m* de terminal

terminal emulation /'tɜːmɪn(ə)l emju ˌleɪʃ(ə)n/ *noun* émulation *f* de terminal

terminal emulation software /ˌtɜːmɪn(ə)l ˌemjʊ'leɪʃ(ə)n ˌsɒftweə/ *noun* logiciel *m* d'émulation de terminal

terminal identity /ˌtɜːmɪn(ə)l aɪ'dentɪti/ *noun* identification *f* d'un terminal

terminal interface /'tɜːmɪn(ə)l ˌɪntəfeɪs/ *noun* interface *f* de terminal; interface *f* pour terminal ◇ **the network controller has 16 terminal interfaces** le contrôleur de réseau possède 16 interfaces pour terminaux

terminal keyboard /ˌtɜːmɪn(ə)l 'kiːbɔːd/ *noun* clavier *m* relié à un terminal

terminal session /'tɜːmɪn(ə)l ˌseʃ(ə)n/ *noun* session *f*

terminal strip /'tɜːmɪn(ə)l strɪp/ *noun* barrette *f* de connexion du terminal

terminate /'tɜːmɪˌneɪt/ *verb* terminer *vt*

terminate and stay resident program /ˌtɜːmɪneɪt ən steɪ 'rezɪd(ə)nt ˌprəʊgræm/ *noun* (*program which loads itself into main memory and carries out a function*) programme *m* résident; programme *m* TSR

terminate and stay resident software /ˌtɜːmɪneɪt ən steɪ 'rezɪd(ə)nt ˌsɒftweə/ *noun* programme *m* résident; programme *m* TSR

termination /ˌtɜːmɪ'neɪʃ(ə)n/ *noun* (*stopping*) arrêt *m*; (*ending*) terminaison *f*

terminator /'tɜːmɪneɪtə/ *noun* **1.** (*LAN resistor*) terminateur *m* de réseau **2.** (*SCSI resistor*) terminateur *m* SCSI **3.** (*end of list*) marqueur *m* de fin de liste ◇ **line terminator** (*connection*) dispositif *m* de fin de ligne

ternary /'tɜːnəri/ *adjective* ternaire

tessellate /'tesəleɪt/ *verb* (*to reduce a complex shape into a collection of simple shapes, often triangles*) présenter sous forme de mosaïque; disposer en mosaïque

test /test/ *noun* (*on a device or program*) test *m*; essai *m* ■ *verb* (*to carry out an examination of a device or program*) tester *vt*; contrôler *vt*; faire un test; faire un essai

test bed /test bed/ *noun* banc *m* d'essai

test data /test 'deɪtə/ *noun* donnée *f* de contrôle

test equipment /test ɪ'kwɪpmənt/ *noun* testeur *m* ◇ **the engineer has special test equipment for this model** l'ingénieur possède un équipement spécialisé pour effectuer les tests sur ce modèle

test numeric /'test njuːˌmerɪk/ *noun* contrôle *m* de numérisation

test run /'test rʌn/ *noun* (*program run with test data*) essai *m*; test *m* d'évaluation d'un logiciel ◇ **a test run will soon show up any errors** un essai fera tout de suite apparaître les erreurs

texel /'teksəl/ *noun* (*collection of pixels treated as a single unit when applying a texture map*) texel *m*

text /tekst/ *noun* texte *m* ◇ **MS-DOS normally operates in a text mode** MS-DOS fonctionne habituellement en mode texte ◇ **people use the text formatter as a basic desk-top publishing program** on utilise le formatage de texte comme programme de base de PAO ◇ **start-of-text (SOT *or* STX)** (code de) début *m* de texte ◇ **text processing *or* word processing** traitement *m* de texte ◇ **text processor *or* word processor** machine *f* de traitement de texte; logiciel *m* de traitement de texte ◇ **the text editor will only read files smaller than 64Kbytes long** cet éditeur de texte ne peut lire que les fichiers de moins de 64Ko

text compression /tekst kəm'preʃ(ə)n/ *noun* compression *f* de texte

text-editing facilities /'tekst ˌedɪtɪŋ fə ˌsɪlɪtiz/ *plural noun* traitement de texte

text-editing function /'tekst ˌedɪtɪŋ ˌfʌŋkʃ(ə)n/ *noun* fonction *f* de traitement de texte ◇ **the program includes a built-in text-editing function** une fonction traitement de texte est intégrée au programme

text editor /tekst 'edɪtə/ *noun* (*screen editor*) programme *m* d'édition de texte ◇ **the text editor will only read files smaller than 64Kbytes long** cet éditeur de texte ne peut lire que les fichiers de moins de 64Ko

text file /tekst faɪl/ *noun* fichier *m* texte

text formatter /'tekst ˌfɔːmætə/ *noun* logiciel *m* de formatage de texte ◇ **people use the text formatter as a basic desk-top publishing program** on utilise le formatage de texte comme programme de base de PAO

text management /tekst 'mænɪdʒmənt/ *noun* gestion *f* de texte

text manager /'tekst ˌmænɪdʒə/ *noun* gestionnaire *m* de texte

text manipulation /tekst məˌnɪpjʊ'leɪʃ(ə)n/ *noun* manipulation *f* de texte

text message /'tekst ˌmesɪdʒ/ *noun* message *m* (écrit); mail *m*

text mode /tekst məʊd/ *noun* mode *m* texte

text processing /'tekst ˌprəʊsesɪŋ/ *noun* traitement *m* de texte

text register /tekst 'redʒɪstə/ *noun* registre *m* de texte

text retrieval /tekst rɪ'triːv(ə)l/ *noun* recherche *f* et extraction de texte

text screen /tekst skriːn/ *noun* (*area to display text*) écran *m* de texte

text-to-speech converter /tekst tə, tʊ spiːtʃ/ *noun* convertisseur *m* texte/signal vocal

texture /'tekstʃə/ *noun* texture *f*

texture mapping /'tekstʃə ˌmæpɪŋ/ *noun* placage *m* de texture

text window /tekst 'wɪndəʊ/ *noun* fenêtre *f* textuelle; fenêtre *f* de texte

TFTP /ˌtiː ef tiː 'piː/ *noun* protocole *m* TFTP

TFT screen /ˌtiː ef 'tiː ˌskriːn/ *noun* écran *m* à transistors à couches minces; écran *m* TFT

thermal inkjet printer /ˌθɜːm(ə)l ˌɪnkdʒet 'prɪntə/ *noun* imprimante *f* à jet d'encre thermique

thermal paper /ˌθɜːm(ə)l 'peɪpə/ *noun* papier *m* thermique

thermal printer /ˌθɜːm(ə)l 'prɪntə/ *noun* imprimante *f* thermique

thermal transfer /ˌθɜːm(ə)l træns'fɜː/, **thermal wax** /'θɜːm(ə)l wæks/, **thermal wax transfer printer** /ˌθɜːm(ə)l wæks ˌtrænsfɜː 'prɪntə/ *noun* (*where the colours are produced by melting coloured wax onto the paper*) imprimante *f* à transfert thermique; imprimante *f* à sublimation thermique

thesaurus /θɪ'sɔːrəs/ *noun* (*file containing synonyms*) thésaurus *m*; dictionnaire *m* de synonymes; dictionnaire *m* par thèmes

thick-Ethernet /θɪk 'iːθəˌnet/ *noun* (*network using thick coaxial cable*) Ethernet *m* câble lourd; câble *m* jaune

thick film /θɪk fɪlm/ *noun* couche *f* épaisse

thimble printer /'θɪmb(ə)l ˌprɪntə/ *noun* imprimante *f* à tulipe

thin-Ethernet /θɪn 'iːθəˌnet/ *noun* (*network using thin coaxial cable*) Ethernet *m* câble fin; câble *m* noir

thin film /θɪn fɪlm/ *noun* (*method of constructing integrated circuits*) couche *f* mince

thin-film memory /ˌθɪn fɪlm 'mem(ə)ri/ *noun* mémoire *f* à couches minces

thin-film transistor screen /ˌθɪn fɪlm træn 'zɪstə ˌskriːn/ *noun* écran *m* à transistors à couches minces; écran *m* TFT

thin window /θɪn 'wɪndəʊ/ *noun* (*single line display window*) fenêtre *f* étroite

third generation /ˌθɜːd ˌdʒenə'reɪʃ(ə)n/ *noun* troisième *f* génération

third generation computer /ˌθɜːd ˌdʒenəreɪʃ(ə)n kəm'pjuːtə/ *noun* ordinateur *m* de troisième génération

third party /ˌθɜːd 'pɑːti/ *noun* tiers *m*

32-bit /'θɜːtiː tuː ˌbɪt/ 32 bits

thirty-two bit system /ˌθɜːti tuː ˌbɪt 'sɪstəm/, **32-bit system** *noun* système *m* informatique de 32 bits

thrashing /'θræʃɪŋ/ *noun* **1.** (*excessive disk activity*) emballement *m*; (*fault in virtual memory system*) pompage *m*; transferts *mpl* de page incontrôlés **2.** pompage *m*; transferts *mpl* de pages incontrôlés

thread /θred/ *noun* (*a program which consists of many independent smaller sections or beads*) programme *m* en chapelet

> 'WigWam makes it easier for a user to follow a thread in a bulletin-board conference topic by ordering responses using a hierarchical indent similar to that found in outline processor.' [*Computing*]

threaded file /θredd faɪl/ *noun* (*file in which an entry contains data and an address to the next entry*) fichier *m* chaîné

threaded language /θredd 'læŋgwɪdʒ/ *noun* langage *m* chaîné

threaded tree /θredd triː/ *noun* arborescence *f* chaînée

three-address instruction /ˌθriː ə'dres ɪn ˌstrʌkʃən/ *noun* instruction *f* à trois adresses

3D /ˌθriː 'diː/ *adjective* à trois dimensions

three-dimensional /ˌθriː daɪ'menʃ(ə)nəl/ *adjective* (*3D*) tridimensionnel *or* -elle; à trois dimensions; 3D

three-dimensional array /θriː daɪ ˌmenʃ(ə)nəl ə'reɪ/ *noun* (*array made up of a number of two-dimensional arrays*) tableau *m* à trois dimensions

3G /ˌθriː 'dʒiː/ *noun* 3G

three input adder /ˌθriː ˌɪnpʊt 'ædə/ *noun* additionneur *m* complet; additionneur *m* à trois entrées

three state logic /ˌθriː steɪt 'lɒdʒɪk/ *noun* circuit *m* logique à trois états

threshold /'θreʃhəʊld/ *noun* seuil *m* ◇ **threshold gate** circuit *m* à seuil ◇ **threshold value** valeur *f* de seuil

throughput /'θruːˌpʊt/ *noun* rendement *m*; débit *m*

thumbnail /'θʌmˌneɪl/ *noun* (*miniature graphical representation of an image*) vignette *f* réduite

TIFF /tɪf/ *noun* format *m* de fichier image; format *m* TIFF

tile /taɪl/ *verb* (*in a GUI: to arrange windows side by side*) disposer en mosaïque; en pavé ■ *noun* (disposition *f* en) mosaïque

tilt and swivel /ˌtɪlt ən 'swɪv(ə)l/ *adjective* (*screen*) orientable

timbre /'tæmbə/ *noun* sonorité *f*

time /taɪm/ *verb* minuter *vt*

time base /taɪm beɪs/ *noun* base *f* de temps

time bomb /'taɪm bɒm/ *noun* bombe *f* logique

time code /taɪm kəʊd/ *noun* code *m* temporel

timed backup /taɪmd 'bækʌp/ *noun* sauvegarde *f* programmée

time division multiplexing /ˌtaɪm dɪˌvɪʒ(ə)n 'mʌltɪpleksɪŋ/ *noun* multiplexage *m* temporel; multiplexage *m* par répartition dans le temps (MRT)

time domain reflectometry /ˌtaɪm dəʊˌmeɪn ˌrɪːflek'tɒmətri/ *noun* test *m* de câble par réflectométrie

time of peak demand /ˌtaɪm əv piːk dɪ'mɑːnd/ *noun* période *f* de demande maximum

timeout /'taɪmaʊt/ *noun* sortie *f* de session

timer /'taɪmə/ *noun* chronomètre *m*; compteur *m*

time-sharing /'taɪm ˌʃeərɪŋ/ *noun* (*of system*) partage *m* de temps; temps *m* partagé

time slice /taɪm slaɪs/ *noun* **1.** (*multitasking system*) tranche *f* de temps **2.** tranche *f* de temps; tranche *f* horaire

time stamp /taɪm stæmp/ *noun* estampille *f*

timing loop /'taɪmɪŋ luːp/ *noun* boucle *f* de temporisation

timing master /'taɪmɪŋ ˌmɑːstə/ *noun* horloge *f* maîtresse

tint /tɪnt/ *noun* teinte *f*; tonalité *f*

tiny model /ˌtaɪni 'mɒd(ə)l/ *noun* (*memory model*) petit modèle *m*

title /'taɪt(ə)l/ *noun* titre *m*; nom *m* ◇ **title bar button** bouton de la barre de titre ◇ **title of disk** nom *or* titre d'une disquette ◇ **title page** (*first main page of a book*) page *f* de titre

title bar /'taɪt(ə)l bɑː/ *noun* barre *f* de titre

T junction /tiː 'dʒʌŋkʃ(ə)n/ *noun* jonction *f* en T

TMSF time format /ˌtiː em es ef 'taɪm ˌfɔːmæt/ *noun* base *f* horaire TMSF

toggle /'tɒg(ə)l/ *verb* (*to switch*) basculer *vi*; valider qc à l'aide d'un commutateur à bascule

toggle switch /'tɒg(ə)l swɪtʃ/ *noun* commutateur *m* à bascule

token /'təʊkən/ *noun* **1.** (*internal code*) jeton *m* **2.** (*control packet*) jeton *m*

token bus network /ˌtəʊkən 'bʌs ˌnetwɜːk/ *noun* (*IEEE 802.4 standard for a LAN*) réseau *m* en bus à jeton

token-passing /'təʊkən ˌpɑːsɪŋ/ *noun* (*controlling access to a LAN*) passage *m* du jeton

Token Ring network /'təʊkən rɪŋ ˌnetwɜːk/ *noun* (*IEEE 802.5 standard*) réseau *m* Token Ring; réseau *m* (en anneau) à jeton ◇ **Token Ring networks are very democratic and retain performance against increasing load** les réseaux Token Ring sont très démocratiques et conservent leurs performances en cas d'accroissement de la charge

tone dialling /'təʊn ˌdaɪəlɪŋ/ *noun* numérotation *f* sur clavier tonal

toner /'təʊnə/ *noun* (*powdered ink for photocopier or printer*) encre *f* en poudre; toner *m* ◇ **change toner and toner cartridge according to the manual** pour remettre du toner ou changer la cartouche, voir la marche à suivre dans le manuel d'utilisation ◇ **if you get toner on your hands, you can only wash it off with cold water** si vous avez du toner sur les mains, il faut absolument les laver à l'eau froide

toner cartridge /'təʊnə ˌkɑːtrɪdʒ/ *noun* cartouche *f* de toner

tool /tuːl/ *noun* outil *m*

toolbar /'tuːlˌbɑː/ *noun* barre *f* d'outils

toolbox /'tuːlbɒks/ *noun* **1.** (*Apple Macintosh: set of utility programs*) Toolbox; (*set of predefined routines*) boîte *f* à outils; (*Apple Macintosh: set of utility programs*) boîte *f* à outils Macintosh **2.** boîte *f* à outils

Toolbox /'tuːlbɒks/ *noun* (*set of predefined routines*) boîte *f* à outils; (*Apple Macintosh: set of utility programs*) Toolbox; boîte *f* à outils Macintosh

toolkit /'tuːlkɪt/ *noun* (*for programs*) outils *mpl*; utilitaires *mpl*

tools /tuːlz/ *noun* (*for programs*) outils *mpl*

ToolTips /'tuːltɪps/ *noun* (*under Windows – line of descriptive text under an icon when the user moves the pointer over the icon*) info-bulles *f*

top down programming /ˌtɒp daʊn 'prəʊgræmɪŋ/ *noun* programmation *f* structurée

top-level domain /ˌtɒp ˌlev(ə)l dəʊ'meɪn/ *noun* domaine *m* de premier niveau

topology /tɒ'pɒlədʒi/ *noun* topologie *f*; configuration *f*; architecture *f* ◇ **if one workstation cable snaps in a star topology, the rest continue, unlike a bus topology** si le câble d'une station d'un réseau en étoile se casse, les autres stations ne sont pas affectées, ce qui n'est pas le cas dans une topologie en bus

TOPS /tɒps/ *noun* (*software that allows IBM PCs and Apple Macintoshes to share files*) logiciel *m* de communication TOPS

touch pad /tʌtʃ pæd/ *noun* pavé *m* tactile; pavé *m* à effleurement

touch screen /tʌtʃ skriːn/ *noun* écran *m* tactile

touch-sensitive keyboard /ˌtʌtʃ ˌsensətɪv 'kiːbɔːd/ *noun* (*thin, flat membrane type keyboard*) clavier *m* tactile; clavier *m* à effleurement

TP *abbr* **1.** (*teleprocessing*) télétraitement *m* **2.** (*transaction processing*) traitement *m* de mouvements

TPI *abbr* (*tracks per inch*) pistes *fpl* par pouce

trace /treɪs/ *noun* (*method of verifying that a program is functioning correctly*) traçage *m* d'un programme

trace program /treɪs 'prəʊgræm/ *noun* programme *m* de traçage

traceroute /'treɪsruːt/ *noun* utilitaire *m* de routage TCP-IP traceroute

trace trap /treɪs træp/ *noun* point *m* de contrôle dans un programme de traçage

tracing /'treɪsɪŋ/ *noun* (*function of a graphics program*) linéarisation *f*

track /træk/ *noun* piste *f* ■ *verb* localiser *vt* ◇ **tracks per inch (TPI)** (nombre de) pistes par pouce

track address /træk ə'dres/ *noun* adresse *f* de piste

trackball /'trækˌbɔːl/ *noun* boule *f* de commande

tracks, minutes, seconds, frames time format /ˌtræks ˌmɪnəts ˌsekəndz ˌfreɪmz 'taɪm ˌfɔːmæt/ *noun* base *f* horaire TMSF

tracks per inch /ˌtræks pɜːr 'ɪntʃ/ *noun* pistes *fpl* par pouce

tractor feed /'træktə fiːd/ *noun* (*feeding paper into a printer*) entraînement *m* du papier par picots

traffic /'træfɪk/ *noun* (*messages and signals*) trafic *m*; mouvements *mpl* ◇ **our Ethernet network begins to slow down if the traffic reaches 60 per cent of the bandwidth** notre réseau Ethernet commence à ralentir lorsque le trafic atteint 60 pour cent de la bande passante

traffic analysis /'træfɪk əˌnæləsɪs/ *noun* analyse *f* du trafic

traffic density /'træfɪk ˌdensɪti/ *noun* densité *f* du trafic

traffic intensity /'træfɪk ɪnˌtensɪti/ *noun* intensité *f* de trafic

trailer /'treɪlə/ *noun* (*final byte of file*) label *m* de fin de fichier

trailer record /'treɪlə ˌrekɔːd/ *noun* (*last record in a file*) enregistrement *m* de fin

transaction /træn'zækʃən/ *noun* transaction *f*; mouvement *m* ◇ **transaction-driven system (TDS)** système *m* transactionnel ◇ **transaction processing (TP)** traitement de mouvements *or* de transactions

transaction-driven system /træn'zækʃən ˌdrɪv(ə)n ˌsɪstəm/ *noun* système *m* transactionnel

transaction file /træn'zækʃən faɪl/ *noun* fichier *m* de transactions

transaction processing /træn'zækʃən ˌprəʊsesɪŋ/ *noun* traitement *m* de mouvements

> 'At present, users implementing client-server strategies are focusing on decision support systems before implementing online transaction processing and other mission-critical applications.' [*Computing*]

transaction record /træn'zækʃən ˌrekɔːd/ *noun* enregistrement *m* d'une transaction

transceiver /træn'siːvə/ *noun* émetteur/récepteur *m* ◇ **radio transceiver** émetteur/récepteur radio

transcribe /træn'skraɪb/ *verb* transcrire *vt*

transducer /trænz'djuːsə/ *noun* transducteur *m* ◇ **a pressure transducer converts physical pressure signals into electrical signals** un transducteur de pression transforme un signal physique de pression en signal électrique

transfer /'trænsfɜː/ *verb* **1.** (*to change command*) transférer *vt* **2.** (*to copy a section of memory*) transférer *vt* ■ *noun* (*between devices or memory*) transfert *m* ◇ **all processing activities have been transferred to the mainframe** toutes les opérations de traitement ont été transférées sur l'ordinateur principal

transfer check /træns'fɜː tʃek/ *noun* contrôle *m* de transfert

transfer command /'trænsfɜː kəˌmɑːnd/ *noun* instruction *f* de transfert; instruction *f* de branchement

transfer control /'trænsfɜː kənˌtrəʊl/ *noun* contrôle *m* de transfert

transfer rate /'trænsfɜː reɪt/ *noun* taux *m*

transfer time /træns'fɜː taɪm/ *noun* temps *m* de transfert

transform /træns'fɔːm/ *verb* transformer *vt*

transformational rules /trænzfə 'meɪʃ(ə)n(ə)l ruːlz/ *noun* règles *fpl* de transformation

transient /'trænziənt/ *adjective* (*state or signal*) passager *or* -ère; de courte durée; éphémère ■ *noun* (*something which is present for a short time only*) effet *m* transitoire

transient area /ˌtrænziənt 'eəriə/ *noun* zone *f* de mémoire des programmes non résidents

transient error /ˌtrænziənt 'erə/ *noun* (*temporary error*) erreur *f* passagère; erreur *f* momentanée

transient read error /ˌtrænziənt 'riːd ˌerə/ *noun* erreur *f* de lecture momentanée

transient suppressor /ˌtrænziənt sə'presə/ *noun* limiteur *m*

transistor /træn'zɪstə/ *noun* transistor *m* ◇ **transistor-resistor logic (TRL)** logique *f* transistor résistance (LTR) ◇ **transistor-transistor logic (TTL)** logique transistor transistor (LTT)

transistor-transistor logic /træn,zɪstə træn,zɪstə 'lɒdʒɪk/ *noun* logique *f* transistor-transistor (LTT)

transition point /træn'zɪʃ(ə)n pɔɪnt/ *noun* point *m* de transition

translate /træns'leɪt/ *verb* (*to convert data*) traduire *vt*; convertir *vt*

translation tables /træns'leɪʃ(ə)n ,teɪb(ə)lz/ *plural noun* tables *fpl* de conversation; tables *fpl* de référence; tables *fpl* d'équivalence

translator /træns'leɪtə/, **translator program** /træns'leɪtə ,prəʊgræm/ *noun* traducteur *m*; programme *m* de traduction

transmission /trænz'mɪʃ(ə)n/ *noun* transmission *f* ◇ **bidirectional transmission** transmission bidirectionnelle ◇ **transmission control protocol (TCP)** (*data transmission protocol*) protocole TCP (de contrôle de transmission) ◇ **transmission control protocol *or* internet protocol (TCP *or* IP)** (*data transfer protocol*) protocole *m* TCP/IP (de transmission de données) ◇ **transmission error** erreur *f* de transmission ◇ **transmission window** fenêtre *f* de transmission

transmission channel /trænz'mɪʃ(ə)n ,tʃæn(ə)l/ *noun* voie *f*

transmission control protocol /trænz ,mɪʃ(ə)n kən'trəʊl ,prəʊtəkɒl/ *noun* protocole *m* de contrôle de protocole; protocole *m* TCP de transmission

transmission control protocol/interface program /trænz,mɪʃ(ə)n kən'trəʊl ,prəʊtəʊkɒl 'ɪntəfeɪs ,prəʊgræm/ *noun* protocole *m* TCP/IP (de communication de réseau)

transmission error /trænz,mɪʃ(ə)n 'erə/ *noun* erreur *f* de transmission

transmission medium /trænz'mɪʃ(ə)n ,miːdiəm/ *noun* support *m* de transmission

transmission rate /trænz'mɪʃ(ə)n reɪt/ *noun* vitesse *f* de transmission

transmissive disk /trænz'mɪsɪv dɪsk/ *noun* disque *m* optique transitif

transmit /trænz'mɪt/ *verb* transmettre *vt*

transmitter /trænz'mɪtə/ *noun* transmetteur *m*

transparency /træns'pærənsi/ *noun* (*for overhead projector*) transparence *m*; (*positive film*) diapositive *f*

transparent /træns'pærənt/ *adjective* **1.** (*program*) transparent *or* -e **2.** (*device or network*) transparent,-e ◇ **transparent interrupts** interruptions transparentes

transparent GIF /træns,pærənt ,dʒiː aɪ 'ef/ *noun* image *f* GIF transparente

transparent interrupt /træns,pærənt 'ɪntərʌpt/ *noun* interruption *f* transparente; interruption *f* contrôlée

transparent paging /træns,pærənt 'peɪdʒɪŋ/ *noun* pagination *f* transparente

transphasor /trænz'feɪzə/ *noun* transphaseur *m*

transportable /træns'pɔːtəb(ə)l/ *adjective* transportable ◇ **a transportable computer is not as small as a portable** un ordinateur transportable n'est pas aussi petit *or* aussi léger qu'un portable

transport layer /træns'pɔːt ,leɪə/ *noun* couche *f* transport

trap /træp/ *noun* (*device or piece of software*) piège *m*

trapdoor /'træp,dɔː/ *noun* point *m* d'entrée dans un système

trap handler /træp 'hændlə/ *noun* manipulateur *m* d'interruption

trashcan /'træʃkæn/ *noun* (*icon which looks like a dustbin*) corbeille *f*

tree /triː/ *noun* arbre *m* ◇ **tree structure** (structure en) arbre *m*

tree and branch network system /,triː ən brɑːntʃ 'netwɜːk ,sɪstəm/ *noun* système *m* arborescent

tree of folders /,triː əv 'fəʊldəz/ *noun* emboîtage *m* de dossiers

tree selection sort /,triː sɪ'lekʃən ,pɔːt/ *noun* tri *m* en arborescence

trellis coding /'trelɪs kɒdɪŋ/ *noun* (*modulating a signal*) codage *m* treillis

triad /'traɪæd/ *noun* triade *f*

trichromatic /,traɪkrəʊ'mætɪk/ *adjective* RVB (rouge, vert, bleu)

trivial file transfer protocol /,trɪviəl 'faɪl ,trænsfɜː ,prəʊtəkɒl/ *noun* protocole *m* TFTP

Trojan Horse /'trəʊdʒ(ə)n hɔːs/ *noun* (*program*) cheval *m* de Troie

troubleshoot /'trʌb(ə)lʃuːt/ *verb* **1.** (*to debug*) déboguer *vt*; (*to locate and repair faults*) localiser et réparer une panne **2.** localiser et réparer une panne

troubleshooter /'trʌb(ə)lʃuːtə/ *noun* (*for debugging*) spécialiste *m&f* en déboguage; (*technician*) technicien/réparateur *m*

true /truː/ *adjective* (*logical condition*) VRAI

TrueType /'truːtaɪp/ (*outline font technology*) caractères TrueType™

truncate /trʌŋ'keɪt/ *verb* **1.** (*to cut short*) tronquer *vt* **2.** (*to give an approximate value*) arrondir par défaut; tronquer *vt* ◇ **3.5678 truncated to 3.56** 3,5678 tronqué *or* arrondi par défaut à 3,56

truncation /trʌŋ'keɪʃ(ə)n/ *noun* (*of value*) troncature *f*

truncation error /trʌŋ'keɪʃ(ə)n ,erə/ *noun* erreur *f* de troncature; erreur *f* d'arrondi

trunk /trʌŋk/ *noun* circuit *m*; faisceau *m* de jonction

truth table /truːθ 'teɪb(ə)l/ *noun* table *f* de vérité

truth value /truːθ 'væljuː/ *noun* valeur *f* binaire; valeur *f* booléenne

TSAPI *abbr* (*telephony services application programming interface*) interface *f* de programmation d'application de services téléphoniques

Tseng Labs /'seŋ læbz/ (*chipset manufacturer*) Tseng Labs

TSR *abbr* (*terminate and stay resident*) programme résident; TSR

TSW *abbr* (*telesoftware*) logiciel *m* téléchargé

TTL /ˌtiː tiː 'el/ *noun* logique *f* transistor-transistor (LTT)

TTL-compatible /ˌtiː tiː el kəm'pɒtɪb(ə)l/ *adjective* compatible LTT

TTL logic /ˌtiː tiː el 'lɒdʒɪk/ *noun* logique *f* transistor-transistor; logique *f* LTT

TTL monitor /ˌtiː tiː el 'mɒnɪtə/ *noun* moniteur *m* TTL

TTY *abbr* (*teletype*) télétype *m*

tune /tjuːn/ *verb* (*a system*) ajuster *vt*; régler *vt*; mettre au point ◇ **to fine tune** régler avec grande précision *or* effectuer un réglage plus fin

tunnelling /'tʌn(ə)lɪŋ/ *noun* tunnellisation *f*

Turing machine /'tjʊrɪŋ məˌʃiːn/ *noun* machine *f* de Turing; simulateur *m* de Turing

Turing test /'tjʊrɪŋ test/ *noun* test *m* de Turing

turn /tɜːn/ *verb* tourner *vt*; retourner *vt*

turnaround document /'tɜːnəˌraʊnd ˌdɒkjʊmənt/ *noun* document *m* circulant

turnaround time /'tɜːnəraʊnd ˌtaɪm/ *noun* **1.** délai *m* d'inversion **2.** temps *m* d'exécution

turnkey system /'tɜːnkiː ˌsɪstəm/ *noun* système *m* clé en main

turtle /'tɜːt(ə)l/ *noun* tortue *f*

turtle graphics /'tɜːt(ə)l ˌgræfɪks/ *plural noun* graphisme généré à l'aide d'une tortue ◇ **the charts were prepared using turtle graphics** la présentation graphique a été préparée avec une tortue

TV /ˌtiː 'viː/ *abbr* (*television*) télévision *f*

TWAIN /tweɪn/ *noun* interface *f* TWAIN™

tweak /twiːk/ *verb* (*make small adjustments*) mettre au point; fignoler un programme

tweening /'twiːnɪŋ/ *noun* (*calculating intermediate images in computer graphics*) transformation *f* sérielle; calcul *m* des déformées intermédiaires ◇ **using tweening, we can show how a frog turns into a princess in five steps** en utilisant le procédé de transformation sérielle nous pouvons montrer comment une grenouille se métamorphose en princesse, en cinq étapes

24/96 /ˌtwenti fɔː ˌnaɪnti 'sɪks/ 24/96

24-bit sample /ˌtwenti fɔː bɪt 'sɑːmp(ə)l/ *noun* échantillon *m* à 16 bits

twisted-pair cable /ˌtwɪstɪd peə 'keɪb(ə)l/ *noun* (*two insulated copper wires twisted around each other*) câble *m* en paire(s) torsadée(s) ◇ **shielded twisted pair (STP) cable** câble en paire(s) torsadée(s) blindé *or* avec blindage ◇ **unshielded twisted pair (UTP) cable** câble en paire(s) torsadée(s) non blindé *or* sans blindage

twisted-pair Ethernet /ˌtwɪstɪd peə 'iːθənet/ *noun* Ethernet *m* à paire torsadée

two-address instruction /ˌtuː ə'dres ɪn ˌstrʌkʃən/ *noun* instruction *f* à deux adresses

2D /ˌtuː 'diː/ (*object in a graphic image that has only the appearance of width and height, not depth*) 2D

two-dimensional /ˌtuː daɪ'menʃən(ə)l/ *adjective* à deux dimensions; bidimensionnel *or* -elle

two-dimensional array /tuː daɪˌmenʃ(ə)nəl ə'reɪ/ *noun* (*ordered structure*) tableau *m* à deux dimensions; tableau *m* bidimensionnel

two-input adder /ˌtuː ˌɪnpʊt 'ædə/ *adjective* additionneur *m* à deux entrées

two-level subroutine /ˌtuː ˌlev(ə)l 'sʌbruːtiːn/ *noun* sous-programme *m* à deux niveaux

two-part /tuː pɑːt/ *adjective* (*paper*) double; en double épaisseur ◇ **two-part stationery** papier commercial, factures, etc., en double épaisseur

two-pass assembler /ˌtuː pɑːs ə'semblə/ *noun* assembleur *m* deux passes

two-phase commit /ˌtuː feɪz kə'mɪt/ *noun* validation *f* à deux phases

two-plus-one-address instruction /tuː plʌs wʌn ə'dres/, **two-plus-one instruction** /tuː plʌs wʌn/ *noun* instruction *f* à deux adresses plus une

two's complement /'tuːz ˌkɒmplɪmənt/ *noun* complément *m* à deux

TX *abbr* (*transmitter*) émetteur *m*

type /taɪp/ *noun* (*shape*) caractères *mpl* d'imprimerie ■ *verb* (*enter data via a keyboard*) saisir des données sur clavier; taper au clavier ◇ **I typed in the command again, but it still didn't work** j'ai retapé la commande, mais ça ne marche toujours pas ◇ **they switched to italic type for the heading** ils ont changé de police de caractères et composé l'en-tête en italique

Type 1 /taɪp wʌn/ *noun* 4 fils, en deux paires de fils solides avec blindage tressé

Type 2 /taɪp tuː/ *noun* 12 fils, en six paires, pour transmission de la voix

Type 3 /taɪp 'θriː/ *noun* 2 fils en paire torsadée pour liaison téléphonique

Type 5 /taɪp 'faɪv/ *noun* câble *m* à fibres optiques de 100–140 microns de diamètre

Type 6 /ˌtaɪp 'sɪx/ *noun* 4 fils, de plusieurs brins chacun, en deux paires

Type 8 /taɪp eɪt/ *noun* câble *m* blindé non torsadé de 4 fils, en deux paires

Type cable /taɪp 'keɪb(ə)l/ *noun* (*specification for cables defined by IBM*) type *m* de liaison (de IBM)

typeface /ˈtaɪpˌfeɪs/ *noun* (*set of characters*) fonte *f*; modèle *m* de caractères; police *f* de caractères; type *m* de caractères

typesetter /ˈtaɪpˌsetə/ *noun* **1.** (*person*) typographe *m*; compositeur *m* **2.** (*device*) compositeur *m*; typographe *m* ◇ **the text is ready to be sent to the typesetter** le texte est prêt à être envoyé au typographe

type size /taɪp saɪz/ *noun* (*size of a font*) corps *m*; taille *f* de caractères

type style /taɪp staɪl/ *noun* style *m* de caractère

U

UA /ˌjuː ˈeɪ/ *noun* agent *m* utilisateur

UART /ˈjuːɑːt/ *noun* émetteur-récepteur *m* universel asynchrone

UART controller /ˈjuːɑːt kənˌtrəʊlə/ *noun* contrôleur *m* d'émetteur/récepteur asynchrone universel

UBC *abbr* (*universal block channel*) canal *m* universel de transmission par blocs

UDP /ˌjuː diː ˈpiː/ *noun* protocole *m* UDP

UHF /ˌjuː eɪtʃ ˈef/ *noun* ultra-haute fréquence

ULA /ˌjuː el ˈeɪ/ *noun* circuit *m* logique non connecté

Ultimedia /ˌʌltiˈmidiə/ (*multimedia concept developed by IBM that combines sound, video, images, and text, and defines the hardware required to run it*) Ultimedia™

ultra- /ʌltrə/ *prefix* **1.** ultra-; hyper-; très **2.** ultra- ◇ **ultra-high frequency (UHF)** ultra-haute fréquence (UHF)

Ultra-2 SCSI /ˌʌltrə ˈtuː es siː es ˌaɪ/ *noun* interface *f* Ultra-2 SCSI

Ultra ATA /ˌʌltrə eɪ tiː ˈeɪ/ *noun* Ultra ATA

ultra high frequency /ˌʌltrə haɪ ˈfriːkwənsi/ *noun* ultra-haute fréquence

Ultra SCSI /ˌʌltrə es siː es ˈaɪ/ *noun* interface *f* Ultra SCSI

ultraviolet erasable PROM /ʌltrəˌvaɪələt ɪ ˌreɪzəb(ə)l ˈpiː rɒm/ *noun* mémoire *f* morte programmable effaçable par ultraviolet

ultraviolet light /ˌʌltrəvaɪələt ˈlaɪt/ *noun* rayonnement *m* ultraviolet; rayons *mpl* ultraviolets

UMTS /ˌjuː em tiː ˈes/ *noun* système *m* moderne de télécommunication avec les mobiles

unallowable digit /ʌnəˌlaʊəb(ə)l ˈdɪdʒɪt/ *noun* (*illegal combination of bits*) chiffre *m* non admissible; chiffre *m* inacceptable; chiffre *m* non autorisé; chiffre *m* non affectable

unary operation /ˌjuːnəri ˌɒpəˈreɪʃ(ə)n/ *noun* (*computing operation*) opération *f* monadique; opération *f* à un opérande

unattended operation /ˌʌnətendɪd ˌɒpə ˈreɪʃ(ə)n/ *noun* (*operation without supervision*) fonctionnement *m* automatique; tâche *f* qui peut être exécutée automatiquement

unauthorised /ʌnˈɔːθəraɪzd/, **unauthorized** *adjective* non autorisé

unbundled software /ʌnˌbʌnd(ə)ld ˈsɒftweə/ *noun* logiciel *m* non compris; logiciel *m* non inclus à l'achat d'un ordinateur

unclocked /ʌnˈklɒkd/ *adjective* (*circuit*) asynchrone; non asservi,-e à l'horloge

uncommitted logic array /ˌʌnkəmɪtɪd ˈlɒdʒɪk əˌreɪ/ *noun* circuit *m* logique non connecté

uncommitted storage list /ˌʌnkəmɪtɪd ˈstɔːrɪdʒ ˌlɪst/ *noun* liste *f* des emplacements disponibles; liste *f* des emplacements non alloués

unconditional /ˌʌnkənˈdɪʃ(ə)nəl/ *adjective* sans réserve; systématique; inconditionnel *or* -elle

unconditional branch /ˌʌnkənˈdɪʃ(ə)nəl brɑːntʃ/, **unconditional jump** /ˌʌnkən ˈdɪʃ(ə)nəl dʒʌmp/, **unconditional transfer** /ˌʌnkənˌdɪʃ(ə)nəl trænsˈfɜː/ *noun* (*instruction*) branchement *m*

uncorrupted /ˌʌnkəˈrʌptɪd/ *adjective* non altéré *or* -ée

undelete /ˈʌndɪiːt/ *verb* (*restore deleted information*) récupérer *vt* ◇ **thankfully we could undelete the files** par bonheur, nous avons pu récupérer ce fichier

underflow /ˈʌndəfləʊ/ *noun* dépassement *m*; débordement *m* négatif

underline *noun* soulignage *m*; soulignement *m*; trait *m* ■ *verb* (*to print or write a line under a piece of text*) souligner *vt*

underlining /ˌʌndəˈlaɪnɪŋ/ *noun* soulignage *m*

underscore /ˈʌndəskɔː/ *verb* souligner *vt*

undetected error /ˌʌndɪtektɪd ˈerə/ *noun* erreur *f* non détectée

undo /ʌnˈduː/ *verb* (*to reverse the previous action*) annuler *vt*; supprimer l'effet; (*function*) annuler *vt* ◇ **you've just deleted the paragraph, but you can undo it from the option in the Edit menu** vous venez de supprimer un paragraphe, vous pouvez annuler cette action avec l'option 'annuler' (undo) du menu Edition

unedited /ʌnˈedɪtɪd/ *adjective* (*text*) non édité *or* -ée; non corrigé *or* -ée

unformatted /ʌnˈfɔːmætɪd/ *adjective* **1.** (*contains no formatting commands*) non formaté *or* -ée; brut *or* -e **2.** (*not formatted*) non formaté ◇ **it is impossible to copy to an unformatted disk** il est impossible de copier quoi que ce soit sur une disquette non formatée ◇ **unformatted text** texte brut

unformatted capacity /ʌnˌfɔːmætɪd kə ˈpæsɪti/ *noun* capacité *f* non formatée

unformatted disk /ʌnˌfɔːmætɪd ˈ dɪsk/ *noun* disque *m* non formaté; disquette *f* non formatée

uni- /juːni/ *prefix* (*meaning one*) uni-

unicast /ˈjuːnikɑːst/ *noun* diffusion *f* individuelle

uniform resource locator /ˌjuːnɪfɔːm rɪ ˈzɔːs ləʊˌkeitə/ *noun* adresse *f* URL

uninstall /ˌʌnɪnˈstɑːl/ *verb* désinstaller *vt* ◇ **uninstall procedure** procédure *f* de désinstallation

uninterruptible power supply /ˌʌnɪntərʌptɪb(ə)l ˈpaʊə səˌplaɪ/ *noun* onduleur *m*

union /ˈjuːnjən/ *noun* (*logical function*) union *f*; opération *f* OU

unipolar /ˌjuːniˈpəʊlə/ *adjective* **1.** (*transistor*) unipolaire **2.** (*transmission system*) unipolaire

unipolar signal /juːnɪˌpəʊlə ˈsɪgn(ə)l/ *noun* signal *m* unipolaire

unipolar transistor /juːnɪˌpəʊlə trænˈzɪstə/ *noun* transistor *m* unipolaire

unique identifier /juːˌniːk aɪˈdentɪfaɪə/ *noun* identificateur *m* unique

unit /ˈjuːnɪt/ *noun* **1.** (*smallest element*) unité *f*; élément *m* **2.** (*single machine*) unité *f*; appareil *m*; dispositif *m* ◇ **arithmetic and logic unit (ALU)** unité arithmétique et logique ◇ **central processing unit (CPU)** unité centrale (de traitement) *or* processeur central

unit buffer /ˈjuːnɪt ˌbʌfə/ *noun* tampon *m* élémentaire

unit record /ˈjuːnɪt ˌrekɔːd/ *noun* enregistrement *m* unique

universal /ˌjuːnɪˈvɜːs(ə)l/ *adjective* universel *or* -elle; standard ◇ **universal asynchronous receiver *or* transmitter (UART)** émetteur/récepteur *m* asynchrone universel ◇ **universal block channel (UBC)** canal universel de transmission par blocs ◇ **universal device (UART, USRT, USART)** dispositif universel ◇ **universal synchronous asynchronous receiver-transmitter (USART)** émetteur/récepteur synchrone asynchrone universel ◇ **universal synchronous receiver *or* transmitter (USRT)** émetteur/récepteur synchrone universel

universal asynchronous receiver/transmitter /ˌjuːnɪvɜːsəl ˌeɪsɪŋkrənəs rɪˌsiːvə trænzˈmɪtə/ *noun* émetteur-récepteur *m* universel asynchrone

universal block channel /ˌjuːnɪvɜːs(ə)l ˈblɒk ˌtʃæn(ə)l/ *noun* canal *m* universel de transmission par blocs

universal device /ˌjuːnɪvɜːs(ə)l dɪˈvaɪs/ *noun* **1.** dispositif *m* universel **2.** dispositif *m* universel

universal mobile telecommunications system /ˌjuːnɪvɜːs(ə)l ˌməʊbaɪl ˌtelikəmjuːnɪ ˈkeɪʃ(ə)nz ˌsɪstəm/ *noun* système *m* moderne de télécommunication avec les mobiles

universal product code /ˌjuːnɪvɜːs(ə)l ˈprɒdʌkt ˌkəʊd/ *noun* code *m* barres

universal programming /ˌjuːnɪvɜːs(ə)l ˈprəʊgræmɪŋ/ *noun* programmation *f* en langage universel

universal resource locator /ˌjuːnɪvɜːs(ə)l rɪˈzɔːs ləʊˌkeitə/ *noun* adresse *f* Web

universal serial bus /ˌjuːnɪvɜːs(ə)l ˈsɪəriəl ˌbʌs/ *noun* bus *m* USB

universal set /ˌjuːnɪˈvɜːs(ə)l set/ *noun* ensemble *m* référentiel

universal synchronous asynchronous receiver/transmitter /ˌjuːnɪvɜːsəl ˌsɪŋkrənəs ˌeɪsɪŋkrənəs rɪˌsiːvə trænzˈmɪtə/ *noun* émetteur-récepteur *m* synchrone universel

universal synchronous receiver/transmitter /ˌjuːnɪvɜːs(ə)l ˌsɪŋkrənəs rɪˌsiːvə træns ˈmɪtə/ *noun* émetteur-récepteur *m* universel asynchrone

UNIX /ˈjuːnɪks/ *noun* (*operating system developed by AT&T Bell*) UNIX

> 'Hampshire fire brigade is investing £2 million in a command and control system based on the new SeriesFT fault-tolerant Unix machine from Motorola.' [*Computing*]

UNIX-to-UNIX copy /ˌjuːnɪks tə ˌjuːnɪks ˈkɒpi/ *noun* utilitaire *m* UUCP

unjustified /ʌnˈdʒʌstɪfaɪd/ *adjective* non justifié *or* -ée

unjustified tape /ʌnˈdʒʌstɪˌfaɪd teɪp/ *noun* (*idiot tape – tape containing unformatted text*) bande *f* de texte non formaté; bande *f* sans paramètres d'impression; bande *f* idiote

unlock /ʌnˈlɒk/ *verb* (*allow other users to write to a file or access a system*) déverrouiller *vt*

unmoderated list /ʌnˌmɒdəreɪtɪd ˈlɪst/ *noun* (*mailing list that sends any material to all the subscribers without a person reading or checking the content*) liste *f* non approuvée; liste *f* non autorisée

unmodified instruction /ʌnˌmɒdɪfaɪd ɪn ˈstrʌkʃən/ *noun* instruction *f* dans sa forme initiale

unmodulated /ʌnˈmɒdjʊleɪtɪd/ *adjective* (*signal*) non modulé *or* -ée

unmount /ʌnˈmaʊnt/ *verb* **1.** (*remove a disk from a disk drive*) retirer un disque dur **2.** (*inform the operating system that a disk drive is no longer in use*) message 'unmount' (qui indique que le disque n'est pas utilisable, que le disque a été retiré)

unpack /ʌnˈpæk/ *verb* (*to remove packed data from storage*) dégrouper *vt*; décondenser *vt*; décomprimer *vt*; décompresser *vt* ◇ **this routine**

unpacks the archived file cette routine permet de décomprimer les fichiers archivés

unplug /ʌn'plʌg/ *verb* débrancher *vt*; déconnecter *vt* ◇ **do not move the system without unplugging it** ne déplacez pas le système sans l'avoir d'abord débranché ◇ **simply unplug the old drive and plug-in a new one** vous n'avez qu'à déconnecter le lecteur et en brancher un nouveau à sa place

unpopulated /ʌn'pɒpjʊleɪtɪd/ *adjective* (*PCB which does not contain any components*) nu *or* -e; non équipé *or* -ée; sans composant

unprotected /ˌʌnprə'tektɪd/ *adjective* (*data that can be modified*) non protégé *or* -ée

unprotected field /ˌʌnprə'tektɪd fiːld/ *noun* champ *m* non protégé

unrecoverable error /ʌnrɪˌkʌvərəb(ə)l 'erə/ *noun* erreur *f* irrécupérable; erreur *f* impossible à corriger

unshielded twisted-pair cable /ˌʌnʃiːldɪd ˌtwɪstɪd 'peə ˌkeɪb(ə)l/ *noun* câble *m* en paires torsadées sans blindage; câble *m* UTP

unsigned /ʌn'saɪnd/ *adjective* (*number system*) sans signe; en valeur absolue

unsolicited mail /ˌʌnsə'lɪsɪtɪd meɪl/ *noun* courrier *m* non sollicité; courrier *m* sans intérêt

unsorted /ʌn'sɔːtɪd/ *adjective* (*data*) non classé *or* -ée; non trié *or* -ée ◇ **it took four times as long to search the unsorted file** il a fallu quatre fois plus de temps pour chercher dans le fichier aux données non classées

unsubscribe /ˌʌnsəb'skraɪb/ *verb* se désabonner

> 'All commercial messages will have to include full details of the sender's name and physical address, as well as an unsubscribe option allowing recipients to stop any further messages.' [*The Guardian*]

unsupported /ˌʌnsə'pɔːtɪd/ *adjective* non renforcé *or* -ée

unzip /ʌn'zɪp/ *verb* dézipper *vt*

up /ʌp/ *adverb* (*working or running*) en bon état de marche ◇ **they must have found the fault – the computer is finally up and running** ils ont sûrement trouvé la source du problème puisque l'ordinateur fonctionne à merveille

UPC *abbr* (*universal product code*) code *m* universel de produits

update /'ʌpdeɪt/ *noun* **1.** (*file*) fichier *m* mis à jour; corrigé *m*; (*system*) nouvelle version *f* (d'un progiciel) **2.** (*action*) mise *f* à jour; correction *f vt* **3.** (*system*) nouvelle version *f* d'un progiciel ■ *verb* /ʌp'deɪt/ (*to change or add specific data in a file*) corriger *vt*; mettre à jour ◇ **we have the original and updated documents on disks** le document original et le document corrigé se trouvent tous les deux sur disquettes

update file /ʌp'deɪt faɪl/ *noun* fichier *m* de mouvements

up/down counter /ʌp 'daʊn ˌkaʊntə/ *noun* compteur *m* incrémenteur/décrémenteur

upgrade /ʌp'greɪd/ *verb* mettre à niveau; optimiser *vt*; améliorer *vt* ◇ **all three models have an on-site upgrade facility** les trois modèles offrent des possibilités de mise à niveau sur site ◇ **they can upgrade the printer** ils peuvent optimiser l'imprimante

upkeep /'ʌpkiːp/ *noun* **1.** (*hardware*) entretien *m*; maintenance *f* **2.** entretien *m*; maintenance *f*

uplink /'ʌplɪŋk/ *noun* (*link from an earth station to a satellite*) liaison *f* terre/satellite

upload /'ʌpˌləʊd/ *verb* **1.** (*to transfer towards another computer or the Internet server, etc.*) télécharger des données vers un autre ordinateur ou serveur **2.** télécharger *vt*; transférer des données ◇ **the user can upload PC data to update mainframe applications** l'utilisateur peut télécharger les données d'un PC sur un gros ordinateur, pour faire la mise à jour des applications

uppercase /ˌʌpə'keɪs/ *noun* majuscule *f*; capitale *f*; haut *m* de casse ◇ **upper case M** M majuscule

upper memory /ˌʌpə 'mem(ə)ri/ *noun* (*IBM PC: memory located between the 640Kb and 1Mb limits*) mémoire *f* haute

UPS /ˌjuː piː 'es/ *noun* onduleur *m*

> 'Magnum Power Systems has launched a new UPS for PCs. The BI-UPS prevents loss of data due to power dips or 'brown-outs' – voltage drops because of circuit overload.' [*Computing*]

uptime, up time *noun* (*time when a computer is functioning correctly*) temps *m* productif; temps *m* de bon fonctionnement

upward compatible /ˌʌpwəd kəm'pætɪb(ə)l/, **upwards compatible** /ˌʌpwədz kəm'pætɪb(ə)l/ *adjective* compatible avec système de niveau supérieur

URL /ˌjuː ɑː 'el/ *noun* adresse *f* Web ◇ **the URL of the Peter Collin Publishing home page is 'http: *or or* www.pcp.co.uk'** l'adresse URL de la page d'accueil de la maison Peter Collin Publishing est la suivante: http//www.pcp.co.uk

usability /ˌjuːzə'bɪlɪti/ *noun* (*ease of use*) facilité *f* d'utilisation; convivialité *f* ◇ **we have studied usability tests and found that a GUI is easier for new users than a command line** nous avons étudié les tests de convivialité et trouvé que l'interface (graphique) GUI est plus facile à maîtriser pour les débutants que les lignes de commandes

USART /'juːzɑːt/ *noun* émetteur/récepteur *m* synchrone asynchrone universel

USB /ˌjuː es 'biː/ *noun* bus *m* USB

use *verb* (*to consume power*) consommer *vt*; (*to operate something*) utiliser *vt*; employer *vt*; se servir de (quelque chose) ◇ **if you use the computer for processing the labels, it will be much quicker** la préparation de ces étiquettes se fera beaucoup plus rapidement avec l'ordinateur ◇

it's using too much electricity l'appareil consomme beaucoup trop d'électricité ◇ **the computer is used too often by the sales staff** les commerciaux utilisent l'ordinateur trop souvent

Usenet /ˈjuːzˌnet/ *noun* (*section of the internet that provides forums also called newsgroups*) réseau *m* Usenet (d'utilisateurs)

user /ˈjuːzə/ *noun* utilisateur *m* ◇ **I found how to solve the problem by asking people at the user group meeting** j'ai trouvé la solution au problème en me renseignant auprès des autres utilisateurs rencontrés à la réunion des membres du groupe ◇ **the style sheet contains 125 user-definable symbols** la feuille de style comporte 125 symboles programmables selon les besoins de l'utilisateur ◇ **the video resolution of 640 by 300, 240 or 200 pixels is user-selectable** l'utilisateur peut sélectionner une résolution d'écran de 640 x 300, 240 ou 200 pixels ◇ **user agent (UA)** (*software – in an X.400 email system*) agent *m* (d')utilisateur ◇ **user datagram protocol (UDP)** (*protocol that is part of TCP/IP*) protocole UDP (d'échange de données utilisateur)

'...the user's guides are designed for people who have never seen a computer, but some sections have been spoiled by careless checking' [*PC User*]

user account /ˈjuːzə əˌkaʊnt/ *noun* compte *m* (d') utilisateur ◇ **I have a new user account on this LAN but I cannot remember my password** j'ai un nouveau compte d'utilisateur sur ce réseau, mais j'ai oublié mon mot de passe

user agent /ˈjuːzə ˌeɪdʒənt/ *noun* agent *m* utilisateur

user area /ˈjuːzə ˌeəriə/ *noun* zone *f* utilisateur; zone *f* pour programme utilisateur

user datagram protocol /ˌjuːzə ˈdeɪtəgræm ˌprəʊtəkɒl/ *noun* protocole *m* UDP

user-definable /ˈjuːzə dɪˌfaɪnəb(ə)l/ *adjective* programmable; paramétrable par l'utilisateur; paramétrable selon les besoins de l'utilisateur ◇ **the style sheet contains 125 user-definable symbols** la feuille de style comporte 125 symboles programmables selon les besoins de l'utilisateur

user-defined character /ˌjuːzə dɪˌfaɪnd ˈkærɪktə/ *plural noun* caractère *m* programmé par l'utilisateur

user documentation /ˌjuːzə ˌdɒkjʊmenˈteɪʃ(ə)n/ *noun* notice *f* d'utilisation

user-friendly /ˌjuːzə ˈfrendli/ *adjective* (*language or system or program*) convivial *or* -e; d'utilisation facile; facile à utiliser; ergonomique ◇ **compared with the previous version this one is very user-friendly** comparée à la version précédente, celle-ci est très facile à utiliser *or* très conviviale ◇ **it's such a user-friendly machine** c'est un appareil vraiment convivial *or* extrêmement facile à utiliser

'ModelMaker saves researchers a great deal of time and effort, and provides a highly user-friendly environment using menus and 'buttons', instant output, and instant access to a wide variety of mathematical techniques built into the system.' [*Computing*]

user-friendly software /ˌjuːzə ˌfrendli ˈsɒftweə/ *noun* logiciel *m* convivial

user group /ˈjuːzə gruːp/ *noun* groupe *m* d'utilisateurs ◇ **I found how to solve the problem by asking people at the user group meeting** j'ai trouvé la solution au problème en me renseignant auprès des autres utilisateurs rencontrés à la réunion des membres du groupe

user guide /ˈjuːzə gaɪd/ *noun* manuel *m* d'utilisation

user ID /ˌjuːzə aɪ ˈdiː/ *noun* (*unique identification code*) mot *m* de passe

user interface /ˈjuːzə ˌɪntəfeɪs/ *noun* interface *f* système/utilisateur

user level /ˈjuːzə ˌlev(ə)l/ *noun* niveau *m* utilisateur

user name /ˈjuːzə neɪm/ *noun* nom *m* d'utilisateur

user-operated language /ˌjuːzə ˌɒpəreɪtɪd ˈlæŋgwɪdʒ/ *noun* langage *m* (d')utilisateur

user port /ˈjuːzə pɔːt/ *noun* port *m* pour périphérique

user program /ˈjuːzə ˌprəʊgræm/ *noun* programme *m* (d') utilisateur

user-selectable /ˌjuːzə sɪˈlektəb(ə)l/ *adjective* (*which can be programmed by the user*) programmable par l'utilisateur; (*which can be chosen or selected by the user*) définissable par l'utilisateur; réglable par l'utilisateur ◇ **this modem has user-selectable baud rates** les vitesses (de réception et de transmission) de ce modem sont réglables

user's manual /ˈjuːzəz ˌmænjʊəl/ *noun* guide *m* de l'utilisateur

user's program /ˈjuːzəz ˌprəʊgræm/ *noun* (*software written by a user*) programme *m* écrit par l'utilisateur; programme *m* d' utilisateur

USRT /ˌjuː es ɑː ˈtiː/ *noun* émetteur/récepteur *m* synchrone universel

utility program /juːˈtɪlɪti ˌprəʊgræm/ *noun* utilitaire *m*

UTP cable /ˌjuː tiː ˈpiː ˌkeɪb(ə)l/ *noun* câble *m* en paire(s) torsadée(s) sans blindage

UUCP *abbr* (*Unix-to-Unix copy*) utilitaire *m* de connexion UUCP

Uuencoding /ˌjuː juː ɪnˈkəʊdɪŋ/ *noun* (*method of converting documents and files to a pseudo-text format*) Uuencodage *m*

UV light /ˌjuː viː ˈlaɪt/ *noun* rayonnement *m* ultraviolet; rayons *mpl* ultraviolets

V

V /viː/ *abbr* (*voltage*) V

V20 *noun* (*processor chips made by NEC, which are compatible with the Intel 8088 and 8086*) processeur *m* V20

V.21 *noun* norme *f* V21

V.22 *noun* norme *f* V22

V.22bis *noun* norme *f* V.22 bis

V.29 *noun* norme *f* V29

V30 *noun* processeur *m* V30

V.32 *noun* norme *f* V32

V.32bis *noun* norme *f* V32 BIS

V.42 *noun* norme *f* V42

V.42bis *noun* norme *f* V.42 bis

V.90 *noun* norme *f* V90

vaccine /ˈvæksiːn/ *noun* (*utility to check a system to see if viruses are present*) logiciel *m* antivirus; utilitaire *m* antivirus

valid /ˈvælɪd/ *adjective* valide

validate /ˈvælɪˌdeɪt/ *verb* valider *vt*

validation /ˌvælɪˈdeɪʃ(ə)n/ *noun* validation *f*

validity /vəˈlɪdɪti/ *noun* validité *f*

validity check /vəˈlɪdəti tʃek/ *noun* vérification *f* de validité des données

valid memory address /ˌvælɪd ˈmem(ə)ri əˌdres/ *noun* adresse *f* valide

value /ˈvæljuː/ *noun* valeur *f*

value-added /ˌvæljuː ˈædɪd/ *adjective* (*with extra benefit for a user*) à valeur ajoutée ◇ **value-added network (VAN)** (*network which offers information services*) réseau *m* à valeur ajoutée *or* réseau à intégration de service (RIS) ◇ **value-added reseller (VAR)** (*buys material and adds other features*) revendeur *m* à valeur ajoutée *or* revendeur à intégration de service

value-added network /ˌvæljuː ˌædɪd ˈnetwɜːk/ *noun* réseau *m* à valeur ajoutée; réseau *m* à intégration de service (RIS)

value-added reseller /ˌvæljuː ædɪd ˈriːselə/ *noun* revendeur *m* à valeur ajoutée; revendeur *m* à intégration de service

VAN /væn/ *abbr* (*value-added network*) réseau *m* à valeur ajoutée; réseau *m* à intégration de service (RIS)

V & V /ˌviː ənd ˈviː/ *noun* vérification *f* et validation; contrôle *m* et validation

vanishing point perspective /ˈvænɪʃɪŋ pɔɪnt pəˌspektɪv/ *noun* perspective *f* fuyante

vapourware /ˈveɪpəweə/ *noun informal* (*products which exist in name only*) rideau *m* de fumée; produits *mpl* fictifs

> 'Rivals dismissed the initiative as IBM vapourware, designed to protect its installed base of machines running under widely differing operating systems.' [*Computing*]

VAR *abbr* (*value-added reseller*) revendeur *m* à valeur ajoutée; revendeur *m* à intégration de service

variable /ˈveəriəb(ə)l/ *adjective* (*able to change*) variable ■ *noun* **1.** (*register or storage location*) variable *f* **2.** (*identifier*) variable *f*

variable data /ˌveəriəb(ə)l ˈdeɪtə/ *noun* données *fpl* variables

variable data type /ˌveəriəb(ə)l ˈdeɪtə ˌtaɪp/ *noun* variable *f* de type non précisé

variable format /ˌveəriəb(ə)l ˈfɔːmæt/ *noun* format *m* variable

variable length record /ˌveəriəb(ə)l leŋθ ˈrekɔːd/ *noun* enregistrement *m* de longueur variable

variable name /ˈveəriəb(ə)l neɪm/ *noun* nom *m* de variable

variable word length computer /ˌveəriəb(ə)l wɜːd leŋθ kəmˈpjuːtə/ *noun* ordinateur *m* à mots de longueur variable

VBScript /viː ˈbiː ˌskrɪpt/ *abbr* (*Visual Basic Script*) (*set of programming commands*) langage *m* VBScript

VBX *abbr* (*Visual Basic Extension*) composant *m* VBX

VCR /ˌviː siː ˈɑː/ *noun* magnétoscope *m*

VDT /ˌviː diː ˈjuː/ *abbr* (*visual display terminal*) terminal *m* vidéo

VDU *abbr* (*visual display unit*) écran *m* de visualisation; écran *m* visuel

> '...it normally consists of a keyboard to input information and either a printing terminal or a VDU screen to display messages and results' [*Practical Computing*]

> '...a VDU is a device used with a computer that displays information in the form of characters and drawings on a screen' [*Electronics & Power*]

vector /ˈvektə/ *noun* **1.** (*address to a new memory location*) vecteur *m* **2.** (*coordinate*) vecteur *m*

vectored interrupt /ˌvektəd ˈɪntərʌpt/ *noun* interruption *f* vectorisée

vector font /ˈvektə fɒnt/ *noun* fonte *f* vectorielle

vector graphics /ˈvektə ˌɡræfɪks/, **vector image** /ˌvektə ˈɪmɪdʒ/ *noun* graphismes *mpl* vectoriels

vector processor /ˈvektə ˌprəʊsesə/ *noun* processeur *m* vectoriel

vector scan /ˈvektə skæn/ *noun* image *f* vectorielle

Veitch diagram /ˈvaɪtʃ ˌdaɪəɡræm/ *noun* diagramme *m* de Veitch

vendor /ˈvendə/ *noun* (*seller*) vendeur *m*

vendor-independent /ˌvendə ˌɪndɪˈpendənt/ *adjective* indépendant, -e du constructeur

vendor-independent messaging /ˌvendə ˌɪndɪpendənt ˈmesɪdʒɪŋ/ *noun* interface *f* normalisée de messagerie

Venn diagram /ˈven ˌdaɪəɡræm/ *noun* diagramme *m* de Venn

verification /ˌverɪfɪˈkeɪʃ(ə)n/ *noun* vérification *f*; contrôle *m* ◇ **verification and validation (V & V)** vérification et validation *or* contrôle et validation

verification and validation /ˌverɪfɪkeɪʃ(ə)n ən ˌvælɪˈdeɪʃ(ə)n/ *noun* vérification *f* et validation; contrôle *m* et validation

verifier /ˈverɪfaɪə/ *noun* (*device*) vérificatrice *f*

verify /ˈverɪˌfaɪ/ *verb* vérifier *vt*; contrôler *vt*

Veronica /vəˈrɒnɪkə/ (*tool that works with Gopher to help a user find information or files on the WWW*) Veronica

version /ˈvɜːʃ(ə)n/ *noun* version *f* ◇ **the latest version of the software includes an improved graphics routine** la dernière version du logiciel comprend une routine graphique améliorée

version control /ˈvɜːʃ(ə)n kənˌtrəʊl/ *noun* utilitaire *m* de suivi de version

version number /ˈvɜːʃ(ə)n ˌnʌmbə/ *noun* numéro *m* de version

vertex /ˈvɜːteks/ *noun* sommet *m*

vertical /ˈvɜːtɪk(ə)l/ *adjective* vertical *or* -e ◇ **vertical format unit (VFU)** unité *f* de formatage vertical ◇ **vertical redundancy check (VRC)** contrôle *m* par redondance verticale

vertical application /ˌvɜːtɪk(ə)l ˌæplɪˈkeɪʃ(ə)n/ *noun* application *f* verticale ◇ **your new software to manage a florist's is a good vertical application** votre nouveau progiciel pour gérer une boutique de fleuriste est une bonne application verticale

vertical axis /ˌvɜːtɪk(ə)l ˈæksɪs/ *noun* axe *m* des ordonnées

vertical blanking interval /ˌvɜːtɪk(ə)l ˈblæŋkɪŋ ˌɪntəvəl/ *noun* délai *m* de retour vertical

vertical format unit /ˌvɜːtɪk(ə)l ˈfɔːmæt ˌjuːnɪt/ *noun* unité *f* de formatage vertical

vertical interval time code /ˌvɜːtɪk(ə)l ˌɪntəv(ə)l ˈtaɪm ˌkəʊd/ *noun* code *m* temporel vertical

vertical justification /ˌvɜːtɪk(ə)l ˌdʒʌstɪfɪˈkeɪʃ(ə)n/ *noun* justification *f* verticale

vertically /ˈvɜːtɪkli/ *adverb* verticalement ◇ **vertically polarized signal** signal *m* avec polarisation verticale *or* signal polarisé verticalement

vertical parity check /ˌvɜːtɪk(ə)l ˈpærɪti ˌtʃek/ *noun* contrôle *m* de parité verticale

vertical portal /ˌvɜːtɪk(ə)l ˈpɔːt(ə)l/ *noun* portail *m* vertical

vertical redundancy check /ˌvɜːtɪk(ə)l rɪˈdʌndənsi ˌtʃek/ *noun* contrôle *m* par redondance verticale

vertical scrolling /ˌvɜːtɪk(ə)l ˈskrəʊlɪŋ/ *noun* défilement *m* vertical

vertical sync signal /ˌvɜːtɪk(ə)l ˈsɪŋk ˌsɪɡn(ə)l/ *noun* signal *m* vidéo vertical

vertical tab /ˌvɜːtɪk(ə)l ˈtæb/ *noun* tabulation *f* verticale

very large scale integration /ˌveri lɑːdʒ skeɪl ˌɪntɪˈɡreɪʃ(ə)n/ *noun* intégration *f* à très grande échelle

VESA *abbr* (*Video Electronics Standards Association*) Video Electronics Standards Association

VESA local bus /ˌviː iː es eɪ ˈləʊk(ə)l bʌs/ *noun* (*standard defined by VESA in an IBM PC*) bus *m* local VESA

vestigial side band /vesˌtɪdʒiəl ˈsaɪd ˌbænd/ *noun* bande *f* latérale résiduelle

V format /viː ˈfɔːmæt/ *noun* (*data organization*) format *m* variable

VFU *abbr* (*vertical format unit*) unité *f* de formatage vertical

VGA /ˌviː dʒiː ˈeɪ/ *noun* (*standard of video adapter developed by IBM*) adaptateur *m* VGA

via /ˈvaɪə/ *preposition* via; par; par l'intermédiaire de; en passant par ◇ **the signals have reached us via satellite** les signaux nous ont été transmis par satellite ◇ **you can download the data to the CPU via a modem** le téléchargement des données sur l'unité centrale peut se faire par l'intermédiaire d'un modem

VidCap /ˈvɪdkæp/ *noun* (*Windows utility to capture a video sequence*) VidCap

video /ˈvɪdiəʊ/ *noun* vidéo *f* ◇ **a printer-readable video image can be sent to a basic laser printer through a video port** une image vidéo imprimable peut être transmise sur une imprimante laser classique par le port vidéo ◇ **digital video camera** caméra vidéo numérique ◇ **infrared video camera** caméra vidéo de vision nocturne ◇ **some instructors monitor their trainees with infrared video cameras** certains instructeurs utilisent une caméra vidéo de vision nocturne pour suivre leurs élèves ◇ **video camera** caméra *f* vidéo ◇ **video card** carte *f* vidéo ◇ **video cassette** vidéocassette *f* ◇ **video compressor** réducteur *m* (de largeur de bande) vidéo ◇ **video expander** déconcentrateur *m* pour transmission vidéo ◇ **video frame** image *f* vidéo ◇ **video image** image *f* vidéo ◇ **video library** vidéothèque *f* ◇ **video nasties** *informal* films *mpl* d'épouvante *or* d'horreur sur vidéocassettes *or* sur bandes vidéo ◇ **video phone** vidéophone *m* ◇ **video player** système *m* vidéo ◇ **video port** port *m* vidéo ◇ **video random access memory (VRAM)** mémoire vidéo à accès aléatoire (VRAM) ◇ **video standards** normes *fpl* vidéo ◇ **videotape** bande *f* vidéo

video adapter /ˈvɪdiəʊ əˌdæptə/ *noun* carte *f* vidéo

video bandwidth /ˌvɪdiəʊ ˈbændwɪdθ/ *noun* largeur *f* de bande vidéo

video board /ˈvɪdiəʊ bɔːd/ *noun* carte *f* vidéo

video buffer /ˈvɪdiəʊ ˌbʌfə/ *noun* mémoire *f* (tampon) vidéo

video capture board /ˌvɪdiəʊ ˈkæptʃə ˌbɔːd/ *noun* carte *f* de capture vidéo

video cassette recorder /ˌvɪdiəʊ kəˈset rɪ ˌkɔːdə/ *noun* magnétoscope *m*

video-CD /ˌvɪdiəʊ ˌsiː ˈdiː/ *noun* CD-vidéo *m*

video clip *noun* clip *m*

video codec /ˌvɪdiəʊ ˈkəʊdek/ *noun* codec *m* vidéo

video compression /ˌvɪdiəʊ kəmˈpreʃ(ə)n/ *noun* compression *f* vidéo

video conferencing /ˈvɪdiəʊ ˌkɒnf(ə)rənsɪŋ/ *noun* vidéoconférence *f*

video controller /ˌvɪdiəʊ kənˈtrəʊlə/ *noun* carte *f* vidéo

video digitiser /ˌvɪdiəʊ ˈdɪdʒɪtaɪzə/ *noun* numériseur *m* vidéo

videodisc /ˈvɪdiəʊdɪsk/ *noun* disque *m* vidéo; vidéodisque *m*

video display /ˈvɪdiəʊ dɪˌspleɪ/ *noun* écran *m*

video editing /ˌvɪdiəʊ ˈedɪtɪŋ/ *noun* montage *m* vidéo

Video Electronics Standards Association /ˌvɪdiəʊ elekˌtrɒnɪks ˈstændədz ə ˌsəʊsieɪʃ(ə)n/ *noun* Video Electronics Standards Association

Video for Windows /ˌvɪdiəʊ fə ˈwɪndəʊz/ (*trade name for a set of software drivers and utilities for Microsoft Windows 3.1*) Video for Windows

video game /ˈvɪdiəʊ geɪm/ *noun* jeu *m* vidéo

video graphics array /ˌvɪdiəʊ ˈgræfɪks ə ˌreɪ/ *noun* norme *f* d'écran VGA

video home system /ˌvɪdiəʊ ˈhəʊm ˌsɪstəm/ *noun* VHS

video interface chip /ˌvɪdiəʊ ˈɪntəfeɪs ˌtʃɪp/ *noun* circuit *m* intégré de carte vidéo

video lookup table /ˌvɪdiəʊ ˈlʊkʌp ˌteɪb(ə)l/ *noun* table *f* de contrôle des paramètres d'écran couleur

video memory /ˌvɪdiəʊ ˈmem(ə)ri/ *noun* RAM *f* vidéo; mémoire *f* vidéo; mémoire *f* image

video monitor /ˈvɪdiəʊ ˌmɒnɪtə/ *noun* moniteur *m*

video RAM /ˌvɪdiəʊ ˈræm/ *noun* mémoire *f* vidéo

video random access memory /ˌvɪdiəʊ ˌrændəm ˌækses ˈmem(ə)ri/, **video RAM** /ˌvɪdiəʊ ˈræm/ *noun* mémoire *f* vidéo

video scanner /ˈvɪdiəʊ ˌskænə/ *noun* scanner *m* vidéo; scanner *m* d'images

video server /ˈvɪdiəʊ ˌsɜːvə/ *noun* serveur *m* vidéo

video signal /ˈvɪdiəʊ ˌsɪgn(ə)l/ *noun informal* signal *m* vidéo

video tape /ˈvɪdiəʊ teɪp/ *noun* bande *f* vidéo

video tape recorder /ˌvɪdiəʊ ˈteɪp rɪˌkɔːdə/ *noun* magnétoscope *m*

video teleconferencing /ˌvɪdiəʊ ˈteli ˌkɒnf(ə)rənsɪŋ/ *noun* visioconférence *f*

video terminal /ˈvɪdiəʊ ˌtɜːmɪn(ə)l/ *noun* terminal *m* vidéo; écran *m* vidéo avec clavier

videotext /ˈvɪdiəʊtekst/, **videotex** /ˈvɪdiəʊteks/ *noun* vidéotex *m*; vidéographie *f* interactive

view /vjuː/ *verb* (*film, etc.*) visionner *vt*; (*display*) visualiser *vt* ◇ **the user has to pay a charge for viewing pages on a bulletin board** l'utilisateur paie un droit pour visualiser le tableau d'affichage

viewdata /ˈvjuːdeɪtə/ *noun* système *m* britannique équivalent au Minitel™

viewer /ˈvjuːə/ *noun* (*person*) téléspectateur *m*

VIM /vɪm/ *noun* interface *f* normalisée de messagerie

viral /ˈvaɪrəl/ *adjective* viral

viral marketing /ˈvaɪrəl ˌmɑːkɪtɪŋ/ *noun* marketing *m* viral

virgin /ˈvɜːdʒɪn/ *adjective* (*tape or disk*) vierge

virtual /ˈvɜːtʃuəl/ *adjective* virtuel *or* -elle ◇ **virtual reality (VR)** (*simulation of a real-life scene*) réalité virtuelle

virtual address /ˌvɜːtʃuəl əˈdres/ *noun* adresse *f* virtuelle

virtual assistant /ˌvɜːtʃuəl əˈsɪst(ə)nt/ *noun* assistant *m* virtuel

virtual circuit /ˌvɜːtʃuəl ˈsɜːkɪt/ *noun* circuit *m* virtuel

virtual community /ˌvɜːtʃuəl kəˈmjuːnɪti/ *noun* communauté *f* virtuelle

virtual device driver /ˌvɜːtʃuəl dɪˈvaɪs ˌdraɪvə/ *noun* module *m* de gestion d'unité

virtual disk /ˌvɜːtʃuəl ˈdɪsk/ *noun* disque *m* virtuel

virtual image /ˌvɜːtʃuəl ˈɪmɪdʒ/ *noun* image *f* virtuelle

virtual machine /ˌvɜːtʃuəl məˈʃiːn/ *noun* (*software that allows a Java application to run on a computer*) machine *f* virtuelle

virtual memory /ˌvɜːtʃuəl ˈmem(ə)ri/ *noun* mémoire *f* virtuelle

virtual memory stack /ˌvɜːtʃuəl ˈmem(ə)ri ˌstæk/ *noun* pile *f* de mémoire virtuelle

virtual reality /ˌvɜːtʃʊəl riˈælɪti/ *noun* réalité *f* virtuelle ◇ **this new virtual reality software can create a three-dimensional room that you can navigate around** ce nouveau logiciel de réalité virtuelle peut créer une pièce en trois dimensions dans laquelle vous pouvez vous déplacer

> 'Autodesk suggests that anyone wishing to build Virtual Reality applications with the Cyberspace Developer's Kit should have solid knowledge of programming in C++ along with general knowledge of computer graphics.' [*Computing*]

virtual reality modelling language /ˌvɜːtʃuəl riˌælɪti ˈmɒd(ə)lɪŋ ˌlæŋgwɪdʒ/ *noun* langage *m* VRML

virtual screen /ˌvɜːtʃuəl ˈskriːn/ *noun* écran *m* virtuel

virtual storage /ˌvɜːtʃuəl ˈstɔːrɪdʒ/ *noun* mémoire *f* virtuelle

virtual terminal /ˌvɜːtʃuəl ˈtɜːmɪn(ə)l/ *noun* terminal *m* virtuel

virus /ˈvaɪrəs/ *noun* (*program which can corrupt data*) virus *m* ◇ **if your PC is infected with a virus, your data is at risk** si vous avez un virus dans votre PC, vos données sont en danger

virus checker /ˈvaɪrəs ˌtʃekə/ *noun* détecteur *m* de virus

virus detector /ˈvaɪrəs dɪˌtektə/ *noun* détecteur *m* de virus

ViSCA /ˈvɪskə/ *noun* protocole *m* ViSCA

visual /ˈvɪʒʊəl/ *adjective* visuel *or* -elle

Visual Basic /ˌvɪʒʊəl ˈbeɪsɪk/ (*programming tool developed by Microsoft*) Visual Basic™

Visual Basic Extension /ˌvɪʒʊəl ˌbeɪsɪk ɪk ˈstenʃ(ə)n/ technologie *f* VBX

Visual Basic for Applications /ˌvɪʒʊəl ˌbeɪsɪk fər ˌæplɪˈkeɪʃ(ə)nz/ (*trade name for a complex macro language developed by Microsoft*) langage *m* VBA

Visual Basic Script /ˌvɪʒʊəl ˌbeɪsɪk ˈskrɪpt/ langage *m* VBScript

Visual C /ˌvɪʒʊəl ˈsiː/ (*trade name for a development product by Microsoft*) technologie *f* Visual C

visual display terminal /ˌvɪʒʊəl dɪˈspleɪ ˌtɜːmɪn(ə)l/, **visual display unit** *noun* (*VDT*) écran *m* de visualisation; écran *m* visuel

visualisation /ˌvɪʒuəlaɪˈzeɪʃ(ə)n/, **visualization** *noun* (*conversion of numbers or data into a graphical format*) visualisation *f*; présentation *f* graphique

visual programming /ˌvɪʒʊəl ˌprəʊˈgræmɪŋ/ *noun* programmation *f* visuelle

VITC /ˌviː aɪ tiː ˈsiː/ *noun* code *m* temporel vertical

VL-bus, VL local bus *noun* bus *m* local VESA; bus *m* VLB

VLSI /ˌviː el es ˈaɪ/ *noun* intégration *f* à très grande échelle

VM *abbr* (*virtual machine*) machine *f* virtuelle

v-mail /ˈviː ˌmeɪl/ *noun* courriel *m* vidéo

voice answer back /ˌvɔɪs ˈɑːnsə ˌbæk/ *noun* répondeur *m* avec message vocal de synthèse

voice coil /vɔɪs kɔɪl/ *noun* bobine *f* acoustique

voice data entry /ˌvɔɪs ˌdeɪtə ˈentri/, **voice data input** /ˌvɔɪs ˌdeɪtə ˈɪnpʊt/ *noun* saisie *f* vocale

voicemail /ˈvɔɪsmeɪl/ *noun* courrier *m* vocal; messagerie *f* vocale

voice output /vɔɪs ˈaʊtˌpʊt/ *noun* sortie *f* vocale

> '...the technology of voice output is reasonably difficult, but the technology of voice recognition is much more complex' [*Personal Computer World*]

voice over Internet protocol /ˌvɔɪs əʊvə ˈɪntənet ˌprəʊtəkɒl/ *noun* voix *f* sur IP

voice recognition /vɔɪs ˌrekəgˈnɪʃ(ə)n/ *noun* (*ability of a computer to recognise words spoken by a human voice*) reconnaissance *f* de la parole; reconnaissance *f* vocale

voice synthesis /vɔɪs ˈsɪnθəsɪs/ *noun* synthèse *f* vocale

voice synthesiser /ˈvɔɪs ˌsɪnθəsaɪzə/ *noun* synthétiseur *m* vocal

VoIP /vɔɪp/ *noun* voix *f* sur IP

volatile memory /ˌvɒləˌtaɪl ˈmem(ə)ri/, **volatile store** /ˈvɒlətaɪl stɔː/, **volatile dynamic storage** /ˌvɒləˌtaɪl daɪˌnæmɪk ˈstɔːrɪdʒ/ *noun* mémoire *f* volatile

volatility /ˌvɒləˈtɪlɪti/ *noun* volatilité *f*

volt /vəʊlt/ *noun* volt *m*

voltage /ˈvəʊltɪdʒ/ *noun* (*expressed in volts*) voltage *m*; tension *f* ◇ **voltage dip** *or* **dip in voltage** baisse *f* de tension

voltage regulator /ˈvəʊltɪdʒ ˌregjʊleɪtə/ *noun* régulateur *m* de tension

voltage transient /ˌvəʊltɪdʒ ˈtrænziənt/ *noun* pointe *f* de tension

volume /ˈvɒljuːm/ *noun* **1.** (*total space*) volume *m*; (*space occupied by data*) volume *m* **2.** volume *m*

volume label /ˈvɒljuːm ˌleɪb(ə)l/, **volume name** /ˈvɒljuːm neɪm/ *noun* nom *m* de volume; étiquette *f* de volume; label *m* de volume

VORTAL /ˈvɔːtəl/ *noun* portail *m* vertical

voxel /ˈvɒksəl/ *noun* voxel *m*

VR /ˌviː 'ɑː/ *noun* réalité *f* virtuelle

VRAM /'viː ræm/ *noun* mémoire *f* vidéo à accès aléatoire

VRC /ˌviː ɑː 'siː/ *noun* contrôle *m* par redondance verticale

VRML /ˌviː ɑːr em 'el/ *noun* langage *m* VRML

VS *abbr* (*virtual storage*) virtualisation *f* du stockage

VSB /ˌviː es 'biː/ *noun* bande *f* latérale résiduelle

V series /viː 'sɪəriːz/ *noun* (*data transmission*) avis *m* de série V ◇ **V.22 BIS** (*1200 bits/second transmit and receive, full duplex*) norme V22 bis (transmission en duplex à 1200 bits par seconde en émission et réception) ◇ **V.23** (*75 bits/second transmit, 1200 bits/second receive, half duplex*) norme V23 (transmission en semi-duplex à 75 bits par seconde en émission et 1200 bits par seconde en réception) ◇ **V.24** (*interchange circuits between a DTE and a DCE*) norme V24 (circuits d'échange entre système central et terminal) ◇ **V.25 BIS** (*automatic calling and answering equipment on a PSTN*) norme V25 bis (équipement d'appel et de réponse automatique sur le réseau public commuté) ◇ **V.26** (*2400 bits/second transmission over leased lines*) norme V26 (transmission à 2400 bits par seconde sur des lignes louées) ◇ **V.26 BIS** (*2400 bits/second transmit, 1200 bits/second receive, half duplex for use on a PSTN*) norme V26 bis (transmission en semi-duplex à 2400 bits par seconde en émission et 1200 bits par seconde en réception sur le réseau public commuté) ◇ **V.26 TER** (*2400 bits/second transmit, 1200 bits/second receive, full duplex for use on a PSTN*) norme V26 ter (transmission en duplex à 2400 bits par seconde en émission et 1200 bits par seconde en réception sur le réseau public commuté) ◇ **V.27** (*4800 bits/second modem for use on a leased line*) norme V27 (modem à 4800 bits par seconde sur lignes louées) ◇ **V.27 BIS** (*4800 bits/second transmit, 2400 bits/second receive for use on a leased line*) norme V27 bis (transmission à 4800 bits par seconde en émission et 2400 bits par seconde en réception sur lignes louées) ◇ **V.27 TER** (*4800 bits/second transmit, 2400 bits/second receive for use on a PSTN*) norme V27 ter (transmission à 4800 bits par seconde en émission et 2400 bits par seconde en réception sur le réseau public commuté) ◇ **V.32terbo** (*pseudo-standard developed by AT&T, among others, that supports transmission at 19200 bits/second*) norme V32 terbo (pseudo-norme mise au point par AT&T, et autres, qui permet une transmission à 19200 bits par seconde) ◇ **V.42 BIS** (*data compression used with V.42 error control*) norme V42 bis (compression de données avec contrôle d'erreurs V42)

VT-52 /ˌviː tiː ˌfɪfti 'tuː/ *noun* standard *m* VT-52

VTR /ˌviː tiː 'ɑː/ *noun* magnétoscope *m*

VT-terminal emulation /ˌviː tiː 'tɜːmɪn(ə)l emjuˌleɪʃ(ə)n/ *noun* (*set of codes developed by Digital Equipment Corporation*) émulation *f* de terminal VT

VxD /ˌviː eks 'diː/ *noun* module *m* de gestion d'unité

Vxtreme /ˌviː eks'triːm/ *noun* (*format used to deliver streaming video sequences over the internet*) format *m* vidéo Vxtreme™

W

W3 *abbr* (*World Wide Web*) Web *m*

W3C /ˌdʌb(ə)l juː θriː 'siː/ *noun* consortium *m* W3C

wafer /'weɪfə/ *noun* (*slice of silicon*) tranche *f* de silicium

wafer scale integration /ˌweɪfə skeɪl ˌɪntɪ 'greɪʃ(ə)n/ *noun* (*chip made of smaller integrated circuits*) intégration *f* sur tranche de silicium

WAIS /ˌdʌb(ə)l eɪ aɪ 'es/ *noun* système *m* WAIS

wait condition /'weɪt kənˌdɪʃ(ə)n/ *noun* **1.** état *m* de latence; état *m* d'attente **2.** état *m* d'attente; état *m* de latence

waiting list /'weɪtɪŋ lɪst/ *noun* (*queue*) file *f* d'attente

waiting state /weɪtɪŋ steɪt/ *noun* (*computer state*) attente *f*

wait loop /weɪt luːp/ *noun* boucle *f* d'attente

wait state /'weɪt steɪt/ *noun* état *m* de latence; état *m* d'attente

wait time /weɪt taɪm/ *noun* délai *m* d'attente; latence *f*

wake-on-LAN /weɪk ɒn/ *noun* réveil *m* par le réseau

wake-up code /'weɪk ʌp kəʊd/ *noun* code *m* d'alerte

wallpaper /'wɔːlˌpeɪpə/ *noun* (*background in a window*) papier *m* peint

WAN /wæn/ *noun* réseau *m* étendu

wand /wɒnd/ *noun* (*bar code reader or optical device*) stylo *m* optique

WAP /wæp/ *noun* **1.** protocole *m* WAP **2.** protocole *m* WAP

WAP browser /wæp 'braʊzə/ *noun* navigateur *m* WAP

WAP markup language /ˌwæp 'mɑːkʌp ˌlæŋgwɪdʒ/ *noun* langage *m* de balisage WAP

warm boot /ˌwɔːm 'buːt/ *noun* (*reloads operating system*) amorçage *m* à chaud; lancement *m* du système à chaud

warmboot /'wɔːmbuːt/ *verb* redémarrer à chaud

warm standby /wɔːm 'stændbaɪ/ *noun* (*secondary backup device*) équipement *m* de secours à démarrage semi-automatique

warm start /wɔːm stɑːt/ *noun* (*of programme*) reprise *f* sur l'instruction d'arrêt; reprise *f* au point d'arrêt

warn /wɔːn/ *verb* avertir *vt* ◇ **he warned the keyboarders that the system might become overloaded** il a averti les opérateurs de saisie d'une surcharge possible du système

warning light /'wɔːnɪŋ laɪt/ *noun* voyant *m* d'alarme

waste instruction /weɪst ɪn'strʌkʃən/ *noun* instruction *f* de remplissage

watermark /'wɔːtəmɑːk/ *noun* tatouage *m* numérique

watt /wɒt/ *noun* watt *m*

wave /weɪv/ *noun* onde *f* ◇ **sound wave** onde sonore

WAVE /weɪv/ *noun* (*analog signal*) WAVE *f*

waveform /'weɪvfɔːm/ *noun* onde *f*

waveform audio /'weɪvfɔːm ˌɔːdiəʊ/ *noun* onde *f* audio

waveform digitisation /ˌweɪvfɔːm ˌdɪdʒɪtaɪ 'zeɪʃ(ə)n/ *noun* conversion *f* d'une onde en numérique; numérisation *f* d'une onde

waveform editor /'weɪvfɔːm ˌedɪtə/ *noun* éditeur *m* d'onde

waveform synthesiser /'weɪvfɔːm ˌsɪnθəsaɪzə/ *noun* synthétiseur *m* d'onde

wavelength /'weɪvˌleŋθ/ *noun* longueur *f* d'onde

wavelength division multiplexing /ˌweɪvleŋθ dɪˌvɪʒ(ə)n 'mʌltɪpleksɪŋ/ *noun* multiplexage *m* en longueur d'onde

wavetable /'weɪvteɪb(ə)l/ *noun* (*memory in a sound card that contains a recording of a real musical instrument that is played back*) mémoire *f* audio wavetable

WDM *abbr* (*wavelength division multiplexing*) multiplexage *m* en longueur d'onde

wearable computer /ˌweərəb(ə)l kəm 'pjuːtə/ *noun* ordinateur *m* vêtement

web /web/ *noun* Web *m* ◇ **once you've created your site, you'll want to upload it to a Web server** vous avez créé votre site, vous désirez maintenant le télécharger sur le Web

web application /web ˌæplɪ'keɪʃ(ə)n/ *noun* application *f* Web

WebBot /'webbɒt/ WebBot *m*

web browser /'web ˌbraʊzə/ *noun* navigateur *m* Web

web cam /web kæm/ *noun* Webcaméra *f*

webcast /'webkɑːst/ *noun* Webémission *f*

'It is spending $450m on a community support programme for developers: webcasts, free on-site training, seminars, roadshows and 125 new books.' [*The Guardian*]

web crawler /'web ˌkrɔːlə/ *noun* robot *m*

web designer /'web ðiˌzaɪnə/ *noun* Web designer *m*

weblog /'weblɒg/ *noun* blogue *m*

webmaster /'webmɑːstə/ *noun* Webmestre *m*; gestionnaire *m* Web

webpage /'webpeɪdʒ/ *noun* document *m* Web

webpage design software /ˌwebpeɪdʒ dɪˌzaɪn 'sɒftweə/ *noun* logiciel *m* de création de document Web

web portal /web 'pɔːt(ə)l/ *noun* portail *m*

web ring /'web rɪŋ/ *noun* anneau *m* de sites

web server /web 'sɜːvə/ *noun* serveur *m* Web

website /'websaɪt/ *noun* site *m* protégé; site *m* sécurisé

WebTV /ˌweb tiː 'viː/ webtélé

webzine /'webziːn/ *noun* magazine *m* en ligne

weighted average /ˌweɪtɪd 'æv(ə)rɪdʒ/ *noun* moyenne *f* pondérée

weighted bit /'weɪtɪd bɪt/ *noun* bit *m* de poids fort; bit *m* lourd

weighting /'weɪtɪŋ/ *noun* pondération *f*; (*sorting of users, programs or data by their importance or priority*) tri *m*

well-behaved /ˌwel bɪ'heɪvd/ *adjective* (*program*) policé; *informal* non bidouillé

wetware /'wetˌweə/ *noun* *informal* matière *f* grise

What-You-See-Is-All-You-Get /ˌwɒt juː siː ɪz ˌɔːl juː 'get/ *noun* ce que vous voyez est tout ce que vous obtenez

What-You-See-Is-What-You-Get /ˌwɒt juː siː ɪz ˌwɒt juː 'get/ *noun* ce que vous voyez est ce que vous obtenez

while-loop /waɪl luːp/ *noun* boucle *f* conditionnelle 'WHILE'

White Book /waɪt bʊk/ *noun* norme *f* Livre Blanc

white pages /waɪt peɪdʒz/ *plural noun* répertoire *m* d'adresses électroniques

white writer /waɪt 'raɪtə/ *noun* imprimante *f* à définition des blancs

whois /'huː ɪz/ *noun* base *f* de données Whois

wide area information server /ˌwaɪd ˌeəriə ˌɪnfə'meɪʃ(ə)n ˌsɜːvə/ *noun* système *m* WAIS

wide area network /ˌwaɪd ˌeəriə 'netwɜːk/ *noun* réseau *m* étendu

wideband /'waɪdbænd/ *noun* (*transmission method that combines several channels*) large bande *f* ◇ **wideband frequency modulation (WBFM)** modulation *f* de fréquence à large bande

widescreen display /ˌwaɪdskriːn dɪ'spleɪ/ *noun* format *m* écran large

Wide-SCSI /waɪd 'skʌzi/ *noun* interface *f* Wide-SCSI (SCSI large)

widow /'wɪdəʊ/ *noun* (*single line*) veuve *f*; dernière ligne *f* d'un paragraphe isolée en tête de page

wild card /'waɪldkɑːd/, **wild card character** /'waɪldkɑːd ˌkærɪktə/ *noun* caractère *m* joker

WIMP /wɪmp/ *noun* environnement *m* graphique WIMP

Winchester disk /draɪv/, **Winchester drive** *noun* disque *m* dur Winchester

window /'wɪndəʊ/ *noun* **1.** (*section of screen*) fenêtre *f* **2.** (*part of document displayed on screen*) fenêtre *f* **3.** (*area of memory*) fenêtre *f* ■ *verb* fenêtrer *vt* ◇ **several remote stations are connected to the network and each has its own window onto the hard disk** plusieurs postes de travail à distance sont connectés au réseau, chacun disposant d'une fenêtre sur le disque dur ◇ **the operating system will allow other programs to be displayed on-screen at the same time in different windows** le système d'exploitation permet d'afficher d'autres programmes simultanément dans des fenêtres différentes ◇ **window, icon, mouse, pointer (WIMP)** environnement *m* graphique WIMP (avec fenêtre, icône, souris, pointeur)

'...when an output window overlaps another, the interpreter does not save the contents of the obscured window' [*Personal Computer World*]

window, icon, mouse, pointer /ˌwɪndəʊ ˌaɪkɒn ˌmaʊs 'pɔɪntə/ *noun* environnement *m* graphique WIMP

windowing /'wɪndəʊɪŋ/ *noun* fenêtrage *m*

'...windowing facilities make use of virtual screens as well as physical screens' [*Byte*]

'...the network system uses the latest windowing techniques' [*Desktop Publishing*]

'...the functions are integrated via a windowing system with pull-down menus used to select different operations' [*Byte*]

Windows /'wɪndəʊz/ (*graphical user interface developed by Microsoft*) Windows™ (de Microsoft) ◇ **Windows for Workgroups™** (*Windows that includes peer-to-peer file-sharing functions*) Windows for Workgroups™ ◇ **Windows NT™** (*GUI derived from Windows*) (système d'exploitation) Windows NT™

Windows 3.1 /ˌwɪndəʊz θriː ˌpɔɪnt 'wʌn/ (*trade name for the first of the new generation of Windows which provided features including OLE and drag and drop*) Windows 3.1

Windows 3.1x /ˌwɪndəʊz θriː ˌpɔɪnt wʌn 'eks/ (*trade name for any version of Windows after version 3*) Windows 3.1x

Windows 3.11 /ˌwɪndəʊz θriː ˌpɔɪnt wʌn 'wʌn/ Windows 3.11

Windows 95 /ˌwɪndəʊz ˌnaɪnti 'faɪv/ (*operating system software*) Windows 95

Windows 98 /ˌwɪndəʊz ˌnaɪnti ˈeɪt/ (*operating system software*) Windows 98™

Windows 2000 /ˌwɪndəʊz tuː ˈθaʊzənd/ (*trade name for a version of the Windows operating system that improves on the speed and features of Windows 98*) Windows 2000

Windows API /ˌwɪndəʊz ˌeɪ piː ˈaɪ/ (*trade name for a set of standard functions and commands defined by Microsoft*) Windows API

Windows CE /ˌwɪndəʊz siː ˈiː/ (*trade name for a software operating system developed by Microsoft*) système *m* d'exploitation mobile

Windows Explorer /ˌwɪndəʊz ɪkˈsplɔːrə/ (*trade name for a software utility included with Windows*) Windows Explorer

Windows for Workgroups /ˌwɪndəʊz fə ˈwɜːkgruːps/ (*trade name for a version of Windows that includes basic peer-to-peer file-sharing functions*) Windows for Workgroups

Windows GDI /ˌwɪndəʊz dʒiː diː ˈaɪ/ (*trade name for a set of standard functions, defined by Microsoft*) Windows GDI

Windows Internet Naming Service /ˌwɪndəʊz ˌɪntənet ˈneɪmɪŋ ˌsɜːvɪs/ service *m* WINS

Windows ME /ˌwɪndəʊz em ˈiː/ (*trade name for a version of the Windows operating system designed for home users*) Windows ME

Windows NT /ˌwɪndəʊz en ˈtiː/ (*trade name for a high-performance GUI derived from Windows*) Windows NT

Windows SDK /ˌwɪndəʊz es diː ˈkeɪ/ (*trade name for a set of software tools*) trousse de développement logiciel

Windows XP /ˌwɪndəʊz eks ˈpiː/ (*trade name for a version of the Windows operating system designed for home and business users*) Windows XP

WINS /wɪns/ *noun* service *m* WINS

Winsock /ˈwɪnsɒk/ *noun* bibliothèque *f* Winsock

wipe /waɪp/ *verb* (*to clean data from a disk*) effacer *vt*; détruire *vt*; blanchir *vt* ◇ **by reformatting you will wipe the disk clean** si vous reformatez, vous détruirez toutes les données du disque *or* vous blanchirez le disque

wire /ˈwaɪə/ *noun* (*thin metal conductor*) fil *m* ■ *verb* (*to install wiring*) câbler *vt*

wire frame model /ˌwaɪə freɪm ˈmɒd(ə)l/ *noun* représentation *f* filaire

wireless access point /ˌwaɪələs ˈækses ˌpɔɪnt/ *noun* point *m* d'accès sans fil

Wireless Application Protocol /ˌwaɪələs ˌæplɪˈkeɪʃ(ə)n ˌprəʊtəʊkɒl/ *noun* (*allows exchanges between a mobile phone and the Internet*) protocole *m* WAP (protocole mondial de communication) ◇ **WAP 1.1** (*for mobile phone*) norme *f* WAP 1.1 ◇ **WAP markup language (WML)** langage WML (de description de pages WAP) ◇ **WAP markup language script (WMLScript)** WMLScript

wireless LAN /ˌwaɪələs ˈlæn/ *noun* réseau *m* local sans fil

wireless markup language /ˌwaɪələs ˈmɑːkʌp ˌlæŋgwɪdʒ/ *noun* langage *m* WML

wireless modem /ˌwaɪələs ˈməʊdem/ *noun* modem *m* sans fil

wireless network /ˌwaɪələs ˈnetwɜːk/, **wireless LAN** /læn/ *noun* réseau *m* local sans fil

wire mesh model /ˌwaɪə meʃ ˈmɒd(ə)l/ *noun* représentation *f* filaire

wire printer /ˈwaɪə ˌprɪntə/ *noun* imprimante *f* matricielle

wire wrap /ˈwaɪə ræp/ *noun* connexion *f* enroulée

wiring /ˈwaɪərɪŋ/ *noun* câblage *m* ◇ **the wiring in the system had to be replaced** il a fallu refaire le câblage du système

wiring closet /ˈwaɪərɪŋ ˌklɒzɪt/ *noun* boîte *f*

wiring frame /ˈwaɪərɪŋ freɪm/ *noun* châssis *m*

WISC /wɪsk/ *noun* ordinateur *m* à jeu d'instructions modifiable

wizard /ˈwɪzəd/ *noun* (*software utility*) sorcier *m* dépanneur

WML /ˌdʌb(ə)l juː em ˈel/ *noun* langage *m* WML

WMLScript /ˌdʌb(ə)l juː em ˈel ˌskrɪpt/ *noun* script *m* WML

word /wɜːd/ *noun* **1.** (*separate item of language*) mot *m* **2.** (*separate item of data*) mot *m* ◇ **words per minute (wpm** *or* **WPM)** (nombre de) mots par minute

word break /ˈwɜːd breɪk/ *noun* coupe *f* d'un mot

word count /ˈwɜːd kaʊnt/ *noun* nombre *m* de mots contenus dans un fichier; nombre *m* de mots contenus dans un texte

word length /ˈwɜːd leŋθ/ *noun* longueur *f* d'un mot

word mark /ˈwɜːd mɑːk/ *noun* marque *f* de mot

word marker /ˈwɜːd ˌmɑːkə/ *noun* (*symbol indicating the start of a word*) marque *f* de début de mot

WordPad /ˈwɜːdpæd/ WordPad

WordPerfect /ˌwɜːdˈpɜːfekt/ (*word-processing application*) WordPerfect™

word-process /wɜːd ˈprəʊses/ *verb* (*to edit, store and manipulate text using a computer*) faire un traitement de texte sur ordinateur ◇ **it is quite easy to read word-processed files** on lit facilement les fichiers après traitement de texte

word-processing /ˌwɜːd ˈprəʊsesɪŋ/ *noun* (*keyboarding, editing, and output of text*) traitement *m* de texte

word-processing bureau /ˌwɜːd ˈprəʊsesɪŋ ˌbjʊərəʊ/ *noun* bureau *m* de traitement de texte

word-processor /wɜːd 'prəʊˌsesə/ *noun* **1.** (*machine*) machine *f* de traitement de texte **2.** (*software*) logiciel *m* de traitement de texte

word serial /wɜːd 'sɪəriəl/ *noun* groupe *m* de mots

words per minute /ˌwɜːdz pɜː 'mɪnɪt/ *noun* mot *m* par minute

WordStar /'wɜːdstɑː/ (*word-processing application developed by MicroPro International*) WordStar™

word time /'wɜːd taɪm/ *noun* temps *m* de transfert d'un mot

word wrap /'wɜːd ræp/ *noun* retour *m* à la ligne automatique

work /wɜːk/ *noun* travail *m*

work area /wɜːk 'eəriə/ *noun* espace *m* de travail; zone *f* de travail

workaround /'wɜːkəˌraʊnd/ *noun* solution *f* de rechange

'This is a known bug… the workaround is to get Outlook Express to prompt you to select an identity when you run it.' [*The Guardian*]

work disk /wɜːk dɪsk/ *noun* disque *m* de travail

work file /wɜːk faɪl/ *noun* fichier *m* de travail

workflow /'wɜːkfləʊ/ *noun* (*software designed to improve the flow of electronic documents*) flux *m* de travaux

workgroup /'wɜːkgruːp/ *noun* (*group of users*) groupe *m* de travail; groupe *m* de projet ◇ **this word-processor is workgroup enabled which adds an email gateway from the standard menus** ce traitement de texte est orienté sur les groupes de travail et comporte un passerelle de messagerie électronique dans le menu courant

workgroup enabled /ˌwɜːkgruːp ɪn 'eɪb(ə)ld/ *adjective* qui permet le travail de groupe; qui facilite le travail de groupe ◇ **this word-processor is workgroup enabled which adds an email gateway from the standard menus** ce traitement de texte est orienté sur les groupes de travail et comporte un passerelle de messagerie électronique dans le menu courant

workgroup software /'wɜːkgruːp ˌsɒftweə/ *noun* logiciel *m* de groupe (de travail)

working /'wɜːkɪŋ/ *adjective* (*which operates correctly*) en état de marche

working in tandem /ˌwɜːkɪŋ ɪn 'tændəm/ *noun* fonctionnement *m* en tandem

working store /'wɜːkɪŋ stɔː/ *noun* mémoire *f* temporaire; mémoire *f* bloc-notes; mémoire *f* banale

workload /'wɜːkˌləʊd/ *noun* charge *f* de travail

worksheet /'wɜːkˌʃiːt/ *noun* (*two-dimensional matrix of rows and columns*) feuille *f* de travail

workspace /'wɜːkspeɪs/ *noun* (*space in memory*) espace *m* de manoeuvre; espace *m* de travail

workstation /'wɜːkˌsteɪʃ(ə)n/ *noun* (*PC*) poste *m* de travail; station *f* de travail ◇ **the archive storage has a total capacity of 1200 MB between seven workstations** sept postes de travail se partagent une mémoire d'archivage d'une capacité de 1200 Mo ◇ **the system includes five workstations linked together in a ring network** le système comprend un réseau de cinq postes de travail reliés en anneau

'…an image processing workstation must provide three basic facilities: the means to digitize, display and manipulate the image data' [*Byte*]

world /wɜːld/ *noun* (*three-dimensional scene displayed on a web site and allows a user to move around*) univers *m*

World Wide Web /ˌwɜːld ˌwaɪd 'web/ *noun* World Wide Web *m*

World Wide Web Consortium /ˌwɜːld waɪd 'web kənˌsɔːtiəm/ *noun* consortium *m* W3C

WORM /wɜːm/ *noun* (*small program that travels across the Internet and replicates itself*) ver *m*

WP /ˌdʌb(ə)ljuː 'piː/ *abbr* (*word-processing*) traitement *m* de texte

WPM, wpm *noun* mots *mpl* par minute

wraparound /'ræpəˌraʊnd/ *noun* (*word-processing*) retour *m* à la ligne automatique

wrapper /'ræpə/ *noun* classe *f* enveloppante

writable instruction set computer /ˌraɪtəb(ə)l ɪnˌstrʌkʃən set kəmˈpjuːtə/ *noun* (*CPU design*) ordinateur *m* à jeu d'instructions modifiable

write /raɪt/ *verb* (*data onto a disk or tape*) enregistrer *vt*; ranger une donnée en mémoire ◇ **access time is the time taken to read from or write to a location in memory** le temps d'accès est le temps requis pour consulter une donnée en mémoire ou pour ranger une donnée en mémoire ◇ **write once, read many times memory (WORM)** disque *m* optique WORM (permettant une seule écriture et des lectures multiples)

write black printer /ˌraɪt 'blæk ˌprɪntə/ *noun* (*printer where toner sticks to points hit by a laser beam*) imprimante *f* à transfert d'encre

write error /raɪt 'erə/ *noun* erreur *f* d'écriture

write head /raɪt hed/ *noun* (*record head*) tête *f* d'écriture

write once, read many times memory /ˌraɪt ˌwʌns riːd 'meni ˌtaɪmz ˌmem(ə)ri/ *noun* disque *m* optique WORM

write-permit ring /ˌraɪt pə'mɪt rɪŋ/ *noun* bague *f* d'autorisation d'écriture

write protect /raɪt prə'tekt/ *verb* interdire l'écriture; protéger contre l'écriture

write-protect tab /ˌraɪt prə'tekt tæb/ *noun* volet *m* de protection en écriture; volet *m* contre l'écriture

writer /'raɪtə/ *noun* scripteur *m*

write time /raɪt taɪm/ *noun* temps *m* d'écriture; temps *m* d'enregistrement

writing pad /ˈraɪtɪŋ pæd/ *noun* tablette *f* à numériser

WWW *abbr* (*World Wide Web*) Web *m*

WYSIAYG /ˈwɪziːeɪg/ *noun* ce que vous voyez est tout ce que vous obtenez

WYSIWYG /ˈwɪziːwɪg/ *noun* ce que vous voyez est ce que vous obtenez

X

X2 *noun* X2

X.25 *noun* (*defines the connection between a terminal and a packet-switching network*) protocole *m* X 25

X.400 *noun* (*defines an electronic mail transfer method*) standard CCITT X 400

X.500 *noun* (*defines a method of global naming*) standard CCITT X 500

XA CD-ROM *m* XA

x-axis /ˌeks ˌaʊt ˈæksɪs/ *noun* axe *m* d'abscisse; axe *m* des X

x-coordinate /eks kəʊˈɔːdɪnət/ *noun* abscisse *f*; coordonnée *f* horizontale

x direction /ˌeks ˌaʊt dɪˈrekʃ(ə)n/ *noun* horizontale *f*

x distance /ˌeks ˌaʊt ˈdɪstəns/ *noun* distance *f* sur l'axe des X

xerographic printer /ˌzɪərəgræfɪk ˈprɪntə/ *noun* imprimante *f* xérographique

Xerox Network System /ˌzɪərɒks ˈnetwɜːk ˌsɪstəm/ (*protocol developed by Xerox*) protocole *m* XNS (pour réseau)

XGA /ˌeks dʒiː ˈeɪ/ *noun* norme *f* XGA de carte graphique couleur pour vidéo sur PC, de IBM

XHTML /ˌeks eɪtʃ tiː em ˈel/ *noun* langage *m* XHMTL

XML /ˌeks em ˈel/ *noun* langage *m* XML

XMODEM /ˈeks ˌməʊdem/ *noun* (*file transfer and error-detecting protocol*) protocole *m* XMODEM

XMODEM 1K *noun* protocole *m* XMODEM 1K

XMODEM CRC *noun* protocole *m* XMODEM CRC

XMS /ˌeks em ˈes/ *noun* spécifications *fpl* de mémoire étendue; spécifications *fpl* XMS

XON/XOFF /eks ˌɒn eks ˈɒf/ *noun* (*asynchronous transmission protocol*) protocole *m* XON/XOFF

X/OPEN /eksˈəʊpən/ *noun* (*group promoting open systems*) groupe *m* X/OPEN

XP *abbr* (*Windows XP*) XP

x punch /ˈeks pʌntʃ/ *noun* (*card punch for column 11*) perforation *f* (de la ligne) 11; perforation *f* X

X-series /ˌeks ˌaʊt ˈsɪəriːz/ *noun* série *f* X

XT /ˌeks ˈtiː/ *noun* (*version of the original IBM PC*) version *f* XT

XT keyboard /ˌeks tiː ˈkiːbɔːd/ *noun* clavier *m* XT

X-Window System /eks ˌwɪndəʊ ˈsɪstəm/, **X-Windows** (*set of API commands and display handling routines*) système *m* X-Window (d'API)

'X is the underlying technology which allows Unix applications to run under a multi-user, multitasking GUI. It has been adopted as the standard for the Common Open Software Environment, proposed recently by top Unix vendors including Digital, IBM and Sun.' [*Computing*]

x-y /ˌeks ˈaʊt waɪ/ *noun* coordonnées *f*

x-y plotter /ˌeks waɪ ˈplɒtə/ *noun* traceur *m* de courbes; traceur *m* de graphiques

Y

y-axis /waɪ 'æksɪs/ *noun* axe *m* de l'ordonnée; axe *m* des Y

y-coordinate /waɪ kəʊ'ɔːdɪnət/ *noun* ordonnée *f*; coordonnée *f* verticale

Y/C video /ˌwaɪ siː 'vɪdiəʊ/ *noun* S-vidéo *f*

y-direction /waɪ daɪ'rekʃən/ *noun* verticale *f*

y-distance /waɪ 'dɪstəns/ *noun* distance *f* sur l'axe des Y

Yellow Book /'jeləʊ bʊk/ *noun* norme *f* ISO 9660

YMCK /ˌwaɪ em siː 'keɪ/ *noun* YMCK

YMODEM /'waɪ ˌməʊdem/ *noun* (*variation of the XMODEM file transfer protocol*) YMODEM

y punch /'waɪ pʌntʃ/ *noun* perforation *f* (de ligne) 12; perforation *f* Y

Z

Z80 /ˌzed 'eɪti/ *noun* (*processor developed by Zilog*) processeur *m* Z80

zap /zæp/ *verb* (*wipe out all data*) faire disparaître de l'écran; nettoyer *vt*; vider l'écran ◇ **he pressed CONTROL Z and zapped all the text** il a tapé CONTROL Z pour vider l'écran

z-axis /zed 'æksɪs/ *noun* axe *m* des Z

z buffer /zed 'bʌfə/ *noun* (*area of memory*) matrice *f* Z

zero /'zɪərəʊ/ *noun* **1.** (*digit 0*) zéro *m* **2.** (*off or false*) zéro *m* ■ *verb* (*to erase*) effacer un fichier ◇ **in Britain, the code for international calls is zero zero (00)** en Grande-Bretagne, l'indicatif des appels internationaux est zéro zéro (00)

zero compression /ˌzɪərəʊ kəm'preʃ(ə)n/ *noun* élimination *f* des zéros

zerofill /'zɪərəʊfɪl/ *verb* garnir de zéros

zero flag /'zɪərəʊ flæg/ *noun* indicateur *m* binaire zéro ◇ **if the result is zero, the zero flag is set** si le résultat est zéro, l'indicateur zéro est activé

zero insertion force socket /ˌzɪərəʊ ɪn ˌsɜːʃ(ə)n fɔːs 'sɒkɪt/ *noun* prise *f* de force d'insertion nulle

zero-level address /ˌzɪərəʊ ˌlev(ə)l ə'dres/ *noun* adresse *f* immédiate; adresse *f* directe

zero slot LAN /ˌzɪərəʊ slɒt 'læn/ *noun* (*LAN that does not use internal expansion adapters*) réseau *m* local sans carte d'extension

zero suppression /ˌzɪərəʊ sə'preʃ(ə)n/ *noun* élimination *f* des zéros

zero wait state /ˌzɪərəʊ 'weɪt ˌsteɪt/ *noun* (*fast enough to run at the same speed as other components*) état *m* sans attente

zettabyte /'zetəbaɪt/ *noun* zettaoctet *m*

ZIF socket /'zɪf ˌsɒkɪt/ *noun* prise *f* de force d'insertion nulle

ZIP /zɪp/ *noun* (*filename extension given to files that contain compressed data*) ZIP ◇ **ZIP disk** (*large disk of 100 or 250 MB*) disque ZIP ◇ **ZIP drive** lecteur de (disque) ZIP

zip file /'zɪp faɪl/ *noun* fichier *m* compressé

ZMODEM /'zed ˌməʊdem/ *noun* (*enhanced version of the XMODEM file transfer protocol*) ZMODEM

zone /zəʊn/ *noun* (*part of a screen*) zone *f*

zoom /zuːm/ *verb* (*to enlarge text or graphics*) faire un zoom; zoomer *vi*

'...any window can be zoomed to full-screen size by pressing the F-5 function key' [*Byte*]

zoomed video port /ˌzuːmd 'vɪdiəʊ ˌpɔːt/ *noun* port *m* zoom vidéo

zooming /'zuːmɪŋ/ *noun* zoom *m*

ZV Port /ˌzed 'viː ˌpɔːt/ *noun* port *m* zoom vidéo